BUILDINGS OF COLORADO

To Kenneth,
Enjoy your
homeland!
July 19, 2003
The Hughes

SOCIETY OF ARCHITECTURAL HISTORIANS

BUILDINGS OF THE UNITED STATES

Buildings of

COLORADO

THOMAS J. NOEL

OXFORD UNIVERSITY PRESS

New York   Oxford

OXFORD UNIVERSITY PRESS
Oxford   New York
Auckland   Bangkok   Buenos Aires
Cape Town   Chennai   Dar es Salaam   Delhi
Hong Kong   Istanbul   Karachi
Kolkata   Kuala Lumpur   Madrid   Melbourne
Mexico City   Mumbai   Nairobi   São Paulo   Shanghai   Singapore
Taipei   Tokyo   Toronto
and an associated company in
Berlin

First published by Oxford University Press, Inc., 1997

198 Madison Avenue, New York, New York 10016

First issued as an Oxford University Press paperback, 2002

Oxford is a registered trademark of Oxford University Press

LIBRARY OF CONGRESS CATALOGING-IN-PUBLICATION DATA
Noel, Thomas J. (Thomas Jacob)
Buildings of Colorado / Thomas J. Noel.
p.   cm. — (Buildings of the United States)
Includes bibliographical references and index.
ISBN 0-19-509076-4
1. Architecture—Colorado—Guidebooks.   2. Colorado—Guidebooks.
I. Title.   II. Series.
NA730.C6N64   1997
720′ .9788—dc21   97-12674

ISBN 0-19-515247-6 (Pbk.)

9 8 7 6 5 4 3 2 1

PRINTED IN THE UNITED STATES OF AMERICA

Buildings of the United States is a series of books on American architecture compiled and written on a state-by-state basis. The primary objective of the series is to identify and celebrate the rich cultural, economic, and geographical diversity of the United States as it is reflected in the architecture of each state. The series has been commissioned by the Society of Architectural Historians, an organization dedicated to the study, interpretation, and preservation of the built environment throughout the world.

Buildings of Colorado has been supported in part by the National Endowment for the Humanities, an independent federal agency; the Bonfils-Stanton Foundation; the Gates Foundation; the Dobbins Foundation; the Colorado Historical Foundation; the University of Colorado at Denver; the University of Missouri; and the University of Delaware.

Foreword

It is with pride and pleasure that the Society of Architectural Historians presents this fifth volume in the monumental series Buildings of the United States.

Heretofore, the United States was the only major country of the Western world that had not produced a publication project dealing with its architectural heritage on a national scale. In overall concept, Buildings of the United States is to a degree modeled on and inspired by Buildings of England, the series of forty-six volumes conceived and carried out on a county-by-county basis by the eminent British architectural historian Nikolaus Pevsner, first published between 1951 and 1974. It was Pevsner himself who—years ago, but again and again—urged his American colleagues in the Society of Architectural Historians to do the same for this country. In method and approach, of course, that challenge was to be as different from Buildings of England as American architecture is different from English. Pevsner was confronted by a coherent culture on a relatively small island, with an architectural history that spans over two thousand years. Here we are dealing with a vast land of immense regional, geographic, climatic, and ethnic diversity, with most of its buildings—wide-ranging, exciting, and sometimes dramatic—essentially concentrated into the last four hundred years, but with significant Native American remains stretching back well beyond that. In contrast to the national integrity of English architecture, therefore, American architecture is marked by a dynamic heterogeneity, a heterogeneity woven of a thousand strands of originality, or, actually, a unity woven of a thousand strands of heterogeneity. It is this quality that Buildings of the United States reflects and records.

Heterogeneity was a condition of American architecture from the first European settlements of the sixteenth and seventeenth centuries. Not only did the buildings of the Russian, Spanish, French, Dutch, Swedish, and English colonies differ according to national origin (to say nothing of their differences from Native American structures) In translation to North America they also assumed a special scale and character, qualities that were largely determined by the aspirations and traditions of a people struggling to fashion a new world in an abundant but demanding land. Diversity marked even the English colonies of the Eastern Seaboard, though they shared a common architectural heritage. The brick mutations of the English prototypes in the Virginia Colony were very different from the wooden architecture of the Massachusetts Bay Colony; they were different because Virginia was a farm and plantation society dominated by the Anglican church, whereas Massachusetts was a communal society nurtured entirely by Puritanism. As the colonies be-

vii

came a nation and developed westward, similar radical contrasts became the way of America's growth. The infinite variety of physical environment, together with the complex origins and motivations of the settlers, made it inevitable that each new state would have a character uniquely its own.

The primary objective of each volume, therefore, is to record, analyze, and evaluate the architecture of the state. All of the authors are trained architectural historians who are thoroughly informed in the local aspects of their subjects. In each volume, special conditions that shaped the state, together with the building types necessary to meet those conditions, are identified and discussed: barns, silos, mining buildings, factories, warehouses, bridges, and transportation buildings take their places alongside the familiar building types conventional to the nation as a whole—churches, courthouses, city halls, and the infinite variety of domestic architecture. Although the great national and international masters of American architecture receive proper attention, especially in volumes for the states in which they did their greatest work, outstanding local architects, as well as the buildings of skilled but often anonymous carpenter-builders, are also brought prominently into the picture. Each volume is thus a detailed and precise portrait of the architecture of the state that it represents. At the same time, however, all of these local issues are examined as they relate to architectural developments in the country at large. Volumes will continue to appear state by state until every state is represented. When the overview and inventory are completed, the series will form a comprehensive history of the architecture of the United States.

The series was long in the planning. The idea was conceived by Turpin Bannister, the first president of the Society (1940–1942). It was thirty years, however, before the Society had grown sufficiently to consider such a project. Alan Gowans, during his presidency (1972–1974), drew up a proposal and made the first of several unsuccessful attempts to raise the funds. The issue was raised again during the presidency of Marian C. Donnelly, when William H. Jordy and William H. Pierson, Jr., suggested to the Board of Directors that such a project should be the Society's contribution to the nation's Bicentennial celebration. It was not until 1986, however, after several failed attempts, that a substantial grant from the National Endowment for the Humanities, which was matched by grants from the Pew Charitable Trusts and the Graham Foundation, made the dream a reality. The final steps to achieving it took place under the successive presidencies of Adolf K. Placzek (1978–1980), David Gebhard (1980–1982), Damie Stillman (1982–1984), and Carol Herselle Krinsky (1984–1986). Development and production of the first books has continued under those of Osmund Overby (1986–1988), Richard J. Betts (1988–1990), and Elisabeth Blair MacDougall (1990–1993), with subsequent development under those of Franklin Toker (1993–1994), Keith N. Morgan (1994–1996), and Patricia Waddy (1996–). Five successive executive directors of the SAH, Rosann Berry, Paulette Olsen Jorgensen, David Bahlman, Susan

McCarter, and Pauline Saliga, were enormously helpful. A series editorial board, including representatives from the American Institute of Architects, the Historic American Buildings Survey, and the Library of Congress, was established. Buildings of the United States is now part of the official mission of the Society of Architectural Historians, incorporated into its bylaws.

In the development of this project, we have incurred a number of obligations. We are deeply indebted, both for financial support and for confidence in our efforts, to the National Endowment for the Humanities, the Pew Charitable Trusts, the Graham Foundation for Advanced Studies in the Fine Arts, and, for this volume, the following generous donors: the Bonfils-Stanton Foundation, the Gates Foundation, the Dobbins Foundation, the Colorado Historical Foundation, the University of Colorado at Denver, the University of Missouri, the University of Delaware, and many members of the SAH. In our fundraising efforts we have benefited enormously from the services of our wonderful director of development, Anita Nowery Durel.

We would also like to express our gratitude to several groups of individuals. First are the current members of our editorial board, listed earlier in this volume, and the following former members: David Gebhard, Sally Kress Tompkins, Alex Cochran, Catherine Bishir, S. Allen Chambers, Jr., John Freeman, Alan Gowans, Alison K. Hoagland, Robert Kapsch, Tom Martinson, and Robert J. Winter. Next are our present and former project and research assistants: Sarah Quail, James Hargrove, Preston Thayer, Marc Vincent, and Robert J. Wojtowicz in the SAH office; Carol Grove at the University of Missouri; and Jhennifer Amundson, Anna Andrzewjewski, Louis Nelson, and Nancy Holst at the University of Delaware. In this regard, we are also very grateful to Dean Larry Clark of the University of Missouri and Dean Mary Richards of the College of Arts and Science at the University of Delaware.

We have tried to establish as far as possible a consistent terminology of architectural history, and the name of J. A. Chewning, mastermind of the series glossary included in every volume, must be gratefully mentioned here. The *Art and Architecture Thesaurus,* a comprehensive publication and database compiled by The Getty Art History Information Program and published by Oxford University Press, has also become an invaluable resource.

Editorial work for this volume was overseen by the series managing editor, Cynthia Ware, with assistance from Janet Rumbarger. The index was compiled by Lynn Stevenson. The maps for this as for earlier volumes were prepared by the computer cartographers at the Geographic Resources Center in the Department of Geography at the University of Missouri–Columbia, thanks to the effort and ability of Christopher Salter, director of GRC; Timothy Haithcoat, program director; Karen Stange Westin and Adrianne Nold, project coordinators; and Norman Bowman, Lisa Cogar, Missey Freese, Steve Marsh, and Joe Walter. Finally, there are our loyal colleagues in this enterprise at Oxford University Press in New York, especially Ed Barry, Claude Conyers,

Karen Casey, Stephen Chasteen, Marion Osmun, and Leslie Phillips.

These volumes deal with more than the highlights and the high points. They deal with the very fabric of American architecture, with the context in time and in place of each specific building, with the entirety of urban and rural America, with the whole architectural patrimony. This fabric of course includes modern architecture, as, on the other end of the scale, it includes pre-Columbian and Native American remains. But it must be said, regretfully, that the series cannot cover every building of merit; practical considerations have dictated some difficult choices in the buildings that are represented in this as in other volumes. There are, unavoidably, omissions from the abundance of structures built across the land, the thousands of modest but lovely edifices, often rising out of a sea of ugliness, or the vernacular attempts that merit a second look but which by their very multitude cannot be included in even the thickest volume.

Thus it must be stated in the strongest possible terms that omission of a building from this or any volume of the series does not constitute an invitation to the bulldozers and the wrecking ball. In every community there will be structures not included in Buildings of the United States that are clearly deserving of being preserved. Indeed, it is hoped that the publication of this series will help to stop at least the worst destruction of architecture across the land by fostering a deeper appreciation of its beauty and richness and of its historic and associative importance.

The volumes of Buildings of the United States are meant to be tools of serious research in the study of American architecture. They are also intended as guidebooks and are designed to facilitate such use; they can and should be used on the spot, indeed, should lead the user to the spot. It is our earnest hope that they will be not only on the shelves of every major library under "U.S.," but also be in many a glove compartment and perhaps even in many a backpack.

Osmund Overby   Adolf K. Placzek
Damie Stillman   William H. Pierson, Jr.

Acknowledgments

Rarely does an author owe so much to so many. Adolf Placzek originally encouraged me to undertake what has been a decade-long project. Osmund Overby, past editor in chief of Buildings of the United States, spent weeks of his time traveling through Colorado with me, poring over maps, scrutinizing structures, and making most helpful organizational suggestions. Kathryn Bishop Eckert, Damie Stillman, Osmund Overby, and David Gebhard graciously reviewed and improved all or parts of this manuscript.

For financial support I am indebted to the Society of Architectural Historians and the organizations whose contributions are acknowledged in the front of this volume. Thanks also to Fernie Baca, Vice Chancellor for Research, and Georgia Lesh-Laurie, Chancellor, University of Colorado at Denver, for a sustained commitment to rewarding student researchers.

Cynthia Ware, editor extraordinaire, greatly improved this work. William P. Bessessen served as a stalwart researcher and fact checker. Colorado architects Edward D. White, Jr., Gary Long and Kathy Hoeft, Victor Hornbein, Rodney S. Davis, Kenneth R. Fuller, G. Cabell Childress, Eugene Sternberg, and others reviewed parts of the manuscript and allowed me to pick their brains and ransack their files. Historians Steve Leonard and Duane A. Smith reviewed and greatly improved this book. Jack Murphy, curator of geology at the Denver Museum of Natural History, generously shared his extensive research on Colorado building stones. Cartographers at the Geographic Resources Center at the University of Missouri–Columbia helped verify site locations.

Many students at the University of Colorado at Denver have worked on various counties over the years, most notably Susan Appleby, Hugh Bingham, Kathleen Chamberlain, Julie Corona, Vanita G. Cosper, Don Ebner, Sharon Elfenbein, Rosemary Fetter, Richard Gardner, Linda Gensmer, Marcia Goldstein, Eric Hammersmark, Rebecca Hunt, Carolyn Keller, Kate Kienast, Myra Kloppel, Marsha Shore Lilli, James McNally, Eric Mogren, Judy Morley, Sharon Newman, Cathleen Norman, Bob Olson, Kevin Rucker, Susan Sanderson, Terrence Shockey, Mary Ellen Silcott, Linda Storey, Marcia Tate, Gerald R. TeBockhorst, Brent Temmer, Jeff Veen, Jeanette F. Walker, Lysa Wegman-French, Chris Whitacre, Nancy Widmann, and Chuck Woodard.

Eleanor M. Gehres and her staff at the Denver Public Library's Western History Department were angels, especially Don Dilley, Bruce Hanson, Augie Mastrogiuseppe, Phil Panum, Kathey Swan, and Kay Wishnia. At the Colorado History Museum Library, photo curator Eric Paddock, manuscripts curator Stan Oliner and Pat Fraker, Rebecca Lintz, and Margaret Walsh were godsends. So was Dick Conn of the Denver Art Museum.

In every county I tried to consult with local architects, historians, and building buffs. This has left me heavily indebted to Bob Griswold, Josie Lobato, Angie Ortiz, Virginia Simmons, Maria Valdez, and the Reverend Pat Valdez for interviews, tours, and manuscript reviews for the San Luis Valley; Rebecca Waugh for Summit and other mountain counties; Rebecca Hunt and Ginny and Larry Steele (Adams); Carolyn Keller and Nan Rickey (Arapahoe); Lois Anderton, Joan Draper, Jeff Limerick, and Jim Noel (Boulder); June Shaputis and Ed Quillen (Chaffee); Tom and Laurie Simmons (Chaffee and Custer); Christine Bradley and Ron Neeley (Clear Creek); Gordon Hodgin and Abbott Fay (Delta); Suzie Appleby (Douglas); Sharon Elfenbein (Eagle and Pitkin); Joseph Martell and Brent Temmer (Elbert); Ed and Nancy Bathke and Mary Davis (El Paso); Cara D. Fisher (Fremont); Lew Cady, Julie Corona, and Chocolate Dan Monroe (Gilpin); Patience Cairns Kemp (Grand); Don Ebner, Rich Gardner, Marcetta Lutz, Francis B. Rizzari, and Dick Ronzio (Jefferson); Nancy Manly and Judge Neil Reynolds (Lake); Duane A. Smith (La Plata and other mining counties); Liston Leyendecker, Eric Mogren, Wayne Sundberg, and Carol Tunner (Larimer); Roberta Cordova (Las Animas), Lyn Deal (Morgan); Emogene and Richard Edwards and Judy Prosser (Mesa); Florence Lister and Jack Smith (Montezuma), Patrik Davis and Kit Moore (Montrose); Doris Gregory, Roger Henn, and Barbara Muntyan (Ouray); Amy Amidon and Roxanne Eflin (Pitkin); Joanne Dodds (Pueblo); Robert C. McHugh, Robert S. Ralston and Joseph Patrick Robbins (Routt); Judge Allen Nossaman (San Juan); Leland Feitz, Bob Lays, Brian Levine, and Wayne, Dorothy and Steven Mackin (Teller); and John Dietz, Robert W. Larson, and Peggy Ford (Weld).

Barbara Norgren and subsequently Dale Heckendorn, keepers of Colorado's National Register, and the State Historic Preservation Office staff have long indulged me and my students. Thanks also to Harold Baer, Don Etter, Roger A. Chandler, Andy Dutton, Dennis Gallagher, Ken Gaunt, Elizabeth Wright Ingraham, Ellen Ittelson, Carol Herselle Krinsky, Jay Mead, Lee Whitely, Rodd Wheaton, Barbara Zimmerman, Dennis Gallagher, the Barrett family (Paul, Janet, Susan, Laura, and Molly), and the Semple family (Janet, Noel, Abigail, and Wynton).

Last and most important of those who enabled me to research and write is my wife, Sumiko.

Thomas J. Noel

Contents

List of Maps

Guide for Users of This Volume

Buildings of Colorado is arranged geographically in four regional sections that cover Colorado's major river valleys: the South Platte, the Arkansas, the Rio Grande, and the Colorado. Each of these regions is subdivided by county and then by town; county tours generally start with the county seat. Larger cities are arranged by neighborhoods. Detailed maps of each region and of many cities, keyed to entries by site numbers, are included. The state maps provided free of charge by the Colorado Department of Transportation are also most useful.

Except for Denver, which is both city and county, cities and towns are treated as subsections within each county. Each community is given a brief descriptive introduction followed by numbered site entries. Ghost towns are treated as numbered sites. The date of founding for a community used here is generally the date the post office opened. Likewise, the closing of the post office is the most reliable single indication of when a town became a ghost. (Ghost towns, of course, are sometimes reoccupied.) In addition to providing historical background, introductions to communities often mention local history museums, hospitable landmarks, and public places with vehicle parking. Because elevation varies dramatically in Colorado and greatly affects both the settings and the buildings themselves, altitude is also noted. Especially at higher elevations, extreme weather, be it snow, hail, or hot sunshine, can visit at unexpected times. Be prepared.

Within each community, sites are in walking or driving tour order. Each entry begins with a two-letter abbreviation of the county name and the number of the site within the sequence for the county. This site number is followed by the current name of the building, with earlier historic names, if any, in parentheses. Next is the date the building was completed, although dates of design, issue of permits, groundbreaking, cornerstone laying, completion, and occupation may in fact stretch over years. The name or names of the architect(s), firm, or builder follow the completion date. Generally buildings are attributed to the architect of record or to the principal of the firm. If it could be determined that the actual designer was a firm member other than these, that person is also listed. This information is followed by the date or dates of major additions or alterations and the names of their architects.

The notation "NR" following the address of the site indicates a listing on the National Register of Historic Places as of 1996. "NRD" denotes a National Register District. NHL (National Historic Landmark) is a rare designation reserved for the most significant sites. For NR or NHL properties, much more information is available from the National and State Register Coordinator, Colorado History Museum, 1300 Broadway, Denver, Colorado, 80202.

Buildings of the United States volumes are intended to include only extant buildings. Some of the structures described here, however, will unfortunately have been demolished or altered beyond recognition by the time this book is in the hands of readers. Changes, errors, and incomplete data, alas, haunt a guide such as this. The author would appreciate hearing about demolitions, alterations, and any other corrections or suggestions. Comments should be sent to Professor Thomas J. Noel, Department of History, University of Colorado at Denver, Campus Box 182, P.O. Box 173364, Denver, Colorado, 80217–3364.

Almost all of the sites are visible from public thoroughfares, and the focus is on public buildings where readers often are welcome inside. We know that readers will respect the property rights and privacy of others as they view the buildings.

Compiling a guidebook such as this requires pruning out many important buildings and keeping descriptions to a modest length. The goal of *Buildings of Colorado* is to introduce readers to a wide variety of representative sites, which may then be explored in much greater detail than is possible here. Happy trails!

BUILDINGS OF COLORADO

Colorado Buildings:
An Introduction

COLORADO'S LANDSCAPE DWARFS ITS ARCHITECTURE. THE eastern high plains, massive central mountains, and western canyons are dramatic settings for buildings. Even the metropolitan strip along the eastern base of the Rockies, where three-fourths of all 4.2 million Coloradans reside, is overshadowed by lofty peaks on the western horizon and fringed on the east by an immense, lonely prairie.

Colorado's 104,247 square miles make it the nation's eighth largest state. If only it could be ironed out flat, Coloradans quip, it would be bigger than Texas. Coloradans are used to a lot of elbow room in their homes, their work places, and their play places. A third of the state is federal land, much of it recreational. This spaciousness is reflected in the architecture: detached single-family housing predominates even in the poorest urban neighborhoods. Outside the cities, residential subdivisions, shopping centers, and office parks sprawl as if there were no end to the land.

Coloradans have rarely recognized natural obstacles to development. They have built in the most hostile environments, where gold, silver, or other natural resources lie. Little of the landscape remains virginal. Roads scale remote and rugged mountains and penetrate isolated prairie and canyon lands. Landscapes are branded not only by roads, but also by railroads, irrigation ditches, power lines, and barbed wire.

With an average elevation of 6,800 feet, Colorado is the highest state. Its backbone, the Rocky Mountains, soars two miles high, with fifty-three peaks over 14,000 feet. The elevation contributes to a climate of extremes—heat waves and sudden cold snaps, high winds and heavy snow loads—which challenge architects. Colorado homes generally have basements which provide both winter warmth and summer coolness. Building codes specify foundations

3

at least three feet deep to reach below the frost line. Architects are also challenged by soils, which range from sandy, melting types to expanding bentonite clay that can wreck foundations.

Dryness—the average annual precipitation is only about seventeen inches—has also influenced Colorado buildings. Much of the state is treeless, and even mountain forests do not produce high-grade hardwoods. So Coloradans have often built with sod, adobe, clay brick, and native stone: granite, limestone, marble, rhyolite, and sandstone. Colorado's expansive, high, dry, sunny environment warrants a special architecture, but Coloradans generally have borrowed styles from elsewhere that are no match for the climate or the setting. This architecture, like settlement generally, is concentrated in the four major river valleys—the South Platte, the Arkansas, the Rio Grande, and the Colorado.

Native Americans

The first builders in the river valleys were Native Americans who used the materials, contours, and colors of the earth. Exactly who these people were, and when and where they first constructed shelters in Colorado, will never be known. Archaeologists are continually finding new pieces in jigsaw-puzzle portraits of prehistoric Coloradans that will never be completed.

The Clovis culture (c. 10,500–9000 B.C.) came to light after spear points were found amid mammoth skeletons at Dent, near Greeley. During the 1930s Regis College Professor Conrad Bilgery, S.J., led a team that first excavated and reported Dent's Clovis spear points, named for similar points found in Clovis, New Mexico. Archaeologists are still debating the details and significance of the scrapers, blades, hammer stones, flake knives, choppers, and bone tools also found at Dent. Alluvial activity has greatly disturbed the site, erasing evidence of whatever shelters these prehistoric peoples may have erected.

The Folsom culture (c. 9000–c. 8000 B.C.) created the distinctive fluted spear points first found south of the Colorado border in Folsom, New Mexico. The Lindenmeier Ranch site, Colorado's most important Folsom find, was a camp and *Bison antiquus* kill site unearthed in 1924. At the Zapata Ranch, just south of the Great Sand Dunes National Monument, archaeologist Dennis Stanford is trying to reconstruct the configuration of a large Folsom community.

The Plano culture (c. 8000–c. 5000 B.C.), named for discoveries on the plains of Texas, is evident in Colorado kill sites. At the ranch of Robert Jones, Jr., near Wray, archaeologists have found a wooden pole, possibly a religious structure similar to the medicine poles erected by historic Native American

Fremont People (A.D. 400–1200) painted these Carrot Man pictographs near Rangely in northwestern Colorado.

buffalo hunters. At various Colorado Plano sites, organized groups trapped and slaughtered entire herds, returning perennially to the same butchering and meat processing stations. Noted Colorado archaeologists such as Joe Ben Wheat and Marie Wormington have identified butchering stations separated from the kill sites. At the Jurgens camp, archaeologists also found tools for grinding seeds and nicotine-coated pipes. Early Native Americans were beginning to feel at home in Colorado, beginning to build long-term shelters.

Prehistoric camps were not confined to the plains. At Caribou Lake, located at 11,000 feet near the Continental Divide, diggers found charcoal, projectile points, waste flakes, and a large knife. The location near Arapaho Pass suggests that Plano people moved from the plains across the high Rockies to upland valleys on their hunting and gathering expeditions.

Between roughly 6000 B.C. and A.D. 1, archaic Native Americans built shelters scattered across the state. During construction of the Colorado–Big Thompson water diversion system, reservoir and pipeline teams unearthed at least forty-two archaic sites in the sagebrush of Middle Park. Traces of firepits, charred rabbit bones, upright ponderosa logs, pine boughs, stone tools, and a jasper quarry led archaeologists to speculate that these people were more permanently settled than earlier hunter-gatherers. Archaeologists further suggested that these archaic Indians lived in wattle-and-daub jacals, constructed of upright pine posts interwoven with branches and plastered over with wet clay.

The Fremont people (c. A.D. 400–1200), named for sites discovered along Utah's Fremont River, left notable art and architecture in the northwestern corner of Colorado. They dug pit houses and constructed masonry homes, granaries, and fortifications. Fremont people fashioned distinctive gray pottery and some of Colorado's most celebrated rock art, which is best seen at Cañon Pintado, now a well-marked site on Colorado 139 about 12 miles south of Rangely.

While archaeologists focus on what they find at Colorado's many prehistoric sites, architectural historians may be interested in the intricate earth excavations done by the archaeologists themselves. At a few places such as the commercial Crow Canyon dig near Dolores, any and all are welcome—for a fee—to observe or to participate in excavations. These excavations are themselves earth sculptures, works of art routinely covered over and hidden.

Henry David Thoreau wrote, "Who does not remember the interest with which when young we looked at shelving rocks, or any approach to a cave. . . . The savage owns his shelter because it costs so little, while in modern civilized society not more than one half the families own a shelter." Unfortunately, no examples of Colorado's oldest extant architecture—Native American rock shelters—have been converted to house museums, but rock shelters were the ancestors of pit houses and elaborate cliff dwellings and pueblo villages. The greatest extant Native American architectural achievements in the United States are the cliff dwellings at Mesa Verde National Park in the southwestern corner of Colorado, the first park devoted to preserving the architectural ruins of a prehistoric people, the Anasazi (Navajo for "ancient ones" or "ancient enemies"). Mesa Verde was also the first World Heritage Site in the United States, so designated in 1978 by the United Nations Educational, Scientific and Cultural Organization.

Between A.D. 1 and 1300, the Anasazi built mud and masonry habitations, first on mesa tops, then in recesses eroded into canyon walls. The cliff villages of Mesa Verde are the best known of many such dwellings scattered throughout Colorado, New Mexico, Arizona, and Utah. These settlements sometimes sheltered several hundred people in structures as high as four stories. The cultural and architectural achievements of the Mesa Verde builders have been compared by architectural historian Vincent J. Scully and others with those of medieval European city builders of the twelfth and thirteenth centuries. The novelist Willa Cather likened Mesa Verde's black-on-white pottery to that of ancient Greece. Although thousands of scholarly reports have surveyed the cliff dwellings, no one has captured their magic as vividly as Cather, in her novel *The Professor's House* (1925):

> Far up above me, a thousand feet or so, set in a great cavern in the face of the cliff, I saw a little city of stone, asleep. It was as still as sculpture— and something like that. It all hung together, seemed to have a kind of composition: pale little houses of stone nestling close to one another, perched on top of each other, with flat roofs, narrow windows, straight walls, and in the middle of the group, a round tower. It was beautifully proportioned, that tower, swelling out to a large girth a little above the

Cliff Palace is the largest of the stone cities preserved in Mesa Verde National Park.

> base, then growing slender again. There was something symmetrical and
> powerful about the swell of the masonry. The tower was the fine thing that
> held all the jumble of houses together and made them mean something.

The Anasazi were cultivators of corn and other crops as well as hunters and gatherers of food. Their remarkably stable and long-lived culture rested on their building abilities. Faced with a dry climate, the Anasazi developed dams and ditches, clay vessels, and stone cisterns. Despite their water-conscious building and culture, the drought of 1275–1300 probably forced them to evacuate their cliff cities. They moved to, among other places, the Rio Grande Valley to build the pueblos still occupied by their descendants.

While the Anasazi culture is enshrined at Mesa Verde, prehistoric Plains Indians left less to inspect. Known sites include caves, rock shelters, pit houses, and earth lodges. Burial sites, sometimes containing multiple corpses and grave offerings, have been discovered in various places, including Denver's suburban subdivisions. Historic Plains Indians, such as the Arapaho and Cheyenne, often used a portable architecture of buffalo hides and pine poles. Only a few tipi rings—either functional or ceremonial—survive as stone circles near Cowdrey in Jackson County, Keota in Weld County, and Virginia Dale in Larimer County. The Utes or their predecessors constructed rectangles, circles, or semicircles made of a course or two of stone that may have been vision quest sites. Circular stone bunkers found in high places were built so Native Americans could crouch under brush and bait to catch eagles for their much-prized feathers.

Historical accounts of Native Americans were first recorded in the 1600s with the Spanish explorations of present-day Colorado. The Spanish reported settlements such as El Quartelejo along the Arkansas River, where Plains Apaches lived in villages and cultivated corn, squash, beans, melons, and sunflowers. The Apaches constructed lodges by making round and rectangular earth pits with posts holding up roofs of brush and mud. During the 1700s the Apache, along with the Comanche, began moving south out of Colorado as Cheyenne and Arapaho pushed in from the east. The Arapaho and Cheyenne occupied eastern Colorado from around 1800 until the 1860s, when they were forced onto reservations in Montana, Oklahoma, and Wyoming.

Since the 1880s only two tribes have had Colorado reservations: the Ute Mountain Utes and the Southern Utes. The Utes, who have inhabited the state for hundreds, perhaps thousands, of years, adapted to the extremes of Colorado climate by developing leather clothing and by using seasonal shelter: tipis for winter and open wood and brush wickiups for summer. Today the Ute Mountain Ute and the Southern Ute reservations, in the southwestern corner of Colorado, are the only refuges left for Native Americans in a state which once hosted not only the Apache, Arapaho, Cheyenne, and Comanche, but also the Kiowa, Pawnee, Shoshone, and other tribes.

Ute wickiup, photographed by John K. Hillers, with the John Wesley
Powell expedition, in 1873

Hispanic Roots

Hispanics, as the *mestizo* peoples carrying both Spanish and Native American
blood often call themselves, were the first Euro-Americans to erect structures
in a state they christened. They named it for the muddy red color of its major
river, the Colorado (Spanish for red, ruddy, or embarrassed). Spanish missionaries, soldiers, and adventurers explored parts of southern Colorado during
the Spanish Colonial period, beginning with Don Juan de Oñate's 1598 settlement of the lower Rio Grande River valley. Two Franciscan friars, Fray Silvestre Vélez de Escalante and Fray Francisco Atanasio Domínguez, made the
most important expedition in 1776. They mapped Colorado for the first time,

and Fray Escalante provided a full report, mentioning Anasazi ruins and the "tents," "huts," and "tiny dwellings" of the Utes.

Discouraged by the dry plains and canyon lands and forbidding mountains, the Spanish did not attempt to colonize the lands that now make up Colorado. Only after the Mexican Revolution of 1821 did Hispanic pioneers settle the San Luis Valley, along the upper Rio Grande. To encourage agricultural settlement, the Mexican government made five large land grants in or near the San Luis Valley. Small adobe plaza towns were established, first along the Culebra River, where San Luis (1851) claims to be the state's oldest permanent town.

The Treaty of Guadalupe Hidalgo (1848), which ended the Mexican-American War, promised U.S. citizenship and property rights to Mexican Americans. In spite of the treaty, much of their property passed into the hands of Anglo settlers. Frequently Anglo town founders ignored previously existing Hispanic communities. Denver, for instance, dates its origins to an 1858 gold strike by U.S. citizens rather than to an 1857 claim known as Mexican Diggings. Yankees did not think much of the indigenous Mexican communities. Francis Parkman, for example, derided Mexican "mud" buildings in his classic, *The Oregon Trail* (1849). Discussing El Pueblo, the 1840s nucleus of the modern city of Pueblo, Parkman, a proper Bostonian, called it "a wretched species of fort, of most primitive construction, being nothing more than a large square enclosure, surrounded by a wall of mud, miserably cracked and dilapidated. . . ."

Other Yankees expressed similar contempt for Hispanic architecture. Delta, a town in west central Colorado, built its first schoolhouse out of adobe, but the pioneers dipped each brick into red paint to make it look like a Yankee brick. Denver passed ordinances requiring that bricks be kiln-fired and measure no more than $8\frac{1}{4}$ by $4\frac{1}{16}$ by $2\frac{1}{4}$ inches. Such laws discouraged the use of traditional sun-dried adobe bricks, which measure roughly 12 by 3 by 6 inches. Such discrimination, intentional or not, discouraged Hispanic building traditions.

A few U.S. citizens had a higher opinion of adobe. Charles and William Bent, two St. Louis traders operating on the Santa Fe Trail, admired structures in New Mexico and used adobe to construct Bent's Old Fort on the Arkansas River in southeastern Colorado. This prairie castle measured 142 by 122 feet and had adobe walls 2 feet thick and 15 feet high. As the regional trade center of the 1830s and 1840s for French, Indian, Mexican, and U.S. trappers and traders, Bent's Old Fort became a model for later structures, ranging from forts on the South Platte to The Fort, a 1960s adobe restaurant in Morrison. The National Park Service reconstructed Bent's Old Fort in 1976 and, like the Bents, used adobe and skilled Hispanic laborers.

Adobe buildings were traditionally organized around plazas, none of which survive intact in southern Colorado. Rail and auto age developments have left

Town plaza of Garcia in the Rio Grande Valley, photographed by Russell Lee for the Farm Security Administration, 1940

only adobe remnants, subjected in many cases to later alterations, ranging from gable roofs to solar panels. Many adobe walls now wear new skins of concrete, stucco, tarpaper, wood, or metal siding.

After 1900 the architecture of Native Americans and Hispanics gained greater respectability. Pueblo and Mission revival, Spanish Colonial, and Territorial styles became the choice for some of the state's finest residential neighborhoods, such as the Broadmoor area in Colorado Springs and Denver's Country Club area. Indigenous southwestern architecture inspired I. M. Pei's National Center for Atmospheric Research (1966) in Boulder. It is clad in bush-hammered exposed aggregate of concrete mixed with the local reddish soil and stone to capture natural colors and textures in modern-day "mud."

Mining-Era Architecture

A different architectural tradition arrived in Colorado beginning with the 1858–1859 gold rush. Although it is stereotyped as Anglo immigration because English-speaking, U.S.-born immigrants predominated, the westward movement was multicultural. In Colorado, German-speaking peoples were the most prevalent nineteenth-century foreign-born group, intermingled with Canadians, English, French, Irish, Scandinavians, Scots, Welsh, Chinese, and others. A few African Americans arrived with the fur trade, cattle drives, and mineral rushes, but many more came with the railroads after 1870. After 1890 southern and eastern Europeans, especially Greeks, Italians, Jews, and Slavs, became more numerous, while Mexicans comprised the largest single immigrant stream by the 1930s.

As this 1879 view of Leadville suggests, many mining towns sprang up without benefit of planning.

Most fortune seekers rushing into Colorado after the 1858–1859 gold strikes built as quickly and cheaply as possible. They used canvas, dirt, and logs from cottonwoods, the only common native tree on Colorado's eastern plains. Under broad-leaved cottonwoods, argonauts (named for Jason and the other sailors of the Argo, who sought the Golden Fleece in Greek mythology) camped, socialized, and slept. To build houses, the pioneers used cottonwood logs for walls and draped cottonwood ridgepoles with split saplings. They piled on sod to complete the roof. When rain or snow fell, muddy water might drip for days indoors, and roofs bloomed with wildflowers.

Saloons epitomized frontier-era structures. As the first and most common public buildings on the Euro-American frontier, they often housed pioneer local governments. Saloons also doubled as theaters, art galleries, and dance halls and even housed church services. Some barkeepers graduated to spiffier structures boasting the finest fixtures in towns—classical mirrored-back bars, plate glass windows, and corbeled brick fronts. This saloon hall legacy was largely erased by the Prohibition era and the tendency of preservationists to save more "respectable" buildings.

Stagecoach stops, another common pioneer building type, have fared better. Many communities have preserved their hewn log stage stops. Denver's Four Mile House and Grand County's Cozens House are particularly well-

Western Mining Corporation, Centennial Mine, Georgetown, by Muriel Sibell Wolle (crayon and watercolor, 12 by 15½ inches) depicts one of many now-vanished mining structures captured in this prolific artist's work between the 1920s and her death in 1977.

preserved museum specimens. These and other surviving stage houses typify the tendency of later residents to dress up log buildings with clapboard siding and Carpenter's Gothic trim.

Log and frame construction dominated early mountain mining towns. Ernest Ingersoll, an eastern journalist who enlisted with the U.S. Geological Survey party mapping Colorado in 1874, wrote in his 1882 bestseller, *Knocking around the Rockies:*

> The miners hastily throw up little log cabins, six or eight logs high, covered with a roof of poles and dirt, and having nothing better than the hard-tramped earth for a floor. In one end is the fireplace (the chimney is outside, like that of a negro's hut in the South), and at the other end are rough bunks, where the owner stuffs in some long grass or spruce boughs or straw, and spreads his bed or blankets. These rude little cabins are packed close together up and down the sides of the gulch, so as to be as near as possible to, and yet out of the way of, the mining. . . . I have known of such a gulch-mining settlement [Leadville] in a single year converting an utter wilderness in the mountains, long miles away from anywhere, into a city of ten thousand, or more.

Miners transformed the landscape radically. Isabella L. Bird, an English world traveler, painted a dark but accurate picture in *A Lady's Life in the Rocky Mountains* (1879):

> Mining destroys and devastates, turning the earth inside out, making it hideous and blighting every green thing, as it usually blights man's heart and soul. There was mining everywhere . . . with all its destruction and devastation, its digging, burrowing, gulching and sluicing; and up all along

the seemingly inaccessible heights were holes with their roofs log supported, in which solitary and patient men were selling their lives for treasure.

The Federal Mining Law of 1872, which is still in effect, regards mining as
the highest and best use of public lands. If miners make certain minimal
improvements they may "patent" (i.e., purchase) their claims. Mining claims,
given grandfather protection even within wilderness areas, pay no royalty for
their use of public lands. Giving miners a free hand has left Colorado with
some unnatural wonders, such as collapsed Bartlett Mountain, with its innards
oozing down Fremont Pass. Its miles of molybdenum mill waste and settling
ponds for the Climax Molybdenum Mine, the largest and richest in Colorado,
have buried the mining towns of Robinson and Kokomo.

Mining towns usually sprang up along creeks where someone found placer
gold. Placer (surface) claims often fronted on the creek and stretched uphill
in rectangles, establishing an unplanned pattern followed by mines and mills,
then residences and businesses. In mining towns—and mining supply towns
such as Denver—local governments struggled to stop private citizens from
erecting structures in public thoroughfares. One of the first ordinances
passed by "The Peoples Government of Denver" in 1861 outlawed "the occu-
pancy of any of the streets, levees or alleys set apart for the use of the public,
and also the erection of buildings in the center of Cherry Creek. . . . Such
possession by individuals of public property is an infringement upon the
rights of the community. . . ." This granddaddy of all Denver ordinances was
the first of many laws passed to address an ongoing struggle between public
and private interests over the location, size, and use of buildings.

Miners founded many Colorado towns and extracted billions in gold, silver,
coal, oil, zinc, lead, molybdenum, and other minerals. If gold and silver mining camps prospered, they generally evolved from log and frame to brick
and stone. Masonry construction was required in commercial cores after fires
destroyed many first-generation wooden buildings. Despite the fortunes taken
out of these towns, most of them are gone today. They were "git-and-git-out"
towns, places to try to make a fortune and then push on. Some towns were
torn done for scrap or to avoid taxes on abandoned buildings. Only traces of
streets and foundations remain amid the scars of deforestation, mine tailings,
and hazardous wastes. Other towns have been victims of weather, fire, or van-
dalism. Ghost town prowling has become a favorite hobby of Coloradans, and
to avoid disappointing tourists, the U.S. Forest Service has stabilized several
ghost towns such as Ashcroft and Independence in Pitkin County. Unfortunately, the Forest Service has also burned down towns to discourage squatters
on public lands.

In some "ghost towns," mining camp structures have been converted to
vacation homes. Such frame dwellings helped inspire a contemporary style

The ghost town of Eureka was captured by Marion Post Wolcott, photographer for the Farm Security Administration, in 1941. The then dying town has vanished, leaving only a few remains, most notably the concrete foundations of the Sunnyside Mill (see Eureka in San Juan County).

that architectural historian David Gebhard named "Mineshaft Modern." Asymmetrical compositions, frequently executed in raw wood with shed roofs; strong, spare lines; and diagonal and vertical patterns characterize this style. Mineshaft Modern log homes likewise are variations on the log tradition introduced by miners.

The Rush to Respectability

During its Native American and Hispanic eras, Colorado remained sparsely populated. The gold and silver rushes after 1858 brought tremendous growth as some 100,000 fortune seekers arrived in Colorado within a few years. A majority became disappointed "go-backs," but enough stayed to justify establishment of Colorado Territory in 1861. After the railroads arrived in 1870 Colorado boomed, becoming the thirty-eighth state in 1876. The population jumped from 34,277 in 1860 to 412,198 in 1890.

Frank E. Edbrooke, Colorado's leading nineteenth-century architect, was caricatured in *The Rocky Mountain News*, 1909, by Frank "Doc Bird" Finch.

Frank E. and Willoughby J. Edbrooke designed Denver's grandest lost landmark, the Tabor Grand Opera House, at 16th and Curtis streets.

During the flush times between 1870 and the silver crash of 1893, a fourth architectural period emerged—the rush to respectability. Coloradans exported pay dirt and imported architects, hoping to catch up with the eastern United States and Europe in matters of taste and refinement. Mining millionaires demanded elegant mansions in fashionable neighborhoods. They frequently left the crude mining towns where they made their fortunes for cities such as Denver and Colorado Springs. There, the mining kings and queens sought architectural refinements to help distinguish themselves from run-of-the-mill miners.

Vernacular mining-era structures gave way in the 1870s to Italianate and other Victorian-era styles. Frame false fronts evolved into elaborate brick facades and metal cornices. Coloradans built modish mansions and commercial blocks, lavishing money on fine masonry, fancy woodwork, and cast iron facades. The Denver Mansions Company, organized by English and Scottish investors in 1878, undertook to satisfy the need for fine homes and commercial structures in Colorado's Queen City. It constructed Denver's first fine hotel, the Windsor, and a pretentious adjacent office block, the Barclay.

Leadville's silver king, Horace A. W. Tabor, exemplified Colorado's rush to respectability. He gave that silver city its Tabor Opera House and Vendome Hotel, then moved to Denver after his 1879 election as lieutenant governor. As Tabor recalled later, "Denver was not building good buildings and I thought I would do something toward setting them a good example." Tabor went to Chicago to interview prospective architects and selected Willoughby J. Edbrooke. Although Tabor initially balked at Edbrooke's $4,500 fee, Willoughby and his brother Frank came to Denver from Chicago in 1879 to design the Tabor Grand Opera House and the Tabor Block. Willoughby soon moved on to design buildings at the University of Notre Dame, the U.S. Government Building for the World's Columbian Exposition, and the Old Post Office in Washington, D.C. Frank stayed to become Colorado's premier nineteenth-century architect. He brought mainstream design influenced by the work of H. H. Richardson and technical achievements such as the steel skeleton skyscraper.

Edbrooke and other architects arriving during the flush 1880s designed fine residences for the moneyed class, who favored Victorian styles and tried to outdo their neighbors by piling on more ornament. The rush to respectability gave Colorado elaborate structures of locally manufactured bricks and locally quarried stone, which made imported, eclectic building designs seem more at home.

Schools, Churches, and Hotels

Schoolhouses were often the first attempt at community cooperation and respectability. Their construction required collective effort, public expenditure, and a consensus on the geographical boundaries of a school district, as Andrew Gulliford points out in *America's Country Schoolhouses* (1990). Schoolhouses also served as lessons in good design, beginning with frame one-room buildings with classical detailing and symmetry. If hamlets prospered, one-room schools evolved into multistory masonry showpieces. During the 1930s

New Deal building programs constructed "PWA Moderne" schools in innumerable communities. When Colorado began consolidating schools in the 1950s, many smaller ones closed. Some were recycled for other community uses, such as museums or community centers.

Churches, the most visible sign of civility in raw western communities, commonly started by holding services in taverns and other public halls, then struggled to build their own small houses of worship. Communities and congregations that prospered erected the stylish, architect-designed masonry churches that still anchor most towns.

Catholic churches, characteristically with crosses atop steeples, spires, and gable ends, tended to Romanesque, Lombard, and Gothic Revival styles. Even adobe churches in southern Colorado generally incorporated, or later added, Romanesque or Gothic elements. The church often became the hub of a parish complex composed of a rectory, a school, a convent, and, in a dozen Colorado towns, a hospital. The bishop in Denver nominally controlled the building and design of Catholic churches, but not until the arrival of Bishop Urban J. Vehr in the 1940s were tight architectural guidelines imposed. Vehr retained one of Colorado's most polished architects, Jules Jacques Benois (Jacques) Benedict, to design brick or stone structures which borrowed, in the Beaux-Arts manner, from the great church styles of Italy, France, and Germany.

Episcopalians commissioned prominent architects to build exquisite, often understated, traditional chapels for their congregations. Sometimes Episcopal parishes hired nationally noted architects, such as Ralph Adams Cram, who designed St. Andrew's Episcopal Church in Denver. Baptists, following national church board recommendations, favored Georgian Revival churches. A church architectural team in Salt Lake City designed for the Church of Jesus Christ of Latter-Day Saints crisp, light-colored structures in a version of Moderne that resembled streamlined Colonial or Georgian Revival styles. Methodists and Presbyterians had more local autonomy and used a wide range of styles, often in vernacular versions.

Churches tended to be traditional, to be "churchy." This stylistic predilection was understandable during the nineteenth century, when churches were seen as the salvation of a godless Rocky Mountain mining frontier. The wilder and more remote the settlement, the more some people—especially women—hungered for houses of prayer such as those they had known in their former homes.

Hispanics and Irish, French and Germans, Scandinavians and Italians often built with memories of their favorite churches in the old country. Jews, coming from a migratory tradition, felt freer to experiment with new and different styles. Their Colorado synagogues ranged from Byzantine Revival, like Temple Aaron in Trinidad, to expressive contemporary forms like Denver's Temple Emanuel.

Churches frequently aspired to architectural grandeur and became neighborhood landmarks. First-generation simple log or masonry churches generally were replaced with finer ones that have endured, probably more often than any other building type. Landmark churches characterize practically every urban neighborhood and rural town. In many small towns, the most endearing building is the little white frame church. Since World War II, houses of worship have become much more avant-garde, allowing architects considerable creativity with new structural methods, materials, and design.

Hotels exhibited not only the latest architectural styles, but also technological advances and new creature comforts. Between the 1880s and the 1920s Coloradans built their grand hotels: the Hotel Colorado in Glenwood Springs, the Broadmoor in Colorado Springs, the Oxford and the Brown Palace in Denver, the Strater in Durango, and the Jerome in Aspen. Such palaces of the public were open to all for haircuts and shoeshines, drinks and gourmet meals in sumptuous surroundings. Inside, everyone could gawk at such wonders as elevators and telephones, hot water showers and flush toilets. Architectural advances such as the steel skeleton and the skylighted atrium lobby were introduced by Frank Edbrooke's Brown Palace Hotel (1892). Between the 1930s and the 1950s the Brown Palace installed the latest marvel—central air conditioning—using the old fireplaces, smoke ducts, and chimney network. Before the advent of the subdivision show home, hotels set the pace for domestic design. After seeing the latest gadgets and design innovations, Coloradans began asking architects to incorporate these marvels in houses.

Cemeteries and Parks

"Of all monuments," Eugène-Emanuel Viollet-le-Duc once observed, "tombs present perhaps the broadest subject for study." Structures for the dead reveal much about the living. Mortuaries, mausoleums, and cemetery parks all strove to provide an elegant, tranquil final neighborhood for a footloose citizenry that hungered for stability and status but rarely found it during their lifetimes.

Mortuaries, an overlooked building type, frequently settle into a community's grand old mansion, like the Hood Mortuary, which moved into the Amy Mansion, Durango's Shingle Style showcase. Long before law firms and other small businesses began adapting large older homes as offices, mortuaries reused them for new commercial purposes. These "funeral homes" laid out corpses in the "funeral parlor" as earlier generations had laid out their dead for viewing in private homes.

Before the 1920s only the wealthiest could afford private mausoleums. During that decade, Americans developed new death styles as well as lifestyles and began to fancy communal mausoleums. From Los Angeles, Chicago, and New York, the fashion swept into the provinces. The new mode of interment was explored by a short-lived Denver magazine, *The Echo,* which aspired to be *The New Yorker* of the Rockies:

> A too blind adherence to the Bible, which remarks that dust to dust returneth, engendered in humanity the misbelief that inhumation in the earth itself was the one divinely appointed means of human sepulcher. . . . In the midst of presentiments of the grandeur of the twenty-first century, the human mind is awakening to the singular repellance of interment in the earth.

Elaborating on how magnificent the final homes of humans could be, *The Echo* noted in this November 1926 piece that although many "community mausoleums" existed elsewhere in the United States, Colorado had none. Responding to the call, Crown Hill Cemetery erected a seven-story "Tower of Memories" in the Denver suburb of Wheat Ridge. This communal mausoleum, a bit of severe classical eclecticism reminiscent of the work of Bertram Goodhue, was begun in 1926, using a grand design by a Kansas City architect. Construction stalled with the 1929 stock market crash; not until 1931 was a cheaper concrete obelisk finally completed—starved classicism on a starved budget.

Denver's Fairmount Cemetery built its 1920s mausoleum more quickly and more elegantly, engaging Denver architects Mountjoy and Frewen to design a Greek temple clad in Colorado Yule marble. Such Neoclassical design prevails in Fairmount Cemetery, largest and grandest of Colorado's cities of the dead. Cemeteries prized various revival styles, ranging from Fairmount's exquisite French Gothic chapel to obelisks and private mausoleums in the Egyptian Revival mode.

Most large Colorado cemeteries borrowed from the 1831 cemetery park prototype, Mount Auburn, in Cambridge, Massachusetts. The concept of a cemetery as a spacious landscape rather than a crowded boneyard quickly became popular in a spacious state whose citizens were keen on elbow room. Of more than 2,000 Colorado burial places reported in the *Colorado Cemetery Directory* (1985), most are spacious rural plots, often now overgrown by tumbleweed or aspen. Fading wooden slabs have grown indecipherable. But the state's great, well-maintained urban cemetery parks, such as Fairmount, Mount Olivet, and Riverside in Denver; Roselawn in Pueblo; Lynn Grove in Fort Collins; and Evergreen in Colorado Springs, are splendid places to study traditional styles. Tombstones and mausoleums often are the well-thought-out and well-designed final monuments of the moneyed class, who saw themselves as guardians of fine taste in a world corrupted by modern design.

Jewish cemeteries, such as Mount Nebo in Aurora and the Emanuel Section of Fairmount, offer tombstone tributes in Art Nouveau, Art Deco, Streamline Moderne, and contemporary styles. Cemetery sculptures, often beautiful compositions trying to capture grief, hope, and love, distinguish even small fu-

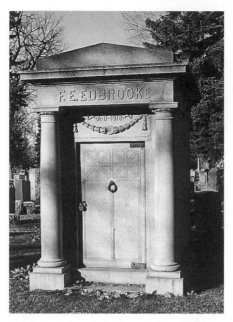

Frank E. Edbrooke's final design may have been his own mausoleum at Fairmount Cemetery in Denver.

neral grounds. In recent decades, both mausoleums and upright headstones have fallen out of fashion, as cemeteries encourage flat grave markers and sparsely landscaped grassy plots that can be trimmed with power mowers. Americans now commonly choose cremation or mausoleum storage compartments resembling the cubicles in high-rise apartment houses.

Cemeteries mirror their communities. Hilltop mausoleum mansions of the elite echo the millionaire's rows where they lived. The poorest people lie in unmarked, low-lying potters' fields. Denver's African American population, concentrated in the northeast quadrant of the metropolis in life, is also consigned to that corner of Fairmount Cemetery. Jews, who once clustered in West Denver's Little Israel neighborhood, have reconvened in the Emanuel Section along the western edge of Fairmount. Other ethnic groups, often by choice, cluster in cemetery sections, where their languages may survive on the tombstones.

Cemeteries, as John Sears notes in *Sacred Places* (1989) became models for private suburbs and public parks. Planners drew inspiration from the winding paths and carriage drives, from landscaping designed for privacy and quiet, and from naturalistic settings that encouraged noble sentiments. By imposing tight design guidelines on construction, landscaping, and behavior, cemeteries also became a prototype for better zoning, an argument for forcing individuals to respect community standards and the common good.

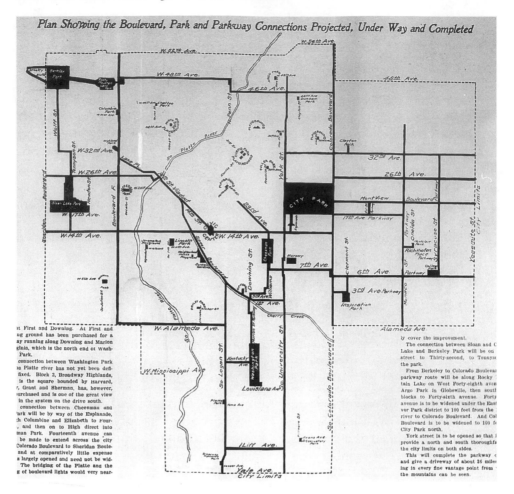

Park planner George Kessler's boulevard, park, and parkway plan for Denver, 1907

Cemeteries served as the first public parks, and to this day Fairmount Cemetery remains the state's largest arboretum. Not until after 1900 and the spread of the City Beautiful movement did many Colorado towns begin to set aside formal parks. Several cities, including Boulder, Colorado Springs, Denver, and Trinidad, developed extensive mountain parks to augment their city parks. Frederick Law Olmsted, Jr., worked in Boulder, which named one park for him. Olmsted, the country's first professor of landscape architecture, also worked for Denver and surveyed on horseback the foothills where he helped to design Denver's mountain park system.

National parks were established at Mesa Verde (1906) and Rocky Mountain (1915). Along with national monuments, forests, grasslands, and wilderness areas, the federal playgrounds occupy almost a fifth of the state. Many local and national parks remained raw land until the 1930s, when the Civilian Conservation Corps (CCC) and Works Progress Administration (WPA) teams constructed roads, trails, shelters, toilets, and other amenities. The CCC helped complete Red Rocks Outdoor Amphitheater and the Winter Park Ski Area for the Denver Mountain Parks. City and federal parks were belatedly joined by state parks. The Colorado Parks and Outdoor Recreation Department, established in 1955, now maintains more than forty parks and recreation areas statewide.

To connect parks and to showcase elite residential districts, some communities also built parkways. George Kessler, the Kansas City parkway master planner, designed a network of Denver parkways with generous green medians and extravagant setbacks. Saco R. DeBoer, a Dutch immigrant, implemented many park and parkway plans and worked as a landscape architect and community planner throughout Colorado. Even before the City Beautiful concept of parkways became popular, many towns constructed irrigation ditches and transplanted local cottonwood, ponderosa pine, blue spruce, or other species to create tree-lined streets. By the 1880s nurseries and mail-order catalogs offered a full range of plant material that could survive Colorado's erratically late and early frosts.

Town Plans

Many Colorado communities were established by railroads acting through subsidiary land development companies that refined the art of town planning, platting, and promotion. Although the Denver Pacific, Kansas Pacific, and Union Pacific received land grants in Colorado, most other railroads did not. This led lines like the Denver & Rio Grande (D&RG) to establish towns to help finance construction and maintenance.

General William J. Palmer of the D&RG acquired a 10,000-acre site for Colorado Springs and produced a promotional brochure to attract well-to-do settlers. Palmer promised that the Colorado Springs Company would use profits from land sales "to pay for all public improvements upon the property such as irrigation ditches, public buildings, ornamenting grounds, opening and improving streets and all other improvements of a permanent character." Colorado Springs started out with one of Colorado's best-planned plats; land near the tracks was set aside for Monument Valley Park and a cemetery (later moved because boosters said it gave railroad arrivals the wrong impression). Palmer and the D&RG also gave land for Alamo and Arcadia parks, for a county courthouse, and for schools.

Most railroads and affiliated land companies, however, did not provide all the services and amenities promised. Those were left to struggling local governments to finance after the railroad and its promoters had pushed on to the next town down the line. Railroad builders were less interested in providing amenities than in procuring land, cash, and other concessions before laying track into any given community. As railroads were the key to prosperity, if not survival, communities offered incentives. Although some town plats initially showed public squares, parks, and generous sites for government buildings and schools, these were generally just window dressing. Even the most essential element of public infrastructure—irrigation ditches—was generally left for private citizens to build. Infant town and county governments struggled to find meeting halls, usually renting space until reluctant and transient populations submitted to financing more elegant and permanent public buildings.

Colorado and other western states were shaped by the federal land ordinances of 1785 and 1789. These federal laws divided the American West into townships of 36 square miles, with each square-mile section containing 640 acres. Quarter-section homesteads of 160 acres are still the basic land unit of many farms and ranches. Even the boundaries of Colorado reflect abstract grid lines drawn in Washington, D.C., rather than determined by natural features. Within the rectangular boundaries of the state, many counties are also rectangles. Nearly every community is a grid. Only in a few of the most vertical mountain mining communities, such as Central City, did nature force town builders to bend their plans. Town grids are repeated in blocks and building lots, in the siting of buildings, and usually in building floor plans. Even the last dwelling places—cemeteries—often succumbed to the economics of the checkerboard.

Grid plans appealed to railroad builders, promoters, and government agents because they made a town instantly comprehensible even to distant buyers and speculators and enabled newcomers quickly to find their way around. In these predictable town plans, street names were often limited to numbers and letters. Main Street typically began at the depot and ran perpendicular to the tracks. On the two parallel streets flanking the tracks were grain elevators, factories, and warehouses. Planned residential areas were platted several blocks away, while shanties, saloons, liveries, and other less reputable structures sprang up close to the tracks.

Blocks in Colorado towns normally measured about 400 by 300 feet, with individual lots 25 feet wide and 125 feet deep. Streets were wide (80 to 100 feet) and alleys narrow (14 to 16 feet). All blocks were generally the same size, with no distinction between commercial and residential. This homogeneity blurred the line between uses to the advantage of town boosters, who hoped that growth would allow commercial and industrial uses easily to displace residential ones. This readiness to sacrifice residential character for "higher and better" uses continues to characterize Colorado communities. Many of Denver's residential neighborhoods, for instance, are zoned to facilitate commercial or multifamily development. Some 13,000 single-family Denver homes sit on land zoned to allow high-rise construction.

Railroads, Automobiles, and Airplanes

Transportation—railroads, automobiles, and airplanes—has shaped the landscape and buildings of Colorado, an isolated state of vast distances and physical obstacles. Swarms of miners first clawed trails into the mountains, sometimes using Indian paths. Miners were followed by toll road builders, then stagecoachers. By 1900 railroads crisscrossed Colorado, ascending even 14,110-foot Pikes Peak and descending into the 1,055-foot-deep Royal Gorge of the Arkansas River.

More than any other nineteenth-century phenomenon, railroads explain the location and development of Colorado communities. In the dry, inland West, the railroad station—not the riverfront or the seaport—is the community nucleus. America's first transcontinental railroads bypassed Colorado and its two-mile-high Rocky Mountain barrier. When railroads did not come to them, Coloradans built to the railroads. Residents donated cash, materials, and labor to construct the Denver Pacific in 1870, giving Denver a lifeline to Cheyenne, Wyoming, and the Union Pacific main line.

Other railroads followed. The Kansas Pacific chugged into Denver from Kansas City and St. Louis. The Colorado Central and the Denver & Rio Grande, two pioneer narrow-gauge roads, tapped mountain mining communities. The Union Pacific (UP); Chicago, Burlington & Quincy (now Burlington Northern); Atchison, Topeka & Santa Fe (Santa Fe); and Chicago, Rock Island & Pacific (Rock Island) built to Denver. Thanks to its spiderweb of steel, the Mile High City emerged as the metropolis of the Rockies by tapping a vast Rocky Mountain and High Plains hinterland. Colorado's other population centers were lesser rail hubs.

To tackle difficult terrain, railroaders used 3-foot-wide narrow-gauge track instead of standard (4-foot, 8-inch) gauge. Narrow-gauge track was cheaper to lay and could handle tighter curves and steeper grades. In climbing the Rockies, railroaders built spectacular tunnels, trestles, and bridges, such as the Georgetown Loop and the Moffat Tunnel, that are among Colorado's noteworthy landmarks.

Railroads shaped the built environment, from the industrial, urbanized corridor along the tracks to agricultural hamlets where discarded boxcars still serve as farm and ranch outbuildings. They introduced new architectural materials, including eastern hardwoods, cast iron fronts, and mail-order trim, to remote corners of Colorado. In cities and larger towns, street railways, as streetcars were first called, shaped growth patterns. Indeed, streetcar suburbanization established the pattern of decentralization often attributed to the automobile.

Passenger depots, and even rural freight depots, were more than commercial and social hubs. Designed by architects or railroad engineering offices, they set building standards for communities. The trains themselves were also

Railroads transformed the landscape as well as the economy of Colorado. This 1,084-foot-long timber trestle served the Colorado Midland's Hagerman Pass route (1890s photograph by W. H. Jackson).

rolling design exhibits, allowing the public to ponder such wonders as George Pullman's palace cars. A half century later, stainless steel locomotives, coaches, diners, and lounge cars of trains like the California Zephyr popularized modern design. The Zephyr, inaugurated in 1934, showcased Streamline Moderne design by Paul Philippe Cret and the Chicago firm of Holabird and Root.

Automobiles have even more drastically transformed Colorado's natural landscape and built environment. Not all highways are ugly. Scenic drives in the Denver Mountain Parks, in Rocky Mountain National Park, and in Colorado National Monument are contoured to complement natural landscapes. Confronted by considerable protest from environmental groups, the Colorado Department of Transportation has made I-70 in Glenwood Canyon one of the world's most beautiful freeways.

Colorado has one of the nation's highest per capita rates of motor vehicle ownership, with one vehicle for almost every adult resident. After being introduced to Colorado in 1899, automobiles caught on quickly. By the 1920s many small towns boasted auto showrooms and gas stations, which often aspired to be stylish. By the 1950s automobiles had become common and auto architecture more prosaic.

Cities and towns were asphalted, and monumental public buildings, businesses, and residences erected by the pioneers were demolished for auto parking, sales lots, and service stations. Despite the sacrifices downtown to accommodate cars, motorists often preferred suburban shopping centers. Since shopping center sales taxes are a major means of financing local governments, localities vigorously promoted construction of new malls, leading to further decay not only in the city core but also in older suburban shopping centers. Following California precedents, Coloradans built and patronized auto-oriented businesses along highway strips, where drive-in banks, restaurants, and theaters proliferated with attendant gasoline alleys of service stations, car dealers, and auto parts stores. As in other places, heavy auto traffic reshaped housing: families abandoned front porches for the quiet and privacy of backyard patios. Garages, once detached like carriage houses, became appendages to houses, and two- and three-car units have became standard in new middle- and upper-class subdivisions. Garages became the front doors to homes, apartment buildings, and office towers.

Acrobatic freeways snaked over, under, and through nineteenth-century urban cores. On the fringes of towns and cities, new suburbs sprouted for miles along freeways. Interstate highways rearranged the landscape with cuts and high fills to keep traffic as straight, level, and fast as possible. Twin freeway tracks, tunnels, overpasses, and the proliferation of roadside development have made highways the most environmentally significant transportation corridors.

In fifty years Colorado's population jumped from 1.1 million (1940) to 1.75 million (1960) to almost 3.3 million (1990). More than 4 million are projected for 2000. Both population and new construction have followed the freeway, just as they once followed rail and streetcar lines. If an interstate came thorough a community, the town usually rearranged itself accordingly. Bypassed communities stagnated, withered, or died. While outlying farming and mining towns bypassed by freeways declined, three-fourths of the state's population settled along the I-25 corridor between Pueblo and Fort Collins.

The detrimental impact of the automobile has led to recent efforts at auto-free environments. Autos have been banned from downtown pedestrian malls, some ski resorts, and some historic districts. Increasingly, planners and architects seek auto-free zones friendly to pedestrians and bicyclists. Oftentimes, car parks are now bermed or buried underground. In the 1990s, new subdivisions in Larimer and Arapahoe counties experimented with designs that severely curb auto intrusions into community life.

While railroads gave birth to many Colorado communities and automobiles reshaped them, aviation has become the latest major urban catalyst. As early as the 1920s airports began appearing in mountain meadows, western plateaus, and eastern wheat fields. Ever since, even the silence of remote wilderness areas has been shattered by the droning of propeller planes and the roar of jets. New airports have transformed Aspen, Denver, Telluride, and Grand Junction, attracting hotels, restaurants, and other businesses that once revolved around train stations.

Denver International Airport (DIA) epitomizes air age development. Coloradans call it the "world's largest airport," both for its 54-square-mile site and its potential for growth. In fact it is outranked in size by the King Kahlid International Airport outside Riyadh, Saudi Arabia, which covers 86 square miles, and by Mirabel International Airport outside Montreal, Canada, which occupies 70 square miles. Nonetheless, DIA is Colorado's biggest building, in terms not only of space but of cost—more than $3 billion. It is also remarkable for its architecture. The terminal roof, made of Teflon-coated fiberglass, consists of transparent, tentlike structures that are translucent by day and glow at night. The cluster of tents is reminiscent of the Arapaho and Cheyenne tipis which once occupied the site.

Tourism

Rail, auto, and air networks have all fostered tourism, Colorado's second largest industry. Much architecture has been designed to attract sightseers, beginning with eastern dudes who came looking for the Wild West. Coloradans indulged tourists with rustic log structures adorned with stone fireplaces and Stick Style trim and furniture. Many fading mining towns and ranches survived by courting tourists, by capitalizing on early twentieth-century America's romance with the great outdoors. During the 1950s tourist architecture began to borrow design elements from Western movie sets. Three towns— Buckskin Joe in Fremont County, Orchard in Weld County, and Ridgway in Ouray County—retain synthetic Hollywood props that have been confused with historic nineteenth-century structures. In Colorado Springs, sightseers swarm to a fake cowboy ghost town and fake Manitou Indian cliff dwellings. Since gambling became legal in Black Hawk, Central City, and Cripple Creek in 1991, alterations of historic buildings have strained design guidelines in these National Historic Landmark towns. Only the facades remain on what are usually mostly new structures. Florid interiors with flocked wallpaper have been crammed with as many slot machines as possible. The Wild West has made a last stand in the imitation Victoriana of these gambling towns.

Colorado's ski resorts have developed an alternative to the false-fronted, Gilded Age, Wild West style: Alpine architecture. By 1900 Switzerland, the world's nineteenth-century pacesetter in tourist promotion, became a model for Colorado. Estes Park and Ouray began puffing themselves as the "Switzerland of America." Shops, hotels, cafes, summer homes, and public structures began wearing the Alpine Style, with its steep-pitched roofs over white stucco and half-timbered walls with window flower boxes. The style bloomed most fully in the 1960s at Vail, the first fully planned tourist town. Since then Vail and other mountain resort towns have moved beyond ersatz Swiss styles to intriguing Modernist and Postmodern architecture.

Growing refinement in designing and redesigning tourist towns has led to improved landscaping, more sensitive treatment of waterways, reduction of auto-related activity, and promotion of public sculpture and pedestrian ambiance. To please locals and tourists alike, Aspen, Boulder, Breckenridge, Crested Butte, Denver, Estes Park, Telluride, and Vail have also experimented with contemporary pedestrian-oriented design that helps to raise statewide design consciousness.

In contrast to master-planned and architect-designed environments are mobile home parks, a growing phenomenon in Colorado, where the gap between the rich and the poor is expanding faster, according to the 1990 census, than in any state except Louisiana, Virginia, and West Virginia. The creation of a huge service class, especially notable around Colorado's affluent suburban communities and mountain resorts, has had an impact on the architecture. Many residents are renters who can hope to buy only inexpensive mobile homes, and roughly one Colorado family in ten resides in this type of housing. Mobile homes are an affordable, innovative, and flexible solution, as Alan D. Wallis pointed out in *Wheel Estate: The Rise and Decline of Mobile Homes* (1991). Yet planners and most architectural historians have ignored them, viewing them with distaste, if not contempt.

The Architects

A few nationally prominent architects have practiced extensively in Colorado, although only Frank E. and Willoughby J. Edbrooke and Herbert Bayer rate separate entries in the *Macmillan Encyclopedia of Architects* (1982). Following the example of Horace Tabor, other capitalists commissioned out-of-state architects instead of local builders. The flush times of the 1870s and 1880s attracted many Illinois architects, including Robert Roeschlaub, Montezuma Fuller, William Lang, Charles and Edward Quayle, and Isaac H. Rapp. The Illinois impact may be seen in Denver skyscrapers, which tended toward the flat-topped Chicago School version rather than the stepbacks and spires of New York City's towers.

The attempt to professionalize Colorado building design and raise architectural consciousness was spearheaded by Jesse B. Dorman's *Western Architect and Building News.* This illustrated monthly extolled architecture as the most democratic and important art form. Dorman's magazine, as architectural historian Richard Brettell put it, was "a rudder guiding the course of the building boom." Although this Denver journal lasted only from 1889 to 1891, it successfully promoted the Colorado Association of Architects, which in 1892 became the Colorado chapter of the American Institute of Architects (AIA). In 1909 the AIA persuaded the Colorado legislature to begin licensing architects.

The Colorado AIA initially welcomed members from Wyoming, New Mexico, and Utah, before these states founded their own associations. A separate Denver chapter was formed in 1960, followed by local AIA chapters for southern, northern, and western Colorado. A short-lived school of architecture at the University of Denver during the late 1940s and the early 1950s was followed in 1962 by one at the University of Colorado, whose College of Architecture and Planning is now on its Denver campus.

By the 1920s Colorado could claim an impressive array of architects. Yet major patrons often have bypassed local talent for national stars. These celebrities sometimes stuck Colorado with such "look-at-me" erections as Philip Johnson's Norwest Bank tower, which defies Denver's Mountain View Ordinance and also disfigures I. M. Pei's Mile High Center, which it wraps. Johnson's fifty-two-story tower is topped by a curved peak which sheds accumulated ice and snow on pedestrians. When told of this, Johnson replied, according to local folklore, "I thought we designed that building for Houston!" Michael Graves's Denver Public Library (1995) is a Postmodern composition using multicolored cast stone with Graves's signature shapes: rectangles, cubes, pyramids, and a drum. The Graves design, done in partnership with the Denver firm of Klipp Colussy Jenks DuBois, reluctantly incorporated Burnham Hoyt's 1955 landmarked library into its village of use-oriented spaces.

After first struggling to establish their profession, Colorado architects began developing, more or less consciously, a regional style. The brothers William E. and Arthur A. Fisher, who dominated both residential and commercial building in Denver between 1910 and 1930, favored the red tile roofs and thick masonry walls of Mediterranean design. This type of construction provided the durable weatherproofing required by Colorado's erratic climate. In a state blessed with 300 days of sunshine a year, one consideration of a new regional architecture has been solar energy. The National Solar Energy Research Institute, opened during the 1970s in Golden with bright hopes, but subsequent federal cutbacks in funding and elimination of the solar design tax credit eclipsed the industry.

Despite efforts to develop a regional architecture, modern Colorado communities differ little from others in the United States. Some regional variation is seen in the predilection for masonry materials. Also somewhat distinctive are the Hispanic towns of southern Colorado and the ski resort towns, where extravagant vacation homes and recreational amenities feature custom designs by many of America's leading architects. In the ongoing search for a Colorado, or at least a Rocky Mountain, style, one of the most successful modes so far has been Southwestern (Mediterranean, Mission, Pueblo, and Spanish Colonial revivals), which suits the region's climatic extremes. Isaac H. Rapp of Trinidad helped to create the Santa Fe Style, refined by the better-known Santa Fe architect John Gaw Meem. Notable Colorado architects such as Thomas MacLaren in Colorado Springs; the contemporary firm of Hurtig,

Architect John Gaw Meem spearheaded the Spanish Colonial Revival and fostered an appreciation of traditional Spanish colonial art. He designed the Colorado Springs Fine Arts Center to house the Alice Bemis Taylor Collection.

Gardner and Froelich in Pueblo; and William and Arthur Fisher, Jacques Benedict, and Burnham Hoyt in Denver have produced notable interpretations of Southwestern styles over the years. Burnham Hoyt's outdoor amphitheater at Red Rocks, Colorado's finest piece of Modernist architecture, integrates minimalist construction with the natural environment. Unfortunately, few other architects have so sensitively accommodated natural terrain and vegetation in their work.

Developing an indigenous style, in the view of some, is not as important as introducing contemporary architecture to Coloradans, who usually have chosen traditional, conservative buildings. Twentieth-century styles—Prairie, Art Deco, International, Streamline Moderne, and Postmodern—have caught on slowly. As early as the 1930s, Modernist concepts, shapes, and materials were introduced by such architects as Robert K. Fuller, Eugene G. Groves, Thompson D. Hetherington, Burnham Hoyt, Glen H. Huntington, and G. Charles Jaka. Yet before the 1950s few architects could make a living by specializing solely in Modernist design. Temple Hoyne Buell, the state's most successful developer-architect, told this author in 1986 with a wink: "We don't fight over architectural styles. The client is always right."

Victor Hornbein, an uncompromising Modernist, responded to Colorado's intense sunshine with roof overhangs that become sheltering eaves and with clerestory windows on flat-roofed, low-slung buildings that hunker down on the prairie to squint at the mountains. Hornbein contended that "creative regional architecture arises out of the use to which the building will be put, . . . the environmental determinants, and hopes that society can sustain itself without the accoutrements of long dead civilizations." Eugene Sternberg, another champion of modernism, argues that "Coloradans should be building into the future, not the past. No gimmickry. No gingerbread. And no false-fronted Postmodernism. Why spend so many resources restoring buildings for tourists instead of allowing a new generation of architects to build for the people who live here?"

Some Modernists have carved special niches: Richard L. Crowther's solar architecture, Thomas E. Moore's innovative precast concrete structural systems, Charles Haertling's organic, sculptural buildings in Boulder, Frederick A. (Fritz) Benedict's distinctive Taliesin designs in Aspen, William C. Muchow's Miesian monuments, Kenneth R. Fuller's service to the profession and to local architectural history and education. Charles S. Sink, who worked for I. M. Pei on several Denver projects, is noted for his command of Modernist architectural concepts, structural systems, and clarity in spatial relationships. G. Cabell Childress has adapted historical and modern styles to fit the peculiar Colorado weather and landscapes. Akira Kanawabe designed low-budget solar structures in the San Luis Valley. Herbert Bayer, the Austrian immigrant and champion of Bauhaus design, helped transform Aspen into a festival of Modernist architecture.

Mrs. L. C. Tuthill, the author of an early survey of U.S. architecture entitled *History of Architecture* (Philadelphia: Lindsay and Blakiston, 1848), dedicated her work "to the ladies of the U.S. of A., the acknowledged arbiters of taste." Women, who often inspired and insisted on fine architecture, have entered the profession. Colorado Women in Architecture counts more than 100 women among some 1,500 licensed architects in Colorado.

Anne Evans was a philanthropist rather than an architect, but her impact has been tremendous. A graduate of the Chicago Art Institute, she spearheaded Colorado's first major preservation effort, the 1932 renovation of the Central City Opera House, a successful summer opera prototype. Perhaps to atone for the sins of her father, a Colorado territorial governor removed from office after the massacre of Arapaho and Cheyenne at Sand Creek, Anne Evans did more than any other Coloradan to make Native American and Hispanic art and architecture respectable. She was one of the first people in the country to perceive Indian crafts and artifacts as art. The Native American art she donated to the Denver Art Museum made possible the first department of Native American art in any art museum. Native Arts is still among the DAM's strongest collections. Alice Bemis Taylor played a similar role in Colorado Springs, where she commissioned John Gaw Meem to design the Fine Arts Center, which she endowed with an outstanding collection of indigenous art and architectural relics.

Historic Preservation

Fast and reckless architecture has more often compromised than complemented Colorado's breathtaking landscape. Although a transient population and the ephemeral nature of much construction may be a national disorder, rootlessness seemed particularly detrimental to good design in the Rocky Mountain West. In the first Western novel, *The Virginian* (1905), a Harvard-educated tenderfoot, Owen Wister, compared pioneer Rocky Mountain towns to decks of cards:

> Scattered wide they littered the frontier. They lay stark, dotted over a planet of treeless dust, like soiled packs of cards. . . . Houses, empty bottles, and garbage, they were forever the same shapeless pattern. . . . They seem to have been strewn there by the wind and to be waiting till the wind should come again and blow them away.

Wister's description still fits many Rocky Mountain towns. The majority of them have blown away with the wind. In Colorado alone, more than 300 post office towns have disappeared from the map, leaving the state with more ghost towns than live ones. Disposable towns as well as disposable buildings have left Colorado with a fragmented architectural heritage.

Colorado's post–World War II energy boom, an echo of the 1870–1893 mining bonanza years, along with the impact of the automobile, led to the alteration or demolition of much of the nineteenth-century built environment. Postwar prosperity, however, bypassed most of the eastern plains and southern Colorado, two generally static or declining agricultural regions. In surviving rural communities, the finest buildings are often stout masonry business blocks, churches, residential foursquares, and bungalows constructed during the flush times between 1900 and 1920. Poverty has been preservation's greatest ally in rural areas, where structures are rarely demolished. Adobe or hewn log residences, when replaced by bigger and newer houses, are typically kept as outbuildings. Even old henhouses, root cellars, and barns are kept by frugal farmers.

Colorado's postwar boom ended with the mid-1980s collapse of oil prices. For the first time since the 1890s, Colorado actually lost population. As in the 1890s, prairie dogs began to repossess subdivisions platted by ambitious developers caught in a recession. Recovery came in the 1990s, but construction levels of the 1970s will probably not be reached until the twenty-first century.

Demolition of Colorado's nineteenth-century architectural heritage sparked a grassroots preservation movement. Starting quietly in the 1960s, architect Edward D. White, Jr., pioneered preservation projects: the Lace House in Black Hawk, the Governor's Mansion and Four Mile House in Denver, and master plans for preserving Central City and Denver's Ninth Street Park, on the Auraria Higher Education Center campus. Passage of the National Historic Preservation Act in 1966 created a federally funded State Historic Preservation Office in each state to identify, designate, and preserve buildings of architectural and historical significance. As a national reaction to urban renewal demolitions and to the American tradition of disposable architecture, the preservation movement found strong support in Colorado. Preservationists drew courage from the environmental movement, which achieved a major success by persuading two out of three Colorado voters to reject state funding for the 1976 Winter Olympics, thus killing that proposal. The 1976 National Bicentennial/Colorado Statehood Centennial celebrations inspired many communities to consider their architectural heritages and undertake preservation efforts.

Reinforcing federal tax laws encouraging historic preservation, the state of Colorado enacted in 1991 a program of state income tax credits for rehabilitation of designated national or local landmarks. Colorado has seventeen National Historic Landmark sites, more than 180 National Register Historic Districts, and more than 950 individual sites listed on the National Register of Historic Places. A major remaining challenge is to preserve newer buildings of outstanding architectural merit that do not meet current National Register guidelines for age and association with august personalities. The State Historical Fund uses tax revenues generated from gaming. As of 2001, some $100 million in gambling taxes had funded more than 1500 preservation projects.

The renewed interest in historic structures has shaped even new buildings, which since the 1980s have often incorporated or echoed traditional shapes, materials, and elements. Neo–revival style subdivisions have replaced ranch houses as the suburban norm. In cities traditionally inspired ornament is reappearing as a reaction to stark, flat-topped parallelepipeds. Even the Greek column and pediment and the Roman arch and dome are making comebacks.

Some eighty counties, cities and towns—notably Aspen, Boulder, Breckenridge, Central City, Crested Butte, Cripple Creek, Denver, Durango, Fort Collins, Georgetown, Golden, Longmont, Manitou Springs, Ouray, and Telluride—have passed local preservation ordinances, often with controls over the demolition or abuse of landmarks. Thanks to such preservation efforts, Colorado's monuments to various cultures and architectural traditions now have prospects for longer and more productive lives.

The South Platte:
The Architectural Mainstream

Here is a land where life is written in water,
The West is where the water was and is,
Father and Son of old, mother and daughter,
Following rivers up immensities
Of range and desert, thirsting the sundown ever,
Crossing a hill to climb a hill still drier,
Naming tonight a city by some river
A different name from last night's camping fire. . . .
> —Thomas Hornsby Ferril, inscription for the murals by
> Allen T. True in the rotunda of the Colorado State Capitol

WATERWAYS ARE NOT ONLY NATURAL BUT ALSO MAN-MADE networks in dry western states such as Colorado. Sparse natural rivers and creeks are rearranged with ditches and dams, tunnels and reservoirs that make it possible to build communities. The water system becomes the ultimate infrastructure. The South Platte River valley exemplifies development written in water.

Pilgrims settling the state's largest utopian colony, Greeley, began by digging communal irrigation canals and side ditches to carry water down every street. Fifty miles farther up the South Platte, the Denver Water Department's tentacles reach over and under the Rockies to divert water intended for the Colorado River drainage into the South Platte system. Ditches and tunnels for water diversion pierce the Continental Divide to capture Colorado River water from the Western Slope and redirect it to the South Platte valley, which has most of the population but only a quarter of the stream flow. Water in Colorado, the saying goes, flows uphill toward money.

The South Platte watershed, with its tributaries, such as the Cache la Poudre and Big Thompson rivers and St Vrain, Boulder, and Cherry creeks, supports almost three-fourths of Colorado's population. The South Platte's 450-mile course carries it through the Denver area, which houses over half the state's residents. Below Denver the river and its tributaries are lined by the major cities of northeastern Colorado, including Greeley, Boulder, Fort Collins, Longmont, and Sterling.

Ironically, the flourishing valley that has become Colorado's agricultural, industrial, commercial, and population center was first named "The Great American Desert." Major Stephen H. Long put that label on his map after the first official U.S. exploration of the upper South Platte in 1820. The river

35

had been named even earlier with the French word for "flat" or "shallow" by two Frenchmen, Pierre and Paul Mallet. In 1739 they became the first known Europeans to cross the Great Plains from the Missouri River to Santa Fe.

After the 1858 gold strikes near the confluence of the South Platte and Cherry Creek, settlers streamed up the river into Colorado. Many began their odyssey at Omaha, near the confluence of the Platte and the Missouri. They followed the Platte to North Platte, Nebraska, where it divides into the North Platte and the South Platte. Both forks originate in Colorado: The North Platte rises in North Park (Jackson County) and the South Platte in South Park (Park County). Immigrant wagon trails, stage lines, railroads, and highways were built into Colorado alongside the South Platte. Railroads introduced an urban, industrialized corridor to the once pastoral riverbanks, which began to bristle with smelters and sugar beet factories, oil refineries, and meat packing plants.

Just above Denver the river flows through Platte Canyon from forested foothills also altered by human settlement. Loggers and miners felled woodlands to timber mines, build settlements, and stoke smelters. Forest fires set by human beings and by steam locomotives often led to the replacement of old growth evergreen forests with aspen, the first trees to take hold on scarred land. Human activity amid montane dark green conifers is often revealed by the lighter green groves of aspen.

The natural landscape has been transformed not only by such obvious destruction but also by the valley's farming and ranching, which have transformed much of what was once virgin prairie. Cattle, which each eat about 35 pounds of grass and drink about 11 gallons of water a day, denuded the prairie and emptied water holes. Native grasses of the eastern high plains, as well as the western canyon lands, vanished, to be replaced by sagebrush, loco weed, tumbleweed, and bare dirt.

Even as settlers diminished the native vegetation, they often yearned for trees. Except for the cottonwoods growing along lowland waterways, prairie vegetation rarely climbed higher than a choke cherry or a scrub oak. Settlers, especially women, planted trees and experimented with seeds and starts, be it a lilac slip or a seed potato. What would grow in the windswept, sunbaked, blizzard-blasted high plains of Colorado? Part of the answer lies in some 40,000 farms and 200 agricultural towns that have been abandoned since 1920. The Great American Desert keeps coming back to haunt those who promoted the high plains as a Garden of Eden. Some contend that the South Platte valley should have been left to the prairie grasses, the buffalo, and the Indians.

Nonnative vegetation prevailed in cities and towns and on farmsteads by 1900. To water the transplants, windmills and water towers were constructed and came to dominate agrarian skylines. By the 1920s Colorado led the nation—even California—in irrigated farm acreage. Frank Zyback, a tenant

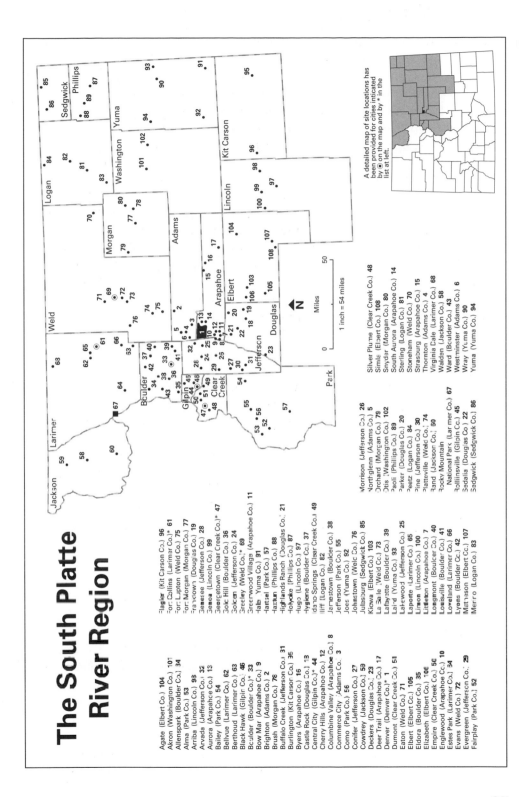

farmer cultivating wheat near Strasburg in eastern Arapahoe County, revolutionized both agriculture and the landscape with his 1952 invention. Zyback rigged up a self-propelled sprinkler on wheels, with lightweight aluminum pipe and rotating sprinkler heads. He patented his center-pivot irrigation device, which can distribute fertilizer and pesticides as well as water. Thanks to these giant sprinklers, irrigated fields now dot the South Platte valley and, to a lesser extent, the Rio Grande and Arkansas valleys, inscribing giant circles in quarter-section plots. In the frontier tradition, this device wastes both land and water, but gets the job done.

Today's air travelers, like the argonauts of 1859, find the South Platte River the main path to Denver. Travelers flying into Colorado along the South Platte see rectangles of spring and summer green, or fall and winter brown. These homestead grids sometimes frame giant circles created by the half-mile-long pipes of sprinkler systems. Along railroad tracks and highways, the big squares and circles sometimes give way to town grids. Between Platte Canyon and Greeley, riverbank development is almost solid, with huge dumps and automobile junkyards that indicate affluence. As the river nears Denver, farms and ranches are displaced by curvilinear subdivisions surrounding older grid neighborhoods. Only the steep, rocky canyon seventeen miles southwest of the city keeps the suburbs from following the South Platte into the mountains. At the center of the conglutination of asphalt and concrete, of clay and brick, is Denver's downtown huddle of fifty-story highrises.

The South Platte valley between Denver and Greeley contains most of Colorado's buildings. These range from high-rise glass and concrete office towers to humble frame, tarpaper, and sod farmhouses. Only a few of the pioneer houses survive, and Indian villages are long gone. Older buildings representing the architectural mainstream are clad in brick and sometimes in imported lumber, as the predominant Anglo-American settlers preferred traditional materials and styles imported from Europe and the eastern United States.

Denver   (DV)

The discovery of golden specks in the South Platte River near its junction with Cherry Creek led to the creation of Denver City on November 22, 1858. Founder William Larimer, Jr., named the town for Kansas territorial governor James Denver to help ensure its selection as the seat of what was then Arapahoe County, Kansas Territory. Larimer platted Denver City with streets parallel to Cherry Creek. Only after Denver began to blossom in the 1870s were outlying areas platted to conform to standard compass-point township lines.

Aggressive town promoters, led by *Rocky Mountain News* editor William N. Byers and territorial governor John Evans, enticed railroads to the isolated town 700 miles from the Missouri River frontier communities. After railroads steamed into Denver in 1870, this crossroads in the middle of nowhere grew into the third largest city in the trans-Missouri West. By 1890 Denver had a population of 106,713, behind San Francisco and Omaha but larger than Los Angeles, Seattle, Phoenix, or any town in Texas.

As in other inland cities without navigable rivers, the railroad station became the nucleus. Railroads hauled gold and silver ores from mountain mining towns into Denver's smelters, producing fortunes that built a grand opera house, elegant churches, majestic hotels, and imposing office blocks. Mining millionaires built brick and stone mansions in the Capitol Hill neighborhood east of Broadway.

Flush times ended with the silver crash of 1893. After federal repeal of the Sherman Silver Purchase Act that year, the price of silver dropped from over a dollar to less than 60 cents an ounce, devastating Colorado's most lucrative industry. Responding to the economic slump and population loss in the mid-1890s, Denver's power elite set about diversifying the city's economy. While still serving a vast, if faltering, mountain mining hinterland, the city also focused on becoming the supply and food processing center for farmers and ranchers on the high plains.

Not content to be the regional metropolis just for Colorado, Denverites used railroads to extend their economic orbit to New Mexico, Utah, Wyoming, and Montana, as well as to western Nebraska, Kansas, Oklahoma, and Texas. Agriculture and food processing, stockyards and meat packing, brewing and banking, manufacturing and service industries became mainstays of Denver's economic base. Federal jobs—civilian and military—have stabilized the boom-and-bust city, especially since the New Deal and World War II. Tourism also emerged as one of the city's most profitable and reliable industries. Tourism and steady, more orderly growth were encouraged by Denver's City Beautiful movement. Robert W. Speer introduced this urban vision of the Progressive Era to Denver after he was elected mayor in 1904. Speer had toured the 1893 World's Columbian Exposition in Chicago and, along with 30 million others, had marveled at the transformation of a swamp on Lake Michigan into an urbane, Neoclassical paradise. He brought the dream home and, as Denver's mayor, set out to turn a dusty, drab, unplanned city into "Paris on the Platte."

Speer served three terms as mayor and died in office in 1918. He first engaged Charles Mulford Robinson, the New York City planner and author of *Modern Civic Art, or the City Made Beautiful* (1903), to prepare a master plan. The 1906 Robinson Plan and George Kessler's 1907 Park and Parkway Plan as later revised and extended by Frederick Law Olmsted, Jr., Frederick MacMonnies, Edward H. Bennett, Saco R. DeBoer, and others, were implemented by "Boss" Speer, who operated both over and under the table. Denver became one of the better examples of City Beautiful planning. These schemes were later expanded with the help of New Deal programs and revived by Denver's first Hispanic mayor, Federico Peña

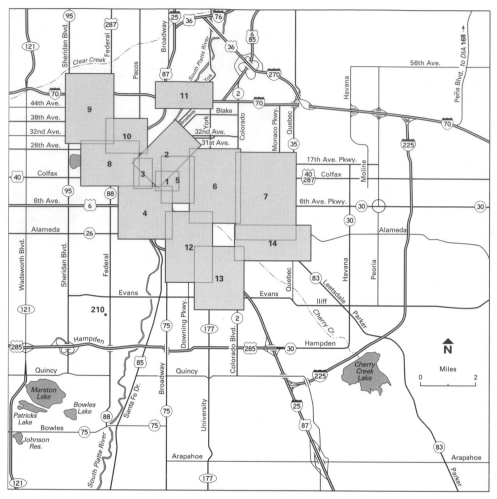

Denver, overview (including DV168 and DV210)

(1983–1991), and first African American mayor, Wellington Webb (1991–present).

Denver's City Beautiful landscape comprises Civic Center Park, surrounded by city, state, and federal office buildings; a network of parkways stretching out from Civic Center via Speer Boulevard to the neighborhoods; neighborhood parks which serve as mini–civic centers surrounded by schools, libraries, churches, and other public buildings; and the Denver Mountain Parks network. Among the last are Winter Park Ski Area, Red Rocks Outdoor Amphitheater, Mt. Evans, and forty-five other parks covering about 13,500 acres in Arapahoe, Clear Creek, Douglas, Grand, and Jefferson counties.

George Kessler, who created the park and parkway plan, was America's foremost parkway planner. Kessler had worked with Frederick Law Olmsted, Sr., on

New York's Central Park, laid out the 1904 Louisiana Purchase Exposition grounds in St. Louis, and given Kansas City, Missouri, a notable park and parkway system. In Denver Kessler abandoned the spoke-and-wheel model of diagonal avenues and connecting outer rings of boulevards. Too many buildings already obstructed that ideal scheme, so Kessler superimposed parkways upon the existing street grid. He placed parks at the highest points for mountain views, as exemplified by Cheesman, Cranmer, and Inspiration Point parks. These spacious parks set high architectural and landscape standards for adjacent private homes and public buildings.

Denver buildings differ from those of many other cities in several ways. Their settings, in this wide-open metropolis unconstrained by any large body of water, are often spacious. Denver has been free to grow outward in every direction, and a western emphasis on elbow room has produced single-family, detached homes, which predominate even in poor, inner-city districts. On the outskirts, residential subdivisions, shopping malls, and office parks sprawl into surrounding counties.

Denver is also distinctively a brick city. Since the nearest forests lie 50 miles away, and clay beds underlie many areas of the city, clay for bricks was often easier to find and use than pine, which in any case was inferior to eastern hardwood. Brick, augmented with reddish local sandstone and, in recent years, tinted concrete, gives Denver a ruddy complexion.

Urban renewal projects, speculation, and rapid and reckless growth spurts have eliminated many notable structures, especially in the central business district and Capitol Hill. Since 1976, however, many nineteenth-century residential areas have been designated for preservation by the City Council on the recommendation of concerned citizens and the Denver Landmark Preservation Commission. The commission reviews alterations requiring a building permit and has ordinance authority to deny demolition in historic districts and to delay for one year destruction of individual landmarks. The commission has overseen designation of more than 260 individual landmarks and some 29 historic districts containing more than 5,000 buildings. Landmark districts include neighborhoods reflecting Italianate and Queen Anne styles, with some Romanesque Revival specimens. Nineteenth-century commercial buildings are represented in the Larimer Square and Lower Downtown historic districts. The central business district is dominated by a generic collection of contemporary concrete and glass high rises.

After 1900 Beaux-Arts, Italian, Spanish, Georgian, Tudor, and other revival styles became popular for residences. The most common type of housing is the one-story classical cottage, followed by foursquares, bungalows, and post–World War II ranch houses. Denverites were slow to experiment with Art Deco and Streamline Moderne styles.

The grid pattern is standard throughout the city, with the exception of some curvilinear post–World War II subdivisions. The pattern of development was determined after 1871 by streetcar lines, which enabled Denver early on to sprawl horizontally into neighborhoods of single-family, detached housing. The pattern of streetcar suburbanization continued with automobile suburbanization. Denver has one of the world's highest per capita car ownership rates—even higher than Los Angeles.

As the most isolated major city in the forty-eight contiguous states, Denver has long aspired to the most advanced transportation systems. In 1994 the city opened the first segment of a light rail system. A year later Denver International Airport opened as the nation's state-of-the-art airport. The early 1900s parkway network is well maintained and remains the best way to tour the city, either on wheels or on foot.

Civic Center

Civic Center (NRD), with its border of city, state, federal, and commercial office buildings, is the core legacy of Denver's City Beautiful era. Charles M. Robinson's 1906 plan used the state capitol as the eastern anchor of a civic mall connected to the central business district by a pedestrian mall along 16th Street. (The latter scheme was not constructed until 1982, with an I. M. Pei design.) Sculptor Frederick MacMonnies refined the Civic Center plan while working on his Pioneer Monument Fountain (1911; see DV013). He introduced the semicircles formed by curving Colfax and 14th avenues between Broadway and Bannock and placed the City and County Building on Bannock opposite the capitol. Frederick Law Olmsted, Jr., also contributed a plan (1912), as did Chicago city planner Edward H. Bennett (1917). Saco R. DeBoer subsequently re-

fined the landscape design for the central park. The park was restored in 1991, but a jagged skyline of glass and masonry skyscrapers around Civic Center has blocked the mountain view and shattered the old dream of classical harmony.

DV001 **Colorado State Capitol**

1886–1908, Elijah E. Myers, Frank E. Edbrooke. E. Colfax to E. 14th aves. between Lincoln and Grant sts.

The main axis of the Civic Center plan is decisively terminated on the east by the capitol, a cruciform building of four stories culminating in a gold dome. Like many domed state capitols of its era, it is inspired by the national Capitol. The exterior walls are Colorado gray granite from the Aberdeen Quarry in Gunnison County. Lighter, cheaper, granite-colored cast iron is used for the three cylindrical stages of the dome. Colorado mining magnates donated the 24-carat gold leaf on the 272-foot-high dome, which was regilded in 1949, 1980, and 1991.

Elijah Myers also designed state capitols for Idaho, Michigan, Texas, and Utah. As in his other statehouses, Myers gave Colorado a classical design of Renaissance origins but with unmistakably nineteenth-century proportions and handling of the orders. Similar, symmetrical bays characterize all four sides, with a west entrance portico overlooking Civic Center. Triple-arched central entrances on each side are topped by triangular pediments with bas-relief sculptures.

The Capitol Board of Managers dismissed Myers in 1889 to save money. Board member Otto Mears explained, "The state has got his plans, and has paid for them. You see we

Inset 1. Civic Center (DV001–DV013)

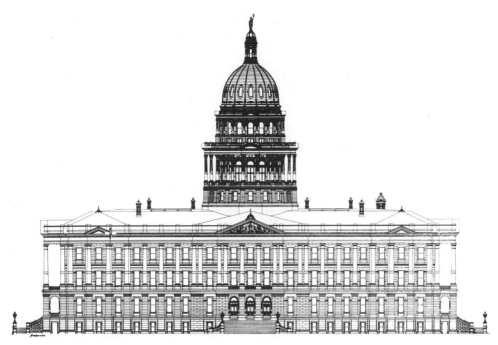

DV001 Colorado State Capitol, elevation, Elijah E. Myers

don't need him." Myers, who was then over sixty, responded that "for a man of my age and experience, this is a most unpleasant occurrence" and returned to his home in Michigan. Frank E. Edbrooke, who had placed second in the original architectural competition, completed the structure, basically following Myers's 1886 design. Edbrooke suggested a gold rather than copper skin for the dome and substituted rich Composite capitals on the porticoes for Myers's more austere Tuscan capitals. The other obvious change was the disappearance of the allegorical female figure meant to represent Colorado with which Myers had crowned the dome. Apparently the legislature, after considerable study of models in various states of dress, could not agree on which was the most shapely.

Capitol interiors feature Beulah red marble and Colorado Yule marble wainscoting and brass fixtures. Of 160 rooms, the most noteworthy are the old Supreme Court chambers, the Senate and House chambers, and the first-floor rotunda, whose walls display murals (1938) by Colorado's premier muralist, Allen Tupper True, and a poem by Colorado poet laureate Thomas Hornsby Ferril.

The capitol complex has grown to include the WPA-funded State Capitol Annex (DV001.1; 1939, Arthur A. Fisher, Sidney Frazier, G. Meredith Musick, Frederick Mountjoy, C. Francis Pillsbury, Charles S. Thomas), 1375 Sherman Street (at East 14th Avenue) (NR), a starved-classical box. The restored State Office Building (DV001.2; 1921, William N. Bowman; 1985, Urban Design Group), 201 East Colfax Avenue, is a Renaissance palace, especially notable for its interior court.

DV002 Old State Museum

1913, Frank E. Edbrooke. Southeast corner of Sherman and E. 14th Ave.

This classical palace with Greek Revival detail is the last work of Frank Edbrooke, who designed it to harmonize with the state capitol, which it faces. In addition to completing the capitol, between 1880 and his death in 1921 Edbrooke's firm, F. E. Edbrooke Architect Co., designed a wide range of buildings, commercial and residential, that

DV002 Old State Museum, perspective, F. E. Edbrooke Architect Co.

per floors threaten to crush anyone walking through the cutout beneath them. The museum was supposed to front on Civic Center Park but the Supreme Court used its clout to flip the plan and take the park frontage. A raised skylight illuminates the subterranean law library, and a mural by Angelo di Benedetto depicts history's great lawgivers. The lack of an easily discoverable entrance may be a commentary on the labyrinthine legal system.

DV004 Denver Public Library

1955, Burnham F. Hoyt, Fisher and Fisher. 1995, Michael Graves with Klipp Colussy Jenks DuBois. 10 W. 14th Ave. (NR)

A large semicircular glass bay on the north side of this full-block complex overlooks Civic Center, whose scale, massing, and colors are reinterpreted in the four-story library building of 1955. Its subtle play on classical composition includes two-story window bands representing a glazed colonnade, with third-story fenestration arranged like a frieze. The reinforced concrete frame is clad with Indiana limestone, shot-blasted to raise the horizontal grain. The foundation veneer is polished, dark green Austrian granite.

set the style of a blossoming city. The square, three-story Old State Museum building is sheathed in polished Colorado Yule marble on a Gunnison granite base. Four fluted marble columns with Ionic capitals support a shallow entrance portico. After the museum moved to 1300 Broadway in 1977, this building was restored as legislative offices. It retains its exquisite marble interior with golden oak and bronze trim.

DV003 Colorado History Museum and Colorado Judicial Building

1977, Rogers-Nagel-Langhart. 1300 Broadway

The Colorado History Museum is a three-story structure of gray brick (a marble skin was cut from the budget) forming a flat-topped triangle with three north terraces descending to an open courtyard. Primary exhibition space for the museum is located below ground, with offices, including the State Historic Preservation Office, on upper levels. Exhibits include a wonderfully detailed WPA diorama of Denver in 1860 and of the Mesa Verde Cliff Dwellings. This museum building is a step down in design, materials, and location from its predecessor (DV002).

The new museum shares its square-block site with the granite-clad, five-story Colorado Judicial Building, which relates to Civic Center with a cut-through opening at ground level. Standing on two legs straddling the first floor, this awkward white edifice disproves the theory that the grand public buildings of the City Beautiful era would inspire other noble structures. The four up-

Michael Graves's seven-story addition to the south has a base of banded granite below a south facade of creamy, fossil-encrusted limestone. Upper stories on the east, north, and west are of cast aggregate stone in greenish and reddish tones wrapping rectangles and cylinders. Unlike the classical composition by Robert A. M. Stern also submitted in the design competition, the Graves design does not respond enthusiastically to either the Neoclassicism of the Civic Center Historic District or the 1955 library. Indeed, his building is "medieval" in having clearly articulated masses that express their functions. His village of different colors and shapes ranges from the copper-clad children's library entry pavilion to the multistory pink stone drum housing adult reading rooms. This distinctive drum, a Graves signature, is centered in the set-back, rectangular massing of the south elevation, where Graves comes closest to Neoclassical harmony with his 13th Avenue facade. Changing colors and textures for various elements enliven the massing and highlight the geometrical shapes of the new structure,

DV004 Denver Public Library

which tripled the library's size. The central great hall and the western history reading room and art gallery are spectacular interior spaces. Graves used warm golden maple for wall panels and his custom-designed tables, lamps, and chairs.

DV005 Denver Art Museum

1971, Gio Ponti with James Sudler Associates. 100 W. 14th Ave., between Acoma and Bannock sts.

Both I. M. Pei and Le Corbusier turned down this commission before it was accepted by Gio Ponti of Milan, a free-spirited creator of everything from factories to espresso machines. Ponti collaborated on his only U.S. building with Denver architect James Sudler to make the museum a dramatic piece of art that demands attention. Their moated castle is clad in custom Corning polished glass tile with seemingly random window slits, some in protruding surrounds. It has been called, by *San Francisco Chronicle* architecture critic Allen Temko, "the largest lavatory in the world." The reinforced concrete frame carries twenty-eight vertical sides rising to crenelated parapets at the roofline. These tall slabs disguise the relative simplicity of the plan, which consists of two squares with cut corners joined at the utility core. A dramatic entrance through an elliptical concrete tunnel sheathed in stainless steel

transports visitors to an airy lobby and stacked, vertical galleries. Each gallery focuses on specific collections, of which the most notable is Native American art. Despite the interior, this building is damned by its slabby exterior walls, which give it the look of a fortress protecting its loot from the hordes. Worse, its huge bulk belittles the City Beautiful idea of generous landscaping and overshadows the nearby City and County Building.

DV006 Byers-Evans House

1883. 1898, addition. 1989, restoration, Long Hoeft Architects. 1310 Bannock St. (NR)

This two-story Italianate house, which shares the block with the Denver Art Museum, was built by William Newton Byers, founding editor of the *Rocky Mountain News*. In 1889 it became home to the family of William Gray Evans, son of Colorado territorial governor John Evans. Restored as a house museum containing many Evans family furnishings, it focuses on Denver history in general as well as the Byers and Evans clans. Different fenestration betrays the 1898 two-story south addition of a library, bathrooms, and bedrooms. In the former servants' quarters and garage, interactive video displays and other exhibits portray the development of Denver.

DV007 **Denver Permit Center** (University of Denver Law School)

1960, Perkins and Will, Temple Hoyne Buell. 1990, James Hartman, Robert Datson, and Robert Root of C. W. Fentress and Associates. Southwest corner of W. 14th Ave. and Bannock St.

A Modernist box was transformed into neo-classicized city offices with a new skin of gray synthetic stone panels to blend with the neighboring City and County Building. The rotunda at the northeast corner entrance salutes the Beaux-Arts Neoclassicism of other Civic Center buildings. As the first work completed after a 1982 city ordinance requiring allocation of one percent of public building budgets for art, this planning, permit, and Denver Landmark Preservation Commission office displays a large mural of Denver street life behind the courtyard information desk and a stainless steel and neon sculpture resembling a car wreck suspended in the rotunda entry.

DV008 **Civic Center Park**

1906, Charles M. Robinson; many revisions. 1991, renovation, Long Hoeft Architects. Colfax to 14th aves. between Grant and Bannock sts.

Between the City and County Building on the west and the capitol on the east, this park is bounded on the north and south by two classical structures inspired by the 1893 World's Columbian Exposition. Enclosing the north end of the axial crossing, the Voorhies Memorial (DV008.1; 1919, William E. Fisher and Arthur A. Fisher), 100 West Colfax Avenue, is a modest copy of the Water Gateway to the 1893 fair. An arcade of Turkey Creek sandstone arcs around a pool and a pair of cherub-on-dolphin fountains designed by Denver sculptor Robert Garrison. In the lunettes of the arcade are murals by Allen True depicting bison and elk in the style and colors of antique Greek vases. The memorial was funded by banker and mining entrepreneur John H. P. Voorhies, who lived across the street. The Greek Theater and Colonnade of Civic Benefactors (DV008.2; 1919, Marean and Norton), West 14th Avenue and Acoma Street, echoes and balances the Voorhies Memorial across the lateral axis of Civic Center. Edward Bennett, the protégé and successor of Daniel Burnham, proposed this despite local critics who complained, "Why the hell does Denver need a Greek theater? We ain't got that many Greeks here!"

The theater's arc responds to the curving wings of the Voorhies Memorial and matches the memorial's Turkey Creek sandstone. Two murals by Allen True, *Trapper* and *Prospector,* depict pioneer types in vivid wilderness settings. The north side is terraced down into an open semicircular arena seating 1,200.

Plans for a sunken sculpture garden solidified with two bronze statues by Denverite Alexander Phimister Proctor, *Bronco Buster* (1920) and *On the War Trail* (1922). On the east side of the capitol is *Closing Era,* a bronze Indian and buffalo crafted for the 1893 World's Columbian Exposition by Preston Powers, who once taught in Denver. Newer memorials and sculptures augment, and in some cases clutter, Civic Center Park.

DV009 **City and County Building Annex No. 2** (Denver Public Library)

1910, Albert Randolph Ross. 144 W. Colfax Ave.

This three-story Greek Revival temple of Turkey Creek sandstone was designed by a New York architect and funded in part by a $200,000 grant from Andrew Carnegie. The main north facade is fronted by giant Corinthian columns culminating in a dentiled cornice. Square pilasters back the columns and continue around the building to divide fenestration bays under a truncated hipped roof. Since the library moved across Civic Center in 1956, the interior has been awkwardly remodeled to accommodate city agencies.

DV010 **City and County Building**

1932, Allied Architects: Roland L. Linder, Robert K. Fuller, et al. 1437 Bannock St.

Balancing the capitol and providing the necessary mass to complete a dominant east-west axis for Civic Center Park, this is the grandest monument of Mayor Speer's City Beautiful. Conceived as part of the original Robinson Plan of 1906, it took twenty-six years to materialize on its full-block site. The design was refined and implemented by a coalition of thirty-nine leading local architects. The Beaux-Arts Neoclassical facade has

DV008 Civic Center Park

DV009 City and County Building Annex No. 2 (Denver Public Library)

DV010 City and County Building, 1941

three-story Corinthian entry columns of travertine atop a grand staircase. Unusual curving wings with engaged Doric columns reach toward the capitol or, some say, toward taxpaying citizens. Dressed Cotopaxi granite forms the base. Upper walls and the entry columns are Stone Mountain, Georgia, granite. Tremendous bronze doors in the pedimented entry portico open to an interior featuring eleven varieties of marble. Colorado travertine panels the main corridors and forms eight 19-foot-tall columns in the second-floor entry rotunda. It and the fourth-floor City Council Chambers are the most elaborate interior spaces.

The gold eagle and carillon clock tower capping this handsome city hall were donated in Mayor Speer's memory by his widow, Kate. The slender bell tower and the building's relatively low profile preserve vistas of the mountains from Capitol Hill.

Despite charges of bad taste and civil liberties suits, the City and County Building has been decorated riotously with colored lights every Christmas since 1932. A $10 million refurbishing in 1991–1992 brightened the interior and restored some features, including the grand lobby, Allen True's mural *The Miners' Court,* and Gladys Caldwell Fisher's life-size bas-relief *Orpheus and the Animals.* In the main entry lobby, 1993 works by Denver artist Susan Cooper depict Denver's architectural heritage.

DV011 Denver Mint

1906, James Knox Taylor, OSA, with Tracy, Swarthwout and Litchfield; several additions. 320 W. Colfax Ave. between Cherokee and Delaware sts. and W. 14th Ave. (NR)

This two-story rectangular fortress inspired by the Palazzo Medici-Riccardi in Florence is clad on the first level in black-flecked pink Pikes Peak granite that contrasts with the Colorado gray granite ashlar above. Marble lunettes, some bearing carved eagles, top high, rectangular windows on the first level, with smaller, paired second-floor windows divided by marble columns and topped by arched marble panels, each inlaid with a single disk. The granite cornice is bracketed above a decorated frieze. Wrought iron is used for the entry lanterns, window grilles, and fencing above a low granite retaining wall. Murals by Vincent Aderente in the

DV011 Denver Mint, c. 1910

main vestibule represent mining, manufacturing, and commerce. Although James Knox Taylor was the supervising architect in Washington, the New York City firm of Tracy, Swarthwout and Litchfield designed the mint. Additions have detracted from this monument to Colorado's gold rush origins, but it remains the city's most popular free attraction and a stately reminder not only of Denver's history but also of the Renaissance origins of banking.

DV012 City Hall Annex No. 1 (Denver University Business School)

1949, Casper Hegner, Thomas Moore, G. Meridith Musick, Dudley Smith. 2002, addition, David Owen Tryba. 1445 Cleveland Pl. (NR)

One of Denver's best International Style buildings comments on its Beaux-Arts neighbors with a studied absence of applied decoration. The roof extends over a fourth-story deck overlooking Civic Center. Solid end walls of dressed white Indiana limestone enclose rectangular planes, while alternating bands of limestone and windows with projecting sun shields along the south facade give the building horizontal orientation.

DV013 Pioneer Monument Fountain

1911, Frederick MacMonnies. Northwest corner of Colfax Ave. and Broadway

Public uproar about honoring "raping, pillaging, lazy, sneaky, dirty redskins" forced Frederick MacMonnies to replace his original heroic Native American figure with one of Kit Carson atop this monument on a triangular site along the north edge of Civic Center. Carson, on horseback, dominates bronze figures of a prospector, a hunter, and a rifle-toting pioneer mother with her infant. The hexagonal granite base also supports a fountain flowing into a pool at the base of the statuary. The monument was restored in 1983.

Downtown

Denver has one of the country's more livable and walkable downtowns. The 16th Street Pedestrian Mall (1982, I. M. Pei and Partners) and the Lower Downtown (LoDo) Historic District, designated in 1988, have reversed deterioration of the city core. Urban renewal in the 1960s erased many of the city's grandest monuments, replacing them with high rises between 14th and 20th streets and Curtis and Larimer streets. Construction tapered off after a new generation of glass and masonry towers arose during the energy boom of the 1970s and early 1980s. LoDo's nineteenth-century red brick, sandstone, and rhyolite commercial buildings of one to seven stories have been rejuvenated with art galleries, night clubs, cafes, and residential lofts. This upscale historic district in what had been Denver's skid row has attracted such major developments as Coors Field, Elitch Gardens amusement park, a projected indoor sports arena, and a planned aquarium.

Broadway, Denver's main north-south axial, cuts across the original, skewed grid of named and numbered streets and divides east and west numbers on the avenues of the cardinal grid. The free 16th Street mall shuttle from the Civic Center RTD Terminal (DV014) at Broadway and 16th Avenue stops at most of the named streets mentioned below.

DV014 **Civic Center RTD Terminal and Denver Post Tower**

1984, Johnson, Hopson, terminal; Hellmuth, Obata and Kassabaum, tower. 1560 Broadway (southeast corner of E. 16th Ave.)

This rare example of courteous, human-scale high-rise architecture is set back to preserve the view of Longs Peak from the state capitol. On the southeast corner, over the bus station, is a pedestrian plaza overlooking Civic Center.

DV015 **16th Street Pedestrian Mall**

1982, I. M. Pei and Partners. Between Broadway and Wynkoop St. at Union Station

After Pei designed the Mile High Center and the Zeckendorf Plaza, his firm was asked to design this granite-paved pedestrian mall to revive downtown's main retail street. Sleek street furniture, fountains, and trees make the spaces people-friendly. The mile-long pedestrian mall connects Civic Center with Lower Downtown.

DV016 **Adams Mark Hotel** (Zeckendorf Plaza)

1958–1960, I. M. Pei and Partners. 350 16th St. (Court Pl. between 15th and 16th sts.)

Winner of a 1959 National AIA Honor Award, this two-block complex for developer William Zeckendorf includes a twenty-two-story hotel, a department store, and a three-level underground parking garage. The hotel, a narrow slab building, has a skin of ruddy exposed precast aggregate panels, pierced on east and west sides by grid windows. Sand and gravel for the aggregate came from the excavation itself. The four-story department store next door, connected to the hotel by both a sky bridge and an underground corridor, is a cube 266 feet on a side with an anodized aluminum grid curtain facade. A hyperbolic paraboloid pavilion with glass curtain walls fronts the 16th Street Pedestrian Mall. In 1996 the paraboloid was demolished and the department store partially gutted to expand the hotel.

DV017 **Curry-Chucovitch-Gerash House**

1888, Frederick A. Hale. 1982, restoration, Edward D. White, Jr. 1439 Court Pl. (NR)

The last remnant of a residential neighborhood, this two-and-one-half-story, side-hall Victorian townhouse stands alone amid asphalt parking lots. Hale, who began his career in Frank Edbrooke's office, used rosy

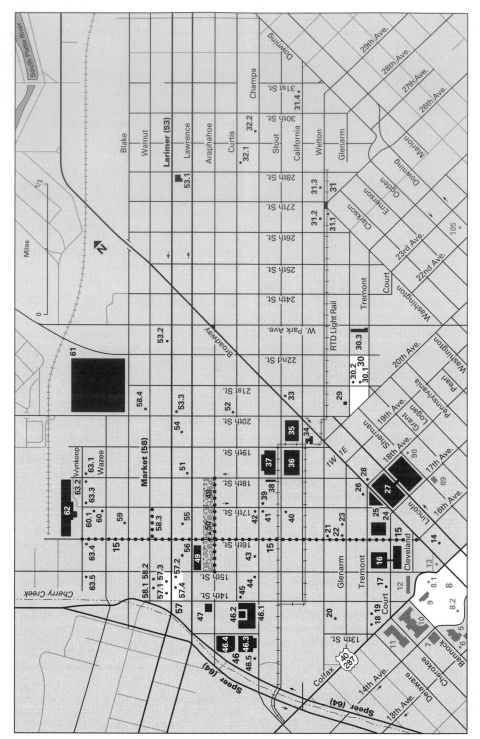

Inset 2. Downtown (DV014–DV064)

50

sandstone in random ashlar with carved stone trim for the facade of the red brick house. The original wooden cornice, with a recessed panel frieze, is topped by a rooftop balustrade above the slate roof. In 1982 Denver's best-known defense attorney, Walter Gerash, restored the house as law offices.

DV018 **Fire Station No. 1** (Firefighters Museum)

1909, Glen W. Huntington. 1326 Tremont Pl.

This Neoclassical fire station was converted in 1980 to a museum with a restaurant in the former upstairs living quarters. Behind the ornate gray brick and light sandstone facade, topped by an elaborate dentiled cornice, the original interior is starkly functional, almost modern, and retains its fire pole amid a wealth of equipment and memorabilia.

DV019 **Ady Terrace** (Tremont Apartments)

1889, Robert S. Roeschlaub. 1332–1338 Tremont Pl.

This two-and-one-half-story Romanesque Revival red brick apartment house is decorated with terracotta foliage. An elegantly curved staircase with an iron railing leads to the horseshoe arch of the entry, with its rough-faced sandstone voussoirs. The L plan creates a courtyard for garden-level entrances and small, wrought iron balconies.

DV020 **Denver Athletic Club**

1889, Varian and Sterner; several additions. 1325 Glenarm Pl. (NR)

The sedate world of eastern men's clubs arrived in Denver with this six-story club house of rough-faced pink sandstone and red brick. A sandstone basement and first floor support a flat facade with round window arches. Recessed spandrels between the second and third floors add horizontal emphasis to the paired brick arches. The 13th Street athletic facilities addition (1973, Rodney S. Davis) and the 14th Street addition (1984, Joel Croenewitt of James Sudler Associates) match the red brick and lines of the original but with Modernist minimalism. Across the street, at 1330 Glenarm Place, is another local landmark, the Denver Press Club (1925, Merrill H. and Burnham F.

DV020 Denver Athletic Club, c. 1910

Hoyt), more notable for its history than its architecture.

DV021 **Masonic Temple**

1890, Frank E. Edbrooke. 1950, W. Gordon Jamieson. 1985, renovation and addition, C. W. Fentress and Associates. 1614 Welton St. (at 16th St.) (NR)

As a secret order that used the symbols of the building art in its emblem and made a ritual of laying cornerstones, the Masons often commissioned fine architectural monuments. Frank Edbrooke, himself a Mason, clad this eclectic Romanesque Revival landmark in red-orange Manitou sandstone with a Pikes Peak granite base. Corner towers are connected by a central arcade echoing the ground-floor arcade. The Welton Street entry is through a 15-foot-wide, elaborately carved Romanesque arch with engaged columns. After a 1984 fire, a new steel frame was erected within the buckled old walls and new stone from the original quarry was sculpted to resemble and replace the granite removed from the first two floors. With the addition of a hipped penthouse and interior rearrangements, the temple has been expanded from five to nine stories. In front of the recessed 16th Street entry, restoration architects erected a freestanding sandstone arch that reflects the round-arched openings in this otherwise chunky vernacular version of Romanesque Revival.

DV022 **Kittredge Building**

1891, A. Morris Stuckert. 511 16th. St. (at Glenarm Pl.) (NR)

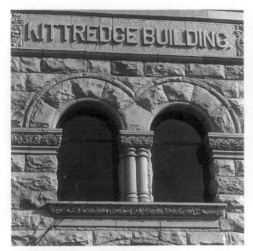

DV022 Kittredge Building

DV023 Paramount Theater

The vernacular Richardsonian Romanesque design of this seven-story antique is rendered in Pike's Peak granite on the first two floors and rhyolite above, with rich detailing. Secondary cornices at the bases of the third, fourth, and seventh stories add horizontal contrast to the general verticality created by the fenestration bays, which are arcaded at the second and sixth stories. The parapet has crenelated moldings and turrets and is broken by the pediment over the slightly protruding entrance bay. Developer Charles M. Kittredge's splendid office block also has a grand entry arch springing from polished granite half columns.

DV023 Paramount Theater

1930, Temple Hoyne Buell. 1631 Glenarm Pl. (NR)

C. W. and George Rapp designed many movie theaters across America in the 1920s, including Denver's only surviving downtown movie palace. Temple Hoyne Buell, then a member of the firm, created this 2,100-seat theater as an Art Deco composition of precast concrete block sheathed in white glazed terracotta trimmed with black marble. The three-story Glenarm Place facade is divided into twelve bays of paired windows, with recurrent rosettes, feathers, and fiddleleaf ferns, which also sprout from the Art Deco interior, although the twenty-rank twin Wurlitzer pipe organs can steal the show. Pilasters are capped by fan-shaped frosted glass

figures, and the sunburst ceiling and the chandelier create a starry effect. The grand, two-story theater entry lobby in the Kittredge Building to the west has been lost, and patrons now enter through the original exit doors on Glenarm Place.

DV024 Republic Plaza

1984, Skidmore, Owings and Merrill. 17th to 18th sts. between Court Pl. and Tremont Pl.

During Denver's flush times, Skidmore, Owings and Merrill opened a Denver office (1977–1988) to design and oversee local and regional projects. The firm offered the client the greatest square footage for cost in a comprehensive package that emphasized quality of materials and design, based on an aesthetic rooted in the International Style. For Republic Plaza, SOM used a monolithic grid of flush-mounted windows and polished Sardinian granite trimmed in narrow bands of aluminum. It is Denver's tallest building, soaring fifty-six stories above the streetscape of open terraces with minimal plantings. Pedestrians in the shadow beneath this monster can at least use its blank facade as a big-screen weather report, reflecting the sun, sky, and clouds it obscures.

Plans to develop the entire block were squelched by bartenders Kenny and Frank Lombardi, who refused $3.5 million for their Duffy's Shamrock Tavern (c. 1906), 1635 Tremont Place, a three-story Beaux-Arts box.

DV024 Republic Plaza
DV025 Brown Palace Hotel, lobby, 1920s

This popular bar and restaurant, with a front bar almost 72 feet long, has been open for decades seven days a week from 7:00 a.m to 2:00 a.m. It offers a historic, human-scale escape from surrounding office towers.

DV025 **Brown Palace Hotel**

1892, Frank E. Edbrooke. 321 17th St., between Tremont Pl. and Broadway (NR)

Henry C. Brown, who homesteaded Capitol Hill, asked Frank Edbrooke to design this $2 million palace. Edbrooke envisioned the three-sided, nine-story hotel with a sky-lighted atrium seventy-five years before John Portman made the Hyatt Hotel atrium a familiar form. To this day, no architect has handled so well the awkward triangular sites created by the meshing of Denver's original mining camp grid with the compass-oriented grids of later additions. By using three grand curves at the corners, Edbrooke wrapped the site effortlessly with red sandstone walls above a Pikes Peak granite base course. The steel and iron frame, clad in terracotta and concrete as well as stone, made this one of America's first fireproof structures, according to a May 21, 1892, cover story in *Scientific American.*

For the exterior, Edbrooke drew inspiration from H. H. Richardson's Marshall Field Wholesale Store and Louis Sullivan's Chicago Auditorium. As in these Chicago landmarks, repetition of arcaded window patterns, multiple cornices, and banding add horizontal emphasis to what was Denver's tallest building. The Brown Palace has expansive ogee entry arches in implied three-story towers and giant arches rising from the fourth through the seventh floors. Stone creatures once swarmed over the exterior, but nearly all were removed after pieces began bombarding the sidewalk. Even the grand stone cornice, inscribed "The H. C. Brown Hotel," has been pared off the Broadway facade, leaving the hotel without a definitive main entrance. Twenty-six medallions of native Colorado animals by James Whitehouse survive on the top-floor fenestration arcade, and the now-closed Broadway entry arch retains some stone trim, including a bas-relief bust of Brown.

The interior still has its opulent 1890s

spaciousness and many antique furnishings. From the overstuffed couches in the lobby, rubberneckers can admire the pastel shades of the skylight and the caramel and cream swirls flowing through 12,000 square feet of onyx paneling from Mexico. The best-preserved chamber, the Onyx Room, has a ceiling mural of cherubs hovering in a heavenly blue sky. In the Tremont Place entrance lobby, two later murals by Allen True contrast the stagecoach and airplane ages. The Ship Tavern, a 1935 celebration of the repeal of Prohibition, was designed by Alan B. Fisher, the son of architect William E. Fisher. The tavern is an inland seaport featuring a fortune in nautical artifacts, ranging from a crow's nest wrapped around the room's central beam to a collection of ships in bottles.

During the 1930s the hotel's high-ceilinged ninth-floor ballroom was converted to two floors of luxury residence suites in Art Deco style. Each hotel room initially had its own fireplace, but the flues and chimneys have been converted to air conditioning ducts, and the 10-foot-high lobby fireplace is now an alcove housing a boutique. The hotel offers free tours, which include a peek into President Dwight Eisenhower's former suite, with its knotty pine paneled walls and lime green tiled bathroom.

DV026 **Museum of Western Art** (The Navarre)

1880, Frank E. Edbrooke. 1983, restoration, C. W. Fentress and Associates with John M. Prosser. 1725–1727 Tremont Pl. (NR)

This rectangular, four-story Italianate structure of red brick is enhanced by projecting full-height bays with pedimented gables. Built as a girls' school, it later became the Navarre, Denver's most notorious department store of vice. It was subsequently rehabilitated as a restaurant and jazz club. In 1983 the Navarre was reincarnated as the Museum of Western Art. The restoration removed a century of additions and revisions and resurrected the double-bracketed cornice and distinctive copper cupola. The building is connected by a legendary basement tunnel to the Brown Palace Hotel across Tremont Place, but the passage is in fact a utility tunnel, too tiny to allow any substantial hotel guest patronage of the Navarre.

DV027 **Wells Fargo Bank, previously, Norwest Bank Center** (Mile High Center)

1956, I. M. Pei and Partners. 1981, Johnson/Burgee. 1700 Broadway

Denver's most conspicuous skyscraper is the 1981 addition to this center, the "cash register" with its arc top, a fifty-two-story shrine to money. It is part of a complex of related structures that occupies three city blocks along East 17th Avenue at the base of the tower. The core is I. M. Pei's Mile High Center at 1700 Broadway, the site of the mansion that housed Capitol Hill developer Henry C. Brown and, later, silver king Horace A. W. Tabor. Developer William Zeckendorf originally complained that Pei "wasted" space on an exhibition hall, plaza, fountains, pools, and shops, but later complimented Pei: "You've doubled the equity." Pei's corner tower features interwoven vertical and horizontal panels. Those covering columns and spandrel beams are dark gray cast aluminum, while panels hiding heating and cooling conduits are off-white porcelain enamel. Pei did much of the design work himself on one of the first of his high-rise commissions.

Pei's barrel-vaulted roofs have been replaced by glazed framed arches that connect the buildings and echo the beak in Philip Johnson's taller structure to the east. The new construction presses setbacks to the limit, sacrificing pedestrian comfort and scale for profitability and impressive size. Inside, an airy, fourteen-story atrium soars above a bar, restaurant, trees, and even some in-house sparrows. The interior is finished in opulent materials such as imported marble and onyx. Especially lavish are the various marble claddings used to customize the bank of elevators in the Neo-Renaissance great hall. The glass atrium arcs at the base mirror the arc at the top, which dropped accumulated snow and ice on the sidewalks below before heating coils were installed.

DV028 **Trinity United Methodist Church**

1888, Robert S. Roeschlaub. 1982, restoration and expansion, Seracuse, Lawler and Partners. 1820 Broadway (NR)

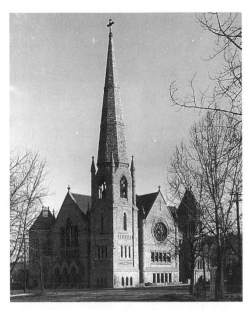

DV028 Trinity United Methodist Church, c. 1890

Trinity United Methodist Church is the finest building of Colorado's first licensed architect. The light weight of volcanic rhyolite from the Castle Rock quarries in Douglas County allowed Robert Roeschlaub to design a 181-foot-high hexagonal corner steeple in stone. The same rhyolite lends multicolored hues and a rough texture to downtown's oldest church. Tooled purple Utah sandstone trim includes three horizontal contrasting stripes in the steeple. This allusion to the Trinity is repeated in the triple-arched entry on Broadway and in Gothic windows arranged in sets of three.

Inside, Roeschlaub's 1,200-seat sanctuary resembles a theater, where a large proscenium arch frames a 4,000-pipe Roosevelt organ. Electric lights on the arch, box seats, and a balcony lend opera hall drama. Most of the stained glass windows are by Healy and Millet of Chicago, fabricators for Louis Sullivan. The solid bronze and oak pulpit commemorates the church's most famous pastor, the Reverend Henry Buchtel, who also served as chancellor of the University of Denver and governor of Colorado.

In 1982 Trinity sold its air rights to a Toronto developer (who never used them) for a $2 million endowment in addition to restoration of the church and construction of a subterranean office, education, and parking complex under a park. This exquisitely designed and preserved church of Denver's oldest religious congregation has superb acoustics, making it a favorite site for public lectures and musical performances.

DV029 St. Andrew's Episcopal Church

1908, Ralph Adams Cram. 1928, Clergy House, Jacques Benedict. 2015 Glenarm Pl. (NR)

Ralph Adams Cram, a high-church Anglican and devotee of John Ruskin, became America's foremost champion of Gothic Revival churches. He designed St. Andrew's as a small, Perpendicular Gothic church on an L plan built of dark red Harvard brick with limestone lintels, tan brick stringcourses, and a slate roof. The interior, dominated by tall brick Gothic arches, has a timbered ceiling and diamond-paned windows with leaded amber glass and exterior wooden Gothic tracery. Works of art include a reredos by Albert Bryan Olsen and a statue of the Virgin by Margaret Buchanan.

DV030 Clements Historic District Area

Glenarm Pl. to Tremont Pl. between 20th and 22nd sts. and several adjacent buildings

This enclave bordering the downtown business district contains restored individual and row houses of the 1880s and 1890s. The Kingston Row (DV030.1; 1890, Arthur S. Miller), 401–415 21st Street (at Tremont Place) (NR), is an ornate, three-story, red brick terrace, designed and built in Queen Anne elegance. At either end are semicylindrical towers topped with slate roofs and matching finials. The fussy facade fenestration ranges from Richardsonian arched windows to diamond-paned dormers to curved glass in the towers. The Thomas House (DV030.2; 1883, William Quayle), 2104 Glenarm Place (NR), reflects the eclectic combination of stylistic elements favored by the middle class. William Quayle, who opened a Denver office in 1880, often worked with his brothers Charles and Edward. In 1900, Quayle moved to San Diego, where his work became more prominent. Like many other houses and school buildings Quayle designed, this one reflects his adroit eclecticism. A 1975 restoration highlighted the finely detailed brickwork, especially on the chimney, and the stone window trim.

Ebert Elementary School (DV030.3; 1924, Mountjoy and Frewen), 410 West Park Avenue (at Tremont Place), is a two-story Renaissance Revival school building of light yellow brick enlivened by concrete moldings with lion heads, human heads, garlands, and a floral frieze. In the library, polychromatic terracotta tiles around the fireplace depict fairy-tale characters. Sympathetic additions have not detracted from this elegant and symmetrical structure.

DV031 Five Points Neighborhood

Bounded by 20th St., 20th Ave., Downing St., and the South Platte River

Five Points is named for the five-way intersection of 27th Avenue, Washington Street, 26th Street, and Welton Street, the main street of Denver's early twentieth-century African American neighborhood. Following a pattern typical of other cities, the area's population was initially white, with many German and Jewish residents. Not until the 1920s was Denver's small and previously scattered black community forced by restrictive housing covenants into Five Points. Italianate houses built in the 1880s, when this was part of the elegant Curtis Park streetcar suburb, linger behind some of the storefronts.

The Rossonian Hotel, formerly the Baxter Hotel (DV031.1; 1911, George Bettcher), 2650 Welton Street, is a restored brick edifice, once home to Denver's premier jazz club. The Ex-Servicemen's Club and Casino Ball Room (DV031.2), 2633–2639 Welton Street, is a two-story brick complex housing the city's first major African American–owned hotel. During the jazz age, this turn-of-the-century commercial building was updated with an Art Deco ballroom. La Paz Pool Hall, formerly Douglass Undertaking Company (DV031.3; 1891; 1916 remodeling, Merrill H. and Burnham F. Hoyt), 2745 Welton Street, is a reminder that Neoclassicism was more than an elitist style for grand public buildings. The single-story, three-bay storefront of flat brick features an urn recessed in the tympanum of the pedimented and pilastered facade. The original business supposedly was founded by a son of abolitionist Frederick Douglass. A typical Italianate house at 3091 California Street, once the home of African American physician Justina

L. Ford, is now the Black American West Museum (DV031.4; 1890; 1991 restoration, C. W. Fentress, J. H. Bradburn and Associates).

DV032 Curtis Park Historic District

Approximately California to Arapahoe sts. between 24th and Downing sts. with exclusions (NRD)

Within the Five Points Neighborhood, this district of Victorian homes includes Denver's first park (1868), a donation to the city from Sanuel S. Curtis, a developer of the pioneer streetcar suburb, Curtis Park. It is Denver's oldest surviving residential neighborhood, developed in the 1870s. Initially a haven for those with the means to move out of the city, Curtis Park evolved into a black, Hispanic, and Japanese neighborhood during the 1920s and 1930s. The David Crowell House (DV032.1; 1873; 1977 restoration, Brian Congleton), 2816 Curtis Street, is a small frame cottage and perhaps the oldest structure in the area. Typical of the larger Italianate homes is that of department store founder John Jay Joslin (DV032.2; 1880), 2915 Champa Street. Since the 1970s the neighborhood has been partly gentrified. The Curtis Park Face Block project restored pedestrian ambiance by reinstalling sandstone sidewalks and street trees. Exterior rehabilitation of forty-three houses in the district won a national AIA Honor Award for preservation architects Gary Long and Kathy Hoeft. They helped rescue two nineteenth-century brick workers' cottages by moving them to the southwest corner of 28th Avenue and Curtis Street, renovating the interiors, and selling them to low-income buyers.

Styles represented within the district include Italianate (2639 Curtis Street), Queen Anne (2663 and 2820 Champa Street), and Carpenter's Gothic (the church at 2501 California Street and houses at 2630 Curtis Street and 2927 Champa Street). Also of note are many eclectic Victorian homes throughout the district, Second Empire designs at 2445 California Street and 2601 Champa Street, and single-story frame cottages at 2913 Curtis Street and 2826 and 2828 Stout Street.

Nearby, along Arapahoe and Lawrence streets, bland blocks of two-story brick townhouses of fireproof concrete construction, originally built as public housing, are being renovated and sold to low-income families as individually owned units. Many of the former tenants have become homeowners, and this changeover, coupled with the addition of gabled terneplate roofs and new window and entry bays to create architectural interest, has bolstered the neighborhood.

DV033 Punch Bowl Tavern

1885. 2052 Stout St.

Darkly romantic murals of mountain scenes adorn the high-backed booths in this narrow bar with a pressed metal ceiling. The murals, according to barstool authorities, were painted, at the rate of a booth a day for a quart a day, by Noel Adams, also known as Chief Sundown. The Punch Bowl, which retains a name from the days when it harbored boxers and their fans, is one of the few old-time saloons in the city to escape urban renewal and gentrification. Originally a cottage, it is scarred with a rough break in the wall where the living room was expanded to become a barroom.

DV034 Holy Ghost Catholic Church

1943, Jacques Benedict and John K. Monroe. 1900 California St. (at 19th St.)

The Lombard-style beige brick and terracotta exterior of this church only hints at the rich interior. Some 300 tons of rose and beige travertine marble from Salida, Colorado, provide a tranquil background for grand wrought iron chandeliers, two banks of predominantly blue stained glass windows, and elaborate dark woodwork. Hundreds of hand-painted glazed tiles are set between carved wooden beams in the coffered ceiling, and an elaborate baldacchino celebrates the role of the church as Denver's daily expositor of the Blessed Sacrament.

Homeless people slept on the golden oak pews until the church sold its rectory, cloister, garage, and air rights to the developer of the adjacent forty-four-story 1999 Broadway Office Tower (1989, C. W. Fentress and Associates). An ambitious glittering green glass tower hovers over the church, like a design intended for Manhattan. The church used the sale proceeds for a restoration and to build Samaritan House (1986, Barker, Rinker, Seacat and Partners), 2301 Lawrence Street, the country's first purpose-built homeless shelter.

DV035 U.S. Custom House

1931, James A. Wetmore, OSA. 1937, addition, Temple Hoyne Buell and G. Meredith Musick. 721 19th St. (at Stout St.) (NR)

The U-shaped custom house is a five-story Italian Renaissance Revival palace cloaked in Colorado Yule marble carved with classical symbols of the federal government's majesty. Colorado's U.S. Senator Lawrence C. Phipps, Colorado Governor Edwin C. Johnson, and Denver Mayor Benjamin F. Stapleton all lobbied heavily for this building, persuading the federal government to substitute snowy white Colorado marble for Indiana limestone despite a $200,000 price increase. Marble was used lavishly inside and out in a building that helped confirm Denver's role as the hub of Rocky Mountain commerce and as a "little Washington" for federal offices.

DV036 City Center Tower

1984, Metz, Train and Youngman. 1801–1863 California St., to Stout St. between 18th and 19th sts.

Above a chocolate-colored Italian marble base, this fifty-four-story tower, which the architects likened to a craggy mountain, has a brown precast cement skin with vertical window bays that step back to profile a pair of interlocked octagons at the pinnacle. An open plaza fronts the southwest corner main entrance.

DV037 **Byron White U.S. Courthouse** (Main Post Office)

1910–1916, James Knox Taylor, OSA. 1922, Tracy, Swarthwout and Litchfield and Maurice Biscoe. 1994, restoration, Michael Barber Architecture. 1823 Stout St. (NR)

Denver's finest Neoclassical building is a five-story Greek temple handsomely masked by a giant colonnade and faced in Colorado Yule marble. On the Stout Street facade of the full-block building, sixteen three-story, fluted Ionic columns form a heroic portico atop a cascading marble staircase. Round-arched first-floor fenestration carries into the interior open courts. The names of post-masters general and of noted Pony Express riders are carved in the marble end walls of the dramatic, vaulted lobby. Gladys Caldwell Fisher, wife of Denver architect Alan Fisher, sculpted the mountain sheep flanking the 18th Street entrance. The Postal Service, banished to a hideous Postmodern address at 20th and Curtis, surrendered this building to the federal judiciary, which lavished millions on an opulent 1994 restoration for the Tenth Circuit Court of Appeals. The courthouse is named for the University of Colorado football star whom President John Kennedy appointed to the U.S. Supreme Court.

DV038 **Ghost Block**

1890, William Lang. 800 18th St. (at Stout St.)

This business block, named for its client, Allen M. Ghost, is the only commercial design by one of Denver's best-known residential architects, who had his office here. A two-story arcade embracing storefront and second-story office windows is highlighted by radiating stone trim beneath a double-corniced third story. Quarry-face brown sandstone laid in a vernacular Richardsonian Romanesque mode exhibits the eccentric, ornate detailing that hallmarked Lang's work. Built at 15th Street and Glenarm Place, the building was reconstructed here after being disassembled stone by stone. The resurrected Ghost Block reopened in 1990 as a popular restaurant featuring Old West food and drink and New West decor.

DV039 **Ideal Building**

1907, Montana Fallis and John J. Stein. 1927, William E. and Arthur A. Fisher. 821 17th St. (at Champa St.) (NR)

For its headquarters the Ideal Cement Company erected the region's first major reinforced concrete structure. The 1927 rear addition employed the same materials. The first two floors are faced with large blocks of dressed Colorado travertine, while the upper floors are clad in brick, now stuccoed. A central two-story arch with an American eagle keystone frames the entry to what was once the Denver National Bank. In conjunction with the 1927 addition, the bank redecorated the two-story lobby, whose ceiling is supported by steel columns simulating marble. Polychrome steel beams divide stained glass skylights, and a mezzanine frieze sculpted by Arnold Ronnebeck addresses the theme of money in history. The bank's huge basement vault has been converted to an intimate private dining room within a subterranean restaurant.

DV040 **Equitable Building**

1892, Andrews, Jacques and Rantoul. 730 17th St. (at Stout St.) (NR)

When it opened, the city's premier office building provided an elegant environment for white-collar workers distancing them-

DV040 Equitable Building
DV042 Colorado National Bank

selves from the grimy smelters and factories where most Denverites labored. Large, smooth granite blocks cover the first two stories of this gray brick edifice. It was Denver's first fine Italian Renaissance Revival structure, enlivened with stone carvings such as the cherubs adorning the stone porch of the fifth floor. The back-to-back, double-E plan not only displays the Equitable Life Assurance Society's logo but also allows light and air into interior offices. Above marble wainscoting, marble chip tiles in Byzantine motifs decorate the vaulted ceilings in a lobby illuminated by a tripartite, transomed Tiffany window. This design by Boston architects is overshadowed but not outclassed by many bland new skyscrapers on 17th Street, "the Wall Street of the Rockies."

DV041 Boston Building

1890, Andrews, Jacques and Rantoul. 828 17th (at Champa St.) (NR)

The Boston firm that designed the Equitable Building produced this combination of Renaissance Revival and Richardsonian Romanesque. A battered stone base rises to round-arched bays on the first, third, fifth, and seventh floors. These arches are repeated in a narrower version on the top story in pairs divided by colonnettes. The cube proportions and absence of recesses or

projections reflect the Renaissance Revival influence, while the arcaded fenestration bays are similar to those of Richardson's Marshall Field Wholesale Store. The huge blocks of red sandstone are from the Kenmuir Quarry near Manitou Springs. Weathering led to removal of the original narrow cornice, carved stringcourses, and trim and smoothing of the originally rough faces of the stone blocks at the base. In 1996–1997 this eight-story office building underwent a conversion to 130 lofts.

DV042 Colorado National Bank

1915, William E. Fisher and Arthur A. Fisher. 1924, Merrill H. and Burnham F. Hoyt. 1965, Rogers-Nagel. 1975, Minoru Yamasaki. 918 17th St. (at Champa St.)

Twenty fluted Ionic columns and bronze window screens front this Colorado Yule marble Greek temple for which William E. Fisher and Arthur A. Fisher prepared more than 135 pages of typed specifications, forty-four architectural drawings on waxed linen, and full-scale models of all ornament. Seerie Brothers, the contractors, provided weekly construction photos to document the progress of the steel frame rising from a 7-foot-thick reinforced concrete slab, 35 feet below grade.

Merrill and Burnham Hoyt designed a flawlessly matched addition along Champa

Street in 1926. They also enlisted Allen True to paint his romantic *Indian Memories* series of lobby murals, a tribute to Native Americans that is reminiscent of Greek art in style and in its depiction of a mythical past.

John B. Rogers and Jerome K. Nagel formed a partnership to design the 1965 addition of two stories above the prominent cornice in a respectful but contemporary manner with a matching white marble skin. Next door at 17th and Curtis, Minoru Yamasaki's twenty-six-story bank tower is sheathed in white marble similar to that of the parent building. Contrasting tinted glass gives the tower symmetry and a sense of proportion and stability. Instead of crowding the site, Yamasaki left a street corner plaza for Harry Bertoia's 1975 sculpture, a 20-foot-high wind chime made of beryllium copper rods with brass top weights. Yamasaki, who is best known as the architect of the World Trade Center in New York City, said he strove to avoid creating another of the "many brutal buildings being built today" by making this one "elegant, delightful and serene."

DV043 Odd Fellows Hall

1887, Emmett Anthony. 1983, renovation, C. W. Fentress and Associates. 1545 Champa St.

One of downtown's finest polished stone facades is crowned by a pressed metal roof with ball finials, a scrolled cornice, and a corner mansard tower. Restored to glory for $3.4 million, the old fraternal hall has new stone street-front columns and a grand, central stained glass window rehabilitated and encased in protective Lexan. Behind a dutiful facade restoration, Curt Fentress rearranged the interior, adding a skylighted atrium, a glass elevator, and a magnificent basement bar.

DV044 Denver Gas and Electric Company (Insurance Exchange Building)

1910, Harry W. J. Edbrooke. 910 15th St. (at Champa St.) (NR)

With 13,000 outlets for light bulbs in the terracotta skin, this is the brightest survivor of the "City of Lights" era, when Denver prided itself on the decorative illumination of its downtown. In this case the illumination was an attempt to brighten the dark public image of a monopoly that rigged elections to maintain its exclusive franchise. Arched tenth-story windows form an arcade beneath the flared cornice. A 1990 restoration uncovered the original entrance and relit the dazzling geometric light display. Harry W. J. Edbrooke, the son of Willoughby, began his architectural career in the Denver office of his uncle Frank.

DV045 Mountain States Telephone Building

1929, William N. Bowman. 14th and Curtis sts.

In a Deco Gothic style that the architect called American Perpendicular, this $11 million terracotta-clad tower with stepped-back massing climbs fifteen stories to a parapet with corner turrets. The tallest office building in the city upon completion, it boasted a base of granite from Platte Canyon quarries, brick made in Denver and Golden, terracotta manufactured by the Denver Terra Cotta Company, and structural steel from the Colorado Fuel and Iron Company in Pueblo. The interior has walls of Colorado travertine, and the ornamental wrought iron was made in Denver. The recessed 14th Street lobby, framed in elaborate terracotta surrounds, has a coffered ceiling, travertine walls, revolving doors in wrought iron housings, and murals by Allen True depicting a history of communication starting with Indian smoke signals.

DV046 Denver Center for the Performing Arts

1978–1979, Kevin Roche of Roche/Dinkeloo. 14th St. to Speer Blvd. between Arapahoe and Champa sts.

Curtis Street, Denver's old theater row, runs from Cherry Creek through downtown high rises to 1880s homes in Curtis Park. All of the old theaters, including the finest building in the city, the Tabor Grand Opera House (1880, Willoughby and Frank E. Edbrooke), once at 16th and Curtis, have been demolished. Their descendant is the Denver Center for the Performing Arts (DCPA). With multiple theaters, a television studio, voice research laboratories, and extensive production, rehearsal, and conservatory space, the DCPA is the second largest theater

DV046 Denver Center for the Performing Arts

complex in the country, after Lincoln Center in New York. It occupies four city blocks and incorporates a grassy park along Speer Boulevard. A barrel-vaulted glass canopy, an evocation of Milan's Galleria, connects an eight-level parking structure to the old auditorium and new theaters and shelters a pedestrian promenade extension of Curtis Street.

DV046.1 Denver Municipal Auditorium

1908, Robert Willison. 1941, G. Meredith Musick and Frederick E. Mountjoy. 1991, restoration, Semple Brown Roberts. 14th and Champa sts.

This historic cornerstone of what has become the DCPA complex opened July 4, 1908, to host the Democratic National Convention. It was second in size only to Madison Square Garden at the time. Its Neoclassical design, in beige brick with terracotta trim, follows that of an auditorium in St. Paul, Minnesota. Along with weekend and evening concerts, it has hosted everything from opera to auto shows, with flags flying from its domes and light bulbs outlining its pediments, domes, dentiled cornice, and quoined corners. The auditorium received a facelift in the early 1990s when part of it reopened as the Temple Hoyne Buell Theater.

DV046.1 Denver Municipal Auditorium, funeral service for Mayor Robert W. Speer, 1918

DV046.2 Temple Hoyne Buell Theater

1991, Beyer, Blinder, Belle, master plan; Van Dyke and Johnson, interiors

Named for the Denver architect and developer whose fortune posthumously helped fund it, this state-of-the-art theater is a 2,834-seat reincarnation of the municipal auditorium's old theater and basketball and wrestling arena. Colorado quartzite lines the walls and the proscenium arch of an interior accented with snazzy blue and purple neon ribbons. The three-level atrium lobby with outdoor balconies is enclosed in glass curtain walls. The Buell is home to the Colorado Ballet and DCPA's Best of Broadway touring presentations.

DV046.3 **Boettcher Concert Hall**

1978, Hardy Holzman Pfeiffer Associates and Hoover Berg Desmond

The Colorado Symphony and Opera Colorado perform in this Postmodern hall, constructed at a cost of $13 million. The rectangular, banded, brick-faced exterior, with its glazed corner lobby, gives little clue to the unique interior. The 2,600 seats are arranged in asymmetrical banks in a 360-degree surround, so that 80 percent of the audience sits within 65 feet of the 2,400-square-foot stage. The boxes have serpentine plastic fronts, and large, brassy sound-dispersion disks suspended from the ceiling give the interior a high-tech gaudiness.

DV046.4 **The Helen Bonfils Theater Complex**

1979, Roche/Dinkeloo. Arapahoe St. and Speer Blvd.

These four theaters with production space and rehearsal rooms are all wrapped in an acrobatic concrete exterior whose curves and angles complement its DCPA neighbors. In a design reminiscent of the architects' United Nations Plaza, a ribbon window set in roughly finished reinforced concrete is shielded by a wide glass canopy which becomes the entry awning. The interior spaces dramatically mix rough concrete, fabric-covered walls, carpeted floors, and mirror and mirror-finish surfaces that add theatrical sparkle. The largest of the four theaters, The Stage, has a seating capacity of 700 around a thrust stage. The Space seats 450 in a pentagonal hall with movable seating on three levels in an evocative echo of London's Old Globe Theater. The Ricketson Theater is a 195-seat end stage, while The Source is an informal 150-seat thrust stage. The resident Denver Center Theater Company is the largest professional resident ensemble between Chicago and the West Coast.

DV046.5 **DCPA Offices** (Denver Police Building)

1940, Earl Morris, G. Meredith Musick, and C. Francis Pillsbury. 1245 Champa St.

The WPA provided $200,000 for this Streamline Moderne structure. Its four-story, steel-frame and reinforced concrete shell is finished in glazed beige brick with concrete trim, subtle horizontal banding in the brick, and rounded corners. DCPA offices, voice laboratories, and studios now occupy the former police offices and jail.

DV047 **Denver Tramway Building**

1912, William E. Fisher and Arthur A. Fisher. 1100 14th St. (NR)

The family of territorial governor John Evans demolished his pioneer home to build the corporate offices of the streetcar monopoly headed by the governor's son, William Gray Evans. Renaissance Revival–inspired trim in white terracotta climbs the eight-story red brick tower, from the grand entry arches to a rooftop frieze with the tramway's *T* monogram. The brass entry lamps hint at the interior opulence of a lobby with pink Tennessee marble floors, a base of green Vermont marble, and wainscoting of white Arizona marble. Marble trim, handsome hardwoods, and bronze fixtures remain throughout much of the tower. The tower and the three-story attached streetcar barns were converted in 1957 to the University of Colorado's Denver campus. After CU-Denver moved out, the complex was further remodeled inside during the 1990s for facilities of the Denver Center for the Performing Arts, Auraria Higher Education Center classrooms, and a luxury hotel.

DV048 **Skyline Park**

1976, Lawrence Halprin and Associates. Arapahoe St. between 15th and 18th sts.

Lawrence Halprin, who designed San Francisco's Embarcadero, among other urban parks, borrowed colors and massing from Colorado's sandstone foothills for this 100-foot-wide landscaped corridor. The park incorporates the Daniels and Fisher Tower in a narrow urban canyon created by stepped, raised planting areas of ruddy concrete. Sunken walkways and courtyards lead to fountains, some with paths through them. Berms of evergreen and deciduous plantings suggesting mountain settings screen the park from the street.

DV049 Park Central

1973, William C. Muchow and Associates. 1515 Arapahoe Street

Skyline Park's 3.1 acres provide a dramatic foreground for one of Denver's more daring cubist exercises. Three towers, of sixteen, eleven, and seven stories, are united by skylit atriums and many angles, including expansive pedestrian stairs and a mountainside observation deck. Black anodized aluminum trims large expanses of black-tinted glass for a dramatic contrast to downtown's red brick and gray concrete.

DV050 Daniels and Fisher Tower

1911, Frederick J. Sterner and George H. Williamson. 1981, restoration, Gensler and Associates. 1601 Arapahoe St. (at 16th St. Mall) (NR)

Succumbing to the national tower-building craze, Denver erected this 372-foot Renaissance Revival tower modeled on the campanile of St. Mark's in Venice, which was undergoing reconstruction at the time. This allowed *The Denver Times* to gloat that Den-

ver's tower, thanks to the flagpole, was six feet taller than the prototype, in an article headlined, "Venetians Erecting a Column Almost Exact Replica of D&F's Tower in Denver."

The 32-foot-square tower, once the corner beacon for the five-story emporium, stands alone today, having escaped urban renewal demolition that erased the rest of what was the city's finest department store. Blond brick and creamy terracotta cover a steel skeleton set on a 24-foot-deep concrete foundation. The lower stories have been refaced to cover the former building juncture. Protruding cornices set off a twentieth-floor arcaded observation deck topped by Seth Thomas clocks with 6-foot hands. A two-and-one-half-ton bell occupies the two uppermost stories. Stairwells and elevator access diminish the tower's sixteen usable floors, which have been converted to offices. During the restoration, workers found an urn containing the ashes of William C. Daniels, the dilettante and dreamer who conceived this tower.

DV051 Denver City Cable Railway Company

1889. 1974, restoration, James Sudler Associates. 1801 Lawrence St. (NR)

A brickmason's tour-de-force, this arcaded edifice features pairs of round-arched windows in round, corbeled insets and a recessed, round-arched entry rising the building's full two stories. The ornate brickwork extends to the triple cornice and the soaring smokestack. Once the powerhouse, corporate offices, and car barns of the Denver City Cable Railway Company, the building has been converted to offices and first-floor retail space in a monument to Denver's once extensive cable car system.

DV052 20th Street Recreation Center
(20th Street Bath House)

1908, Robert Willison. 1011 20th St. (at Curtis St.)

To scrub away some of the city's pungent frontier heritage, Mayor Speer proposed this brick box with sparse Neoclassical frosting. Still open to the public for swimming, billiards, basketball, aerobics, and arts programs, it commemorates the progressive commitment of the City Beautiful era to improving the lives of all citizens.

DV053 Larimer Street

"I am Denver City," William Larimer wrote to his family after founding the town on November 22, 1858, by jumping the claim of another town company. A tour of Larimer Street provides a quick profile of Denver's growth, from tiny, century-old cottages to modern high rises. Upper Larimer Street still has quaint one- and two-story masonry buildings. Sacred Heart Church (DV053.1; 1879, Emmett Anthony), 2760 Larimer (NR), uses Carpenter's Gothic woodwork to enhance the brick exterior of a traditional cruciform church with the steeple above the Larimer Street entrance. Now painted and with the octagonal masonry tower replaced by a diminutive wooden steeple, it is Denver's oldest church building still regularly used for religious services.

The two-story Italianate El Bronco Bar (DV053.2; 1879), formerly Christopher Columbus Hall, an ethnic saloon where Italians gathered, at 2219 Larimer, is the oldest saloon in Denver still operating in its original location. La Casa de Manuel restaurant (DV053.3; 1889), 2010 Larimer, is a one-story building, stark on the exterior but rich inside with large-scale paintings by José Castillo, a Denver artist, depicting the settlement of the West from a Hispanic perspective.

DV054 Sakura Square

1972, Bertram A. Bruton. 1900 block of Larimer St.

After the Denver Urban Renewal Authority razed the area known as Japan Town, a Buddhist temple bought back its square-block site and hired Bertram Bruton, a Denver African American architect, to design a tower for subsidized housing and a shopping complex. Bruton also revamped the exterior of the existing Tri-State Buddhist Temple (1949), 1947 Lawrence Street, to make it compatible with the new full-block development, a center for Denver's Japanese community. The twenty-story Tamai Tower, honoring longtime Tri-State Buddhist Temple pastor Yoshitaka Tamai, has recessed apartment balconies in a textured concrete fa-

cade. A bermed courtyard and mini-park create intimacy, as does the walled temple courtyard with its Japanese garden and shrine of St. Shinran.

DV055 Tabor Center

1984, Kohn Pedersen Fox Associates. 1600 Larimer St.

This superblock replaces the noble old Tabor Block (1880, Willoughby and Frank E. Edbrooke), erected by silver magnate Horace A. W. Tabor. Along the 16th Street Mall, a three-story, glazed galleria (Urban Design Group) bridges Lawrence Street with a span of shops 500 feet long. Exposed steel construction harks back to cast iron storefronts and public market structures. Behind the thirty-two-story office tower adjoining the nineteen-story Westin Hotel, at 17th and Larimer, prefabricated metal hindquarters mark the point where Tabor Center abandoned plans for a second, forty-story office tower after the 1983 oil crash.

DV056 Writer Square

1981, Barker, Rinker, Seacat and Partners. 1500 block of Larimer St.

This full-block development has been applauded as a well-designed downtown residential-retail complex. Its graceful archways, corbeled brick trim, and people-oriented scale mesh with neighboring Larimer Square. A courtyard and passageway separate the twelve-story office building at the corner of 16th and Larimer streets from a lower-rise complex of town houses with commercial spaces on the ground level. Open space, red brick, and greenery make this a bold departure from cold, fortress-like architecture epitomized by Larimer Place (1980), just across the street.

DV057 Larimer Square Historic District

1870s–1880s. 1965, Langdon Morris. 1990s, Semple Brown Roberts. 1400 block of Larimer St. (NR)

This block of Larimer Street is a creative adaptation and reuse of antique buildings with iron storefronts, metal cornices, and cut stonework. The deep, narrow commercial structures on both sides of the street have been opened up to daylight with cutthroughs, recessed facades, interior courts, and open basements. This effort to spare one block of old Denver from bulldozers proved successful enough to inspire the rejuvenation of the rest of lower downtown.

DV057.1 Crawford Building

1875. 1439–1441 Larimer St.

After its restoration this elaborate Second Empire brick commercial building was renamed to honor Dana Crawford, who spearheaded Larimer Square's rehabilitation. The two-story building has ornate iron columns from Chicago, second-story lintels with scalloped and broken pediments, and a grandiose, bracketed cornice and curved pediment parapet. The 25-by-36-foot facade is probably Denver's finest Second Empire front, although it lacks the typical mansard roof. Denver has few Second Empire structures, as that style was superseded by Italianate, Queen Anne, and Romanesque Revival in the 1870s when the city's first great building boom began.

DV057.2 Granite Hotel (Clayton Building)

1882. 1456–1460 Larimer St.

This masonry gem, whose pink, purple, and gray stone skin shines in sunlight, is located on the site of city founder William Larimer's 1858 log cabin. Carved, dressed, and quarry-face granite, rhyolite, and sandstone rise to a large, bracketed cornice topped by a balustrade. Rejuvenated for retail and office purposes, this landmark retains its original skylight, stained glass windows, and cast iron columns.

DV057.3 Gallup-Stanbury Building

1873. 1445–1451 Larimer St.

In the Tambien Saloon, opened on this site by Avery Gallup and Andrew Stanbury, western artist Charles Stewart Stobie raffled several of his landscapes and Indian portraits to help pay his bar tab. The original false-fronted saloon was replaced by this Italianate building, three stories of brick decorated with stone and cast iron pilasters that blossom into metal flowers.

DV057.4 Kettle Arcade

1873. 1990, remodeling, Semple Brown Roberts. 1426 Larimer St.

This arched passageway was the shop of George Kettle, gutted in 1990 to create better access to an interior court for Larimer Square. Kettle adorned his shop's 20-foot-wide front with a cut stone facade and fancy molded cornice. A mural (1988, Evans and Brown) of early Denver characters adorns the fine new vaulted ceiling.

DV058 Market Street

Between the 1870s and 1912, Market Street was Denver's red-light district. Today many of the old taverns, whorehouses, and warehouses have been rehabilitated. The Colorado Bakery and Saloon (DV058.1; 1866, Frederick C. Eberley; 1890; 1989 restoration, Larry Nelson), 1440–1444 Market, is a particularly fine restoration of a very early store front. The tall, arched, second-story windows, cast iron fronts, and bracketed metal cornice typify the first generation of Denver's brick business buildings. Next door at 15th and Market is the Wells Fargo Depot (DV058.2; c. 1870). The much-altered one-story red brick building on a rough-faced rhyolite foundation has unusual pointed-arch windows. A row of buildings, Market Center (DV058.3; 1890s; 1980s restoration) in the 1600 block of Market Street, has been recycled for retail and office use, providing a striking masonry foreground for high-rise glass and concrete towers. One former brothel, the Mattie Silks Building (DV058.4; 1886), 2009 Market, commemorates Colorado's most notorious madam in a two-story Italianate house now converted to other business.

DV059 Cactus Club

1990, Peter H. Dominick, Jr. 1621 Blake St.

A first-rate example of infill in the Lower Downtown (LoDo) Historic District, this private clubhouse squeezed into a narrow vacant lot between two larger structures artfully echoes surrounding buildings. Highlights of green and purple glazed brick in the geometric decoration of the gray brick facade distinguish the two-story, neo-Victorian building. For the facade the architect chose terracotta, marble, granite, tile, sandstone, and metals—all materials borrowed from older buildings in the district, most notably the two-story Oxford Hotel addition (DV060).

DV060 Oxford Hotel

1890, Frank E. Edbrooke; 1902 addition. 1983, restoration, William Muchow and Associates. 1600–1612 17th St. (at Wazee St.) (NR)

The suavely restored Oxford is now one of Denver's finest hotels as well as the oldest. Frank Edbrooke designed what may have been the city's first steel-skeleton building two years before his masterpiece, the Brown

DV060 Oxford Hotel, c. 1912

Palace Hotel, at the other end of 17th Street. The original five-story, red brick structure was built on a U plan a block from the railroad station. Edbrooke's two-story addition (1902) on Wazee Street used the same facade detailing.

To celebrate repeal of Prohibition in 1933, the Oxford had Charles Jaka design a Streamline Moderne cocktail lounge, the Cruise Room. Flowing lines shape the front bar, booths, and even the ceiling. The walls are paneled with Denver artist Alley Henson's beaverboard bas-relief portraits of characters from various nations offering toasts in their own languages. The Oxford Hotel Annex (DV060.1; 1912, Montana Fallis and Robert Willison), 1628 17th Street (NR), is the same height as the hotel, but the entire facade is elaborately detailed white terracotta, an echo of the belle époque.

DV061 Coors Field

1995, Hellmuth, Obata and Kassabaum. 2001 Blake St.

After HOK's Oriole Park at Camden Yards in Baltimore won the architectural World Series, that Kansas City firm's Joseph Spear and Bradley Schrock designed a second old-fashioned-looking ball park for the Colorado Rockies, a National League expansion team established in 1993. The four-story curved brick entry has a clock cornice flying the flag in a salute to traditional baseball parks such as Brooklyn's Ebbbets Field. The red brick walls relate to the surrounding warehouse district and incorporate one old building. Coors Field combines high-tech modernism with nostalgic elements such as a grass playing field, a hand-operated scoreboard, and "knothole" peeps at the field through the main (20th and Blake sts.) entrance. Brick pilasters are topped by forty terracotta columbines (the Colorado state flower) by Denver sculptor Barry Rose. Another piece of public art is the gleeful sculpture *Evolution of the Ball* (1995, Lonnie Hanzon), a large psychedelic baseball on a stretch of tilted railroad track supported by columns with 108 glazed terracotta balls, ranging from mud balls to cheese balls. The entire stadium is sunken behind red brick walls no higher than 60 feet to minimize obstacles to mountain and city views.

DV062 **Union Station**

1881, William E. Taylor. 1895, Van Brunt and Howe. 1912, Gove and Walsh. Wynkoop and 17th sts. (NR)

Jay Gould, the New York tycoon, and local entrepreneur Walter Scott Cheesman put together a multiblock parcel to give Denver a consolidated train station. Rough-faced pink-gray rhyolite from Castle Rock and pale gray sandstone trim from Morrison sheathed the original Second Empire edifice, by William Taylor, a Kansas City architect. After a fire in the early 1890s, the Kansas City firm of Van Brunt and Howe rebuilt the central clock tower, switching from Second Empire to the more up-to-date Italianate. Their tower was demolished for the 1912 expansion by Gove and Walsh in the Beaux-Arts Renaissance Revival mode, with an exterior clad in granite and terracotta textured and colored to look like granite.

Amtrak and the Winter Park Ski Train still use this station, whose basement is occupied by a huge model railroad layout duplicating many Colorado trainscapes. Union Station remains the anchor of 17th Street, which has been lined since the 1880s with the city's tallest hotels and office buildings. The depot's sunlit great hall, with its grand, three-story round-arched windows, evokes the golden age of railroading when Union Station was the heart of the city.

DV063 **Wynkoop Street Warehouses**

1880s–1920s. 1980 and 1990s, rehabilitation. Cherry Creek to 19th St.

Opposite Union Station is a row of four-to-six-story fortresses of stout masonry, built to hold tons of agricultural and mining machinery, foodstuffs, clothing, and other merchandise. Following the high standards set by H. H. Richardson's celebrated Marshall Field Wholesale Store in Chicago, Denver's wholesale merchants hired leading architects to design these stylish brick and stone warehouses, which also served as sample rooms and corporate headquarters. Since the 1980s most of them have been converted to offices, lofts, and retail outlets. *New York Times* architecture critic Paul Goldberger called the Wynkoop Street warehouse row one of Denver's finest architectural legacies.

DV063.1 **18th Street Atrium** (Bourk-Donaldson-Taylor Building)

1920. 1984, John Novak of the Urban Design Group. 1639 18th St. (at Wynkoop St.)

By lifting the ceiling a few feet and restoring the skylight, the Urban Design Group resurrected this handsome four-story, brown brick warehouse trimmed sparingly in terracotta. The original owners, Bourk, Donaldson, and Taylor, wholesale produce brokers, put their monogram just below the fourth-story roundels. It now contains offices wrapped around a spacious central atrium supported by the original massive wooden beams. Decorative polychromatic brickwork in geometric patterns is even more flamboyant on the old Littleton Creamery, now the Ice House Lofts (1903, Gove and Walsh) across Wynkoop.

DV063.2 **Wynkoop Brewing Company** (J. S. Brown Mercantile)

1899, Gove and Walsh. 1988, restoration, Joe Simmons. 1634 18th St. (at Wynkoop St.) (NR)

One of the city's more elaborate warehouses rises to fifth-story round arches that echo the large, recessed street windows. Exterior walls are red pressed brick, with sandstone trim and a rough quartzite foundation. The original interior was finished in Oregon pine and oak, with maple floors. In 1988 this heavy-duty building was remodeled for Denver's first brew pub, including a second-floor pool hall. Pressed metal ceilings reflect sound downward to keep brewpub and pool hall commotion from disturbing the upper-level lofts.

DV063.3 **Streetcar Stables Lofts** (Denver City Railway Company)

1883, Harold and Viggo Baerresen; 1892, remodeling. 1994, Urban Design Group. 1635 17th St. and 1734–1736 Wynkoop St. (NR)

On rainy days, whiffs of horse manure still haunt this brick and timber storage barn and corporate offices for the city's pioneer horse streetcar firm. But the fourth-story false front of brick exemplifies the ambitious facades of the Gilded Age. A $9 million project carried out in 1993–1994 brought retail development to the ground floor with forty-three lofts above.

DV063.4 Tattered Cover Books (Morey Warehouse)

1896, Gove and Walsh. 1628 16th St.

Denver's largest wholesale firm erected this warehouse of 253,000 square feet, designed by Aaron Gove and Thomas F. Walsh, the architects of many warehouses surrounding their best-known work, the 1912 portion of Union Station. The brick exterior is distinguished by horizontal banding on the first story, recessed upper-story windows, and a bracketed metal cornice. A grand second story entrance from the 16th Street Viaduct (demolished in 1993) led to oak-finished offices on the second floor. Chester S. Morey presided over a wholesale food empire of 500 employees and eighteen branches in Colorado, Nebraska, New Mexico, and Wyoming. Morey's building was remodeled in the early 1990s as a branch bookstore, coffee bar, offices, and warehouse of The Tattered Cover, founded in 1974 by Joyce Meskis as a tiny bookshop. The Tattered Cover has grown into a giant with some 500,000 titles in stock, earning praise from *The New York Times* as "the best general bookstore in the U.S."

DV063.5 Edbrooke Lofts (Spratlen-Anderson Warehouse)

1906, 1910, Frank E. Edbrooke; 1990. 1450 Wynkoop St. and 1626–1638 15th St.

The original four-story, red brick Spratlen-Anderson Warehouse had paired, double-hung windows in vertical bays with recessed paneled spandrels. A two-story 1910 addition employs paired, round-arched windows separated by roundels, a device Edbrooke also used in the Brown Palace Hotel. Denver developer-preservationist Dana Crawford led the project for conversion to the spacious Edbrooke Lofts in the early 1990s.

DV064 Speer Boulevard

1907–1918. University Blvd. to Irving St. (NR)

George Kessler's 1907 park and parkway master plan made Speer Boulevard the key diagonal. It follows Cherry Creek from University Boulevard to the creek's confluence with the South Platte River and then crosses the river and the tracks on a viaduct into northwest Denver. Jerome Smiley, in his *History of Denver* (1901), described Cherry Creek as a "miserable and sandy waste" lined with dumps and used as a sewer. Kessler's imaginative plan transformed the creek into the centerpiece of a tree-lined boulevard. The plan left little triangular land parcels where this only major diagonal in the city met the grid. Some of these have been dedicated as mini-parks complementing several larger parks along Speer Boulevard.

Designation of Speer Boulevard in the 1980s as both a National Register and a Denver landmark ended the street widening that had reduced its grassy, tree-shaded edges. Restoration of the historic lighting, bridges, and landscaping on Speer stimulated restoration of the entire parkway and park system along City Beautiful lines. Various ramps off Speer lead to a paved creekside trail to Denver's birthplace, Confluence Park. One of the loveliest stretches of the Cherry Creek Greenway is Creekfront Park (1992, Robert Karns) at Speer Boulevard and Larimer Street, with a water garden and a path from downtown under Speer to the Auraria Higher Education Center campus.

Auraria

Auraria (from the Latin word for gold) was established a month before Denver, in October 1858, by William Greene Russell. Russell's party of friends and relatives from Georgia were the prospectors who first found gold in the South Platte near its confluence with Cherry Creek in July 1858. Their discovery triggered the Colorado gold rush. After the Russells left to join the Confederacy, Denver annexed their town in 1860.

Denver's oldest neighborhood, bounded by Cherry Creek, West Colfax Avenue, and the South Platte River, evolved into a mixed residential, retail, and industrial area after the railroads arrived. Auraria became the victim of the Denver Urban Renewal Authority in the 1970s, when much of the neighborhood north of West Colfax Avenue was de-

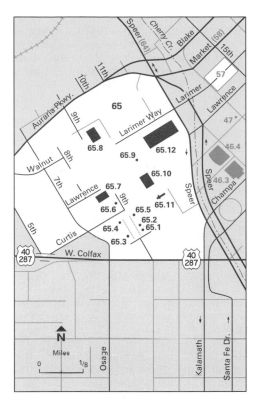

Inset 3. Auraria Higher Education Center Campus (DV065.1–DV065.12)

molished to clear land for the 171-acre Auraria Higher Education Center. South of the campus, many 1880s Italianate homes, modest red brick housing, churches, and businesses linger. Elitch Gardens (1995,

Davis and Associates), Denver's grandest amusement park since its 1890 opening, moved to a riverside site in Auraria in 1995. Elitch's lofty observation tower, roller coaster, and Ferris wheel give Denver one of America's dizziest skylines.

DV065 **Auraria Higher Education Center Campus**

1976, Jacques Brownson, master plan. Bounded by Speer Blvd., W. Colfax Ave., 5th St., and Auraria Pkwy.

An instant campus designed as a 171-acre urban renewal project features generally bland red brick boxes that keep the focus on several landmarks and on the restored residences of 9th Street Park. Designers of the low-budget campus are striving for Ivy League landscaping, and an urban forest is rising around the two-to-five-story complex. The campus is shared by the Community College of Denver, Metropolitan State College of Denver, and the University of Colorado at Denver. With more than 34,000 students, it is the most populous campus in Colorado. Jacques Brownson, who worked and studied with Ludwig Mies van der Rohe, designed the master plan for the campus to utilize the existing street and utility grid.

The campus incorporates the 9th Street Historic Park (1976 restoration, Edward D. White, Jr.), 9th Street between West Colfax Avenue and Curtis Street (NR), a novel project that preserved one of Denver's oldest intact residential blocks of middle-class housing. Restored exteriors and renovated interiors now contain offices for the Auraria

DV065 Auraria Higher Education Center Campus

Higher Education Center. The pavement of 9th Street has been replaced with grass, but the granite curbs and flagstone sidewalks have been preserved. Among the brick dwellings, two frame houses predate an 1874 Denver ordinance mandating brick construction as protection against fire.

The Knight House (DV065.1; 1885), 1015 9th Street, is one of Denver's finest Second Empire specimens, while the Madden-Schultz Duplex (DV065.2; 1890, Jason J. Backus), 1045–1047 9th Street, is the simple, two-story brick house of William F. Schultz and Eugene Madden, the Larimer Street saloonkeeper who served as the district's longtime councilman. The Smedley House (DV065.3; 1872), 1020 9th Street, a very early frame residence with its original bracketed eaves, housed one of Denver's pioneer dentists, whose descendants also distinguished themselves in that profession. It served for many years as Casa Mayan restaurant, a social center for the Hispanic community. Restraint heightens the impact of the detail on the Davis House (DV065.4; 1873), 1068 9th Street, an Italianate dwelling with Carpenter's Gothic woodwork. Houses at 1061 and 1024 9th Street are in the same style, but less assertive. The Mercantile Cafe (DV065.5; 1906, Frederick C. Eberley), 1067 9th Street, originally the Groussman Grocery, is a two-story corner store with distinctive brickwork detail. The streetside parapets are embellished by globe finials and central arches, with the corner cut for the store entrance. The Golda Meir House (DV065.6; 1911), 1146 9th Street, is a single-story, flat-roofed duplex of pressed red brick, a type so humble and common that it is generally overlooked. This dwelling, elevated by the brief residency of a Jewish American who became the first female prime minister of Israel, was moved to the park from the working-class neighborhood of "Little Israel" on West Colfax Avenue.

DV065.7 St. Cajetan's Center (St. Cajetan's Catholic Church)

1926, Robert Willison. 9th and Lawrence sts.

The first church for Spanish speakers in northern Colorado is stucco and red tile in the Spanish Colonial style. Curvilinear parapets, twin bell towers, and round arches make this a larger, refined version of smaller

country churches in the San Luis Valley. With its credit union and health care station this church did much to improve the physical, spiritual, and economic health of the community. It has been revamped inside as a lecture and concert hall, but faithfully restored outside.

DV065.8 Auraria Student Union and Shopping Mall (Tivoli-Union Brewery)

1881. 1890, Frederick C. Eberley; subsequent additions. 1980s, renovation, Hellmuth, Obata and Kassabaum. 900 block of Larimer St. (NR)

The original structures of this complex were part of or later incorporated into the Tivoli-Union Brewery, which went out of business in 1969. The tallest building (1890) was one of the first breweries in Colorado and has the oldest wells in Denver. The West Denver Turnhalle Opera House (1882, Harold W. Baerresen) and its horseshoe-shaped balcony await restoration. Frederick Eberley designed the distinctive Italianate tower (1890) that still crowns the brewery. The bottling and storage building at the corner of 9th and Walnut was a later addition. The Auraria Higher Education Center encouraged private developers to renovate the brewery as a retail mall during the 1980s. Students voted in 1991 to use the Tivoli also as an expanded student center, a plan rejected by a less preservation-minded student body in the 1970s.

DV065.9 Student Art Gallery (Emmanuel Sherith Israel Chapel)

1876. 1976, renovation, Gale Abels and Associates. 1201 10th St. (NR)

Rhyolite stonework shines on this simple Gothic Revival chapel built for an Episcopalian congregation. In 1903 the growing "Little Israel" community along West Colfax Avenue purchased the church, whose service as a synagogue is commemorated by the Star of David on the roof and a Hebrew inscription over the door, while Gothic-arched windows recall its original Episcopalian affiliation.

DV065.10 Auraria Library

1977, Helmut Jahn. Between 10th and 11th sts. and Curtis and Lawrence sts.

Helmut Jahn of Chicago designed this two-story, 187,000-square-foot building of reinforced concrete with a white-painted aluminum skin that makes it easy to find on a red brick campus. The interior space is organized into 30-foot-square bays by circular concrete columns, and enhanced by two interior courtyards, three open stairways, and large window areas. Windows on the south and west walls have adjustable aluminum sunscreens that add to the horizontal feel of the structure and contribute deep shadow lines.

DV065.11 St. Elizabeth's Catholic Church

1898, Frederick W. Paroth. 1062 St. Francis Way (NR)

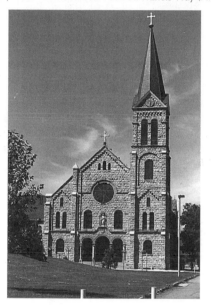

This Romanesque Revival church of rough-cut Castle Rock rhyolite has a dominant single corner spire soaring 162 feet. The interior was once embellished with statues and woodwork carved in Germany but has been remodeled. The church, now used by both the Auraria campus and the community, was Colorado's German national parish, where use of the German language and customs were sanctioned. Germans, counted as the largest foreign-born group in Colorado until 1910, made this church the spiritual center of the Auraria neighborhood with its many breweries and saloons. A curving arcade and cloisters join the church

with the St. Francis Conference Center (1980, Marvin Hatami), which has contrasting expanses of glass and stark brick walls.

DV065.12 North Classroom Building

1990, Hoover Berg Desmond. Speer Blvd. to 11th St. between Larimer and Lawrence sts.

The architects designed the circulation system of this two-block-long classroom building to provide light and views for orientation. The corridors wrap the outside of the building, and stairs are on the outside, enclosed in glass block for visibility. An atrium running the length of the south side provides space for lounging, studying, and eating, with access to outdoor terraces. The oversized clocks on the exterior, according to architect George Hoover, "are to give a sense of going to school, of getting to class on time."

DV066 Buckhorn Exchange Restaurant

1886. 1000 Osage St. (northeast corner of W. 10th Ave.) (NR)

In 1893 Henry Zietz moved his legendary tavern from Market Street into this typical two-story brick commercial building. Buffalo Bill and presidents from Theodore Roosevelt to Ronald Reagan drank and dined here on the wild game, which ranges from rattlesnake steaks to saucy Rocky Mountain oysters.

Wildlife murals by Noel Adams decorate the exterior. The interior is jammed with around 300 stuffed animals and birds, ranging from jackalopes to a golden eagle, from prairie dogs to a giant bison head. Besides doubling as a natural history museum, the Buckhorn is also packed with antique guns, trappers' tools, and an assortment of western Americana. The Zietzes supposedly brought the white oak front bar with hand-carved oak leaves and acorns from the family tavern in Essen, Germany.

DV067 La Mariposa Health Station

1974, Robert Engelke. 1020 W. 11th Ave. (southwest corner of Kalamath St.)

Society's concern with the health of its poorest members is celebrated in this two-story

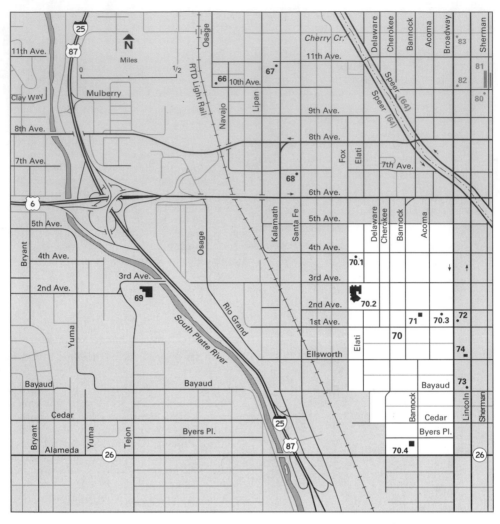

Inset 4. Baker area (DV066–DV074)

stuccoed cinderblock monument, whose sloping walls accented with glazed tile, buttresses, deep reveals around small windows, and red tile roofs honor the Central American heritage of the surrounding Chicano neighborhood.

DV068 Byers Branch Library

1918, Varian and Varian. 1992, restoration, Stanley Pouw Associates. 675 Santa Fe Dr. (southwest corner of W. 7th Ave.)

This treasure chest in the Renaissance Revival style is cement-covered brick trimmed with Turkey Creek sandstone. Named for William N. Byers, the founder of the *Rocky Mountain News* and Denver's greatest booster, it is a single-room library. The large, finely crafted space has a fireplace under a vaulted ceiling, with basement meeting, storage, and office spaces. Denver artist Carlota Espinosa painted the large mural, *Pasado, Presente, Futuro* (1975), capturing the full sweep of Mexican-American history. As a center for children and for programs in English as a second language, it has been the cornerstone of the revived, Spanish-accented business district on Santa Fe Drive.

DV069 **Denver Wastewater Management Building**

1993, Michael Barber Architecture. 2000 W. 3rd Ave.

Motorists on I-25 and the 6th Avenue freeway may slow down to gawk at this Neo–Art Deco daydream, which designer Paul Todd says is "in the spirit of the 1930s Works Progress Administration." The eight-story, precast concrete concoction has step-backed elevations, 1,100 concrete panels set in slightly indented and projecting patterns, and a barrel roof. In front, on the old 3rd Avenue Bridge (1924), is a colossal water sculpture, *Bridge of Recycling Fountains* (1993, Laura J. Audrey), consisting of two rows of twenty-nine stainless steel columns on a bridge over the South Platte River.

DV070 **Baker Historic District**

W. 5th Ave. to W. Alameda Ave. between Broadway and Fox St. (NRD)

This middle-class neighborhood has many elegant, if generally small, Queen Anne homes, as well as some notable larger houses and institutions. The Mary Coyle Chase House (DV070.1; 1891), 532 West 4th Avenue, is a typical small, two-story dwelling with brick skin and stone trim, fishscale-shingled front gable, and ornate, wooden-columned front porch. Here the journalist wrote her Pulitzer Prize–winning play *Harvey* (1944), which introduced the world to an imaginary six-foot-tall rabbit. The Fairmount Elementary School (DV070.2; 1924, Harry James Manning; 1971, Slater, Small, Spenst), 520 West 3rd Avenue, is a two-story, L-plan structure of dark red brick in the Collegiate Gothic style, with elaborate gray stone trim and terracotta relief plaques. A Mother Goose mural by Allen True decorates the kindergarten. The Art Deco Denver Fire Station No. 11 (DV070.3; 1936, Charles F. Pillsbury), 40 West 2nd Avenue, has stepped red brick piers with wrought iron lanterns framing the original wooden bay doors. The former Byers Elementary School (DV070.4; 1902, Gove and Walsh), now condominiums (1982, Charles Nash), 108 West Byers Place, is a discreet, four-story Mission Revival building. Chalk boards, desks, and other academic souvenirs have been retained as interior decor.

DV071 **St. Peter and St. Mary Episcopal Church**

1891, Boal and Harnois. 126 W. 2nd Ave. and Acoma St.

Like a Richardsonian suburban railway station, this exquisite stone structure looks natural. Rough gray rhyolite walls hide under the sloping eaves of steep-pitched hipped roofs, and the facade evokes a hillscape. Inside, the nave's open trusses, exposed rafters, and beaded roof decking suggest a beautifully crafted boat.

DV072 **Mayan Theater**

1930, Montana S. Fallis, facade. 1985, restoration, Midyette-Seieroe. 110 Broadway

This and the Mayan Theater in Los Angeles may be the only surviving examples of movie palaces extensively decorated in Pre-Columbian motifs. Rescued from the wrecking ball in 1984, the theater has technicolor terracotta ornament and hand-painted and stenciled walls. Also rejuvenated are the facade's terracotta Indian chief and Aztec and Mayan polychrome trim by Julius P. Ambrusch of the Denver Terra Cotta Company. This exotic facade fronts an older red brick theater, the homey Queen Theater.

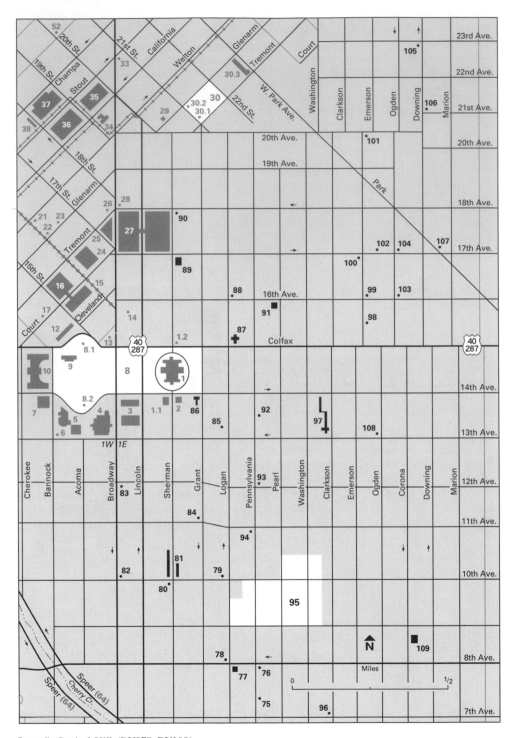

Inset 5. Capitol Hill (DV075–DV109)

74

DV073 **Ross-Broadway Branch Library**

1952, Victor Hornbein. 33 E. Bayaud Ave. (northwest corner of S. Lincoln St.)

Looking like a Wrightian residence, this horizontal structure of red brick has a concrete base and sills. A flat, projecting roof suspended from steel I-beam rafters shades the clerestory window bands. Corner windows descend from clerestories to frame solid brick wall panels. Golden oak trim inside and out frames glass panels with a whimsical arrangement of colored glass rectangles suggesting a Piet Mondrian painting.

DV074 **South Broadway Christian Church**

1891, Edwin J. Miller and Wenzel J. Janisch. 23 Lincoln St. (northwest corner of Ellsworth Ave.)

The dominant element of this Romanesque Revival church, a crenelated square bell tower surmounted by a smaller round turret, soars above walls of quarry-face rhyolite with round arches. Carved stone adorns the gable peaks, buttress caps, and recessed entrance. Decorative wood accentuates the steep peaks of rhythmic rows of gables and dormers.

Capitol Hill

Denver's millionaires built their showplace homes, schools, clubs, and churches here, surrounded by lawns along gridded, tree-lined streets with flagstone sidewalks. Some smaller homes, modest apartments, and nineteenth-century institutional and commercial buildings also survive amid commercial intrusions, parking lots, and high-rise apartments in this architecturally rich and diverse neighborhood around the gold-domed state capitol (DV001).

DV075 **Grant-Humphreys Mansion**

1902, Boal and Harnois. 770 Pennsylvania St. (NR)

Excluding ostentation, Denver's best-known Neoclassical residence has a monumental semicircular portico supported by four two-story fluted Corinthian columns. Built for James B. Grant, a smelter owner and Colorado governor, the peachy brick house employs lavish terracotta trim in window surrounds, balustrades, cornices, corner pilasters, and frieze. This early use of terracotta as a substitute for decorative stonework set an example widely copied. Interiors are on a grand scale, featuring exotic woods, plaster trim, and a sunroom addition. Second owner Albert E. Humphreys, an oil tycoon who later become embroiled in the Teapot Dome scandal, added a two-story, ten-car garage, complete with gas pump, for his fleet of Rolls-Royces. His son, Ira, donated the house in 1976 to the Colorado Historical Society, which uses it as a house museum and a party house.

DV076 **Malo Mansion**

1921, Harry James Manning. 500 E. 8th Ave. (southeast corner of Pennsylvania St.)

One of the city's finest Spanish Colonial Revival mansions, this twenty-three-room, two-story stucco villa exults in finely crafted detail, such as the hand-painted rosettes on the overhanging eaves. Oscar Malo, a president of the Colorado Milling and Elevator Company, also had the architect include rose patterns in stained glass throughout. A sensitive 1980s rear upper-story addition does not detract from this refined specimen.

DV077 **Governor's Mansion** (Cheesman-Evans-Boettcher Mansion)

1908, Marean and Norton. 1980s, restoration, Edward D. White, Jr. 400 E. 8th Ave. (southeast corner of Logan St.) (NR)

A wrought iron fence with cannonball finials on the brick posts guards the formal, late Georgian Revival house of Alice Cheesman, widow of the real estate and water tycoon who founded what is now the Denver Water Department. Her daughter, Gladys, and son-in-law, John Evans II, also lived briefly in the mansion before it was sold in 1926 to Claude Boettcher. After his death the Boettcher family donated it in 1958 as the governor's residence.

Deep red brick walls are almost lost amid rich white wooden frosting under a hipped roof with prominent gabled dormers. The pedimented, dentiled cornice provides a strong shadow line. Massive, two-story fluted Ionic columns guard the west side portico. The pompous entry has grouped columns supporting a porch that becomes a balustraded second-story balcony. Pilasters echo

DV075 Grant-Humphreys Mansion

DV076 Malo Mansion   DV077 Governor's Mansion (Cheesman-Boettcher Mansion)

the porch columns and define the corners. A semicircular sunroom added by the Boettchers overlooks Governor's Park.

DV078 **Providence House** (Sayre's Alhambra)

1892. 801 Logan St. (northwest corner of E. 8th Ave.)

Hal Sayre, a mining engineer who made his fortune in the Central City gold rush, built this twenty-five-room beige brick house with ogee-arched transom cutouts supposedly inspired by the Spanish Alhambra. Unrestored and little altered, it is now one of the more dignified shelters for Denver's homeless.

DV079 **Dorset House**

1937, S. Arthur Axtens. 1001 Logan St. (northwest corner of E. 10th Ave.)

Capitol Hill boasts several dozen intact Streamline Moderne and Art Deco apartment houses. This representative, three stories with a flat roof, has a yellow wire-cut brick skin. Streamline Moderne detailing includes raised horizontal banding and long fenestration bays of glazed yellow brick. Large steel casement jalousie windows are grouped vertically by size for a symmetrical, machine age appearance. The curved entry corner has side lights and a shallow transom in a faux stone surround beneath a cantilevered stainless steel canopy.

DV080 **Crawford Hill Mansion**

1906, Boal and Harnois. 1990, Peter Dominick, Jr. 969 Sherman St. (southwest corner of E. 10th Ave.)

This French-influenced Renaissance Revival show house wears a mansard roof and symmetrical facade with pedimented dormers flanked by ocular windows. Large brick pillars hold decorative wrought iron gates fronting the formal entry bay. A two-story east portico with a third-floor balcony is supported by tall Ionic columns. Inside, steel framing allowed rooms to be laid out functionally without concern for load-bearing walls. Mrs. Crawford Hill, Denver's society queen, reigned here long after her husband's death. After her death in 1955, this formal mansion and gardens became the Town Club until it was converted in 1990 to law offices.

DV081 Poets Row Apartments

1930s, Charles D. Strong. 1000–1055 Sherman St.

Similar height, massing, and styling characterize these nine three-story apartment buildings. The 1931 Robert Frost and Louisa May Alcott Apartments use terracotta surrounds for visual interest in eclectic edifices. Subsequent constructions reflect Art Deco influence in vertical brick piers and heavy use of terracotta spandrels and door surrounds, or favor Art Moderne touches that include contrasting horizontal brick banding and rounded corners. Charles Strong, who organized citywide cooperatives and bartering arrangements during the Great Depression, is better remembered as a social activist than as an architect.

DV082 Gart Brothers Sports Castle
(Cullen-Thompson Motor Company)

1926, Jacques Benedict. 1000 Broadway (northwest corner of E. 10th Ave.)

Denver's premier automobile showroom is a three-story Deco Gothic building dressed in terracotta. Splendid stained glass windows, including transoms with Chrysler's winged wheel logo, are framed by fluted pilasters that culminate in rooftop finials. Converted to a sporting goods store in the 1970s, the building now contains an artificial ski slope on the interior auto ramp and a rooftop tennis court.

DV083 Howard Lorton Showroom

1923. 1982, addition, Callister, Fatley and Bishoff. 1160 Broadway (southeast corner of E. 12th Ave.)

DV082 Gart Brothers Sports Castle (Cullen-Thompson Motor Company)

This former Studebaker and Franklin automobile showroom sporting an ornate terracotta facade with green and white floral spandrels has a contemporary north addition in russet brick. The addition's San Francisco architects matched the old showroom's cornice line and massing but used a dramatic, truncated corner display window framed by a three-story concrete arch. The glazed opening allows passing motorists a peek at display floors joined to the old showroom by a central staircase. Although quite different in design, the structures complement each other.

DV084 Sheedy Mansion

1892, E. T. Carr. 1975 restoration, Dan Havekost. 1115 Grant St. (northwest corner of E. 11th Ave.) (NR)

This eclectic mansion, notable for fine interior woodwork by carpenter Joseph John Queree, housed Dennis Sheedy, a self-made rancher, banker, and businessman. "A love of nature prompted me to furnish each room with a distinctive wood," Sheedy explained, "and I carried out the idea to include the furniture." After Sheedy's death in 1927, his home became the University of Denver's Lamont School of Music. Both the house and the matching carriage house were renovated in the 1970s for business use but retain many lavish elements of decor

DV086 First Baptist Church   DV087 Basilica of the Immaculate Conception, under construction

such as the sheepskin wall covering in the entry. On the exterior, asymmetrical but harmonious massing is emphasized by several open porches, towers, turrets, balconies, a courtyard, and a porte-cochère. Elegant detailing extends to the pressed red brick walls and red sandstone trim of this three-story mansion reminiscent of the years when Grant Street was millionaires' row.

DV085 Denver Women's Press Club (Burr Studio)

1910, Varian and Varian. 1325 Logan St.

This picturesque English cottage has dark red brick walls and restrained ornament with bracketed hoods over the entrance and grouped front windows. The entrance hall has a low ceiling and small open staircase to a balcony overlooking the two-story, skylighted studio. George Elbert Burr, one of America's foremost etchers of natural scenes, built this as a home and studio after settling in Denver in 1906. After he moved to Phoenix, Arizona, in 1924, this became the Denver Women's Press Club.

DV086 First Baptist Church

1938, G. Meredith Musick. 230 E. 14th Ave. (southwest corner of Grant St.)

The thin Protestant spire on this Georgian Revival church rises triumphantly above heavier neighboring domes and towers.

"The idea of a cock atop the weather vane mounted on the steeple's zenith became a matter of strong contention among the trustees of the church until I reminded them that the cock had long been a Protestant symbol for Christ at the last supper," wrote the architect in his autobiography, *Wayfarer in Architecture*. The red brick walls and Indiana limestone trim are complemented by the immense polished red granite columns of a pedimented entry portico. Dense landscaping of the narrow street margins has enhanced this landmark.

DV087 Basilica of the Immaculate Conception

1906–1912, Leon Coquard; Gove and Walsh. Northeast corner of Logan St. and E. Colfax Ave. (NR)

Denver's finest example of French Gothic architecture is constructed of gray Bedford, Indiana, limestone over brick above a foundation of granite from Gunnison, Colorado. Matched spires with open bell towers, 210 feet high, flank a large rose window with stained glass angels playing classical instruments. A full-range carillon of fifteen bells occupies the east tower. Inside, the vault of the nave soars 90 feet. The highly detailed main altar, 30 feet high, is of Carrara marble, as are much of the statuary, the pulpit, and the bishop's chair. Leonardo da Vinci's *The Last Supper* inspired the altar table bas-relief, while Bartolomé Estéban Murillo's *Immacu-*

late Conception was the model for the central statue above the altar. The exquisitely detailed stained glass was made by the F. X. Zetter Royal Bavarian Art Institute in Munich. The cathedral was elevated to a minor basilica in 1979 and underwent a $2.5 million restoration for the 1993 visit of Pope John Paul II. That project included a meditation garden with a wonderful bronze sculpture, *The Assumption of Mary,* which brings needed tranquility to worldly East Colfax Avenue.

DV088 International House (Fisher House)

1896, Frank E. Edbrooke, Willis A. Marean. 1600 Logan (NR)

Daniels and Fisher Stores Company millionaire William Garrett Fisher favored the popular Neoclassical style for his three-story, $50,000 mansion. Willis A. Marean, then a young architect with the large Edbrooke firm, apparently did much of the work on this show home. Exterior walls are smooth sandstone with similar stone arches, cornices, and stringcourses. The distinctive two-story, semicircular entry portico on the west is topped by a balustraded balcony. The cornice of the portico wraps the living quarters above the second floor and continues as the cornice for a wide portico on the south. Woodwork in the reception hall is walnut, mahogany, and oak with rosewood and bird's-eye maple used elsewhere. A single-story ballroom and art gallery, paneled in Argentine mahogany, join the main building on the north. Stone lions still guard the entry.

DV089 Central Presbyterian Church

1892, Frank E. Edbrooke. 1660 Sherman St. (southeast corner of E. 17th Ave.) (NR)

Red-orange sandstone from Redrock Canyon in Colorado Springs faces and trims this nearly square edifice. The presiding element is a 196-foot square belfry, with tall, thin lantern openings topped by round arches. A cross-gable roof covers the three-story church. The carved exterior sandstone, stained glass windows, and golden oak interior woodwork are adorned in floral motifs reminiscent of Art Nouveau. Unfortunately much of the exterior sandstone trim has been lost, leaving defoliated stubs.

As is typical of Presbyterian churches, few religious images appear in the interior, which resembles that of an opera house. The sense of theater is enhanced by curved seating rows, balconies, and boxes, a sloping floor, and two false fireplaces. Ranks of brightly painted organ pipes are augmented by simulated ones, their effect enhanced by three arches. The basement has been converted to a shelter for the homeless and an exhibition space with a display on the church's history since its founding in 1860.

DV090 Rocky Mountain Shrine Consistory

1906–1907, Baerresen Brothers. 1770 Sherman St. (southeast corner of E. 18th Ave.)

A fanciful Moorish shrine with exotic onion domes and a roof balcony, this five-story red brick building has contrasting creamy terracotta trim, most notably the horseshoe-shaped window arches. Harold W., Viggio, Albert T., and William J. Baerresen, sons of a noted Danish designer of ships and shipyards, established a successful architecture firm in Denver. Between 1884 and 1928 they designed and constructed many of the city's buildings. This is the most remarkable example of their work in Denver. In 1996 it became the home of an African American theater group.

DV091 Temple Center (Temple Emanuel)

1899, John J. Humphreys. 1924, T. Robert Wieger. 1595 Pearl St. (NR)

Exotic influences in this beige brick synagogue celebrate Judaism's Near Eastern origins. The east facade features minaret-like towers with walkways and Turkish-style copper domes, which are repeated atop two pavilions on the north side and a third on the south. The central and north towers are octagonal and taller than the third, which fronts a rectangular addition with buttressed corners. Stone trim, striated brick banding, and a red tile roof enhance the composition. Floral and geometric motifs prevalent in Islamic architecture are evident in rows below the eaves, in the door panels, and in the extensive stained glass windows, as well as in the interior carved wood paneling and stenciling. After serving Colorado's largest Jewish congregation, the building is now owned by the City and County of Denver and used as an events center.

DV092 **Molly Brown House**

1890, William Lang. 1340 Pennsylvania St. (NR)

"Typical Brown luck. We're unsinkable!" Molly Brown told the crowd waiting in New York City to meet survivors of the 1912 *Titanic* sinking. The irrepressible wife of a successful miner from Leadville was snubbed by Denver society but accepted on the East Coast and in Europe, and her story eventually inspired a Broadway play and movie. Molly never sank, but her house almost did. After her death in 1932, it became a home for wayward girls, then a target for demolition. Historic Denver, Inc., was formed in 1970 to rescue and restore this example of Queen Anne Style, built in rough-faced pink and gray rhyolite. As one of America's most flamboyant self-made women, Molly would probably be tickled pink to know that her home is now a popular house museum, faithfully restored from the anaglypta-covered entry hall to the stone lions in front. Interiors are fussy and rich with carved woodwork and a wealth of furnishings from the Brown era. The two-story carriage house has been converted to a gift shop and visitor reception area.

DV093 **Dunning-Benedict House**

1890, William Lang. 1200 Pennsylvania St. (northeast corner of E. 12th Ave.) (NR)

One of the finest houses of Denver's leading nineteenth-century residential architect is this Richardsonian Romanesque design, with that style's typically heavy, asymmetrical massing. Three stories of rough gray rhyolite rise to gabled roofs with four prominent chimneys. The balustraded entry porch has stout stone posts with foliated capitals. A crenelated parapet on a corner tower is echoed by a two-story bay on the south with its crenelated parapet around a small balcony. The stained glass is extravagant, especially in the large peacock window on the north wall. The two-story carriage house has been connected to the dwelling by a later addition.

Walter Dunning's house illustrates William Lang's exuberance and penchant for eclectic combinations of historicist detail from various periods. The Benedict clan, including a Colorado Supreme Court justice and several prominent attorneys, lived here for several generations. This jewel was converted to apartments and, more recently, to offices.

DV094 Croke-Patterson-Campbell Mansion

1887, Isaac and Edgar J. Hodgson. 428–430 E. 11th Ave. (southwest corner of Pennsylvania St.) (NR)

The chateau of Azay-le-Rideau supposedly inspired this three-story red sandstone dwelling. The irregular plan includes an attached, similarly styled carriage house connected through a small courtyard. The steep slate roof bristles with crockets, finials, roundel dormers, and corner towers, although much carved sandstone decoration has disappeared.

Thomas B. Croke was a schoolteacher and clerk who invested in railroads and agriculture. His experiments with irrigated farming on 3,500 acres north of Denver in what is now the suburb of Northglenn proved remunerative enough to pay for this $100,000 mansion. Later it became the residence of Thomas M. Patterson, owner of *The Rocky Mountain News* and a U.S. senator, and then of Patterson's son-in-law, Richard C. Campbell. Several deaths here have inspired persistent rumors that the house is haunted.

DV095 Quality Hill Historic District

Bounded by Logan and Washington streets between East 9th and 11th avenues

The Quality Hill Historic District displays a variety of styles and periods in its single-family and apartment houses. A cornerstone of the district is the Craig House (1914, Jacques Benedict?), 605 E. 9th Ave. (northeast corner of Pearl St.), a trim, two-story townhouse that borrows casually from Classical Revival styles with a tiled hipped roof and broad, overhanging eaves above a dentiled cornice. The Granada, 607–615 East 10th Avenue, and the Cardenas, 707–715 East 10th Avenue, four-story apartment buildings designed by Walter Rice and dating from 1925, flaunt ornament loosely based on Moorish and Spanish Colonial designs, including tile pent roofs, iron balconies, curvilinear parapets, and arched bays whose white plaster contrasts dramatically with the red brick walls.

DV096 Zang Mansion

1903, Frederick C. Eberley. 709 Clarkson St. (northwest corner of E. 7th Ave.) (NR)

Built for Adolph J. Zang, the son of the founder of the Zang Brewing Company, this monochromatic Neoclassical Revival mansion of gray brick trimmed in graystone rebukes its less formal neighbors. The two-story, semicircular portico that proclaims the main entrance is supported by two massive Ionic columns. The front dormer in the hipped roof gives access to a small terrace from the third-floor ballroom. Behind splendid oak doors, the interior, now converted to offices, features stained and painted glass windows, painted and gilded ceilings, five ornate fireplaces, a Tiffany chandelier, and twelve varieties of wood in beautifully carved woodwork.

DV097 St. John's Episcopal Cathedral

1911, Gordon, Tracy and Swarthwout. 1313 Clarkson St. (NR)

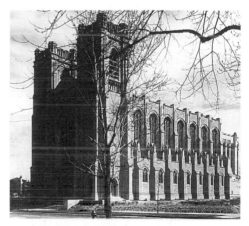

The New York City firm that won a national architectural competition for the design of this cathedral accommodated the surrounding residential neighborhood with a low, generously landscaped English Gothic Revival design clad in random-coursed Indiana limestone. A carillon of fifteen bells is housed in matching square, castellated towers flanking the north entrance. The fifty-one stained glass windows range from Gothic Revival to contemporary in style. A rosebush in the Adam and Eve window was added when a seductive Eve proved distracting to churchgoers. The altar, altar screen, and reredos, carved from Salonica oak, are from the congregation's first church at Broadway and Welton, which was destroyed by fire.

A taller central tower, transepts, and south additions included in the original design were never completed. The attached Parish House (1928, Merrill H. and Burnham F. Hoyt) is of particular interest for its Gothic Revival St. Martin's Chapel, with a magnificent wooden reredos by sculptor Arnold Ronnebeck. Across the street at 13th Avenue and Washington Street, a Public Service Company substation (1990) camouflaged by brickwork and triangular pediments echoes the lines of the cathedral rectory.

DV098 Zang House

1889, William Lang. 1532 Emerson St. (NR)

Adolph Zang (see also DV096) commissioned this tall, narrow townhouse with a rough-faced rhyolite facade. Its steep-gabled front is embellished by a corner oriel win-

dow with a conical roof. The parapeted gable end is topped by a carved stone griffin that lends a Gothic shiver to the asymmetrical and sharply vertical facade. Three more of William Lang's townhouses (1889–1890) survive two blocks west in the 1600 block of Washington Street, including his own home at 1626 Washington, with a dressed sandstone facade and stepped front gable end.

DV099 Bouvier-Lathrop House

1890, Robert G. Balcomb and Eugene R. Rice. 1600 Emerson (northeast corner of E. 16th Ave.) (NR)

The fussy facade of this eclectic brick creation bulges beyond the insistent rectangle of the plan and the rusticated stone corseting. Robert Balcomb, a carpenter, came to Denver in 1885 and joined Eugene Rice the following year in a partnership to design and construct residential buildings. Rice, trained in architecture at Cornell University, set up his own practice in 1897. Next door, at 1610 Emerson, Balcomb and Rice also designed the Flower-Vaile House (1889) (NR). Its three stories of pressed brick with stone trim rise above a rusticated stone base in another weighty Queen Anne embodiment of opulence.

DV100 Perrenoud Apartments

1902, Frank S. Snell. 836 E. 17th Ave. (southwest corner of Emerson St.)

Billed on its opening as Denver's "swellest yet" apartment house, this building has an exterior simplicity that hides elegantly appointed interiors. The four-story dwelling, built at a cost of $125,000, has six units per floor, each with six to eight rooms arranged around four light courts. The main entrance leads into a grand hallway with marble wainscoting, French plate glass mirror walls, and a Tiffany skylight. The central lobby rotunda has a fireplace and an ornate brass grille elevator cage. The billiard room, ballroom, and bowling alley, as well as a private garage, were once attended by uniformed staff. The building is now condominiums, but the occupants are still screened by a committee like the one dominated by socialite Adele Perrenoud, an original resident for whom the building was named.

DV102 Edbrooke House

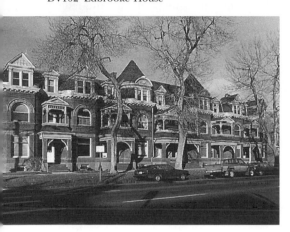

DV104 Grafton Apartments (Aldine Apartments)

DV101 **New Terrace**

1889. 900–914 E. 20th Ave. (southeast corner of Emerson St.) (NR)

These Queen Anne rowhouses employ projecting and recessed bays to define eight units distinguished by a variety of facade detailing, roof shapes, and a large central pavilion with a pyramidal roof. Fireplaces and woodwork remain intact, and staircases still lead to shared plumbing on the second floor, old-fashioned washstands flanked by separate toilet and tub rooms. Despite minor changes and loss of some elements over time, this fanciful terrace still flaunts an exuberance to lure Denverites accustomed to single-family, detached dwellings.

DV102 **Edbrooke House**

1893, Frank E. Edbrooke. 931 E. 17th Ave.

Denver's style-setting architect of the late nineteenth century designed this house for himself. Queen Anne massing is highlighted by skillfully employed Neoclassical detail. Raised brick courses accentuate the window arches, and grouped Doric columns distinguish the pedimented porch. Smaller Tuscan columns accent the set-back second-story porch above it. Stone banding at the main-floor sill level is integrated into the porch balustrade, while a second-story band becomes the common sill of three windows that paraphrase Palladio. The Edbrooke-designed house next door to the east (1896) has been converted to a bed and breakfast inn.

DV103 **Bailey Mansion**

1889, William Lang. 1600 Ogden St. (northeast corner of E. 16th Ave.) (NR)

The largest of William Lang's surviving residential designs combines Queen Anne massing with Richardsonian detailing and materials. Gabled bays extend from a central hipped element, and grouped windows are divided by heavy piers and transom sills. Smooth horizontal banding restrains the rough surfaces of beige Longmont sandstone at lintel and sill heights. Massed columns support two porch roofs with pedimented gables above the entry steps. A finely detailed chimney fronts a third-story recessed porch on the rounded south bay. The cantilevered north gable incorporates a bay window below and chimney above into a single composition. The interior also reflects Lang's penchant for rich and varied materials and detailing. The house, built for businessman George B. Bailey, has been restored for offices.

DV104 **Grafton Apartments** (Aldine Apartments)

1890, James Murdoch. 1001–1021 E. 17th Ave. (northeast corner of Ogden St.) (NR)

These six townhouses have three-story brick bays with recessed entry porches, round bay windows, and second-story balconies. Curved porch brackets and round-arched windows on the second floor contrast with pedimented third-floor dormers and conical turrets punctuating a mansard roof. Dentiled cornices and brick and stone banding give horizontal emphasis, while multiple chimneys with corbeled tops add verticality to the lively facade. Built for Albert Brewster, whose initial appears in the trim, the apartments next belonged to U.S. Senator Thomas M. Patterson, who changed their name to the maiden name of his wife. Conversion to condominiums in 1980 led to interior renovation and exterior restoration.

DV105 **Gebhard-Smith-Brantigan House**

1884, Henry Gebhard?. 2253 Downing St. (northwest corner of E. 23rd Ave.) (NR)

This Italianate domicile with a two-story polygonal bay and decorative brick chimneys was restored in the 1980s by Dr. Charles Brantigan for his medical offices. The porch has ornate columns and bracketed eaves. Large brackets along the eaves of the truncated hipped roof divide the facades into window bays, with different lintel treatments on each level. Incised geometric patterns distinguish both the ornate wooden trim and the stone lintels. The house is one of many historic structures in the San Rafael Historic District (NRD), which extends from East 20th to East 26th avenues, between Clarkson and Downing streets.

DV106 **American Woodmen Building**

1950, Gordon D. White. 2100 Downing St. (northeast corner of E. 21st Ave.)

Founded in Denver in 1901, the Woodmen became a leading African American fraternal, charitable, and insurance society with a national membership and branches in other cities. Their headquarters is a late example of Streamline Moderne uncluttered by additions and sheathed in snowy terracotta. Across the street, at 2123 Downing Street, is the eclectic Victorian Ferril House (1889, Franklin Goodnow), home of Thomas Hornsby Ferril, Colorado's foremost poet.

DV107 **Rosenzweig-Cleworth House**

1882, Charles L. Dow, builder. 1129 E. 17th Ave. (northeast corner of Park Ave.) (NR)

Leopold Rosenzweig's two-and-one-half-story Italianate house has restored Eastlake porch framing, a dentiled frame cornice, and bracketed eaves. The tall, evenly spaced windows are topped with stone arches. Also on the site are a gabled barn and a coal shed. Publisher Charles Cleworth restored this and neighboring residences, including the tiny, steep-roofed 1882 cottage at 1732 Downing Street, and converted them to a distinctive office complex.

DV108 **Cornwall Apartments**

1901, Walter E. Rice. 921 E. 13th Ave. (northwest corner of Ogden St.) (NR)

The name belies the predominant Mediterranean Revival mode of this apartment-turned-condominium. Column capitals, cornices, architraves, friezes, wrought iron, and other ornament give a highly decorative appearance to an early example of this style in Denver. Tile roofs on the corner towers form semisheltered roof garden rooms connected with open promenades. Each apartment originally opened onto the ornately columned balconies over the entrances. Walter Rice was an engineer and inventor who designed and mass-produced his own terracotta trim and frankly advocated simple buildings sugar-coated with terracotta frosting.

DV109 **Dora Moore School** (Corona School)

1889, Robert S. Roeschlaub. 1993, restoration and additions, Stanley Pouw Associates. 846 Corona St. (NR)

Robert Roeschlaub organized one of his finest schools around a central court, with square corner entry towers topped by bell-shaped domes with nipple finials. The brick walls blend into rich layers of stone trim and a terracotta frieze. A strong cornice separates the two-and-one-half-story base from the towers and parapeted gable dormers. Two large additions, each reflecting its own era, complement the original.

When the school board announced plans to demolish their school, students here

DV109 Dora Moore School (Corona School)

helped persuade the Denver Landmark Preservation Commission and the Denver City Council to declare it the first locally landmarked school. Roeschlaub, Colorado's leading institutional architect of the nineteenth century, designed at least a dozen Denver schools, including the Emerson School (1884), East 14th Avenue and Ogden Street, which features a large south wall sundial reminiscent of the one installed on the 1993 addition to Dora Moore.

DV110 Stoiber-Reed-Humphreys House

1908, Marean and Norton. 1022 Humboldt St. (NR)

Red-haired Etta Stoiber, reputedly an ex-madam and the widow of Edward G. Stoiber, a wealthy silver magnate, built this thirty-room, three-story Italian Renaissance Revival mansion, sometimes called Stoiberhof. Its rough-faced gray stone walls hide such amenities as a basement swimming pool and a barbershop. Rebuffed by snobbish local society, Etta Stoiber constructed a 12 foot high spite wall of rhyolite around her property and a wrought iron gate at the foot of the entry stairway. This is the largest of several mansions in the Humboldt Street Historic District, which extends from East 10th to East 12th avenue on the west edge of Cheesman Park. The district's twenty-six large houses include Georgian Revival and late nineteenth-century Italianate as well as early twentieth-century eclectic examples, with several notable variations on the four-square type.

DV111 Bridaham House

1905, Sterner and Williamson. 350 Humboldt St.

The Greek Revival went out of style by the 1860s but continued to appear in banks, churches, and post offices. This is a rare Colorado residential example of what architectural historian William Jordy calls "Greek Survival." Bringing the glory that was Greece to Denver, this brick temple sits well back on three lots, behind an iron fence with brick piers topped by concrete cannonball finials. Behind an entry court balustrade, the two-story portico is supported by six large Doric columns, with triglyphs and mutules on the entablature. This house is a cornerstone of Park Club Place, bounded by Downing and Humboldt streets and East 4th and East 1st avenues (NRD). It was developed by investors such as Mayor Robert W. Speer, whose house (1912, Marean and Norton) is at 300 Humboldt Street.

DV112 Biscoe House

1908, Maurice Biscoe. 320 Humboldt St.

Maurice Biscoe, a Beaux-Arts-trained architect, went to Denver to represent the New York firm of Gordon, Tracy and Swarthwout in the construction of St. John's Cathedral. He stayed in the Mile High City to design fine residences, including his own, a two-story, L-plan house in Mediterranean Revival style with modest but pleasing detail.

DV113 William E. Fisher House

1910. William E. Fisher. 110 Franklin St.

Architect William Fisher designed his own house in the "Spanish style," which he and his brother, Arthur, considered appropriate for Denver's climate. The two-story Spanish Colonial Revival abode, with stucco walls and a red tile roof, is oriented to the south side garden where the pillared and pilastered entry is off the driveway, while the street side has a single-story columned porch with a roof balustrade. The Fishers ran Denver's most prolific architecture firm from 1905 until William committed suicide in 1937 in this house.

The Fishers helped design, in collaboration with Frederick Law Olmsted, Jr., the surrounding Country Club Place (1909),

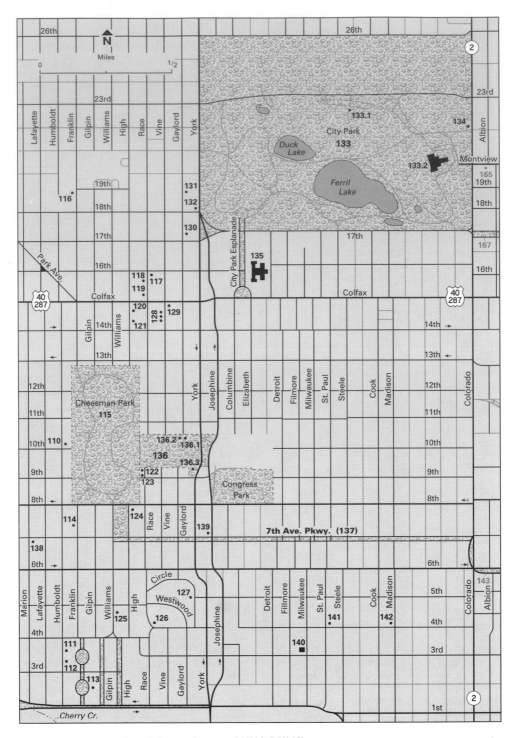

Inset 6. Cheesman Park and City Park areas (DV110–DV142)

86

which stretches from Franklin to Race street between East 1st and East 4th avenues. Fisher and Olmsted laid out extra long blocks with landscaped medians. For the entry gates on East 4th Avenue, Fisher used stucco and red barrel tile, in keeping with a Spanish theme.

DV114 **Ries House**

1935, Henry Eggers and Stanley Morse. 737 Franklin St.

Jane Silverstein Ries, grande dame of Colorado's landscape architects, transformed this house by designing a unique and all-encompassing garden. Her campaign to replace lawns and "useless" banks with terraces and walled gardens is reflected in much area residential landscaping as well as her own home.

DV115 **Cheesman Park**

1898, Reinhard Schuetze. E. 8th to E. 13th aves., between Franklin and Race sts. (NR)

Once the city cemetery, this fine urban park follows Reinhard Schuetze's 1898 plan. Curvilinear walks and drives and perimeter trees border an expanse of lawn that carries the eye to the mountain view. A formal hilltop garden and reflecting pool surround the Colorado Yule marble Cheesman Pavilion (1910, Marean and Norton). A block long esplanade (1912) between Williams and High streets joins the south end of the park to the East 7th Avenue Parkway (DV137).

DV116 **Mullen Nurses Home**

1920s, Temple Hoyne Buell. 1895 Franklin St. (at E. 19th Ave.)

Jagged parapets of red brick provide an organic, ivy-like edge to this four-story, beige brick residence for student nurses. The Art Deco relief ornament continues in the entry surround and provides striking vertical accents on the flat walls. Raised plaster designs on walls and ceilings and strong geometric patterns in floors make the interior as exotic as the exterior. Numerous additions to the mother hospital, St. Joseph's, have obscured some views of this marvel.

DV117 **Castle Marne** (Raymond House)

1890, William Lang. 1572 Race St. (southeast corner of E. 16th Ave.) (NR)

William Lang's flowery stone detailing embellishes this three-story rusticated rhyolite domicile with trim of Indiana limestone, which is much easier to carve than rhyolite. A fanciful, if superfluous, colonnette supports the keystone of the transom arch on the parlor window beside the carved golden oak entry. On the north side, in another typical Lang detail, stone trim frames a round, stained glass window above two round-arched openings whose awkward junction is disguised with a baroque bouquet in limestone.

This Richardsonian Romanesque edifice, built for $40,000, features exquisite stonework even for the nine limestone chimney pots. Rough stone balustrades crown the porch and the southwest corner tower. With a two-story 1920 addition, the house and carriage house were converted to thirty-one apartments. Restored in 1989 as a bed and breakfast, it is one of the finest of many elegant structures in the Wyman Addition, a large, mixed-use local landmark district stretching roughly from York Street to Franklin Street between East 13th and East 17th avenues.

DV118 **Unity Temple of Practical Christianity** (Delos Chappell House)

1895, Frank S. Snell?. 1555 Race St.

Reflecting the shift from Queen Anne and Richardsonian exuberance to more cautious, classical styles after the silver crash of 1893, this two-and-one-half-story red brick domicile is predictable in its boxy shape and classical detail. The dignified interior, with its original hardwood trim, has been home since 1936 to the Unity Temple, whose minister welcomes visitors of all persuasions, even architecture enthusiasts.

DV119 **Milheim House**

1893. 1515 Race St.

This two-and-one-half-story house of red pressed brick was moved in 1989 from 1355 Pennsylvania Street. The current owners acquired John Milheim's house for a song on the eve of its scheduled demolition. They spent almost $400,000 to transport the 583-ton structure seventeen blocks and replant the early foursquare. Its exterior embellishments look back to the Queen Anne Style, as does the exquisite original woodwork inside.

DV120 Olmsted House

1892, David W. Dryden? 1460 High St.

A great gambrel gable with an arched cutout for a Palladian window soars over one corner of this exuberant pile. A smaller gable frames a round-arched balcony window. The asymmetrical, two-story tan brick dwelling has a rough sandstone base and a shingled superstructure. Clarence H. Olmsted's eclectic Dutch Colonial is on a block of jolly Victorians, including the Bohm Mansion (1895), now the Holiday Chalet Hotel Apartments, 1820 East Colfax Avenue. The Holiday Chalet is the largest of these extravaganzas, a sprawling, asymmetrical, three-story mansion with unusual stepped parapets that suggest the Jacobethan Revival.

DV121 Sykes-Nicholson-Moore House

1897, Varian and Sterner. 1410 High St.

The Reverend Richard E. Sykes, minister of the First Universalist Church, built this two-story Colonial Revival mansion of pale brick. The second owner, Meredith Nicholson, wrote the suspense novel *The House of a Thousand Candles* (1905), using the house as a setting. The Nicholsons added the semicircular two-story solarium to the south, echoing the curve of the columned entry porch on the west. They had carved into the mantelpiece words from Ralph Waldo Emerson: "The ornament of the house is the guests who frequent it." After stints as a rooming house and a halfway house, the building was restored as a school for maids and butlers.

DV122 Toll House

1912, William E. Fisher and Arthur A. Fisher. 919 Race St.

This large, two-story stucco house in the Mediterranean Revival Beaux-Arts tradition has two wings angled to face the mountains.

DV122 Toll House, c. 1912

The carriage house supposedly was built a block away, at 777 Vine Street, because Mrs. Toll did not want horses and their flies and droppings anywhere near the house. The carriage house was enlarged to become the Henry W. Toll, Jr., House (1920, William Fisher).

DV123 Benton House (Livermore House)

1911, Maurice Biscoe and Henry H. Hewitt. 901 Race St.

This red brick Georgian Revival house has white-painted wood trim, fluted pilasters, and a fine Georgian entrance. The second-story balustrade once extended around all four sides below dormered third-story servants' quarters. Variegated brick end walls rise into large double chimneys. The formal house hides an underground garage and has Cheesman Park as its back yard. It is part of Morgan's Addition, a Denver Historic District extending from East 8th to East 9th Avenue between Race and York streets, on the east side of Cheesman Park. The houses represent many 1920s and 1930s interpretations of revival styles.

DV124 Kohn-Dobbins-Dominick House

1925, Jacques Benedict. 770 High St.

This Beaux-Arts palazzo was commissioned by the founding president of the American Furniture Company. Landscaping by Saco R. DeBoer remains in evidence behind tall fencing and shrubbery. Architect Peter Dominick, Jr., has preserved the mansion as his family home. Other nearby Beaux-Arts Renaissance Revival palaces designed by

Jacques Benedict are the Sullivan House (1926), 801 Race, and the Neusteter-Bailey-Chenoweth House (1921), 817 Race.

DV125 Architects' Small House Service Bureau Model House

1920s. 456 Williams St.

This symmetrical facade minimizes historicist detail to flirt with Modernist simplicity. The east side of Williams Street contains other variations on this approach of the ASHSB, whose Mountain Division was established in Denver in the early 1920s by ten leading local architects. The ASHSB designed and built "no frills" houses that excluded "meaningless ornamentation." Plans for sixty different houses were designed and marketed in an attempt to provide affordable architect-designed housing. The double allée of elms along Williams between Cheesman Park and 4th Avenue is an unusual variation on the standard parkway planting strip.

DV126 General Electric Demonstration House

1935, Lester L. Jones. c. 1952, addition, Victor Hornbein. 450 Race St.

General Electric, in collaboration with *Architectural Record* and *Time* magazine, staged a heavily publicized nationwide design contest during the 1930s to promote modern residences that accommodated GE appliances.

This brick house, built to showcase new electric marvels, is self-consciously Modernist in its composition of cubes juxtaposed with a cylinder in the manner of Le Corbusier. Victor Hornbein's addition extends the brick walls and multipaned windows while protecting design integrity. Hornbein added projecting eaves and wooden sunscreens and joined the two parts with a pergola that wraps the original chimney. The landscaping for the difficult, pie-shaped lot was designed by Jane Silverstein Ries, who softened the lines and created privacy.

DV127 Reed House

1931, Harry James Manning. 475 Circle Drive

Colorado's grandest Tudor Revival mansion is a towering dream of steep-pitched slate roofs; four immense, ornate chimneys; and numerous dormers and gables. The glazed tapestry brick walls with limestone trim and half-timbered gable ends soar above two and one-half acres of walled gardens, with a separate garden house by Saco R. DeBoer. A greenhouse, terrace, fountain, swimming pool, and interior elevator were added in 1955–1956. Mary Reed commissioned the house shortly after the death of her husband, Verner Z. Reed, who made fortunes in both Cripple Creek gold and Salt Creek, Wyoming, oil. This is the largest and finest house in the Country Club Historic District, bounded roughly by First and Sixth avenues between University Boulevard and Downing Street. Its high-style Tudor Revival design helped make vernacular Tudor Revival, often marketed as "English bungalow," one of the most popular local styles of the 1930s.

DV128 Vine Street Houses

c. 1890, William Lang. 1415, 1429, 1435 Vine St. (NR)

This trio of Lang residences shows a progression from the asymmetry of the Tedford House (1889), at 1415 Vine, with its off-center porch tower, to the studied symmetry and crisp gables of the Grove House (1890) at 1435. In between, 1429 Vine (1890), dominated by a gable with Queen Anne detailing, is stronger and cleaner than 1415. The conversion of this group to multiunit dwellings has complicated the understanding of their interiors, but the surviving stair halls are labyrinths of lavish, dark woodwork.

DV129 Weicker Depository

1925, William E. and Arthur A. Fisher. 2100 E. Colfax Ave. (southeast corner of Vine St.)

This mock tower, an apparition transplanted from Florence, reaffirmed Denver's aspirations of transporting Old World grandeur to the nouveau-riche Rocky Mountain West and gained national coverage in *Architectural Record*. Ogee-arched openings grace the travertine sheathing of the first two levels, and six upper brick levels rise to a flared, crenelated parapet of what is still used as a warehouse.

DV130 Baerresen House

1904, Harold W. Baerresen. 1718 Gaylord St.

The oldest of the four Baerresen brothers designed this Dutch Colonial house with a plethora of Neoclassical elements. Harmony is achieved by topping the pairs of triple Ionic entry columns with pairs of triple balcony balusters.

DV131 Denver Museum of Miniatures, Dolls, and Toys (Pearce-McAllister Cottage)

1899, Frederick J. Sterner. 1880 Gaylord St. (NR)

Frederick Sterner used the Dutch Colonial mode for this two-story brick house, which Harold Pearce built as a wedding present for his bride. The plan is a modified T, with a two-story servants' wing at the rear. The wood-shingled cross-gambrel roof with three evenly spaced shed dormers overhangs a full-length, balustraded entry porch. The offset doorway is flanked by side lights and pilasters. A glazed conservatory was added to the southeast corner around 1926.

Pearce, one of many British investors in Colorado railroads, mining, and smelting, married the daughter of Dr. William Bell, vice president of the Denver & Rio Grande. The couple occupied the house until returning to England in 1907. Henry McAllister, general counsel for the D&RG, purchased the house, and his family donated it to the Colorado Historical Society in 1971. It is now a house museum, with the miniatures museum upstairs and a cast iron cat still prowling the roof ridge.

DV132 Smith House

1902, William E. Fisher and Daniel Riggs Huntington. 1801 York St. (northwest corner of E. 18th Ave.) (NR)

A French influence shows in the roundel roof windows and ornate voussoirs of this three-story mansion and two-story carriage house built by Frank L. Smith. Gray brick on a steel frame is ornamented with white terracotta under tiled hipped roofs, with fine interior woodwork. The letter *S* appears repeatedly in the plasterwork, making it clear that the family wanted to be remembered. One of a row of notable residences along the west edge of City Park, this Beaux-Arts mansion and its prominent carriage house served a long stint as a boarding house before both underwent 1980s restoration for office use.

DV133 City Park

1882, Henry F. Meryweather. 1890s, Reinhard Schuetze. York St. to Colorado Blvd. between E. 17th Ave. and E. 26th Ave. (NR)

City Park is Denver's largest (317 acres) and most elaborate, with notable buildings, sculpture, a zoo, and a natural history museum. Harry Meryweather, a city civil engineer, laid out the park in the Olmsted tradition, using a romantic, informal plan of looping drives and walks around lakes. Landscaping ranges from dense tree planting and shrub massing to grassy expanses. George Kessler, the Olmsted brothers, and Saco R. DeBoer also had a hand in shaping City Park. The Pavilion (1896) and the Floating Bandstand (1896; 1929, Fisher and Humphreys) at the west end of Ferril Lake were restored in the 1990s as part of a local historic district that includes the park superintendent's house (1893) near the McLellan Gate (1903) on York Street.

City Park is formally approached from East Colfax Avenue by City Park Esplanade (1905), guarded by the Sullivan Memorial Gateway (1917, Leo Lentelli, sculptor), with heroic twin figures atop tall columns representing mining and agriculture. Unfortunately, the 12-foot-high figures, made of concrete reinforced with steel, have become crumbling lepers that the city plans to replace with fiberglass clones. Edward H. Bennett, the Chicago city planner and architect who designed that city's Grant Park and provided one of the schemes for Denver Civic Center, planned the fountain and gateway of the Esplanade, which is also the main artery through the campus of East High School. The north end of the Esplanade enters City Park at the Thatcher Memorial Fountain (1918, Lorado Taft, sculptor), a composition of granite, bronze, and water culminating in an 18-foot female figure armed with a sword and shield. The Sopris Gateway (1912, Frank E. Edbrooke), East 17th Avenue between Detroit and Fillmore streets, commemorates Richard Sopris, a mayor of Denver and the city's first park commissioner.

The Denver Zoological Gardens (DV133.1; 1896), which supposedly began when Denver's park superintendant was given a troublesome pet bear cub, has become a large complex of architectural habitats for animals. Bear Mountain (1918) (NR)

was the creation of zoo director Victor H. Borcherdt. It is made of structural steel and concrete to resemble a hogback west of Denver, with barless bear pits and native landscaping. Newer attractions include Northern Shores (1989, Alan Petersen), with subterranean polar bear pool viewing, and the huge glass pyramid housing Tropical Discovery (1993, Anderson, Mason, Dale). The Denver Museum of Natural History (DV133.2; 1908, Frederick J. Sterner; many additions), 2001 Colorado Boulevard, is Colorado's most popular and distinguished museum. The original classical temple on a hill is now hidden under precast concrete and glass additions.

DV134 Fire Station No. 18

1912, Edwin H. Moorman. 2205 Colorado Blvd. (northwest corner of E. 22nd Ave.)

This fire station on the east edge of City Park set a fine standard for bungalows, the most common house type in the Park Hill neighborhood across the boulevard. Edwin Moorman's design bristled with porticos, pergolas, gabled projections, and extended, bracketed Craftsman rafter ends. The simpler building actually erected retains the dark red Harvard brick, columned pergola, Palladian window, and many Craftsman details.

DV135 East High School

1925, George H. Williamson. City Park Esplanade and E. Colfax Ave.

Sited on a parkway next to City Park, East High exemplifies the Progressive era's fondness for erecting showcase public buildings

DV134 Fire Station No. 18, design, 1912

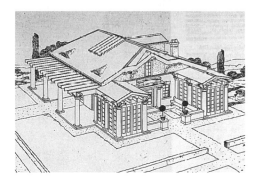

in grand settings to teach public lessons in fine design. Mottled red brick trimmed with pale gray terracotta sheathes this eclectic adaptation of the English Jacobean style to a school distinguished by a bell tower vaguely reminiscent of Philadelphia's Independence Hall. The four-story, H-plan building with a 162-foot-high tower is remarkable for its 25 percent window-to-floor-area ratio, designed for natural light. Minimal interior remodeling has left in place the gray Ozark marble of the main lobby and the replica of Michelangelo's *David,* a tribute to triumphant youth.

DV136.3 Denver Botanic Gardens House

DV136 Denver Botanic Gardens

1959, Garrett Eckbo. 909 York St.

The Boettcher Foundation, whose money came in large part from the Ideal Cement Company, funded this complex and encouraged use of concrete throughout. Even the dendriform lamps are concrete "trees" with globe lights posing as fruits. San Francisco landscape architect Garrett Eckbo planned the twenty outer acres with sculpture, water features, and plantings that have grown to include Colorado high plains, Alpine, Japanese, rose, and vegetable gardens. The main entrance to the conservatory and education building is through a central court, with raised planting beds around a waterfall and pool.

The most striking edifice in the botanic gardens is the Boettcher Conservatory (DV136.1; 1964, Victor Hornbein and Edward D. White, Jr.), 1005 York St., made of faceted Plexiglas panels between interlaced concrete arches that arc 50 feet above tropical gardens. Here some 600 species are cultivated amid waterfalls and pools constructed in a sloped, naturalistic environment. The raw concrete Boettcher Memorial Center (DV136.2; 1971, Victor Hornbein and Edward D. White, Jr.) is Wrightian in concept and human in scale. It is finely detailed in its flagstone paving and trim, oak doors in steel frames, and geometric stained and leaded glass in door and window openings. A sunken walled garden on the east and south sides of the building provides direct outside access for lower-level offices, meeting rooms, and classrooms.

The Denver Botanic Gardens House (DV136.3; 1926, Jacques Benedict), 909 York St. (NR), a splendid Beaux-Arts villa at the southeast corner of the botanic gardens, lies behind a tree-shaded garden. Of brick and stucco under green-tiled gables, the house is meticulously finished with details such as bronze lighting fixtures with matching switchplates and an arched, carved stone living room fireplace. The main staircase, with its wrought iron balustrade, winds gracefully up from the entry. A second stairway, hidden behind bookshelves in the library, leads down to the wine cellar and up to the master bedroom. Elements of various revival styles enhance this beauty. Stucco walls, grouped windows, irregular massing, and the steep-pitched roof suggest Tudor, but the generous, round-arched first-floor windows are more Mediterranean. Many original furnishings and textiles remain in this gift to the botanic gardens from Mrs. James J. Waring in memory of her father, Henry M. Porter. Mrs. Waring lived next door to the west in an equally exquisite 1922 Benedict masterpiece which also has a romantic central oriel window.

Northeast Denver

Denver's magnificently planned, planted, and maintained parkways are best seen in Northeast Denver (north of Alameda Avenue Parkway and east of University Boulevard). The suggested route, with detours off the connecting parkways to see notable buildings, follows 7th Avenue Parkway to 6th Avenue Parkway (with a side trip on Clermont Street Parkway) to Monaco Street

Parkway, Montview Boulevard, Forest Street Parkway, and 17th Avenue Parkway. East Alameda Avenue Parkway is a less lavish latter-day (1970s) rendition.

DV137 East 7th Avenue Parkway

1914, Saco R. DeBoer. Williams St. to Colorado Blvd. (NR)

East 7th Avenue Parkway's median plantings range from larch trees to floral extravaganzas, while the planting strip borders a variety of houses, including a most notable collection of Jacques Benedict's Beaux-Arts designs. The area along 7th Avenue between Logan Street and Colorado Boulevard, bounded for the most part by East 6th and 8th avenues, is Denver's largest local historic district. It comprises some 927 buildings, from grand mansions and apartment houses on the west end to modest bungalows on the east end.

DV138 Brown-Garrey-Congdon House

1921, Jacques Benedict. 1987, restoration, Edward D. White, Jr. 1300 E. 7th Ave. Pkwy. (southeast corner of Marion St.)

This long, narrow, Chateau Style townhouse is one of the finest of many splendid homes in the 7th Avenue Parkway Historic District. A steep tiled roof with roundel dormers covers the two-story stuccoed masonry walls with a brick base and brick trim on tall, narrow fenestration bays. A two-story, semicircular conservatory bay overlooks the walled back gardens.

DV139 Schwalb House

1921, Marean and Norton. 2325 E. 7th Ave. Pkwy. (northwest corner of Josephine St.)

Carl Philip Schwalb's home, with its unusual range of classical to Art Deco terracotta trim and fancy green roof tiles, was built as a show home for products of his Denver Terra Cotta Company. To expand his firm's palette of colors and range of textures and shapes for trim and roof tiles, Schwalb toured Europe and returned with samples and ideas. His three-story red brick house in a Georgian Revival style has parapeted gable ends incorporating paired chimney stacks. The symmetrical facade fits the center-hall plan with a sunroom on the west balanced by an open porch on the east. Among the few changes have been conversion of former third-floor servants' quarters, with their three large, fanlighted dormers, to children's bedrooms.

DV140 Ross Cherry Creek Library

1962, Paul R. Reddy. 1993, remodeling, Michael Brendle. 305 Milwaukee St.

Deconstructivism came to Denver with this facelift of a boxy, International Style branch library. The new facade is a jumble of raw concrete slabs, tilting I beams, and purely decorative metal braces painted a bloody red. Spare parts spill out the front door, and wacky angles and exposed innards prevail inside in the cutout spaces and dramatized ductwork.

DV141 Masonic Temple (Harman Town Hall)

1891, Franklin E. Kidder and John J. Humphreys. 400 St. Paul St. (northeast corner of E. 4th Ave.)

This two-story brick hall, later stuccoed, was the town hub of a streetcar suburb platted by homesteader Edwin P. Harman. His town of Harman was annexed to Denver in 1895 and has evolved into the Cherry Creek North neighborhood, characterized by upscale shops and aggressive upgrades of small cottages to "pop tops," solar homes, and condominium complexes.

DV142 Crowther House

1974, Richard L. Crowther. 401A Madison St. (northwest corner of E. 4th Ave.)

Capitalizing on Colorado's 300 days of sunshine a year, Denver architect Richard Crowther became one of the nation's first and most articulate champions of solar architecture. After starting his career developing neon signs for a New York advertising agency, he designed his first solar projects, the Ford Rotunda Building (1935) for the San Diego World's Fair and his own passive solar residence (1944) in San Diego. He moved to Denver in the 1940s to give Lakeside Amusement Park a facelift. He stayed to design solar homes at 180 South Dahlia

Street; 100 and 101 South Eudora Street; 370, 378, and 386 Grape Street; and 379, 387, and 395 Hudson Street, all in 1950–1951.

Crowther's own gray and white concrete house sits on an elevated northwest corner in a complex of solar homes he also designed. Its bermed landscaping softens and brings to earth unusual geometric shapes oriented toward the sun and mounted with solar collectors. Other nearby Crowther solars are the duplex at 300 Monroe Street (1967), 500 Cook Street (1972), 310 Steele Street (1975), 419 St. Paul Street (1974), 435 St. Paul (1975), and 2735 East 7th Avenue Parkway (1962).

DV143 East 6th Avenue Parkway

1909–1912. Colorado Blvd. to Quebec St.

Although the 1885 prospectus for the suburb of Montclair (see DV151) shows a tree-lined parkway with a generous median strip where 6th Avenue is today, this parkway was developed relatively late, without sidewalks and with residential fences intruding on 30-foot-deep, city-owned planting strips. The original canopy of elms is being replaced with honey locusts and other trees. The 88-foot median contains an Olmstedian plant palette, with mass shrub plantings alternating with specimen evergreen trees. Most parkway residences were built after 1910, providing a smorgasbord of twentieth-century styles.

DV144 Clermont Street Parkway and Cranmer Park

E. 6th Ave. Pkwy. to E. 1st Ave. between Bellaire and Cherry sts. (NR)

Epitomizing a City Beautiful scene, this parkway, with its spectacular median flower beds, leads to a hilltop park offering fine mountain viewing. Denver Manager of Parks and Improvements George Cranmer, whose house (DV145) borders the east edge of the park, maximized the panoramic views by declaring that trees could not be planted to grow above the sight line from an open flagstone terrace at the top of the hill. The terrace's stone disk sundial and inlaid terrazzo mountain finder provide modest decoration and useful information.

DV145 Cranmer House

1917, Jacques Benedict; additions, Burnham F. Hoyt. 200 Cherry St.

George Cranmer, Denver's powerful and visionary manager of parks improvements between 1935 and 1947, made use of New Deal funding and labor to realize many City Beautiful goals. These range from Red Rocks Outdoor Amphitheater to Winter Park Ski Area. He had Jacques Benedict design his own residence, of generous proportions. This one-and-one-half-story stuccoed Italian Renaissance Revival villa with cast stone trim looks across Cranmer Park to the Front Range of the Rockies. Round arches predominate in the facade with a pedimented doorway opening into a vaulted entry hall. Benedict designed many details, such as the iron chandeliers of the arched ceiling, the massive stone fireplace anchoring the north wall of the living room, and the sunroom with Palladian windows that are echoed in the trim of the interior walls. Benedict was also responsible for the early buildings of Graland School on the south side of Cranmer Park.

DV146 Groves House

1938, Eugene G. Groves. 330 Birch St.

Moderne takes an interesting twist in this reinforced concrete house of a leading International Style architect. The vaulted living room is clearly articulated outside in an elongated cement dome. South of the dome is a roof terrace with a concrete balustrade reached by an exterior stairway. Corners are rounded, and the design also borrows Pueblo Revival massing and detailing in the flat roofs and low parapets. Even details

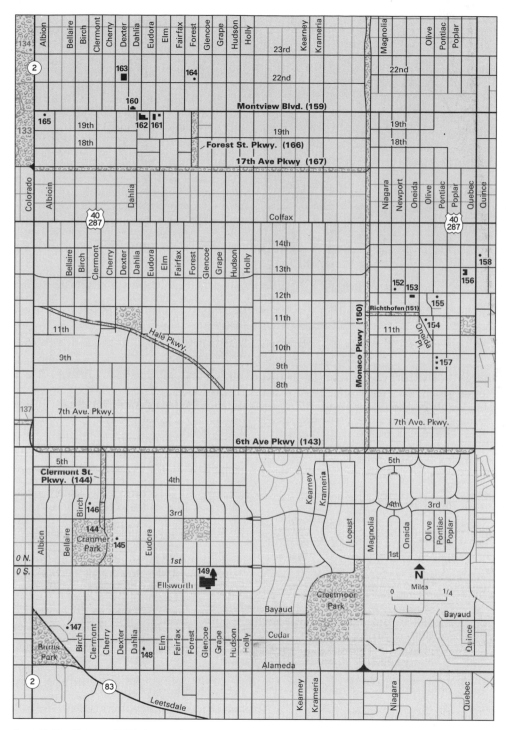

Inset 7. East Denver (DV143–DV167; for DV168 see the overview map on p. 40)

ranging from window mullions to kitchen cabinets are concrete.

DV147 Shangri-la House

1937, Raymond Harry Ervin. 150 S. Bellaire St.

Built for local theater mogul Harry Huffman, this flamboyant house was inspired by set designs for the monastery in the 1937 movie version of *Lost Horizon*. The west elevation reveals a chevron motif and stylized flower pattern in a vertical Art Deco panel above the terrace. The entrance rises through the white stucco wall to exaggerated eaves with ribbed soffits. Flat, projecting roofs and bright aluminum banding provide strong horizontal accents.

DV148 Joshel House

1954, Joseph P. Marlow. 220 S. Dahlia St. (NR)

Joseph Marlow, an admirer of Bauhaus design, reduced this house to the basics. A wide, recessed carport on the northwest corner incorporates the main entrance, combining porch, garage, and porte-cochère. The two-story south elevation is two horizontal ribbons of glass, separated by a band of wooden louvers. Marlow set the two-level house with a single flat roof plane into the south hillside, protected on the north by sculpted evergreens that provide a windbreak, privacy shield, and insulation—the same treescaping he used for his own International Style house (c. 1949) at the southeast corner of Oneida Street and East 12th Avenue. A delicate steel modular frame defines this dwelling's pure rectangularity.

DV149 Temple Emanuel

1960, Percival Goodman. 51 Grape St.

Percival Goodman, a New York architect and professor at Columbia University, coauthored the classic planning text *Communitas* (1947). Goodman, who is noted for synagogues in other cities, designed this for Denver's oldest Jewish congregation. It has high walls of coursed red Lyons sandstone. The east entrance, in a recessed courtyard, uses the same sandstone for paving, floors, and walls inside and out to link interior and exterior. Vertically stepped walls provide tall, narrow, recessed window bays, which cast interesting shadows. Low gables with pointed, projecting roof ends radiate from a pentagonal clerestory with multiple, sharply pointed bays. Contemporary leaded, stained glass panels from France fill high openings under the eaves above the simple sandstone walls. Ten squares of pink marble from Mount Sinai house the Torah scrolls, while the Feiner Chapel (1989) contains a Torah, an ark, and rabbi's chairs from a synagogue destroyed by the Nazis.

DV150 Monaco Street Parkway

1911. Between E. 6th Ave. Pkwy. and Montview Blvd. (NR)

Monaco Street Parkway's median and curbside plantings front a parade of fine homes. Several Spanish Colonial Revival haciendas are typified by the Vandermoor House (1929), at 1400 Monaco. Tudor Revival and Georgian Revival homes of the 1920s and 1930s are also common. An isolated experiment with Modernism is the Streamline Moderne house (1936) at 1521 Monaco, enhanced by black-painted trim such as the brick speed lines and entry fanlight surrounds on a crisp white stucco background. The industrial age is also suggested by the curved corner living room topped by an outdoor deck with curved steel railings.

DV151 Richthofen Parkway

c. 1912. Monaco St. Pkwy. to Oneida St.

This parkway is named for a German emigré, the Baron Walter B. Von Richthofen, who in 1885 founded the suburban town of

Montclair. The core of that neighborhood makes up the Montclair Historic District, along Olive and Oneida streets between 7th and 12th avenues, an unusual Denver historic district of a few scattered large Victorian homes on one-block tracts infilled with newer residences, including many that are modest and modern. The older houses were built in the late nineteenth century as show homes to attract homebuilders, but the crash of 1893 froze development until after 1900. Thus the neighborhood is a catalog of area styles from the 1880s to the present, with a preponderance of 1950s brick houses incorporating bungaloid and ranch house elements. The three-story brick house at 740 Olive Street is the restored home (1897; 1987 restoration) of architect Harlan Thomas, who served as a Montclair mayor. True to George Kessler's 1907 scheme, Richthofen Parkway terminates in a park.

DV152 Bershoff House

1900; 1994, James S. Bershoff. 1200 Niagara St. (northeast corner of E. 12th Ave.)

"Pop tops," one of the more controversial developments in many older neighborhoods, are epitomized by this two-story addition to a small, stuccoed brick cottage. "Rather than match our old house, I wanted to be honest about this. This is a new house that landed on top of an old one," explained resident and architect James Bershoff. With studied asymmetry, the addition is twisted, and the third-story windows and skylights are placed off center and rotated to form diamonds rather than squares. Bershoff reconciled the original and the new with a uniform stucco skin, reinstallation of part of the original hipped roof, and a roof cap which recapitulates the design below.

DV153 Montclair Civic Building
(Molkerei)

c. 1899. 6820 E. 12th Ave. (in Montclair Park)

Here cattle were stabled below and tuberculosis patients housed upstairs, where they could lounge on open-air sun porches, drink fresh milk, and breathe the barnyard effluvium. Originally known by the German word for dairy and modeled after German health spas offering the milk cure, this three-story

clapboard structure with a rhyolite foundation and brick columns has a screened porch on three sides. Tuscan columns and the Eastlake trim on the north entry and overhead balcony are among the few pieces of ornament on a utilitarian edifice that found reuse as one of Denver's first community centers.

DV154 Richthofen Fountain

1901, Harlan Thomas. Richthofen Pkwy., Oneida St., and Oneida Pl. (NR)

To refresh beasts of burden and honor Baron Walter von Richthofen, his widow built this fountain of Pikes Peak granite. Later her ashes were interred in a bronze repository in the fountain wall. Besides the name *Richthofen,* the foundation is inscribed with a line from Samuel Taylor Coleridge's *The Rime of the Ancient Mariner* to emphasize the bucolic nature of Montclair as a model streetcar suburb: "He Prayeth Well Who Loveth Well Both Man and Bird and Beast."

DV155 Richthofen Castle

1887, Alexander Cazin?. 1910, addition, Maurice Biscoe. 1924, addition, Jacques Benedict. 7020 E. 12th Ave. (at Olive St.) (NR)

Walter von Richthofen erected this rhyolite castle as the show home of Montclair. Alexander Cazin, a fellow German, may have designed this mock medieval fortress with its third-story tower, turrets, and gables. On the northwest corner is a red sandstone bust of Frederick Barbarossa, the medieval ruler who first tried to unify Germany. The original castle, a prickly Prussian affair, was re-modeled and enlarged in 1910 for a new owner, Edwin B. Hendrie. Maurice Biscoe and, later, Jacques Benedict softened the lines with half-timbered and stuccoed west and south wings (1924) and transformed the crenelated roofline with shingled gables and a cap for the central tower. Inside the thirty-five-room castle is an entry hall with dark oak paneling and hand-tooled leather walls and a parquet-floored music room seating 150. The gatehouse to the east has been divided from the property and converted to a separate residence.

DV156 St. Luke's Episcopal Church

1890, James Murdoch. 1270 Poplar St. (southeast corner of E. 13th Ave.)

Rough-faced rhyolite walls pierced by lancet windows and a square corner tower with a tall, shingled steeple distinguish this church. Despite additions, St. Luke's, with its mini-buttresses, fine stonework, and stained glass windows, remains a countrified example of an English Gothic Revival chapel.

DV157 Tuberculosis Houses

1907–1911, Charles M. Kittredge and Dennis Tirsway, builders. 928, 940, 956 Olive St.

The dry, sunny Colorado climate attracted more settlers than even the gold and silver rushes. One of the most innovative designs for tuberculosis patients was these single-story homes featuring screened porches where patients—or anyone exposed to tuberculosis—slept in the fresh air. Subsequent owners have enclosed the sleeping porches of a floor plan that was surprisingly modern, with all rooms opening off a central space with a single, central fireplace. Ten-foot ceilings, many windows, and large doorways made for a bright, open house, in contrast to the bungalows being built at the same time. Other examples of dramatically updated "TB houses" are at 721, 920, and 928 Newport Street.

DV158 False-Fronted House

1925; 1980s. 1340 Quebec St.

The owner of this tiny cinderblock and stucco cottage stuck a fanciful Italianate frame face on the outer edge of the front porch. An elaborately bracketed cornice and trim dress the false front rising above the humble house to which it is connected by glass side walls under a gable roof.

DV159 Montview Boulevard

1892–1907. Monaco St. Pkwy. to Colorado Blvd. (NR)

Houses in European revival styles line this eastern approach to City Park and the Denver Museum of Natural History. As one of the first boulevards, Montview lacked the median of later parkways but included the generous, city-owned setbacks that front homesites. Tudor and other English revival styles are the most common along Montview, mixed with Spanish Colonial, bungaloid, and Modernist examples.

DV160 Park Hill Branch Library

1920, Merrill H. and Burnham F. Hoyt. 1994, restoration, David Owen Tryba. 4705 Montview Blvd. (northeast corner of Dexter St.)

This Carnegie branch library, a domestic-scale example of the Italian Renaissance Revival style, honors Montview Boulevard's grand but residential scale. The library, built for $27,000, is enriched by details such as the balustraded motif used in the ribbon windows. The diamond-paned leaded windows are echoed by the decorative diamonds of the paneled door. An unfortunate 1964 remodeling was happily undone in a 1994 restoration. Once again, the interior gives its original impression of natural light and spaciousness, with dark woodwork and ceiling beams for contrast.

DV161 Blessed Sacrament Catholic Church

1912, Harry James Manning. 4930 Montview Blvd. (southeast corner of Eudora St.)

The architect at first designed a $250,000 Gothic Revival cruciform church with twin spires soaring over Montview Boulevard. This cathedral-sized fantasy remains only a beautiful drawing in the parish files, as financial troubles shrank the building to its current proportions.

DV162 **Montview Boulevard Presbyterian Church**

1910, William N. Bowman; several additions. 1980 Dahlia St. (southeast corner of Montview Blvd.)

Inspired by English Gothic Revival architecture, this complex of rusticated rhyolite buildings, which the architect kept low to blend into a residential neighborhood, sets a style followed by neighboring churches. The Castle Rock rhyolite quarries were reopened for the south addition along Dahlia with its grandiose, Gothic-arched entry.

DV163 **St. Thomas Episcopal Church**

1908, Manning and Wagner. 2201 Dexter St. (northwest corner of E. 22nd Ave.)

This splendid Spanish Colonial Revival specimen has a Churrigueresque entry surround of cast stone leading to a rustic, wood-beamed, open-truss nave. Stucco walls and red tile roofing characterize the church, auxiliary buildings, and cloister, which frame a courtyard. Endearing details such as the three stepped cutout arches of the bell tower are beautifully executed.

DV164 **House**

1906. 2205 Forest St. (northwest corner of E. 22nd Ave.)

The stuccoed and half-timbered second story, exposed roof beams and rafter tails, triangular knee braces, sloping foundation, and full-length wraparound porch make this red brick bungalow a picture-perfect example of the Craftsman style. The slightly pitched roof, shed dormers, and slanting porch roof seem to squint into the morning sun.

DV165 **House**

1921, Jacques Benedict. 4050 Montview Blvd.

This beautifully proportioned Tuscan-style house uses red brick for understated trim as well as the skin. The interior is lavish in details, with molded plaster ceilings and faux marble columns. The three-story carriage house, now stuccoed, has been converted to a separate residence at 1955 Albion Street. Note also the full-size Burlington freight car and caboose in the garden of the

half-timbered Tudor Revival house at 1980 Bellaire Street (corner of Montview Boulevard).

DV166 **Forest Street Parkway**

1913. From Montview Blvd. to E. 17th Ave. (NR)

Three blocks of landscaped parkway are lined by a variety of well-maintained homes ranging in size from cottages to mansions. The two-story brick house (1930, G. Charles Jaka) on the southeast corner of Forest and 18th Avenue, is notable for its plain composition, carved wooden window surrounds, and a concave masonry entry arc at the intersection of the perpendicular wings. The grandest residence, the Peter H. Holme House (1929, Burnham F. Hoyt), 1750 Forest Street Parkway, is a Tudor mansion with angled, balancing wings occupied since 1991 by architect Curt W. Fentress.

DV167 **East 17th Avenue Parkway**

1911. Colorado Blvd. to Monaco St. Pkwy.

Frederick Law Olmsted, Jr., was among the planners who made this an early model for Denver parkways with its generous 115-foot-wide landscaped median and 20-foot-wide planting strips. Clustered trees and shrubs alternate with sections of grass and flower beds to provide a flow from forest to meadow and back again. The Obrecht House (1888), 5238 East 17th Avenue Parkway, is a venerable Queen Anne farmhouse thought to be the oldest residence on the parkway. As City Beautiful planners hoped, the city's parkway plantings inspired private homeowners to respond with notable landscaping of their own.

DV168 **Denver International Airport**

1995, C. W. Fentress, J. H. Bradburn and Associates. East of Denver on I-70 exit 284 to Peña Blvd.

The Teflon-coated fiberglass roof of the Denver International Airport terminal reflects both the snowcapped Rockies and Indian tipis that once occupied the site. Nautical illusions also are fostered, not only by the billowing white roof but by the crow's nests of its masts. The roof, draped on steel cables, borrows conceptually from the tensile structures of European architects such

DV168 Denver International Airport

as Ove Arup and Frei Otto and from Kenzo Tange's fabric roof for Tokyo's Olympic Stadium, as well as San Diego's convention center and Vancouver Place in British Columbia. The translucent material admits diffused daylight and glows at night. DIA may be seen as a sculptural adventure in Expressionist architecture whose pedigree can be traced to Eero Saarinen, the Finnish architect who influenced John Dinkeloo and a Dinkeloo protégé, James H. Bradburn. Yet the tensile fabric roof "sculpture"—the largest fully integrated one in the world— also happens to be a cheap way to enclose such a massive space.

Reconciling the airy tents with the banal concrete bulwarks of the terminal, parking garages and concourse buildings presented an architectural challenge. Unharmonious shapes, colors, and materials mar this $5 billion "campus," but it is enhanced by Denver's one-percent-for-art ordinance, which applies to construction budgets for new buildings costing $1 million or more. Much of the art is directional, including elaborate granite and tile floor patterns and "paper airplane" ceiling mobiles that point the way out of an underground people mover. The terminal building showcases local materials, including Colorado Yule marble and red sandstone.

In this artsy terminal the most animated and appropriate artifacts are house sparrows flitting about the tent tops and food courts. Budget constraints postponed plans for extensive landscaping with native plants and a resident herd of buffalo as well as a rail connection with downtown Denver. Nevertheless, this opened as the country's largest and most technologically advanced airport with its automated baggage handling and a 54-square-mile site that is larger than Chicago's O'Hare and the Dallas–Fort Worth airport sites combined.

Northwest Denver

Anglo settlement in Northwest Denver began after 1858, when Denver founder William H. Larimer waded across the South Platte River to stake out "Highlands." This area began to thrive during the 1880s following construction of streetcar lines and viaducts over the South Platte River and railroad tracks. A wave of Italian immigrants between the 1880s and 1920s established "Little Italy" there, although Spanish-speaking settlers have been most numerous since 1950. The ethnic peoples of Northwest Denver have added to a colorful collection of churches, cafes, bars, and housing.

DV169 Confluence Park

1976. Northwest end of 15th St. Bridge over the South Platte River

Following a 1965 flood, the trashy confluence of Cherry Creek and the South Platte was converted into a park celebrating Denver's birthplace. Paved paths follow the

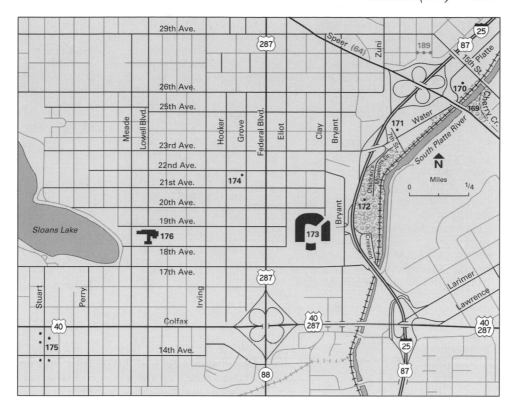

Inset 8. Northwest Denver (DV169–DV176)

South Platte and Cherry Creek to other waterways and waterside parks. Confluence Park, with its grassy amphitheater, vegetation, and stepped masonry landing, became the prototype for a statewide network of greenways. As in similar programs nationwide, old railroad beds and bridges have been converted to pedestrian use, as has Colorado's oldest metal vehicular bridge in public use, the 19th Street Bridge (1888, Missouri Valley Bridge and Iron Company), which has ornate cresting and a wooden sidewalk.

DV170 **REI Denver Flagship Store, previously Forney Transportation Museum** (Denver Tramway Company Powerhouse)

1901, Stearns Rogers Co. 2000, restoration and expansion, Mithun Partners. 1416 Platte St.

This Neoclassical temple of technology bordering Confluence Park has red brick walls with roundel windows and corbeled arches. It housed the coal-fed power plant that generated electricity to move Denver's trolleys. The rejuvenated Platte Valley Trolley (1989, Denver Rail Heritage Society), starts here for a trip to the Zang Brewery site, the Children's Museum, and Mile High Stadium.

DV171 **Zang Brewmaster House**

1889, William Quayle. 2345 7th St. (NR)

Zangs, the biggest brewery in the Rockies before Prohibition, no longer exists, but the two-story Queen Anne house of the brewmaster is easily visible from I-25. From a rough red sandstone foundation, the red brick walls with carved red sandstone trim rise to corbeled chimneys. The hipped roof has decorative gabled projections featuring paneled bargeboards and fishscale shingles. The wooden front porch and balcony have turned balusters and posts with carved foliage and grape clusters. Less elaborate by comparison is the nearby worker housing, formerly the Rocky Mountain Hotel and now the Zang Brewing Company Bar and Restaurant (1871; additions), 2301 7th Street (NR).

DV172 Children's Museum

1984, Russell Seacat of Barker, Rinker, Seacat and Partners. 2121 Children's Museum Dr. (at the Platte River Greenway)

Corrugated metal painted bright blue-green is used for three industrial-looking, Postmodern buildings in a loose U plan with solar glazing above the front entrance. Denver's Children's Museum, modeled after the Boston prototype, opened in a modest storefront in 1973 and graduated to this $2.8 million, 25,000-square-foot playground located between the Platte River Greenway and I-25. Russell Seacat designed this as a skeleton with flexible interior space for hands-on exhibits.

DV173 Mile High Stadium

1948, Stanley E. Morse. 1977, movable stands, James Tolle. 2001, demolished. W. 17th to W. 20th Ave. between Elliot and Bryant sts.

One of America's ugliest stadiums, stuck in an ocean of asphalt parking, began with Stanley Morse's original two-tiered, 10,000-seat grandstand on the north and west side. In 1961 25,000 seats were added for the opening season of the Denver Broncos football club. The city bought the stadium in 1968 and ultimately expanded it to 75,000 seats. The 1977 addition included the "floating" east side seating, which is hydraulically lifted and moved on a cushion of water to open up the field for baseball. Next door is the better-designed McNichols Sports Arena (1975, Charles Sink and Associates), 1635 Clay Street, an enameled metal oval popularly known as "Big Mac."

DV174 Neef House

1886. 2143 Grove St.

Frederick Neef of Neef Brothers Brewing Company built this brick Queen Anne Style house. Eastlake bargeboard on the entry porch is repeated on the two-story front bay and in the main front gable, lending symmetry to a house with exuberant and varied detail, including an attic oriel window tucked under the front gable, stained glass transoms in a variety of ornate window surrounds, and curlicues in the wrought iron fence.

The Neef House is the handsomest edifice in the Witter Cofield Historic District, bordered roughly by West 21st and West 25th avenues between Federal Boulevard and Irving Street. In this Denver Landmark District, named for the two men who platted it, most of the 216 structures are single-family 1880s residences. Queen Anne Style dwellings, ranging from cottages to large, elaborate homes, are the most common. Homes built after 1910 are mostly modest bungalows.

DV175 Stuart Street Houses

1890, Lang and Pugh. 1389, 1390, 1435, 1444, 1471 Stuart St. (NR)

William Lang and his partner, Marshall Pugh, designed these eclectic Romanesque Revival and Shingle Style houses shortly before the silver crash of 1893 precipitated Lang's suicide and lowered Denver's architectural aspirations. Ralph Voorhees, a real estate developer and state legislator, commissioned them as show homes for his West Colfax subdivision. Voorhees lived at 1471 Stuart, which, like the others in the group, is a three-story mass of rough-faced rhyolite with a shingled upper story. These homes are romantically asymmetrical and culminate in third-story towers, steep-pitched gables, and rustic stone chimneys. The Frank W. Smith House, at 1435 Stuart, has tall windows, soaring stonework, and an open, three-story tower that give it a church-like verticality. The house at 1444 Stuart is a splendid Shingle Style home with rectangular ribbons of shingles completely wrapping the top two stories. Curving corners, deeply recessed sets of round and rectangular ribbon windows, irregular massing, and the heavy stone arches add distinction.

DV176 Lake Junior High School

1926, Merrill H. and Burnham F. Hoyt. 1820 Lowell Blvd.

This Tudor Revival masterpiece, with towers, chimney, and patterned brickwork, is supposedly modeled after a part of Windsor Castle but also features an Arabic minaret and dome. The expansive building, constructed for $829,000, occupies a 3.5-block hilltop site looking west onto Sloan's Lake in a parklike setting designed by landscape architect M. Walter Pesman. The school is relatively unaltered, its exquisite brick detail emphasized by the absence of other materials.

DV177 Heiser House

1893. 3016 Osceola St. (northeast corner of W. 30th Ave.)

Herman H. Heiser, a maker of custom saddlery, placed his monogram in the floor tiles of the front porch of his two-story Queen Anne residence. Particularly impressive is the entry door with leaded glass side lights and transom and the tower at the southwest corner. Interior woodwork, paneling, and doors are beautifully matched, with different woods in each room. The restored house has a four-car garage added in 1989, meticulously detailed to match even the narrow mortar joints of the house.

DV178 Sears, Roebuck House

1908. 3401 Stuart St.

Between 1908 and 1940 the Modern Homes Department of Sears, Roebuck and Company sold a million homes nationwide in 450 ready-to-assemble designs. One of the many options was this foursquare, constructed of rough-faced concrete blocks made by a contraption sold by Sears. One of the few known surviving mail-order homes in Denver, this has five bedrooms, one bath, and solid oak flooring and woodwork. Lena and John Otte, the brother and sister who assembled this house, also purchased from Sears the leaded art glass windows, beveled plate glass in the front door, "palace car" mirrored mantel ($10.53), a complete plumbing system ($34.44), and a hot water heating system ($209.14). The Ottes lived in an outbuilding, the current garage, while Lena, clad in overalls, did much of the construction. John helped on weekends. The original Tuscan porch col-

umns have been replaced by cast stone railings and pillars that match the house.

DV179 Cox "Gargoyle" House

c. 1889, David Cox, Sr. 3425 Lowell Blvd.

Stonemason David Cox designed and built his two-story home and decorated it with fanciful carved creatures that add a Gothic creepiness. Constructed of alternated broad and narrow courses of rough-faced sandstone block, the dwelling is notable for Cox's craftsmanship, as expressed in the stone balustrade of the porch and grouped columns with carved capitals, the carved stone of the gable panel and finial, floral friezes and dragon downspouts, and the faces topping the window spandrels. Cox erected for his daughter the Cox Foursquare (1903) next door, at 3417 Lowell Boulevard, with 18-inch-thick wall panels of dressed buff sandstone.

DV180 Walker House

1885, David Cox, Sr. 3520 Newton St.

This house in the Queen Anne Style minus the usual fancy wood trim was built for John Brisben Walker, a northwest Denver developer who also owned Red Rocks and sold it to the city for use as an amphitheater park. Walker later moved to New York City, where he owned *Cosmopolitan* magazine until he sold it to William Randolph Hearst. Reversing the usual Denver pattern of brick houses trimmed in stone, this gray rhyolite domicile is trimmed in red brick.

DV181 Elitch Gardens Theater

1890, Charles Herbert Lee and Rudolph Linden. Southwest corner of W. 38th Ave. and Tennyson St. (NR)

From the beginning, when Phineas T. Barnum and Tom Thumb supposedly helped John and Mary Elitch open their gardens, performing arts were important to Denver's oldest and largest amusement park. Some of Denver's first moving pictures as well as summer stock theater played in this octagonal board-and-batten theater surrounded by a two-story porch. This all-wooden early example of the Western Stick Style has been closed since the 1980s. In 1995 Elitch's

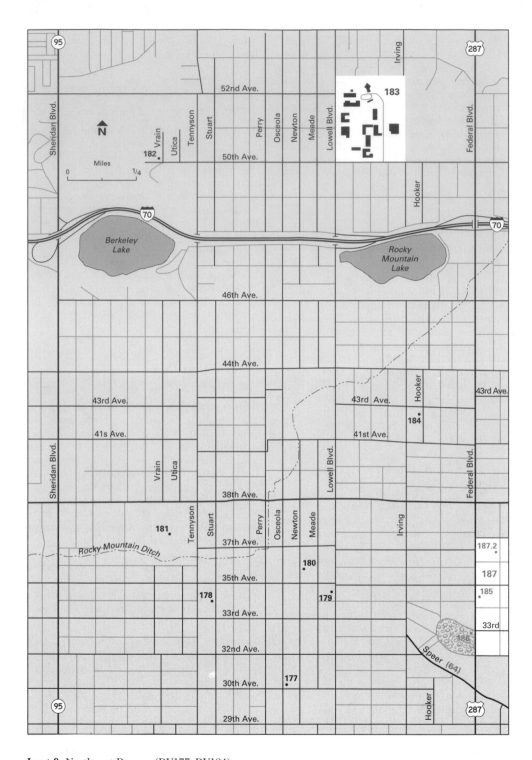

Inset 9. Northwest Denver (DV177–DV184)

moved into the Auraria neighborhood, to an expanded site along the South Platte River, leaving behind this landmark theater.

DV182 El Jebel Shrine and Clubhouse

1925, William N. Bowman and T. Robert Wieger. 4625 W. 50th Ave. (northwest corner of Vrain St.)

A Beaux-Arts palace in Moorish drag, this complex of stucco over brick has decorative tile trim and roofing and, along with seven other window types, ogee arches. An open observation deck under an octagonal cupola crowns the square, balustraded tower. Inside the three-story building, the decor is even more exotic: murals and mosaics adorn the ballroom and an auditorium guarded by two plaster lions.

El Jebel was founded in 1887 by Mortimer J. Lawrence. A Denver chapter opened in 1888 for this "brave, fun loving, adventuresome band of men," still noted for sponsoring hospitals for crippled children. The Shriners left their 1906 home at 18th and Sherman (DV090) in 1929 for this exotic, $225,000 replacement and the adjacent 193-acre golf course. During the Great Depression, El Jebel sold the golf course to the city of Denver.

DV183 Regis University

1888, W. 50th Ave. Pkwy. to 53rd Ave. between Lowell Blvd. and Irving St.

Founded in Las Vegas, New Mexico, in 1877 as the College of the Sacred Heart, this Jesuit school moved to its 40-acre north Denver site in 1887. Edward Barry, a scholastic trained in architecture, worked with Denver architects Henry Dozier and Alexander Cazin on Old Main (1888), a three-story tan and red sandstone and rhyolite hall with a mansard roof. Renamed Regis in 1921 to honor a seventeenth-century French Jesuit, the college grew slowly despite impressive grounds arranged around the typical tree-lined quadrangle lawn. Carroll Hall (1923) was the only other distinguished building until the 1950s. Since then this university of about 5,000 students has thrived, and the campus has filled with newer buildings. On the campus one of the most impressive new structures is the Coors Life Directions Center (1987), 3539 W. 50th Avenue, whose parapeted gable ends and steep-pitched roofs allude to the Collegiate Gothic style of Carroll Hall. Saco R. DeBoer provided a 1923 master plan that has been partially implemented but abandoned on the eastern edge of the campus along Federal Boulevard, where a commercial strip prevails.

DV184 The Victorian Theater (Bungalow Theater)

1911, George Swartz. 4201 Hooker St.

The basement of this bungalow was converted to a theater by a tuberculosis victim who found solace in Shakespeare. His daily recitations attracted a neighborhood audience to whom his wife and daughters served grape juice and homemade cookies. As audiences grew, Swartz accommodated them by

DV183 Regis University, c. 1925

DV185 Milton House

DV186 Woodbury Branch Library

building his 150-seat basement theater. Among 800 plays produced during Swartz's twenty-year occupation were every one of Shakespeare's dramas. In the 1950s R. Paul Willett reopened the space as the Gaslight Theater, which staged plays in an informal atmosphere, a tradition continued by The Victorian Theater.

DV185 **Milton House**

1916, Glen W. Huntington. 3400 Federal Blvd. (northeast corner of W. 34th St.)

Glen Huntington, the designer of this early Prairie Style residence, was a Denver admirer of Frank Lloyd Wright. He used a flat roof, overhanging eaves, and window bands to create a horizontal emphasis which departed radically from the popular styles of the day. Small-paned, rectangular windows and rectangular ornamentation on the fascias of the eaves add to the studied, geometric composition. The open, multilevel interior was also far ahead of its time. Originally stucco, the house was faced in stone during the 1950s.

DV186 **Woodbury Branch Library**

1912, Jacques Benedict. 1992, restoration, David Owen Tryba. 3265 Federal Blvd.

Fronting Highland Park and Federal Boulevard is a beautifully proportioned Italian Renaissance palace in miniature. Roger W. Woodbury, first president of the Denver Public Library board, suggested the Florentine style for this branch library, partly funded by Andrew Carnegie, whose portrait hangs above one of two original fireplaces. The single story of beige brick atop a full basement is trimmed with elaborate terracotta pilasters and medallions, while triple arches grace the central entry. The ceiling's ornately carved open trusses and silver birch decking shine after a 1992 restoration that undid many "improvements" to resurrect the original inspired design. Tryba, a Denver architect, added a rotunda at the rear that opens to an outdoor stage. In this addition he used the same large, arched openings that distinguish the original facade.

DV187 **Potter Highlands Historic District**

Zuni St. to Federal Blvd. between W. 32nd and W. 38th aves. (NRD)

This large district of 667 buildings is a fairly intact ensemble of late Victorian dwellings. Planting strips and flagstone sidewalks front evenly set-back homes. Large Victorian residences, like the Mouat House, now the Lumber Baron Bed and Breakfast (DV187.1; 1890; 1994 restoration, David Anderson), 2555 West 37th Avenue, and the Sayre-Brodie House (DV187.2; 1886), 3631 Eliot Street, advertised Mouat's lumber company and Brodie's Lyons sandstone business. Interspersed are plainer Queen Anne examples, as well as foursquares, classical cottages, bungalows, and a few frame farmhouses. The Edbrooke Foursquares (DV187.3; c. 1904, Frank E. Edbrooke), 2501, 2511, 2519, and 2525 West 32nd Avenue, were con-

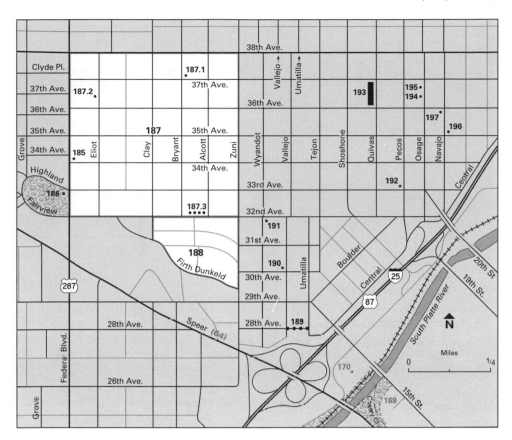

Inset 10. Northwest Denver (DV186–DV197)

structed as a family complex for John W. Prout, a mining man and geologist in the first graduating class of the Colorado School of Mines. The small rear yards were joined and had a common carriage lot and driveway, which helps to explain the lack of garages. These early foursquares, with little ornamentation other than the Tuscan porch columns and bracketed cornices, represent Edbrooke's shift from embellished Victorian designs to Neoclassicism.

DV188 Highland Park Historic District

1874. Zuni to Clay sts., between W. 32nd Ave. and Dunkeld Pl. (NR)

The town of Highlands originally stretched from Zuni to Lowell Boulevard between West 26th and West 38th avenues, including Highland Park, the oldest of thirty-six north Denver subdivisions annexed to Denver in

1893. On the southeast corner of what is now the large Potter Highlands Historic District, William J. Palmer and Dr. William A. Bell of the Denver & Rio Grande Railroad laid out the Highland Park subdivision in 1874. In a rare departure from the grid, Highland Park's irregular streets follow the land contours. Today, Highland Park, also known as Scottish Village because of its curving lanes with Scottish names, illustrates over 100 years of low-cost housing built on tiny lots, atypical in a city generally given to much larger lots and houses.

DV189 Stonemen's Row Historic District

1891–1893. W. 28th Ave. between Vallejo and Umatilla sts. (NRD)

Stonemasons who prospered during Denver's 1880s building boom built houses for their own families in this block. Designs came from several architects: 2753–2755 Umatilla and 2112–2114, 2118–2120, and 2140 West 28th Avenue are by Balcomb and Rice; 2122 West 28th Avenue is by the Baerresen Brothers; and 2128 West 28th Avenue is by J. H. Barnes. These flat-roofed duplexes are harmonious in repetition of Richardsonian elements, such as the triangular roof pediments, with enough variety of texture and materials to avoid monotony. The quarry-face sandstone and rhyolite mixed with red brick, combined with the weight of the Romanesque Revival elements, makes these small units seem bigger than they are. The back yards overlook the Platte Valley from a precipitous bluff offering a spectacular vista of downtown.

DV190 Asbury Methodist Church

1890, Franklin Kidder and John J. Humphreys. 2215 W. 30th Ave. (northwest corner of Vallejo St.)

On a prominent hillside visible from downtown, this Richardsonian Romanesque edifice stands in rough-faced gray sandstone. The wide entry arch is in the base of a corner bell tower, with an open belfry under a steep polygonal cap. The tower's narrow, arched openings are divided by stone pilasters, grouped at corners. The design may be inspired by H. H. Richardson's Trinity Church in Boston, with arched, tripartite window bays centered in each street elevation. Red sandstone bands visually hold the large expanses together. Inside, the renovated pipe organ (1875) is said to be the oldest in continual use in Colorado.

DV191 Chapel of Our Merciful Savior

1890, James Murdoch. 2224 W. 32nd Ave. (southeast corner of Wyandot St.) (NR)

A soaring steeple atop a buttressed corner bell tower distinguishes this red brick Gothic Revival chapel. Rosy, rough-faced stone trims the entrance, centered in the gabled narthex beneath a rose window. Inside, original carved wooden statues, pulpit, baptismal font, and pews survive under a hammerbeam ceiling. The marble angel holding a shell for holy water was sculpted by Elsie Ward Hering, a Denver student of Augustus Saint-Gaudens.

DV192 St. Patrick Catholic Church

1907–1910, Manning and Wagner. 3325 Pecos St. (northwest corner of W. 33rd Ave.) (NR)

Father Joseph P. Carrigan defied his bishop to build this parish complex after a tour of California's eighteenth-century Franciscan missions. The priest worked with Harry James Manning, a leading Denver architect then in partnership with Francis C. Wagner to produce a Mission Revival design executed in smooth-dressed light brown stone with red barrel tile roofs. Although Carrigan was dismissed for insubordination, his church stands, recently restored. A curvilinear parapet and square, domed towers overlook the sheltered entrance. The inner courtyard is rimmed by the church, sacristy, a two-story rectory, and a small library. Plaster walls, open beams, and other Mission Revival elements also characterize the interior. In 1989 the parish was closed, and the property became Our Lady of Light Monastery for Capuchin Poor Clare nuns, noted for their twenty-four-hour prayer vigils and their heavenly cookies. A block southeast, at 3233 Osage Street, the original red brick Romanesque Revival St. Patrick's Catholic Church (1883) was converted to the parish school and then to the Original Mexican Cafe.

DV193 Bryant-Webster Elementary School

1930, G. Meredith Musick. 1992, additions, JH/P Architecture. 3635 Quivas St. (NR)

Perhaps the most unusual school design in Denver, this Art Deco fantasy culminates in a five-story entry tower. Expressionist designs in the purple-brown brick subtly portray buffalo, kachinas, and other motifs found in

DV193 Bryant-Webster Elementary School

Navajo textiles, Pima baskets, and Pueblo pottery. Other southwestern motifs such as the running zigzag patterns in the frieze and stepped diamonds are hallmarks of the Pueblo Deco style. The varied shapes and sizes of brick, requiring special molds and clays, were manufactured by the Denver Clay Pipe and Brick Company. Leone Bradbury painted an Indian pueblo mural for the first grade classroom, and an artist from San Ildefonso Pueblo decorated the burned clay tiles in the interior. This experiment in cross-cultural architecture, which originally cost the Denver Public Schools $250,000, including design fees, has aged well with the help of sympathetic additions.

DV194 Damascio House

1895, Frank Damascio. 3611–3615 Osage St.

Frank Damascio, one of Colorado's many Italian stonemasons, helped build the Brown Palace Hotel, the Basilica of the Immaculate Conception, and other Denver landmarks. In this eclectic house for his family, he used red and gray stone in alternating courses of rough- and smooth-faced stone. A central bay rises full height to a polygonal flared roof topped by a finial. Round and pointed arches of rough stone lead to recessed porches, with small, decorative turrets at each side of the front facade.

Fancy stone posts and wrought iron fencing guard the front yard. Built as a double, this house later served as a convalescent hospital run by the builder's daughter, Elisa Damascio Palladino.

DV195 Cerrone's Grocery (North Denver Mercantile Company)

1893, Frank Damascio. 3617 Osage St.

Frank Damascio and his partner, Horace Palladino, designed and built this single-story brick box with 15-foot ceilings for their North Denver Mercantile Company. Brick pilasters rise above the roof to bracket a narrow, corbeled cornice. Since the 1920s the Cerrone family has operated one of Denver's last old-fashioned neighborhood groceries with its original hardwood floor, wooden display cabinets, and chopping blocks guarded by a statue of the Blessed Virgin.

DV196 Hannigan-Canino Terrace

1890. 3500 Navajo St. (northeast corner of W. 35th Ave.) (NR)

Although single-family housing has always dominated even poor neighborhoods in Denver, perhaps a hundred terraces such as this were built in the city's blue-collar districts. Its ten apartments have basement-to-parapet brick fire walls between every two units in a structure of simple massing and ornament. The two stories of red brick are topped with a flat roof and a corbeled cornice. Ten recessed bays are separated by pilasters, and door and window openings are arched. Each apartment contains a living room and small kitchen on the first floor, with a closed stairway leading to upstairs bedrooms. Built without bathrooms and central heat, the units have been individually remodeled to include these conveniences.

Irish immigrant Frank Hannigan built these units at the time of a large influx of his countrymen. Second owner Joseph Canino, who remodeled the corner unit as a storefront space and apartment in 1935 to accommodate his meat market and family, represented a later wave of Italian immigrants. These two ethnic groups slowly improved their economic conditions and

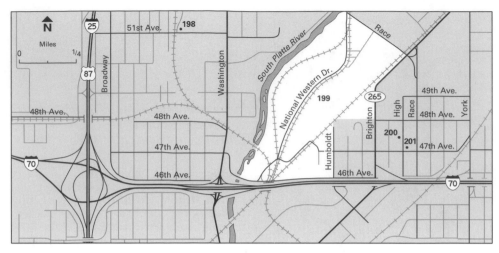

Inset 11. Northwest Denver (DV198–DV201)

moved on, to be succeeded by a third ethnic community, Hispanos.

DV197 Our Lady of Mount Carmel Catholic Church

1904, Frederick W. Paroth. 3549 Navajo St. (southwest corner of W. 36th Ave.) (NR)

Still reigning over the neighborhood known as Little Italy, Mount Carmel was Colorado's first Italian national parish. The Romanesque Revival design in brick has twin towers capped by copper domes. A large rose window is centered in the front gable above a niche for a statue of Our Lady of Mount Carmel. The 1,000-pound bell, the "heartbeat" of north Denver, once regulated life as church bells did in the old country. The interior is decorated by marble statues brought from Italy and mural paintings on the walls and ceiling. In the alley behind the church, proud craftsmanship can be seen in the red brick chimneys with blond brick crosses inset.

DV198 American Smelting and Refining Company, Globeville Plant

1889. 495 E. 51st Ave. off Washington St.

From the 1880s to around 1910 smelting was Denver's largest single industry. Of a dozen smelters which once darkened the skies but enriched the residents of the Mile High City, this is the sole survivor, its giant stack and nineteenth-century brick industrial structures separated by chain-link fencing and barbed wire from a surrounding wasteland. ASARCO was convicted in 1993 of polluting Globeville, the working-class town to which it gave birth, and ordered to begin a $38 million cleanup.

DV199 Denver Union Stockyards

1889. Bounded by I-70 on the south, the South Platte River, Race Court, and Brighton Blvd.

This complex includes the four-story Exchange (1899), housing livestock firms and the Stockyards Inn. A plain office building with a brown brick base and three upper stories of red brick, it was originally dressed up by a triple round-arch entry below four three-story Ionic columns supporting a curvilinear, scrolled parapet. Nearby, at East 46th Avenue and Humboldt Street, is the National Western Auditorium (1909), a two-story, parapeted red brick oval structure with an entry pavilion distinguished by curtain window walls. Augmented by numerous additions, including a major 1993 expansion, the complex houses the National Western Stock Show, a celebration of Denver's cow town heritage, for ten days every January.

DV200 **Elyria School**

1924, Wilson and Wilson. 4725 High St.

This Beaux-Arts design, a one-story blond brick structure with a red tile roof, shows how delightful and intimate a school building can be. Its U-shaped plan opens to the neighborhood rather than shutting it out, as do modern fortress schools. Generous round-arched windows with graceful fanlights front the two ends of the *U*, smiling on the sidewalk of this working-class district of modest cottages. Abandoned and sold in 1979, the school was reopened in 1989 by Su Teatro, a Hispanic theater company.

DV201 **Elyria Branch Library**

1920, Harry James Manning. 1901 E. 47th Ave. (northeast corner of High St.)

Akin to nearby Elyria School, this Beaux-Arts design is the last of Denver's eight Carnegie libraries, built for $16,500. The red stucco building with large, round-arched, fanlighted windows once had a red tile roof, a fireplace, and murals by Albert Olsen portraying the adventures of Don Quixote. It was closed as a library in 1952 and converted to an art gallery.

South Denver

The town of South Denver sprouted along the Broadway streetcar line and grew to be the largest of the streetcar suburbs annexed by Denver. Incorporated in 1886, South Denver stretched from South Alameda to Yale avenues between Colorado Boulevard and Pecos Street. This white, middle-class town was annexed to Denver in 1893. Well preserved for the most part, South Denver has Denver's best collection of bungalows and its first International Style dwelling, the Hegner House (1935, built by Casper F. Hegner), 3525 East Dakota Avenue (northwest corner of South University Boulevard.)

DV202 **South Downing Street–South Marion Street Parkway**

1913. Speer Blvd. to Washington Park

This six-block piece of Denver's original parkway network includes the now-covered City Ditch (see DV204.1) in its median strip. It is formally planted and lined by a few notable buildings, including Steele Elementary School (1913, David Dryden; 1929, Merrill H. and Burnham F. Hoyt), 320 South Marion Street Parkway, whose exotic polychrome tilework gives it a Middle Eastern air.

DV203 **South Downing Street Waiting Station**

1904. Southeast corner of S. Downing St. and E. Bayaud Ave.

This open wooden structure of turned posts and bracketed crossbeams has glazed interior partitions and a shake shingle roof with a slight Japanese flair. Neighborhood volunteers help maintain this quaint station, far removed from the slick modern metal and glass bus stop shelters of which it is an ancestor.

DV204 **Washington Park**

1899, Reinhard Schuetze. 400 S. Marion St. Pkwy. (NR)

This 160-acre park with Grasmere Lake and Smith Lake as its centerpieces is connected by a Great Meadow reminiscent of London's Hampstead Heath. The narrow, rectangular park is relieved by looping roadways, paths, and City Ditch (DV204.1; 1860s), which makes the lakes and greenery possible. This irrigation channel originates as a diversion of the South Platte River in Waterton Canyon and ends in City Park's Ferril Lake. Within the park it is kept open as a landmark that historian Louisa Ward Arps called "the oldest working thing in Denver." Buildings include the twelve-sided Shelter House (1912) on the east side of the Great Meadow and a picturesque, late nineteenth-century farmhouse and barn expanded as the park headquarters and maintenance center. *Wynken, Blynken, and Nod* (1919), a sculpture by Mabel Landrum Torrey, stands at the southwest corner of Exposition Avenue and Franklin Street, next to the Eugene Field Cottage, the poet's residence and a rare example of simple 1880s frame cottages that were once common in Denver. It was trans-

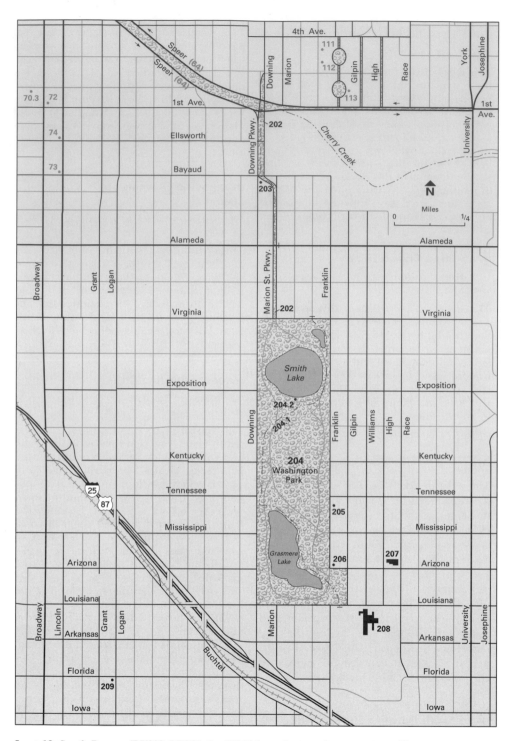

Inset 12. South Denver (DV202–DV209; for DV 210 see the overview map on p. 40)

112

planted from its original site at 307 West Colfax Avenue. The Boat House (DV204.2; 1913, Jacques Benedict; 1987 restoration, Anthony Pellecchia Associates) is on the south shore of Smith Lake. The two-story facade, a mix of Prairie Style, Italianate, and Arts and Crafts elements, is outlined with electric lights, creating a dreamy nocturnal reflection.

DV205 Sink House

1986, Charles S. Sink. 1050 S. Franklin St.

Charles Sink raised this glassy house a story above street level to capitalize on the view of Washington Park and the Rockies beyond. One of the few conventional elements is the gable roof, with a prominent single chimney ending in the same slope to emphasize the angle. The house has a glass skylight, glass block, ceramic tile, and mirrors to add to the illusion of space. The architect-owner studied with Walter Gropius at Harvard and began his career working for I. M. Pei on Pei's Denver projects. Sink's other designs include One Cheesman Place (1968), East 13th Avenue and Williams Street, a twenty-story luxury apartment building with a structure entirely of post-tensioned reinforced concrete and views south over Cheesman Park through floor-to-ceiling glass.

DV206 Causey-Sutherland House

1913. 1198 S. Franklin St.

This storybook Tudor Revival country manor of dark red brick has a fabulous "thatched" roof of curvy, irregularly patterned shake shingles. Roofing, brickwork, and ornamental details are carefully matched in the carriage house, garage, and walled garden and gazebo.

DV207 Washington Park Community Church

1917, Marean and Norton. Northwest corner of Arizona Ave. and Race St.

This church and the arcaded gallery that fronts it frame a cloistered garden. The church has a central domed bell tower. Earth-colored brick with terracotta trim and Doric columns distinguish this refined composition looking back to the Romanesque.

DV208 South High School

1926, William E. Fisher and Arthur A. Fisher. 1700 E. Louisiana Ave. (southeast corner of S. Gilpin St.)

Overlooking Washington Park is this three-story Italian Renaissance Revival school building with red brick walls trimmed in yellowish terracotta under a red tile roof. The main entrance has a loggia of five arches with griffins and grotesques perched above to keep students in line. A large, square tower, banded with several bracketed cornices, features a clock face. Inside, the study hall is guarded by an owl, a crowing cock, a parrot, and a penguin exemplifying wisdom, early rising, recitation, and deportment. The Denver School Board set high design standards in the 1920s and hired Denver's leading architects, granting them artistic freedom, a policy that proved its worth in South High.

DV208 South High School

DV209 Sarah Platt Decker Branch Library

1913, Marean and Norton. 1993, restoration, David Owen Tryba. 1501 S. Logan St.

This fanciful recreation of an Elizabethan cottage has leaded, diamond-paned windows and a gable roof of green tile with ornate chimneys. Red brick wall contrast with creamy terracotta trim. Over the fireplaces are murals by Denver artist Dudley Carpenter, *The Pied Piper of Hamlin* and *The Lady of the Lake and the Sword Excalibur.* Inglenook seating by the fireplaces, a high, open-beam, vaulted ceiling, and teddy bears galore make this a much-loved neighborhood haven. It is named for a Denver clubwoman who championed causes ranging from women's suffrage to branch libraries. Next door, in Platte Park, 1510 South Grant Street, is the James A. Fleming House (1882). Fleming, the mayor of South Denver before its annexation to Denver in 1893, used his stone house, with its three prominent round, conical-capped towers, as the town hall.

DV210 Teikyo University Old Main
(Loretto Heights University)

1890, Frank E. Edbrooke. 3001 S. Federal Blvd. (NR)

A traditional idea of what a college should look like is epitomized in towering Old Main, originally the centerpiece of a Catholic women's college run by the Sisters of Loretto. Old Main's grand stone entry arch bears the Latin inscription *Fides-Mores-Cultura* under an open bell tower that dominates the southwest Denver skyline. For this four-story administration building, Frank Edbrooke used rough red Manitou sandstone and the Richardsonian Romanesque style. The building has a cross-gable roof punctuated with dramatic dormers and carved stone crosses on the gable ends. Perpendicular gabled bays at each end form a modified H plan. A heroic statue of the Blessed Virgin rests in a grotto above the entrance. The chapel addition (1910) contains eighteen stained glass windows made in Munich, Germany. Teikyo, a multibranch, international Japanese university that took over the school in 1989, has diplomatically preserved Old Main and other landmarks, including the nuns' graveyard, on the 160-acre campus.

DV211 University of Denver Campus

1890. 2199 S. University Blvd. and E. Evans Ave.

Founded in 1864 as the Colorado Seminary by territorial governor John Evans, DU is Colorado's oldest institution of higher education. University Hall (DV211.1: 1890, Robert S. Roeschlaub), 2199 South University Boulevard, is robustly symmetrical, with stone porch entrances nestled into the junctures of gabled bays and circular stair towers whose function is expressed by staggered windows that climb with the stairs inside. Various steep-pitched roofs culminate in a central bell tower with an octagonal cap and flagpole. Red sandstone is used for the trim as well as the skin of this formal yet friendly hall.

Across the circular campus entry drive, Iliff School of Theology (DV211.2; 1892, Fuller and Wheeler), 2201 South University Boulevard, has an arcade of eight Gothic windows above the pointed-arched entry of polished stone. This ornate and detailed entry bay dresses up the plainer polygonal wings of a four-story edifice of rough-faced stone with Richardsonian aspirations, complemented by a contemporary addition.

When fire destroyed the Buchtel Memorial Chapel (DV211.3; 1917, Thomas Barber), its ruins were left as a striking sculptural piece. The central water gardens (1967, Garrett Eckbo) and Evans Memorial Chapel (DV211.4; 1874) lend serenity to the campus core. The brown sandstone Gothic Revival Evans chapel is the original part of what later became the larger Grace Methodist Church. It was moved to DU in 1960 when the church, with its later additions, was dismantled. Mary Reed Library (DV211.5; 1932, Harry James Manning) is the Collegiate Gothic anchor of the campus, with a west side terrace and a "peak finder" guide to the Front Range, which shimmers in the distance. Its bulwark, 14,264-foot Mt. Evans, was renamed upon his death in 1897 for DU's founder.

DV212 Buchtel House

1906, Frederick T. Adams, builder. 2100 S. Columbine St. (NR)

One of the earliest and largest Denver bungalows, this is also one of the boldest, with its white brick and massive knee-brace brackets. A wide-eaved dormer and windows lend a lively symmetry to the facade of the two-story dwelling. Henry A. Buchtel, a governor of Colorado, chancellor of the University of Denver, and pastor of the downtown Trinity United Methodist Church, wanted a fashionable bungalow for entertaining as well as for a family home. The builder, inspired by Greene and Greene's Pasadena, California, homes, used a modern, open plan that can accommodate 150 guests at a reception. Since 1985, the University of Denver Women's Club has made Buchtel House its home and opened it for public use.

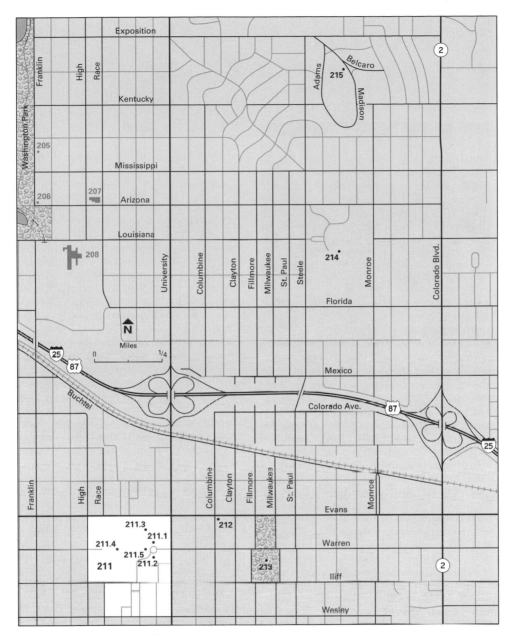

Inset 13. South Denver (DV211–DV215)

DV213 **Chamberlain Observatory**

1890, Robert S. Roeschlaub. 2930 E. Warren Ave. in Observatory Park (NR)

Humphrey B. Chamberlain, a wealthy real estate promoter and amateur astronomer, made a gift of this observatory to the Univer-sity of Denver. The building, of rough-faced, random-coursed red sandstone with an iron dome, is an elegant combination of forms and styles. Roeschlaub's prototype was an 1887 observatory for Carleton College in Minnesota. In Denver he added gabled wings and a protruding entrance bay and had his name as well as the donor's carved into the linear pediment over the round-arched entry.

DV214 St. Thomas Seminary Chapel

1926–1931, Jacques Benedict. 1300 S. Steele St. (NR)

On what was then a farm, Bishop John Henry Tihen opened a seminary in 1908. He engaged Jacques Benedict to design its first grand structure, the Philosophy Building (1926). The twelve-story Renaissance Revival Tihen Tower (1927), also by Benedict, is guarded at each corner by 12-foot-tall angels carved by Enrico Licari. Attached to the tower is Benedict's awesome St. Thomas Chapel (1931). In this exquisite Renaissance Revival church, Benedict employed over two hundred different shapes, sizes, and colors of brick. Arabesque patterns in pearl, gold, and red enhance the terrazzo floor. Eighty-five arched windows of various sizes include seventeen from the Munich stained glass studios of Franz Meyer. The marble altar was carved in Italy from eighth-century designs, and carved, pierced rafters support a coffered tile ceiling. After the seminary closed in the early 1990s, the Archdiocese of Denver moved its offices there.

DV215 Phipps House (Belcaro)

1932, Charles A. Platt; William E. Fisher and Arthur A. Fisher. 3400 Belcaro Dr. (NR)

One of the last and best designs by the New York master of country houses, Belcaro (beautiful dear one) is Denver's grandest residence, a symmetrical Georgian design with eight massive chimneys. On a low hilltop of what was once a much larger estate, the fifty-four-room, 33,123-square-foot mansion, built for $301,063, retains some of its gardens and its huge, enclosed tennis court. The Fisher firm slightly revised Platt's design for the house, especially its "Italian" tendencies.

The poured concrete building is clad in red brick, with dressed Indiana limestone trim and a slate roof. Beyond the entry, with its columns and broken pediment, are a reception area and stair hall finished in Colorado travertine from Wellsville. The oak paneling of the billiard room was transplanted from a Jacobean house in London. This room, the paneled dining room, and some interior fixtures were provided by Charles Roberson, who also furnished interiors for Edsel B. Ford's home in Detroit and William Randolph Hearst's castle at San Simeon.

The ivy-covered Tudor Revival tennis house was designed by John Gray of Pueblo, the initial project architect replaced by Platt and the Fishers. The glass-and-tile-roofed, 423,000-cubic-foot structure is, like the mansion, clad in brick and Indiana limestone. Exposed steel beams appear in the barrel vault over the court, which has a loggia entrance trimmed in wrought iron. The tennis house has a two-bedroom second-floor apartment, dressing rooms, kitchen, soda fountain, and fireplace lounge. In the lounge a large mural by Allen True depicts Phipps family members skiing at the Winter Park Ski Area, which they helped develop. Carved into the fireplace mantel for this millionaire clan to ponder is the motto, "Why should life all labour be."

Annette Hoyt Flanders of New York designed the 8.5-acre gardens in collaboration with Platt, who was also renowned as a landscape architect. The estate, now reduced to five acres, was given in 1964 to the University of Denver for use as the Lawrence C. Phipps Memorial Conference Center.

Lawrence C. Phipps, a multimillionaire vice president and treasurer of Carnegie Steel in Pittsburgh, moved to Denver for his wife's health. He served as a U.S. senator (1918–1930) and invested successfully in many local ventures. The Phipps family's Belcaro Realty and Investment Company be-

DV215 Phipps House (Belcaro)
DV216 Four Mile House

DV216 **Four Mile House**

1859; additions. 1976, restoration, Edward D. White, Jr. 5000 E. Exposition Ave. (NR)

Denver's oldest extant building is this hewn log cabin of ponderosa pine, refined over the years with clapboarding, additions, and a two-story Victorian center section of brick. Built as a stage stop along Cherry Creek and the Smoky Hill Trail, it rests on giant cottonwood logs with broadaxe scars. With the help of drawings by the Historic American Buildings Survey, the house has been restored as a museum, with 7-acre grounds

gan developing the area surrounding the estate in 1931 as one of Denver's posher residential enclaves, with Belcaro as the centerpiece.

Inset 14. South Denver (DV216–DV218)

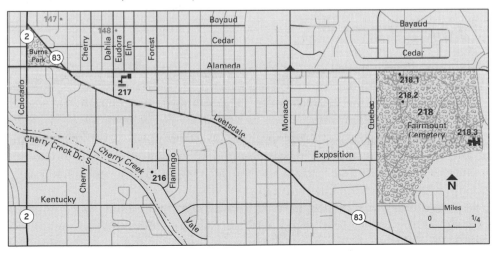

comprising a living history farm. Among numerous reconstructed outbuildings are a three-hole privy complete with window and roof vent. The City of Denver owns and operates this retreat to the rural past.

DV217 Jewish Community Center

1962, Nathaniel Sachter and Robert Max Morris. 4800 E. Alameda Ave.

This novel concrete structure under a linked barrel-vault roof descends a steep south hillside in multiple levels. Although dramatically modern, the utilitarian structure is clad in traditional local red brick and native pink sandstone. The center surrounds an outdoor garden with shelters formed by columns terminating in flattened hyperbolic parabolas. In the entry a repoussé frieze in bronze by Angelo di Benedetto welcomes patrons to extensive recreational facilities, including a vaulted natatorium.

DV218 Fairmount Cemetery

1890, Reinhard Schuetze. 430 S. Quebec St. (near E. Alameda Ave.)

Fairmount is Colorado's most populous cemetery and a peaceful place to study history and architecture. Fairmount's founders promised to abandon the "mournful effects of the old style cemetery" for the rural cemetery park initiated at Mount Auburn Cemetery in Cambridge, Massachusetts. Fairmount recruited Reinhard Schuetze, a native of Holstein, Germany, who had studied landscape architecture and engineering at the Royal Academy in Potsdam. Bringing to Denver the concept of romantic landscape, he planted more than 4,000 trees in Fairmount, which is still the state's largest and most diverse arboretum. Schuetze, Colorado's first landscape architect, subsequently designed or redesigned many Denver parks.

Many well-known Coloradans dwell in this necropolis, where a number erected obelisks and Greek temple mausoleums as their final earthly homes. Frank E. Edbrooke probably designed his own relatively modest Neoclassical mausoleum, as did architect-developer Temple Hoyne Buell, whose final mansion is a polished granite crypt with elaborate wrought iron doors. Buell, a multimillionaire by the time of his death, topped his mausoleum with two Egyptianesque female figures in gilded cast iron, *Princess* and *Pauper.*

Henry T. E. Wendell was the designer of the Richardsonian Romanesque gate lodge (DV218.1; 1890), on East Alameda Avenue, and the Ivy Chapel (DV218.2; 1890), a fine, frilly, French Gothic apparition. The communal Mausoleum (DV218.3; 1930, Mountjoy and Frewen) is a huge Greek temple with a granite veneer. Inside, fine stained glass windows, Alabama white marble walls, Tennessee pink marble floors, and soft recorded music create a celestial atmosphere.

Adams County   (AM)

Fort Convenience, the adobe fur trade fort built in the 1820s by Pierre Louis Vasquez at the confluence of Clear Creek and the South Platte River, was the county's first Euro-American structure. This mud fort had melted by 1858 when Captain Jack Henderson set up a ranch on a small island in the Platte. Henderson's Island became a popular stop along the Platte River Road, where immigrants traded weary stock for those refreshed by grazing in the grassy river bottom. Other ranchers and farmers also settled in the Platte bottomlands, raising food for Denver and the mining camps.

Adams County was created in 1902 and named for Colorado governor Alva Adams. As the county seat, voters selected the farm town of Brighton on the South Platte River, which meanders through the western end of the county. This western part has evolved into large Denver suburbs, such as Commerce City, Northglenn, Thornton, and Westminster. Adams County also has small, unincorporated towns that maintain much of their rural character. The eastern third of the county remains sparsely populated and agricultural.

Gravel dredging and heavy industry have become the chief economic resources. More recently, residents concerned about polluted water and the degraded landscape have begun a cleanup. Once neglected riverfronts and creekfronts are being incorporated in a greenway system of foot trails and parks.

Brighton

Brighton (1871, 4,982 feet) was first named Hughes Station for Bela M. Hughes, president of the Denver Pacific Railroad. By 1879 Daniel F. Carmichael had purchased much of the area and renamed it for his wife's hometown of Brighton Beach, New York. Incorporated in 1887 with about 175 residents, it became the seat of Adams County in 1902.

The Brighton Creamery, the Kuner-Empson Cannery, the Great Western sugar beet factory, and other agribusinesses emerged as the major employers. Truck farming remains a profitable business, and Hispanic, Italian, and Japanese American families raise much of the fresh produce grown in the area. During the harvest season, roadside vegetable stands garnish major highways.

AM01 **Brighton Municipal Building** (Adams County Courthouse)

1906, John J. Huddart. 1939, remodeling, Richard O. Perry and Lester L. Jones. 22 S. 4th Ave. (southeast corner of Bridge St.)

The original courthouse, three brick stories with limestone trim, once had a steep tile roof and a cupola. A 1939 WPA renovation removed these, along with the top-floor courtroom, and added a carefully detailed west addition and new main entrance in a full-height, pedimented portico. Trim on the addition is concrete that closely resembles the original limestone, with recessed brick spandrels and a foundation of green-glazed brick.

AM02 **City Events Center** (Presbyterian Church)

1886. 147 S. First Ave.

This small, steep-gabled church of pressed brick with Carpenter's Gothic details has a wooden steeple surmounting a secondary gable over the entry bay. The open belfry wears a steep pyramidal cap. Trim is simple, with individual lancet windows divided by pilasters. Following the congregation's relocation in 1987, the building was saved from demolition by the city of Brighton and adapted by the Adams County Historical Society for use as a special events center.

AM03 **Armory**

1921, John J. Huddart. 300 Strong St. (southeast corner of Cabbage Ave.)

Posing as a medieval castle, this cinderblock edifice has a recessed central entry flanked by square concrete pilasters and topped by a concrete lintel, with arcaded windows above. Square towers of rough stucco frame an open-trussed, barrel-vaulted roof. Similarly designed state armories also guard Cañon City, Craig, Fort Morgan, Greeley, and other Colorado cities.

AM04 **Brighton Depot Restaurant** (Union Pacific Depot)

1907. 269 E. Bridge St. (northeast corner of Cabbage Ave.)

The single-story depot, the town's third, served as the center of commerce in early Brighton, when the railroad was the main form of transportation. Like other vernacular Prairie Style depots, this 80-by-24-foot building is covered with shiplap siding above vertical boards. A trackside bay has sawn gable trim, and large brackets support the wide roof overhang. Moved a block south from the tracks, it is now a restaurant, expanded into an attached Burlington Northern boxcar.

AM05 Heritage Community Center
(Brighton High School)

1927, Robert K. Fuller. Southeast corner of 8th St. and Bridge St. (NR)

Red and beige brick walls, creamy terracotta trim, and red tile roofs provide the elements of a Spanish Colonial Revival treatment for this school. The three arched entries in separate bays are edged in molded and patterned terracotta, and doorways are flanked by round terracotta columns with owl capitals. Blind arches above the transomed double doors are tiled and contain terracotta plaques. Fenestration across the north facade of the two-story main building is also arched, although the largest windows have been bricked in. The building has been recycled as a community center.

AM06 Hall of Justice

1961, C. Francis Pillsbury. 1931 E. Bridge St.

A Denver architect designed this courthouse as a 50,856-square-foot, two-story drum. Its dark brown brick is broken first by a horizontal fenestration band, then by vertical panels of white-painted cinderblock with raised patterns that section the segmental bays. Originally constructed on stilts to allow parking under the structure, it was enclosed five years after it opened to provide ground-level facilities.

AM07 First Presbyterian Church

1987, Arthur Everett of Everett Zeigel Architecture. 510 S. 27th Ave.

With its tiered triangular dormers rising out of moundlike massing, this fantastic hilltop structure is reminiscent of resorts such as San Diego's Hotel Del Coronado. The dormers dramatize a triangular profile, created by a tall, pyramidal roof rising to a large,

AM07 First Presbyterian Church

central cross. Beneath is a square, red brick building, its first story sparsely adorned except for soldier brick courses. An exposed wood truss supports the 50-foot-high roof and crowns the sanctuary and fellowship hall.

AM08 Van Aire

c. 1967. Between 157th and 160th aves. and Gun Club and Harvest rds., 5 miles east of Brighton

This subdivision of 90 homes is Colorado's premier "fly-in" community, one of over 100 nationwide. "Garages" on the sprawling ranch houses are oversized for the small aircraft that provide the preferred mode of transport. The cul-de-sac streets are laid out around a 4,000-foot-long runway. Two-acre lots and $200,000-to-$500,000 homes include an ownership share in the runway and adjoining taxiways. The location is six miles north of Denver International Airport.

Commerce City

Commerce City (1952, 5,150 feet) amalgamates several earlier settlements: Adams City, Derby, Irondale, and Rose Hill. Rose Hill centered on the Rose Hill Grange Hall and Rose Hill Hebrew Cemetery (1892), 6841 East 62nd Avenue. Commerce City was incorporated in 1952 to block Denver's northward expansion. Louis Vasquez's fort is thought to have been in the vicinity of 72nd Avenue. Irondale, which is commemorated only by a sign along the railroad tracks, was originally a housing development for workers at Charles Kibler's Stove Works.

Old-timers include the Fernald Farmhouse (1882), 7131 Colorado Boulevard, with stuccoed brick walls two feet thick. The Conoco Refinery (c. 1930) remains the state's largest refinery and supplies 15 percent of all gasoline used in Colorado from the Brighton Boulevard plant. Other prominent landmarks include several grain silos belonging to Conagra. The Rocky Mountain Arsenal (1942, U.S. Army), Quebec Street to Buckley Road, between East 56th and East 88th avenues, saturated with defense industry chemical byproducts and with Shell Oil Company pesticides, is being cleaned up as a wildlife refuge. With a 1990 population of almost 20,000, Commerce City is outgrowing its reputation as the armpit of the metropolis, preferring to be known as "Denver's no-nonsense industrial suburb."

AM09 **Riverside Cemetery**

1876, Harvey C. Lowrie. 5200 Brighton Blvd. (at Welby Rd.) (NR)

Colorado's first cemetery park lies mostly in Adams County, with a portion in Denver. Harvey Lowrie, a civil engineer and the Denver municipal surveyor, laid out its curvilinear carriage drives and landscaped grounds beside the South Platte River. Rather than "a boneyard [that is] the most shunted and neglected suburb of the city—given over to owls and bats," the original Riverside Prospectus called for "a much frequented and delightful park."

The original Gothic Revival stone caretaker's cottage (c. 1880) survives, along with a Mission Revival crematorium and office (1903, Frank E. Edbrooke). The 25 foot high monument of cattle baron John Wesley Iliff, a classical female figure atop a granite column, stood as the centerpiece of Riverside inside the now vacant central circle, Block 7. As railroads, industry, stockyards, and smelters moved into the area, Denverites sought newer, more fashionable, and more pastoral burial grounds. Iliff's family moved his monument to Fairmount Cemetery. Even after death, prominent pioneers did not want to be found on the wrong side of the tracks. Yet some 66,000 remain

AM09 Riverside Cemetery, Lester Drake monument

interred in Riverside, which is a treasury of early and eccentric tombstones and mausoleums.

Fairmount Cemetery Association bought Riverside in 1890 and has operated it since. One of the many unusual monuments is a five-foot-high limestone replica of the log cabin of miner Lester Drake. Exquisite details in the solid stone cabin include a pick and shovel beside a door with the latchstring out. Many other intriguing old markers survive, reflecting the generally sentimental and traditional tastes of Colorado's pioneers.

Thornton

Thornton (1953, 5,268 feet) is a city of more than 55,000 residents initially developed by Sam Hoffman, who began by building 300 speculative single-story ranch houses. Governor Daniel Thornton and actress Jane Russell presided at the grand opening. The town is named for him, Russell Boulevard for her. The Thornton Town Center, with such marvels as Bigg's Hypermarket (1990), built as Colorado's largest supermarket, is a $12 million, 100-acre project that gave Thornton what many other suburbs lack—a downtown.

AM10 **Thornton Town Center**

1989, L. J. Hooker Development. 10001 Grant St.

This "new generation" mall contains both municipal and commercial services. A massive, one-story, ordinary mall is distinguished by adobe-colored brick accented with aqua tile trim and roofing. The huge, barrel-vault roof arches over front and rear entries and in between becomes a skylight for the 100,000-square-foot atrium. The Town Center contains the metro area's largest supermarket and Cactus Moon, a high-tech country and western night club with a 6,000-square-foot, horseshoe-shaped dance floor adorned by a revolving glass saddle chandelier. From a mechanical horse you can rope a frisky mechanical calf in this neon-trimmed Old West wonderland.

Northglenn

Northglenn (1959, 5,460 feet) is a city of over 30,000 with curvilinear residential streets laid out according to a master plan by the Denver city planning firm of Harman, O'Donnell and Henninger. The original community focal point, the Riverdale Grange Hall (1909), has been moved to neighboring Thornton and replaced as the activity center by the Northglenn Mall (1968), 10590 Melody Drive and I-25. The Earl Stonehocker Farmhouse (1901), 3190 East 112th Avenue, was preceded by the earlier frame homestead house across the ditch.

AM11 **Graystone Castle**

1984. 83 E. 120th Ave., at I-25

Complete with conical towers and crenelated parapets, this six-story medieval castle of rough-faced concrete block guards the north entrance of the metropolis. Fake stone lions and a porte-cochère mark the entrance to this fanciful hotel complex, which one critic likened to a camouflaged grain elevator.

AM12 **St. Stephen Lutheran Church**

1964, Charles A. Haertling. 10828 Huron St. (at Kennedy Dr.)

Four concrete catenary roofs with 120-foot spans rise into a central spire, creating a concave dome centered over the altar of this church in the round. The Boulder architect, an admirer of Frank Lloyd Wright and Bruce Goff, created organic architecture according to Goff's definition: "that which grows from within outward through the natural use of materials so the form is one with function." This eye-catching church in an open field has been likened to everything from a sagging tent to soaring sculpture that suggests the snowcapped Rockies.

Westminster

Westminster (1911, 5,280 feet) was named for the university established there in the 1890s. The school failed, but its towering Old Main became a focal point for the town that grew up in its shadows. Originally called DeSpain Junction, then Harrisburg, it was incorporated as Westminster in 1911. The agricultural nature of the early settlements has given way to suburban development. The Westminster Mall, at West 88th Avenue and Sheridan Boulevard, City Hall, and City Park Recreation Center help to anchor and define what is now Colorado's tenth largest city.

AM13 **Belleview College** (Westminster University)

1892–1907, E. B. Gregory with Stanford B. White. 3455 W. 83rd Ave. (NR)

The pioneer monument that gave Westminster its name is superbly sited atop one of the most prominent hills in the metropolis. Square towers adorned with smaller circular towers and turrets add romance to an irregular, multistory Richardsonian Romanesque edifice in rough-faced red sandstone. New Yorker Henry J. Mayham conceived and bankrolled the project, recruiting his friend Stanford White, one of H. H. Richardson's most prominent associates, to redesign work begun by a Denver architect. Construction commenced on the 640-acre site in 1892, but the silver panic of 1893 intervened. After it was finally completed and opened in 1907, "the Princeton of the West" struggled with economic and staffing difficulties, culminating in a fatal switch to all-male enrollment on the eve of the draft for World War I.

The floundering university formed a real estate company that sold lots and residences around the campus but did not bring financial salvation. A local fundamentalist sect, the Pillar of Fire Church, purchased the campus for $40,000 in 1920. The church still owns and operates a seminary and KPOF, the oldest religious broadcasting station in Colorado, on this campus. The Westminster Law School, a survivor of the original dream, lasted until its 1957 merger with the University of Denver College of Law. This fabulous Romanesque Revival apparition is well preserved but diminished by shiny metal roofing that would appall H. H. Richardson and Stanford White.

AM14 **Bowles House**

1871–1876, Edward Bowles. 3924 W. 72nd Ave. (at Newton St.) (NR)

This two-story vernacular Italianate house has red sand brick walls 18 inches thick. Twin chimneys rise above the hipped roof with its central gable and widely spaced, carved double brackets under the overhanging eaves. Double brick banding adds horizontal contrast to the tall, narrow windows, with arched openings on the first floor. Restored by the Westminster Historical Society for use as a museum, it commemorates the pioneer settler who donated a depot site for the Denver, Western & Pacific Railroad, assuring Westminster's role as a commuter suburb of both Denver and Boulder.

AM15 **Pleasant DeSpain School**

c. 1892. 1926 addition. 7200 Lowell Blvd. (NR)

Originally constructed in vernacular Romanesque Revival style as a single-story red brick building, this school building was modified at the time of a later addition to include Craftsman elements and was faced with beige brick accented in red. The addition doubled the space and added indoor plumbing to the school, named for 1871 homesteader Pleasant DeSpain. An educational complex that developed to the north and east includes Westminster's first high school (1929) and a junior high school (1949).

AM16 **Arabian Horse Center**

1984, Hoffman Reed Partnership. 12000 Zuni St.

This exotic, sand-colored complex is the international headquarters for the Arabian Horse Association, Registry and Trust. The $6 million center includes offices, a library, an art gallery, a film room, and an archives in a Middle East–influenced structure with rich interior appointments. Ogee arches decorated with subtly colored tiles frame terraces and a reflecting pool on a linear axis. The same decorative tiles are inset into floors in a central, glass-roofed atrium supported by ogee arches with flat-roofed square bays, offering spectacular mountain views from the west-sloping hillside.

AM16 Arabian Horse Center

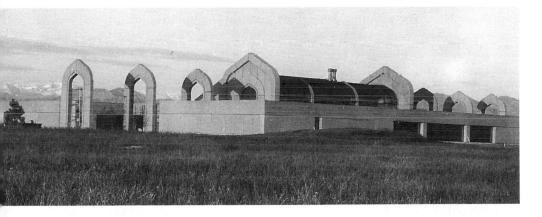

AM17 **City Park Recreation Center**

1986, Barker, Rinker, Seacat and Partners. 10455 Sheridan Blvd.

Located in the 120-acre City Park, landscaped by Royston, Hanamoto, Alley and Abey, the recreation center is a combination of rectangular bays organized around a tall, gabled, full-length galleria with clerestory windows above flat roofs. A fountain plaza entrance capitalizes on panoramic views from the hilltop site. The building veneer is square red brick set in sailor courses, with soldier courses around the windows. A round balcony in the center of the galleria has a curved staircase descending to locker rooms beneath a cross gable in the concrete-tiled roof. The swimming pool is composed of three curved shapes on different levels connected by waterfalls. A rock climbing wall was hand built by Mount Everest climber Edward Webster.

AM18 **Westminster City Hall**

1988, Murata, Outland, Thomas Partnership. 4800 W. 92nd Ave. (southeast corner of Yates St.)

A reference to Big Ben and Westminster Abbey as well as an echo of the nearby Westminster University tower, the city hall's 136-foot clock and bell tower is the new symbol of this city. It crowns a beige brick complex trimmed with horizontal bands of red brick and green glass. The 73,000 square feet of office and public space are distributed over three stories. In front of City Hall, George W. Lundeen's larger-than-life sculpture, *Promise of the Prairie*, depicts a pioneer couple with a barefoot child.

AM19 **West Park Place**

1987, Allen and Phillip Architects, Inc. 8700 Turnpike Dr., near Sheridan Blvd. and U.S. 36

This six-story cubistic office complex has a stepped facade rising from a brick base with Neo-Victorian detailing to reflective glass curtain walls. Corbeled red brick and modern tinted glass make it a pleasing compromise between old and new.

Arapahoe County   (AH)

Arapahoe County, Kansas Territory (1855), initially constituted much of what is now east central Colorado. After the 1858–1859 gold rush brought in an estimated 50,000 settlers, it was subdivided into smaller counties. The final surgery came in 1902, when Denver and Adams counties were carved from its northern half. Littleton replaced Denver as the county seat.

Settlement by English-speaking peoples began with the gold rush. By the early 1860s the Platte River Improvement and Lumber Company employed thirty men cutting timber to build Denver and Littleton. Even after the railroads arrived in the 1870s and granite quarries opened in the Platte Canyon, most construction was frame, exemplified by the Fred Bemis House, now on the grounds of the Littleton Historical Museum (AH09).

Once a sparsely settled collection of hamlets, ranches, and farms, Arapahoe is now the third most populous county in Colorado with more than 400,000 residents. Even so, it has preserved many of its pioneer buildings. Notable collections have been moved to the grounds of Strasburg's Comanche Crossing Museum (AH60) and to the Littleton Historical Museum. Despite a proliferation of shopping malls, Littleton has retained much of its nineteenth-century Main Street. The Arapahoe Greenway (AH12) uses the banks of the South Platte River and some of its tributaries for a series of paved trails and parks that connect with those of neighboring counties.

During the 1920s Arapahoe County became the place for Denver's fashionable suburban homes, built in expensive residential enclaves such as Cherry Hills and Greenwood Village. Country villas and suburban ranch houses have since replaced working ranches in much of the county, which is heavily developed in its western end. Ambitious commercial architecture and landscaping characterize business parks such as the Denver Technological Center (AH24) and Greenwood Plaza (AH26), with its Museum of Outdoor Art.

Littleton

The county seat (1861, 5,362 feet) is named for Richard S. Little, a surveyor, who laid out a tidy country town reminiscent of his native New England next to his Rough and Ready Flour Mill (1867). The Denver & Rio Grande arrived in 1871 and built a depot, followed by the Atchison, Topeka & Santa Fe, making Littleton an early rail suburb of Denver.

Local lumber, hardware, and tin shops provided materials for homebuilders. The Denver & Rio Grande, which developed rhyolite quarries at Castle Rock in Douglas County, provided that stone for upscale residences designed by Denver architects such as Robert S. Roeschlaub and Jacques (Jules Jacques Benoit) Benedict. Most early structures, however, were vernacular frame without great pretensions, a type well displayed in the living history farmhouse preserved at the Littleton Historical Museum.

AH01 RTD Light Rail Station, previously Denver & Rio Grande Depot

1875. Southwest corner of S. Rio Grande and W. Crestline aves. in Town Center Park

One of Colorado's oldest depots, this rectangular single-story beauty is of ashlar rhyolite hauled by the D&RG from the Castle Rock quarries in Douglas County. The once-standard small-town design has a side-gable roof of new corrugated metal, with overhanging eaves supported by elbow brackets with acorn finials. In 1981 Littleton restored the depot, now in the Town Center Park, to its 1910 appearance.

AH01 Denver & Rio Grande Depot, c. 1910

AH02 Santa Fe Arts Center (Atchison, Topeka & Santa Fe Depot)

1888. 2107 W. Powers Ave. (NR)

The railroad's in-house architects provided the plans for this one-story wooden depot with vertical board-and-batten siding and a gable roof. Like the nearby D&RG depot, it is a simple rectangle enhanced by a trackside bay window and ornate elbow bracketing for its overhanging eaves. Transplanted from its original location near Main Street it has been restored and recycled as an art gallery with an 1898 caboose for company.

AH03 Littleton Public Schools Administration Building (Littleton High School)

1920, Robert K. Fuller. 5776 S. Crocker St.

Breaking with the Beaux-Arts tradition, Robert Fuller incorporated zigzags, chevrons, and stylized floral ornament into this three-story, polychromatic brick building with terracotta eagles guarding the entry. In 1956 it became Grant Junior High School and has since been converted to the administrative headquarters of the Littleton Public Schools.

AH04 **Town Hall Arts Center** (Littleton Town Hall)

1920, Jacques Benedict. 2450 W. Main St. (NR)

One of the more exotic designs of a fanciful architect, this two-story brick hall has a stone facade supposedly modeled after the Palazzo della Regione in Vicenza, Italy. Three large Gothic-arched openings at street level are topped by ogee-arched windows with bas-relief terracotta spandrels and banding adorned by Colorado's state flower, the columbine. Exquisite details include the polished stone exterior, double-bracketed cornice, balconies, and cast iron lamps designed by the architect. When the larger Littleton Town Center (1976, Michael Barber) opened at 2255 West Berry Avenue, this treasure was recycled as the Town Hall Arts Center, providing performing arts and gallery space.

AH05 **Littleton Carnegie Library**

1917, Jacques Benedict. 2707 W. Main St.

A Beaux-Arts jewel showcased at the west end of Main Street, this beige brick landmark nods to the Renaissance Revival in recessed openings with fanlighted arches framed by fluted Ionic pilasters. Decorative terracotta printers' marks and a griffin frieze hide below the cornice. After a new library opened in 1965, this became the police building, then a restaurant.

AH06 **Little House**

1884, Robert S. Roeschlaub. 5777 S. Rapp St.

Town founder Richard S. Little hired a leading Denver architect to design this two-story, nearly square house, with rhyolite walls 15 inches thick and rhyolite trim. Its hipped roof is fronted by gables on protruding bays. In the 1930s, the house was remodeled by owner Harleigh R. Holmes, Sr., who replaced original windows with large metal casement units. Holmes pioneered development of a front-wheel-drive axle system for small trucks made by Littleton's Coleman Manufacturing Company.

AH07 **Columbine Mill Brewery** (Columbine Mill)

1922. 5798 S. Rapp St.

Littleton's "skyscraper" is a heavy wood-frame mill sheathed in corrugated metal panels with a 64-foot-tall grain storage elevator, sited beside the mill ditch. Extensively remodeled for use as a restaurant and brewpub, this is the sole surviving flour mill of the many that made Littleton northern Colorado's early grain milling center.

AH08 **Arapahoe Community College**

1974, Eugene Sternberg. 5900 S. Santa Fe Dr.

Concrete Brutalism arrived in Colorado with this boxy, four-story compound housing an entire campus. The architect calls it "a strong, dependable, brutal and honest form looking towards the future." Geared to working students, it was one of the first community colleges to include a day care center and

AH09 Littleton Historical Museum, McBroom Cabin exhibit

a central "family room" learning resources center. Recessed, bunkerlike windows and the stark gray concrete hulk cry out for a massive planting of fast-growing ivy.

AH09 Littleton Historical Museum

1970. 6028 S. Gallup St.

Beautifully sited overlooking Ketring Lake, this museum complex of historic buildings and a living history farm adjoins Gallup Park and the Carmelite retreat (AH10). The core structure is the converted one-story Ketring House (1950, Joseph P. Marlow). Native rhyolite and glass walls under cantilevered projections of the flat roof blend into the lakeside cottonwood grove, including one giant tree, 110 feet high and 31 feet in circumference. The McBroom Cabin (c. 1860) is a hewn log, side-gabled, one-room dwelling built by pioneer Isaac McBroom. The Fred Bemis House (1889), representing second-generation housing, is a small, one-story clapboard farmhouse with decorative shingles. Among other attractions are a hewn log, one-room schoolhouse (1864), an icehouse (1910), an operating blacksmith shop, gardens, livestock, and a restored windmill.

AH10 Carmelite Convent (Benedict House)

1912, Jacques Benedict. 6138 S. Gallup St.

After marrying socialite June Brown, architect Jacques Benedict moved into an old farmhouse on the south shore of Ketring Lake. Over the years he transformed it into this Beaux-Arts villa, incorporating Italianate, Gothic Revival, and Romanesque Revival elements. A demanding architect who supervised workmen closely, Benedict had artisans on scaffolds hand paint the ceiling and worked with landscape architect Saco R. DeBoer on the extensive grounds. A Chicago native, Benedict was the first Colorado architect trained at the Ecole des Beaux-Arts in Paris, and he worked with Carrère and Hastings in New York City at the time they designed the New York Public Library (1909). A flamboyant character noted for inspecting buildings while wearing white gloves, he designed some of Denver's grandest Beaux-Arts residences and churches, as well as Littleton's landmark town hall (AH04), public library (AH05), and First Presbyterian Church (1929), 1609 West Littleton Boulevard. After his death in 1948, a cloistered order of Roman Catholic nuns, the Carmelites, moved into this suburban retreat of an architect who had been a notorious bon vivant. The red brick and round arches of the original house are echoed in the new chapel and other additions to the Carmel of the Holy Spirit.

AH11 Riverfront Festival Marketplace

1984, Barker, Rinker, Seacat and Partners. Southwest corner of S. Santa Fe Dr. and Bowles Ave.

Sited along the Arapahoe Greenway and designed to look like an old waterfront terminal, this large market hall has a cruciform, skylit roof and vaulted ceilings. Despite splendid interior space and the prize-winning design, it succumbed to the 1980s oil bust and awaits reuse.

AH12 Arapahoe Greenway

1980s, Robert M. Searns/DHM. Along the South Platte in Arapahoe County

This paved, landscaped trail along the South Platte River connects with the metropolitan network started by Denver in 1976 to rehabilitate trashy waterways as recreational and scenic amenities. Littleton's stretch of the greenway includes the 625-acre South Platte Park (1975), with seven lakes in former gravel pits restored by Littleton's Cooley

AH12 Arapahoe Greenway, *Coming Home*

Gravel Company. Other attractions are the Theo L. Carson Nature Center (1991), a two-story spruce log house with a massive fireplace of sandstone from Lyons in Boulder County, and Hudson Gardens (1995, Douglas G. Rockne, landscape architect), 6115 South Santa Fe Drive, a 27-acre botanical garden. The eight-foot-wide Arapahoe Greenway interconnects these and serves as a local stretch of the Colorado Trail, leading west into Platte Canyon. The parks and greenway are irrigated by solar-powered pumps and enhanced by *Coming Home* (1987, Susan Grant Raymond), a bronze sculpture at the southwest corner of South Santa Fe Drive and Prince Street.

AH13 Denver Mormon Temple

1986, Bobby R. Thomas and LDS church architectural staff. 2001 Phillips Circle near S. University Blvd. and County Line Rd.

This modern celebration of Colorado's long and active Church of Jesus Christ of Latter-Day Saints is a Mormon Moderne design of precast stone with a soaring, streamlined tower capped by a statue of the angel Moroni. On a 7.5-acre site, the dramatically horizontal, terraced building with its single, stepped spire contains fifty-four rooms, including four ordinance rooms and six sealing rooms.

Columbine Valley

Columbine Valley (1959, 5,280 feet), modeled after the Thunderbird Country Clubs

in Palm Springs and Phoenix, is wrapped around the Columbine Country Club and Golf Course. The Clubhouse (1955, C. Francis Pillsbury) is California ranch style with large expanses of glass, patios, and stone and brick walls under a cedar shake roof. Many of the surrounding homes are similarly styled, with a minimum of 1,400 square feet of interior space, large patios, and attached multicar garages.

AH14 Bowles House

c. 1884, Robert S. Roeschlaub. 3600 W. Bowles Ave.

Andrew Jackson Downing called the American farmer "a man of nature" whose dwelling should suggest "simplicity, honesty of purpose, frankness, and a hearty genuine spirit of good will." This amiability is expressed architecturally by a generous porch and many chimneys to embody hospitality, suggesting that Robert Roeschlaub had read Downing when he designed one of Colorado's first important country homes. The original owner, rancher Joseph W. Bowles, established a 2,000-acre spread along the west bank of the South Platte River. To celebrate his prominent pioneer role, he had Roeschlaub design this front-gabled, L-plan house in pink Castle Rock rhyolite. Built in the fashionable Queen Anne Style, it had hot and cold running water on both floors, gas lighting, a furnace, and extensive landscaping. The house has been home since 1935 to the Paul Wolf family, who raise horses and other livestock at what they call Willowcroft.

AH15 Light of the World Catholic Church

1989, Karl A. Berg of Hoover Berg Desmond. 10306 W. Bowles Ave.

Honored by a national AIA award, this radically contemporary hilltop church was designed, according to the founding pastor, "from the inside out." The result is a dramatic, skeletal church of modest materials: brick, drywall, laminated timber, and glass blocks. Yet it embraces the traditional forms of the baptistery, cloister, colonnade, chapel, gallery, and steeple.

Bow Mar, 5200 Lakeshore Drive

Bow Mar

Bow Mar (1958, 5,500 feet) is located between and named for Bowles and Marston lakes in southwest suburban Denver. Lloyd J. King, founder of Colorado's King Soopers grocery chain, purchased the 575-acre parcel in 1947. He hired Denver landscape architects and city planners Harman, O'Donnell and Henninger to design a suburban community of one-acre house lots centered on Bowles Lake, with its sandy beaches, docks, and wildlife sanctuaries. Today Bow Mar is an upscale suburban retreat of about 850 residents. The subdivision show home (1948, Harman, O'Donnell and Henninger), 5200 Lakeshore Drive, drew inspiration from a popular 1948 comedy film starring Myrna Loy and Cary Grant, *Mr. Blandings Builds His Dream House*. This Colonial Revival ranch house captures a fine view of the lakes and the mountains beyond with a large picture window. It is the prototype for the subdivision's single-story, side-gabled, low-slung houses, characterized by contrasting combinations of wood, brick, and stone, picture windows, and minimal decorative detail.

Englewood

Several earlier settlements consolidated in 1903 as Englewood (1903, 5,306 feet), the largest town in the county until overtaken by Littleton after World War II. Streetcar lines and train service, most memorably the horse-drawn Cherrelyn streetcar serving the South Broadway commercial district, enabled Englewood to become a major early Denver suburb. During the early 1990s, Englewood gave a facelift to this commercial strip and transformed trashy Dry Creek with paved paths and parks.

AH16 **Arapahoe Acres**

1949, Eugene Sternberg. Dartmouth to Bates aves. between Merion and Franklin sts.

Eugene Sternberg provided the master plan and first five designs for this 100-house development featuring winding streets and grouped driveways to reduce the intrusion of paved areas. Careful siting maximizes privacy, southern exposure, and mountain views. Clean, contemporary designs, characterized by clerestory windows and outdoor patios in cohesive landscaping, set the standard for later designs by other architects. Among Sternberg's other communities is Orchard Hills (1962), a 150-acre development of individually owned homes around a common lake and green space, at Belleview Avenue and Dayton Street in Littleton. As part of the Mile High Housing Association Cooperative Sternberg designed his own home (1951) in the 2400 block of South Dahlia Street in southeast Denver, where thirty-two Sternberg houses in a simple contemporary style surround a communal park.

AH17 **Brown House**

c. 1900, George H. Williamson. 2303 E. Dartmouth Ave. (northwest corner of Dartmouth and University Blvd.) (NR)

David W. Brown, a founder of the Rocky Mountain Fuel Company, spent some of his coal fortune on this three-and-one-half-story stuccoed brick house. The rambling Queen Anne dwelling showcases vernacular framework in its octagonal tower, multiple low-pitched rooflines with extended overhangs, and first- and second-story porches. An entrance under a porte-cochère leads to an interior resplendent with oak, walnut, and cherry woodwork in eighteen rooms reached by a spiral staircase. Arched interior doorways, pocket doors, chandeliers, six fireplaces, and a third-story "ballroom" enhance this landmark, now surrounded by post–World War II developments.

AH18 Englewood Post Office

1939. 3330 S. Broadway

This typical New Deal–era post office is notable for its lobby mural, Boardman Robinson's *Colorado Stock Sale* (1940). One of sixteen Colorado post office murals by the Federal Artists Project, it depicts a horse sale, focusing on the facial expressions of the buyers and sellers. In this last mural of a distinguished career, Robinson, then the director of the Broadmoor Art Academy in Colorado Springs, provided a splendid counterpoint to the many auto sales lots lining South Broadway.

AH19 Commercial Federal Bank
(Englewood Savings and Loan)

c. 1965, Charles Deaton. 3501 S. Broadway

Passing motorists cannot miss this 32-foot-high, 10,000-square-foot white ellipsoid. Architect Charles Deaton, most famous for his flying saucer house in Genesee in Jefferson County (JF45), worked out the design for this in clay, then in plastic, before doing the architectural drawings. Steel bars support the 8-inch-thick concrete shell, which Deaton described as a "strictly non-representational form." This marvel is set in a park along Dry Gulch.

AH20 Skerritt House

1860s; additions. 3560 S. Bannock St.

Under numerous additions and remodelings lies the vernacular farmhouse of Thomas Skerritt, the founder of Englewood. White shiplap siding, double-hung windows with semicircular head trim, and fishscale shingles in the gables mark the oldest portion of the house, the hub of Skerritt's 640-acre Shadyside Ranch. Landscaped lawns, flower beds, and orchards are gone now, as are the antelope Skerritt used to shoot from his front porch. In their place lies one of the busiest intersections in the metropolis, Hampden Avenue (U.S. 285) and Broadway, which Skerritt laid out with his oxen and plow.

AH21 Cinderella City

1968, James E. Johnson Associates. 701 W. Hampden Ave (northeast corner of West Hampden and Santa Fe Ave.)

Englewood sold its old city park and frog pond to developer Gerry Von Frellick for $1 million. Von Frellick turned it into a 60-acre shopping mall, which opened as "the world's largest shopping complex under one roof." An 8,000-vehicle, double-deck parking lot helped draw the masses to Colorado's first enclosed shopping mall, whose centerpiece was a 30-foot-high fountain. Larger and even slicker subsequent malls, however, have outshone the one-time fairy tale prince, now turned back into a frog.

AH22 Atchison, Topeka & Santa Fe Depot

1915. 1994, Erickson Architects. Northeast corner of W. Dartmouth Ave. and S. Galapago St.

One of the Santa Fe Railroad's characteristic Mission Revival depots, this elongated frame rectangle with a symmetrical stucco facade, projecting eaves, and corbeled brackets under curvilinear parapets was abandoned in 1979. Originally the waiting room and baggage rooms were separate buildings joined by a breezeway. The depot was moved here in 1994 from Hampden Avenue and Santa Fe Drive and restored as a home for the Englewood Historical Society.

AH23 Campbell House

1974, Eleanor Campbell. 3962 S. Chase Way

Situated on a one-and-one-half-acre site on the north edge of Pinehurst Country Club, this 16,000-square-foot home, designed in the Italian Renaissance style, was altered after the owner, Eleanor Campbell, read an issue of *National Geographic* featuring Japanese temples. Her husband, owner of a furniture store chain, helped furnish the house and gardens. A *torii* gate, the traditional entrance to a Shinto temple, guards the circular drive entrance. The 2,800-square-foot master suite and loggia with 16-foot-high entrance and glass floor overlook an indoor-outdoor swimming pool over which they are cantilevered. Multipitched hipped roofs are tiled and have raised corner points. The walls have large areas of glass overlooking gardens, including a moated teahouse. Mrs. Campbell was the architect, interior and landscape designer, general contractor, and construction supervisor.

Next door is the Vaile-Norgren House (1911, Temple Hoyne Buell), 3982 South Chase Way, overlooking the large land holdings that became Pinehurst Country Club and the surrounding subdivisions. The two-story log house with hipped roof elements is two older log buildings bridged by a crossing wing with elaborate carving.

AH24 Denver Technological Center

1963, Harman, O'Donnell and Henninger. East side of I-25 between Belleview and Orchard aves.

Colorado's first distinctive office park was the brainchild of engineer and developer George M. Wallace, who wanted a "campus for the creative worker." The Denver architects and planners landscaped grassy open space around lakes and planted more than 10,000 trees. (At least 30 percent of each building site is open space.) Parking and utilities are hidden off tree-lined, 30-acre "superblocks." The sixty-eight buildings on DTC's 947 acres generally represent striking contemporary architecture and interior design. One of the few complaints has been the lack of interconnecting pedestrian paths.

Notable structures include the four-story glass office building (1982, C. W. Fentress and Associates) at 116 Inverness Drive East, one of the first buildings of its kind in the United States, a completely glass-sheathed, monolithic, geometric composition that shows no exposed structure and no window mullions. In a form that Charles Jencks has called "slick tech" it revisits the theories of Philip Johnson and Henry-Russell Hitch-cock's 1932 discourse on the International Style. One DTC (1985, C. W. Fentress and Associates), 5251 DTC Parkway, is a thirteen-story office tower sheathed in reflective bronze glass dressed up by burgundy, mahogany, and gray Dakota granite and stainless steel banding, with a three-story, glass-enclosed lobby and a landscaped outdoor plaza.

AH25 Seventeen Mile House

c. 1866. 8181 S. Parker Rd. (Colorado 83) (NR)

Located 17 miles southwest of Denver along the Cherry Creek trail, this gold rush–era roadhouse and stage station began as a one-story hewn log inn. It was enlarged to two stories and clapboarded during the 1870s. The L-shaped addition on the northwest dates from the 1920s. The large cottonwood next to the house was supposedly planted to hide the grave of a murdered man. Unkempt, the building is threatened by surrounding development.

Greenwood Village

An affluent suburb on the south side of Cherry Hills, Greenwood Village (1950, 5,422 feet) was one of the first places in Colorado to promote cluster housing and commons, epitomized by developer Robert B. Bogg's subdivision at the northwest corner of South Clarkson and East Orchard Road. Now a community of some 8,000, it contains a model upscale development of the 1990s, the Preserve at Greenwood Village, where half-million-dollar homes have replaced a large prairie dog colony. To appease enraged animal rights activists, developer Walter Koelbel laid nature trails through the development and created a 45-acre "nature preserve"—minus the prairie dogs.

AH26 Greenwood Plaza

1970, John Madden Company. West of I-25 between Belleview Ave. and Arapahoe Rd.

Greenwood Plaza is a 1970s office park that incorporates fine art as well as architecture and landscaping. The Museum of Outdoor Art (1982), 7600 East Orchard Road, exhibits the work of Henry Moore and Red Grooms, as well as paintings, collages, tapestries, and an exhibit of street lamps from designs by Michelangelo. Set amid fountains and lush lawns, this artsy 400-acre complex includes the 20,000-seat Fiddler's Green Outdoor Amphitheater (AH26.1; 1988). Harlequin Plaza (AH26.2; 1981, Gensler and Associates), 7600 East Orchard Road, is based on the visual theme of Picasso's portrait of clowns, *Les Harlequins*. This 18-acre plaza consists of office buildings with glass curtain walls and ceramic tile bases. It is set in a 5,000-square-foot plaza of black and white terrazzo diamonds with seven life-size sculptures of harlequins by American sculptor Harry Marinsky.

Nearby Carrara Place (AH26.3; 1982, Murata Outland Associates), 6200 South Syracuse Street, is a six-story office and parking structure with an exterior skin of Carrara marble. A large atrium and interior courts invite sunlight into the building. Greenwood Plaza's Tuscan theme is continued in MCI Plaza (AH26.4; 1984, Kirkham, Michael and Associates), 6312 South Fiddlers Green Circle, where two six-story office towers are placed at right angles and connected by a glass-domed atrium. Tuscan travertine marble and copper roofing enhance the building, which has terraced bridges connecting the two wings. The Gulf Mineral Resources Company Headquarters (AH26.5; 1983, Skidmore, Owings and Merrill), 6200 South Quebec Street, is an energy-conservative complex of precast concrete and glass. Two-and three-story buildings are stepped to exploit the sloping terrain and mountain

AH26.4 MCI Plaza

views. Skylights and exterior courtyards leave no part of the interior more than 20 feet from natural light. A computer senses natural light levels and adjusts supplemental artificial light. In dramatic contrast to this sophisticated office park is the adjacent William McKinley Carson Park, maintained by Greenwood Village, at 6000 South Quebec Street, with a 1940s farmhouse surrounded by old apple trees and rusting farm machinery.

AH27 Inverness Business Park

1980s. East of I-25 at County Line Rd.

Inverness Business Park comprises 900 acres centering on eighteen-hole Inverness Golf Course. American Express, Citicorp, Conoco, Diners Club, Eastman Kodak, Hewlett Packard, John Deere, Martin Marietta, Honeywell, Merrill Lynch, and Pentax are among the tenants. The sleek Inverness Hotel Denver (1989, Knud Frus) is a $53-million, 353,000-square-foot hotel and conference center designed by a Danish architect. An elevated site and prow-shaped end distinguish the eight-story office building (1993, Joseph Poli of Pouw and Associates) at the entrance to the park. Buff-colored precast concrete has stringcourses to resemble limestone. A rectangular tower of reflective glass is attached by a curved, covered walkway to the parking garage. Concrete columns around the recessed entry portico are clad in metal, and the entrance has a beveled concrete surround in a curving glazed grid.

AH28 **Happy Church** (Beau Monde Shopping Mall)

1985, Tatman Associates. 8081 E. Orchard Rd. (at I-25)

A 200,000-square-foot, high-end shopping center was failing in 1984 when a large and growing congregation's plans for a new church were rejected by Greenwood Village. The solution: converting this "European-style" mall, with its rust-colored brick floors and walls, marble fountains, and Tuscan columns and wrought iron lamps, to a house of the Lord. Pastor Wallace Hickey's Happy Church purchased the mall for $7.8 million in 1989 and converted it to a spiritual supermarket.

AH29 **Cherry Creek Schoolhouse**

1874. 9300 E. Union Ave. (NR)

Relocated on the campus of a huge modern high school, this one-room clapboard schoolhouse has been restored as Greenwood's oldest building and a living history exhibit.

AH30 **Curtis School**

1914. 2349 E. Orchard Rd. (NR)

This one-story brick and shingle building with rough-faced sandstone trim, hipped roof, symmetrical, gabled entrance bay, and central belfry now houses the Greenwood Village Cultural Arts Center.

AH31 **Koelbel Public Library**

1992, Barker, Rinker, Seacat and Partners. 5955 S. Holly St. (at E. Orchard Ave.)

Named for a major donor, Greenwood developer Walter Koelbel, this $6 million, 45,000-square-foot structure is a welcome understatement among the many grandiose homes and office towers surrounding it. Patrons enter through the upper level of what appears to be a low, red brick building enhanced by a course of red sandstone. A gray concrete tile roof is accented by copper trim and downspouts. The rotunda entry is bright and open, enhanced by white marble tile and murals. The bay windows incorpo-

rate inviting seats, and low doorways guard the children's area.

Cherry Hills Village

Cherry Hills Village (1920s, 5,381 feet) is named for the cherry orchards it displaced in the 1920s. Early plans by Saco R. DeBoer called for a quaint business section patterned after Henry Ford's Greenfield Village in Deerfield, Michigan. Commercial development was subsequently rejected in what is now a 6.5-square-mile residential community bordered by Denver, Englewood, and Greenwood Village. By the mid-1980s, Cherry Hills ranked as the third wealthiest suburb in the United States, behind Kenilworth, Illinois, and Hunter's Creek near Houston, Texas.

From the beginning, homebuilders here have been urged to follow fashionable revival styles. Unpaved streets, bridle paths, and mansions on large lots still characterize the suburban enclave of about 6,000 people. The neighborhood's centerpiece is the Cherry Hills Country Club, but it also claims two of Colorado's oldest private schools, Kent Country Day and St. Mary's Academy. St. Mary's, founded in downtown Denver in 1864, moved into the Hickman Mansion at 4545 South University Boulevard and has added contemporary buildings that include a $435,000 addition (1964, John Milan) to the 24-acre campus.

AH32 **Foster-Buell Mansion**

1916, William E. Fisher and Arthur A. Fisher. 2700 E. Hampden Ave., near 4100 S. University Blvd.

Rising two and one-half stories on a hilltop, this Georgian Revival showplace is red brick laid in English bond. The gabled roof is covered in Pennsylvania slate with four large chimneys. Eight imposing columns support the front porch, which is formed by an extension of the rooflines. Saco R. DeBoer's landscaping, featured in a 1924 *Country Life* article, consisted of formal gardens, an octagonal gazebo and fireplace for the summer garden, a lily pond, and an entry forecourt and garden wall to mask the four-car garage and caretaker's cottage. From Alexis C. Foster, a banker and businessman, the house passed to leading architect and developer Temple Hoyne Buell, who was active from the 1920s to the 1980s.

AH33 Gano-Bradley Mansion

1920, William E. Fisher and Arthur A. Fisher. 4100 S. University Blvd.

Clothier George Gano and his wife fashioned their thirty-two-room mansion after an English manor house. Elizabethan, Jacobean, and Tudor elements adorn the two-story house of hand-molded brick under a steeply pitched roof with multiple cross gables. The round-arched entry shelters a heavy board-and-batten door with hand-wrought iron fittings. The interior is adorned with oak-beamed ceilings, leaded and stained glass windows, hand-wrought iron fixtures, and five fireplaces. Robert Bradley, who bought the house in 1962, reported poltergeists in the parlor and bats in the attic of what has become one of Colorado's most storied "haunted houses," appropriately shrouded by a grove of cottonwood trees.

AH34 Cherry Hills Country Club

1923, Merrill H. Hoyt; many additions and remodelings. 4125 S. University Blvd.

James Steck's 80-acre farm became a country club and golf course that helped lure affluent Denverites to the suburbs. A prominent 1920s golf course architect, William S. Flynn, laid out the greens. Hoyt's elongated, angular, Tudor Revival clubhouse is on a hilltop, with dining areas and a lanai overlooking the course and the mountains beyond. The steeply pitched roof has multiple cross gables and is overshadowed by large, elaborate brick chimneys with multiple shafts. The random brick first-story walls contrast with stucco cladding and half-timbering on the second story. An expensive 1961 facelift by local architect Edwin Francis and Cannell-Chaffin Interiors of Los Angeles was followed by another, five years later, by architect Alan Peterson.

AH35 Taylor House

1990, James S. Bershoff/OZ Architecture. 1000 E. Quincy Ave.

This updated Shingle Style design uses traditional elements such as towers, rounded corners, ribbon and eyebrow dormers, broad, overhanging rooflines, and white cedar shingles. The owners are New Englanders whose homes back east are McKim, Mead and White designs inclued in Vincent Scully's two books on the Shingle Style. The massing and details of East Coast forebears are incorporated in this 5,000-square-foot, two-story home, but more glazing adds brightness and mountain views. A gatehouse serves as a detached garage and privacy shield.

Aurora

(Note: Although the part of Aurora north of East Colfax Avenue lies in Adams County, everything within the city limits is treated in Arapahoe County.)

Aurora (1891, 5,342 feet) was founded as Fletcher by Denver developer Donald K. Fletcher. The town's original boundaries were Yosemite and Peoria streets, between 6th and 26th avenues, on the eastern edge of Denver. Much of Fletcher consisted of land granted to the Union Pacific Railroad, whose tracks ran along Smith Road to the north. The railroad subsequently sold the land to homesteaders. During the early 1890s the Colfax Trust Company built speculative houses on and along Galena Street, around the east end of the Colfax Avenue trolley line.

Aurora reached a population of 202 by 1900. After Donald Fletcher absconded with city funds, citizens renamed their town in 1907 for the Roman goddess of the dawn. Aurora grew slowly until the 1920s, but by the end of that decade Fitzsimons Army Hospital and the Denver Municipal Airport had helped boost the population to 2,295. Greater growth came with the establishment of Lowry Army Air Field, Buckley Army Air Field, and the Rocky Mountain Arsenal. Following the opening of Lowry Field in 1938, its eastern edge, Havana Street, began to develop as a commercial strip, drawing business south from Aurora's original main street, East Colfax Avenue.

After 1945 many ex-servicemen returned

to the clear, sunny place where they had trained to raise their families. Aurora developed its own water department and began annexing neighboring developments such as the Hoffman Heights subdivision (1953), a large tract stretching from East 6th Avenue to 13th Avenue between Peoria and Potomac Streets. Developed on the old Cottonwood Ranch, Hoffman Heights boasted 1,705 homes by 1956. The first of many large postwar subdivisions, it helped Aurora's population to quadruple by 1960. By 1980 Aurora had become the state's third largest city, with 158,588 residents. Expansion finally slowed enough during Colorado's 1980s recession to allow rattlesnakes to retreat ahead of the advancing developments. By the 1990s the ambitious city of approximately 250,000 had annexed more than 100 square miles in Adams, Arapahoe, and Douglas counties, becoming Colorado's largest city in terms of square miles.

City administrative facilities have followed the southeast shift of the population center from original quarters around Emporia and East Colfax Avenue to an impressive new complex, east of the Aurora Mall (1976), 15000 East Alameda Avenue (at Chambers Road). Aurora's master plan calls for a low-rise core and diversified activity centers. A quest for community roots and identity led to the establishment of the Aurora Historical Commission in 1970. It has established a history museum and a program of land-marking structures for preservation to increase historical consciousness and a sense of place in Denver's largest suburb.

AH36 **Aurora History Museum** (Municipal Justice Center)

1978, Rogers-Nagel-Langhart. 15001 E. Alameda Dr.

The old justice center is a composition of strong angles and sheer planes that relate well with the Aurora Public Library, the original building in this county government complex. Three red brick bays, progressively taller and narrower, extend north to join the new justice center next door. The south parapets are uniformly clipped, and the entry is in a glazed facade within the diagonal

northwest wall. After county officials moved into the new justice center, this became the headquarters and exhibition space for the Aurora History Museum, a city agency.

AH37 **Aurora Municipal Justice Center**

1989, Skidmore, Owings and Merrill; senior designer, W. Kenneth Wiseman. E. Alameda Dr. and S. Sable Blvd.

An apparition on the prairie, this $21 million Neo–Renaissance Revival palace features a 65-foot-high, 72-foot-diameter precast concrete dome, covered in metal painted to resemble oxidized copper. Exterior walls are paneled in gray precast concrete resembling stone with horizontal banding. Windows have applied painted iron sunbursts. The main (west) entry features a traditional open court, wood and brass accents, and a terrazzo sunburst floor in the lobby. Gracefully curving stairs lead to a gallery around the domed rotunda, which is washed with light from high east windows to celebrate Aurora, goddess of the dawn. Municipal courts, police headquarters, and an expanded detention center occupy wings in the 190,000-square-foot facility.

AH38 **Aurora Public Library**

1982, Brooks Waldman Associates with Warner, Burns, Toan, Lunde. 14949 E. Alameda Dr.

An abstract metal sculpture accents the angled glass and metal entrance to this three-story structure of buff brick and concrete set into a hill. The multipitched roof has large skylights and is surmounted by a diamond-shaped light tower over the central interior staircase. A sharp prow extension on the south is matched by a corresponding cutback into the facade to create a walled courtyard. The main interior floor is cut away on the northwest corner to overlook the lower level and provide a sense of openness.

AH39 Aurora Public Market

1989, Gail and Robert Karn with Flickinger and Associates Ltd. 14100 E. Exposition Ave.

This Postmodern rendition of a traditional covered farmers' market draws on Aurora's agricultural heritage. Its single story of open interior space is enclosed by industrial brick and concrete walls, covered by a metal roof with a central double gable and exposed trusses, and lighted by clerestory windows. Evenly spaced stall fronts with European-

AH40 Delaney Round Barn

AH41 Buckley Air National Guard Base

style pull-down shutters are protected from the elements by shed canopies.

AH40 Delaney Farmhouse and Round Barn

1890s, John Delaney. 170 S. Chambers Rd.

In 1870 John and Bridget Gully Delaney from Tipperary, Ireland, settled a homestead that is now a 160-acre Aurora City Park site on two waterways, Tollgate Creek and the Highline Canal. The round frame barn (c. 1900) (NR), the only one left in Colorado, has a conical roof and prominent ball finial which emphasize its shape. A variety of outbuildings, including a railroad boxcar and a cinderblock silo, document farm and ranch activities over the past century. John Delaney's clapboard farmhouse (1892) has been restored to its 1910 appearance.

The park also contains the Thomas Gully farmhouse, 200 S. Chambers Road (NR), moved in 1983 from its original location and restored. The Gully family lived in the original single-room clapboard house until a one-and-one-half-story, two-room addition was constructed across the front gable end. The full-width front porch is a good vantage point for watching the front yard prairie dog colony. Restored to its 1870s appearance, this plain house, distinguished by Greek Revival vernacular elements, is the oldest dwelling in Aurora.

AH41 Buckley Air National Guard Base

1942, U.S. Army. 18500 E. 6th Ave.

The base landmarks, visible from throughout the metro area, are six giant white "golf

balls," radar towers (1970) consisting of vinyl-covered geodesic domes protecting large parabolic dishes. Inflexible as the Maginot Line, the dishes are permanently pointed to the north.

AH42 Coal Creek School

1922. 17700 E. 8th Ave. (northeast corner of Telluride St.)

Shielded from subdivision by the Springhill Golf Course, this simple clapboard box is set on a concrete footing and covered by a front gable roof with clipped peaks. A shed-roofed south entry leads to a cloakroom and a well-preserved single classroom heated by a large potbelly stove. Outbuildings include twin outhouses, a windmill, and a small shed and corral for horses that some students rode to school.

AH43 Hoffman Heights Subdivision

1950–1954. E. 6th Ave. to E. 13th Ave. between Peoria and Potomac sts.

Sam Hoffman, a Russian Jewish immigrant who learned plastering and cement finishing in Detroit, titled himself the Henry Ford of the homebuilding industry. Like Levittown, his mass-produced housing was designed to give middle-class families the opportunity of home ownership. In a 1953 *Business Week* interview, Hoffman declared: "Frank Lloyd Wright builds houses around the personalities of the people who live in the house; I build houses around people's pocketbooks."

His $10,000 homes were available in several one-story ranch house plans. Well built of good red and yellow brick and timber, these hip-roofed houses were "modern" in eliminating front porches and adding backyard patios, one and two-car attached garages, large picture windows, and two bathrooms. Some 400 of the 1,700 homes were sold before construction began. Although most have been modified, 12540 East 7th Avenue remains true to its original plan.

AH44 Fire Station No. 1–Martin Luther King Municipal Center and Branch Library

1978, Victor Hornbein. 9801–9859 E. 16th Ave. (at Del Mar Pkwy.)

Updated Prairie Style in red brick trimmed with concrete, this understated structure has wide, overhanging eaves from a flat roof sheltering clerestory window bands. The building's composition as a series of linear pavilions one and two stories tall, its varied setbacks and roof heights, and its prominent cantilevered roofs create interesting shadow patterns. The library is reminiscent of the architect's Denver Public Library Ross-Broadway Branch (DV073). Around the corner at 1633 Florence Street is Hornbein's Aurora Mental Health Center (1978), with his distinctive flat roof and cantilevered eaves stretching into entry canopies.

AH45 Smith House

1910, Joseph Wilson. 1983 restoration, Long Hoeft Architects. 412 Oswego Court (NR)

William Smith arrived from Scotland and bought 320 acres along the Highline Canal bounded by today's Moline and Potomac streets and 1st and 6th avenues. Some 47 acres of his farm are now occupied by a residential area, Del Mar Park (1957), but Smith's foursquare farmhouse still stands and has been restored.

The house is beige pressed brick under a hipped roof with overhanging eaves bracketed at the corners. A porch extending from the pedimented entry gable wraps the west corner. Decorative detail includes the original stained and leaded glass, a tiger oak fireplace surround, a Texas pine stairway, and a built-in china cabinet. Smith founded the Aurora public schools in 1885 and served as secretary of the school board until 1935. His daughter, Margaret, occupied the house until her death in 1982.

AH46 China Place Restaurant (Valentine Diner)

c. 1947, Valentine Diners. 9842 E. Colfax Ave.

Delivered already assembled by a manufacturer in Wichita, Kansas, this tiny, enameled steel diner served hamburgers before sundown on the day it was installed. The fare changed in 1978, when Mr. and Mrs. Albert Chan renamed the diner, but the original logo, a heart pierced by an arrow, can still be found just inside the door.

The diner epitomizes East Colfax Avenue, which calls itself "America's Longest Main Street." The venerable and varied commercial strip, faded since its glory days as U.S. 40, is the metropolitan area's principal east–west artery and Aurora's first main street. In Aurora, buildings on East Colfax include Denver's oldest country and western nightclub, The Zanza Bar, and the adjacent Cactus Motel. The two-story Victorian brick Cottonwood Motel (1898), 9200 East Colfax Avenue, built as a hotel for trolley line workers, is senior among many motels on East Colfax.

AH47 **Aurora Fox Arts Center** (Fox Aurora Theater)

1946. 1982 renovation, Baer and Hickman. 9900 E. Colfax Ave.

The distinctive cylindrical second-story facade of ribbed metal panels above a cantilevered canopy and dramatic vertical sign remain from the original movie theater. Quonset construction developed by the military for temporary structures has proved durable; in fact, almost indestructible. Streamline Moderne Carrera glass and the metal marquee were later additions. A fire in 1981 closed the theater and led to its rebirth as Aurora's arts center.

AH48 **Official Emissions Testing Station** (Hanna's Super Shell Station)

c. 1930. 9445 E. Colfax Ave.

Representing the commerical use of Pueblo Revival style, this diminutive structure with a single service bay and an office has a parapet with round vigas extending from concrete stuccoed walls. The gas pumps are gone and the building, most appropriately, has been rehabilitated for exhaust emissions inspections.

AH49 **William M. Smith High School**

1931, Eugene G. Groves. 10000 E. 13th Ave.

Constructed of poured-in-place concrete reinforced with steel, this brick-clad two-story school has double front doors in a wide surround centered in a symmetrical main facade. The doors originally had stained glass panels, and borders of leaded glass outlined upstairs windows. Red brick is trimmed in a lighter brick and beige sandstone in varied horizontal and vertical patterns, with darker brick in first-floor spandrels.

AH50 **Novelty Windmill** (Hart House)

c. 1920. 11937 E. Colfax Ave.

A two-story frame hexagonal windmill house and substantial Dutch Colonial Revival dwelling were the center of a group of thirteen cottages built by former Fitzsimons Army Hospital patient Col. Arthur L. Hart for rental to hospital workers and tourists. It is now the centerpiece of a mobile home park.

AH51 **East 70 Drive-in Theater**

1947. 12800 E. Colfax Ave.

Colorado's first drive-in theater opened July 4, 1947, with *A Night in Casablanca* and *Sunbonnet Sue*. This state-of-the-art drive-in offered portable battery chargers, windshield washing, a children's playground, baby bottle warmers, and in-car heaters.

AH52 **University of Colorado Health Sciences Center, previously Fitzsimons Army Hospital**

1918, T. Robert Wieger. 1941, main building, additions. E. Colfax Ave. and Peoria St.

The original, World War I–era hospital was built on the 595-acre Gutheil Tree Nursery after the Denver Chamber of Commerce purchased the land and leased it to the U.S. Army for $1 per year. A. H. Gutheil's home, with alterations, became the base commander's residence. Dedicated as Army Hospital No. 21 in 1918 and named for First Lieutenant William T. Fitzsimons, M.D., the first U.S. officer killed in World War I, Fitzsimons consisted of forty-eight temporary buildings that housed servicemen suffering from pulmonary-respiratory ailments caused by chemical warfare. Denver architect T. Robert Wieger of the U.S. Army Corps of Engineers helped supervise construction of the huge medical complex.

The Streamline Moderne 610-bed main building (1941) is reinforced concrete with cream-colored limestone trim and eleven varieties of buff brick used on walls, col-

AH52 Fitzsimons Army Hospital, 1947

umns, and stairways. The south facade is symmetrical, with a ten-story stepped tower above the main entrance and wings extending north, east, and west. Rounded corners, horizontal banding, and simple massing suggest a monolithic permanence. Many aluminum Art Deco fixtures and some buildings with screen porches remain, remnants of Fitzsimons's origin as a pulmonary treatment center. Abandoned by the army in the 1990s, the complex is now a University of Colorado facility.

AH53 RTD Bus Maintenance Facility, East Metro Division

1980, Rogers-Nagel-Langhart. E. Colfax Ave. and I-225

This Brutalist design of ribbed precast concrete panels harmonizes with the nearby concrete monster, I-225. Landscaping on the building's sloping, earth-filled roof verges has been removed, adding to the starkness. Pointed prows of enameled aluminum panels extend in bays on the north and south to serve as entrances, reception and office spaces, and a cafeteria. Large panels of glass brick, forming "the largest air-based solar space heating system in the world," let in light along the sides of the huge garage.

AH54 State Highway Department (KOA Radio Station)

1924. 18500 E. Colfax Ave.

This elegant, two-story brick office building with terracotta trim has an entry bas-relief depicting the sun and mountains, radio waves radiating from the nearby tower, and a portrait of the building. Of interest inside are the geometric, multihued flooring and scrolled metal stair rail.

AH55 1300 Block of Dayton Street

Early in the century Edward and Rose King built several houses, primarily Craftsman-inspired, on this block. The first was the clapboard, hip-roofed bungalow (1908) at 1360 Dayton, which still has a chicken coop in the backyard. They also erected another clapboard bungalow (1910) at 1356 Dayton, in an area Rose remembered as having "wide board sidewalks, no trees, tall weeds, and good pheasant hunting to the south." The one-and-one-half-story house has square porch posts with brackets at the eaves and decorative pierced wood scallops on the front gable. King, a salesman for a lumber company, used mahogany woodwork inside the two-story stuccoed brick house (1912) at 1390 Dayton. After his death, his wife took in tuberculosis patients as boarders to pay off the mortgage. The house retains its original French-style front door, built-in china cabinet, ceiling beams, and two-story sleeping porch.

AH56 Galena Street District

E. Colfax Ave. to E. 25th Ave.

The middle-class vernacular homes in this local landmark district were built from 1889 to the mid-1930s. The Milliken House (AH56.1; 1893), 1638 Galena Street, sold for $5,000 in 1893, the highest price recorded for a home in Fletcher in the 1890s. During the 1920s H. M. Milliken, an early Aurora mayor, replaced the original porch with a two-story affair wrapping front and side, with fluted Doric columns and an upper balustrade of turned posts and ball finials.

The Fletcher/Aurora Centennial House (AH56.2; 1890), 1671 Galena Street, is a two-story brick featuring gabled ends in projecting bays which intersect hipped roof elements in a generally square plan. The asymmetrical front features a pedimented porch roof with turned columns and dentiled eaves. Fishscale shingles complement the upper gable and a pair of round-arched windows. Built as Blanche A. Wilson's house, it is one of the oldest in Aurora. It has escaped significant alteration and has been restored as a house museum.

South Aurora

AH57 Melvin Schoolhouse Museum-Library

1922, Ren and Henry DeBoer. 4950 S. Laredo St. at E. Smoky Hill Rd. (NR)

Aurora's first municipally designated landmark was displaced in 1950 when Cherry Creek Dam was built, flooding the old town of Melvin. Hauled to the southwest corner of Quincy Avenue and Parker Road, it became the Emerald Isle Tavern. Cherry Creek Valley Historical Society moved it to the current site on the Smoky Hill High School campus, where it was restored by the community in 1977–1978. The square bell tower, lost during the building's wild times as a tavern, has been replaced with a replica, and the linoleum flooring, kitchen, and other developments of the tavern era have been removed to create a sparkling restoration.

AH58 Plains Conservation Center

1969. 21901 E. Hampden Ave.

Reconstructed sod buildings, an agricultural museum, and 2,000 acres of virgin prairie sustaining deer, antelope, burrowing owls, prairie dogs, and rattlesnakes make this a wonderful retreat into the past. Exhibits include a tipi and a Grange museum. A facsimile sod house, one-room school, and blacksmith shop have been constructed from "bricks" cut out of the prairie. Measuring two feet by one foot by three inches, these bricks were stacked, grass side up, around a packed earth floor. Minimal wood framing forms doors and windows, set in place as the walls rose. Cottonwood poles and willow brush were topped with lightweight strips of sod for a roof. Mud was used to fill exterior crevices, and plaster or lime to plaster inside walls.

AH59 Regis Jesuit High School

1991, David Owen Tryba. 16300 E. Weaver Place

This Postmodern monument atop a hill is a pageant of striped and checkered masonry, glass squares, and mullioned windows. A pedimented chapel with abstract campanile, modeled after St. Clara's Church in Assisi, dominates the 94,000-square-foot school. David Owen Tryba, one of Denver's best young architects, designed a medievalish village consisting of a classroom wing, rotunda library, and gymnasium, organized around a formal courtyard. Narrow pilasters project from the convex exterior of the library rotunda, and protruding ribs in the chapel's gable roof meet buttresslike piers in the upper walls, providing vertical tension. Horizontal stripes of dark brown and tan brick relate to the surrounding prairie as well as to the Italian church that inspired Tryba.

Strasburg

Strasburg (1870, 5,756 feet), on the Adams–Arapahoe county line, was originally called Comanche. It was renamed in 1875 for John Strasburg, section foreman of the Kansas Pacific Railroad (KP, later part of the Union Pacific), whose crew once raced to build 10.25 miles of track in a day. Strasburg's crew worked its way east from Denver, the other west from Kansas City. They met here for their reward, a keg of beer. Strasburg claims that it, not Promontory Point, Utah, was where the transcontinental rails first met, since the KP actually bridged the Missouri River, while the UP did not and relied on a ferry. This tiny prairie town, like many others, blossomed during the first two decades of the twentieth century, when a boxcar was parked along the tracks as the first depot (1911) and the grain elevator (1916) was erected.

AH60 Comanche Crossing Museum

1970s. 56060 E. Colfax Ave., I-70 exit 310 (NR)

Oil and ranching tycoon Philip Anschutz gave this two-acre tract to the local historical society, which has constructed an ambitious museum complex. All seven buildings, including the wooden windmill (c. 1890) with adjustable wooden slats, have been moved to the grounds. Two steel storage buildings house a large collection of antiques, including architectural pieces such as Strasburg's first post office and the back bar and soda fountain from Doc Taylor's drugstore.

The Living Springs School (AH60.1; 1891) is a one-room, lap-sided schoolhouse built for $750 by local cabinetmaker E. J. Smith. The porch shows some Victorian frills with its machine-turned posts, curvilinear brackets, and fishscale gable shingles. Moved to the museum grounds from the now vanished stage stop 12 miles north, it has been restored for interpretive programs. It shares the site with Wolf Creek School (AH60.2; 1904), a tiny, one-room clapboard structure.

Strasburg Depot (AH60.3; 1917) replaced the original boxcar depot of the Union Pacific Railroad. This one-story frame building has a hipped roof with intersecting gables and wide eaves supported by heavy open brackets. Decorative roof cresting is about the only ornament. The 41-foot caboose was donated by the Union Pacific, which has made a policy of donating old equipment and depots to local museums.

The Weaver Store (AH60.4; 1907), 1407 Main Street (northeast corner of Railroad Avenue), a two-story frame, false-fronted landmark that was once the town hub, epitomizes the multifunctional role of the country store. The owners, Mr. and Mrs. D. H.

Weaver, according to Emma Mitchell's *Our Side of the Mountain* (1968), "would gladly serve meals, since there was no restaurant for a time. If they didn't have what was wanted, they would get it. . . . Mr. Weaver installed a telephone switchboard in his store which consisted of a series of knife switches. Rural lines were built using the barbed wire fences. At a gate or crossing, two by fours were nailed to the fence post to raise the wire for crossing below. . . . The second floor was used for parties, box socials, dances, meetings, and elections."

Byers

Byers (1868, 5,202 feet) was established along the Kansas Pacific Railroad and named for promoter William N. Byers, founder of Denver's *Rocky Mountain News*. After the railroad arrived in 1870, this became a rail and agricultural hamlet, with a general store, blacksmith shop, and saloon. Efforts to transform Byers into a suburban residential community for Denver began early. The *Rocky Mountain News,* on May 16, 1888, announced free rail excursions from Denver to look at Byers Town Company lots and proclaimed this "the longest ride and biggest lunch yet offered by real estate men in Denver."

After 1950 oil wells began to replace windmills on the horizon with discovery of the Peoria oil field and erection of a $2 million natural gas production plant. Even the 264-acre steel and glass Interstate Dog Track (1970) had three oil wells. Byers's long-anticipated boom as a Denver suburb may be generated by the 1995 opening of nearby Denver International Airport.

AH61 Snow House

c. 1910, George A. Snow, builder. 256 McDonnel St.

George Snow, a New Yorker who homesteaded in Byers in 1879, put together one of the county's largest sheep and cattle ranches. His story-and-a-half clapboard house has a hipped dormer and large front porch spanning the living room. Despite various modernizations of the house and site, the original iron twist-and-flame fence still fronts the property. Snow served as the Byers postmaster (1897–1910), built the bank (1910), and organized the Byers Presbyterian Church (c. 1911), at Sherman and Front streets. This Prairie Gothic brick and clapboard church has a steep gable roof and a square corner belfry. Built during flush times on the high plains, it boasted 132 opera chairs, electric lighting, and an organ.

The Snow Ranch Barn (c. 1890, George A. Snow, builder), four miles south on Arapahoe County 173, is a vertical clapboard barn with a cupola-crowned, gambrel roof and an overhang on the north side to cover the hay pulley. Five small four-paned windows look out of the east and west sides. This relic of a once common building type is the only early structure left on a ranch the Snow family held until 1957, when it became part of the vast Bradbury Land and Cattle Co.

Deer Trail

Deer Trail (1875, 5,183 feet) was named for the trail along Bijou Creek, first used by deer and other game, then by stagecoaches and the railroad. A depot and a stockyards helped make this a ranching center. The Arapahoe County Fairgrounds here are a legacy of the 1869 rodeo, which locals claim was the world's first with recorded rules and prizes. The largest edifice in this town of about five hundred is the huge black water tower standing on steel legs.

AH62 Deer Trail Museum (Kansas Pacific Depot)

1870. 2nd Ave. and Fir St. in City Park

This venerable one-story frame depot with a side-gabled roof and heavy decorative brackets was moved here and restored as a local history museum.

Douglas County   (DA)

Established in 1861 with the South Platte River as its west border, Douglas County encompasses rolling prairie and pine-timbered hills. The mountainous southwest quadrant lies within the Pike National Forest. A once rural county originally known for its Black Forest pineries and its rhyolite quarries, Douglas supplied lumber and a popular building stone for the nineteenth-century Front Range building boom.

Silas W. Madge, while digging around his mesa-top ranch two miles south of Castle Rock, found hard, pink and gray lava rock approximating granite. To capitalize on this large rhyolite formation, he opened a quarry in 1872 and arranged to have the Denver & Rio Grande Railroad build a spur line. Rhyolite soon became Colorado's favorite building stone, especially in towns along the railroad. Reopened for restoration projects, the original quarry is now operating as the Hallet Quarry. When the Santa Fe Railroad arrived in Castle Rock in 1889, it opened the Santa Fe Quarry on a nearby mesa top. The O'Brien (1881) and other quarries also produced the fine-grained volcanic stone, colored from near white to pink, gray, and tan. This stone is very strong for its weight and, since it hardens with exposure to air, weathers well. It appears in many notable Colorado landmarks, including Denver's Trinity Methodist Church and Union Station. The growing popularity of Portland cement and terracotta closed these quarries in the first decade of the twentieth century.

Since World War II, thoroughbred horse and cattle ranching, dairying, clay mining, explosives manufacture, and the Martin Marietta missile plant have been major employers. Sandwiched between the expanding metropolitan areas of Denver and Colorado Springs, Douglas became the second fastest-growing county in the United States during the 1990s.

Castle Rock

Castle Rock (1871; 6,202 feet) was first settled as an agricultural community to support mining camps and Denver. Hungry early travelers supposedly called the butte northeast of town Pound Cake. Better known as Castle Rock, it gave its name to the town at its base, which became the Douglas County seat in 1874. Castle Rock became best known for nearby rhyolite quarries. Many residents could not afford the fine local stone: Castle Rock's modest early homes are typified by the one-story frame Wilson Cottage (1897) at 704 Wilcox Street. Early commercial architecture is commemorated by the shed with false front at 313 3rd Street.

More grandiose new developments on the outskirts of town are epitomized by Castle Pines, an upscale 1980s residential enclave in the rolling foothills and meadows five miles north of Castle Rock. Its master plan calls for architect-designed custom houses and townhouses on 2,700 of approximately 6,000 acres. Castle Pines Village, west of I-25 on Happy Canyon Road, boasts two golf courses designed by Jack Nicklaus.

DA01 Douglas County Administration Building

DA01 **Douglas County Administration Building**

1982, Hoover Berg Desmond. 301 Wilcox St.

A radically Modernist replacement of a Victorian courthouse destroyed by fire, this won a national AIA award for the innovative Denver firm that designed it. The architects were inspired by the memory of the old courthouse and the architectural context, but were driven by a small budget. A stark box of smooth-faced concrete block, the building is a study in minimalism adorned only by contrasting rough-faced block for the foundation, stringcourses, and window trim. White glazed block "dentils" are the only cornice ornament. The Douglas County Executive Building (1994?), 101 3rd Street, is a much more successful combination of contemporary cinderblock and traditional rhyolite.

DA02 **Old Stone Church Restaurant** (St. Francis of Assisi Catholic Church)

1888, John Baptiste Ehmanon, builder. 210 3rd St. (corner of Jerry St.)

John Baptiste Ehmanon, a parishioner and stonemason, used local rough-faced rhyolite to build Castle Rock's first Catholic church, with a rose window and a projecting vestibule. After the parish moved to a larger church in 1966, this one was restored outside and remodeled inside to become a popular restaurant and bar, retaining its 1920s stained glass windows.

DA03 **Masonic Hall** (First National Bank of Douglas County)

1904, George Louis Bettcher. 300 Wilcox St. (northeast corner of 3rd St.)

This two-story building constructed with alternating wide and narrow courses of rough-faced rhyolite housed a bank until it closed in 1933. The Masons purchased it in 1937.

DA03 Masonic Hall (First National Bank of Douglas County)

Although the cupola is gone, the corner entrance behind arched openings is still there, as are the fan transoms of the arched second-story windows. Decorative fleur-de-lis medallions anchor tie rods between the floors, and a paneled frieze rises to a bracketed and dentiled cornice.

DA04 Keystone Hotel

1904, James and Francis Fetherolf. 219–223 4th St. (northwest corner of Wilcox St.)

This two-story hotel with storefronts, faced with rough rhyolite, has housed saloons, a dance hall, apartments, the Castle Cafe, and Hi's Western Store. The builders, James and Francis Fetherolf, originally operated the hotel and the downstairs saloon, where they discouraged cowboys from riding their horses into the bar. The cornice is gone and, in a 1946 remodeling of the building as apartments, the first-floor windows were sealed up with rhyolite to match the walls.

DA05 Town Hall (Douglas County High School)

1911. 1989, renovation, Ronald Abo. 620 Wilcox St.

Originally this building was faced entirely in rhyolite, but a 1936 gymnasium addition and remodeling added a blond brick facade. Art Deco is suggested by the cream, gold, orange, and red brickwork, the rhyolite diamonds inset in the brick frieze, and the tapered brick pilasters. A $1.8 million 1989

renovation transformed the old high school, which had become a junior high, into the town hall and school district headquarters.

DA06 Denver & Rio Grande Depot

1875, Benjamin J. Hammar, builder. 420 Elbert St. (NR)

Hammar, a leading pioneer stonemason who did much early work with locally quarried rhyolite, built this 24-by-40-foot single-story structure with thick gray rhyolite walls. The gable roof has wide, overhanging eaves on all sides supported by elaborate, diagonally braced brackets with ball pendants. Closed in 1965 and moved from its trackside location in 1970, the building served as an arts center and a senior center before its latest reincarnation as the Castle Rock Museum.

DA07 Christ Episcopal Church

1907; many additions. 615 4th St. (northeast corner of Lewis St.)

Local stonemason Charles Heub used rough-faced, uncoursed local rhyolite from the Santa Fe Quarry for this small chapel with stained glass lancets and a steep gable roof that has become the focus of a well-orchestrated complex of related gabled structures. The nave was constructed in 1906–1907 and the sanctuary added in 1911. A narthex of dark stained wood with a stone west wall provides entry on the south end and defines the style of later additions. A garden-level parish hall connects to the north wall of the Education Wing (1966, G. Cabell Childress), with pointed-arched windows and rhyolite facing.

DA08 Cantril School

1897. 1931 and 1950s, additions. 320 Cantril St. (NR)

Rough-faced blocks of rhyolite make Cantril School, atop Schoolhouse Hill on a full block with a playground, a showcase for the local stone. The first courses are the rare and more precious pink stone and the upper courses are the more common gray stone. Two stories tall, the building has an irregular plan, intersecting hipped roofs, and wide, bracketed eaves. The square three-story bell tower with paired, round-arched openings in each face echoes the entry arch. A similar entry farther north serves the auditorium and meeting room addition of 1931, constructed to blend with the original. The interior has 12-foot ceilings and oak floors, woodwork, and wainscoting. The building is one of the community's finest structures.

DA09 Cantril House

c. 1910. 221 Cantril St. (southwest corner of 3rd St.) (NR)

William W. Cantril's two-story foursquare is a rare brick residence in the older part of a frame and stone town. It is distinguished by plain, overhanging eaves from a hipped roof, arched windows, and raised stringcourses of stone at the sill levels of both floors. A rear addition matches the size and style of the original, now converted to the Cantril House Apartments for senior citizens.

DA10 Hammar House

1887, Benjamin J. Hammar, builder. 203 Cantril St. (northwest corner of 2nd St.) (NR)

Benjamin Hammar, a stonemason for the Denver & Rio Grande Railroad who worked on many depots (see DA06), later owned the Castle Rock Stone Company and the Santa Fe (railroad) Quarry. His story-and-a-half house of pink and gray rhyolite has steep-pitched side gables and a distinctive cross-gabled front entry with a frame porch topped by a small balcony. The T plan has a clapboarded frame north wing. The stone portion of the house has smooth stone sills and arched window tops with raised keystones. Reveals below the lintels are incised with Eastlake carving. Inside, original pine floors, woodwork, and cupboards remain in this well-preserved house. After Hammar departed, this was the home and office of Dr. George E. Alexander from 1902 until his death in 1947.

DA11 Dyer House

c. 1875, Samuel Dyer, builder. 208 Cantril St. (northeast corner of 2nd St.)

One of the oldest clapboard structures in town was built by the son of Father John Dyer, the famed pioneer Methodist preacher. The middle section, with modified shed roof and triangular dormer, was the first of three stages. The front section, with high gable roof and a porch with decorative bracketed beams, came next, and finally a rear addition that now contains a kitchen and bath. A 35-foot-deep well under a screen trap door on the back porch supplied water, and the stone outbuilding near the back door stored milk, meat, and coal.

Franktown

Franktown (1861, 6,120 feet) grew up around a stage stop on the Smoky Hill Trail. Frank Gardner first claimed the area, named Frank's Town for him. Gardner built a large hotel with a second-floor dance hall above guest rooms and a dining hall, which became the social center. A sawmill and several other roadhouses served the town, which was the first county seat (from 1861 to 1864).

DA12 Pikes Peak Grange Hall No. 163

1909. 3093 Colorado 83 (Parker Rd., 1 mile north of Franktown) (NR)

From its 1867 founding as the Patrons of Husbandry, the Grange organized rural folk for political, economic, and social reasons, including the formation of cooperatives and the Montgomery Ward mail order house. The national organization, whose membership peaked at almost two million in the 1870s, appealed to Coloradans. Of almost 500 Colorado halls, this one, built by Grange volunteers, is one of the few still active. Typical of pioneer vernacular construction, it is a simple, front-gabled clapboard structure. A side-gabled dining room wing was built in 1916 and a shed addition stage and modern coal furnace were added in 1938. Two transomed 9-foot-tall doors open into the meeting room, which has a 12-foot ceiling paneled in pressed metal and wainscoted in pine. Grange meetings and potluck suppers in this well-maintained hall perpetuate a long tradition of social and political solidarity among farmers and ranchers.

Parker

Parker (1873, 5,870 feet) originated with the Twenty Mile House on the Smoky Hill Trail. The original 1863 log cabin stage stop stood 20 miles southeast of Denver on Cherry Creek. James S. Parker, for whom the town is named, converted the Twenty Mile House into a depot for the Denver & New Orleans Railroad when it chugged into Parker in 1882. Little remains of the Twenty Mile House except a small remnant now used as a garage. Parker's population has skyrocketed from about 1,000 residents in 1960 to around 6,000.

DA13 Fonder School

1883. 1981, restoration, Bernard Wayne Lorance. 5219 Colorado 83 (Parker Rd.)

So that his wife would have a place to teach Franktown children, Hubert Fonder and some neighbors erected this school along the banks of Cherry Creek using local rhyolite and pine. A cross gable joins two front-gabled wings, one of rubblestone and one half-timbered, flanking the side-lighted entrance. The stone gable end also has a transomed door centered in it, with the lintel inscribed "1883." After closing as a school in 1949, it was restored in 1981 for community use.

DA14 Ruth Memorial Methodist Episcopal Church

1913, William Holmes. 19670 F. Main St. (Parker Rd.) (NR)

Circuit-riding sky pilots (as westerners called their traveling ministers) led services in this church, named for Ruth Heath, whose father donated the land and $1,000. Contractor William Holmes supervised locals who donated their labor as well as supplies and furnishings. The frame church, with horizontal wood siding and a wide pointed-arch window in the front gable end, is a variant of the Gothic Revival style. Under a steep-pitched roof, the transomed doors are in the base of a square, open corner bell tower. Since a 1980s restoration, the building has been used for gatherings and meetings.

Highlands Ranch

Highlands Ranch (1980, 4,563 feet), formed after the subdivision of the 22,000-acre ranch for which it is named. Within less than a decade it became the most populous community in Douglas County. John W. Springer established one of Colorado's most noted horse and cattle ranches here in 1898. Phillips 66 oil tycoon Waite Phillips bought the ranch in 1920 and acquired many adjacent properties. Frank Kistler became the owner in 1926 and had Jacques Benedict enlarge and Tudorize the old stone ranch house. The ranch was purchased in 1937 by U.S. Senator Lawrence C. Phipps. His family sold off 1,500 acres on the western edge of the ranch in 1970 for what is now part of Chatfield Reservoir State Park, which offers a marina, stables, and the arboretum of the Denver Botanic Gardens. The Chatfield Dam and State Recreation Area (1976, U.S. Army Corps of Engineers) is at the confluence of the South Platte River and Plum Creek, southwest of the intersection of Colorado 470 and U.S. 85 (Santa Fe Drive).

Oil billionaire Marvin Davis and the Highland Ventures group purchased the rest of Highlands Ranch from Phipps's heirs in 1978 for $13 million. A week later they sold it for twice that price to Mission Viejo, a California-based subsidiary of Philip Morris, Inc. Development began in 1981 with plans calling for an ultimate population of 90,000 in some 36,000 living units. A 1988, $435,000 show home, architect Karen Keating's "Professional Woman's Dream Home," has four bedrooms, three and one-half baths including a 325-square-foot master bath boasting two walk-in closets, and a laundry room on the second floor. The home's "Old English" design, mixing Tudor and bungalow features, characterizes many homes in Highlands Ranch.

DA15 **Highlands Ranch Headquarters**

1891–1911. 1932, Jacques Benedict. South end of Broadway at County Line Rd.

The 20,000-square-foot, two-and-one-half-story Tudor Revival manor house of Highlands Ranch includes an octagonal cobblestone windmill added during the 1930s. Rancher John W. Springer built the house and added to it over twenty years, accounting for approximately 60 percent of the building today. Second owner Frank E. Kistler engaged Jacques Benedict to remodel the house in the Tudor Revival style. The sprawling, irregular "castle" lies under shake shingle roofs bristling with a multitude of dormers, finialed gables, decorative chimney stacks, and a central, square, four-story tower with a crenelated parapet. Three-and-one-half-foot-thick rhyolite walls rise to upper walls clad in stucco and half-timbering. Fenestration includes varied use of arches and mullions in many small-paned casements, with lancet windows in the tower. A two-level balustraded terrace surrounds the main entrance. Surrounding frame barns, sheds, a shop, and several bunkhouses survive along with the ranch house, which is now a centerpiece and events center for Colorado's largest subdivision.

DA16 **Highline Canal**

1883. Begins south of Chatfield Reservoir at the Arequia rail siding of the DSP&P just above Kassler in the South Platte Canyon and runs through Douglas, Arapahoe, and Denver counties for 80 miles to the Rocky Mountain Arsenal in Adams County

Built by English capitalists, the Highline Canal was an engineering marvel using topography and natural flow to water the southeast quadrant of the metropolitan Denver area. Unlike canals in the eastern United States, this often dry western irrigation ditch was never used for transportation. Today the service road along the canal has been converted by the Denver Water Department

to a meandering trail where hikers, bikers, roller bladers, and joggers enjoy the cottonwood-lined banks inhabited by racoons, foxes, rabbits, and waterfowl.

Sedalia

Sedalia (1871, 5,860 feet) was established near the site of D. C. Oakes's 1859 sawmill, which exported lumber to Denver. Cattle roundup pens and a road along Plum Creek brought people here, as did an early livery stable and feed store and both the D&RG and Santa Fe railroads. The town took its name from another Santa Fe Railroad cowtown, Sedalia, Missouri. A devastating 1965 flood washed away the Presbyterian church and the original Grange hall.

DA17 **Cherokee Ranch** (Charlford Castle)

1924–1927, Burnham F. Hoyt. 6113 N. Daniels Park Rd. (NR)

The original owner of this twenty-room mansion, Charles A. Johnson, and his wealthy wife, Alice Gifford Phipps, gave architect Burnham Hoyt free rein to create a fifteenth-century Scottish castle on a bluff overlooking the Plum Valley. Hoyt's crew of thirty Cornish stonemasons used rhyolite found on site to build a fantasy that blends beautifully with its surroundings. Hoyt later turned the quarry into a water cistern. Chisel marks reveal that all the stone arches were carved by a single workman, the capitals by another, and the ledges by a third.

The multigabled manor has a high, half-timbered facade. Vermont slate covers the roofs, which bristle with turrets, four towers rising as tall as three stories, and dragon-head gargoyles. Crenelated parapets hark back to storybook medieval warfare with boiling oil and arrows, and the circular stairs built into the turrets spiral downward in counterclockwise rotation to give the advantage to defenders in hand-to-hand combat. The 25-by-40-foot great hall is dominated by round arches of stone and oak, a vaulted oak ceiling with carved rafters, and a musicians' balcony at the rear.

Tweet Kimball acquired the 2,000-acre ranch complete with castle and 6,642-foot Cherokee Mountain for $135,000 in 1954.

The original white frame ranch house (1889) is now headquarters for her 6,000-acre ranch specializing in Santa Gertrudis cattle.

DA18 St. Philip-in-the-Field Episcopal Church

1872, Newton Grant, builder. 1889, William Curtis. 5 miles south of Sedalia on Colorado 105 (NR)

This single-story frame church has a steep, front-gable roof with a Celtic cross above a protruding vestibule centered in the east facade. Shiplap siding is broken by three Gothic windows on each side. The spectacular site is framed by a wrought iron fence with red sandstone piers. Built in 1872 as a Methodist church, it was acquired in 1886 by Episcopalians, who had architect William Curtis draw expansion and remodeling plans for carpenter John Harris of Castle Rock to implement. The well-maintained building is surrounded by a cemetery where many Douglas County pioneers are interred amid lilacs and cedars.

DA19 Roxborough State Park

1975. South end of Roxborough Park Rd.

Magical red rock planes and the relatively sheltered site attracted prehistoric peoples, who left multiple archaeological sites within this park. Henry S. Persse, a pioneer settler, and fellow investors planned a large resort that never developed, although Roxborough did become a favorite outing place for Denverites.

A single kiln near the park entrance is the last remnant of the Silica Brick and Clay Company operation of 1904–1913. Of the Persse homestead, a sandstone house (c. 1903) with a metal roof remains, along with a barn constructed of old hewn and newer peeled logs with saddle notching, and two pole log sheds. These ruins lent inspiration for the George T. O'Malley Visitors' Center (1985, G. Cabell Childress Architects), a rustic textured and tinted concrete structure nestled into one of the rock formations and adorned with Frederick Myers's sculpture, *Kokopelli*, the humpbacked Indian flute player whose figure also shapes the courtyard. Residents of upscale subdivisions on the park's east, north, and west sides closed

DA19 Roxborough State Park, Visitors' Center

access to the park in 1981, trying to create a private enclave from public land. Public protest finally reopened this 1,500-acre state park, easily accessible for year-round use.

Deckers

Deckers (1896, 6,400 feet) is a fishing resort, earlier known as Daffodil, on the South Platte River where Steve Deckers opened a tavern, gas station, general store, and modest rental cabins. These were spared by the floods that washed away many pioneer structures. Lost Valley Ranch (1883) is a rustic log dude ranch 10 miles southwest of Deckers. Since 1898, Denver has eyed this spot near the confluence of the north and south forks of the South Platte for a dam. In 1990, after $40 million had been spent on Two Forks Dam, planned as one of the West's largest dams, the Environmental Protection Agency rejected the project, which would have flooded Deckers.

DA20 Cheesman Dam

1905, Charles L. Harrison. 13 miles southwest of Deckers via S. Deckers Rd. and U.S. Forest Service Rd. 211

This National Engineering Landmark is a most effective and beautiful stone dam incorporating existing rock features and a natural rock spillway. Charles Harrison, who previously worked on the Pennsylvania Railroad and the Panama Canal, used granite blocks averaging four to six tons each and quarried at the site. The dam is 176 feet thick at the base, 18 feet wide at the top, and 221 feet high. The first major on-stream municipal water storage in the Rockies, this is also the first major U.S. dam to use the gravity-arch concept, which makes it possible to construct safer and stronger dams. Walter Scott Cheesman (1838–1907) presided over the Denver Union Water Company before it became the city-owned Denver Water Department in 1918. The pristine waters of the 875-surface-acre lake, set in Pike National Forest, are part of Denver's water supply.

DA21 **Greenland Ranch**

1890s. Exit 167 from I-25 west to Douglas County 74

The 11,000-acre spread of Greenland Ranch is the county's largest undeveloped private land parcel. Spectacularly sited in high rolling hills and meadows south of Larkspur, this cattle ranch was put together by Frank Kirk, who persuaded every cowboy in sight to homestead a claim and sell it to him. In this way he acquired about 12,000 acres for Charles and Augustus Kountze, founders of Denver's Colorado National Bank.

Greenland was a popular overnight stop for stagecoaches traveling between Denver and Colorado Springs. The remains of a hotel, livery, and railroad stock-loading station are visible. The L-plan frame ranch house near the railroad tracks has corbeled brick chimneys, decorative shingle patterns in the gable ends, and bracketed porch posts. Antique outbuildings include the large frame barn and square frame silo with hipped roof. In 2000 a coalition of conservation groups acquired the ranch and surrounding 21,000 acres to preserve as open space.

Jefferson County (JF)

Established in 1861 as one of Colorado's seventeen original counties, Jefferson chose its oldest town, Golden, as the county seat. The county is watered by mountain streams flowing into the South Platte River. Ranching, farming, lumbering, and coal mining, the primary pioneer occupations, have been replaced by business, industry, and government offices, most notably the giant Federal Center in Lakewood and the Adolph Coors Company brewery. Jefferson County contains many of Denver's fastest-growing suburbs. Proliferating subdivisions and shopping centers lap into the foothills, where only a few backwater hamlets still contain tumbledown cabins untouched by modern times. Several small mountain communities remain summer home havens. On its western edge, this suburban county retreats into Pike and Roosevelt national forests and the Lost Creek Wilderness Area.

Jefferson will soon displace Denver as the most populous county in Colorado. Of 438,430 residents in 1990, 126,481 lived in Lakewood, 89,235 in Arvada, and 29,419 in Wheat Ridge. Golden is hemmed in by mountains that have curbed its growth. With about 14,000 residents, it is now smaller than the unincorporated mountain town of Evergreen, which is spreading like wildfire through the forests from which it takes its name. The Jefferson County Open Space Program and the Jefferson County Historical Commission identify, acquire, and attempt to preserve parklands and historic structures threatened by development.

Denver Mountain Parks, which occupy some 9,000 acres in Jefferson County, feature picnic shelters by architect Jacques Benedict, a leading proponent of a rustic Rocky Mountain style. The versatile Benedict mastered a range of styles. His Denver mansions and churches drew on the richest traditions of European architecture, while his rustic mode for picnic shelters and mountain cottages was derived from a studied and sensitive response to the region, a subject on which he lectured at the 1922 national AIA convention. Among other delights of the Denver Mountain Parks is Red Rocks Outdoor Amphitheater (JF39), Colorado's best example of Modernist architecture.

Golden

Squeezed into a narrow valley between North Table Mountain and South Table Mountain on the east and Lookout Mountain on the west, the county seat (1859, 5,675 feet) has remained a small town physically isolated from Denver's sprawl. The town, reportedly named for prospector Thomas L. Golden, began as a business venture of the Boston Company, which was one of the better-organized and better-capitalized early colony builders. Despite the hilly terrain, the company imposed the usual grid pattern on the townsite, which is bisected by Clear Creek.

Golden became an industrial center, with clay, coal, copper, and iron mines, as well as smelters, brickyards, and railyards. As Denver's early-day rival, it even reigned as the territorial capital from 1862 to 1867. After losing both that designation and railroad dominance to Denver, Golden became famous for locally made pressed fire bricks. Rich and varied local clay deposits also made it a center for the manufacture of drainpipes, pottery, and porcelain. Golden grew slowly after its initial boom, with a stable population of around 3,000 until the 1950s. Much of the main street (Washington Avenue) and the 12th Street residential district remain fairly intact. The Colorado School of Mines Campus in the center of town covers a range of building styles, from Romanesque Revival to stark solar boxes. The largest structures in town are the concrete-block buildings of the Adolph Coors Company. The Coors brewery (1873) has been the town's largest employer since the 1930s.

Hospitable landmarks include the Dove Inn (1868, Ebenezer T. Osborne, builder), 711 14th Street; the Barnes Mansion (1865, George Morrison, stonemason), a bed and breakfast at 622 Water Street; and Rock Rest Tavern (c. 1907), 16005 Old Golde Road, a cobblestone restaurant and dance hall.

Golden's history and some of its demolished landmarks are colorfully portrayed in the five-panel 1993 mural by Robert Dafford on the renovated Foss Building, 1224 Washington Avenue (northwest corner of 13th Street). The Opera House, now the Ace High Tavern (1879, Milliken and Lee, builders), 1212–1216 Washington, a two-story brick building that originally had an ornate, pressed metal cornice, first-floor offices, and a second-story opera hall, awaits restoration, but the nearby Woods Mortuary (1872, Joel W. Smith and Frederick H. Taft, builders), 1100 Washington, never sacrificed its Victorian dignity.

Washington Avenue is spanned by an old-fashioned welcome arch, reading, "Howdy Folks! Welcome to Golden Where the West Lives," erected in 1949 by the Chamber of Commerce. In 1992 the city spent $2 million on a facade restoration and streetscaping for Washington Avenue, which retains a few noteworthy residences such as the Boatright House (1901, Perre O. Unger, builder), 1518 Washington, a finely crafted foursquare, and the Tudor Revival Ryland House (1939, Donald Weiss), 1701 Washington. Washington Avenue's 1990s restoration makes downtown livelier competition for a neo-Victorian shopping mall and an 800-acre theme park a mile south at Heritage Square (1957).

JF01 **Mount Olivet Cemetery**

1892. W. 44th Ave. near I-70

This silent, subterranean city of more than 100,000 opened in 1892 on what had been the Clear Creek farm of Bishop Joseph P. Machebeuf, the French missionary who brought Catholicism to northern Colorado. Among many fine monuments, the finest is the mausoleum of the Reed family. This $250,000 votive chapel of St. Benedict above the family burial crypt was carved in Carrara marble by Raffaello Romanelli in Florence, Italy. It is a rich interpretation at small scale of the late Gothic style of the cathedral of Milan. Bronze doors and grillwork and the stained glass windows, which shed soft light on the relief carving clustered around the three altars on the interior, were also made in Italy. Work on the chapel began following the death of gold and oil millionaire Verner Z. Reed in 1919, and the chapel was shipped to Colorado and dedicated in 1923. The elegant landscaping is by Saco R. DeBoer.

JF02 **National Renewable Energy Research Facility and Visitors' Center**

1993, Anderson and DeBartelo. 1617 Cole Blvd.

On a sunny flank of South Table Mountain, this complex includes the Solar Energy Research Facility, a dramatic stadium of a building stepped back to catch the sun on each level. The center, which was founded in the 1970s, incorporates many state-of-the-art laboratories and demonstrations, as well as a visitors' center.

JF03 **Colorado Railroad Museum**

1959, Robert Richardson. 17155 W. 44th Ave.

Railroadiana galore, including architectural bric-a-brac, make this large museum a joy for rail enthusiasts. A replica railroad depot is jammed with ephemera, photos, paintings, books, models, and other artifacts. The large grounds hold more than sixty-four pieces of vintage rolling stock and a half-mile track for mini-excursions. Museum founder Robert Richardson selected the Allen Lewis farmhouse (1863), the county's oldest, for the curator's house, although numerous alterations hide its antiquity.

JF04 **American Mountaineering Center** (Golden High School)

1923, Eugene Groves. 1995, restoration, Barker, Rinker, Seacat and Partners. 710 10th St. (northeast corner of Washington Ave.)

The American Alpine Club (AAC) left New York City in 1993 to move into this former junior high school, which it shares with the Colorado Mountain Club. Built as Golden High School, the three-story Beaux-Arts school building is blond brick with terracotta trim, including polychrome columbines blooming at the entrance. The building and landscaped grounds, which occupy a full block, were restored for $500,000 and now house the AAC's 18,000-volume library, a mountaineering museum, a bookshop, and a 300-square-foot scale model of Mount Everest. Gerald R. Cassidy's 1925 painting *Dawn of the West,* in the main hall, depicts a pioneer family finding gold at the future site of Golden on Clear Creek, to the dismay of Indians in the background.

JF05 **Stewart Block**

1892, James Nankivell and Robert Jones, builders. 922 Washington Ave. (northwest corner of 10th St.)

This two-story, red brick corner grocery, named the E. E. Stewart Block on the stone corner entry entablature, was operated for four decades by Elvyn E. Stewart. The keystones of the Washington Avenue second-story windows are carved with the initials of the Golden Knights of Pythias Lodge, which met upstairs. The Indian mural painted by John Walker on the south wall is the remnant of an 1891 advertisement for Rocky Ford Cigars.

JF06 **Coors Building**

1906, Perre O. Unger and William A. Wortham, builders. 1120 Washington Ave.

This two-and-one-half-story, mansard-roofed commercial emporium in pressed red brick is one of the city's best-preserved and least altered. Adolph Coors built it as a bottling plant and saloon. It was renovated in 1992 as part of the Silverheels Restaurant, which also occupies the adjacent Territorial Capitol building.

JF07 **Loveland Block–Territorial Capitol**

1863–1866, Duncan E. Harrison, builder. 1991, renovation, Andrews and Anderson. 1122 Washington Ave. (northwest corner of 12th St.)

The Colorado Territorial Legislature met here in 1866–1867, supposedly because William A. H. Loveland offered the legislators use of his building and townsfolk offered free firewater and firewood. Loveland, Golden's prime promoter, also presided over the Colorado Central Railroad, which hoped to make Golden, not Denver, the rail hub of the Colorado Territory. This two-story, red brick structure, built in stages, was designed with a mansard roof and generous, round-arched window and door openings. After the territorial government moved to Denver, the Jefferson County government met here until the first courthouse was built in 1877. The third floor and mansard roof have been removed and the main street facade remodeled with new windows and doors. After a 1991 renovation, the venerable hall re-opened as a bar and restaurant.

JF08 **Everett Block**

1873, Baker Brothers. 1200 Washington Ave. (southwest corner of 12th St.)

Francis E. Everett built this two-story brick building with stone trim to house his bank. He served as mayor of Golden (1881–1888) but committed suicide when it became known that he had defrauded bank customers. One of the finest structures on Golden's main street, the Everett Block echoes the Second Empire style. George Morrison (see entry for the town of Morrison, Jefferson County), with contractor John H. Parsons, built the stone horseshoe arches and stone courses for merchant Francis Everett. After considerable abuse and the collapse of a central wall in 1984, the block has been beautifully restored by Frederick A. (Heinie) Foss for use as the Henry J. Foss Clothing Co.

JF09 **Table Mountain Inn**

1924, Tracy Quick. 1993, restoration. 1310 Washington Ave.

Built as a hotel, this structure was remodeled in 1993, using the distinctive massing of the Pueblo Revival style in battered walls, blunt angles, and stepped parapets. Tile floors, unpainted wood columns, wooden bracket capitals, and vigas also helped to transform this once nondescript hotel complex. Arched facade openings, outdoor landscaping, and patios make the inn a key piece in the revival of Golden's main street.

JF10 **Adolph Coors Company Brewery**

1873. 13th and Ford sts., 2 blocks east of Washington Ave.

The tiny brewery that Adolph Coors and a partner, Jacob Scheuler, established in an old tannery in 1873 has become a 3,400-acre plant extending six miles along Clear Creek below Golden. The main plant claims to be the world's largest single brewery. "I like functional buildings with no frills," William Coors, Adolph's grandson, explained. "There never have been any architects, only our own engineers and contractors." In 1910 the brewery shifted from brick to concrete structures. Many new, raw cement buildings are built of 20-by-20-inch precast concrete wall sections. The oldest surviving brewing structure is the 1934 brewhouse. Coors weathered Prohibition by making malted milk, butter, near beer, and porcelain. The Coors complex still produces a high-grade porcelain for scientific and industrial uses ranging from missile nose cones to ceramic tiles. The brewery has been a tourist destination since 1874, when Adolph Coors converted the grove along Clear Creek into a beer garden and bathhouse where visitors could drink, eat, swim, hear music, dance, and tour the brewery. Although the beer garden is gone, tourists can still inspect the brewery and sample its wares free of charge.

The brewery's dance pavilion (1874) was converted into the Coors family home in 1882. In 1903 Denver architect Harold W. Baerresen remodeled elaborately and added onto the house for Louisa Webber Coors, Adolph's wife. The two-story eclectic frame home features classical columns and Palladian windows, as well as attic dormers and gables, skylights, and leaded glass windows. Over the decades, it has been enlarged to twenty-two rooms and moved three times to accommodate growth in what is now America's third largest brewery. Louisa Coors also transformed the grounds into a rose garden and added a large greenhouse still maintained by the family, along with the mansion itself, located on a railroad spur and hemmed in by large brewery buildings.

JF11 **Foothills Art Gallery** (First Presbyterian Church)

1872. 1889, addition, James H. Gow, builder. 809 15th St. (southwest corner of Washington Ave.) (NR)

The Reverend Sheldon Jackson, a notable pioneer Presbyterian preacher, worked with parishioners to build this structure of local sandstone and Golden pressed red bricks. The Queen Anne Style church has an irregular plan, Gothic-arched doorways and windows, and a distinctive two-story, square, closed corner bell tower. The Rubey House (1899, Perre O. Unger) next door at 1510 Washington Avenue, now the gallery gift shop, was the work of a prominent local contractor who built many of the town's landmarks. The congregation moved to new quarters in 1958, and a decade later the Foothills Art Center recycled this lovely landmark as a gallery.

JF12 **Astor House Hotel Museum**

1867, Seth Lake. 822 12th St. (NR)

Seth Lake constructed rough stone walls, up to 18 inches thick, with stone from a quarry a few blocks away at the west end of 12th Street to build what is now the oldest stone hotel in Colorado. For the foundation, he dug a trench, filled it with boulders, and then tamped in local fire clay. The two-story building bears little resemblance to its New York City namesake. One of its few architectural refinements is a reconstructed frame balcony forming a porch over the entrance. Window and door trim consists of heavy, hand-hewn square logs. Additions dating from 1892, of local pressed brick, have fine, round-arched windows on both stories beneath a mansard roof with pedimented dormers. On the eve of demolition in 1972, Golden voters rescued it, allowing the Golden Landmarks Association to convert it to a municipal museum.

JF13 **12th Street Historic Residential District**

11th to 13th sts. between Arapahoe and Elm sts. (NR)

Astor House is a gateway to this historic district, which contains some of the oldest residences in Colorado. These small masonry homes, some dating to the 1860s, are of greater historical than architectural interest, as some have lost their design integrity. George West, a town founder and founder of the still published *Golden Transcript*, built the West House (1871) at 1018 12th Street. West's two-story pressed red brick house is the oldest among twelve significant and thirty-three contributing homes in the fifty-seven-structure district. John H. Parsons, who did much construction in early Golden, built his own large brick and stone Parsons House (1869) at 1011 12th Street. The Guy Hill School (1876), in a pocket park at 12th and Ford streets, is a one-room, lap-sided school moved here in 1976. The otherwise unremarkable post office (1940, WPA), 619 12th Street, houses Kenneth Evett's 1941 WPA mural, *Building the Road,* depicting construction of U.S. 6 through Clear Creek Canyon.

JF14 **Calvary Episcopal Church**

1867, John H. Parsons. 1300 Arapahoe St. (NR)

A tall, stately steeple, sharply pitched roof, and Gothic-arched openings framed in stone distinguish this tiny brick church, one of the first Gothic Revival edifices in Colorado. Built as a chapel for the Episcopal college that evolved into the Colorado School of Mines, it is Golden's oldest standing church.

JF15 **Colorado National Guard Armory**

1913, James H. Bryant and Joseph C. Taylor. 1301 Arapahoe St. (NR)

This three-story fortress with its 65-foot-high square tower was built by Golden contractor James H. Gow with 3,300 wagonloads of river rock from nearby Clear Creek. Locals boast it is the largest cobblestone structure in the world. Built by the National Guard Corps of Engineers, it initially had dormitories, a mess hall, drill hall, weapons storage rooms, a hospital, and an auditorium, but has been converted to shops and offices.

JF16 Colorado School of Mines

1869. W. 6th Ave. (U.S. 6) to Illinois St. between 10th and 19th sts.

"The World's Foremost College of Mineral Engineering," as this school calls itself, started in 1869 as an Episcopal school, St. John's in the Wilderness. Five years later Colorado Territory adopted the foundling institution, which is still a state school. Three early Second Empire mansard-roofed brick buildings have disappeared, although Jarvis Hall (1878, Duncan E. Harrison, builder) survives off campus as a private apartment house at 921 19th Street. Notwithstanding an 1894 master plan by Robert S. Roeschlaub and a 1950 plan by Fuller, Fuller and Fuller, campus architecture is discordant, offering decade-by-decade examples of the latest institutional styles, ranging from the Romanesque Revival favored by the Roeschlaub plan to stark solar. Much work here has been done by Fuller, Fuller and Fuller, a Denver firm comprising three generations of the same family. As the descendant of the old Roeschlaub and Fuller firm, it is the state's oldest architecture firm. Besides developing the 1950 master plan, which called for Modernist buildings, the Fullers designed Alderson Chemical and Petroleum Engineering Hall (1953), Coolbaugh Chemistry Hall (1952), Nathaniel Hill Metallurgy Hall (1958), Paul Meyer Physics Hall (1963), and Volk Gymnasium (1957). Other notable construction includes the Steinhauer Field House (1937, Jacques Benedict), George R. Brown Geology Hall (1979, Lamar Kelsey), Green Center (1970, Kenneth R. White), and a five-story Modernist, solar dormitory (1979, John D. Anderson). Since 1985 many campus buildings have been restored on the exterior and renovated inside.

JF16.1 Berthoud Hall

1937, Temple Hoyne Buell. Northwest corner of 16th and Illinois sts.

Four stories with two-story wings, Berthoud Hall, built as a WPA project, houses the Geological Museum, whose treasures include six murals by Irwin D. Hoffman depicting the history of mining from prehistoric times. Hoffman painted the series for the 1939 Golden Gate Exposition in San Francisco. This yellow brick edifice is lavishly trimmed in terracotta with exuberant Beaux-Arts detailing bordering on the rococo for extravagant entry surrounds, pilasters, spandrels, and wide, double-bracketed eaves.

JF16.2 Hall of Engineering

1894, Robert S. Roeschlaub. 15th and Arapahoe sts.

The oldest structure on campus, this three-story building of local red pressed brick with a rhyolite foundation has sandstone trim for the round entry arch, corbeling, cornice, and stepped parapet. This building is one of the best works of prominent Golden contractor Herbert Tracy Quick, father of Tracy Quick, a Golden architect.

JF16.3 Guggenheim Hall

1905, James Murdoch. 1500 Illinois St.

At the upper (west) end of the main campus axis, this administration building was erected with an $80,000 donation from smelter magnate and U.S. Senator Simon Guggenheim. A small, gold-domed cupola atop a square bell tower distinguishes the three-story gray brick building with side bays culminating in curvilinear parapets with roundels. This eclectic building has been restored as the campus centerpiece.

JF16.4 Stratton Hall

1902–1904, Harlan Thomas. 14th and Cheyenne sts.

Harlan Thomas, who also did design work for Colorado State University in Fort Collins, designed a three-story building of gray Golden-made brick on a Lyons sandstone base and the first steel-frame construction on the campus. The foundation was made with crushed slag from the remains of the Golden Smelting Works. Remarkably unchanged, this classic, named for mining millionaire Winfield Scott Stratton, a trustee and benefactor of the school, still has its original skylight and distinctive curvilinear parapets with quatrefoil windows.

JF17 Coors House

1910–1919, Jacques Benedict. 1817 Arapahoe St.

Herman F. Coors, a son of Adolph, built this stone and stucco cottage for his family. A two-story house on an irregular plan, it includes a variety of arched and square-top windows. A stone wall surrounds the four-lot site, where the gardener's and carpenter's houses have been converted into separate residences. Jacques Benedict's octagonal entry has massive walnut beams joining at the center of a dome. Walnut beams also grace

JF19 Jefferson County Courthouse

the 18-foot living room ceiling. Benedict's trademarks—stone trim and fireplaces, beveled windows, French doors, and exquisite woodwork—enhance the little-altered interior.

JF18 Jefferson County Human Services Center

1990, C. W. Fentress, J. H. Bradburn and Associates. 900 Jefferson County Pkwy.

The circular wings of this 132,000-square-foot semicoliseum reach out to visitors because, as architect C. W. Fentress put it, "we wanted people who are having a difficult time in life to feel welcomed by it." The $60 million, four-story complex of brick and glass houses two dozen once-scattered social service agencies. A two-story solarium inside provides circulation and views of a colonnaded, landscaped plaza. Polished maroon granite bands are cut and shaped to complement the golden brick on the exterior, which borrows its color from the grasses of the surrounding foothills.

JF19 Jefferson County Courthouse

1993, C. W. Fentress, J. H. Bradburn and Associates. 100 Jefferson County Pkwy.

The county's grandest, most overbearing structure, sited on a prominent hillside, won a national AIA citation, but local critics have been less kind to the building they call the "Taj Mahal." Soaring above raw prairie hills and arroyos, this 531,000-square-foot, $102 million monument of tan and brown cast stone culminates in a 130-foot-high glass-domed atrium from which four wings arc through landscaped courtyards. The glazed rotunda and plaza recall monumental public buildings of the past, while the grand atrium is reminiscent of a John Portman hotel lobby. Trimmed in brass and cherry wood, this interior space presents a grand view. Balconies extend in semicircular bays from the upper three floors, and neutral colors are sparked by bands of blue, green, and rose terrazzo and bits of red granite in the floors. To one side are county administrative offices; opposite are twenty-eight courtrooms. The buff precast concrete exterior has darker squares and crosses inset to humanize its massive scale. Golden's original brick courthouse could fit inside the grandiose atrium.

Some of the building's critics blasted the county for abandoning downtown Golden for a suburban site. In addition, the building's high cost sparked a taxpayer revolt. Jefferson County voters ousted the county commissioners responsible for it and overwhelmingly supported a tax limitation amendment to the state constitution.

JF20 Lookout Mountain

1 mile west of Golden

Lookout Mountain, one of the most prominent foothills of the Rockies, is part of the system of Denver Mountain Parks and a fashionable residential area. Long a lure for sightseers, it became the first notable mountain auto drive with the completion of the Lariat Loop Road (1914, Frederick Law Olmsted, Jr.). In the Olmsted tradition, this road uses rather than abuses the topography. The many curves, hairpin turns, and dips follow the contour of the mountainside. Native stone is used for park structures, including the guardrails, springhouses, and entry arch. The rustic stone style is also seen in the shelters, campsites, comfort stations, the nearby Mother Cabrini Shrine, founded as an orphanage in 1903, and the Buffalo Bill Grave and Museum complex (JF21).

JF21 Buffalo Bill Grave and Museum

1921, Edwin H. Moorman. 987 Lookout Mountain Rd.

The City and County of Denver maintains this museum in a two-story rustic log and slab lodge with a second-story balcony, Stick Style trim, and stone chimneys. Built of undressed pine logs and hand-split shingles, the interior is animated by stuffed wildlife illuminated by pine-branch chandeliers. A bland new museum addition (1978) next door helps house a large collection of Buffalo Bill memorabilia, as well as paintings by western artists Charles S. Stobie, Charles Schrevogel, and Robert Lindneux.

JF22 Jefferson County Nature Center (Boettcher Summer Home)

1916, William E. Fisher and Arthur A. Fisher. 900 Colorow Rd. (NR)

Charles Boettcher, Colorado's greatest industrialist, erected this Tudor Revival country estate built of local granite and pine. The 10,000-square-foot home seems to grow out of its craggy hilltop site, with its profile softened by clipped gables, a shake shingle roof, and stone walls. A carriage house, well house, barn, and gazebo further enhance the 110-acre site. In 1975 the summer lodge reopened as the Jefferson County Outdoor Conference and Nature Center. The Fishers' elevation drawings for this wonderful, understated "cottage" adorn the upstairs meeting rooms. The 110-acre surrounding ponderosa forest offers nature trails and fine views.

JF23 Mount Vernon House (Robert W. Steele House)

1860, George Morrison. 1 mile south of Golden at I-70, Jefferson County 26, and Mount Vernon Canyon Rd. (NR)

At the mouth of the Mount Vernon Canyon route into the mountain gold fields, stonemason George Morrison built this two-story house with 22-inch-thick walls of rough-faced native sandstone and shingle cladding on the second story. After Morrison moved on to found the nearby town named for him (see below, Jefferson County), this became the home of Robert W. Steele. Steele was elected governor of Jefferson Territory, an extralegal territory never recognized by Congress which preceded the official 1861 creation of Colorado Territory. The enthusiastic but stillborn Jefferson Territorial government met in the front hall under 12-foot-high ceilings. "Governor" Steele, a great admirer of George Washington, envisioned creation of Mount Vernon City, which existed from 1860 to 1885. The house served over the years as a general store, roadhouse,

JF23 Mount Vernon House (Robert W. Steele House), east elevation

post office, saloon, and Wells Fargo stage stop. Designated Colorado's first HABS site and Jefferson County's first National Register site, it became the house that moved a freeway when I-70 was constructed around it during the 1960s.

JF24 **Rooney Ranch**

1860, Alexander Rooney. Rooney Rd. and W. Alameda Pkwy. (NR)

Rancher and stonemason Alexander Rooney constructed many of the fourteen structures on this 200-acre ranch, still owned by his descendants. Alexander built the two-story, front-gabled main house (1860) with 18-inch-thick walls of native sandstone quarried from the hogback behind the house. A small springhouse (1860s), barn (1890, enlarged 1936) with a gambrel roof, and other outbuildings are made of uncoursed rubblestone with uniform asphalt roofs.

Lakewood

Lakewood (1892, 5,440 feet) was platted in 1889 by William A. H. Loveland, the ubiquitous pioneer who also promoted Golden, built railroads, and in 1878 became the owner of the *Rocky Mountain News*. Lakewood first flourished as a health spa with the opening of the Jewish Consumptive Relief Society in 1904. Started as a tent colony, the JCRS evolved into a major tuberculosis sanatarium. Lakewood's isolated sanatariums, turkey farms, and ranches were never the same after the start of World War II, which brought construction of the Denver Ordnance Plant. This $35 million federal complex behind chain link and barbed wire fences was built on the Hayden Ranch, a tract bounded by West 6th and Alameda avenues, between Kipling Street and Union Boulevard. To connect the plant with downtown, West 6th Avenue was rebuilt as Colorado's first freeway, an artery which fostered postwar suburban growth. After peace came in 1945, the plant became the Denver Federal Center, the nation's second largest concentration of federal workers. The complex incorporates major offices for some thirty agencies with about 10,000 employees, of whom 317 can fit into a subterranean bomb shelter to keep the federal government humming in a post–nuclear war world.

Lakewood did not incorporate as a city until 1969, but thereafter began an aggressive annexation campaign that has made it the fourth most populous city in Colorado. The old main street, West Colfax Avenue, has been replaced by Union Boulevard with its concentration of government and private office buildings. Lakewood's grand old mansion, Belmar (1930s, Jacques Benedict), a replica of the Petit Trianon at Versailles, once stood at 739 Wadsworth Boulevard. After demolition in 1970, the 750-acre estate was subdivided for Belmar Park, with its large Kountze Lake; Villa Italia shopping center; the glassy Lakewood Municipal Center (1983, William C. Muchow and Associates), 445 South Allison Parkway; and Historic Belmar Museum and Village, a preserve for landmarks in the path of development. Now a city of more than 130,000, Lakewood consists primarily of post-1940 subdivisions and shopping centers with some architecturally notable enclaves and a handful of landmarks, including the home of town founder William Loveland (1888), at 1435 Harlan Street, a brick vernacular home with Italianate trim. For a pristine recreation of the rural ideal, see the White Fence Farm, a farmhouse/restaurant and model farm complete with petting zoo, all in patriotic Colonial Revival beneath an oversized American flag at 6263 West Jewell Avenue.

JF25 **Lakeside Amusement Park**

1908. 1940s, renovation, Richard Crowther. 4601 Sheridan Blvd.

This once grand turn-of-the-century amusement park is the centerpiece of the one-square-mile town of Lakeside, which has thirteen residents, a shopping center, and a 37-acre lake. The amusement park wraps around Lake Rhoda, which Lakeside founder Ben Karsner named for his daughter, the current owner. The park's lavish 150-foot Tower of Jewels, lit with 16,000 light

JF26 American Medical Center (Jewish Consumptive Relief Society)   JF27 Casa Bonita

bulbs, is a square campanile with Venetian and Moorish overtones. It retains some of its original Victorian decor, as well as the 1940s Streamline Moderne redesign by Richard Crowther. Fresh from working on San Francisco's Golden Gate Exposition, Crowther added modern lines, colors, and sparkle to the aging park. Edward Vettel of the famed family of roller coaster engineers designed the Cyclone Roller Coaster (1940). Queasy visitors prefer the 22-inch-gauge train that has been carrying visitors around the lake since 1908.

JF26 **American Medical Center** (Jewish Consumptive Relief Society)

1904; additions, various architects. 6401 W. Colfax Ave. (NRD)

In 1904 Dr. Charles D. Spivak established a tent colony tuberculosis sanatarium that evolved into a nationally prominent 105-acre campus with thirty-four buildings of various ages, styles, and functions surrounding a central rectangular lawn. Red tile roofs, brick and stucco walls, exuberant terracotta trim, and a Beaux-Arts aura are the most common denominators. The well-preserved core of the campus survives as a general medical and research center. The Isaac Solomon Synagogue (1911, William E. and Arthur A. Fisher), a small red brick and creamy terracotta building with ogee arches, has

been converted to a museum. The Fishers also designed the Neusteter Rehabilitation Building (1926), the Texas Pavilion for Women (1927), and the TriBoro Dining Hall (1936). Harry James Manning designed the post office and cooperative store (1926). The JCRS was renamed the American Medical Center in 1954 when part of the grounds were sold off for the JCRS Shopping Center (1957) on West Colfax Avenue.

JF27 **Casa Bonita**

1974, Philip H. Phillips. 6715 W. Colfax Ave.

An old store in the JCRS Shopping Center has been remodeled into a south-of-the-border fantasy. The 82-foot-high pink stucco bell tower with a balustraded observation deck is a three-tiered, Spanish Baroque apparition crowned by a life-size warrior with spear, shield, and plumed helmet. Inside, under a high black ceiling simulating a tropical night, the decor caters to the romantic stereotypes of Mexico cherished by North Americans. A Spanish tile floor winds through a jungle of concrete palm trees, plastic ferns, and strolling, strumming mariachis. Tables overlook a three-tiered fountain on a lagoon, where diners can choose a thatched roof cabaña or a ferny grotto. Smiling señoritas deliver the margaritas, while fire jugglers dive off cliffs into the lagoon. This 52,000-square-foot complex—

with a tropical jungle, 30-foot waterfall, pirates' hideout, and other marvels—is the largest link in a chain of Casa Bonitas.

JF28 **The Glens**

1923, Glen Creighton and Saco R. DeBoer. W. Colfax to W. 6th aves. between Estes and Garrison sts.

Saco DeBoer, Colorado's premier landscape architect, planned this 80-acre "Park for Happy Homes" with curvilinear streets. This "residence park," with a community center and park, attracted middle-class residents whose preferences did not run to the fanciful English country mansions and cottages that promoter Glen Creighton fancied.

JF29 **Davies Chuck Wagon Diner**

1957. 9495 W. Colfax Ave.

Of perhaps 4,000 diners that sprang up along U.S. roadsides between the 1920s and 1950s, less than 1,000 survive, including two in Jefferson County (see also JF42). Brent Davies built what became one of Lakewood's first designated landmarks in 1989. This chrome home on the range is a fully equipped, stainless steel, 46-ton diner delivered to this site by rail from a New Jersey manufacturer. Inside, the 1950s Deco decor exults in aluminum fixtures; pink, gray, and white formica counters; individual jukebox selectors in each booth; and mirrored walls. Thanks to a life-sized palomino horse on top of the building and a 36-foot-high cowboy chef in a white apron and white hat on the neon sign, this 1950s time capsule is impossible to miss.

JF30 **Lakewood Heritage Center, previously Belmar Village Museum**

797 S. Wadsworth Blvd.

Of the once fabulous estate of *Denver Post* heiress May Bonfils Stanton Berryman, little remains except for the calf barn, caretaker's cottage, and auction house, which are now the core of Lakewood's municipal museum complex. Exhibits include the Peterson House (c. 1886) (NR), a typical L-shaped shiplap farmhouse that was moved here, a wealth of agricultural apparatus, and Ralston Crossing Schoolhouse (c. 1869).

JF31 **Stone House**

c. 1870; 1975 restoration, Langdon Morris. W. Yale Ave. and 2800 S. Estes St. (NR)

Eighteen-inch-thick cobblestone walls with windows and doors framed with Morrison sandstone are eye-catching features of this stone farmhouse. Joseph Hodgson, a New Yorker who had joined the California gold rush, built the side-gabled house, with a rear attached shed of the same carefully matched Bear Creek river rock, on his 640-acre Bear Creek farmstead.

JF32 **Chatfield Dam and State Park**

1977, U.S. Army Corps of Engineers (dam). Southwest corner of S. Wadsworth and Deer Creek

This 147-foot-high, earth-fill flood control dam on the South Platte River inundated much of the 1870s ranch of Isaac W. Chatfield at the confluence of the Platte, Plum Creek, and Deer Creek. A visitors' center, picnic areas and museum, and the Denver Botanic Gardens Arboretum make this a favorite recreation area.

JF33 **Ken-Caryl Ranch Manor House**

1914. 14432 W. Ken-Caryl Rd.

The huge Ken-Caryl subdivision formed from this 28,000-acre ranch typifies the fate of many ranches in the Denver metropolitan area. Chicagoan John C. Schaeffer, owner of the *Rocky Mountain News* from 1913 to 1926, established this Hereford ranch, which he named for his sons, Ken and Caryl. During the 1970s the Johns Manville Corporation of New York City bought the Ken-Caryl Ranch for $7.5 million and moved its world headquarters to the grounds. Manville developed the ranch as a subdivision. The first homes opened in 1976 for a subdivision planned to accommodate an estimated 18,000 residents, an office park, and a shopping center.

The two-story manor house, for all its size and grand hilltop location, is a simple vernacular white clapboard home with some Georgian Revival detailing. The 8,000-

square-foot house has a distinctive two-story south portico with a giant order of Doric columns and attic dormers. It is now a restaurant, with many private rooms in the little-altered original room configuration. The large sunroom is now a piano lounge. The Dutch Colonial barn (1917) is the Equestrian Center for Ken-Caryl subdivisions.

Also on the ranch are the ruins of Robert Bradford's two-story stone house, stage stop, and inn (1859), once a separate 385-acre ranch now developed as Ken-Caryl's North Ranch. Bradford built the house as an inn along his toll road from Denver through this area and up Turkey Creek Canyon to the mines in South Park. A few other structures sprang up nearby to make up "Bradford City," of which only the crumbling walls of Bradford's home survive amid expensive new suburban homes. Restrictive covenants overseen by the Architectural Control Committee require large lots and spacious homes of at least 2,200 square feet on the first floor, with exteriors "of natural materials with no pastel or bright colors permitted."

This sheltered scenic mountain valley between a hogback and foothills has long attracted home seekers. A major prehistoric rock shelter was discovered on the ranch along with a fire pit, animal bones, scraping tools, and projectile points.

JF34 Lockheed Martin (Martin Marietta) Astronautics (Johns Manville World Headquarters)

1976, The Architects Collaborative. 12275 Colorado 121

The September 1977 *Architectural Record* praised this joint design of Harry Weese, T. C. Enradi, Robert Geddes, William Le Messurier, Sheelhe and Gebharts, and landscape architect Hubertus J. Mittman for its "low, wide feel" and for "occupying the site sparingly" yet "as splendidly as a Greek temple." The machine age building of glass and aluminum makes no concessions to natural materials or shapes. A skyscraper lying on its side in a spectacular natural foothills setting, it is now a part of the Martin Marietta complex.

Morrison

Morrison (1873, 5,800 feet, NRD) was established by George Morrison, a Scottish stonecutter from Montreal. In 1864 Morrison homesteaded this area along Bear Creek, where he found fine red sandstone and opened one of Colorado's first quarries. After the Denver, South Park & Pacific Railroad arrived, as many as six quarries provided pinkish-red sandstone for buildings statewide. Morrison and former governor John Evans, principal backer of the Denver, South Park & Pacific, founded the Morrison Stone, Lime, and Town Company. Morrison remains a quaint little town protected from a sea of suburban development by the Morrison Hogback on the east, Red Rocks Park on the north, and steep foothills on the west. The stone ruins of a proposed summer White House (1919, Jacques Benedict), a

JF34 Martin Marietta Astronautics (Johns Manville World Headquarters)

never-completed marvel based on Prince Ludwig's castle in Bavaria, are a reward for a short hike to the top of Mt. Falcon.

JF35 Standard Station

1927. 101–103 Bear Creek Ave.

Twin curvilinear parapets over twin service bays are separated by a central bell tower in this distant echo of Padre Junipero Serra's San Diego mission. Clad in stucco under blue roof tiles, this gas station has been reincarnated as an art gallery, a bakery, and an automobilia shop.

JF36 Cliff House Lodge

1873, George Morrison. 121 Stone St. (corner of Mt. Vernon Ave.)

Stonemason and quarry owner George Morrison built this two-story family home with

JF38 The Fort

JF39 Red Rocks Outdoor Amphitheater

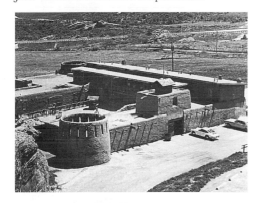

red and white sandstone in a smooth ashlar forming two-foot-thick walls. Details include arches, dentils, and a pediment on the slightly pitched front gable. An attached house in rough-faced red sandstone has matching sills and roofline. After Morrison's death in 1895, James Swanson converted the two houses to the Cliff House hotel. Now operated as a bed and breakfast, this double house is in fine condition amid dense, attractive landscaping.

JF37 Morrison Schoolhouse

1875, George Morrison. 226 Spring St. (NR)

Expressing the elevated goals of public education, this is an impressively vertical composition, once heightened by an open bell tower. Large blocks of rough-faced red Morrison sandstone frame pairs of square-top windows, trimmed in the same sandstone. The building was used as a school until the 1950s and is now a private home with a garage and deck addition.

JF38 The Fort

1963, Bill Lumpkins. Colorado 8, just north of U.S. 285

For this restaurant replica of Bent's Fort (OT11), owner Sam Arnold commissioned Bill Lumpkins, a leading Santa Fe architect. Craftsmen used local red earth and straw to make the 80,000 bricks for this adobe castle with a single large entry gate, round corner tower, and upstairs accommodations resembling those of Bent's Fort. Ox blood was used to seal the tile floors and give them a lustrous, rich red color. The interior incorporates many other southwestern details, including the Padre Martinez chairs and the southwestern cooking of Sam and Carrie Arnold.

JF39 Red Rocks Outdoor Amphitheater

1941, Burnham F. Hoyt. In Red Rocks Park on northwest side of Morrison

The ultimate beauty of this acoustically superb outdoor theater is the natural setting of massive sandstone and metamorphic rocks tilted upward by volcanic action. The May 1945 *Architectural Forum* praised "the admirable restraint with which architect Burnham Hoyt has preserved the original flavor of a majestic setting." Collaborating with nature, Hoyt used the local juniper tree as landscaping and native red sandstone for the drainage and ledgelike outdoor seating. The wonderful simplicity of this design has been marred by a few subsequent additions such as a stage covering which partially blocks the view of Denver and the High Plains. The surrounding 1,640-acre Red Rocks Park also offers hiking trails and the Pueblo Concession House (1931, W. R. Rosche), a two-story structure mixing a Mission Revival parapet and Pueblo Revival vigas on the facade of a visitors' center, cafe, and museum. The AIA selected Red Rocks as the Colorado entry for its centennial exhibition at the National Gallery of Art in 1957.

JF40 Red Rocks Civilian Conservation Corps Camp

1938, Civilian Conservation Corps. Colorado 74 and Red Rocks Park

About 125 young men, the CCC laborers who constructed Red Rocks, lived here in what is now one of the nation's best-preserved CCC camps. The simple frame cottages and barracks are still used to house Denver Parks and Recreation employees working at nearby Red Rocks Amphitheater, as well as a small CCC museum.

JF41 Tiny Town

1915, George Turner. 10 miles west of Morrison off U.S. 285 on Turkey Creek Canyon Rd.

George Turner, owner of Turner Moving and Storage in Denver, designed and built Tiny Town in a picturesque forested foothills valley. Some of its 125 buildings survived fires and floods, but not the moving of U.S. 285 in 1949. Bypassed, the town faded until 1989, when volunteers restored and reopened it. Hobbyists built and rebuilt more than one hundred of the miniature landmarks at varying scales, including replicas of the Stanley Mill outside Idaho Springs, the Arvada Flour Mill, and The Fort Restaurant in Morrison. A 15-inch-gauge train, capable of carrying small children, has also been restored for excursions through this Lilliputian village.

Conifer

Conifer (1865, 8,270 feet), originally known as Bradford Junction, was a stage stop on the Denver and South Park Toll Road. It evolved into a town renamed for the surrounding evergreen forest, now diminished by residential development and a huge shopping center. Old Bradford Junction is commemorated by a hexagonal, stone-walled, cupola-topped well (1861) at the junction of Barkley Road and Colorado 73 next to an old elliptical-roof frame barn. Another antique, Medlen School (1886), 2 miles south of U.S. 285 on South Turkey Creek Road, with hewn logs under clapboards, is a one-room school being restored by the Jefferson County Historical Society.

JF42 Coney Island

1966, Lloyd Williams and Marcus R. Shannon. 25877 Conifer Rd. (at U.S. 285)

West Hollywood's "Tail O' the Pup" has a companion in Colorado's most delicious example of roadside architecture: a 14-ton hot dog measuring, from wiener tip to wiener tip, 42 feet, in a 34-foot bun. The prefabricated diner, originally located at 4190 West Colfax Avenue and Raleigh Street in Denver, sits on a concrete base with a wood frame and stucco facade. Stainless steel interior fixtures were custom made to fit inside the structure. The hot dog is complete with bright yellow mustard and green relish that pick up autumn aspen and the evergreen trees on surrounding mountainsides.

Designer Marcus R. Shannon patented

this design (April 12, 1966, #204,372) for what he and partners hoped would be the Boardwalk Coney Islands, Inc., chain of sixteen such dogs in Denver. Plans fizzled. Beverly and Jan Slager purchased the hot dog in 1970 and moved it here, where it thrives in near-original condition.

JF43 **Meyer Ranch** (Midway House)

1889. 9345 U.S. 285 (NR)

Midway between Denver and Bailey on an old toll road, this way station has evolved into an elegant Queen Anne house with multiple gables, porches, bays, and Carpenter's Gothic trim. The 1870s barn, of hand-hewn log post-and-beam construction with wooden pegs, still stands behind a super-wide garage which houses an airplane. Norman and Ethel Meyer bought this ranch in 1950 and have elegantly restored the two-and-one-half-story clapboard ranch house. Jefferson County Open Space has purchased the ranch to preserve this landmark in its current rural setting.

Genesee

JF44 **Genesee Mountain Park, Subdivision, and Office Park**

Exit 252 off I-70

The park is approached from I-70 via Genesee Overpass (1970, Frank Lunberg). The Colorado Department of Transportation engineer made this simple pillarless concrete bridge into a frame for a spectacular view of the snowcapped Continental Divide. Genesee Mountain Park (1914, Frederick Law Olmsted, Jr., and others) was the first of some forty-five Denver Mountain Parks covering about 15,000 acres in Jefferson, Clear Creek, and Douglas counties. Best known as the home of Denver's municipal buffalo herd, Genesee Park is a ponderosa-clad landscape centered on Mt. Genesee. The park is now surrounded by a well-planned residential community and a small office park and shopping center. The one-story frame Oxley Homestead House (c. 1922), at Currant Drive and Genesee Vista Road, onetime center for a turkey farm, has became the community center for one of the first and best-known master-planned mountain subdivisions. Tight covenants outlaw groomed grass, fences, and individual mailboxes, while protecting native animals and plants.

JF45 **Chief Hosa Lodge**

1918, Jacques Benedict. 27661 Genesee Dr. at exit 253 off I-70

On a south-sloping hillside in Genesee Mountain Park, Jacques Benedict's rustic mountain cabin combines timber and native stone. A steep-pitched roof with massive end chimneys of rough stone, dormers, and clipped gables top a rough, coursed-stone lodge consisting of two connected cottages with a west-facing courtyard and a rustic stone arcade. Benedict fitted the one-and-one-half-story lodge to its forested site by using tree branch gable supports, rock walls, log railings, and tree bark (now asphalt) shingles. Inside, the stone walls rise to exposed log ceiling beams in rooms warmed by three large stone fireplaces, lighted by arched stone windows, and furnished in a rustic style. This is one of the earliest and most accessible examples of Benedict's Rocky Mountain style, as he described it in *Denver Municipal Facts* (March 1919): "Hosa Lodge was always there. It lay about before one's eyes as surface rock and spruce trees growing on the very ledge upon which it stands today, as a sort of collection of waste material at hand. We simply piled up the rock in layers, leaving some openings for light. We laid felled trunks across the top and called it a lodge, and it suffices. It remains rock and red bark like its setting."

JF46 **Deaton House**

1966, Charles Deaton. On Mt. Genesee overlooking I-70

"People aren't angular. So why should they live in rectangles?" asked Charles Deaton, who calls himself a "sculptural architect." The Denver architect built this "flying saucer" or "clamshell" house as his home and studio. It is a habitable sculpture on a reinforced concrete pedestal. Precast columns support a double shell of concrete sprayed on a welded steel frame. In this elliptical, three-story, cement and glass house, the doors, windows, walls, closets, and furniture are all curved, except for a few straight lines in the kitchen. The 3,000-square-foot house, built for $100,000, starred in the Woody Allen movie *Sleeper.*

Evergreen

Evergreen (1876, 7,040 feet) is named for its forests of large and abundant spruce, fir, and ponderosa pine. Originally logging attracted settlers, who operated a half-dozen sawmills along Upper Bear Creek. Governor John Evans and other prominent Denverites built rustic summer homes in the area. Tourism began to boom after 1919, when Denver Mountain Parks bought the 420-acre Dedisse Ranch on Bear Creek. Denver built Evergreen Dam (1927) to create Evergreen Lake as the centerpiece of a mountain park noted for fishing and ice skating. Since World War II, Evergreen has boomed as a year-round home for many who work downhill in Denver. Still unincorporated, it is now a city of some 16,000.

Notable structures vary from Buffalo Park School (1877), a restored one-room, hewn log school now on the campus of Wilmot Elementary School, at 5124 South Hatch Drive, to multimillion-dollar mountain estates. The Fillius Park Picnic Shelter (1918, Jacques Benedict) (NR), on Colorado 74, a massive stone structure with open wicker-work below the log roof and a stone fireplace, exemplifies Benedict's Rocky Mountain style. The lovely drive along Upper Bear Creek Road west of Evergreen winds through a fine collection of rustic mountain mansions.

JF47 **Evergreen Episcopal Conference District** (Stewart Hotel)

1865. Colorado 74 (NRD)

Some twenty-two rustic structures make up this summer retreat center and church music school. Robert Stewart converted a gable-roofed frame bunkhouse for sawmill laborers into a hotel for vacationers by adding two wings and dormers. The vertical slab siding, with an inlaid cross, was added in 1897 when builder John (Jock) Spence (see

JF51) remodeled the building to accommodate the Mission of the Transfiguration (1899). Spence also added the 35-foot-high bell tower (1911) of large, unfinished pine logs topped by a Celtic cross which originally stood on the Church of the Holy Redeemer in New York City. The lovely little stone library (1921) on the campus became Evergreen's first public library. Stewart's Hotel was converted to a performing arts center for the Evergreen Players and the Jefferson Philharmonic.

JF48 **Jefferson County Public Library**

1993, G. Cabell Childress. 5000 Colorado 74

Cabell Childress, a Denver architect known for his fine drafting skills, designed this one-story library as a modern variation on mountain architecture. The building displaced some large old spruce trees, the old Evergreen School (1922), and Evergreen High School (1948, S. Arthur Axtens). Childress used burnt orange brick with metal and gray slate for the roof. Two tall chimneys for working fireplaces, four gabled skylights, and a circular corner tower under a conical roof are the defining elements. The porte-cochère under a cross gable clearly marks the entrance.

JF49 **Evergreen Lake Skating and Boat House**

1993, Murata Outland Associates. East end of Upper Bear Creek Rd. and Colorado 74 at west end of Evergreen Lake

A contemporary version of rustic mountain architecture, this community center and skating and boating house is built of peeled logs, with prominent dormer windows in the gabled roof. A glass pavilion and open decks overhang the lakefront. The stone-clad cement base, wrought iron tree branch door handle, wrought iron chandeliers, raw wood interior, and massive fireplace make this a fine modern edition of the area's rustic style. The $1 million, 5,000-square-foot structure was prefabricated in Montana, where logs were cataloged by size and position and then trucked to Evergreen for assembly. Boardwalks extend out over the adjacent wetlands. Although elegant and of indigenous materials, this grand new facility seems less appropriate than the log Warming House (1934, CCC), so carefully and unobtrusively snuggled into the south shoreline.

JF50 **Keys on the Green Restaurant and Evergreen Golf Club**

1925, Jacques Benedict. 29614 Upper Bear Creek Rd.

This peeled log octagon is wrapped around a massive central circular stone fireplace. The dovetailed, notched, horizontal logs support a hogan-like conical log roof. Interior walls are the same massive logs. Light fixtures are made of gnarled tree branches hung from alternate ceiling bays between dormers. The wood flooring is laid diagonally to emphasize the octagonal shape. Despite many unfortunate additions, Jacques Benedict's original design for this clubhouse is still discernible and appealing.

JF51 **Hiwan Homestead Museum**

1884–1914, John (Jock) Spence. 4208 S. Timbervale (NR)

One of Colorado's prized mountain vernacular dwellings, this peeled log house with tall chimneys and octagonal two-story towers is the best surviving work of Evergreen's master builder, the Scottish carpenter Jock Spence. As ownership changed, Spence added on various specialized rooms with built-in bookcases, hutches, and a staircase of quarter logs. The last of the seventeen rooms was an octagonal tower for the study and private chapel of Winfred Douglas, an Episcopal priest who did much to promote rustic and Native American arts and crafts. The most striking room, the chapel, has a

vaulted and beamed ceiling, hand-hewn logs, and much detailed workmanship by Spence. The builder's trademark, a carved stairstep design, can be found more than two hundred times throughout the complex. Eyebrow dormers, diamond-paned windows, log decks with hand-carved owls, and seventeen fireplaces add to the ambiance. In 1975 Jefferson County rescued the house from demolition by the developer of the surrounding Hiwan subdivision and opened it as a museum.

JF52 **Everhardt-Herzman Ranch**

1861. 1994, restoration, Edward D. White, Jr. 6309 Lone Peak Dr., 4.5 miles southeast of Evergreen Lake (NR)

In the middle of an open meadow stands one of the oldest ranch houses in Colorado. Johnny Everhardt, a logger, built the hewn log cabin with simple notched corners cut flush to accommodate clapboarding which was never applied. Chinking between logs is augmented on the interior walls by the use of ponderosa saplings. The double-crib horse barn and hayloft are 1860s buildings of closely spaced round logs with saddle-notched corners. They were joined by a common roof about 1870. Among the nine historic ranch structures are a hand-dug, stone-lined well; a bunkhouse; a log turkey shed; a root cellar foundation; and the ruins of an antique logging truck. Sometime after Everhardt filed a claim on the site in 1872, he sold the cabin to Charles and Matilda Herzman. The ranch remained in the Herzman family for almost a century. Owners John and Dorothy Hall began restoration in the early 1990s along lines suggested by

Denver preservationist and architect Edward White.

JF53 Bells of Granite Glen Museum

1920, Arthur H. Jones. 30213 Upper Bear Creek Rd.

The Jones family lived in tents on the site while this large, three-story house of log and local granite was being constructed. Winston Jones, whose father designed this mountain mansion, began collecting bells in 1925 and now has some 5,000, including school bells, locomotive bells, hotel desk bells, mine warning bells, and Molly Brown's Chinese dinner gong. Bells filled the house and overflowed into the grounds, inspiring the Joneses to open their house as a museum in 1957.

JF54 Mayo House

1920, Jacques Benedict. 32743 Upper Bear Creek Rd. (north side behind large wrought iron gate reading "Rosedale")

Jacques Benedict designed this house to look like a medieval monastery, complete with an arcaded cloister, steep-pitched front gable, and octagonal Gothic Revival tower. Uncoursed native rhyolite and log half-timbering characterize the rough-hewn exterior of a sophisticated design. This fanciful mountain home merited publication in *The Western Architect*. Descendants of the original owner, Paul T. Mayo, still reside here.

JF55 Davenport House

1987, E. Fay Jones. 285 Potato Patch Circle, off Upper Bear Creek Rd.

Architectural illustrator Lawrence Davenport asked one of Frank Lloyd Wright's best-known disciples to design a house centered on a studio and set on a granite outcropping. Jones responded with a compact design with steep-pitched roof planes to shed snow and repeat the bold angles of the surrounding terrain. Amid spruce and aspen, the roof rises sharply from almost ground level to twin peaks fifty feet tall. The east entry and west porch floors are similar jutting points of stone protected by overhanging tall gables. Wooden balconies penetrate the glass end walls, visually linking the interior and the outside. Inside, the granite-

paved entry descends a short flight of broad stairs to the living and dining room and bedrooms. The second-floor studio is open to the living room below, revealing the dynamic roof structure with high clerestories. The 48-foot rise of the chimney above the fireplace and the multilevel profile of the balusters reinforce the vertical rush.

JF56 Greystone Manor

1916, Maurice Biscoe. 34001 Upper Bear Creek Rd.

Beautiful, red-haired Genevieve Chandler Phipps, following her sensational divorce from U.S. Senator Lawrence Phipps, asked Maurice Biscoe, a Denver architect, to design this Adirondack-style retreat with the help of craftsman Jock Spence. The 10,000-square-foot main house has walls of lichen-covered rough stone block in random courses. It features skylights, a ballroom, spiral staircases, and diamond-paned leaded glass windows. A 3,013-square-foot guest house and a carriage house, now with an office wing, are among the six outbuildings. The estate, in its prime, had a stable, creamery, and blacksmith's shop on more than 1,200 acres. After stints as Elmer Wilfley's cattle ranch and as Colonel William R. Sandifer's dude ranch, it is again a private estate overlooking Bear Creek.

JF57 Jefferson County Outdoor Laboratory (Dodge Ranch)

1907, Jock Spence. 201 Evans Ranch Rd., off Upper Bear Creek Rd. (NR)

Originally part of the Evans Ranch (JF58), the Dodge Ranch grounds include the original homestead cabin, a 1907 guest house, a root cellar, and a carriage house. During the 1940s the Dodge family converted this to a dude ranch, which has since become the school district's outdoor laboratory.

JF58 Evans Ranch

1870s. Upper Bear Creek Rd. (NR)

At the upper end of Upper Bear Creek Road, in Clear Creek County but accessible only from Jefferson County, this is one of the county's oldest and most historic ranches. One of the smallest buildings is the most notable: the Anne Evans Cabin (1910,

Jock Spence; 1924, Merrill H. and Burnham F. Hoyt; 1992, Long Hoeft Architects) (NR).

Anne Evans, daughter of Governor John Evans and a philanthropist who contributed much to preserving regional art and architecture, had the cabin built and used it until her death. Originally a simple, gable-roof structure with walls of flush upright logs splined together, it has been enlarged and expanded over the years and now has screened porches. In their 1924 major reconstruction and expansion, brothers Merrill and Burnham Hoyt installed artist Josephine Hurlburt's wooden sculptures of abstract eagles in the east and west gable ends. Once a summer house, it is now the mountain home of Jan and Frederick Mayer. Kathy Hoeft and Gary Long, Denver preservation architects, reconstructed the structure in 1992, replacing the original primitive stone roof with slate. Published in *House Beautiful, American Home,* and *Architectural Record* as a model mountain summer house, it incorporates not only the eagle sculptures but an overmantel mural by Allen True. Bedrooms are on an upper level, and the living room, dining room, and kitchen are below. A tunnel-like entry of upright logs at the upper level leads to a grand wooden staircase that descends to the lower-level public areas. Perched on a ridge, it uses natural stone and vegetation as landscaping.

Pine

Pine (1882, 6,770 feet) once housed lumbermen but is now a mountain resort. Hospitable landmarks are the Bucksnort Saloon off Elk Creek Road in nearby Sphinx Park, a small log cabin with numerous additions, including outdoor decks and a satellite dish, and Meadow Creek Bed and Breakfast (1929), 13438 U.S. 285. The latter is a large, two-story rustic stone house on 35-acre grounds adorned by two barns, a smokehouse, and the original 1916 cabin.

JF59 **Pine Valley Ranch**

1927, Jacques Benedict. Elk Creek Rd.

On one of his firm's ice farms, Denver Ice Company president William A. Baehr built this $1.5 million lodge in a style that archi-

tect Jacques Benedict called Colorado Alpine. Using native stone and spruce, an army of sixty men supposedly took only ninety days to construct the twenty-seven-room lodge, complete with wrought iron fixtures, hand-etched log paneling, log vergeboards, railings, and balconies. Two octagonal roof towers, tall stone chimneys, and multiple steep-pitched gables enliven the long, irregular front facade. Baehr had an observatory built in 1937 some 200 feet above the main lodge. After the Baehr family sold the ranch in 1956, it became a private fishing lodge and conference center. The Jefferson County Open Space Program bought the 820-acre ranch in 1986 to convert it to a public park.

Buffalo Creek

The town of Buffalo Creek (1878, 6,750 feet) was established along the Denver, South Park & Pacific Railroad, whose grade and stone trestle and bridge foundations are still evident. The firm of Serrie and Geddes, leading early-day stonemasons and contractors in Denver, opened a large granite quarry here. They produced stone cemetery markers and building stone used for, among many other landmark structures, Cheesman Dam (see Douglas County).

JF60 **The Blue Jay Inn**

1880. Jefferson County 126 and S. Wellington Rd. (NR)

Innkeeper Joseph Bailey moved two, two-story log hotels together to form a T-shaped boardinghouse for lumbermen. John J. Jerome bought the inn around 1900 and, perhaps with the help of Denver architect Frederick J. Sterner, converted it to a resort. They added the clapboard siding and full-length, shingled, wraparound veranda. In 1907 the Girls Friendly Society bought it as a summer vacation retreat. Since 1948 Katherine Ramus has operated the inn, which is heated only by a double fireplace, as a summer resort.

JF61 Green Mercantile

1898. 17706 Jefferson County 96 (NR)

The original store and its large sign, "J. W. Green Dealer in Everything," burned in 1898 along with many other wooden buildings in this tiny lumber and resort hamlet. Green, a native of Virginia, rebuilt the store in 1898 with chunks of granite from the nearby Serrie and Geddes Quarry. The huge blocks were hoisted into place by a team of mules, a jim pole, and six strong men. The two-story, rock-faced stone building with walls two feet thick shows few changes. Inside, many original fixtures remain, as does the 14-foot-high pressed metal ceiling and the family of the original owner, represented behind the counter by J. W. Green's grandson, Donald. The store has been the community center, post office, polling place, dance hall, and, until the Colorado & Southern abandoned the line in 1938, ticket office for the narrow-gauge railroad.

Arvada

Arvada (1871, 5,337 feet), with its own large performing arts complex and a rejuvenated downtown, is one of Denver's more progressive suburbs. Long an agricultural town of several hundred, it became one of the county's fastest-growing communities after World War II. With a population of more than 90,000, Arvada is now Colorado's sixth largest city. Despite its transformation, Arvada retains a sense of identity and community pride not always found in suburban areas. This is reflected in the town's renewed commercial core, its cultural facilities, and its tidy residential neighborhoods.

JF62 Arvada Flour Mill Museum

1925, Eugene Benjamin. 5580 Wadsworth Blvd. (Colorado 121) (NR)

The 30-foot-tall wooden structure was built to receive and process wheat, then package, store, and distribute the flour marketed as Arva-Pride. Corrugated metal siding and roofing has helped this three-story, gambrel-roofed antique survive. In 1980, three decades after the mill closed, the Arvada His-

torical Society restored and reopened it as a museum.

JF63 The Festival Playhouse (Clear Creek Valley Grange Hall)

1876. 5665 Olde Wadsworth Blvd.

Local stone from F. Dusing's quarry and lumber from a Turkey Creek mill were used for this small, front-gabled hall. One of the oldest grange halls in the country, it has been moved, stuccoed, decked, and converted to a theater.

JF64 Arvada Tavern

1910, John E. Borba, builder. 5707 Wadsworth Blvd.

A former blacksmith shop turned neighborhood bar with a venerable shuffleboard table, this small, two-story gray brick building is full of old-timers and folklore. Following a typical pattern, the blacksmith shop evolved into an auto repair garage during the 1920s. After the repeal of Prohibition in 1933, when it became a tavern, the outdoor stairs were moved indoors and the chimney was removed.

JF65 Arvada Water Tower

1910. Allison St. and Reno Dr.

A metal tank atop steel beams with cross bracing, this is the town's most conspicuous landmark. Abandoned in 1975, it was painted with "Olde Town Arvada" to advertise downtown's renaissance.

JF66 Arvada Center for the Arts and Humanities

1976, Seracuse Lawler with Perkins and Will. 6901 Wadsworth Blvd.

This arts complex opened with a 2,000-seat amphitheater, a 500-seat theater, and generous gallery, studio, meeting, and exhibition space. Exhibits include the restored walls of an 1864 hewn log cabin. Set in a large city park on a south-facing slope, the asymmetrical, Postmodern building had plenty of room to expand, which it did in 1992. An enlarged amphitheater features a work by Clarice Dreyer, a thicket of aspen branches in cast aluminum attached to sky-blue walls.

The $10 million 1992 expansion also added a sculptural bird sanctuary by Dreyer composed of birdhouses and birdbaths decorated with flowers, foliage, and tree branches. Other public art added in 1992 includes Vito Acconci's $84,000 *Ribbon Wall,* an earth sculpture snaking through the new addition, and a five-acre environmental art park.

JF67 Shrine of St. Anne Catholic Church

1920, Harry James Manning. 7555 Grant Place (at Wadsworth Blvd.)

Inspired by the Shrine of Ste.-Anne-de-Beaupré in Quebec, this beige brick church brings a sophisticated Lombard design, colorful terracotta trim, and a landmark bell tower to Arvada. Inside are the wrist bone of St. Anne and rose-colored windows that shed dim, blood-red light under a barrel-vaulted ceiling.

JF67 Shrine of St. Anne Catholic Church

Boulder County (BL)

The discovery of gold in Boulder Creek and its tributaries led to the creation in 1861 of a county stretching from the eastern high plains to 14,256-foot Longs Peak and the Continental Divide. Mining, agriculture, and the University of Colorado provided the economic base, now bolstered by expanding scientific, commercial, and manufacturing enterprises. Roosevelt National Forest, Indian Peaks Wilderness, and Rocky Mountain National Park, all located in the mountainous western half of the county, make tourism another important part of the economy.

Boulder County is named for the rocky creek that flows from the Continental Divide through mining towns to the county seat of the same name. The city of Boulder, the county's oldest and largest community, has set a national example in growth management. Boulder's controls, however, have merely diverted growth to the surrounding communities of Louisville, Longmont, Lafayette, and Broomfield. While Boulder's population has remained fairly steady, the county grew from 131,889 in 1970 to 225,329 in 1990.

County builders have used pink sandstone from quarries around the town of Lyons. This gorgeous stone, often set in sun-catching rimrock and hogbacks, is a remnant of the sandy beaches of the great inland sea now replaced by the prairie ocean.

Boulder

The county seat (1859, 5,363 feet) is insulated by greenbelts from the suburban sprawl of metropolitan Denver. Boulder's ongoing debate over building limits began early, with the original, 1859 town plat. Town founders staked out a community stretching two miles along Boulder Creek. Instead of the standard 25-by-125-foot lots, lots measuring 50 by 140 feet were offered to buyers at $1,000 each.

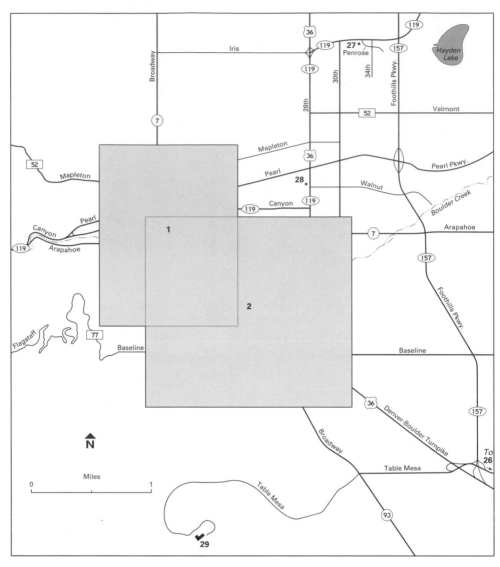

Boulder, overview (including BL27–BL29)

Amos Bixby, a booster and the editor of *The Boulder Valley News,* complained that this town plat was the work of those who wanted "to make a 'big thing' for themselves." Bixby favored "giving away alternate lots to those who would build on them, or doing most anything to attract population and capital. Unfortunately," he complained, "the high-priced party prevailed, but the lots were not taken at $1,000 each," thus crushing "the hope and reasonable expectation . . . to have centered here the men of money and enterprise and thus to have made Boulder what Denver afterward became, the leading town of the territory."

Ultimately Boulder is indebted to English city planner Ebenezer Howard, author of *Garden Cities of To-morrow* (1898). Howard, shocked at London's cancerous growth, argued that communities should limit their

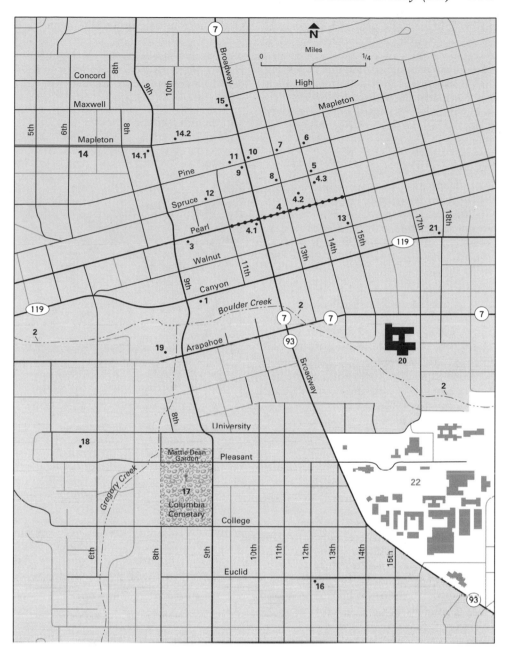

Inset 1. Downtown area (BL1–BL21)

growth and decide on an optimum size. Growth could be curbed through communal ownership of a surrounding "greenbelt." To implement such a plan, Boulder began acquiring the state's earliest mountain park system in 1898, and later augmented it with more acreage, including farm and ranch lands on the plains.

The town hired Frederick Law Olmsted, Jr., America's premier landscape architect, to provide a master plan, *The Improvement of Boulder* (1910), and pursued Olmsted's suggestions for a park system, to include a floodplain park along Boulder Creek and an "urban forest" in the foothills. One city park is named for Olmsted. Another, Flagstaff, displays fine Civilian Conservation Corps craftsmanship in its roadway, picnic facilities, and outdoor arena. The Flatirons, massive, tilted stone slabs that have become Boulder's emblem, are also preserved as a mountain park.

The town grew slowly but steadily by balancing mining and agricultural interests and by donating land for the University of Colorado, founded in 1876. Seventh Day Adventists chose Boulder as the site of their third "sanatarium" during the 1910s, following the original in Battle Creek, Michigan, and a second in St. Helena, California. These health resorts had their own dairy farms, food factories, and bakeries. Not only the infirm but people wishing to maintain their health were welcomed for treatment and education. This sanatarium, at the base of Mt. Sanitas, became the Boulder Memorial Hospital in 1961.

Expansion of the University of Colorado's scientific research programs after World War II helped to attract large plants such as IBM, Ball Aerospace, the National Bureau of Standards, the Rocky Flats Nuclear Weapons Plant, and the National Center for Atmospheric Research. A giant U.S. West Advanced Technologies Research Center and other federal and private industries continue to seek out Boulder, giving the city a steady, prosperous job base. The post–World War II population of 12,000 has increased to some 84,000 today, not including most of 25,000 students at the University of Colorado.

At 5,354 feet, Boulder has imagined itself closer to heaven than the rest of metropolitan Denver. Not only in careful planning, but also in emphasizing parks and historic preservation, Boulder pursues a higher quality of life. One result is a number of striking public, commercial, and residential buildings, often designed with open space, the city's solar energy ordinance, and a view of the surrounding greenbelts in mind. A handful of notable local architects, including Charles Haertling, James M. Hunter, and Hobart Wagener, have contributed to Boulder's rich contemporary architecture.

BL01 Boulder Public Library

1961, James M. Hunter Associates. 1992 addition, Midyette-Seieroe-Hartvonft and Associates. 1000 Canyon Blvd.

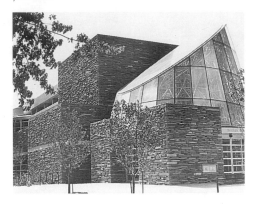

Responding to its floodplain site, the original public library building spans Boulder Creek and offers glass-walled views of creek and greenway. The 53,000-square-foot 1992 addition along Arapahoe consists of a three-story sandstone cube fronted by a truncated, skewed glass cone over the doors. The dramatic entry previews the interior, including a children's library with an outdoor terrace. Lyons sandstone, laid in rough vertical ashlar courses, helps to unify the two strong, glassy contemporary designs, as does the glass-walled Boulder Creek bridge, which houses the library shop and coffee bar. Aquariums inside the library allow a closer look at some of the aquatic life in Boulder Creek.

BL02 Boulder Creek Greenway

1970S. Along Boulder Creek as it flows through the city

A paved greenway links the library and creekside parks, such as the Boulder Creek Fish Observatory (c. 1980), 28th and Arapahoe, which has viewing portholes built into a cement wall below creek level. Central Park, at the southeast corner of Broadway and Canyon Boulevard, contains the old number 30 locomotive (1898) of Boulder's narrow-gauge line, the "Switzerland Trail," which served mountain towns west of the city from 1898 to 1919.

BL03 National Guard Armory

1898, George Hyder. 934 Pearl St.

Smooth and rough pink sandstone trims this fancy, two-story brick edifice posing as a Romanesque fortress. A grand, stepped-arch entry in a protruding central bay is repeated by second-story arches amid elaborate brick courses, corbeled brick, and a crenelated parapet. Hardwood floors used for drills also made it ideal for weekly dances and for basketball games. At one time it was converted to a laundry and, more recently, to offices.

BL04 Pearl Street Pedestrian Mall

1977, Sasaki, Walker, Dawson and DeMay with Everett Zeigel Architecture. Pearl St. between 11th and 15th sts.

In the 1970s Boulder closed a section of its major retail street to motor vehicles and landscaped it with plants, sculpture, and pedestrian amenities. The mall attracts shoppers, tourists, business people, students, unofficial performing artists, sidewalk vendors, and people watchers. At 646 Pearl, Frenchman Anthony Arnett built Arnett House (1877), the town's finest early Queen Anne Style house, with a fanciful, three-story mansard tower, and the demolished Arnett Hotel (1875), 1025 Pearl. Also of note are the venerable Macky Building (1860), 1242 Pearl, and the Citizens National Bank (1899; 1976, restoration and addition, Everett Zeigel Architecture), 1426 Pearl, an Italian Renaissance Revival gem with fluted columns on an exuberant facade.

BL04.1 Boettcher Hardware

1878. 1142–1148 Pearl St. Mall

Charles Boettcher, who built Colorado's largest and most diversified industrial empire, started out with this corner store and the slogan "Hardware, Hard Goods and Hard Cash." Boettcher, a German immigrant, lived at 925 Pearl Street. After he

moved on to Leadville and then Denver, the upper floor of his hardware store was converted to a theater, a frivolity on which he would have frowned.

BL04.2 Boulder County Courthouse

1933, Glen H. Huntington. 1300 Pearl St. Mall

This Art Deco replacement for an Italianate courthouse destroyed in 1932 by fire was considered shockingly ultramodern when built. The stepped-back building, designed by the son of Denver architect Glen Wood Huntington, uses sandstone blocks taken from bridge abutments of the dismantled Switzerland Trail railroad. The blocks were trucked to the site, then sized and cut on the courthouse lawn. International Style wings (1962, Hobart Wagener) now enclose a small courtyard on the north. Rather than make further additions, the county moved expanding offices into the Elks Lodge (1904), a two-story brick building with garland frieze and stone trim at 2045 13th Street.

BL04.3 Boulder Theater

1936, Robert Otto Roller. 2032 14th St. Mall

Robert Roller, with his brother Carl, formed a Kansas City architecture firm that designed over ninety theaters in Missouri, Kansas, Oklahoma, and Texas, as well as now-demolished movie palaces in Pueblo and Colorado Springs. Their Art Deco theater for Boulder has a stucco facade and upper-level vertical panels of polychrome terra-cotta. Yellow and white fans above blue and green bases rise from the protruding marquee, which is trimmed in bands of neon. The theater incorporates brick from the demolished Curran Opera House (1906), which stood on the site. The interior retains some Art Deco murals of desert plants in pastel shades, under walls painted with southwestern designs. Upstairs, the balcony has a Deco mahogany bar put into use when this movie house, closed in 1982, reopened as a cabaret with live concerts in 1988.

BL05 First Methodist Church

1891, Harlan Thomas. 1914, addition. 1960, sanctuary, Hobart Wagener. 1401 Spruce Ave. (northeast corner of 14th St.)

Boulder's First Methodist congregation, established in 1859, built this Romanesque Revival church for $22,500. The walls, of rough ashlar sandstone from the Green Mountain Quarry, have matching extruded mortar joints and contrasting buff limestone trim. Intricate stone carving is best seen in the decorative buttresses at the street corner entrances of the three-story tower. A north wing was added in 1914, but the most interesting expansion came in 1960, when Hobart Wagener designed a massive new sanctuary on the east. Six repeating gables faced in screens of precast concrete and glass block echo the pitch of the original roof. New stone panels match the old walls and

spring in low arches at street level to light the basement.

BL06 St. John's Episcopal Church

1902–1905, Henry M. Congdon and Son. 1965, chapel, Hobart Wagener. 1986, parish hall, James Phelps Toohey. 1419 Pine St. (northeast corner of 14th St.)

A New York firm produced this classic English-influenced Gothic Revival design, executed in rough-cut ashlar blocks of local sandstone, with a prominent, crenelated corner tower finally finished in 1921. Additions to the east borrow the original steep roof pitches, shake shingles, and even the stonework of Wagener's chapel. Both new and old interiors have Edgar Britton's stained glass windows.

BL07 Victoria Bed and Breakfast (Dwight-Nicholson House)

c. 1875. 1889–1895, addition, Balcolm and Rice. 1305 Pine St.

Carpenter Jason L. Dwight is thought to have built the original small frame house as well as the stone carriage house. An elaborate 1890s renovation greatly enlarged the house and dressed it in Colonial Revival guise for Colonel John H. Nicholson. Improvements included a new entrance in a central enclosed and pedimented bay of the full-width porch, fronted by a Palladian window. Carved wood trim, roof cresting, and a recessed second-story patio fronted by arches further distinguish this resplendent house, reborn as a bed and breakfast.

BL08 Hotel Boulderado

1906, William Redding and Son. 1989, addition, James Reich Magee. 2115 13th St. (northwest corner of Spruce Ave.)

When no private parties expressed interest in building downtown lodging, a spirited public subscription drive bankrolled this Mission Revival hotel, which was city-owned until 1940. Five-story red brick walls rise to distinctive central curvilinear parapets flanked by square corner towers. After repeal of local prohibition ordinances in 1967, the city's first bar, the Catacombs, opened in the hotel basement in 1969. Under a stained glass barrel vault, a mezzanine with a cherry wood railing overlooks the lobby. An ornate, five-story cherry staircase provides fine viewing of the atrium's Craftsman interior, complete with the original desk, safe, Otis elevator, and fountain for Arapahoe Glacier water. Filling out the block, a $4.2 million north wing addition (1989) uses a contemporary but sympathetic design with similar broad eaves, red brick skin, and sandstone trim.

BL09 **First Congregational Church**

1906–1908, Thomas MacLaren and T. D. Hetherington. 1128 Pine Ave. (southwest corner of Broadway)

In a district of fine old churches, this English-inspired Gothic Revival design, like St. John's Episcopal church a block east, is clad in quarry-face sandstone. A square corner tower with a crenelated parapet soars above the red tile roof, dominating the irregular massing.

BL10 **Trinity English Lutheran Church**

1929, Margaret Read. 1966, sanctuary, and 1989, additions, Robert Sass. 2200 Broadway, northeast corner of Pine Ave.

A modest Gothic Revival church of uncoursed, narrow blocks of red sandstone, Trinity English Lutheran has an expansive north addition (1989) that is sympathetic to the original and yet makes a contemporary statement. Along the west street front, the original parapeted gable end is repeated by the 1980s addition to the north and a gabled face dormer in the crossing roofline above a panel of stained glass. The sanctuary (1966, Robert Saas) is topped by a futuristic, freeform spire with narrow, vertical bands of stained glass.

BL11 **Carnegie Library**

1906, Thomas MacLaren. 1125 Pine St. (NR)

As the "Athens of the Rockies," Boulder relished the Greek Revival style of its first grand library. The restored oak ceiling beams and wainscot, marble fireplace, and pine floors shine once again. After the opening of the new main library (BL01), this became the

BL11 Carnegie Library

local history branch, with a collection that includes a wealth of material on Boulder buildings.

BL12 **Squires-Tourtellot House**

1865. 1019 Spruce St. (NR)

Believed to be the oldest residence in Boulder, this two and one half-story, front-gabled, New England–type farmhouse is constructed of local fieldstone. Frederick A. Squires, first president of the Boulder City Town Company, lived here with his family and that of his brother-in-law, Jonathan A. Tourtellot. The Tourtellot and Squires Addition, roughly from 8th to 11th between Pearl and Pine, was platted in 1870. The house, with minimal exterior changes, is now offices.

BL13 **Main Post Office**

1910, James Knox Taylor, OSA, and Benjamin C. Viney. 1932–1933, 1959, additions. 1905 15th St. (northwest corner of Walnut St.) (NR)

The Office of the Supervising Architect in Washington worked with local architects such as Benjamin Viney. With hooded dormers and a metal hipped roof, the tan brick post office is defined by recessed two-story panels separated by pilasters, and Renaissance Revival and classical detailing in terracotta and limestone. The additions have flat roofs, with solar panels added in 1980.

As with other post offices, the style shows the aesthetic conservatism characteristic of government buildings. The design is consistent with the classicism preferred by James

Knox Taylor, expectedly symmetrical, sophisticated, and refined in the federal image. The lobby's marble wainscoting reflects comparatively generous pre-1929 budgets for federal buildings.

BL14 Mapleton Avenue Historic Residential District

Broadway to 4th St. between Maxwell and Spruce sts.

The Mapleton Avenue district lines a hilltop parkway with a landscaped median of grass, shrubs, and trees. Two post-1890 residences, the Culbertson House and Ivycrest, have mistakenly been attributed to H. H. Richardson even though he died in 1886 and no Boulder sites are listed in Jeffrey K. Ochsner's *H. H. Richardson: Complete Architectural Works* (1982). The district's cornerstone is Mapleton Elementary School (BL14.1; 1888), southwest corner of Mapleton Avenue and 9th Street, made of uncoursed rough sandstone block with red grapevine mortar joints. An octagonal shingled cupola tops the entrance tower. The Culbertson House (BL14.2; 1900), 1001 Mapleton Avenue (northwest corner of Broadway), was built by Charles Culbertson, general manager of the Colorado & Northwestern Railway (later the Denver, Boulder & Western Railroad). The house is a red brick two-and-one-half-story stretched foursquare with paired dormers in the hipped roof. The eaves are dramatically extended and finished in tongue-in-groove beaded boards. Ivycrest, formerly Prospect Heights (1890), 1040 Mapleton Avenue, a two-and-one-half-story Shingle Style country house, curves along the brow of a hill overlooking downtown. The first level, of rough sandstone, is topped by banded courses of painted wood shingle and multiple gable roofs. Two full-height polygonal bays distinguish the west facade. A low retaining wall along the sidewalk is topped by an ornamental iron fence, and a broad, two-story porch on the east affords a spot to enjoy the view.

BL15 Boulder Valley Eye Center

c. 1971, Charles A. Haertling. 2401 Broadway (northwest corner of Maxwell Ave.)

Architectural Forum marveled at this optometrists' office, bizarrely shaped in white sprayed concrete, with odd exterior projections along Broadway that form enclosures for eye examination charts. Charles Haertling (1928–1984) used foamed concrete injected into formwork and then sprayed with gunite. Of his bulbous buildings, he declared, "There's more excitement and movement in curves than in straight lines."

BL16 Boulder Museum of History (Harbeck House)

1899. 1206 Euclid Ave. (southeast corner of 12th St.)

This two-story dwelling of regular, square-cut, quarry-face ashlar sandstone sits behind the fine stone wall of its wraparound porch on a large corner lot. Pairs of Tuscan columns supporting the balconied and balustraded porch suggest foursquare houses, as do the symmetrical attic dormers. Four tall chimneys of the same stone used for the skin and the trim soar above a hipped roof with hipped dormers. Inside are a Tiffany stained glass window, an Italian tile fireplace, and collections and exhibits on Boulder's history.

BL17 Columbia Cemetery

1870. 8th to 9th sts. between Pleasant and College sts.

Moss rock entry gates guard this historic cemetery, now a park. The open irrigation ditch is still in use. The Mattie Dean Garden, made up of six lots across the street from the north side of the cemetery kept as a wooded wild garden, was left to the city as open space on the owner's death in 1981. Tom Horn, the notorious bounty hunter, is buried here.

BL18 Goss House

1988, Anthony Pellecchia. 543 Pleasant St.

Anthony Pellecchia, a Philadelphia-trained protégé of Louis I. Kahn, started this project as a renovation of an 1880s mansard-roofed house. In the end he tore down the old house to build a Postmodern replacement "in the spirit of the original." A two-story bay with horizontal bracing overlooks a sunken terrace garden.

BL19 Highland School

1891, Varian and Sterner. 1923, addition. 885 Arapahoe Ave. (NR)

Highland School was enlarged in 1923 to its current H plan. A grand, ogee-arched entry surround adorns the south facade. The red brick Romanesque Revival building features round arches in gray sandstone, with the entrance inset in a central protruding bay with a pedimented dormer. A central bay to the north connects the addition, with its banded fenestration. Brick, stone, and overhanging eaves are matched in the addition, which is distinguished by different stonework in the foundation and window treatment. A first-rate restoration as a residential complex includes beautifully landscaped grounds.

BL20 Boulder High School

1938. Earl Morris, Francis W. Frewen, and Glen H. Huntington. 1604 Arapahoe Ave.

Banded windows and a heroic bas-relief sculpture over the entry distinguish this three-story Streamline Moderne building wrapping an interior courtyard. The exterior masonry is local red quartzite, laid up in an uncoursed ledgerock pattern with concrete trim. Sympathetic additions in the same Lyons sandstone and raw concrete repeat the original angles and curves. The entry panel bas-relief, *Strength and Wisdom,* by Denver sculptor Marvin Martin, barely survived removal orders from the Boulder school board, which condemned the figures in the composition as "squat, exaggerated, massive and modern."

BL21 Woodward-Baird House

1871. 1733 Canyon Blvd. (NR)

The one-and-one-half-story balloon frame of this house was later infilled with brick behind vertical board-and-batten siding. The side-gable roof has a rear shed extension, with a 6-foot-deep porch along the front facing Canyon Boulevard, once a rural road that evolved into the Switzerland Trail railroad. Since 1978 Historic Boulder has owned this relic of Boulder's mining camp days.

BL22 University of Colorado Boulder Campus

1876; many additions. From Broadway on the west to 28th St. on the east and Arapahoe Ave. on the north (NRD)

This campus sits on a hill south of town whose gentle northeastern slope allowed lawns and trees to be watered by a gravity-operated system of open irrigation ditches, still in use. Old Main was first supplemented by Victorian Cottage No. 1 (1876) on Broadway and the President's House, now the Koenig Alumni Center (1884, Ernest P. Varian), near the corner of University and Broadway. The Woodbury Arts and Sciences Building (1890, F. A. Hale), east of Old Main, was originally a men's dormitory.

The campus grew slowly and haphazardly until 1918, when Charles Z. Klauder of Philadelphia designed a master plan. He laid out the campus, with a parklike quadrangle at its center, on a Beaux-Arts site plan with a cardinal axis but departed from the Collegiate Gothic style he and his partner, Frank Miles Day, had used at Cornell, Princeton, and Wellesley. Inspired by the foothills setting, he developed a picturesque but unpretentious "Colorado style" that borrows from the Tuscan hill country of northern Italy: an innovative combination of robust stone walls, arcades, towers, and sloping roofs accented by ornate stone chimneys. His buildings are uniformly of local pink Lyons sandstone with red tile roofs. The last building on campus built from his drawings is Sewell Hall (1937; 1946 addition). Since his death in 1938, Klauder's plan has been followed or at least used as a starting point for most subsequent buildings on the campus.

Design direction was provided in the late

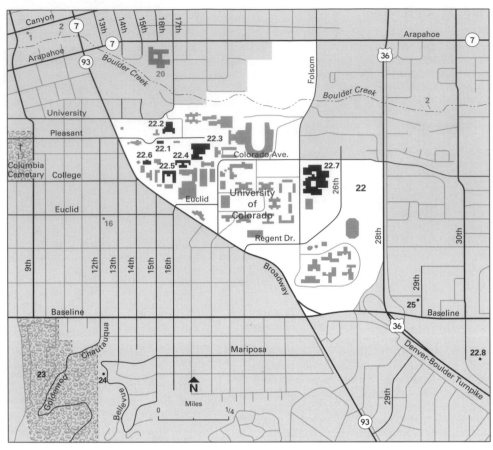

Inset 2. University area (BL22–BL25)

1950s by Hideo Sasaki, who steered large-scale growth to the south and east of the original campus. Despite many architectural departures during the tremendous expansion of recent decades, including a new research campus, CU-Boulder is probably Colorado's best example of a large, planned community in a memorably consistent style. Thomas Gaines, in his book *The Campus as a Work of Art* (1991), ranks CU-Boulder among the nation's best-designed campuses.

BL22.1 Old Main

1876, Erastus H. Dimick

An octagonal, four-story mansard tower crowns this three-story red brick Italianate hall, which initially housed the school's president, three professors, students, and janitor.

Old Main is now restored as, among other things, the Campus Heritage Center, housing a campus diorama and a collection of architectural records.

BL22.2 Macky Auditorium

1909, Gove and Walsh. 1987, restoration, Midyette-Seieroe

Crenelated corner towers surmounted by slightly taller engaged octagonal towers distinguish this red sandstone building with its churchy facade. Macky was designed by the same firm that designed the campus power plant (1910) and in a similar Gothic Revival style. It was the last of the Victorian buildings constructed before Klauder's plan was adopted by the university's board of regents in 1918.

BL22.3 Norlin Library

1939, Charles Z. Klauder

The library, at the east end of Norlin Quadrangle, was designed to be a central focus of the university, in the tradition established by Thomas Jefferson at the University of Virginia. It is named for George Norlin, CU president from 1919 to 1939.

BL22.4 Ekeley Chemical Laboratories

1898, Ernest P. Varian

The university's chemistry laboratories began as a three-story brick building to which Charles Klauder added sandstone wings in 1925. The original core was replaced with an exposed concrete and sandstone building by Johnson Hopson Associates in 1973.

BL22.5 Hellems Arts and Sciences Building

BL22.7 Engineering Sciences Center

BL22.5 Hellems Arts and Sciences Building

1921, Charles Z. Klauder

Charles Klauder's first building for the campus is composed of two symmetrical end pavilions linked by ground-floor colonnaded porticoes, augmented by long wings that frame the Mary Rippon Outdoor Theater (1937), used for CU's summer Shakespeare festival.

BL22.6 Guggenheim Geography Building
(Guggenheim Law School)

1908, James Murdoch

This gift to the university from U.S. Senator Simon Guggenheim has a Greek-inspired classical facade, echoed in its dignified, spacious interiors. Murdoch also designed a nearly identical Guggenheim Hall, built a decade later, for the University of Northern Colorado in Greeley.

BL22.7 Engineering Sciences Center

1966, William C. Muchow and Associates. Additions, Sasaki Walker Associates; Wagener and Associates; Rodney Davis; G. Cabell Childress; C. W. Fentress, J. H. Bradburn and Associates; and others. Colorado Ave. between Folsom St. and Regent Dr.

This center is among the most spectacular of the university's newer buildings. William Muchow and later architects used the traditional campus Lyons sandstone and red tile roofs to accent cement buildings. They departed from Charles Klauder's rural Italian style with soaring, shed-roofed buildings that have been characterized as Mineshaft Modern but draw inspiration from Klauder's Ketchem Engineering Building.

BL22.8 Environmental Hogan Complex

1989, Dennis Holloway. South end of 30th St.

Hidden between the golden brick towers of Williams Dormitory (1969, Hobart Wagener), Boulder's only high rise, and a pretentious new mansion for the university president lies this group of three experimental houses by CU environmental design professor Dennis Holloway and Navajo graduate students. It includes a traditional domed hogan, a hogan with a heat-collecting sunroom, and a hogan attached to what looks like a conventional solar house. The project explores the possibilities of developing new, energy-efficient housing from traditional forms. Under provisions of the 1987 Indian Housing Act, Navajo students lived in the houses and reported on their experience and on the buildings' performance.

BL23 Chautauqua Park

1898. 1981, restoration, Alan Zeigel of Everett Zeigel Architecture. 9th St. and Baseline Rd. (NR)

Of hundreds of Chautauquas established nationwide by the 1920s, this claims to be the last one active west of the Mississippi River. Founded in 1876 on Lake Chautauqua, New York, the initial religious programs came to include educational, recreational, and political themes, as the nation's first mass education and entertainment experiment spread across the country to become a cultural institution. In 1898 a group of Texas educators agreed to arrange and fund Chautauqua programs in return for Boulder's donation of 75 acres, an auditorium, a dining hall, water, and electricity. Cottages were privately owned, and profits were put back into permanent facilities.

Today's 91-acre grounds retain the small frame cottages and lodges facing inward to create a rhythmic pattern along the streets and lanes. The standardized front and side setbacks without fences or sidewalks are in marked contrast to the tight urban residential grid to the north across Baseline Road. The original accommodations consisted of striped tents on wooden platforms, later aug-

BL23 Chautauqua Park, dining hall

mented by frame cottages. The Chautauqua Community House (1918, A. E. Saunders), at the corner of Wild Rose and Morning Glory drives, is a three-story stucco hall with foundation and exterior chimney of native rubblestone. The Dining Hall (1889; 1985, OZ Architecture) is a two-story frame structure with a second-story wraparound veranda beneath pedimented gables and towers with vernacular classical details. The rustic stone entry gate and streetcar shelter at 12th Street and Baseline Road survive in skeletal form.

The auditorium (1898, Franklin E. Kidder and Eugene R. Rice; 1983 restoration, OZ Architecture) (NR) is a prefabricated paneled structure that was erected in sixty days for its opening on July 4, 1898. This polygonal frame building with four observation towers framing a pedimented front typifies Chautauqua resort architecture. The main floor exterior is sheathed in vertical board-and-batten siding with Neoclassical detail. Inside is a huge, primitive, barnlike hall under a maze of exposed rafters.

BL24 Willard House

1963, Charles A. Haertling. 125 Bellevue Dr.

Perched on the edge of a hill with a jagged mountain backdrop, this angular stucco composition has a sculptural wooden roof whose eaves tip upward like the wings of a bird. Other Haertling houses in Boulder include the Brenton House (1978), 3752 Wonderland Hill Avenue; the Clamshell House (197?), 65 Bellevue Drive; the Gill House (1974), 730 15th Street; the Jorgenson House (197?) at 780 Flagstaff Road, with white concrete cylinders supporting cantilevered rooms under a flared copper roof; the Leaneagh House (1980), 52 Boulder View Lane; the Menkick House (1969), 165 Greenrock Drive, a sod-roofed, moss rock dwelling built against a 50-foot-rock; the Knudson House (1959), 420 Christmas Tree Drive; and the Volsky House (1963), 711 Willow Brook Drive, featured in the August 5, 1966, issue of *Life* magazine.

BL25 Office Building

1960s, Hobart Wagener. 737 29th St.

This unusual three-story post-and-beam office building is cantilevered over a pond on concrete stilts. It is an unusually candid structure whose structural elements are the only ornament.

BL26 East Boulder Recreation Center

1992, Barker, Rinker, Seacat and Partners. 5660 Sioux Drive (off 55th St. between Baseline Dr. and S. Boulder Rd.)

Set in an expanse of open fields, this barn-like, Postmodern complex has a central octagonal superstructure with clerestory windows and a cupola over the aquatic center. Glass lobby walls allow visual access to the center, which has a mushroom-shaped waterfall in the children's pool, a serpentine water slide, jacuzzis, sauna, and sun deck. Wings extending from the central "water world" contain a rock climbing wall, a dance studio, craft rooms, a senior wing, and a commons.

BL27 Geological Society of America

1973, Everett Zeigel Architecture. 3300 Penrose St.

With glass offices tucked under massive eaves, this cast-in-place concrete building is strikingly handsome, partly because of detailing such as the textured aggregate finish and incorporation of geological specimens.

BL28 Last American Diner

1978, Henry Beer of Communication Arts. 1996, demolished. 1955 28th St.

Designer Henry Beer describes this former restaurant as "a truck stop made out of a truck." The stainless steel facade was made by Freuhauf Fabricators, a Denver truck manufacturer. The interior's pink and gray color scheme and extensive use of vinyl and laminate, roller-skating wait staff, bright neon signage, and asphalt landscaping made this a nostalgic salute to diners past before it closed as a restaurant in 1996.

BL29 National Center for Atmospheric Research

1967, I. M. Pei and Partners. West end of Table Mesa Dr.

I. M. Pei, the Canton-born master of Modernism educated at MIT and Harvard, designed one of Colorado's finest complexes, sited in a Boulder mountain park. Pei, who also designed major projects in downtown Denver, appreciated the spectacular natural setting on an otherwise undeveloped mesa with foothills beyond. "We found we had to return to elemental forms," he said. Studies of cliff dwellings at Mesa Verde and pueblos such as Taos led Pei to a loosely neo–Pueblo Revival structure using colors, textures, and massing borrowed from the setting. A nearby quarry yielded a distinctive reddish aggregate that was mixed with concrete for the walls. When it was bush-hammered, the aggregate fractured so as to give a stony look like that of the surrounding soil and the giant, upended stone slabs known as the Flatirons.

BL29 National Center for Atmospheric Research

Pei's design achieves simplicity of form despite a complex, seven-story arrangement of clusters of small offices linked to centralized laboratories and libraries. Exhibits include interactive displays, scale models, and simulations that allow visitors to play with the weather. Views from the spectacular site are exploited with terraces and openings at the corners of each tower cluster. The building is placed on the southeast end of the site to maximize its visibility, and the entrance, amid trees and large boulders, does not scar the topography. Visitors are welcome to tour the exhibits inside and the center's outdoor nature trails.

BL30 Walker Ranch Historic District

1869–1930, James A. Walker, builder. 7.5 miles west of Boulder via Flagstaff Rd. (Bear Canyon) (NRD)

Ruins of fourteen slab, log, hewn log, and frame buildings in what is now a Boulder County Park of 2,566 acres reflect the organization and vernacular construction typical of pioneer ranches. In 1882 James Walker patented the original 160 acres where he had long been squatting and had built a hewn log cabin (c. 1869) and livestock barn (1880). Later he built a house (1881), wagon barn (1885), turkey house (c. 1885), and, at a safe distance, a "gas house" (1914) for storing the family's first automobile. Ruins also include a sawmill, the Langridge Cyanide Mill, and Arapaho Indian sites.

BL31 Ryssby Swedish Evangelical Lutheran Church

1882, L. P. Kimmons, builder; Charles Olson, stonemason. North of Boulder approximately 5.5 miles on U.S. 36, then east on Nelson Rd. approximately 4 miles, then south on 63rd St. (NR)

On a 3-acre hilltop in open farmland sits a tiny church of random-coursed tan sandstone. It has a square narthex and smaller wooden tower protruding from the west gable end that replaced a larger stone tower destroyed by lightning in 1914. Lancet arches top all openings, creating a Gothic vernacular spirit. Swedish immigrants, who named this now-dispersed agricultural colony for their hometown, are memorialized on the gravestones behind the church.

Allenspark

Allenspark (1896, 8,520 feet), named for early homesteader Alonzo Allen, is located at the foot of Longs Peak on the eastern edge of Rocky Mountain National Park. Following a flurry of gold mining between 1903 and 1912, the town languished. Today it is primarily a tourist destination in summer, when the 600 permanent residents host several thousand guests. Of various rustic log structures, the most notable are the rambling, three-story Allenspark Lodge (c. 1935, Richard Isles) and the log slab St. James-on-the-Mount Episcopal Chapel (1925), now the Allenspark Community Church.

BL32 Bunce School

1888, J. H. Bunce and V. H. Rowley, builders. Colorado 7, 3.8 miles south of Allenspark (NR)

This school, in a wooded setting with the Continental Divide as a backdrop, is named for its builder. The broadaxe-hewn logs are square-notched at the corners and rest on stone rubble piers. Corrugated metal covers the front-gable roof, the windows have the standard schoolhouse symmetry, and the trim is simple and spare. One of two remaining log schools in Boulder County, this is a well-preserved example of the type. After the school closed in 1940, the building became a community center.

BL33 St. Catherine's Chapel at St. Malo

1934, Jacques Benedict. Colorado 7, 4.4 miles north of Allenspark

In a free Romanesque Revival style, this picturesque roadside chapel on a modified cruciform plan is built of massive boulders under steep-pitched roofs. On its rocky crag ("Upon this rock I will build my church"), which is incorporated into the structure, the chapel marks the entry road for St. Malo, a Catholic summer camp, mountain retreat, and conference center on 160 acres adjoining Rocky Mountain National Park.

Eldora

Eldora (1897, 8,700 feet), historically known as Happy Valley and Eldorado Camp, sprang up after a gold strike on Spencer Mountain. Eldora is a good example of a mining town that became a resort. Miners' cabins were converted to summer houses after the Switzerland Trail railroad arrived in 1905, and by the 1920s tourism had replaced mining as the economic base.

The Eldora Historic District centers on Eldorado Avenue, the main street, whose buildings are of log construction, as this mining camp never graduated to the masonry town stage. The Gold Miner Hotel (1897), northwest corner of 6th and Klondike, a hewn log boarding house with a clapboard front, reopened as a bed and breakfast in 1984. False fronts attached to the log commercial buildings used milled lumber from five local sawmills. Early miners' cabins, such as 601 Washington (1878), are single story, with corner-notched logs and no foundations. Later tourist cabins are distinguished primarily by porches. Newer log homes make the community a showcase for the evolution of rustic log architecture. The town has been little affected by the Eldora Mountain ski area, seven miles away and over a ridge, unique in being served by a Regional Transportation District bus line and for its night skiing.

Gold Hill

Gold Hill (1863) was born following 1859 placer and lode gold strikes on the hill for which the community was named. Profitable gold soon played out, and a forest fire, which sent the populace deep into the mines for safety, destroyed much of the original town. Tourism developed following World War I, and by the 1930s the town had become a summer resort and, more recently, a remote suburb of Boulder. It remains a log village of dirt streets at the end of a bumpy mountain road.

The original townsite contained 17 blocks of mostly 50-by-100-foot lots along Gold Run Creek. The earliest buildings are log, single story and rectangular, with gable roofs, like 210 and 240 Horsfal Street. Wood-frame construction came later, along with more sophisticated hipped roofs and stylistic embellishments such as decorative shingle and turned porch posts. The Gold Hill Historic District, including Main, Pine, College, and Horsfal streets, contains log and vernacular frame buildings, many set on stone foundations.

BL34 **Bluebird Inn** (Wentworth House)

1873, Charles Wentworth. Main St.

This two-story, hewn log miners' boarding house has gabled attic dormers and a shed-roofed front porch held up by log posts and guarded by log railings. Eugene Field stayed at the Wentworth and celebrated it in his *Little Book of Western Verse* (1889):

. . . The bar wuz long 'nd rangy, with a mirrer on the shelf,
'Nd a pistol, so that Casey, when required, could help himself;
Down underneath there wuz a row of bottled beer 'nd wine,
'Nd a kag of Burbun whiskey of the run of '59;
Upon the walls wuz pictures of hosses 'nd of girls,—
Not much on dress, perhaps, but strong on curls!

Next door is the rustic one-story Gold Hill Inn (1920s), originally the dining hall for the Bluebird Inn. It is built of round logs with overlapping saddle-notched corners and a massive river rock fireplace and exterior chimney. The quaint interior with its log walls and open-beam ceiling, its memorabilia and its mismatched chairs and tables, makes it a popular and unique restaurant.

BL35 Snowbound Mine

1900–1936. Boulder County 52 between Gold Hill and Sunset (NR)

Sunshine Canyon shelters this mine, first located in 1877 but not worked much until 1900. Of twelve historic structures, the Shaft House (1917) is the largest. Its modified T plan is built around the shaft opening, topped by a headframe of 10-inch-square beams rising 25 feet. Heavy frame walls are covered by horizontal fir planks with narrow fir strips, once tarpapered. Steep gable roofs are covered in corrugated metal panels held down by narrow wood strips along the seams. Inside are a blacksmith shop, ore assay and sorting office, and tracks to the dump. Machinery was driven by the 10-foot-wide, 23-feet-long, 70-horsepower boiler.

Hygiene

BL36 Church of the Brethren

1880. 17th Ave. (Colorado 10) (NR)

The town of Hygiene (1878, 5,090 feet) grew up around the church built by Dunkard preacher Jacob S. Flory. Flory also built a sanatarium, Hygiene House (now gone). The random-coursed native stone church with a simple, front-gable roof was built at a cost of $2,000. The plain plaster walls and hand-hewn pine floor reflect the austerity of the Dunkard sect, founded in Germany in 1708 and named for its practice of triple-immersion baptism. Although regular services were discontinued in 1907, the site continues to be used by the Northern Colorado Church of the Brethren as a community center and burying ground.

Jamestown

BL37 Jamestown Mercantile

c. 1896. Main St. (NR)

Jamestown (1867, 6,920 feet) was once called Elysian Park for its mountain setting, where galena gold ores were discovered along James Creek in 1864. Two strikes in 1875 and a third boom in 1882 produced a peak population of perhaps 1,000. An 1883 town plat attempted to bring order to a conglomeration of saloons, dance halls, parlor houses, and gambling dens, many of which were washed away by an 1884 flood. A vernacular frame store of two and one-half stories nestles into the hillside on its stone foundation. Its pedimented false front has a round-arched window centered in the gable peak. It has the prototypical recessed central entry, transomed glass display windows, and kickplates. Above the general store and post office was the Odd Fellows Hall. To the west is the 1935 town hall.

Lafayette

Lafayette (1889, 5,237 feet) was named for 1870s pioneer Lafayette Miller, whose wife, Mary, owned the land on which the town was built. Coal was discovered on the Miller farm in 1884, and Lafayette became a major coal town. Most of the mines closed by 1950, but Lafayette is now booming again as a bedroom community of Denver and Boulder.

Although little remains of the mines, individual buildings representing the mining era have been preserved in a National Register district honoring coal miners. Notable structures include the Boulder Valley Grange Hall (1900), 3400 North 95th Street; the Rocky Mountain Fuel Company Store (1901), 400 East Simpson Street; the Miller House (1889), 409 East Cleveland Street (at Michigan Avenue); and the Sonic Drive-In, 50 Waneka Parkway.

BL38 Miners' Museum (Lewis House)

c. 1890. 108 E. Simpson St. (southwest corner of Harrison St.)

This single-story, gable-roofed, L-plan house with a small south addition was originally located at the nearby Gatfield Mine. It is covered in narrow clapboard siding, dressed up by a bay window and turned porch balustrade spindles. It was moved here and placed on a Lyons sandstone foundation around 1910. William E. Lewis, a miner, bought it in 1913, and it remained in his wife's possession until her death in 1975. Since then it has been converted to a museum of coal mining history. The back yard contains an old outhouse and a much rarer sight: a decaying coal shed surrounded by a pile of clinkers.

BL39 Congregational Church

1892. 300 E. Simpson St. (southeast corner of Gough St.) (NR)

This simple white frame church sits on a base of Lyons sandstone under steep gable roofs minus the steeple, which was destroyed in 1901. The three gables with bracketed eaves on the facade shelter a shallow porch. Town founder Mary Miller provided most of the construction funds and paid the minister's salary for years. The building served as an emergency hospital during the 1918 influenza epidemic and has been the community library since 1923.

BL40 Lafayette Boarding House

1900. 600 E. Simpson St. (southeast corner of Finch St.) (NR)

Of several boarding houses in town, this two-story frame box with narrow clapboard siding, simple trim, and a wide shed porch is the most prominent and least altered. Miners found furnished rooms and meals here for $6 a week. Accommodations included the old washhouse, which is still out back.

Longmont

Longmont (1872, 4,979 feet) was founded by members of the Chicago Colorado Colony, who named it for Longs Peak, the 14,255-foot landmark on the western horizon. Boulder County's second largest city has a strong agricultural base as well as significant industry and commerce, although the once mighty Great Western Sugar and Kuner-Empson canning factories are both defunct.

The 1870s two-story frame house of colony treasurer John Lawrence Townley is on its original site at 239 Pratt Street, next to the Denio Flour Mill in Old Mill Park. A brick Moderne building at Main Street and 6th Avenue, a former auto dealership, features contrasting horizontal banding and a facade combining convex and concave curves. Across from it is a sinuous brick sculpture (1991, Kenneth Williams), installed as part of a relandscaping of Main Street. The frame Colorado & Southern Railroad depot now serves as a retail store at 2nd Avenue and Main Street, while the nearby Chicago, Burlington & Quincy depot, in local sandstone, is now the freight office for the Burlington Northern.

BL41 Dickens Opera House

1881–1882. 1905, rear addition. 1986, rehabilitation. 300 Main St. (northeast corner of 3rd Ave.) (NR)

This two-story opera house with commercial storefronts sits directly across Main Street from the 1880 Imperial Hotel. The building, of brick detailed in lighter-colored stone trim, retains its original corner entrance beneath a smaller pediment in a secondary cornice. The narrow Main Street facade has three bays crowned by a central pediment and a bracketed cornice. Inside, the porcelain tile floor, marble staircase with ornamental iron baluster, and woodwork have been restored. A splendid, hand-carved Honduran mahogany bar has been added.

William Henry Dickens brought respectability to town when his opera house opened on February 2, 1882, with Will Holland's *The Greek Twins*. Dickens's house (1904), 303 Coffman Street, one block west of Main, was the scene of his murder in 1915 and subsequently became a hospital and, more recently, a boarding house.

BL42 Cannery Apartments (Empson Cannery)

1887, Benjamin C. Viney; additions. 15 3rd Ave. (NR)

John Empson commissioned Luther Burbank to develop a smaller, sweeter pea for canning that helped the Empson Cannery to thrive. Expansions of his original cannery, probably designed by local architect Benjamin C. Viney, housed equipment that included mechanical "viners," developed and patented by Empson to do the work of 600 hand shellers. Empson died in 1926, and his packing empire was purchased by Kuner Pickle Company in 1927 to become Kuner-Empson.

The two-story, 72-by-327-foot brick warehouse on the eastern edge of the site was constructed in three phases, beginning with the north half in 1901. Foot-thick walls support the gabled wooden roof sheathed with metal. Astride most of the ridgeline is a 9-foot-wide glazed monitor. The factory closed in 1970 and was later redeveloped into the Cannery Apartments, with a second apartment building and clubhouse mimicking the warehouse.

BL43 East Side Historic District

Collyer St. from 4th Ave. north to 6th Ave. and Emery St. from 5th Ave. to Longs Peak Ave. (NRD)

The sixty-seven contributing structures in this predominantly residential historic district represent a range of Victorian styles, from small vernacular cottages to elaborate Queen Anne and Italianate houses of brick and frame construction. This was Longmont's most fashionable neighborhood until wealth generated by the sugar factory that opened in 1902 expressed itself on the city's West Side.

BL44 Landmark Apartments (Longmont College)

1886, Frederick A. Hale. 546 Atwood St. (southeast corner of 6th Ave.) (NR)

The south wing of a much larger building proposed for the Presbyterian synod of Colorado, this vertical vestige is somewhat oddly proportioned. The Italianate three-bay facade has a central projecting two-story pavilion with full-height pilasters and a parapeted pediment for the steep hipped roof, which retains its iron cresting. Light stone trim, with some carving, dresses the patterned brick walls above a rough red sandstone foundation.

After serving as the Longmont Academy and, briefly, Longmont High School, the college was the charge of the Sisters of St. Francis from 1906 to 1948. The sisters added a three-story south side sleeping porch, subsequently enclosed, in 1907. In 1948 the building was converted to the Landmark Apartments.

BL45 St. Stephen's Episcopal Church

1881. 470 Main St. (NR)

This tiny brick chapel has a steep, front-gable roof covered in metal panels above a narrow narthex. Tall and narrow Gothic-arched windows trimmed in stone are evenly spaced between stepped buttresses. The chancel, which appears to be an addition, has a window composed of arches within arches. The rectory and fellowship hall have been converted to commercial use since the church closed in 1972. Surrounded by a spruce grove, St. Stephen's seems somewhat incongruous and hemmed in, as do many cathedrals in larger cities.

BL46 West Side Historic District

1877–1920. Roughly from 3rd to 5th aves., between Grant and Terry sts. (NRD)

In this district incorporating parts of the Thompson Park and Central School neighborhoods, 118 of 136 predominantly residential buildings are designated as contributing structures. Although the West Side was part of Longmont's original town plat, many of its historically significant buildings date from after 1900. The larger houses of merchants and sugar plant foremen are along the western end of 3rd Avenue and Pratt and Bross streets. Twentieth-century examples include the foursquare Emmons House (1903), 858 3rd Avenue, and a 1900 Tudor Revival house at 1206 3rd Avenue. Dutch Colonial, Mediterranean, and Classical Revival styles are also represented, as well as classical cottages, bungalows, and Craftsman houses. Stylistic interpretations are generally simple and reticent, reflecting the conservative bent of the inhabitants.

BL46.1 Callahan House Community Center

1892, James Wiggins, builder. 312 Terry St.

Thomas M. Callahan, one of the founders of the Golden Rule Stores, which evolved into the J. C. Penney Company, built one of Longmont's finest mansions. This two-and-one-half-story Queen Anne Style house is frame faced with red brick on a foundation of Lyons sandstone. Although the carriage house is original, the main dwelling's two-story rear addition, second-story balconies, wraparound porch, and porte-cochère were turn-of-the-century additions. In 1908, the Callahans had a Chicago landscape firm plant the formal Italian garden. Mitchell and Halback, also of Chicago, redecorated the interior. They Neoclassicized the house, using a different exotic hardwood in each downstairs room and leaded glass windows. When Callahan retired to California in 1938, he donated the house to Longmont, which has used it ever since as a community center.

peaked in 1909 at 753,287 tons. Transportation was never a problem in Louisville, since it lay on the Colorado Central's Boulder-to-Longmont line, constructed in 1872–1873. The town's first plat ran two blocks deep for four blocks along the west side of the tracks, and additions until after World War I almost always developed north, west, and south toward the coal mines. The business district centered on Main Street, while saloons were limited to a strip between Front Street and the tracks.

With rapid expansion of suburban housing in recent years, Louisville has become one of the fastest-growing towns in metropolitan Denver. A historic district of seventy mostly frame buildings represents development before 1920.

BL47 **Hover Mansion**

1913–1914, Robert S. Roeschlaub, Robert K. Fuller, Frank S. Roeschlaub. 1309 Hover Rd.

This brick Jacobethan house, set on a hill surrounded by large lawns and mature trees, was designed as the retirement home of Charles Lewis Hover (1867–1958), general manager of Empson Canning Company. The rambling, two-story dwelling has multiple bays and gabled wings forming a modified U plan. Gable ends and dormers all have parapeted brick faces fronting the roof of large asbestos shingles laid in a diamond pattern. Creamy limestone trim frosts windows, parapets, and the flattened entry arch above the recessed porch. The drive passes between brick piers with wrought-iron gates and under a porte-cochère. On the east, a wide, polygonal bay beneath paired dormers and a balustraded terrace suggest a country house, although suburban sprawl now occupies 141 of the original 160-acre grounds. Several frame outbuildings on the remaining 20 acres include a garage, a barn, and a two-story Victorian cottage (c. 1900).

Louisville

Louisville (1878, 5,350 feet) was platted by Louis Nawatny after coal was discovered in 1877. Production from three dozen mines

BL48 **Pine Street Junction** (Lackner's Tavern)

c. 1900. 1006 Pine St. (NR)

This single-story commercial building with shiplap siding has a clipped corner entry accented by a large sunburst. Window sizes have been changed and a south side beer garden has been added, but the original ornate bar and back bar remain inside. An even grander rococo mahogany back bar may be found at the Old Louisville Inn, a small, venerable, frame saloon at 740 Front Street.

BL49 **Steinbaugh Hardware** (National Fuel Company Store)

c. 1905. 801 Main St. (NR)

At 4,600 square feet, this is the largest of Louisville's historic commercial buildings. It was built as a company store by Dr. Charles F. Wolfer, converted to a grocery in 1909, and to a hardware store in 1974. The two-story false front hides a gable roof that is hipped at the rear. The second-story fenestration is a narrow band, trimmed top and bottom with molding. Although the storefronts were modified after World War II, the interior retains its original mezzanine and staircase, with a balustrade of turned spindles.

BL50 Louisville History Museum (Jacoe Store)

1903. 1001 Main St. (NR)

In contrast with the large company store, this 830-square-foot frame emporium on a side street needed a false front to make it plausible and a side extension to increase the stockroom. Eliseo Jacoe, who rented the store, made it a gathering spot for Louisville's sizable Italian community.

BL51 Nyland Collaborative Community

1993, Barker, Rinker, Seacat and Partners. 2 miles west of Louisville at 3525 Nyland Way South

With 42 houses on 43 acres this was the largest cooperative community in the United States when built. Cooperative member and resident Ronald Rinker, of the prominent Denver architecture firm, spearheaded communal planning. The Danish-inspired plan limits parking to the periphery with pedestrian-only approaches to homes. Members take turns doing the cooking for the entire community in the 7,000-square-foot community house. Despite frequent meetings the community cannot always reach consensus; diverse color schemes reflect one area of disagreement.

Lyons

Lyons (1882, 5,374 feet), in the valley where North and South St. Vrain creeks meet, is noted for its quarries of red sandstone, which town founder Edward S. Lyons exported to Denver for that city's flagstone sidewalks. Platted in 1882 as the Lyons Townsite and Quarry Company, Lyons began to grow after an extension of the Denver, Salt Lake & Pacific Railroad (Moffat Road) arrived in 1884 to transport the stone to markets nationwide. As the stone business subsided, tourism entered the picture, and the town became known as the "Double Gateway to the Rockies," for the two roads up the scenic North and South St. Vrain canyons to Rocky Mountain National Park.

Many of the town's sandstone buildings, dating from the 1870s to 1917, are part of a National Register district of fifteen buildings constructed by local craftsmen from the local sandstone, which is called red, although it is usually more pink, orange, or gray. These vernacular designs range from a dynamite shed (1892), 427 High Street, to the Montgomery School (1917), 5291 Ute Road. The oldest is the Griffith Evans Homestead (early 1870s), a mile northwest of Lyons, with a two-story house and a complex that served as a stage stop, inn, butcher shop, and blacksmithy. Residences at 409, 413, and 425 Seward Street are vernacular types with gable roofs and stone gable ends. Commercial buildings of Lyons sandstone, such as the McAllister Saloon (1881), 450 Main Street; the 1890s General Store, 415 Main Street; and the Lyons General Store (1884), 426 High Street, have flat roofs behind parapets and storefronts with recessed entries. The Turner-Stevens Building (1917), 401 Main Street, is a former bank and garage with decorative cornice. One of the few non-sandstone buildings is the Meadow Park Picnic Shelter (1933, WPA), 600 Park Drive, built of rounded stones from St. Vrain Creek. The Sandstone Park and Visitors' Center (1991), southeast corner of Broadway and 4th Avenue, has sculpture, a fountain, and picnic tables made of local sandstone, as well as displays on the quarries. The public restroom provides a showcase for sandstone colors and patterns.

BL52 Lyons Redstone Museum (Lyons High School)

1881. 340 High St. (northeast corner of 4th Ave.)

The former high school, with its frame second story (1900) covered in pressed metal panels to resemble the Lyons sandstone of the first floor, has a belfry atop the gable roof. This L-plan structure is the largest of the historic sandstone buildings, easily visible on the hill north of Main Street (Colorado 7). In 1979 it reopened as a museum with local history exhibits, including material on some thirty local quarries.

BL53 First Congregational Church

1894. 717 4th Ave. (northwest corner of High St.) (NR)

"The Old Stone Church," perhaps the most outstanding of the town's historic sandstone buildings, was built by the stoneworkers who worshipped here, led by their fellow mason and pastor, the Reverend Henry Harris. Twenty-inch-thick walls of hand-cut block rise from a stone foundation. A 42-foot-tall square tower at the southeast corner, distinguished by irregular coursing, houses the entrance, recessed into a round arch with radiating voussoirs. A corbeled course supports the frame-enclosed belfry, which is topped by a swordlike finial.

BL54 **Lyons Depot Library**

1885, Mark W. Boyd, builder. 400 block of Broadway (Colorado 7) (NR)

This typical small-town, late Victorian depot is a horizontal, single-story structure under a long gable roof with a polygonal south side bay. The walls, under a roof of galvanized metal strips pressed to simulate shingles, are local sandstone. A brick chimney astride the ridge rises from the wall between the central office and west passenger waiting room, with outlets on each side for wood stoves. A later frame addition on the east nearly doubles the size of the depot.

The Union Pacific took over the depot and branch line in 1888, followed by the Burlington in 1895, and subsequently by a Burlington subsidiary, the Colorado & Southern. In 1908 the depot became a meeting place for the Stanley Auto Line, which ferried guests to the Stanley Hotel in Estes Park. Abandoned in 1960, the old depot was remodeled in 1977 as a library.

BL54 Lyons Depot Library

Ward

Ward (1863, 9,258 feet) was named for Calvin Ward, who found gold here in 1860. Remnants of its bonanza days include the Community Church, originally the Ward Congregational Church (1890s), 41 Modoc Street (NR), a clapboard Carpenter's Gothic charmer with its wavy bargeboard and rose window. The Switzerland Trail's Ward Depot is now the Ward Store and Cafe, and the former Ward School (1898), 1 Columbia Street (NR), is now the Town Hall. The Modoc Mill (c. 1890), next to Duck Lake, 4 miles north of Ward (NR), is one of the best surviving examples of a stamp mill, where thirty large lead and metal stamps once pulverized gold ores. In 1988 it was rehabilitated as a private residence.

Gilpin County (GL)

"The Little Kingdom" of Gilpin is a vestigial mining realm still wearing its golden era garb. The Central City–Black Hawk–Nevadaville National Historic Landmark District has 418 contributing structures out of a total of 472. This small county named for Colorado's first territorial governor, William Gilpin, was once the richest and most populous in Colorado.

Gilpin County proved to be Colorado's mother lode after John H. Gregory's May 6, 1859, find on a tributary of North Clear Creek. Horace Greeley, who was among 10,000 people pouring into Central City that summer, wrote back to his newspaper, the *New York Tribune,* that "the entire population of the valley sleeps in tents or under booths of pine boughs, cooking and eating in the open air. I doubt there is as yet a table or a chair in these diggings, eating being done around a cloth spread on the ground, while each one sits or reclines on mother earth."

By 1867 Bayard Taylor described the county's principal towns as having "a curious, rickety, temporary air, with their buildings standing as if on one leg, their big signs and little accommodations, the irregular streets, and the bald, scarred and pitted mountains." Mountain City, the original settlement in Gregory Gulch, was soon overrun and annexed by Central City. Mines, homes, and businesses sprawled into nearby American City, Apex, Black Hawk, Eureka, Gold Dirt, Missouri City, Mountain City, Nevadaville, Nugget, Russell Gulch, Tip Top, and Wideawake. To build these towns, timber the mines, and stoke the smelters, hillsides of fir, pine, and spruce were sacrificed. In one of the first environmental abuse suits, Secretary of the Interior Carl Schurz charged in 1877 that Nathaniel P. Hill had fueled his Black Hawk smelter with wood stripped from public lands. Not only was the natural setting ravished, but much of the built environment was ripped down later, during the 1930s and 1940s. Towns such as Nevadaville were virtually demolished to avoid taxes, maintenance, and liability and to make a few dollars on used lumber, brick, and hardware.

Stone foundations, structures, and walls have persisted in Black Hawk and Central City because of the widespread use of yellowish local metamorphic rock. This dry rock work is generally attributed to Cornish immigrants, although Austrian, German, and Irish stonemasons are also listed in the 1880 and 1900 censuses for Central City. The Cornish "Cousin Jacks" constructed tight retaining walls that still keep buildings from sliding down the county's precipitous canyons. The Cornish boasted that "at the bottom of every mine—all over the world—lies a Cornishman." In Colorado, they introduced what became the standard miner's lunch pail. This tin bucket held tea or coffee in the bottom, then a dish of soup and a Cornish pasty on top, a three-course meal heated over a miner's candlestick.

Black Hawk and Central City differ from most Colorado towns, where freestanding buildings with lawns are typical. Here, contiguous buildings share common walls along picturesque streets that curve with the hillside contours.

Gilpin County produced more than $200 million in gold, but only a few small, sporadically productive mines and mills survive amid the ruins of mineshafts, headframes, cabins, and metal-sheathed mills. By the 1890s Cripple Creek outshone Gilpin County, and of twenty-three communities that sprang up during flush times, only Black Hawk, Central City, and Rollinsville survive as post office towns.

Gilpin County perked up when gambling became legal on October 1, 1991. In 1990 voters statewide approved an amendment to the state constitution allowing limited stakes gambling ($5 per bet) in Black Hawk, Central City, and Cripple Creek, with the provision that gambling profits could be taxed to support preservation and other community improvements.

The marriage of gambling and historic preservation has been rocky. Gambling is nothing new to Central City: gaming halls existed from the beginning and as late as the 1940s financed a free school lunch program. Gambling's impact in the 1990s appears to be less beneficial, as the built environment is transformed by monstrous new three- and four-story casinos overwhelming old Victorian facades. Older structures recycled as casinos have generally been gutted of their historic interiors, even though Central City's 1991 preservation ordinance differs from many such ordinances across the nation in allowing interiors as well as exteriors to be designated for preservation. Examples of well-preserved interiors are the Teller House Bar and the Gold Coin Saloon.

Central City

The county seat (1859, 8,496 feet) sparkled as the first hub of the Rocky Mountain gold rush and Colorado Territory's most populous city during the 1860s. Within weeks after John Gregory's 1859 strike, canvas, slab, and hewn pine shacks climbed the rocky hillsides like stairs. Locals joked that "a fella can't spit tobaccy juice out his front door without putting out the fire in his neighbor's chimney." Nevertheless, it was fire that erased much of the ephemeral pioneer town in 1874. Many downtown commercial buildings were quickly rebuilt and still wear the date 1874. Reconstructed with brick and native rock, the business district survives largely intact. Central City's population, which peaked in 1900 at 3,114 and hit a rock bottom of 226 in 1970, had bounced back to 335 by 1990.

GL01 **Gilpin County Historical Society Museum** (Gilpin County High School)

1870, Newton D. Owen. 228 E. High St.

Some 250 students once squeezed into the ten oak-wainscoted classrooms of this sturdy sandstone structure. This Italianate landmark served as the grade school until 1901, when Clark Elementary School opened nearby at 142 Lawrence Street. After Clark opened, the older school became the high school until its 1966 closing. Then the Gilpin County Historical Society converted the structure, which had been condemned because of a broken boiler, to a museum. Clark School, a sophisticated building with ornate brickwork, dignified Beaux-Arts touches, and a well-preserved interior, is now an annex of the county courthouse.

GL02 **St. Paul's Episcopal Church**

1873, Newton D. Owen. 220 E. High St.

Local stonemasons labored on this sandstone landmark with its lancet openings and spired belfry. The church was designed by a local amateur architect and built by a local stonemason and contractor, M. H. Root.

GL03 **Raynold's Beehive**

1863. 123 Lawrence St.

This survivor of the 1874 fire became a "beehive" of activity after it was rebuilt with imported brick to house the Hazard Powder Company and its agent, J. O. Raynold. Its brick facade, front gable, and shuttered windows stand out in a town of rough stone buildings, epitomized by the granite house next door. In 1992 the Beehive became part of a three-story casino.

GL04 **Masonic Temple** (Register-Call Building)

1862. 109 Eureka St.

Colorado's second oldest newspaper, the *Central City Register-Call*, published weekly since 1862, was issued until 1996 from this

Central City

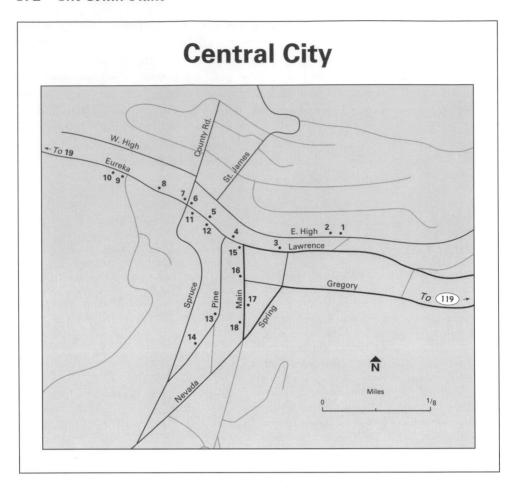

three-story granite building. When the newspaper ran into red ink, it sold the building to the Masons, who added the third-story lodge hall and leased space to the newspaper. Central City's pioneer photographer, Joseph Collier, whose work documents the rapid, early evolution of the county, had a studio here. In one of the few structures to survive the 1874 fire, heavy metal fire shutters guard the door at the top of the wooden steps of Register Alley.

GL05 Washington Hall

1861, William Z. Cozens. 117 Eureka St.

This simple hall started out as a hewn log jail constructed in 1861 by Sheriff Billy Cozens, a skilled carpenter whose own modest

board-and-batten house survives at 201 East First High Street. After clapboard siding and a second story were added in 1864, it was named Washington Hall. The Miners' Court, and later the Territorial District Court, convened here, as did other county agencies and several religious congregations before they erected their own churches. Crowded political meetings wore out the second floor, which collapsed in 1871, depositing 200 Republican conventioneers in the clerk and recorder's office below. The hall was rebuilt to withstand much heavier loads. In 1900, when county offices were moved to the new courthouse, Central City bought Washington Hall as a city hall. The cramped first floor houses an antique safe, while the upstairs houses the Gilpin County Art Association Gallery.

GL06 St. James Methodist Church

1872. 123 Eureka St.

"I asked a miner if there was any church," A. D. Richardson wrote of Central City in his 1869 account, *Beyond the Mississippi*. The miner replied: "No, but we are going build one before next Sunday." Steepleless St. James is a reminder of how miners hustled to give instant cities respectability. St. James traces its origins to a July 10, 1859, service, making it the oldest Protestant congregation in Colorado. An earlier log church burned down and two false starts delayed efforts to erect a grander replacement. Among stalwarts in the congregation was Aunt Clara Brown, a former slave turned washerwoman, who had held services in her home and helped build this bulwark of native stone with Gothic and round-arched openings. M. H. Root, a local stonemason, constructed the church. Inside it is adorned with stenciled wallpaper and has an 874-pipe, tracker action organ that was operated by water power until 1932. The well-maintained sanctuary, illuminated by beautifully detailed stained glass windows, seats 400 in eighty oak pews.

GL07 Gilpin County Courthouse

1900, Baerresen Brothers. 203 Eureka St.

This vernacular rendition of an Italian villa in pressed and cornered brick is dominated by square corner towers and a recessed central loggia and entry. The little-changed interior contains courtrooms and is replete with many-pointed deer and elk heads, golden oak woodwork, and imposing dark wood display cabinets for mineral specimens. The Baerresens designed a similar courthouse for Otero County.

GL08 Thomas House

1874. 128 Eureka St.

One of the town's most elegant frame houses follows the Classical Revival style with its pedimented doorways and windows, a Tuscan-columned, full-length porch, corner pilasters, a low, pedimented roofline, and symmetrical dignity. Built by one of the Hendrie brothers, who operated the foundry across the street, it was purchased by Benjamin P. Thomas. The interior furnishings, virtually unchanged since 1917, inspired the Gilpin County Historical Society to open it as a house museum.

GL09 McFarlane Foundry Rehearsal Center

1881. 1994, remodeling, Rodney S. Davis and Partners. 200 Eureka St.

The McFarlane Foundry was the oldest machine shop and foundry in Colorado, a predecessor of the huge Hendrie and Bolthoff Mining Machinery Company. Its rubblestone ruin was incorporated by the Central City Opera House Association into a rehearsal center. This $2 million, state-of-the-art center has a large performance hall, an elegant lounge, and recital and rehearsal rooms. The restoration was an especially challenging project for the architect, who had to underpin the foundry's native granite walls in order to incorporate them and had to contend with building over Eureka Gulch and its wooden flume. Rodney Davis sensitively incorporated ancient wooden doors and shutters as well as foundry tools and ruins. New and old corrugated and pressed metal helps blend old spaces into new ones in this exquisite, reborn building. Despite a few roof vents for height and light, the understated, one-story structure fades into the surrounding aspen forest.

GL10 **McFarlane House**

1873. 222 Eureka St.

Peter McFarlane, who was a proprietor of the foundry, owner of the Central City Opera House, and a mayor of Central City, built this simple, boxy, two-story clapboard house with rear additions. The house has been cutesified with gingerbread eaves and shutters.

GL11 **Central City Opera House**

1878, Robert S. Roeschlaub. 124 Eureka St.

A dynamite blast traditionally launches the Central City Opera season as the town revels in its best-known landmark. Built of local brick and stone, the opera house seats 500 on the lower floor and 250 in the balcony.

The Gilpin County Opera Association raised money by popular subscription to build Colorado's first notable theater. While many wanted a pretentious opera house, Robert Roeschlaub, his daughter Alice later claimed, "stood fast for a different type— one that would be in harmony with the great mountains surrounding it, an expression of the new and simple West." One-foot-thick stone and firebrick side walls lack decorative elements, which are saved for the front. The symmetrical facade, faintly Chateauesque, has arched openings, a balcony cantilevered over the entrance, and corner pavilions ris-

GL11 Central City Opera House, 1950s

ing to a tripartite mansard roof with a central roundel. Inside, two grand staircases spiral from the lobby to the balcony.

After the 1878 grand opening, the house survived by hosting political rallies, wrestling matches, lectures, high school graduations, and funerals. The association sold it to Peter McFarlane in 1900, and he converted it to a movie house, which closed in 1927. The abandoned, deteriorating opera house was acquired in the early 1930s by philanthropist Anne Evans and Ida Kruse McFarlane, Peter McFarlane's daughter-in-law. They founded the Central City Opera House Association, which staged a glorious 1932 reopening with Lillian Gish starring in *Camille*. Despite uncomfortable seating and distant restrooms—reminders of the building's primitive rural origins—the house has thrived, inspiring similar restorations in Aspen and Telluride.

GL12 **Teller House**

1872, Newton D. Owen. 110 Eureka St.

President Ulysses S. Grant stepped out of a stagecoach on April 28, 1873, to find the Teller House walk paved with silver bricks. Townsfolk quickly took up the $12,000 silver carpet after the cigar-chomping Civil War hero left. The hotel was named for one of its builders, Henry Moore Teller. As Colorado's most distinguished politician, Teller served the state's first and longest senatorial term and as U.S. secretary of the interior. Teller and his partners spent $107,000 on the site and the four-story, red brick hotel.

Newton D. Owen, a local carpenter-contractor responsible for the Gilpin County High School and St. Paul's Church, built a hotel that looked, as one observer put it, like a New England factory. The pride of the Teller House was not its exterior, or its 150 small, unheated rooms without baths, but its magnificent public spaces. Besides the lobby, with its elegant mineral display cases, the first floor housed a bank, bar, library, post office, and skylit dining room.

Anne Evans bought the deteriorating, largely abandoned hotel in 1933 and began restoration. In 1936 Herndon Davis, a Denver artist, painted a woman's face on the barroom floor, drawing inspiration from Hugh d'Arcy's poem. This barroom is also graced by *Apollo, Venus with Apple, Leda and the Swan,* and five other murals of life-size Greek goddesses and gods. The murals, found underneath layers of wallpaper during the 1930s restoration, are the work of Charles St. George Stanley, as restored by Paschal Quackenbush, who added two figures. Each mural, patrons report after much study, has a deliberate distortion.

Evans arranged for the Central City Opera Association to operate the hotel as a bar, restaurant, and museum. In 1991 the Teller House underwent a $7.6 million restoration and the installation of 361 one-armed bandits, eighty-two video poker games, and six blackjack tables. A Swiss casino firm assumed a lease to restore and operate the Teller House. Accustomed to rehabilitating European casinos, the Swiss eagerly took on what they described as "the youngest building we've ever restored."

GL13 St. Mary's of the Assumption Catholic Church

1892, Frederick W. Paroth. 135 Pine St.

The guardian angel of Central City replaced an earlier frame church dedicated in 1861. Bishop Joseph P. Machebeuf laid the cornerstone for a larger house of God in 1872. Twenty years later it was finally finished after a struggle with Irish malcontents who wanted to call it St. Patrick's. Gothic-arched windows, a steeply pitched roof, gables, and bell tower echo the steep hillside site. Inside the 90-by-42-foot brick and granite structure, 400 worshipers could gather under the 31-foot-high stenciled ceiling. One side altar statue portrays St. Barbara, the patron saint of miners.

GL14 St. Mary's Convent

c. 1875. 205 Pine St.

Restored in the 1940s by Colorado Springs philanthropist Julie Penrose as a private residence, this is a good example of Second Empire vernacular with its mansard roof, dormer and bay windows, and window hood ornaments. The convent housed the nuns who taught at St. Aloysius School. Pine Street neighbors to the south included sisters of a quite different order who staffed several brothels, including that of Central City's most celebrated madam, Lou Bunch.

Today these former houses of ill repute are prim and proper, restored to architectural and moral respectability.

Uphill behind the convent and church, atop 150 rickety steps, stood St. Aloysius Academy (1873). Opened by the Sisters of Charity of Leavenworth, it closed in 1917. Ida Kruse McFarlane, a graduate of St. Aloysius, purchased the land and remains of the school, hoping to build a public park and overlook (Central City had neither). Instead she devoted her energies to teaching and to restoring the Central City Opera House. Only after her death did friends realize her dream with the Ida Kruse McFarlane Memorial Overlook (1940, Burnham Hoyt), designed to incorporate the school's masonry ruins. The Celtic cross atop the viewing wall once crowned the academy bell tower.

GL15 First National Bank Block

1874. Southwest corner of Main and Eureka sts.

On the town's most prominent corner sits a brick bank with arched doorways and second-story window trim and a flat roof in the Italianate mode. The pioneer telephone exchange, post office, and offices of doctors, lawyers, and mine owners lay behind the heavy plate glass windows. With a three-ton fireproof and burglar-proof Herring safe, this stronghold of capital attracted miners who lined up to sell dust to gold buyers.

GL16 Elks Lodge

1874. 111 Main St.

Originally the Mullen Building, this became Lodge 557 of the Benevolent and Protective Order of Elks in 1902. The fraternal order added the third-story lodge hall, a bastion of the strongest and most enduring of the mining town fraternities, which served as surrogate families for many bachelor miners. Of the twenty-three fraternal organizations with fifty-three individual lodges that once were active in Gilpin County, this is one of the few survivors.

Somehow a huge stuffed elk with a seven-foot rack was carried up the narrow staircase and planted in the middle of the lodge room, where the Eastlake back bar is adorned with two smaller elk heads. The false-front brick cornice bears a white frame pedimented entablature with classical garlands and a central clock. Windows, especially a third-floor oriel and a second-story round-arched opening with leaded glass lights, brighten the facade.

GL17 Gold Coin Saloon and Lady Luck Casino

1897. 118–122 Main St.

Italian immigrants opened this two-story red brick commercial building as the Gold Coin, long celebrated as the most authentic old-time saloon in a town of many antique watering holes. The Coin's swinging doors open into another world. The authentic entry foyer has a shoeshine chair and cigar display case behind a golden oak Eastlake screen with acorn finials. The inner sanctum is warmed by an ancient potbellied stove on a diagonally laid pine plank floor, and tinny music from a player piano bounces off the tongue-and-groove wooden ceiling. The interior was carefully measured and photographed for restoration as the centerpiece of the three-story casino opened around it in 1992. Gambling, however, has been banished from this sanctuary with its Neoclassical back bar.

GL18 Harrah's Glory Hole Saloon (Meyer Building)

1864. 129 Main St.

Reflecting the shifting fortunes of a mining town, this structure has seen a wide variety of uses over the years. Its two-foot-thick stone side walls survived the 1874 fire, although the rest of the structure was gutted. Various restaurants, a funeral parlor, the post office, and the *Gilpin County Observer* were here before 1897, when Ignatz Meyer added a second story, put his name on the cornice, and reopened the building as a saloon.

In 1992 the old two-story building was enveloped inside a four-story brick building to become what was then the largest casino in Colorado. The $13 million Glory Hole Saloon and Gaming Hall incorporates restored Main Street facades and a handsome new brick and stone rear entrance on Pine Street opposite St. Mary's Church. The old back bar was preserved and doubled in length, while the tiny upstairs living quarters were rehabilitated as private dining rooms. New pressed metal ceilings, Victorian wallpaper, heavy velvet draperies, and fake palm trees adorn this gambling haven, where the saloon's old potbellied stove reappeared with perpetual cellophane flames. Amid all the Victoriana, an escalator incongruously carries customers to 535 slot machines and twelve card tables.

GL19 Cemeteries

West end of Eureka St.

Gilpin County has many more residents below ground than above. Over a dozen cemeteries served this once frenetic collection of mining towns and camps. Dynamite was used to blast burial space out of the stony terrain, and mourners might spend more time examining the new hole in the ground for gold than in burying the deceased.

Six cemeteries are concentrated on this flats at the headwaters of Eureka Gulch, 2 miles west of Central City near Russell Park and the Boodle Mine: City, Catholic, Ancient Order of Foresters, Independent Order of Odd Fellows, Knights of Pythias, and the Improved Order of Red Men. Their tombstones reflect life and death in a mining town. In 1879, for instance, records of the Catholic Cemetery list thirty-eight burials; eleven of the dead were under one year old and four were "killed in a mine." About one death in ten came in a mine mishap, while one in twenty were killed by "miner's con [sumption]."

GL20 Nevadaville

1859–1921. 1 mile southwest of Central City

By 1880 Nevadaville was a town of 1,084, but today only a few structures and residents remain. This predominately Cornish and Irish community contained many mines and mills, of which the most notable is the huge, open-pit mine known as the Glory Hole. Most surviving structures are of native yellow rock with brick fronts. They include a ramshackle barn labeled City Hall (c. 1870) across Main Street (Gilpin County 1) from the town's grandest edifice, the two-story Masonic Temple (1879). Kramer's Saloon (1876) and the Bon Ton Saloon (1880s) are hangovers from livelier times when thirteen saloons lubricated Nevadaville.

GL21 Russell Gulch

1859–1943. 3.5 miles southwest of Central City via Virginia Canyon Rd.

William Green Russell, whose South Platte River strike launched the Colorado rush, soon moved on to more profitable diggings. He uncovered a rich lode in June 1859, and by September, men were at work in Russell Gulch, producing $35,000 a week. The miners of Russell Gulch formed one of the first major northern Colorado water projects, the Consolidated Ditch Company (1859). Once a town of around 600 residents, it is largely in ruins today, with perhaps a dozen year-round residents. Some fifty homes remain, as do a three-story brick schoolhouse (c. 1890) and a fine, blond brick Odd Fellows Hall (1895), which dominates the main street.

Rollinsville

Rollinsville (1860, 8,420 feet) was named for John Quincy Adams Rollins, a miner and promoter, who erected the Rollins Steam quartz mill here on South Boulder Creek. Today this ramshackle crossroads retains a tavern and the ruins of the mill, an icehouse, an assay office, and some modest homes.

GL22 Stagecoach Tavern

1868. Colorado 119

Dominating the landscape and social life of Rollinsville, the two-story board-and-batten inn has sheet metal pressed and painted to look like brick on the second story under a metal roof. Apparently built as the Toll Gate Barn of the Butterfield Stage, it has accommodated a hotel, grocery, general store, and several taverns over the years. In the tongue-and-groove-walled, hardwood-floored hayloft/dance hall, wood pins and mortising are still visible. The back bar is an 1860s mahogany classic supposedly brought from Missouri by covered wagon, while the barroom chandeliers are constructed from pulley wheels of the now demolished Rollins Steam Quartz Mill.

GL23 East Portal of the Moffat Tunnel

1927, George Lewis, chief engineer. 12 miles west of Rollinsville

This 6.2-mile-long rail passage under the Continental Divide, a National Engineering Landmark, was built by the Moffat Railroad. It was the longest tunnel in the Western Hemisphere when completed, although only half the length of the Simplon tunnel (1906) through the Alps between Switzerland and Italy.

Floods such as an 1,800-gallon-per-minute flow from Crater Lake, 1,300 feet overhead, drowned out hopes for a natural rock tunnel and made a steel and concrete lining necessary. The 1928 grand opening gave Denver a long-awaited direct rail route through the Rockies. The Denver & Rio Grande Railroad acquired the Moffat in 1947 and still uses the tunnel. Rail fans gather to see the great canvas curtain, designed to improve ventilation and keep out animals, raised and lowered as trains rumble through the pedimented concrete entry.

The Moffat Tunnel considerably shortened the original 26-mile roadbed between what are now its east and west portals. This abandoned rail route is now a summer jeep road and winter excursion for cross-country skiers and snowmobilers. The ride, which climaxes with the Corona Station, atop 11,600-foot Rollins Pass, includes Needles Eye Tunnel, 19.8 miles west of Rollinsville, and a view of an unusual square water tower, 8.7 miles west of Rollinsville.

Black Hawk

Black Hawk (1860, 8,042 feet), "The City of Mills," was named for a pioneer quartz mill built by the Black Hawk Company of Rock Island, Illinois. Strategically located at the confluence of Gregory Gulch and North Clear Creek, this mill town became the county's ore processing hub. Colorado's first great successful smelter, Nathaniel P. Hill's Boston and Colorado Smelter, opened in 1868 and salvaged the sputtering gold rush by applying a process imported from Swansea, Wales, to cook recalcitrant Colorado gold ores. By the 1870s, fifteen stamp mills were crushing ores for twenty-five smelters that darkened Black Hawk skies with sulfurous smoke. To feed the smelters, much of Gilpin County was deforested for charcoal. Twenty-four hours a day Black Hawk throbbed to the beat of the stamp mills, where huge steel- or iron-tipped lead weights pulverized ore.

Black Hawk became a grimy mill town, and also the county's railhead following the arrival of the Colorado Central in 1872. This narrow-gauge line ran until 1941, by which time all the major mills were closed. In 1900 it housed 1,200; by 1990 the population had fallen to 225. Never having suffered a serious fire, Black Hawk boasts a large number of 1860s and 1870s wooden structures. Gambling began to change the scene in 1991, replacing old retail shops and mill sites with gambling joints that a modern-day William Blake might also characterize as "dark Satanic mills."

GL24 **Lace House**

1863. 1976, restoration, Edward D. White, Jr. 161 Main St.

Lavish decorative wood detail makes this a fine example of how Carpenter's Gothic trim could enhance a miner's shack. On a stone foundation, the two-story, vertical board-and-batten dwelling has a steeply pitched roof, gable finials, pointed windows, lace cutout porch trim, and bargeboards dripping with wooden scroll-sawn icicles. It

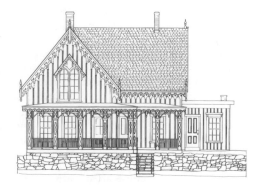

GL24 Lace House, elevation

was donated in 1974 to the town of Black Hawk for use as a museum that has become one of the most photographed examples of Gothic Revival architecture in the Rockies. The Lace House is evidence that even remote frontier towns aspired to the picturesque domestic styles popularized by Andrew Jackson Downing.

GL25 **Gilpin Hotel**

1870. 111 Main St.

This three-story brick hotel incorporates an older wooden building that is said to have housed the first town newspaper and schoolhouse. The stone cellar houses the Mine Shaft Bar. In 1991–1992 the Gilpin Hotel was rehabilitated for a casino career. The buildings on either side, neo-Victorian casinos (1992–1993) of brick and stone, draw some inspiration from this venerable hotel.

GL26 **Bull Durham Casino** (Fick's Carriage Shop)

c. 1877. 110 Main (northeast corner of Gregory St.)

William Fick, a Prussian immigrant, built heavy-duty "Black Hawk Wagons" with large double wheels for mountain use. His thriving wagon-building, repair, and blacksmith shop occupied this two-story granite building with a fancy brick front. After the auto age eroded business, another owner made a few dollars by allowing the large Bull Durham sign to be painted across the facade. It is one of the few remaining signs of thousands painted nationwide by traveling crews of the American Tobacco Company. After a women's organization complained about the bull's conspicuous private parts, the company sent an employee around the country to paint a fence over the offending apparatus. The sign and the building were restored for a 1991 recycling as a casino.

GL27 **Knights of Pythias Hall**

1864. 101 Gregory St.

J. E. Scobey's Billiard Saloon occupied this early brick commercial structure before the Knights of Pythias purchased it in 1885. The second-story round-arched windows were matched by arched windows on the first floor before conversion to solid plate glass storefronts. The building is now completely surrounded by the giant, four-story Bull-whackers Casino (1992), which has preserved only the facade of the old hall. Here, and in many other casinos, cheap contemporary rooftop screens hiding mechanical systems wreck any neo-Victorian illusions perpetrated by the rest of the building.

GL28 **Rohling Block**

1868. 160 Gregory St.

J. H. Philip Rohling, a Prussian immigrant who became a merchant and mayor of Black Hawk, operated a dry goods store in this two-story, red brick landmark with its distinctive arched windows and doorways. In 1991 it became the Rohling Inn Casino.

GL29 **Crook's Palace**

1900. 200 Gregory St.

In claiming to be Colorado's oldest establishment of its type, the Palace traces its ancestry to a demolished 1860s saloon on the same site. A classic storefront adorns this tiny, old-time saloon with matching front and back bars decorated by Corinthian pilasters and egg-and-dart cornice trim. Richard Hicks painted the frilly, mock-Victorian wall murals with trompe-l'oeil genitalia. The pine floor is worn white, the brass footrail is shiny with use, and the seats have been contoured by regulars. From the barstools

GL29 Crook's Palace

old-timers squinted at the daily changes in gold and silver prices scribbled on a chalkboard. Nowadays gamblers, also struck with gold fever, stare into slot machines.

GL30 **City Hall Annex** (First Presbyterian Church)

1863. 211 Church St.

One of the town's oldest landmarks, this board-and-batten church overlooks Black Hawk from a prominent hillside perch. It has lost its steeple, but its windows with pedimented hoods and steeply pitched roof still point to heaven. It was sold to the schoolhouse next door for use as a gym in 1906, but was vacant after the school closed in 1960 until the 1990s, when it became Black Hawk town offices.

GL31 **Black Hawk Schoolhouse**

1870, State of Colorado standard design. 221 Church St.

This two-story clapboard structure has an entry portico beneath a pedimented window in the central bay, but drops its Greek Revival aspirations in the two simple vernacular wings. Imposing for its commanding site on Bates Hill rather than its design, the schoolhouse is propped up by a massive stone retaining wall. It was revamped as the police department in the mid-1990s.

GL32 Bobtail Mine

1862. 400 Gregory St.

One of the oldest and richest mines in Colorado, this jackpot still pays off today as tourists clamber aboard donkey-pulled ore carts for mine tours. The tunnel reaches the main Bobtail gold vein 1,100 feet into Bobtail Hill, a lode that produced some $5 million before owners switched to mining tourism in the 1950s. The town's distinctive dry-wall rock construction can be seen in the mine portal and foundation of the mine office.

GL33 Golden Gilpin Mill

1880s–1920s. 1 mile north of Black Hawk on Colorado 119

Of Black Hawk's mighty mills, which made it the 1870s smelting capital of Colorado, this remnant is the sole survivor, near the Black Hawk terminus of the Gilpin County Tram, whose roadbed is visible on the west side of the highway.

Clear Creek County (cc)

Gold miners settled in this county on the eastern flank of the Continental Divide as early as 1859 after a major gold strike by George Jackson led to the birth of Idaho Springs, the first county seat. Fifteen miles farther up Clear Creek, Georgetown sparkled as Colorado's first silver city and captured the county offices in a hotly contested 1868 election. Despite the subsequent decline in Georgetown's wealth and population, the larger community of Idaho Springs never regained political hegemony. After peaking at more than 8,000 in the 1880s, the county's population sank to 2,000 during the 1930s before slowly recovering to reach 8,000 in the 1990s.

The county is named for its major creek, the first great golden stream of the Colorado gold rush. Two dozen mining camps sprouted along the creek and its tributaries during the 1860s, leaving Clear Creek rarely clear until mining played out in the early 1900s. Only Berthoud Falls, Dumont, Empire, Georgetown, Idaho Springs, Lawson, and Silver Plume survive in a county that once hosted two dozen mining towns.

A narrow-gauge railroad crawled up Clear Creek to service the mines and bring in tourists. Double- and triple-header steam trains climbed a steep terrain via engineering wonders such as the famous Georgetown Loop, which was abandoned in the 1930s when the WPA helped replace some of the railbed with the roadbed of U.S. 40. The handsome stone retaining walls and bridge abutments of the rail grade may have inspired the fine stonework on the rims and parapets of U.S. 40's many tunnels.

Skiing at Berthoud Pass, Loveland Valley, and Loveland Basin areas has become the county's economic mainstay. Auto roads climb through mining-era ruins to the summits of Berthoud, Loveland, and Guanella passes; to St. Mary's Glacier; and to the summit of 14,264-foot Mt. Evans. Little new construction has taken place in a county where three-fourths of the land is in public ownership, including the Arapaho National Forest and the Mount Evans Wilderness Area. In 1984 the Colorado Historical Society restored the Georgetown Loop narrow-gauge train excursion between Georgetown and Silver Plume. Most of the I-70 traffic bypasses still slumbering towns such as Georgetown, Idaho Springs, and Silver Plume, which contain some of Colorado's oldest and best-preserved mining-era architecture. Georgetown, the Georgetown Loop Railroad and Lebanon Mine, and nearby Silver Plume make up a National Historic Landmark District.

Georgetown

Georgetown (1860, 8,519 feet) has an elegance that makes it strikingly different from most raw mining settlements. Gentrification began with town founder George Griffith, who brought his wife and family to settle in "George's Town." Other women also arrived early, encouraged, according to legend, by free town lots. They insisted on painted houses, gardens, churches, schools, an opera house, and other refinements that made Georgetown unusually genteel for a mining town.

In 1860 Griffith discovered gold near where the Griffith Mine portal still stands at the east end of 11th Street. Four years later, after discovery of the Belmont Lode,

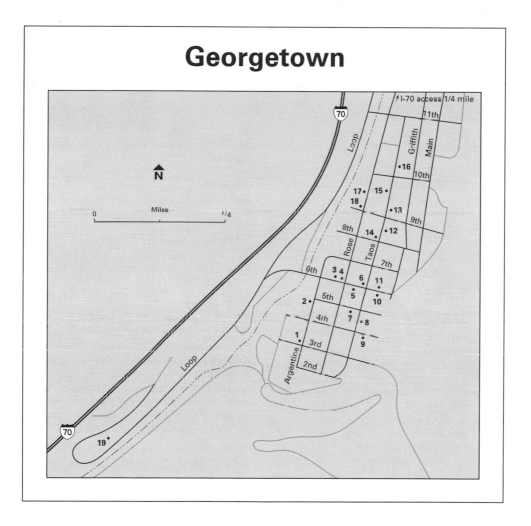

Georgetown became Colorado's first silver city and the supply town for many surrounding silver mining districts. After the 1893 silver crash, Georgetown declined and has seen little new construction since.

Whereas most mining towns squandered little, if any, land on parks, Georgetown set aside a full block, between Taos and Rose streets from 10th Street to Park Street, as City Park, with a bandstand, playground, and iron gates. Tree-lined streets and gardens mixing wild and cultivated flowers also make this town exceptional among usually bleak, functional mining communities.

Historic Georgetown, Inc., enacted one of the first and toughest local preservation ordinances. To keep development from creeping up the surrounding mountainsides, in the 1980s the town bought out a condominium developer on the Guanella Pass Road. Since the 1970s Georgetown has lost only two of 211 nineteenth-century structures in the downtown historic district. Nearly all buildings are compatible, although the Williamsburg-like Colonial Revival post office was a blunder, sent to the wrong address.

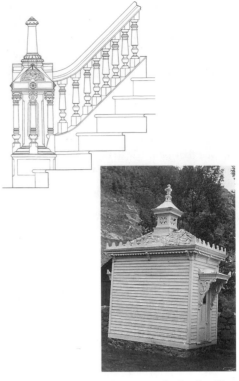

CC01 Hamill House Museum, stair detail, office building (above); outhouse (below)

CC01 **Hamill House Museum**

1867, Joseph Watson, builder. 1879, Robert S. Roeschlaub. 305 Argentine St. (northwest corner of 3rd St.) (NR)

Free off-street parking behind the house at the west end of 4th Street makes this a good starting point for a walking tour of Georgetown. A two-story Gothic Revival showcase, this has always been Georgetown's finest residence. Mine mogul William A. Hamill, an Englishman, bought the residence from its builder, his brother-in-law, and hired Denver architect Robert Roeschlaub to enlarge the house. Roeschlaub added the central and back wings, along with the solarium, bay windows, and matching oriels.

A granite wall surrounds a lawn with a large metal fountain in front of the carriage house and office (1880–1881), two miniaturizations of the Chateau Style. In contrast with the clapboard house, the carriage house is rubblestone granite, while the office is ashlar granite with raised quoins. The resplendent office interior has a huge wall safe, walnut woodwork with burl veneer, and a grand staircase to upstairs rooms under a crested hipped roof.

Hamill, a member of the state legislature, was also the wealthiest man in town, thanks to the Pelican and Dives mines. He supposedly lit his cigars with ten-dollar bills. The Georgetown Society acquired his house in 1971 and has expertly restored and furnished it as a house museum. The solarium is memorable, and the six-seat outhouse in back is Colorado's finest with its proud cupola and three walnut seats in front for the Hamills. On the other side, three plain pine seats accommodated servants who, archaeologists report, used their holes to hide broken Haviland china, empty liquor bottles, and other incriminating evidence.

CC02 **Clear Creek County Courthouse**

1978, Phillips, Brandt and Reddick. 405 Argentine St. (southwest corner of 5th St.)

A contemporary county complex matches the white horizontal clapboard of the old Clear Creek County Courthouse (1868, John Fillius and J. G. Mahaney, builders), a two-story building across Argentine Street. The older courthouse was built as the Ohio Bakery and has now been recycled as a visitors' and community center. Next to the new courthouse is the stone jail (1883), containing two cells and a watchman's area behind the original iron padlock.

CC03 **Masonic Hall**

1891. 608 6th St.

One of the town's largest and most ornate structures is distinguished by its central roofline pediment with three tiny round-arched windows, echoing the five larger second-story windows below with their stained glass tops. Almost six feet of corbeling, a diapered frieze, and a cornice heighten the facade. Arches with articulated keystones adorn the second floor, where the Masons still convene above the first-floor stores.

CC04 **Ram Bar and Restaurant** (Fish Block)

1889. 1981, restoration. 606 6th St. (northwest corner of Rose St.)

Charles R. Fish built this two-story, red brick commercial edifice for the Bank of Clear Creek County. Since the 1960s, it has been a legendary bar and restaurant, the Red Ram. Corbeled and diapered brickwork and a pressed metal frieze top the facade. The sturdy granite foundation forms the walls of the basement hall. A balcony with tables lines the west wall overlooking a mounted ram's head and a golden oak back bar whose mirror is framed by 10-foot Ionic columns and a classical entablature.

CC05 **Kneisel and Anderson Store**

1883. 511 6th St.

The oldest continually operated business in town was begun by Henry Kneisel. Grand-daughters of Emil Anderson, Kneisel's son-in-law, still operate this old-fashioned general store behind the one-story, red brick

storefront with an ornate frieze, corbeling, and metal cornice. Kneisel, as mayor of Georgetown, oversaw installation of the sandstone sidewalks and City Park.

CC06 **Silver Queen** (Cushman Block)

1875, W. H. J. Nichols. 500 6th St. (northwest corner of Taos St.)

William Cushman's imposing three-story brick Italianate commercial structure culminated with a third-floor opera house. Although the third floor was declared structurally unsound shortly after it was built, it did not collapse until 1969, finally relenting under heavy snow loads. The rubble was cleared away and the roof lowered, leaving this building with especially broad eaves and an oversized cornice. Since the 1950s it has housed the Silver Queen restaurant, saloon, and beer cellar, as well as the Clear Creek National Bank.

CC07 **Alpine Hose Company No. 2**

1875. 507 5th St. (NR)

The town's second volunteer brigade erected this two-story, false-fronted clapboard firehouse, adding the 65-foot-high battered frame tower (1880), for which William Hamill (see CC01) donated the bell. Small windows under the bell are for the fire watchmen. As in other small towns across America, the fire department was socially active, staging Christmas and July Fourth celebrations and firemen's balls. The Alpines covered Georgetown with glory by winning Colorado's first statewide tournament, where they ran 700 feet with their hose cart in thirty seconds, capturing first prize (a silver tea set and a brass cannon).

CC08 **Grace Episcopal Church**

1869. 408 Taos St.

Colorado's oldest operating Episcopal church is an early example of Carpenter's Gothic with its clapboard siding and plain wooden trim, lancet windows, front-gable faux quatrefoil, and crosses atop a steeppitched shake shingle roof. After a windstorm blew the church over and knocked off the bell tower, the church was reinforced with tie rods, and the bell tower was reerected on the ground beside the church. The tracker organ in a solid oak case is said to be the state's oldest operating pipe organ.

CC09 **Maxwell House**

1867; 1890–1891. 409 4th St.

This encyclopedic example of High Victorian gingerbread is one of Colorado's most photographed homes. A multihued paint job highlights the profuse detail. Originally this was the simple frame house of grocer B. F. Potter. Frank A. Maxwell, a later owner, added the front section, wings, and much

CC09 Maxwell House

CC10 Hotel de Paris, dining room, 1954

of the decorative trim in 1890–1891. He also added a third-story tower, balconied porch, and second-story dormers to complete this exuberant example of the Second Empire style.

CC10 **Hotel de Paris**

1875–1890. 409 6th St. (NR)

Louis Dupuy, a Frenchman from Alençon, built this hotel with its two-foot-thick rubblestone walls, plastered and painted to look like ashlar stone. In 1875 Dupuy opened the small Delmonico Bakery (today's dining room) and later acquired two adjacent storefronts and made additions to the back. The fronts are skillfully tied together with a dentiled and bracketed cornice, wrought iron railing, and windows hooded with elaborate flattened arches. Although the marble busts of Molière and Voltaire are gone, a statue of justice and a soldered zinc lion and seated stag still guard the 10-foot-high stone wall around the very early outdoor cafe.

After Dupuy's death, it was learned that he was Adolphe François Gérard, a deserter from the U.S. army. His hotel has been owned since the 1950s by the Colorado chapter of the National Society of the Colonial Dames of America and operated as a museum. The Dames found in "French Louis's" ample wine cellar boxes of twenty-eight different fine French wine labels that could be applied to bottles filled locally. The well-preserved interior with its library and salons features walnut woodwork and alternating light maple and dark walnut floor boards.

CC11 **Town Hall** (Star Hook and Ladder)

1886. 404 6th St.

Thanks to the vigilance of the Stars and its three other volunteer fire companies, Georgetown never burned down. It still has a large number of frame structures, including this two-story shiplap structure with wooden trim, which, after a 1960s restoration, became the town hall.

CC12 **First United Presbyterian Church**

1874. 1974, restoration. 812 Taos St.

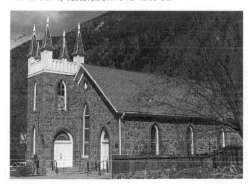

A two-story square bell tower at the northwest corner, topped by a wooden turret with eight pinnacles, distinguishes this uncoursed granite building, home of a congregation founded by Reverend Sheldon Jackson. Pointed-arched doors and windows are outlined in red brick. The remodeled interior, with flat white plaster walls and ceiling, is lighted by stained and frosted glass windows. The walnut pews were divided in 1965 to form a center aisle.

CC13 **Buckley House**

c. 1880. 910 Taos St.

Bernard Buckley's two-and-one-half-story white clapboard dwelling is an engaging, eclectic specimen of Carpenter's Gothic with its steep-pitched roof, gables, dormers, and bays, adorned by scroll brackets and cutout vergeboard.

CC14 **Old Georgetown School**

1874–1875, W. A. Lewis. 809 Taos (northwest corner of 8th St.)

The finest and most conspicuous structure in Georgetown when built, this two-story, red brick ruin awaits restoration. The "state approved standard design" brass plaque on the front means this was an architect's design for a building type used throughout the state. This school is one of the few survivors of an early model with Italianate elements: wide, double-bracketed eaves, carved keystones on both round and flattened arches, and boxy symmetry. Pilasters mark the building corners and flank the central entry bay, which lies under a large gable dormer in the truncated hipped roof. The school closed in the mid-1930s after the WPA built a less distinguished replacement at 4th and Taos streets, which was Victorianized with clapboard and wood trim in the early 1990s.

CC15 **McClellan House**

1866. 1929, restoration, Benjamin Draper. 919 Taos St.

Job and Erskine McClellan constructed this two-story house with vertical sawn boards. Flattened tin cans have been applied over the butt joints. A very early vernacular dwelling, this has homemade Carpenter's Gothic detail with wood quoins, lintels, frieze, and ornamental shingles. McClellan's Opera House (1869, burned 1892), next to the Hotel de Paris on 6th Street, was reputedly Colorado's first.

CC16 **Old Missouri Hose Company**

1875. 1004 Taos (northeast corner of 10th St.)

This clapboard-fronted structure with board-and-batten sides rises to two stories across the front with a third-story open bell tower trimmed in the Italianate style.

CC17 **Long-Hoeft House** (Church-Hamilton House)

1876, Robert S. Roeschlaub. 1980s, restoration, Long Hoeft Architects. 921 Rose St.

A crackerjack example of Gothic Revival, this two-story vernacular clapboard dwelling was restored by preservation architects Gary Long and Kathy Hoeft to become their home. Robert Roeschlaub showed solar sensitivities in orienting the main rooms to the south to catch the late-rising and early-setting sun in this deep mountain valley. Spear-point finials emphasize the steepness of the roof and the verticality of the composition.

CC18 **Bowman-White House**

1892. 901 Rose St. (northwest corner of 9th St.)

John Henry Bowman, a silver-mine owner, built this two-story frame residence with Italianate and Queen Anne touches. The L plan wraps a square entry tower at the inside corner. Wood trim is particularly profuse on the porch, including unusual spoolwork and a hooded dormer with a double sunburst. Purchased in 1974 and restored by Historic Georgetown, Inc., the property also now houses two transplants, a log trapper's cabin (1860s) and the Tucker-Rutherford Miner's House (1870s).

CC19 **Georgetown Loop Railroad**

1880s; 1980s. Georgetown to Silver Plume (NHL)

This is the railroad that moved a highway. I-70 was blasted out of a mountainside instead of ripping up the Clear Creek Valley in order to protect the ruins of the engineering marvel. Two miles—and a rise of 638 feet—separated Georgetown and Silver Plume. Robert Blickensderfer, a Union Pacific engineer, designed the original 4.47 miles of track, which used two hairpin turns and looped over itself to cut a 6 percent grade to 3.5 percent. At the Devil's Gate Viaduct, a 300-foot bridge spanned the track and Clear Creek 95 feet below. Sightseers from all over the globe came to gawk, if not to "do the loop" on "that famous knot in a railroad." Mining and tourism had both played out in 1939 when the Colorado and Southern Railway, last operator of the Georgetown Loop, abandoned the line, scrapping the Devil's Gate Viaduct for $450.

CC16 Old Missouri Hose Company

CC17 Long-Hoeft House (Church-Hamilton House)

For $2 million, the Colorado Historical Society rebuilt the loop in 1984.

The resurrected train stops at the Lebanon Mine (1870s) for an underground mine tour. The site includes the 1970s restorations of the 1870s Lebanon Mill, the office of mine manager Julius Pohle, a change room, and a blacksmith shop. The Pohle-Toll House (1878) resembles Gothic Revival designs that Andrew Jackson Downing published in several editions of his *Cottage Residences* beginning in 1842. It has narrow windows, pendant ornaments for windows and gables, and overhanging eaves.

Silver Plume

Silver Plume (c. 1870, 9,118 feet) is noted for its silver mines and granite quarries. While merchants and mine owners gravitated to Georgetown, Silver Plume housed most of the mines and miners. The town, named for ore so rich that silver flakes broke off in feathery plumes, runs the length of a narrow, steep-sided valley. Some 1,500 people lived here in 1890, ten times the present population.

Small vernacular frame homes reflect the limited space in the narrow valley and the meager wages of miners. Most homes have fewer than four rooms, with ornament limited to pediments over doors and windows, suggesting a Greek Revival influence. Relatively stable property values and lack of development pressure have left much of Silver Plume's nineteenth-century architecture intact, making it one of Colorado's best-preserved mining towns.

CC20 **Silver Plume Depot**
1884. 1985, restoration. I-70 and Mountain Ave. (NR)

Shipped in pieces to the site by rail, the original board-and-batten depot served until its abandonment in 1939. Moved from the west end of town in 1965 and restored for the revived Georgetown, Breckenridge & Leadville Railroad, it has been augmented by new construction, including shops and garages (1986).

CC21 **Jailhouse**
1881. Northwest corner of Main and Garfield sts.

This small, square, one-story granite dungeon with two-foot-thick walls was built into a hillside. Originally used by the security guards hired by British mine investors, the jail became town property upon Silver Plume's incorporation in 1880. Facilities were spartan, and prisoners had to be taken for meals to a nearby boarding house. It became a dog pound after human offenders were moved to the county jail in Georgetown.

CC22 **Rowe Museum** (Schoolhouse)
1894, William Quayle. North side of Main St., east of Garland St.

William Quayle, a prominent Denver architect who later became even better known in San Diego, designed this two-story, red brick school trimmed in sandstone, which was supposedly constructed in eight weeks by Silver Plume contractors Sopp and Truscott. Its bricks, made from clay dug and fired at the east end of town, are laid up in common bond atop a granite foundation. A central gable, deep, bracketed eaves, fancy metal cornice, ornate banding, tall windows with arcaded transoms on the second floor, and a boxy symmetry give the school an Italianate air. The simple interior boasts one extravagance, an elaborate, machine-turned stair balustrade. Large windows light the four classrooms, which were used until 1959. People for Silver Plume purchased the building in 1975 and developed a museum

CC22 Rowe Museum (Schoolhouse), elevation

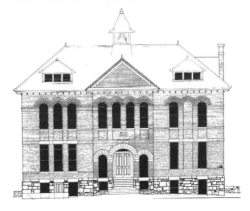

named for longtime mayor George Rowe, whose collection of Silver Plume memorabilia is housed here.

CC23 **Arts at Silver Plume** (St. Patrick's Catholic Church)

1876; 1884. 417 Main St.

After St. Patrick's was miraculously spared from a fire in 1884, the largely Italian congregation turned its small Gothic chapel ninety degrees to form the rear vestry of a larger church constructed that year. Above doors hand carved in Italy, the clapboard church now has a peculiar new bubble window in the rose window opening. It has been recycled as an arts and crafts shop, and its nave, sanctuary, and minuscule choirloft have been restenciled in original colors and patterns.

CC24 **K. P. Cafe** (Knights of Pythias Hall)

c. 1875; moved 1895. 429 Main St. (northwest corner of Silver St.)

In 1895 the Knights of Pythias bought the east end of this two-story frame false-front and moved it here from Brownsville, a town that once existed a mile west. The west section of the building was added in 1903 by the Knights, who met in the upstairs hall until 1944. A heavy, bracketed cornice unites the two slightly askew all-wood structures. The south facade is nearly all glass to snatch sunshine and provide a view of funky Main Street and the mine-splotched mountains.

CC25 **Buckley's Old Store**

1884. 432 Main St.

Alice and Jeremiah Buckley bought this general store and dynamite dealership in 1902. Now restored, the building houses residents and a studio behind one of the town's best-preserved facades. A bracketed cornice tops the false front on an asymmetrical arrangement of business and living quarters with separate entries. Buckley's new general store and gas station is at the I-70 off ramp.

CC26 **Sopp and Truscott General Store**

1978, Pat Pickering. Southeast corner of Main and Daily St.

A modern reproduction, this building has a false front with bracketed double cornice that wraps the corner, above a cutaway angled storefront entrance. The gable roof has a standing-seam metal roof, and a window on Daily Street is topped with a molded pediment.

CC27 **Little Town Hall–Hose Company No. 1**

c. 1886. 360 Main St.

Home for the town offices as well as the town's fire hose cart and pumper, this one-story building has a typical false front hiding a gable roof. The town also uses the Big Town Hall (1884), a two-story false front at the east end of Main Street. Next door is a narrow-gauge caboose used on the line serving Silver Plume.

Idaho Springs

Idaho Springs (1859, 7,540 feet) was established after George A. Jackson, attracted by the hot springs that gave the town its name, camped here in January 1859 and struck placer gold in Chicago Creek near its confluence with Clear Creek. A swarm of miners established mines, mills, and outlying camps for which Idaho Springs emerged as the core supply town. In 1863 Dr. E. M. Cummings opened a commercial hot springs, which has evolved into the Indian Hot Springs Hotel and Resort.

Since 1900 Idaho Springs has stabilized at a population of about 2,000. Strung out along the narrow stretch of Clear Creek Canyon, the town retains a well-preserved commercial main street (Miner Street), a National Register District. Several parallel avenues are lined by mostly turn-of-the-century cottages, foursquares, and Queen Anne Style homes. Colorado Boulevard, the I-70 business route, retains many impressive residences such as the Cooper House (1905), 1122 Colorado Boulevard, a Classical Revival frame house occupied until the late 1920s by novelist Courtney Riley Cooper.

During the 1980s, Idaho Springs installed a greenway walk under I-70 to Clear Creek for its most prominent landmark, the restored Charles Taylor Water Wheel (1907), near Bridal Veil Falls south of I-70. The 50-foot-high wheel once powered Taylor's five-stamp ore concentrator south of Idaho Springs along Ute Creek. Taylor, a blacksmith and engineer, may have designed and built the wheel himself. Following his death in 1946, it was moved to its present site as an ornament.

CC28 Carnegie Library

1904, Sidney Varney and Silas Knowles, builders. 219 14th Ave. (northwest corner of Miner St.)

Built according to Carnegie Library specifications by local brickmasons, this virtually unaltered gem retains the original floor plan, golden oak card catalog, shelving, and portrait of Andrew Carnegie, who donated $10,000 and the plans. The two-story gray brick classical temple has fluted Doric columns flanking the east entry portico. The lower south entrance is off a mini-park with a Spanish *arrastra* (an animal-powered drag with a large boulder for crushing ore).

CC29 Underhill Museum

1912. 1416 Miner St.

James Underhill, a mining man and professor at the Colorado School of Mines, constructed this vernacular brick home and office with corbeled cornice. After his death, the one-story structure became the home and museum of the Historical Society of Idaho Springs.

CC30 Hanchett Building

1890, Silas Hanchett, builder. 1431–1435 Miner St.

The most imposing facade in town consists of large display windows with patterned sill plates and a recessed doorway framed by cast iron pilasters from the Colorado Iron Works in Denver. Arched second-story windows have stained glass lunettes. A high metal cornice has ornate end brackets and a decorated frieze beneath a central pediment. Hanchett made his money from the Lamartine Mine and constructed this building as income property, while living in the two-and-one-half-story brick house at 1003 Colorado Boulevard (1890).

CC31 Brunswick Flat

c. 1890. 1991, restoration. 1502–1506 Miner St. (northeast corner of 15th St.)

Tall, ornately framed Italianate windows in brick brighten the upper-story apartments of this two-story red brick building. It has cast iron storefronts with large plate glass windows on the ground floor and is crowned by a handsome corbeled cornice and sawtooth frieze.

CC32 Buffalo Bar (Normandeau Building, Rohner's Bar and Billiard Hall)

1881; 1906. 1617 Miner St.

Edward and William Normandeau built this one-story brick building as a dry goods store

CC35 Argo Mill

which John Rohner bought in 1906 and remodeled, adding the elaborate front with its six courses of stepped brick, bracketed metal cornice, and paneled Adamesque frieze with decorative swags. A large, long building with back rooms, it was restored in the 1970s to become once again a popular bar, restaurant, and billiard hall with many antique furnishings, including an Eastlake back bar.

CC33 City Hall

1894; moved, 1986. 1711 Miner St. (southeast corner of 17th St.)

Constructed as the Grass Valley School House at 2325 Miner Street, this building was moved here in 1986 and restored as the city hall. The two-story red brick edifice with hipped roof has a large corner bell tower and asymmetrical plan.

CC34 Rock Eyrie

1881, Robert S. Roeschlaub? 1828 Illinois St. (southeast corner of Virginia St.)

This two-to-three-story random-coursed native granite house is built on a promontory overlooking the town. Posing as a medieval castle, it has round towers on the south corners, the smaller tower on the west having a conical stone cap. A heavily crenelated parapet surrounds the roof beneath two brick chimneys with corbeled throats.

CC35 Newhouse Tunnel and Argo Mill

1893–1910. 2350 Riverside Dr. (NR)

Conceived by Samuel Newhouse (1853–1930), a New York entrepreneur, this $5 million tunnel served many mines and intersected numerous veins of ore with a 21,968-foot bore that ended in Eureka Gulch, just west of Central City in Gilpin County. The tunnel is 8 feet tall and wide and without shoring, as it is carved from solid rock. Two seven-ton Westinghouse electric locomotives moved three-ton ore cars until a serious accident closed the tunnel for good in 1943.

The Argo Mill at the Idaho Springs mouth of the Newhouse Tunnel opened in 1913. The seven-story, steel-frame mill with corrugated metal covering is terraced up the mountainside along Clear Creek and surrounded by tailing dumps. It is open to tourists, as is the nearby Edgar Mine of the Colorado School of Mines.

CC36 Indian Hot Springs

1869; additions. 302 Soda Creek Rd.

Harrison Montague built the stone and frame center portion of the current lodge and a natatorium and baths using the hot mineral waters of Soda Creek. Another $300,000 in improvements included twenty-four cottages (c. 1912), a two-story, thirty-two-room main lodge (1905), and a dining room (1924). Water ranging from 104 to

112 degrees F. is used for a large, plastic-domed pool and for various private baths, including some subterranean stone caverns with chest-deep pools and a mud bath.

CC37 Stanley Mines Mill

1 mile west of Idaho Springs along Clear Creek, U.S. 6 and I-70

Claims owned by the Stanley Mines extended from the top of the ridge north of Clear Creek to the top of the ridge south of the creek and over into Spring Gulch. Cornish miners organized in 1864 what became the Stanley Little Mattie Group to work nearby rich lodes. The large, metal-clad frame mill and its extensive tailings bespeak the production volume. The adjacent two-story frame house presumably was for the manager. Efforts to revive the Stanley mill in recent decades have led to its stabilization and improvement.

CC38 Mount Evans Highway

1927

At the time of its construction, this was the world's highest paved auto road. It passes a new U.S. Forest Service visitors' center and some rustic picnic shelters before reaching the remains of Crest House (1941, Edwin A. Francis; Justus Roehling, builder; NR) at the 14,264-foot summit. A 1979 propane fire destroyed all but the outer walls of this two-story structure of stone, wood, and glass combining organic and Modernist elements. It housed a coffee shop and gift shop and served as a staging station for search and rescue operations.

CC39 Squaw Mountain Fire Lookout

1936, Civilian Conservation Corps. End of Squaw Mountain Rd. off Colorado 103

Battered stone walls above a square concrete base form one-room living quarters. The wood-frame lookout above has a cantilevered catwalk around a central enclosed room with large glass panels on all sides, topped by a hipped roof. Also on the site atop Squaw Mountain are a peak locator on a stone pedestal and a stone pit toilet with a shed roof of flat stones. No longer used as a fire lookout, the structure now serves as an information booth and welcome center.

Empire

Named by New Yorkers for their native state, Empire (1860, 8,601 feet) remains a quiet town of about 400, little affected by modern developments. North of town, beyond the current dump, are the ruins of Upper Empire or North Empire, the original mining town that was overshadowed by the current townsite along U.S. 40. Early vernacular frame buildings include the Mint Saloon, 13 East Park Avenue (NR), and a Carpenter's Gothic cottage (1881), 167 Park Avenue (U.S. 40), now the Mad Creek Bed and Breakfast. The Town Hall (c. 1880s?), Park Avenue (U.S. 40), is a two-story clapboard building with a cupola and siren on top. As much city business is conducted in the downstairs Hard Rock Cafe, which has been here since 1932, as in the upstairs town hall.

CC40 Peck House

1860s. 83 Sunny Ave. (NR)

James Peck arrived in Empire in 1862, struck it rich with the Pay Dirt Mine, and built the home now celebrated as Colorado's oldest operating inn. The two-story clapboard hotel with its full-length front veranda overlooks the town of Empire from a splendid hillside site. The original four-room house (now the reception, bar, and kitchen area) is a front-gabled structure on the west side of the current hotel. The large, two-story, side-gabled addition (c. 1881) contains twelve bedrooms and a downstairs billiard room, library, office, and women's lounge. The west wing addition (c. 1958) houses a new kitchen and dining room.

The hotel, opened in the 1860s, became a stage stop on the Georgetown–Middle Park run over Berthoud Pass. During the quiet decades for mining, it became a boardinghouse that was often vacant. In 1958 Louise C. Harrison and Margaret Collbran reopened it as a hotel, bar, and restaurant after installing central heating and plumbing and carrying out an extensive restoration and refurnishing. Harrison, the granddaughter of brewer Adolph Coors, tells the story in her book, *Empire and the Berthoud Pass* (1964).

CC41 Red Men Hall

1898. 125 W. Park Ave. (U.S. 40)

The local chapter of the Improved Order of Red Men, a nineteenth-century fraternal organization founded in Baltimore in 1833 to preserve the culture of the American Indian, built this two-story, clapboard, balloon-frame hall. Now restored, it has an enclosed exterior staircase that leads to the upstairs museum containing dioramas, kachinas, artwork, and historical exhibits.

CC42 Guanella Ranch

1862; additions. U.S. 40, 1 mile west of Empire

Five generations of the Lindstorm and Guanella families have lived in this slab log ranch house with its oversized third-story dormers and a broad, wraparound porch. Pressed metal ceilings and many old elements and furnishings fill this house, which has also served as an inn, a brewery, and a tavern.

CC43 Urad Mine

1914. 7 miles west of Empire on Jones Pass Rd. turnoff from U.S. 40

The Climax Molybdenum Company won the first National Environmental Protection Award for reclamation efforts at the Urad Mine, an old gold and silver mine that became one of America's first molybdenum mines in 1914. After closing the strip mine in 1974, Climax brought in topsoil and reforested. On the back side of the area, however, scars remain both from Urad operations and from Climax's newer, still operating Henderson Mine nearby.

Dumont

Dumont (1861, 7,950 feet) was known as Mill City until 1879. Surviving buildings include the one-room Dumont Schoolhouse (1904) and the Green Dumont Stage Station, now a museum. Mill City Road House (1860), U.S. Highway 40 near Mill Creek Road, to the east of the current post office, is a one-and-one-half-story hewn log structure said to be one of the oldest buildings in Clear Creek County. The L-plan structure has notched corners, and the intersecting frame gable roofs have rough overlapping boards in the gable ends. Used as a gift shop and post office until the late 1950s, it is currently boarded up and deteriorating.

Park County (PK)

The 9,000-foot-high, mountain-rimmed valley that makes up most of Park County is the cradle of the South Platte River. Its early name was Bayou Salado, for its salt deposits. French trappers and traders called it *parc* (park, or pen for wildlife).

Yankees renamed it South Park and made it one of Colorado's original 1861 counties. Gold strikes in 1860 brought hundreds of settlers; some gold has been mined here ever since, along with other minerals. The Denver, South Park & Pacific Railroad (DSP&P) arrived in the 1880s, bringing flush times and some 5,000 residents. By 1890 decline had begun as the South Park mines played out and the county's elevation, averaging two miles high, discouraged agriculture. Of seventy-one small railroad, mining, and ranching communities, less than a dozen survive as post office towns.

Since the 1880s, Park County has escaped a major boom; it remains a nearly empty empire with only two traffic lights. It has no major mines, ski areas, or industries, only scattered cattle, dude, and hay ranches, summer cabins, and fishing resorts. Half of this huge county is within national forests. Travelers reaching the summits of Hoosier, Kenosha, and Ute passes are rewarded with breathtaking views of vast, relatively flat South Park, stretching some fifty miles north to south and twenty-five miles east to west. Only recently, Denver's growth has crossed the eastern edge of this county, whose population jumped from 2,185 in 1970 to 7,174 in 1990.

Fairplay

Fairplay (1860, 9,953 feet) was organized as the "Fairplay Diggings" by miners squeezed out of the nearby mining camp of "Grab-all." Fairplay prospered and became the county seat, while most other mining towns became ghosts. Mining continued until the 1970s, when the last large dredge boat working streams around the town was dismantled and shipped to South America. Telltale gravel mounds still disfigure strands of the Upper South Platte. Fairplay, whose population has been static at around 400 for decades, turned to tourism. The town's most unusual structure is the Prunes Memorial (c. 1930), a crude downtown monument of rocks framing a memorial case and bas-relief of a burro that lived to be sixty-three years old. This is a tribute to the beasts of burden who hauled building materials into remote mining camps and brought out ore.

Fairplay, Prunes Memorial

PK01 South Park City Museum

1959, Edward L. Bunts. 4th and Front sts.

Log and frame buildings from throughout the county have been brought together at South Park City, a re-created mining frontier town. Edward Bunts, a Colorado Springs architect, planned this extension of Front Street as a dirt lane with plank sidewalks lined by thirty-two relocated historic structures maintained by the South Park County Historical Society. As Colorado's best single collection of early mining camp architecture, it contains the V-notched, hewn log Park County Courthouse (1862), moved from Buckskin Joe; a stage house (1879) of 18-inch-thick spruce logs from the top of Mosquito Pass; the Greek Revival Bank of Alma (1870s); and the Garo Schoolhouse (1879). Buildings representative of mining frontier towns include a mortuary conveniently located between the doctor's and dentist's offices. A false-fronted saloon from Alma, Rachel's Place, has an unusual Neo-Gothic back bar. The Sumner Brewery (1873) and Sumner Saloon (1879) are both National Register structures built by Leonard Sumner of red sandstone quarried on nearby Red Hill. The brewery, in its original location, has a three-story facade of rough rubblestone smoothed over with tinted mortar and a bowed parapet. Rubblestone in undulating courses forms the other three sides of this much-altered antique. Displays inside depict early mining artifacts and tools. Sumner Saloon is a one-story frame building with a false front, adorned by a double Carpenter's Gothic cornice with double brackets. Near the entrance to South Park City is Memorial Chapel (1867), a squared log structure built as a hotel, which Father John L. Dyer turned into Fairplay's first house of worship.

PK02 Park County Library (Park County Courthouse and Jail)

1874, George W. Nice. 418 Main St. (NR)

Colorado's oldest continuously used courthouse hosts ceremonial trials once a year in what is now the county library. Rough, uncoursed granite walls wrap this two-story antique. Smoothly carved arches for openings and wide, double-bracketed eaves lend Italianate elegance. In the little-altered interior, the county clerk's vault holds a run of *The Fairplay Flume and Park County Republican,* plus other prized library possessions. The separate, one-story jail is of the same uncoursed, rough granite with a steel door and window bars. The buildings share the large block with the graves of the burro Shorty and his canine companion Bum.

PK03 Fairplay Hotel

1922. 500 Main St.

A replacement for two earlier hotels that both burned, this two-story clapboard and shingle inn has a concrete base clad in cobblestone that rises, as pillars of a now-enclosed front porch, into roof parapets. The dark wood interior is brightened by large, square, six-over-one windows. Squeaky

floors reveal the presence of visitors in the venerable parlor, upstairs bedrooms, dining room, and the Silver Heels Saloon. The latter has cast iron swivel barstools and a brass rail at a pilastered front bar with Adamesque trim. Half of a mahogany back bar, made in St. Louis by Brunswick in 1883, has Corinthian capital columns and an Adamesque frieze below the classical cornice. The saloon's huge cobblestone fireplace is decorated with a bull's head in honor of the county's cattle ranchers.

PK04 Sheldon Jackson Memorial Chapel

1874. 6th St. (southeast corner of Hathaway St.) (NR)

The Reverend Sheldon Jackson, an illustrious pioneer Presbyterian circuit rider, built this splendid board-and-batten example of Carpenter's Gothic. Lancet arches form the windows and doorway and grace the open bell tower. The steeply pitched roof stretches skyward in a lacy, vertical composition. This tiny Gothic Revival gem is enhanced by a well-kept garden and picnic pavilion behind a jacal fence of tree branches. The pavilion faithfully replicates the steep bell tower with its dripping bargeboard, hexagonal cap, and finial. Of twenty-two Colorado churches founded by Sheldon Jackson, this is one of the finest of the sixteen still standing. In 1877 Jackson moved to Alaska, where he achieved further fame as a pioneer circuit rider and church builder.

PK05 Leavick

1896–1899. 2 miles south of Fairplay, turn west and proceed 11 miles up Horseshoe/Four Mile Creek on Park County 18

This ghost town, with ruins of the Hilltop and Dauntless mines and mills, was named for the mining man who brought in a spur of the DSP&P. After the Last Chance Mine was discovered near here on Mount Sheridan, it attracted prospectors, mills, and a little community that had a post office for only three years. The best-preserved buildings, including a one-room trapper's cabin and the Hoffman Brothers Blacksmith Shop, have been moved to the South Park City Museum (PK01).

Alma

Alma (1873, 10,355 feet), named for an early woman settler, claims to be the world's highest incorporated town. Its smelter and various mills made it a pioneer mining hub that remains a frame and log town of one- and two-story nineteenth-century structures. Besides the grand Queen Anne dwelling on the hill at 48 North Pine Street, there are several two-story, clapboard-fronted hewn log buildings, including one at 241 Main Street with a two-story bay window and second-story rear door for access in deep snow.

PK06 Alma Fire House and Mining Museum

c. 1880s. Northwest corner of Main and Buckskin sts.

Vertical boards make a false front for a peeled log cabin with unnotched corners that houses artifacts squeezed in around a shiny red and chrome manually drawn water pumper.

PK07 Town Hall (Alma Schoolhouse)

1928. 59 E. Buckskin St.

Vaguely Mission Revival, this one-story stucco building has a two-story entry tower. Matching wings wear crenelated parapets responding to the central bell tower. Colorful tile arches tie newer corner entrances to the central entry.

PK08 Silver Heels Tavern

1920s. 11 Main St.

The full-width front porch of the Silver Heels Tavern is part of a one-story horizontal shiplap facade on a stuccoed cinderblock building forming a balustraded false balcony. The false front has Carpenter's Gothic brackets supporting a modest board cornice with a central pediment. A plank floor, balcony, and old-fashioned high-back booths under a pressed metal ceiling embellish the interior. Silver Heels, a legendary prostitute with a heart of gold, nursed local miners through a smallpox epidemic.

PK09 Buckskin Joe

1861–1866. 2 miles west of Alma on Buckskin Rd.

Nothing is left of the former county seat but a cemetery that is being reclaimed by aspen, evergreens, and wildflowers. In much better shape is the nearly intact nearby Paris Mill (1890s–1950s) and the still working Home Sweet Home Mine, which claims to be the only rhodochrosite mine in the United States. A well-preserved *arrastra*, an ore-crushing device fashioned from natural stone, may be found near the town on Buckskin Creek.

PK10 London Mine and Mill Complex

1931–1980s. 1 mile south of Alma, turn right on U.S. Forest Servide Rd. 438 (Mosquito Pass)

The old mining town of Park City lies one mile up this dirt road. A mile farther west, the London complex stretches for several miles along the road and Mosquito Creek. The North and South London Mines, opened in 1883, were connected to the railroad spur up Mosquito Creek by a 4,500-foot aerial tramway, remnants of which can still be seen. Production of 100 tons per day justified a custom gold mill, which operated into the 1980s. The rough, four-wheel-drive road to Leadville over 13,186-foot Mosquito Pass meanders through many other mining ruins.

Bailey

William L. Bailey, who settled here in 1864, founded a remote ranch that has become Bailey (1878, 7,750 feet), a town of several hundred residents. Timber resources attracted settlers and the DSP&P, which arrived in 1878, and sawmills and lumberyards proliferated. Today Bailey is a small-town hub for many summer homes and resorts.

PK11 McGraw Park

1972. Downtown Bailey

Town founder William Bailey and his brother-in-law, the Reverend John Dyer, the energetic Methodist minister who wrote *The Snow-Shoe Itinerant*, built a two-story cabin on Main Street in 1864 for Dyer's sister, Elizabeth L. Entriken. The Entriken Cabin, moved to McGraw Park in 1973, now houses historical artifacts, memorabilia, and photographs. The park also contains the Bailey Public Library, a Colorado & Southern Railroad caboose, and a one-room schoolhouse (1899) moved from near Shawnee. The Keystone Bridge (c. 1865, Keystone Bridge Company, Pittsburgh), relocated here after service in both Leadville and in Platte Canyon, is a DSP&P bridge now used as a pedestrian

bridge. The only Keystone Company bridge in Colorado, it is a wrought and cast iron through truss single-span design.

PK12 Estabrook Historic District

4.2 miles southeast of Bailey on Park County 68 (NR)

This summer resort originated with the 1874 ranch of Joseph A. Estabrook. After the DSP&P arrived in 1878, railroad backers Charles B. Kountze and his brother-in-law William Bart Berger bought the ranch and converted it to a family retreat. Kountze, with his brothers and brother-in-law, founded the Colorado National Bank. Since the 1860s the Bergers and Kountzes have been prominent in Denver banking and social circles, often retaining leading architects to design their banks, homes, and summer places. The Kountze House (1902, William E. Fisher and Daniel Riggs Huntington) is a two-story, slab-sided house with a wraparound veranda with hand-carved porch posts and a stable on Craig Creek. The Rivercliff Ranch consists of a two-story granite house (c. 1930) and an old barn, a corral, and an icehouse. The Bergers' Estabrook Ranch House (1874 with additions) exemplifies the western Rustic Style with its steep-pitched roof, gabled dormers, diagonal and vertical slab construction, and wraparound porch with ornamental log railings. Most other Estabrook structures are in the same style: timber-framed buildings sheathed with thin semicircular or elliptical sections of log covered with bark. Whole or partial bark logs are also used for fences, railings, and

PK12 Estabrook Historic District, Estabrook Ranch House, 1890

trim. These structures fit unobtrusively into the mountain forests. Only the rail bed, frame and shingle depot, and one single-span bridge survive of the Denver, South Park & Pacific, which allowed city folks to get "back to nature."

PK13 Glen-Isle Resort

1900. U.S. 285, 1.5 miles west of Bailey (NR)

Willis M. Marshall, president of the Central Bank of Denver, and some Denver partners bought a 160-acre tract and sent a crew of twenty-five men to build this lodge overlooking an island in the South Platte. Spared major remodeling, this rustic riverside resort has a three-story, slab log and shingle main lodge with a round, three-story corner tower. Split lodgepole pine logs laid vertically sheathe the lower exterior walls, with square shingles above. Unpeeled logs likewise serve as trim and railings, while the windows have distinctive diamond panes. A broad, shed-roofed veranda wraps three sides of the lodge, with log furniture from which guests may survey the North Fork of the South Platte River cascading through the front yard or towering evergreen trees shading a log gazebo. Outlying cabins have similar vertical slab and shingle exteriors under forest-green composition roofs. Inside the main lodge, the dining room has a high, beamed ceiling and central fountain with a trout pond.

PK14 Shawnee Trading Post

c. 1900; rebuilt 1918 after a fire. Off U.S. 285, 6 miles west of Bailey

This white clapboard general store is the liveliest place in a sleepy hamlet overlooking the Platte Valley and the Fitzsimmons Ranch. The overnight stage stop and DSP&P depot are gone, and only the stone foundations survive of the Shawnee Lodge, which fell to fire in 1929. The Grandview Hotel (1886) has been restored as a bed and breakfast.

PK15 Christ of the Rockies

1934. U.S. 285, 13 miles west of Bailey

This railroad stop, originally named in 1885 for DSP&P agent David N. Cassells, became

PK15 Christ of the Rockies in fabrication, 1934

a Catholic summer camp called Santa Maria. On the hill behind the camp the statue of Christ, made by Denver's Northwestern Terra Cotta Company, stands 33 feet high on a 22-foot-high pedestal, second in size only to the Cristo in Rio de Janeiro. It is a colossal copy of a statue by New York sculptor Harriet Frismuth for the John K. Mullen family plot in Mount Olivet Cemetery near Golden.

PK16 Webster

1877–1909. U.S. 285, 12 miles west of Shawnee

A small town grew up at the stage and, later, railroad stop, where Emerson and William Webster operated the Hall Valley and Webster Pass wagon road to Montezuma, Breckenridge, and the Summit County mines. Today the cemetery, ruins of charcoal ovens, and frame and log cabins linger in an easily accessible ghost town.

Jefferson

Jefferson (1861, 9,500 feet) began as an 1860s gold-mining camp and was revived in 1879 by the arrival of the DSP&P, whose

PK16 Webster

depot (1879) along U.S. 285 has been lovingly restored. This clapboard station is typical of hundreds of small-town depots with its simple, side-gable construction, bracketed eaves, signboards, and station agent's bay window. The well-maintained Jefferson Schoolhouse (c. 1900) is a one-story, lapsided structure with an enclosed entry and open mansard bell tower.

Como

Como (1879, 9,800 feet) was named for the lake in their homeland by Italian miners who worked coal mines near this DSP&P town and division point. From here a narrow-gauge branch climbed over Boreas Pass to Breckenridge and the Summit County mines, while the main line headed southwest over Trout Pass to Buena Vista, Leadville, and Gunnison. Around 1890, some 400 people lived in this town, subsequently ravaged by several fires and now mostly empty.

PK17 Como Roundhouse and Depot

1880–1881. East end of 7th St. (NR)

This six-stall roundhouse of rough stone with decorative stone pilasters and arches lost a later frame addition with seven more locomotive stalls in a 1935 fire that started in a bird's nest. Of the wrought iron turn-

table only the pit survives. The chimneys have flat-topped spark arresters for locomotive smokestacks. This handsome if dilapidated tombstone to the days of narrow-gauge steam railroading is being slowly restored. The adjacent depot (1880), east end of 6th Street (at Rowe Avenue) (NR), is a one-story frame rectangle with an ell addition. It has lost many original features, such as a polygonal bay, but three brick chimneys survive.

PK18 Depot Hotel

1897. East end of 5th St. (NR)

This two-story, hip-roofed hotel replaced a more elaborate predecessor, the Palace, destroyed by fire in 1896. The current brick hotel aspires to a Neo-Georgian plan and

PK17 Como Roundhouse

style with two rectangular, two-story sections connected by a central, one-story wing. Closed in 1938, it reopened in 1979 and has been subjected to minimal "improvements."

PK19 **Boreas Pass Section House**

c. 1884. 9 miles northwest of Como (NR)

Between Como and Breckenridge, the old DSP&P rail grade was converted to a dirt auto road by the U.S. Army Corps of Engineers after the railroad abandoned the line in 1937. Atop 11,498-foot, blizzard-blasted Boreas Pass, a small community hung on for only a few years. Of a post office, frame depot, stone engine house, turntable, water tank, section house, and 957-foot-long snow shed, only the log section house and one cabin still stand. Both are being restored by the U.S. Forest Service.

Hartsel

Hartsel (1875, 8,860 feet) was founded by Sam Hartsel, who introduced shorthorn cattle to Colorado at his ranch here. The Hartsel stage stop evolved into a station for the Colorado Midland Railroad, a standard-gauge line from Colorado Springs whose rail bed and passenger and freight depots survive on the south side of Main Street (U.S. 24). The South Park Mercantile (1906) is a Mission Revival, one-story store with curvilinear front and side parapets and red tile roof. The Swift Meat Packing Company of Chicago built the store after acquiring the old Hartsel Ranch and operated it until 1916, when the federal government began breaking up Swift's meat-packing monopoly. Today this old-time general store with a soda fountain, as well as an old schoolhouse, an antique saloon, and other pioneer buildings linger in a town where cattle are still driven down the main street.

PK21 **Salt Works Ranch**

1864. 13 miles west of Hartsel

Salt springs, marshes, ponds, and Salt Creek gave South Park its early name of Bayou Salado. Charles Hall, a New Yorker, homesteaded here in 1862 and opened a salt factory in 1864. Its square, 60-foot-high stack of battered stone rising above the two-story frame factory at its base is South Park's tallest landmark. Although the saltworks closed in 1883, six generations of the Hall family have operated the site as an 8,000-acre cattle ranch.

Jackson County　(jc)

Young (1909) Jackson County comprises most of North Park, the high, isolated headwaters of the North Platte River. The park, which spills into Wyoming, is the northernmost of Colorado's four large, mountain-rimmed central valleys. It is defined on the east by the Medicine Bow Mountains, on the south by the Rabbit Ears Range, on the southeast by the Never Summer Range, and on the west by the Park Range. These forested mountains and foothills descend to dry grasslands and sagebrush on a valley floor that the Indians called the Buffalo Pen. White settlers have made the 1,628-square-mile county a livestock pen, noted for its cattle ranches.

Jacques Bijeau, Jim Bridger, Old Bill Williams, Jim Baker, and other legendary mountain men hunted in North Park as early as the 1830s. Rabbit Ears Pass and Willow Creek Pass on the south (now traversed by U.S. 40) and Cameron Pass on the east became the principal routes into the county. The early gold mining towns of Pinkhampton and Teller have vanished, leaving only scars in the landscape.

Ranchers began to settle by the 1880s, and the railroad spur (1911) from Laramie, Wyoming, made coal mining and logging important. Lumber mills are still active at Gould and Walden.

Of some 1,600 residents, half reside in the county seat of Walden. Hay ranching is the mainstay, with cattle and sheep also important. Oil and coal production, and a little gold mining, boost the economy. Recreation has become a tourist draw in a county with abundant public lands, including the Mount Zirkel Wilderness Area, the North Sand Hills Recreation Area, several wildlife refuges, Routt National Forest, and Colorado's only state forest. Antelope, bear, beaver, deer, and recently introduced moose make this county popular with wildlife lovers—and hunters.

Functional metal, stone, and wood-sided buildings are battened down against the winds and blizzards. The county offers Colorado's finest tipi ring site northwest of Cowdrey and vintage ranch complexes such as the Big Horn.

Walden

Located, as the county seat, in the center of North Park, Walden (1881, 8,099 feet) was named for Marcus Aurelius Walden, a pioneer postmaster. The county remained largely wild until the Laramie, Hahn's Peak & Pacific Railroad arrived from Wyoming in 1911. This road, which was soon swallowed by the Union Pacific, opened up North Park for coal mining and logging. Until it closed in 1994 a large Louisiana Pacific lumber processing plant was Walden's major employer. As the only town of any size in all of North Park, this is the center for logging, ranching, farming, and tourism.

Main Street notables include the three-story, solid sandstone Odd Fellows Hall (1912, William H. Bowman), 450 Main Street, with its crenelated parapet; the First National Bank (c. 1918), 476 Main, a one-story red brick and white terracotta Beaux-Arts structure; and Jack's Auto Parts, formerly F. W. Smith Livery (c. 1910), 528 Main, with shiny new steel siding over an old frame barn enhanced by a stepped false front and side dormers. A fine stone cottage (c. 1920), 413 LaFever Street opposite the courthouse, with white quartz doorway and window trim and quoins under a steep-pitched roof, is a home worthy of Snow White and the Seven Dwarfs. The Kohlman Ranch (1879), 2156 Colorado 14, and the Wattenburg Ranch (1884), 15760 Jackson County 12 West, maintain historic structures. Despite a fine site on the edge of a bluff, Walden is swallowed by its environment—the vast prairie and the big sky. The smallness and fragility of the town are accentuated by the picturesque Walden Cemetery at the south end of Main Street.

JC01 Jackson County Courthouse

1913, William N. Bowman. 404 4th St. (at LaFever St.)

Dominating this sagebrush hamlet on a hilltop site, the three-story Neoclassical courthouse is made of large blocks of rough-faced native sandstone with dressed stone quoins and two-story Ionic columns of cracked concrete. Pediments and balusters dress up the roofline. The interior retains the original woodwork, signage, and floor plan.

JC02 **North Park Pioneer Museum**

1883, Norell and Johnson, builders. 365 Logan St.

Located behind the county courthouse, this was the home of State Representative Vic Hansen, who donated the hewn log house to the city and moved it here in 1961. Hansen and many other Swedes, including the builders of this low-slung cabin, settled early in North Park. Swedes had developed the cabin of horizontal logs with notched corners by the end of the Bronze Age and later introduced it to the United States, where it competed with English frame and clapboard.

JC03 **St. Ignatius Catholic Church**

1952, John K. Monroe. 4th and LaFever sts.

A bluff-top site near the courthouse was donated for this brick and stucco church. The simple, handsome interior features a wall of Lyons sandstone behind the altar and golden oak floors and pews.

Cowdrey

Cowdrey (1882, 7,910 feet) was named for homesteader Charles Cowdrey and his wife, Julia, who was killed by a board blown off their roof. This small cattle and supply town near the confluence of the North Platte, Michigan, and Canadian rivers is wrapped around the Cowdrey General Store, a two-story stucco building with vigas. Another exotic structure, .4 mile west of town, is a house made of three geodesic domes interconnected by a skin of pink stucco.

JC04 **Big Horn Ranch**

1903. 1 mile west of Cowdrey on Jackson County 6W along the Union Pacific Railroad and North Platte River

Colorado industrial tycoon Charles Boettcher established this ranch in 1903. The most conspicuous building is one of the largest stock barns in the West, a 100-foot-long, L-shaped frame barn with a red-painted exterior under a gambrel roof. The loft accommodated community dances and parties. The Big Horn Land and Cattle Company, a 100,000-acre spread, is one of the state's largest and best-known outfits. This well-kept complex in a verdant meadow along the North Platte includes a hewn log cabin among numerous frame outbuildings.

JC05 **Placer Creek Tipi Ring Site**

6 miles west of Cowdrey on Jackson County 6W, then 2.3 miles north on Jackson County 3 (Independence Mountain Rd.)

The 30-mile-wide, 8,000-foot-high North Park valley provides a magnificent setting for fourteen stone circles on the southwest side of the road. The circles are grouped along the crest of an open, grassy ridge a quarter mile northeast of Placer Creek. The windy, south-facing site provided good visual scouting, as well as relief from summer insects and winter snow. The stones were probably ritualistic rather than functional, as no known painting or photograph of early tipis shows stones sealing their bottom edges. The stone circles, some with a stone-lined firepit in the center, measure about ten to fifteen feet in diameter. No doubt these stones have been rearranged by visitors and archaeologists, but they remain a magical remnant and are among the best and oldest building footprints left by the Ute Indians.

JC06 Pearl

1889–1919. 2 miles south of the Wyoming border and about 20 miles northwest of Cowdrey

Several private summer residences are among a dozen buildings left in this ghost of a mining town founded by three Chicago capitalists. Lumber for construction was hauled sixty miles from the LaFever Saw Mill on the upper Michigan River, and by 1903 there were sixty houses, four stores, four lodges, two hotels, and a newspaper in addition to the twelve mines producing copper sulfides, silver, and gold. A copper smelter was constructed on a hillside south of town in 1905, but it never operated, since declining mine production doomed the town to an early death. The smelter's concrete foundations are still visible, as are a few stretches of boardwalk and the ruins of log and frame houses. The town was named, apparently, for Pearl Wheeler, the first postmistress. The Wolverine Mine, largest and most productive of a dozen mines, is now a large ruin spilling out its mechanical guts.

Rand

Rand (1882, 8,620 feet) was first called Stringtown, then Rosebud, and finally named for pioneer Jack Rand. It is a tiny ranch town with a few log and frame structures. The Rand Hotel/Store (c. 1906, J. W. Welch), 124 Rand Street, is the town hub. This two-story box under a hipped roof, like many other early buildings, has been given a rustic veneer of slab and frame siding.

Larimer County   (LR)

One of Colorado's seventeen original counties, Larimer consists of irrigated valleys and level plains in the east that climb to foothills and Rocky Mountain National Park on the west. Beginning in the early 1800s fur trappers and miners explored the Cache la Poudre and Big Thompson canyons, principal passageways into the northern Colorado Rockies. No major mineral discoveries were made until "black gold" was struck in the Wellington Oil Field in 1923. Subsequently petroleum became a subsidiary product in a county that is primarily agricultural and the home of the state agricultural college.

Today Larimer is one of the more prosperous and progressive counties in Colorado. It has attracted many new industries and residents, especially to Fort Collins and Loveland. The county has restricted growth by promoting nature preserves in the Cache La Poudre and Big Thompson canyons. Rustic structures compete with tawdry ones for tourists in the resort communities around Rocky Mountain National Park.

Many buildings in the county are faced with sandstone quarried at Bellvue and Stout, west of Fort Collins; at Arkins, west of Loveland; and at Pinewood Springs, whose rose-red granite is still widely used and is featured in Denver's 16th Street Pedestrian Mall (1982). Limestone is also quarried at Laporte, home of a giant cement plant (1923).

Fort Collins

The county seat (1873, 4,984 feet), on the Cache la Poudre River, started in 1864 as an army post named for Lieutenant Colonel William O. Collins. The army left in 1867, but the town persisted, thanks to pioneers such as Elizabeth ("Auntie") Stone, who opened her cabin as the first hotel and school. Fort Collins replaced Laporte as the

Fort Collins

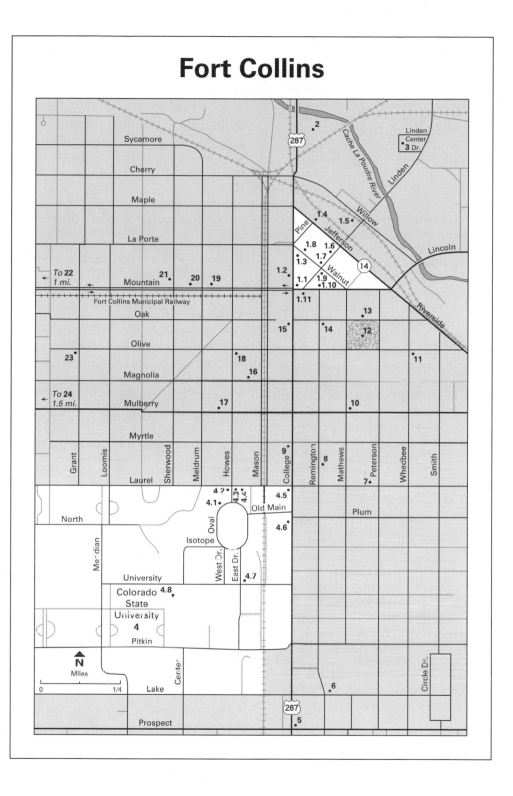

Larimer County seat in 1868 and two years later was selected as the site of the state agricultural college. When the railroad arrived in 1877, it provided an outlet for local produce, livestock, and quarried stone.

In the original plat, streets paralleled the Cache la Poudre River, but Franklin C. Avery platted the "new" town west of College Avenue and south of Mountain Avenue in 1873 using compass points. Avery laid out broad, tree-lined streets, explaining, "People need wide streets and land's cheap." By the 1880s Fort Collins had become a progressive town with electric lights and a municipal waterworks. The city's first resident architect, Montezuma W. Fuller, arrived from Nova Scotia in 1880. Before his death in 1925, Fuller designed more than 300 local homes, schools, churches, and commercial buildings. His own home and some of his surviving work are among many local buildings landmarked by the city of Fort Collins.

Fort Collins grew from an agricultural and college town of 14,937 in 1950 to a city of 87,758 in 1990. The small agricultural college became Colorado State University (CSU) in 1957. Today, with more than 20,000 students, it is the second largest university in the state. Giant new regional industrial plants such as Hewlett-Packard and Anheuser-Busch have also made this one of Colorado's fastest-growing communities.

Despite its swelling population, Fort Collins has preserved much of its original commercial core and nineteenth-century neighborhoods. Its Landmark Preservation Commission (1969) and Historic Preservation Office have designated two dozen local landmarks and the Old Town Historic District. City Hall set an example for preservationists by converting the abandoned Great Western sugar beet plant, at Eastview Drive and North LeMay Avenue, to city offices. College Avenue, the main street, still has diagonal parking and at-grade railroad tracks, giving Fort Collins a small-town feeling.

Fort Collins became nationally noted as an example of how to manage rapid growth after its *Land Development Guidance System* (1981) required landscaping for parking lots, strict sign controls, and neighborhood hearings on new developments. Developers were encouraged to build neighborhoods mixing residential, retail, and industrial structures such as Scotch Pines (1980s), at Drake and LeMay.

LR01 Old Town Fort Collins

Bounded by East Mountain Ave. on the south, College Ave. on the west, and Jefferson St. on the northeast (NRD)

Old Town Fort Collins has thirty-eight historic structures and sensitive infill centered on a 1980s pedestrian plaza. Autos are consigned to a four-story brick and red-tinted concrete parking garage (1985) at Mountain Avenue and Remington Street.

LR01.1 Avery Block

1897, Montezuma Fuller. 106 E. Mountain Ave. (northeast corner of N. College Ave.) (NR)

Franklin C. Avery, a surveyor from New York, came west to help Horace Greeley's Union Colony establish Greeley. In 1872 he was hired by the Larimer County Improvement Company to replat Fort Collins. He stayed on to spearhead the city's growth and built this two-story brick and stone commercial center. Architect Montezuma Fuller, who would open his own office upstairs, designed a three-sided building to fit the triangular site. The principal tenant, the First National Bank, has a red sandstone facade with engaged columns and pilasters and a lion's head keystone atop the round entry arch, marked by a prominent tower. Its two wings sport a brick facade with sandstone trim under a pressed metal cornice. The Town Pump (1936), Fort Collins's oldest operating saloon, is a tiny antique barroom in the northwest wing of the block.

LR01.2 Opera House Block

1881. 1917, Ansel Pierce. 117–131 N. College Ave. (NR)

Like other western "cities" rushing to respectability, Fort Collins had to have an opera house. Although no full-scale opera was ever staged there, the upstairs hall accommodated traveling theatrical companies, local talent, balls, motion pictures, and high school graduations. Ansel Pierce's 1917 renovation of this 100-foot-long, three-story commercial structure gave it a "modern" buff brick veneer with terracotta Art Nouveau ornament and second-story leaded glass transoms. The storefronts have been rejuvenated and the building reanimated with a stained glass galleria.

LR01.3 Commercial Bank and Trust

1907, Arthur M. Garbutt. 146 N. College Ave.

This one-story brick building with quartzite trim is a miniature Neoclassical gem. Pilasters divide three recessed, arched bays beneath a second-story brick false front with a large pediment and inscribed frieze. Since the 1970s restaurants have occupied the interior, which retains its Ionic pilasters, oak wainscoting, fireplace, and walk-in vault.

LR01.4 Union Pacific Depot

1911, Office of the Chief Engineer, UP, Omaha. 200 Jefferson St.

Beneath a cross-gable roof, the well-preserved one-story brick depot retains its old fenestration, much original woodwork, tile floors, and a refurbished molded ceiling in what is now a bar and restaurant.

LR01.5 Northern Colorado Feeders Supply

c. 1900. 359 Linden St.

Stepped parapets and a brick and stone storefront anchor the steep-pitched metal roofs of this combined grain elevator and feed store. Nearby along the same railroad tracks two other venerable mills survive, the restored Harmony Mill and Ranch Way Feeds.

LR01.6 Reed and Dauth Block

1881, William Quayle. 223 Linden St.

William Quayle, who worked in Denver, Fort Collins, and San Diego, produced this two-story brick building. Following a 1983 reconstruction, it once again sports round-arched windows, hewn keystones, and a cast-iron-columned storefront. Quayle also designed the Jefferson Block (1881), a brick commercial row at 209–227 Jefferson Street.

LR01.7 Linden Hotel

1883, William Quayle. 1995, restoration. 201 Linden St. (north corner of Walnut St.)

William Quayle designed this eclectic Victorian edifice as the Loomis and Andrews Block, housing a Masonic lodge on the third floor and the Poudre Valley National Bank on the first. He used local sandstone trim and ornamental stone pilasters beneath an elaborate pressed metal cornice. Note the distinctive clipped corner entry with a two-story oriel crowned by a prominent corner tower with a bell-shaped hood. This became the Linden Hotel in 1904 when the matching wings were added.

LR01.8 Old City Hall Museum

1881, John F. Colpitts, builder. 1981, restoration. 232–234 Walnut St.

After removing a modern metal front from a building that been stripped of its tower and trim, Theodore and Karene Will carefully built a replica facade as part of a conversion to office and residential use. The brick facade now sports a reconstructed tower with mansard roof, and arched doorway and fire truck entrances. Replicas of the original cornices, upper-level window trim, and other architectural details likewise have reappeared. In back, note the saw cut in one of the original bars of the old jail and the rooftop deck of the renovated upstairs living

LR01.7 Linden Hotel, c. 1935

LR01.9 Miller Block, sketch, c. 1890

quarters. This was the city hall until 1957 and a fire station until 1974.

LR01.9 **Miller Block**

1888, John F. Colpitts, builder. 162 Linden St. (south corner of Walnut St.)

One of Old Town's premier structures, this Italianate red sandstone edifice with buff sandstone trim has handsome faces on both Linden and Walnut streets. Both elevations are graced by an elaborate galvanized iron cornice, cresting, and a decorative pediment. Locally made cast iron columns and lintels enhance the exterior. Inside, one of the first Howe truss systems in Colorado supports the second floor, leaving the entire first floor free of posts. Frank C. Miller, a Danish immigrant, built his business to sell both wet and dry goods. His liquor business evaporated in 1896 when the town went dry. His son Frank briefly operated the business after his father's death, then joined a Wild West show, where his feats of marksmanship earned him a niche in *Ripley's Believe It or Not.*

LR01.10 **Hohnstein Block**

1904. 220 E. Mountain Ave. (at Remington St.)

This two-story Italianate commercial building reemerged in the 1980s from behind a modern metal screen to rejoin its Victorian neighbors. One of Colorado's first brewpubs, Coppersmiths, reigns behind the restored facade of former storefronts. Besides considerable interior remodeling to accommodate the brewing apparatus, there are a new side entrance of terne roofing and glass and a rear elevation which includes a beer garden on the pedestrian mall.

LR01.11 **Kissock Block**

1889, Montezuma Fuller. 115–121 E. Mountain Ave. (NR)

Fake stone panels were ripped off this two-story building in a 1983 restoration that retrieved a red brick and native sandstone edifice with cast iron storefront columns. John A. C. Kissock erected this for his title abstract company, among other businesses. Kissock is known as the father of Fort Collins's sewer system because he persuaded officials to install a sewer under Mountain Avenue on a trial basis after he paid engineers to do the feasibility studies and cost estimates.

After an 1895 fire, the Odd Fellows reconstructed the building and converted the second story to their Grand Hall, a social center for community banquets, balls, and concerts. Brick pilasters divide the facade into three two-story bays and continue through the storefront cornice and the protruding cornice atop the building to end in rounded finials.

LR02 **Fort Collins Municipal Power Plant and Fountain**

1936, Burns and McDonell Engineering. 430 N. College Ave.

This Streamline Moderne industrial relic, with boxy setbacks and creamy terracotta trim, commands an expansive site along the Cache la Poudre River graced by an Art Deco fountain (1938, WPA). The plant was sensitively adapted in 1992 by the Colorado State University Mechanical Engineering Department as a testing facility for alternative fuels.

LR03 **The Mission**

1989, John Dengler and Associates. 400 Linden Center Dr. and Linden St.

The Mission, which started as a project of local Catholic community service agencies and was built with multidenominational support, incorporates men's, women's, and family quarters as well as a cafeteria, a job bank, and an elderly outreach program. The architects used gable roofs to give the Postmodern building a residential look. The beige brick and sandy stucco and a skeletal bell tower subtly suggest a southwestern mission.

LR04 Colorado State University

1878; numerous additions. College Ave. to Shields Rd. between Lake and Laurel sts.

The cornerstone of the main building of Colorado State Agricultural College was laid in 1878 amid a prairie dog colony on the south side of Fort Collins. In 1970 the Second Empire landmark burned during a Vietnam War protest. The loss of Old Main left few nineteenth-century structures on a spacious campus to which more than fifty new buildings have been added since the college became Colorado State University in 1957.

Architect Harlan Thomas, who graduated from CSU in 1894, designed several of its buildings, of which only the Mechanical Arts Building remains. Thomas moved on to Denver and then Seattle, where he headed the University of Washington architecture school. The old campus is wrapped around the Oval, on Howes Street south of Laurel Avenue at the north end of the campus. The oval drive encompasses a vast lawn divided by a tree-lined central walk. Surrounding buildings are buff brick with discreet accents of gray sandstone and terracotta in various classical styles. Besides individual landmarks listed below, The Oval contains the old Beaux-Arts library (1927, Eugene Groves), now the Music Building. The finest Renaissance palace occupying the most favorable site is, of course, the Administration Building (1924, Eugene Groves). East of it stands the old Student Union, built with PWA funding. No structure on The Oval is taller than the towering elm trees, and the horizontal, open expanses reinforce the human scale. Southwest of the bucolic old campus, a mass of new buildings reflects the school's growth. The 500-acre main campus is augmented by the 1,700-acre Foothills Campus two miles west, largely devoted to engineering research. Pingree Park, 54 miles west in Roosevelt National Forest, is a summer campus for forestry and the biological sciences.

LR04.1 Ammons Hall

1922, Eugene Groves. The Oval (NR)

Built as a women's gymnasium and social center, this beige brick structure with Renaissance Revival elements departs markedly from the original Romanesque Revival campus style. An implied arcade along the front and parapeted sides connects the four corner pavilions set around a central skylight. Not only an architectural but a social departure, Ammons Hall was named not for CSU's first woman professor, Theodosia G. Ammons, but for her brother, Colorado Governor Elias M. Ammons. Also known as the Women's Club Building, it is similar in concept to Ida Noyes Hall at the University of Chicago.

LR04.2 Danforth Chapel

1954, James M. Hunter. Southwest corner of W. Laurel and S. Howes sts. on The Oval

High walls of thin-coursed rough sandstone and an east wall of opaque glass in a wooden screen stretch from a flagstone floor to exposed ceiling beams on the interior of the Danforth Chapel. A cantilevered altar of black marble and full-height stained glass panels create ascetic simplicity. Double doors beneath a pergola are of hammered bronze with bas-relief angels wearing jeweled halos. A freeform sandstone wall holds back the hillside on the east, defining a small meditation garden.

LR04.3 Guggenheim Hall

1910, James Murdoch. Southeast corner of Laurel Ave. and Howes St.

Simon Guggenheim Hall of Household Arts was donated by the scion of the Philadelphia smelting family who procured a U.S. Senate seat from Colorado. The two story buff brick Neoclassical facade is highlighted by a full-height pedimented entry portico with heroic Corinthian columns in gray sandstone.

LR04.4 Mechanical Arts Building

1885. 1894, Harlan Thomas. South side of W. Laurel St. on The Oval

This two-story red brick and sandstone building was remodeled in 1891 in the Richardsonian Romanesque style by Harlan Thomas, then a twenty-one-year-old student who would graduate in 1894. Originally called the Industrial Arts Building, with "forge room," "molding room," and "modern machines" areas, it is now shops, offices, and workrooms for the building trades and mechanical engineering. Wall cases display antique tools. Next door to the east is a functional industrial shop with stepped flat roofs and a traditional brick facade. Industrial glass walls brighten this WPA-built piece of classicized Bauhaus design.

LR04.5 Botanical and Horticultural Laboratory

1890, O. Bulow. Southwest corner of College Ave. and Laurel St. (NR)

This one-story red soft brick building sits above a raised basement of projecting rough-faced sandstone, with sandstone and darker brick highlights. The roof is a combination of gable and hipped elements, forming a gablet in the rear. The vine-covered entry and ornate, colored glass window give the Queen Anne front facade an inviting, domestic aura.

The laboratory, which originally cost $3,900, was refurbished in 1894 for the Domestic Economy Department, then for the music conservatory. Since 1964 it has been office space. Behind is a potting shed, built from bricks salvaged from the original claim shanty (1874), which held the land until the Agricultural College could be built.

LR04.6 Spruce Hall

1881, Hiram Pierce, builder. 1990, renovation and addition, Pellecchia-Olson Architects. Southwest corner of College Ave. and Plum St. (NR)

The oldest building on campus, just north of the former site of Old Main, is Romanesque Revival with red brick walls accented by bands and panels of a darker red brick. A sandstone staircase climbs to the recessed entrance, whose arch echoes those of the paired windows. The 1990 two-story north addition uses the same brick colors and patterns, but in concrete instead of sandstone and with Postmodern design details.

LR04.7 Student Services Building

1930s? South of The Oval on East Dr.

Located between classic academic edifices on the Oval and modern ones on the south and west part of the campus, this Streamline Moderne structure reflects the transition to modern architecture with its irregular plan, rounded corners, flat roofs, and stepped-back massing. Panels of stucco are set into the corners and flank the third-story windows across the main facade. Numerous terraces and the multipaned steel casement windows add interest to the clean lines of this cream brick building. Unusual circular stepped-back towers house interior staircases.

LR04.8 Morgan Library

1965, James M. Hunter. Southwest corner of University Ave. and Centre Ave.

The design of a Boulder architect, the library was conceived as a series of modular themes that could be repeated. The original L-shaped building had adjoining two- and three-story wings enclosing a courtyard on the northeast. Each level has a protruding zigzag roofline of concrete, breaking up the courtyard elevation and providing visual interest. Recent additions have filled in the courtyard and extended the building to the west.

LR05 Taco Bell (Mawson House)

c. 1930. 1993, Architecture One. 1530 S. College Ave. (northeast corner of Prospect Rd.)

A fairytale lesson in preservation perseverance is this single-story yellow brick house with a Mission Revival red tile roof and round-arched windows in a modified U plan. It may set new standards for fast food restaurant chains invading residential neighborhoods. At the urging of the Fort Collins Planning Department, Taco Bell remodeled the home of lumber magnate Irl Mawson rather than demolish it and erect the chain's standard "Santa Fake"–style eatery. The Mawson House's fine arched side windows have become order and pickup stations, with the company logo on a discreet front yard sign. Inside, the original fireplace, oak front door, and picture window are preserved.

LR06 Old Fort Collins High School

1924, William N. Bowman. 1400 S. Remington St.

This school exhibits an irregular plan with parapeted wings on both sides of a center gable, a three-story columned portico, and a prominent central cupola. Red brick with tan stone quoins covers the three-and-one-half stories. Numerous rear additions do not detract from the front facade. The students and athletic teams are called Lambkins, commemorating the days when Fort Collins was a major lamb feeding center.

LR07 Laurel School and Historic District

1906, Montezuma Fuller. 330 E. Laurel St. and E. Laurel between Matthews and Peterson sts.

This two-story brick building on a rectangular plan has a low hipped roof, a boxed and bracketed cornice, and a decorative frieze. Of the four schools that Montezuma Fuller designed in Fort Collins, the Laurel School (now Centennial High) is the only one remaining. Fuller also designed the German

LR09 Offices (Beebe Clinic)

Congregational Church (1904), 201 Whedbee Street.

The surrounding Laurel Street School Historic District, East Oak Street south to Lake Street and Remington Street east to Whedbee Street, with some exclusions (NRD), is a residential neighborhood platted in 1873. It is characterized by wide streets, mature landscaping, and uniform setbacks and spacing. Of some 665 buildings, 549 are considered to contribute to the historic character of the district. The clapboard Coy House (1876), 401 Mathews Street, constructed by carpenter Grant Ferguson, is the oldest house in the district. Styles range from river rock Craftsman, at 628 East Elizabeth, to the hooded Germanic cottage at 503 Mathews, with its Flemish flared eaves. A hospitable landmark offering a good look at the interior of a typical district foursquare is the Elizabeth Street Guest House (1905, M. G. Conley, builder), 202 East Elizabeth Street (northeast corner of Remington).

LR08 Metcalfe House

1900, William Metcalfe, builder. 634 S. Remington St.

Showcasing local building stone, this one-story dwelling has alternate courses of smooth and rough-faced red sandstone with carved sandstone trim and an elegant sandstone gable dormer.

LR09 Offices (Beebe Clinic)

1939. 605 S. College Ave. (southwest corner of Myrtle St.)

The best Streamline Moderne specimen in town sports a neon accent strip, brick speed lines, corner windows, and curved windows of glass block on its single story. Built as a medical clinic, it has been little altered on the exterior despite conversion to real estate offices.

LR10 Baker House

1896, Montezuma Fuller. 304 E. Mulberry St. (NR)

This two-and-one-half-story brick house with a virtually unchanged front facade is trimmed in rough-faced sandstone and brick banding. A semicircular turret pokes out of the steep, gabled roof. A single-story porch wraps the southeast corner, with nine square wooden piers supporting the curved roof. Frederick Baker, the builder and a mayor of Fort Collins, fancied this later adaptation of the Queen Anne Style with triple front gables and a two-story rounded bay.

LR11 St. Andrews Episcopal Church
(Bethlehem Evangelical Lutheran Church)

1914, Montezuma Fuller. 300 Whedbee (southeast corner of Olive St.)

Buff-colored, rough-faced sandstone distinguishes this small church with a central entry and traditional bell tower. Said to mirror churches in Germany, it has a horseshoe-shaped balcony inside, buttresses, and slight Gothic arches.

LR12 Library Park

Mathews to Peterson sts. between Oak and Olive sts.

The new and old libraries and several pioneer structures enrich this park. The original Carnegie Library (1904, Albert Bryan) of rough-faced red sandstone from the Stout Quarry is now complemented by the boxy, cantilevered $1.4 million Fort Collins Public Library (1975, Alan Zeigel). The old library became the Fort Collins Museum, showcasing local history and a fine collection of Folsom points from the Lindenmeier site, 28 miles northwest of the city.

Library Park's Pioneer Courtyard contains three transplanted early-day log structures, as well as stone hitching posts and architectural bric-a-brac. The Antoine Janis Cabin (c. 1859), a hewn log cabin from Laporte, has been spruced up with a fine sandstone chimney and shake shingle roof. The Auntie Stone Cabin (1864) started out as the community's first private home and served as an officer's mess for the old fort, the town's first schoolhouse, and the home of the city's pioneer woman settler, Elizabeth Stone.

LR13 Andrews House

1889, Montezuma Fuller. 324 E. Oak St. (northwest corner of Matthews St.) (NR)

Eastlake elements such as the porch spoolwork and apron dress up this single-story, red brick home beneath a steep roof with

LR13 Andrews House

shingled gables and an eyebrow dormer. The Charles Andrewses moved next door to 322 Oak Street in 1893 after Montezuma Fuller completed that house. The small, elegant house at 324 Oak is now used by the CSU history department for seminars and meetings.

LR14 Andrews-McHugh House

1884, Lars Kemoe and Montezuma Fuller. 202 S. Remington (southeast corner of Oak St.) (NR)

Stonemason Lars Kemoe started this house with its two-story tower and facade of large, rough-faced sandstone blocks and lighter sandstone trim. Even the chimney and tower cornice are built in the handsome stone. Charles Andrews, cofounder of the Poudre Valley National Bank, bought the house and had Montezuma Fuller complete it. Third owner Jesse Harris, real estate developer and horse breeder, sold the house in 1899 to Dr. P. J. McHugh. McHugh converted the two-story stone carriage house into a private hospital, which he operated until his death in 1920. As both Harris and McHugh were mayors of Fort Collins, the house is sometimes called "The House of Mayors."

LR15 Fort Collins Post Office

1912, James Knox Taylor, OSA. 201 S. College Ave. (corner of Oak St.)

James Knox Taylor, Supervising Architect of the Treasury in Washington, probably never saw this or hundreds of other federal buildings for which he is the architect of record. He sanctioned for Fort Collins a typically noble Beaux-Arts post office with Renaissance Revival details and classical propor-

LR15 Fort Collins Post Office

tions. Built for $100,000 on the site of the Fort Collins Military Cemetery, it is a concrete shell faced with coursed limestone from Bedford, Indiana, punctuated by massive arched windows. Above the transom level and beneath a slightly hipped red tile roof, small rectangular windows are grouped in threes amid frieze carvings, including the seal of the United States in Alabama marble. Large, ornate medallions over the two main entrances carry the letters *US* flanked by cornucopias. After the post office moved to modern quarters in the 1970s, its old home was renovated for shops, offices, and an art gallery.

LR16 **Fuller House**

1895, Montezuma Fuller. 226 W. Magnolia St. (near northwest corner of Howes St.) (NR)

The Queen Anne Style home of Fort Collins's first architect is a two-story brick with an asymmetrical facade and ornate front porch. Fuller used raised stringcourses, shingled gables, and corbeled chimneys of tapestry brick. The rising sun motif of the porch gable is repeated in an elaborate Eastlake screen on the gable end.

Montezuma W. (Monty) Fuller, who practiced in Fort Collins from 1880 until his death in 1925, was a carpenter, builder, and architect. Many of his buildings, both commercial and residential, still stand. His son Robert, after practicing with his father for a few years, moved to Denver, where he joined Robert Roeschlaub. The Roeschlaub-Fuller firm, the oldest in Colorado, is perpetuated

by Montezuma's grandson, Kenneth, and great-grandson, Robert, contemporary Denver architects.

LR17 **Office Building**

1987, James Cox. 212 W. Mulberry St.

This small frame engineering office garnered awards as one of Fort Collins's finest contemporary commercial structures. With its cross-gable roof and narrow windows, it fits unobtrusively into a residential neighborhood.

LR18 **Anderson House**

1901, Montezuma Fuller. 300 S. Howes St. (near southeast corner of Olive St.) (NR)

This may have been the prototype for a design by Fuller which won second prize in a contest sponsored by *Carpentry and Building* magazine in 1902. His two-story frame residence for Peter Anderson on a rough-cut local sandstone foundation has a restored clapboard exterior under a hipped roof. Five bays behind the long porch of the main (west) facade and a two-story south bay enliven the rectangular plan. An arched, sidelighted doorway gives a Palladian look to the second level of the west face. Fuller designed this house for a Norwegian immigrant who parlayed his start as a harness maker into interests in ranching, freight transport, banking, livestock, and the local beet factory of Great Western Sugar. Anderson's Farm Implement Store, beautifully restored in 1993, still stands at 222 Walnut. Peter Anderson's farm near the sugar beet plant became Andersonville, where he built small frame houses for Hispanic workers.

LR19 **Avery House**

1879, Franklin C. Avery. 328 W. Mountain Ave. (near northwest corner of Meldrum St.) (NR)

Franklin Avery, who laid out Fort Collins, may have designed his own house from a pattern book, although architect Montezuma Fuller worked on matching additions. One-foot-thick walls of rough-faced tan sandstone quarried near Bellvue are trimmed in red sandstone. This Chateauesque cottage has tall chimneys and a high gable roof with bargeboard eaves, a

LR19 Avery House

conical-roofed turret, and a porch with sandstone balusters and pillars. The carriage house echoes the exuberance of the style in diminished scale. Avery's cottage is restored on a quarter-block site, shared by a gazebo rebuilt to Avery's original design and a rough-faced sandstone fountain. With sympathetic additions over the years, it is now the Avery House Museum.

LR20 Robertson House

1893, Pierce and Loveland. 420 W. Mountain Ave. (NR)

Queen Anne massing gives this two-story house an asymmetrical front elevation of red brick above a sandstone foundation, with sills and lintels of the same stone. The irregular floor plan features a two-story polygonal bay on the west. A wraparound front porch, reconstructed as part of an exterior restoration in 1991, is pedimented over the entrance and has turned and bracketed roof supports and a decorative wooden screen beneath the eaves. The carriage house (1906) has been remodeled to fit the earlier style of the house.

LR21 Bouton House

1895, Harlan Thomas. 183 N. Sherwood St. (NR)

One of the handsomest domiciles in town, this two-and-one-half-story balloon-frame house has beautiful proportions and Colonial Revival details. Jay H. Bouton (or Boughton), an attorney, businessman, judge, and politician, spearheaded the cul-

tural crusade to erect the Opera House (LR01.2). The ground-floor wraparound veranda features decorative urn finials on its baluster railing. The second floor overhangs the first, and the roof is a complex combination of hip and gable elements incorporating third-story overhanging front gables with Palladian windows. A barn and a root cellar survive in back.

LR22 Fort Collins Municipal Railway

1908. 1801 W. Mountain Ave.

In 1919 the city purchased the Denver and Interurban's Fort Collins operations and dropped the old Woeber cars in favor of lighter, more efficient Birney safety cars. One of these short, open cars, Birney Safety Street Car no. 21, was restored for service in 1985, when the Fort Collins Municipal Railway Society revived streetcar service from City Park to downtown via the grassy median of West Mountain Avenue. For car no. 21 a new barn (1983) was constructed in City Park. The elderly but well-kept Mission Style brick trolley barn (1907), 330 North Howes (southeast corner of Cherry Street), is still owned by the city and used as a storage facility.

LR23 Reinholtz-Forney House

1919. 309 S. Grant St.

This house combines Beaux-Arts and Prairie Style elements in its central classical portico flanked by a symmetrical composition of grouped casement windows, cast iron roof balustrade, and low hipped roof with wide, overhanging eaves. A south wing has an enclosed porch. J. D. Forney, who invented and manufactured farm welding equipment, housed his collection of vintage vehicles in Denver's Forney Transportation Museum.

LR24 Maxwell House

1899, R. G. Maxwell, builder. 2340 W. Mulberry St. (NR)

Above a cut stone foundation, brick walls rise one-and-one-half stories to a cross-gable roof. Decorative bargeboard graces the projecting eaves of the shingled gable ends. Stone walls guard the early farmhouse and grounds, which contain a circular, rough-cut sandstone well house. R. G. Maxwell was a founder of the Empire Grange (1904), nearby at 2306 West Mulberry Street, for which he donated the land.

Bellvue

Bellvue (1882, 5,124 feet) occupies a site where fur trappers buried excess supplies and gunpowder. This was the cache for which the Cache la Poudre River is named. Merchant Jacob Flowers founded the town in 1882 as a supply center for the mountain mining camps of Lulu City and Teller City.

LR25 **Bingham House**

1864, Samuel Bingham. 4916 Larimer County 52E

Samuel and Eliza Bingham came from Missouri in 1864 with their cattle, children, and two wagons. They built a two-story frame house, using simple, front-gable construction. A newer house in front now obscures one of the oldest residences in northern Colorado. The Bingham Hill Cemetery (1862), northeast corner of North Overland Trail and Bingham Hill Road, contains more than 120 graves of settlers and later inhabitants identified in Rose L. Brink's book *Bingham Hill Cemetery* (1988), including various Binghams.

LR26 **Senior Center** (Flowers Grocery)

1887, Jacob Flowers. Southwest corner of Larimer County 52E and Larimer County 23

Town founder Jacob Flowers built this tiny, one-story store of rough-faced stone. After conversion to a Grange hall, it was last recycled in 1977 as a senior center.

Berthoud

Berthoud (1875, 5,030 feet) was founded by the Colorado Central Railroad and named for that road's chief surveyor, Edward L. Berthoud. Unlike pre-railroad towns such as Bellvue, Berthoud was laid out on a grid plan. The old depot, with an entry addition, has been converted to the Lions Clubhouse, 600 3rd Street (northeast corner of Massa-

chusetts Avenue), but the original town hall (c. 1900), 328 Massachusetts Avenue, is still just that, with a newer library addition.

LR27 **Bimson Blacksmith Shop Museum**

1893, A. G. Bimson. 224 Mountain Ave. (NR)

Alfred G. Bimson, a mayor of Berthoud as well as an artisan, constructed this flat-roofed shop, which he operated until 1943, of rough-hewn stone. Now converted to the Little Thompson Valley Pioneer Museum, the variegated pink sandstone building with red sandstone accents is a strong and simple statement of its original purpose.

Estes Park

Estes Park (1875, 7,522 feet), at the main entrance to Rocky Mountain National Park, is named for Joel Estes, who settled in this broad mountain valley in 1859. An abundance of game attracted sportsmen, most notably Irishman Thomas Wyndham-Quinn, fourth Earl of Dunraven, who attempted to make Estes Park his private game preserve. Local settlers frustrated these plans, and ultimately Dunraven sold his 6,000-acre spread. English world traveler Isabella Bird also fell in love with the mountain-rimmed park and described its spectacular scenery and rustic structures in *A Lady's Life in the Rocky Mountains* (1879).

By 1876 the village of Estes Park had emerged where the Fall and Wind rivers join the south fork of the Big Thompson River. A tourist town from the beginning, it blossomed with the establishment of Rocky Mountain National Park in 1916. By the 1960s Estes Park had become an ugly duckling among Colorado resort towns, a hodgepodge of candy and curio shops. Confronted by stiff competition from Aspen, Breckenridge, Telluride, Vail, and other mountain resorts, Estes Park belatedly reformed itself.

Urban renewal began on July 15, 1982, when Lawn Lake Dam on Fall River burst, inundating much of the town. It was the coup de grâce for many struggling creekside businesses. Survivors rallied behind the Estes

Park Urban Renewal Authority to build Riverfront Plaza (1988) and Riverwalk (1990) along the Big Thompson and Fall rivers, adorned with well-landscaped parking lots, waterfalls, pools, native plants, boulders, and life-size outdoor wildlife sculptures. Elkhorn Avenue, the main street, underwent a $1 million streetscaping in 1987, introducing trees, rock gardens, Victorian lighting, and new patios and rear entrances on the Riverwalk. Some historic businesses remain, including Grubb's Livery (c. 1890), East Riverside and Elkhorn Avenue, and MacDonald's Book Shop, which started out as a family home and general store (1908), 152 East Elkhorn Avenue. The Continental Hotel (c. 1890), 110 West Elkhorn, has become Lonigan's Saloon, a romper room filled with electric games, pool tables, televisions, and even a basketball hoop. The Community (formerly Presbyterian) Church (1908), 157 West Elkhorn, has become the guiding light for the Old Church Shops. The Coffee Bar (1901), at East Elkhorn and Virginia Drive, began as a hay and grain barn and a general store. In 1986 the owner costumed the exterior with a gaudy, neo-Victorian frame facade in five pastel colors.

LR29 Park Theatre

The Park Theatre's beacon was added in 1922, crowning Estes Park with a clapboard tower 67 feet tall. Traces of light bulbs outline the tower and its red neon heart, making this a tourist grabber in the Coney Island tradition. In recent years, the closed theater has become the centerpiece of the Park Theatre Mall with frontage on Elkhorn Avenue.

LR28 Estes Valley Public Library

1991, Roger Thorpe Associates. 333 E. Elkhorn Ave.

Roger Thorpe, an Estes Park architect, conceived this impressive earth-bermed, Wrightian addition to the town hall. Native stone walls and pillars, redwood panels, and windows are sheltered by a gently sloping, dark green roof with projecting, bracketed eaves. Intensive treescaping helps conceal the juncture with the less distinguished town hall. The old library (1922; demolished 1992), 225 East Elkhorn, was a single-story stucco structure with stone trim and exposed log trusses under a hipped roof. Constructed by town volunteers in Bond Park, it was graced by a stone fireplace and built-in window seats.

LR29 Park Theatre

1914, J. L. Jackson and L. H. Bond, builders. 130 Moraine Ave. (NR)

LR30 Elkhorn Lodge District

c. 1877. 530 W. Elkhorn Ave. (Colorado 24) (NRD)

The thirteen lodge buildings in this small historic district include six log structures, seven modern but compatible buildings, and a campground for recreational vehicles. The William James family started a cattle ranch, but soon began taking in lodgers, who became their major source of income. The original frame ranch house (1877), with several chimneys and porches, is now the Olde Lodge. The Main Lodge (1901; additions, 1908 and 1912) is a rambling, two-story log structure with two double-decked front porches. It includes a large, half-timbered dining room, a ballroom, and the tiny Corral bar. The twenty-acre site includes a heated outdoor pool and the large, century-old Elkhorn Stables. The old casino and coach house (1890) has been converted to a restaurant.

LR31 Stanley Hotel

1906–1909, T. Robert Wieger. 333 Wonder View Ave.
(NRD)

Freelan O. Stanley and his twin brother, Francis, developed a photographic dry plate process allowing film to be sold in rolls, which they sold to George Eastman. They were also the inventors of the steam-powered automobile named for them. After contracting tuberculosis, Freelan moved to Colorado in 1903 for the climate cure. He bought 1,400 acres from Lord Dunraven to build his summer home and this magnificent hotel complex, one of the finest examples of Georgian Revival in Colorado.

Freelan, who fancied himself an architect, helped T. Robert Wieger design the 150-room complex. Twelve buildings are arranged in a row facing south across a meadow with unobstructed views of the surrounding mountains. The large scale and the sophisticated style of these white clapboard structures contrast markedly with the rugged setting.

From a rough-cut sandstone foundation the main hotel rises to fourth-floor dormers and double octagonal cupola. The symmetrical plan includes three wings, intersecting in an II pattern, with the side wings treated as bays. The pedimented entry bay descends to a generous veranda where guests may sit in bentwood chairs and gaze across Estes Park to Longs Peak. Six sets of paired, turned columns support the veranda's balustraded roof. Fenestration is consistent and highlighted by arched tops, fanlights, Palladian accents, and pedimented and ocular windows.

Inside, the Dunraven Tavern, MacGregor Dining Room, a music room, billiard room, and the many lounges and meeting rooms generally echo the Georgian Revival theme. Stanley himself designed the kitchen, one of the first all-electric kitchens in the country. The spacious, sunny lobby is laced with feathery arches and columns and has a grand staircase.

On the east side of the hotel, the Manor House (1912) mirrors the detail of the hotel in diminished scale. Stanley Hall, a 450-seat concert hall that was originally a casino, has a large pedimented and columned porch. A second smaller porch on the west side has triple sets of pillars supporting its roof. The Carriage House, east of Stanley Hall, initially sheltered the resort's fleet of customized Stanley Steamer "mountain wagons" that each carried a dozen passengers. Tourists might also enjoy the hotel swimming pool, tennis court, bowling alley, golf course, croquet courts, and an orchestra promenading around the grounds.

After Stanley sold the hotel in 1926, it weathered hard financial times when its frame construction made it hard to maintain and insure. Closed during World War II, it afterward opened intermittently during the summers. After a 1980s renovation, it is now open year round and enjoying a renaissance. Despite protests in the 1980s, a shopping center was constructed at the base of the 125-acre hotel site, compromising the view of the hotel and obscuring its entrance.

LR32 Stanley House

1905, T. Robert Wieger and Freelan O. Stanley. 411–415 Wonder View Ave.

Instead of dying of tuberculosis as his doctor predicted, Freelan Stanley lived to be ninety-one and become a community patriarch responsible for developing the Estes Park power company, waterworks, and sewer system. An inventive and promotion-minded genius, Stanley helped put Estes Park on the map as a tourist town. His home, in a high-style Georgian Revival mode, was the prototype for the Stanley Hotel.

LR33 Lord Dunraven's Cottage

1874. 890 Fish Creek Rd.

After his first hunting trip to Estes Park in 1872, Lord Dunraven had this cottage built. The irregular stone and frame house has a combination hip and gable roof which resembles a witch's hat. This many-angled house became the home of Theodore Whyte, the agent who tried to buy all of Estes Park for Dunraven.

LR34 MacGregor Ranch

1873, Alexander Q. MacGregor. 180 MacGregor Ave.
(NRD)

This 3,600-acre ranch bordering Rocky Mountain National Park contains forty-one structures. The ranch house, milk shed, chicken house, barn, and "loafing shed" are

LR34 MacGregor Ranch, house

original, while the smokehouse and root cellar are reconstructions. Alexander Mac-Gregor, an attorney, and Clara Marie Heeney, who came to Estes Park on a sketching expedition, met in 1872 and married. With his wife's help, MacGregor frustrated the Earl of Dunraven's plans to make Estes Park his private hunting preserve by exposing phony homestead claimants who were holding the land. MacGregor set up a law practice and a ranch, while his wife became the town's first postmistress. The MacGregor House (1873) is built around a log cabin that is the oldest structure, while the MacGregor Ranch Museum (1896; remodeled 1920s) is the newest and largest of the family residences, with the MacGregor *XIX* brand incorporated in the slab siding. Inside, family memorabilia and many original fixtures and furnishings are now museum exhibits. MacGregor was killed by lightning in 1896, but his son Donald took over the ranch and operated it with his wife until 1950. The family raised hay, cattle, and oats and took in a few paying dudes. Their daughter, Muriel, kept the ranch going until her death in 1970, while her cattle and cats ran wild, generating many complaints. Muriel doted on her parents and grandparents, for whom she built a rock mausoleum on the ranch. Now a living history museum, this is one of Colorado's best-preserved pioneer ranches.

LR35 Baldpate Inn

1917, Gordon and Charles Mace. 7 miles south of Estes Park at 4900 S. Colorado 7 (NR)

Tucked into an evergreen forest on the north slope of Twin Sisters Peak, this three-story, hand-hewn lodge is a rustic relic. Named for the then popular mystery novel, *Seven Keys to Baldpate*, it boasts "the world's largest key collection." Third-story dormers and exposed rafter ends cap the second-story balcony, which has been enclosed to enlarge second-floor guest rooms. Rustic furnishing and the uneven, creaking floors add to the charm.

LR36 Mills Cabin Museum and Nature Center

1885, Enos Mills. 9 miles south on Colorado 7 (NR)

At age fifteen, Enos Mills ran away from his family's Kansas farm for the Rockies. He built this rectangular, one-story cabin of chinked, notched logs with framed cutouts for the door and windows. Mills supported himself by guiding tourists up Longs Peak and by writing magazine articles and a dozen books on the joys of nature and mountaineering. No one did more to create Rocky Mountain National Park, established in 1915. Even more important, Mills promoted the idea that mountains should be treated as recreational rather than extractive resources. He also extolled rustic architecture, using sticks and poles to make the furnishings in his Long's Peak Inn, which stood across the highway from his cabin before it was destroyed by fire.

Laporte

Laporte (1860, 5,060 feet), the oldest community in the county, started with the 1859 cabin (now in Fort Collins Library Park, LR07) of Antoine Janis, a trader and interpreter. Sam Dion Cabin (c. 1858), 2710 Overland Trail, built by another French trader, is a well-kept, hewn log link to the pioneer era. Other early structures are the Milk House, 5101 North U.S. 287, and Pleasant Valley Schoolhouse no. 7 (1867), a two-room school of native sandstone from the nearby Stout quarries. A newer, larger landmark is the Ideal Cement Plant (1923), 4629 North Overland Trail. The Old Fort Collins Municipal Waterworks (1883, Russell and

Alexander, builders), Overland Trail, is a one-story, double-gabled brick and stone Italianate structure. The original pump house, with additions on its north side, functioned until 1904. It and the surrounding quarter section of open land are still owned by the city of Fort Collins.

Loveland

Loveland (1877, 4,982 feet), founded by the Colorado Central Railroad and named for its president, William A. H. Loveland, has the grid plan of a railroad town. It became a large agricultural center after the Great Western Sugar Company built a plant (1901). Since 1985, Loveland has become a national center for sculpture. The Art Castings of Colorado Foundry (1972), 511 South 8th Street, attracted sculptors such as Dan Ostermiller, George Lundeen, and George Walbye, who helped Loveland's Sculpture in Benson Park (at West 29th and Beech streets) program become a notable exhibition. Peter Toth's towering tree sculptures add further interest to the "Sweetheart City." More than fifty local houses, including that of town founder David Barnes, are featured on a Chamber of Commerce tour brochure. Most are early twentieth-century brick homes with relatively sedate Classical Revival designs. Hewlett-Packard's 575,000-square-foot Loveland plant (1974) is the leading local employer. Although Loveland's population soared from 6,773 in 1950 to 37,352 in 1990, it has maintained a small-town scale. The Municipal Building (1987, Midyette Seieroe and Associates), southeast corner of 2nd Street and Washington Avenue, set an example for architectural recycling by using the Washington School (1905), a two-story Mission Revival building, as a core with tasteful additions in a park setting.

LR37 **Colorado & Southern Depot**

1902, C. B. Martin. 405 Railroad Ave. (NR)

Low, intersecting hipped roofs unite the brick passenger depot with freight offices, both executed in buff brick. The depot has wide eaves and eyebrow dormers. The entry arcade is hidden by a restaurant and retail addition.

LR38 **Loveland High School**

1919, Robert K. Fuller. 211 W. 6th St.

The high school, now a grade school, is a restrained example of Collegiate Gothic in brick and terracotta by one of Denver's leading architects.

LR39 **Post Office**

1937. 501 Cleveland Ave. (southwest corner of 6th St.)

On St. Valentine's Day customers flock here for a Loveland postmark for their Valentine messages. Over the entry of this starved-classical box of gold-speckled brick with sandstone trim, a bas-relief locomotive, plane, and ship speed the mail to its destination. Inside, a 1938 WPA mural by Russell Sherman, *Industries around Loveland,* portrays farmers working wheat and sugar beet fields and the local sugar beet refinery.

LR40 **Rialto Theater**

1920, Robert K. Fuller. 228–230 E. 4th St. (NR)

This 1,014-seat theater is a creamy terracotta Art Deco gem with three glass arcs at street level. Terracotta medallions portray Venetian ships, knights on horseback, and peacocks. A second-story frieze adorns the facade, which also has windows on the second floor. After several modernizations, the theater closed in 1977 and was converted to a retail mall with offices in the balcony. The city of Loveland acquired it in 1987 and used volunteer labor and contributions of the Friends of the Rialto Theater to complete a full restoration in 1993. The Art Deco interior has also been revived. The project has been an example for other successful restorations that have made 4th Street an unusually vibrant and intact main street, including the Beaux-Arts First National Bank, now the Interweave Press, 201 4th Street.

Rocky Mountain National Park

(*See also* Grand County.)

LR41 Headquarters and Visitors' Center

1966, Taliesin Architects. 3 miles west of Estes Park on U.S. 34 (NRD)

The Wrightian tradition as perpetuated by the Taliesin School lives in this unobtrusive, low-slung, flat-roofed structure of moss rock which wraps a Cor-ten steel truss system enveloping the upper floor. A stamped Cor-ten steel fascia tops the building, and the same material is used for balcony railings. The V-shaped stone buttresses harmonize with triangular steel sections. Moss rock panels form the interior walls of the auditorium and lobby. The $575,000 building was designed for the north side of the road, but a powerful park superintendent moved it to the south side, so visitors enter at the rear and rarely see the original facade.

LR42 Bear Lake Comfort Station

1941. West end of Bear Lake parking lot (NR)

A fine example of the National Park Service's rustic architecture, this humble frame structure blends into its natural environment. The concrete foundation is faced five feet high with massive boulders and rounded rocks. A shake shingle roof, projecting log ridgepole and half-log rafters, and a small stone chimney reinforce the rustic character of this rest stop on a forested slope.

LR43 Fall River Road

1922. 9.5 miles between Horseshoe Park and Fall River Pass–Trail Ridge Rd. (NR)

The first auto road across the northern Colorado Rockies was begun in 1913 with convict labor and completed nine years later. Because of its narrow track with steep switchbacks and hairpin curves, it was converted to a one-way motor nature trail in 1968. The partially paved route is lined with ruins of three convict labor camps. At the northwest corner of Willow Park is the Willow Park Patrol Cabin and Stable (1924), a two-room saddle-notched log cabin with exposed logs, rafters, and decks inside what were the kitchen and mess hall for Fall River Road construction crews. Near the 11,749-foot-high junction of Fall River and Trail Ridge roads is an enduring piece of Alpine architecture, Timberline Cabin (1925), a small, low-slung, functional pile of local rock with logs and rocks holding down the roof. Fall River Pass Ranger Station (1922) is a 16-by-20-foot rubblestone cabin dug into the rocky tundra slope under closely spaced log pole rafters, with a trap door in the roof for access in deep snows.

LR44 Moraine Lodge and White Cabins

1910. Bear Lake Road (NRD)

In 1935 the National Park Service purchased the two-story log lodge and converted it to a visitors' center. Built into the slope of a glacial moraine, it has a concrete foundation covered by uncoursed rubblestone. Log walls and an overhung shingle roof, the generous porch, and the stone chimney make this a picturesque addition to a scenic mountain meadow. Inside are mounted wildlife specimens, dioramas, fireplace lounge, and shops. Five small rustic cabins nearby include the William Allen White Cabin (c. 1914), where the famed Kansas journalist summered until his death in 1944.

Virginia Dale

LR45 Virginia Dale Stage Station

1862. U.S. 287, 5 miles south of Wyoming (NR)

Jack Slade built this station and named it for his wife. His hewn log structure is divided by upright logs into three sections under a low gable roof. It has several additions. The Overland Stage Company hired Slade to build and run this stop to keep him from robbing it. A notorious gunman, Slade was described by Mark Twain in *Roughing It* (1872) as an "ogre who, in fights and brawls and various ways, had taken the lives of twenty-six human beings." Since the stage abandoned it in 1869, the ramshackle structure has been a post office, general store, dance hall, and women's clubhouse. It is thought to be the last intact stage stop on the Overland Trail.

Weld County   (WE)

Weld County (1861), named for Lewis L. Weld, the first secretary of Colorado Territory, is one of the richest agricultural counties in the United States. It has led the state in production of barley, beans, oats, sugar beets, hay, and cattle. Wheat, corn, hogs, and sheep are also important commodities. The South Platte River and several major tributaries—the Cache la Poudre River, Boulder Creek, St. Vrain Creek, the Big and Little Thompson rivers—facilitate irrigated farming.

Greeley, the county seat, was founded as the core of the 72,000-acre Union Colony, the most successful agricultural colony in Colorado. Farming and ranching were furthered by the sugar beet factories at Eaton, Fort Lupton, Greeley, Johnstown, and Windsor, as well as the huge Monfort cattle feedlots.

A long Native American history surfaced in 1932 at Dent, a stop on the Union Pacific near Greeley. A flood unearthed woolly mammoth bones with fluted Clovis points among them, suggesting that prehistoric people lived and hunted in the region more than 10,000 years ago. Much later, Native Americans traded at four fur trade forts—Jackson, Lupton, St. Vrain, and Vasquez—erected along the South Platte River during the 1830s.

Surviving vernacular architecture, ranging from cattle herders' line camps to granaries to rammed earth houses, shows how settlers built in the Great American Desert. Among local architects was a pioneer woman in the field, Bessie Smith of Greeley.

Greeley

Greeley, the county seat (1870, 4,663 feet), began as the communitarian dream of Nathan C. Meeker, agricultural editor of the *New York Tribune*. Meeker and *Tribune* editor and onetime U.S. presidential candidate Horace Greeley helped make Greeley the West's second most celebrated colony (after Salt Lake City). Meeker, who admired the French utopian socialist Charles Fourier, had helped plant the Trumbull Phalanx, a utopian community near Warren, Ohio. For his Colorado experiment, which he called the Union Colony, he recruited sober-minded colonists of good character able to buy $155 memberships. The colony, Meeker declared, "will be for the benefit of all the people, not for schemers and speculators." Each family would own a "comfortable, if not elegant home, surrounded by orchards and ornamental grounds."

The site surrounding the confluence of the Cache la Poudre and South Platte rivers was purchased from the Denver Pacific Railway, which had already launched the neighboring town of Evans. The promised utopia disappointed some, including Anne M. Green, who wrote: "We pitched our tent, which was almost daily blown to the ground.

Greeley

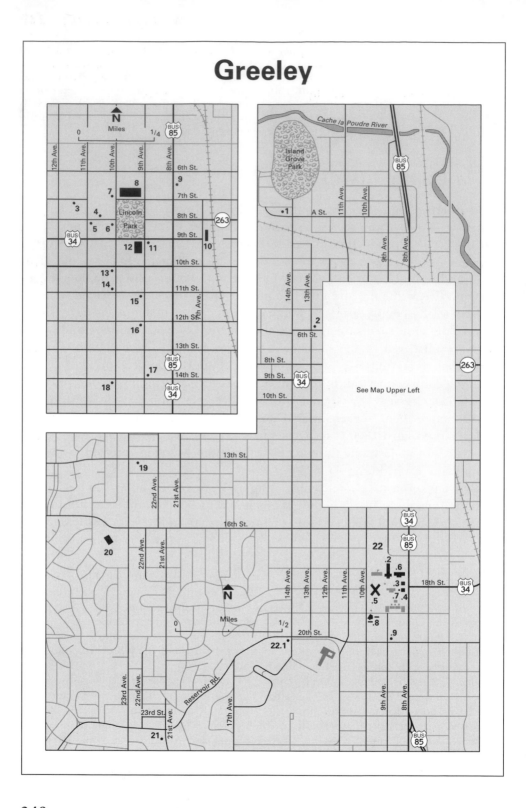

[I] wept and prayed for a change [in my] wretched life. . . ." Another critic complained that the pioneer town looked like "dry goods boxes scattered across the Plains of the Almighty."

Despite some desertions, Greeley within a year attracted some 1,500 settlers. They laid out 100-foot-wide streets and blocks 400 feet square with a 10-acre central square (Lincoln Park). Meeker initially named the north-south streets for trees and began planting each street with its namesake tree, but ran heavily into debt after failed experiments with magnolias, oaks, and other trees unhappy with the Colorado climate. Supposedly to pay his debts, Meeker became the Ute Indian agent in Rio Blanco County, where he was killed by Utes.

To water their patch of the Great American Desert the Greeley colonists built irrigation ditches. Although communal dreams were soon abandoned, the settlement remained a model of irrigated farming. In 1877 Greeley permanently replaced Evans as the county seat. In 1889 the town succeeded in capturing the state normal school for teacher education, which has evolved into the University of Northern Colorado, with some 11,000 students. Another key to the city's growth has been the Great Western Sugar Company plant (1902, The Dyer Company), at 13th Street and 1st Avenue, whose towering smokestacks and storage elevators make it the city's skyscraper.

Much of the nineteenth-century down-

WE.01 Centennial Village Museum, Wagon House

town has been lost, although close-in residential neighborhoods remain fairly intact. Glen Mere Park on the north edge of the university campus clings to a garden suburb plan of the 1930s formulated by the Greeley Garden Club. East Greeley, which has an industrial district along the railroad tracks, is heavily Hispanic. Broad, tree-lined streets of the original plat (1st to 14th avenues and 1st to 16th streets) survive, as does one of the 1870 ditches, Ditch No. 3, part of Meeker's dream for utopia on the South Platte.

WE01 Centennial Village Museum

1976. 1475 A St. (northwest corner of A St. and 14th Ave., on the south side of Island Grove Park)

This reconstructed village emphasizes agricultural and ethnic architecture. Buildings moved in from throughout northeastern Colorado are arrayed around a central gazebo and gardens behind the frame Union Pacific Depot (1910), typical of those built in small towns across the West. The two-room beet workers' shack (c. 1920), board and batten with a slightly bowed roof, is typical of houses built by immigrants known as Germans from Russia, descendants of German farmers recruited to settle in the Volga Valley of Russia during the time of Catherine the Great.

The Wagon House (1917) is a 9-by-14-foot transition between a prairie schooner and a mobile home. A Swedish-American clapboard house (1909), an adobe outbuilding, an octagonal frame granary, and a replica stone house accompany the Italianate Hall House (1885, Robert Hall, builder) and the Queen Anne Style Stevens House (1900), a Sears, Roebuck mail-order house. The first Weld County Courthouse (1861–1863), a hewn log cabin from Evans, shows how unsatisfactory cottonwood logs were for building: as they dried, they twisted, bent, stretched, and wrecked the chinking.

WE02 Project Head Start Center (North Ward School)

1916. Northeast corner of 6th St. and 13th Ave.

This beige brick school has twin villa towers flanking the west entrance, a curvilinear parapet on the south, and Craftsman-style brackets under broad eaves with exposed rafter ends. The building was expanded with a sizable 1933 addition and is now a Head Start Center. A design twin, somewhat larger, is the East Ward Elementary School, now the Sunrise Community Health Center (1916), 1028 5th Avenue (northeast corner of 11th Street) (NR).

WE03 Woodbury House

1871, Joseph A. Woodbury. 1124 7th St. (NR)

Woodbury, a pioneer, carpenter, contractor, and Greeley mayor, built this frame Carpenter's Gothic cottage with a central gable and steep roof. The Gothic Revival style is characteristic of early Greeley homes, although the Tuscan-columned porch is a newer addition. A similar design in masonry is the David Boyd House (1879), 1312 11th Street, home to the author of the 1890 *History of Greeley and the Union Colony*.

WE04 Old Greeley High School and Grade School

1895, Harlan Thomas. 1902, Robert S. Roeschlaub. 1015 8th St., between 10th and 11th aves. (NR)

These two schools are massive rectangular-plan buildings of red pressed brick, joined by a connecting passage, with raised full basements, red sandstone foundations and trim, and red mortar. Architect Harlan Thomas gave the high school round-arched windows with inscribed spandrels and a bracketed cornice above a garland frieze. A single-story apsidal bay on the north housed the public library until 1907. Robert Roeschlaub of Denver designed a simpler, harmonious two-story addition to the west which has recessed, flat-topped windows but uses the same brick and trim with Georgian Revival elements. Both schools were restored in 1982 for professional offices.

WE05 Boomer House

1889. 1024 8th St.

This two-story Carpenter's Gothic cottage with fanciful bargeboard, arched gable truss, and elaborate spoolwork housed William Boomer, a pioneer farmer and a mayor of Greeley. The gable over the front entry porch is repeated above the second-story windows with a sunburst tympanum.

WE06 Park Congregational Church

1906, T. Robert Wieger. 803 10th Ave. (southwest corner of 8th St., on west side of Lincoln Park)

This Tudor Revival exterior was constructed around an existing 1880 church. Buff pressed brick walls rise out of a raised sandstone foundation. The sanctuary is up a half-flight staircase to a porch with a triple Tudor arch and massive stone columns. The gable end above the entry is capped by a metal Norman cross, and a small, round turret projects from the northeast sanctuary corner. The bell tower has a stepped parapet, which extends around the education wing to the south. The dark-stained oak interior is lit by fine stained glass and has an open-beamed ceiling and a floor sloped to the chancel on the west. Since the Congregationalists moved elsewhere in 1956, this has become the Greeley Foursquare Church.

WE07 Union Colony Civic Center

1988, Robert Shreve, ARIX. 701 10th Ave. (northwest corner of 7th St.)

A local firm designed this angular red brick and glass complex housing a $9.2 million civic center, with the 1,700-seat Monfort Concert Hall and 240-seat Hensel-Phelps Theater and a recreation center to the north. Entered through a small ticketing area, the building opens to an expansive atrium with a southeast glass wall and sweeping stairway to two balcony levels.

WE08 **Greeley Municipal Center**

1969, Carpenter, Williams, Johnson. 919 7th St. between 9th and 10th aves. along north side of Lincoln Park

This one- and two-story precast concrete complex with exposed aggregate wall panels includes city offices, the fire and police offices, the library, and the Greeley Municipal Museum. The city council chambers and municipal courtroom are in a separate pavilion attached by a glass passage. The tawny-colored composition mixes Neoclassical, Meso-American, and Prairie Style elements, including overhanging eaves with modified dentils.

WE09 **Good Times Saloon** (State Armory)

1921, John J. Huddart?; Major A. R. Young, superintendent of construction. 614 8th Ave.

This two-story beige brick hall with square, parapeted corner towers and a classical terracotta entry flanked by paired pilasters is similar to those in Brighton, Cañon City, Fort Morgan, and elsewhere. While an armory, this became a popular place for parties and dances. Now recycled as a restaurant and bar, it retains the armory theme with a B-17 bomber suspended over the rear dance floor and numerous missiles, part of a submarine, and other weapons as part of the thematic decor. In addition, hundreds of antiques and four bars make this an offbeat museum. The interior of the large, long building retains the original hardwood floors, staircases, and balcony rails.

WE10 **Amtrak Depot** (Union Pacific Depot)

1930, Gilbert Stanley Underwood. 902 7th Ave. (at 9th St.) (NR)

Gilbert Underwood, a prominent Los Angeles architect, also designed UP depots for Omaha, Nebraska, and Topeka, Kansas, as well as famous rustic lodges for Bryce Canyon, Grand Canyon, Yosemite, and Zion national parks. Underwood's custom design for Greeley framed a one-story polychromatic brick depot with twin parapeted entry bays bearing the UP emblem in terracotta medallions atop elaborate surrounds. The railroad abandoned the building in 1983, but both the exterior and the interior, with its fine stenciled designs and wooden trusses, ticket counter, and benches, have been resurrected by the city for Amtrak service.

WE11 **Coronado Building**

1905, Bessie Smith. 900–920 9th Ave. (southeast corner of 9th St. Mall)

This sleek, two-story brick building has ornate corbeling and diapered panels, with sandstone trim that becomes bands of sills and lintels for the upper story added about 1909. Scars show where a protruding cornice once adorned this handsome structure. Bessie Smith, Greeley's pioneer woman architect, was the daughter of a local contractor who trained with the Denver architecture firm of Baerresen Brothers.

WE12 **Weld County Courthouse**

1915, William N. Bowman. 1965, 1973, restorations. 9th St. and 9th Ave. (NR)

Indiana limestone with terracotta trim covers the four stories and basement of this dignified Beaux-Arts classical edifice. Eight three-story columns with Ionic capitals front the recessed second-story balcony. Triangular pediments top flanking bays whose recessed fenestration is edged by engaged Doric columns. The roof balustrade frames a central round clock tower. The stonework emphasizes the round-arched doors and windows at ground level. Inside, an elaborate ironwork staircase graces the opulent lobby. Interior stair treads, wainscoting, columns, some floors, and one courtroom are finished with white Colorado marble.

The courthouse is flanked on its south and west sides across a courtyard by two- and three-story contemporary buildings faced with wide, horizontal bands of brick and rough-formed concrete and joined by elevated crosswalks.

WE13 **Greeley City Hall** (United Bank)

1970. 1000 10th St. (southwest corner of 10th Ave.)

This contemporary rendition of a Neoclassical treasury is a two-story drum with a dark glass curtain wall fronted by a full-height, glistening white precast concrete arcade. The basement is exposed on the west by a balustraded light well. A central lobby fountain helps diffuse the echo effects of the round plan. Originally a bank, the building now houses the city hall.

WE14 **First Baptist Church**

1910, T. Robert Wieger. Northwest corner of 10th Ave. and 11th St. (NR)

This classical temple in beige brick on a raised foundation has paired engaged Ionic columns and a pedimented parapet above the entry bay. The sanctuary is in near-original condition, with a beamed ceiling and apse with leaded, patterned stained glass flanked by organ pipes. The organ was purchased in 1927 from Denver's Orpheum Theater.

WE15 **Southard House**

1907, Bessie Smith. 1103 9th Ave. (southwest corner of 11th St.)

One of Greeley's most exuberant frame houses, a three-story Colonial Revival mansion with columns on both the east entry and semicircular sitting porches and paneled corner pilasters. was built for Samuel H. Southard, who moved to Greeley in 1877. Palladian windows in the roof dormers and an enriched cornice complete the detailing. In contrast, the White-Plumb Farmhouse (1906), 4001 10th Street, also by Bessie Smith, is a simple frame vernacular construction.

WE16 **Wolff-Lemmon House**

1886. 1203 9th Ave. (southwest corner of 12th St.)

This trim, two-story Queen Anne Style house of red brick has elaborate sweeping curves incorporated in the bargeboard trim of the gable ends. A second-story sleeping porch and two first-story porches amid many gables, bays, and projecting elements add outdoor access.

WE17 **Meeker Memorial House Museum**

1870, Arthur Hotchkiss; various additions. 1324 9th Ave. (NR)

Town founder Nathan Meeker, whose many enthusiasms included adobe construction, built a boxy, two-story adobe house on a quarter-block site donated by the Union Colony. The low, truncated hipped roof with a widow's walk and other eclectic design elements confuse the style, and the adobe has been painted with dark lines to imitate stone construction. After Meeker's death in 1879, his wife and daughters ran this as a boarding house. The city acquired it in 1927 for use as a house museum.

WE18 **Glazier House**

1903, Joseph A. Woodbury, builder. 1403 10th Ave. (southwest corner of 14th St.) (NR)

Jeweler I. O. Glazier commissioned this two-story frame Queen Anne Style house with two-story bays projecting on three sides, multiple gables, and a hexagonal tower above a corner of the front porch. The porch roof is supported by Tuscan columns, and the gable ends are faced with decorative shingles. Now housing the Hospice of Weld County, it retains its original cedar lap siding, oak woodwork, and stained glass in the west wall of the dining room.

WE19 **First Christian Church**

1966, James Johnson. 2230 13th St. (southeast corner of 23rd Ave.)

A Neo-Expressionist shake roof sweeps down from a high peak to flare into wide, overhanging eaves, a form made possible by laminated wood arches. Clerestory windows lighten the composition. Single-story support buildings with low, pitched roofs extend the horizontality of the flaring eaves.

WE20 Cottonwood Square Shopping Center

1975, John Todd, developer. Southwest corner of 23rd Ave. and 16th St.

In this unusually discreet, well-designed mixed-use complex in a residential neighborhood, second-story apartments under uniformly sloped roofs face elegantly landscaped 17th Street. The shops and offices on the first floor face the rear, opening onto a shopping center with many landscaped parking islands to mediate the usual asphalt eyesore. Burnt-orange brick, shake shingle roofing, and dense landscaping characterize the entire project.

WE21 Miller House

1945, J. Palmer Boggs. 2319 21st Ave.

This horizontal house with a low, south-sloping roof was built of dirt dug from the site, shoveled into wooden wall forms, and packed with long hand tampers. The original owners, attorney David Miller and his wife, Lydia Alles Miller, helped found the American Historical Society of the Germans from Russia (see WE01) and built this house to commemorate rammed earth houses in the old country. Several other rammed earth buildings, including a school, were built in this Alles Acres subdivision. Built on concrete foundations, these houses typically have 18 inch thick walls which deaden sound and retain warmth in winter and coolness in

WE22.5 University of Northern Colorado, Gunter Hall of Health

WE22.9 University of Northern Colorado, Faculty Club House

summer. Louvered transoms facilitate heat transfer throughout the house.

WE22 University of Northern Colorado

8th to 10th sts. between 16th and 20th aves.

Colorado's first normal school for teacher training, approved by the state legislature in 1889, originally accepted any student a faculty member vouched for and offered remedial courses as needed. Students who agreed to teach after graduation in Colorado schools paid no tuition. The initial 40-acre campus on Rattlesnake Hill grew to a square mile. Enrollment surpassing 10,000 students led to a new West Campus (1960), 10th to 17th avenues between 20th and 24th streets, on what had been the Petrikin Farm. West Campus structures are more notable for size than style, with a few exceptions such as the Patton House (WE22.1; c. 1916), at the southwest corner of 14th Avenue and 20th Street, an attractive, unmuddled bungalow used for the School of Nursing.

On the tree-shaded original campus, many Collegiate Gothic and Neoclassical landmarks survive. Carter Hall (WE22.2; 1907, Robert S. Roeschlaub; 1939, Frederick W. Ireland, Jr.) was built as the library but was later converted to the administration building. Ireland's addition buried the Neoclassical original under blond brick Moderne additions, including curving two-story reading rooms, and a terracotta entry. Guggenheim Hall (WE22.3; 1913, James Murdoch), a four-story Neoclassical building originally for industrial arts and now housing the fine arts department, has a twin on its south side, Crabbe Hall, formerly the

Home Economics Building (WE22.4; 1919, Thomas P. Barber), named for third UNC president John G. Crabbe. Gunter Hall of Health (WE22.5; 1928, William N. Bowman) is a Collegiate Gothic gymnasium with crenelated parapet and paired gables. The four-story corner tower partially obscures a smaller octagonal tower, which bristles, like its parent, with turrets and parapets. Kepner Hall (WE22.6; 1910, Thomas P. Barber; 1924, wings, William B. Ittner; 1985, Manning, Knapp and Watson) is a three-story red brick Collegiate Gothic building with Lyons sandstone trim. It underwent a $4 million remodeling in 1985 to become the College of Business and now has a wonderful lobby sculpture that plays on classical ruins. The Roudebush Home Economics Practice Cottage (WE22.7; 1915, Thomas W. Barber) is a single-story bungalow named for home economics professor Margaret M. Roudebush. From the same era, Belford, Gordon, and Decker halls (WE22.8; 1921), by St. Louis architect William B. Ittner, are women's dormitories posing as gambrel-roofed barns. Denver architect Robert F. Linstedt designed similar-looking dorms in 1957–1958. Faculty Club House (WE22.9; 1930, 1947, Frederick W. Ireland, Jr.) is a three-and-one-half-story Tudor Revival building with half-timbered walls on the upper floors over brick trimmed in limestone below. It is a faculty residence as well as a clubhouse.

WE23 **SLW Ranch**

1885. 27401 Weld County 58½, 8 miles east of Greeley via U.S. 24 (NRD)

One of Colorado's best-preserved and most storied ranches has earned a Barn Again award from the National Trust for Historic Preservation and a Centennial Farm award from the Colorado Historical Society. Among the seventeen contributing outbuildings of this working ranch along Crow Creek are the Ranch House (1885), bunkhouse (1890), blacksmith shop (1880s), concrete silo (1918), and a dairy barn (1900). The most notable building is a barn (1885) with a three-story cross-gambrel roof and two vented cupolas.

The ranch was started in the 1880s by Lord Lyulph Ogilvy, the Scottish Earl of Airlie, who helped establish the vast Prairie Cattle Company of Colorado and Wyoming. In 1888 Ogilvy sold his ranch and became a writer for *The Denver Post*. The ranch became the Percheron-Norman Horse Company, a major supplier of workhorses for farmers and city dwellers. In 1899 it became the SLW Ranch, which is still in family hands with Stow Witwer, who raises Herefords, hay, corn, and grain for winter feed.

Stoneham

Activity in Stoneham (1888, 4,600 feet) centers on the P&M Recreation Hall (1920s), a vernacular wooden structure with a false front and a magnificent back bar inside. A few trees, houses, a four-story metallic grain elevator, and one of the loveliest of the white churches of the Colorado high plains mark this oasis in the middle of nowhere. St. John's Catholic Church (1914) is a tidy clapboard Gothic prayer, rising symmetrically through a similarly pitched entry, church, and closed bell tower to a stark wooden cross.

WE24 **Uhl Ranch Line Camp**

c. 1867, O. E. Jones. East side of Weld County 149 near Uhl Reservoir

One of Colorado's last line camps, this was once part of the huge John Wesley Iliff Ranch, which stretched almost from Greeley to Julesburg on the northwest bank of the

WE23 SLW Ranch

WE24 Uhl Ranch Line Camp

South Platte. Cowboys in line camps attempted to keep cattle from wandering off the ranch, especially into Nebraska, where state law allowed farmers to pen stray cattle to avoid damage to crops. Cattleman O. E. Jones framed this dirt-floored 16-by-24-foot cabin with lumber hauled in from Nebraska, then built exterior walls of evenly coursed rubblestone gathered from the nearest rock cliff. Under a low, gabled roof, the three log roof beams project beyond the exterior walls. The off-center door has a wooden frame and windows amount only to small portholes with board shutters fastened by leather hinges. The cabin has been well maintained since 1944 by David E. and Jeanne Uhl of the Cedar Creek Ranch.

WE25 **Keota**

1888–1973. Weld County 390

Keota is now nearly a ghost, despite the attractions listed in a 1911 billing in the *Keota News:* "At an elevation of almost 5,000 feet, where the air is pure and health giving, where we have no cyclones or hot winds; where we have the beautiful Rocky Mountains only 80 miles away as a background and where the soil is rich and the water is of the purest and in abundance. Doesn't it appeal to you, Mr. Man looking for a home, as a good place to drop anchor." Within the memory of 1990s resident Roger Myers, some 1,000 people lived here. The ruins of fireplaces, sidewalks, fire hydrants, a large hilltop school, and main street buildings are being repossessed by the prairie. Several fading landmarks include a Methodist church (1918).

WE26 **Missile Silo**

1960s. 5 miles northeast of Keota at junction of Weld County 104 and Weld County 11

Power lines and a 12-foot-high chain-link fence around a cement pad with a weather station give away the location of one of many nearby underground missile silos built and filled with a deadly payload during the Cold War. About fifty MX and Minuteman III underground missile silos were constructed in Colorado by the U.S. Air Force 90th Strategic Missile Wing. Each silo contains a precast cement canister 100 feet long planted into the ground atop a shock absorber, then filled with a missile and capped with a cement lid 12 feet in diameter. In the underground command center, the "umbilical cords" have been cut since the end of the Cold War to defuse these instruments of Armageddon.

Eaton

Eaton (1883, 4,839 feet) was platted by Benjamin Eaton, who later became governor of Colorado. A Great Western Sugar Company beet refinery dates from 1902. The town thrived on sugar beets and is notable for frame foursquares, such as those at 16 Cheyenne Avenue and 120 Maple Avenue, although the type was usually executed in brick in Colorado. At 421, 432, and 434 Cheyenne Avenue are single-story bungalows built in 1910 for Great Western Railroad employees. The Town Hall (1927) is Beaux-Arts classical with mismatched Colonial Revival bell towers. A fairly intact main street (1st Street) features turn-of-the-century structures such as the Corner Pocket (1898), northeast corner of 1st Street and Elm Avenue, a grocery store converted to a pool hall, bar, and restaurant. The First National Bank (1911), northwest corner of 1st Street and U.S. 285, retains some of its original elegance under a stucco job. East Eaton, a neighborhood of Hispanic agricultural workers also known as Rag Town, has a wonderful vernacular chapel and some interesting residences adorned by, among other things, bathtub madonnas.

WE27 **Farr House**

1890. 208 Elm Ave.

W. J. Farr, Eaton's first mayor (1902–1903) and proprietor of the Owl Creek Ranch and cattle feedlot, had this two-story Shingle Style frame dwelling built for his family. Prominent gables on front and sides are finished in decorative shingle patterns, and a bracketed hood above three second-story windows in the front gable brings the upper peak out flush with the eaves. Paired first-floor bay windows are hidden behind the enclosed front porch. A polygonal oriel on the left side houses the stair landing. The carriage house at the rear has an unusual double four-gabled roof.

WE28 **Victorian Veranda Bed and Breakfast** (Smillie House)

1894. 515 Cheyenne Ave.

Rancher and hardware store owner Jack W. Smillie built this two-story clapboarded frame house with Carpenter's Gothic detailing. Its irregular plan, steep roof, balconies, bays, and wraparound veranda epitomize the Queen Anne Style. During the 1930s, it was nicknamed the "Beehive House" because some thirty-five people lived here. Restored and opened in 1989 as a bed and breakfast, it has the original woodwork and many antiques, including some fine Eastlake pieces.

WE29 **St. Michael's Catholic Church**

1930. 490 Wall St.

A generic clapboarded frame dance hall was converted into a Catholic chapel for Rag

Town, the working-class district on the east side of Eaton. This tiny church is distinctive for its homemade bell tower and spire, a frame box cutout and cone miniature reminiscent of the spires of churches in southern Colorado and northern New Mexico.

Evans

Evans (1869, 5,063 feet) was established along the Denver Pacific railway and named for its president, former territorial governor John Evans. This townsite was a part of the 900,000-acre grant received by the railroad. Although Evans was the first railroad boom town and county seat, it was eclipsed by its neighbor on the north, Greeley, which permanently replaced it as the county seat in 1877. Unlike Greeley, which was dry, Evans allowed bars and was generally more relaxed than its utopian neighbor.

WE30 **Evans Historical Museum**

1887, James Henry, builder. 1985, moved and restored. Northeast corner of Golden and 38th sts.

The museum, a well-preserved clapboard Carpenter's Gothic cottage in the municipal building complex, houses community treasures. The symmetrical facade has a pedimented porch joining two bay windows under a hipped roof with shed dormers. Inside, first-floor rooms open off a central hallway.

La Salle

La Salle (1886, 4,676 feet), at the junction of the Union Pacific's South Platte and Cheyenne, Wyoming, lines, has a skyline of water tank and grain elevators. The old two-story brick railroad hotel (c. 1889), 111 1st Street, is now the Armadillo Inn.

WE31 **Union Pacific Depot**

c. 1910. 101 Todd Ave. (northeast corner of Main St.)

Restored and now recycled as the La Salle Community Center, this depot has lap siding above vertical boards. Gracefully arched brackets for the wide eaves and a central second-story dormer characterize this hand-

WE31 Union Pacific Depot

WE33 Fort Vasquez

some design, which came from the UP head-quarters in Omaha.

Platteville

Platteville (1875, 4,820 feet) arose as an agricultural center near the site of a now-reconstructed 1830s fur fort (WE33). One of its landmarks is the huge Public Service Company Fort St. Vrain Nuclear Plant, the only one ever built in Colorado, now being converted to a steam plant after multi-million-dollar misadventures with nuclear energy.

WE32 First United Methodist Church

1929. Northeast corner of Main St. and Elizabeth Ave.

This building of dark red wire-cut brick has a tower front with a square entry and bronze paneled doors. The nearby St. John's Evangelical Lutheran Church (1926), 306 Byers Avenue, is a frame building with a square central belfry.

WE33 Fort Vasquez

1835. U.S. 85, 1 mile south of Platteville (NR)

Fort Vasquez, a Colorado State Historical Society Branch Museum, offers exhibits, tours, information, and two WPA murals depicting the fur trade era. The adobe fort is a WPA reconstruction, updated slightly over the years. Once the fort had twelve rooms clustered against the stout walls

around a central open plaza. The gunports did not exist in the original, which was built by Andrew Sublette and Pierre Louis Vasquez and abandoned in 1842. Walls 2 feet thick and 14 feet high enclose a space approximately 105 feet north to south and 120 feet east to west, with two corner watch-towers.

Fort Lupton

Fort Lupton (1869, 4,914 feet) traces its origins to a fur trade fort established in 1836 by Lancaster P. Lupton, a West Point graduate who left the army to join the fur trade. The adobe outpost along the South Platte River was abandoned in 1844, but the farm center established about a mile south in the 1860s boomed after Great Western opened a sugar beet plant (1920, James Stewart and Company). Abandoned in 1953, the plant was dismantled in 1966. Other agribusiness and surrounding oil and natural gas fields have sustained this town.

WE34 La Familia Restaurant (Otteson Feed Mill)

1916. 815 E. 7th St.

Twin round tile elevators and a square corrugated metal one soar over the two front-gabled sheds that were converted to a Mexican restaurant in 1989. This new use provides a rare opportunity to inspect a vernacular building type with minimal exterior and interior changes.

WE34 La Familia Restaurant (Otteson Feed Mill)

WE35 **Fort Lupton Museum and Recreation Center** (Fort Lupton Library)

1929, John J. Huddart. 453 1st St. (northwest corner of McKinley Ave.)

This miniature Renaissance Revival villa has a beige brick skin with red brick banding and trim and bright blue terracotta accents. Fanlight windows, a metal cornice, and the roof parapet remain unaltered.

Johnstown

Johnstown (1903, 4,820 feet) thrived after construction of a Great Western sugar beet plant (1926). An antique main street has turn-of-the-century commercial buildings such as the two-story brick Eureka Block (1907), the *Johnstown Breeze* newspaper office at 7 South Parish Avenue, and the old depot nearby.

WE36 **Big Thompson Valley Ranch (Brush Ranch)**

1865, Jared Brush. 24308 Weld County 17 (NR)

Brothers Jared, John, and William Brush left Missouri for Colorado in 1859 with a train of mules. They tried mining, then switched to homesteading on the Big Thompson River. Their ranch supplied beef and hay to mountain mining towns. The Brush ranch house and barn are among the oldest pioneer structures in Weld County. The saltbox house has horizontal board siding and a full-width front porch with squared columns. Well-tended and expanded by additions, the Brush house still sits on its original stone foundation. The square barn (1865), with notched and pegged beams, board-and-batten siding, louvered vents, and pigeon-holes, is in near-original, unpainted state.

WE37 **Dearfield**

1911–1953. 27 miles east of Greeley on U.S. 34

After reading Booker T. Washington's *Up From Slavery,* Oliver T. Jackson established Dearfield as Colorado's only African American colony. Jackson had worked at the Colorado State Capitol as a messenger for Governor John Shafroth, who helped him realize his dream of an agricultural community where "our people can get back to the land, where they naturally belong, and to work out their own salvation from the land up." Jackson's niece, Jennie, operated the lunch counter until 1953, when she became the last black to leave Dearfield. Her counter, with a faded sign, lingers. Windowless and doorless homes, a school, a store, and a few frame homes are tumbling back into the prairie.

WE37 Dearfield, lunch counter

Morgan County   (MR)

During the 1860s Fort Morgan guarded the South Platte River route through the center of this agricultural county. Like the fort and the county seat, the county is named for Colonel Christopher A. Morgan, a Civil War veteran who never saw his namesake. Ranching prevailed until the 1880s development of major irrigation canals off the South Platte. During the subsequent agricultural boom, Morgan County was formed in 1889 from the southeastern portion of Weld County.

Morgan County has been among the top five statewide producers of grain corn, beans, sugar beets, and cattle, as well as natural gas and oil. Of some 22,000 residents, about 9,000 live in Fort Morgan and another 4,000 in Brush.

Fort Morgan

The county seat (1884, 4,330 feet) began as a frontier outpost of sod and adobe buildings around a parade ground. Abner Baker, a member of the Greeley Union Colony, platted a town near the abandoned fort in 1884. The community developed after 1900 primarily as a livestock, truck gardening, and irrigated farming center. The skyline is dominated by the gleaming white sugar bins of the Great Western Sugar plant (1906). These round towers in a stepped, graceful composition hover above the gabled, red brick, four-story plant, one of the last operating among a dozen sugar refineries that once hummed in South Platte valley towns between Brighton and Sterling.

Fort Morgan is perfumed by a major meat packing plant and various feedlots. Extensive oil and natural gas development have augmented the agrarian economy to make this a livelier town than many on the high plains. Fort Morgan Junior College occupies a small campus on the east side of town. Unusually progressive commission government established municipal utilities and a brightly lit commercial core for the "City of Lights," which welcomes visitors, especially on the first Wednesday in August with its "Howdy Day." The town's pride and progressive spirit are reflected in the original Classical Revival city hall (1908, Marean and Norton), 110 Main Street (NR), still owned by the city as income property. Next door is the towering 1903 standpipe of the municipal water company.

MR01 **Morgan County Courthouse**

1936, Eugene G. Groves. 225 Ensign St. (corner of Main St.)

A central, flat-topped tower and two-story pilasters with stepped capitals surmounting the plain parapets distinguish this vertical Art Deco composition in blond brick with terracotta insets. Inside, offices on a linear plan flank a central hall with terrazzo floors. This trim Moderne monument replaced a more ornate Beaux-Arts courthouse (1906, Thomas Barber), part of which it incorporates.

MR02 **Farmers State Bank**

1930, Eugene G. Groves. 300 Main St. (southwest corner of Kiowa Ave.) (NR)

The Denver architect of the county courthouse also created this classically derived, single story building of buff Indiana limestone in smooth ashlar blocks. The little-altered bank combines a vertical Art Deco feeling with horizontal zigzag banding above windows. Both street elevations have slightly protruding central bays with modest raised parapets and dentiled cornices. On the narrow west facade, double doors are recessed between flat, fluted pilasters with plain plinths and stylized capitals, and the entry and window transoms feature carved floral patterns. Art Deco facades also grace the

Municipal Fire and Police Building (1937, Walter H. Simon), 120 Main Street; the Club Tap Room (1930), 212–214 Main Street; and the Stapleton Building (1930s), 316 Main Street.

MR03 **Post Office**

1917, James A. Wetmore, OSA. 1972, renovation. 300 State St. (northeast corner of Kiowa Ave.) (NR)

The pedimented portico, front door fanlight, and rooftop balustrade of the post office say Federal Revival style, which is usually associated with eastern Colonial Revival architecture but is rarely seen in western states. A coffered barrel vault fronts the entrance, whose leaded transom and tall, flanking windows reaffirm the Colonial Revival appearance. The side elevations have arched windows with side lights which echo the entry. A later rear addition matches the light tan brick and the Flemish bond pattern of the original. The interior has been unfortunately remodeled.

James A. Wetmore served as acting Supervising Architect of the Treasury from 1912 to 1913 and between 1915 and 1934. In 1915 Secretary of the Treasury William McAdoo recommended that more rational financial criteria be applied to public building projects. This post office was built just before standards were implemented to limit size and level of ornamentation of post office buildings with an eye to postal receipts and site value.

MR04 **Fort Morgan Library and Fort Morgan History Museum**

1916, William Redding and Son. 1975, Edward Warner. 414 Main St. (southeast corner of Bison Avenue, in City Park)

Built with a $10,000 grant from the Carnegie Foundation, the library has been completely remodeled as a wing of this library-museum complex designed by Edward Warner, a Denver architect and son of Fort Morgan town founder George Warner. While the original library was the typical Carnegie Beaux-Arts model, the much less fussy new building is a severe, two-story grouping of rectangular boxes. Inside, the museum displays models and dioramas of Fort Morgan's nineteen sod, lumber, and log structures arranged

around the parade ground and a soda fountain and exhibits from the Hillrose Drug Store (1924–1972).

MR05 **Warner House**

1886. 508 Sherman St.

George W. Warner, secretary-treasurer for the Fort Morgan Land and Canal Company and founding editor of the *Fort Morgan Times,* moved from his downtown tent into this pressed brick dwelling. Over the years, the original four-room homesteader house evolved into a two-story Queen Anne dwelling with multiple roof gables and a prominent octagonal entry turret rising above a wraparound porch. Warner designed this transformation to accommodate his growing family and to provide a show home for the subdivision of his 160-acre farm, a development he promoted with a twenty-two-page pamphlet, *An Oasis in the Desert.* Warner's subdivision is now part of the Sherman Street Historic District, Sherman Street between Platte and Beaver avenues (NRD). This small district consists of four prominent houses and related outbuildings constructed between 1886 and 1926.

MR06 **Bloedorn House**

1926, Mountjoy and Frewen. 440 Sherman St.

John H. Bloedorn, president of the Farmers State Bank, built the landmark bank building at 300 Main Street (MR02). His wife, after seeing a Mountjoy and Frewen house in Denver, had that firm build a similar Georgian Revival residence. Featured in *Country Homes* magazine in 1928, it is easily the finest home in Fort Morgan, complete with third-floor ballroom. The brick house is a symmetrical design with pedimented entry portico and center hall plan under a side-gable roof with matching chimneys in each gable end. The mansion sits behind a brick post and wooden lattice fence, surrounded by a large lawn and formal gardens.

MR07 **Graham House**

1914, John J. Stein and William J. Westfall. 428 Sherman St.

Denver architects designed this two-and-one-half-story foursquare, which has the gabled dormers and hipped roof typical of that form and Craftsman details. The gabled entrance portico extends across the right side of the main facade as an open porch leading to a side pergola and terrace. A second pergola in the garden proceeds to a secluded gazebo. Prominent tripartite windows, symmetrically placed in the brick facade, have multiple lights above large single panes. The interior is richly appointed in walnut and oak.

MR08 Curry House

1898, Charles Eyser, builder. 404 Sherman St.

James P. Curry, a rancher and president of the First National Bank of Fort Morgan, built this two-and-one-half-story clapboard Queen Anne Style house. An irregular plan is enhanced by elaborate wood trim, especially on the first- and second-story porches. Curry's humble origins as a sheepherder and cowboy are commemorated by the battered frame water tower and frame outhouse in the back yard near the two-story barn and attached carriage house. Local historian Lyn Deal has re-created the old front porch on what is now her house.

MR09 Fort Morgan Power Plant

1923, George Cox. Riverside Park (NR)

The original municipal power plant and its huge black stack, built next to City Hall, were an eyesore, so city superintendent George Cox, a civil engineer, designed this state-of-the-art plant in a park setting. Cox

MR09 Fort Morgan Power Plant

sheathed his concrete post-and-beam structure with curtain walls of red and buff brick and a Tudor arch entry. Stone-capped pediments and pilasters with inset terracotta diamonds add Art Deco stylishness to a handsome facade. The building has a matching stepped rear addition, also designed by Cox. Many generous, symmetrically placed steel windows amplify the plant's light, open modernity. Since being replaced in 1952, it has been used as maintenance, storage, and offices by the Fort Morgan Parks Department. The well-preserved and landscaped plant is at the entrance of a large park located between I-76 and the South Platte River at the Rainbow Arch Bridge.

MR10 Rainbow Arch Bridge

1923, Marsh Engineering Company. Colorado 52 (NR)

Engineer James B. Marsh of Des Moines patented the rainbow or Marsh arch design in 1912. Although expensive to construct, this graceful and innovative concrete and steel design was used throughout the country. When it was built to bridge the South Platte River, this single Colorado example of the type was said to be the longest such bridge in the world. Its eleven spans arch gracefully over the roadbed from below-grade piers. The three southern spans have been reinforced by steel tension rods, and a second bridge was built in 1963 to relieve traffic volume on the narrow roadbed. Now designated a Civil Engineering Landmark, the bridge has been converted to a pedestrian crossing with the original cast iron lamps recast and reinstalled in 1995.

Brush

Brush (1882, 4,231 feet) began as a cattle shipping point on the Burlington Railroad named for cattleman Jared L. Brush. Unlike many small towns on the high plains, this one prospers. It is still a major cattle raising, feeding, and shipping center. People who like the small-town lifestyle have been creative about making their livings here. Since 1986, for example, the Superior Livestock Company has marketed cows on television with video auctions. One of the first care centers for Alzheimer's patients works because of the small-town setting, and a local greenhouse grows tomatoes using excess power from a nearby plant. The old downtown hotel has been converted to senior apartments and a community center. The town cherishes its elderly buildings, such as the frame John J. Wylie House (1882) at 105 North Railway Street and the Kneval School in Brush Memorial Park.

MR11 Central School

1928, Mountjoy and Frewen. 411 Clayton St.

Frederick Mountjoy and Francis Frewen headed a Denver firm that specialized in school buildings throughout the state and developed an impressive body of work in smaller towns. Their classically oriented designs are exemplified by this two-story, symmetrical school building, of beige brick and terracotta trim under a red tile roof, with one-story wings forming an I plan. The most striking feature is a pressed metal frieze, fully three feet wide, with bas-relief floral patterns and lamps of learning, rising to a cornice adorned with egg-and-dart trim, dentils, and foliate scrolled brackets. This spectacular, silvery frieze and cornice wrap all four sides of the central building and become a draped cornice on the wings.

MR12 All Saints Lutheran Church of Eben-Ezer

1918, Baerresen Brothers. 122 Hospital Rd. (NR)

Two Danish immigrants, the Reverend Jens Madsen and his wife, Anne Marie, established the Eben-Ezer Sanatarium for tuberculosis patients in 1903. The 35-acre grounds came to include landscaped, curving walks to the many house tents. Madsen and the Baerresens, Danish-born Denver architects, designed a chapel incorporating Danish Gothic features, most notably the stepped parapets and triangular roof windows. Red brick walls rise to a gable roof with three triangular dormers on each of the long sides. The stepped gable ends are composed of alternating piers and recessed panels capped in Del Norte rhyolite, with a

cross at the apex. Walls are banded and trimmed in the same stone, as are the keystones of the Gothic-arched surrounds framing stained glass windows. The pulpit and lectern are part of the chancel wall, and the altar is built of brick topped with stone slabs. Similarly designed Elim Hospital (1915) was demolished in 1969. The story of what is now the Eben-Ezer Lutheran Care Center for the elderly is told in Madsen's autobiography, *Retrospective Musings of an Old Man.*

Orchard

Orchard (1882, 4,400 feet) grew up near a large cottonwood grove shading the South Platte River, where Lieutenant John C. Frémont and a party of twenty-six men camped in 1842. Thereafter known as Frémont's Orchard or just Orchard, this tiny town starred as one of the sets in the television miniseries based on James A. Michener's epic novel about Colorado, *Centennial* (1976). The original town buildings were augmented with plywood facades covered in foam brick siding. Some of these sets remain, in deteriorating condition.

MR13 Stoll Sod House

c. 1893. West of Orchard on the Marvin Etchison Ranch

Homesteader William Stoll built this rare two-story sod house, a remnant of the days when cheap, fireproof sod was used for pioneer homes. Sod bricks were cut with a special plow and laid grass side down a few courses at a time to allow for drying and settling. Openings were left for doors and windows to be framed and filled later. When the walls were completely dry, the sides were straightened and excess grass removed with a large knife. Walls could then be plastered. With walls 18 to 24 inches thick, "soddies" were cool in summer and warm in winter. While early soddies often had roofs of brush and soil, this one was roofed with milled lumber and shingles and boasted carbide lights, a front room and front porch running the length of the house, and a frame kitchen wing. Both stories had hardwood floors, with three bedrooms and hall above. Now the hipped roof is in pieces and the house is deteriorating.

Snyder

MR14 Nick's Place

c. 1890. Near Colorado 71 and Morgan County W

Snyder (1882, 4,175 feet), on the South Platte River and Union Pacific tracks, is noted for its old-time saloon, Nick's Place, the most famous bar, hamburger restaurant, and dance hall in Morgan County. Nick Dimitroff, a Bulgarian immigrant, owned and operated this bar for fifty-four years before his death at age ninety-three in 1974. A bachelor, he lived next door, where he raised the onions, peppers, and lettuce to garnish his hamburgers. Nick's is a combination of two old storefronts with pressed metal ceilings and a classic Brunswick Collender mirrored back bar.

Logan County   (LO)

This high plains agricultural county carved from Weld County in 1887 is bisected by the South Platte River and the riverside trail that brought the first settlers in the 1860s. The river and extensive irrigation systems have made this one of the richest agricultural counties in Colorado, notable for its production of livestock, hay, corn, and wheat.

Logan County boasts the largest city in northeastern Colorado, the county seat of Sterling, which has a population of some 10,000. Otherwise the county is sparsely settled with small towns, farms, and ranches. The town of Iliff commemorates Colorado's cattle king, John Wesley Iliff, whose immense ranch occupied much of the northwest bank of the South Platte.

Since the 1950s numerous oil and natural gas fields have been discovered and tapped here, in the heart of the Julesburg-Denver Basin. Oil derricks have compromised the bucolic landscape, but the leases have sustained many a farmer and rancher while livestock and farm prices fell. The sugar beet industry, once in the lead, has soured with the closing of the Great Western refinery at Sterling. Cattle raising, with a large meat processing plant in Sterling, remains a mainstay.

Sterling

The county seat (1884, 3,935 feet) was founded as an agricultural colony in 1873 and incorporated eleven years later. The first irrigation ditch and the post office arrived in 1874, when the town was laid out by a railroad official who named it for his home-town in Illinois. Sterling moved three miles south to its present location in 1887, when the Union Pacific Railroad agreed to make this its division point on the line to Denver. The original street grid parallels the diagonal tracks; later additions to the town are compass-oriented.

When the Chicago, Burlington & Quincy

Railroad also came to Sterling, the town's role as a major trading center for northeastern Colorado and the hub of the Julesburg-Denver Basin was confirmed. Sterling also attracted business with one of the first rail bridges over the South Platte. A sugar beet factory (1905) fueled further growth. It attracted Germans from Russia (Russian immigrants of German descent), who lived in small frame houses, such as the one at 530 Washington Street. The industrial northside "Russian Town" also houses the large Sterling Beef Company packing plant (1966) and other industries.

Since the 1980s Sterling has become noted for its tree stump sculpture. Bradford H. Rhea started the fad by carving many fanciful subjects from dead trees, including *Sky Grazers* (1984), consisting of five giraffes formed from a multitrunk tree in Columbine Park on 3rd Street. Such public art has further enhanced a tidy and progressive city. Sterling's most memorable modern building, the Memorial Auditorium (1932), an expressionist Art Deco design by Denver architect Temple Hoyne Buell, burned in the 1970s. A splendid auto showroom, Bill's General Motors Dealership, catercorner from the courthouse, is a polychromatic and plate glass monument to the 1920s, still in Cadillac condition. One of Sterling's many fine early twentieth-century homes, the 1912 foursquare built by banker John Lutin at 516 South Division Street, has been converted to the Crest House Bed and Breakfast.

LO01 Logan County Courthouse, c. 1910

rado Yule marble and ornate tile floors, its golden oak trim, wrought iron staircase, and brass railings. The interior restoration also revived many rich classical details, replaced 4,000 broken floor tiles with hand-cut duplicates, and refurbished the original golden oak jury chairs.

Denver architect John Huddart, who trained in England and as a draftsman for Frank Edbrooke in Denver, designed government buildings over a span of four decades in Colorado, Nebraska, Oklahoma, and Wyoming, including a number of Colorado county courthouses.

LO02 First Presbyterian Church

1919, J. C. Fulton; Wilson and Wilson, supervising architects. 130 S. 4th St. (NR)

J. C. Fulton, a Uniontown, Pennsylvania, architect, gave this church an imposing dome that echoes that of the county courthouse across the street. The church's speckled buff brick walls combined with a limestone base and limestone trim follow a Classical Revival design, with modified Roman, Greek, and eclectic detailing. The entry facade is perfectly symmetrical, with a two-story portico flanked by four fluted columns with Ionic capitals. The semicircular golden oak auditorium, with all of its 500 seats within 40 feet of the pulpit, has a wrapping balcony. Large, leaded stained glass windows light the auditorium. Stained glass also colors the rotunda, where two large urns with bas-reliefs of children listening to Jesus are the work of the noted local sculptor, Mabel Lan-

LO01 Logan County Courthouse

1909, John J. Huddart. Main to Ash sts, between 3rd and 4th streets (NR)

Occupying a full, tree-shaded block, this Neoclassical edifice has a metal-clad dome and many protruding bays. The formal, three-story design is executed in beige-white brick, with terracotta for quoins, keystones, and trim. The pedimented north entry with its ornate medallion and exaggerated keystone is flanked by pairs of columns with Ionic capitals. Stained glass skylights brighten the four-story interior rotunda, restored in 1984, returning luster to its Colo-

drum Torrey, a student and protégé of Lorado Taft.

LO03 I&M Building

1920, Eugene G. Groves. 223 Main St. (NR)

Isabel and Mildred, daughters of banker George A. Henderson, were celebrated by this beauty, a two-story commercial building a half block wide and 20 feet deep. The first floor has large expanses of glass between classical limestone pilasters. Limestone bas-reliefs at the northeast and northwest corners contain images of an Indian, an eagle, buffalo, cattle, and wheat sheaves under a balustraded second story faced in brick. A wrought iron and glass awning tops the main entrance. Second-story brickwork on the narrow north facade is in mosaic patterns. The interior retains its marble floors, oak woodwork and wainscoting, ornate cast plaster ceiling, and the original elevator. Sound as well as beautiful, the building was designed for possible expansion to five stories.

LO04 Sterling City Hall

1912, John J. Huddart. 214 Poplar St.

This well-maintained gem, with double doors in front for a horse-drawn fire wagon, retains its original Georgian Revival detailing and interior tile floors and woodwork. The arch above the wagon doors is echoed in a tripartite window symmetrically bracketing the hooded and fanlighted entrance. The building is now used for offices and military recruiting, and the fire truck stall

LO04 Sterling City Hall, c. 1920

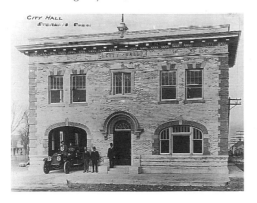

is converted to a lounge.

LO05 Post Office and Federal Building

1931, James A. Wetmore, OSA. 3rd and Poplar sts. (NR)

This combined federal and post office building is a typically eclectic example of late Beaux-Arts classicism. The building is constructed in reinforced concrete on a steel skeleton over a concrete foundation. The first floor is veneered in sandstone, and the upper floors are faced in light tan brick spotted black with manganese and applied ornament of cast stone, terracotta, and cast iron. A flat roof replaces the original hipped roof. Six pairs of grand pilasters at the second- and third-floor levels carry a Doric-derived triglyph and metope frieze and separate bays of paired windows with relief spandrels.

LO06 Union Pacific Depot

1903. 1923, wings. 1986, restoration, Ronald K. Abo. 113 N. Front St. (northwest corner of Main St.) (NR)

The unknown architect of this railroad depot tended toward Tudor Revival style in combining buttressed and parapeted gable ends with a square entry tower and large, full-arched waiting room windows. A prominent chimney and steeply pitched roof add to the verticality, making this an elegant departure from typically horizontal depots. The exotic facade fronts a typical linear plan with a two-story central section flanked by asymmetrical single-story wings added in 1923. The hipped roofs extend generously over knee brackets. Pressed red brick is complemented by gray Fort Collins stone and white-painted wood trim. The three-story entry tower has a corbeled arcade above recessed panels with banded stucco circles on the second level. Below, the front door is flanked by side lights and flared stone buttresses and topped by a banded arch with prominent keystone. The central waiting rooms retain their elegant golden oak interiors. Originally at 240 Front Street, where it served both the Union Pacific and the Burlington, the building was moved in 1984 and recycled as a museum and events center.

LO07 **Great Western Sugar Company Plant**

1905. End of S. Front St. at the railroad tracks

Built by the Sterling Sugar Company and later acquired by Great Western, this plant, originally furnished with machinery moved from Saginaw, Michigan, had a capacity of 600 tons per day. Production had been increased by 1960 to 2,175 tons per day. The four-story factory, with white concrete storage elevators looming above, is unique in its construction on a floating concrete slab. The site includes a three-story superintendent's house with shingled dormers and a two-story office, both constructed around 1900. Closed in 1989, the plant was converted to beet storage for the working sugar plant in Fort Morgan.

LO08 Northeastern Junior College Library

LO08 **Northeastern Junior College Library** (Logan County Poorhouse)

c. 1900. 3rd St. and Sidney Ave.

The college opened its doors in 1941 but did not acquire its own building until 1945, when it purchased the county poorhouse. This elegantly dormered three-and-one-half-story buff brick structure with a porch retains its original windows and interior woodwork. It is now offices for Northeastern Junior College, which consists primarily of contemporary brick and glass buildings on a campus in east Sterling.

LO09 **Harris House**

c. 1910. 102 Taylor St. (northwest corner of S. Division St.) (NR)

The Palladian window in the front dormer distinguishes this two-and-one-half-story buff brick foursquare. A low hipped roof, compass-point dormers, wide eaves, large windows with sandstone lintels, and a wrapping porch dominate the exterior, creating a horizontal feel, despite the house's height and traditional massing. A matching carriage house reflects the strong, symmetrical geometry of the house. The original owner, W. C. Harris, was a prominent rancher who opened one of the county's first feedlots in 1906 and pioneered the use of agricultural byproducts to feed livestock.

LO10 St. Anthony's Catholic Church

LO10 **St. Anthony's Catholic Church**

1911, The Black Hills Company, Architects. 329 S. 3rd St. (NR)

Masses in Sterling were celebrated in Chicago, Burlington & Quincy Railroad construction tents before St. Anthony's was built. The Deadwood, South Dakota, architects used pressed brick on a stone foundation and lighter brick trim. The cruciform plan features unmatched towers flanking the main entry's compound round arch with tympanum and half pillars, all within a Gothic arch. Round-arched windows are accented by light-colored voussoirs and filled with leaded stained glass.

LO11 **Overland Trail Museum**

1936, WPA. 1965, addition. 1989, addition, Baer and Hickman Architects. I-76 and U.S. 6, in Centennial Square

Commemorating the emigrant stream that traveled the Platte River Road, WPA workers constructed this museum as a replica of Fort Sedgwick in Julesburg. They used local sandstone for the uncoursed rubble walls and corner towers with gunports. The same fieldstone was used for 1965 and 1989 additions, the latter designed by a Denver firm. Myriad outbuildings are filled with farm equipment, lawn mowers, and many other artifacts, including a stagecoach. Also on the grounds are the Carpenter's Gothic Stoneham Evangelical Lutheran Concordia Church (1915) and the one-room frame Stony Buttes School (1911) with accompanying outhouses, all moved from rural sites. Exhibits of native grasses are featured in the landscaping.

LO12 Luft House

1902, Hoffman brothers, builders. 1429 Colorado 14 (NR)

Originally home for the brothers who built it, this is a three-story, multigabled frame house with Colonial Revival detailing but irregular Queen Anne massing. Roof cresting is highlighted by an antique lightning rod. The house became a rooming house and then the Stone Mortuary before 1925, when Conrad Luft, Sr., moved it from its town location on Poplar Street next to the post office. The horse and wooden roller took ten days to reach the new site 1.5 miles away on a 40-acre farm on Sterling Ditch No. 1. As many as seventeen family members lived under the roof. The last was Marie Luft, Conrad's daughter, who occupied the house alone through the 1980s, making a minimum of alterations.

Iliff

Iliff (1882, 3,833 feet) was named to honor cattle baron John Wesley Iliff. Although platted in 1871, for years it remained little more than a railroad siding to load cattle. Most of its buildings, like its people, are gone, but the old town well is still in the middle of Main Street in front of the post office.

LO13 Iliff Line Camp

1889, Charles Fitch and brothers, builders. 2.5 miles west of Iliff off Logan County 970

One of Colorado's last line camps sheltered cowboys working some 50,000 head of cattle on the huge Iliff spread. Stone walls 2 feet 8 inches thick have kept this small building standing.

Merino

Merino (1883, 4,035 feet) amounted to a single store until the arrival in 1907 of a newspaper to puff the town, the *Merino Breeze*. Soon after, a doctor and "veterinary dentist" came to town. His services provided a boost in amenities, replacing those of the former blacksmith dentist. A few miles west, along the South Platte River, lay the adobe ranch house of Godfrey's Station, which Indians, after an unsuccessful 1864 attack, called "Fort Wicked." Merino is now a stable farm town of about 230 people.

LO14 Davis House and Barn

1887. 13066 Logan County 8

Homesteader Hugh Davis's one-and-one-half-story frame dwelling is the oldest house in town. Davis, who arrived in Colorado in 1875, constructed the barn with lumber that had to be freighted across the treeless plains from Sidney, Nebraska.

Peetz

Peetz (1908, 4,432 feet), named for homesteader Peter Peetz, embraced a 1907 homesteaders' haven of sod houses known as Sodtown. After the claims were proven, soddies were often replaced with cement houses, of which a few remain. Overlooking the primitive buildings and lack of timber, the *Peetz Gazette* once boosted the town with the banner headline: "Peetz Biggest Town For Its Size In The State." The Chicago, Burlington & Quincy water tank (c. 1900), southeast corner of town next to the grain elevators, is said to be the last railroad water tank in northeastern Colorado. Another local landmark in this community of about 180 is the Minuteman missile silo 1.5 miles outside of town. Buried under the rolling prairie behind a chain-link fence, the now defused missile sits beneath bristling power poles and electronic antennae.

LO15 Sacred Heart Catholic Church

1964, Henry De Nicola. Colorado 113

In 1914 German Catholics built a small, high-spired frame church, which was dismantled in 1963 and replaced by this contemporary brick church. Six stained glass windows by Belgian artist Bradi Barth incorporate bits of local color: the creation scene includes the cat that became the artist's constant companion as she worked, while another window includes the old frame church in the background.

Sedgwick County   (SW)

Sedgwick County (1889), in the extreme northeastern corner of Colorado, was named for General John Sedgwick, whose name had also been given to a fort built nearby in 1864. Sedgwick County has been the major gateway to Colorado for travelers following the South Platte River, the first stagecoach line, the Union Pacific Railroad, and today's I-76.

Besides the county seat of Julesburg, the only lively town is Sedgwick. Ovid (1907, 3,521 feet), which sprang up around the Great Western Sugar Company plant (1926), has dwindled to a town of some 350 since the plant closed. Agriculture is the mainstay: wheat, feed corn, hay, sugar beets, and livestock. Like most other high plains counties, Sedgwick has been stable in population during the twentieth century since peaking in 1900 at 2,744, about half that number residents of Julesburg.

Julesburg

Englishman William A. Bell, a Cambridge graduate and railroad investor and promoter, watched Julesburg, the county seat (1860, 3,477 feet) being born. "Townmaking is reduced to a system," he explained, in *New Tracks in North America* (London, 1870): "A long freight train arrived, laden with frame houses, boards, furniture, palings, old tents, and all the rubbish which makes up one of these mushroom 'cities.' Jumping off the train with these properties, the railroad guard called out with a flourish, 'Gentlemen, here's Julesburg.'"

Although "end-o-track" and "hell-on-wheels" Julesburg is gone today, the town's rail origins permanently shaped it. Born a stagecoach town named for stage stop operator Jules Beni, it became a typical railroad town after the Union Pacific transcontinental line arrived in 1867. The town grid is askew, aligned diagonally with the cardinal points to front the tracks. The current town is the fourth reincarnation of a community that refused to die. It was burned down by Indians and had to move several times to oblige stage and rail lines. Julesburg always popped up again, tough as a thistle.

This much-moved town has lost several landmarks, including the Brown Hotel, the Opera House, and Fort Sedgwick, which was abandoned in 1871. The most famous structure in the county, known as the Italian Caves (1887–1910), is now a ruin. Uberto Gibello, a homesteader who worked as a stonemason and well digger, burrowed into the ground like a prairie dog to build his Julesburg home, several shrines, and outbuildings connected by a maze of tunnels that kept him out of the sunbaked, windblasted climate.

SW01 **Fort Sedgwick Depot Museum**

1929. 202 W. 1st St.

The Fort Sedgwick Historical Society maintains this UP depot, a side-gabled polychrome brick structure with terracotta trim under a new shake shingle roof. After the UP abandoned passenger service, the society reopened this handsome one-story depot as a museum in 1976. Its collection of artifacts and documents includes material on Native American, agricultural, and railroad buildings.

SW02 **Chaka Theater**

1919, A. E. Lanning, builder. 215 Cedar St.

Although altered many times, the Chaka Theater retains much of its original terracotta facade with porthole windows, a curvilinear parapet roofline, and an arched entry. The Art Deco trim is highlighted with floral-based electric lights. The original domed, pressed metal ceiling has been covered with Celotex to aid acoustics. Another acoustical addition has been a "cry room" for babies in one of Colorado's last small-town, family-owned movie theaters.

SW03 **Julesburg Library–Pioneer Museum**

1936. 320 Cedar St.

The WPA Moderne library, a one-story cubistic composition, echoes the similarly styled courthouse (1938) across the street.

SW04 **St. Anthony's Catholic Church**

1948, John K. Monroe. 606 W. 3rd St.

One of the raunchiest towns in Colorado, Julesburg needed religion. After first meeting in the UP section house, Catholics built a church of rough-faced cast stone, then replaced it forty years later with this building. The vernacular brick church combines lancet windows with a half-timbered entry portico and front gable. John Monroe, a Denver architect and assistant of Jacques Benedict, designed many churches for the Archdiocese of Denver. In this one he used Mission Style beams to decorate the vaulted ceiling. The recessed niches for the statues of St. Anthony and the Blessed Mother reinforce the Mission Style, which is otherwise used lightly in this church.

Sedgwick

Unlike Julesburg, Sedgwick (1883, 3,500 feet) was platted on the standard compass point township plan, rather than on a diagonal to mesh with the UP tracks. Yet U.S. 138 (Railroad Street) is a diagonal along the tracks, as is Elevator Road on the other side of the tracks.

SW05 **Sedgwick Hotel** (Farmers State Bank)

1920. 100 Main St.

This two-story, red and tan brick building was the town's grand hotel, with the bank on the street floor. It has housed everything from a beauty shop to a church, from the Lions Club to RD's Tavern. Bright white terracotta trim outlines an ogee arch doorway with finials that are repeated in the roof parapet. Decorative terracotta tiles and zigzag brickwork further enrich this vernacular example of Art Deco.

SW06 **Old Post Office** (First National Bank)

1909, J. F. Wren, builder. 27 Main St.

This one-story, pressed brick building with stone trim has classical pilasters, a ball finial cornice around the entry, and a modest brick frieze. From 1938 to 1995 it was the post office, resplendent inside with the original rose marble counters, oak woodwork, and embossed metal ceiling.

SW07 **Sedgwick High School**

1920, Wilson and Wilson. 300 5th St.

The most striking elements of this two-and-one-half-story, red brick and white stucco school with terracotta trim are two bays flanking the Gothic-arched entry, which rise above the roofline as stepped parapets. Closed in 1966 and now surrounded by weeds, it remains a dramatic red and white apparition.

Phillips County   (PL)

The Lincoln Land Company, a subsidiary of the Chicago, Burlington & Quincy (now the Burlington Northern), created the major towns of Amherst, Holyoke, Haxtun, and Paoli in 1887 when the railroad built through this prairie region. Following its formation in 1889, Phillips produced wheat, grain corn, hay, pinto beans, barley, and livestock. The tiny town of Amherst boasts the largest grain elevator (1945–1946, with additions) in northeastern Colorado. Like most high plains counties, Phillips has lost population and gained relatively little new construction since World War II. Roughly half of the 4,000 residents live in the county seat of Holyoke. That town, thanks to one man's foresight and generosity, has become a model community.

Holyoke

The county seat (1887, 3,746 feet) was named by the general superintendent of the Burlington Railroad for his son-in-law, Edward A. Holyoke. This division point on Frenchman Creek was laid out on a grid. Grain elevators are the skyscrapers in Holyoke, which is still focused on its main street, Interocean Highway (U.S. 385). The Burge Hotel (1912), 230 North Interocean Highway, has a huge stone fireplace and tablet honoring the "Knights of the Grip," the traveling salesmen who spiced small-town life. A main street mansion converted to a nursing home has a large sign: "Love is Ageless. Visit Us."

PL01 Holyoke Library (Heginbotham House)

1918–1920, Michael McEachern, builder. 539 S. Baxter St. (northeast corner of Jules St.) (NR)

This two-story Craftsman house, built for $75,000 and considered the finest in the region, is tapestry brick with half timbering, gable brackets, exposed rafters, a tile roof, a porte-cochère, and a matching garage. Extensive English-style gardens include a formal sunken walled garden, border gardens, a lily pond, a sun court, and trellis gateways.

Will E. Heginbotham presided over the Holyoke National Bank, the only one in the county to survive the Great Depression. He built the house and lived in it until his death in 1968. He served as Holyoke town clerk and city manager, manager of the Phillips County fair, and founder of the Melissa Memorial Hospital. A quiet, retiring man whose only hobby was gardening, he left his entire $4 million estate in trust for the improvement of the town of Holyoke and Phillips County. He donated his home for use as a library, which opened in 1976.

Interest on Heginbotham's estate has funded a $300,000 school auditorium, the Phillips County Historical Museum, at the southeast corner of Denver Street and Campbell Avenue, and other civic amenities. The town of Haxtun has received a $90,000 Olympic-sized swimming pool, a modern medical center, and various other improvements. Executors of the estate have also followed Heginbotham's directions to fence and maintain cemeteries and provide low-income housing, better health care, and recreation facilities throughout Phillips County.

PL02 Phillips County Courthouse

1935, Eugene G. Groves. 221 S. Interocean Highway

The first courthouse, the Burlington Railroad Eating House, was replaced by this two-story Moderne building. Facing of black-spotted white brick is trimmed with local sandstone and terracotta decorative blocks. Inside are the original steel doors with brown enamel, terrazzo lobby floor, and decorative Nuwood ceilings.

Haxtun

PL03 Haxtun City Hall (First National Bank)

1917. 145 S. Colorado Ave. (corner of Letcher St.) (NR)

Haxtun (1888, 4,028 feet), laid out as a grid by a subsidiary of the Burlington railroad, blossomed by 1920 into a town of 1,118 people, its peak population. Its elegant city hall, built as a bank, is a survivor of that era. White marble trim adds Colonial Revival frosting to the red brick, single-story building with a prominent corner clock. A pediment over the entry transom is repeated in a larger edition overhead at the cornice level. Paired marble pilasters on the face and single ones on the other elevations give the building a light verticality. Inside, the original terrazzo floors, marble baseboards, hardwood counters, two safes, leaded and etched glass windows, and high, open-beam ceilings are intact. After the Great Depression wiped out the bank's assets, the building was restored as the city hall in 1939.

Paoli

PL04 Paoli Pool Hall

1911. U.S. 6

Strategically located across the street from major grain elevators, this simple box has always been a pool hall, restaurant, and recreation center. It is notable for its diagonal oak floor, wrought iron swivel chairs, big, solid oak tables, stainless steel bar footrail, and a Neoclassical mahogany back bar from the Brunswick Balke Collender Company. Old-timers here recall when this pool hall was the hub for the local jackrabbit roundups, which exterminated rabbits by the millions.

The town of Paoli (1888, 3,898 feet) was named by a railroad official for Paoli, Pennsylvania, and the nineteenth-century Italian hero who fought against French domination.

Yuma County (YM)

Yuma County (1889) borders on Nebraska and Kansas and takes its name from the town of Yuma, the first county seat. Wide, high prairie is broken by the sometimes dry Arikaree River and two forks of the Republican River. The Republican's north fork flows through Wray, and its south fork fills the county's largest body of water, Bonny Reservoir, in the southeast corner. Center-pivot irrigation systems fed by the Ogallala Aquifer have made Yuma County one of the nation's top producers of corn, sorghum grain, soybeans, sugar beets, and wheat. The county is also known for dry-land farming, cattle and hogs, the Beecher Island battlefield, pheasant hunting, and prairie chickens, whose spring mating dance rivals any nightclub exhibition.

Evidence of early Native American habitation was revealed by "blow-outs," wind-enhanced erosion that was most severe during the drought years of the Dust Bowl. Etienne B. Renaud, a Parisian archaeologist, first classified and reported on the early, parallel-flaked projectile points he named Yuma points. The 1973 discovery of a well-organized bison butchering site in bottomland along the Arikaree River led a Smithsonian Institution anthropologist to date Paleo-Indian occupation back more than 10,000 years.

Despite optimistic names like Happyville (1910–1922) and Heartstrong (1921–

1940), at least forty towns are dead or dying. The town of Yuma and the county seat, Wray, are holding their own in this county of about 9,000 people.

Wray

The county seat (1882, 3,516 feet), located in the valley of the north fork of the Republican River, has a more sheltered and moister climate than the surrounding high plains. Limestone cliffs to the south and sand dunes to the north frame a tree-shaded oasis. The town began as a Burlington railroad stop named for James Thomas Wray, cattle foreman on the nearby I. P. Olive Ranch. Unlike most plains towns, Wray has maintained a steady population of around 2,000 in an unusually progressive community with a notable new consolidated school. The Wray Museum, 205 East 3rd Street, houses a fine collection of artifacts, including the famed Yuma points. The town's grand old "mansion," Quiggle Mansion (1903), is at the southeast corner of 4th and Ash streets. The sandstone Yuma County Courthouse (1903), 310 Ash Street, has many brick additions. The Bank of Wray (1887), southwest corner of 3rd and Main streets, is a single-story brick building with arched windows and corner doorway and egg and dart terracotta trim.

YM01 Wray Elementary and High School

1985, Anderson Mason Dale. 30074 Yuma County 35

"Prairie grain storage vernacular" is the label Denver architect John Anderson favors for this school, published in *Architectural Record* in 1987. Tall silos and grain elevators inspired the massing, while the stuccoed walls borrow their color from the surrounding wheat fields. The walls and columns are striped like the strata of the nearby limestone cliffs. This Postmodern complex sprawling over 70 acres is wrapped around a central three-story bell tower. Separate elementary and high schools, with individual libraries and a shared music room in octagonal pavilions, flank an arcaded cross-axial

spine. A series of courtyards clarify relationships between the buildings. A perpendicular loggia connects the 458-seat auditorium-gymnasium-cafeteria, which also doubles as a community performing arts center. Low-tech construction systems, like stuccoed masonry block walls, standing-seam steel roofs, and wood roof trusses, used local labor to reduce costs and strengthen the agrarian economy.

YM02 Beecher Island Battle Ground

1924–1958. Yuma County KK

Beecher Island was built around a combined post office and store near the site of an 1868 battle between the U.S. army and bands of Cheyenne and Arapaho. Lieutenant Frederick H. Beecher and the Cheyenne warrior Roman Nose both lost their lives in this ten-day siege, ended by the arrival of U.S. cavalry. Today this semi–ghost town consists of abandoned frame cottages and an unlikely collection of three Sunday schools, the oldest and largest built in 1891. An obelisk commemorates the battle site on an island that the Arikaree River has since washed away. The Rosencrans Ranch on Willow Creek, 6 miles east of Beecher Island, has a rare two-story sod ranch house.

Hale

Hale (1890, 3,600 feet) is distinguished by the antiquated frame general store, where the clerk presides primarily over fishing gear. Because of its isolated location, high winds, intense summer heat, and sudden storms, the tourism expected to follow completion of Bonny Dam (1951, U.S. Bureau of Reclamation) never arrived. Bonny Reservoir State Park, 2 miles west of Hale at the confluence of the south fork of the Republican River and Landsman Creek, is surrounded by a natural area and a state recreation area that include camping and picnic facilities and an airstrip.

Joes

YM03 **Mennonite Brethren Church**
1918

Joes (1912, 4,270 feet) was established by C. N. and Joseph White, who named it Three Joes for three men by that name among the small band of settlers. The post office shortened it to Joes. Its Mennonite Brethren Church is a picturesque prairie frame church in the German tradition. An unusual full-length front porch gives it the air of a boardinghouse and divides the first floor from the gabled second story, with its two Gothic-arched windows below a small rose window. Painted the traditional white, the church is not as well kept as a tidy adjacent cemetery.

Laird

Laird (1887, 3,400 feet) was established around the first Colorado depot of the Chicago, Burlington & Quincy Railroad. The C Bar C Land and Cattle Company platted the town and named it for Congressman James Laird of Nebraska. Today the depot is gone, but the town lingers.

YM04 **Octagon House**
c. 1880. 37586 Yuma County 355

This two-story masonry octagon has a single-story rectangular addition to the south and a shed-roofed porch wrapping six sides. The stuccoed walls rise to a truncated polygonal cap with a central brick chimney. Windows are tall and narrow, with boxed eaves. Round porch posts appear to be alternating smooth and rough-faced sections of stone rising from a solid balustrade. Although lacking the observation cupola that is an element of other octagon houses, this is a vernacular example of the romantic house type popularized by New York lecturer and writer Orson S. Fowler beginning in 1849.

Yuma

Yuma (1885, 4,132 feet) developed from a railroad camp near the grave of an Indian teamster named Yuma, who died while working on the original roadbed in the early 1880s. Yuma's grave was rediscovered in 1920, when a new roadbed was built, and now has a historical marker. The railroad proved to be a lifeline in many ways. Sometimes it provided the only source of drinking water and of fuel (in the form of coal or railroad ties). The railroad also paid farmers for train-killed animals, which they could then butcher and eat, a hard-times expedient for more than one farmer. Although it lost the designation of county seat to Wray in 1903, Yuma is now a prosperous, tidy town with large cattle and hog feedlots and packing plants.

YM05 **Black School Museum**
1881. 4th and Detroit sts.

Relocated and rehabilitated in 1991, this simple frame schoolhouse is now a museum in a lakeside park that includes the Wray Museum and Community Hall, two one-story modern brick buildings.

YM06 **Tumbleweed Hotel** (Lett Hotel)
1916. 204 S. Ash St. (southwest corner of 2nd Ave.) (NR)

John A. Lett, an Irish immigrant, built this two-story clapboard hotel solid enough to withstand a tornado that blew it off its foundation a month after it opened. The white paint, hipped roof, and large, wrapping porch with Tuscan columns were common in hotels of eastern Colorado's small prairie towns. This one boasted the area's first steam heat and hot and cold running water.

Kit Carson County   (KC)

The Chicago, Rock Island & Pacific Railroad, the driving force behind settlement, created and promoted most of the towns in this county on the Kansas border, which came into existence in 1889. Of thirty-seven post office towns, only six still appear on highway maps. Some architectural treasures survive, such as the Immanuel Lutheran Church (1926), one of the larger frame prairie churches, north of Bethune. Water from the Ogalalla Aquifer has sustained wheat, corn, sunflowers, and other crops. Cattle are also a major industry. County seat Burlington has created a historic village to attract tourists.

Burlington

The county seat (1888, 4,163 feet) was apparently named for Burlington, Kansas, from which many early pioneers came. Of some 7,000 county residents, about 2,900 live in this ranching and farming hub. Burlington boasts a good collection of antique buildings, salvaged throughout the region for Old Town Burlington, and the Kit Carson County Carousel at the county fairgrounds. The business district has many facades featuring brickwork panels and geometric decoration typical of the early twentieth century.

KC01 Old Town Burlington

1988. I-70 and S. 14th St.

The 80-foot-long, round-roofed Pizel Barn (1937) is the anchor structure of a group of transplanted buildings on a 15-acre site north of I-70, opened as Old Town in 1988 for Burlington's centennial. The barn has been restored inside and out as a museum and community hall. The half-million-dollar project, a partnership between local and state government, was a pioneer effort to draw tourists to the high plains. Grounds now include the false-fronted frame newspaper office of the *Burlington Blade*, the county's pioneer jail, a clapboard saloon with false front and second-story porch, and a one-room schoolhouse (1911) from the town of Cope. Also noteworthy are a sod house and the Rock Island Railroad depot from Bethune, the white frame Methodist Episcopal church, and the old grocery from the defunct border town of Kanorado.

KC02 Kit Carson County Fairgrounds Carousel

1905, Philadelphia Toboggan Co. Northwest corner of Colorado Ave. and 15th St. (NHL)

One of seventy-four carousels built by the Philadelphia firm, this has its original forty-six hand-carved animals in three stationary rows. These richly detailed wooden creatures include a seahorse, a lion, a tiger, a zebra, a camel, a giraffe, and many horses marching counterclockwise on a 45-foot-diameter platform within a twelve-sided building (1928). Real antlers adorn the deer, and many of the horses have horsehair tails. Inside the carousel is a 1912 Wurlitzer Monster Military Band Organ, a restored and functional 100-key instrument with 200 pipes. Built for Elitch Gardens in Denver, the carousel operated there until 1928, when it was sold to Kit Carson County. In 1931, with the Great Depression and dust storms devastating the county, the fairgrounds closed and the carousel building was used for feed storage. Restoration began in 1976, and several years later locals and visitors could once again ride at 15 miles per hour to waltzes played by a mechanical band on Colorado's most celebrated merry-go-round.

KC03 Burlington State Armory

1926, Sidney G. Frazier. 191 14th St. (NR)

Architect Sidney Frazier drew plans for this armory while employed by the Colorado National Guard. The building is the only state armory in east central Colorado, for which Burlington remains the major population center. The small wage paid to guard members became very important in helping residents weather the Depression years. The armory was also used for community gatherings and events. The vaulted guard hall is fronted by a two-story Collegiate Gothic wing above a raised basement. The main facade is rigidly symmetrical, with a crenelated parapet and a pair of narrow polygonal towers flanking the central entry bay. Stone trims windows and surrounds the double doors. A corbeled cornice of red brick is topped by diaper detailing in the parapet frieze.

KC04 Winegar Building

1907, 494–498 14th St. (southeast corner of Martin St.) (NR)

One of the largest buildings in Burlington is this two-story commercial structure of locally fired yellow brick. Classical detailing includes a central pediment containing the name and construction date in the parapet. Flat pilasters with Ionic capitals divide the street facades into vertical bays, and brick corbeling accents stone trim. A 1917 rear addition housed a creamery with apartments above. It and a full-width front porch with enclosed second-story access to flanking open balconies were removed in 1996. A. R. Winegar was one of the founders of the Kit Carson Land Company, an early settler, developer, and businessman.

KC05 Sim Hudson Motor Company

1922. 1332 Senter Ave.

The town's only Art Deco monument was remodeled in 1932 to its current appearance, with a dressing of cream and ivory stucco, large plate glass windows, and indirect lighting. The design features vertical piers with stylized leaves in relief, elongated vertical lights and indentations in the parapet, rounded corners, and painted signs on the facades. The rectangular massing could be called Pueblo Deco.

Flagler

Flagler (1888, 4,931 feet) was named for Henry M. Flagler, a railroad tycoon who also made fortunes as a Standard Oil executive and as a developer of Florida resorts, in the vain hope that he would invest here. The Rock Island's rails followed prairie trails into this town, where a wooden water tower and pumphouse were the first constructions.

KC06 Municipal Building (Hotel Flagler)

1909, William H. Lavington and W. L. Price, builders. 311 Main St. (NR)

This two-story, red brick box, now stuccoed, has a front porch with a balustraded second-story balcony supported by square, fluted columns. Converted to a hospital in 1937 by Dr. W. L. McBride, it became the Flagler Municipal Building in 1967. Two years later the library moved in with its Hal Borland Room, commemorating the noted writer, novelist, poet, and naturalist who grew up in Flagler and spent his last years with the *New York Times*. The collection includes all forty-four of Borland's books as well as numerous articles and artifacts donated by his widow after his death in 1978. One of Borland's classic accounts of life on the high plains, *Country Editor's Boy* (1970), vividly describes the town which his father, editor of the local paper, boosted as "the Best Little City in Eastern Colorado, a community of tree-shaded streets and municipal power and water." In his book Borland recalled that "waves of homesteaders had lonelied out or discouraged out or dried out."

Lincoln County (LN)

This rural county has about twenty ghost towns, five lively towns, and the dying towns of Bovina, Boyero, Karval, and Punkin Center. I-70 serves as a lifeline to a shriveling number of farms, ranches, and residents. From a peak population of 8,272 in 1920 the county has declined to half that number. Hugo, a town of 600, has been the seat since the county's formation in 1889, although Limon is now three times larger.

Hugo

The county seat (1871, 5,046 feet) was named for pioneer Hugo Richards, an official of the Holladay Overland Express and Mail Company. Hugo started out as a stagecoach stop, but after the Kansas Pacific arrived in 1870, it became an important cattle shipping point. Its finest hour came when President Theodore Roosevelt, passing through on a campaign train, was persuaded to stop for a steak and coffee breakfast with cowboys assembled for the spring roundup.

LN01 **Lincoln County Services Complex**

1993, Donald W. Figert. 1st St. and 3rd Ave.

This Postmodern version of the county courthouse is a stark, elongated, single-story brick shed with a standing-seam metal roof. Ornament consists solely of the pedimented entry from the previous courthouse (1923) with its Ionic columns and round-arched portal, flanked by antique globe streetlights. Inside is a model of the old Neoclassical courthouse, demolished in 1992.

LN02 **Lincoln County Museum** (Hill House)

1879. 617 3rd Ave. (southwest corner of 3rd Ave. and 7th St.)

William Hill, the town's first postmaster and a land promoter who laid out Hill's Addition in 1877, brought his bride to a two-story, front-gabled frame house. They subsequently expanded the structure with single-story additions. From 1907 until 1972 it belonged to the Peter Hedlund family before its conversion to the county museum. Although full of antiques, old costumes, and fancy goods, it remains a simple frame house with a screened porch.

LN03 **Union Pacific Roundhouse**

1907, Union Pacific. Northwest end of 3rd St. and 3rd Ave.

This semicircular, eight-bay roundhouse is a one-story brick building with a stepped parapet and four round-arched windows. Bay doors have been covered in plywood since a farm implement dealer converted the building to tractor storage.

Arriba

Arriba (1887, 5,228 feet), from the Spanish for high ground, was founded and named by the Chicago & Rock Island Railroad. Although fading, it boasts one of the most ambitious hotels on the rural high plains.

LN04 **Tarado Mansion** (Adams Hotel)

1907, Minnie Adams; relocated and remodeled. Southwest corner of I-70 Arriba exit and Colorado 63

A primitive vernacular replica of Mount Vernon, this hostelry began life as Minnie Adams's boarding house, with twenty-two rooms, each barely large enough for a single bed and a closet. After I-70 bypassed the hotel, the owners dismantled and moved it piece by piece to the interstate exit. Originally L-shaped, it was reestablished on a new rectangular concrete foundation with a basement. Its one-story wings at either end faintly echo the arcaded wings at Mount Vernon. Six massive, square, two-story porch columns ape the plantation style, and a hexagonal cupola copycats Mount Vernon's crowning element. Instead of third-story dormers on the shallow hipped roof, the Arriba model has an oversized wooden roof cresting. It has been renamed Tarado (Tara of Colorado).

Genoa

Genoa (1889, 5,602 feet) originated with the Chicago & Rock Island Railroad and is fading with the railroad's demise. Its forlornness is epitomized by the frame Lutheran Church (1918), on 2nd Street, steepleless and abandoned.

LN05 **World's Wonder View Tower**

1927, Charles Gregory. .5 mile west of Genoa on I-70 exit 371

This zany twenty-room museum of curiosities houses three two-headed calves, 20,000 arrowheads, antique guns, and mammoth bones. The stuccoed, six-story frame tower supposedly gives a view of six states. The museum walls are of local fieldstone and concrete several feet thick. Although the cafe, theater, and rooftop dance pavilion are gone, a second owner has kept this homemade roadside attraction open as a museum.

LN06 **Sod House**

1888. 1 mile north of Genoa on Colorado 109

Unique for its two-story construction, this venerable vernacular house is still occupied by owner Floyd Howe. The outside of the thick walls has been stuccoed. Henry Isaac filed on this homestead the year before the Rock Island Railroad arrived in 1889. Lumber was hauled from Denver in wagons, and the sod was cut from a nearby wetlands. Railroad workers occupied curtained cubicles on the upper floor. It is now an outbuilding on the L. H. Hardy farm.

Limon

Limon (1888, 5,366 feet), named for a railroad foreman, prospered as the junction

point of the Union Pacific and the Chicago, Rock Island & Pacific railroads. Here, where the Smoky Hill trail split and the Rock Island Rocket passenger train divided, I-70/U.S. 40 and U.S. 24 now part company, with some traffic heading for Denver, some for Colorado Springs. Although this is the county's only sizable town, the only high rises are the grain elevators, including a white-painted concrete one marked with the town's name.

After a tornado leveled much of the town in 1991, reconstruction was carefully master planned with the help of a consortium of architects, landscape architects, and planners. The reborn Main Street mixes a new library and senior center with an old Masonic temple (1919), the Moderne Lincoln Theater, 245 E Avenue, and the tiny, cast stone Limon National Bank (c. 1905), 179 E Avenue. What remains of the downtown reveals its early twentieth-century roots, although alterations compromise the integrity of most buildings.

LN07 **Limon Heritage Depot Museum, Schoolhouse, and Railroad Park**

899 1st St.

The Rock Island depot has been repeatedly devastated by natural causes and repeatedly rebuilt. Despite the loss of architectural integrity, it retains the elongated look of a depot, with its trackside bay and antique rolling stock, including a dining car. The two-block site of the Rock Island's now vanished roundhouse, water tower, and shops has been converted to a park. Among the attractions is the last of the county's sixty-eight one-room schoolhouses, a relocated front-gabled model with a protruding entry and shiplap siding, dating from 1905.

LN08 **Town Hall**

1991, Tom Morris. 100 Civic Center Dr., south end of E Ave.

A daring Denver architect designed this contemporary, functional building of masonry, steel, and glass. Its walls are of gray, split-faced block accented by charcoal-colored stripes. A two-story glass front bespeaks open government, while the symmetrical one-story cinderblock wings and a clock tower on the gable roof are traditional elements. A tornado-inspired Postmodern piece nearby is the Limon Volunteer Fire Department (1990, Dennis Humphries of Pouw and Associates), 130 C Avenue (northeast corner of 1st Street), of plain-faced, load-bearing concrete block interspersed with colored tiles.

LN09 Spaid Motor Company

1928. 1948, remodeling. 900 Main St.

Particularly notable for its dramatic, curvilinear parapet fronting a truss roof, this Mission Revival showroom aspires to capture the fancy of passing motorists. Most exterior detail and a long canopy have been removed, the display windows have been closed, and the exterior has been repainted for conversion to retail use.

Washington County　(ws)

Huge herds of Texas longhorns began cropping the grass in Washington County in the early 1870s, and dry-land farmers arrived with the railroad in the 1880s. One of the biggest jokes among early farmers was the story of an emigrant who shipped a stump puller from his home in the East. This county, created from eastern Weld County in 1887, consists of rolling prairie broken by the passage of the South Platte River through the extreme northwestern corner. Irrigated farming and, since the 1950s, oil and natural gas have sustained the economy during tough times. The population dropped from a 1920 peak of 11,208 to 4,812 in 1990, with 1,599 in Akron, the county seat.

Typical of many small farm towns struggling to stay alive is Last Chance. It has never rated a post office but was put on the state highway map when the Last Chance Cafe and Gas Station opened in 1926 in an old one-room school hauled in from Anton. A Dairy King and two gas stations also found enough business along the main street, U.S. 36, until I-70 opened 40 miles to the south. A few years later I-76 was built 30 miles north. Bypassed by both freeways, Last Chance now has a single gas station left, and even its future seems dicey: the office is a mobile home.

Akron

The county seat (1882, 4,462 feet), platted as a railroad grid town, was christened by a Burlington official's wife for her Ohio hometown. As the Greek word for high point or summit, Akron seemed appropriate for this division point on the crest of the divide between the South Platte and Republican rivers. Heavy 1880s emigration led to the opening of a U.S. Land Office here. A quarry and brick kiln helped local architecture progress beyond the sod house and canvas stage.

The 1890 prospectus of the Akron Town Site and Improvement Company projected Akron as neatly arranged like a New England village. The prospectus explained that with "more American NERVE and ENTERPRISE than can be found anywhere else, Akron only ten years hence will be a city of 50,000. . . . God has placed the elements of UNLIMITED mineral and agricultural wealth around us." Akron's busted dreams are epitomized by the boarded-up, two-story Burlington Hotel (1915), northwest corner of Adams Street and Railroad Avenue, with a 1922 arcaded stucco addition to the original gabled boarding house.

WS01 Public Library

c. 1931, M. S. Beach, builder; 1958 renovation. Northeast corner of 3rd and Main sts. (Colorado 34)

This symmetrical red brick box with an unusual front corner parapet and a hexagonal roof has round-arched windows slightly recessed into individual bays. The entry vestibule extends at an angle across the corner.

WS02 Burlington Depot Museum

1928. Adams Ave. and Railroad Ave.

This typical small-town depot is a single-story, rectangular brick box with brick quoins dominated by an overhanging hipped roof. Fenestration is set into stuccoed upper wall panels above brick courses whose top ledge serves as sills. The same red and black brick and distinctive roofline are used for the one-story Burlington dormitory (1945) a block away, although the latter is

WS03 First United Presbyterian Church

distinguished by a large, semicircular bay. The depot and dormitory are being restored as a museum.

WS03 First United Presbyterian Church

1887. 1981, restoration. Southwest corner of Ash and 3rd sts.

The original white clapboard Queen Anne Style church, with its crested and dormered mansard bell tower, has a south side addition (1930) and educational wing (1952). A gabled entry bay extending from the bell tower base features an unusual bracketed bay with a stained glass window.

WS04 United Methodist Church

1920. Northwest corner of Main and 3rd sts.

A tease of Art Deco in the polychrome brick pattern, piers, parapets, and commanding square corner tower add interest to this fine church. Terracotta Gothic arches frame the doors and large stained glass windows.

WS05 Washington County Courthouse

1909, John J. Huddart. 2nd and Ash sts.

This overblown red brick foursquare with a hipped roof and gabled and pedimented dormers centered in each side is a variant of the basic courthouse design John Huddart used elsewhere, here distinguished by a prominent, domed cupola astride the ridgeline. The small, protruding entry surround is topped by a balustraded second-floor balcony. Much of the original interior survives, including woodwork, high ceilings, and wide, creaking stairs to the second-floor courtroom and third-floor jury deliberation rooms.

Just south of the courthouse at Main and Ash streets is a two-story stone jail with a similar foursquare plan that suggests that John Huddart designed it as well. The jail was rehabilitated as the county museum in 1958, and the frame Prairie View Schoolhouse was moved next door as part of the museum complex.

WS06 Yeamans Hardware

1885, Patrick Daugherty, builder. Northeast corner of Main and 1st sts.

Akron's oldest business was opened by brothers Edward and Charles Yeamans in this false-fronted, one-story frame structure with pressed metal "brick" siding. This general store had a mortuary in the basement. Between two vintage glazed storefronts, the traditional recessed double-door entry leads to an ancient interior crammed with antiques. The Yeamans have moved into a newer brick store next door and maintain this as a museum annex.

WS07 Central Great Plains Field Station

1907. 4.5 miles east of Akron on U.S. 34

The U.S. Office of Dry-Land Agricultural Investigations established this facility as the Akron Dry-Land Field Station. The staff planted 5,000 trees in the county and introduced drought-resistant strains of grain, particularly winter wheat. Three combined office and laboratory foursquares with pedimented dormers and wide, columned porches, numerous barns and sheds, and a 1975 administration building occupy the 64-acre tract.

Otis

Otis (1886, 4,335 feet) was founded by the advancing Burlington line and platted and developed by that railroad's acreage arm, the Lincoln Land Company. *The Otis Clipper* thrived by publishing notices required for

final proof on homesteads, preemptions, and timber claims. The two-story buff brick Otis Hotel (1920), 110 S. Washington St., is abandoned, and the town's sporadic activity centers on the large steel grain storage bins and the Otis Pool Hall (c. 1920), southeast corner of 1st and Washington sts. The last is a one-story corner billiard hall of white-painted brick that also serves as the town cafe, video store, and informal community center. Its plate glass storefront with central recessed entrance hides beneath a metal-clad canopy incorporating a swamp cooler.

WS08 Otis Water Tower

1918, Chicago Bridge and Iron Works. 302 E. 1st Ave.

Although a new tower went up in 1978, the town has kept as its landmark this 50,000-gallon cylindrical steel tank with a hemispherical bottom and a conical top, to which an antenna was later added. Standing 110 feet tall on four webbed steel legs, it carries the town's name high above the treeless plains. The tank and associated waterworks served a population that peaked at over 1,000 in the early 1920s.

WS09 Summit Springs Battlefield Site

5 miles east of Colorado 63 on Washington County 2, 32 miles north of Akron

Markers on this enclosed one-acre site commemorate the last battle on the Colorado plains, fought here between the Cheyenne Indians and the U.S. 5th Calvary, on July 11, 1869. Some 300 cavalrymen, under General Eugene A. Carr, and more than 100 Pawnee scouts surprised 450 warriors led by Chief Tall Bull (Tatonka Haska). In a battle lasting less than an hour, fifty-two Cheyenne, including Tall Bull, were killed, seventeen taken prisoner, and many ponies and buffalo robes confiscated before the encampment was burned. One of the scouts present at the battle was Buffalo Bill Cody, who later reenacted the battle as a regular feature of his Wild West Show.

A large stone slab commemorates an unknown fifteen-year-old Cheyenne herd boy slain here. An anonymous Indian artist's sketchbook captured at Summit Springs, which portrays Indian life and war with the bluecoats, is now in the Colorado History Museum in Denver.

Elbert County (EL)

Elbert County (1874) is named for Colorado territorial governor Samuel Hitt Elbert, the son-in-law of an earlier territorial governor, John Evans. Evans's Denver & New Orleans Railroad ran from Denver through Elizabeth and Elbert, towns he also named for in-laws, in the west end of the county.

Relatively high, wet terrain makes Elbert one of the more verdant of the high plains counties. The west end of the county is carpeted by the ponderosa pine of the Black Forest, and early sawmills and lumberyards in the towns of Elbert and Elizabeth supplied pioneer Denver and Colorado Springs, as well as the frame towns of the plains. Rolling prairies flow eastward out of the pine forests, creating expansive pastoral vistas of Pikes Peak to the southwest, and a landscape dotted with villages, farms, and ranches.

With a population under 10,000, this county is dominated by its natural landscape rather than its built environment. In a largely unpopulated setting, long, unbroken barbed wire fences are often the only evidence of human presence. This may change: the county's population jumped from 6,850 in 1980 to 9,646 in 1990. As metropolitan Denver residents move to "the country," subdivisions are sprouting amid the sunflowers.

Kiowa

The county seat (1859, 6,408 feet), on Kiowa Creek, originated as a Pony Express and Butterfield Overland stagecoach stop. While Elbert and Elizabeth battled it out for county seat honors, Kiowa officials quietly built a two-room courthouse and began holding trials.

EL01 Elbert County Courthouse

1912, John J. Huddart. 751 Ute Ave., at Comanche St. (Colorado 86) and Pawnee St.

This two-story Renaissance Revival brick structure built on a conventional rectangular floor plan has a hipped roof and plain cornice. Parts of the interior retain the original woodwork and details. The Hungate-Dietmann Memorial Marker (1939, Pioneer Women of Colorado), on the courthouse lawn, commemorates the slaughter of the Hungate (1864) and Dietmann (1868) families by Arapaho Indians.

EL02 Masonic Temple

1911. 304 Pawnee St.

This two-story vernacular clapboard building has an arched main doorway emblazoned with the symbol of freemasonry, a letter *G* within the jaws of an engineering instrument. The Masonic temple also served as Kiowa's movie theater from the 1930s until 1955.

EL03 Hitching Post Bar (Kiowa Mercantile)

c. 1880. 222 Comanche St. (Colorado 86)

This two-story clapboard box with frame brackets and cornice is thought to be the oldest building in town. It has served many functions over the years, primarily as the town's general store, before becoming a tavern.

EL04 St. Mark's Presbyterian Church

1907. 231 Cheyenne St.

Local carpenters and stonemasons built this Queen Anne Style church with a gable and open bell tower of vertical lap siding. The foundation and first story are of sandstone quarried southeast of Kiowa.

EL05 Kiowa Town Hall (Kiowa State Bank)

1907. 228 Comanche St. (Colorado 86)

This structure of concrete, chicken wire, plaster, and stucco is a Lilliputian Greek temple with square columns imitating the Ionic order, mutules on the front cornice, and a broken dentiled pediment framing a bas-relief urn over the front door. After closing as a bank, it became the Bank Restaurant and then the town hall.

EL06 Elbert County Library (St. Ann Catholic Church)

1903. 331 E. Comanche St.

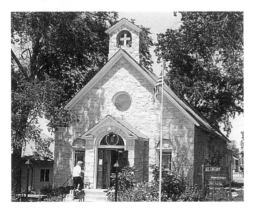

A fine example of vernacular stonework, this one-story church with a steep, gabled roof has walls of rough-cut, uncoursed local sandstone in a soft yellow shade. The stone is used for the building and the surrounds of Gothic-arched windows and blind round arches on the facade. St. Ann's depended on circuit-riding missionaries from Denver for masses and other services until 1970, when it became the public library.

EL07 Elbert County Museum (Kiowa High School)

1921, William F. Pigg. 700 E. Comanche St.

This two-story building has elements of the Spanish Colonial Revival style in its red tiled roof, entry tower, stuccoed brick walls, round-arched windows, and curvilinear parapets. It was replaced by a new high school building in 1985 and became the Elbert County Museum in 1991.

EL08 Carnahan Ranch

1860, Carnahan family, builders. 28773 Elbert County 25–41, 6 miles southwest of Kiowa

Carnahan Ranches, Inc., raises Limousin cattle on a 3,200-acre spread. The oldest building on the property is the 1860 log cabin of ranch founder Jacob Dietrich. Houses and other buildings date from 1874 to the 1950s. In the 1930s the ranch hosted a Civilian Conservation Corps camp. The most impressive older building is the large barn visible from Elbert County 25–41, the road connecting Kiowa and Elbert. This 1917 structure lacks the gambrel roof of classic barn architecture, but its roof crest is lined with lightning rods and louvered vents. The barn consists of a hayloft and gigantic double doors at the east and west ends. According to Charles Carnahan, his grandfather traded a team of draft mules for the lap siding, which came from Missouri. The granary (1885) was once a schoolhouse. The family resides in an 1880 frame house with three front dormers.

Agate

Agate (1876, 5,458 feet) was originally known as Gebhard for local rancher Henry Gebhard and was renamed for the chalcedony agate stone found in the area. Another local legend has it that a large, A-frame gate at the townsite suggested the name for this town of around 400. The Agate Community Church (1921), northeast corner of 1st Avenue and Monroe Street, built by a Baptist congregation, is a one-story vernacular frame structure with stained glass windows and a gable roof crowned by a mock bell tower.

EL09 **Agate Hotel**

c. 1910. 1st Ave.

The Agate Hotel, a leftover from Agate's days as a passenger stop on the Union Pacific Railroad, was built as a house by Minnie Peterson. The two-story, stuccoed brick building with a hipped roof is one of the few foursquares in the county. When the Great Depression and dust storms swept down on the area, Minnie Peterson converted her residence to a boarding house. Today the hotel stands unoccupied and decaying behind a chipped, faded sign.

EL010 **Beuck Land Company Ranch**

1874, August Beuck. 7 miles southwest of Agate

August Beuck, a Dane, immigrated to Agate in 1874 to establish this ranch. The frame ranch house (c. 1878) has later additions and log and frame outbuildings under newer metal roofs. Beuck continued purchasing land until 1910, when his 18,060 acres were divided between his two sons, whose descendants still own and operate it. The nearby ghost town of Beuck (also known as Buick) began its short life along the Union Pacific tracks around 1908 but withered and died during the 1920s.

Elbert

Begun as a sawmill settlement, Elbert (1860s, 6,715 feet) moved to its current site in 1882. Located in the county's "rain belt" at the edge of the Black Forest, Elbert was a premier potato growing district until a blight wiped out crops in the late 1920s. Since then, farming around Elbert has centered mainly on dry-land crops such as hay, grain, and wheat. After a flood in 1935 wiped out half the town, the Denver & New Orleans Railroad pulled up its tracks and discontinued service. The unincorporated, dirt-streeted town lingers on with only a handful of residents. A blond brick one-story post office (1930s), northeast corner of Main Street and Lavell Avenue, was originally the bank. A most interesting house is the two-story, cross-gabled Carpenter's Gothic cottage (1890s), 24163 Eccles Street (northwest corner of St. Claire Avenue), with 1980s wood gingerbread trim more exuberant than the Victorian original.

EL11 **St. Mark's Presbyterian Church**

1880, Taylor Green. 225 Main St. (NR)

A square corner bell tower entry dominates this unusual white frame church. Six classical columns support the bell-shaped roof over the exposed bell. A brick chimney pokes through the gabled roof beside the tower, which dominates this small town. The well-preserved church, which has elegant double-hung stained glass windows in Gothic-arched moldings, was designed and built by a member of the congregation. Since the site donated for the church is on a hillside, a long wooden staircase (1899) was built to provide a Main Street connection.

EL12 **Garage** (Elbert County Bank)

1907. Main St., .5 block north of St. Mark's Presbyterian Church

This vernacular red brick structure replaced the original 1890s wood-frame bank. A stepped parapet and corbeled brickwork survive, although whitewashed garage doors have replaced the bank's formal entrance and large plate glass window. Former Elbert schoolteacher and school superintendent J. E. Mayer opened the bank in 1907 and carried many townspeople, farmers, and ranchers through hard times. With Mayer in charge the bank survived a flood in 1935, as well as several holdups, but closed when he retired in 1947. Shortly thereafter the single-story, rectangular building was converted to a garage, now stuffed with farm implements and tractor parts.

EL13 **Denver & New Orleans Section House**

1882. 38 Main St.

This plain, two-story clapboard house with side gables is the only remaining structure of the railroad that helped put Elbert on the map.

EL14 **Garage** (Sacred Heart Catholic Church)

1914. .4 mile east of Elbert at 7217 Elbert County 98

This once elaborate clapboard church has a distinctive recessed Gothic arch centered in the front gable beneath a handsome square bell tower, with the bell hidden behind louvered, pointed-arched shutters. The gable faces are adorned with fishscale shingles. The Gothic-arched windows are now broken and boarded up, the tiny rose window in the front gable is gone, and sheet metal is peeling off the spire and bell tower. The church closed in 1959, to become the only garage in Colorado with a bell tower and cross.

Elizabeth

Elizabeth (1859, 6,478 feet) began as a small hamlet after brothers named Weber started a sawmill. In 1881 John Evans named the town, by then a stop on his Denver & New Orleans Railroad, for his sister-in-law, Elizabeth Gray Kimbark Hubbard. Today Elizabeth is luring city dwellers from Denver forty miles away, including artists such as the watercolorist Buffalo Kaplinski, who converted an old farmhouse to his home and studio. Black Forest Potters have an adobe studio at the southwest corner of Main and Chestnut streets.

EL15 **Wildflower Tack Shop** (Odd Fellows Hall)

1897. 122 Main St. (southeast corner of Colorado 86)

A parapeted false front and elegant corbeling distinguish this vernacular commercial building of red brick. Stepped side walls hide the slightly sloping roof. The Odd Fellows still use the upstairs hall for fraternal and community functions.

EL16 **Elizabeth Library** (Adventist Church)

1900. Northeast corner of Poplar and Pine sts.

Rough-cut, uncoursed local sandstone forms the walls and the large corner bell tower of this church, which has a steeply pitched shake shingle roof. The church was built by Seventh Day Adventists but was purchased by a Presbyterian congregation around 1903. After the Presbyterians built a new church in 1924, this became the Elizabeth Library, then a private residence.

EL17 **Bank**

1907. 188 Main St. (northeast corner of East Broadway), 1 block south of Colorado 86

One of the more ornate structures in Elbert County, this one-story stone building combines a Neoclassical arcaded entry with a decorative parapet adorned with cannonball finials. The abandoned bank hides its slow demise behind two juniper trees.

Matheson

Matheson (1886, 5,786 feet) was named for its original settler, Duncan Matheson, a young Scottish immigrant who raised sheep on the site. After the Chicago, Rock Island & Pacific Railroad arrived, the town gained a post office and a general store and became a trading center for livestock and dry-land crops. The railroad discontinued service in 1980, darkening any hopes for the town's further growth. The Beaux-Arts classical schoolhouse (1920) on the hill south of town is now part of a cattle business.

Simla

Simla (1887, 5,966 feet) started as a Chicago, Rock Island & Pacific siding, which a railroad official's wife named after a town in northern India. In 1907 Michael Altman, from nearby Ramah, was encouraged to move his saloon, the Lumberjack, to Simla. Soon afterward Altman persuaded several Colorado Springs investors to help him lay out a town. Simla, like Agate and other Elbert County railroad towns, became an agricultural trade center. Once the largest pinto bean shipping point in the Pikes Peak region, it is a tidy town of some 500 souls.

EL18 Big Sandy School

1968, Bourn and Dulaney. Southwest corner of Fox and Pueblo sts., .5 mile south of U.S. 24

This red brick, one-story school for kindergarten through twelfth grade is designed to keep students of the same age group together and avoid cross traffic among classrooms. Four round "pods" with cedar shake roofs are connected by short passages around a center pod, forming a cloverleaf. Each of the outlying pods houses grades of a different age group, while the center contains conference rooms and administrative offices.

The Arkansas:
Agrarians and Argonauts

> These planks that were a town
> Lie warping in the sun
> As if a barrel tumbled down the peaks
> Were shattered into staves.
> You always wish these wasted towns were older. . . .
> —Thomas Hornsby Ferril, "These Planks"

FLOWING 1,450 MILES FROM THE HIGH ROCKIES TO MEET THE Mississippi below Little Rock, the Arkansas tumbles from the highest point in Colorado, Mt. Elbert (14,433 feet), in the Sawatch Range above Leadville, to the lowest place, Holly (3,350 feet), near the Kansas border.

The upper Arkansas first became known to the United States when President Thomas Jefferson asked Zebulon Pike to explore the southern frontier of the Louisiana Purchase in 1806. Thirteen years later the river was established as the boundary between the United States and New Spain. After the Mexican revolution of 1821, it became the border between the United States and Mexico. Traders and trappers used it as a major route into the Rockies, especially after Charles and William Bent built Bent's Fort in the 1830s, at a site on the Arkansas near present-day La Junta in Otero County.

The Bents experimented with raising crops at their adobe castle and found that with irrigation the Arkansas Valley could be productive. For centuries the Arkansas Indians in Oklahoma and Arkansas had farmed the banks of the river named for them. In southeastern Colorado, Apache Indians had grown corn along the river's banks before they acquired horses and became nomadic hunters. These ancestral Apaches built distinctive, five-sided earth lodges. They began with five poles stuck in the ground and joined at the top by horizontal poles. Vertical logs were then piled against this framework, and a log and sod roof were added to pentagonal lodges that resembled the Mandan lodges immortalized in George Catlin's paintings.

By the 1840s settlements such as El Pueblo (the predecessor of the modern-day city of Pueblo), Greenhorn, and Hardscrabble had emerged as small agricultural and trade centers with a diverse population of U.S. citizens, Native

278

The Arkansas River Region

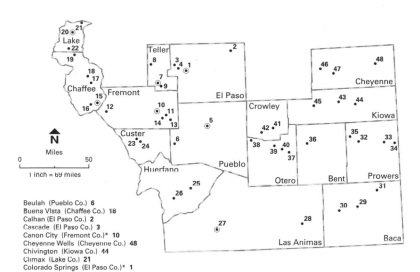

N

Miles

0   50

1 inch = 69 miles

Beulah (Pueblo Co.) **6**
Buena Vista (Chaffee Co.) **18**
Calhan (El Paso Co.) **2**
Cascade (El Paso Co.) **3**
Canon City (Fremont Co.)* **10**
Cheyenne Wells (Cheyenne Co.) **48**
Chivington (Kiowa Co.) **44**
Climax (Lake Co.) **21**
Colorado Springs (El Paso Co.)* **1**
Cripple Creek (Teller Co.)* **7**
Crowley (Crowley Co.) **42**
Eads (Kiowa Co.) **43**
Florence (Fremont Co.) **11**
Florissant (Teller Co.) **8**
Fowler (Otero Co.) **38**
Granada (Prowers Co.) **33**
Granite (Chaffee Co.) **19**
Haswell (Kiowa Co.) **45**
Holly (Prowers Co.) **34**
Howard (Fremont Co.) **12**
Kim (Las Animas Co.) **28**
Kit Carson (Cheyenne Co.) **47**
La Junta (Otero Co.) **37**
La Veta (Huerfano Co.) **26**
Lamar (Prowers Co.) **32**
Las Animas (Bent Co.) **36**
Leadville (Lake Co.)* **20**
Manitou Springs (El Paso Co.) **4**
Nathrop (Chaffee Co.) **17**
Ordway (Crowley Co.) **41**

Poncha Springs (Chaffee Co.) **16**
Portland (Fremont Co.) **13**
Pritchett (Baca Co.) **30**
Pueblo (Pueblo Co.)* **5**
Rockvale (Fremont Co.) **14**
Rocky Ford (Otero Co.) **39**
Salida (Chaffee Co.)* **15**
Silver Cliff (Custer Co.) **24**
Springfield (Baca Co.) **29**
Swink (Otero Co.) **40**
Trinidad (Las Animas Co.)* **27**
Twin Lakes (Lake Co.) **22**
Two Buttes (Baca Co.) **31**
Victor (Teller Co.) **9**
Walsenburg (Huerfano Co.) **25**
Westcliffe (Custer Co.) **23**
Wild Horse (Cheyenne Co.) **46**
Wiley (Prowers Co.) **35**

A detailed map of site locations has been provided for cities inticated by ⊙ on the map and by * in the list at left.

279

Americans, French trappers, and Mexicans. With the 1858–1859 gold strikes on the South Platte, the Arkansas became the major southern route to the Colorado gold fields. Prospectors followed the Arkansas to its headwaters and found the yellow metal in what they called California Gulch. There the town of Oro City shone with million-dollar brightness during the 1860s but had died by the 1870s when silver strikes in the area gave birth to Leadville.

When the Civil War brought a blockade of the Mississippi River and cut off the Arkansas River as a southern route into Colorado, traffic switched north to the South Platte route. Not until the 1880s arrival of the Santa Fe Railroad and the development of irrigated farming did the southeastern Colorado high plains along the Arkansas begin to prosper.

Although the Santa Fe Railroad turned south at Pueblo to head for its namesake city, the Denver & Rio Grande Railroad and later U.S. Route 50 continued to follow the Arkansas westward and upward to Leadville, Colorado's largest silver city. From this two-mile-high city on the headwaters of the Arkansas, ores and wealth flowed downstream to enrich Salida, Cañon City, and Pueblo, the regional metropolis.

East of Pueblo, the southeastern quadrant of Colorado is dry agricultural land sustained by the Arkansas River's muddy milk. On the plains, the river has few reliable tributaries. Most of the other streams have at some time dried up, as have many of the towns. Surviving communities are visible miles away because of their grain elevators, reinforced concrete skyscrapers for winter wheat and other crops. The other hallmark tower of a living town is the classic, round-bottom water tank on huge metal stilts. These elevated tanks often carry a town's name and its Christmas star.

Once the Arkansas was bordered by short-grass prairie that could support buffalo, cattle, and sheep. Indeed, large ranches preceded the influx of homesteaders arriving with the Santa Fe and Missouri Pacific railroads in the 1880s. Homesteaders found it difficult to coax a crop from the dry land, and, once broken, the soil blew away with spring winds. Yet high crop and livestock prices, especially during World War I, created flush times until the 1920s and 1930s. Many sodbusters gave up during the "dirty thirties," when the Dust Bowl and the Great Depression depopulated much of rural southeastern Colorado. Tumbleweed and sneezeweed reclaimed many homesteads and even whole towns. This part of the valley is now a land of porcupine grass and rattlesnake grass, which rustles and rattles as you walk through it.

Arkansas River architecture, like the river itself, straddles Yankee and Hispanic cultures. Spanish Southwestern styles in stucco and adobe are seen along with the more conventional brick, frame, and prefabricated built environment. Some of the valley's best buildings are made with the sandstones native to the lower Arkansas and the fine granite quarried near the headwaters of a major tributary, the South Arkansas River, on Monarch Pass.

During the 1860s and 1870s the first generation of U.S. settlers on the eastern plains employed simple building types reflecting their determination to survive. Besides wood, which had to be hauled in, builders used sod, or dug into the ground. Roofs were sometimes just sod laid over wood sheathing covered with tarpaper. Doorways were on the south or east, away from the prevailing winter winds. Animals needed shelter as well. Barns and outbuildings were usually of the same material as the houses but were also built of more innovative materials, including baled Russian thistle or straw covered with chicken wire.

Although less intensely developed than the South Platte River valley, the Arkansas too is scarred. Leadvillites and other settlers on the Arkansas headwaters deforested much of the valley. When the federal government prohibited cutting live trees, fires blamed on the Ute Indians produced "dead trees" that could be used as charcoal for smelters. The deforestation of the upper Arkansas, which has never recovered its rich spruce and fir forests, caused floods. The 1921 flood of Pueblo, the second worst in Colorado history, resulted in the uninspired solution of a huge dam and a monstrous concrete canal to channel the river through downtown Pueblo.

In the lower Arkansas Valley, the federal government bought back land from bankrupt farmers and ranchers between 1938 and 1942. The Soil Conservation Service planted shelter belts of cottonwoods, elms, and osage orange trees to keep more soil from blowing away. Much of this abandoned acreage has been set aside as part of the Comanche National Grassland. Scattered through Baca, Las Animas, and Otero counties, this 419,000-acre tract of noncontiguous parcels is administered by the U.S. Forest Service, which is allowing native flora and fauna to repossess ghostly prairie homesteads with tattered windmills.

In 1989 the state of Colorado designated the river from Granite to Lake Pueblo State Park as the 148-mile-long Arkansas Headwaters Recreation Area. Waters that once helped miners wash silver and gold out of the high Rockies are now used by whitewater rafters and fishermen. Below the Royal Gorge and Cañon City, the Arkansas is still a working river, the lifeblood of farmers in southeastern Colorado.

Leadville, Buena Vista, Cañon City, Florence, Pueblo, and Lamar, the major towns of the valley, all peaked before World War II, and their architecture reflects their fortunes. They are railroad towns of red brick with stone trim, spared the post–World War II boom that transformed many northern Colorado communities. In both the farm communities of the lower Arkansas and the mining towns of the upper Arkansas, life was precarious. The Arkansas Valley has more dead towns than live ones and is haunted by architectural ruins.

El Paso County   (EP)

A bristling military presence, elegant homes and public buildings of Colorado Springs, the well-preserved resort town of Manitou Springs, and Colorado's ultimate resort hotel distinguish El Paso County's built environment. One of the original counties of 1861, El Paso emerged as a series of towns along the Denver & Rio Grande Railroad. Railroads, ranching, and resorts initially attracted investors, settlers, tourists, and health seekers. I-25, which follows the north-south route the D&RG blazed through the county in the 1870s, serves as the modern development corridor.

Between World War II and the 1980s, the county struck gold in defense dollars spent at Fort Carson, Peterson Air Force Base, the North American Air Defense Command, the Air Force Academy, and the Consolidated Space Operation Center. A recent boom in high tech industries has also helped make Colorado Springs the second largest city in the state.

The county includes 14,110-foot Pikes Peak and its extensive foothills and spectacular stone formations, epitomized by the Garden of the Gods. West of "the Springs" on Colorado 24 (the old Colorado Midland Railroad route), are Manitou Springs and smaller communities such as Cascade and Green Mountain Falls. A dozen agricultural hamlets linger on the high plains. Their simple architectural honesty is an antidote to tourist attractions such as Santa's Workshop and North Pole and the fake Manitou Cliff Dwellings.

Colorado Springs

The county seat (1871, 6,012 feet) was planned by General William Jackson Palmer, whose equestrian statue (1929, Nathan D. Potter) is at Nevada and Platte avenues. Palmer, founder and president of the Denver & Rio Grande Railroad, planted his model town just outside the boundary of extant Colorado City so that he could more easily acquire and control real estate—the same strategy he and the D&RG would use in Pueblo, Antonito, Durango, and many other Colorado towns.

Palmer envisioned Colorado Springs as the state's elite residential city. Smoke, sweat, and noise would be banished to Denver, Colorado's rail hub, and Pueblo, the manufacturing center. Palmer's chief construction engineer, William H. Greenwood, platted a city of seventy blocks, each 400 feet square, with broad avenues lined by irrigation ditches, planting strips, and parks. After

Greeley, this was perhaps Colorado's best-planned city.

The first stake was driven in 1871 at the southeast corner of Pikes Peak and Cascade avenues. Palmer took aesthetic advantage of the setting by aligning Pikes Peak Avenue and the Antlers Hotel with Pikes Peak and setting aside frontage on Fountain Creek as a park. He hired John Blair, who had worked on Chicago parks, to help design parks, trails, and bridges for Colorado Springs, Manitou Springs, and his own estate at Glen Eyrie, on the northwest edge of town. Initially, Colorado Springs attracted English settlers and wealthy tuberculosis patients, who helped build fine institutions and neighborhoods. The ideal of broad, tree-shaded avenues is perpetuated in the residential North End Historic District (EP25).

In the 1870s Palmer brought Philadelphia architect George L. Summers to Colorado Springs, establishing a genteel tradition continued by Thomas MacLaren, the city's best-

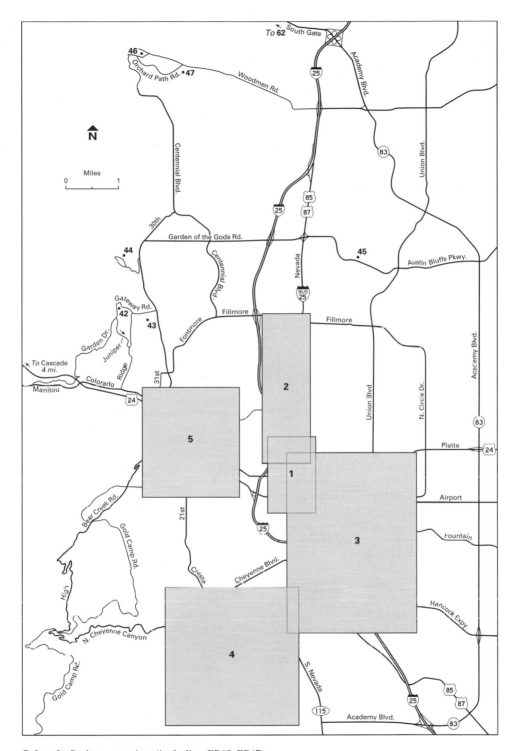

Colorado Springs, overview (including EP42–EP47)

known architect. Born in Scotland and educated in London and on the Continent, MacLaren moved to Colorado Springs for his health early in the twentieth century. He designed many notable residences, churches, and public buildings in Colorado Springs and elsewhere in Colorado. MacLaren, working alone and with various partners, including Thomas P. Barber, Charles S. Thomas, and Thompson D. Hetherington, favored traditional revival styles that reflected his classical British training. Thomas P. Barber, also English-born, practiced here along with his younger brother, William. Barber designed public buildings around the state, including school buildings in Greeley and Boulder, before moving to Los Angeles, where he designed the Methodist Church in Hollywood. Charles S. Thomas, the son of an English stonemason, was a popular Colorado Springs architect who also served as a mayor of the city from 1917 to 1919.

Local artisans also contributed to the county's many fine buildings. Artus and Anne Van Briggle of the Van Briggle Art Pottery made building tiles and trim as well as prized pottery. The Van Briggles, like many others, came to Colorado Springs hoping to recover from tuberculosis. The Hassell Iron Works of Colorado City, which was founded in 1887 and produced iron goods until the 1920s, provided superb woven-wire fencing, iron castings, structural iron, and ornamental ironwork, still found in fences and roof cresting of Colorado Springs houses. The Hassell House, 1422–1424 Wood Avenue, displays the firm's "double daisy" iron fence. Limestone from quarries around Manitou Springs and sandstone from Red Rock Canyon were used throughout the county and elsewhere in the state. Despite the availability of fine stone, frame construction has been more prevalent, perhaps because Colorado Springs never suffered a major fire.

General Palmer provided land for Evergreen Cemetery, the Colorado College, and Colorado School for the Deaf and Blind. He also donated the land and funding to maintain a park system which started with Alamo Park (now the courthouse square) and Acacia Park in 1871. The system grew to include Monument Valley Park (1907, Edmund C. van Diest), along Monument Creek, incorporating the Horticultural Society Garden and a "geological column" displaying samples from local rock formations. Palmer Park, on the bluffs northeast of the city, commemorates the city founder as part of a 1,638-acre park system also encompassing mountain parks and drives, including the Garden of the Gods.

Palmer found a successor in Spencer Penrose, the bon vivant whose Broadmoor Hotel and many philanthropic donations to the city reinforced Palmer's original dream of a cultural, residential, and recreational haven. Neither man could foresee the post–World War II growth which has created a city of some 300,000.

EP01 Colorado Springs Pioneers Museum (El Paso County Courthouse)

1903, Augustus J. Smith. 215 S. Tejon St. (NR)

Augustus Smith, according to Manley and Eleanor Ormes's 1933 *Book of Colorado Springs,* was "not only prodigal, but wanton in his use of forms, undoubtedly lacking discrimination with materials." Despite such criticism and later demolition proposals, this $420,000, three-story palace survives on a spacious, landscaped block. The Renaissance Revival design on a U plan is muddled by an exotic entry portico and the awkward central clock tower rising three more stories to an ornate domed cupola, an element that anticipated a never-built fourth-story addition. Rough-cut blocks of Pikes Peak granite, a distinctive pinkish stone speckled with black mica, were used for the foundation. Rhyolite and cast stone were used for the upper levels. Hand-carved Indian heads—each one different—decorate the keystones of the first-floor window arches. Inside, scagliola columns of various orders rest on marble floors. Decorative painted ornament remains on the coffered ceilings, and murals of historical scenes adorn the walls. An Otis birdcage elevator remains in operation as an alternative to the wide stairways. A medical history exhibit on the second floor includes a Gardiner Sanitary Tent,

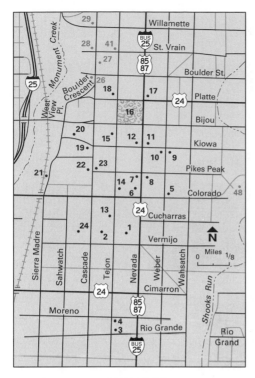

Inset 1. Downtown (EP01–EP24)

invented by a local physician and once the most common building type in Colorado Springs. Gardiner's one-room hexagonal frame shelters for tuberculars, supposedly modeled after Indian tipis, were efficient, comfortable, and well-ventilated. The Colorado Springs Pioneers Association (1909) acquired this building following the completion of a new courthouse nearby and restored it in the 1980s as a history museum.

EP02 **El Paso County Judicial Complex**

1979, Edward L. Bunts, Robert Muir. 20 E. Vermijo Ave. (northwest corner of Tejon St.)

Spacious grounds and courtyards lead west from the Pioneers Museum to a plaza between the Modernist courthouse and jail. Prefabricated aggregate panels prevail in the new county buildings, but a visual highlight is the polished granite that girds the inset first story of the courthouse, with curved corners that soften the sharp edges of the rest of the complex.

EP03 **Colorado Springs Day Nursery**

1922, William Stickney. 104 E. Rio Grande St. (northeast corner of S. Tejon St.) (NR)

Beneath four ornate compound chimneys and a steep, multigabled roof, this three-story Tudor Revival structure has variegated brick walls, half timbering, and sandstone trim. Brick and stone Tudor arches above the original oak doors lead to an interior decorated and scaled for children, with Mother Goose murals by Allen Tupper True, a Colorado Springs native.

EP04 **Boys Club**

1907, F. R. Hastings. 105 E. Moreno Ave. (southeast corner of S. Tejon St.)

Alice Bemis Taylor, who donated the Day Nursery, joined other wealthy donors to raise $6,000 for the adjacent Boys Club. The Penrose family donated a gymnasium (1910) designed with Modernist massing, although the trim details and entry surrounds are Tudor-influenced, as is the variegated brick skin, which matches the Day Nursery. Remodeled most recently in 1984, the gym is now office space.

EP05 **Fire Station No. 1**

1925, Thomas MacLaren. 29 S. Weber St. (northeast corner of Colorado Ave.)

This symmetrical Beaux-Arts station has a central arched doorway between two truck bays and a Mediterranean-style upper facade, complete with balconies. This elegant fire station reflects the community's pride and its fondness for traditional architecture.

EP06 **Municipal Utilities Building**

1931, T. D. Hetherington. 18–20 S. Nevada Ave.

Zigzag Moderne is rare in conservative downtown Colorado Springs, but after years of designing in traditional styles in the offices of Robert Roeschlaub and Thomas MacLaren, T. D. Hetherington broke loose with this solo effort. The terracotta facade of the rectangular, two-story building rises in piers culminating in a castellated parapet. Low-relief terracotta trim provides embellishment in patterns that also appear in the

EP01 Colorado Springs Pioneers Museum (El Paso County Courthouse)

EP03 Colorado Springs Day Nursery

EP07 Mining Exchange Building, 1940s

metal entry canopy. This building represented an unusual $110,000 public investment in municipally owned utilities in a conservative city.

EP07 **Mining Exchange Building**

1901. 8 S. Nevada Ave. (southwest corner of Pikes Peak Ave.)

Winfield Scott Stratton, who made millions in Cripple Creek gold mines, built this golden brick temple of capitalism to facilitate stockholder investment in Cripple Creek. Five stories in the Beaux-Arts Neoclassical style culminate in a bracketed, carved Indiana limestone cornice protruding boldly from the plane of the facade. Piers separate fenestration bays, with swags in heavy relief decorating spandrels between the floors. The first level has been resheathed in travertine.

EP08 **Post Office and Federal Courthouse**

1908–1910, James Knox Taylor, OSA. 1939, 1963, 1967, additions and renovations. 201 E. Pikes Peak Ave. (southeast corner of Nevada Ave.) (NR)

The rigidly symmetrical post office facade, sheathed on all four sides in pink Pikes Peak granite, rises two stories, fronted by pilasters dividing fenestration bays. The taller, first-level openings have rounded tops. The composition and ornament are Neoclassical. Pilasters carry an Ionic frieze and projecting cornice, with a balustrade around the flat roof, whose original tin was replaced in 1961. First-floor keystones form corbels to support the second-story stringcourse. Two main entrances are between large arched windows, with relief sculpture in the transoms and flanking cast iron fixtures.

James Knox Taylor, formerly chief draftsman, was promoted to Supervising Architect of the Treasury following architectural training at MIT and a partnership from 1884 to 1892 with Cass Gilbert in St. Paul. Taylor oversaw design of many government structures across the country, including the Denver Mint (DV011) and main post office (DV037). Most of the interior of the El Paso post office has been closed to the public after extensive remodeling in 1967 blocked off the original light court, and a 1936 mural by Frank Mechau was moved to the Denver Federal Building.

EP09 **First Baptist Church**

1891, L. B. Valk and Son. 317 E. Kiowa St. (southeast corner of Weber St.)

A square, Neo-Romanesque tower surmounted by a smaller, subordinate round turret distinguishes this wonderful church designed by a Brooklyn architecture firm. Irregular massing is capped by a roofline punctuated with a row of gabled dormers and a small cupola over the gable crossing. Rough sandstone arches frame windows vibrant with naturalistic flora created by the Omaha Art Stained Glass Company. Although the exterior, of Kansas City pressed brick and red sandstone, remains little altered, the interior has been considerably reworked.

EP10 **City Auditorium**

1922, Thomas MacLaren and Thomas D. Hetherington. 221 E. Kiowa St. (southwest corner of Weber St.) (NR)

The last Neoclassical civic building constructed in downtown Colorado Springs is a massive, square temple of blond brick with limestone trim with pilasters and a colossal, nonfunctional Ionic portico at the second-floor level above the canopied entrances. The unadorned roofline, minimal decoration and fenestration, and rounded corners anticipate Modernism. Architect Charles S. Thomas, as mayor of Colorado Springs, initiated plans for this 3,000-seat facility.

EP11 **City Hall**

1904, Thomas MacLaren and Thomas P. Barber. 212 E. Kiowa St. (northeast corner of Nevada Ave.)

This Beaux-Arts Neoclassical box occupies a corner site with a standard reproduction of the Statue of Liberty on the landscaped grounds. The formal, symmetrical composition is of gray granite, rough-faced to the base of the raised first floor. Four two-story Ionic columns support the entry portico, rising to a pediment that is repeated above the central entry doors and single windows at each end of the facade. The interior lobby is wainscoted in green marble, and the grand double stairway has a stained glass skylight. Like so many city halls, this one is now largely devoted to courtrooms.

EP12 Colorado Springs Company

1913, Nicholas Van den Ahrend. 130 E. Kiowa St. (northwest corner of Nevada Ave.)

The Dutch architect gave this five-story buff brick structure exotic window shapes and vibrant dark green terracotta trim in patterns reminiscent of Art Nouveau. Raised parapets at the corners of this flat-roofed structure are treated as towers. French doors form fourth-floor windows, and the entrances are set into Gothic arches at mid-level between the basement and the first floor. The YMCA, the second occupant of the building, altered the interior, but some of the original has survived, including an operational 1913 birdcage elevator and fragments of woodwork. Since the YMCA moved out, a two-story gymnasium has been converted to two levels of offices around a skylit atrium. In the basement pub the large blocks of sandstone used for the foundation are visible, as are the walled-in brick arches of basement door and window openings.

EP12 Colorado Springs Company, 1950

EP13 Alamo Hotel

1890, Thomas P. Barber. 128 S. Tejon St. (northwest corner of Cucheras Ave.) (NR)

This four-story Romanesque Revival edifice is pressed brick with sandstone trim on multistory bays and pilasters that terminate in arches. A pediment with an implied arcade breaks the cornice to give the effect of a tower. Although more than half of this building is gone, parts of the elegant lobby remain in the most recent conversion to offices. The street on the south side has been closed and made into a pedestrian mall. The south side of the old building is obscured by the addition of a contemporary entrance lobby and elevator shaft.

EP14 Hibbard and Company Department Store

EP14 Hibbard and Company Department Store

1914, Charles S. Thomas. 21 S. Tejon St.

This narrow, four-story commercial building of deep red brick has rich white terracotta trim, including pilasters and raised garlands and swags on the spandrels. The bracketed cornice is crowned by a stepped parapet. Inside, an elevator operator greets customers and announces each floor and its attrac-

tions, and 1930s pneumatic tubes serve as interfloor communication to a central accounting desk. This splendid department store, now operated by the third generation of Hibbards, specializes in hard-to-find items and is itself of an old-fashioned, vanishing breed.

EP15 DeGraff Building

1897, Thomas P. Barber. 116–118 N. Tejon St. (NR)

The parapet of this brick building was removed and the sandstone trim chipped back flush for the 1968 addition of a rock aggregate veneer. Restoration fourteen years later replaced the lost sandstone trim with pink concrete and reinstated the eight-foot-tall curvilinear parapet, complete with date stone. Storefronts have been restored and large awnings added. The resurrected lobby and original oak staircase are once again lit by the original skylight. Built by rancher and investor David DeGraff, this was an early home for the YWCA and later became offices and retail space.

EP16 Acacia Park

Nevada Ave. to Tejon St. between Bijou St. and Platte Ave.

This square-block park combines an old band shell and shuffleboard and horseshoe courts with new raised planter beds and a new clubhouse. The Renaissance Revival Acacia Park Hotel (1907, Robert and Bischoff, Thomas MacLaren), 104 East Platte Avenue, restored for senior housing in 1987, looks south onto the park.

EP17 William J. Palmer High School

1940, Edward L. Bunts and Burnham F. Hoyt. Northeast corner of Nevada and Platte aves.

This International Style school, designed by a noted Denver architect and Edward Bunts of Colorado Springs, combines round and rectangular shapes in an asymmetrical composition. Sandstone frames bands of windows along the west facade, which curves into the multilevel southwest corner entrance, with its curved metal canopy. Vertical panels of glass block are used to light stairwells. Additions fill the block, echoing the red brick, fenestration, and massing of the original but introducing terracotta and concrete trim.

EP18 El Paso Club

1883, James Ellis. 1891, Thomas P. Barber. 30 E. Platte Ave. (northwest corner of Tejon St.)

This clubhouse, built originally as a residence, displays a profusion of ornament, including curvilinear gable ends on south-facing dormers and a dragon finial from the Hassell Iron Works atop the corner tower. A single-story wing with Neoclassical detailing extends from the west side of the large Queen Anne Style house. The building became the clubhouse of the oldest (1877) private men's club in the Rockies, whose membership has virtually defined the power elite of Colorado Springs. Despite additions and remodelings, the clubhouse has maintained a domesticity that contrasts pleasantly with neighboring commercial and public buildings.

EP19 Carnegie Public Library

1905, Calvin Kiessling. 20 N. Cascade Ave. (southwest corner of Kiowa St.)

In the *Colorado Springs Gazette Telegraph* for March 12, 1905, the Boston architect described this Carnegie library as "a forceful adaptation of . . . what is commonly known as the Néo-Grec style," continuing: "With an exterior expressing the intents and purposes of the building, aided by the concentration of solids and voids in groups, an extraordinarily ample fenestration is secured without impairing the solidity or monumental character of the building."

The walls are of pressed Roman brick in a gray color, with trim of Platte Canyon granite, Pueblo sandstone, and ivory white terracotta. The formality of the design defers to the entry, with its overdoor anthemion. The building now serves as the library's local history section, attached to the northwest corner of the newer and otherwise unremarkable Penrose Public Library, a sprawling, two-story building at 20 North Cascade.

EP20 St. Mary's Catholic Cathedral

1903, James Murdoch, L. A. Pease, and Thomas P. Barber. 22 W. Kiowa St., 1 block west of Cascade Ave.

Built on a cruciform plan, this modified Gothic Revival church has prominent, uneven bell towers topped by steep polygonal spires. Red brick is accented by limestone ornament, which also frames the facade's large rose window and towers flanking a gabled parapet above a statue of St. Mary in a niche. Inset windows beneath the bell towers were once entrance doors, closed off by the 1968 addition of a contemporary entrance ramp and stairway, which provide a meditation area between church and street. The center landing of this new entrance features a bronze railing by Edgar Britton, a prominent Colorado sculptor. As was the case with many other financially struggling Catholic parishes, the basement (1891) was used as a church while fund raising for a more formal church dragged on. The superstructure of St. Mary's was not completed until 1898, and the bell towers were not added until 1903.

EP21 Giuseppe's Restaurant (Denver & Rio Grande Depot)

1887, Frederick J. Sterner. 10 S. Sierra Madre St.

The rambling Queen Anne passenger depot has been restored as a restaurant decorated with railroadiana. Inside, the hexagonal tile floor, curved oak ticket counter, stained glass windows, and wood-paneled ceiling survive. Originally planned as an adjunct to the now demolished Antlers Hotel, the structure bristles with gabled train sheds, dormers, porches, and a cupola. All rooflines except the cupola repeat the same 45-degree pitch. Castle Rock rhyolite and rust-colored sandstone compose the exterior walls. In a typical Queen Anne treatment, various wood surfaces and detailing—shingles, siding, and half timbering—decorate the upper structure. Sympathetic 1901, 1911, and 1919 additions complement the original better than the 1980s restaurant additions.

EP22 Palmer Center

1991, Klipp Colussy Jenks DuBois; master plan, Kohn Pedersen Fox. Cascade Ave. between Colorado and Pikes Peak aves.

This $85 million high-rise hub of Colorado Springs, a collaboration of Denver and New York architects, is the latest attempt to enhance the original site of the splendid old Antlers Hotel (demolished in 1963), whose twin towers once framed Pikes Peak.

The new Antlers Doubletree Hotel is flanked by sixteen-story towers joined to the hotel by two-story wings that define a central entrance court framed on Cascade Avenue by an elevated pergola. The design-integrated Norwest Bank Tower, on the south end, is reminiscent of the Deco Gothic skyscraper style. This richly detailed Postmodern edifice wears an acid-etched precast concrete skin resembling limestone with traditional stonelike detailing and granite ac-

EP21 Giuseppe's Restaurant (Denver & Rio Grande Depot), c. 1890

EP22 Palmer Center, Norwest Bank Tower

cents. A triple cornice steps up to a hip-roofed penthouse. The lobby's coved and domed ceilings, granite and marble accents, and multicolored granite floor are reminiscent of the elegant Antlers Hotel.

On the north end, an identical base is used to incorporate the sixteen-story Holly Sugar Building, the centerpiece of the 1960s complex on this site, with its thin, vertical bands of stone and glass jutting skyward. Across the street from the underground parking entrance on Pikes Peak Avenue, the polychrome stag's head in the terracotta parapet of the Antlers Garage recalls another era.

EP23 **Cheyenne Hotel**

1901. 2–8 E. Pikes Peak Ave. (northeast corner of
Cascade Ave.)

This three-story commercial corner of red
and yellow brick housed offices of the Chicago, Rock Island and Pacific Railroad before conversion to a hotel in 1909. Above
the first floor, pilasters separating window
bays culminate in third-story arches. A terracotta bust of a Cheyenne Indian guards the
northeast corner entrance, to what became,
in 1994, the Phantom Canyon Brew Pub.

EP24 **Pikes Peak Center**

1982, John James Wallace Associates; Clifford S. Nakata Associates; Artec. 190 S. Cascade Ave. (northwest
corner of Vermijo Ave.)

The focal point of this multipurpose arts
center is the 2,100-seat El Pomar Great Hall,
fan-shaped for optimum acoustics. A movable orchestra canopy and curving walls
tilted over the balconies project and diffuse
sound to three audience levels and cantilevered box seats. The center's irregularly
massed concrete exterior faces the Colorado
Springs Pioneers Museum through the
courtyard of the county government complex.

EP25 **North End Historic District**

Nevada to Wood aves. between Madison and Uintah
sts. (NRD)

Colorado Springs's North End Historic District is a residential area comprising 657
contributing properties, with only nineteen
intrusions. Homes built between the 1870s
and the 1920s display a high standard of
residential construction. Detached, two-
story frame residences, typically carpenter
built, have standard 25-foot setbacks and
planting strips, giving a spacious feeling to
the street facades. The wide north-south
streets contribute to the parklike setting,
as do landscaped medians along Nevada,
Cascade, and Wood avenues. Several houses
have impressive ornamental iron fences, and
many sport small-paned decorative windows.
Houses built before 1920 commonly have
sleeping porches to accommodate consump-
tives. Styles are overwhelmingly English, with
some Craftsman bungalows and examples of

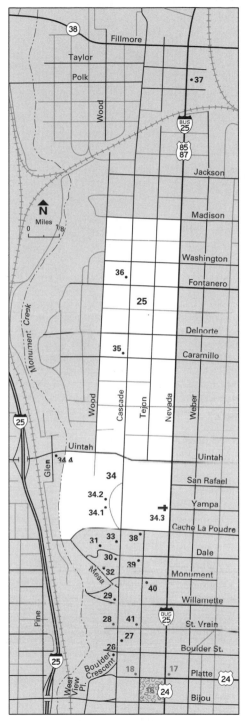

Inset 2. North End (EP25–EP41; for EP42
through EP47 see the overview map on p. 283)

more modern design. A few former carriage houses have been converted to residences. Although the development of the Broadmoor area lured some residents away, this remains a neighborhood of well-maintained, distinguished homes.

Cascade Avenue, the district's main north-south avenue, divides Colorado Springs addresses into east and west street numbers. Houses on Cascade represent a range of residential styles, from Colonial Revival at 1230 North Cascade to Shingle Style at 1530 North Cascade, both 1892 designs by Colorado Springs architect E. C. G. Robinson.

EP26 Boulder Crescent Place

1894–1910. 9 and 11 W. Boulder Pl.; 312, 318, and 320 N. Cascade Ave. (NRD)

This mini-district of five houses on small lots reflects a rise in land values that followed the 1890 Cripple Creek bonanza, which created many fortunes spent on fine houses in Colorado Springs. The residences make use of the pattern-book styles popular at the time. The large houses embrace Queen Anne and Dutch Colonial styles, displaying decorative shingles, dentil trim, cornices, columns, and leaded and beveled glass windows.

EP27 McAllister House

1873, George L. Summers. 423 N. Cascade Ave. (NR)

Smaller than later homes in the area, this English-influenced brick cottage with Carpenter's Gothic trim was constructed by Winfield Scott Stratton, a carpenter who later became a mining millionaire. George Summers, a Philadelphian, designed this first substantial house in Colorado Springs for Major Henry McAllister, Sr., a Civil War assistant to General Palmer who was later recruited to direct the Colorado Springs Company. Major McAllister not only landscaped his own property but planted some 5,000 cottonwoods along the ditches bordering Cascade Avenue and other streets of the bare prairie village.

After facing winds in Colorado Springs powerful enough to derail trains, McAllister insisted on double-thick walls of Philadelphia brick, the local brick at the time being too soft and crumbly. The steep, clipped gable roof, tiny dormer, prominent bays,

and stone quoins, lintels, and sills distinguish this quaint dwelling. One of the three oldest residences in the Pikes Peak region, it may be the only remaining residential work by George Summers. The El Pomar Foundation purchased the home for the Colonial Dames of Colorado, who operate it as a house museum.

EP28 Hearthstone Inn (Bemis House)

1885, W. F. Ellis, Jr. 506 N. Cascade Ave. (northwest corner of St. Vrain St.) (NR)

Once home to Colorado philanthropist Judson Moss Bemis, this and its next-door neighbor have been converted to a hostelry, joined at the rear through a former outbuilding. Both houses are clapboard in the Queen Anne Style, with elaborate shinglework on the Bemis House. Dormers and gables in the deep-pitched roof and a wraparound porch capitalize on views of the neighborhood and of Monument Valley Park. Judge Bemis, one of thousands who flocked to Colorado Springs for a tuberculosis cure, founded the business administration and banking schools at The Colorado College. His daughter, Alice Bemis Taylor, continued her father's support of the college and led the crusade to build the Colorado Springs Fine Arts Center.

EP29 Cascade Park Apartments (Hagerman Mansion)

1885, C. S. Wright. 1927, Benjamin Lefkowsky. 610–624 N. Cascade Ave. (northwest corner of Willamette Ave.) (NR)

Sphinxes guard the entry of the pink rhyolite mansion built for James John Hagerman, who spent a fortune he made in Michigan iron mills to construct the Colorado Midland Railroad from Colorado Springs to Grand Junction. Flemish gables crown Tudor-arched windows and dormers in this three-story house, whose grounds once occupied the entire block.

During the 1920s Benjamin Lefkowsky purchased the estate and added L-shaped stuccoed wings to both sides of the house. On the north side, he built a similarly massed Decoesque apartment house. He also converted the carriage house to residential units. By incorporating similar design elements and scale, Lefkowsky accomplished the change without destroying the mansion's character.

EP30 Gwynne-Love House

1886, Willard B. Perkins. 730 N. Cascade Ave. (southwest corner of W. Dale St.) (NR)

This large Queen Anne house has a hexagonal three-story tower on the southeast corner. Four stone chimneys further emphasize the vertical. Rough-cut pinkish ashlar rhyolite sheathes the first floor while wood shingles, half-timbered gables trimmed with molded bargeboards, and twin oriel windows adorn the upper two levels.

EP31 Colorado Springs Fine Arts Center

1936, John Gaw Meem. 30 W. Dale St. 1 block west of Cascade Ave. (NR)

John Gaw Meem, who worked primarily in New Mexico, refined the Santa Fe Style with Pueblo Revival and Spanish Colonial elements. The most modern of his designs, this arts center integrates Southwestern, Modernist, Art Deco, and classical elements in a monolithic, poured concrete structure. The building earned a silver medal in 1940 at the Fifth Pan American Congress of Architecture in Uruguay.

The stepped pueblo form blends into a bluff overlooking Monument Valley Park, once the spectacular site of the mansion built by Spencer Penrose. When the Penroses built El Pomar (EP55), they made the old mansion a home for the Broadmoor Art Academy, Colorado's first notable attempt to attract and cultivate artists and the predecessor of the Fine Arts Center. Meem's building was designed as a home for the extensive art collections of Alice Bemis Taylor, who financed most of its cost. He worked closely with Taylor and later married her niece, Faith.

Native rock sheathing the foundation contrasts with raw concrete walls, which retain markings from their forms. Columns, doors, and windows are classically grouped in threes, fives, and sevens. Aluminum is used for sleek door and window moldings as well as loggia and balcony railings and the *canales* draining the flat roofs. Traditional Pueblo and Navajo designs have been abstracted into Art Deco metal ornament, highlighting the building's streamlined yet classic proportions. Ink-on-linen drawings in the John Gaw Meem Archives at the University of New Mexico's Zimmerman Library specify the incorporation of art as well as of custom designs ranging from bookcases to door handles. Boardman Robinson's murals grace spandrels above the five main entry doors, and Frank Mechau's frescoed horses adorn the frieze facing the courtyard.

An auditorium lies at the center of the plan, which includes a director's quarters, music room, studio spaces, and the outdoor sculpture garden. Hispanic religious folk art is exhibited in a reconstructed chapel. Despite the building's large size, Meem pro-

EP31 Colorado Springs Fine Arts Center

vided a human scale often missing from such sculptural approaches to Modernism.

EP32 Tilley House

1952, Gordon Ingraham and Elizabeth Wright Ingraham. 30 W. Mesa Rd.

Built into the hillside between retaining walls of surrounding properties, this simple, tile-block house with its outdoor deck enjoys a southern exposure. Elizabeth Wright Ingraham, architect and granddaughter of Frank Lloyd Wright, collaborated with her husband on the Wrightian design of this house and designed several other Prairie Style residences, including a house in the Cole Heights neighborhood of Colorado Springs (1987), 3450 Broadmoor Valley Road.

EP33 American Numismatic Association Money Museum

1967, Carlisle B. Guy and Associates. Addition, Leland B. Roberts. 818 N. Cascade Ave. (near northwest corner of W. Dale St.)

One of the world's most extensive collections of coins and paper money is displayed in this boxy abstraction with a set-back second level. A framework of steel girders at the front of the second level is repeated in a smaller structural grid in a cutaway portion of the roof near the recessed entrance. This is also the international headquarters of the American Numismatic Association, including its research library.

EP34 The Colorado College

1874; numerous additions. Nevada Ave. to Monument Creek between Uintah and Cache la Poudre aves.

The Colorado College, opened in 1874 as a Congregational school, has the largest endowment and the best academic reputation of Colorado's four-year colleges. The senior building on the compact campus is The Gothic Revival Cutler Hall (see below). The styliistic range also includes Palmer Hall (1903, Andrews, Jacques and Rantoul), 1025 N. Cascade Avenue (NR), an imposing exercise in the Romanesque Revival style with rough-faced sandstone covering a steel frame; Bemis Hall (1908, Maurice Biscoe), 920 North Cascade, a Tudor Revival dormi-

tory with steep-pitched dormers and gables; and the angular Modernist Tutt Library (1962, Skidmore, Owings and Merrill; 1980, addition, Carlisle B. Guy and Associates), the largest building on campus.

EP34.1 Cutler Hall

1878, Peabody and Stearns. 912 N. Cascade Ave. (NR)

Prolific Boston architects who also designed the original Antlers Hotel (1883) in Colorado Springs were responsible for this Gothic Revival structure of rough-cut Castle Rock rhyolite. It rises two stories above a raised basement to a steep gabled roof with parapeted ends culminating in chimney stacks. An open bell tower with flying buttresses sits astride the ridgeline in the center of the symmetrical facade. A quatrefoil and an astrolabe globe cap the triple Gothic arch entry. Four fine, fierce tigers (1930, Chicago Art Bronze Works) guard the flagpole. These Colorado projects and other commissions in the Midwest led Peabody and Stearns to form an office in St. Louis under the direction of Pierre Furber.

EP34.2 Montgomery Hall

1891, Douglas and Hetherington. 1030 N. Cascade (NR)

Rough-cut rhyolite sheaths the first two levels of this three-story residence hall on a rectangular plan. Half timbering on the attic level and dormers rhythmically punctuates the steep hipped roof in an Elizabethan manner.

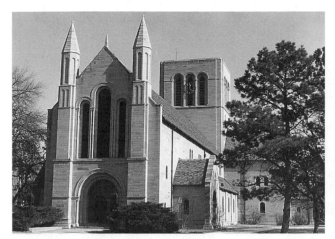

EP34.3 The Colorado College, Shove Chapel

EP34.4 The Colorado College, Old Van Briggle Art Pottery Factory

EP34.3 Shove Chapel

1931, John Gray. 1010 N. Nevada Ave.

Creamy stone sheathes this chapel, which is aligned with Cutler Hall to form the east anchor of the campus axis. This Collegiate Romanesque bulwark is dominated by a square bell tower with a 17,322-pound carillon. The sparse interior, with slate floor and stone walls under an open-beamed ceiling, features stained glass windows by Reynold, Francis and Rohnstock of Boston and ceiling paintings by Robert Wade, also of Boston.

EP34.4 Old Van Briggle Art Pottery Factory

1907, Nicholas van den Ahrend. 1125 Glen Ave. (southeast corner of W. Uintah St.)

Posing as a Hudson River mansion, this factory wears a handsome red brick skin with decorative tile ornament as well as wide, open-rafter eaves, dormers, gables, and two massive kiln chimneys. Now used by the college as offices and a maintenance facility, it was built for the pottery founded at the turn of the century by Artus Van Briggle, the son of a Dutch immigrant. He and his wife, Anne, used Chinese glazing techniques and Art Nouveau designs for a prized line of art pottery. Nicholas van den Ahrend often incorporated Van Briggle tiles into his architectural designs, including this Art Nouveau treasure.

EP35 Sharp House

1913, Nicholas van den Ahrend. 1600 N. Cascade Ave. (northwest corner of Camarillo St.)

Arthur Sharp of the Exchange National Bank occupied this gray brick mansion with a local brown sandstone base, terracotta trim, a green tile roof, and arcaded porch. It is an eclectic mix of Mediterranean, Tudor, and Craftsman elements. Among many interior features are tapestry wallpaper, lavish mahogany and oak woodwork, and seven Van Briggle ceramic tile fireplaces. A large carriage house, pergola, and stone and iron fence augment the property, now occupied by the American Red Cross.

EP36 Wheeler House

1889, Frank E. Edbrooke. 1908 N. Cascade Ave. (northwest corner of Fontanero St.)

Although he owned elegant summer residences in Aspen and Manitou Springs, this mansion remained home for railroad and silver mining millionaire Jerome B. Wheeler. Of the rough-faced sandstone and Shingle Style houses once so popular, this is one of the last survivors on Cascade Avenue.

EP37 Navajo Hogan

1936, John Aaron, builder. 1989, restoration. 2817 N. Nevada Ave. (NR)

North Nevada Avenue evolves from a street of fine homes along a landscaped median to a commercial strip above Jackson Street. Its prize piece of roadside Americana is this restaurant and bar mimicking a traditional Navajo dwelling. Thick, hand-hewn pine slabs were fitted on site to form a domed roof. Around 1940 a second hogan was added to the east of the first, with a pentagonal addition at the rear for an office. Neon zigzags along the eaves and outlines the 17-foot-tall Navajo sign. Next door, El Sombrero, 2821 North Nevada Avenue, is a tiny cinderblock restaurant under a huge concrete sombrero.

EP38 Plaza Hotel

1900, Walter W. and Guy F. Atkinson. 830 N. Tejon St. (NR) (southwest corner of Cache la Poudre St.)

This Renaissance Revival structure with Spanish and Mission influences is clad in St. Louis–made pressed brick in a buff color. It rises four stories to hipped roofs with overhanging eaves. The principal facade of the H-shaped building has protruding bays on each side with an arcade spanning the opening. Two fenestrated arches in each bay carry the rhythm across the entire facade. Twin square open towers are the most prominent elements. The hotel resembles Thomas MacLaren's later Cragmor Sanatarium (EP45), supporting speculation that he was at least consulted on its design. It is now William I. Spencer Center of The Colorado College.

EP39 All Souls Unitarian Church

1892, Walter F. Douglas. 1984, addition, Elizabeth Wright Ingraham. 730 N. Tejon St. (southwest corner of Dale St.)

The heavy massing of this church is relieved somewhat by the large, round-arched windows and the three-story stone bell tower with a bell-shaped roof. The exterior is shingle and "green stone," a greenish-to-reddish sandstone found near Manitou Springs. The addition uses stucco instead of natural stone but, according to its architect, Elizabeth Wright Ingraham, tries to "keep the spirit of the original by incorporating its banding, shadow lines, overhang, stained glass, fenestration, and roof pitch." Ingraham also designed the Vista Grande Community Church (1985) at the southwest corner of Montebello Drive and Union Boulevard, with dramatic concrete paneled walls topped by a barrel vault of ribbed copper supported by laminated oak beams and an interior lighted by glazed end walls and a narrow, full-length skylight.

EP40 Grace Episcopal Church Complex

1926, Frohman, Robb and Little. Southeast corner of Monument and Tejon sts.

A soaring, turreted bell tower with four ornate spires caps this Gothic Revival church by Boston architects known for their ecclesiastical works, including the Episcopal Cathedral in Baltimore, Trinity Chapel in Hartford, Connecticut, and the National Cathedral in Washington, D.C. For Grace Episcopal Church, they used rough-faced stone, buttresses, and recessed Gothic-arched openings to unify an asymmetrical design in one of Colorado's finest rhyolite structures.

The lovely chapel of rough-faced rhyolite (1894, Thomas MacLaren) that originally housed the congregation, seven blocks south at 217 East Pikes Peak Avenue, has been converted to a restaurant.

EP41 First Congregational Church

1889, Robert S. Roeschlaub, Henry Rutgers Marshall, and Joseph Dozier. 500 N. Tejon St. (northwest corner of St. Vrain St.)

An oversized square tower and massive, rough stone porch columns are striking features of this landmark, built on a Greek cross plan. The enormous rhyolite columns and spandrels of the curved, south-facing porch lend an earthiness to this church, whose pastors initially also served as presidents of nearby Colorado College. Henry Rutgers Marshall, a prominent New York architect and author, worked with two Denver architects on a design reminiscent of

H. H. Richardson's work in its bold textures, massive stonework, and tight craftsmanship.

EP42 Hidden Inn

1915. 1999, demolished. Garden of the Gods, northeast corner of Gateway Rd. and Garden Dr.

The Garden of the Gods, a 1,350-acre city park (1909), features large natural weather-carved sculptures of red sandstone. The Pueblo Revival style Hidden Inn (1915) offered snacks, curios, views, and interpretive materials on the park's megalithic monuments. This fine period piece was replaced by a new visitors' center (1995, Gaede and Larson), 1805 30th St. (at Gateway Rd.)

EP43 White House Ranch (Rock Ledge)

1874, Robert Chambers. Southwest corner of 30th St. and Gateway Rd. (NR)

On the southeast side of the Garden of the Gods, Robert Chambers designed and built Rock Ledge as his home, with a dam and reservoir to facilitate cultivation of fruit and vegetables for sale to the Antlers Hotel. His square, one-and-one-half-story Italianate vernacular house, of rough sandstone block, has a cross-gable roof with pendant gable trim. The 160-acre ranch is now a living history museum operated by the city of Colorado Springs. The ranch also contains Orchard House (1907, Thomas MacLaren), the Dutch Colonial Revival house of General

William Palmer's brother-in-law, William Sclater, author of *A History of the Birds of Colorado* (1912).

EP44 Glen Eyrie

1901, Frederick J. Sterner. 3820 N. 30th St. (NR)

William Palmer began building his estate in the 1870s on 2,225 acres at the mouth of Queen's Canyon, which he named for his wife, Queen Mellen Palmer. Originally a frame structure, it has evolved through several additions, most notably Denver architect Frederick Sterner's 1901 scheme, which wrapped it in 24-inch-thick stone walls. Stones from Bear Creek Canyon west of Colorado Springs were carefully selected for their color and moss covering, wrapped in burlap, and packed in barrels of sawdust for a wagon trip to the site. Sterner favored the Tudor Revival style but also incorporated Flemish arches and stepped gable ends. The irregular massing, multiple gables, chimneys from twenty-four fireplaces, protruding bays, turrets, and castellated parapet give the feeling of a small Tudor village.

Palmer ultimately spent more than $1 million on his manor house, for which he imported such elements as an old church roof from England. The estate is self-contained, having its own electric generator, water supply, heating plant, and even a rustic, one-room school for the Palmer children and those of the family's servants. The Navigators, a Christian missionary group, now own and use Glen Eyrie as their headquarters and offer public tours and accommodations.

EP45 Cragmor Sanatarium, University of Colorado at Colorado Springs, 1920s

EP45 Cragmor Sanatarium, University of Colorado at Colorado Springs

1914, Thomas MacLaren. Austin Bluffs Pkwy. and Meadow Lane

Today's campus for the University of Colorado at Colorado Springs is built around the deluxe tuberculosis sanatarium known as the "asylum of the gilded pill." This state-of-the art sanatarium and its many wealthy patients did much for the local economy before it closed in 1964. The three-story structure was donated to the university as an administration building. It is of uncoursed, stuccoed stone with a flat roof, four corner

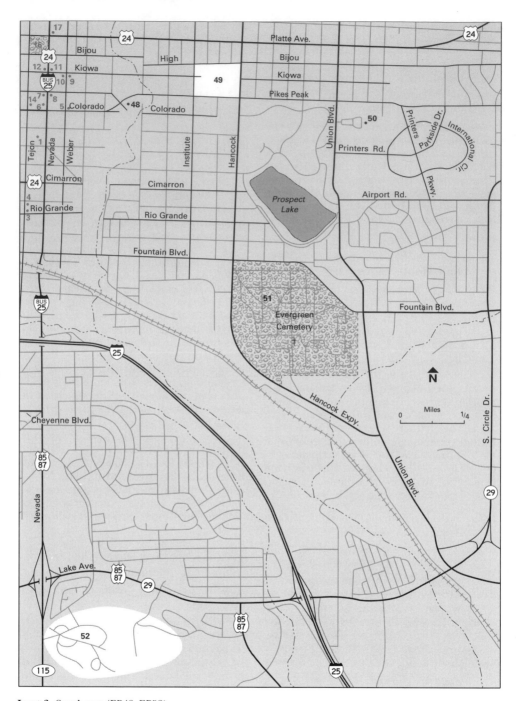

Inset 3. Southeast (EP48–EP52)

towers, and high parapets to provide privacy for the rooftop sun deck. Pyramidal tower roofs echo the hipped roofs of enclosed multistory bays that were once open sleeping porches. The old landmark rises above the 400-acre campus of many large, newer horizontal brick and concrete structures.

EP46 **Mount St. Francis Mother House** (Woodmen of the World Sanatarium)

1910–1920, Thomas MacLaren and Charles S. Thomas. 7550 Assisi Heights at Woodman Rd. and Orchard Path Rd.

The Woodmen of the World, a fraternal group, erected twenty Craftsman buildings on 112 acres for a tuberculosis sanatarium. The Sisters of St. Francis purchased it in the 1950s, after drug treatment for the disease became common and sanatariums were no longer needed. A recent $7 million renovation and restoration (Downing, Thorpe and James) added a nursing home center and restored some of the original native granite buildings topped with red tile roofs.

EP47 **Woodmen-Roberts Elementary School**

1990, Clifford Nakata. 8365 Orchard Path Rd.

This one-story structure of buff-colored brick matches the color of the nearby sandstone "mushrooms," as the curious natural stone formations are called. The classrooms are clustered around a central skylit library. The school's low profile is dramatized by a freestanding bell tower.

EP48 **Atchison, Topeka & Santa Fe Depot**

1917, E. A. Harrison. 555 E. Pikes Peak Ave. (southeast corner of Corona St.) (NR)

This $325,000 palace of hard-burned red brick has flat-roofed, single-story wings flanking a two-and-one-half-story central section under a multigabled green tile roof. Tudor-arched windows in parapeted dormers and bays, and cast stone and terracotta trim reinforce the Jacobean Revival style. After a decade of abandonment and decay, a 1979–1981 restoration transformed the depot into the centerpiece of a small business park of office buildings in red brick and cream concrete. Inside, the grand old waiting room, with its 28-foot ceiling and original tile floor, and the adjoining Harvey House Restaurant, with bright floral tile and a molded plaster ceiling, have been trashed to create office cubicles.

EP49 **Colorado School for the Deaf and Blind**

1876. 33 N. Institute St.

Jonathan R. Kennedy persuaded Colorado's territorial legislature to establish this school by demonstrating the abilities of his three deaf children to the members. William Palmer donated the original 35-acre hilltop site, which grew to include a 200-acre farm. The buildings generally reflect styles popular for institutions in the period of construction, from no longer extant Italianate buildings to a Neoclassical administration building (1906, Charles S. Thomas. Most of the twentieth-century buildings are stone and/or brick and flirt with the Collegiate Gothic style. Lamar Kelsey went Modernist in his preschool (1967). G. Cabell Childress designed a Postmodern addition (1984) to Wark Auditorium (1922) that incorporates the distinctive stone trim, steep roofs, and parapeted gables characteristic of most structures on this handsome campus.

EP50 **Union Printers Home**

1892, Meredith and Mau. 101 S. Union Blvd. to Printers Pkwy. between Pikes Peak Ave. and Parkside Dr.

This Chateau Style castle has rough red sandstone walls with white rhyolite trim accenting corner towers, dormers, and parapets. A wing (1917) and a sanatarium (1932, D. Y. Murphy and Bros.) are among various additions. The tower clock is stopped at eight o'clock, commemorating the union victory of an eight-hour work day. Set amid expansive landscaped grounds, this edifice embodies the dream of comfortable, dignified retirement for union members.

EP51 **Evergreen Cemetery**

1875. 1992, restoration, Long Hoeft Architects. 1005 S. Hancock Rd. (at Fountain Blvd.) (NR)

Evergreen Cemetery, on a ponderosa pine–clad hill called Mount Washington, contains

EP50 Union Printers Home

graves moved from the original City Cemetery, which was visible from the D&RG depot and discouraged health seekers and tourists. William Palmer selected a large block of untrimmed Pikes Peak granite for his headstone. Author Helen Hunt Jackson and many other Colorado Springs celebrities rest in this 220-acre cemetery. The rustic Romanesque Revival chapel (1906, L. A. Pease) is of Manitou Springs green stone.

EP52 Myron Stratton Home

1913, George E. Barton and Maurice B. Biscoe. 2525 S. Nevada Ave. (at Colorado 115 just south of Lake Ave.)

Winfield Scott Stratton used his Cripple Creek gold fortune to build this haven for the elderly poor named in honor of his father. The wrought iron entry gates carry a bronze tablet with the inscription "In as much as ye have done it unto one of the least of these my brethren, ye have done it unto me (Matthew 25:40)." Vast, landscaped grounds are settings for handsome stucco Mediterranean-style villas such as Washington Hall and Independence Hall (both 1913) and eleven other structures.

EP53 Broadmoor Hotel

1918, Warren and Wetmore; additions. 1 Lake Ave.

Spencer "Spec" Penrose, the black sheep of a prominent Philadelphia family, bought the land for this luxury hotel complex in 1916 for $90,000 in cash. Once a dairy farm, the site, with its man-made lake, had earlier been transformed into a resort by Count

EP53 Broadmoor Hotel

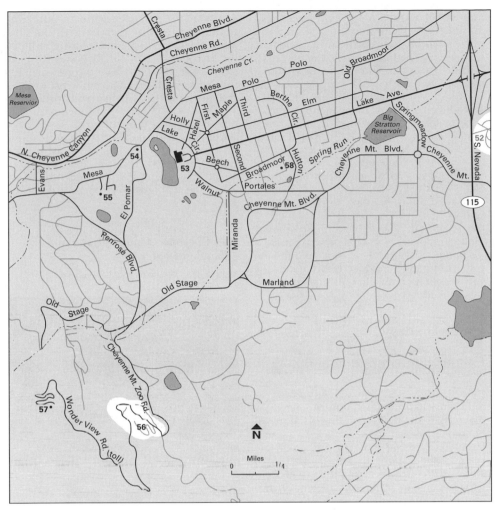

Inset 4. Southwest (EP53–EP58)

James Pourtales, another eastern adventurer. Penrose hired Whitney Warren and Charles D. Wetmore, whose New York firm built New York City's Ritz-Carlton and Biltmore hotels. They designed a hotel in an Italianate style, nine stories with a tower and decorative frieze, of pink stucco with red tile roofs. Penrose lavished $3.1 million on the hotel before its 1918 grand opening. He adorned it with fine domestic and imported art, including the seventeenth-century Venetian fountain in the entry garden and five carved heads of Bacchus, each lusty in his own way, over the five main entry arches.

The Tavern (1918) is a wood-paneled retreat hung with original Toulouse-Lautrec posters. Thousands of liquor bottles line the walls leading to the restrooms, and Penrose boasted of being present when most of them were opened. At the Tavern's north end is the Garden Room (1953), a glass-roofed, stone-floored dining patio with luxuriant plantings. The Broadmoor Casino, now the Golf Clubhouse (1898, Thomas MacLaren), enveloped by a new south wing of the main hotel, is the oldest structure in the complex, moved to its present site in 1916.

A lakeside walkway helps to integrate the original hotel with newer structures such as Broadmoor South (1961). The Broadmoor

West (1976, Carlisle B. Guy and Associates), an understated addition, uses the original's pinkish stucco and red tile in a contemporary design. The International Center (1961, Carlisle B. Guy and Edwin A. Francis), under a hyperbolic paraboloid roof, houses the Golden Bee Pub in the basement with a splendid, ornate African mahagony back bar and matching furnishings. The Carriage House Museum (1936, A. G. Jan Ruhtenberg) houses twenty-eight vehicles, ranging from an 1850 Concord stagecoach to a car that belonged to Spencer Penrose's wife, Julie, a 1928 Cadillac customized in Paris with solid silver handles, unborn calfskin upholstery, and a speaking tube to direct the chauffeur. The 2,400-acre Broadmoor Hotel complex also contains a ski area, a shopping village, and its own greenhouse. Long Colorado's premier resort hotel, the Broadmoor perennially outshines competitors in guidebook ratings.

EP54 Pauline Chapel

1918, Thomas MacLaren. 4 Park Ave., on west side of Broadmoor Hotel complex at southwest corner of Mesa Ave.

Julie Penrose, who donated the money to build this chapel, wanted it to be named for her granddaughter. According to Marshall Sprague's *Newport in the Rockies,* "The good fathers . . . made haste to discover a deceased Saint Pauline in Rome." This small stucco structure sits across the street from Broadmoor West in a grove of blue spruce and pine. Spanish Baroque details include a front facade statue of St. Paul with a tarnished steel halo.

EP55 Penrose House, previously El Pomar Center

1909, Horace Trumbauer. 1917, remodeling, Thomas MacLaren. 1661 Mesa Ave. (NR)

Named for an apple orchard in which Grace Goodyear Depew and her second husband, Ashton Potter, built the original structure, this hacienda was purchased by Spencer and Julie Penrose in 1916. Thomas MacLaren's sympathetic additions to the Depews' house (1909, Horace Trumbauer) have blended Beaux-Arts Neoclassical and Southwestern styles in what is now a 37,000-square-foot, three-story showplace. The white stucco villa

with a red tile roof opens onto a south-facing fountain courtyard and terraced gardens. Penrose died in 1939, but his empire building is continued by his El Pomar Foundation, a $100,000,000 philanthropy which has funded many fine public buildings in Colorado. After 1945 El Pomar was acquired by the Sisters of Charity of Cincinnati, who operated it as a retreat house. In 1992 the order sold it to the El Pomar foundation, which spent $3 million on a first-rate restoration to create its center. The 18-acre grounds were designed by the Olmsted firm to include the teahouse, fountains, and sunken gardens.

EP56 Cheyenne Mountain Zoo and Education Center

1926. 4200 Cheyenne Mountain Zoo Rd.

After a monkey from the Broadmoor Hotel menagerie bit a guest, the monkey and its companions were moved to this nearby Cheyenne Mountain site, which still maintains a lively primate population. Spencer Penrose founded this zoo, which remains privately owned. A large stone, stucco, and half-timbered lodge serves as the education center. Other structures have been built in the Pueblo Revival style, incorporating passive solar features to help warm animals in this unusual montane setting.

EP57 Will Rogers Shrine of the Sun

1937, Charles S. Thomas. Wonder View Rd. above Cheyenne Mountain Zoo

Refreshed by a facelift in 1995, this five-story medieval tower of rough-faced granite, with buttressed corners and crenelated parapet, perches on the side of Cheyenne Mountain overlooking Colorado Springs. No wood or nails were used in the structure, which features floors of red Italian marble and terrazzo. A spiral stairway connects the four rooms, which are filled with memorabilia honoring Will Rogers, the cowboy humorist. The fourth floor observation alcove displays local history murals by Randall Davey of Santa Fe. A bronze bust of Will Rogers (1935) by Jo Davidson stands in the front courtyard. Spencer and Julie Penrose are buried here in what was initially planned as their private shrine and mausoleum. Penrose dedicated the tower to Will Rogers after Rogers died in a plane crash in 1935.

EP58 The Colorado Springs School
(Claremont)

1907, Thomas MacLaren. 21 Broadmoor Ave. (southwest corner of Hutton) (NR)

Colorado's copy of the Grand Trianon at Versailles has brick masonry walls completely clad in white terracotta. The flat roof has a balustraded parapet, and Ionic pilasters flank the arched French doors in the facade. A colonnaded portico and wings enclose the rear paved court. The formal entrance is through a domed rotunda, with interior rooms finished with wood paneling and plaster relief moldings.

Charles and Virginia Baldwin sent Thomas MacLaren to France to study the Trianon at Versailles before erecting this scaled-down copy as their home. Stanford White may have been consulted, having just finished Rosecliff in Newport, Rhode Island,

but his murder in 1905 precluded any planned involvement. The October 1910 issue of *Architectural Review* commended MacLaren for combining modern architectural technology and fine French classical design in the house, which is now a private school.

Colorado City

Colorado City (1860, 6,012 feet) was El Paso County's first Anglo-American settlement. It rivaled Denver and briefly captured the territorial capitol, but after the 1870s it was eclipsed by Colorado Springs, which annexed it in 1917. Colorado City became a smelting center, processing most of the gold ore pouring out of Cripple Creek. Although the Golden Cycle mill was dismantled in 1949, mountains of smelter waste at the base of the Golden Cycle smokestack (1906), south of Highway 24 near 21st Street, remain Colorado City's most massive monument.

"None of the refined gold was left here," according to William "Big Bill" Haywood, a labor organizer in Colorado around the turn of the century. Haywood described it as "a forlorn little industrial town of tents, tin houses, huts, and hovels, bordered by some of the grandest scenery in nature." Of some 6,500 remaining structures, about a fourth are nineteenth-century working-class frame cottages. Some feature ornate wrought iron fences from Colorado City's Hassell Iron Works.

EP58 The Colorado Springs School (Claremont)

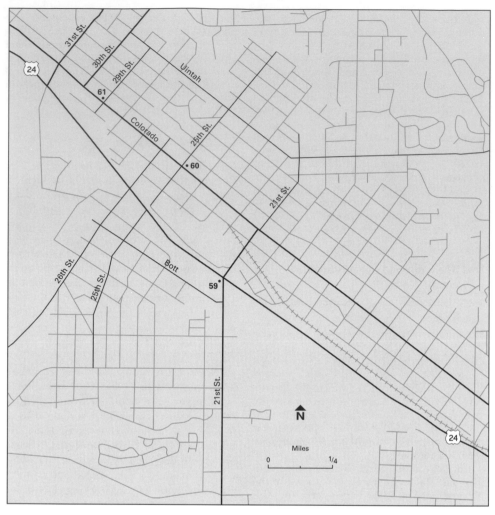

Inset 5. Colorado City (EP59–EP60)

The Old Colorado City Historic Commercial District, Colorado Avenue to Pikes Peak Avenue between 24th and 27th Streets (NRD), includes side streets north to Pikes Peak Avenue. Western commercial vernacular brick structures with sandstone trim generally extend to lot lines, creating a densely built environment of rhythmic rooflines and fenestration levels. This density is alleviated on the east end by Bancroft Park, with Dr. Garvin's Cabin (1859), a rustic log cabin with a frame false front, and a stone band shell (1929). A hospitable landmark is the Holden House (1902), 1102 West Pikes Peak Avenue, now a bed and breakfast, a comfortable restored Victorian house distinguished by turret and finial.

EP59 **Van Briggle Art Pottery** (Colorado Midland Terminal Railroad Roundhouse)

1889. 600 S. 21st St. (southwest corner of U.S. 24) (NR)

The Colorado Midland Railroad, the first standard-gauge line to be built through the Rockies, used rough-faced brown sandstone in ashlar blocks for this roundhouse with shops. Arches top columns along the concave, parapeted facade, with corresponding arched windows in the convex back wall. The Midland used the building until the railroad's demise in 1949. Since 1954 the structure has housed the manufacturing and sales areas for Van Briggle Art Pottery. Pikes Peak Ghost Town occupies the former Midland Shops to the west of the parking lot. Although Colorado has no shortage of authentic ghost towns, this Hollywood version, complete with talking mannequins, saves the less adventurous tourist the time and trouble of back-country travel.

EP60 Waycott Opera House

1901. 2432 W. Colorado Ave. (northeast corner of 25th St.)

The opera house, which once contained a large theater, may have been designed by Ernest and R. H. Waycott, the contractors and proprietors. Clever murals that mimic the third-story fenestration mask removal of the original second-story bay windows. The first level is now a multiroom maze filled with antiques and architectural souvenirs in what has become a bar and restaurant.

EP61 Old City Hall

1888. 2902 W. Colorado Ave. (northwest corner of 29th St.) (NR)

Colorado City's first city hall is a two-story building with a square, three-story tower at the southeast corner. Originally incorporating the jail, firehouse, and city offices, it became a school soon after a second city hall was built closer to the commercial strip. The sides and rear are brick, but the facade, now attractively restored, is rough gray stone with orange sandstone trim around the segmental-arched openings. The interior has been adapted for commercial use.

EP62 U.S. Air Force Academy

1958, Skidmore, Owings and Merrill. I-25 (9 miles north of Colorado Springs)

Colorado Springs captured the U.S. Air Force Academy in 1954 by offering an 18,500-acre foothills site forested in ponderosa pine. This extensive open space surrounds well-planned residential, commer-

cial, and public facilities as well as the campus itself. The academy's boxy buildings around a formal plaza by landscape architect Dan Kiley helped confirm Modernism as an acceptable style for the federal government, to the disappointment of traditionalists and many military top brass who wanted this to look more like West Point or Annapolis.

Skidmore, Owings and Merrill, whose interpretation of spare, contemporary design was highly regarded at the time, won the commission to design the campus despite competition from several prominent architects. Eero Saarinen wanted the job. So did Frank Lloyd Wright, who thought that the federal government owed him at least one large project. Wright, who proposed building the academy with a local sandstone, condemned SOM's design as "a factory for birdmen." SOM, however, impressed the air force with its design for Oak Ridge, Tennessee, and the high quality and speedy completion of that federal project. Since 1955 the campus has emerged as an equal to West Point and Annapolis and has drawn Colorado Springs development northward.

Walter Netsch of the SOM Chicago office did the design work (1954–1957) with help from Gordon Bunshaft of SOM's New York office. Nathaniel Owings declared the academy design "styleless" and "timeless," but it has become perhaps America's best and purest example of the International Style. Its horizontal skyscrapers—glass and metal boxes—flaunt a hard geometry and concede nothing to the awesome setting. Although part of the campus is off limits to tourists, it has become one of Colorado's most popular man-made attractions. Free public tours begin at the Barry Goldwater Visitor Center, North Entrance exit from I-25.

EP62.1 Academy Chapel

1963, Skidmore, Owings and Merrill

Soaring above the horizontal campus, the chapel's seventeen spires consist of tetrahedral frames made of aluminum-clad steel pipe and stained glass panels. Principal architect Walter A. Netsch, Jr., gave this $3.5 million marvel separate Catholic, Protestant, and Jewish worship spaces. The glistening aluminum and glass abstraction, a dramatic Modernist reinterpretation of Gothic verticality, is Colorado's most famous church.

EP62.1 U.S. Air Force Academy Chapel

EP62.2 **Academy Superintendent Residence** (Carlton House Complex)

1930, 1937, Richard S. Requa and George Washington Smith. Pine Valley (NR)

This complex in the Spanish Colonial style, as popularized by its two Southern California architects, was designed for the widow of Cripple Creek mine and mill owner Albert E. Carlton. After he died, Ethel Carlton went into a building frenzy, transforming a simple country cottage her husband had built into an elaborate residence that locals dubbed the Ritz-Carlton. Designed as a setting for entertaining, it incorporates guest houses and outbuildings connected by courtyards. The main house (1930) is a rambling abode, with walls of stucco over structural clay tile, a type of construction patented by Richard Requa. Requa, a San Diego architect, defined and championed Spanish-American architecture in books and articles as well as his buildings. After Mrs. Carlton moved out in 1950, the complex became the private Pine Valley Club. The Air Force Academy acquired it in 1955 and converted it to housing for the base superintendent and visiting dignitaries.

EP63 **Shepard's–McGraw-Hill, Inc.**

1990, Michael Barber Architecture. 555 Middle Creek Pkwy., 2.3 miles west of Colorado 3

This unusual office building appears as rectangular units around a central atrium capped by a raised circular glass roof. Dubbed "the flashcube" because of the glow from the atrium at night, it has recessed courts on north and west sides leading to entries. Three tall, rectangular bays protrude on both east and south walls, with large fenestration bands that cut through floor levels. The stepped-back massing and irregular rectangularity give the structure a neo–Pueblo Revival flair, reinforced by dark inset panels at the frieze level which can be read as vigas.

Calhan

Calhan (1888, 6,507 feet) was founded by a Rock Island railroad contractor named Callahan, but its name was shortened by the U.S. Post Office. Slovaks began homesteading around Calhan in the 1890s. The farm community, which peaked in the early 1900s at about 900, had a 1990 population of 562.

EP64 **St. Mary's Eastern Orthodox Church**

1932, The Reverend Michael Zoharkov. Colorado 24, 5 miles north of Calhan at the southeast corner of Calhan and Ramah rds.

Michael Zoharkov, a carpenter-priest, designed and supervised the construction of this frame Eastern Orthodox church on the Andrew Trojanovich farm near Calhan. The church replaced an earlier St. Mary's (1905), now a nearby ruin and cemetery on a lonely hilltop. The new clapboard church has an open-front bell tower and a matching cupola centered on the roof, both crowned by large Orthodox crosses, recalling a distant but never forgotten Slovak homeland.

Cascade

Cascade (1887, 7,370 feet), named, like the nearby creek, for the many waterfalls in this scenic canyon, was promoted as a resort town by the Colorado Midland Railroad. The Cascade Community House (1927), U.S. 24 near Pikes Peak Road, was built as a Spanish Colonial Revival hacienda for the town hall, post office, general store, refreshment parlor, garage, and filling station. The Eastholme Hotel (1885), 4445 Hagerman Avenue, is a Victorian boarding house with a full-length double-deck front porch, converted to a bed and breakfast in 1988. Santa's Workshop and North Pole (1956), Pikes Peak Toll Road, houses figures of Santa and his elves in a village of brightly painted Swiss chalets with gingerbread trim frosting the steep-pitched roofs, dormers, and flower boxes. Modeled after the North Pole Village in Whiteface Mountain, New York, which was popularized by a 1953 *Saturday Evening Post* article, this tourist attraction is wrapped around a concrete North Pole with white-painted snow that never melts.

EP65 **Chapel of the Holy Rosary**

1930, Charles S. Thomas. 4435 Holiday Trail at Fountain Ave.

This Neo-Romanesque country chapel of local stone has a Tuscan red tile roof, open bell tower, and round-arched openings. Uncut, uncoursed red sandstone, from nearby Pyramid Mountain, forms the walls while

EP65 Chapel of the Holy Rosary, 1930s

uncoursed ashlar from another quarry is used for the arches, buttresses, and corners. Hidden amid ponderosa pines on the much-advertised road to Santa's Workshop, it is a memorial to Thomas and Mary Green Cusack. Cusack, who made a fortune by erecting billboards in Chicago, bought extensive summer home property in the picturesque mountain resort of Cascade. The chapel contains glass and bronze stations of the cross and Carrara marble statues.

EP66 **Congregation of the Holy Cross Novitiate** (Marigreen Pines)

1923, Ralph Zimmerman. U.S. 24

Designed by a Chicago architect and built by local architect-contractor Charles Thomas, this brick Italian villa under a tile roof has an implied arcade topped by a second-story balcony, between two protruding bays. Marble floors and fireplaces adorn the interior. Thomas Cusack bought Rock Haven (c. 1885), the original house still on the grounds, as his family summer house and added Marigreen Pines, a much larger and more elaborate house. A daughter, Anne Cusack Johnson, gave this 50-acre site to the Holy Cross Fathers in 1977 for use as a residence and training retreat for novice clerics.

EP67 **North American Air Defense Command**

1961–1966, U.S. Army Corps of Engineers; Parsons Brinckerhoff with A. J. Ryan and Associates. 3.5 miles west of Colorado 115

Here, in a sci-fi fantasy burrow inside the granite bulwark of Cheyenne Mountain, the United States and Canada monitor the skies for enemy missiles. NORAD is perhaps the most unusual small town in the state, complete with heating and power plants, fire and police departments, health and consumer services, and recreational facilities. Its huge, blast-proof steel gates can snap shut in thirty seconds. A cavernous 4.5-acre community, created by removing 693,000 tons of rock, consists of fourteen metal buildings, eight of them three stories tall, and all cushioned atop springs made of 3-inch-diameter steel and shock absorbers to ease vibrations from enemy warheads. Two rock-walled reservoirs hold 1.5 million gallons of drinking water and 4.5 million gallons for industrial use. Six locomotive-size diesel engines, with fuel reserves for thirty days, power an air filtration system for emergency use. A complex communications network connects this center with outposts throughout North America and enables the president of the United States to launch nuclear Armageddon from this control center. NORAD's fantastic structure can house some 425 of the 1,100 men on round-the-clock duty, as well as several hard rock miners who continually patrol the cave to tighten the 100,000 rock bolts that pin wire fabric mesh to cavern walls. As the development of more powerful missiles and the end of the Cold War have made this facility obsolete, it has become as useless as the Maginot Line.

EP68 Fountain Valley School

1930. 6155 Fountain Valley School Rd.

In 1930 faculty from the Old Farms School relocated from Connecticut to a 1,600-acre ranch near the town of Fountain, now a suburb of Colorado Springs. The school took the name of its new location and moved into the John R. Bradley Hacienda (1927, Addison Mizner), a stuccoed Spanish Colonial Revival home wrapped around its courtyard. Mizner, the society architect who defined the style of Palm Beach, Florida, and planned the community of Boca Raton, designed this home for a Palm Beach friend. "Casa Serena" was set in a valley and designed with a Moorish tower, originally built for water storage. Los Manos tiles manufactured by Mizner Industries in Florida were used inside and out.

Elsewhere on the campus, the stuccoed Pueblo Revival style and massing of John Gaw Meem appear in his Elizabeth Sage Hall (1930), which is reminiscent of his plaza buildings in Santa Fe. Meem's other work for the campus includes Penrose Hall, a soft-edged, two-story structure with an entry *zaguan* and stepped-back upper-story massing. The Spanish Colonial theme is continued in the Carlton Chapel (1960s, Carlisle B. Guy and Associates), with its stepped parapet rising to a bell tower. Open-beam ceilings predominate in the interiors of these buildings, as does a feeling of casual ele-

EP68 Fountain Valley School, Penrose Hall

gance. Guy, who studied with Meem, designed five buildings for the campus. The Frantantschi Campus Center (1990, Johnson, Nestor, Mortier, Rodriguez) is a bright, exquisitely detailed contemporary version of Pueblo Revival Style. The Visual Arts Center (1991, Michael Collins) is housed in a 1928 remodeling of a stock barn.

Manitou Springs

Manitou Springs (1871, 6,412 feet) has the natural mineral springs for which Colorado Springs is named. It was established as a resort town by Colorado Springs founder General William Palmer and Dr. William A. Bell, vice-president of the D&RG. They platted the 640-acre site as a railroad resort for the wealthy. Bell insisted on "streets and roads adapted to the contour of the ground" and lots "of large size and of necessity irregular . . . mostly intended for villa sites." A shortage of buyers inspired subdivision of the original large lots to accommodate more modest dwellings.

To supplement the natural beauty of the wooded hillsides, landscape architect John Blair planned meandering roads and paths, two stone footbridges (1906–1907), and rustic seats placed to capture the views. Many of the older structures were built by the Scottish brothers Angus, Archibald, and James Gillis, who used Queen Anne prototypes found in pattern books. They used Manitou's native red sandstone and Manitou green stone, green sandstone from the

Yount Quarry northwest of town, as well as limestone and pink and gray Pikes Peak granite.

By 1900 the "Saratoga of the West" boasted some fifty springs, whose "magic waters" allegedly could cure everything from heartbreak to wrinkles. During the early 1990s the Mineral Springs Foundation restored Manitou's eight public springs, bringing back not only the flowing liquid but the fanciful gazebos that sheltered the springs.

Of 1,001 buildings in the historic core of the town, 752 are deemed contributing structures in the Manitou Springs Historic District, U.S. 24 to Iron Mountain Avenue between El Paso Boulevard and Ruxton Avenue (NRD). Hospitable landmarks include Grays Avenue Hotel (1875), 711 Manitou Avenue, and the Stagecoach Inn (1880), 702 Manitou Avenue. Streamline Moderne surfaces enhance Al and Betty's Cafe, 108 Manitou Avenue, a rounded curiosity with a corner glass brick window that claims to be the "Home of the Fastest Coffee Pot in the West." Of several Pueblo Revival motels, El Colorado Lodge (1927), 23 Manitou Avenue, is the least altered.

EP69 **Briarhurst Manor** (Bell House)

1888, Frederick J. Sterner. 404 Manitou Ave. (U.S. 24) (NR)

Queen Anne Style massing and Tudor Revival elements characterize this English country house built of rough-faced Peach Blow sandstone and trimmed with fancy bargeboards with arched cutouts and half-timbered gable ends. The multigabled slate roof wears a roof comb and stone mythological creatures. A multitude of chimney pots serve eleven fireplaces copied from originals in English castles. Sterner, an Englishman who moved to Denver in 1880 and practiced there until he moved to New York in 1909, was patronized by Colorado Springs Anglophiles, among them Manitou Springs co-founder William Bell. The son of a London society doctor, Bell recruited D&RG investors among his father's patients. He attracted so many immigrants that the Colorado Springs and Manitou Springs area was dubbed "Little London." After Bell and his

EP69 Briarhurst Inn (Bell House), c. 1910

wife had returned permanently to their much larger manor in England in 1920, Briarhurst was converted to a restaurant by chef Sigfried Krauss and his wife, who respected the ornament and plan of the original house.

EP70 **Red Crags**

1889, Henry Van Brunt. 302 El Paso Blvd. (northwest corner of Rockledge Lane)

Rising in a fine example of the Shingle Style four stories above its red sandstone foundation, this house commands a south-facing slope overlooking Manitou Springs. Shingled walls are pierced by large arched windows and several decks. Commissioned by William Bell to house potential investors, it is now a bed and breakfast.

Henry Van Brunt, who designed several buildings at Harvard University and in Cambridge, Massachusetts, moved his practice to Kansas City, Missouri, in 1886 and established a reputation for fine residential design. He also designed several stations for the Union Pacific Railroad, served as national AIA president in 1899, and wrote many articles relating to his profession.

EP71 **Onaledge, Rockledge, and Craftwood Inn**

1912, Rolland Bautwell. 336, 328, and 404 El Paso Blvd.

These three Arts and Crafts houses are stone-faced with Neo-Tudor detailing and stucco and half timbering. Onaledge, with its splendid hardwood interior and terrace garden, is now a bed and breakfast. It had originally served as a guest house for Rockledge, which remains secluded and is just visible over a rise from the road. Rolland Bautwell, an Englishman devoted to the ideas of John Ruskin, also designed the Craftwood Inn (1912), 404 El Paso Boulevard, as a sales showroom for his copper work. Since 1940 this small Manitou greenstone structure has been a fine restaurant, specializing in wild game. Uncoursed walls are topped with a clipped gable roof and are half-timbered in the gable ends. Inside the Craftwood Inn, leaded glass windows, beamed ceilings, the original fireplace hood, and several small lanterns reflect Bautwell's craftsmanship,

EP72 First Congregational Church

1880, Angus Gillis and George W. Snyder. 101 Pawnee Ave. 1 block south of Manitou Ave. (NR)

Colorado's oldest Congregational church is a one-and-one-half-story vernacular Queen Anne Style structure of rough reddish stone with a cross outlined in neon atop its open bell tower. Gothic arches frame all structural openings, and a steep gable roof covers an interior with walnut beams, pews, and paneling lit by stained glass windows.

EP73 Jerome B. Wheeler Building

1888. 717–719 Manitou Ave. (NR)

A recessed entrance, two large Neo-Romanesque stone arches, and plate glass storefronts distinguish the street-level facade of this bank. Extensive Peach Blow sandstone trim, now mostly missing from the upper two stories, still adorns the first level. Above a dentiled cornice at first-floor height, pilasters flank three bays on the second and third levels, and stone banding adds tension at the third story. The massive detail of the ground level contrasts with the more austere upper floors. From here, Jerome B. Wheeler directed his Colorado investment empire. His bank was on the first floor, his business offices were on the second, and the third was originally Wheeler Music Hall, a space with fine acoustics and a 15-foot ceiling.

EP74 Manitou Town Clock

1890. Corner of Cañon and Manitou aves.

In the triangular plaza that marks the Y intersection of Manitou and Cañon avenues, Jerome Wheeler installed this cast iron clock to commemorate completion of the now-razed Manitou Mineral Water Bottling Company. The four-faced clock, topped by a statue of Hygeia, daughter of Aesculapius, god of medicine, was restored in 1991.

EP75 St. Andrew's Episcopal Church

1904, Henry A. Macomb. Manitou Ave. at Cañon Ave.

This English Gothic Revival structure of rough green sandstone has a roof of slate imported from England. Inside, leaded windows with painted and stained glass signed "E. Frampton, 110 Buckingham Palace Rd., London, England" illuminate a lovely chapel beneath a dark coffered ceiling. The original church (1880), 116 Cañon Avenue, is a plain frame structure, a striking contrast to this fine stone edifice by a Philadelphia architect.

EP76 Barker House

1872. 819 Manitou Ave. (southwest corner of Manitou Ave.)

With its exotic, mismatched octagonal corner towers, this clapboard complex reflects Manitou's architectural evolution from primitive frame to fashionable Queen Anne Style. C. W. Barker started out with two frame houses to which he added a central lofting peak and other additions. The fourth-story pedimented gables and second-story porches strive to bring symmetry to an altered but still striking landmark, now a retirement home.

EP77 Manitou Arcade

1930, M. F. Yount. 924 Manitou Ave. (to Cascade Ave.)

M. F. Yount, owner of the Green Stone Quarry near Manitou, built this full-block arcade with square columns of rough-cut stone from his quarry. The gable roof has exposed beams, truss work, and bracketed eaves. Alpine and English elements compete

EP78 Manitou Spa

sick, a student of Thomas Hart Benton, painted the interior mural, *The Legend of Bubbling Springs*. The lobby floor is patterned in 24-inch diamonds in dark and light terrazzo, and the walls have 7-foot-high marble wainscoting.

The post office occupies the former site of Jerome Wheeler's manor house, Windemere. Several of the estate buildings remain, including the bowling alley (1891) at 36 Park Avenue, and the livery barn, converted to apartments, at 42 Park Avenue. The Wheeler Spring, drilled by Wheeler's son-in-law in 1920 and later donated to the city, bubbles from a retaining wall of Manitou sandstone next to the post office.

in this amusement center, which houses many games, some antiques in themselves. Original fenestration and floor plans survive, as do copper light fixtures and roof drains.

EP78 **Manitou Spa**

1920. 934 Manitou Ave. (NR)

This vaguely Spanish Colonial Revival structure of stuccoed concrete is three stories with a central tower capped by a pyramidal tile roof. The sun deck above the entrance and a flat-roofed third-story setback relieve the overall squareness, as do several hipped tile roofs. Inside, a vaulted ceiling covers the mineral spring, and the walls are decorated with murals depicting local legend and history. The second floor was for the baths, and the third floor had private bedrooms, since converted to apartments.

EP79 **Post Office**

1940, Louis A. Simon, OSA. 307 Cañon Ave. (between Cascade and Park aves.) (NR)

This small Georgian Revival post office has Doric columns and a golden eagle entablature around the entrance. The single story of rough-faced Manitou green sandstone sits under a side-gable roof of flat red tile with a dentiled cornice and a wooden cupola centered on the apex. Original brass lamps and railings flank the marble steps leading to the central entry, and the shiplap-sided gable ends have fan windows. Archibald Mu-

EP80 **Gillis House**

1878. 106 Ruxton Ave.

Symmetrical porches and dormers flanking a central, protruding bay enhance this modest frame duplex. Details such as the clapboard first level, decorative shingles, and bracketed second-story bay window in the central bay are typical of the many Manitou Springs houses built by Angus, Archibald, and James Gillis. A planing mill they built in 1888 supplied lumber and decorative trim for their many projects. This house is said to be a reproduction of their family home in Nova Scotia.

EP81 **Montcalm Castle** (Miramont)

1889–1897, The Reverend Jean Baptiste Francolon. 9 Capitol Hill Ave. (NR)

Castellated battlements, Flemish stepped gables, Queen Anne shingled dormers, ogee arches, Moorish doors and windows, Elizabethan half timbering, and other elements vaguely Byzantine, Chateau Style, Queen Anne, Romanesque, and Tudor haunt this 14,000-square-foot castle, which might be used to define the word *eclectic*. Father Jean-Baptiste Francolon, a French priest, helped design this four-story edifice on a steep hillside as his residence. He explained that no one style would do: "Romanesque style was too uniform, Ionic too classic for romantic Manitou, Gothic too pious for a residence, Moorish too pagan for a clergyman, and Colonial out of order for a mountain region." Angus and Archibald Gillis and stonemason William Frizzell worked from Father Francolon's drawings and instructions, which constantly changed. The sandstone and granite exterior, rumored to resemble the cleric's family chateau in France, has ten entrances and sixty windows, while the twenty-eight rooms feature oak woodwork, carved stonework, and stained glass. By 1904, Father Francolon had converted his fantasy into the Montcalm Tuberculosis Sanatarium, staffed by the Sisters of Mercy. Converted to apartments during World War II, the house has been refurbished as a museum by the Manitou Springs Historical Society.

EP82 Manitou Cliff Dwellings Museum

1906. .5 mile north of Manitou Springs on U.S. 24

Virginia McClurg, a grande dame of Colorado Springs, spearheaded designation of Mesa Verde as a national park in 1906. After a falling out with others involved in Mesa Verde's preservation, she used her considerable energies to construct this replica of native American cliff dwellings in a natural sandstone cliff. A viga-studded, Pueblo Revival structure houses employees, including native Americans who dance, make pottery and beadwork, talk with tourists, and pose for photos. Various Native American architectural styles are arbitrarily combined and used in this fake cliff dwelling in a town named for an Algonquin god of healing unknown to any Colorado tribe.

EP83 Pikes Peak

15 miles west of Colorado Springs (NR)

America's most famous mountain, Pikes Peak (14,110 feet) is generally visible from many places on the Front Range of the Rockies and the eastern plains. The peak, which juts out into the plains, served as a point of orientation for indigenous peoples long before Zebulon Pike saw in 1806 what the Spanish already had named El Capitan. Dr. Edwin James, of the Stephen Long expedition, led the first successful recorded climb in 1820. The Manitou & Pikes Peak Cog Railway reached the summit in 1891, and Spencer Penrose built a highway to the top in 1915 that is today's auto toll road. At Glen Cove is the Half-way House (c. 1890), a rustic two-story, hewn log way station that served a stage line and then the auto road. Despite new Swiss gingerbread and a chalet balcony, the old building, with foundation, walls, and chimneys of Pikes Peak granite, is intact. Atop the peak, a new Summit House (1964), built to replace more elaborate ancestors, sits above the retaining wall of the original cog railway depot.

Pueblo County   (PE)

James P. Beckwourth, Joseph Doyle, "Uncle Dick" (Richens L.) Wootton, and other mountain men built an adobe trading post in 1842 near the confluence of Fountain Creek and the Arkansas River. They called it El Pueblo (Spanish for village). El Pueblo was abandoned in 1854 after Chief Tierra Blanco and his band of Utes attacked on Christmas Day and killed or captured all occupants.

Six years later, the Pikes Peak gold rush gave birth to another settlement on the site, a new town which became Colorado's industrial giant and gave its name to the county created in 1861. Although Pueblo became a great smelting and steel city of immigrant populations, the county also harbors some of Colorado's oldest agricultural hamlets—Autobees (now part of Boone), Doyle, and Green-horn. Although christened the Great American Desert by explorer Stephen Long, the Arkansas River Valley has become famous for irrigated farming of corn, sugar beets, melons, and other crops. Present-day rural Pueblo County retains its ag-ricultural and ranching heritage. Spanish adobe, as well as Anglo brick, frame, and stone, characterize the county settlements.

Pueblo

The county seat (1860, 4,695 feet), a sleepy trading post, awakened in 1872 to the steam whistle of the Denver & Rio Grande. Rising with the railroad age, Pueblo had put up 185 new buildings by the end of 1873. By the 1880s, the D&RG and its subsidiary, the Colorado Fuel and Iron Company (CF&I), transformed the outpost at the junction of

Pueblo, overview (including PE21, PE24, and PE38)

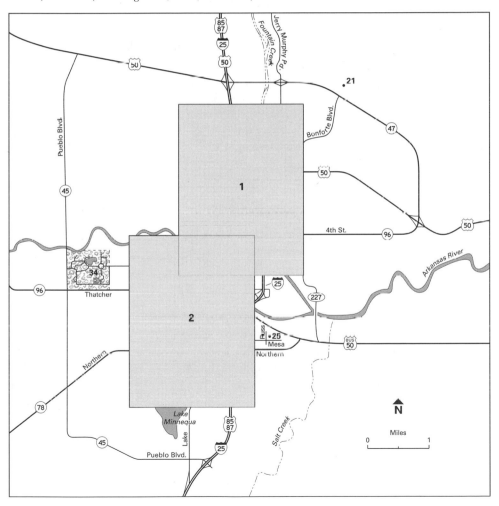

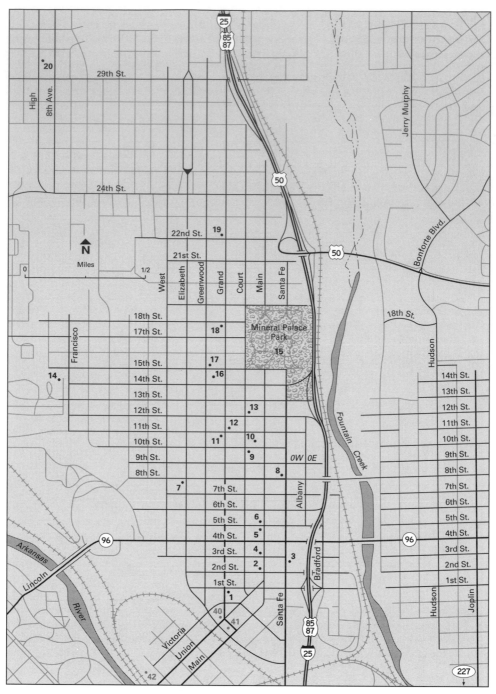

Inset 1. Downtown and North Side (PE1–PE20; for PE21 see the overview map on p. 313)

Fountain Creek and the Arkansas River into the Pittsburgh of the West.

Architect and Builder magazine noted in 1891 that Pueblo's "massive monuments of imperishable stone [put it] far ahead of many cities of a larger population." Many masonry edifices survive, giving Pueblo an unusually rich building stock of older homes, public buildings, and commercial structures. As Colorado's industrial giant, Pueblo developed many ethnic, working-class neighborhoods. Italians initially clustered around the steel mill in Bessemer, while many Slavs worked at the Philadelphia Smelting and Refining Company and lived nearby amid the cottonwoods lining the Arkansas River in the area known as the Grove. More recently, Hispanics settled in Peppersauce Bottoms and along Salt Creek. Greeks, Japanese, and others also staked out turf in the Steel City.

Modern Pueblo is an amalgam of four communities, an evolution that accounts for some of its odd street patterns and conflicting grid plans. Pueblo was platted in 1860 on the north bank of the Arkansas River near the site of El Pueblo. General William Palmer platted South Pueblo on the south side of the Arkansas in 1873. It grew to include the fashionable residential district on the southern bluffs. Central Pueblo grew up between Pueblo and South Pueblo on the north bank of the river. These three municipalities were consolidated in 1886 and joined in 1889 by Bessemer, the steelworkers' town which grew up farther south, around the CF&I steel mill.

Pueblo at one time aspired to replace Denver as the state capital and, in an effort to outdo Denver, hired Louis Sullivan to design its Grand Opera House. This 1889 landmark burned in 1922. Pueblo's hopes of displacing Colorado's Queen City were also short-lived. Until the 1960s Pueblo was the second most populous county in Colorado, but it did not share in Colorado's post–World War II boom. Now that the steel mills are modernized and only partly in use, the air is clearer and sweeter in the steel city. Pueblo is today capturing new industry, retirees, and tourists.

DOWNTOWN AND NORTH SIDE

Pueblo's relatively compact downtown is walkable, while the near north side features fine homes around the fabulous Rosemount Mansion, in an area south of 24th Street, between West Street and Santa Fe Avenue.

PE01 El Pueblo Museum

1950s?, 1992. 324 W. 1st St. (southeast corner of Grand Ave.)

The Colorado Historical Society's Pueblo Museum occupies the rehabilitated Pueblo Housing Authority Headquarters adjacent to the 1842 Fort Pueblo site. This one-story building, stuccoed to resemble adobe in a neo-Aztec mode, houses exhibits on local history, including a replica of the original one-story trading post of El Pueblo, with its two rounded, crenelated towers.

PE02 American Furniture Company (Mechanics and Masonic Hall)

1890–1891, Francis W. Cooper. 207–211 N. Main St. (NR)

This five-story commercial building has long punctuated the Pueblo skyline. Pioneer architect Francis W. Cooper also had a hand in the design of many other important downtown structures. The pressed brick and red sandstone building features a central two-story bay window framed in copper. Other notable details include the row of arched windows and a broken stringcourse along the fourth story, the decorative brickwork on the fifth story, and the large fan of carved stone in the center section of the cornice.

PE03 Sangre de Cristo Arts and Conference Center

1972, Hurtig, Gardner and Froelich. 210 N. Santa Fe Ave.

Built into the west side of Goat Hill, where Italian immigrants once lived and raised goats for milk and cheese, this acrobatic two-building complex is dramatically Modernist. Raw concrete in graceful curves and angles gives it power and substance, while richly colored red-orange bricks relate to the nearby landmarks in one of the oldest parts of town. Funded by the U.S. Economic Development Administration and the Pueblo County Commissioners, the center embraces a 7,000-square-foot conference facility, a 500-seat theater, a dance school, the Three Peaks Gift Shop, and a children's museum. Four galleries and the Francis King Collection of southwestern art make it the focal point of the fine arts in southeastern Colorado. Despite its massive size, the center beautifully captures the warmth, earth tones, and irregular shapes of the southwestern landscape.

PE04 **S. H. Kress Store** (Business and Technology Center)

1930, George E. Mackay. 301 Main St. (northwest corner of 3rd St.)

Samuel H. Kress's five-and-dime empire peaked at 264 stores, designed by an in-house architecture department. This Art Deco delight is yellow brick with polychrome terracotta trim and ornament, including modernistic Rocky Mountain bighorn sheep heads adorning the third-story frieze.

PE05 **Old Federal Building** (Post Office)

1897, William Aiken, OSA. 421 N. Main St. (southwest corner of 5th St.) (NR)

This federal building, sited at the prime intersection in downtown Pueblo, is a fine

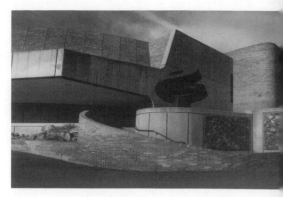

PE03 Sangre de Cristo Arts and Conference Center

specimen of Beaux-Arts Renaissance Revival. The modified Italian palazzo combines Florentine and Federal Revival elements. The four-story gray brick building with a rectangular rear wing is sheathed in Bedford, Indiana, limestone. An embossed U.S. seal graces each of the bronze window guards of the main floor, and the American eagle in various poses and scales of justice are carved into the stone trim.

PE06 **First National Bank**

1914, Schmidt, Garden and Martin. 501 Main St. (northwest corner of 5th St.)

A Chicago firm noted for its Prairie Style designs created this seven-story red Manitou sandstone headquarters for the Thatcher family's statewide financial empire, which

PE06 First National Bank, c. 1915

included thirty-two banks. John A. Thatcher, a Pennsylvanian who opened a general store in Pueblo in 1863, became, with help from his brother Mahlon, southern Colorado's leading entrepreneur. The Thatchers invested in banking, real estate, cattle, and railroad enterprises.

Little altered, this cornerstone of downtown, built on a Pikes Peak granite foundation, has a tall ground floor with a mezzanine. On the arcaded first floor, smooth sandstone columns carry elaborately carved Sullivanesque spandrels. Above the first-floor cornice, smooth sandstone walls rise to a frieze with floral carving. The flat, overhanging eaves are trimmed with ornate metal antefixes. In the well-preserved lobby, murals by Holsing and Company of Chicago illustrate the Thatchers' various business interests, from cattle to smelting. Here, the Thatchers posted a guard with a machine gun. (The bank was never robbed.) Since 1982 the building has been the Pueblo headquarters of Colorado National Banks.

PE07 Eighth Street Baptist Church

1891. 1907, rebuilt. 600 W. 8th St. (southwest corner of Elizabeth St.)

Pueblo's African Americans, many of whom worked in nearby mansions, used this church as a social, recreational, and cultural as well as religious center. They constructed their humble brick church with a stone foundation, an abbreviated tower inset at the northeast corner, and Gothic-arched windows with wood tracery and leaded glass.

PE08 Young Women's Christian Association

1935, Walter De Mordaunt. 801 N. Santa Fe Ave. (northwest corner of 8th St.) (NR)

This Mission Revival villa with low-pitched tile roofs and rooflets has a square, four-story corner tower and a third-story loggia whose round arches reflect the entry. The sturdy, 14-inch-thick masonry walls are faced with stucco. Inside are original oak woodwork, wrought iron fixtures, red tile floors, fireplace, and swimming pool. Mahlon Thatcher's wife, Luna, a supporter of the YWCA and other women's organizations in Pueblo, provided funding for this building.

PE08 Young Women's Christian Association

PE09 First Presbyterian Church

1890. Southeast corner of Court St. and 10th St.

Of the many Colorado churches founded by the Reverend Sheldon Jackson, this is the oldest and one of the finest. A tall, shingled steeple beckons worshippers of fine period architecture to this red sandstone landmark indebted to the Richardsonian Romanesque style. The Thatcher family donated the Tiffany glass for the Gothic-arched windows. Dark red mortar joints blend with the rich red-orange stone laid in a variety of sizes and shapes to provide a wealth of restrained detail.

PE10 Pueblo County Courthouse

1908–1912, Albert W. Ross and G. Wroe. 10th to 11th streets between Court and Main sts. (NR)

A New York City firm designed this courthouse in the Beaux-Arts Neoclassical tradition. It is faced with Turkey Creek white sandstone in smooth-faced ashlar over two-foot-thick brick walls. Pikes Peak granite is used for the foundation and the grand entry stairs.

On a landscaped full city block, the courthouse reigns over downtown Pueblo. The south and north elevations are distinguished by central and end bays with fluted Corinthian columns supporting dentiled pediments. Immense casement windows stretch from floor to ceiling, giving maximum light and a sense of spaciousness to the interior. The center bay is capped by a dome sheathed in copper with eight ocular windows.

PE10 Pueblo County Courthouse, c. 1912   PE13 Bowen Mansion

In addition to onyx and marble floors and decorative bronze hardware and fixtures, the interior is distinguished by the stencil murals of J. Charles Schnorr depicting the history of the area. Schnorr's portraits of community leaders hang on the walls of the rotunda, the County Commissioners' Chamber, and the courtrooms.

PE11 Sacred Heart Cathedral

1912, Robert Willison and Montana S. Fallis. 1025 N. Grand Ave. (southwest corner of 11th St.) (NR)

A soaring corner spire rises above this cruciform church with two square towers flanking the triple arched entry beneath a large rose window. The French Gothic Revival edifice, designed by Denver architects, is speckled blond brick with terracotta trim, a red tile roof, and a foundation of Turkey Creek sandstone. The strong vertical emphasis of Gothic architecture is articulated here by crosses, pinnacles, a steep-pitched roof, and pointed arches, as well as the octagonal spire. The stained glass windows were designed and crafted by the Emil Frei Studio in St. Louis. The church became a cathedral in 1942 when the Diocese of Colorado was divided and Pueblo became the seat for the Diocese of Southern Colorado. The cathedral received a major remodeling and renovation in 1989 that added a fine, glassy south pavilion.

PE12 Pueblo School District Administration Building

1978, Hurtig, Gardner and Froelich. 315 W. 11th St. (northeast corner of Grand Ave.)

Grassy berms, low walls, and pleasant landscaping set the scene for this irregularly massed, multilevel modernistic structure with flat roofs and a curved brick wall between the entrances, on the site of the demolished Centennial High School (1876). Kenneth Williams, who has adorned many Pueblo walls and buildings with three-dimensional murals, used the beige brick of the building to create a bas-relief in the curving brick entry wall.

PE13 Bowen Mansion

1892, Francis W. Cooper. 229 W. 12th St. (northeast corner of Court St.) (NR)

Thomas Bowen, a lawyer, judge, and U.S. senator, built this asymmetrical, three-story dwelling of red brick trimmed with sandstone and undulating shingle. A corner tower with a bell-shaped roof, fluted chimneys, and a steep, multigabled roofline give this Queen Anne house a verticality that keeps it competitive with larger nonresidential structures downtown, where it is a rare survivor of a once elegant residential neighborhood.

PE14 Colorado State Hospital Superintendent's Residence

1934. 13th and Francisco sts. (NR)

This formal, two-story residence was built during an era when the officers and staff of such an institution were required to live on the grounds. Until this hospital was established in 1879, mentally ill patients were sent to out-of-state asylums. This was until 1961 Colorado's only state facility for the mentally ill. Vaguely Southwestern Style features include the red tile roof, white stucco finish, cast concrete pilasters framing the windows and entry, wrought iron window grates, and arched entry. Now a conference center and museum, the house is part of a vast, tree-shaded campus of predominantly rectangular red brick buildings, many decorated with horizontal courses of contrasting concrete and brick.

PE15 Mineral Palace Park

1896. Between 15th and 19th sts. from Court St. to I-25

King Coal and Queen Silver once reigned in the Colorado Mineral Palace, which was the centerpiece of this park. Built as Colorado's answer to the World's Columbian Exposition, this masterwork of Pueblo architect Otto Bulow was razed in 1942. (A model is in the El Pueblo Museum.) The triple-arched stone bridge over Lake Clara to the band shell remains, as does the Pavilion (1936, Robert Burris, draftsman), which now houses the Pueblo Art Gallery but once served as a boathouse. Alterations by the Civilian Conservation Corps streamlined the surviving Victorian buildings.

PE16 Rosemount Mansion (Thatcher Mansion)

1893, Henry Hudson Holly. 419 W. 14th St., between Grand Ave. and Greenwood St. (NR)

Commanding an entire square block on a hillside, Rosemount is a magnificent late Victorian specimen designed by a New Yorker acclaimed for his writings as well as his architecture. The 24,000-square-foot mansion, built by entrepreneur John A.

PE16 Rosemount Mansion (Thatcher Mansion)

Thatcher, is a three-story brick shell faced with rough, rose-colored rhyolite and accented by smooth stone stringcourses. The red Vermont slate roof is hipped, gabled, and detailed with eyebrow dormers, a dentiled cornice, and columned chimneys serving ten fireplaces. The veranda has golden oak ceilings and is accessible from inside through 10-foot-high sash windows.

In 1967 the mansion was donated to Pueblo for use as a house museum. Many of the furnishings, including furniture designed by the architect, still grace the thirty-seven rooms. Interior marvels include the 9-by-13-foot stained glass window, *Kingdoms of Nature,* by Charles Booth of New York; bird's-eye maple, oak, and mahogany woodwork; Tiffany lighting; and hand-decorated ceilings. An elaborate intercom system of speaking tubes makes the kitchen the communications center. An elevator (1914) reaches the third floor maids' chambers and a huge walk-in cedar closet. The third floor houses the Andrew McClelland Collection of World Curiosities, ranging from fine paintings to an Egyptian mummy. The carriage house, with six stalls, built to match the house, has been a restaurant since 1981.

PE17 Beaumont House

1889, A. Morris Stuckert. 425 W. 15th St. (northeast corner of Greenwood St.) (NR)

Allen J. Beaumont, an English-born attorney, commissioned a house described by the *Pueblo Chieftain* on March 10, 1889, as a "commanding and beautiful structure . . .

of pink lava stone." A. Morris Stuckert, a Denver architect, gave the one-and-one-half-story house a porch with twin semicircular bays on the east facade and a complex gable roof. A two-story stone and wood turret, large, arched stained glass windows of diverse shape and treatment, and decorative shingles further distinguish this Queen Anne Style eyecatcher. Stuckert also designed the nearby Pryor House (1889), 1325 Greenwood Street (NR), a more traditional and vertical Queen Anne design held to earth by a heavy sandstone first story and corner tower.

PE18 Ascension Episcopal Church

1913, Wetherell and Gage. 400 W. 18th St. (southwest corner of Grand Ave.)

The Norman simplicity of this buttressed brick church earned it a photographic spread in *Architectural Record* for January 1917. The architects, a New York firm, kept the elevations low in deference to the elegant residential neighborhood around Rosemount. The interior is rich in dark wood, from the open ceiling beams to the hand-carved choir screen and reredos with Biblical scenes. A complementary Neo-Norman church office and rectory next door at 410 West 18th Street has a steep-pitched roof and half-timbered entry with an oriel window. The garden includes a columbarium (1986) with brick wall art by Pueblo artist Kenneth Williams.

PE19 Octagon House

1888, Patrick P. Mills. 2201 Grand Ave. (northwest corner of 22nd St.) (NR)

This two-story brick and clapboard dwelling is a side-gabled house hiding behind a large, semioctagonal front porch topped by a semi-octagonal second story, capped by a smaller, full-octagon third-story tower. It was one of the show homes of Dundee Place (NRD) a historic district of eighteen square blocks. Patrick Mills, perhaps the first architect to open an office in Pueblo, designed the first seven model homes, including this one for realtor John L. Streit.

PE20 Star-Journal Model Home

1926, Walter De Mordaunt. 2920 High St. (NR)

This vernacular version of an English country home represented the Anglophilic fashions of the 1920s. The *Pueblo Star-Journal*, like newspapers across the country, publicized model homes, not only for design but for state-of-the-art appliances and construction techniques. The well-preserved two-story brick house has blocks of sandstone randomly set into the brick exterior and a steep-pitched roof which sweeps down over the arched entry door.

PE21 University of Southern Colorado

1965, Caudill Rowlett Scott. 2200 Bonforte Blvd. (at Colorado 47)

A strangely ethereal city of concrete boxes surrounded by sagebrush, this 847-acre campus sits on a mesa northeast of Pueblo. Precast concrete panels studded with a local aggregate form the "modified pueblo" structures of this starkly Modernist complex, softened somewhat by curving paths and outdoor sculpture, such as the nine-foot-high aluminum *Paper Airplane*.

BESSEMER, THE GROVE, AND SOUTHEAST

Developed as an industrial area in the 1880s, Bessemer was named for the inventor of the blast furnace. Today most of Bessemer's smelters, mills, and factories are dead. The

Colorado Fuel and Iron Company, whose huge plants and soaring smokestacks still dominate the cityscape, is making a comeback with updated rail, rod, and bar mills. Northern Avenue, an I-25 exit, is Bessemer's main street. From Northern Avenue, Santa Fe Avenue leads to the Grove, a small area bounded by Plum Street, the Rio Grande yards, I-25, and the Arkansas River. The Grove's ethnic history is reflected in three Catholic churches within three blocks on Clark Street: Croatians, Slovaks, and Slovenians attended St. Mary's; Italians congregated at Mt. Carmel; and Slavs worshiped at St. Anthony's.

PE22 **Minnequa Elementary School**

1978, Hurtig, Gardner and Froelich. 1708 E. Orman Ave., between Logan and Cedar and Jones aves.

Brown fired-clay blocks sculpted into neo-Southwestern motifs adorn this yellow brick school, which was created by an unusually close and innovative alliance of architect, artist, and brickmaker. Pueblo's premier architecture firm commissioned Kenneth Williams, then potter-in-residence at the Sangre de Cristo Arts Center, to design and fabricate the large bas-reliefs with the help of Summit Brick and Tile Company. This contemporary structure, built at a cost of $1.2 million, fits in well with the tiny but proud Pueblo Revival cottage across the street at 1717 East Orman Avenue.

PE23 **Colorado Fuel and Iron Company**

1901–1903. Abriendo Ave. (northeast corner of Canal St.), via I-25 exit 97A

CF&I's administrative building (c. 1901) and the dispensary next door feature the curvilinear parapets, stucco walls, and refined details of the Mission Revival. This genteel architectural facade for a tough, dirty business typifies the efforts of company president John C. Osgood. Between 1901 and 1903 Osgood pumped $24 million into building elegant company buildings and expanding and modernizing the steelworks, which grew to include the Guggenheims' giant Pueblo plant. Osgood's improvements

are what visitors see today as mostly decaying, abandoned works.

From around 1910 to the 1950s, CF&I was one of the largest steel makers in the West and Colorado's single largest industrial plant. Some 6,000 to 7,000 employees produced as much as 600,000 tons of steel annually, to be made into the rails and barbed wire that tamed the West. CF&I coal mines, limestone quarries, coking plants, and other operations, including many company towns and the model town of Redstone (Pitkin County), reshaped the landscape.

PE24 **Gus' Place**

c. 1905. 1201 Elm St. (southwest corner of Mesa St.)

Colorado's best-known blue-collar saloon is a small, one-story brick corner tavern that blends into a working-class neighborhood. Gus Masciotra went to work at the nearby CF&I steel mills at age fourteen and saved enough to buy this house. In 1926 he added a grocery. When happy days returned with the end of Prohibition in 1933, Gus opened a tavern in the front of the grocery. He also dispensed beer in buckets to go, from a takeout window on the north wall that has been filled with glass blocks. In 1937, 1939, and 1941 *Ripley's Believe It or Not* pronounced Gus' the national leader for beer sales per square foot.

Inside, booted steelworkers have worn out two steel bar rails. A section of the second is mounted in a wall trophy case. Clean design prevails in this little-altered saloon, which displays the green, white, and red colors of the Italian flag on its front awning, in the ceiling tiles and the linoleum floor, and even in the neon on the mahogany back bar.

PE25 **Edison School**

1909, J. M. Gile. 1923, 1952, additions. 1110–1130 Russ Ave. (northeast corner of E. Mesa Ave.) (NR)

The six Edison School structures, initially designed as cubical units connected by breezeways, are vaguely Italianate. Gathered around a handsome, twin-towered Italian Villa Style main building, this complex of one-story, hip-roofed structures in blond brick was based on the concept of the "Pueblo unit schoolhouse," developed by school board member Dr. Richard W. Cor-

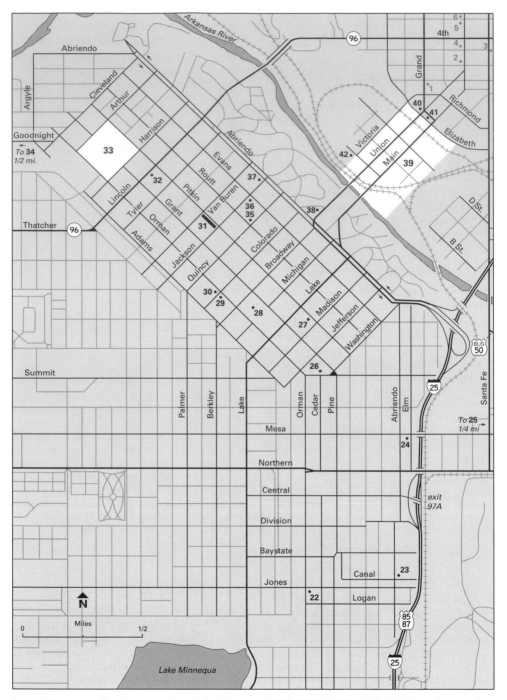

Inset 2. Bessemer, the Grove, and South Pueblo area (PE22–PE37, PE39–45; for PE38 see the overview map on p. 313)

win. In a typical Progressive-era experiment with improving public buildings, Dr. Corwin specified high windows on three sides of each detached unit, allowing good ventilation and diffuse lighting to eliminate "objectionable reflections or cross-lights."

PE26 St. Michael's Eastern Orthodox Church

1924. 801 W. Summit St. (at Cedar St.)

Orthodox crosses atop the spire and gilded onion domes distinguish this plain brick church. After the 1921 Arkansas River flood destroyed the first church, its gilded onion dome was saved and reused for this church.

SOUTH PUEBLO

A fine residential district occupies the bluffs looking north onto the Arkansas River. It includes three National Register districts (Adams Avenue, Argyle Avenue, and Pitkin Place) and some notable public buildings. From the 1st Street–Union Avenue exit off I-25, Union Avenue leads first to the railroad depot district, then continues south across the river to the residential area, where it becomes Broadway, the area's main street, with a well-preserved Standard Station (northwest corner of Broadway and Evans) and a fire station, Hose Company No. 3 (116 Broadway), now converted to a firefighters' museum.

PE27 Old Central High School

1882, C. R. Manning. 431 E. Pitkin Ave. (at Madison St.)

This handsome Italianate two-story edifice is of rough-faced light pink rhyolite with creamy, smooth Manitou sandstone trim. A central 80-foot bell tower is topped by a mansard roof with a pediment that mimics the main entry below it. Superintendent of Schools Preston Search initiated here the Search, or Pueblo, Plan, one of the earliest attempts at individualized education in the United States. This noncompetitive program was designed to benefit gifted as well as slow learners by allowing students to advance at their own pace. The plan provided for free textbooks, a student savings plan, and guest speakers on such subjects as personal hygiene and industrial education. After the new high school replaced it in 1905, the stone schoolhouse became an elementary school. Scheduled for demolition in 1979, it was rescued in 1980 to house the Pueblo Ballet.

PE28 Central High School

1906–1912, Robert S. Roeschlaub. Orman Ave. to Grant Ave. between Broadway and Michigan St. (NR)

Fluted Ionic columns grace the entry of this beige brick, stone-trimmed school building in the Beaux-Arts Neoclassical mode. North and south wings end in gracefully curved four-story bays crowned with balustrades. Robert Roeschlaub planned a never-built central dome to cap his classical Roman temple of learning. Some recent rear additions (Hurtig, Gardner and Froelich) complement the complex on its spacious site, as does the former 1926 junior high school (now the Keating Educational Center) across Orman Avenue, which architecturally echoes Roeschlaub's work.

PE29 Stickney House

1889, William H. Ward and F. A. Hale. 101 E. Orman Ave. (at Colorado Ave.) (NR)

William Ward, a New York architect, worked with a Pueblo colleague on this romantic, two-and-one-half-story monument of rough Manitou red sandstone. Romanesque detailing is evident on the main facade, the end gable, and two oriels bridged by a shingled panel. Other notable design features include the irregular, gabled roofline, a second-story oriel that serves as the base of a third-story balcony, and the flattened stone entry arch.

PE30 Orman-Adams Mansion

1890, William Lang. 102 W. Orman Ave. (at Colorado Ave.) (NR)

Second only to Rosemount among Pueblo mansions, this may be the only work in Pueblo by Denver architect William Lang. The Richardsonian Romanesque show house uses red sandstone both as sheathing and as ornament, including fancifully carved gargoyles and cherub faces. Governor James B. Orman built the house, which was later the home of Governor Alva Adams and his son, U.S. senator Alva B. Adams. The lavish mansion has expansive grounds and a similarly styled carriage house.

PE31 Pitkin Place Historic Residential District

1891–1911, George W. Roe and E. W. Shutt. 302–326 W. Pitkin Ave. (NRD)

This row of seven Victorian residences adorns the avenue named for Colorado governor Frederick W. Pitkin, who retired to Pueblo in 1883. Pitkin helped develop this subdivision for wealthy Puebloans, including many associated with the steel industry. Subtly repeated design elements—pink stone, decorative shingling, brick, and roof tex-

PE30 Orman-Adams Mansion, 1890s

PE31 Pitkin Place Historic Residential District, 1 Pitkin Place

tures, as well as similar setbacks and massing—give harmony to the block. The houses are also similar in their stone archways, arch-topped windows, Doric columns, and chimney style and placement. The exception is the sixth home, a 1911 bungalow, one of the earliest in the region. Because of its scale, height, and columned veranda it fits pleasingly into the block.

PE32 Phelps House

1938. 1984, remodeling, Hurtig, Gardner and Froelich. 420 Lincoln St.

This neo-Pueblo Revival house of stucco over brick combines irregular massing and buttressed and battered walls with such fanciful touches as vigas and a small exterior ladder that connects the first story with a stepped-back second level. The design incorporates small-paned windows and a curvilinear roofline. The owner, James Vernon Phelps, and his family have made their home and its walled garden a showcase for southwestern art.

PE33 Pueblo Community College

1937, Walter De Mordaunt and John Gray. 900 W. Orman Ave.

This eclectic campus, begun in 1931, is to some degree unified by its Southwestern Style architecture. The 115,000-square-foot Academic Building (1991, Manning, Knapp with Hurtig, Gardner and Froelich) blends Postmodern, Southwestern, Mediterranean, and Mission Revival styles. The building is brightened by a red tile roof and by columns banded in terracotta and turquoise applied by Pueblo artist Judy Williams. Beige brick and stucco and arcades with massive Roman arches complement buildings of the 1937 campus.

PE34 City Park

1903. 800 Goodnight Ave. (between Pueblo Blvd. and Calla Ave.)

City Park, along with the newer Lake Pueblo State Park, occupies part of Charles Goodnight's vast Rock Canyon Ranch. The only remnant of the ranch is the Goodnight Barn (1871), .6 mile west of the intersection of West Highway 96 and Goodnight Avenue, at the west end of the Valco Sand and Gravel plant. This rare early example of masonry construction is built of rough limestone blocks, now under a corrugated metal roof with a pigeon tower. Goodnight, with partner Oliver Loving, blazed the Goodnight-Loving Trail from Texas through New Mexico, Colorado, and Wyoming, roughly along the route of today's I-25. During the 1860s and 1870s this was a major cattle trail.

City Park encompasses 161.5 acres. The WPA built many of the granite retaining walls and buildings such as the golf course clubhouse (1938), the adobe Girls' Recreation Lodge (1940), and the original Pueblo Zoo buildings. The 1985 Zoo Education Building (Hurtig, Gardner and Froelich) has an Aztec flair. The City Park Carousel (1911) (NR), "county fair model number 72" of Charles W. Parker Amusement Devices, Abilene, Kansas, has thirty-six hand-carved, brightly painted horses pulling chariots and a band organ. It was restored in 1985.

PE35 King House and Carriage House

1891, Miles McGrath, builder. 229 Quincy St. at Routt Ave. (NR)

Splendidly trimmed in red sandstone and Carpenter's Gothic ornament, this three-story, multigabled red brick residence is notable for its large front porch and third-story octagonal tower with a bell-shaped roof. A tiny, second-story porch is suspended from the southwest corner eaves. The variety of window shapes makes this a good example

of the Queen Anne Style. The charming, whimsical nature of this house is accentuated by a matching carriage house and a Queen Anne playhouse. The owner, Dr. Alexander King, a native of Glasgow, Scotland, came to Pueblo as a physician for CF&I and served as mayor of Pueblo.

PE36 First Congregational Church

1889, C. H. Stickney. 228 W. Evans Ave. (at Jackson St.) (NR)

The *Colorado Chieftain* for October 3, 1889, described this Romanesque Revival church as "a regular little gem in church architecture, complete and perfect in every respect." It elaborated: "The walls are built of pink stone, cut to represent the natural fracture of the rock, and consequently do not present any of the parallel lines and right angles which are usually seen in cut stonework." This red sandstone is showcased in a tower on the northeast corner. The arch of the entrance is echoed in a large arched window on the north wall, and the apse has a row of Tiffany stained glass windows.

PE37 Abriendo Inn (Walter House)

1908, 1912, P. C. Pape?. 300 W. Abriendo Ave. (at Jackson St.) (NR)

Martin Walter's unusually large and elaborately detailed foursquare has that form's typical hipped roof with central dormers and broad, bracketed eaves above a dentil bed molding. The full-length front porch, supported by ornate Ionic columns, extends beyond the house to frame the driveway entrance in a porte-cochère. Walter and his two brothers came from Germany to establish Walter's Brewery, which, at its high point, distributed twenty-seven different brands of beer in seven western states. The brewery closed in 1975, and much of it has been destroyed. The house reopened in 1989 as a bed and breakfast with many original interior fixtures.

PE38 McClelland Public Library

1965, James M. Hunter. 100 E. Abriendo Ave.

This Modernist library is sited on a prominent hillside. James Hunter, a Boulder architect, used a splashing fountain to separate the parking lot from the glazed, concave facade. The two-story building of brick, pre-cast concrete, and glass expands northward beyond the well-designed, welcoming service desk. The library is named for Andrew McClelland, a wholesale grain and flour dealer who parlayed South Pueblo real estate into a fortune. He and his wife, Columbia, also donated the McClelland Orphanage, a Colonial Revival complex at 415 East Abriendo Avenue, extending to Lake Avenue and Madison Street.

PE39 Union Avenue Historic Commercial District

Roughly Arkansas River to Elizabeth Ave. between Victoria and Oneida aves. (NRD)

As the main street for South Pueblo, Union Avenue is lined with exuberantly styled two- and three-story retail stores and offices. A 1921 flood inundated the Union Avenue area, destroying or damaging many structures. Of eighty-seven survivors in the district, seventy have been listed as contributing from an architectural and historical viewpoint.

Along Union Avenue are several pressed metal fronts, including one with a notable Schlitz logo atop the Schlitz Beer Hall (c. 1880), 223 South Union. Elaborate Italianate buildings at 222 South Union (1881) and 226–228 South Union (1887) have been spruced up. The Gold Dust Block, 130 South Union (at D Street), is an elegantly restored three-story brick mortuary close to the site of an old hanging tree. The McLaughlin Building, 330 South Union (at B Street), serves as a large, imposing cornerstone for the district.

PE40 Hotel Vail

1911, J. M. Gile, Robert S. Willison, and Montana S. Fallis. 217 S. Grand Ave. (southwest corner of Union Ave.) (NR)

John E. Vail's hotel, dedicated on September 11, 1911, was Pueblo's grandest. It was designed by a local architect, J. M. Gile, and Robert S. Williams and Montana S. Fallis of Denver. The five-story, white brick Renaissance Revival building has a recessed central bay with an Ionic-columned and balustraded entry porch between bays with storefronts

PE40 Hotel Vail

distinguished by stained glass transoms with V monograms. The foundation and parts of the building are concrete, while the Neoclassical trim is speckled terracotta, rising to a heavily dentiled and bracketed cornice and balustrade. After several decades of disuse, the monument was restored in 1984 by the Pueblo Housing Authority for use as assisted living housing, with the Pueblo County Historical Society museum and library in the basement. The main floor lobby still reflects the hotel's original elegance, most notably in the great Beulah red marble columns topped with hand-carved wooden scrolls.

PE41 Pueblo City Hall

1917, W. E. Stickney. 1919, Godey and Haskins. Union Ave. and City Hall Place

Built after the 1886 consolidation of Pueblo, Central Pueblo and South Pueblo, City Hall's original building occupies the west half of a block facing Union Avenue. Exterior brick is trimmed with terracotta, which is used in a prominent second-floor cornice, thus diminishing the third level. Pilasters divide fenestration bays on the lower levels in this modest exercise in Neoclassicism. Memorial Hall, a 1919 addition, echoes the scale and rhythm of City Hall, including the cornice, but is much more decorative. Entirely sheathed in creamy terracotta, it features a slender cupola and engaged columns with Ionic capitals and decorative spandrels between the first- and second-level windows. President Woodrow Wilson made his last public address here in 1920.

PE42 **Union Depot**

1890, Frank V. Newall. 1992, restoration. Victoria and B sts. (NR)

Like many American railway stations of its time, this one is designed in a picturesque mode. The Neo-Romanesque castle fronts on B Street with rectangular wings flanking a central entrance surmounted by a six-story mansard clock tower. Frank Newall, a Chicago architect, used large, rough-faced blocks of red Manitou sandstone laid in both broken and continuous courses. Bays are defined by round-arched windows, while third-story dormers punctuate the steep-pitched roof.

Inside, cast iron columns are painted and decorated to look like wood. Stained glass Art Nouveau transoms, rich golden oak wainscoting and parquet ceiling, and hexagonal ceramic tile floors enhance this period piece. The Victorian interior was updated by an Art Deco soda fountain. Now without passenger service, this is the least changed of Colorado's large railway stations.

Beulah

Beulah (1873, 6,200 feet) is a small town and summer resort in a secluded valley with the Beulah Marble Quarry at the west end. Beulah red marble, known for its striking color and swirling patterns, was used for the wainscoting of the Colorado State Capitol in Denver. Prominent Pueblo families built summer homes in Beulah, notably along Pine Drive. Pueblo Mountain Park (1920), a 600-acre park owned by the City of Pueblo,

has various CCC and WPA facilities. Cascade Trail was laid out by landscape architect Frank H. Culley. Structures include the rustic Pueblo Community House, of massive local stones; the Pueblo Revival Horseshoe Lodge; a summer camp; and a rustic picnic pavilion. The 3-R Ranch, once owned by Pueblo business magnate James N. Carlile, is a working cattle operation with a rustic ranch house and a barn with stone corrals. The KK Ranch, Bed and Breakfast, and Carriage Museum (1871), 8987 Mountain Park Road, is a 67-acre spread incorporating renovated rough-cut lumber ranch structures and fifteen restored antique carriages and sleighs.

PE43 **Ben Butler Ranch House**

c. 1880. Roughly 25 miles southeast of Pueblo on the Huerfano River, just southwest of the Vertrees Reservoir

Built on land that was once part of a Spanish grant of some 91,000 acres, this 1880s ranch house is the largest adobe building in the county, with walls 18 inches thick and three tall chimneys of native stone. Only the eastern wing is of wood-frame construction. The foundation is native stone, and rafters in the north half are unpeeled logs, while those of the south half are milled lumber. The barn and other outbuildings are of native stone laid in irregular, noncontinuous courses and are topped by gable roofs. Benjamin Franklin Butler, a Civil War general, Massachusetts governor and congressman, and presidential nominee, purchased the ranch in 1885.

Teller County (TL)

Ironically, the great Pikes Peak gold rush, which gave birth to Colorado, bypassed the richest goldfields of all, hidden just west of the peak. Cowboy Bob Womack scratched around the high-country cow pastures for years, theorizing that the surface gold he found would lead to richer deposits. In 1891 he found a pay streak. During the subsequent gold rush, Cripple Creek was founded and soon became the fifth largest city in the state and the seat of the county created in 1899 and named for U.S. Senator Henry M. Teller.

Cripple Creek emerged an instant city with two dozen satellite gold camps in a

Cripple Creek

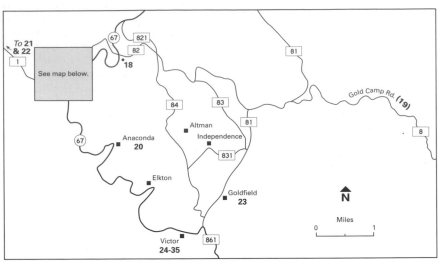

To **21 & 22**
1
67
821
82
• **18**
See map below.
81
Gold Camp Rd. **(19)**
84
83
81
67
Altman
Anaconda
Independence
20
831
Elkton
Goldfield
23
N
Miles
0   1
8
Victor
24-35
861

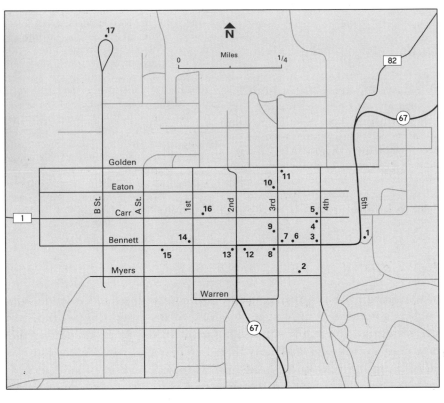

• **17**
82
N
Miles
0   1/4
67
Golden
11
•
10
•
Eaton
B St.
A St.
1st
16
•
2nd
3rd
5
•
4th
5th
Carr
9
•
4
•
7 **6**
• •
3
•
1
•
Bennett
14
•
13
•
12
•
8
•
15
•
Myers
2
•
1
Warren
67

24-square-mile district that called itself "the world's greatest gold camp." In 1900 some 500 mines surrendered more than $18 million in gold, outproducing Australian, Canadian, Russian, South African, and U.S. rivals. Cripple Creek's golden age is commemorated today by blast-and-pray prospect holes, mine headframes, and immense mine waste dumps and mill tailings. Ubiquitous saloons were sometimes the last surviving structures, as is the case with the log and frame Grand View Saloon in Midway and another in Altman. Three railroads rushed in: the Florence & Cripple Creek, the Colorado Springs & Cripple Creek District, and the Colorado Midland with its Midland Terminal extension from Divide to Cripple Creek. All three railroad grades have been converted to auto roads: the Phantom Canyon Road from Florence, the Gold Camp Road, and Colorado 67, which squeezes through the Midland's old one-lane timbered railroad tunnel.

Of the fifteen towns in the Cripple Creek District, only Cripple Creek, Goldfield, and Victor survive. Three other county towns—Woodland Park, Divide, and Florissant—originated during the 1870s as stops along the Ute Pass trail to South Park, Leadville, and Aspen. This route was used in the 1880s by the Colorado Midland, the first standard-gauge line to cross the Rocky Mountains.

Railroads eventually carried $800 million in gold ore out of the district, which produced some forty millionaires. As in many other mining camps, profits flowed downhill out of the mining town to centers of capital, services, and supplies. Cripple Creek gold built many lavish houses on Denver's Capitol Hill and in the North End and Broadmoor neighborhoods of Colorado Springs.

The Cripple Creek District boasted around 13,000 residents in 1900. As the high-grade ore became more costly to mine and a 1903–1904 labor war crippled mining operations, gold production slipped, but the annual output did not fall below $1 million until 1945. Mining has revived somewhat since the 1970s with the introduction of cyanide leaching to wring more gold from huge turn of the century mill dumps.

After the 1903–1904 strike, Cripple Creek shriveled and smaller towns and camps fell to fire, weather, or the hands of man. Rather than pay taxes on vacant structures, many owners dismantled them and sold off the scrap. In 1990, 4,610 people lived in Woodland Park, 584 in Cripple Creek, and 258 in Victor. Tourism has replaced mining as Teller County's chief industry, particularly since the introduction in 1991 of limited-stakes gambling in Cripple Creek.

Cripple Creek

The county seat (1891, 9,494 feet) is named for a rocky trickle notorious for crippling humans and animals. Cripple Creek lies on the lip of the crater of an extinct volcano whose lava extrusions contained gold veins that formed a "bowl of gold." This discovery by Cowboy Bob Womack led Horace W. Bennett and Julius A. Myers to replat part of their Broken Box Ranch as a city, which by 1900 had 10,147 residents, three railroads, and two electric streetcar lines. Even two fires in the same week, which leveled downtown Cripple Creek in 1896, did not check growth. Residents rapidly rebuilt with fireproof brick from six local brickyards. Prominent Denver architects John J. Huddart and

Thielman Robert Wieger apparently designed many of the new red brick and stone commercial buildings. Nearly all carry the date 1896.

After a statewide vote, gambling became legal in Cripple Creek's commercial core in 1991. A modern-day gold rush took place as long-desolate downtown commercial lots sold for as much as $2 million each. Old structures, and a few new ones, were made into thirty-one casinos before gambling fever subsided. Casino builders often demolished everything but the streetfront facade and built a completely new structure behind it. Inside, split-level design and mirrored walls visually expanded interiors jammed with slot machines. Fanciful, neo-Victorian interiors sport wood trim, chandeliers, pressed metal ceilings, and carpets in hues of lavender and mauve. Honky-tonk piano players and cocktail waitresses outfitted in dancehall finery add to the carnival.

A share of the gambling proceeds is earmarked for historic preservation and guidelines enforcing, for example, the three-story height restriction downtown and a buffer zone in which commercial buildings are reserved for non-gambling uses. Despite housing, parking, and policing headaches, optimists contend that gambling revenues will help pave Cripple Creek's dirt side streets and may even bring a stoplight to the town. Locals and tourists want to preserve the town's historic scavengers—a herd of semi-wild burros—who roam the streets, chomping, braying, and glaring at tourist cameras.

The entire town has been designated a National Historic Landmark District. Bennett Avenue, Cripple Creek's main street, is bordered by red-brick commercial buildings with glazed storefronts and recessed entries. Many facades show fine face brick, often with exuberant detailing—sandstone pilasters, decorative friezes, and egg-and-dart molding. The once solid row of storefronts along Myers Avenue are mostly gone, replaced by weedy vacant lots. During the 1930s and 1940s, hundreds of frame and brick homes were demolished. Yet a core residential district survives along Carr, Eaton, and Golden avenues on the north side

of Bennett. One of the more ornate Victorian homes, 315 East Eaton, has been converted to a bed and breakfast.

TL01 Cripple Creek District Museum (Midland Terminal Depot)

1896. East end of Bennett Ave. (Colorado 67) and 5th St.

At the bottom of Tenderfoot Hill, this three-story depot welcomed as many as eight daily passenger trains until 1949. To fit its hilly site, the depot has two track-side stories and three stories on the town side. The stationmaster and his family lived on the top floor, while passengers, below, used separate men's and women's waiting rooms. Rough-faced sandstone walls rise to red pressed brick on the second and third stories. The town-side entrance is at the base of a square, off-center bay. On the track side, a round two-story bay wears a conical roof. Sandstone quoins and trim detail the depot, as do the round-arched entry and paired upper windows beneath brick dentils and corbeling. Decorative rafter ends and bracing under the gable ends and an open third-story balcony on the west facade lend a little airiness to this heavy building. Inside, golden oak staircases, wainscoting, and trim are well preserved.

The depot reopened in 1953 as a museum with a good collection of photographs, mining equipment, furniture, household goods, and a model of the underground workings of the Cripple Creek District's Portland Mine. Just north of the museum, the relocated Bull Hill Station (c. 1895) has been converted to the ticket booth and gift shop for the 2-foot-gauge Cripple Creek and Victor Railroad (1967). This steam train goes halfway to Victor along the original Colorado Midland railroad bed. Passengers are treated to views of mine dumps, headframes, and the snowcapped Sangre de Cristo Range 60 miles to the southwest.

TL02 Old Homestead Museum (Parlor House)

1896. 353 E. Myers Ave.

This restored brothel has a prominent bay window, complemented by a small, roofed porch, that lends demure elegance to an ordinary brick house. Adamesque swags, garlands, and tassels adorn the bay, front porch, and pressed metal cornice. The rooms are furnished with period antiques. The Homestead is now a museum with tours conducted by costumed guides.

Teller County's finest whorehouse had, according to the 1900 manuscript census, a resident cook, a housekeeper, two chambermaids, two butlers, and a musician. Five female "boarders" had rooms upstairs, with one room for viewing only. The downstairs features a fancy sitting room, two parlors, a dining room, and a kitchen. This is the last remnant of the notorious Myers Avenue redlight district, a five-block strip of some fifty gambling houses, saloons, sporting houses, and brothels. At 320 East Myers are the stone ruins of the Grand Opera House.

TL03 Elks Lodge (Gold Mining Stock Exchange)

1896, John J. Huddart and T. Robert Wieger. Northwest corner of E. Bennett Ave. and 4th St.

As if to reassure investors, this sturdy red brick and sandstone Romanesque Revival building radiates wealth and permanence. From a stone-arched, recessed entry a central bay rises above the sandstone cornice, dentils, and frieze to a prominent parapet. Ten years after it closed in 1903, the exchange became the Elks Club. The floor of the large, high-ceilinged exchange hall still contains electrical outlets for communications with exchanges in Colorado Springs, Denver, Chicago, and New York. The Elks maintain a bar, dining rooms, ballroom, and meeting rooms on the second floor and a grand hall and sleeping rooms on the third.

This stock exchange is a reminder that Cripple Creek was not a poor man's camp: mining by the 1890s had become big business, controlled largely by out-of-town capitalists, while the miners were reduced to $3-a-day drudgery. These economic circumstances are evident in the district's architecture, which is characterized by modest homes rather than mansions.

TL04 Cripple Creek High School

1899, T. E. McNulty, builder. Southwest corner of 4th St. and Carr Ave.

An Italian Villa Style tower crowns this two-story red brick school. It has been converted to a hotel, with original fixtures such as the blackboards and desks as decor. The upstairs auditorium has housed meetings and socials.

TL05 St. Andrew's Episcopal Church

1896. Northwest corner of 4th St. and Carr Ave.

After meeting in various saloons, this congregation of "Whiskeypalians" graduated to a brick church on this corner in 1893. After Cripple Creek's 1896 fire, the Reverend Charles Y. Grimes and his flock rebuilt in brick and stone. Gothic arches grace the Queen Anne massing, capped by the three pedimented peaks of the front facade. The basement chapel has walls of reputedly high-grade gold ore. Stephen Mackin, a Cripple Creek artisan and hotelkeeper, designed the memorial stained glass windows.

TL06 City Hall

1898. 343–345 E. Bennett Ave.

After the fire of 1896, Cripple Creek's city hall was rebuilt with a fire station as its most prominent feature. The red pressed brick building has a corbeled parapet, and double brick rows serve as stringcourse and trim for the arched windows, rough-faced stone windowsills, and large front doors. City offices remain, but now the firehouse is a visitors' center displaying an antique fire engine, a Linotype machine from an early Cripple Creek newspaper, and a cell from the town jail.

TL07 Becker and Nolon Block

1896. 1991, restoration, David Langley. 301 E. Bennett Ave. (northeast corner of 3rd St.)

Saloonkeeper Johnny Nolon made this Neoclassical brick building the most popular watering hole and gambling hall in Cripple Creek. After Nolon left for the goldfields of Nevada in 1904, David Moffat converted it to the Cripple Creek State Bank. The original second-story dentiled cornice, Adamesque frieze, and elaborate pilasters still distinguish this building, which returned in 1991 to its original use.

TL08 Weinberg Block

1896. Southwest corner of E. Bennett Ave. and 3rd St.

Solomon, Harry, Fred, and C. L. Weinberg's haberdashery boasted a Georgian Revival corner tower on a two-story brick commercial building, reopened in 1992 as the Bowl of Gold Casino.

TL09 Imperial Hotel and Casino

1896, J. M. Roseberry, builder. 133–137 N. 3rd St. (between Bennett and Carr aves.)

This three-story, red brick building, originally the Collins Hotel, has round-topped windows, dentils, bracketed frieze, and unobtrusive egg-and-dart trim. Windowsills and door stoops are of rough-faced sandstone. Wayne and Dorothy Mackin purchased the boarded-up, run-down hotel for $18,000 in 1946 and outfitted the rooms with brass beds and antique furnishings. Over the years they acquired the attached two-story red brick Pittsburgh Block (1896) fronting on Bennett Avenue. It was converted to additional hotel rooms, offices, and commercial space before becoming the Imperial Casino in 1991. Melodramas have been performed since 1948 in the basement Gold Bar Room Theater, including revivals of antique plays staged under the supervision of Dorothy Mackin, author of *Melodrama Classics* (1982). The Red Rooster piano bar, in what was originally the hotel sample room where merchants could display goods, inherited both its antique bar and its name from a tavern in Twin Lakes (Lake County). Creaky floors and stairs and uneven ceilings attest to the difficulty of erecting stable, squared-up buildings on such a steep slope.

TL10 St. Nicholas Hotel (St. Nicholas Hospital)

1898. Northwest corner of 3rd St. and Eaton Ave.

During Cripple Creek's heyday, the Sisters of Mercy opened this hilltop hospital, built in the Italian Villa Style of red brick with stone trim and a two-story, columned entry porch. One of the sisters is said to have directed construction of the three-and-one-half-story building, which incorporated steam heat, electricity, and a surgery department. One of the twenty-six hospital rooms was elegantly furnished by mine owner Albert E. Carlton for his employees. After the nuns left in 1925, several doctors operated this as a private hospital until 1960, then sold it to the county for $1. In the 1980s it became the St. Nicholas Hotel, with a Celtic cross still atop the rooftop cupola.

TL11 St. Peter's Catholic Church

1897. 318 N. 3rd. St.

Erected atop the highest hill in town, supposedly to remind people of the steep climb to heaven, this red brick Romanesque Revival church has a three-story bell tower capped with a steeple. It replaced a smaller 1892 church on the same site. Cripple Creek's wealthiest mining millionaire, the so-called Midas of the Rockies, Winfield Scott Stratton, gave Father Thomas Volpe the money to erect the church. The red brick convent and rectory which once hugged the south side of the church are gone.

TL12 Phenix Block

1896. 1996, restoration. 232 E. Bennett Ave.

Radical remodeling of this commercial block removed everything but the front to build a casino. The restored facade incorporates three storefront display and transom windows and recessed doorways. Wood dentils mark the first- and second-story heights beneath a metal cornice with brick corbeling.

TL13 Palace Hotel

1896. 1993, David M. Barber. Southwest corner of Bennett Ave. and 2nd St.

After a wooden predecessor was dynamited to create a fire break during the 1896 fires, this three-story, red brick hotel with sandstone trim and a frame porch was erected as a replacement. Above the storefronts the eighteen-room hotel has round-topped windows and a bracketed metal cornice.

The Palace had been boarded up for several years when the Lays family bought it for $55,000 and reopened it in 1977. The hotel houses a restaurant, a casino (1993), summer vaudeville, and, according to one of the owners, a ghost—a feminine apparition believed to be Kitty Chambers, owner of the hotel from 1908 to 1918, who died in room 3.

TL14 Teller County Courthouse

1904, Augustus J. Smith. Northwest corner of Bennett Ave. and 1st St.

This three-story structure, built for $68,000, has a limestone base and walls mixing brown half-bricks with red full bricks. Arched brick doorways, patterned brick quoins, egg-and-dart trim, sandstone sills, and second-story

blind arches decorated with Adamesque wreaths and garlands adorn the building, as do herringbone brick spandrels and a double-dentiled cornice. The little-altered interior has creaky wooden floors, golden oak wainscoting, lath and plaster walls, and operable lunette transoms. Antique radiators, brass fixtures, and signage make this a vintage home for the county and district courts, tax assessor, and social services. A golden oak staircase leads upstairs to the original oak-trimmed courtrooms, which are exquisitely preserved.

TL15 Teller County Sheriff's Office and Jail

1901, Matthew Lockwood McBird. Southeast corner of W. Bennett Ave. and A St.

The county jail's steel-barred windows and stout orange brick walls atop a gray granite foundation discourage escapes. Neo-Romanesque touches include the round-topped windows and arched doorways, red sandstone trim, and the corbeled corner roof turrets. With an eye toward the likely expertise of the anticipated clientele, the city spent $25,759 for an interlocking push-button cell system and a steel cross-grid in the concrete floors, all of which remains. Some, including inmates of this antique prison, have suggested converting it to a gambling parlor. Matthew Lockwood McBird, the son of Denver architect Matthew John McBird, may also have designed buildings for the Woods brothers, who founded Victor. When replaced by a new facility in Woodland Park, this became a jail for sale.

TL16 Miller-Robinson House

1897. 127 W. Carr Ave. (NR)

Charles N. Miller, a gold broker, built the finest residence in town, this two-story Queen Anne house subsequently owned by William Robinson, a mayor of Cripple Creek and publisher of the *Cripple Creek Gold Rush*. Built on two lots, this example of Victorian residential architecture has three fishscale-shingled gables decorated with scalloped bargeboard. Two balustraded porches grace the front of the house. The first-floor porch is decorated with latticework, cutout frame arches, and spindles. The second-floor porch has a triple-arched cutout gable.

TL17 Hospitality House (Teller County Hospital)

1901, C. E. Troutman. 1992, restoration, David M. Barber. North end of B St.

After decades of neglect and abandonment, this two-story white elephant with Neoclassical trim was acquired by the Mackin family during the 1970s. They converted it to a hotel and headquarters for a mobile home park. The large hospital has a glass-enclosed two-story front porch framed between wooden Ionic columns and a grand, pressed red brick entry arch. A discreet rear addition and the eighteen original rooms, restored by Colorado Springs architect David Barber, use a hospital theme to tickle the fancy of tourists wanting "intensive care."

TL18 Mollie Kathleen Mine

1891. Tenderfoot Hill, 1 mile northeast of Cripple Creek on Colorado 67

The Mollie Kathleen mine surrendered more than $2 million from its ten levels after Mollie Kathleen Gertner opened it in 1891. Since it switched to mining tourists' pockets in the 1950s, it has become a popular mine tour. Visitors ride the "skip" 1,000 feet underground to inspect a hard rock gold mine, now owned by a grandson of Verner Z. Reed, who was one of Cripple Creek's millionaires.

TL19 Gold Camp Auto Road (Colorado Springs and Cripple Creek Railroad Bed)

1901, 1922. Between Colorado Springs and Cripple Creek

The last of three railroads to reach the mining district is a notable piece of civil engineering. Shunning the stream bed construction of many other narrow-gauge mountain railroads, it built along mountainsides and canyon walls, requiring much cut-and-fill work. It snaked over the south slope of Pikes Peak and through the town of Cameron to reach Cripple Creek and Victor. President Theodore Roosevelt, after taking the trip, is said to have declared, "This is the ride that

bankrupts the English language!" W. D. Corley bought the railroad bed in 1922 and turned it into the Gold Camp Road for motorists, who still thrill at its hairpin curves and dizzy dropoffs.

TL20 Anaconda

1893–1917. 2 miles south of Cripple Creek on Colorado 67

Anaconda, founded near the Anaconda Mine, had a 1900 census population of 1,059. Cribbing and mill house ruins linger at the Doctor Jack Pot, Fauntleroy, Mary McKinney, and other million-dollar holes. Anaconda's main street was lined with false-fronted frame buildings, including the *Write Up the Camp* newspaper office. Today only the foundation of the jailhouse, fire hydrants, and evidence of streets survive. The Cripple Creek & Victor narrow-gauge excursion ends here near the only frame structure still wearing a roof. Cripple Creek's last operating mill, the Carlton Mill (1951), on the southwest side of Colorado 67, 1 mile southwest of Anaconda, processes 1,000 tons of ore per day, dumped by trucks into the sixteen bins that face the highway. The 414-by-463-foot, L-shaped prefabricated steel structure claims to be the largest custom gold refinery in the world. During the 1980s it was reopened by the Texas Gulf and Golden Cycle Mine as a cyanide leach operation. Waste from this mill has buried the old town of Arequa, which is now beneath a cyanide leach pad.

Florissant

This ranching community (1872, 8,178 feet) was founded by James Costello, who named it after his home in Missouri. The Colorado Midland Railroad built a depot here in 1887 on its line to Leadville and Aspen. Florissant thrived as a supply and lumber town during the Cripple Creek bonanza days. The Florissant Fossil Beds National Monument, 3 miles south on Florissant Road, contain remnants of a subtropical forest of moss, ferns, and sequoia trees that flourished here over 50 million years ago. Volcanic eruptions covered this paradise with boiling mud and molten lava, pressing down layers of ash to preserve insects, leaves, flowers, and the trunks of giant sequoia trees in fossilized form. Following its discovery in 1874, plundering and commercialization damaged the site before it was declared a national monument in 1969.

TL21 **Florissant School**

1887, Elias Ashley, builder. 2009 Teller County 31 (NR)

This one-story schoolhouse, built for $884, doubled as the Florissant Grange Hall. The frame L-plan structure has pedimented window moldings and the original school bell. Inside are the original wainscoting, teacher's desk, piano, and students' desks. Also on the property are a teacher's residence, two outhouses, the foundation of an early post office, and a small, gable-roofed building that was the school cafeteria.

TL22 **Hornbeck House**

1878. 2 miles south of Teller County 1 (NR)

Adeline Hornbeck built this homestead house with the help of her three sons. The one-and-one-half-story structure, of massive squared logs with V notches, has a steeply pitched cedar-shingled roof with board-and-batten gable ends. The main floor contains a bedroom, parlor, kitchen, pantry, and well room in a T plan. The National Park Service moved a bunkhouse and barn to the site and reconstructed the rustic pole fence for what is now a house museum.

TL23 **Goldfield**

1895–1932. 1.5 miles northeast of Victor

Once a town of some 2,000 and the ore shipping center of the district, Goldfield has shrunk to thirty or forty homes on a mostly bare grid of dirt streets. The city hall and fire station (1899), a two-story, raw frame structure at Victor Avenue and 9th Street (NR), has been installed on a new foundation and its bell tower reinforced and roofed. The first floor housed the fire cart and horses; city offices were upstairs. The flat-roofed building has ornate wooden quoins.

Victor

After the Cripple Creek rush began, Frank M. and Harry E. Woods of Denver platted Victor (1893, 9,693 feet) and named it for an early homesteader, Victor C. Adams. While mine owners and businessmen gravitated to Cripple Creek, Victor's working-class residents built clapboard and brick houses in the shadows of headframes and huge mine dumps. Underground blasting shook the town, and heavy ore wagons rumbled continually through the streets.

In August 1899 a fire ravaged Victor, destroying fourteen blocks and leaving 3,000 homeless. The town quickly rebuilt, replacing ramshackle wood structures with dignified Neoclassical brick commercial buildings and modest masonry houses. By 1900 its 4,986 residents made it the eighth most populous city in Colorado. As many as fifty-eight trains a day moved through the city, bringing in mining machinery and supplies and taking out gold ore to the huge smelter complex in Colorado City. Like Cripple Creek, the town has been in decline since World War I. Several historic saloons, such as Zeke's Place (c. 1910), South 3rd Street, have survived, but churches have had a harder time. The Church of Christ Scientist (c. 1900), fronted by a Greek classical facade with Doric columns supporting a pediment, has been boarded up with bark slabs.

Victor's heyday was described by schoolteacher Mabel Barbee Lee in *Cripple Creek Days* (1958): "As I looked out upon it from my classroom window, high on a hill, the beauty of the land overwhelmed me. Famous gold rich mountains rimmed the north with their tall smokestacks. A maze of roads wound in and out among the cribbings piled with waste rock. Small cabins were clustered around them in the open spaces, merging the camp with its mines. Absurd, cracker-box houses with tiny windows and crisscrossing stovepipes clung to the steep slopes of the lopsided streets."

The Victor Downtown Historic District (NRD) covers six blocks, bounded roughly by 5th and 2nd streets between Diamond and Portland avenues. It contains sixty-six business buildings with classical, Romanesque Revival, and Renaissance Revival aspirations, typically with recessed center doorways and large display windows. The residential area is composed of modest brick and frame houses, including three bed and breakfast inns, the Portland Inn (1896), 412 West Portland Avenue; the Kessey House (1901), 216 South 3rd Street; and the Midnight Inn (1899), 4th Street and Spicer Avenue.

TL24 Visitors' Center

1894. Victor Ave. between 2nd and 3rd sts.

Gracefully arched wooden brackets and wide eaves enhance this one-story frame train station, moved here from Alta Vista. The hipped roof, vertical board-and-batten siding, and simple design make this a picturesque starting point for a walking tour of Victor.

TL25 Elks Lodge No. 367 (Armory Hall)

1892. Southeast corner of 3rd St. and Diamond Ave.

This armory became home for the state militia, sent in to crush striking miners, before the Elks purchased it in the 1920s. This large, three-story brick structure combines Italianate and Neo-Romanesque elements. Arched windows and doorways are of rough-faced red sandstone. A leaded glass fanlight crowns the double-doored front entrance. A stepped brick parapet and long porch mark the front of the building. The porch is supported by square concrete pillars topped by pediments, apparently a later addition. The Elks, who still meet here, have preserved the splendid interior with its hardwood trim and many original fixtures.

TL26 City Hall

1900. Northeast corner of Victor Ave. and 5th St.

This elaborate, two-story brick building features sandstone quoins and an arched sandstone entry in a central bay. Brick dentils and sandstone egg-and-dart trim embellish the exterior, as do the roofline brackets and frieze. The most prominent feature is a brick bell tower surmounted by a domed cupola.

Although the fire department has moved out, the large double firehouse doors remain, as do city offices and wall maps of the mazelike mining claims, shafts, and tunnels underlying "The City of Mines."

TL27 First Baptist Church

1898. Northwest corner of 4th St. and Portland Ave.

A square, three-story corner bell tower and the original pump organ distinguish this stone Romanesque Revival church built by Victor's founders, Frank and Harry Woods, who taught Sunday school here.

TL28 New Victor Hotel (Bank Block)

1900. 1992, restoration, Jones Dernbach Associates. Northeast corner of Victor Ave. and 4th St.

This bank building sat atop its own gold mine. While excavating for this four-story structure in 1899, the Woods brothers discovered a 20-inch-wide vein of high-grade ore. Mining continued far underground during and after construction. The bank and the mine lasted until the Great Depression. Later reincarnated as the New Victor Hotel, this beige brick structure with orange brick trim still contains the pressed metal ceiling, 12-foot-high plate glass windows, an ornate elevator, and the office suite used by the Woods brothers. In 1993 a $1 million restoration revived the building as a thirty-room hotel with a bank vault in the lobby.

TL29 Gold Coin Club

1899–1900, Frank M. and Harry E. Woods, builders. 413 W. Diamond Ave.

Town founders Harry and Frank Woods built the Gold Coin Club for their employees' recreation, supposedly patterning the interior of their grandiose hall after the New York Athletic Club. The Colonial Revival building has Ionic columns supporting a second-story porch under a pediment and a decorative frieze. Inside, the club originally contained a ballroom, gymnasium, bowling alleys, pool room, dining rooms, and a library. After the 1903–1904 labor strike closed the Gold Coin, it was used as a hospital and later as a private residence. Currently used for apartments, it stands across Dia-

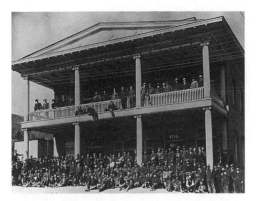

TL29 Gold Coin Club, c. 1900

mond Avenue from the crumbling ruins and collapsing shafts of the Gold Coin Mine.

TL30 Isis Theater

c. 1896. 109 S. 3rd St.

This one-story brick theater received an Art Deco facelift in stucco during the 1920s, when it was also given its current name. The original movie theater interior survives, complete with the wooden proscenium arch, in what is now a large antique shop.

TL31 Lowell Thomas Museum

1899. Southeast corner of Victor Ave. and 3rd St.

Built as the Reynolds Block, this two-story brick building with large, square, plate glass windows has egg-and-dart detailing and window surrounds of rough-faced stone. The building housed Tomkins Hardware, the Victor Mining Stock Exchange, Victor Dry Goods, and the Hackley Furniture Store over the years before its conversion to a museum commemorating Victor's most famous resident, who worked at the *Victor Record* before attaining international fame as a radio correspondent.

TL32 Masonic Temple

c. 1910. 114–116 S. 4th St.

One of Victor's more ornate buildings has a central, pedimented, triple-arched entry flanked by two slightly projecting pedimented two-story bays. The brick structure

with red sandstone trim is capped by a wooden frieze and multiple cornices.

TL33 Midland Terminal Railroad Depot

1895. 230 N. 4th St. (southeast corner of Granite Ave.)

One of Victor's first brick structures and its only surviving railroad depot has a hipped roof with wide, bracketed eaves to shelter waiting passengers. The bay window gave station workers a clear view of the tracks. Large, arched freight doors allowed baggage carts to be easily maneuvered. Inside, the ticket sales window, telegraph window, passenger waiting area, and freight and baggage storage areas remain much as they were from 1894 to 1949, when the Midland Terminal Railroad provided passenger service.

TL34 Miners' Union Hall

c. 1899. 118–122 N. 4th St.

Bullet holes still scar this building, where, on June 6, 1904, striking members of the Western Federation of Miners, Local No. 32, were attacked by the state militia. Arched window openings and red sandstone trim enhance the Italianate design of this brick building, whose lower story is finished with more recent wood planking.

TL35 Victor Mines

Victor displays some particularly fine examples of the soaring headframes of mineshafts. Closest to town, at the northeast end of 3rd Street, is the Strong Mine (1892), whose dumps, mill structures, and metal headframe are still erect. Behind the Strong is Winfield Scott Stratton's Independence Mine (discovered July 4, 1901), which ultimately produced more than $28 million in gold. The pulley wheel is still atop the wooden headframe with sheet metal skin. North of the Independence, higher on Battle Mountain, are the Portland No. 1 and No. 2 (1892) headframes and mill houses. Together with the now demolished Portland No. 3, they produced more than $60 million in gold from some 75 miles of underground workings. The Portland and the Independence, the two richest and most celebrated gold mines in Colorado, were consolidated in 1915 when both were already in decline. Lessees have continued to operate the mines intermittently and now include heap leaching firms that reprocess the waste rock and mill tailings.

West of the Strong Mine, the Ajax Mine (1895) has a restabilized headframe and a new hoist, part of a 1970s rehabilitation program for one of the last gold mines, which did not close until the 1980s. The shaft has been repaired and retimbered to the 3,100-foot level at a cost of $300 per foot. These four mines are among the most easily visited of approximately one hundred whose headframes or mill houses may still be seen and identified in the Cripple Creek District.

Fremont County   (FR)

Explorer John C. Frémont gave his name to one of Colorado's pioneer counties, although he failed to negotiate its awesome Royal Gorge of the Arkansas River. In the Arkansas River valley, a few pre–gold rush settlements, including Hardscrabble, an 1844 adobe plaza town, have disappeared. Cañon City, the county seat, was platted in 1859 and served as a supply center for mountain mining towns. Oil and coal, both discovered in the Cañon City–Florence area in the early 1860s, ultimately proved to be the richest natural resources.

Cañon City sandstone quarries, the Wellsville granite quarry near Howard, the Cotopaxi quarries, known for blue, red, gray, and pink granite, and the Cowan Brothers Travertine Quarries, 2 miles northwest of Cañon City, are among a dozen prominent county stone suppliers. The Ideal Cement plant at Portland has fed construction projects across the state since the 1890s. Abundant clay deposits supplied brickyards that manufactured brick for both Fremont County and the nearby Cripple Creek gold district.

The Denver & Rio Grande reached Cañon City in 1874. This railroad, by a marvelous feat of engineering, squeezed through the bottom of the Royal Gorge and on to Leadville. Along with the Arkansas River and U.S. 50, the D&RG still serves as the urban corridor of Fremont County. Cañon City has been the site of the state penitentiary since 1871. The largest of all federal prison complexes, opened in 1993 in Florence, has pumped new life and dollars into the economy. In the United States, with more than a million citizens behind bars, prisons have become a big business.

Voluntary visitors come to see the 8-mile-long, 1,000-foot-deep Royal Gorge and its suspension bridge, the biggest spectacle of the Arkansas Headwaters Recreation Area, which stretches from Leadville to Pueblo. Three roadways from Fremont County to the historic Cripple Creek Mining and Gaming District—the High Park Road, the Shelf Road, and the Phantom Canyon Road (the old Florence & Cripple Creek roadbed), form the Historic Highways and Byways "Gold Belt Tour."

Apple orchards, which once blanketed the valley, have largely disappeared, but other agriculture, along with mining, prisons, and tourism, has given Fremont

County steady, if unspectacular, population growth to 32,273 residents in 1990, roughly a third of whom live in Cañon City.

Cañon City

The county seat (1859, 5,343 feet) lies in a broad valley where the Arkansas River emerges from the Royal Gorge. Born as a supply camp for the upper Arkansas River mines, Cañon City led an up-and-down adolescent career during local gold, coal, oil, tin, and zinc booms. The D&RG, which demanded and received $50,000 in bonds and town lots before building to Cañon City, made the town a rail hub.

Cañon City was a contender for the Colorado state capital until it backed Denver's bid in exchange for the state penitentiary site. Its citizens reckoned that the state prison would be better attended than the other possible second prize—the state university. Furthermore, prisoners, who would provide cheap labor, building stone, and road work, were thought to be more productive than professors and students.

A fairly well-preserved main street and residential areas reflect past economic booms. The Downtown Historic District, 3rd to 9th streets between Main and Macon streets (NRD), contains eighty brick and stone commercial buildings, some by local architects C. C. Rittenhouse, D. A. Bradbury, Dryden and Helm, S. S. Nichols, D. G. Scott, and Smith Patton. Street-level modernization has marred many Main Street landmarks, such as the Central Block (1901), the Burrage Building (1888, C. C. Rittenhouse), and the Wilbar Building (1895).

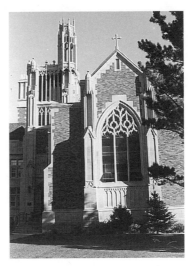

FR01 Holy Cross Abbey

with cast stone trim, some in the French Flamboyant mode, and distinguished by a cantilevered tower on the southeast corner. Gothic Revival influences are revealed by the massing, buttressing, pointed-arch window treatments, and filigree. The interior has the stark look of sudden budget cuts but retains a mini-museum and an 18,000-volume library. Unfortunately, the architectural quality of other structures on the 225-acre campus does not come near that of this well-landscaped medieval apparition. Closed in 1984 because of low enrollments, the campus is currently used for community college classes as well as for retreats conducted by the few remaining monks.

FR01 Holy Cross Abbey

1924, Joseph Dillon and L. A. Des Jardins. 2 miles east of Cañon City on Royal Gorge Blvd. (U.S. 50) (NR)

Benedictine monks built this $500,000 Collegiate Gothic abbey as the showpiece of a boys' college preparatory school. The imposing, three-and-one-half-story abbey, built on a Latin cross plan, is a steel-frame structure clad in gold and brown brick decorated

FR02 Graydene-Smith House

c. 1885. 2650 E. Main St.

Colonel and Mrs. F. E. Graydene-Smith patterned their turreted and towered thirteen-room mansion after the castles of her English homeland. Built of gray sandstone quarried by convict labor, it incorporates Neo-Romanesque elements such as thick, rough-faced stone block in the walls and round-arched doorways and windows. The

Cañon
City

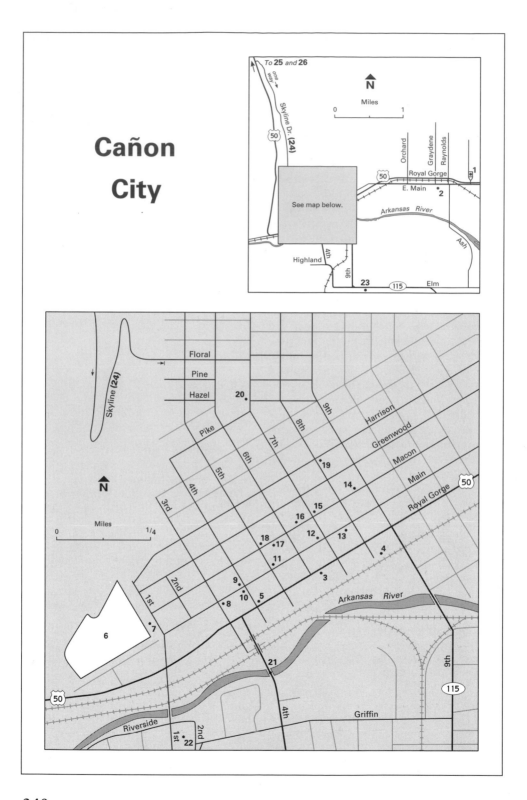

manor has been well maintained as a residence.

FR03 Cañon City Municipal Building and Museum

1927, Eugene Groves. 612 Royal Gorge Blvd. (NR)

Cañon City's municipal building is a two-story Moderne structure in wire-cut brick with a terracotta portico for the recessed entrance. Fasces alternate with the torch of justice on the terracotta frieze. City offices are on the lower floors. Upstairs is a collection of Fremont County artifacts, including the animal trophy collection of Dallas De Weese, an early promoter of Cañon City. Other exhibits and fossils illustrate extensive discoveries of dinosaur remains from local digs, which since 1878 have provided skeletons to the Carnegie Museum in Pittsburgh, the Peabody Museum at Yale, and the Denver Museum of Natural History. The museum complex includes the Rudd Cabin (1860), the 28-by-20-foot hewn log home built by Anson Rudd, a pioneer settler, and

his later house (1881), a two-story structure of uncoursed rubblestone quarried by convicts for Rudd, who donated the land for the state penitentiary and became its first superintendent.

FR04 Municipal Court and Police Station (Denver & Rio Grande Depot)

1909. 816 Royal Gorge Blvd. (U.S. 50)

Metal fascias in a diamond and oval pattern adorn the wide eaves on this elongated, low-slung station, a harbinger of Modernism. Chocolate brown wire-cut brick with Indiana limestone trim is overshadowed by the red tile hipped roof and ornate roof brackets rising out of pilasters. Eaves overhang from hip-roofed wings on east and west, extending from a central, slightly higher gable with parapeted ends. The well-landscaped and well-preserved building is now converted to municipal use.

FR05 Clelland-Peabody House

1880. 403 Royal Gorge Blvd. (northwest corner of 4th St.)

This Second Empire mansard-roofed dwelling belonged to James Clelland, an early Cañon City merchant also responsible for the Clelland Block at 404 Main Street. James Peabody, a Cañon City mayor who later

FR03 Cañon City Municipal Building and Museum

FR04 Denver & Rio Grande Depot, 1910

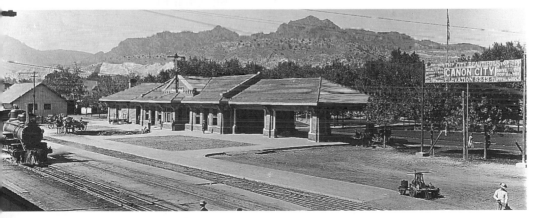

served as Colorado governor (1902–1904), also lived in the house, which has two grand parlors and splendid fireplaces. In the early 1990s the city restored it for Chamber of Commerce offices and a visitors' center, as part of the $2.4 million River Station Project, which also rehabilitated the nearby bungaloid Atchison, Topeka & Santa Fe depot (c. 1915), catercorner across 4th Street.

FR06 Colorado State Penitentiary

1869. West end of Main St. at 1st St.

An octagonal stone guard tower overlooks the curve in U.S. 50, and other stone guard huts and observation posts command the hill above this prison. The state penitentiary was sited, not accidentally, against a hogback of lime and sandstone. This location made it possible to put prisoners to work on the traditional rock pile, quarrying the beige sandstone not only for their own confinement but also for buildings throughout the town. The lime was sold for smelter flux and used to build paved roads with convict labor statewide. Before the practice was abandoned, prisoners built many roads, including Cañon City's spectacular Skyline and Royal Gorge scenic drives.

The Women's Prison, a two-story stuccoed stone compound, was rehabilitated as the Colorado Territorial Prison Museum in 1988. Its thirty-two cells are now crowded with exhibits of prison industries, such as quarrying and making license plates, and with examples of "behavioral control devices."

FR07 Colorado Department of Corrections Office (Warden's House)

1901. Main and 1st sts.

Inmates constructed this two-story, hip-roofed, Queen Anne Style house of brick with stone trim. It is overshadowed by its three-story round corner tower decorated with an inset stone lion's head and topped by a domed roof. An open, circular porch around the tower base and a trio of stained glass windows lend a residential ambiance to a home hemmed in by the prison's 20-foot high, 4-foot-thick stone wall topped by barbed wire. Besides two cat-sized stone lions on the front walkway, the Warden's House is also guarded by the State Armory (1921,

Major A. R. Young, construction superintendent), across the street. This unusually well-preserved, still functioning armory, following a design used statewide, is a two-story brick barrel-vaulted structure fronted by formidable square corner towers and a peaked parapet.

FR08 Catlin Building

1888. A. C. Jansen, builder. 304 Main St. (southeast corner of 3rd St.)

W. C. Catlin, the owner of the most prominent local brick factory, displayed his product in this handsome two-story building with decorative peaked stone lintels and a narrow, bracketed metal cornice.

FR09 Strathmore Hotel

1874, William H. McClure, builder. 323–331 Main St. (northwest corner of 4th St.)

This three-story, L-shaped hotel has housed the Fremont and First National banks behind its 12-foot-high storefronts with colored glass panels framing the transoms. The brick exterior is crowned with an incised garland frieze and dentiled cornice with finials. Although the upper-story windows retain their arched trim, most street-level openings have been altered and have lost their original colored glass transoms.

FR10 Raynolds Bank Building

1882–1883, L. A. Allen, builder. 330–332 Main St. (southwest corner of 4th St.) (NR)

This two-story business block, Gothic Revival in style with an arresting corner tower, is clad in rough pink Castle Rock rhyolite trimmed with smooth local "prison stone." A splendid corner entrance pediment is supported by granite pillars and topped by a second-story turret crowned with the slender, 20-foot-tall spire, a reconstruction of the original. Besides the bank of Frederick A. Raynolds, the edifice originally housed the McGee Mercantile before becoming the aerie of the Fraternal Order of Eagles in 1962.

FR11 Annex Building–Opera House

1903, Lyman Robison, builder. 505–507 Main St.

Even in a row of fine Victorians with strutting cornices, this exuberant Neoclassical brick, stone, and metal composition stands out. The tripartite facade is distinguished by a bracketed broken cornice with a central pediment. The second story, whose triple-arched central window is flanked by paired windows and pilasters with granite shafts, contains an opera hall with a proscenium stage and a balcony under a skylighted, pressed metal ceiling.

FR12 Hotel Saint Cloud

1879. 1886, moved to Cañon City. 627–631 Main St. (northwest corner of 7th St.) (NR)

As the silver mining era faded in Silver Cliff (Custer County), the original site of this three-story brick hotel, the building was dismantled and hauled into Cañon City to reopen as the Hotel St. Cloud. Notable guests have included Buffalo Bill Cody, Calamity Jane, and western movie idol Tom Mix, who briefly made Cañon City a mini-Hollywood. The mansard roof is pierced by dormer windows and a central pavilion that divides the building's facade into three bays. Rough-cut stone marks the corners and the window tops above the first floor. The hotel also boasted the town's first elevator and elegant interior details, such as the pressed metal ceiling in the Silver Lining Saloon.

FR13 Acme Building

1890. 722–724 Main St.

Four wooden bay windows dominate the Acme Building's upper story, above transomed display windows and recessed entrances divided by cast iron pillars made by the Hassell Iron Works in Colorado Springs. The main facade of this brick building is clad in rough-faced red sandstone. Tenants have ranged from a grocery to a mortuary, from a bicycle shop to a dance studio.

FR14 Atwater House

1898. 821 Macon Ave.

Queen Anne massing focused on a square corner tower distinguishes this two-story brick home with sandstone foundation, windowsills, pediments, and stringcourses. A polygonal, two-story bay flanks the west side, while a three-story turret stands at the southwest corner. Double and triple fluted colonnettes with Corinthian capitals support the front porch roof. Originally owned by Samuel H. Atwater, a realtor, the house deteriorated after conversion to a tuberculosis sanatarium but has now been restored as a private residence.

FR15 First Presbyterian Church

1901, Bradbury and Rittenhouse. 700 Macon Ave. (northeast corner of 7th St.) (NR)

Soaring over an elegant residential neighborhood, this church's octagonal shingle-clad belfry culminates in an octagonal spire and nine finials pointing heavenward. The red and buff stone base springs into the tower and other airy turrets and finials. The graceful, irregular plan has been marred by several ground-floor additions. This vertical Queen Anne Style composition contrasts well with the stocky Romanesque Revival red sandstone First Baptist Church (1890) on the opposite corner.

FR16 Fremont County Courthouse

1960, Lester Jones of Nixon and Jones. 615 Macon St.

Architect Lester Jones, of a Boulder firm, used a Usonian design for this low-slung courthouse spreading across a full-block site. The asymmetrical plan has single-story wings extending east and southwest from a central two-story core. A relief diamond pattern in weathered copper covers the battered second-story walls, with small, narrow clerestory windows under canopies of the same copper with triangle patterns. Copper fascia trim also edges wall panels, spandrels, and the overhanging flat roofs of the wings. First-floor walls, capped and edged in smooth limestone, are paneled in irregular slabs cut from amorphous volcanic rock. The main entrance is through a glass curtain wall divided by slab columns. The deep-set doors have vertical full-height glazing paired with geometric-relief oak panels and hardware in triangular shapes. The exterior stone walls continue into the lobby, where an open stairway above a rock garden leads to second-floor courtrooms.

FR17 Cañon City Public Library

1902, C. C. Rittenhouse. 516 Macon St.

Red sandstone sandwiches beige-colored stone on the walls of Cañon City's Carnegie library. Pilasters further define the symmetrical facade and highlight the transomed bays. Stone dentils and scalloped woodwork highlight the bracketed eaves of this one-story edifice with a low hipped roof broken by a gable that accents the central entrance. More homey, romantic touches are provided by the two rustic chimneys and the cozy fireplaces and golden oak woodwork of a little-altered interior. A modern two-story addition is fortunately hidden behind the original.

FR18 Old Post Office and Federal Building

1931, James A. Wetmore, OSA. 505 Macon Ave. (northeast corner of 5th St.) (NR)

This Beaux-Arts federal building, which borrows from McKim, Mead and White's Boston Public Library, has a smooth limestone foundation and terracotta skin covering reinforced concrete and hollow tile, under a red Spanish tile roof. The south front is typical of late Italian Renaissance Revival structures, as are the rich facade details in terracotta. The fanlight arch of the front entry, capped by a terracotta keystone, is echoed in six multipaned front windows, which are supported by a set of balusters and separated with pilasters and medallions under a wide, dentiled cornice. Large corner windows have molded sills supported by corbels and triangular pedimented heads. Oversized iron lanterns flank the main entrance in a rigidly symmetrical facade. The richly detailed lobby has Neoclassical ceiling mold-

ing, oak paneling, and marble bordering the terrazzo floor, with marble stairs to a small second floor that once housed offices. This late example of Beaux-Arts Neoclassicism is a throwback to an earlier era of monumental proportions, excellent detailing, fine materials, and high levels of craftsmanship. When the post office moved elsewhere in 1990, this little-altered landmark became the Fremont Center for the Arts.

FR19 Christ Episcopal Church

1902, Thomas MacLaren. 800 Harrison Ave. (southeast corner of 8th St.)

This T-plan English Gothic Revival church, built in ashlar stone and covered by a steep-pitched roof, was designed by the architect of a number of buildings in English period revival styles in Colorado Springs. This church is distinguished by a thin stone belfry.

FR20 St. Scholastica Academy Fine Arts Building

1897. Hazel Ave. and 7th St.

Benedictine nuns from Chicago took over a financially ailing military school in 1890 and transformed it into a school for young ladies. The three-story east classroom building, now used for the fine arts, still stands amid newer campus structures. Designed in a typical turn-of-the-century institutional mode, the brick building has heavy-hooded, round-topped windows and a mansard roof with pedimented dormers suggestive of the Italianate style and Carpenter's Gothic detailing on the entry porch.

FR21 4th Street Bridge

1891, Bullen Bridge Company. 4th St. (NR)

A venerable crossing of the Arkansas River built by a Pueblo company, this all-steel truss bridge with cantilevered wooden sidewalks leads to the old South Cañon City residential neighborhood and some notable nineteenth-century houses.

FR22 Robison Mansion

1884, Marean and Norton. 12 Riverside Dr. (southeast corner of 1st St.) (NR)

One of Colorado's best-preserved Second Empire edifices is located on a two-block site. Lyman Robison, owner of mines in Cripple Creek and Leadville, built this 6,000-square-foot, three-story residence of native sandstone and pressed brick from the local Catlin brickyard. Wrought ironwork tops the cornice, while tall, narrow windows capped by ornamental lintels pierce the mansard roof. Two-story bay windows project from the east and west sides of the house, and a two-story porch supported by classical columns stretches across the front. The interior has three fireplaces, seven bedrooms, two bathrooms, a solarium, and a carved walnut staircase. On an expansive, well-landscaped, tree-shaded site beside the Arkansas River, the residence and its two-story carriage house have been restored, the latter as a restaurant.

FR23 DeWeese House Lodge

c. 1886. 1226 Elm Ave.

Dallas DeWeese, who platted the surrounding Lincoln Park neighborhood thirty years earlier, built this two-story, thirteen-room log house with gables, balconies, decorative shingles, and ornamental porch columns that relieve the dark wood and heavy massing. De Weese was a noted hunter who collected big game trophies from all over the world and contributed specimens to the Denver Museum of Natural History and other institutions. In appreciation, the Dall sheep, a snowy white mountain beast, was named for him. His Queen Anne Style house was designed as a hunting lodge. It is now a bed and breakfast inn.

FR24 Skyline Drive

1905. 2.5 miles west of Cañon City on U.S. 50

One of the best-preserved early scenic drives for motorists, Skyline Drive was built for $6,400 by convict labor as a 2.5-mile excursion along the ridge of Cañon City's western hogback formation, with its precipitous dropoffs and fine views. Opened as a two-way buggy drive, it was later converted to a paved, one-way auto road with deep dips and steep hills. The arch (1932) at the west entrance contains rocks from every U.S. state and was also built by convict labor.

FR25 Buckskin Joe

1958. 5 miles west of Cañon City on U.S. 50

This mock western town borrowed its name from the original Buckskin Joe in Park County. Among the buildings relocated in the 160-acre theme park are an old-time jail, saloon, assay office, hardware store, livery stables, opera house, and the store and post office allegedly operated by silver tycoon Horace A. W. Tabor in the original Buckskin Joe. This reconstructed main street has served as a set for *Cat Ballou, The Duchess and the Dirtwater Fox,* and other movies. The "frontier town" is open summers only and features mock hangings, gunfights, and stagecoach and burro rides. Such Wild West attractions have been augmented in recent years by a nearby recreational vehicle park, rafting, jeeping, and helicopter tours.

FR26 Royal Gorge Bridge and Incline Railway

1929, George Cole. 8 miles west of Cañon City via U.S. 50 (NR)

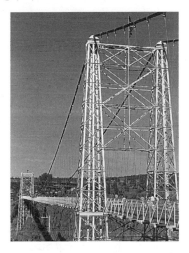

Architect George Cole of the Royal Gorge Bridge and Amusement Company designed and supervised construction of the 1,220-foot-long "World's Highest Suspension Bridge" with a view of the Arkansas River 1,053 feet below. The three-quarter-inch steel cables are composed of 2,100 strands of wire anchored in the canyon's granite walls and suspended from four towers rising 75 feet above the roadway. In 1931 Cole built an incline railroad to carry passengers from the rim to the canyon floor and back again. The D&RG track in the bottom of the gorge boasts its own engineering marvel, a hanging bridge suspended over the river from the canyon walls. The suspension bridge, incline railway, aerial tram, and surrounding 5,000-acre park are owned by Cañon City. Some 500,000 visitors annually come to this bridge, which goes nowhere but provides a fine view, not only of a natural wonder but also of some awesome engineering.

Florence

Florence (1873, 5,187 feet) was founded by James McCandless, who named it for his daughter. Eleven years earlier, oil bubbling to the surface of Oil Creek had inspired Alexander M. Cassidy to dig a well. He found the first oil field in the Rocky Mountain West and supposedly the second in the country. At one time 75 wells pumped 3,000 barrels of crude oil daily, and Standard, United, and other national firms had storage and processing facilities here. Until it ceased production in 1988, Oil Well No. 42 (1889), north of Florence on Cyanide Avenue, was said to be the oldest continuously producing commercial well in the world. Continental Oil Company (Conoco), which started here as the Arkansas Valley Oil Company, still dominates the skyline with its refinery stacks. Oil wells, coal mining, and a nearby Portland cement plant made Florence one of Colorado's major industrial centers by the early 1900s. Today Florence boasts the largest federal prison complex in the United States, which is the town's major employer.

Old Florence, between 2nd Street and the D&RG tracks from Crawford to Santa Fe avenues, is blessed with large old brick homes as well as brick commercial buildings with ornate classical stone trim dating to the town's 1892–1920s boom era. An unusually intact Main Street includes a Decoesque theater, the Rialto (1923), a Sulllivanesque Masonic temple (c. 1905), and the Oasis Tavern in the Vannest Building (1895), of rough-faced local sandstone.

FR27 Gumaer House

1893. 225 E. Main St. (Colorado 115)

Romanesque Revival and bungaloid elements, an unusual mix, prevail in this large clapboard house on a rough-faced red sandstone foundation culminating in porch balustrades. Tuscan columns and a portecochère add classical touches to the home of cattle baron and business tycoon Augustus R. Gumaer. In 1994 it was converted to a funeral home.

FR28 McCandless Building

1894. 109–111 E. Main St.

Florence's founder, James McCandless, constructed this three-story red brick structure, distinguished by an intact storefront with recessed entrances between cast iron pillars from the Riverside Ironworks of Kansas City. Above a full-width clerestory, upper floors contain a two-story interior atrium with a third-story balcony. This commercial building has housed various businesses, including a hotel. It belongs to a block of fine commercial buildings, among them the prototypical corner First National Bank (c. 1900), with its entry flanked by fluted columns and Greek classical detailing.

FR29 Hotel Florence

1906. 201 W. Main St. (southwest corner of Santa Fe Ave.)

Built for mercantile use, this two-story red brick hotel with an elaborately corniced corner entry is trimmed with stone banding and has arched, paired second-story windows. In the 1990s, after a stint as a nursing home, it was refurbished and reopened as a hotel.

FR30 Denver & Rio Grande Depot

c. 1910. South end of Pikes Peak Ave. (at Railroad St.)

Florence's D&RG depot, a long, low brick building with a red tile roof, is now the Florence Senior Center. Elongated wings, wide eaves, and a paneled frieze give it a Prairie Style horizontality.

FR31 **Florence Pioneer Museum**

1894, Philip Griffith, builder. Pikes Peak Ave. and Front St.

This somber, gray facade of rough-cut ashlar sandstone belies an exciting past. The two-story corner commercial structure was once a saloon, with gambling in the basement and a bordello upstairs. It also served as a hay and grain barn, a draft office during World War I, and an Eagles Lodge Hall. Today the Pioneer Museum exhibits historic mining and oil drilling equipment, radios, clothing, and firearms. Florence's original jail (c. 1875), relocated behind the museum, is constructed of 2-by-6-inch wood slabs criss-crossed at the corners and has 6-by-6-inch barred windows.

FR32 **Florence Mortuary** (McCandless House)

1889. 120 N. Pikes Peak Ave.

Town founder James McCandless moved his family to this Queen Anne Style house of brick with stone trim after succeeding in several commercial enterprises, including oil and Portland cement. The three-story house with semicircular entry and window bays and a second-story porch tucked under the eaves has been modified for use as a funeral home. McCandless, who became the town's key businessman and a state senator, originally built and occupied the log cabin (c. 1869) at 209 North Petroleum Avenue.

FR33 **Post Office**

1936, Louis A. Simon, OSA. 121 N. Pikes Peak Ave. (southwest corner of W. 2nd St.) (NR)

This L-shaped light brick box of classical proportions is stripped of ornament but hints at Art Deco inspiration. Recessed rectangular windows are outlined by stepped brick courses, and the concrete face around the front door is fluted and extends to include two adjacent windows. A cast panel of zigzag pattern tops the door.

Inside, the original tile floor, tile wainscot, and fluted ceiling molding are intact, as is a 1937 WPA mural in vivid pastel shades, *Antelope Grazing,* by Olive Rush, who also painted murals for the La Fonda Hotel and the Public Library in Santa Fe, New Mexico;

the State College of New Mexico; and the post office in Pawhuska, Oklahoma.

FR34 **Robinson House**

1897. 529 E. 2nd St. (northwest corner of Crawford Ave.)

Profuse Carpenter's Gothic detail makes this blond brick Queen Anne Style house the finest in town. A turned-spindle porch fronts the house, and an octagonal, bell-shaped tower topped by an ornate lightning rod flanks the southeast side. A front oriel with flanking balconies gives the structure an exotic flavor. Thomas Robinson, a superintendent for the United Oil Company, also invested in the Florence and Cripple Creek Railroad. Beautifully maintained and landscaped, the house benefits from the quaint open concrete ditches that still irrigate this part of town.

FR35 **Federal Correctional Complex, Florence**

1993, LKA. Partners with Lescher and Mahoney DLR Group. Colorado 67, 2 miles south of Florence

As prisons have become a major growth industry since the 1980s, Florence welcomed the largest one ever built in the United States. It is actually four separate prisons designed to hold 2,350 people in what looks more like a community college than a corrections facility. The Postmodern design dresses up brick and concrete boxes with pediments, brick banding, blind roundel windows, and blue-green metal roofs. This $196 million complex, a joint venture of architects from Phoenix and Colorado Springs, has a "super max" for the nation's most dangerous convicts.

FR36 **Phantom Canyon Road**

1892. Fremont County 67–Teller County 86, between Florence and Victor

James McCandless and other local promoters built this wagon road to Cripple Creek, which David Moffat and local businessmen converted in 1894 to the Florence & Cripple Creek Railroad bed. The railroad shipped foodstuffs and supplies to Cripple Creek and carried ore to seven gold processing mills in

Florence until a 1912 flood washed out the line. The narrow, serpentine route, requiring eighteen bridges and forty-two trestles, was converted in 1938 to an auto trek as a WPA project. The Adelaide Bridge (1894, R. W. Stewart, chief engineer) is a 210-foot, three-span steel deck railroad viaduct to Adelaide (1894–1901), 11.5 miles north of Florence, one of a dozen Fremont County ghost towns.

Howard

A sign announces Howard (1877, 6,720 feet) as "The Home of 150 Nice People and a Few Soreheads." The Howard Bridge (1924, Minneapolis Steel and Machinery Company), off U.S. 50 over the Arkansas (NR), is a single-span, Warren pony truss structure. The Stout House (c. 1880, William Stout), located on the west side of U.S. 50 at mile marker 236 east of the town limits, is a two-story stone Italianate home built by a Tennessean who came west after the Civil War to establish a homestead and orchard. A fine old schoolhouse, on Cherry Creek Street (Fremont County 47), and other relics make this a rewarding side trip into the past.

Portland

This company town (1899, 5,100 feet), named for its cement plant, has a D&RG railroad spur to ship Portland cement to construction projects across the state. Portland cement has been manufactured here since 1898, using local deposits of lime, silica, and gypsum. In 1901 James McCandless of Florence, Lyman Robison of Cañon City, and other local businessmen incorporated the Portland Cement Company, later purchased by Charles Boettcher. Boettcher's Ideal Cement built a $10 million plant here in 1948 and a third plant in the 1970s. Small concrete-block dwellings built by the company cluster around a shady town park with concrete benches and tables made to demonstrate how attractive and durable the material can be. Concrete was also used to build the stylish three-story corporate headquarters, with its curvilinear parapeted gables, and the giant cylindrical and rectangular components of this dormant plant.

Rockvale

Like neighboring Williamsburg, Coal Creek, and several other county towns, Rockvale (1882, 5,350 feet) began as a coal camp. Remnants of the commercial district include the diminutive Rockvale Town Hall (1913), southeast corner of Railroad and Mesa streets, with its pressed concrete false front and wood-framed bell tower. The two-block downtown district of May and Knob streets includes the wood-frame vernacular St. Patrick's Church (1891).

Chaffee County   (CF)

This county, with the mighty Mosquito Range on the east and the soaring Sawatch Range to the west, originated with mining camps on Cache, Chalk, and Trout creeks and the Arkansas River. Chaffee County was carved from Lake County in 1879 and named for U.S. Senator Jerome Chaffee. County government originally sat at Granite, where the gold rush began in 1860. After Granite's mines, smelter, and population played out, the county moved its offices to Buena Vista in 1880 and to Salida in 1928.

The Denver & Rio Grande; Denver, South Park & Pacific; and Colorado Midland railroads all laid track through this crossroads county. Salida and Buena

Vista emerged as gridded and gritty railroad towns. The railroads were attracted not only by precious minerals. Fine building stone abounded: Salida granite, Maysville marble, and limestone from the Monarch and Kalbaugh quarries near Monarch Pass.

This montane county contains more 14,000-foot peaks than any other in the United States and also has river valley ranching and farming. Tourists fancy its mining-era ghost towns, especially St. Elmo, Vicksburg, and Winfield. The Arkansas River delights fishermen, kayakers, and white water rafters, while the mountains offer skiing, hiking, hunting, camping, and hot springs. San Isabel National Forest and the Collegiate Peaks and Buffalo Peaks wilderness areas occupy roughly three-fourths of the county. Of some 13,000 county residents, 5,000 live in Salida and another 1,800 in Buena Vista.

Salida

The county seat (1880, 7,036 feet) takes its name from the Spanish word for exit because of its location at the west end of the Arkansas River canyon. D&RG town developer and former territorial governor Alexander C. Hunt laid out a V-shaped town grid bounded by the converging Arkansas and South Arkansas rivers and the tracks hugging the riverbanks. The D&RG built a splendid depot, roundhouse, hotel, hospital, and shops at Salida, a strategic division point for trains headed south over Poncha Pass to the San Luis Valley, west over Marshall Pass, or north to Leadville. The large, two-story Queen Anne Style depot at the foot of F Street (the main street) was replaced by a 1930 Streamline Moderne depot, itself now gone. Local granite quarries and three brickyards fed a building boom that continued until the early 1900s.

Salida became a major rail, smelter, and supply town, with a population peaking at 5,065 in 1930. A low rate of growth since then has left Salida with one of Colorado's most intact downtown historic districts. First Street's fine collection of masonry commercial buildings includes the Salida Mail Building (1880), 127 East 1st, with a magnificent red brick facade, stone trim, and griffins topping the parapet; the Union Block (1880s), 130 West 1st, now the Salida Sweet

Shop, with an old-time soda fountain; and a homey, two-story clapboard bed and breakfast. Salida is most remarkable for fine, elaborately fronted double houses and terraces and small apartment buildings with Neo-Romanesque detailing. These include the A. M Carpenter Terrace (1903), 223–249 E Street, and the Swallow Apartments (1909), 348–350 F Street, perhaps by the same architect or builder.

CF01 **Manhattan Hotel**

1901. 228 N. F St. (on the Arkansas River) (NR)

At the downtown end of the F Street Bridge (1907, Pueblo Bridge Company) (NR) and Riverside Park, this brick castle for travelers sports heavy stone trim and a stony parapet of pyramidal finials. Ground-floor display windows are divided by iron columns and

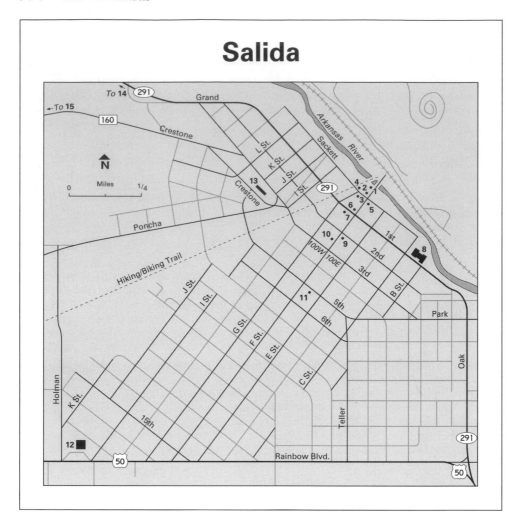

rough stone pilasters, the latter rising through elaborate ornamental brickwork to peaked finials. Round windows are set in the diapered brick frieze, which turns into a corner tower with a fine view of Haight Pavilion, a small frame observation shelter atop Tenderfoot Hill across the Arkansas.

CF02 Palace Hotel

1909. 204 N. F St. (north corner of Sackett Ave.)

Stone banding enlivens this red brick facade with first- and second-story dentils and corbeling on the third-story cornice. The

stepped parapet has recessed blind lunettes. Inside the venerable lobby are the original oak reception counter with a brass rail and transomed windows, under a 14-foot-high pressed metal ceiling.

CF03 Mon-Ark Shrine Club (Laura Evans Parlor House)

c. 1900. 129 W. Sackett Ave.

Laura Evans, who lived to the age of ninety, ran a "female boarding house" from the 1890s to 1950 in this plain, two-story, red brick building. Stucco now coats the facade and the bulging stone window trim, banding, and cornice. The one-story frame apartments across the street contain six small rooms used by Madam Evans's less popular boarders. The Shriners have converted the notorious bordello to their temple.

CF04 **Salida Performing Arts Center** (Salida Steam Plant)

1892. 200 W. Sackett Ave. (NR)

Various additions have made what was originally a small frame structure into a large complex of two, two-story buildings of local red brick with recessed brick panels between brick pilasters and round windows in the gables. The plant provided electricity for Salida from 1887 until it shut down in 1958. The 75-foot stack has been removed, and the complex was recycled in 1989 as a summer stock theater for the Powerhouse Players.

CF05 **Victoria Hotel and Tavern**

1886. 143 N. F St. (south corner of Sackett Ave.)

A typical commercial building, this two-story red brick hotel trimmed in brick and stone has a splendidly preserved corner saloon. After a 1979 renovation, the hardwood floor, pressed metal ceiling, mahogany back bar with festoons and garlands, and antique Walter's Beer clock match fairly well a large old photograph of the interior kept on the wall to settle arguments about how things used to be.

CF06 **A. T. Henry Building**

1886. 102–104 N. F St. (north corner of 1st St.)

A. T. Henry's handsome, red brick commercial block originally housed the Chaffee County Bank and other substantial businesses. Typical of Italianate commercial buildings, it has elongated, double-hung windows topped by stone arches on the second story and a bracketed metal cornice. A rooftop pediment framing a sunburst design marks the corner entry, and a secondary cornice tops transomed plate glass display windows. Even the metal rooftop finials survive on this cornerstone of the downtown district.

CF07 **Unique Theater** (Salida Opera House)

1889. 129 W. 1st St. (Colorado 291)

Window trim still shadows this stuccoed facade, which hides the once grandiose arched entrance and third-story stained glass windows of the opera house. The second story had fanlighted windows in the central and side bays. The massive, metal-bracketed cornice with a raised central pediment remains a reminder of the elegant detailing smothered under stucco. After the original wooden opera house burned in 1888, townsfolk subscribed $30,000 for this proof of Salida's sophistication. It has been converted to a movie house with a typical marquee on a facade begging for restoration.

CF08 **Heart of the Rockies Medical Center** (Railroad Hospital)

1900. 1st and B sts.

Of extensive railroad facilities in Salida, this is one of the few remnants, built and sustained for decades by monthly deductions from railroad workers' paychecks. Today the building is the centerpiece of a regional medical center. The two-story beige brick edifice has classical brick quoins, fluted cast iron porch columns, a balustrade surmounting the porch, and a garland frieze. Landscaped grounds with two fine antique fountains help incorporate newer two-story wings.

CF09 **Knights of Pythias Hall**

1895. 201 F St.

Another impressive commercial corner, this has a first floor constructed of rough-faced stone blocks, with stone stringcourses elaborating the second story. The metal cornice is ornamented with floral swags and egg-and-dart molding, and a corner clock recalls the time when the First National Bank occupied the ground floor.

CF10 **Sandusky Block**

1907. 222 F St.

This symmetrical, light brick beauty has first-story stone columns and second-story brick pilasters with detailed classical capitals. Square, transomed storefront windows are echoed by large, square-paned second-story windows. A generous brick cornice is a lively collage of banding, central name panel, and two lunettes with classical garlands. S. W. Sandusky opened a dry goods business at this location, which operated until 1930. The building was restored in 1985. Next door, the equally exuberant Strait-McKenna Building (1902) is a brickmason's tour de force with its diapered and corbeled frieze.

CF11 Gray Cottage

1882. 125 E. 5th St. (NR)

Profuse Carpenter's Gothic detail inspired the *Salida Mountain Mail* to call this house "a daisy," "first rate in every respect," and "the neatest home in the country." Garret and Julia Gray, enriched by their Madonna Mine on Monarch Pass, piled ornament on this eclectic clapboard cottage with pineapple pendants at the entry.

CF12 Salida Hot Springs

1937, WPA. 410 W. Rainbow Blvd.

Located in the heart of Centennial Park, Colorado's largest indoor hot springs pool was built by 200 WPA workers to channel hot, clear, odorless spring water into a 25-meter lap pool, a wading pool, and six private hot tubs. The original two-story Mission Revival facade of pink stucco has lost its rounded parapet and upstairs windows during remodelings, which also added a gable roof. Adjacent Centennial Park hosts the Salida History Museum, Chamber of Commerce Information Center, recreational facilities, and a D&RG caboose.

CF13 Chaffee County Courthouse

1932, Walter De Mordaunt. 104 Crestone Ave.

A dentiled terracotta cornice is the icing on this yellow brick Art Deco creation. It defers to classicism with fluted terracotta pilasters, travertine marble entry surround, and symmetrical plan with a center bay. In a 1968 judicial and jail annex, the pilasters are repeated in brick, as is the symmetrical, vertical massing. Inside the original courthouse are wrought iron stair railings, heavy glass

CF13 Chaffee County Courthouse

light fixtures, carved floral ornamentation, and floors and trim of travertine from the nearby quarry town of Wellsville. Walter De Mordaunt's Art Deco designs for stained glass windows were rejected by security-minded county commissioners. The architect nevertheless gave Chaffee County a dramatic courthouse with an especially notable interior.

CF14 Ohio-Colorado Smelting and Refining Company Smokestack

1917, Emil Bruderlin. 2 miles north of Salida on Chaffee County 150 via Colorado 291 (NR)

Although dwarfed by the 1,245-foot-high International Nickel Company smokestack in

Ontario, Canada, and the 600-foot power company stacks in Craig, Colorado, this is the tallest edifice in southern Colorado and the tallest smelter stack left in the state. Most of these towering monuments to ore processing, once the state's major industry, have been razed.

Emil Bruderlin, a structural engineer, designed this 365-foot-high stack to disperse the noxious fumes created in the processing of gold and silver ores after area residents and farmers claimed that a shorter (85-foot) stack built in 1901 was ineffective. (The short stack was razed in the late 1920s to provide brick for homes in Salida.) It took two years, $43,000, and 264 railroad cars of brick to build the new stack. After the smelter closed in 1920, this stack twice came within twenty-four hours of demolition before being rescued by the Salida Museum Association. It is built of large, glazed face bricks fronting common bricks strengthened with steel rods on a four-tiered octagonal brick base. The concrete foundation is sunk 32 feet into the ground. The stack is 42 feet wide at the base and 17 feet wide at the top, where the lip of the stack has embedded silver dollars. Eighty acres of furnaces, blowers, and railroad facilities which surrounded the stack are mostly gone, as is the surrounding community known as Smeltertown.

CF15 **Chaffee County Poor Farm Bed and Breakfast** (Chaffee County Poor Farm)

1892, Lawrence Brothers, builders. 8495 Chaffee County 160 (NR)

Three miles north of Salida on the banks of the Arkansas River, the former county poor farm sits on a scenic, 11-acre site. The plain, two story, T-plan house is of red brick on a stone foundation with hipped roofs. Its thirteen rooms once housed the county's hardship cases, who earned their living by working the 120-acre farm. The frame barn (1892) on a stone foundation survives, as does the old icehouse, now remodeled as a cottage, and the one-story, red brick pest house by the river. From 1944 until 1963 the local Grange used this as its hall. In 1982 Herbert and Dorothy Hostetler converted it to a bed and breakfast.

Poncha Springs

Poncha Springs (1877, 7,469 feet), like the nearby pass and mountain, takes its name from the Poncha Hot Springs. Poncha Pass, the northern gateway into the San Luis Valley, attracted stage lines and the D&RG, while the town of Poncha Springs, originally called South Arkansas, became a way station on the South Arkansas River. James P. True platted the townsite and opened a general store in 1879.

CF16 **Hutchinson Ranch**

1874; additions. 9104 E. U.S. 50, 2 miles east of Poncha Springs (NR)

A two-story frame house built in 1874 is the old timer on this ranch. It is sheathed with vertical board-and-batten siding and adorned with bargeboard and a carved entry hood. Ranch outbuildings lolling about in a meadow along the South Arkansas River include a log granary, bunkhouse, blacksmith shop, and corrals. Joseph S. Hutchinson, a Civil War veteran who became a mine superintendent at Granite, started this cattle ranch with his wife, Annabelle.

CF17 **Town Hall** (Poncha Springs Schoolhouse)

1883, C. B. Frunash, builder. 330 Burnett St. (NR)

Light stone quoins and a belvedere-type bell cupola distinguish this two-story Italianate schoolhouse of red brick. Within the L plan are classrooms with 12-foot-high-pressed tin ceilings, slate blackboards, Oregon fir floors, and pine trim and wainscoting. Today the well-preserved schoolhouse contains a museum and town offices in a park shaded by large old cottonwoods.

CF18 **Jackson Hotel**

1878. 220 Main St. (U.S. 285), at U.S. 50 (northwest corner of True Ave.) (NR)

For the town's principal hostelry, Henry A. Jackson brought in the lumber and furnishings, even the rosewood piano, by oxcart. The two-story L-plan structure accommodates thirty-one guest rooms. The hotel has a gable roof with overhanging eaves and decorative brackets, lap siding, and a second-story balcony to capitalize on splendid views of the Arkansas Valley and surrounding mountains. The corbeled brick chimney and frame outside stairs are two clues to its antiquity.

CF19 Monarch

1879–1903. On the D&RG and U.S. 50

Monarch, formerly called Chaffee, takes its name from 11,312-foot Monarch Pass, four miles to the west. This tiny D&RG railroad town, which boasted the biggest limestone quarry in the state, is now gone. The Madonna Mine, oldest and richest of Chaffee County mines, is one of many historic structures along U.S. 50 as it climbs Monarch Pass. The Monarch Ski Area is on the east side of the pass, and the Monarch Pass Visitors Center is at the top. The latter is an earth-sheltered structure with a granite and glass front for a U.S. Forest Service information station and the Monarch Aerial Tramway.

Nathrop

Nathrop (1879, 7,690 feet) was founded by and named for Charles Nachtrieb, who established an adobe home and flour mill (1868) here. The spelling of his name was not the only casualty; Nachtrieb himself was shot in the back in 1881 by a disgruntled employee. The town became an important rail stop for the Denver, South Park & Pacific, which followed Chalk Creek west to the Alpine Tunnel. Nathrop has boomed since the 1980s as a launch site for Arkansas River rafters and kayakers.

CF20 Nathrop Schoolhouse

1881, Richard Weeks. 11405 Chaffee County 197B

Richard Weeks of Buena Vista was paid $2,175 to design and erect this one-room school with a stone foundation and a teacher's platform. The conventional lap-sided structure is enhanced by round-arched wooden window and door trim and the

CF18 Jackson Hotel

usual open bell tower. Since the school closed in 1946, the building has served as a community center.

CF21 St. Elmo

1880–1952. 16 miles west of Nathrop on Chaffee County 162 (NRD)

St. Elmo, one of the West's best-preserved ghost towns, hosted several hundred miners from the 1880s to the 1910s. Sited on Chalk Creek in a spectacular and isolated mountain valley, this mining and milling town is surrounded by deep forests, which inspired its original name, Forest City. The second name came from pioneer storekeeper Griffith Evans, who fancied Augusta Jane Evans's sentimental novel, *Saint Elmo*. He hired L. C. Cornwell, a civil engineer, to survey the site and design a town plan. Cornwell imposed a gridiron of right-angled streets and rectangular blocks that ignored both branches of Chalk Creek and equally serpentine Grizzly Creek, as well as the hilly outskirts of town. Because the plan was impractical and rendered many lots useless, even the town fathers came to ignore it. Buildings were allowed in street right-of-ways, creating irregular setbacks and roadways.

Carpenter Frederick W. Brush built many of the commercial and residential buildings in St. Elmo. Two fires during the 1890s destroyed much of the business district, including the opera house. Forty-three nineteenth-century structures survive in this rare concentration of log and balloon-frame buildings that were the town's first and only generation of architecture.

Log cabins varied with the regional and ethnic origins of their builders. The McKenzie-Ottoson House (c. 1885), on the east side of Poplar Street across from the Pawnee Mill, is made of peeled logs joined in saddle notches with mud chinking. It has gable ends dressed with vertical planks, showing an Anglo propensity for making the gable end the facade. The Helmer-Savard House (c. 1888), on the south side of Gunnison Avenue four doors west of 1st Avenue, is a side-gabled house with board-and-batten gable ends and V-notched logs.

Decades after everyone else left, one family, the Starks, stayed on to run their store and guard the town against the depredations that leveled the nearby towns of Alpine, Hancock, Iron City, and Romley. Only after Tony Stark was taken to the state mental hospital in Pueblo and his wife, Annabelle, to a Salida nursing home did St. Elmo become a ghost. In recent decades, some of the old homes have been converted to summer cabins, whose residents have restored the plank sidewalks, town halls, school, jail, and Home Comfort Hotel. In the surrounding Chalk Creek Mining District, many mine, mill, railroad, and house ruins linger.

CF22 Pawnee Mining and Milling Company

1880. Northeast corner of Poplar St. and Main St.

Of many mill buildings once in and around St. Elmo, this is the best preserved, thanks to gamblers who feed the Colorado Historical Society's preservation fund. The vertical slab log complex includes a stamp mill, barn, stable, blacksmith shop, and ore wagon scales.

CF23 St. Elmo General Store (Miners Exchange)

1880. Near the northwest corner of Main St. and Poplar St.

The faded name on the clapboard false front of the Miners Exchange recalls earlier times, when this one-story, round log building with a tin gable roof did double duty as a bank and a saloon. The proprietor kept cash on hand to cash miners' paychecks until the last and most lucrative mine, the Mary Murphy, closed in 1922. Instead of the usual bracketed Italianate false front, this building has relatively simple cornice and window treatment.

CF24 Pat Hurley's Saloon

1892. North side of Main St., second building west of the Miners Exchange

A large curvilinear parapet once topped the false front on one of the most impressive edifices in town. All that is gone, but pedimented windows still adorn the second story of this gambling saloon with raw vertical plank sides, where the town's Saturday night dances were held upstairs. During Prohibition, Hurley's was rehabilitated as the St. Elmo Mercantile.

CF25 Town Hall

1880s. South side of Main St., three doors west of 1st St. opposite the Home Comfort Hotel

The clapboard front and vertical plank sides of St. Elmo's town hall (c. 1885) and jail (c. 1881) are covered by a tin gable roof with a square, open bell tower. Storefront windows and a transomed double door allow light into the otherwise windowless shack. The jail, attached to the town hall via a heavy wooden door, still has a tiny exercise area and two windowless wooden cells with a ball and chain.

CF26 Home Comfort Hotel

c. 1885. North side of Main St. opposite Town Hall

The struggle of St. Elmo's last residents, the Stark family, with the deep snows and bitter cold that lock in the town from October to June are evoked by this two-story, raw plank, false-fronted structure with frame additions connecting the adjacent front-gabled cottage. Annabelle, the last of the Starks, maintained the Home Comfort as a sixteen-room boarding house, general store, post office, telegraph desk, and cabin rental agency until the 1950s. Melanie Milam restored the Home Comfort and the huge antique "Home Comfort" cook stove, which gave its name to the hotel it heats.

CF25 Town Hall (far left)   CF26 Home Comfort Hotel

CF27 **Schoolhouse**

1882. North end of 1st St.

To face the country weather, this white clapboard one-room schoolhouse has half-size windows, a narrow door, and a small, low belfry. On its elevated position on a hill overlooking the town, the school embodies mining town hopes for permanence and gentility.

Buena Vista

Buena Vista (1879, 7,954 feet), with its splendid view of the Collegiate Range to the west, lives up to its name. Pioneer prospectors, the story goes, named the peaks for their girfriends: Mt. Flossie, Mt. Fannie, Mt. Daisy Mae, Mt. Lulu, and so forth. After Buena Vista developed aspirations to respectability the peaks were renamed Oxford, Harvard, Yale, Princeton, and Columbia in 1896 by I. D. Whitney, a professor of the Harvard University Mining School. Cottonwood Creek and the Arkansas River converge here, as did three railroads. Buena Vista became a raucous center for railroaders, teamsters, cowboys, and miners. The town later lost ore processing, smelting, and railroad business, as well as population and the county seat, to faster-growing Salida.

Buena Vista was laid out as a typical grid railroad town. Unlike most mining towns, which did not "waste" land on parks, Buena Vista created McPhelemy Park, on West Main Street at U.S. 24, a tree-shaded retreat along Cottonwood Creek. Another attraction is the Old Midland Railroad Scenic Route, an abandoned standard-gauge rail grade with spectacular views and stonework, as well as four short, in-line tunnels blasted through solid rock.

Today, agriculture, the state reformatory, and tourists sustain Buena Vista. The well-kept downtown boasts Italianate masonry buildings with elaborate metal cornices. The Buena Vista Hotel (1879), 301 East Main Street, supposedly built by seventy people in one day as the Railroad Hospital and Black Hills Club Room, has been restored as Buena Vista Square. Other Main Street landmarks include the Webb Hotel (1885), 414 East Main, with its cast iron–columned storefront, now a bed and breakfast inn. Palace Manor, as "Cockeyed Liz" Marshall called her bordello, is an Italianate double two doors west of the courthouse. The barrel-vaulted, 600-seat Orpheum Opera House (1910), 411 East Main Street, with a cast stone facade and an exterior in need of restoration, was originally a livery stable, converted most recently to a bank. The so-called Wedge Building (1883), 111 East Main Street, is a two-story brick flatiron building with decorative brick frieze and cornice. Built as a dry goods store, it still has the oversized corner canopy added when it was a gas station before recent conversion to offices.

CF28 **Buena Vista Heritage Museum** (Old Chaffee County Courthouse and Jail)

1883, George E. King. 501 E. Main St. (NR)

For a safe full of county records stolen from Granite in a successful effort to capture the county seat designation, Buena Vistans erected this two-story brick courthouse inscribed in stone, "Dedicated to Justice 1882." Leadville architect George E. King produced the design, executed by local builder Diedrich Fisher, who also built an early Fremont County courthouse in Cañon City. Fisher constructed this courthouse and the matching jail for $50,000. He used red brick with hand-tooled sandstone from the Ruby Mountain Quarry near Nathrop for the foundation, quoins, and trim. The classic Italianate edifice has central, pedimented bays on each side and a high-hatted octagonal cupola. Edward Kruger, a German tinsmith, produced the paneled and bracketed cornice and the metal roof for the cupola with its stag weathervane. After Buena Vista lost the county seat to Salida in 1928, this became a school, to which the WPA added

a gym in 1937. Since the 1980s, the courthouse has been restored and occupied by the Buena Vista Heritage Museum. The second floor contains a display with scale models of the Alpine Tunnel and the three railroads that chugged into Chaffee County.

CF29 **Buena Vista Town Hall** (Bank of Buena Vista)

1883. 210 E. Main St. (northwest corner of Railroad Ave.)

Double entry doors grace the corner entrance of this two-story brick Italianate building with carved stone trim. The corner entrance is advertised by a pediment rising above the bracketed metal cornice. After the Great Depression closed the bank, it became a welfare center for distributing food and clothing before being reborn as the town hall, still with two original walk-in safes.

CF30 **Lariat Saloon**

1885. 208 E. Main St.

This handsome red brick building is crisply decorated with light-colored stonework very similar to that on the town hall next door. The upper-story windows have stone trim carved with garlands, and the pilasters have carved stone block capitals. The large, ornate, dentiled and bracketed metal cornice has a central signature pediment. Like most other buildings constructed during Buena Vista's 1880s boom, it is Italianate in character. Inside what has been the Lariat Saloon since the 1930s, local cattle brands have been burned into the knotty pine wall paneling.

CF31 **Wright-Sindlinger House**

1881. 400 W. Main St.

A rare Colorado vernacular example of the Second Empire style, the Wright-Sindlinger House has multiple dormers capped by the dentiled cornice that wraps the entire mansard roof. Stone trim distinguishes arched windows on the first floor, and the dormers have unique teardrop-patterned windows. Attorney William D. Wright built the house, which was later acquired by lumberyard owner D. C. Sindlinger. After stints as a rooming house and a restaurant, it has been restored as a private residence. A similar Second Empire home, now the Centennial Manor Apartments, is at 508 West Main Street.

CF32 Visitors' Center (St. Rose of Lima Catholic Church)

1880. 343 S. U.S. 24 in Forest Square Park

Built in an effort to civilize a raunchy railroad town, this clapboard Carpenter's Gothic church retains a shamrock cross on its open bell tower. Parishioner James Mahon hauled lumber donated by Thomas Starr's Poncha Springs Mill, and priest and parishioners constructed their church. A symmetrical plan, nice detail, generous landscaping, and good maintenance make this a gold star example of white frame country churches. On the eve of the church's demolition in the 1970s, a savior arose in the form of a church member and preservationist who arranged to move the church to Forest Square Park for use as a visitors' center.

CF33 Grace Episcopal Church

1889, Lannan Brothers, builders. Southwest corner of W. Main and Linderman Ave. (NR)

Intricate board-and-batten siding sheathes this frame church with a rose window, Gothic lancets, and Carpenter's Gothic detailing on the frame buttresses and arched entry hood. The steep gable roof is capped by a square, open belfry. Inside, exposed timber trusses are trimmed with turned pendants and curved brackets and accented by a Gothic arch setting off the chancel. The church was consecrated on September 13, 1889, by a congregation founded in 1882.

CF34 Vicksburg

1881–1885. Chaffee County 390, 8 miles west of turnoff from U.S. 24 (NR)

Vicksburg and nearby Winfield lie along a gentle dirt road lined with mining ruins. Vicksburg, arguably the most orderly and best-planned mining town in Colorado, has a grand allée of Balm-of-Gilead trees which were planted after an early-day fire denuded the area. The trees shade seven evenly set-back hewn, slab, or peeled log cabins with low-pitched roofs. One miner's cabin (1880s, George Anderson) has been set aside as a museum by the Clear Creek Canyon Historical Society of Chaffee County. Named for pioneer storekeeper Vick Keller, this mining camp claimed several hundred residents in the early 1880s. Although the town lost its post office after only four years, a few residents have maintained the tiny wooden water flumes (1883) lining both sides of Main Street, complete with boxes for cold water food storage. Residents are not allowed to winter in Vicksburg; rock slides and avalanches have narrowly missed the town on either side.

CF35 Winfield

1881–1912. Chaffee County 390, 4.5 miles west of Vicksburg (NR)

Set in an open mountain meadow, this town lacks the tree-shaded orderliness of Vicksburg, but the Clear Creek Canyon Historical Society has overseen equally diligent care of four cabins and the tiny, false-fronted frame Winfield Schoolhouse, now the Winfield Museum. Across from the schoolhouse-museum is the Ball Cabin, typical of early miners' homes.

Granite

Granite (1868, 8,920 feet) was the first Lake County seat (1868–1878) and, for one year, the first seat for Chaffee County. Granite lies at the junction of the Arkansas River and Cache Creek, where argonauts first found pay dirt in 1860. The stage stop and town hub for the upper Arkansas Valley until eclipsed by Leadville to the north and Buena Vista to the south, it retains a hewn log blacksmith shop and livery stable (1870s) and several antique log and stone structures. On a hillside overlooking the town and fronting the old stage road is the white clapboard Granite Schoolhouse (1888), with its steep gable roofs, shed additions, and outdoor privies.

Lake County   (LK)

Lake County (1861) lured miners after 1860 gold strikes on the headwaters of the Arkansas River. Oro City, the initial camp on California Gulch, boomed briefly during the 1860s and became the first county seat. It was replaced by nearby Leadville after rich silver finds gave birth to that two-mile-high city.

Besides silver and gold, Lake County has produced zinc, lead, and molybdenum, ultimately the richest mineral resource of all. Between the 1950s and the 1970s, the Climax Molybdenum Mine produced more than half the world's supply. The molybdenum market collapsed in the 1980s, and by 1990 Lake County fell to its lowest population since 1870—6,007. Only two towns survive, Leadville and Twin Lakes.

Much of Lake County is two miles high or higher. Despite a growing season of forty-three days, which wags claim never come in a row, there is some ranching and hay farming. Mountain sports are popular in a county walled in by the Mosquito Range on the east and by the Sawatch Range, with Colorado's highest peaks, on the west. The World War II army ski troops of the Tenth Mountain Division at Camp Hale trained on a nearby hill which evolved into the Ski Cooper winter sports area. San Isabel National Forest and the Mount Massive Wilderness Area occupy about half the county. Recreational activities generated rustic resort architecture, which is showcased in the Twin Lakes and Inter-Laken historic districts.

Leadville

The Lake County seat (1877, 10,152 feet) was born in a prospector's pan. The initial settlement of Oro City sprang up in 1860 along California Gulch as a gold camp. A decade later the black sand that had gummed gold miners' operations proved to be high-grade silver ore of lead carbonate and gave birth to Colorado's greatest silver city. By 1880 Leadville's 14,820 residents out numbered those of every Colorado city save Denver. Two dozen surrounding camps and towns popped up as its satellites.

Charles Boettcher, the German immigrant who became Colorado's most prominent industrialist and philanthropist, got his start selling hardware in Leadville. Upon his arrival in 1879, Boettcher found "The Magic City" infested with "any number of reckless people, lounging around doing nothing, just living on excitement. . . . People were living right on the streets. Many had tents, log cabins, or mere shelters covered with brush. The place was so crowded you could barely wedge your way through." Author Helen Hunt Jackson described Leadville as "a Monaco gambling room emptied into a Colorado spruce clearing."

By the time it was two years old, Leadville had thirty sawmills and four brickyards to feed a building boom. Frame construction and the need for charcoal to fuel eighteen smelters denuded this mountain valley of its once dense spruce forests. A century later aspen trees are slowly reforesting the two-mile high site, for which Colorado's two highest peaks, Mt. Elbert (14,433 feet) and Mount Massive (14,421 feet) form an awesome backdrop.

In 1896 Leadville built one of Colorado's most fantastic structures, the Ice Palace, which masqueraded as a castle on a three-acre site. This frame and ice-block sculpture

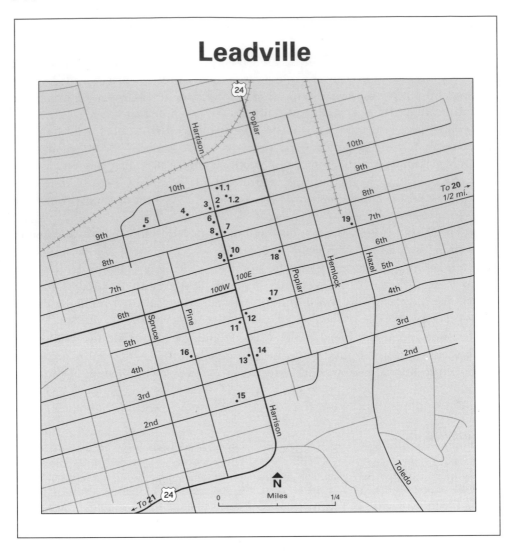

Leadville

measured 325 by 180 feet with 90-foot-high crenelated entry towers. Dedicated, like prototypes in Moscow, Quebec City, and St. Paul, to winter fun, it contained skating and curling rinks, a dance floor, a restaurant, and gaming rooms. An early spring thaw melted this fantasy.

The highest and wildest of America's silver cities, Leadville still looks like a mining town. Pell-mell expansion over surrounding mine tunnels left the city plagued by disappearing back yards, sinking streets, and black holes that swallow everything thrown into them. After the last smelter closed in 1961, the slag pile at the south end of Harrison Avenue was used instead of sand and salt to fight ice and snow on the streets in winter.

Leadville has been a "git-and-git-out" town, where miners took out what they could find but put very little back into the community. The three railroads that rushed in during the early 1880s have all pulled out. Not until 1951 did Leadville build a citywide sewer system, and not until the 1980s were the sidewalks on Harrison Avenue aligned, in a main street facelift that unearthed multiple levels of wooden sidewalks. Residents distinguish between the sunny and shady sides of the street, the climate being such that people on one side could be mowing their lawns while those on the other shovel snow.

Leadville's population sank by 1990 to 2,629, but the callused mining town refuses to knuckle under. One of Colorado's few National Historic Landmark Districts, Leadville is gradually recycling its rich history and architectural heritage to attract tourists. The main street, Harrison Avenue (U.S. 24), is lined with rare (for Colorado) Second Empire buildings, while residential side streets feature extravagant Carpenter's Gothic homes, such as those at 119 West 3rd Street and 208 West 6th Street; Mollie May's Brothel, at 131 West 5th Street; and the House with an Eye, named for its eyebrow dormer with an eye painted on the window glass (1879, Eugène Robitaille), 134 West 4th Street. The town is particularly notable for many frame miners' cottages with exuberant Carpenter's Gothic entries, porches, and bays on the facades of what might otherwise be called shacks.

LK01 Healy House and Dexter Cabin Museum

1878; 1879. 912 Harrison Ave.

Smelter tycoon August R. Meyer built the older of these houses, the white clapboard Healy House (LK01.1), enhanced by an Italianate bracketed and balustraded porch, shutters, pedimented lintels, and a bay window. After conversion to a boarding house in the 1890s, it received a third-story addition. Leadville schoolmarm Nellie A. Healy inherited the house in 1912 and provided rooms for her fellow teachers. Since 1947 the Colorado Historical Society has operated it as a house museum, remarkable for its top-of-the-town site and its interior. Exquisite Victorian furnishings demonstrate how quickly settlers in successful mining communities acquired comforts, luxuries, and bric-a-brac.

The Dexter Cabin (LK01.2), moved to the grounds from 110 West 3rd Street in 1947, is a two-room, hewn log cabin with a corbeled brick chimney and lavish interior. James Viola Dexter, a wealthy mine owner and dilettante, installed floors of black walnut and white oak, a Lincrusta-Walton anaglypta wall covering, and an orgy of Victorian artifacts.

LK02 Heritage Museum (Carnegie Library)

1904, Herbert C. Dimick. 192 E. 9th St. (northeast corner of Harrison Ave.)

Herbert Dimick, a Leadville architect, designed this two-story brick library, trimmed in gray sandstone but without the Neoclassical detailing usually found on Carnegie buildings. Round-arched doors and windows and the rough-faced sandstone base are its most ornate features. When a new, Modernist library opened at 1115 Harrison, this became a museum housing dioramas and artifacts of Leadville's early days.

LK03 Taylor House

1895, Herbert C. Dimick. 100 W. 9th St.

Herbert Dimick designed this two-story Queen Anne house on the most prominent hill in town for druggist George E. Taylor. The semicircular front porch with a domed roof topped by a semicircular bay is its most striking feature. Bargeboard pediments on the entry porch, over the second-story bay, and atop the second-story dormer lend symmetry to this clapboard house with elaborate shingle trim.

LK04 National Mining Hall of Fame and Museum (Lake County High School)

1900. 120 W. 9th St.

Rising above boxy school and museum additions, the ornate, pedimented dormers of the original Lake County High School building sport urn finials and corbeled compound brick chimneys. During the 1980s the abandoned school became a major mining museum. A bronze miner sculpted by Lori Atz greets visitors at the main entrance. The museum's Hall of Fame contains exhibits on famous miners such as prospector-turned-journalist George Hearst and Meyer Guggenheim, whose mines and smelters launched a family fortune that enriched eastern U.S. and European cities but gave nothing back to Leadville.

LK05 King House

1880, George E. King. 212 W. 9th St.

Local architect George King liked mansard roofs and put them on Leadville's best-known Second Empire landmarks, including the county courthouse, destroyed by fire in 1942. King capped his own modest house with a mansard roof and used another for its square tower. "Mr. King drew the plans for nearly all Leadville's best buildings," reported the *Leadville Weekly Democrat*, January 1, 1881. "As an architect he has no superior in our city." He experimented on his own house, which has second-story windows similar to those he used on the Tabor Grand Hotel and third-story roundels like those he used for the Delaware Block.

LK06 Englebach-Furman House

1895, Herbert C. Dimick (?); Francis Colahan, builder. 815 Harrison Ave.

August L. Englebach of the Englebach Machine Manufacturing Company built this house, which the *Leadville Herald Democrat* called "a fine sample of a modern dwelling, the round tower and ornamental woodwork

being in the best style of the building art." Besides the conical-roofed three-story corner tower, this frame Queen Anne house has roof cresting with finials, a pediment above the entrance, and diamond shingle trim. Owner-occupant Evelyn Furman is the author of several books about the Tabors and Leadville.

LK07 City Hall (Post Office)

1904. 800 Harrison Ave. (northeast corner of 8th St.)

A steep hipped slate roof with tiny hipped dormers, broad eaves, and snow catchers lends a Chateauesque air to this otherwise Neoclassical federal building with a dentiled cornice, slightly arched second-story windows, and round-arched first-floor windows with fanlights and keystones. The *Leadville Herald Democrat* praised the new building, with its handsome red and yellow brickwork and granite banding, but condemned as a waste of taxpayers' money the basement "lounging room for [mail] carriers and elegant marble wainscoted lavatory with a $600 shower bath." After the post office moved out in the 1970s, the city government moved in. Much of the marble and golden oak interior remains, as do the large interior transoms that brighten city offices.

LK08 First Presbyterian Church

1889. Eugène Robitaille, builder. 801 Harrison Ave. (northwest corner of 8th St.)

Eugène Robitaille, who came from Quebec in 1879, designed and made unusual Carpenter's Gothic trim for this granite-based, red brick Queen Anne church with that style's characteristic corner tower dominating the composition. Atop the tower, an open belfry and its bowed balustrade are clad with shingles under a flared pyramidal spire. The bells were moved to the congregation's new church. Its graceful predecessor has been converted to a visitors' center.

LK09 Tabor Grand Hotel

1885, George and John King. 1992, restoration. 701 Harrison Ave.

Named in honor of Leadville silver king and mayor Horace A. W. Tabor, the Tabor Grand Hotel became the Vendome Hotel in 1893

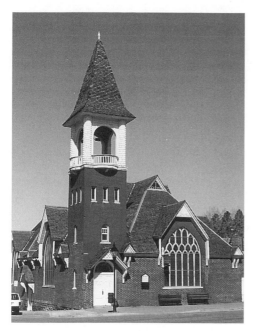

LK08 First Presbyterian Church

before closing in the 1970s. Repeated stripping of the building by short-term owners ended with the 1989 collapse of the northwest corner, exposing the naked interiors of rooms. A $3.1 million restoration in 1992 rehabilitated not only the fallen corner but the entire four-story red brick edifice for first floor retail space and thirty-eight upper-story units of low-income housing. An octagonal corner tower above the mansarded fourth floor is the outstanding feature of this exquisite Second Empire landmark. De-

LK09 Tabor Grand Hotel

tails include wooden pilasters mimicking cast iron storefronts, prominent fourth-floor dormers, and a bracketed metal cornice. The southwest corner room has an eccentric observatory jutting out over the sidewalk.

LK10 Delaware Block

1885, George King. 700 Harrison Ave. (northeast corner of 7th St.)

An iron-crested mansard roof over the angled corner entry and paired segmental-arched windows distinguish this three-story, red brick commercial building in the Second Empire style. The original owners, from Delaware, spent $80,000 to erect a first–rate business block, which their heirs sold in 1946 for half that amount. A $1 million restoration in the 1980s converted fifty offices to thirty-six hotel rooms with twelve-foot ceilings and six-foot windows. A mansard half-roof and elaborate geometric frieze adorn the Harrison Avenue facade, while the cornice is crowned by a broken pediment with the building's name inscribed.

LK11 Western Hardware Store

1880. 431 Harrison Ave. (southwest corner of 5th St.)

Built as the Manville and McCarthy Hardware and Miners Supply Company, this has been Western Hardware since 1920 and a fine example of an old-time hardware store. The two-story brick building has a cast iron storefront, bracketed cornice, and paired windows with segmental arches. Inside, in the north wall under a dentiled cornice, are more than 1,000 tiny drawers that offer a fortune in fixtures. The original counters, nail bins, and hardwood floors survive, as do the 15-foot ceilings of the full basement and first and second floors.

LK12 American National Bank

1891, Jerry Irwin, builder. 422 Harrison Ave. (southeast corner of 5th St.)

A turnip dome topped by a flagpole rises above the rounded corner entrance of this three-story Romanesque Revival bank building of red brick with a rough sandstone base and sandstone trim. Once the proudest bank in town, it is now a humble second-hand store.

LK13 Silver Dollar Saloon

1883, George King. 315 Harrison Ave.

An 1879 frame saloon was replaced by this two-story brick building with a bracketed metal cornice. The interior is unusually well preserved, although barn wood now hides the Italianate exterior. An oak Eastlake partition separates the old-fashioned antechamber from the main barroom. A classical cornice, frieze, beadwork, dentils, and Tuscan columns frame a diamond-dust back bar mirror. Beyond the main barroom and through swinging bat-wing doors are a dance hall and back rooms. The McMahon family, owners since 1943, have filled this 1880s interior with antiques, art, and animal trophies.

LK14 Tabor Opera House

1879, J. Thomas Roberts, builder. 308–312 Harrison Ave.

One memorable night in 1882, Oscar Wilde stepped onto the stage of the Tabor Opera House wearing a dark velvet suit, knee britches, and a Lord Byron collar. His full, sensuous lips parted in a smile, and he began to lecture the miners of Leadville on "The Practical Application of Aesthetic Theory to Exterior and Interior House Decoration, with Observations on Dress and Personal Ornament."

Like Wilde's lecture, this Italianate opera house, allegedly constructed in a hundred days, epitomizes the mining frontier's rush to respectability. The three-story brick building incorporates a central pedimented pavilion with a round-arched, fanlighted entry beneath a balcony. The entry is flanked by storefronts with their own recessed central entries. Flattened-arch sandstone window tops adorn the third floor, while round arches with carved keystones grace second-floor windows. The little-altered interior contains a wobbly wooden balcony with some 700 Andrews patent cast iron, plush-upholstered opera chairs, which were lugged over Weston Pass in wagons. Briefly known as the Weston Opera House, then as the Elks Opera House, the building was

acquired in 1955 by local resident and author Evelyn Furman, who opened it for tours and performances.

LK15 Pioneer Bar and Brothel

1882. 118 W. 2nd St.

The oldest continually operating brothel in Colorado died in 1970 with its last madam, Hazel Gillette "Ma" Brown, who wore cat's-eye spectacles set with real diamonds. Her house, built as the Pioneer Billiard Hall, is a two-story brick structure with rough stone quoins, banding, and window trim. It has a metal frieze and dentiled cornice with a rectangular parapet hiding behind a neon sign. A separate corner entrance leads to the upstairs rooms of this abandoned, decaying bordello. Next door is the Pastime Club, the sole survivor of some twenty-five saloons on once-notorious West 2nd Street.

LK16 St. George's Episcopal Church

1880, W. P. Westworth. 200 W. 4th St. (northwest corner of Pine St.)

W. P. Westworth, a Boston architect, is said to have modeled this high-style Gothic Revival church after St. George's in New York City. The small frame building has a double-pitch roof with a decorative truss in the steep peak that flows gracefully into the bargeboards. A central, open belfry under a flaring, pyramidal cap is crowned by a botonné cross. The roof flares over side wings with wooden buttresses dividing paired Gothic lancets framing stained glass windows. The rose window, framed within a wooden Gothic arch, contains four smaller circular colored glass windows. The tracker organ, made by the Ryder Company of Boston, was brought in pieces over Mosquito Pass by oxcart.

LK17 Tabor House

1877. 116 E. 5th St.

Horace Austin Warner Tabor became Leadville's mayor and most famous citizen following a propitious grubstake that paid off with the Little Pittsburg mine. He lived with his first wife, Augusta, in this two-story clapboard cottage, moved here in 1879 so that the Tabor Opera House could be constructed on its original site. A narrow sawtooth molding runs around the eaves and up into the front gable, where it culminates in a turned pendant at the roof peak. Triangular pediments top the narrow windows, and a mansard bay extends from the front gable end. The dwelling was restored in 1952 as a house museum.

LK18 Annunciation Catholic Church

1880. 609 Poplar St. (southwest corner of E. 7th St.)

The silvery metal-clad octagonal steeple of Annunciation Catholic Church is 150 feet high, the tallest landmark in town. It tops an arcaded belfry and buttressed tower at the corner of a red brick, stone-trimmed church with stained glass Gothic-arched win-

dows and paintings decorating the vaulted ceiling.

LK19 Leadville, Colorado & Southern Depot

1893, Union Pacific Railway. Northwest corner of E. 7th and Hazel sts.

Wide, bracketed eaves distinguish this one-story red brick depot with gabled dormers and corbeled chimneys. Built while the Union Pacific owned the DSP&P, the depot, along with the line, later became part of the Colorado & Southern and finally of the Burlington Northern. Burlington diesel standard-gauge locomotives, not the steam engine on exhibit outside the depot, are used for the Leadville, Colorado & South-

LK14 Tabor Opera House

LK16 St. George's Episcopal Church, 1941

LK20 Matchless Mine, Baby Doe Tabor outside her cabin, 1935

ern's 23-mile scenic excursions to Fremont Pass. The LC&S facilities also include an antique frame roundhouse with three stalls.

LK20 Matchless Mine Museum

1878. 1.1 mile east of Harrison Ave. on E. 7th St.

The gabled mine building with metal roof and vertical board siding became the home of the second Mrs. Tabor following Horace's death in 1899. Elizabeth McCourt Doe Tabor (known as Baby Doe), generally regarded as the most beautiful woman in Colorado, retired to this shack at the Matchless Mine, where she lived for the rest of her life, impoverished by the loss of the family fortune in the silver crash and depression of 1893. Her frozen corpse was discovered here in 1935. Besides her cabin, the site includes the blasting powder magazine, hoist room and blacksmith shop, and the shaft and headframe amid dumps and tailings. Since 1953 the Matchless has been open for tours.

LK21 Leadville National Fish Hatchery

1889. 6 miles southwest of Leadville on U.S. 24 and Colorado 300 (NR)

The eyebrow dormers, Carpenter's Gothic porch, and decorative fountain are gone, but the rough-faced native red sandstone building, outlying pools, and secondary buildings are still interesting features of the second oldest operating federal fish hatchery in the United States. "No matter how hard we try, we can't raise fish dumb enough for everybody to catch," is the superintendent's response to fishermen who come here to complain about their luck. Inside, parquet-floored rooms with exhibits front the maze of raceways for tiny trout. On the grounds are the remains of the Evergreen Hotel (1880s), a resort on the Evergreen Lakes that burned down in 1894.

Climax

Climax (1887, 11,320 feet) was named for the Denver, South Park & Pacific depot (1881) atop Fremont Pass, which became the first office of the Climax Molybdenum Mining Company. The Climax Mo-

lybdenum Mine (1916) turned low-grade molybdenum ore into Colorado's richest mine and mill operation. Molybdenum, used as an alloy to harden steel, became crucial during World War I for armor plating and during the 1920s for automobile steel. World War II triggered much greater expansion, and for several decades Climax produced more than half of the world supply of molybdenum, along with byproducts of tungsten, lead, and iron pyrite. Production peaked at 50,000 tons per day in what claimed to be the world's largest underground mine.

As the use of steel and molybdenum mining declined, this company town was dismantled, and many dwellings were moved to Leadville in the 1960s to become the nucleus of the West Park suburb. In 1982 Climax ceased production and laid off 3,000 workers, retaining only a skeleton crew. Hollowed-out Bartlett Mountain and miles of waste dumps and tailings ponds remain as Colorado's most spectacular unnatural wonder.

Twin Lakes

Twin Lakes (1879. 9.210 feet) (NRD) developed as a resort on the north side of the lower of two lakes. The D&RG stagecoach service from that railroad's depot at Granite enhanced access, as did the opening of the Independence Pass road to the Aspen mines. This hamlet of small log and slab homes has a beautifully restored schoolhouse (1895), the rustic Nordic Inn (c. 1910), and the two-story frame Holt's Hotel (1898).

The Mt. Elbert Pumped-Storage Power Plant (1975, U.S. Bureau of Reclamation) incorporates a fine museum and visitors' center into the voluminous space enclosed in raw concrete, with huge windows overlooking Twin Lakes. This fourteen-story structure, mostly underground on the edge of the lake, is the showpiece of the Frying Pan Arkansas Water Diversion Project, which diverts water from the Frying Pan River on the Western Slope to the agricultural communities of the Arkansas River Valley. The Twin Lakes Dam (1898) enlarged the two natural lakes as an irrigation reservoir.

LK22 **Inter-Laken Resort**

1880s. South of Twin Lakes off Colorado 82, 2 miles by foot on the Colorado Trail (NRD)

James V. Dexter developed this resort on the south side of the Twin Lakes. The Inter-Laken Hotel (1880) is a two-story log building, cruciform in plan, with board-and-batten facing on the north facade and an imposing corbeled brick chimney. A hexagonal outhouse (1880s) has six stalls numbered to correspond to rooms in the hotel. Other structures on the site include a single-story building for servants' quarters, with rooms arranged along a central hall, and a hewn log barn with a door and hayloft at each end. The hewn log Dexter Summer House (1895) has a mansarded second floor topped by an enclosed observation cupola, flanked by two corbeled chimneys. A mansarded veranda with decoratively trimmed posts extends around all four sides, and the interior is grandly furnished in walnut and bird's-eye maple.

Custer County (CR)

With the 1876 Battle of the Little Big Horn vividly in mind, legislators honored General George A. Custer when they created this county in 1877. Settlement has always been concentrated in the Wet Mountain Valley, framed on the west by the Sangre de Cristo Range and on the east by the Wet Mountains.

Rosita, the county's first large mining camp, blossomed briefly during the 1870s and withered quickly after a silver strike gave birth to nearby Silver Cliff. Silver Cliff, third largest city in the state by 1880, demanded that it be made the state capital. As a consolation prize, in 1886 Silver Cliff captured the county seat from fading Rosita.

Silver Cliff's failure to establish successful ore processing facilities led to its demise. It lost even the county seat to nearby Westcliffe, which the D&RG made its Custer County terminus. After the D&RG abandoned rail service in 1937 and mining activity diminished, farming and ranching became the mainstay of this small, sparsely populated county. Among the many ghosts is Colfax, a colony (1870–1879) of the German Colonization Society of Chicago, led by Carl Wulsten, a temperamental idealist. The county's population peaked in 1880 with 8,080 residents and had sunk by 1990 to 1,926 residents.

Westcliffe

The county seat (1881, 7,888 feet) was founded by Dr. William A. Bell, vice president of the D&RG, who purchased several ranches and established a cheese factory in the town he named for Westcliffe-on-the-Sea in his native British Isles. He also brought in a D&RG rail spur to tap the resources of the area. Ignored by the railroad, nearby Silver Cliff lost population and even buildings to Westcliffe. St. Luke's Episcopal Church and a hotel "with the pictures still hanging on the walls" were hauled into what is still the largest town in Custer County.

CR01 **Hard Times Hotel** (Wolff Building)

1887. 201 2nd St. (southeast corner of Rosita Ave.) (NR)

William Wolff amassed a fortune in mining and built the first hotel in Westcliffe, a two-story brick affair with a rough-faced sandstone facade trimmed with the same stone in smooth and cross-hatched blocks. The front parapet is supported by full-height corner pilasters and has a central signature pediment. Two 8-foot-high windows flank the door, all with round-arched surrounds of stone blocks. A low stone wall in front of the building retains iron rings for hitching horses. Formerly the National Hotel, the building has been restored and renamed the Hard Times Hotel.

CR02 Westcliffe State Bank Building

c. 1900. 201 Main St.

Exemplifying Gilded Age facadism, this one-story, gracefully aged building has a smooth-faced brick front and cheaper brick side walls. An elaborate cast iron cornice with dentils and modillions ornaments the facade, as does a secondary cornice with inset brick panels. The iron shopfront has fluted pilasters supporting a narrow cast iron band of floral emblems and a metal doorsill stamped "Colorado Iron Works, Denver."

CR03 Custer County Library and Community Building

1990, John Hurtig. 209 Main St.

One of the few contemporary buildings in Westcliffe incorporates an older building into its structure, and its facade pays homage to the town's architectural heritage. The library portion to the east is new construction, while the community center is in an old drugstore. John Hurtig, a Pueblo architect, gave the building a roof parapet with a cast concrete capstone, a brick cornice, and brick stringcourses at lintel and sill levels, as well as a round-arched entry transom.

CR04 Hope Lutheran Church

1917, John Reininga. 312 S. 3rd St. (northwest corner of Powell Ave.) (NR)

The Reverend John Reininga, who designed this picturesque church, also carved the ornate altar for his German congregation. The cast stone exterior walls rise into a 96-foot spire with gables over the belfry. The little-changed, traditional interior retains four-

CR04 New Hope Lutheran Church
CR05 Westcliffe School

teen splendid stained glass windows, including a triple-panel Biblical scene.

CR05 Westcliffe School

1891. 302 S. 4th St. (northwest corner of Powell Ave.) (NR)

Fieldstone walls and contrasting lava stone quoins distinguish this one-room school. Fishscale shingles adorn the bell tower and front and back gable ends. Evenly spaced double-hung windows, accented with brick lintels, provide illumination for young scholars. After closing in 1953, this schoolhouse was restored as part of the town's centennial celebration for use as a museum and community center.

CR06 Custer County Courthouse

1929, John J. Huddart. 205 S. 6th St.

A year before he died, John Huddart designed this, the last of his many county courthouses. The two-story brick building is an Art Deco departure for Huddart, who, like Frank Edbrooke, in whose office he trained, generally used period revival styles. Terracotta trim and polychromatic brick brighten somewhat the rather stark facade with urn finials. Among those unimpressed with this newfangled design was the county sheriff, who specified local fieldstone and a much plainer style for the sheriff's office, which was added to the northeast corner in the 1930s.

CR07 Beckwith Ranch

1860s. 6.2 miles north of Westcliffe on Colorado 69

The red-roofed buildings of the Beckwith Ranch have long been local landmarks. The vaguely Italianate ranch house with square tower, ornate balcony, bay window, and porte-cochère is one of the county's more elaborate early residences. The main house is flanked by small frame dwellings and outbuildings, as well as two clapboard barns with louvered cupolas. The complex exemplifies a growing ranch which, with rural frugality, kept the older structures, including the bunkhouse across the road, as new ones were added. Elton T. Beckwith, a native of Maine, drove cattle herds to Colorado in 1869 to feed the miners. By 1880, the Beckwith Cattle Company was running 2,000 head of cattle and breeding blooded horses.

Silver Cliff

Silver Cliff (1878, 7,982 feet) was established as a result of silver discoveries in the nearby cliffs. In 1880 Silver Cliff boasted a population of 5,040, twenty-five saloons, twenty groceries, three hotels, and four newspapers. The silver panic of 1893 dealt a major blow, as did several serious fires. In 1929 the final indignity came when the county seat was transferred to Westcliffe. Today this is a hamlet of around 300 residents. Silver Cliff boasts the only geodesic dome bar in the United States, the Silver Dome Saloon and Music Hall (1984, Charles Behrendt), 611 Ohio Street and Colorado 96.

CR08 Town Hall and Fire Station Museum

1882. 606 Main St.

Following two major fires, this two-story hall was built for duty, for public meetings and as a "pleasant place for the reception of brother firemen who frequently visit the city." The false-fronted building, topped by a gabled bell tower and bracketed cornice, has three round-arched, double-door entrances. After a new town hall was erected next door, this became a museum for mining, firefighting, and other artifacts.

CR09 Rosita

1873–1966. Custer County 328 (Rosita Rd.), 15 miles southeast of Silver Cliff

Rosita, now a ghost town, was founded by prospectors who named it for its small wild roses. Rosita peaked in 1877 with a population of around 1,500 before newer mining settlements seduced many residents, who often took their houses with them. Today, amid newer vacation and retirement homes, almost nothing remains of the original settlement except for the hewn log assay office and the picturesque Rosita Cemetery.

CR10 Bishop's Castle

1969, James Bishop. 6 miles north of Lake San Isabel on Colorado 165

A large iron dragon poking its head over 70-foot-high castle walls makes Custer County's most unusual building easy to find. Since 1969 Jim Bishop of Pueblo has been building this medieval-inspired stone castle, complete with gatehouse, arched openings, flying buttresses, towers, and a projected moat and drawbridge. Working without blueprints or architectural training, Bishop built with scavenged stone and decorated his castle with wrought iron from his father's ornamental iron shop in Pueblo.

CR11 Mingus Homestead

1913. 1.2 miles east of Colorado 165 on Ditch Creek Rd. (NR)

For his homestead ranch, Alan Mingus built a one-and-one-half-story, four-room house of logs with a stone foundation and gable roof. His two-story, gabled barn has log walls covered with vertical boards. Outbuildings include a gabled shed with log foundation and milled lumber walls and an outhouse of vertical boards with a special child's potty seat.

Huerfano County   (HF)

A solitary black volcanic butte on the east side of I-25 known as Huerfano (Spanish for orphan) gave its name to the county, established in 1861. The Spanish Peaks, known to the Utes as Huajatolla, or "Breasts of the Earth," are the county's other landmarks. The Wet Mountains on the north and the Sangre de Cristo and Culebra ranges on the west guard this scenic county, which includes much San Isabel National Forest land.

A misty history has left little except adobe ruins and the graveyards of more than fifty vanished towns, including Badito, the original county seat. The old Spanish fort 7 miles south of Badito on Oak Creek was an outpost of New Spain, abandoned after the Adams-Onis Treaty of 1819 established the Arkansas River as the boundary between the United States and Mexico.

The Cucharas (Spanish for spoon) River nourishes the only two incorporated towns: Walsenburg and La Veta. Redwing, with its post office in a silvery Airstream trailer, and Gardner are tiny but living hamlets on the Huerfano River. Cuchara, a Hispanic community founded in the 1860s on the upper Cucharas River, is becoming a resort town.

During the coal mining boom of the early 1900s, Huerfano County's population climbed as high as 17,000. After natural gas and fuel oil began to replace coal heating during the 1930s, the coal industry declined. All that remains are abandoned coal camps with concrete foundations and steps that lead nowhere. With the mines closed, the county has returned to the agricultural pursuits that first sustained settlers. Huerfano County has shrunk to 6,000 residents, of whom roughly half are Spanish surnamed.

Walsenburg

The county seat (1858, 6,185 feet), originally named La Plaza de Los Leones for founder Don Miguel Antonio Leon, was transformed by the 1870 arrival of ambitious German settlers who replatted and renamed it. Among the newcomers was storekeeper Frederick Walsen, who became the first mayor and opened a pioneer coal mine.

Walsenburg replaced Badito as the county seat in 1872 and, following the D&RG's arrival in 1876, evolved into a rail and coal mining hub. By 1900 the U.S. census taker found twenty-six different nationalities among the residents of Walsenburg, who worked in mines with names such as Ideal and Sunshine. A mile west of town, visible from U.S. 160, lie ruins of the giant power plant for the Walsen and Robinson Mine.

Notable Huerfano County characters fill the colorful mural on the exterior of 418 Main Street, a 1991 project of the Walsenburg Arts Council, painted by Jason Crum, Dean Fleming, and Ken Martinez. The well-preserved, Beaux-Arts Neoclassical red brick and white terracotta First National Bank of Walsenburg (1904) is at 501 Main Street. At 724 7th Street, the Bonicelli Gas Station (1925) retains some of its original Spanish Colonial Revival flair, while the Streamline Moderne Vogue Super Service Station (1939), 300 Main Street, uses glazed tile block and glass brick with rounded windows. The coal mining era lingers in the form of blue-collar taverns and modest homes, including tiny brick duplexes at 1003 and 1007 West 7th Street. Adobe outbuildings and garages are reminders of the town's Hispanic origins. Among the region's vernacular attractions is the Roadside Shrine, overflowing with pastel plastic flowers in a large natural grotto on U.S. 160, 7 miles west of Walsenburg.

HF01 **Huerfano County Courthouse and Jail**

1904, C. A. Henderson. 401 Main St. (U.S. 160) (NR)

C. A. Henderson, an architect from Pueblo, designed the county courthouse, which still dominates Walsenburg's downtown, reflecting in its rich detail and shiny silvery roof the county's more opulent days. The exterior of the symmetrical, two-story building is rough-faced local sandstone that rises to a central, four-story bell tower bristling with pedimented dormers, a rooftop finial,

and minarets. Large stone blocks are used for both the skin and the surrounds of the arched second-story and round tower windows, the open entry porch, and the retaining walls around the courthouse square. Similarly Romanesque Revival in inclination is the adjacent jail (1896), of the same stone and with the same dominant square tower. The steel cells and steel beds are still in the jail, which in 1994 became the Walsenburg Mining Museum, digging into the past of "The City Built on Coal."

HF02 **Visitors' Center** (Colorado & Southern Depot)

1910. 112 E. 4th St.

The restored Colorado & Southern depot, across Main Street (U.S. 160) from the courthouse and next to still-used tracks, is a bungaloid station building of wire-cut red brick with crisp white frame trim and a multigabled green tile roof. Inside, the original ticket window and waiting room survive, recycled to provide tourists with literature and guidance. A side room houses the Colorado Barbed Wire Collectors Museum, displaying several hundred different styles of the fencing that made farming and ranching possible on the treeless Great Plains.

HF03 **Post Office**

1934, Louis A. Simon, OSA. 204 E. 6th St. (northeast corner of S. Russell St.)

This modest red brick post office in a simplified Georgian Revival style has an arched, fanlighted entry and keystoned lintels. Inside is the moody 1937 mural, *The Spanish Peaks,* by Ernest L. Blumenschein, a founder of the Taos, New Mexico, art colony. The mural depicts the saddle shaped peaks in silvery snow, with a foreground of Ute tipis and a Hispanic sheepherder.

HF04 **Walsenburg Middle School** (Walsenburg High School)

1933, Isaac H. Rapp. 415 Walsen Ave.

In one of his last designs, Isaac Rapp, known for his work in Trinidad (see Las Animas County), used red brick with cast stone frosting for a vaguely Collegiate Gothic school

HF04 Walsenburg Middle School (Walsenburg High School)

building with buttresses, an ornate parapet, and slender, octagonal towers and a grand, Gothic-arched entry.

HF05 St. Mary's Catholic Church

1900, Patrick P. Mills. 121 E. 7th Ave.

A 1931 windstorm blew off St. Mary's original tall steeple. Now only a cross and stumpy fragment and a miniature metal spire top the crenelated bell tower. Local brick, now stuccoed, forms the walls of this cruciform church with a steep-pitched roof and Gothic-arched openings. Three large, stained glass windows from the Royal Bavarian Studios in Munich are said to have cost almost as much as the entire church. An unusual paneled oak ceiling further distinguishes this church, sometimes called Our Lady of the Seven Dolors. St. Mary's School (1912), after the 1922 addition of six classrooms and an auditorium, was the largest parochial school in Colorado, with classroom space for 1,250 pupils. The Mission Revival rectory (1919) stands on the site of the 1882 adobe church, which replaced the original adobe-covered jacal church of the 1870s.

HF06 Medical Office (Community House)

1929. 129 E. Kansas Ave.

A later version of the settlement houses that provided shelter, activities, and social services, this handsome structure is sheathed in beige wire-cut brick. It has blind round arches above the second-story windows and bracketed canopies over the entries. The facade has a bay topped by a second-story balcony. A flat roof, angled corners, and streamlined stone banding give a modern jauntiness to what is now a medical office.

HF07 Lathrop State Park

1962. 3 miles west of Walsenburg on U.S. 160

Colorado's first state park, named for the first director of the state parks and recreation board, has a visitors' center with a remarkable mural painted by Paul Busch in 1972. Depicting settlement waves from prehistoric Native Americans to Hispanics and twentieth-century miners and ranchers, the mural spotlights historical figures such as Juan de Oñate, Chief Ouray, Zebulon Pike, Kit Carson, General William J. Palmer, and Frederick Walsen.

La Veta

La Veta (1862, 7,013 feet) stands against the backdrop of the Spanish Peaks, which soar 6,000 feet above the surrounding plains. John Francisco, a Virginian, and John Diagre, a French Canadian, purchased the townsite from owners of the Vigil and St. Vrain Mexican land grant. Their adobe trading post, Fort Francisco, became the nucleus of a settlement first known as Francisco Plaza. Prospectors renamed it La Veta (Spanish for *vein*), for a gold vein on nearby Spanish Peaks. This scenic village is graced by twenty-seven vernacular buildings constructed by local masons of sandstone from the nearby Piñon Hills Quarry. Even outbuildings were

La Veta, stone barn

made of this soft yellow stone, including such notable examples as the stone barn at the northwest corner of 4th and Oak streets (1895, E. R. Coleman, builder). One of the few frame buildings in town is the false-fronted general store (1905), now an art gallery, at 220 South Main Street.

HF08 **Masonic Temple** (Dotson and Company)

1889, W. S. Bellard and ? Davidson, builders. 210 Main St. (Colorado 12)

Warm sandstone in regular courses of rough-faced, square-cut ashlar blocks forms the walls of this two-story commercial structure. The same stone is used for the facade, the trim, and even the false front.

HF09 **La Veta Bank Building**

1903, Coleman Brothers. 222 S. Main St.

The Colemans, local stonemasons who built many La Veta structures, left their name in the stone to prove it. Although of rough-cut sandstone, this bank is refined by smooth stone quoins, pilasters, and window and entry detailing.

HF10 **La Veta Hardware**

1911. 300 S. Main St.

One of the largest of La Veta's sandstone buildings was originally a general store. The 18-inch-thick stone walls of the two-story building are squared rubblestone on the sides but regular and coursed on the facade. Details of the metal frieze are highlighted by colorful paint under the stone corbeling.

HF11 **Francisco Plaza**

1860s. 312 S. Main St. (NR)

This plaza is enclosed on three sides by one-story adobe buildings with 18-to-25-inch-thick walls and on the fourth side by a fence. The small, dirt-floored rooms open inward on the plaza, with no windows or doors in the outward-facing walls. The chimneys survive, although the original flat roof has been replaced by a metal gable roof and porches have been added, along with other Territorial Style elements. John Francisco

built this as his home, trading post, and granary. When the D&RG reached La Veta in 1876, the rooms were converted to a hotel, telegraph offices, and depot. In 1957 the fort became a museum. On the grounds are the Ritter School (1876), a one-room log schoolhouse moved here from its original site 5 miles east on the Cucharas River; a clapboard Presbyterian church (1893) used since 1973 for the summer theatricals of the Spoon River Players; and a tiny stone building that was once the town hall (1912). A saloon (1888), the Hiram Vasquez Blacksmith Shop (1863), and other buildings have been moved to this museum complex, which is open from Memorial Day to Labor Day.

HF12 **1899 Inn**

1909. 314 S. Main St.

A hospitable, full-length front porch and generous dormers in the mansard roof distinguish this vernacular stone dwelling. Despite the name, it was built in 1909. The 18-inch stone walls shelter six guest rooms. The inn was earlier the Lamme Hospital (1912–1940s) and then a boarding house before conversion to a bed and breakfast in 1981.

HF13 **La Veta Pass Narrow-Gauge Railroad Depot**

c. 1877. 13 miles west of La Veta on the south side of the old La Veta Pass Rd. (NR)

One of Colorado's oldest depots is built of the handsome local sandstone, later stuccoed and painted white. Sited on the east side of La Veta Pass near the ruins of a turntable, this single-story, L-shaped station continued to serve wagons and trucks after the narrow-gauge railroad abandoned it.

HF14 **Farisita**

1923–1988. Colorado 69 and Huerfano County 620

Asperidon Faris, a Lebanese merchant, established a 160-acre ranch, with a store and post office, and gave it the feminine diminutive form of his name, for his daughter, Jeannette. She recalled: "Dad sold everything in his store, from christening clothes to coffins. The walls of the basement were four to five feet thick." The now abandoned Faris store and house survive, along with a barn whose Gothic window suggests religious use.

Las Animas County   (LA)

Colorado's largest county ranges from broken prairie in the east to the high mountains of the Culebra Range in the west. Settled in the 1860s by agrarians, it proved to have some of the richest coal pockets in the Rockies. Las Animas became Colorado's fourth most populous county by 1910, but labor wars and the switch to natural gas as heating fuel ended the bonanza days of "black gold." The county is haunted by about one hundred dead coal camps, including the remains of Cokedale, a company town, and spooky Ludlow, with its sad monument to the slain wives and children of striking miners.

Many communities had predecessor Hispanic settlements whose history lingers in adobe ruins and cemeteries. Typical of these towns is Aguilar. Platted as a D& RG coal town in 1892, it replaced what had been the tiny mission and trading post of San Antonio Plaza (1867). Today Aguilar, with its many abandoned old buildings and a ghostly main street, epitomizes the fading towns of Las Animas County.

Agriculture has replaced coal as the lead industry. More than 2.5 million acres are classified as range land, while another 100,000 acres are farmed in this high and dry county. The federal government has preserved picturesque San Isabel National Forest in the northwestern corner of the county, and, in the east, the Comanche National Grasslands.

Trinidad

The county seat (1859, 6,025 feet) is strategically sited on the Purgatoire River at the northern base of Ratón Pass on the Mountain Branch of the Santa Fe Trail. According to one story, sheepherder Gabriel Gutierrez named the place for a sweetheart left behind in New Mexico, Trinidad Baca. To console himself, he opened a tavern that helped attract other settlers, including Anglos. The Goodnight-Loving Cattle Trail ran through town, and Trinidad became headquarters for the Prairie Land and Cattle Company's vast land holdings. The settlement grew slowly and did not incorporate until 1879, in part because litigation of Mexican land grant claims kept ownership of many lots cloudy until the mid-1870s. Despite its hilly site at the base of Fisher's Peak, Trinidad is laid out on a grid.

Trinidad boomed between the 1880s and the 1920s, when the thriving coal industry made it Colorado's fourth largest city. Trinidad is noted for its red brick streets and sidewalks, some of the bricks stamped "Trinidad." Perhaps no town in Colorado has more fine stone structures, many constructed with the local golden sandstone by master masons such as Trinidad stonemason-architect Charles Innes. The town's golden age is also preserved in the architecture of the brothers Isaac Hamilton Rapp, Jr., and William Morris Rapp, who practiced in partnership first with C. W. Bulger (1889–1902) and later with A. C. Hendrickson. The Rapps, not to be confused with the early twentieth-century Chicago firm that specialized in theaters, rose to prominence in Trinidad, where they did much work in the Victorian, Pueblo Revival, and Mission modes before moving on to Santa Fe. In New Mex-

Trinidad

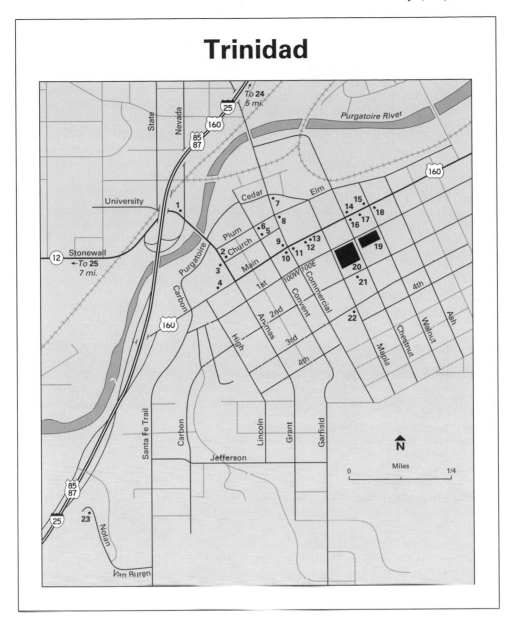

ico thcy pioneered the Santa Fe Style, which was refined and popularized by John Gaw Meem, as Carl D. Shephard points out in *Creator of the Santa Fe Style* (1988). The Rapps designed the original La Fonda Hotel and the Museum of New Mexico in Santa Fe, as well as the New Mexico Building for the 1915–1917 Panama-California Exposition in San Diego's Balboa Park.

Since the 1930s Trinidad has lost population and two fabulous Pueblo Revival buildings, the Santa Fe Railroad depot and the Cardenas Hotel. Despite thsse losses the town is unusually rich in late nineteenth-century Victorian and early twentieth-century architecture, as highlighted in the Corazón de Trinidad (heart of Trinidad) Historic District (NRD), which includes virtually all of downtown Trinidad. Survivors include the Toltec Hotel (1911, Frank E. Edbrooke), 126–128 North Commercial Street, a clean design with the old Toltec logo on the plate glass windows; an elegant stone waterworks (1879, Charles Innes), 201 West Cedar Street; and Zion Lutheran Church (1889, C. W. Bulger and Isaac H. Rapp), 613 Prospect Street (southwest corner of Pine Street), a small, richly detailed brick and frame church. Handsome red brick buildings in predictable styles house the Trinidad State Junior College (1925).

LA01 Colorado Visitors' Center

1986. 309 Nevada Ave. (northwest corner of University St.)

Trinidad's red brick, Romanesque Revival architecture is updated in this Postmodern tourist haven, easily identifiable by its three-story observation tower with a pyramidal roof. Horizontal wings recall the demolished Santa Fe depot, which stood on this site, while the tower echoes those on the nearby five-story Schneider Brewery.

LA02 Carnegie Library

1904, John G. Haskell. 202 N. Animas St. (northeast corner of W. Church St.)

A skin of Trinidad sandstone, from the nearby James Radford Quarry, and two-story Ionic columns like those of City Hall across the street are used in this standard Carnegie design. On the site where Gabriel Gutierrez is said to have built Trinidad's first cabin, this library has a pristine interior sparkling with the original high ceilings, stained glass lunette windows, golden oak card catalog, and wrought iron book racks.

LA03 City Hall

1909, John Conkie. 135 N. Animas St. (opposite W. Church St.)

Square corner towers dominate this three-story hall of rough-faced stone with the entry recessed behind two-story black granite Ionic columns. This unusual design honors a local tradition of building in rough-faced Trinidad sandstone, although such Neoclassical compositions usually call for smooth, polished stone. Rough-faced stone also serves as base and trim on this building, with a rooftop balustrade to emphasize its fierce symmetry.

LA04 West Theater

1908, Issac H. Rapp. 423 W. Main St.

Edward West had Trinidad's leading architect design this three-story, red brick theater with its first-story balustrade and second-story round arches. Alterations and additions intrude on the interior, which retains its three tiers of seating and double-decker boxes. Nearby, at the northeast corner of Animas and Main, is the West Block (1889), a three-story brick building faced with native sandstone and with newer brick corbeling in place of the original stone cornice.

LA05 Holy Trinity Catholic Church

1885, Charles Innes. 135 W. Church St. (northeast corner of Convent St.)

The successor to a simple white adobe chapel, this monument of rough-faced local stone exults in round arches, buttresses, and minarets. The soft golden sandstone helps unify an awkward combination of a cruciform plan with Georgian massing and a mix of Romanesque details with a diminutive Gothic steeple added in the 1890s. The chapel has a 60-foot barrel-vaulted ceiling, marbleized wood-paneled walls, and splendid stained glass.

LA06 Schneider Brewery

1888. 240 N. Convent St. (southeast corner of W. Plum St.)

A Tuscan-style double penthouse distinguishes this otherwise ordinary six-story brick edifice, which acquired many additions as the town and its thirst grew. Henry Schneider founded the brewery, which marketed its beers throughout the southwest. Schneider's survived Prohibition to become one of the last hometown Colorado breweries. Closed around 1960, it is abandoned and neglected.

LA07 Children's Museum (Firehouse No. 1)

1888, Bulgar and Rapp. 314 N. Commercial St. (southeast corner of Cedar St.)

Light sandstone quoins contrast dramatically with the red brick skin of this narrow, two-story building with an asymmetrical bell tower. The city hall, city jail, and other city offices as well as Trinidad's fire department were housed here until the new city hall opened in 1909.

LA08 First Presbyterian Church

1902, Theodore S. Hawley. 224 N. Commercial St. (southeast corner of Elm St.)

The Reverend Theodore Hawley, who had an architecture degree from Carthage College in Illinois, designed this fortresslike Gothic Revival brick church. The squat corner building with its stepped parapet still lacks a projected tower that would have made it more graceful. The stonemason, William McDonald, also worked on the Carnegie Library (LA02).

LA09 Columbian Hotel

1879, John Conkie. 111–119 N. Commercial St. (northwest corner of Main St.)

Originally called the Grand Union Hotel, this three-story brick landmark trimmed in white stone was renamed in honor of the 1893 World's Columbian Exposition. Heavily hooded and elongated windows in sets of two and three, polished stone quoins, an ornately bracketed cornice above a decorative frieze, and the flat roof with overhanging eaves are typical of the Italianate style. A terrazzo-floored lobby leads to a Rococo ballroom, a ladies' "retiring room," and a gaming room, saloon, and smoking parlor. Sadly, this 100-room grand hotel has been vacant since the 1970s.

LA10 Trinidad Opera House

1882, Solomon, Henry, and Samuel Jaffa, builders. 100–116 W. Main St. (southwest corner of Commercial St.)

The Trinidad Opera House has a smooth sandstone skin stretched tightly up the two-story facade and decorated with hand carved geometric patterns. The same handsome stone is used for the window trim, brackets, cornice, pediments, and a flattened arch entry, although modernized storefronts mar the street level. A central stairway leads to the 710-seat, second-floor opera hall with an oval stained glass skylight, a glorious space now divided into rental rooms. The builders, brothers Solomon, Henry, and Samuel Jaffa, three pioneer Jewish merchants, used the corner storefront for their shop in what is sometimes called the Jaffa Opera House. An embodiment of Trinidad's aspirations, the building also represents the contribution of Jewish merchants to cultural life on the frontier.

LA11 **First National Bank**

1892, C. W. Bulger and Isaac H. Rapp. 100 E. Main St. (southeast corner of Commercial St.)

Stone faces hide in the facade of this five-story Richardsonian Romanesque landmark of Trinidad sandstone. The round arches that dominate the street fronts are repeated on upper stories. An asymmetrical, pedimented gable end heightens the verticality of the composition. Gargoyles, twin polished stone half columns at the entrance, and a balustraded stone balcony are among many fine details. Frank Bloom ran his Bloom Land and Cattle Company, stretching from New Mexico to Montana, from this bank, of which he was vice president. This $70,000 edifice was lauded by Denver's *Western Architect and Building News* for its use of local sandstone, not only in masonry but as "cut and dressed stone trimmings." In the upstairs photography studio, with its skylight and carbide lamps, Glenn Aultman continued the business established by his father, which documented life in Trinidad and Las Animas County throughout the twentieth century in one of Colorado's most important photographic collections.

LA12 **Masonic Temple**

1911, Isaac H. Rapp (?). 132–136 E. Main St.

This three-story beige brick building is rich in Neoclassical terracotta detail, including Adamesque garlands and wreaths in the blind arches over the second-story windows, Ionic capitals atop the brick pilasters, second- and third-story dentiled cornices, and the cap on the parapet.

LA13 **Colorado Building**

1903, John Conkie. 150 E. Main St.

Beneath a fancy pressed metal cornice, this two-story brick commercial building with Chicago windows once housed a leading Trinidad department store. Now it is a museum honoring illustrator and town benefactor Arthur Roy Mitchell. A local cowboy trained as an artist in New York City, Mitchell returned to Trinidad and gained fame driving around in his Ford automobile to paint outdoors. The "Model A Cowboy" painted over 150 covers for pulp western magazines.

LA14 **Post Office**

1910. James Knox Taylor, OSA. 301 E. Main St. (northeast corner of Chestnut St.) (NR)

Paired sandstone Ionic columns support the pediment of the entry portico on this monumental one-story temple of tan brick. In the tympanum is a bull's-eye window with compass keystones. The arched windows and oversized keystones are characteristic of the Beaux-Arts classicism espoused by James Knox Taylor, as are the rigidly symmetrical elevations, massive proportions, and fine detailing. The base and front and side steps are gray granite. The post office replaced an outstanding early residence on the block of Main Street known in the late nineteenth century as Millionaire's Row.

LA15 **Mullare-Murphy Funeral Home** (Chappell House)

1883, Charles Innes. 335 E. Main St. (northwest corner of Walnut St.)

Charles Innes, a leading Trinidad stonemason and amateur architect, worked with Delos Chappell, Trinidad's city engineer, on this two-story stone mansion. The two also collaborated on the city's original waterworks (1879), whose pumphouse survives at the intersection of Cedar and Convent on the banks of the Purgatoire River. In this mansion, rough-faced stone forms the foundation and walls, while elaborate Eastlake wooden trim and frame gables, porches, and siding make the superstructure seem light by contrast.

LA16 **Baca House Museum**

1870. E. Main St. (southeast corner of Chestnut St.) (NR)

Merchant and mill owner John S. Hough built this house, which was sold a year later to early settler Felipe Baca, a rancher and state senator. The two-story adobe house, the town's oldest residence, has characteristically thick walls but incorporates a Territorial Style frame hipped roof, pedimented windows, and shutters, and a balustraded front porch. At the rear is an adobe barn, now the Pioneer Museum. With the neighboring Bloom Mansion, it is part of a full block of property acquired in the early 1960s for a museum complex operated by the Colorado Historical Society.

LA17 **Bloom Mansion Museum**

1882; 1963 restoration. E. Main St. (southwest corner of Walnut St.) (NR)

Frank and Sarah Bloom selected their Second Empire house design from a magazine and had a local contractor build it. The three-story home bristles with cresting and a weathervane atop the metal-clad fourth-story mansard tower. The red brick is frosted with white stone quoins, while the first floor is wrapped in an elegant frame veranda. The Colorado Historical Society has fastidiously restored the mansion as a house museum in conjunction with the Baca House next door.

LA18 **Roberto's Restaurant** (First Christian Church)

1890, The Reverend John Stevens. 400 E. Main St. (southeast corner of Walnut St.)

Allegedly designed and built by the pastor, a stonemason, this became the church for a Spanish-speaking Presbyterian congregation in 1922 and later a warehouse. In the 1970s it was converted to a restaurant. The church combines Romanesque Revival and Queen Anne details and uses local sandstone to advantage in walls skillfully rounded at the corners, stone diapered trim, and stone scrollwork.

LA19 **Veterans Memorial Square**

c. 1937, WPA. Southeast corner of Chestnut and 1st sts.

Set on a steep hillside, this complex resembles a frontier fort, with separate small buildings surrounding a central quadrangle. Each unit was originally assigned to honor a different veterans' organization; a larger building at the northeast corner contains a gymnasium. Several of the buildings are now connected for use as county social services offices. As in other WPA projects, the rough-faced stone blocks are set with exaggerated mortar joints.

LA20 **Las Animas County Courthouse**

1912, Isaac H. Rapp, William M. Rapp, and A. C. Hendrickson. Southeast corner of E. 1st and S. Maple sts.

The courthouse, a Beaux-Arts monument of Bedford, Indiana, limestone with creamy terracotta trim, occupies a full-block site. Beneath a rooftop balustrade, two-story Ionic columns dominate a three-story facade. The full basement emerges along the bottom of the hilly site on the north side, where the main entrance lies. Inside, white marble walls, ornate plaster trim, gilded iron stair railings, and golden oak woodwork survive, as does a mural depicting local history, painted by Angelo di Benedetto.

LA21 **Van Vleet House**

1904. 212 S. Chestnut (southwest corner of E. 2nd St.)

In this Shingle Style dwelling, the third-story shingled gable and dormer ends are cantilevered over the sandstone walls below. Flared bargeboard on the gables and dormers echoes the entry pediment trim, as does the use of paired brackets. Walls of irregular coursed ashlar sandstone are matched by the massive stone columns of the wraparound porch. The third-floor ballroom, actually a multipurpose room, a two-lane basement bowling alley, and a swimming pool were among the amenities enjoyed by the Van Vleets in livelier times.

LA22 Temple Aaron

1889, C. W. Bulger and Isaac H. Rapp. 407 S. Maple St. (southwest corner of E. 3rd St.)

An exotic, red brick synagogue with base and trim of rough-faced white stone, Temple Aaron has one octagonal front tower with a pressed metal onion dome and a second, square tower with a pyramidal cap. The central rose window and pediment are flanked by minarets. Round and ogee arches add to the eclectic display. Slightly projecting two-story bays with flattened arches, echoed by the flattened entry arch, add symmetry. Inside one of the oldest synagogues in Colorado are a hand-carved pulpit and a pipe organ said to have been brought west by wagon train.

LA23 Trinidad Country Club

1922, Isaac H. Rapp, William M. Rapp, and A. C. Hendrickson. 142 Nolan Way

As published in the January 1923 issue of *Architectural Record*, this one-story stucco "adobe" clubhouse with vigas, log porch posts, rounded corners, flat roofs, and an entry bell tower exemplified the early Santa Fe Style, combining Pueblo Revival and Mission Revival elements. The towers at the front corner were borrowed from the old church of the Acoma Pueblo in New Mexico.

Soft, irregular lines are epitomized in the parapet, which rises and falls along the roofline, becoming higher at corners and where it is integrated into chimneys. A. C. Hendrickson did most of the design work on this project for the firm of Rapp and Hendrickson. Still a clubhouse for what is now a municipal golf course, it has been somewhat altered but retains the corner fireplace and ceiling beams inside. It commands an impressive site, seeming to grow out of the local clay atop a mesa overlooking Trinidad.

LA24 El Moro

1876–1933. 5 miles north of Trinidad on Colorado 239 (intersection of El Moro Rd. and Rd. 75.0)

The town of El Moro was created when the D&RG arrived in 1876. This once busy railroad town became one of the most notable communes of the 1960s, an artists' colony called Drop City, a community of geodesic dome homes largely deserted by 1970.

LA25 Cokedale Historic District

Colorado 12, 7 miles west of Trinidad (NRD)

Touted by the American Smelting and Refining Company as a model company town, Cokedale, founded in 1906, was designed by James Murdoch, a Denver architect, to include housing and public and commercial buildings. These masonry buildings served workers in the nearby mines, coal washery, and coke ovens. The town plan had three rows of houses, with public buildings at each end, paralleling Reilly Creek. Prototype house plans placed 12-foot-square room units under hipped or pyramidal roofs with shed porches over entry doors. The primary construction material was cinderblock made from waste coke dust, with walls finished in heavy, pebbled stucco. Over 100 of the original buildings survive, although many have been remodeled and enlarged since they were sold following the 1947 shutdown of mining operations. The large school, mercantile, boarding house, and mine office buildings still anchor the plan, and the former Gotlieb Mercantile is now a museum. Despite some demolitions, this one-time town of 1,100 is the most intact Colorado coal camp. Across the highway are dormant coke ovens, a silent reminder of Cokedale's past.

Kim

Kim (1917, 5,690 feet) is on the site of a farming village, founded around 1893, which failed because the settlers knew little about dry-land farming. Olin D. Simpson started the present town when he built a post office–store on his homestead and named it for Rudyard Kipling's boy hero. Today, Kim is surrounded by acreage reclaimed from the Dust Bowl as the Comanche National Grasslands.

As is true of some other tiny, poor towns, Kim's most impressive structures are masonry monuments to the WPA. The County Garage (1938) and the Kim High School and Kim Elementary School (c. 1939, WPA), 425 State Street, are constructed of local sandstone. The school complex consists of a pair of flat-roofed classrooms flanking a two-story, hip-roofed gymnasium, which now houses the Kim Activity Center. The vernacular Romanesque Revival gym with its random stone coursing looks as if it might have been a project to teach masonry techniques to novices. The more refined classroom buildings have stepped parapets and façades that hint at Art Deco.

LA26 **Ludlow Tent Colony Site**

1913–1914. End of Delaqua Canyon Rd., 12 miles north of Trinidad and 1 mile west of exit 27 from I-25 (NR)

In the winter of 1913 the United Mine Workers erected near this railroad depot a tent city for 1,500 people evicted from company housing during a strike. In the spring of 1914, the Colorado National Guard crushed the strike, shooting many unionists and setting fire to the tent city. The conflict was exacerbated by hired thugs and detectives employed by the Colorado Fuel and Iron Company, whose principal stockholder was John D. Rockefeller, Jr. Two women and eleven children suffocated in the fire, and in all an estimated 100 people lost their lives in one of the bloodiest episodes in American labor history. Ruins of several buildings linger along the railroad tracks, and a granite statue (1918) of a mining family by sculptor Hugh Sullivan marks the site of the doomed tent city.

LA27 **Ratón Pass**

I-25, 13 miles south of Trinidad (NHL)

Originally saddled by a toll road through the ranch (1866–1893) of Richens L. "Uncle Dick" Wootton, Ratón Pass is now crossed by I-25 as it climbs across the Colorado–New Mexico border. Near the top of the pass and visible (but not accessible) from I-25 is Wootton's ranch, from which he collected his tolls between 1866 and 1880. His rectangular two-story stuccoed masonry house has disappeared. Wootton died here in 1893 and is buried in Trinidad. The ruins of several coal camps also may be seen from I-25 as it slithers over the pass, named by Spaniards for its prolific community of ground squirrels. Remnants of a church six miles below the summit are a relic of the coal camp called Morley.

Baca County (BA)

Named for Felipe Baca, a pioneer settler in Trinidad, this county (1889) forms the southeast corner of the state, bordering on Kansas, Oklahoma, and New Mexico. Sanora Babb, who wrote of her 1920s childhood here in *An Owl on Every Post* (1970), observed: "While other parts of the United States moved swiftly ahead, the hopeful or desperate people who filed claims on these high western grazing lands were plunged a hundred years backward in our history, to live and struggle again like the early settlers. . . ."

One of the counties hardest hit by the droughts that created the Dust Bowl, Baca has never really recovered. The number of post offices has dropped from forty-nine to ten. "We have more ghost towns here than up in the mountains," one inhabitant explained, "but we don't have the remains. They mostly blowed away, burned up, or got plowed under."

Springfield

The county seat (1887, 4,365 feet) was named for Springfield, Missouri, home of some early settlers. The town is small and growing smaller with agricultural hard times. Once a thriving producer of broom corn, Springfield now houses about a third of Baca County's 4,500 residents. It became the birthplace for the militant American Agricultural Movement during the 1970s after the foreclosure auction of cofounder Jerry Wright's farm attracted 250 angry protestors and national television coverage of a near-riot.

Native sandstone used in several buildings comes from The Cedars Quarry near the Las Animas County line, southwest of Pritchett. This stone is the basis for a masonry tradition throughout the southeast corner of the state dating from early Anglo settlement and extending through the WPA projects of the 1930s and 1940s. The honey-to-rust-colored stone has been used to build in both rough fieldstone and quarried and polished blocks. "Welcome to Springfield" is painted on the 200-foot-tall water tank in the block-square city park, where an antique tractor takes the place of the usual cannon.

BA01 **Baca County Courthouse**

1930, Hutchison Architects. 1935, WPA. Main to Colorado sts., between W. 6th and W. 7th aves.

The county courthouse, sited in a tree-shaded public square, is a Beaux-Arts Renaissance Revival composition in blond brick. Purple and blue terracotta trim highlights egg-and-dart detail in the dentiled cornice above second-story blind arches with floral medallions and Adamesque wreaths. This

impressive facade transformed the 1916 courthouse, a plain, two-story brick box with hipped roof whose stuccoed walls now form the central portion of the building. The wing on the west, constructed of rough-faced local sandstone blocks in the plain but meticulous style of the WPA, now houses the Baca County Museum. Additional WPA projects on the courthouse grounds include a small building on the northwest corner and a low wall around the entire block. The library is in a 1985 addition to the north. On the inside, tile work on the staircase of the front bay is noteworthy.

BA02 **Masonic Temple** (Rock School)

1889, M. Gaffney, builder. 281 W. 7th St. (northeast corner of Tipton St.) (NR)

A well-preserved, front-gabled, one-room school constructed of the local sandstone, this is the oldest schoolhouse in the county. The dressed stone block walls have raised quoins. A band course above the raised basement incorporates the lintels of recessed windows. Random-coursed walls change to regular courses of smaller stones in the gable ends. The stonemason and fellow workers labored for a dollar a day on the building.

which was constructed for $2,000. After closing in 1921, it served as a community center until the Masons acquired it and made it their meeting place.

Pritchett

Pritchett (1927, 4,827 feet), named for Dr. Henry S. Pritchett, a director of the Santa Fe Railroad, relieved neighboring Joycoy (1915–1927) of the post office when the railroad completed a spur from Springfield. The town is visible from some distance because of three ten-story white grain elevators towering above the plains. Gracefully curving Modernist lines, flat tops, and unadorned, curved surfaces give a spare, Art Deco look to these co-op elevators at the only railhead for many miles. Despite these cathedrals of the plains, the town of 153 is wrestling with oblivion. Boarded-up brick and frame one- and two-story buildings from the early twentieth century include the polychrome brick Colorado Hotel.

Two Buttes

Two Buttes (1910, 4,125 feet) is named for the twin-peaked butte 20 miles north, a prominent landmark in an otherwise level landscape. The doors of the Methodist Church open wide every Sunday morning, and the proprietor of the Two Buttes Grocery bills his customers once a month. Next to the grocery is the frame Library and Museum. The town boasts a two-story community center (1936, WPA), northwest corner of 5th and C streets, constructed of rough-faced sandstone blocks with exaggerated mortar joints. Its second-level balcony overlooks the gymnasium floor. The entry features the low, stepped parapet that is a signature of WPA work in the area, as well as a curved reception and ticket desk opposite the doors.

Prowers County (PW)

Prowers County, established along the Kansas border in 1889, contains Colorado's lowest altitudes. Its prairie bottomland supports irrigated and dry-land farming and ranching. Trail City, one of the wildest Colorado cattle towns, flourished during the 1880s on the National Cattle Trail, but it is now a ghost. Prowers County commemorates the huge cattle kingdom of John Wesley Prowers, whose 20,000-head herd once occupied much of the Arkansas River valley. Indigenous vernacular structures in Prowers and adjacent counties of southeastern Colorado are of an earth-tone sandstone used for everything from commercial buildings to barns in this largely treeless country of short-grass prairie and big sky.

Lamar

Promoters named the county seat (1886, 3,622 feet) for U.S. Secretary of the Interior Lucius Quintius C. Lamar in hope of procuring federal patronage for the town. The Santa Fe Railroad ran excursions to Lamar and sold $45,000 worth of land the first day. "Only five short weeks ago," marveled *The Prairie Farmer* in May 1886, "only a single log building [lay] down by the cottonwood belt that fringes the stream [Arkansas River]. Today there are five and twenty buildings complete and town lots selling for $400 to $600 a piece." Lamar emerged as the largest city on Colorado's southeastern plains, a position it still maintains with a 1990 population of 8,343.

PW01 Big Timbers Museum

1929. 2 miles north of Lamar at junction of U.S. 50, U.S. 287, and Colorado 196

White terracotta banding and trim distinguish this Beaux-Arts brick box, which resembles a post office. Built to house repeater equipment for Denver–Kansas City long distance telephone cable, it was donated in 1966 by the American Telephone and Telegraph Company to the Prowers County Historical Society. The society converted it to a museum named for cottonwood groves along the Arkansas River. Many of these trees, some with circumferences of 18 feet, were cut down for building material and fuel, but some of the monarchs survive.

PW02 Lamar Tire Service (Shamrock Station)

1932, W. G. Brown. 501 N. Main St. (northwest corner of Sherman St.)

Petrified wood from Two Buttes in Baca County covers the east and south elevations of this gas station, with logs four feet in diameter framing the front service bay, doorway, and window. The thick log specimens, said to be 150 million years old, were stacked vertically to culminate in a spiky, irregular parapet. W. G. Brown, a Lamar lumber dealer, conceived and executed the design to immortalize an otherwise standard concrete block Shamrock Station. The "Petrified Wood Gas Station" earned a listing in *Ripley's Believe It or Not* and survives as a tire service shop.

PW03 Colorado Welcome Center
(Atchison, Topeka & Santa Fe Depot)

1893. Northeast corner of S. Main and Beech sts.

PW03 Colorado Welcome Center (Santa Fe Depot)

This standard Prairie Style depot, resembling those in Rocky Ford (Otero County) and Las Animas (Bent County), remains in its original location and is used by Amtrak's Southwest Chief. In 1990 Lamar rehabilitated its depot as a tourist center and offices for the Chamber of Commerce, completely gutting and reconfiguring the interior for constructive reuse. Adjacent Santa Fe Park boasts Santa Fe Locomotive 1819 and the Madonna of the Trail Monument (1926), sculpted by A. Leimbach of St. Louis, one of a dozen stone statues commissioned and donated by the National Society of the Daughters of the American Revolution for sites across the U.S. This westward-facing woman, clutching a baby and a rifle with another child clinging to her skirt, honors pioneer mothers.

PW04 Payne Hotel (Davies Hotel)

1902. 122 N. Main St. (southeast corner of Poplar St.) (NR)

Lewis Davies commissioned this three-story hotel of rough-faced local sandstone with banding at sill and lintel levels in a slightly lighter sandstone. Balconies once fronted the second and third levels above the entry. The three facade bays are divided by square piers with a parapet topping the center bay.

Davies met arriving trains and personally escorted travelers to his hotel. He also rented the rooms in shifts to sugar factory workers and slept at his desk when he had no bed for himself. The hotel held overflow from the local hospital during the 1918 influenza epidemic. Noteworthy and notorious guests included Governor Alva Adams, Tom Mix, and the Fleagle brothers, who robbed a local bank and killed four people in 1928. Renamed the Payne Hotel in 1943, the building was renovated for offices around 1975.

PW05 Lamar Theater

1920s. 219 S. Main St.

Art Deco triumphs behind the Lamar Theater's plumed neon marquee on a prow-like canopy. Blue glazed block used on the street level rises through a white stuccoed upper wall in vertical relief panels culminating in rounded and square peaks above the parapet.

PW06 Prowers County Courthouse

1928, Robert K. Fuller. 301 S. Main St. (NR)

Combining Neo-Renaissance and Neoclassical elements with Moderne massing, this three-story, rectangular courthouse of Indiana limestone sits on a granite-walled basement. The symmetrical north facade has full-height pavilions projecting from each end with vertical, windowless bays. The smaller upper panels have carved bison and corn motifs, while the central entablature features four bewigged judges. Over centered double doors of bronze with leaded glass panes, the pediment is ornamented with an eagle crowned by a nine-petaled flower and an engraved entablature. Inside are brass chandeliers, ceiling stenciling to echo exterior details, and local cattle brands incised in the friezes. The well-preserved interior retains its terrazzo floors and staircase, brass and wood fixtures, and coffered ceilings. The elaborate courtroom on the third floor has its original dark walnut furnishings and a stenciled, barrel vaulted ceiling. The Postmodern Prowers County Jail (1992) is on the south end of the courthouse block.

PW07 Post Office

1936, Louis A. Simon, OSA; Walter De Mordaunt. 300 S. 5th St. (NR)

One of Colorado's few Southwestern-style post offices, designed by a Pueblo architect selected by the Office of the Supervising Architect, has an asymmetrical stuccoed facade, red tile roof, and heavy wooden shutters. Above a red brick base, square pilasters with molded capitals divide recessed bays that include the transomed double-door entry. Inside, a beamed ceiling, tile floor, and marble wainscot have survived remodelings. The growing popularity of the Spanish Colonial style and the reduced interest in classicism in the late 1930s led to a greater use of regional styles in federal buildings, although this look is more typical of post offices in southern California than of Colorado. Irregular volumes and the asymmetrical plan disguise a basic rectangular shape.

PW08 Eighth Street Arms Apartments (Junior College of Southeastern Colorado)

1937, 1940, WPA. 8th to 9th sts. between Chestnut and Walnut sts.

A block on the south edge of town was developed for a two-year college, with its single building reflecting the WPA's trademark stone construction and low, stepped parapets. The original building is two stories in a shallow U plan, with a single-story porch, now converted to stairways and decks. The 1940 addition on the west is a gabled two-story structure with a single-story, hip-roofed wing extending south. Two blocks of playing fields for the Lamar High School Savages are enclosed by a low stone wall north of the campus. These were laid out by the WPA in 1940. The buildings were remodeled into apartments after the renamed Lamar Community College moved to a 1960s brick and concrete campus at 2400 South Main Street.

PW09 Willow Creek Park

1933, WPA. Parkway Dr. and S. 1st St.

The first WPA project in Colorado created a park and provided flood control along Willow Creek. A tapering, Decoesque 28-foot-high observation tower constructed of the local sandstone commemorates Zebulon Pike's camp near here (1806). The WPA also endowed this park with a rustic native stone and viga community/recreation building and a monumental outdoor picnic deck and outdoor fireplace.

Granada

Granada (1873, 3,484 feet), created by the Santa Fe Railroad, was a terminus until the railroad pushed on to La Junta in 1875. The town was moved from the mouth of Granada Creek, for which it was named, to its present location in 1876.

PW10 Octagon House

c. 1890. 410 Hoisington St.

This single-story brick house has a truncated octagonal roof. A gabled wing extending west is stuccoed, and the house has been painted white. Note the keystoned triangle trim above the windows.

PW11 Amache Japanese Relocation Camp Site

1942. 1 mile southwest of Granada via Prowers County. FF and 23

After the Japanese bombed Pearl Harbor, the U.S. government interned Japanese-Americans with as little as one-sixteenth Japanese blood, outdoing Hitler, who defined Jewish ancestry as a one-eighth portion. Between 1942 and 1945, 7,657 Japanese-Americans were held in what quickly became the tenth largest city in Colorado. The self-sufficient camp produced a surplus of crops and livestock. The internees transplanted small cottonwoods and willows from the Arkansas River banks to their bleak concentration camp, where they lived in wooden barracks buildings. They worked in factories and on farms and participated in scrap drives and other activities to help win the war. Only a few foundations survive today, along with the cemetery.

Holly

Holly (1880, 3,397 feet) was named for pioneer Hiram S. Holly, whose 50,000-acre ranch sprawled along the Arkansas River bottomlands from Granada to the Kansas line. The town was the first home of the Holly Sugar Company before it expanded

PW11 Amache Japanese Relocation Camp, 1943

and moved to Colorado Springs. The Holly City Buildings are of hand-sawn stone from a quarry ten miles north that produced building stone as soft as wood that hardened after quarrying. No buildings remain of Amity (1894–1937), 5 miles west of Holly, a Salvation Army colony for working men from large eastern cities.

PW12 Holly Land and Cattle Company Buildings

1880s. South end of Main St.

The town of Holly grew up around this ranch headquarters, a three-story masonry building with a shingled mansard roof that was then the largest building in town. A two-story gabled and dormered ranch house of native sandstone and a barn, both south of the tracks, are remnants of a huge ranch that supported some 15,000 cattle. Also on the south end of Main Street is the vacant AT&SF depot, the Santa Fe's standard small-town design blending Mission and Prairie Style elements in red brick with terracotta trim.

PW13 Holly Schools Complex

1922–1964, various architects. 200 block of N. Main St.

Buildings housing the town's school system, elementary through high school, comprise works designed by notable Colorado architects over a period of forty years. The Elementary School (1922, Mountjoy and Frewen) is a good example of that Denver firm's Neoclassical design and symmetrical planning, although it has lost its protruding cornice. Its raised interior hallway sits above a novel concrete ventilation duct running the long axis of the building, which draws air in through roof vents and windows and exhausts it through ports at the sides. The Community Gymnasium (1939, WPA) has lower wings with stepped parapets at either end of a tall, gabled central portion. The native stone walls are smooth blocks, with rounded corners beside the entrances. The Anna Bryce School (1957, C. Francis Pillsbury) houses classrooms and administrative offices in a single-story International Style building of light brick, also by a Denver architect. The newest building is the Junior-Senior High School (1964, Nixon and Jones), conceived by Boulder architects as a group of bermed polygonal pods connected to a central gymnasium by glass-walled corridors.

PW14 Holly Sugar Plant

1905. North of U.S. 50 at the west edge of town

The Holly Sugar Company opened this plant as its first and namesake location, only to move the machinery from here to Sheridan, Wyoming, in 1915. The company survives, but not in its hometown. The plant's brick buildings include a four-story rectangular silo and two processing buildings that exhibit attractive recessed paneling and corbeling. They were recycled as storage for the adjacent horse racing track, Gateway Downs.

PW15 Douglas Crossing Bridge

1936, WPA. Prowers County 28 over Two Butte Creek, 19.5 miles southwest of Holly (NR)

This is one of the finest of Colorado's WPA bridges. It has six 14-foot round arches springing from battered piers with alternating narrow and wide stones. An eight-man crew used stone hauled by teams from a nearby quarry to build the $20,000 structure and another single-span bridge 50 yards north over another gully.

Wiley

PW16 District 13 School

1938, WPA. Southeast corner of Main and 6th sts.

"Down Wiley way it's kids and hay" is the motto of this town. Its single-story, four-room school building is topped by a stepped stone parapet and faced with slabs of fieldstone with narrow limestone window trim. The random slabs make for a rustic look that is not typical of WPA work. Large wrought iron hinges distinguish double entry doors under a bracketed canopy. Wiley (1907, 3,731 feet), with its unusually wide main street and sandstone curbing, was named for William M. Wiley, a town promoter and head of the Holly Sugar Company. This farming center and poultry shipping point thrived after the Santa Fe Railroad arrived.

Bent County (BN)

Named for Bent's Fort (now in Otero County), Bent County (1874) is a nearly perfect rectangle of rolling, open land. Thanks to the Arkansas River and the huge John Martin Reservoir (1948), irrigated farming is the mainstay, with some ranching and oil production. Recent restorations have resurrected Boggsville, the pioneer settlement and original county seat. A dozen other towns have disappeared, leaving Las Animas as the only sizable town. The 1990 population of about 5,000 is the lowest since 1910 in this parched and sparsely settled agricultural county.

Las Animas

The county seat (1886, 3,893 feet) was named for El Río de Las Animas Perdidas en Purgatorio (river of lost souls in purgatory), or, in French, Purgatoire River, which flows into the Arkansas River nearby. The town grew up along the Atchison, Topeka, & Santa Fe railroad tracks during the early 1870s and eventually wrested the government seat from Boggsville, two miles south along the Santa Fe Trail. A fabled cow town, Las Animas was where herds driven up from Texas met Santa Fe cattle cars headed to Kansas City and Chicago stockyards. Now more economically diversified, the community is home for about half the county's residents. Area history is the focus of the Kit Carson Museum, 9th Street and Bent Avenue. The post office (1937, Louis A. Simon, OSA), 513 6th Street, is a yellow brick example of starved classicicism.

BN01 Bent County Courthouse

1887, Holmberg Bros. Carson to Bent aves. between 7th and 8th sts. (NR)

Colorado's oldest active courthouse is symmetrical on all sides, with recessed bays and a roofline of hipped and mansard elements, now missing its original iron cresting. The two-story red brick building has an elevated basement of rough-faced sandstone block and tooled sandstone trim in the same beige color. The vernacular composition combines round arches with molded and dentiled cornices and lintels, a pediment above the en-trance, and large, open corner towers with mansarded caps. The effect is vertical and elegant despite problematic additions and alterations outside. Some of the original interior remains.

To the north on the square-block grounds, the sheriff's office and jail (1902) has the look of a late Victorian home, except for the heavy metal window grids. South of the courthouse is the Santa Fe depot, which has the same plan and appearance as the depot in Rocky Ford (Otero County), with a low hipped roof and dormers over projecting polygonal bays. The north side of the red brick Prairie Style depot boasts a substantial porte-cochère with stone support pillars. With the courthouse in the background, this must have been an impressive scene for early rail travelers.

BN02 Las Animas Middle School (Bent County High School)

1913, James Larson. 1939, addition, John Gray. 1214 Thompson Blvd. (U.S. 50), between Poplar and Cottonwood aves.

The two-story brick school with an elevated basement of rough-faced stone block has a central portico with six two-story fluted columns culminating in Ionic capitals. The window bands have molded and bracketed lintels, and above are a frieze, a bracketed cornice, and a plain parapet. Paneled vertical piers mark the corners. The gymnasium-auditorium addition is Moderne.

BN03 Columbian School

1916, Nels T. Nelson, W. F. Mowbray, and F. W. Foote, builders. 1946, addition. 1026 W. 6th St.

This single-story brick school on a rectangular plan has a central open courtyard and a two-story gymnasium on the north. The Mission Revival style is evident in the curvilinear parapets with quatrefoil ornaments and in the arcade on three sides of the courtyard. The two-story addition at the northeast corner is larger but sympathetic, with light and dark beige brick contrasting subtly in tone to highlight brick patterns in the full-height entry surrounds. The nearby cottage, built for band practice, has been remodeled for classrooms. Builder Nels T. Nelson, who came from Sweden via Ishpeming, Michigan, built many stone buildings in Fort Lyon, Las Animas, and Cripple Creek.

BN04 Boggsville

1862–1890s. 2 miles south of Las Animas on Colorado 101 (NR)

Thomas O. Boggs, son of a Missouri governor and grandson of Daniel Boone, worked at Bent's Fort and married the fourteen-year-old stepdaughter of Charles Bent. Boggs established this ranch along the Santa Fe Trail on the banks of the Purgatoire River, near its confluence with the Arkansas River. The oldest unfortified permanent white settlement in southeastern Colorado, it served as a trading post, a post office, and the first county seat. Boggsville also became an agricultural center with a general store, stage stop, and school among more than twenty structures. After the Santa Fe Railroad built two miles north, Las Animas replaced Boggsville as the county seat.

Abandoned in the mid-1890s, the 110-acre townsite is now undergoing restoration as a historical park operated by the Pioneer Historical Society of Bent County. Archaeological and historical research conducted in consultation with Long Hoeft Architects has been used to restore and re-create the adobe Boggs House (1866) and a wing of the Prowers House (1867). These Territorial Style dwellings have Greek Revival details and lines painted on the adobe to suggest formal stone construction. Plans call for re-creating Kit Carson's last house, the pioneer school, sheep quarters, a general store, and other structures of this pioneer outpost along the Santa Fe Trail.

BN04.1 Boggs House

BN04.1 Boggs House

1866, Thomas Boggs. Colorado 101, 1.75 miles southeast of Las Animas

The Boggsville Revitalization Committee began restoration of this Territorial Style adobe house in 1985. A concrete foundation, brick chimneys, and a new roof were added to the U-plan house, and the old adobe was stabilized and covered with a lime plaster. Sections of the interior have been left unaltered to show the original stone foundation, pine roof, and 30-inch-thick adobe walls.

BN04.2 Prowers House

1867, John W. Prowers. Colorado 101, 1.75 miles southeast of Las Animas

John Prowers, the cattle king of southeastern Colorado, built a twenty-four-room, two-story adobe ranch house which also served as a stage stop, a hotel, and the first county courthouse. A third of the building—one wing—still stands and has been stabilized and restored. Prowers came to Colorado to join the Bents at Bent's Fort in 1857 and started his ranch in 1862. He introduced eastern pedigreed cattle to the area and built up the largest ranch in the Arkansas Valley, which stretched over much of Bent County and into what is now Prowers County, to the east.

BN05 Veterans Administration Medical Center (Fort Lyon)

1867; many additions. 4 miles east of Las Animas via U.S. 50 and Colorado 183

Established in 1860 below the confluence of the Purgatoire and Arkansas rivers, this was originally called Fort Wise but was renamed Fort Lyon in 1861 and moved 20 miles upstream to its present site on higher ground. Abandoned in 1889, the fort was resurrected by 1906 for a U.S. Navy tuberculosis sanatarium, and many hip-roofed frame buildings were built on the grounds. Of the older buildings, a dozen examples of stone and frame construction remain, arranged formally along straight roads in a 189-acre historic district.

The small, stone Kit Carson Memorial Chapel (c. 1867) was originally one of several officers' quarters built northeast of the parade grounds. In mid-May of 1868 an extremely ill Kit Carson was brought to these quarters, which then housed the post surgeon. Here Carson died of a ruptured aneurism, ending a long career as trapper, scout, and one-time commander of Fort Garland. The simple, front-gabled building was previously a blacksmith shop, then a meeting hall and museum, until its 1959 conversion into a small chapel.

Within the larger historic district, between A and C streets and from 1st Street to the East Service Road, is a second, 20-acre district of 1930s brick buildings belonging to the Veterans Administration Medical Center complex. These are uniformly Georgian Colonial Revival, with hipped and gable roofs originally of slate and detailing in brick, wood, and terracotta. They surround three sides of an open quadrangle with sanatariums on the north.

Otero County   (OT)

Bent's Fort, an important early trading post in the American Southwest, attracted Native Americans, Hispanics, French trappers and traders, and Yankees, making this area the commercial hub of southern Colorado during the 1830s and 1840s. Otero County, carved from the western portion of Bent County in 1889, was named for Miguel Otero, a founder of the county seat of La Junta. In this prairie county hugging the Arkansas River, the agrarian economy includes ranching, farming, and packaging frozen foods. Major crops are flower and vegetable seeds, hay, lettuce, dry beans, and Rocky Ford melons and cantaloupes.

La Junta

The county seat (1875, 4,066 feet) was originally King's Ferry, established in the 1840s as a place for Santa Fe trail travelers to cross the Arkansas River. The early 1870s railroad tent camp called Otero was renamed La Junta (Spanish for junction) because both the Santa Fe Trail and railroad routes forked here, with branches to Pueblo and Trinidad. Livestock shipping developed after the Santa Fe steamed into town, and La Junta has been an agricultural center ever since, housing about a third of the county's 20,000 residents.

The grand old courthouse, centerpiece of a tree-shaded square, 2nd to 3rd streets between Colorado and Santa Fe avenues, was demolished for a boxy replacement that is monumentally nondescript. The Kit Carson Hotel (1896, John Gwyn; remodeled, 1906, 1933), northeast corner of Colorado Avenue and 2nd Street, is brick with Art Deco detailing added in a 1933 remodeling. East of Colorado Avenue on 3rd Street, the

Rourke Opera House, now the Fox Theater (1913, George W. Roe), 11 East 3rd Street, retains original Moorish elements despite remodeling. The three-story Masonic temple (1924, George W. Roe), on East 3rd Street, has a polychrome brick frieze in a diamond pattern and an inset, pedimented bay with four Ionic columns in the upper south wall. The stately First Presbyterian Church (1905, George W. Roe), southwest corner of 3rd St. and Santa Fe Avenue, has been reduced to a first-floor video store. La Junta has demolished or mutilated many of its landmarks. Happy exceptions are two large catercorner Victorians in the elegant Colorado Avenue residential district that have been refurbished as bed and breakfast inns: the Jane Ellen Inn, a foursquare at 722 Colorado Avenue, and My Wife's Inn (1898), a more ostentatious Queen Anne Style house at 801 Colorado Avenue.

OT01 Atchison, Topeka & Santa Fe Depot
1954. U.S. 50 north of Colorado Ave.

This Streamline Moderne composition of single-story rectangular brick boxes has a flat roof that extends in wide overhangs supported by round steel posts. It replaces a grandiose 1892 three-story station that incorporated a Harvey House restaurant. A minimalist approach also characterizes the starkly Modernist passenger waiting room and ticket office inside.

OT02 Atchison, Topeka & Santa Fe Offices

1914. 402 Santa Fe Ave. (southwest corner of 4th St.)

The Santa Fe's modified Mission-Prairie Style is apparent in this administrative center, which was designed as three stories although only two were built. The red brick upper floors are on a base of light sandstone that is echoed in the stone frieze and in the Santa Fe cross logo, in terracotta, set into corner bays.

OT03 Post Office

1915, Oscar Wenderoth. Northwest corner of 4th St. and Colorado Ave. (NR)

This sparkling, two-story Renaissance Revival edifice with a coffered soffit in the overhanging, bracketed eaves has rough stuccoed walls and a limestone foundation and trim. Windows flanking the entry bay on the main floor have elaborate, round-arched surrounds, while the second-level fenestration features iron-balustraded balconets. Three arches centered in the symmetrical east facade lead through decorative metal gates to a recessed entry portico. Marble wainscot, plaster relief detail, and terrazzo floors shine in the full-height lobby, which features a coffered ceiling and second-floor balustraded balcony.

OT04 San Juan Avenue Historic District

San Juan Ave. between 5th and 6th sts. (NRD)

This small residential district consists of the east side of San Juan Avenue for the full block and a single house on the northwest corner of 6th Street. One- and two-story masonry houses built between 1896 and 1905 represent a gamut of historical vernacular styles, with uniform setbacks, low retaining walls along the sidewalks, mature trees, and a single remaining stone hitching post disguised as a tree stump. The houses at 509, 521, and 522 San Juan Avenue were designed by John Gwyn, a local architect also responsible for the Chestnut Apartments (1908) at 4th Street and Santa Fe Avenue.

OT05 Finney House

1899, Walter Dubree. 608 Belleview Ave. (NR)

Just outside the San Juan Avenue Historic District in another block of large, dignified old homes is this two-story brick Queen Anne Style house. It is overlaid with Neoclassical trim and fronted by an overscaled, two-story porch with columns and pediment. The block contains another Queen Anne house augmented with Neoclassical elements, the Rourke House (1898), 619 Carson Avenue (northeast corner of 7th Street) (NR). It has a round corner tower and a second-story porch that becomes an attic balcony. Both residences were constructed by Blankenship Brothers. The Hart House (1898, George Burnett), 802 Ratón Avenue (NR), is a purer example of the Queen Anne Style.

OT06 Otero Museum Complex

Southwest corner of 2nd St. and Anderson Ave.

This project of the Otero Museum Association brings together many elements of the area's past, including transportation artifacts and two historic buildings, in a complex set in a working-class residential neighborhood. Nancy Wickham moved her tiny Wickham Boarding House for railway workers from the former end-of-track town of Granada in 1875 to La Junta. The one-story house, now moved to the museum site, has vertical board-and-batten siding, a side-gable roof, and a full-width front porch. The Sciumbato Grocery (1908), 706 2nd Street (NR), is a frame false-fronted structure with typical display windows. Now restored as the principal structures of the Otero Museum, the house and store display some original furnishings, an extensive railroad memorabilia collection, and furnishings of a vintage doctor's office.

OT07 **Offices** (Lincoln School)

1937, Walter De Mordaunt and John Gray. 317 W. 3rd St. (NR)

The architects, a Pueblo firm, gave a Spanish Colonial look to this handsome brick school with its arcaded entry. Aztec accents grace the auditorium and library. The latter is also enhanced by murals by Robert Wade.

OT08 **Koshare Indian Museum**

1944, Damon O. Runyon. 115 W. 18th St. (northwest corner of Santa Fe Ave.)

This stuccoed cinderblock Pueblo Revival complex on the Otero Junior College campus surrounds a kiva that is 60 feet in diameter with a roof formed by 637 layered logs. The Nebraska architect supposedly studied Indian kiva roofs and designed the span using toothpicks and a teacup. This museum complex was developed by Explorer Scouts under the direction of James F. "Buck" Burshears (1909–1987), who in 1933 began studying and performing traditional Indian dances and making costumes. Burglar bars on the lower windows of the viga-studded museum building are designed to resemble corn plants. They guard a fabulous collection of Native American artifacts, including San Ildefonso Pueblo pottery and Taos School paintings by, among others, Ernest L. Blumenschein and Joseph Henry Sharp.

OT09 **Atchison, Topeka & Santa Fe Hospital** (Mennonite Sanatarium)

1884–1907. 401 Smithland Ave.

A rooftop balustrade is about the only hint of elegance left in this deteriorated two-story beige brick complex, which opened as a tuberculosis sanatarium and later became a hospital for railroad workers. It stood vacant for many years until purchased by the Elks, who are slowly renovating it as a bingo club. Part of the neglected three-block grounds are occupied by a housing project.

OT10 **North La Junta School**

1914, Walter Dubree. Northwest corner of Main and Trail sts. (Colorado 109 and 194) (NR)

This prominent school set on spacious grounds in the unincorporated community north of the Arkansas River closed in 1985. Although rather plain in style, the red brck building, two stories on a raised concrete basement, is distinguished by banded peach and buff brick and stone trim beneath the overhanging eaves of a low hipped roof. Boys and girls have separate entrances. Next door to the east is the original frame school, now the Fort Bent–North La Junta Community Building.

OT11 **Bent's Old Fort**

1828–1834. 1976, reconstruction, George Thorson and National Park Service staff. 8 miles northeast of La Junta on Colorado 194 (NR)

Learning from the durable and fire-, heat-, and cold-resistant adobe buildings of Taos and Santa Fe, brothers William and Charles Bent and their partner, Ceran St. Vrain, imported Mexican artisans to construct an adobe trading fort. They used local clay, mixing in straw and lamb's wool to help hold together their mud fortress on the north bank of the Arkansas River, then the boundary between the United States and Mexico. Like the original, this 1976 replica has catercorner towers with cannon slits. Bent's Fort was the largest of all the fur trade posts, measuring about 130 by 180 feet with walls 2 feet thick and 15 feet high. The heavy planks of the main gate were covered in sheet iron, with a tower above and double doors so that traders could deal through a wicket. Cactus planted atop the adobe walls also reinforced security. Inside, the courtyard is flanked by 38 rooms, with shed roofs over log and adobe walls. These interior rooms have been reconstructed and furnished to illustrate the fur trade era.

William Bent married a Cheyenne, Owl Woman, an alliance that fostered trade with her tribe. Apache, Arapaho, Comanche, Kiowa, and other Plains tribes also traded at Bent's Fort, exchanging buffalo robes, beaver pelts, and deer hides for goods from St. Louis. The fort also attracted French *coureurs du bois* and traders from Mexico. As many as 100 men worked at the fort during its 1840s heyday, when it boasted such refinements as an icehouse and a rooftop billiard room.

Bent's Fort helped shape the American Southwest in several ways. The Bents introduced ranching and farming to southeastern Colorado and replaced heavy Conestoga wagons with light Studebakers in the Santa Fe Trail trade. Little but foundations of the first fort remained by the 1970s, when the National Park Service began reconstruction in what had become a cornfield. Drawings by Captain James Abert, a U.S. Army engineer, and archaeological research guided the $3 million reconstruction. Living history exhibits and staff storytellers breathe life into this replica of the most celebrated adobe fort of the American Southwest.

Fowler

Fowler (1882, 4,341 feet) was named for Orson S. Fowler, who set up the Fowler Ditch Company, acquired large real estate holdings, and platted the town. He was also a professor who specialized in phrenology, physiology, and horticulture. The town's original grid paralleled the railroad tracks, but additions on the south, east, and west are aligned to compass points. Structures of interest include the Fowler Auto Camp (1933), north side of U.S. 50 at the east town limit, a few small frame cottages and a store, now closed, in a complex converted to a small recreational vehicle park. The First National Bank (1905), 115 Main Street, is a two-story building of beige brick with stucco and terracotta trim. A large, round-arched entry and rough-faced sandstone first floor survive on a much-altered post office (1890s), 123 Main Street.

OT12 Town Hall (Atchison, Topeka & Santa Fe Depot)

1913. Northeast corner of Main St. and Santa Fe Ave.

A red cross, the Santa Fe Railroad's distinctive logo, and yellow terracotta trim the four parapeted gable ends of this single-story red brick depot. A standard small-town depot design developed around 1909, it has several siblings along the line from Kansas City to Pueblo. Shallow arches top the transomed waiting room windows, and the walls below the sills are slightly battered. Dark red brick and cream terracotta lend a Jacobethan ambiance to what is now a spiffy town hall. The Santa Fe depot (1912–1913) at 212 North Grand Street in Manzanola, the next town east, is a twin, now used as a community center.

Rocky Ford   *mom's birthplace*

In Rocky Ford (1871, 4,178 feet) George Washington Swink (1836–1910) first planted watermelons as a crop in 1877 and helped to develop the hybrid orange-fleshed cantaloupe in 1884, as well as the honeydew melon, developed in 1916. Melon production peaked at 3,000 railroad carloads in 1928. Today, Rocky Ford melons are grown in several states, but the town remains the "Melon Capital of the World" by virtue of being the seed source. The Holly Sugar Company, which George Swink also helped found in Rocky Ford in 1900, was another major producer until the 1960s.

Originally founded at a stony ford of the Arkansas River in 1871 by storekeeper Asa Russell, the town was moved three miles south to meet the Santa Fe Railroad's route to Pueblo. Swink, who joined Russell in 1874 as a partner in his store, laid out the present town on his own homestead. The original six-block plat, following the diagonal of the tracks, was expanded with additions platted along compass points. Main Street's one- and two-story commercial buildings exhibit noteworthy brickwork in the elevations above storefronts. So does the First Presbyterian Church (c. 1906), 303 South 9th Street. Rocky Ford's large new water tank atop Play Park Hill is emblazoned with the high school team name, The Meloneers. The Arkansas Valley Fair Grounds, located north of town on a part of Swink's 1876 timber claim, retain a 300-foot-diameter octagonal frame exhibition hall (1901).

OT13 Chamber of Commerce (Atchison, Topeka & Santa Fe Depot

1907. 1989, renovation, Tom Morris Architects. 105 N. Main St.

A one story, 30-by-160-foot Prairie Style structure with a hipped roof and projecting bays on three sides of the waiting area was the standard Santa Fe design for larger towns, used for Rocky Ford's third depot. Red sandstone trim provides subtle contrast to the red brick. Railway Express built a separate freight depot to the west, augmenting the station's own baggage wing. Tom Morris, a Denver architect, redesigned the depot as an information center and Chamber of Commerce offices, with a new band shell for the adjacent town park.

OT14 Odd Fellows Hall

1892. 200 S. Main St. (southeast corner of Front St.)

This two-story brick commercial block houses the Northrop King fruit and vegetable seed company in the storefront space below the second-story fraternal hall. Its parapet features the fancy brickwork showcased in many other downtown buildings, with a carved stone plaque showing the name and date of construction. Horizontal bands of rough-faced stone accent second-floor sills and lintels.

OT15 Rocky Ford Historical Museum (Rocky Ford Library)

1909, Walter Dubree. Sycamore Ave. between 10th and 11th sts. (NR)

At the south end of a full-block site that is now Library Park, with a new library (1979) at the northwest corner, Rocky Ford's Carnegie library is a single story of gray brick above a raised basement of rough-faced cast stone block. Its Greek Revival design probably originated in Carnegie Foundation of-

fices. The north entrance of the rectangular building is centered in a slightly protruding bay with a cornice supported by pairs of wooden Doric columns. The Rocky Ford Museum, which had been housed in the basement since 1950, now occupies the whole building. A Postmodern addition (1990) and a wall to the south enclose a rear courtyard.

OT16 Scouting Clubhouse

1923, Walter Burchett, builder. 91 Play Park Hill, west end of Play Park Hill on the south end of Main St., next to the golf course

This clubhouse on the bluff overlooking the town was conceived specifically as a meeting place for scout troops. Its rustic vernacular style owes much of its charm to the masonry walls of rounded river rock set in mortar. The flat roof has a crenelated parapet, giving the appearance of a fort. Subsequent additions, including screened porches along the north and east sides, have expanded the original small rectangle.

OT17 Rocky Ford High School

1963, Caudill Rowlett Scott and Paul S. Pierson, associated architects. West of Play Park Hill golf course between Washington Ave. and Cottonwood Lane

The high school's single-story runs of brick classrooms enclose a south-facing courtyard on three sides in the manner of an early Spanish fortification. Connecting interior hallways look onto the courtyard through large, full-height windows. Within the courtyard, the gymnasium is located in a bermed building covered in a shallow hyperbolic paraboloid, with window bands filling the remaining walls.

OT18 Post Office

1935, Louis A. Simon, OSA. 401 N. 9th St.

This symmetrical brick box, typical of the small-town post offices of its time, has a broken pediment and urn topping the central entrance. It retains its tile floors, wainscot, and most of the original woodwork and features a mural by W. Victor Higgins of

Taos, New Mexico, *The First Crossing at Rocky Ford.*

OT19 American Beet Sugar Plant

1898–1900. North of Chestnut Ave. between 1st and 3rd sts.

A steel skeleton and brick skin form the original building of this complex, whose 1,000-tons-per-day capacity jumped to 3,350 tons with the addition of two more buildings. All three have paneled brick walls and stepped parapets fronting barrel-vault roofs. This factory, now closed, once employed 400 workers earning an average of 35 cents per hour. In the 1920s during an average day they sliced 1,650 tons of beets and during an average year converted 200,000 tons of beets into 35 million pounds of sugar. The six conjoined storage elevators attest to the former importance of the sugar industry in the Arkansas River Valley.

Swink

OT20 Holly Sugar Company Plant

1906. N. Swink Dr. at Sugar Rd.

Swink (1900, 4,118 feet) changed its name from Fairmount in 1906 to honor George Washington Swink, father of melon cultivation in the Arkansas Valley and cofounder of the Holly Sugar Company. Fields of colorful zinnias surrounding the town provide seed packaged by the D. V. Burrell Seed Company. The white Holly Sugar stack is the town sentinel. This plant processed 1,200 tons of beets per day. It closed in 1959, and the machinery was removed. The plant building, superintendent's residence, and administrative offices remain, the last converted to apartments.

Crowley County   (CW)

Created from a portion of Otero County in 1911, this high plains county began to be settled in 1887, when the Missouri Pacific line from Kansas City was extended to Pueblo. The MP fostered many towns of which Sugar City, Ordway, Crowley, and Olney Springs remain in a county whose population has dwindled to fewer than 4,000 people and some 70,000 cows. Sugar City's huge American Beet Sugar Company plant was dismantled in 1949. Between Sugar City and Ordway, the large reservoirs at lakes Henry and Meredith hold water diverted through the Colorado Canal from the Arkansas River to quench the thirst of cattle and crops, of ranchers and farmers.

Ordway

The county seat (1890, 4,312 feet) was named for George N. Ordway, a Denver president of the company that developed the area. The town's showplace was a large frame house boasting twenty-five rooms, forty-eight windows, and, oddly, fifty-three doors. It was dismantled in 1931, and the materials were reused to build several smaller farmhouses. A livestock hub, Ordway has a 60,000-head feedlot, its largest industry.

CW01 Crowley County Courthouse

1915, J. M. Gile. Northeast corner of 6th and Main sts.

Posing as a large dwelling, this foursquare courthouse has conventional Georgian Revival detailing, a concrete foundation, a glazed brick base, buff brick walls, and a wide, sturdy porch to give it a domestic appeal. Horizontal banding at the corners gives the effect of quoins. A much larger rear addition is one of the clues that this is more than a large house.

Crowley

CW02 **Crowley County Heritage Center**
(Crowley School)

1914. 1993, restoration. 300 E. Main St.

Crowley (1914, 4,275 feet) was named for state senator John H. Crowley, who developed the town and irrigated farming in the area. Its elementary school is a striking one-and-one-half-story building of pressed red brick dominated by a shingled, central bell tower, with four smaller corner towers and round-arched openings. The school has dou-bled as a community center hosting, among other things, Presbyterian church services, Commercial Club meetings, World War I Red Cross classes, and a hospital during the 1918 influenza epidemic. Bunker-like concrete additions flanking the entrance were removed during the 1993 restoration. The upstairs classrooms and entry hall retain their original woodwork. Next door, at 200 East Main Street, is the two-story red brick high school (1921, W. E. Stickney), a Mediterranean Revival Beaux-Arts building with a curvilinear parapet, currently scheduled for renovation as a senior residence.

Kiowa County   (KW)

Dry-land farmers and ranchers have replaced the Kiowa tribe in Kiowa County (1889), a rural region of small, unincorporated communities. Eads, the county seat, has a stockyard and grain elevators and is the primary rail shipping center for a county once served by the Burlington, the Missouri Pacific, and the Rock Island railroads. The 1990 population of 1,688 is the lowest since 1910, when the agricultural boom began. Discovery of the Brandon Oil Field and McCalve Gas Field in the 1950s brightened hopes for faltering farmers.

Eads

The county seat (1887, 4,213 feet) was founded with the arrival of the Missouri Pacific Railroad and named for James B. Eads, a noted Civil War army engineer who built the Eads Bridge, the first bridge across the Mississippi River, at St. Louis. Although not incorporated until 1916, Eads became the county seat in 1902, replacing Sheridan Lake, where the courthouse mysteriously burned in 1900. Eads's current population hovers at around 800, and its dominating structures are the towering grain elevators near the railroad. The old Eads State Bank, 1300 Maine Street, is now the home of the Kiowa County Historical Society, and the Missouri Pacific depot, 100 East 15th Street, survives as another of the well-maintained downtown buildings. The WPA-built former city hall (c. 1937), now a Masonic lodge, is stone with a later brick addition.

KW01 **Kiowa County Courthouse**

1956. 1305 Goff St. (northeast corner of 14th St.)

At its dedication in 1956 a county commissioner apologized for this modest, two-story, flat-roofed brick building with ribbon windows: "After six years of drought we did not have the courage to ask you folks to become saddled with a burden of indebtedness. . . . Your county officials did the very best that they know how to do and they hope from the bottom of their hearts that you like what they have done. . . . As you probably know, $192,000 is not a great deal of money with which to build a building of this size." The site of the razed 1904 red brick courthouse next door became the parking lot for the new courthouse.

Chivington

KW02 **Sand Creek Massacre Site**

9 miles northeast of Colorado 96 via Kiowa County 54 and W

A small historic marker is the only structure commemorating the site, now on private farmland, that once held an encampment of Southern Cheyenne and Arapaho, mostly old men, women, and children. They were massacred on November 29, 1864, by the Third Colorado Regiment, under the command of Col. John M. Chivington, a former minister. When asked by a subordinate if they should kill children, Chivington responded, "Nits make lice." Of almost 900 soldiers, 10 were killed and 38 wounded. Of some 500 Indians, more than 137 were killed and many of their bodies mutilated.

The unincorporated town of Chivington (1887, 3,890 feet), named for the colonel, was at one time a freight division for the Missouri Pacific. Today Chivington is on the edge of the grave, if not a ghost town, with only birds and rodents attending the ruins of a two-story Italianate schoolhouse.

Haswell

Haswell (1903, 4,538 feet) has a small, relatively unchanged business district representative of the restrained vernacular favored in the early twentieth century. The cross-gabled, frame Homestead House, moved in 1913 to Main Street north of the tracks, is highlighted by a simple bracket in the peak of the front-gabled porch. The L&M Market (c. 1907), on the north side of Colorado 96, is a narrow, deep, brick edifice with a two-story front section that hosted dances upstairs. A wide porch shelters the south storefront. Of the same vintage is the stuccoed Haswell Hotel (c. 1907), formerly the Holly Hotel, on the east side of Main Street south of the highway. A hipped roof and wide front porch with tapered square masonry supports give this brick foursquare hotel a homey air.

KW03 Booster Hall

1914–1915. Thomas B. Singer, builder. North of Colorado 96 at east end of town

Built as a multifunctional hall for educational and social purposes, this stuccoed cement-block meeting hall has long hosted monthly dances. The dominant hipped roof has a small, peaked dormer in the front, above the gabled canopy with tapered supports that shelters the transomed double entry.

KW04 Post Office

1909. West side of Main St., south of Colorado 96

This single-story brick structure, now stuccoed, with flat roof and entrance in a cut corner, was built as a bank, which failed in 1927. It became the post office in the 1960s. Shallow, blind arches top a pair of large windows in the street facade, and a decorative, corbeled cornice runs across the parapet.

KW05 Methodist Church

1916. Thomas B. Singer, builder. West side of Main St. at south end of town

This cross-gabled church has a square bell tower with a spire in the inside corner of the intersecting wings with the entry in its base. Modest detail on the stuccoed masonry building includes shallow triangular pediments above the entry and a small tower window. Large steel windows with a grid of small panes provide ample, uncolored light.

Cheyenne County (CH)

Cheyenne County, established in 1889, lies in rolling plains along the Kansas border. The town of Kit Carson became an early supply town on the Smoky Hill Trail, a gold rush and immigrant route that crossed the county. Livestock raising and dry-land farming have become the principal industries, and millions of dollars in winter wheat are harvested each year. In 1894 land near Cheyenne Wells was deeded to the state by the Union Pacific Railroad to use as an experimental farm. Here, John "Uncle Johnnie" Robinson and other state agricultural agents tried different dry-land crops, planted a successful orchard, and built several adobe buildings to demonstrate that farmers could survive here. The Cheyenne Wells (1968) and Sorrento (1976) oil fields have sustained the economy in recent decades.

Cheyenne Wells

The county seat (1876, 4,296 feet) was named for wells Cheyenne Indians had dug on the original townsite five miles north on the Smoky Hill Route. The town moved here to accommodate the Kansas Pacific Railroad and developed a water system (1887), a hotel (1888), and streetlights fueled from nearby gas wells. Such progressive and aggressive leadership enabled Cheyenne Wells to capture and keep the county seat and otherwise to dominate the county from the beginning. About half of Cheyenne County's 2,400 residents live here.

CH01 Cheyenne County Courthouse

1908, John J. Huddart. 51 S. 1st St. (NR)

Aspiring feebly to Georgian Revival, this overblown foursquare is three brick stories tall. It has four attic dormers, a pedimented entry, decorative keystones over first-floor windows, brick pilasters, and white-painted eaves and frieze. Inside, light from original fixtures still shines on much of the original woodwork, mosaic tile vestibule floor, and coffered-ceilinged courtroom with a portrait of George Washington. A new wing and a 1983 renovation complement the original. In this sparsely populated county, the courthouse still houses many of its original functions, as well as the social service department, the county extension agent, and the weed control office. One of a number of Colorado county courthouses designed by Denver architect John Huddart, this is a relatively sparse, simple building exemplifying the early twentieth-century reaction to Victorian styles.

CH02 Eastern Colorado Historical Society Museum (Cheyenne County Jail)

1894, Robert S. Roeschlaub. 85 W. 2nd St. (NR)

This forbidding brick fortress embodies the concept of law and order, functioning as an unmistakable symbol as well as a place of imprisonment. A Romanesque Revival structure with an octagonal two-story tower and irregular plan, it has heavy brick corbeling and chimneys. The Citizens Brick Company of Cheyenne Wells constructed the building, which in 1905 was covered with stucco scored to resemble large stone blocks. Interior spaces include the sheriff's living quarters and office, steel men's and women's cells installed in 1937, a lean-to addition (1920s), and a restored carriage house. Robert Roeschlaub, a versatile Denver architect who specialized in institutional structures, also designed a now-demolished jail for neighboring Lincoln County. In 1961, after the county built a new jail, the Cheyenne Wells Business and Professional Women converted this unique landmark to a museum.

CH01 Cheyenne County Courthouse

CH03 Masonic Temple (Forker Building)

1907. 200 E. 1st St.

This two-story block of cast stone built by automobile maker Walter Chrysler's father-in-law, George Forker, has arched, double-sash second-story windows with decorative keystones above a typical transomed store-front. The structure survived a 1910 fire and became the Masonic temple.

Kit Carson

Kit Carson (1869, 4,285 feet), named for the western scout and guide, began as a Kansas Pacific railroad settlement with a large number of tents and dugouts. The original (1869) town stood three miles west of the present site on the banks of Sand Creek. The track and the town moved here in 1882. North of town in open prairie is the Old Trail Monument (1954, Gerald Maydew), commemorating the Smoky Hill Trail. Built 34 feet high of 110 tons of local fieldstone, it resembles the fireplace and chimney of a burned-out house with a wagon wheel cemented into the pyramidal top.

CH04 Union Pacific Museum (Union Pacific Depot)

1906. Northwest corner of U.S. 287 and Park St., in the town park

Small-town depots such as this anchored isolated prairie towns, as railroads delivered food, clothing, coal, and even shelter (in the form of mail-order houses). This passenger depot, with its distinctive radiating wooden screens in the gable peaks, was moved here for preservation as a museum, with UP caboose 25400 on display.

CH05 Kit Carson Pool Hall, Silver Spoon Saloon, and Recreation Parlor

1916. Northwest corner of 2nd and Main sts. (NR)

This commercial block is a single brick story above a concrete basement which resounds with the crackling of billiard balls. Above the requisite transomed storefront with recessed central entrance, a shallow, stepped parapet contrasts with decorative patterns in a darker brick frieze. A barbershop, community meeting rooms, and liquor store have also been tenants here.

Wild Horse

CH06 Wild Horse Community Association Building

1921. Ivan Nilsen, builder. Southeast corner of 5th and Main sts.

Wild Horse (1877, 4,470 feet) was named for nearby Wild Horse Creek, where both red and white men found wild ponies. The first substantial building erected after a 1917 fire leveled the town was the Community Association Building. It was built with donated local labor, and the $4,000 cost for materials was financed by selling shares in the association. The one-story, rectangular hall has a red brick parapet, window trim, and quoins that contrast with the gray brick walls. The round-arched, recessed entry is below a raised central section of the parapet, which hides the peak of a shallow gable roof. Lightning shortened the chimney in 1954, and the building has since been stabilized with wood beams and tie rods. Most other structures in this dying town are in similar disrepair.

CH07 Aroya

1889–1965

CH07 Aroya, schoolhouse

Founded near where the Union Pacific tracks cross the often dry Big Sandy River and given the misspelled Spanish name for a dry gully, Aroya, like so many other small high plains towns, is struggling to stay on the map even though the post office has closed. As if to signal the town's distress, resident sculptor Owen Moreland used scrap iron and other rusting relics of the plains to construct a 35-foot-high lighthouse that has become the town's landmark. The notable schoolhouse, now abandoned, is a clapboard building with a hipped roof rising to an open bell tower with a flagpole and separate, arched entrances for boys and girls at the front corners. Many western schools did away with the eastern school custom of separating the sexes; this is a rare Colorado example of front-door discrimination.

The Rio Grande:
The Adobe Frontier

Walk quietly, Coyote,
The practical people are coming now
Into the juniper, into the sage arroyos,
Where the smoke is sweeter than anywhere
And the mud is ready for building . . .
While the Puritans over in England
Are getting ready to whisper,
"There is a way and we will build a ship,"
People in motion are . . . along the Rio Grande. . . .
                    —Thomas Hornsby Ferril, "Nocturne at Noon—1605"

T HE RIVER THE SPANISH CALLED EL RIO GRANDE DEL NORTE, the nation's third longest, guided the first Euro-American settlers into Colorado. Don Juan de Oñate in 1598 claimed the entire drainage for Spain, "from the leaves of the trees in the forest to the stones and sands of the river."

The Rio Grande's headwaters converge in Colorado, in the area known as the San Luis Valley, which was one of the most remote reaches of Spain's global empire. The valley is walled on the west by the San Juan Mountains and on the east by the Sangre de Cristo Range. These 14,000-foot ranges frame the dry valley, which lies at 8,000 feet and has average annual precipitation of about eight inches. Rainfall often proves to be an illusory virga, evaporating before it reaches the earth. The area was never economically important to Spain, or, after the 1821 revolution, to Mexico.

In 1806 President Thomas Jefferson assigned U.S. Army Lieutenant Zebulon Pike to explore the southern boundary of the Louisiana Purchase. Only after Pike and other U.S. explorers, traders, and trappers repeatedly poked into the San Luis Valley did Mexico become concerned. To promote settlement and limit Yankee encroachment, the Mexican government made five land grants, including the gigantic Conejos and Sangre de Cristo grants of 1833 and 1843. A few parties of farmers from New Mexico arrived in the 1840s but were pushed back by the Utes, who had inhabited the valley for hundreds of years.

In 1848 the United States took possession of the San Luis Valley after winning the Mexican War and established a fort in 1852 to police the Utes. Fort Garland provided more protection for Mexican-Americans than Spain or Mexico ever had and made possible permanent settlements such as San Luis

The Rio Grande Region

Saguache
• 36
• 30
• 37 • 34
• 29
• 35 • 32
• 27
• 33
• 28
• 31
Mineral
Rio Grande
Conejos
• 26 • 24 • 25
• 2 Alamosa
• 3
4 ⊙ 1
• 6 • 8
17
• 23
• 11 • 14 5
19 • 20
• 13 • 7
18 • 15 • 21
• 13 • 10
22 • • 16
• 9
Costilla
12

Alamosa (Alamosa Co.)* **1**	Del Norte (Rio Grande Co.) **24**
Antonito (Conejos Co.) **16**	Fort Garland (Costilla Co.) **8**
Blanca (Costilla Co.) **6**	Garcia (Costilla Co.) **9**
Bonanza (Saguache Co.) **30**	Hooper (Alamosa Co.) **2**
Capulin (Conejos Co.) **17**	La Garita (Saguache Co.) **33**
Center (Saguache Co.) **31**	La Jara (Conejos Co.) **19**
Chama (Costilla Co.) **7**	Las Sauses (Conejos Co.) **20**
Conejos (Conejos Co.) **15**	Manassa (Conejos Co.) **21**
Creede (Mineral Co.) **27**	Mineral Hot Spings (Saguache Co.) **34**
Crestone (Saguache Co.) **32**	Moffat (Saguache Co.) **35**
	Mogote (Conejos Co.) **18**
	Monte Vista (Rio Grande Co.) **25**
	Mosca (Alamosa Co.) **3**
	Ortiz (Conejos Co.) **22**
	Saguache (Saguache Co.) **29**
	San Acacio (Costilla Co.) **11**
	San Francisco (Costilla Co.) **12**
	San Isidro (Costilla Co.) **10**
	San Luis (Costilla Co.) **5**
	San Pedro - San Pablo (Costilla Co.) **13**
	Sanford (Conejos Co.) **23**
	Sargents (Saguache Co.) **36**
	South Fork (Rio Grande Co.) **26**
	Viejo San Acadio (Costilla Co.) **14**
	Villa Grove (Saguache Co.) **37**
	Wagon Wheel Gap (Mineral Co.) **28**
	Waverly (Alamosa Co.) **4**

▲
N

Miles
0 _____ 50

1 inch = 61 miles

A detailed map of site locations has
been provided for cities inticated
by ⊙ on the map and by * in the
list at right.

(1851). Most of the Mexican land grants, however, passed into the hands of non-Hispanic newcomers through proceedings in the Yankee courts. Both through the legal process and in other ways, land granted to New Mexican farmers and ranchers has been gobbled up by non-Hispanic newcomers. Land grabbers have ranged from the first Colorado territorial governor, William Gilpin, to the billionaire Malcolm Forbes, who acquired the largest private estate in Colorado, the 240,000-acre Trinchera Ranch.

Mormon settlements at La Jara and Manassa, and Anglo, German, Japanese, and Scandinavian settlers added to the valley's diversity. Yet Spanish language, culture, and architecture linger in the valley, which sometimes seems more New Mexican than Coloradan.

The San Luis Valley has funneled Hispanic art, architecture, culture, and people northward into the rest of Colorado. Hispanics, many with roots in "El Valle," have become the state's largest ethnic minority. But not until development of the Santa Fe Style in the early 1900s did Hispanic architecture become respectable. By the 1950s it had become common throughout Colorado in derivative styles, especially in ranch houses.

Hispanic towns in the Rio Grande Valley dug irrigation ditches and set aside grazing fields and hunting areas that allowed poor farmers and ranchers to survive in a tough country. Adobe structures, following older Spanish custom, were built around plazas, which provided protection and promoted community.

Churches were the cornerstones of these plazas. Hispanic churches, unlike Native American structures, which hugged the ground, challenged the landscape with vertical lines, asserting spiritual as well as physical dominion. No matter how simple the valley churches, they share the Renaissance ideal of symmetry and perspective. Each is properly viewed from its gateway, and inside, the main altar is set opposite the main door and framed as the focal point. Church spires still preside over many of the smaller Hispanic towns. Sometimes a morada (Spanish, dwelling) sits next to the church. These are small halls where the Penitentes, a radical Catholic men's group, meet to do penance.

A few churches are still decorated with *retablos* (paintings on wood panels) and *bultos* (statues carved of wood), although Anglo collectors have acquired many of these treasures, just as Anglo settlers acquired the land. Like the kachinas of the Pueblo tribes, these santos, or statues of saints, are functional; they are carried out of the church in processions to bless the fields, to bring rain, and to ward off harm. If effectual, as Father Thomas J. Steele, S.J., notes in his book, *Santos and Saints,* traditionally "the santo would be rewarded with a new dress or costume jewelry, a vigil light, or some other small token of gratitude." If the santo did not perform, "it might be 'punished' by being turned to the wall, put out of sight, or deprived of some ornament." Saints, at least in folklore, not only healed people but restored leaky church roofs and crumbling adobe walls.

Adobe is an ancient building material dating back at least to the Egyptians, who built the pyramids at Saqqara using sun-fired bricks of clay with chopped straw or coarse grass stubble. Adobe was also used in what is now Iraq earlier than 3000 B.C. From Iraq and Egypt, adobe made its way around the Mediterranean world to Spain, then to New Spain. Mud had been in use among Precolumbian Native Americans, who soon began using adobe bricks as well.

In New Mexico and southern Colorado, adobe bricks are about twelve inches long, six inches wide, and three inches thick. They are made by mixing clay and water, then adding straw for reinforcement. Originally made by hand, adobe bricks are now formed in wooden frames but are still sun dried. Adobe thinned with water is used as mortar, and as plaster to patch walls. Building walls are replastered more or less regularly, sometimes with animal blood mixed into the water to harden the plaster. Adobe structures are ideally two bricks thick to keep winter heat in and summer heat out.

Sometimes logs, not adobe bricks, formed the structure under mud plaster. The oldest type of Hispanic log structures, jacales, were made of posts planted upright with their feet in a trench and their tops lashed together and capped with a horizontal bond beam. They were often plastered with adobe and roofed with whatever was at hand. Jacales were used as the first fences and corrals as well as houses. Variations using horizontal logs are called *fuertes*. As towns grew more permanent, adobe brick structures generally replaced cruder jacales and *fuertes*, which often were reused as outbuildings.

In the San Luis Valley the oldest adobe structures are Territorial, as buildings erected after 1848 and the establishment of U.S. territories (and architectural influence) are known. Territorial adobe buildings have log roof beams that do not extend beyond the walls, unlike the distinctive vigas of the Native American Pueblo style. As Indians had only stone tools, they did not cut roof beams flush with the walls as Hispanics did, but let the ends protrude. While Native Americans used round logs, Hispanics often squared logs on two sides, leaving the sides round. They also laced peeled limbs (*latías*) together in a herringbone pattern across the ceiling beams to form a ceiling. They might paint doors blue, the color associated with the Blessed Virgin, to keep out the devil.

Hispanic adobe buildings of the 1850s–1880s originally had flat roofs, but, confronted by the harsh Colorado climate, many residents added pitched roofs later to provide better insulation and drainage. Early adobe buildings had few openings and little or no ornamentation. Later Territorial adobe structures are distinguished from the earlier, simpler Hispanic adobe by the presence of such architectural details as brick corbeling, pedimented wooden door and window frames, and Italianate or Victorian elements.

Modest adobe houses commonly began as a single room. As the family grew, additional rooms were added. Larger structures were often a series of self-contained rooms, each with exterior, but not interior, doors. After making two or three additions in a row, builders sometimes added the next rooms to form an L shape, then a U shape, and finally perhaps a four-sided structure with a central courtyard that echoed the community's larger plaza plan.

Adobe construction prevailed until the 1880s, when the influx of Anglo settlers and railroads carrying lumber, bricks, quarried stone, and other materials led to a hybridization of Hispanic and Yankee architecture. Many adobe buildings hid their mud origins under concrete stucco, frame, tarpaper, or metal siding. Earlier Hispanic settlements were displaced by railroad towns, such as Alamosa, Antonito, Del Norte, and Monte Vista. Many of the valley's Mexican towns are gone. The adobe plazas romanticized by guidebooks have disappeared, but in some towns pre-1880 churches and older nearby adobe buildings are clues to where the plaza once was. Today abandoned churches, cemeteries, and adobe ruins, with a few newer adobe solar structures, highlight the architecture of a rural area that is the poorest region in Colorado in terms of per capita income. Many mobile, prefabricated, cinderblock, and low-budget homes are scattered among the adobe buildings, which include a number of tiny churches.

Alamosa County   (AL)

The last county (1913) created in Colorado received the same name as the county seat, Alamosa (Spanish for cottonwood tree grove). The town was founded by the Denver & Rio Grande Railroad in 1878 as its regional headquarters. Ultimately as many as 700 railroaders worked in Alamosa, which quickly became the hub of the San Luis Valley.

Half the county's population has been centered in Alamosa since the 1880s. The rest of this relatively flat county is occupied by farms, ranches, fifteen ghost towns, and the 1930s Farm Security Administration Resettlement project of Waverly. Tiny Hooper and Mosca are the only post office communities beside Alamosa. Farmers rely on artesian wells for center-pivot irrigators and on canals from the Rio Grande and its tributaries for grain, hay, and vegetable raising.

The Great Sand Dunes National Monument is guarded by the snowcapped massif of 14,345-foot Blanca Peak (Sierra Blanca), Colorado's fourth highest mountain. Standing by itself west of the rest of the Sangre de Cristo Range, The Blanca massif inspired Franklin Rhoda, surveyor for the Hayden expedition of 1874, to report, "Such a beautiful subordination of parts we have not seen before anywhere among the mountains of Colorado." When the first recorded expedition climbed Blanca in 1874, its members found a stone breastwork—presumably the work of either Utes or Spaniards.

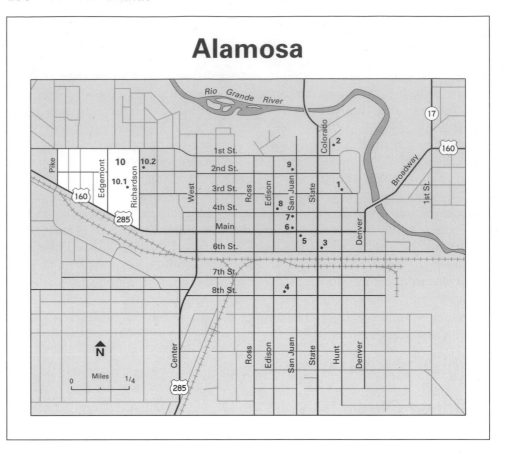

Alamosa

The county seat (1878, 7,574 feet) was established after the D&RG land company bought a 1,608-acre townsite on the west bank of the Rio Grande and laid out a grid city promoted as a new Garden of Eden. Town founder Alexander C. Hunt, a former territorial governor of Colorado and president of the D&RG Construction Company, brought in many of Alamosa's early frame and log buildings on flatbed rail cars from Fort Garland, the previous end-of-track town, and plunked them down on newly platted lots. A few of these structures survive south of the tracks, at 312 and 411 8th Street and 621 9th Street. Where the east end of 9th Street terminates in the D&RG yards is a communal outdoor adobe oven.

In this semiarid country, the most conspic-uous landmarks are water tanks: Alamosa's old rocket-shaped tank (1920s), fed by six deep artesian wells, is now rivaled on the skyline by a 1980s onion-shaped tank. This new bright blue and white tank is an indica-tion of Alamosa's steady, if slow, growth to a 1990 population of 7,579. Growth in and around the city in recent decades is at least partly due to innovative new agricultural industries. Rakhra Mushroom Farms, which opened during the 1980s, is now one of the largest employers. Another local entrepre-neur used the hot springs on his spread to start the San Luis Valley Alligator Ranch, 2 miles south of Hooper.

Nineteenth-century Alamosa favored Vic-torian architecture, but since the 1920s the town has taken a fancy to Hispanic styles. Local architects such as Philip Gallegos and Akira Kanawabe have used adobe and stucco in Southwestern designs, particularly for residential work.

AL01 **Alamosa Visitors' Center**

1951. North end of Hunt St. in Cole Park

In a city park along the Rio Grande, the Chamber of Commerce operates this tourist center in a replica of the second D&RG Alamosa depot, which burned down on Christmas Day in 1907. This clapboard Queen Anne model combining passenger and freight depots is similar to the depots in Crested Butte, Mancos, and other towns, which used the same basic plan although each depot received some individualized ornament. Crested, high-pitched roofs with flared and bracketed eaves cover this gabled structure. The square trackside bay rises into a large dormer so the stationmaster could watch the tracks from his second-story living quarters. D&RG narrow-gauge engine 169, an 1870 Baldwin steam locomotive with a diamond stack and a wooden cow catcher, is on exhibit with an 1880 sleeping car.

AL02 **Alamosa Senior Center** (Hunt House)

1879. Near northeast corner of 1st St. and Colorado Ave.

Town founder Alexander C. Hunt built this large clapboard house with Carpenter's Gothic detailing, a second-story portico on the east, and a two-story bay on the south. Over the years the house has been remodeled inside to accommodate a funeral home, a nursing home, and, since the 1970s, a senior center, but the exterior retains much of its rich Italianate trim and dripping vergeboard.

AL03 **County Social Services Office** (Denver & Rio Grande Depot)

1908. 610 State Ave. (northeast corner of 6th St.) (NR)

Alamosa's third and last D&RG passenger station is a two-story beige brick Beaux-Arts box with a red tile hipped roof. Wide eaves, a low roofline, wings, and a suspended metal entry canopy give it a low-slung, Prairie Style profile. During the 1980s this standard L-plan depot was converted to offices for Alamosa County Social Services. The now bleak

trackside terrain surrounding the depot once bustled, amid much smoke, steam, and racket. Only five derelict bays survive in what was once a fifteen-stall roundhouse, and little is left of machine shops so fully equipped they could make a new engine boiler.

AL04 **Old City Jail**

c. 1880. Behind 713 8th St., south side of alley between Edison and San Juan aves.

Best seen from the alley, the first town jail retains its telltale 2-by-6-inch board walls and iron bars. This one-story calaboose later became the city animal pound and is currently used for storage.

AL05 **Masonic Temple**

1887. Southeast corner of Main St. and San Juan Ave.

Cast iron fronts such as this, as their New York City developer James Bogardus pointed out, could be raised higher than heavier masonry walls, and the slender cast iron columns made larger display windows possible. Inside, smaller columns also meant wider vistas for displaying merchandise. This two-story brick Italianate showplace houses the Masons above leased commercial space on the street level. Below a prominent bracketed and stepped cornice, fifteen engaged Corinthian columns are joined by shallow arches above tall, double-hung windows.

AL06 **Manders Building**

1891. 703 Main St. (northwest corner of San Juan Ave.)

Rough-faced rhyolite from quarries at Del Norte (Rio Grande County) distinguishes this two-story commercial building with a corner entrance. Paired second-story windows under a bracketed metal cornice have single-light transoms and shallow round arches. Like the Masonic temple catercorner, it is scarred by remodeled storefronts.

AL07 **Alamosa County Courthouse**

1937, George C. Emery. Southwest corner of San Juan Ave. and 4th St.

Alamosa County took twenty-four years to build a courthouse, but this splendid red

AL07 Alamosa County Courthouse

brick Southwestern Style government center was worth the wait. Three two-story rectangular structures form a *U* around a north-facing arcaded courtyard. Gable roofs with curvilinear brick parapets and skirt roofs above some windows are covered in the same red tile. Terracotta Indian head medallions enhance the doorways. The round arches of the arcade are repeated atop windows and doors. Interior ceilings are beamed with heavy timbers and finished with beaded tongue-in-groove paneling in knotty pine, while the walls are softly textured like plastered adobe. Much of the original design survived an extensive interior remodeling and updating (1978–1981, Riley Williamson; Gathers and Associates). These Denver architects also produced the fine modern annex at 402 Edison Street, using similar red brick and roof tiles.

AL08 **Sacred Heart Catholic Church**

1927, Robert Willison. 727 4th St. (northeast corner of Edison Ave. and 4th St.)

The square, flat-topped twin turrets of this brick Neo-Romanesque church were intended for steeples that never materialized. Robert Willison, a Denver architect, used a cruciform plan for this church, which was "Hispanicized" in 1953 with a coat of stucco. Inside, a vaulted ceiling soars above the golden oak pews and oak floor. A young German artist, Joseph Steinhage, painted the large Christ on the sanctuary ceiling over the altar and the mural behind the altar in 1942. This 78-by-138-foot church with transepts and a rounded apse is the nucleus of a parish complex that includes a rectory and convent (1927, Robert Willison), a school (1963), and a parish hall (1976). A stuccoed arcade connects the two-story, stuccoed brick rectory (1939) to the church. A block east, at 401 4th Street, St. Thomas Episcopal Church (1923, William E. Fisher and Arthur A. Fisher), with its walled courtyard, is another example of Hispanicized redesign, while the First Baptist Church (1907), catercorner across State Street, stuck to its Queen Anne principles.

AL09 **Cottonwood Inn Bed and Breakfast**

1908. 123 San Juan Ave. (northwest corner of 2nd St.)

This comfortable, one-and-one-half-story frame bungalow originally built by an Alamosa lumber dealer has Tuscan columns fronting a wide, balustraded porch. Gabled dormers with diamond shingling extending from the hipped roof on three sides have paired, board-trimmed windows and boxed eaves. The interior is refurnished but still has the original pine woodwork, built-in cabinets with leaded glass, and parlor fireplace.

AL10 **Adams State College**

1925. North side of U.S. 285, between Richardson and Pike aves.

State Senator William H. ("Billy") Adams of Alamosa, who had only a grade school education, persuaded his fellow legislators to create the Adams State Normal School, which opened in 1925 to train teachers. The school built stucco Southwestern Style structures until after World War II, when, like schools across the country, it experienced tremendous expansion. Enrollment climbed from 349 in 1952 to 1,250 in 1960 to well over 3,000 by the 1990s. Since the 1950s the campus has acquired many flat-roofed, rectangular Modernist buildings of red sandstone, concrete, and glass, exemplified by the library (1973, Lamar Kelsey). One wing of the Student Union (1970s, Henry Koch) breaks out of its boxiness with a barrel-roofed ballroom that critics likened to a cow shed or potato cellar. Architects Bunts and Kelsey of Colorado Springs added Modernist structures of concrete and Lyons sandstone, including the Social Science and Education Building (1967).

AL10.1 **Richardson Hall**

1923, William N. Bowman. Edgemont Blvd. and 3rd St.

Richardson Hall was named for the college's first president (1925–1950), Ira L. Richardson, who worked closely with William Bowman, a Denver architect. The original two-story Colonial Revival building, of red pressed brick with light-colored, cast stone trim, is topped by a domed octagonal tower of three stories. Richardson Hall, expanded by a south wing (1929) for an auditorium and gymnasium and a later north wing, initially housed the entire college and is still the administration building. The second-floor library, a large hall with a domed ceiling supported by exposed, arched trusses on Corinthian columns, has become the Luther E. Bean Museum, which holds notable southwestern and local collections.

AL10.2 **President's House**

1929, William N. Bowman. 1401 2nd St. (northeast corner of Richardson Ave.)

This seventeen-room house, designed with considerable input from President Richardson, was originally Colonial Revival red brick. Influenced by the Spanish heritage of the San Luis Valley, Richardson later remodeled the house in the Spanish Colonial Revival style with stucco, a red tile roof, and wrought iron trim. Many elements from razed campus buildings have been incorporated in the interior. On the north side of the walled grounds, the Casa del Sol Apartments (1929, William N. Bowman), a two-story faculty residence with a stucco exterior

under red tile gable roofs, defers to the presidential hacienda.

Hooper

Hooper (1891, 7,553 feet) was named for Major Shadrach K. Hooper, D&RG general passenger and ticket agent. Major Hooper launched the first massive national promotion of Colorado tourism. He hired Colorado writers such as William E. Pabor, Patience Stapleton, and Stanley Wood for the Rio Grande's "Literary Department" and photographers William Henry Jackson and George L. Beam to produce images for thousands of brochures, postcards, calendars, panoramic views, guides for health seekers, and collections of poetry such as *Rhymes of the Rockies*. His town—a dusty shadow of its former self—could use Major Hooper's hoopla today. Main Street's deserted buildings include the two-story, false-fronted Reddin's Grocery (1911), once the hub of this tiny town, a frame building with metal siding stamped in a brick pattern. The one-story, false-fronted Town Hall (c. 1910) has a corrugated metal roof and pressed metal sides stamped to look like stone.

Mosca

Mosca (1888, 7,550 feet) takes its name from the Spanish word for fly and from nearby Mosca Pass. The D&RG abandoned this town after World War II. Little is left except for forlorn, false-fronted frame buildings, including a fading town hall.

AL11 **Mosca United Methodist Church**

1894. Southwest corner of Barker and 4th Ave.

This narrow, front-gabled building with clapboard siding and overhanging boxed eaves was erected for $178. An open cupola added in 1943 houses the bell from a disbanded Baptist church. The parsonage (1897), converted to a Sunday school in 1943, now has a layer of plaster over its frame construction. Inside the church, the beaded board ceiling is set in large diamond patterns, with the same beaded board used for the original pulpit.

AL12 **Great Sand Dunes National Monument**

1932. Colorado 150, 21 miles east of Mosca

For thousands of years prevailing westerlies have blown sand into this natural trap on the west edge of the Sangre de Cristo Range, creating approximately 39 square miles of dunes that rise 700 feet above the valley floor. Although the sands look white or tan, under a microscope they are multicolored. Some grains are volcanic, from the San Juan Mountains across the valley; others have been formed by streams tumbling out of the mountains. The high water table helps to keep the sand moist and stable. Legend populates this giant sandbox with lost sheepherders, Spanish suits of armor, and webfooted horses.

Archaeological exploration has found evidence of habitation by hunters of the prehistoric Folsom culture, named for archaeological discoveries in Folsom, New Mexico. More recently the Utes occupied the area. An astonished Zebulon Pike described these dunes in the journal of his 1806–1807 expedition as looking "like the sea in a storm." The dunes were designated as a national monument in 1932, but not until the 1960s were a visitors' center, campground, and amphitheater added for tourists visiting North America's largest inland dunes.

AL12.1 **Monument Headquarters** (Superintendent's Residence)

1939, WPA (Kenneth Saunders). Colorado 150 (NR)

This one-story adobe structure resembling Territorial Style buildings exemplifies the National Park Service predilection for vernacular, rustic structures built of local materials. A WPA project designed by a team from the Santa Fe regional office led by architect Kenneth Saunders, it includes a walled courtyard and entrance station, overseen by a long veranda on the side of the house. The low gable roofs have protruding vigas. The former living room has been converted to the superintendent's office.

AL13 **Great Sand Dunes Country Club and Inn** (Zapata Ranch)

c. 1876, 1990s. 5303 Colorado 150 (NR)

Archaeologists Dennis and Peggy Stanford of the Smithsonian Institution have unearthed numerous Folsom sites on and around the Zapata Ranch. Fine Folsom spear points and other stone tools led them to speculate that a band or two of Folsom people camped around a lake here some 11,000 years ago, living in hide-draped pole shelters. The Trujillo family homesteaded here in 1864 and began raising sheep, only to be driven out by cattlemen, who have operated a ranch here since the 1870s. By 1879 a post office had opened at the ranch. Several old log structures include ruins of an unusual five-sided chapel and morada.

Spectacularly sited at the base of the Sangre de Cristo Range near the Great Sand Dunes, the fifteen-room log inn has singlestory gabled wings extending from the twostory building. Outbuildings are also constructed of notched-corner logs, except for an old barn made of two railroad boxcars. A new swimming pool now occupies the old corral of what has become a luxury resort and buffalo ranch.

Waverly

AL14 **Farm Security Administration Resettlement Project**

1937–1941. Colorado 370, 11 miles southwest of Alamosa via U.S. 285

The frame Waverly School (1890), on the south side of Colorado 370, and the Christian Reformed Church, on the north side, are still the nucleus for the widely scattered remnants of what became a New Deal settlement. The San Luis Valley Farms project, one of 149 such projects nationwide, resettled farmers hard hit by the Depression. The federal government constructed irrigation ditches and laterals and built farmsteads on 80- or 160-acre parcels. These eighty-six farm sites, interspersed among privately owned farms, attracted families, primarily from southeastern Colorado, between 1938 and 1940. Each family received a house with running water and REA electricity, as well as a barn, a shed-roofed chicken house, a hog house, and an outhouse.

The basic dwelling was a single-story, three-bedroom frame structure on a concrete foundation with drop siding under a cross-gable roof. A small wooden porch sheltered the main entrance, and twelve-pane, double-hung windows were standard. Some of these simple rectangular houses can still be seen, although most have been altered.

Costilla County (CT)

Costilla (Spanish, rib) County is centered on the Culebra (Spanish, snake) River, a tributary of the Rio Grande. It is the oldest continually inhabited county in the state and has the highest percentage (80) of Spanish-surnamed residents.

Farmers and ranchers came in the 1850s to what is still a rural area with only one incorporated town, the county seat of San Luis. When designated one of the original seventeen counties in 1861, Costilla had almost 2,000 residents. From a peak population of 7,533 in 1940, the county dropped to 3,190 residents by 1990. Its eastern half climbs the wild, rugged Sangre de Cristo Range, said to have been named by a Franciscan padre to whom the sunset glow on the snowcapped peaks suggested the blood of Christ. The flatter, western half of the county, bordered by the Rio Grande, has a few small family farms and ranches. Although one of the poorest Colorado counties in per capita income, it is rich in vernacular adobe architecture.

San Luis

The county seat (1851, 7,965 feet), the oldest permanent town in Colorado, also claims the state's oldest operating water ditch and only common, the Vega. The Spanish named the town (originally La Plaza de San Luis de la Culebra) and the valley for King Louis IX of France, because the town of San Luis was founded on his feast day, June 21. Farmers and cowboys from New Mexico first settled on Culebra Creek in 1846. Initially driven off by hostile Ute Indians, they returned to found San Luis on April 5, 1851. A flour mill soon made the town an agricultural hub for the valley.

The Vega (Spanish for fertile plain; 1863), on the east side of town, is a communally owned grazing land similar to those of New England and old Mexico. This 633-acre common was created by the original town ordinance, which specified that "all the inhabitants shall have use of pasture, wood, water . . . not interfering with the rights of others." Another communal enterprise was the San Luis People's Ditch (1852), the oldest continually used irrigation ditch in Colorado, which carries water from Culebra Creek to the town and outlying residents.

San Luis is surrounded by small family farms and ranches, including the Gallegos Ranch (1860; see CT09), the Ortega Farm (1869), and the Rio Culebra Ranch (1863), all still operated by descendants of founding families. Not incorporated until 1968, San Luis remains an informal town lacking such refinements as mail delivery and regular street addresses. The Plaza de San Luis de la Culebra Historic District, Colorado 159 and Main Street (NRD), has a few old adobe structures still in place—often behind newer storefronts. Deep window and door reveals characterize antique structures with 18-inch-thick adobe walls that support ceilings bearing as much as a foot of dirt insulation.

CT01 Costilla County Courthouse

1883, Farrington and Rucker, builders. Northeast corner of Main and Gaspar sts.

County commissioners specified that this single-story, side-gabled structure with an open bell tower be built "of Chicago lumber with good substantial adobe walls." Golden stucco ties together various cinderblock and cast stone additions. This small, informal courthouse blends into the streetscape instead of dominating its surroundings, as courthouses usually do.

CT02 **Malouff Department Store** (Bank of San Luis)

1911. 351 Main St.

Four heavy Doric columns support the temple front of a masonry bank which became a store with apartments upstairs. Stucco layers applied over the years have helped integrate what was originally a jarring architectural departure from indigenous adobe. The bank's basic disharmony is compounded by its siting at a slight angle to adjacent main street frontages, perhaps a grid-minded Anglo builder's attempt to straighten out the town.

CT03 **R&R Supermarket** (Salazar Store)

1857. 359 Main St. (southwest corner of 4th St.)

This is said to be the oldest continually operated store in Colorado, although an 1895 fire destroyed everything but the 2-foot-thick adobe walls. Solar panels added in the 1970s are among the many alterations that have transformed the original one-story, 20-by 40-foot building. Vigas protrude from the stuccoed adobe, topped by small, stepped parapets above the second-story front. Milled beams support a porch that extends out over the sidewalk, with a balcony above for the second-story rooms of the venerable Don Carlos Hotel.

CT04 **San Luis Cultural Center**

1938, WPA. 1980, Akira Kanawabe. 401 Church Pl., southeast of the church

The San Luis Cultural Center, built by the WPA as a community center, began as a one-story, flat-roofed adobe structure studded with vigas. In 1943 the facility became the San Luis Institute of Arts and Crafts, a branch of Adams State College. Adams State gave the building back to the community

CT04 San Luis Cultural Center

after World War II, and it was converted to the Centennial High School. In 1980 a $1 million federal project remodeled and expanded the old high school into a cultural and commercial center. Akira Kanawabe, an Alamosa native and leading local architect, retrofitted the complex with 2,600 square feet of solar paneling whose two sloping wedges overshadow the original horizontal Pueblo Revival building with their vertical, angular lines. The cultural center houses a museum, a library, an auditorium, and a large diorama of the town as it appeared in 1887. Upstairs, the adobe-walled, pine-plank-floored Morada Room contains a collection of religious art.

CT05 **Sangre de Cristo Catholic Church**

1886, The Reverend Jean-Baptiste Pitival. 400 Church Pl.

Facing south toward the former plaza, this adobe church, designed by a French priest, has Gothic elements, including lancet windows. The front-gable roof rises in a steep pitch to a soaring bell tower. The transept was added around 1900, and tan cement stucco has been applied to the adobe. A small chapel added in the rear has a wooden altar homemade with mail-order materials. A large, two-story brick rectory (1920s) at the northeast corner of the church uses both Craftsman and Mediterranean elements and two shades of brick. An adobe storage building at the northwest corner of the church displays a vibrantly colored exterior mural (c. 1987) depicting members of the parish meeting Jesus. The original chapel (1854) stands a half block away, at the northeast corner of Main Street and Church Place, near a stone barn that belonged to the church. Charles Jaquez converted the old chapel to a grocery and subsequently to the family home. Ghost marks on the adobe facade reveal where round-arched openings once were.

CT06 El Convento Bed and Breakfast

1905. 512 Church Pl.

Built of adobe as a parochial school, this became home for the Sisters of Mercy when a new school opened one block north. After the sisters closed the school and departed, the parish converted the building to a bed and breakfast inn in 1980. A crafts shop occupies the former first-floor chapel. The exterior is stuccoed on the first floor, with wooden shingles on the frame second story. On the second floor, the nuns' nine cells have been converted to four large guest rooms decorated with antique hand-carved furniture and religious folk art.

CT07 Zegob Grocery

1905. 404 Church Pl.

A clapboard false front adorns this two-story store of white painted adobe, one of several opened in southern Colorado by a family of Lebanese merchants.

CT08 Stations of the Cross Shrine

1989, 1992. Corner of Colorado 159 (Main St.) and Colorado 142

The only major shrine built in Colorado in decades is a notable work of art as well as the centerpiece of a spiritual and artistic renaissance in San Luis. From Main Street, a rustic double-span bridge carries Highway 142 over Culebra Creek to the trailhead for the pilgrimage up La Mesa de la Piedad y de la Misericordia (hill of piety and mercy). The shrine, sited on a rocky hillside of sagebrush and yucca, was the dream of Father Jose Maximo Patricio Valdez, pastor of Sangre de Cristo Catholic Church. Volunteers constructed the 1.5-mile walk with fourteen stations of the cross, consisting of evocative bronze sculptures (1989, Huberto Maestas) on pedestals of native volcanic stone. The landscaped trail winds its way up a hill to a sculpture of Christ's resurrection, a grotto shrine, and a mesa-top Knights of Columbus Environmental Education Building (1994, Arnold Valdez). The latter is an arc of glass framed in a neo–Pueblo Revival structure overlooking the town below. Also atop the mesa is La Capilla de Todos los Santos (1995, Arnold Valdez and Michael Bertia), with twin domed bell towers at the entry and four larger domes over the sanctuary, transepts, and apse of a finely detailed adobe chapel.

CT09 Gallegos Homestead

1925. Gallegos Ranch, south side of Colorado 142, 1 mile west of San Luis

An example of how additions can expand an adobe home as a family grows, Corpus Gallegos's two-story stuccoed adobe has an added gable roof and three wood-frame dormers above the wide, stuccoed front porch. A small balcony in the middle of the east facade as well as additions on the south side and rear modify the original plan of rooms arranged on either side of a central hallway.

Blanca

Blanca (1908, 7,746 feet) was named for nearby Mount Blanca, a huge, snowcapped massif soaring to 14,345 feet with four lower shoulders over 14,000 feet high. Blanca became the northernmost terminus and home base of the San Luis Southern Railway (1910–1959), which joined the D&RG here. This standard-gauge road ran 31 miles south through Ojito, San Acacio, Mesita, and Jaroso in Costilla County but never reached its projected terminus, which was Taos, New Mexico. The town well pavilion, made of rubblestone, remains at the northeast corner of Broadway Avenue and Main Street (Colorado 160). St. James the Less Catholic Church (1938), northeast corner of 9th Street and Broadway, is adobe with Gothic-arched windows and a blind rose window. The diminutive model next to the church, which is carried in processions to represent the community, is typical of those found beside the mission churches of the San Luis Valley.

CT10 Blanca School

1910, Morris and Price, builders. Northeast corner of 10th St. and Broadway Ave.

One of the town's more notable structures is this two-story school, a vernacular interpretation of Beaux-Arts Mediterranean Revival style in stuccoed adobe, under a hipped roof with hipped dormers and a cupola bell tower. It is now falling into ruins. The gymnasium next door, now used as a garage, also shows adobe under crumbling stucco. It has a barrel-vault roof and a front parapet of five rounded adobe arches, slightly irregular as if hand formed.

Chama

This Culebra Creek community (c. 1864, 6,420 feet), settled by families from Chamita, New Mexico, has some of the valley's least altered adobe buildings. In the Lobato-Mascarenas House (1880), northeast of Costilla County L.7 and 22.3, across from the old post office, typical alterations have been made to a single-file-plan adobe house. A gable roof, corbeled brick chimneys, and a skin of concrete stucco have been added, along with rough-faced quoins. Two wedge-shaped buttresses on the east side stabilize the 18-inch-thick walls.

CT11 Old Post Office

1932. Southeast corner of Costilla County L.7 and 22.3

This small adobe structure on a concrete foundation is finished in textured stucco. The parapet around the flat roof has a curvilinear arc over the central entrance and stepped-up sections at the corners. The building is now in ruins but is far more noteworthy than its replacement.

CT12 SPMDTU Concilio No. 31

c. 1920. Southwest corner of Costilla County L.7 and 22.3

Another good example of vernacular adaptations, this hall has stuccoed adobe walls and side-gable roofs. The Sociedad Protección Mutua de Trabajadores Unidos (united workers' mutual protection society), a fraternal and insurance society, opened Chama's Concilio (meeting hall) No. 31 on October 7, 1920. Except for the large headquarters in Antonito, in Conejos County, where the organization was founded in 1900 (see Conejos County, CN04), the local meeting halls tended to adopt the human scale of the village moradas.

CT13 Immaculate Conception Church

1938. Costilla County 22, 1 mile north of Costilla County L.7

This large adobe structure, built in the Territorial Style as a replacement for an 1864 church, has a Gothic-arched entry and window openings. In the transepts stained glass lancet windows adorn adobe gable ends. The double-tiered bell tower has louvered, Gothic-arched openings in its wood shingle cladding and a polygonal roof.

Fort Garland

The army post of Fort Garland (1858, 7,936 feet) replaced Fort Massachusetts (1852–1858), 8 miles north on Ute Creek. Initially built to provide protection from the Utes, the fort attracted settlers and merchants. The D&RG arrived in 1878, and "Garland City" briefly flourished as an end-of-track town. It was described by settler John Morgan, whose account was published almost a century later in *Colorado Magazine* (November 1948). "Garland is emphatically a railroad town," he wrote in 1878. When the railroad pushed on to Alamosa, he explained: "Garland begins to move forward, and on every hand we see men tearing down the frail wooden structures with which it is built, and starting westward with them. Soon Garland will be a thing of the past and only battered oyster cans, cast-off clothing, old shoes, and debris will mark the site of where once stood a flourishing city, with its hotels, its stores, its théatre comique, etc."

The original adobe Holy Family Church (c. 1894) sits beside its 1950 replacement of stuccoed cinderblock with a curvilinear parapet and twin front bell towers. The adobe Hoaglund Store (1880s), on the north side of the fort, with its Victorian storefront and stepped, capped parapets on the side walls, exemplifies the Territorial Style.

CT14 **Fort Garland Museum**

1858. 1948, reconstruction. West side of Colorado 159, 1 mile south of U.S. 160 (NR)

Fort Garland's low-slung, one-story adobe structures are wrapped around a courtyard shaded by towering cottonwood trees. The original fort, whose parade grounds have been invaded by Colorado 159, was named for Brigadier General John Garland, military commander of the Department of the Army of New Mexico. The original buildings had adobe walls, sod roofs, and (only in the officers' quarters) board floors. The Colorado Historical Society acquired the site in 1945 and has converted five of the original structures, including the officers' quarters and a barracks, to a regional museum. Exhibits and rooms reflect San Luis Valley history. The commandant's quarters have been restored to reflect the 1866–1867 period, when Colonel Kit Carson commanded the garrison.

Garcia

Garcia (1849?, 7,693 feet; on Costilla County B, .8 mile west of Colorado 159 and 18 miles south of San Luis) was originally called La Plaza de los Manzanares. According to local historians Olibama López Tushar and Virginia McConnell Simmons, this, not San Luis, is the oldest permanently occupied settlement in Colorado. Tushar wrote in *The People of El Valle* (1978) that her ancestors, Manuel and Pedro Manzanares, settled here in 1849 with their families. The plaza that once organized the community is lost among newer structures and adobe ruins.

CT15 **La Morada de Garcia**

c. 1860. West of Costilla County C, .15 mile north of Costilla County B

This stuccoed adobe hall, a gathering place for members of the Penitente sect, has been reinforced with a concrete apron and buttresses. The gable roof is sheathed in metal, with adobe gable ends. The L configuration shelters a statue of Jesus dragging a cross. The Penitentes, an all-male sect once outlawed by the Catholic Church for their practice of extreme penance with self-flagellation and even crucifixions, have in recent years been accepted as a social, political, and spiritual fraternity. This reconciliation, aimed at encouraging men to participate in church activities, is demonstrated by this morada's location next to Sacred Heart Church.

San Isidro

San Isidro (c. 1853), also known as Fuertocito (little fort) for a vanished log structure, is a hamlet of a few farms, ranches, and houses, many of adobe. The Sanchez House (1890), Costilla County K.5, .2 mile east of Costilla County 22.3, is a one-and-one-half-story, L-shaped Territorial adobe with stuccoed walls. It has been altered, but its flat-roofed adobe storage shed reflects the original profile. The Madrid House (c. 1936), across Costilla County K.5 from San Isidro Church, has textured stucco-over-adobe walls, stepped parapets, and vigas. Vernacular Prairie Style influence can be seen in the entry door and several windows of narrow

CT16 San Isidro Church, altar

panes surrounding a large center pane, with other windows massed along the south side for solar gain.

CT16 San Isidro Church

1900. North of Costilla County K.5, .3 mile east of Costilla County 22.3

New stucco covers the adobe walls, and new shake shingles cover the roof and open bell tower of San Isidro Church. Inside, beside a potbellied stove, the wooden altar is painted to look like white marble. The altar is adorned with a hand-carved wooden statue of St. Isidore of Madrid, the plowman whose fields were tilled by an angel while he prayed.

San Acacio

San Acacio (1909, 7,820 feet) was also known as New San Acacio after it relocated around the railroad depot. The move was promoted by the Costilla Estates Development Company, which invested $327,000 in a 31-mile railroad as part of a speculative real estate venture in irrigated cropland. The company founded three agricultural colonies, New San Acacio and nearby Jaroso and Mesita, and also built a reservoir above

San Francisco. Its headquarters, the Sanchez Ditch Building (1909), north of Colorado 142 and 1 block west of the depot, is a bungalow with a simple gable roof that represents an alternative to adobe, a local vernacular tradition of building in smooth rubblestone.

CT17 San Luis Valley Southern Railroad Depot

c. 1910. Colorado 142

This two-story rectangular station building of stucco over frame is the largest of three built by the Costilla Estates Development Company. The railroad, which hauled livestock, crops, and locally mined minerals, provided daily freight and passenger service until 1946, then wheezed on with an intermittent schedule until 1959. The depot has a shingled hipped roof with overhanging eaves and exposed rafter ends. The roof shape is repeated in three hipped canopies, supported by large, flanking brackets, over the main entry. Trackside, a full-height rectangular bay gave sight lines along the right of way. With several small additions, the depot was converted to a bed and breakfast in 1993.

San Francisco

CT18 San Francisco Catholic Church

c. 1950. Near the intersection of Costilla County J.2 and J.8

This remote valley town (1854, 9,200 feet) was named for St. Francis of Assisi. The 1854 plaza is gone, but venerable adobe buildings survive. The church is one of the county's newest, a replacement for a much older structure that stood next door. The stuccoed cinderblock building has large, steel-framed, clear glass windows and a likeness of St. Francis of Assisi in the rose window of the main bell tower and entry. A glass block cross lights the stairwell of the bell tower on the southwest corner.

CT19 San Francisco Morada

1880. Costilla County J.2, .6 mile east of Costilla County J.8

This traditional linear-plan adobe is the valley's largest morada. The main meeting room and a combined storage and meeting room have separate exterior doors on the south. The interior also houses an oratory chapel with a *fogon*, or corner fireplace. In the 1930s the Penitentes replaced the original flat roof with a gable tarpaper one, installed wood planking over the earthen floor and a kitchen addition (1934) with shed roof, and stuccoed the exterior.

San Pedro–San Pablo

CT20 San Pedro y San Pablo Catholic Church

1915. 1930, reconstruction. West side of Costilla County 21, 1 mile south of Colorado 142

The adjoining towns of San Pedro and San Pablo (1851, 8,100 feet) share this tall adobe church with a concrete foundation and gable roofs that cross over the transept. Its eastern orientation, cruciform plan, and adobe construction continue the tradition of two former churches on this site. Gothic influence shows in the pitched roof, vaulted ceiling, rose window, and pointed windows. The altar and plaster statues inside replace original hand-carved santos. Although the windows have been enlarged, the choir loft and bell tower rebuilt, and acoustical tile added to the cross ribbed ceiling, the church remains picturesquely vernacular.

Viejo San Acacio

Viejo San Acacio (1853, 7,820 feet) was founded only after efforts in the 1840s to establish a town here on Culebra Creek failed because of resistance from the Ute Indians. Settlers were finally successful, according to local folklore, because their patron, San Acacio, a Roman soldier, appeared on horseback and frightened away the Utes. Townfolk built a chapel in thanksgiving. Its ruins linger east of the present church, between the graveyard and the irrigation ditch. The town has been called Viejo (old) San Acacio since the establishment in 1904 of new San Acacio.

CT21 Viejo San Acacio Chapel

c. 1856. Costilla County 15, .8 mile south of Colorado 142

This chapel, which has 18-inch-thick adobe walls, is said by some to be older than the "oldest church in Colorado" (in Conejos; CN01). It lies on the southwest corner of what was the old plaza. Like other early churches in the San Luis Valley, this originally had a flat roof supported by vigas 16 inches in circumference. Around 1910 it was replaced with a pitched roof supported by a system of pitched rafters and tie rods. Evidence of the old flat viga roof was discovered during reconstruction in 1989.

A relatively fresh coat of adobe plaster glistens on the bulky composition bolstered by huge buttresses reminiscent of the old adobe church of El Rancho de Taos in New Mexico, made famous by Georgia O'Keeffe's paintings. A shake shingle roof is crowned by an open wooden bell tower with a bronze bell (1910). Painted panels fill one-over-one double-hung windows, with a lancet window in the east gable and a round window in the sacristy on the west. Inside, new peeled log columns and beams support the roof and choir loft. When the floor was replaced in 1990, graves in the earth beneath it were marked to avoid placing any bracing on them. The altar is a raised wooden platform in the apse with a hand-painted reredos (1989) by Maria Romero Cash. The adobe-walled church courtyard and cemetery overlook the tiny village of Viejo San Acacio with its dirt lanes and sparkling water ditches.

CT21 Viejo San Acacio Chapel

Conejos County   (CN)

Hispanic folklore has Our Lady of Guadalupe, the patroness of Mexico, guiding colonists to the banks of the Conejos (Spanish, rabbits) River, which runs fast as a jackrabbit down from the San Juan Mountains into the Rio Grande. When Hispanic settlers first rested on the cottonwood-shaded bank of the Conejos in 1854, one of their oxen refused to go any farther. The owner cajoled and cursed, pushed and pulled, but the beast would not budge. Finally someone pointed out that the statue of Our Lady of Guadalupe, which the creature was carrying, had fallen off on that spot. After this sign from heaven, the colonists settled there on the north side of the Conejos River. That summer they built Guadalupe, said to be the oldest town in Conejos County, dug the Conejos Ditch, and built a small chapel for Our Lady of Guadalupe.

This was the first permanent settlement on the Conejos Land Grant, awarded by the governor of New Mexico in 1833 to Seledon Valdez and other residents of Taos County, New Mexico. The Conejos grant covered some 1,600 square miles between the Rio Grande on the east and the San Juan Mountains on the west, from the La Garita Mountains on the north to the round-topped Mount San Antonio just south of the Colorado–New Mexico boundary. The grant was ultimately disallowed in a Santa Fe courtroom in 1895 despite the testimony of Crecencio Valdez, the son of Seledon, that his father had given the Conejos grant deed to Lafayette Head and Alexander C. Hunt to be recorded. That was the last seen of the document. Head spearheaded development of Conejos County and became the first lieutenant governor of Colorado. Hunt, who would become a territorial governor, promoted the Denver & Rio Grande Railroad and its development of the San Luis Valley.

Among U.S. citizens who moved into the valley were Mormons, who planted farming communities at La Jara, Manassa, Romeo (formerly Romero), and Sanford. The D&RG arrived in 1880 and created the new railroad town of Antonito. Thanks to the D&RG connections to stockyards in Denver and elsewhere, Conejos County became the sheep-raising center of Colorado. Between 1900 and 1950 the county grew steadily, peaking at around 12,000. Since then, falling farm and livestock prices have caused a decline in population to a 1990 count of 7,453. Adobe ruins and graveyards mark the sites of many abandoned communities. Of thirty-seven post office towns once active in the county, most are fading or gone. The county perked up in 1971 with the reconstruction of the D&RG route to Chama, New Mexico, as the Cumbres & Toltec Scenic Railroad, America's longest and highest steam-powered narrow-gauge line.

Conejos

A flour mill, a sawmill, and a famous church helped make this unincorporated hamlet (1854, 7,882 feet) the county seat. It still retains some of its original plaza configuration with a modern county courthouse that replaces an old one destroyed by fire in the

1970s. The Garcia House (1860s), built by Castelar Garcia, on the southeast edge of Conejos Plaza, is a single-story adobe house, which now lies behind a prominent stone and iron fence. An example of late Territorial adobe, it has a hipped roof and mud-plastered walls. A newer front entry porch with Victorian bracketed supports and other updatings camouflage its antiquity.

CN01 Our Lady of Guadalupe Catholic Church

c. 1926. Conejos Plaza

The original church (1858), a replacement for a chapel dedicated in 1856, was a 16-by-30-foot jacal of cottonwood posts with cross-beams at the top and an adobe plaster skin. A second adobe church (c. 1879) enlarged upon the original structure, but burned down in 1926. Some of the ruins were incorporated into the current church, with a 1948 facade whose curvilinear parapet is flanked by twin 56-foot towers wearing domed metal caps. This entry facade has a rose window and a niche for a statue of Our Lady of Guadalupe. Raised bands of red and gray brick adorn the facade and outline round-arched windows. Inside, the wooden pulpit and altar have been painted to look like marble, and the walls are furnished with some notable folk art, such as the crucifix in the south transept.

Antonito

Antonito (1880, 7,888 feet) was established by the D&RG a mile away from the county seat of Conejos as a railroad ploy to gain control of trackside real estate. D&RG promoters platted Antonito as a grid with Main Street a block west of and parallel to the tracks. Antonito was an Anglo community that soon became the commercial hub of the valley, even though Conejos retained the county seat. Although the town is heavily Hispanic today, it was built primarily by Anglo-Americans whose institutions included a Presbyterian church, the Palace Hotel, and a now vanished opera house.

Antonito's population peaked at around 1,300 in the 1940s. Subsequently the large sheep-raising industry declined, and Antonito became a sleepy, Spanish-accented town sustained by farming and ranching, the Cumbres & Toltec Scenic Railroad, and the Gerfco Cellite and Johns-Manville crushed perlite plants (1959), 2 miles south of town on U.S. 285. These plants make perlite of volcanic rock from open-pit mines near No Agua, New Mexico. When heated, the perlite explodes like popcorn and then is crushed, sized, and blended for use as, among other things, a soil conditioner and a lightweight aggregate used in concrete and plaster.

CN02 La Virgen de Guadalupe Shrine (Castillo Castle)

1988, Cono Espinosa. Northwest corner of 10th Ave. and State St.

After returning from the Vietnam War, a disabled veteran built his residence of recycled lumber, aluminum cans, and rubblestone. The irregular, two-story structure is topped by an open wooden tower housing a homemade statue of the Virgin of Guadalupe. Some of the poles bristling around and above the virgin form a surrealistic cross in a glittering fantasy reminiscent of the Watts Towers in Los Angeles.

CN03 **St. Augustine Catholic Church**

1889. Northwest corner of 8th Ave. and Pine St.

This parish church has exterior walls of random stone beneath adobe. Gothic-arched stained glass windows are separated by shallow buttresses. The main entry doors and altar are hand-carved work that complements the modern golden oak pews. Spanish-born Father Felix Lopez, the pastor since 1971, has painted murals on the front wall inside the church. His sculptures and a fountain adorn the gardens he has planted around the rectory. The two-story gray brick rectory, attached to the church at the southwest corner, was built as a small monastery that has been converted to community use.

CN04 **SPMDTU Concilio No. 1**

1925. 603 Main St. (U.S. 285)

La Sociedad Protección Mutua de Trabajadores Unidos (united workers' mutual protection society) was founded in Antonito in 1900 by seven Hispanic laborers, including Celedonio Mondragon, the first president. The SPMDTU promoted Spanish language and culture, fought discrimination, and provided social activities and low-cost group insurance. From this headquarters, the organization established sixty-three other chapters throughout Colorado, New Mexico, and Utah, with a peak membership of around 2,500. About a dozen chapters remain active.

Members constructed this two-story Mission Revival hall of adobe with a bright white concrete stucco finish. It includes a 100-by-49-foot meeting hall with a stage, in addition to offices. Shallow-arched steel trusses span the hall. A mural on the back wall of the stage of a field worker offering the valley's

produce was painted by two Adams State College students who signed themselves Los Muralistas del Valle. In 1981, a mural depicting boxers was painted on the south exterior wall by Edward Chacon.

CN05 **Palace Hotel**

1890. 433 Main St. (U.S. 285)

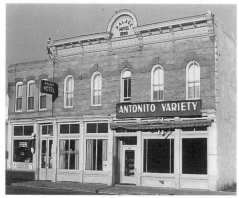

Rhyolite fronts this two-story brick building, rectangular in plan, with typical storefronts retaining metal kickplates below and transoms above. A central entrance leads into the businesses and the hotel. The second story has five narrow, double-hung windows with round-arched tops. Radiating voussoirs of darker rhyolite are joined across the facade by a stringcourse of the same stone, which is also used for sills. The parapet has a bracketed and dentiled cornice of pressed metal with a central arched pediment to crown Antonito's prime example of Victorian commercial architecture.

CN06 **Warshauer Mansion**

1913, George F. Harvey, Jr.. 515 River St. (NR)

Antonito's show home, designed by a Denver architect and built by Denver contractor Samuel A. McDonald, is a Craftsman house which replaced an 1890 Queen Anne dwelling destroyed by fire in 1912. It rises two stories over a full basement on a modified H plan, with walls of beige pressed brick set in stretcher bond. Gable ends under the flared red tile roof are stuccoed above a dentiled frieze and set off by bargeboards. The five chimneys are symmetrically placed.

Wooden trim milled in Iowa enhances the

interior with its fancy paneled walls and ceilings. The house included central vacuum cleaning, internal communication, and fire control systems as well as steam heat, all unusual luxuries for the place and the period. Jens Eriksen of Denver, who had been trained in Copenhagen, painted the interior murals, and William Ernst of Denver originally landscaped the full-block site.

Frederick B. Warshauer, a German immigrant who became a successful sheep rancher, lumberman, and banker, committed suicide at the zenith of his career in 1913. Subsequently the house has been used as a convent, a restaurant, and a private residence. Other large old homes in the neighborhood include the Jordan House (1917), at the southwest corner of River Street and 4th Avenue, and the McGregor House (c. 1900), at the northwest corner of 6th Avenue and River Street.

CN07 **Denver & Rio Grande Depot**

1880. Southeast corner of Front St. and Lobatos Rd.

This typical small depot of locally quarried volcanic stone blocks has a modified hipped roof with eaves supported by decorative wooden trusses. Hipped dormers poke out of projecting bays on the east and west sides. Companion buildings once included a bunkhouse (c. 1881) of squared logs, a frame section house (1882), and an engine house. Antonito was a busy rail center where the D&RG's "Chili Line," bound for Santa Fe, New Mexico, and the Durango-bound San Juan Extension divided. Besides the depot and much intact track, the only other remnant is the freight house, which has been converted to a private residence.

CN08 **Cumbres & Toltec Scenic Railroad**

1880; 1971. From Antonito to Chama, New Mexico (NR)

The D&RG built this narrow-gauge line as the first part of its San Juan Extension to the rich mines of the San Juan Mountains. The 64-mile stretch between Antonito and Chama, which crosses the state border nine times, was restored as a summertime passenger excursion by the states of Colorado and New Mexico in 1971. A National Historic Civil Engineering Landmark, this serpentine line slithers along a granite shelf 1,000 feet above Toltec Gorge and climbs 10,015-foot-high Cumbres (Spanish, summit) Pass. It is the highest still-used passenger railroad in the United States. To cross some of the wildest and most remote terrain in Colorado, the D&RG used numerous cuts and fills, tunnels, and trestles and, as protection against snow, built on south-facing slopes and erected wooden snowsheds on Cumbres Pass.

Some of the water tanks, old depots, snowsheds, and other structures along the line have been stabilized. The frame depot at Antonito (1971) is less distinguished than the rhyolite original (CN07). The passenger coaches made in the Antonito shops during the 1980s loosely resemble their antique ancestors. Much original rolling stock and a typical railroad yard, including one of the few operational coaling towers in the country, may be found in Chama. In Antonito, Engine No. 463 (1903, Baldwin Locomotive Works, Philadelphia) (NR), restored by actor-singer Gene Autry, is a rare remnant of the Rio Grande's K-27 series, whose outside frame and Mikado wheel pattern allowed a much larger firebox. Coupled with a compound cylinder system that reused exhaust steam to power the drivers on the recovery stroke, this design doubled the tonnage a locomotive could pull over this route's 4 percent grades. A splendid guide to structures along the line, as well as the rolling stock, landscape, and history, is Doris B. Osterwald's *Ticket to Toltec: A Mile by Mile Guide for the Cumbres & Toltec Scenic Railroad* (1976).

Capulin

CN09 **St. Joseph Catholic Church**

1912, Justo Duran, builder. 14 Church Rd.

Capulin (c. 1867, 7,810 feet) named for the native chokecherries, is a relatively prosperous hub for surrounding ranches and farms. Townsfolk used horse teams to haul buff-colored sandstone from Hot Creek Quarry 12 miles to the west for stonemason Justo Duran of Monte Vista. He constructed this house of God with rough-hewn blocks and corner pilasters extending through the gable roof and topped by carved stone crosses. A wooden cross tops the closed bell tower. The wooden altar, acquired in 1924, is intricate in detail and elaborately painted to resemble several colors of marble. Stained glass windows fill Gothic-arched openings, and a small Gothic window lights the wooden choir loft above the entrance.

The former cloister (1928) of the Benedictine sisters who taught in the parish school has become the rectory. Its two stories of gray cast stone blocks join the church at the northwest corner. This rectory has round-arched windows on the first floor. The two-story stone parish office meets the church at the southwest corner, creating a complex footprint and an interesting intersection of walls around the apse. The preceding church (1878), of adobe, stood on the west side of the church cemetery.

Mogote

Mogote (1856, 7,900 feet), an unincorporated hamlet on the Conejos River, was named by New Mexican farmers for a small, triple-peaked mountain nearby that reminded them of bundled sheaves of grain. Although the post office closed in 1920, a few descendants of the original settlers remain here at the base of picturesque Conejos Canyon, with its scattered dude ranches, summer cabins, and a trout hatchery.

CN10 Presbyterian Church

1895. 500 feet south of Colorado 17 on Conejos County 9

This L-shaped, single-story structure of adobe has a steep-pitched, pyramidal bell tower angled across the northeast corner of the hipped roof. A gabled wing extends north from the west end. A canted gate at the northeast corner of the lot leads through a picket fence, under an arch with the fading inscription "Dios es Amor." The long-abandoned church and an attached flat-roofed adobe school are falling into ruins amid traces of a garden.

CN11 Menkhaven

1931. 20900 Colorado 17, 20 miles west of Antonito

Eighteen rustic cabins along the Conejos River are clustered around a two-story, hewn log lodge with gable roof and shed additions. The lodge's sunken corner fireplace of rubblestone is surrounded by rustic rocking chairs, on a ground floor whose unevenness is attributed to winter heaving. Complex roof framing highlights a slab-sided addition at the southwest corner with a south sunroom bay that has been extended to the second floor. A stairway of half logs, with a balustrade of peeled branches, leads to the upstairs living quarters. The 15-acre dude ranch was started by Gladys, Dutch, and Hazel Menke, daughters of a local businessman. Two of them briefly basked in vaudeville glory on Broadway and later brought entertainment stars to their ranch as guests and performers.

CN12 Rainbow Trout Lodge

1925. Colorado 17, 35 miles west of Antonito

Texas oilman William B. Hamilton and some cronies built what they claimed was Colorado's largest log cabin. This two-story, hewn log lodge, with a double-faced fireplace of random-coursed smooth river rock, was built by local stonemason Jose Santiago Valdez. It was originally surrounded by several canvas-top cabins, which have been replaced by rustic log cabins. Nearby is the older Conejos Ranch, first homesteaded in 1894, with a two-story, hewn log lodge (c. 1910) set into a south-facing hillside above the Conejos River.

CN13 Guadalupe

1854. 1 mile north of Conejos on the north bank of the Conejos River

Guadalupe may be the first Hispanic settlement in the county. During the late 1850s many residents moved a mile south to Conejos, a higher, flood-free site on the other side of the Conejos River. Jose Maria Jaquez is said to have built the first house in Guadalupe in 1854, and his family joined him there. Father José Montaño built the first primitive jacal Church of Our Lady of Guadalupe in 1854. Guadalupe houses were rectangular or square jacales, with walls of logs set vertically in trenches, tied at the top and plastered inside and out with adobe mud. These were later replaced by horizontal-log and adobe buildings. By 1855 settlers had constructed a communal irrigation ditch from the Conejos River. A year later the town had a flour mill and a second ditch. Today roughly two dozen structures, many of adobe, linger.

La Jara

La Jara (1880, 7,602 feet), named in Spanish for the local willows, started with a D&RG water tank before a station was built in 1883. The La Jara Town Company platted areas on both sides of the tracks for an agricultural community. An artesian well was drilled on the east side of the tracks for the new business area along a main street stretching east from the depot. Stock raising and farming were augmented as warehouses were built for storage and shipping. Extensive Mormon settlement is commemorated by a handsome Mormon Moderne church. From a peak of around 2,000 in the 1930s, population has dwindled to about 700.

The Conejos County Agricultural Museum, 2 miles south of La Jara on U.S. 285 at the County Arena Grounds, is a casual collection of farm machinery, including harvesters, tractors, and giant hay derricks.

CN14 **Town Hall** (Denver & Rio Grande Depot)

1911; 1970. Broadway and Main St. (NR)

This elongated, rectangular station building influenced by the Prairie Style has a hipped roof with 4-foot eaves. Recessed entry porticos occupy the southeast and southwest corners. The southern half of the structure once provided living space for the agent on a second story. Stone veneer wraps the base and rises into the square columns of the entry porticos. The depot became the town hall in 1970.

CN15 **La Jara School**

1930s?. Northeast corner of Poplar and Main sts.

This two-story, red brick school building is an unusual local example of vernacular Streamline Moderne style. The design employs curves and horizontal lines, with a cantilevered entrance canopy trimmed in bright aluminum. Ribbon windows and glass block, as well as the flat roof, further accent the horizontality.

CN16 **Church of Jesus Christ of Latter-Day Saints**

1949. 716 Broadway

This asymmetrical, two-story structure of red brick has a large bay extending from the east end of a cross-gabled wing with a portico on the south side. The building is trimmed in wood and cast stone and employs ornamentation and shapes in streamlined versions of classical elements. A thin, copper-clad steeple rises from the gable end of the projecting bay. The building has a prosperous look in a less than prosperous area.

Las Sauses

Las Sauses (1863, 7,500 feet) took its Spanish name from a willow slough near the confluence of the Rio Grande and the Conejos River. Never platted or incorporated, this tiny village sprang up close to an early ferry over the Rio Grande, Stewart's Crossing. Some crumbling adobe structures remain, as does one large ranch house, Cross Arrow (1901, Denver Concrete Contractors).

CN17 **St. Anthony of Padua Chapel**

1928. Conejos County 28

This mission church, which has no running water and no well, incorporates walls of the first (1880) church on the site. It is stuccoed adobe with a gable roof, an open bell tower, and stained glass windows. The flat ceiling of narrow beaded boards extends over the tiny choir loft at the rear with its propane-fired ceiling heater.

Manassa

Manassa (1879, 7,683 feet) was founded by Mormon colonists and named for one of the sons of Joseph in the Old Testament. Hispanics at Los Cerritos, 3 miles southeast, supposedly tried to stop the colony by dam-ming the north fork of the Conejos River, but the Mormons cleared the river and built a successful agricultural town.

CN18 Jack Dempsey Home and Museum

1966. Main St. (Colorado 142) in City Park

The single-room, side-gabled house that was the birthplace of the world champion boxer has been moved from its original location to the town park. A stone fireplace dominates the east gable end, with entry doors on the north and south. Since 1966 the house has been a museum with free admission to exhibits memorializing the "Manassa Mauler."

CN19 King Turquoise Mine

1890. Colorado 142, 9.5 miles east of Manassa

In 1890 Perrine King rediscovered this prehistoric mine once worked by Native Americans. King dug pits on the south side of the highway to mine high-grade turquoise. His family continues the operation on a limited basis today, using an unpatented claim filed on Bureau of Land Management land. Of the four main shafts, the deepest is about 130 feet.

Ortiz

CN20 San Gaetano y San Juan Nepomucen Catholic Church

1938. 6 miles southwest of Antonito via U.S. 285 and Conejos County C

Ortiz (1871, 7,950 feet) was named for Nestor Ortiz, a prominent storekeeper and sheep rancher. This tiny village in a small valley near the Colorado–New Mexico border is proud of its church, a building of white stucco over concrete. A curvilinear parapet rises from corner piers to meet the projecting bell tower at the apex of the gable end. The frame belfry has a pyramidal cap topped by a wooden cross embellished with nails and painted bloodstains. It was made

and installed by Benito Archuletta, caretaker of the church since 1956.

The gently curved apse has a detailed mural, painted in 1990 by Michael Derry, a local artist, who portrayed the community as background for a heroic figure of the Virgin blessing the churches at Conejos and Ortiz. Round-arched stained glass windows shed light on a large wood stove, made from a 100-gallon oil drum, which heats the church. The church is dedicated to Saints Cajetan and John Nepomucen, the latter being the patron of the Penitente sect. Nepomucen's statue over the altar depicts him in his typical pose—with a finger raised to his lips.

Sanford

CN21 Pike's Stockade

1807, Zebulon M. Pike; 1960s, reconstruction. 4 miles east of Sanford on Colorado 136 (NHL)

On his expedition in 1806–1807 to determine the southern boundary of the Louisiana Purchase, Zebulon Pike and his men crossed the Sangre de Cristo Range and constructed a crude fort. Pike raised the American flag there, on Spanish territory, and was arrested and taken to Mexico. He was released five months later and escorted back to the United States. During the 1960s the Colorado Historical Society reconstructed Pike's Stockade in a picturesque cottonwood grove on the north bank of the Conejos River. The location and dimensions were determined by studying Pike's journals (although some say the actual site was about half a mile away, on higher ground, near McIntyre Hot Springs).

In the interest of permanence, the reconstruction substituted oak logs on a concrete foundation for the original horizontal cottonwood logs with notched corners. The wall heights vary, with sharpened poles to protect the lower sections. A flagpole stands at the center of the enclosure, and picnic tables furnish the surrounding park. The closest town, Sanford (1881, 7,560 feet), was established by Mormon colonists and named for Silas Sanford Smith.

Rio Grande County (RN)

Created in 1874, Rio Grande County emerged as a supply center for the mining rushes to the San Juan Mountains. Del Norte quickly claimed the county seat, although Monte Vista ultimately became the larger town. The eastern half of the county is level agricultural land watered by the river for which it is named, while the western half is montane forests, mostly within the Rio Grande National Forest. The Monte Vista National Wildlife Refuge is a haven for birders, who flock there in March looking for whooping cranes among the thousands of migratory sandhill cranes.

Hispanic farmers and ranchers first settled the county, but most of their architecture is gone, except for a few remnants such as a venerable jacal at Haywood, 5 miles northwest of Monte Vista. After the 1870s influx of Anglo miners, mining and agriculture blossomed. Mining has declined since 1900, although a major gold and silver mine was worked at Summitville until 1992. Agriculture remains the mainstay in a county known for its production of barley, hay, potatoes, oats, lettuce, and livestock. From an 1880 population of 1,944 the county has grown steadily to a current count of around 11,000, of whom roughly 2,000 live in Del Norte and 5,000 in Monte Vista.

Del Norte

The county seat (1872, 7,882 feet) was founded at a crossing on the often frisky Río Grande del Norte. It supplanted a preexisting Hispanic town of La Loma de San Jose, founded 3 miles to the east in 1859 by Juan Bautista Silva and a settlement party from Santa Fe, New Mexico. Del Norte became primarily an Anglo supply town for the San Juan mining regions, a role enhanced by the 1881 arrival of the Denver & Rio Grande Railroad. A visitor information center occupies the D&RG caboose at the corner of Grande Avenue and Spruce Street. Many buildings here use lightweight, tough rhyolite, the volcanic stone found locally in light pink to white colors.

RN01 **Rio Grande County Museum** (Barlow and Sanderson Stage Depot)

1874. In Centennial Park, southeast corner of Spruce and 2nd sts. at the D&RG tracks

Barlow and Sanderson, the last major Colorado stagecoach company, used this one-story, hand-hewn cabin of Douglas fir logs with notched corners and overlapping exterior boards. It was moved to this cottonwood-shaded park across from the Town Hall in 1973, placed on a stone foundation, and converted to a transportation museum.

RN02 **Del Norte Town Hall** (D&RG Depot)

1886. 140 Spruce St. (in Centennial Park)

This depot has upstairs living quarters and the standard first-floor trackside bay. Although much altered, the interior still has a section of the original ticket counter and the original wainscoting and fenestration. The simple exterior, stuccoed with a heavy texture above grooved horizontal boards, hints at the Prairie Style.

RN03 **Del Norte Mineral Well**

1897. Columbia St. and Grande Ave. (U.S. 160)

This open pavilion of rough-faced pink rhyolite, constructed by convicts from the state penitentiary at Cañon City, initially stood over a public well and fountain whose mineralized water was touted as curative. It has been moved from the town's main intersection but still has the original pyramidal roof of decorative wood shingles.

RN04 Windsor Hotel

c. 1872. Southeast corner of Grande Ave. (U.S. 160) and Columbia St.

Local rhyolite was used for this plain, two-story, vernacular Italianate hotel, one of the oldest still operating in Colorado.

RN05 Stone Quarry Building

c. 1876. North side of Grande Ave. (U.S. 160), west of Columbia St.

Rhyolite from several local quarries is show-cased in the exterior and interior walls of this two-story edifice, which once housed the offices of U.S. Senator Thomas Bowen. The otherwise flat-roofed structure has gable ends for a barrel-vaulted back room. Thick stone walls create three distinct 14-foot-high storefronts, now modified, with a west section not built until 1913. Over the storefronts is an intact, dressed stone second story with tall, shallow-arched windows. Besides shops, the building now houses a bed and breakfast inn that incorporates a former barbershop, a small adobe house, and an adobe wall with old gates from Taos, New Mexico, to form a courtyard in back.

RN06 Holy Name of Mary Catholic Church

1898. Southwest corner of Pine and 6th sts.

A large, open bell tower crowns this rhyolite block church. Round-arched windows and a rose window are set with stained glass. The elaborate, columned altar is flanked by two statuary niches displaying life-size figures. A transverse chapel at the southwest corner of the church joins it to the Spanish Colonial Revival rectory, forming a courtyard.

RN07 Assembly of God Church
(Methodist Church)

1876. Northeast corner of Pine and 7th sts.

Suffragette Susan B. Anthony gave the dedication address for this church, whose rhyolite walls are topped by a wooden superstruc-

ture. Beneath the open belfry, a diamond window is centered above the transomed double entry. The voussoirs of the tall, flat-arched windows are of the same dressed stone used for the sills and quoins.

RN08 Rio Grande County Museum

1987, Jack Rominger. Northeast corner of Oak and 6th sts.

This single-story contemporary musuem has an irregular plan of rectangular spaces under flat roofs that draws on traditional adobe construction. Stuccoed frame walls enclose wings and bays that extend from a narrow, clerestoried, central-gabled gallery opening onto east and south walled courtyards. The south side gallery is a glass wall opening onto a Spanish-style courtyard with slat-roofed loggias supported by peeled log columns. Architect Jack Rominger, a Del Norte native retired from an architectural practice in Palo Alto, California, designed this small museum for artifacts of Native American, Hispanic, and Euro-American cultures.

RN09 Del Norte High School

1919, Mountjoy and Frewen. Southwest corner of Oak and 9th sts.

In a typical but handsome design, the Denver architects used two stories of dark red brick on a rectangular plan with a rough rhyolite base rising to the sill level of the first floor. Raised, brick-trimmed courses of rough stone, brick piers and quoins, recessed brick spandrels, and window arches of tapestry brick enliven the facade with a Neo-Tudor touch.

RN10 Del Norte Grade School

1942, Walter H. Simon. South end of Oak St.

Beige rhyolite enhances this two-story school by a Denver architect. The double-door entry is centered beneath a tall, narrow window that imparts Art Deco ambiance, as does the name in Moderne metal letters.

RN11 Presbyterian College Dormitory

1884. Southwest corner of 6th and Cherry sts.

The Reverend George Darley of the Home Missionary Movement founded the Presbyterian College of the Southwest in 1883. This square, three-story frame structure with a mansard roof remains. The old Presbyterian Chapel (1895), Spruce Street between 6th and 7th streets, with its rough-faced rhyolite walls and tall, Gothic-arched, stained glass windows, has been incorporated into a new community church. The New England Protestants who built the college were not well received by Catholic Spanish-speaking locals, and the school closed in 1901.

RN12 Rio Grande County Courthouse

1939–1954, Walter H. Simon. Southeast corner of 6th and Cherry sts.

Pueblo Revival massing and rough-faced rhyolite in random courses characterize this three-story building designed by a Denver architect. Like much WPA work, it was built with local materials, in this case stone cut on the grounds. Construction, interrupted by World War II, was not completed until 1954.

RN13 St. Joseph Hospital

1954, Gordon Sweet. 1280 Grande Ave. (U.S. 160)

Gordon Sweet, a Colorado Springs architect, designed this hospital as flat-roofed, single-story, rectangular modules of red brick trimmed in gray limestone radiating from a taller entrance bay. In a limestone-paneled wall, a tall, multipaned window with a subtle cross motif lights the waiting area. Brick wings with mansard roofs contain a nursing home and a small brick chapel. This stylish contemporary structure occupies the site where St. Joseph's first opened in 1907 in a converted house.

RN14 Montoya House

c. 1864. 16095 U.S. 160

This large adobe house behind a willow windbreak began as the small store and rear living quarters of pioneer Luis Montoya, a successful sheep rancher. With the addition of a large dance hall, now the living room, and separate living quarters for residents and visitors, the house became a social club.

The rambling, multigable roof reveals the gradual expansion of the building, which also encloses a well and a former courtyard. A glazed sun porch has been added to the west wall, and a potato cellar east of the house has been converted to an earth-sheltered dwelling.

RN15 Haywood Jacal

1860s. 5 miles northwest of Monte Vista beside U.S. 160

On the D&RG siding known as Haywood is one of the best surviving examples of a Hispanic jacal, built of upright poles lashed together and plastered with adobe. Now used as stables on the Haywood Ranch, it is a semi-ruin with abandoned electrical wiring and part of a stovepipe chimney.

RN16 Seven Mile Plaza

1860s. 7 miles east of Del Norte at junction of Rio Grande County 5N and 5W on the Rio Grande River

Seven Mile Plaza consists of the ruins of an adobe trading post and several outbuildings. It lies midway between Del Norte and Monte Vista and is named for the distance from each.

RN17 St. Francis of Assisi Catholic Church

1881. One mile west of Seven Mile Plaza

Concrete footings help support the thick, stuccoed adobe walls of this church, with the few openings deeply inset. A shingled bell tower is topped by a pyramidal roof and cross. The sacristy and a storeroom flank the rounded apse as shed additions to the transepts. Inside are a small vestibule under the choir loft, stained glass windows in pink and blue, and a wooden altar painted to look like marble.

Monte Vista

Monte Vista (1881, 7,663 feet), originally known as Lariat, prospered after the 1881 arrival of the D&RG and the introduction of irrigated farming. Monte Vista became an important shipping point for livestock and crops, primarily barley and potatoes. The countryside is filled with cylindrical, corrugated stainless steel barley silos with conical tops, while Monte Vista itself is dominated by the rectangular tower of the Adolph Coors Company's ten-story barley elevator.

Monte Vista's prosperous agrarians and merchants developed one of the San Luis Valley's finest residential neighborhoods. Bounded by Prospect and 4th avenues, between Washington and Dunham streets, this area offers well-maintained examples of various ages and styles of residential construction, ranging from small brick and cast stone cottages to large period revival homes. Many of the commercial buildings, generally designed by the local contractors who constructed them, are of gray rhyolite from a quarry 7 miles south of town.

RN18 **Colorado State Veterans Center, Homelake**

1891; additions. Northwest corner of Rio Grande County 3E and Sherman Ave., 3 miles east of Monte Vista

Locals donated the 500-acre site for structures that span a full century of construction, many of them four-unit cottages that began to be built in 1907. The main office (c. 1892), originally the superintendent's house, is two stories of rough-faced rhyolite with expansive, balustraded porches on all four sides. Round arches and Neoclassical columns set the tone for several other buildings sharing the grassy grounds and circular drive. These include a chapel, an old dining hall, a pool hall, and an open pavilion

RN17 St. Francis of Assisi Catholic Church

(1892) with stout stone pillars supporting a wooden hipped roof.

Rows of cottages and dormitories with white stucco walls and green-painted trim, materials also used for facilities such as a women's lounge and a shop, dominate the center. A single-story hospital and nursing home (1928) of beige wire-cut brick replaced the original hospital east of the office. Its hipped roof with exposed rafter ends shelters battered buttresses at the corners that emphasize a low profile and solid appearance. A cemetery and several outbuildings of the Homelake Farm as well as the Homelake State Wildlife Area surround this antique institution.

RN19 **Visitors' Center** (Public Library)

1895. Southeast corner of Jefferson St. and 1st Ave.

This tiny, single-story building of rough-faced pink rhyolite could have housed a modest collection and a librarian of small proportions. The entry of its glazed storefront is centered under an etched glass transom. An elegant cornice tops the west facade. In 1987 the Monte Vista Historical Society made this its headquarters. Next door to the south is a newer library building (1904, John J. Huddart), a single-story, red brick box atop a raised full basement, a typical Carnegie design in Beaux-Arts Neoclassical dress.

RN20 **Mansion Antiques** (Sylvester House)

1913. 1030 Park Ave.

This large house, built by rancher L. D. Sylvester. is a classic Craftsman design from its ribbon of attic shed dormer windows to the massive front porch braces. Yellow, orange, red, and brown glazed brick is trimmed with local sandstone in unusual triangular insets and T shapes under the windows and at the base of the wooden roof braces. Wide eaves with exposed rafters, half timbering, and stained glass windows in geometric designs further adorn the house. The interior retains its dark ceiling beams, beveled glass, built-in wooden furniture, and a Van Briggle tile fireplace. A matching carriage house echoes the materials, style, and shallow roofline of the dwelling, which now contains an antiques gallery.

RN21 **Monte Villa Inn** (El Monte Hotel)

1930, E. Floyd Redding. 925 1st Ave. (NR)

After helping his father design the Hotel Boulderado (BL08) in Boulder, E. Floyd Redding, a Denver architect, chose a Spanish Colonial Revival style for this three-story edifice. The H plan is set in a concrete foundation with brick walls covered in stucco under a flat roof. Vigas, a curvilinear parapet, and tiled pent roofs at the top of the third story reinforce the Southwestern theme, as does the main entry marquee of projecting log ends supported by decorative scroll ironwork.

A 1973 single-story concrete addition contains a new lobby. The old main entrance vestibule, hall, former lobby, office, and women's bridge room have been transformed into the main dining room, making

use of the original textured walls and rich, dark woodwork. Simple columns rise to a coffered ceiling with a central stained glass skylight. The mezzanine, wrought iron staircase, and Otis elevator also remain.

RN22 **J. J.'s Lounge** (Armory)

1922, Mountjoy and Frewen. Washington St., north of 1st Ave.

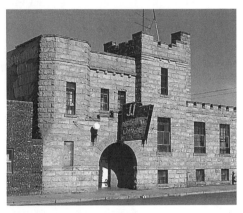

A medieval fortress that once protected the interests of Anglo capitalists, this two-story pile of rough-faced rhyolite has become a Hispanic nightclub. A recessed entry hides in the shadows of a massive round arch, under a crenelated tower and parapet, capping this bastion of social control built for strike-breaking troops. It has fallen to the enemy: celebrating members of the working class.

RN23 **Post Office and Federal Building**

1933, James A. Wetmore, OSA. Northeast corner of Washington Ave. and 2nd St. (NR)

Late Beaux-Arts classicism influenced the massing of this monumental, two-story red brick building with central entry loggia and wings. Six fluted, full-height Ionic columns front the recessed entry of three bronze doors topped by transoms with wrought iron grilles. Both limestone and terracotta are used for detail, including a dentiled cornice below a parapet with antefixes. Red tile covers the metal hipped roof. Inside, most of the original bronze detail and dark-stained woodwork remain, augmented by a 1980s mural by Thomas Lockhart depicting local history.

RN24 United Methodist Church

1924, C. J. Anderson. Southwest corner of Washington St. and 2nd Ave.

Breaking with ecclesiastical tradition, the Methodists used a Beaux-Arts Neoclassical design in purple-brown brick trimmed with pink rhyolite. The nearly square building is set on a raised basement faced in rhyolite blocks. The facade is symmetrical, with five single entrance doors on a deeply recessed porch between four brick columns with dressed stone bases.

RN25 First Presbyterian Church

1899, James Campbell, builder. Northeast corner of 2nd Ave. and Broadway

Constructed by a local stonemason of coursed gray rhyolite blocks from the local Myers Stone Quarry, the First Presbyterian Church has a cross-gable roof with parapeted gable ends and a square, open bell tower. Church members, including Swedish immigrant Charles Ydren, carved the interior woodwork and installed cabinetwork imported from Sweden. This church replaced a frame one, from which the 1888 cornerstone was taken. The manse (1906), to the east, is a plain, two-story foursquare of yellow brick, with an enclosed sun porch on the second floor over a balustraded porch.

RN26 St. Joseph Catholic Church

1922, Bernard Noriega, builder. 359 Patterson St.

Stone blocks and bricks from two predecessor churches are combined in this unique structure, rising skyward to curvilinear parapets on the facade and bell tower. Brick trim on stone surfaces reverses the stone-trimmed brick that prevails in Colorado, where stone is considered fancy and brick ordinary.

RN27 Bowen Community Church

1909. 10 miles south of Monte Vista on Colorado 370, 2 miles east of Colorado 15

RN27 Bowen Community Church

Originally Methodist but now eager for any worshippers, this church stands alone and unused beside a back road. Its white-painted grooved siding rises into a soaring, flared spire topped with a Scandinavian metal ornament. Strikingly simple, it is a stark tombstone for the deceased agricultural town of Bowen (1883–1901).

South Fork

South Fork (1876, 8,190 feet) was built around a large lumber mill that still sustains the hamlet. An old general store and an abandoned D&RG water tank survive from the glory days of narrow-gauge steam railroading. Here U.S. 160 intersects the scenic Silver Thread Byway (Colorado 149), which leads to Wagon Wheel Gap and the mining town of Creede in Mineral County.

RN28 Holy Family Mission Church

1940. South of U.S. 160, on the east edge of South Fork

Behind the large sawmill that dominates the town with huge piles of lumber and logs, a white bell tower sticks up like a hand at the back of the classroom. It belongs to this adobe church with Gothic-arched openings and a rose window under a steep pitched roof with exposed rafter ends and overhanging eaves. The square corner bell tower is topped by an octagonal closed carillon with a roof surmounted by a cross. The church, strong in design and well maintained, is a good example of modern-day vernacular adobe construction.

RN29 Spruce Lodge

1925. 29431 West U.S. 160

The owners of a local lumber mill built this boarding house for mill customers. Peeled logs form the two-story main lodge, which has a hipped roof and a two-story front porch. The porch is enclosed with large windows and raised, with a central wooden stairway and entrance. The lobby features a fireplace of glazed river rock. In the 1970s a two-story chalet building was built on the west, with a cross-gable roof and two large shed dormers to accommodate second-floor lodgings. The upstairs areas are reached by stairways and balconies set under the over-hanging eaves. Unpeeled logs are used for rustic stick balustrades. The small cottage nearby, sided in vertical logs, is one of a few surviving mill worker homes.

RN30 Summitville

1876–1947. 45 miles south of Del Norte via U.S. Forest Service Rd. 330

Summitville produced Colorado's largest gold boulder, now on display at the Denver Museum of Natural History (DV133.2). Among the surrounding ruins, one of the best-preserved structures is the Elmwood Telephone Line Cabin, used by telephone company repair workers. Part of the town was razed to excavate a 45-acre pit mine where Galactic Resources of Vancouver opened a heap leaching cyanide gold recovery operation. This operation used cyanide-laced water to extract gold from ore, leaking thousands of gallons into the Alamosa River and killing all the fish within 17 miles. Galactic declared bankruptcy in 1992, leaving the state and the federal government with a $64 million mess.

Mineral County (ML)

Silver, gold, zinc, lead, and copper gave Mineral County its name, but logging, ranching, and tourism have sustained its economy. Rio Grande National Forest and the Big Blue, La Garita, Weminuche, and Wheeler wilderness areas cover 90 percent of the land, supporting camping, hunting, fishing, and other tourist activities that have supplanted mining. Since Mineral County was formed in 1893, settlement has been mostly confined to the county seat of Creede, the only lively town in a county that once boasted fourteen.

Ranches line the Rio Grande and some of its tributaries, which have worn twisting paths through rocky terrain softened somewhat by sagebrush and upland forests. Some hay and cattle ranches take in tourists, and rental cabins are scattered along Colorado 149, the county's main thoroughfare. Winter tourism revolves around the Wolf Creek Pass Winter Sports Area, which leads Colorado ski areas in snowfall with more than 400 inches a year. U.S. 160 crosses the Continental Divide at Wolf Creek Pass through a concrete snowshed to protect vehicles. The last mine, the Homestake, closed in 1985. The population countywide has fallen from an 1890s peak of more than 2,000 to about 500 year-round residents, 75 percent of whom live in Creede.

Creede

"Holy Moses!" shouted Nicholas C. Creede upon striking a silver lode on Willow Creek two miles above its junction with the Rio Grande. His discovery in 1889 of what became the Holy Moses Mine started a rush that brought an estimated 10,000 people into this remote chasm and led to the establishment of Creede (1891, 8,852 feet), which soon replaced Wason as the county seat. Creede also struck pay dirt with the Amethyst Mine. He sold his Holy Moses (whose ruins may still be seen 3 miles up East Willow Creek) to David H. Moffat, president of the D&RG, which built a spur line to Creede in 1891 from Wagon Wheel Gap. Seven camps thrived in the extremely narrow gorge of Willow Creek: Amethyst, Bachelor, Creede, Jimtown, North Creede, Stringtown, and Weaver.

As Richard Harding Davis marveled in *The West from a Car Window* (1892), Creede had "hundreds of little pine boxes of houses and log-cabins, and the simple quadrangles of four planks which mark a building site. . . . There is not a brick, a painted front, nor an awning in the whole town. It is like a city of fresh card-board."

This "card-board" town squeezed in between towering basaltic spires was scorched by fires and drowned by several major floods. But nothing stopped the eternal hubbub of mining and ore processing, of gambling and carousing in some thirty saloons strung out along Willow Creek. Creede attracted a rogue's gallery of western characters, including Poker Alice Tubbs, Bob Ford, Calamity Jane, Bat Masterson, and Soapy Smith. Cy Warman, editor of *The Creede Candle*, wrote of the frenetic frontier boom town that "it's day all day in the daytime, and there is no night in Creede."

In the awesome canyons surrounding this resilient silver city, the principal mines lie on Campbell Mountain and Bachelor Hill, north of town, while many smaller headframes and mill ruins perch on steep canyon walls. Awesome milling and mining structures top the five-to-seven-story-high cribbing at the upper end of Main Street for the

Amethyst, Last Chance, and Commodore mines. Creede's subterranean heritage—some 2,000 miles of underground mining tunnels—is commemorated by an underground community center, mining museum, and fire station (1993–1994), 9 Canyon Road at the northwest end of town. Much of modern Creede spills south, to more open terrain to capture more sunshine, leaving the old town to its narrow, spooky canyon.

ML01 Mineral County Museum (Denver & Rio Grande Depot)

1891. 109 S. Main St. (in City Park)

Built as a replacement for the town's original tent depot, this single-story, board-and-batten model has a cross-gable roof with shake-shingled ends, a steep, shingled gable over the entry bay, and a smaller gable over a protruding telegrapher's bay. David Moffat of the D&RG claimed that this spur line paid for itself within the first four months of operation. Other depots, at South Creede and North Creede, have been demolished. The D&RG hung on until 1932, when it abandoned passenger service. In 1965 the Creede depot, with its matching privy (1891) and a new City Park Gazebo (1976), became a museum run by the Creede Historical Society.

ML02 Elks Lodge No. 506

c. 1892, Charles Ewry, builder. 102–110 Main St.

A second-story frame oriel above the clipped corner distinguishes this large, two-story red brick commercial building. Constructed as the Ewry Building, it houses the Elks lodge, with the town's oldest bar, on the second floor. Four first-floor storefronts flank a round-arched central entry. Rough stone sills and lintels decorate second-story windows below a diapered frieze and corbeled cornice. A mural, *The Four Seasons,* was painted in 1992 by Creede artist Stephen Quiller.

ML03 Creede Community Church (Congregational Church)

1905. Northeast corner of Creede Ave. and 4th St.

ML03 Creede Community Church (Congregational Church)

The ungodly town of Creede, one of the wildest in Colorado, inspired Congregationalists in Denver to donate a circus tent for services. That tent evolved into this serene, red brick Queen Anne Style church with trim of local sandstone, a steep, pyramidal roof, and a stocky, shingled corner belfry tower. The so-called Akron, or fan-shaped, seating plan common to many U.S. church buildings of the period was used in a square hall with corners cut off by entrances and the fellowship room. The same subtle Gothic arch distinguishes the entry, the bell tower openings, and the stained glass windows, which were donated by the town fraternal lodges.

ML04 **Creede Consolidated School No. 1 Complex**

1947, Jerry Crawford. 210–408 La Garita Ave.

Creede's high school and library (1947) is a rustic structure of logs used horizontally, vertically, and at various diagonals. The roof and entry are gabled. The same Denver architect used a similar log design for his adjacent Lamb Elementary School (1963), but added clerestory ribbon windows. Crawford also designed the gym and recreation center (c. 1970) for this complex, whose school library doubles as the public library.

ML05 **Quiller Gallery** (Creede Boarding House)

c. 1900. 110 N. Main St.

Built after one of Creede's fires with a mixture of cinders from the fire and cement placed between two-by-six timbers, this two-story commercial building with transomed glass storefronts was dressed up with an elaborate pressed metal facade. Thin pilasters and ornately scrolled panels frame the two upstairs windows beneath a 3-foot frieze and cornice of metal pressed to look like rough stone with dentils, scallops, and a blind balustrade. The building has housed a grocery, a saloon, the Silver Threads Clothing Store, and, since 1974, the gallery of local artist Stephen Quiller. Quiller "re-silvered" the fa-

ML05 Quiller Gallery (Creede Boarding House)   ML07 Creede Repertory Theater

cade with aluminum, to revive the exuberance of this Gilded Age silver city.

ML06 Creede Hotel

1892. 120 N. Main St.

Philip Zang of Denver's Zang Brewing Company built and owned what was originally called Zang's Hotel. This one-story frame building became the annex of a later two-story frame building next door. The original second-story porch, complete with rocking chairs overlooking Main Street, provides a covering for the sidewalk. At the rear of the hotel, a stone and brick structure that was once a brothel now houses the proprietors. The high-ceilinged dining room has chandeliers and a ceiling heater. The annex houses a restaurant in what was the rowdy Creede Hotel Bar, where the decor was mostly mineral specimens. This is the oldest hotel in town, with four quaint rental rooms still available upstairs.

ML07 Creede Repertory Theater

1894. 1993, renovation, Long Hoeft Architects. 124 N. Main St.

In 1966 student actors began staging summer plays in a ramshackle collection of one-, two-, and three-story buildings and additions, sheathed in corrugated metal and frame siding, which step back to a fourth-story penthouse. Crudely remodeled after a 1970 fire, the funky old movie theater was given a low-budget, high-tech facelift and interior renovation by Long Hoeft Architects of Denver and Georgetown. Their Mineshaft Modern design cleverly rearranges traditional elements and materials seen on the town's old-timers. They reformed and strengthened the structure, clad it in pressed metal siding—a cheap, common, traditional mining town solution—and added a second-story porch similar to that of the neighboring Creede Hotel.

ML08 Pappy's Place (Western Federation of Miners Hall)

c. 1900. 128 N. Main St.

During its campaign for an eight-hour workday, $3-a-day wages, and safer mining conditions, the WFM built this single-story gabled building. Like the builders of the Creede Boarding House (ML05), they used wood frames to form walls made of concrete and cinders and rubble from one of Creede's many fires. A stepped false front on the gable end frames a transomed single door between two large, transomed shop windows. A later porch on the south, covered by an extension of the roof, is supported with turned posts fronting what is now a fast food restaurant.

ML09 Masonic Temple

1892. 131–133 N. Main St.

Supposedly the first masonry structure in a town of canvas and raw pine, this two-story commercial building was built with sand bricks made at the Wason Ranch. With its fancy brick frieze, corbeling, and window trim, it is very similar to the building immediately to the south, differing chiefly in the enclosed outside staircase on its north wall.

ML10 Tomkins Brothers Hardware

1892. 127 N. Main St.

Red brick walls 17 inches thick on a 3-foot-wide stone foundation, steel ceiling girders, and posts of Oregon pine help to explain the longevity of this ornate, two-story business block. Storefronts rise to paired, shallow-arched windows on the upper floor, beneath a bracketed cornice of the now stuccoed facade. With the hardware store, which is still in business, the building until 1925 also housed a bank, of which the teller window and vault remain. Another section of the building, old Firehouse No. 1, was resurrected in 1992 as a bed and breakfast inn.

ML11 Old Miners Inn (Miners and Merchants Bank)

1892, W. F. Nichol. 107 N. Main St.

The town's first allegedly fireproof edifice, erected after a fire in June 1892, used cinders and rubble from the fire as well as cement, a precedent for several other buildings. This single-story structure has rough sandstone trim, with a capped parapet above a corbeled frieze. Storefronts and recessed entry bays with tall transoms front the building. After the bank closed it served as a post office until 1976, when the Old Miners Inn opened here. This rustic saloon is filled with antiques, including the hotel's old walk-in safe, now used as a beer cooler. Crude frame additions (1990s) that climb two stories above an otherwise one- and two-story town led Creede finally to consider zoning.

ML12 Sunnyside Cemetery

c. 1891. Off Bulldog Mine Rd., .5 mile west of Creede

The small Carpenter's Gothic Immaculate Conception Catholic Mission (1897) was moved from Creede to this hillside to make room for a new log church (c. 1974) at the northwest corner of Main and 3rd streets. Amid the tombstones behind the old church, a miniature model of the church serves as a mausoleum for the Kiner family. In the "shotgun cemetery" (Creede's Boot Hill) 30 yards north a wooden marker commemorates saloonkeeper Bob Ford, who killed Jesse James before dying of a gunshot wound himself.

ML13 Ryder-Hall House

1885. 178 U.S. Forest Service Rd. 502, on the west side of East Willow Creek in North Creede

Prospector Haskell Ryder constructed what is purportedly the oldest house in town. It is a front-gable, hewn log cabin with sheet metal roofing and improvised log and frame outbuildings snuggled into a rock cliff along East Willow Creek. The poet Walter Hall and his wife Nancy later lived here and tried to promote Creede as a haven for artists, writers, and actors. The dirt road continues up the creek past ruins of mines, including the Holy Moses, 2 miles up the canyon, on a 17-mile self-guided tour of the Bachelor Historic District.

ML14 Wason Ranch

1871. 2.3 miles southeast of Creede on Colorado 149 and the Rio Grande

Martin Van Buren Wason established the first ranch in the area, 6 miles above Wagon Wheel Gap. Following the stampede to Creede, he built a courthouse and platted

Wason (1891–1904) as an 80-acre townsite. Although designated the first county seat when Mineral County was created in 1893, Wason was short lived. Boosters from Creede hauled off the county records and also took the courthouse, plank by plank, to Creede, where it burned in 1946.

Wason's ranch house is a two-story stuccoed frame building, L shaped with a gable roof and a full-height gabled bay in the middle of the facade. Hipped roofs cover single-story porches between the bay and both ends of the building. The tall, narrow windows have pedimented lintels. Among various outbuildings are small rental cabins, updated with kitchenettes and large picture windows framing the jubilant, trout-filled Rio Grande.

Wagon Wheel Gap

Wagon Wheel Gap (1875, 8,390 feet), which started as a stage stop on the Rio Grande route into the San Juan mining regions, took its name from a pile of broken wagon wheels found along the old road. J. C. McLellan opened a hotel in 1881, and General William Jackson Palmer and the D&RG arrived in 1883 to promote the area as a spa, touting its natural hot springs and the spectacular mountain setting. Among the nearby tourist attractions is the Wheeler Wilderness Area, with unusual formations of volcanic tuff carved by wind and rain into fantastic shapes likened to temples and castles. The stone domes and pinnacles have been fenced off to prevent vehicular intrusions into an area accessible only by foot trails and served by a 1920s rustic shelter.

ML15 Denver & Rio Grande Depot

1883. Colorado 149, 13 miles southeast of Creede (NR)

An elegant if standard frame depot has the rectangular trackside bay required for the agent. The two-story passenger section of the depot is 26 feet by 37 feet, with a single-story freight wing. The cross-gable roof has a brick chimney slightly off the ridgeline. The bracketed entry canopies are flared extensions of the main roof. Clapboard siding

ML15 Denver & Rio Grande Depot

rises from vertical board sheathing, and the shingled gable ends feature sunburst designs above paired windows. Indoor plumbing is one of the few modifications to what has been a private residence since the 1970s.

ML16 4UR Ranch

1890s. South off Colorado 149, 1 mile northwest of the D&RG depot

General Palmer and the D&RG founded this resort along Goose Creek near the railroad. Its remnants include some early log accommodations, a one-story lodge of stuccoed concrete with a curvilinear parapet, and old-fashioned hot springs plunge pools lined in concrete with amethyst crystals set in the rims. Somewhat incongruously, the ranch also hosted a company town where an intact fluorspar mine and mill are still surrounded by clapboard cottages, a bunkhouse, and a foreman's residence. Halfway up a scenic hillside is the one-room clapboard Wagon Wheel Gap Schoolhouse (c. 1927), distinguished by a balustraded entry porch and an open bell tower with a pyramidal cap. The school was moved to this site and restored on a new concrete foundation.

ML17 La Garita Ranch

c. 1895. 9 miles southeast of Creede off Colorado 149

This 2,500-acre ranch along Bellows Creek near its confluence with the Rio Grande was purchased by U.S. senator Lawrence C. Phipps of Denver in 1908. The private re-

treat of the Phipps family for a half-century, it is now a dude ranch. Part of the two-story log main lodge dates back to 1885. Besides three log guest lodges—the Biltmore, the Ritz, and the Waldorf—La Garita has a large recreation hall, heated swimming pool, spa, sauna, stables, and fish house. Recently the Phipps family subdivided part of the ranch for a planned development, Wagon Wheel Estates. An easement for the main ranch and a 1,000-acre setting have been donated to the Nature Conservancy, which will oversee its preservation.

ML18 Spar City

1892–1895. 7.3. miles southwest of Creede along Colorado 149

This settlement along the Rio Grande, a stagecoach suburb of Creede, swelled to some 600 residents before the 1893 silver crash sank the community. In 1905 a group of Kansans bought the abandoned site for summer residences. These flatlanders restored two hand-hewn log cabins with double porches, the two-story log Coinage Hotel, and the jail with its original bars.

ML19 Antelope Springs

1876–1903. 12 miles southwest of Creede at the confluence of Trout Creek and the Rio Grande

This stage stop, also known as Antelope Park, was named for a salt lick that attracted deer, antelope, and other creatures. The Texas Club (Freeman Ranch) (1866) is a two-story log lodge with porches on the south and west sides and a rock fence in front. The oldest building in the county, it is now surrounded by summer homes in a compound known as the Texas Club or Antelope Park Club. Several other summer resorts are scattered around this wild and remote mountain valley.

ML20 Ruby Lake Cabins

1894–1935. 11 miles southwest of Antelope Park via Colorado 149 to Fern Creek Sheep Driveway

Nestled against the snowy white bosom of the Continental Divide, this resort began in 1894 as a homestead cabin. The land and lake were acquired by Clayton Wetherill in 1911. He ran it as a trout ranch where Teddy

Roosevelt's son, Quentin, is said to have helped build the still existing "dugout cabin" in 1915. A cook shack (1934) and bunk cabin (1935) were added for summer guests of Eugenia Wetherill, Clayton's wife, whose neighboring Wetherill Ranch (1917) has typical single-story rustic rental cabins under green shingle roofs. Art dealer C.

Bland Jameson traded two Charles Russell paintings for the land in 1959 and sold it to the U.S. Forest Service in 1970. At that time, the San Luis Valley Historical Society managed to save the buildings by fighting for a special use permit reversing the Forest Service policy of burning down buildings on newly acquired lands.

Saguache County (SH)

Saguache (Ute, blue earth) County (1867), with its sagebrush flats and montane borders, spans the northern end of the San Luis Valley. On the east it climbs to the crest of the 14,000-foot Sangre de Cristo range; on the west it rises into the Cochetopa Hills and the 14,000-foot San Juan Mountains. Parts of the Rio Grande, Gunnison, and San Isabel national forests; the Great Sand Dunes National Monument; and the La Garita Wilderness Area occupy more than 60 percent of the county.

Gold mining first attracted U.S. citizens to Kerber Creek in 1866, giving birth to Bonanza and several other towns. These gold camps soon fizzled, and the county shifted to lumbering. Over half of its twentieth-century industrial plants have been sawmills and planing mills. Saguache is also an agricultural county noted for lettuce, potatoes, barley, hay, oats, and livestock. Tourism and hunting are the current bright spots in an economy which, in recent decades, has been as flat as much of the terrain. Of fifty-eight post office towns which flowered with mining, lumbering, and agricultural booms, only seven remain.

Saguache, the county seat, holds the greatest architectural interest, along with Crestone, an old mining town that has been reborn as a religious center with exotic monasteries and places of worship. As Saguache County has minimal building regulations, it has been a haven for alternative housing types, ranging from stucco-clad straw bale houses at Crestone to solar adobe buildings in some rural areas. The county's modest vernacular architecture is enhanced by the high desert landscape framed by towering snowcapped mountains.

Saguache

The county seat (1867, 7,697 feet) was born in a gold rush and sustained by its grain mills and livestock ranches. Otto Mears, the "Pathfinder of the San Juans," founded one of several flour mills here, built area toll roads, and helped bring the Los Pinos Ute Indian Agency here. In this sleepy nineteenth-century town, buildings have long life expectancies. The largest edifice on 4th Street, the main street, is the two-story Italianate Masonic temple neighboring the vernacular Art Deco Ute Theater and the false-fronted office of *The Saguache Crescent*, one of Colorado's last newspapers set in metal type on a Linotype machine. Housing ranges from a hewn log, L-shaped house, on the northwest corner of 3rd Street and San Juan Avenue, to a split-level cottonwood tree house behind the St. Agnes Catholic Church.

SH01 **St. Agnes Catholic Church**

c. 1950. Southeast corner of Gunnison Ave. (U.S. 285) and 6th St.

Unusual Art Deco–inspired ornament of raised panels with raspberry-colored paint appears on the north entry facade of this stuccoed adobe structure. Around and above the door, in the stepped gable end wall, a stylized cross incorporates a stained glass window. Flanking the entrance are two additional stained glass windows, surrounded by Y-shaped panels reminiscent of chalices. An open bell tower sits atop a rear corner.

SH01 St. Agnes Catholic Church

SH02 **Saguache County Museum**

1908. Southwest corner of U.S. 285 and San Juan Ave.

This one-story, gable-roofed adobe building originally housed the school and then the undersheriff who guarded the jail next door. Its thick walls have been patched with concrete and painted to look like stone blocks. The jail to the south, with a center block of steel cells and a separate cell for women, was described when it was built in 1908 as "a marvel of protective confinement." The original cell graffiti remain in this jail, which once accommodated the cannibal Alfred Packer. Beginning with a nutmeg grater and one display case in 1959, the museum has grown into a large operation with artifacts spilling out into the yard. Outdoor exhibits include a "Chapel of Ease" (privy), the back side of which consists only of a chicken wire screen.

SH03 **Courthouse Annex** (Saguache Elementary School)

1915, Harry James Manning and Francis W. Frewen. South side of Christy Ave., between 6th and 7th sts.

The Mediterranean Revival influenced this pressed red brick H-shaped structure with gabled wings. The first story of the two-story building has a series of round-arched openings separated by flat pilasters that are echoed in the north gable ends of the wings. Decorative patterns in the brick, brick banding, and concrete panels add distinction, as does the red tiled roof, crowned by an octagonal chimney and a cupola.

SH04 **Community United Methodist Church**

1873. 601 Christy Ave. (northeast corner of 6th St.)

A tall, square, closed bell tower caps the entry bay of this white frame church, which was moved from the nearby townsite of Milton in 1885. The steep-pitched gable roof is covered in red metal, and shallow-arched wood moldings top the windows and doors. The church has modest additions on the north side.

SH05 **U.S. Forest Service Ranger Residence**

c. 1938. 450 Christy Ave. (northeast corner of 5th St.)

This single-story Pueblo Revival house, viga-studded with recessed wooden window lintels, faces south on a slightly elevated site, with a bunkhouse for summer workers. Several tall garage bays and thick columns flanking the entry punctuate the stucco walls.

SH06 **Saguache County Courthouse**

1910, John J. Huddart. 501 4th St. (southwest corner of Christy Ave.)

This design, like John Huddart's other Colorado courthouses, aims for a functional interior and an impressive exterior. The two-story, vernacular Neoclassical structure has a raised basement and dormered attic for extra space. Beige brick walls with limestone trim rise to a standard dentiled cornice and a pediment over the entry.

SH07 **Saguache Hotel**

1910. 413–415 Main St.

The thirty-room, two-story Saguache Hotel, composed of two rectangular wings forming an L shape, suggests the Prairie Style with low hipped roofs and hipped dormers spaced along the roofline. Boxed eaves overhang the red brick walls, and a porch with square wooden columns and a wooden plank floor runs south from the intersection of the wings and around the southeast corner of the hotel to the entrance. Florence Gellatley Means, who bought the hotel in 1935 and made it a success, tells that story in *But What, My Dear, Do You Know about Hotels?* (1992). Now vacant, the building appeared as the Independence Hotel and Saloon in the 1987 PBS American Playhouse production *Land of Little Rain*.

SH08 **Saguache County Bank**

1880, 1913. 311 Main St.

Established as the Pioneer Bank of Saguache County, with Isaac Gotthelf as president, this narrow, single-story brick bank was given a facelift in 1913, when the Denver Terra Cotta Company applied a classical pedimented facade of terracotta, limestone, and marble. Elegant columns flank the entry in an elaborate composition for so small a structure. Since 1927 the building has been used as a store, a cold storage locker, and a residence.

SH09 **Saguache Town Hall**

1915, H. W. J. Edbrooke. 504 San Juan Ave. (northwest corner of 5th St.)

Blueprints and specifications by the Denver architect, who was Frank E. Edbrooke's nephew, are available from the town clerk inside. This reinforced concrete Prairie Style hall replaced an adobe town hall. The narrow, two-story building has a red brick veneer with raised soldier courses to define the second story with its overhanging eaves. Square windows alternate with panels of aggregate to give the impression of a wide frieze under a green tile roof. The first-floor fenestration is evenly spaced, with the entrance door set between two tall windows on the narrow south facade. The jail has

been moved to the new sheriff's office next to the courthouse, but the venerable Charpiot walk-in safe remains behind the clerk's desk.

SH10 **Settle House**

1860s. 305 San Juan Ave.

Andrew Settle's U-shaped, single-story Territorial adobe house, said to have been built as a fort, may have been the first dwelling in town. Four entrances open onto the porch that wraps the north facade. The porch columns have Eastlake brackets under the eaves. The thick walls and multiple entrances are traditional adobe design elements, now clad in concrete, although the hipped roof, with antefixes, scroll finials, and four corbeled red brick chimneys, is definitely European in inspiration.

SH11 **Robertson Flour Mill**

1873, Enos Hotchkiss. West of Saguache County 46 (Baxter Rd.), .5 mile south of Saguache County Z (Denver Ave.) (NR)

Abandoned since 1925, this is one of few remaining water-powered gristmills in Colorado. The three-story, hand-hewn log structure is nearly 30 feet square and covered with vertical board-and-batten siding that uses wooden pins and square nails. Towers in the gable roof provided room for the machinery, whose wooden components were replaced by a roller system in 1886, when George Robertson purchased the mill. The south end had a water wheel, now dismantled, and the two-story north end had a loading dock. The mill house was made by combining two older cabins with a covered breezeway. The mill, on private, fenced property in a willow grove, is only partially visible from the road to the north.

Bonanza

SH13 Bonanza

1880–1938. Saguache County LL 56

Bonanza was founded after prospectors struck pay dirt in the Bonanza Mine. By the mid-1880s the town had more than 150 buildings and an estimated 1,000 people. By 1890 the gold boom was over. Raw pine boards turned gray, and weeds climbed the rusting mine machinery. The population in 1890 was 118 and a century later is only 16. Mining town life here was well described by resident Anne Ellis in her book, *The Life of an Ordinary Woman* (1929). Frame buildings and ruins line the main street, and traces of mines, mills, and smelters survive in town and in the surrounding foothills of the San Juan Mountains. The two-story, chinked log Kempner House (1880s), Saguache County LL 56, 10.8 miles northwest of U.S. 285, a T-shaped, cross-gabled house, provides local historian Helen Kempner with a fine view down the Kerber Creek Valley.

Center

Center (1898, 7,645 feet) is a stable agricultural town of about 1,500 residents named for its location in the center of the San Luis Valley. James L. Hurt platted a grid community, which, after the San Luis Central Railroad arrived in 1913, became a major lettuce- and potato-growing center. Besides early twentieth-century bungalows and cottages of stucco or frame construction, Center has a north side development of public housing units, plain duplexes grouped around a central open space, and an extensive mobile home community. Predominantly Hispanic farm workers form a major underclass whose marginal resources are reflected in their homes, bars, and businesses. More prosperous-looking farm-houses may be found on the outskirts of town.

SH13 City Hall Complex

c. 1938. 400 block of Worth Ave.

Interconnected stuccoed concrete buildings of one and two stories, arranged on an irregular plan and aspiring to the Pueblo Revival style, house the legal and social service agencies of the town, as well as the library. The core of the complex is a WPA-built community center.

SH14 Coin-o-Matic Laundry

c. 1910. 395 Worth Ave. (northwest corner of 4th St.)

This rectangular corner commercial structure with pediments over both front and side entrances has the pretensions of a bank. The single story of beige brick is trimmed with projecting courses and accented by brick panels of another color.

SH15 Haskin Medical Building

c. 1920s. 220 Worth St.

The Haskin Medical building, a rectangular, single-story structure covered in beige stucco, combines elements of Streamline Moderne and Pueblo Revival. The parapet has rounded corners and steps up above the entry, where the door is recessed beneath a semicircular, cantilevered canopy. Built as the office of a prominent physician, John W. Haskin, the building now houses an office of the Saguache County Public Health Department.

SH16 American Legion Hall

1920s. 204 Worth St. (southeast corner of 2nd St.)

This narrow, single-story building has a para-peted flat roof and a central entrance recessed beneath an unadorned round arch. Blind arches painted red and window trim painted blue are patriotic complements to the white stucco exterior.

SH17 Haskin Elementary School

1919, Mountjoy, French, and Frewen. 550 S. Broadway Ave.

SH17 Haskin Elementary School

Dominating the west end of Center, this large, two-story red brick building designed by Denver architects is visually enlarged by a high parapet and square corner towers. White stucco spandrels and ornamental panels, located between brick piers, are outlined with raised courses of red brick, providing lively elevations. Bands of windows appear modern for the design, and may be updated replacements. To the south and connected by a covered walkway is the less inspired Skoglund Middle School, a tribute to Modernist minimalism.

SH18 **Ford House**

1982, Belinda Zink. 50501 Saguache County C

This group of domes takes its form from computer-designed balloons sprayed on site with gunite reinforced with metal fibers. The two-story central structure has skylights and a secondary garage wing amorphously joined on the west side. Flared bays wrap large windows and sliding doors on the first floor, while the main entry is a Pueblo Revival–style bay. Two separate, smaller domes stand behind the main structure, with a bank of freestanding solar panels to the west. A stucco southeast wall has a wooden gate beneath a stucco arch. Owner David L. Ford and his wife worked closely with Belinda Zink on the design.

SH19 **Mobile Home**

1970s. 691 W. Saguache County 112 (northeast corner of Jackson St.)

Many coats of tarpaper around the base and thick white paint have softened the lines of this streamlined mobile home, with a small wooden porch covered by purple clematis. The structure is well attached to the site and is acquiring the melted lines of adobe buildings.

Crestone

Crestone (1880, 7,863 feet) was founded as a gold mining camp on a spectacular foothills site at the base of the Sangre de Cristo Mountains. As miners rushed in and gold poured out, the D&RG built a spur from Moffat. The town, located on the edge of a land grant, was named for the jagged, 14,294-foot Crestone (Spanish, cock's comb) Peak towering over the east edge of town. Galena, the main street, is dominated by the two-story false-fronted frame San Luis Valley Bank and Assay Office (1886), at the southeast corner of Alder and Galena streets, with a corner storefront that now houses the Twenty-First Amendment Liquor Store. Willow-shaded side streets lead to perhaps fifty log and frame cottages.

In recent decades Crestone has attracted religious communities and groups, including Zen Buddhist and Carmelite monasteries and actress Shirley MacLaine's New Age retreat. Environmentalist Maurice Strong has been instrumental in attracting diverse groups to the area, including the Aspen Institute for Humanistic Studies and a Colorado College extension campus. The private estate of Najeeb Halaby contains a prayer tower inspired by an ancient Assyrian ziggurat design, with a spiral stairway contained by stuccoed walls rising to an open prayer platform.

SH20 **Community Building** (Crestone School)

1880. Cottonwood St. and Carbonate Ave. (NR)

This single-story, two-room structure was originally sheathed in board and batten but was covered with clapboard at the time of a kitchen addition. The south entrance is in a gabled vestibule, with a door enlarged to accommodate funerals. The windows have pedimented lintels. In 1976, after the open belfry began to deteriorate, the bell (1912, C. B. Bell Company, Hillsboro, Ohio) was moved to a nearby rock pedestal. Since its 1949 closing the school has become a political, social, and religious center.

SH21 **Crestone Mountain Zen Center** (Lindisfarne Celtic Monastery)

1970s, Sim van der Ryn and Keith Critchlow. South end of Camino Baca Grande

The main stone, log, and glass structure of this retreat, designed by Sim van der Ryn, is sunk into a stony, southwest-facing hillside. The central kitchen with its greenhouse extension is the heart of the complex, which includes an earth-sheltered library under a pyramidal skylight and a two-story polygonal

guest wing on the west. Farther up the hill is the meditation and ceremonial building, designed by Keith Critchlow, with two joined domes covered by rolled roofing over a framework of arched timbers. The timbers rise at oblique, intersecting angles to a central fiberglass skylight. Lack of windows makes the structure introspective, as are the smaller retreats surrounding the two main structures and a 41-foot-high stupa. Built as the Lindisfarne Celtic Monastery, it became a retreat for Zen Buddhists who fled the 1959 Chinese takeover in Tibet.

SH22 **Haidakhandi Universal Ashram Temple**

1980s. South end of Camino Baca Grande

Beneath an elaborate brass spire a small shrine and sunken courtyard perch on a rocky, west-facing slope. Symmetrically designed as a structure within a structure, this domed and stuccoed frame temple houses a statue of the Murti or Divine Mother. Red terne roofs slope away from the central spire to cover a surrounding corridor. The gabled entry bay with stained glass in an arched transom leads to a sanctuary. The ashram also has a learning center, with the library in a modified geodesic dome.

SH23 **Carmelite Monastery**

1982. West end of Rendezvous Way, 1.5 miles south of Crestone

The Carmelites' peeled log chapel and monastery, sited on a sandy sagebrush swell, are

SH23 Carmelite Monastery

joined by an elevated, buttressed footbridge. In a contemporary interpretation of a walled Norman enclave, polygonal roofs atop square and round elements are joined by tan stucco walls. The earth-sheltered chapel, which has a dramatic pyramidal tower over the corner altar, is illuminated by stained glass panels depicting the monastic life. Spread about the hillside are passive solar hermitages with wooden or stucco walls, some earth sheltered and earth roofed.

La Garita

La Garita (1858, 7,840 feet) was settled by Hispanics who named it for nearby La Garita (Spanish, lookout) Peak in the San Juan Mountains and began raising cattle, sheep, and crops. Newer log buildings include the La Garita Cash Store and Post Office, while the old adobe school, with its trefoil gable ends, is now a private house. A 155-acre ranch has been converted to the Wild Iris Inn Bed and Breakfast, 38145 Saguache County E-39, for tourists and outdoors-people interested in the La Garita Wilderness Area. Also nearby are the Carnero Creek Pictographs, fifty-four figures in red hematite on rock, painted by Native Americans.

SH24 San Juan Art Center (Capilla de San Juan Bautista)

1873, 1912. 8 miles west of U.S. 285 (NR)

Exemplifying the mix of Hispanic and Yankee elements in San Luis Valley structures, this cruciform one-and-one-half-story chapel has 20-inch-thick stuccoed adobe walls under a shingled gable roof with solar heating panels and a two-story belfry. Red brick outlines the rose window and lancet windows that frame smaller, plain glass replacement windows. The lancet shape is repeated in the belfry openings. The interior has a high, pressed metal ceiling, hardwood floor, and stuccoed walls. Nearby are the ruins of an adobe convent and a Hispanic cemetery with hand-carved grave markers.

SH25 SPMDTU Concilio No. 16

1910s?. Saguache County 41G

A low, front-gable roof tops this abandoned hall of the workers' society, the Sociedad Protección Mutua de Trabajadores Unidos. The narrow, deep adobe building has small windows widely spaced along the sides and double doors centered in the main south facade.

Mineral Hot Springs

Mineral Hot Springs (1911, 7,740 feet), on the D&RG, was named for several hot springs known to the Utes long before the area was homesteaded in the 1880s. Of thirty-seven hot springs, the Chamberlain (c. 1912) was one of the first developed for tourists, but is now part of the Chamberlain Swine Farm. The town is in ruins, and the old Mineral Hot Springs Hotel, a one-story frame shack, houses hog farm workers.

Moffat

Moffat (1890, 7,561 feet), platted by the D&RG, was named for the railroad's one-time president David H. Moffat. Since the railroad withdrew, the town has lost most of its population. The Bank of Moffat (1897), on Moffat Way, the main street, with its original name still barely visible in fading paint, is a single-story frame building with a gable roof, retrofitted with large barn doors as the town garage. The abandoned Town Hall (c. 1892), on Moffat Way, is a tiny, false-fronted frame box. The forlorn Moffat Hotel (c. 1906), at the northwest corner of Moffat Way and Broadway, is a two-story red brick building with beige brick quoins and courses. The simple design, with a hipped roof and symmetrical fenestration, looks like an elongated foursquare.

SH26 First Baptist Church

1911. 1 block south of Moffat Way

The two-story, cast stone First Baptist Church has a roof covered in scalloped metal panels. Small Palladian windows in the north and south gable ends have round-arched, stained glass transoms in the center and stained glass panes on the sides. The double-hung

SH26 First Baptist Church

windows below have matching stained glass. A steeple with a double flared cap serves as an unusual top for the corner bell tower, with the entrance in the base. Like the gable ends above the eaves, it is covered in silver-painted metal panels stamped in a geometric design, making this a shimmering, if abandoned, town sentinel.

Sargents

Sargents (1880, 7,929 feet) was established as a D&RG station for helper locomotives on the west side of Marshall Pass. Many railroad ruins, including a round frame water tank and some new homes, are scattered around the current town hub on U.S. 50, Dotty's General Store.

SH27 Old Agency Fortified Site

21 miles southwest of Sargents on the east side of McDonough Reservoir No. 2; accessible by foot from U.S. Forest Service Rd. 855

In 1973 Ray D. Lyons of the Colorado Archaeological Society followed up local tales of a "robber's roost" and discovered this rock fort, used by Native Americans for an estimated 4,500 years. Utes, although not usually fort builders, may have erected or enhanced this fortification during their encounters with palefaces.

Overlooking the site of the 1870s and 1880s agency, this fort measures about 600 feet long and 200 feet wide atop a narrow natural stone rampart. Inside is a 20-by-25-foot room, with an entry area to the west separated by a low rock wall with access at each end. Rock walls with wooden supports rise 6 feet to enclose the space where the natural stone does not rise that high. Four guard pits lie along the entry trail, which climbs across a talus slope, and two more mark the trailhead.

Villa Grove

Villa Grove (1894, 7,980 feet), established by the D&RG at the north end of the San Luis Valley, has remained a community hub and a stop for travelers. False-fronted frame stores and shops line Main Street (U.S. 285).

SH28 Valley View Hot Springs

c. 1920s. 5 miles south of Villa Grove via U.S. 285, then 8 miles east on Rd. GG

Now part of a large ranch, this resort retains antique one-story octagonal cottages, both hewn log and clapboard, and a large concrete hot springs pool. Since the 1960s, it has been a popular if offbeat spa where bathing suits are optional. The elevated site, in the foothills of the Sangre de Cristo Mountains, offers a spectacular view of the San Luis Valley. A dirt road leads 2 miles north to the ghost town of Orient, once a major iron ore mine of the Colorado Fuel and Iron Company.

The Colorado:
The Western Slope

Here was the glint of the blossom rock,
Here Colorado dug the gold
For a sealskin vest and a rope of pearl
And a garter jewel from Amsterdam
And a house of stone with a jig-saw porch. . . .
Here's where they cut the conifers and ribbed
The mines with conifers that sang no more,
And here they dug the gold and went away,
Here are the empty houses, hollow mountains,
Even the rats, the beetles and the cattle
That used these houses after they were gone
Are gone; the gold is gone,
There's nothing here,
Only the deep mines crying to be filled.
　　　　　　—Thomas Hornsby Ferril, "Ghost Town"

T HE COLORADO RIVER HAS ITS SOURCE IN ROCKY MOUNTAIN
National Park, on whose southwestern border lie the first of many man-
made diversions in its course. With its tributaries the river drains all of
Colorado west of the Continental Divide. For 1,500 miles it flows through the
driest part of the United States, watering not only Colorado's Western Slope
but also Utah, Arizona, Nevada, and southern California. Dams and diversions
keep the muddy red waters, which gave both the river and the state their
name, from reaching the blue Pacific.

The mighty Colorado carved out the Grand Canyon and conquered the
great deserts of the Southwest, but it is now threatened by diversions and
salinity, by the silting and evaporation that diminish its many dammed reservoirs. Even in the moisture rich high Rockies, the Colorado flows through a
hydraulic landscape of dams and ditches, of headgates and tunnels, of measuring stations and holding basins. Much of its water is directed under the
Continental Divide to Denver, the Eastern Slope of Colorado, and, ultimately,
the Atlantic Ocean.

On its course through Colorado, the river runs through rocky and forested
terrain which provided material for the houses of stone and jigsaw lumber
observed by Colorado poet Thomas Hornsby Ferril. Such buildings can be
found in the towns along the upper Colorado and its major tributaries, the
Fraser, Blue, Eagle, Roaring Fork, and Gunnison rivers. These old stone and

The Colorado River Region

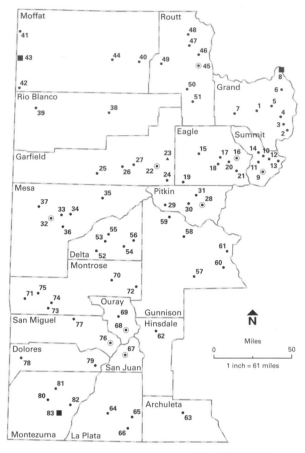

Moffat
- 41
- ■ 43
- 44 40
- 42

Routt
- 48
- 47
- 46
- ⊙ 45
- 49

Rio Blanco
- 39
- 38
- 50
- 51

Grand
- 8
- 6
- 5
- 7 1
- 4
- 3
- 2

Garfield
- 25
- 27
- 26 22
- 23 ▲
- 24
- 19

Eagle
- 15
- 17 16
- 18 20
- 21

Summit
- 14 10
- 12
- 11 13
- 9

Mesa
- 37
- 33 34
- 32
- 36
- 35

Pitkin
- 31
- 28
- 29 30
- 59
- 58

- 55
- 53 56
- 52 54

Delta
Montrose
- 70
- 71 75
- 74
- 73
- 72

- 61
- 60
- 57

Ouray
- 69
- 68 ⊙
- 76 ⊙
- 67 ⊙
- 79

San Miguel
- 77

Gunnison
Hinsdale
- 62

Dolores
- 78

San Juan

- 81
- 80
- 82
- 83 ■
- 64
- 65
- 63

Archuleta

Montezuma La Plata
- 66

N

Miles
0 _____ 50
1 inch = 61 miles

A detailed map of site locations has been provided for cities inticated by ⊙ on the map and by * in the list at right.

Aspen (Pitkin Co.)* **28**
Avon (Eagle Co.) **17**
Basalt (Eagle Co.) **19**
Bayfield (La Plata Co.) **65**
Beaver Creek (Eagle Co.) **18**
Bedrock (Montrose Co.) **71**
Breckenridge (Summit Co.)* **9**
Brown's Park (Moffat Co.) **41**
Carbondale (Garfield Co.) **24**
Cedaredge (Delta Co.) **55**
Cimarron (Montrose Co.) **72**
Clark (Routt Co.) **47**
Clifton (Mesa Co.) **33**
Collbran (Mesa Co.) **35**
Cortez (Montezuma Co.) **80**
Craig (Moffat Co.) **40**
Crested Butte (Gunnison Co.) **58**
Delta (Delta Co.) **52**
Dillon (Summit Co.) **10**
Dinosaur (Moffat Co.) **42**
Dinosaur National
  Monument (Moffat Co.) **43**
Dolores (Montezuma Co.) **81**
Dove Creek (Dolores Co.) **78**
Durango (La Plata Co.) **64**
Eagle (Eagle Co.) **15**

Fraser (Grand Co.) **3**
Frisco (Summit Co.) **11**
Fruita (Mesa Co.) **37**
Glenwood Canyon (Garfield Co.) **23**
Glenwood Springs (Garfield Co.)* **22**
Granby (Grand Co.) **5**
Grand Junction (Mesa Co.)* **32**
Grand Lake (Grand Co.) **6**
Gunnison (Gunnison Co.) **57**
Hahns Peak (Routt Co.) **48**
Hayden (Routt Co.) **49**
Hot Sulphur Springs (Grand Co.) **1**
Hotchkiss (Delta Co.) **54**
Ignacio (La Plata Co.) **66**
Keystone (Summit Co.) **12**
Kremmling (Grand Co.) **7**
Lake City (Hinsdale Co.) **62**
Lay (Moffat Co.) **44**
Mancos (Montezuma Co.) **82**
Marble (Gunnison Co.) **59**
Meeker (Rio Blanco Co.) **38**
Mesa Verde
  National Park (Montezuma Co.) **83**
Minturn (Eagle Co.) **20**
Montrose (Montrose Co.) **70**
Montezuma (Summit Co.) **13**
Naturita (Montrose Co.) **73**
Norwood (San Miguel Co.) **77**
Nucla (Montrose Co.) **74**
Oak Creek (Routt Co.) **50**
Orchard City (Delta Co.) **53**
Ouray (Ouray Co.)* **68**
Pagosa Springs (Archuleta Co.) **63**
Palisade (Mesa Co.) **34**
Paonia (Delta Co.) **56**
Parachute (Garfield Co.) **25**
Pitkin (Gunnison Co.) **60**
Rangely (Rio Blanco Co.) **39**
Red Cliff (Eagle Co.) **21**
Redstone (Pitkin Co,) **29**
Rico (Dolores Co.) **79**
Ridgway (Ouray Co.) **69**
Rifle (Garfield Co.) **26**
Rocky Mountain
  National Park (Grand Co.) **8**
Silt (Garfield Co.) **27**
Silverthorne (Summit Co.) **14**
Silverton (San Juan Co.)* **67**
Snowmass (Pitkin Co.) **30**
Steamboat Springs (Routt Co.)* **45**
Strawberry Park (Routt Co.) **46**
Tabernash (Grand Co.) **4**
Telluride (San Miguel Co.)* **76**
Tincup (Gunnison Co.) **61**
Uravan (Montrose Co.) **75**
Vail (Eagle Co.)* **16**
Whitewater (Mesa Co.) **36**
Winter Park (Grand Co.) **2**
Woody Creek (Pitkin Co.) **31**
Yampa (Routt Co.) **51**

wood dwellings may seem worlds apart from the slick new resorts of western Colorado. But since countercultural shabbiness became architecturally fashionable in the 1960s with developments such as California's Sea Ranch, newer resorts have been borrowing elements from older farms, ranches, and mining towns. From the pioneer generation of Euro-American architecture, Mineshaft Modernists borrow shed roofs, raw lumber, native stone, and straightforward design.

Sometimes builders look back even farther, to Native American tipis. For thousands of years Ute Indians have endured the drastic climatic variations and stony, vertical landscape they called the Shining Mountains. Unlike the Anasazi and Fremont peoples, who may have been their ancestors, the Utes did not stay in one place long enough to develop extensive agriculture or architecture. They borrowed tipis from Plains Indians, who derided the mountain tribe as "bad lodge makers." By using tipis for winter and wickiups for summer the Utes responded to the extremes of subzero winter blizzards and blazing hot summer days.

Today much of western Colorado's ordinary built environment is lumber and plywood from local aspen and pine, or sheetrock made from local gypsum. Sand and gravel, now Colorado's most profitable mining products, are used to make cinderblock, concrete, and cast stone. With most nineteenth-century quarries now closed, brick and cement plants supply materials for much of the masonry construction.

Mining, which originally led to development of the Western Slope and long dominated its economy, has collapsed. High elevations generally limit farming to cold-weather crops such as carrots, lettuce, peas, potatoes, spinach, and turnips, although the lower Colorado River valley does sustain some fruit orchards. Hay is now the main crop, and cattle and sheep raising are also important.

Many mines and mills, ranches and farms have succumbed to the new bonanza: tourism. Western Colorado's great condominium market opened with the development of Vail in the 1960s. The condominium and time-share revolution in housing, which required the rewriting of Colorado statutes to clarify ownership and responsibility, has helped make the winter sports industry western Colorado's leading source of income. "A whole new group of persons, not necessarily looking for a tax write-off," observed *The Denver Post* in July 1964, "find that they can own a condominium in the Rockies as a second home . . . and make money from it when they're away. It's a new concept in Colorado tourism and the cash registers are ringing."

Contemporary visitors were not the first to prospect western Colorado for scenery and recreation. Visitors have long been attracted by the awesome mountains, mesas, and canyons as well as precious metals. America's second national forest, White River (1891), embraced old mining areas in Eagle, Lake, and Pitkin counties as lands to be preserved and used for recreation.

This conservation thrust, reinforced by subsequent creation of many more national forests and wilderness areas, has made western Colorado a playground for sightseeing, hunting, hiking, fishing, and camping, as well as winter sports.

Mines and ranches are being displaced by the recreational landscape. Now skiers, mountain bikers, four-wheelers, snowmobilers, and condominium developers are leaving their marks on a fragile land. No one has dared to call ski areas environmental eyesores, although they are now the most prominent and largest scars on the mountainsides. The federal government owns all the ski area leases and about three-fourths of the Western Slope, but has permitted mining, logging, skiing, and other uses that sometimes clash with preservation goals.

Although most counties along the Colorado River are now thriving on tourism and recreation, many fringe areas have never recovered from the mining busts. In southwestern Colorado near the Utah border, towns such as Uravan and Vancorum sprang up in the 1950s on a diet of radium, uranium, and vanadium. Now they are radioactive, starving ghost towns awaiting Environmental Protection Agency Superfund cleanups. In northwestern Colorado decaying towns and scarred landscapes reflect the coming and going of oil and coal booms. The oil shale bust of the 1980s left modern ghosts of prefabricated metal and plywood, littered with old cars rather than old wagons. A few residents hang on, not in shacks and cabins, but in mobile homes.

Mobile homes tucked into mountain valleys and desert canyons are an architectural reminder that the recreational boom on the Western Slope has created a vast new service economy. Transient communities house carpenters and maids, ski lift operators and waitresses, nannies and gardeners who work in resort areas with multimillion-dollar homes. While the resort homes are empty most of the time, these mobile home clusters teem with workers. They have an even slimmer chance of striking it rich than the miners who first settled the Western Slope in equally transient and underpaid hordes. Like the Utes, they live in cheap, functional, mobile dwellings that few consider architecture.

Grand County   (GA)

A stream trickling out of Rocky Mountain National Park joins its first major tributaries—the Fraser and the Blue rivers—to become the Colorado, the mightiest canyon cutter in the world. Below Grand Lake the Colorado River valley widens into Middle Park, which occupies most of Grand County. Middle Park is rimmed by the Continental Divide on the east, the Rabbit Ears Range on the northwest, the Gore Range on the southwest, and the Williams Fork Mountains on the south.

An influx of settlers in the 1870s led to the establishment of a county named for the Grand River, as the upper Colorado was called until 1921. The elevation severely limits farming, but ranching has been a mainstay of the economy. Reforestation hides most of the scars of a once significant lumbering industry. Roughly 55 percent of the county is national forest land or in Rocky Mountain National Park.

As a transmontane, freeway-less county spared intensive development, Grand retains much of its pioneer log and frame architecture. The Coulter, Cozens, 4 Bar 4, Gaskill, Kauffman, and Pinney Ranch log stage houses survive along the Berthoud Pass route (later U.S. 40), established during the 1870s. David Moffat's railroad, the Denver, Salt Lake & Pacific, climbed over Rollins Pass and crossed the county in 1906. This 11,680-foot-high pass, often closed by snow, was replaced in 1928 by the 6.2-mile-long Moffat Tunnel, with its east portal on the other side of the Continental Divide, in Gilpin County (GL23) and its west portal in Grand County (GA05).

The iron horse promoted tourism in a county famous for dude ranches. The Holzwarth Ranch (1917) in Rocky Mountain National Park is preserved as a rustic ranch which worked dudes as well as livestock. Hay racks, barns, and antique outbuildings dot a county with lush meadows and rich hayfields, grazed by fat cattle.

Since the 1960s skiing has been Grand County's major source of revenue. Ski area development has produced innovative contemporary vacation houses, condominiums, and commercial structures, some with solar features. The county has grown gradually from its 1874 establishment to a 1990 population of 7,966.

Hot Sulphur Springs

The county seat (1874, 7,670 feet) is named for a hot spring that was a campsite for John C. Frémont on his 1853 expedition. Frémont was followed by other Euro-Americans who took a dip in what the Utes called "The Big Medicine"—sulfur-scented water that comes out of the earth as hot as 120 degrees F. Ute legends credit the water's magical properties to an old chief who came here to die. With the Great Spirit's guidance, he built magic fires within the springs, then drank and bathed in what had become a fountain of rejuvenation.

Such magic attracted *Rocky Mountain News* founding editor William Newton Byers, who built a log lodge and platted a town of twenty-two blocks in 1874. Interesting pioneer buildings often have been replaced by blander structures. The outdoor pool is supplemented by four smaller steam and soaking rooms built into the rock hillside.

Hot Sulphur Springs hosted Colorado's first major winter sports carnival in 1911. Today this sleepy town, in contrast to the county's faster-growing southeast corner around the Winter Park Ski Area, is a bucolic backwater of fewer than 400 residents.

GA01 Grand County Museum
(Schoolhouse)

1924. 110 Byers Ave. (U.S. 40)

This substantial brick country schoolhouse with a square, open bell tower became the county museum in 1976. The fenced museum complex incorporates the 1891–1902 Grand County Courthouse and County Jail, both of hewn logs. Two iron cells and iron bunks remain in the jailhouse. Other buildings moved into this museum complex include a sod-roofed blacksmith shop and a second school (1920) that was used between 1942 and the 1960s to house migrant lettuce workers.

GA02 Grand County Courthouse

1937, Robert K. Fuller. Southwest corner of Byers Ave. (U.S. 40) and Maple St.

This example of starved classicism is a lean, two-story, yellow brick box. Robert Fuller, a Denver architect, made the design subtly interesting by using the same wire-cut golden brick for corbeling, pilasters, soldier courses, diapering, and sloping brick sills. Aluminum Art Deco entry lamps and window screens and restrained zigzag patterns in the sparse terracotta trim add modernity. The original courthouse has been doubled in size by a sensitive 1969 addition that uses similar brick and styling.

GA03 Riverside Hotel

1903. 1983, restoration. 509 Grand Ave.

A clapboard structure expanded over the years with the same primitive planking, the Riverside Hotel is somewhat more elaborate inside, where a huge fireplace warms a tiny lobby decorated with animal horns and old rocking chairs sit in a quaint saloon. The ramshackle, twenty-two-room hotel was given a rustic look in 1983 by owner Abraham Estaban Rodriguez, who took out "everything that was tin and plastic," restoring a frontier simplicity to this two-story antique, which follows the riverside contour to minimize excavation.

GA04 Berthoud Pass

U.S. 40, southeast of Hot Sulphur Springs

Edward L. Berthoud, an engineer and surveyor in Golden, blazed an 1861 toll road with mountain man Jim Bridger over this 11,307-foot pass. Their dirt road to Hot Sulphur Springs became a stage road in 1874 and the first paved road over the Continental Divide when U.S. 40 was completed in 1938. The current two-lane highway offers beautiful views plus the excitement of hair-pin curves and occasional avalanches and rock slides. The Berthoud Pass Inn (1950), U.S. 40 atop Berthoud Pass, is a homely complex that replaced earlier structures of more appealing design, beginning with the first Berthoud Pass Inn, which L. D. C. Gaskill opened in 1876 as a stage stop. Berthoud Pass Ski Area, atop the pass, boasted Colorado's first rope tow in 1937, followed by the first double-seat chair lift. During the 1940s Berthoud attracted a third of Colorado's skiers but has since been dwarfed by nearby Winter Park and other newer, much larger areas.

Winter Park

The town and ski area of Winter Park (1939, 9,110 feet), the largest and fastest-growing community in the county, began as a construction camp for the west portal of the Moffat Tunnel. Reborn as a ski area, it has boomed since the 1950s, becoming a sophisticated resort with variations of Mineshaft Modern architecture, such as Portal Place and Chalet Blanc.

GA05 Winter Park Ski Area

1940. U.S. 40, 7 miles north of Berthoud Pass

Denver parks manager George Cranmer planned and implemented this Denver Mountain Park. The U.S. Forest Service and ski enthusiasts began laying out runs as early as 1933. A year later the D&RG constructed a depot and began transporting skiers. Rope tows were installed in 1939 by WPA and CCC workers with contributions of additional labor, money, and materials from volunteers organized by George Cranmer. Officially dedicated in 1940, it has become a large, high-tech, popular winter sports complex, emphasizing family and handicapped skiing. The success of Winter Park has led to the creation of an ancillary ski area, Mary Jane (named for Mary Jane Creek), and the smaller ski areas of Idlewild and Silver Creek.

Balcony House (GA05.1; 1955) is a two-story warming house with a large sunny-side balcony at the base of the ski runs and several additions. It became a prototype for the solar-oriented warming houses now stan-

GA05 Winter Park Ski Area

dard in Colorado ski areas. D&RG caboose no. 1448 (GA05.2; Burnham Shops, Denver, 1945) was put on display in 1989, two years after the D&RG replaced cabooses with ET's (end-of-train devices). Parked at the base of Winter Park ski runs next to a new, high-tech lift, this bright yellow steel caboose houses an information booth and mini-museum.

The entrance to this winter sports haven is near the west portal of the Moffat Tunnel (GA05.3), whose buttresses give it a sphinxlike aura. The tunnel's east portal is on the other side of the Continental Divide in Gilpin County (GL23).

GA06 **Village at Winter Park**

1982, 1984. Near U.S. 40 at base of ski area

This Postmodern complex at the ski area base does not fit the topography and site as well as earlier lumber and stone structures such as Balcony House (GA06.1). Eschewing natural wood and stone, the architects used two corrugated metal boxes on concrete bases. The larger box (Hoover Berg Desmond, 1982), painted black, houses the children's center, a medical clinic, and conference rooms. The smaller box, painted a baby blue, is the new West Portal Railroad Depot (1982, Muchow, Haller and Larsen), a replacement for the original tiny, asbestos-sided depot. The two cubistic corrugated metal hulks are connected by a shopping mall. The landscaping and the shapes are

interesting, but the village ultimately challenges rather than complements the surrounding spruce-clad mountainsides.

Fraser

Fraser (1905, 8,550 feet), established as a railroad town, is the self-proclaimed "Icebox of the Nation," chilled by frigid air that flows down from the surrounding peaks. It was named for a river, which in turn was named for a pioneer settler, Reuben Frazier, whose name was misspelled by post office officials. Solar and frame condos perch prominently on south-facing hillsides.

GA07 **Cozens Ranch House Museum**

1874, William Zane Cozens. 1991, restoration, Long Hoeft Architects. 77849 U.S. 40 (NR)

Grand County's vernacular log and frame architecture is well represented by the Cozens Ranch Museum. William Cozens, the fearless pioneer sheriff of Central City, married Mary York, the first white woman in these parts. She insisted that they leave the wild mining town for a better place to raise a family. Across Berthoud Pass, in then unsettled Grand County, the Cozens clan started this pioneer cattle, hay, and potato ranch.

The original hewn log house under board-and-batten siding was enlarged in 1876 with a rear stage stop and a small post office on its south side. Travelers used the six tiny rooms over the stage stop as a hotel. Cozens welcomed stagecoaches but not railroads. He is said to have fired on the railroad survey crew from his rocking chair on the front porch, shooting out the stakes they planted in his hay meadow. That is why, the tale goes, the railroad tracks are still out of firing distance from the Cozens Ranch, hidden across the valley in the woods.

Mary Cozens, a devout Catholic, donated the property to the Jesuits upon her death, and from the 1920s to the 1980s the order used it as a church and retreat known as Maryvale. In 1990 the Grand County Historical Association spent $300,000 to restore the complex, converting it to a museum. The unusually sensitive restoration retained the cold storage room, post office equipment, and backyard family cemetery. The rooms have been painted and papered to replicate early interior design, leaving samples of the original lath and plaster walls and wallpaper. One exhibit is a scale model of the ranch and outbuildings at their peak around 1900, when this was a 600-acre spread.

GA08 Evans Barn

1904. 4 miles northwest of Fraser, on U.S. 40 and .3 mile west on Grand County 5

This gracefully aging two-story, hewn log barn, beautifully sited in a meadow on the homestead of Michael Evans, served as the town hall of Eastom (an early, now vanished settlement) and as a dance hall. Windows on all sides and the front Dutch doors suggest original use by human beings as well as livestock.

GA09 4 Bar 4 Stage Stop and Barn

1880s. 3.4 miles northeast of U.S. 40 on Grand County 5

Richard W. McQuery and his clan built these two structures of round logs hewn only at the crudely notched corners. Both are now ruins, abandoned and sinking into the earth. The stage stop retains an unsteady second-story porch and vestiges of the first-floor accommodations.

GA10 Fraser Mercantile

1904. Northwest corner of Eisenhower Dr. and Railroad St.

A classic, false-fronted clapboard store originally known as Cozens Mercantile, this store is most celebrated for President Dwight Eisenhower's patronage during his vacations at the nearby Byer's Peak Ranch to fly fish the Fraser River. Behind the store is a Postmodern open waiting shed for Amtrak passengers.

Tabernash

This village (1904, 8,320 feet), begun as a siding for the railroad, is still a repair shop and crew change point for the D&RG. Tabernash was named for a Ute chief killed for raiding ranches, rustling, and telling William Cozens and other palefaces to get out of Middle Park.

GA11 YMCA of the Rockies Snow Mountain Ranch

1907. 4 miles west of Tabernash, west off U.S. 40 at the end of Meadow Lane

The Rowley Ranch House (1907; restored 1982) serves as a museum and nature center for a 3,000-acre recreational haven with campsites, cabins, and a main lodge. The log Rowley Ranch House has a low-pitched roof supported by a central log wall. The museum complex includes a horse-powered hay stacker, a one-room trapper's cabin of chinked logs with a sod roof built into a low hillside, an outhouse, a milking shed, a root cellar, a smokehouse, a logger's cabin, a hog house, a rhubarb patch, a barn full

GA11 YMCA of the Rockies Snow Mountain Ranch, Rowley Ranch House

of antique machinery, and a new outdoor chapel.

Granby

Founded as a railroad town near the confluence of the Colorado and Fraser rivers, Granby (inc. 1905, 7,965 feet) was named for Colorado's U.S. District Attorney, Granby Hillyer, to flatter law enforcement officials concerned about the collection of roadhouses that first sprang up there. Granby became a national center for head lettuce cultivation in the 1920s, but the business had declined by the 1950s, when one lettuce warehouse became the Windy Gap Inn. Granby is now a supply, ranching, and tourist center with approximately 1,000 residents.

GA12 **Amtrak Depot**

1907. 1 block south of U.S. 40 in center of town

This replica of an old-style clapboard depot has bracketed eaves and fishscale shingles on its cross-gable ends. Double hung windows and large, arched transoms in the north and south gable entrances make it a bright, see-through, glass and frame passenger station. On old-fashioned curved oak benches inside, passengers await trains that, according to a railroad attendant, are "usually three to five hours late." The old depot, now a freight and storage shed, is next door.

GA13 **C Lazy U Ranch**

1925. 6.5 miles west of Granby on Colorado 125

Six major resorts make Granby the state's dude ranch capital. The C Lazy U, often rated as one of the finest in Colorado, offers an elegant modern two-and-one-half-story main lodge of glass and hewn logs which complements 1920s cabins and a horse barn on this 2,000-acre haven for "pampered dudes."

GA14 **Lake Granby Pumping Plant**

1951. U.S. 40 at the head of Lake Granby

This giant, boxy concrete and glass brick station is a good example of industrially inspired International Style, complete with a turbine pump fan to serve as an entry sculpture. Besides three stories above ground, the 189-foot-high structure has five floors underground, plunging deep into Lake Granby to pump water up to Shadow Mountain Reservoir for the Colorado–Big Thompson (C-BT) Project. This plant, open daily for tours in the summer, is a $10 million showpiece of the C-BT's Northern Colorado Water Conservancy District. Largest of all Colorado water projects, C-BT consists of 12 reservoirs, 100 miles of canals, 34 miles of tunnels, and 6 power plants that took twenty-seven years and $163 million to complete.

Grand Lake

Colorado's largest natural body of water is a 400-foot-deep glacier-made bowl of sparkling water that reflects the surrounding mountains. The Utes, awed by its white mists, called it Spirit Lake, or White Buffalo Lake. Its water was perfectly clear and drinkable before the Bureau of Reclamation built dirty, shallow Shadow Mountain Reservoir and pumped its water back through Grand Lake and into the Alva Adams Tunnel under Rocky Mountain National Park to the Big Thompson River and the Front Range.

Founded as a mining settlement, the town of Grand Lake (1879, 8,396 feet) captured the county seat from 1881 to 1888. It lost this honor to the original county seat, Hot

Sulphur Springs, after a deadly shootout among county commissioners which damaged Grand Lake's reputation. Nevertheless, hunters, fishermen, and prospectors gravitated to this early mountain resort platted in 1881 as a 160-acre grid around a town square.

Now bypassed by the main highway, this end-of-the-road town retains rustic public buildings and private cabins. Most were constructed before 1929 of the straight, skinny lodgepole pines that still envelop this sleepy summer resort with its sandy beach and a few new summer homes. Many of the finer structures are clustered on the southwest edge of the town and the lake, which is rimmed by log and log slab siding boathouses. Hemmed in by the lake, Rocky Mountain National Park, and national forests, this village of 250 people, with its rough-hewn log and slab structures and wooden sidewalks, seems frozen in an earlier time.

GA15 **Grand Lake Cottage Camp**

c. 1917. 820 Grand Ave. (southeast corner of Vine St.)

This primeval motel is a long, narrow, slab-sided shed with covered stalls for autos alternating with four tiny court units. Georgia Estlick, who had a home nearby, ran the pioneer auto camp. Her father, contractor Preston H. Smith, whose clapboard carpenter shop survives at 401 Ellsworth (northwest corner of Lake Avenue), may have been the builder.

GA16 **Corner Cupboard Inn** (Grand Central Hotel)

1880. 1028 Grand Ave. (southwest corner of Pitkin St.)

A plain building with an ambitious name, the Grand Central Hotel housed the first school in Grand Lake shortly after Winslow Nickerson opened the hotel in 1880. The original hewn log hotel with its large stone fireplace and chimney on the east end of the structure is now the Corner Pub. The

side-gabled building has received various functional additions over the years. It is now a long, low, board-and-batten-clad structure devoid of architectural pretensions. Inside, a simple column and brace arrangement keeps the ceiling fairly even though the floor is not.

GA17 **Town Square**

1881. 1000 Grand Ave. to Park Ave. between Garfield and Pitkin sts.

Many Colorado towns sold off their original platted public squares, but Grand Lake's Town Square remains a public park that has been used for fish frys, rodeos, and buffalo barbecues. Town volunteers built the central Community House (1922), now used as a summer theater. A 1995 addition erased the stone chimneys and quaint rusticity of what is now a larger, reconfigured building. Other structures on the square include a combined library and fire station, a bandstand, an ice rink, and the old log Presbyterian Church.

GA18 **Humphreys Store**

1881. 1100 Grand Ave. (southeast corner of Pitkin St.)

The core of this two-story slab and log building is the original 1881 store of James Carins, who stuck it out following the 1880s mining bust and removal of the county seat to Hot Sulphur Springs. Horizontal and vertical lodgepole slab siding recesses into a second-story porch on the west side, and a covered porch shelters the sidewalk. This pioneer commercial building houses a store and a soda fountain.

GA19 **The Rapids Lodge**

1913, Laps Ish. 209 Hancock Ave.

Lodgepole slab walls in vertical and diagonal sections adorn the original rustic lodge of this resort. Under a new metal roof, The Rapids still welcomes diners and overnight guests. Laps (for Lapis Lazuli because of his deep blue eyes) Ish, a miner, built the lodge with the help of his son, Guy. Prominent third-story dormers provide a peaked theme repeated in small separate cabins. The little-altered structure sits in a spruce and lodgepole pine grove on the north inlet of Grand Lake, where Ish harnessed rapids with a water wheel and electric generator to make The Rapids the first electrified resort in the county.

GA20 **Grand Lake Yacht Club**

1912, Aaron Gove and Preston H. Smith. 1128 Lake Ave.

During the first week in August the Grand Lake Yacht Club hosts the world's highest official yacht regatta. "Snotty yachties," as locals put it, incorporated the club in 1902 and began racing here for the Lipton Cup in 1913 after the English tea baron, Sir Thomas Lipton, donated a sterling silver cup. The two-and-one-half-story clubhouse and anchorage is a dark, weathered wooden structure that aspires to Victorian rusticity, with clapboard on the first floor, vertical slab log siding on the second, and multipane

casement windows in sets of threes. An enclosed observation deck tops the double-decker waterfront porch.

GA21 **Kauffman House Museum**

1892, Ezra Kauffman. 407 Pitkin St. (northwest corner of Lake Ave.) (NR)

Ezra Kauffman, an expert log cabin builder, practiced his craft on many cabins around Grand Lake. He sawed and hewed the logs by hand, leaving a rounded bark exterior but an inside wall so smooth it could be papered. In his own house, tin cans were tacked over the cracks in the chinking to improve insulation. The original square, two-story house has several additions and a large front porch. Kauffman made it both his home and a hotel until his death in 1920. In 1973 it became the museum and office of the Grand Lake Area Historical Society.

GA22 **Spider House**

c. 1896, Warren G. Gregg. 62 Main St.

Warren Gregg, a cabinetmaker, built this hewn log dwelling with a two-story front porch adorned by fan-shaped saplings that resemble spiderwebs. Well preserved under a new metal roof, it retains its spidery trim, clipped gables, and log-framed bay window.

GA23 Grand Lake Lodge

1924, Frank I. Huntington. 1 mile north of Grand Lake, then east off U.S. 34 (NHL)

Roe Emory had Frank Huntington, the Grand County engineer, build the main lodge and almost 100 smaller cabins and outbuildings as the Rocky Mountain National Park resort of the Chicago, Burlington & Quincy Railroad, which shuttled tourists here in motorbuses from its railheads. Sited on a forested hill overlooking Grand Lake, the 300-foot-long main lodge of logs atop a river rock foundation has a two-story sun porch with peeled log railings and posts. Inside, the original peeled log construction and trim are especially notable in the large, open-beamed lobby and dining hall.

GA24 Grand River Ditch

1894–1936, J. J. Argo. From the east side of Grand Lake over slopes south of La Poudre Pass into Baker Creek (NR)

This 17-mile-long irrigation ditch has scarred the landscape for so long that it has been designated a landmark. Engineer J. J. Argo started the ditch just above Grand Lake and took it eastward over the divide. Chinese, Japanese, Mexican, and Scandinavian laborers dug the ditch by hand through the Never Summer Range to catch snow melt. Their work camps of saddle-notched and V-notched log huts are in ruins, but the ditch is still used by its builder, the Water Supply and Storage Company of Fort Collins. A striking landscape feature, the ditch is historically important as one of the first of many devices to divert Colorado River water over the Continental Divide to Eastern Slope users.

Kremmling

Kremmling (1885, 7,322 feet) began with the general store of Kare Kremmling at the junction of the Blue and Colorado rivers and solidified as a town with the 1905 arrival of the railroad. It remains the supply town for a large, sparsely settled area of hay and livestock ranches. Notable buildings include the Dan Hoare Blacksmith Shop, northeast corner of 2nd Street and Central Avenue, with shiplap siding and a false front.

GA25 McElroy Livery Stable

1904. 4th St., .5 block north of U.S. 40

This well-maintained example of a round log barn has been reborn as a museum. The two-story, gable-roofed building has a gabled vent in the center of the roof ridge and a faded "LIVERY" sign on the front. One block west, at 3rd Street and U.S. 40, a similar barn has been dressed up with a curvilinear parapet and pressed metal siding to become the Mt. Wolford Masonic Temple, an example of how refined a barn can become.

GA26 Town Square, City Park, and Visitor Information Cabin

U.S. 40 between 3rd and 4th sts. and Central Ave.

The Louisiana Pacific and Tri-River lumber companies, the town's largest employers in the 1980s, helped renovate two log cabins in the Town Square. One is a new visitor information center, a twin of the old jail next door, which has been rehabilitated as a museum.

Rocky Mountain National Park

See Larimer County for background on the park.

GA27 Holzwarth Ranch Historic District

1917. 8 miles north of Grand Lake on Trail Ridge Rd. (NR)

John Holzwarth, Sr., a Denver saloonkeeper forced out of business by statewide prohibition in 1916, homesteaded here in 1917. When the Fall River Road to Rocky Mountain National Park opened in 1920, the Holzwarths began taking in visitors for $2 a day. The original, 1917 "Mama Cabin" soon had baby buildings, of which an icehouse, a woodshed, a taxidermy shop, guest cabins, tent cabins, and the 1945 Rose Cabin survive in a lush meadow on the headwaters of the Colorado River. John Holzwarth, Jr., ran the dude ranch until 1973, when it was acquired by the National Park Service. Known as the Holzwarth Trout Ranch and most recently as the Never Summer Ranch, the Holzwarth spread exemplifies dude ranches where city slickers exulted in rusticity. The National Park Service has restored the hewn, V-notched log structures with simple gable roofs.

GA28 **Shadow Mountain Lookout**

c. 1933, Civilian Conservation Corps. On Shadow Mountain Trail (NR)

The CCC built this fine fortress, the last fire detection tower left in the park, in the rustic style of the National Park Service. The three-story tower overlooking Shadow Mountain Lake and Recreation Area is 13 feet square at its base. Battered, uncoursed rubblestone supports the third-story overhanging log porch of a frame and glass lookout.

GA29 **Trail Ridge Road**

1933. Grand Lake to Estes Park (NR)

When the park was newly established, Superintendent Oliver Toll toured the 40-mile route of the proposed Trail Ridge Road with Arapaho Indians to collect their place names. They called it the Dog Trail, for the beasts of burden who helped them travel it. Also known as the Ute Trail, for the other tribe that pioneered the route, it was a foot and wagon road before it became a major tourist drive in the 1930s. Landscape architect Charles Eliot protested: "It is much better to build no roads than to run the risk of destroying wilderness areas." National Park Service director Horace Albright countered that such roads served "the great mass of people who because of age, physical condition, or other reason would never have an opportunity to enjoy, close at hand, this marvelous mountain park."

W. T. Lafferty, district engineer for the Bureau of Public Roads, helped two private contractors build the road with curves, switchbacks, and rustic stone retaining walls designed to do as little violence to the landscape as possible. Log cribbing, hand-laid rock walls, and trenches help prevent erosion. The highest continuous paved highway in the United States, this two-lane scenic drive climbs from forested mountain valleys to alpine tundra as high as 12,183 feet. Snowplows open the road for Memorial Day and snowstorms close it soon after Labor Day.

GA30 **Alpine Visitor Center**

1965, William C. Muchow and Associates. Trail Ridge and Fall River rds. at Fall River Pass

Designed to sustain terrific winds and blizzards, this large structure uses a steel frame and concrete shell, sheathed in a rubblestone veneer and held down by a lattice of large logs on the roof.

Summit County (ST)

"What a wonderful transformation has been wrought by man in this wonderful minerals section!" exulted the *Summit County Journal* in 1916. The *Journal* marveled further that once only Utes had lived in a landscape where there were "no great white and brown dumps, no fuming smoke stacks, no rumbling mills, no clanking dredges."

Not everyone exulted in the transformation mining had brought to the Alpine tundra and forests of Summit County. Industrial-strength gold grubbing left Summit County with what Breckenridge novelist Helen Rich, in *The Willow Bender* (1950), called "upside-down streams and inside-out mountains." Brutal earth movers—nine monster dredge boats—operated between 1898 and 1942 on the Swan and Blue rivers and in French Creek. Even today's riverfront landscaping and a fine new hike-bike system cannot hide all the scars left by ravenous gold boats that even invaded the city limits to chew up part of Breckenridge.

Before these gold dredges turned riverbeds into rock piles, high-pressure hydraulic hoses washed away hillsides, burying the first county seat, Parkville, in its own mineral waste. During the 1960s Kokomo, Recen, and Robinson were smothered under mine tailings of the Climax Molybdenum Mine. Although environmentalists have been quick to condemn past mining practices, few commit the modern-day sacrilege of calling Summit County's ski runs scars on the land.

Skiing began in the 1860s with Scandinavian miners and the "snowshoe itinerant," Father John L. Dyer, whose church in Breckenridge has a stained glass portrait of him on skis. During the 1930s a rope tow was installed on Breckenridge's Barney Ford Hill and another during the 1940s on Dillon's Cemetery Hill. The modern Breckenridge Ski Area opened in 1961 and in 1978 installed Colorado's first Alpine slide, a summer toboggan run on a 2,600-foot-long dual track made by Demay of West Germany. Steady expansions made Breckenridge one of Colorado's largest ski areas by the 1980s.

As Summit became the fastest-growing county in Colorado during the 1970s, some environmental protection was provided by the federal government, which owns 81 percent of the land, including Arapaho National Forest and the Eagles Nest Wilderness Area. Relics of the pioneer period have been preserved by the Summit Historical Society, which maintains a dozen structures, including the cabin museum of naturalist Edwin Carter.

Summit County's economic ups and downs match its spectacular peaks and valleys. As one of the original counties created in 1861, Summit once comprised Colorado's entire northwest quadrant. During its flush mining days the original county had fifty-five post office towns, most of which are gone. A few sunburned, wind-blasted miners' cabins now shelter only weathered steel-toed boots, rusted tin cans, broken dishes, and assayers' crucibles. Agriculture was not a viable alternative for one of Colorado's highest counties; surviving communities have capitalized on "white gold"—fine powder snow—to draw skiers. They have succeeded beyond even gold rush expectations: Summit is now Colorado's most popular ski county and a major American playground.

Breckenridge

The county seat (1860, 9,603 feet) was named for U.S. Vice President John C. Breckinridge but changed the spelling of its name after he joined the Confederacy. Prospectors first prowled the confluence of the Blue and Swan rivers and French Gulch in 1859. Fearing the Utes and the weather, they built a stockade called Fort Mary B, for Mary Bigelow, the only woman in the party.

After obtaining a post office in 1860 and capturing the county seat from Parkville in 1862, Breckenridge began a series of bonanzas and busts. Gold in the 1860s, silver in the 1880s, and turn-of-the-century gold dredging bankrolled rosy times. During hard times, some who had built homes and

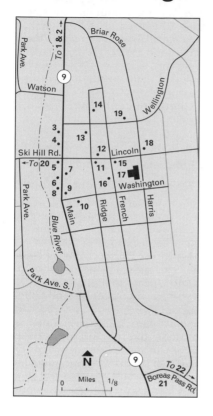

Breckenridge

institutions on the outskirts of town moved them closer to the center. As many structures had no foundations, Breckenridge could accommodate its shrinking and stretching with this game of musical buildings. To this day, bed and building hopping continues to be common in a town with roughly 1,400 residents and some 23,000 bed pillows, the indicator by which the tourist bureau attempts to keep track of the town's accommodations.

Since the Breckenridge Ski Area opened in December 1961, the town's building stock has grown tremendously. A 1980 National Register District designation has helped preserve approximately 250 structures in the center of town. Hospitable landmarks include a half-dozen nineteenth-century dwellings converted to bed and breakfast inns.

ST01 Ben Stanley Revett House (Swan's Nest)

1898, Ben Stanley Revett. 50 Summit County 315, 4 miles north of Breckenridge on Colorado 9, then 1 mile east

On the Swan River, which his firm was dredging for gold, Ben Stanley Revett, a graduate of the Royal School of Mines in London, built an expansive frame house befitting his flamboyant lifestyle and immense girth. Swan's Nest has extra-wide doors, a grand entry hall, four family bedrooms, quarters for his Japanese gardener and Filipino house servants, two indoor bathrooms, and a billiard room. His frame "nest" consists of a central section under steep-pitched roofs with five dormers above the broad central veranda, flanked by two-story wings.

Finding stones for the massive fireplace was no problem: the view from the veranda across the now defunct croquet and tennis courts ends in massive rock piles left by Revett's dredge boat operations. After Revett and his gold boats disappeared, the house sat vacant and vandalized, once selling for $466 in back taxes before its 1978 restoration as a resort.

ST02 Swan River Dredge No. 4

1899–1904, Bucyrus Company. 3 miles north of Breckenridge on Colorado 9, 2.7 miles east on Tiger Rd.

California redwood and Oregon pine were used for this 100-foot-long gold boat, a steam-powered outfit operated by a three-person crew. The surviving hull, along with the ponds and the mounds of waste rock the dredge created on the Swan River, are now part of a park (1991). Ruins of another dredge may be seen on French Creek, 5 miles southeast up French Gulch Road. The Gold Dredge Restaurant (1993, Baker + Hogan Associates), 180 West Jefferson Street, is a full-scale concrete replica of an old gravel gobbler.

ST03 Choy's Chinese Laundry

1880s. 107 N. Main St.

This broadaxe-hewn log building with a clapboard facade and a modest vernacular pediment and cornice trim had a laundry on the first floor and quarters for the owner and three assistants on the second floor.

ST04 **Gold Pan Restaurant and Saloon**

1879. 103–105 N. Main St.

Originally one story with a false front, the oldest tavern in town now occupies two antique two-story structures that seem to lean on each other. The buildings are both clapboard and show similar window and cornice treatment. An earlier occupant, the respectable Palace Restaurant, featured a large aquarium filled with trout in a front window, often broken during recent decades by rowdy regulars of the Gold Pan Saloon. The restaurant, with its rumpled asphalt "brick" siding on the north side exterior, is connected by an open passageway to the raw barroom side, where ore car track serves as the bar footrail. A gold pan made into a clock adorns a classic Brunswick mahogany back bar with Ionic columns framing the large, diamond dust mirror.

ST05 **Watson's Clothing and Gents' Furnishings**

c. 1883. 101 S. Main St.

This all-wood Italianate false-fronted building has wooden "cast iron" pilasters and "stone" quoins—Carpenter's Gothic icing on a gingerbread facade. The side walls are sheathed with corrugated sheet metal siding. Inside, the original counter and some other fixtures are still in use.

ST06 **Miners Home Saloon**

1880. 123 S. Main St.

Once a false-fronted saloon, this frail-looking example of vernacular architecture has been a millinery shop, a goat barn, and a boutique named Skinny Winter. The balloon-frame structure has an outside stairway, now enclosed, which was a common arrangement to save precious interior space.

ST07 **Finding Hardware and Mining Supplies**

1885, Elias Nashold. 120 S. Main St.

Charles A. Finding built the only stone commercial false front in town, later adding pressed metal above that imitates the rough red sandstone at street level. Quartzite rubblestone was used for the side walls. Elias Nashold, a successful local carpenter-contractor, was responsible for the design and construction of many Breckenridge landmarks.

ST08 **Bunchman-Taylor Building**

1990, Jon Gunson Architects. 125–135 S. Main St.

"Harmony but not duplication" of historic styles is architect John Gunson's goal. He disagrees with those who "want time to stand still in a Breckenridge of 1890." This two-story brick Neo-Victorian mini-mall and his Towne Square, at the northeast corner of Main and Lincoln streets, Gunson calls "contemporary renditions of historic buildings." Above round-arched windows and corbeled cornices the horizon is framed in open steel beam friezes and gables. Tighter 1992 town guidelines for the downtown historic district frowned on such loose interpretations of historical styles, and especially on Gunson's split-level structures with garden courtyards.

ST09 **Masonic Temple**

1892. 136 S. Main St. (northeast corner of Washington Ave.)

This barnlike hall, a two-story frame building, has pedimented second-story window lintels on its exaggerated false front. The members of Breckenridge Lodge 47 have convened here since purchasing the building in 1906, using the venerable outdoor stairs to reach the upstairs hall and leasing out the storefront space.

ST10 **Ford House**

1882, Elias Nashold. 111 E. Washington St.

Barney Ford, a runaway mulatto slave, discovered gold on what is now called Barney Ford Hill. His Oro Mine, later consolidated with the Wellington Mine, became one of the county's biggest and longest-lived producers. Supposedly run out of Breckenridge by its many Confederate sympathizers, Ford moved to Denver, where he became a prominent innkeeper. He returned to Breckenridge in 1880 to open Barney Ford's Chop House (demolished), at 201 South Main Street (northeast corner of Washington Avenue), and built this modest frame house with a spacious yard.

ST11 Offices (Bank of Breckenridge)

1880. 100 S. Ridge St. (southeast corner of Lincoln St.)

Picture perfect, this two-story clapboard built for $3,000 has a bracketed wooden cornice and elongated four-over-four windows with Neoclassical pediments. Built as the Bank of Breckenridge, it later served as the Engle Brothers Exchange Bank and the post office, before conversion to office space.

ST12 Summit County Courthouse

1909, John J. Huddart. 208 E. Lincoln Ave. (northeast corner of Ridge St.)

An observation tower and a four-sided dome top the county courthouse, whose north and south entry pediments feature painted mining and railroad scenes in bas-relief on pressed zinc. Pedimented entry bays, balanced fenestration, and gray sandstone and gray brick trim lend the red brick building the Neoclassical dignity characteristic of

ST13 Carter Cabin Museum

Huddart's courthouses. Such details as the miniature concrete pilasters set into the brick just below the architrave were spotlighted in a 1987 renovation by Baker + Hogan Associates, which preserved the large, octagonal main-floor hall, the golden oak stairwell and woodwork, the high, pressed metal ceiling, chandeliers, and other furnishings of the upstairs courtroom.

ST13 Carter Cabin Museum

1875, Edwin P. Carter. 111 N. Ridge St.

Naturalist Edwin Carter began collecting and preserving local wildlife specimens in 1868. He housed them in this log cabin with a shed addition and ornate porch posts with four-leaf clover cutout brackets. In 1900 Carter's heirs sold his incomparable collection of Colorado specimens for $10,000 as the core collection of the Denver Museum of Natural History. His rustic, hewn log cabin, set in a large meadow, exemplifies the mining camp stage of log architecture. In 1993, the town of Breckenridge and the Summit Historical Society paid $1 million for this little cabin—and the large open field where it sits—preserving one of the most developable sites in Breckenridge as open space and a natural history house museum.

ST14 Brown House Restaurant (Brown House Hotel)

1898, Thomas Brown. 208 N. Ridge St.

Thomas and Maude Brown's 1898 addition transformed a foursquare into a rectangular hotel. Atop a stone foundation with log crossbeams are a maze of rooms on the first and second stories. Now an upscale restaurant, the house remains architecturally ambivalent, with both classical foursquare simplicity and romantic Italianate bracketing, cresting, and porch trim.

ST15 St. John the Baptist Episcopal Church

1881, Elias Nashold. 100 S. French St. (southeast corner of Lincoln St.)

Congregationalists built this church before selling it for $350 to Episcopalians, who moved it to the present site. The clapboard building with a steep gable roof, corniced windows, and a small, hip-roofed open belfry might be mistaken for a country schoolhouse except for the cross on top.

ST16 St. Mary's Catholic Church

1881. 109 S. French St. (northwest corner of Washington St.)

This small Carpenter's Gothic church has a central, open belfry (1899) with shingle siding and four pedimented gables. Father Thomas M. Cahill and his parishioners built the shell in twelve days, but immigrant miners probably took longer to paint the interior ceiling stenciling. During the 1890s depression, the church was dragged downhill from the southeast corner of High and Washington streets. Next to the church, Benedictine nuns and monks built and staffed St. Joseph's Hospital and St. Gertrude's Convent and Academy in efforts to civilize and Christianize the mining town. One German monk complained that "all the roustabouts, rascals, loose women, adulterers, etc., etc., find their way to Breckenridge."

This same Father Rhabanus Gutmann called St. Mary's a crude church with makeshift furnishings, "a disgrace to the name of St. Mary." Today it has been elegantly restored. Next door stands the much larger frame, metal-roofed 1985 church, for which priest and parishioners once again donated material, money, and labor.

ST17 Colorado Mountain College (Breckenridge School)

1909, Eagleton and Mountjoy. 103 S. Harris St.

The facade of this red pressed brick school designed by Denver architects sports curvilinear parapets, third-story roundel windows with stained glass, and round-arched second-story windows. The town's investment of $20,000 in a fashionable building reflected hopes that prosperity had come to stay. In 1920 a gym, auditorium, and indoor swimming pool were added on the west. Over the years, the school "modernized" with interior elements such as acoustical tile. Built as a kindergarten-through-twelfth-grade school, the building later became a firehouse and then the town hall before the new town hall opened on Ski Hill Road. It is now renovated as a home for the public library and Colorado Mountain College.

ST18 Briggle House

1896. 104 N. Harris St.

William Harrison Briggle, a cashier at the Engle Brothers Exchange Bank, and his bride Kathleen built this Victorian frame cottage around a one-room, hewn log cabin

ST17 Colorado Mountain College (Breckenridge School)

ST19 Father Dyer Methodist Church

that is now the south parlor. Some semicircular windows still contain the original wavy glass. The house was the Mars Hotel, a crash pad for hippies, during the 1970s, before its restoration as a house museum by the Summit Historical Society. The Briggle House stands next to the Alice G. Milne Memorial Park (1991, Baker + Hogan Associates), featuring an 1880 clapboarded log house with newspaper insulation and the original icebox; the tiny board-and-batten Eberlein House (1877); and a Carpenter's Gothic outhouse.

ST19 Father Dyer Methodist Church

1880; 1967 restoration. 310 Wellington Ave.

Father John Lewis Dyer's achievements in Colorado mining towns are chronicled in his reprinted 1890 autobiography, *The Snow-Shoe Itinerant*. Called "father" because he was an old man with white hair, Dyer advocated muscular Methodism and helped build the church himself. Efforts by his fellow "sky pilots" to steer people to heaven by enforcing Colorado's saloon-closing law led to retaliation: the belfry of this church was dynamited. After being rebuilt with a new spire and an open, square bell tower, it was moved in 1977 from 107 North French Street to this site. Tasteful additions match the original Carpenter's Gothic elements

Father Dyer found a worthy successor in the Reverend Mark Fiester, the pastor who restored and enlarged this church, adding the stained glass window which depicts Dyer on "snowshoes" (i.e., skis).

ST20 Lomax Gulch Placer Mining Museum Complex

1860s, 1986. 301 Ski Hill Rd

One of the first placer mines to use hydraulic mining techniques, these 1860s diggings are now the centerpiece of a 4.9-acre park where visitors can practice gold panning, hydraulic mining, and ore processing The complex includes the old assay office from Tiger, spared that ghost town's 1972 burning by the U.S. Forest Service to discourage squatters. The Summit Historical Society moved the assay shack from the Tiger townsite, 4.6 miles east of Colorado 9 on the Swan River, to house an extensive mineral collection and equipment used to demonstrate assay techniques. Another refugee relocated here, the Giger Barn, originally stood on French Street. It is a classic carriage barn with folding doors and a separate door for the horse. The 8-by-10-foot bachelor miner's log cabin with its single window came from Ridge Street. Other exhibits range from a giant nozzle used to wash away hillsides to a sluice and flume that deliver mud and sludge laced with "free" gold to fascinate tourists.

ST21 Boreas Pass Road

East off Main St. at the south end of Breckenridge

This dirt road between Breckenridge and Como in Park County follows the bed of the Denver, South Park & Pacific, a narrow-gauge railroad winding up 5-percent grades and tight S curves. The 64-mile roadbed is said to include 435 curves, with the longest straight stretch only 1.6 miles long. Completed in 1882, the line was abandoned in 1937. Ruins of the engine house, boarding house, and snow sheds atop the 11,482-foot pass are disappearing, but the section house has been restored, as has the Baker Water Tank (1882), 6.6 miles east of Breckenridge, a 9,305-gallon redwood cylinder moved here in 1910 from its original site on the Denver, South Park & Pacific near the Alpine Tunnel.

ST22 Washington Mine

1880. Summit County 518 via Boreas Pass Rd., 1.1 miles east of Breckenridge on Barney Ford Hill

This prospect hole proved rich enough to justify six tunnels by 1911. Hard-rock miners dug gold, lead, and silver here for eighty years. In 1984 the Summit Historical Society restored the above-ground shaft house, change room, equipment, and part of one shaft for hard-hat tours.

ST23 **Copper Mountain Ski Resort**

1972. I-70 and Colorado 91, 15 miles southwest of Dillon

At the confluence of Tenmile and West Tenmile creeks, John S. Wheeler established Wheeler in 1880. This mining district crossroads was restaked in 1972 as the Copper Mountain Ski Resort. Named for an old, low-yield copper mine, Copper Mountain has functional rather than stylized structures produced by in-house designers relying heavily on precast concrete that withstands extreme freeze-thaw cycles.

During the 1980s architectural diversity came with a new conference center, condominiums, an athletic club, a golf course, and a chapel (1976, Taniguchi and Associates), a Mineshaft Modern design combining a box and a modified A frame. Elsewhere on the grounds, an old barn and log cabin remind skiers and golfers of a very different lifestyle here a century ago.

Dillon

Dillon (1879, 9,156 feet) is said to have been named for Thomas Dillon, a wandering prospector. Like him, the town has been migratory. Originally on the Snake River, it was moved to the Blue River and then to a trackside location after the D&RG and DSP&P arrived in 1882.

During the 1940s the Denver Water Department began buying land and water rights to build a reservoir. While drowning the old townsite, the dam (1963) created 25 miles of shoreline, now dotted with new development. Many town buildings were moved uphill to the Fred Phillips Ranch to escape a watery grave. Dillon's population, as well as its location, has fluctuated with mining and transportation changes. After

the railroads abandoned Dillon, the town declined until I-70's 1.7-mile-long Eisenhower Tunnel (1973) under the Continental Divide brought skiers to Summit County and started an avalanche of development.

ST24 **Summit Historical Museum** (Dillon Schoolhouse)

1883. 403 E. LaBonte St.

Used as a church after its 1910 retirement as a school, this clapboard schoolhouse crowned by an open bell tower with a shingled, flared roof was relocated here in 1961. Recycled as a museum and home for the Summit Historical Society, it is furnished with such antique tools of the trade as McGuffey readers and McGuffey desks. The school sits beside two relics moved from nearby Keystone, the one-and-one-half-story log Myers Ranch House (1885) and a 14-by-18-foot "honeymoon cabin" (1930s), which originally sat along U.S. 6.

Frisco

Thick stands of evergreens shaded the confluence of Tenmile and North Tenmile creeks, where "Frisco City" (1879, 9,907 feet) was platted as a stop for the DSP&P and the D&RG railroads. Frisco blossomed as a rail, ranching, and mining hamlet, but wilted after the railroads pulled out in 1937.

Fading Frisco came to be known as "Junk Junction" until completion of Dillon Reservoir and I-70's Eisenhower Tunnel triggered a new boom. The old rail depot was replaced by the Frisco Marina, and the town flaunted its shoreline location by adding a sailboat to its logo. During the 1980s, landscaping, a greenway and parks, and a historical park transformed the town, while its rail heritage was celebrated with the installation of a D&RG baggage car (1880) at 303 Main.

ST25 **Frisco Funtastic Fungrounds**

1990, Robert Leathers. Southeast corner of 8th Ave. and Pitkin St.

Robert Leathers, a prominent playground designer from Ithaca, New York, interviewed Frisco children before creating this huge wooden fantasy next to the elementary school. The stockade-like design, constructed by town volunteers, is unified by triangular towers atop a maze of wooden playground apparatus. Leathers has also created playgrounds for Denver, Idaho Springs, Manitou Springs, and Steamboat Springs.

ST26 **Frisco Historic Park**

1983, Dokken Crowe Architects. 120 Main St. (corner of 2nd St.)

To clear land for development, members of several endangered architectural species were moved to this park behind the old schoolhouse. The schoolhouse (1900) (NR) was built as a saloon but served as a school from 1902 to 1958. Restored to house the Frisco Historical Society Museum, the one-room school has an Italianate open bell tower borrowed from a demolished school in Breckenridge. Dovetailed corners enhance the design, as do gingerbread and scalloped shingles in the front and rear gables. Five other historic buildings include the log jail (1881, J. Scott and William Meyers), which stood three blocks to the east, and Bill's Ranch House (c. 1890), with its finely detailed joints and corners. The Staley House (c. 1908) is a log home with a frame front.

Keystone

After the DSP&P arrived in 1883, Keystone (1879, 9,250 feet) hummed as the railhead for the logging and mining towns of Argentine, Chihuahua, Montezuma, and Saints John (named for two saints, John the Baptist and John the Evangelist). After the railroad pulled out in 1937, it became a ghost. Resurrection came in 1970 when the Ralston Purina Corporation opened the Keystone Ski Area and Resort.

ST27 **Keystone Resort**

1970. U.S. 6, west side of Loveland Pass

The first Colorado ski resort built after passage of the Environmental Protection Act (1969) incorporated runs, lifts, and facilities that purport to caress rather than scar the terrain. Runs were not totally cleared of trees but made to go around and through them. High-speed quad chair lifts and gondolas whisk skiers up the slopes day and night, as thirteen trails are lit until 9:00 p.m. The Keystone complex now includes Arapahoe Basin Ski Area (1946), North America's highest lift-served area, with enough snow for skiing into May. This comprehensive, single-owner resort has developed related resort and residential areas, including a golf course designed by Robert Trent Jones, Jr. With few older buildings to consider, Keystone Resort's design opportunities have been wide open, and it is a well-planned resort. The Keystone Conference Center (1989, Michael Barber Architecture), a 56,000-square-foot convention center trying to hide in a grove of lodgepole pine, is sheathed in "aspen tree gold" precast concrete panels. The Keystone Science School (1880s; 1976), a rustic campus of old log and frame cabins lining the Keystone rail grade, is an informal setting for the study of the environment and field trips into the spectacular surrounding mountains.

Montezuma

Montezuma (1865, 10,280 feet), begun as a lofty silver mining center on the headwaters of the Snake River, once boasted 100 structures, of which perhaps one-fourth survive. The rustic town is threatened by Keystone Resort, which is creeping up the Snake River. Cabins and a few public lodges generally are built into south-facing slopes for warmth and sunshine.

ST28 Montezuma Schoolhouse

1884. Webster Ave., one block east of Main St.

This one-room clapboard school on a stone foundation has a vestibule, cupola, and "boys" and "girls" outhouses affixed to the rear. Thirty-two years after closing in 1958, the school was acquired and restored by the Summit Historical Society. Inside is a wainscoted classroom with blackboards, desks, vintage texts, and a 1958 Dupont Explosives wall calendar. Montezuma used the school as a polling place, wedding and dance hall, and town center. Verna Sharp, the last schoolmarm to preside on the elevated teacher's platform, authored a history of the community and its environs.

ST29 Saints John Smelter

1869, Boston Silver Mining Association. 1 mile south of Montezuma in the ghost mining town of Saints John

One of the largest early smelters is a ruin today. Near remnants of a smelter stack, a hillside powder house (1872) remains, built of super-strong brick supposedly brought from Swansea, Wales. Ore processing efforts here were undermined by newer, improved smelters elsewhere and by the hostile climate at 10,800 feet.

Silverthorne

Silverthorne (1962, 8,790 feet) traces its origins and misspelled name to Judge Marshel Silverthorn's 1881 placer claim on the Blue River. This crossroads did not boom until the 1950s, when it became a construction camp for the Dillon Dam and the Roberts Tunnel, which divert Blue River water under the Continental Divide to metropolitan Denver. Silverthorne has since become Summit County's largest town and a mix of fast-food restaurants, trailer parks, factory outlet

stores, and houses ranging from dilapidated shacks to million-dollar resort homes. In the 1980s the town used vastly expanded tax revenues to begin belated planning and beautification projects such as the spectacular new town hall and the Blue River greenway.

ST30 The Mint Saloon

1880s. 321 Blue River Pkwy. (Colorado 9)

This barnlike clapboard hall with sheet metal roofing was transplanted from the dammed and drowned town of Dillon. The false frame front and second-story pedimented windows do not redeem this ramshackle deportee with its many liquor signs and shed additions. The shell, which once housed Jim Ryan's Saloon, still draws locals fond of the cheap food and beverages, as well as the nostalgic ambiance flowing from a splendid old back bar. Next door is a similar transplant, the Old Dillon Inn (1880s), also a large frame false-fronted bar and restaurant.

ST31 Silverthorne Town Hall, Library, and Police Complex

1989, Dokken Crowe Architects. 601 Center Circle

Beautifully landscaped into the rocky bank of the Blue River, this 17,000-square-foot Postmodern structure houses city offices, the library, and the police station. The Frisco architects used plenty of glass to admit daylight and visually incorporate the Blue River greenway setting. Angular lines and stark, steep gables characterize the facade and beamed entry pavilions. Inside, Dokken Crowe attempted to create "a playful and somewhat ethereal atmosphere conducive to enhancing employee morale and productivity during the long winter months."

Eagle County (EA)

High on the headwaters of the Colorado River, Eagle County boasts North America's largest ski area and some compelling contemporary resort architecture. The first tourist of note, Sir St. George Gore, eighth baronet of Manor Gore, County Donegal, Ireland, arrived in the 1850s. Jim Bridger, the mountain man, guided Lord Gore's forty-one-man retinue, including his chef, gun bearers, and a trout fly artist, as well as 112 horses, several milk cows, twelve yoke of oxen, six wagons, twenty-one carts, and hunting hounds, into virgin wilderness.

The Utes must have been astonished. Gore is said to have slept in a green-and-white-striped silk tent complete with a carpet and a fur-lined commode. He dined al fresco using his English pewter plate and silver goblet, but barely tasted the vast amount of wild game he and his party slaughtered. The Gore Range, which guards the eastern boundary of Eagle County, commemorates this celebrated visitor, who also gave his name to a creek that flows through what is now the town of Vail. There modern-day tourists emulate Gore's penchant for conspicuous consumption.

Twenty years after the Lord Gore pageant, Eagle County captured America's

Eagle County, I-70, west side of Vail Pass

imagination when the 1873 Hayden Survey led to widespread reproduction of William Henry Jackson's photographs and Thomas Moran's paintings of the Mount of the Holy Cross. Within the shadows of Holy Cross, the ungodly mining town of Red Cliff sprang up in 1879 after silver strikes brought the first wagon road over Tennessee Pass from Leadville. Two years later the Denver & Rio Grande Railroad followed the wagon road into Red Cliff and continued down the Eagle River Valley to meet the Colorado River.

A century later, completion of I-70 opened Eagle County, which is guarded on all sides by 10,000-foot passes. The highway, with its cantilevered curves of earth-toned concrete, spacious median, and Taliesen-designed hike-bike path, is an architectural and engineering gem. This attractive, quick route over 10,066-foot Vail Pass triggered a boom; the county population climbed from 4,677 in 1960 to 21,928 in 1990. New condominiums, multimillion-dollar homes, and commercial development proliferate, binding Vail, Beaver Creek, Avon, and Arrowhead into a lavish mountain suburbia with some contemporary work by nationally noted architects such as William Turnbull, Robert Venturi, and Harry Weese.

Eagle

The county seat (1887, 6,600 feet) was named, like the county, for the Eagle River, whose tributaries supposedly resemble the feathers in an eagle's tail. Eagle's population has soared to over 1,600 with the booming ski industry, propelled by a 1986, $6 million runway expansion of the 1947 airport to lure jetsetters. The main street, Broadway, is lined with turn-of-the-century brick commercial buildings, usually with tall, narrow, double-hung windows, often with arched tops and radiating brick voussoirs. At 201 Broadway the Diamond J Bar, earlier known as the Eagle Bar, Dempsey's, Louisa's, Spooky's, Jack's Bar, and the Copper Eagle, has recently acquired a two-story false front of barn wood. Inside are a spacious dining room, bar, dance floor, orchestra platform, pool area, and a meeting hall used by Eagle town officials and the police department, who have tiny offices next door.

The residence at 308 Broadway (1914), a one-story house with a hipped roof and dormers, has a front porch with fancy columns. At 405 Broadway is a house of rough-faced cast stone (1911) with neo-Victorian ornament. The bank (1912) at Third and Broadway has been unfortunately modernized. Less altered are the terracotta-trimmed

buff brick Dice Brothers commercial building (1904) at 221–225 Broadway, the brick Community House (1900) at 2nd and Broadway, and the two-story log house at 332 Howard Street. The Eagle County Historical Society Museum is housed in a gambrel-roofed dairy barn (1882) moved in 1984 to Chambers Park for restoration as a museum and visitors' center near the picturesque Eagle County Rodeo Grounds.

EA01 Eagle County Courthouse

1932. 1991, addition, G. Cabell Childress. 500 Broadway

This three-story, buff brick courthouse with Art Deco spandrels and a third-story parapet occupies a full block shared with a 1980s lawn sculpture—a giant, oxidizing metal eagle. The little-altered interior of the 1932 structure still has original aluminum fixtures, signage, and doorway eagle medallions. For the sympathetic Postmodern addition Cab Childress used brick trimmed with Indiana limestone and a traditional copper and slate roof and incorporated a dozen eagles, including a seven-foot-tall one on the new east facade terminating Broadway.

EA02 Eagle County Justice Center

1985, William C. Muchow and Associates. 885 Chambers Ave.

On the northeast outskirts of town along I-70, this raw concrete solar structure was described by *Architecture* magazine (August 1986) as "a low-slung building with linear massing parallel to the land's contours . . . remarkable mainly for its peak-roofed, glazed entry before which two free-standing fluted columns stand at sentry duty." William Muchow, a devout Postmodernist, described the layout as "traditional for a jail" but said he tried to make it "a somewhat happy place" by using skylights for daylight.

Vail

Vail (1962, 8,150 feet) is the largest ski area in North America. The Gore Creek Valley was remote ranching country in 1940 when Colorado Highway Department engineers built a paved road over a pass named for Colorado Highway Department Chief Engineer Charles D. Vail.

During the 1950s Peter Seibert, a veteran of the U.S. Army's Tenth Mountain Division ski troops and a ski school director at Loveland Basin, discovered the slopes of Vail Mountain. Seibert, with friends and investors, paid $44,000 for the 520-acre Hanson Sheep Ranch and opened it five years later as Vail. Seibert enlisted Milwaukee architect Fitzhugh Scott, who in 1961 built the first house in Vail, a chalet that served as the corporate headquarters for the development

Vail, Alpine Standard station

partnership and also housed the town's only indoor bathroom.

Scott designed much of early Vail, developing a composite Alpine style, using white stucco with dark wood trim, balconies, window flower boxes, setbacks, crafted details, and steeply pitched roofs. The style seemed appropriate: skiing was then more European than American, and foreign-accented émigrés staffed the ski school and many of the lodges and shops. The Aspen Ski Area, which had been open since 1938, also looked to European ski resorts as models for its early development. Vail's version of the Alpine Style survives in the pioneer 1962 gas station at the southwest corner of Frontage Street and Vail Road. This stuccoed, half-timbered affair even has a stone chimney and a fireplace. The $1 million Lodge at Vail (1962, Fitzhugh Scott), 174 East Gore Creek Drive, next to chairlift no. 1, experienced unexpectedly sudden success. It inspired construction of Christiana-at-Vail (1965, Fitzhugh Scott), 356 East Hanson Ranch Road, and Gasthof Gramshammer (1964), 231 Gore Creek Drive at Bridge Street, operated by Austrian skiing star Pepi Gramshammer and his wife Sheika.

Critics snickered at Vail as "instant Alpine," "pseudo- Bavarian," "Swiss schmaltz," and "transplanted Tyrolean." Others called it—in honor of Fitzhugh Scott—"Milwaukee Swiss." This ersatz style, as even Peter Seibert admitted, "may not have been brilliant, but it was fairly safe." The somewhat standardized forms with individuality in details provided what architect Scott called "a background for outdoor activity." Winding pedestrian streets drew people to the town center, aiding this New World resort in its pursuit of Old World ambiance.

Trucks waddled over Vail Pass carrying giant cranes and huge slabs of precast concrete to erect a city that quickly eclipsed Eagle and Red Cliff. A major 1969 expansion—Lionshead at Vail—introduced ski runs, gondolas, and a concrete commercial cluster reminiscent of the work of Le Corbusier and the Modernist architecture of French Alpine resorts such as Chamonix. Development pressures grew so great by the

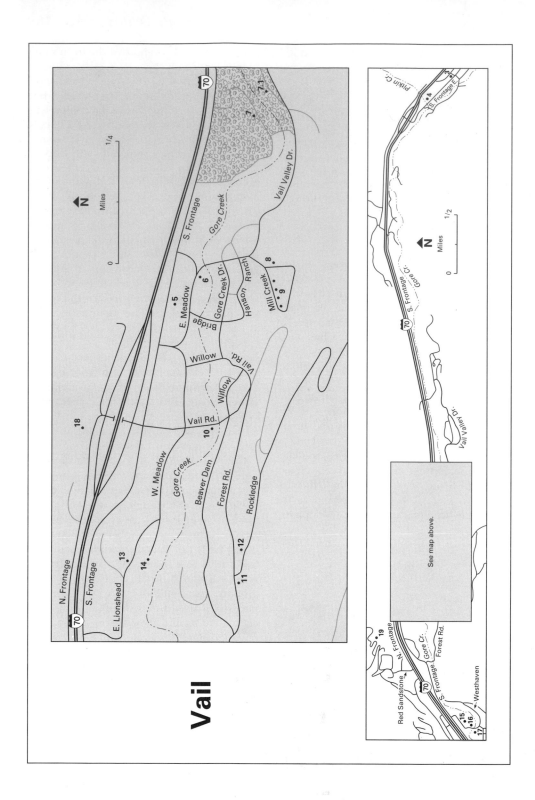

Vail

mid-1970s that Vail put a moratorium on building until design guidelines could be fully articulated. The resulting *Vail Village Urban Design Guide Plan* constrained some architectural creativity to help control growth and promote continuity of style and materials. It imposed height limits and promoted housing in the upper stories of shops in the village center. Succumbing to developers, Vail has since allowed eight-story condominiums to overshadow its landmark three-story Alpine clock tower and covered bridge.

Vail has pioneered state-of-the-art ski technology. Its four-passenger Bell gondolas, made in Lucerne, Switzerland, were the first used in America. During the 1980s four-passenger Vista Bahn chair lifts were installed to whisk skiers 2,000 vertical feet in nine minutes. To help pay for these conveyances, lift tickets, which cost $5 in 1962, have soared to more than $50.

The town is plowed with Unimogs, snowplows made by Mercedes-Benz, and policed by officers driving Saabs. Vail Mountain is blessed with an average of 300 inches of snow a year but was nearly bare of snow for the 1962 grand opening. Desperate, Seibert and his fellow investors called in Southern Ute Indians from Ignacio, Colorado. The Utes, led by Minnie Cloud, did rain dances, and a blizzard followed. Since then Vail has pioneered the use of snow-making machines.

King of the ski hills, it boasts 15 square miles of champagne powder, varied terrain, and famous back bowls that have attracted world championship races. With more than 4,000 permanent residents and 25,000 tourists at the Christmas peak, Vail is a city with taxes, potholes, air pollution, and Colorado's third largest urban bus system. Shangri-la now has a Safeway supermarket and a cemetery. Vail's phenomenal success inspired many other resorts, including Beaver Creek and Arrowhead at Eagle, where Peter D. Seibert, Jr., strove to do what his father did with a remote mountain sheep ranch. Vail's early architectural style, borrowed from Europe, has become a springboard to the Postmodern and avant-garde styles which now predominate.

EA03 **Bus Stop** (Kiahtipes Summer Ranch House)

c. 1930. East Vail I-70 exit to Bighorn Rd. near Pitkin Creek

This log structure with the Circle-K brand on the chimney has been restored for use as a bus shelter. The simple notched corner joints are similar to those of the Bauldauf Cabin (1906), 3160 Katsos Ranch Road (at Frontage Road), a two-story, hewn log ranch house now used as the Vail Mountain School.

EA04 **Pitkin Creek Park Condominiums and Shops**

1979, Briner and Scott. 4000 Bighorn Rd., East Vail

Simple textured plywood sheathes this angular compound that combines street-floor shops with two floors of affordable condominium housing. The housing units, under steeply pitched shed roofs, have generous balconies and fireplaces. This is a rare alternative for employees of Vail businesses to the usual long commute from mobile home parks or distant communities with affordable housing.

EA05 **Vail Transportation Center**

1975, James T. Ream and Associates; Royston-Hamamoto, Alden Beck, landscape consultants. 1990, remodeling and expansion, Michael Barber Architecture. 352 E. Meadow Dr. (at Bridge St.)

A small, man-made mountain camouflages the largely sunken, five-story parking garage, bus terminal, and visitors' center, which should be the arriving motorist's destination, since Vail is a pedestrian town. It is topped by an information kiosk and the Vail bus depot. Tourists might well start here at the Colorado Ski Heritage Center (1990, Michael Barber Architecture), a spacious storefront museum whose exhibits trace skiing back to Scandinavia 2,000 years ago. The public plaza in front of this center leads to Vail's famous covered bridge, clock tower, and a landscaped hike-bike trail.

EA06 Vail Athletic Club and Spa Condominiums

1976–1978, Pierce, Briner and Scott. 352 E. Meadow Dr. (southwest corner of Vail Valley Dr.)

Like many well-designed, understated Vail buildings, this one is bigger than it seems to be. Textured beige stucco and low-lying forms are further integrated with the site by close-planted trees and a deck over Gore Creek. This contemporary, sprawling, multistory development includes a hotel, condominiums, restaurant, and health club.

EA07 Ford Park and Amphitheater

1987. 601 Vail Valley Dr.

Former President Gerald Ford and his wife, Betty, lent support to an outdoor theater and a surrounding park and garden named for the couple, who have a home in the Vail Valley. The informal Ford Park Amphitheater (1987, Morter Fisher Architects), 400 Vail Valley Drive, with half its seating on grassy berms, is partially covered by a series of wooden roof planes that frame the surrounding hillsides. The Betty Ford Alpine Rock Garden was designed by Marty Jones. Nearby in the park is a one-room, hewn log schoolhouse (1922) that now serves as the Gore Creek Museum. The Vail Nature Center (EA07.1), 601 Vail Valley Drive in the park, was originally the Anholtz farmhouse (c. 1930). The two-story, gabled house was moved to Ford Park and given two additions and solar panels.

EA08 Goltra House

1970, 1980–1981 (additions), Harry Weese and Associates. 385 Mill Creek Circle

Chicago architect Harry Weese, a noted Modernist, designed this L-shaped house in a meadow overlooking the Gold Peak ski runs. Asked to build a vacation home that could comfortably sleep twenty-five, Weese, who also designed the Armstrong House in Vail, departed from Vail's usual styles with a boxy composition of vertical red cedar siding reminiscent of mining town structures. Exterior facades employ white trim to highlight rectangular windows, bays, and balconies. The outdoors is brought into the design with a double deck, skylights, a two-story south window, and pillow-level sliding windows.

EA09 Mill Creek Circle Houses

1960s

For their own residences, many Vail town founders chose lots along Mill Creek at the end of the Gold Peak ski run. These unpretentious, functional houses are now endangered, eminently replaceable by larger, glitzier homes. Fritz Benedict, a well-known Aspen architect, designed 375 Mill Creek Circle, demolished in 1995 for a larger residence, in the Prairie Style. Fitzhugh Scott's Tyrolean design (1965), 304 Mill Creek, has a battered stucco base, solid plank walls, painted shutters, and window flower boxes.

EA10 Vail Interfaith Chapel

1976, 1978 (enlargement), Pierce, Briner and Scott. 19 Vail Rd.

This version of a Tyrolean chapel uses Vail's prescribed white stucco and dark wood trim in a stark, emphatically Modernist church. The 500-seat interior is modernized Gothic

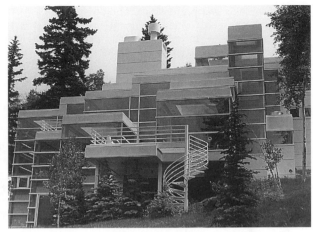

EA11 Brant House   EA12 Tennenbaum House

made possible by glue-laminated arches, but generic enough to accommodate seven different denominations that moved out of restaurants and bars where they had been meeting amid the lingering Saturday night fumes.

FA11 **Brant House**

1976, Robert Venturi of Venturi, Rauch and Scott Brown. 338 Rockledge Rd.

Robert Venturi's version of a chalet has inspired delight and derision. Built against a steep hillside, this redwood house expresses the change of grade with its design, while suggesting the designs of Charles F. A. Voysey, the English architect and designer. The sides of the first two stories are recessed, making the structure appear taller than it is. The upper story overhangs the lower stories and features a large, arched dormer window on each slope of a hipped roof. Vail's most widely acclaimed contemporary structure has its own cable chair lift from the garage to the second floor of the house. The top-floor living room with its warm redwood vaulting, according to Venturi, as reported in *Three Centuries of Notable American Architects* (1981), borrows not only from Voysey, but also from the vaulted interiors of eighteenth-century Polish synagogues.

EA12 **Tennenbaum House**

1988, Ed Niles. 307 Rockledge Rd.

Typical of the second-generation homes that have replaced Vail's original smaller houses, this huge, high-tech composition designed by a California architect rejects Alpine antecedents. Its green glass cubes, framed in white metal, pose a question: Do Malibu oceanside homes work on Vail's mountainsides? So many locals threw verbal stones at this glass house that the Vail Town Council, Planning and Environmental Commission, and Design Review Commission conducted what Mrs. Tennenbaum, in the June 30, 1989, issue of *Vail Trail*, called "an architectural witch hunt." This eyecatcher revives the International Style in the Postmodern tradition of Richard Meier.

EA13 **Dobson Ice Arena**

1979, Everett Zeigel Architecture. 321 E. Lionshead Circle

This rink of glue-laminated timber and raw cement received a regional AIA award from a jury that praised its low, earth-sheltered profile, designed to reduce the bulk of the 40,000-square-foot structure. The column-free interior accommodates a variety of events, as well as an Olympic-sized, year-round skating rink. It honors John A. Dobson, a Vermonter who built Vail's Covered Bridge Store and in 1966 was elected the town's first mayor. During his nine years in office, Dobson also wrote melodramas for the Vail Players, often poking fun at the town's problems and pretensions. The open space on Lionshead Circle contains a large bronze sculpture of children leaping in play by Colorado sculptor Susan Grant Raymond.

EA14 Vail Public Library

1983, Snowden and Hopkins. 292 W. Meadow Dr.

Various awards, including national AIA honors and recognition in *Solar Age* magazine (September 1985), were lavished on this earth-shelterd, sod-roofed $2.4 million library. Almost hidden amid 60-foot-high spruce trees, the down-to-earth design, in redwood siding and native stone, is a sharp departure from the Carnegie Greek temple libraries of yesteryear. Inside is a fireplace for cozy reading and storytelling. The north facade, on East Lionshead Circle opposite Dobson Arena, uses the library's landscaped berm, earth architecture, and stone wall to define a plaza, and the building opens on the south to the Gore Creek greenway. A glass galleria connects a two-story office wing with the library.

EA15 Colorado Mountain College

1983, Briner and Scott. 1310 Westhaven Dr. in the Westin Hotel Complex

Reminiscent of Bauhaus designs, this large, angular building is capped by skylights which slope heavenward as steeply as the surrounding hills.

EA16 Millrace Condominiums

1986, Robert L. Arnold Associates. 1360 Westhaven Dr., West Vail

This winner of an AIA Western Mountain Region award clusters plaster and wood-paneled stacked units with contrasting industrial metal–railed balconies around a carefully landscaped watercourse and central pool.

EA17 Coldstream Condominiums

1986, Morter, Fisher; Robert L. Arnold Associates. 476 Westhaven Dr., West Vail

James Morter's rendition of a European village, this condominium complex in a bend of Gore Creek won a regional AIA award. Its stacked townhouse units cluster around a Vail-style clock tower but are oriented toward the river, large evergreens, and the winter sun.

EA18 Mountain Bell Microwave Tower

1972, Rogers-Nagel-Langhart. I-70 near Vail Dr.

This $2.7 million utilitarian sculpture on the north side of I-70 is Vail's most visible landmark, a 110-foot-high, shed-roofed structure used to transmit telephone signals over the mountains. "Vail did not want the visual pollution of just another steel phone tower with microwave horns," architect John Rogers explained in 1990. "So we preserved the natural landscaping and nearby aspen. We used native gravels for the tower's rusticated precast concrete skin."

EA19 Potato Patch Club and Condominiums

1978, Pierce, Briner and Scott. 950 Red Sandstone Rd.

On what was once a south-facing hillside potato farm, this collection of townhouses climbs a steep hill across I-70 from Vail Village. Exaggerated shed roofs and arched chimney covers update the Alpine Style. In an effort to keep housing affordable, Vail required homebuilders in portions of the Potato Patch and Sunburst Drive on the south side of the Vail Valley Golf Course to construct attached secondary residences half the size of the primary residence. An example of this "low-income" housing is the Gary Bossow House (1984, Robert K. Fuller), 758 Potato Drive. Fuller, a fourth-generation member of Denver's pioneer Roeschlaub-Fuller firm, used vertical redwood planks for this multilevel duplex.

Avon

Avon (1884, 7,430 feet) was a D&RG rail town christened by a homesick English pioneer, William H. Nottingham, for the Avon Valley of his youth. The Nottingham Ranch House (c. 1898), 55 Village Road, is a two-story, L-shaped, hewn log house with a gable roof, stone chimney, expansive veranda, and log outbuildings, restored in 1989 as a restaurant. Until the 1970s Avon consisted of a few ramshackle structures, including a post office, a log general store, and a one-room schoolhouse surrounded by ranches and potato and lettuce farms. With the ski boom, Avon gained a jetport, stylish new office buildings, shopping malls, and condominiums. The Avon Station Mobile Home Park houses hundreds of construction and service workers for Vail, Beaver Creek, and Arrowhead who cannot afford to live in the communities where they work. Avon's population has grown to over 2,000. Mayor Allen Nottingham, grandson of the town's founder, admitted to the *Rocky Mountain News* on February 5, 1989, "The vacant lots make us appear to be incomplete, but we hope to see the town developed to its capacity." *Skiing* magazine sniffed in November 1987 that Avon resembled "a municipal yard sale, a desperately uncoordinated checkerboard" crowned by "a great concrete toad [the Peregrine Hotel]."

Beaver Creek

Former president Gerald Ford, Beaver Creek's best-known resident, presided at the July 28, 1977, groundbreaking by Vail Associates for the resort town of Beaver Creek (1980, 8,100 feet). Despite opposition from environmentalists, this 5,000-acre, $600-million haven opened with 25 miles of ski trails and six chair lifts. Beaver Creek's 1979 design regulations aimed "at establishing a compatibility between buildings and the natural environment, fulfilling the expectations of visitors as a retreat to the mountains, respecting the historic precedent of mountain buildings and resort communities in both Colorado and Europe, and utilizing energy conservation and solar energy applications."

The ski area won national design awards in 1991 and 1992 from *Snow Country* magazine, which praised the use of natural con-

tours and minimal visual impact on the landscape. Beaver Creek's hotels and condominiums, even swankier than Vail's, bristle with gables, dormers, bays, and chimneys under "spruce blue" manufactured stone roof tiles. Beaver Creek cascades through the town center, which is landscaped with sculpture, boulders, and pansies, poppies, and aspen. The stepped massing, steeply pitched roofs, and vertical lines of many structures visually echo the surrounding mountain valley. Deluxe private homes above the town center, like that at 222 Elk Track Road, employ natural materials and ingenious design in the pursuit of elegance and comfort.

EA20 Beaver Creek Clubhouse

1985, Morter, Fisher with Eric Erickson. 103 Offerson Rd.

This starkly Modernist three-story complex, a collaboration of Vail and Los Angeles architects, earned the praise of *Architecture* magazine in May 1986 for its massing, proportion, detailing, and strong relationship to its site on Beaver Creek Golf Course. The course, designed by Robert Trent Jones, Jr., spills down the valley, which is lined with luxury homes. The rustic Holden Barn (c. 1904) and picturesque farm implements adorn this exquisitely manicured golf course.

EA21 Beaver Creek Hyatt Regency Hotel and Conference Center

1989, Hornberger, Warstell and Associates. 136 E. Thomas Pl.

Copper-topped towers and prominent chimneys, as well as steeply pitched roofs, round-arched windows, and myriad dormers and gables lend a medieval mien to this contemporary chalet designed by a San Francisco firm.

EA22 Beaver Creek Interfaith Chapel

1988, Zehren and Associates. Northwest corner of Vail Dr. and Gore Creek

This Neo-Norman church of rough-faced stone with an off-center bell tower, slatelike

EA22 Beaver Creek Interfaith Chapel

roof, and large, creekside deck cost $1.3 million. Round-arched windows with clear glass, golden oak pews, and a peaked ceiling with exposed beams enhance a simple nave, while the sanctuary is dominated by a novel baptismal font—a jacuzzi bordered by large slabs of native stone.

EA23 Centennial Condominiums

1983, Turnbull and Associates. 180 Offerson Rd.

William Turnbull, one of the internationally noted architects of Sea Ranch in California, designed this multistory, stepped structure to mirror its setting by climbing a mountain valley, a solution that captured an award from *Progressive Architecture*. In summer its textured stucco mass is anchored by light-colored boulders in the landscaping; in winter the building seems to melt into the snow.

EA24 Ford House

1983, William Haynes

Former president Gerald Ford's home is typical of many in the Beaver Creek Valley in displaying considerable individuality while meeting the community's design guidelines. It and neighboring homes were described in the October 1988 issue of *Snow Country* magazine: "Often massive in scale and borrowing selectively from the traditions of Alpine architecture, the homes of Beaver Creek are unique in American ski resort architecture, most of them costing in excess of a million dollars to build on mountainside land that has been rationed as carefully as Beverly Hills homesites."

EA25 De la Lama House

1981, Victor de la Lama. Elk Track Rd.

This Mexican architect designed his own home of raw wood and glass in shed-roofed modules set amid aspen trees. "Many mountain houses tend to have similar envelopes," Vail architect Fitzhugh Scott told *Snow Country* magazine (October 1988), but de la Lama's house was an "outstanding design departure."

EA26 Spruce Saddle Warming House

1980, Bull, Field, Volkmann and Stockwell. Centennial Express Ski Run

Capitalizing on its site atop the Centennial Express ski run, this building has glass sides, framed at the corners by huge, vertical logs, that capture spectacular views. Ceiling beams unify the multilevel interior.

Basalt

The standard-gauge Colorado Midland Railroad, steaming out of Colorado Springs through Leadville, reached this point at the confluence of the Roaring Fork and Frying Pan rivers in 1886. Railroaders founded Basalt (1887; 6,624 feet), named for the nearby mountain of basaltic lava. The CM also stopped at the Peach Blow Quarry (1909–1915), 7 miles east on the Fryingpan River, the largest of several quarries supplying peachy-red sandstone used in nearby Aspen and Glenwood Springs and as far away as Chicago.

EA27 Bank of Basalt (Colorado Midland Depot)

c. 1890. Railroad (Main) St. and Midland Ave.

This elegant little depot with its bracketed eaves and pediments above doors and windows, sits on the main street, which is still called Railroad Avenue even though the depot is now a bank. A CM caboose serves as the Chamber of Commerce and Information Center at the corner of Midland Avenue and Colorado 82, and a rusting iron CM trestle still spans the Roaring Fork River on the south edge of town.

EA28 **Gilman**

1886–1977. Colorado 24, 6 miles south of Minturn

Perched precariously atop the Eagle River Canyon at 8,970 feet, Gilman is one of Colorado's newest ghost towns. Named for mining man Henry M. Gilman, it mushroomed as fortune seekers from Leadville poured into the Battle Mountain District, named for an 1849 battle between the Utes and the Arapaho. On a shoulder of Battle Mountain, 600 feet above the river and the D&RG tracks, the town of Gilman flourished on a diet of silver, zinc, copper, lead, and a little gold. A tram carried ore and supplies to and from the railroad at the foot of the canyon, while passengers climbed the steep grade on a stairway. The New Jersey Zinc Company purchased Gilman and nearby mines in 1912, creating a company town which by the 1930s produced 85 percent of Colorado's copper and 65 percent of its silver. During the 1930s and 1940s boom, Gilman's population climbed back almost to 500, where it had peaked in the 1890s. After the Eagle Mine closed in 1977, residents were evicted from the drab, typical company town in a spectacular natural setting. Like many closed mines, the Eagle continues to be a source of water pollution, spilling acids, arsenic, and other hazardous wastes into the Eagle River. Although placed on the Environmental Protection Agency's Superfund cleanup list in the 1980s, Gilman still awaits a prescribed $100 million cleanup.

Minturn

Minturn (1885, 7,817 feet), named for a railroad official, grew up around a D&RG roundhouse and remains a blue-collar town strung out along the tracks. Locals once worked on the railroad, in Battle Mountain mines, and at lumbering, but most now labor in nearby resort communities. Many small, well-kept old houses enhance this town of 1,000. The roundhouse and railyards, although diminished, remain busy. Despite its humdrum architecture, the new Turntable Restaurant next to the yards features historical memorabilia and railroadiana. A Lionel D&RG circles the ceiling, a model of the famous Red Cliff Bridge spans the restroom entrance, and photographs by William Henry Jackson line the walls. This cafe-museum is attached to the large D&RG dormitory and offers a year-round haven for railroad workers and the general public with the front-door invitation, "Come on in or we'll both starve."

The Battle Mountain Trading Post, 1031 South Main, and the Eagle River Hotel (1894), 145 North Main, are notable for their goods and services as well as for their antiquity. The latter has been redesigned in Southwestern adobe style as a bed and breakfast inn.

EA29 **Tigiwon Shelter**

1933–1934, Civilian Conservation Corps, 6 miles west off Colorado 24 between Gilman and Minturn at trailhead to Mount of the Holy Cross and Notch-Top Mountain

This huge log structure with notched corners has a side-gable roof that extends low over a front porch and an open-rafter interior hovering over a massive stone fireplace. It is all that materialized from numerous plans to erect a shrine and pilgrimage center to commercialize the Mount of the Holy Cross. President Herbert Hoover declared the mountain a national monument in 1929, but in 1950 it was demoted to become again part of the White River National Forest. Notch-Top Mountain offers the best view of Holy Cross, a 13,976-foot granite peak with a cross-shaped crevasse immortalized by photographer William Henry Jackson, painter Thomas Moran, and poet Henry Wadsworth Longfellow: "There is a mountain in the distant west / That, sun-defying, in its deep ravines / Reveals a cross of snow upon its side.   "

Red Cliff

Red Cliff (1879, 8,750 feet) was founded after silver strikes on Battle Mountain drew a swarm of miners from Leadville. They found a place level enough to plat a town where the Eagle River Canyon broadened at its junction with Homestake and Turkey creeks. By 1881 Red Cliff boasted a railroad, a sawmill, five hotels, and an opera house.

Despite its fast start, Red Cliff never exceeded a population of 900 and, in 1921, lost the county seat to Eagle. The town has become a home not only for miners, but also for maids, bartenders, and construction workers laboring elsewhere. Metal-roofed, slab-sided buildings cling to the mountainside in disarray. Miner's shacks, log cabins, vernacular false-fronted commercial buildings, and a one-room schoolhouse make this a more authentic relic of the mining frontier than more fashionable mining towns reborn as ski resorts with streets of cute, colorfully frosted gingerbread buildings.

EA30 Red Cliff Bridge

1940, King Burghardt. 1985. U.S. 24, 1 mile west of Red Cliff (NR)

Highway Department staff engineer King Burghardt designed Red Cliff's sole claim to architectural grandeur. This spectacular 318-foot silvery span over the Eagle River and twin D&RG tracks is the only cantilevered steel arch bridge left in Colorado. Fortunately, the highway department has never altered this graceful giant with its decorative concrete portal obelisks.

EA31 Camp Hale

1942–1946. U.S. 24, 11 miles south of Gilman (NR)

During World War II the small mountain valley known as Eagle Park, on the D&RG line between Leadville and Redcliff, and the surrounding peaks became the training camp for the U.S. Army's first and only ski troops, the Tenth Mountain Division. Named for Colorado Spanish-American war hero General Irving Hale, the camp replaced an iceberg lettuce farm on the valley floor of the upper Eagle River. Constructed in 1942 to house 735 officers and 13,500 enlisted men, the base was leveled to its concrete foundations in 1965. Many veterans who trained here, including Vail's Peter Seibert, returned to Colorado after the war to launch ski areas at Aspen, Vail, and elsewhere.

Garfield County   (GF)

Garfield County's main street, the Colorado River, has cut into the Flat Top Mountains the 2,000-foot gorge of Glenwood Canyon. This corridor for Amtrak and automobiles allows passengers a grand view of the cliffs of sandstone, limestone, and granite.

White settlers came in search of gold, silver, and coal in 1881, the year President James A. Garfield was assassinated, hence the county name. The mineral search shifted during the 1920s to oil shale and in the 1950s to radioactive metals. A much bigger boom came in 1980 with Exxon's $5 billion Colony Oil Shale Project. Exxon exited abruptly in 1982, laying off 2,100 workers. Hundreds of others also left, unable to afford even cheap prefabricated and mobile homes.

While flirting with various metals and oil shale, Garfield has been steadily supported by coal mining, tourism, and agriculture. River valley farmers and ranchers raise hay, potatoes, strawberries, sheep, and cattle. Skiing, hunting, river rafting, fishing, and the Glenwood Hot Springs, Colorado's most popular watering hole, make tourism the county's major draw. To build the Hotel Colorado and the Hot Springs Lodge, Walter A. Devereux, a mining engineer trained at Columbia University, opened up the Peach Blow Quarry on the Frying Pan River in nearby Eagle County. The stone, colored a rich golden-orange like peach blossoms, was used widely, especially along the line of the Colorado Midland Railroad,

Glenwood Springs

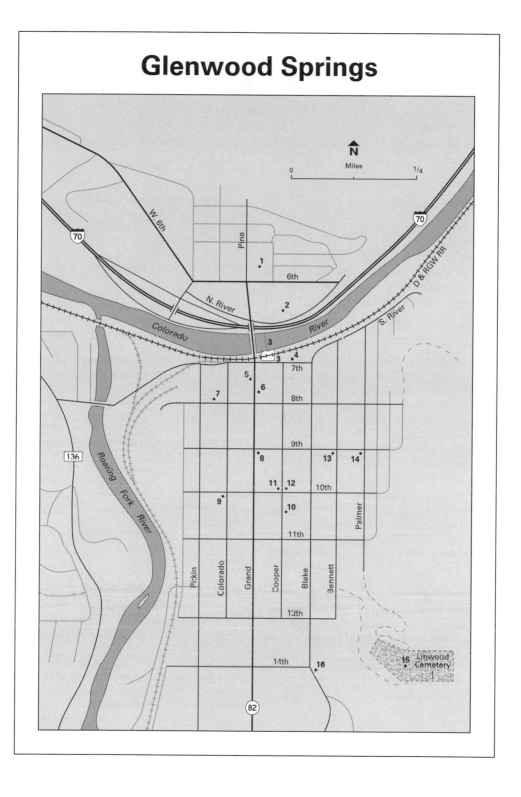

which served the quarry on its route between Colorado Springs and Grand Junction.

Deer, bear, and elk have attracted hunters, including President Theodore Roosevelt, whose ghost haunts local folklore. Three fish hatcheries and the Rifle Gap State Recreation Area help lure fishermen. The small Sunlight Ski Resort borrows its name and site from one of the county's many abandoned coal camps. Glenwood Springs, the county seat and only sizable city, has half the county's 30,000 residents.

Glenwood Springs

A huge hot springs pool, a restored Victorian bathhouse, and a grand hotel make the county seat (1883, 5,765 feet) Colorado's favorite place to "take the waters." The Yampah (big medicine) attracted the Utes for centuries before Captain Richard Sopris found the hot springs. Taken ill, Sopris soaked in the Ute medicine springs and was healed. On the south side of Glenwood Springs he also encountered the solitary, symmetrical mountain named for him.

Prospectors staked out a townsite at the confluence of the Roaring Fork and the Colorado rivers in 1878. Mining engineer Walter Devereux arrived in 1883 and transformed the town into a hot springs spa. In 1887 the D&RG blasted its way through Glenwood Canyon, and the Colorado Midland arrived via the Roaring Fork valley. Both railroads promoted Glenwood as a tourist destination, while also tapping the rich coal deposits nearby.

Glenwood Springs has a residential district of note along Colorado Avenue between 7th and 12th streets. Among various bungalows, the finest is a Craftsman example, with river rock porch pillars and graceful gables, at the southwest corner of 11th Street. The Talbot House (c. 1900), 928 Colorado, is a frame Queen Anne. At 1008 Colorado, an oddly massed house enlarges upon a small Victorian brick cottage with a shingled second story opening onto second- and third-story porches.

GF01 Hotel Colorado

1893, Theodore von Rosenberg. 526 Pine Ave. (NR)

Walter Devereux's 200-room Italian Renaissance Revival hotel has square corner towers with Palladian belvederes, a design that Theodore von Rosenberg, Devereux's Viennese architect, may have borrowed from the Villa Medici outside Rome. Massive fanlighted, round-arched windows flood the first floor with light. Rising six stories, the honey-colored brick beauty has a foundation, first-story facing, and trim of Peach Blow sandstone. The hotel's U-shaped plan shelters a central court with terraced formal gardens, a Florentine-style fountain and trout pool, and outdoor cafe. During World War II the U.S. Navy converted it to a convalescent hospital. A 1980s restoration revived the Palm Room, with 18-foot-high windows; the 5,000-square-foot Devereux Room, with its barrel-vaulted ceiling; a large ballroom; and the spacious lobby.

Distinguished guests have included Theodore Roosevelt, who stayed here on hunting trips. During his 1905 visit, the president posed on the front lawn with an enormous bear he had killed. Then and there, if local folklore can be believed, his daughter, Alice, coined the term "teddy bear."

GF02 Hot Springs Bath House and Pool

1891, Theodore von Rosenberg. 1993–1994, restoration-expansion, Caudill Gustafson Ross and Associates. 401 N. River St. (southeast corner of Grand Ave. and 6th St.)

The Viennese architect hired by Walter Devereux designed this Romanesque Revival bathhouse with a skin of Peach Blow sandstone. The original upstairs smoking parlor, reading room, and casino are now rehabilitated as private health club facilities. The basement Roman baths with porcelain tubs and the plebeian wooden bathhouse have not survived. An addition borrows the pitches of its gables and mansard from Rosenberg's original, with a sandstone base and stuccoed walls that carry the style better than the boxy 1950s additions on the east. The pool (1888, Theodore von Rosenberg) is fed by hot mineral waters. The 405-foot-long main pool and warmer 100-foot pool are promoted as the world's largest natural outdoor hot springs.

GF03 Two Rivers Park and River Walk

1985. Grand and River sts.

A pedestrian bridge (1985, Hauter and Associates) over the Colorado River leads to a paved trail along it and its tributary, the Roaring Fork River. A covered rest area at the south end has red roof tiles like those of the nearby train depot. A train-watching deck has a display guide to rail sights and signals. Another riverside building is the Glenwood Springs Center for the Arts, originally the Glenwood Electric Company (1886), 601 6th St.

GF04 Amtrak Depot (D&RG Depot)

1904, Theodore von Rosenberg? 413 7th St. between Cooper and Blake sts.

This red brick station is trimmed in rough-faced purple, gray, and red sandstone which also forms the first-story walls. Above a rough stone base with round-arched windows, ornate brickwork with Neoclassical wooden trim focuses on a central entry canopy with Ionic pilasters, under a red tile hipped roof with wide, flaring eaves and clipped gables.

The dominant design elements, twin towers with open viewing porches, echo the towers of the Hotel Colorado. The depot's stonework and some details also relate to the hot springs resort just across the river. Inside, some of the original oak wainscoting and brass fixtures survive between a linoleum floor and lowered acoustic tile ceiling. The trackside facade features a five-bay window with curved glass corners.

GF05 Silver Club Building (O'Neil Saloon)

c. 1885. 715 Grand Ave.

A pedimented parapet over the corner entry and a Palladian window distinguish this two-

story sandstone-trimmed brick building on an alley corner. Amid the north side potpourri of round-arched windows, a fading sign painted on the brick reveals the building's past as Ballie's Garage. The subterranean restaurant has a brick floor and exposed brick walls. This corner building introduces a row of altered Victorians, beginning with the Palace Hotel (c. 1885), and the Italiannate edifice at 717 Grand Avenue, which retains its original storefront under arched second-story windows and a bracketed cornice. The Parkinson Building (c. 1900), 719 Grand Avenue, has been muddled through extensively remodeling, as has 712 Grand Avenue (c. 1898), with sandstone banding poking through grotesque stuccoing.

GF06 Doc Holliday Tavern

1900, 724 Grand Ave.

A 10-foot neon six-shooter identifies this classic saloon, a long, narrow brick building that shares a cornice with a twin structure to the north, on which it leans. The massive cherry and mahogany Brunswick back bar, complete with bullet holes, may help to explain why the plank floor tilts to the northwest corner, where the exterior wall and foundation are sinking. A huge stone fireplace supplements the potbellied stove. The interior is decorated as a shrine to the gunslinging dentist and gambler, creating a rowdy ambiance enhanced by two pool tables.

GF07 Garfield County Courthouse

1928, Robert K. Fuller. 1983, addition, Henningson, Durham and Richardson. 109 8th St. (northwest corner of Colorado Ave.)

The original, south half of the county courthouse features terracotta trim, pilasters, spandrels, pediments, and an entry adorned with the torch of liberty, the scales of justice, spread eagles, and a longhorn cow skull. The blond brick building displays a careful geometric discipline related to the Prairie School. After the 1983 renovation and expansion, which added a stark northern half to the original Neoclassical box, a local resident complained that the building looked "somewhat like a wedding cake constructed by two bakers from opposite schools of design."

GF08 White River National Forest, U.S. Forest Service Headquarters

1918. Southeast corner of Grand Ave. and 9th St.

Inside this two-story blond brick Neoclassical building is a mural map of the region by Frank Mechau. Mechau, a Glenwood Springs native, studied art in Denver, Chicago, New York, and Paris. His romantic, stylized western scenes reflect his interest in Cubism and Chinese and Japanese art. Under New Deal arts programs he painted murals for post offices in Washington, D.C., Texas, and Nebraska as well as Colorado, then headed the Columbia University Art Department before his death in 1946.

GF08 White River National Forest, U.S. Forest Service Headquarters

GF09 Frontier Historical Museum

1905. 1001 Colorado Ave. (southwest corner of 10th St.)

This home on a quiet, tree-shaded street was converted in 1963 to a house museum with collections of old photos, animal skulls, and hats. The basement houses the Frontier Historical Society's archives, while the master bedroom features a model coal mine jammed with memorabilia. An oversized dormer and awkward-looking new brick columns on the full-length front porch make the house less graceful than many neighboring Victorian and bungalow dwellings.

GF10 First Presbyterian Church

1886. 1949, additions. 1016 Cooper Ave.

The oldest church in town, this lovely eclectic chapel has a stone foundation rising two feet out of the ground to meet the flared skirts of a shake shingle superstructure. The stark interior has exposed rafters and a contemporary altar.

GF11 First Church of Christ Scientist

1916, 1927. 931 Cooper Ave. (northwest corner of 10th St.)

This clapboard church, classical except for its Gothic-arched windows, is simple in the best Christian Science tradition. Tasteful traditional elements such as the columned porch, bracketed eaves, and pilasters, as well as the matching rear reading room added in 1927, adorn this distant relative of a Greek temple, which bows to its more imposing residential neighbors.

GF12 Kaiser House

1902. 932 Cooper Ave. (northeast corner of 10th St.)

This Queen Anne Style frame dwelling features a quarter-round front porch, conical corner tower, and multigabled and dormered roof. Originally the home of Frederick Kaiser, who helped bring electric power to Glenwood, it was restored in 1987 as a bed and breakfast. A hot tub, elegant interior woodwork, and marble bathrooms grace the guest rooms, which are brightened by antiques and a palette of pastel colors. Other fine residences line Cooper Avenue, including an overgrown bungalow at 1032 Cooper and a quaint cottage at 717 Cooper.

GF13 Taylor House

1904. 903 Bennett Ave. (southwest corner of 9th St.) (NR)

U.S. Representative Edward T. Taylor fathered the Taylor Grazing Act, a major piece of New Deal legislation that reshaped the livestock industry and much of the western landscape. The Taylor Act regulated livestock grazing on public lands for the first time, stipulating that the U.S. Forest Service impartially rent grazing rights to cattle and sheep ranchers. This ended bitter sheep-versus-cattle wars and curbed environmental abuses such as overgrazing. Coloradans of the Western Slope reelected Taylor to the House of Representatives seventeen times, keeping him in office from 1908 until his death in 1941. After the city of Glenwood decided not to buy the Taylor home for $1 for use as a library and museum, it became an apartment house.

This overgrown foursquare with third-story dormers and various bays is more important for its former occupant than its architecture. Numerous changes to the original design, as well as the addition of asbestos siding, have cheapened the house. The Colonial Revival front porch attempts elegance with its tri-clustered Tuscan columns and pilastered and pedimented entry, as does the elaborately carved foyer with its mahogany piers, brackets, spindles, and egg-and-dart trim. Far humbler cottages around Congressman Taylor's domicile include two vernacular Victorian cottages at 727 and 729 Bennett. A more polished foursquare with a heavy Doric porch and Craftsman ornament is the B. T. Napier House (1912), 930 Bennett.

GF14 **Starr Manor**

1901. 901 Palmer Ave. (southwest corner of 9th St.) (NR)

Wonderfully preserved, this impressive frame Queen Anne Style house has a wrap-around porch and multigabled roof with spindles, pendants, and sunburst detailing. A jumble of angled dormers and various window types punctuate vertical boxcar board siding and decorative second-story shingling. At the second story the rounded entry bay becomes a rounded window bay aligned with third- and attic fourth-story pedimented dormers, which have elaborately framed windows.

GF15 **Linwood Cemetery**

1886. On Jasper Mountain, .5 mile walk starting at 12th St. and Bennett Ave.

John "Doc" Holliday, the gunslinger, came to Glenwood hoping for a hot springs tuber-

culosis cure. It did not work. Belatedly realizing that Doc's tomb could become a tourist shrine, townsfolk put up a monument in 1958. It explains that Doc, still a slippery presence, lies "someplace in this cemetery." Small white marble headstones grace the African-American section. Now a dead and dry cemetery, Linwood has reverted to a natural landscape of wildflowers, juniper, sage, gambel oak, and wild grasses in dusty red earth, on a hill that offers a fine view of the town.

GF16 **Colorado Mountain College**

1981, Peter Dobrovolhy. 1400 Blake Ave.

Low-slung and stepped into a south-facing hillside, this is a notable passive solar structure. This Postmodern frame and glass building is "Old Main" for CMC's Glenwood Springs campus, which started in 1969 in the Hotel Colorado. Within an exposed aggregate block and steel structure, the central, enclosed courtyard has a jungle of plants under fuchsia-colored ductwork.

GF17 **Cardiff**

1887–1918. 3 miles south of Glenwood Springs on Garfield County 163 (Airport Rd.)

Little remains of the once large rail complex of the Colorado Midland Railroad except for a loading mill and a few shacks. In 1910 Cardiff, a CM division point, was a smoky village of 462 where coal brought by the railroad was fed into ovens to be cooked into coke. At Cardiff, ruins of about 50 of some 200 beehive ovens once connected by a stone wall still line a half-mile stretch of former railroad grade. Colorado Midland trainmen tweaked the curiosity of tourists by telling them that the ovens were used to heat the water for "Glenwood's so-called natural hot springs." Last owned by the Colorado Fuel and Iron Company, which closed them in 1915, the Cardiff ovens produced over 1.3 million tons of coke for smelters in Colorado and Utah.

Glenwood Canyon

The Colorado River dug this 12.5-mile-long chasm through gray Mississippian and green-gray Devonian limestones, brown Ordovician dolomite, and light and chocolate-banded Cambrian quartzites to reach the foundation of pink Precambrian granite. This natural masonry, exposed and sculpted over the past 40 million years, dwarfs sensational highway and railroad design in the 2,000-foot-deep chasm. The Denver & Rio Grande Railroad first blasted, tunneled, and bridged its way through the south wall of the canyon in 1887, followed by a northside 1890 wagon road that evolved into U.S. 6, then I-70.

GF19 Grizzly Creek Rest Area

GF18 I-70 in Glenwood Canyon

1993, Joseph Passonneau and Edgardo Contini

Construction finally began on I-70 in Glenwood Canyon in 1980, after more than twenty years of studying natural obstacles and of legal battles with environmentalists. Colorado Department of Transportation engineers and the architects, Joseph Passonneau of Washington, D.C., and Edgardo Contini of Los Angeles, reduced the environmental impacts, protected vegetation, and made this a beautiful ribbon of highway whose concrete is colored to match the craggy cliffs. The four-lane freeway flows through the canyon, sometimes rimming the river, sometimes floating over the treetops. An army of workers sculpted and stained newly blasted rock to match the patina of the unmolested canyon walls. Cantilevered, cliff-hugging lanes, over 6 miles in 40 bridges and viaducts, twin 4,000-foot-long tunnels, and an interwoven bike path complement the river's work. Some 140,000 native trees and shrubs were planted to enhance this showpiece freeway. The project, which cost $500 million, was the final, 12.5-mile segment of the 43,000-mile, $115-billion interstate highway system mandated by Congress in 1956.

GF19 Grizzly Creek Rest Area

1991, Philip E. Flores Associates, Inc. 6 miles east of Glenwood Springs on I-70

"Instead of the usual pit stop," supervising landscape architect Philip E. Flores explained, "our design team tried to provide an inspirational respite." The designers aug-

mented Grizzly Creek with artificial pools and waterfalls and an island and replaced an old gas station, orchard, fruit stand, and mobile home park with native plants. The new concrete, glass, and tile comfort station (1991, David Davis) is solar-warmed and lighted and earth-sheltered, with stepped walls, terraces, and rock gardens that harmonize with the strata of the canyon. To protect Grizzly Creek and the Colorado River, which converge here, the toilets are waterless, self-composting Clivas-Multrum devices.

Carbondale

Carbondale (1888, 6,181 feet), named for a coal mining town in Pennsylvania, became a railroad town that tapped many area coal mines. Basking in the glow of nearby Aspen, it has a handsome, healthy main street of one- and two-story buildings. The post office (1987), 655 Main Street, is a one-story, cubistic red brick building with deeply recessed banks of windows, finished at the top with an oversailing course. Inside is a mural relocated from the Glenwood Springs post office, Frank Mechau's *Wild Horse Race* (c. 1936). Mechau called the colorful tempera on canvas "a drama of forms and force, of colors and textures, with a lightning line sewing the cyclone chaos together." The old blacksmith shop (1890s), 26 South 3rd Street, is now a restaurant with a lawn sculpture contribution to Main Street. The old

D&RG depot (c. 1888), 97 North 3rd Street, now serves as an American Legion post, with the flag rising out of a red, white, and blue trash drum.

GF20 Colorado Rocky Mountain School

1953. 1493 Garfield County 108

The Bar Fork Ranch Barn (1895), "the largest log barn in Colorado," has been capped with a shiny corrugated metal roof and converted to the office, auditorium, library, and classrooms for a preparatory school. More recent additions to this ranch campus include a beehive-shaped brick and adobe art studio inspired by both Navajo hogans and the area's beehive coke ovens. Rustic log and frame construction are used in other one-story classrooms and dormitories, including two octagonal structures.

Parachute

Parachute (1886, 5,095 feet) took its name from the creek that joins the Colorado River here. The creek's forks supposedly resemble the cords of a parachute. Renamed Grand Valley between 1904 and 1980, it is the birthplace of the oil shale industry and a classic twentieth-century boom-and-bust town. Pioneer Michael Callahan used local shale to build his fireplace. He invited everyone in for a housewarming, during which his chimney caught fire. The house burned down, but Callahan and his guests had discovered "the rock that burns." The Piceance Basin area north of Parachute contains the world's largest oil shale reserves, enough to provide fuel for the United States for decades—If environmentally and financially sound methods could be found to squeeze the oil, a few ounces per ton, out of the shale.

Inflated and deflated by oil shale booms and busts over the years, Parachute grew once again after Exxon announced in 1980 its $5 billion Colony Oil Shale Project in partnership with TOSCO, another oil company. Exxon's 1982 abandonment of its project and UNOCAL's (formerly Union Oil of California) 1991 abandonment of a $650 million Parachute Creek Shale Oil Program

let this town down without a parachute. As the hardest-hit victim of the oil shale bust, Parachute now strives to capture I-70 tourists with a spiffy new visitors' center (1991).

One silver lining of the 1980s oil recession is the town of Battlement Mesa, across the Colorado River from Parachute. Planned for 25,000 oil shale workers and named for the rocky parapets rimming the horizon, it is now marketed as a retirement center, capitalizing on the first-rate infrastructure installed by Exxon during the flush times. Battlement Mesa has new sewage, library, public safety, and recreation facilities, as well as the Bea Underwood Elementary School (1982, Caudill, Gustafson and Associates).

GF21 Bank Saloon (Garfield County Bank)

c. 1890. Southeast corner of 1st St. and Parachute Ave.

The most elegant structure in town, this one-story brick corner bank with flattened-arch openings, a diapered frieze, and a corbeled cornice closed in 1937. After its rebirth as the town saloon and social center, it hosted Sunday morning services for Catholic masses and baptisms. The teller cages have been placed behind the bar, and the walk-in safe now chills beer instead of bucks.

GF22 Battlement Mesa Schoolhouse

1897, 1907. 7201 Rd. 300, at Stone Quarry Rd., next to new St. John Middle School, via Battlement Mesa Pkwy. from I-70 (NR)

This two-room school with a flagpole atop its open belfry is made of hand-hewn blocks of sandstone from nearby Stone Quarry Creek. The same stone forms a 1907 rear addition. This schoolhouse and community center was used for meetings, weddings, potlucks, rallies, and funerals. The school closed in 1957 but was restored in 1983.

Rifle

Rifle (1884, 5,345 feet), named for Rifle Creek, was originally a cow town which claimed to load more cattle into rail cars than any community in Colorado. The Rifle Bridge over the Colorado River (1909,

Charles G. Sheely), 1 mile south of Rifle off I-70 (NR), is the longest (430 feet) pinned truss auto bridge left in the state. The handsome double span has been closed to motor traffic and reserved for pedestrians.

A D&RG parlor car at the I-70 entrance road was purchased by the Chamber of Commerce for $1 and converted to a tourist center. The old City Hall, 337 East Avenue, has been converted to the Rifle Creek Museum. The United Methodist-Presbyterian Church (1890s), northeast corner of East Avenue and 4th Street, is a Queen Anne church of tawny local sandstone with a three-story belfry. The Red Lion Pub (1902), northwest corner of Railroad Avenue and West 3rd Street, has an elaborate frieze and metal-bracketed cornice atop two stories of local beige sandstone cut in large, rough-faced blocks.

GF23 Odd Fellows Hall

1895. 401 Railroad Ave. (northwest corner of 4th St.) (NR)

This ramshackle, two-story frame hall has Greek Revival aspirations in its pedimented facade. The Odd Fellows continue to meet upstairs in this unusual survivor of boom-town frame architecture, which has generally been replaced by masonry.

GF24 Post Office

1940, Louis A. Simon, OSA. Southeast corner of Railroad Ave. and E. 4th St. (NR)

The most detailed and complete of five small Colonial Revival post offices in the state is a red brick jewel, beautifully polished. Framed by two giant lilacs and brass and copper lanterns, granite steps lead to a Georgian Revival entry with a cast iron eagle perched below thirteen stars in the arched transom. Fluted wooden columns and leaded windows flank doors leading to an interior sparkling with the original brass-bordered terrazzo floor, travertine wainscoting, wood paneling, and golden oak writing stands. George Vander Sluis of the Colorado Springs Fine Arts Center painted the 1942 mural, *Colorado Landscape,* above the postmaster's office door. Beyond the style, uncommon in this part of the country, the exceptional detailing for so small and late a post office is noteworthy.

GF25 Rifle Gap State Recreation and Reservoir Area (*Valley Curtain* Site)

10 miles north of Rifle on Garfield County 325 at the junction of East and West Rifle creeks

CCC labor refined this Rifle city park, which has become a state recreation area. It gained fame as the setting for the most extravagant art happening in Colorado. New York artist Christo Javacheff, who wrapped the Pont Neuf in Paris and has decorated California coastlines, draped the canyon of Rifle Creek with a bright orange curtain. Christo and his assistants took two years to install the 1,368-by-365-foot nylon curtain across the V-shaped canyon and Colorado 13. After a lavish grand opening, however, the curtain was shredded by a harsh critic—Mother Nature.

Silt

Silt (1898, 5,432 feet) was named for the soil deposited here by the Colorado River. At the Silt Wickiup Village, Ute Indians built their traditional shelters by lashing poles to trees and covering them with animal skin and brush. Silt had wooden water pipes and only one paved street until the 1980s oil shale boom. Of several venerable frame buildings in town, the most striking is a three-story shingled Victorian structure at 777 Main Street, with a full-length veranda and a second-floor porch. Local landmarks include an old bank and the Antlers School

(1887), a two-room schoolhouse with an enclosed bell tower.

GF26 Silt Historical Park

1981. 8th and Orchard sts.

Strategically located beside the D&RG tracks and the Cactus Valley Ditch, this building collection includes the first Silt Public Library, the hand-hewn two-story log Sallee House (1914, Leander Sallee), the one-room Jake's Pool Hall, a blacksmith shop, a country store, a cow camp cabin, and agricultural, logging, and mining equipment. The Austin School (1913) is a one-roomer where twelve grades were taught.

Pitkin County (PT)

Prospectors poked into the Roaring Fork River country as early as the 1870s. Their finds gave birth to the towns of Ashcroft, Aspen, and Independence and led to the creation in 1881 of a county named for Governor Frederick W. Pitkin. After the 1893 silver crash, Aspen and Pitkin County faded, except for some ranching, haying, and coal mining. Of thirty-four mining, ranching, and railroad communities that once had post offices, only Aspen, Redstone, Snowmass, and Woody Creek survive.

In 1938 the opening of the first ski tow attracted people seeking something more than the weary little rooms at the Hotel Jerome, Aspen's only inn. André Roche, a noted Swiss skier, laid out the Aspen Mountain ski run. Friedl Pfeifer, a former director of the Sun Valley ski school, helped build the Bavarian-Highlands Lodge (1938, Gordon Kauffman), 5.5. miles up Castle Creek Road from Colorado 82. Now a private residence on the Highlands Ranch, it was designed to house potential investors as well as guests. James Bodrero, an artist for Walt Disney Studios, developed an Alpine style for the lodge.

Alpine became the dominant style for two decades. In Aspen, as in its later interpretation in Vail, it is characterized by low-pitched gable roofs, numerous horizontal wood balconies decorated with cutout trim, and wooden window shutters, often painted bright red or chocolate brown. Walls were often stucco, sometimes with false half timbering or log treatment.

World War II curtailed the ski resort business as many good skiers, including Friedl Pfeifer, joined the U.S. Army's Tenth Mountain Division of ski troopers. After the war ended in 1945, many of the division's veterans became interested in developing skiing in Pitkin County. The success of the pioneer ski lift on Aspen Mountain inspired W. V. N. Jones to develop Aspen Highlands Ski Area (1958, Fritz Benedict), 1600 Maroon Creek Road. Benedict, who, along with Austrian designer Herbert Bayer, shaped Pitkin County's renaissance, designed some of the original structures, including the triple A frame lodge of wood and glass. Its roofline is, according to Benedict, "an interpretation of an unusual nearby mountain called Maroon Bells."

Since the 1950s ski resorts have transformed Pitkin County into a national pacesetter for the architecture of affluence. Meadows rimmed by mountains provide a majestic setting which has inspired some of America's greatest architects. This silver mining region reborn as a recreation center has become a case study in the struggle to reconcile architectural creativity, historic preservation, and intense developmental pressures.

Aspen

The county seat (1880, 7,908 feet) offers architecture enthusiasts a wealth of Victoriana, Alpine shops and chalets, sleek Bauhaus-influenced structures, raw Mineshaft Modern curiosities, and various Modernist and Postmodern residences. Some of America's most expensive resort structures and private homes have been designed by internationally known architects and a notable stable of some hundred local firms.

Colorado's most affluent and architecturally distinctive town started out in 1879 as a tent-and-shack mining camp called Ute City. Silver seekers from Leadville struck pay dirt in the broad valley where the Roaring Fork of the Colorado River is fed by Castle, Hunter, and Maroon creeks. After the Utes were dispossessed, the town was platted and incorporated as Aspen. Aspen Mountain south of town and Smuggler Mountain to the east boasted fabulously wealthy mines such as the Durant, the Little Nell, the Midnight, the Mollie Gibson, and the Smuggler, which produced the world's largest silver nugget, 93 percent pure and weighing 2,060 pounds.

From the beginning Aspen seemed ambitious. Its broad (70-to-80-foot-wide) streets were laid out with a compass rather than on the stream-oriented plat of many mining camps. Townsfolk planted street trees and formed a literary society and a glee club. The Denver & Rio Grande arrived from Glenwood Springs in 1887, followed a year later by the Colorado Midland from Leadville. Aspen's population peaked in 1893 at around 12,000 as the town briefly surpassed even Leadville in silver production to become the nation's number one silver city.

After the 1893 silver crash, little was built until the late 1940s, when the ski era dawned. Newcomers acquired silver bonanza structures for back taxes unpaid since

1893. Since the 1950s steady growth has brought Aspen back from a 1930s low point of 700 residents to a 1990 population of 5,049.

Walter and Elizabeth Paepcke of Chicago established a home in Aspen in 1945. Paepcke, board chairman of the Container Corporation of America, brought the Bauhaus designer Herbert Bayer and an intellectual and social elite to town. Paepcke began quietly buying up property, hoping to control growth and restore the Victorian townscape. In an *Aspen Times* notice, he offered free paint to any residents who would confer with Herbert Bayer on color schemes. Few did. Some locals resented Paepcke and also Walter Gropius, whose town plan, commissioned by Paepcke, recommended that Aspenites "restore the best of the old, but if you build, build modern" to avoid "an antiquarian museum of tacky, nonsensical historical imitations."

Most railroad, smelter, and mine structures had vanished by 1972, when Aspen established a local Historic Preservation Committee. The Main Street and Commercial Core District (Bleeker Street to Durant Avenue between Monarch and Hunter streets) contain some 280 contributing historic buildings. More than 150 locally designated landmarks range from four-story business blocks to simple miners' homes, such as the hand-hewn Callahan Log Cabin (1885), 205 South 3rd Street; the clapboard Thomas Hynes Cottage (1885) (NR), 303 East Main, and the quaint, clapboard Italianate Cameron Cottage (1883), 201 East Hyman Avenue.

PT01 **Aspen Institute**

1949. 3rd and Gillespie sts.

The Aspen Institute originated with the 1949 Goethe Festival, an international celebra-

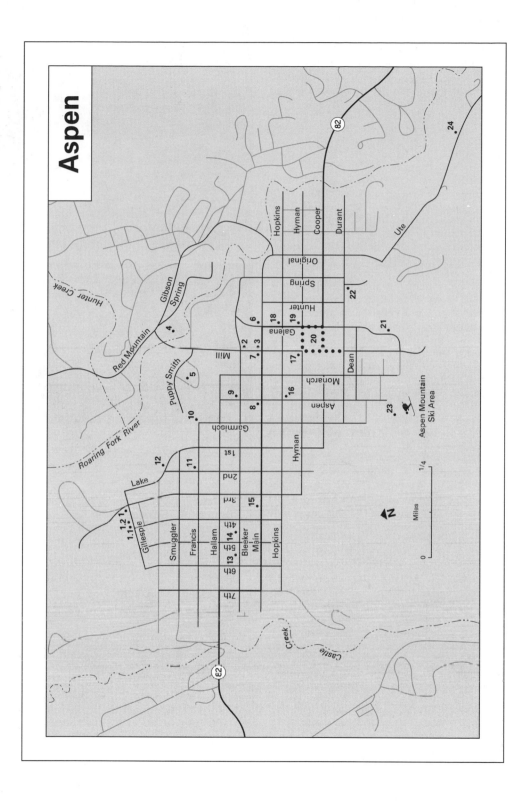

Aspen

tion of the author's birth bicentennial. By honoring the German cultural giant, the institute hoped to heal some of the wounds of World War II and acknowledge German cultural contributions. Highlighted by Albert Schweitzer's only public appearance in the United States, the conference inspired creation of an institute devoted to the arts, humanities, and sciences.

Elizabeth Paepcke and her husband recruited Herbert Bayer to design many of the institute's structures. Bayer (1900–1985) immigrated to the United States when Adolf Hitler closed the Bauhaus school. Bayer had studied mural painting with Wassily Kandinsky as well as graphic design, photography, and typography. He found design work with the Container Corporation of America, where he promoted avant-garde advertising, such as CCA's "Great Ideas of Western Man" series. After Bayer retired to California, his brother-in-law, Taliesen-trained architect Fritz Benedict, continued his work for the Aspen Institute and elsewhere in the Aspen area. Although Bayer never officially completed architectural training, he is one of Colorado's most influential Modernist master builders. His work in Europe, New York, Chicago, and Colorado and on the West Coast is documented in the Bayer Collection and Archives at the Denver Art Museum.

Following his move to Aspen in 1946, Bayer worked on designs for everything from Aspen ski posters with the famous snowflake logo to town plans and the "Ski Colorado" logo. He chaired the city-county planning commission, focusing on both new design and historic preservation. For the Aspen Institute, he designed the Boettcher Seminar Building (1953), the Marble Sculpture Garden (1955), the Grass Mound (1955), the Health Center (1957), the Paepcke Monument (1960) and Paepcke Memorial Building (1963), Anderson Park (1962), and Trustee Houses (1964). Bayer also spearheaded the 1951 creation of Aspen's International Design Institute, which strove to convince business people and corporations that good design was good business and that America needed to excel culturally as well as militarily and financially.

After Paepcke died in 1960, Robert O. Anderson followed him as the Aspen Institute's director and perpetuated and expanded the original dream. Elizabeth Paep-

PT01 Aspen Institute, Boettcher Seminar Building (top); Marble Sculpture Garden (bottom)

cke, who kept a house in Aspen until her death in 1994, spearheaded projects such as the creation of the 25-acre Aspen Center for Environmental Studies and a nature preserve around Hallam Lake.

PT01.1 Aspen Music Tent

1965, Herbert Bayer. 2000, replacement, Harry Teague. 4th and Gillespie sts.

In 1941 Walter Paepcke commissioned Eero Saarinen to design a tent large enough for a full orchestra and an audience of 2,000 people. Saarinen's orange and beige tent was a circular tensile fabric affair put up only during the summer music festival. Bayer's 1965 replacement, like the original, incorporates Aspen's fresh air and mountain scenery into the performances. Bayer landscaped the tent with small water channels recalling the once ubiquitous water ditches that provided irrigation in Aspen.

PT01.2 Joan and Irving Harris Concert Hall

1993, Harry Teague. 4th and Gillespie sts.

Next to the music tent lies what violinist Pinchas Zukerman calls "the first concert hall of the twenty-first century." To keep this 500-seat auditorium from upstaging the Aspen Music Tent, Harry Teague buried it underground behind aluminum and glass garage doors and a roof of tilted white planes that shape sound below and reflect the multiangled surrounding hills. Teague told *The New Yorker* (September 6, 1993) that he designed the $7 million hall to be a "virtually soundproof" space for listening and recording. "People have been listening to music in the tent through storms, the screeching of magpies, even a shooting," he explained. "It's lousy acoustically, but it's an icon that had to be respected. The new hall is like a cadenza to the tent. Whereas the tent is perfectly symmetrical, the hall is asymmetrical. Symmetry is the enemy of good music."

PT02 Rio Grande Transportation Center

1990, Rogers-Nagel-Langhart with Gibson and Reno. Southeast corner of Mill and Bleeker sts.

Beneath a clock tower, this design minimizes four levels of below-grade parking behind a gabled facade reminiscent of the D&RG railroad terminal that originally sat here. The garage borrows its overhanging roof and red brick and stone facade from nearby historic structures. The transportation hub, which accommodates autos, buses, and a bike trail, opens onto a civic plaza.

PT03 Pitkin County Library

1991, Caudill, Gustafson, Ross and Associates. Northeast corner of Mill and Main sts.

For this library Samuel J. Caudill, a veteran Aspen activist-architect, chose the flattened roofs, overhanging eaves, and rectangular banded windows of the Prairie Style instead of something more indigenous. The red

brick library, with its distinctive entry clock tower, shares a plaza with the 1984 Justice Center, including jails and a juvenile center, by the same architects. Confronting the buildings from across the plaza is an equestrian *Don Quixote*, made of chrome car bumpers.

PT04 Aspen Art Museum

1886. 1987, renovation, Caudill, Gustafson, Ross and Associates. 590 N. Mill St.

From Rio Grande Park a trail of outdoor sculpture wanders over the iron railroad bridge (1911) above the Roaring Fork River to the grassy grounds of the art museum, which is housed in a converted brick hydroelectric generating plant. A Modernist brick addition with clerestory windows and a corrugated metal roof typifies Samuel Caudill's sympathetic treatment of additions to historic structures, which he explains as "interjecting innovative technology and detailing, overlapping of building facades, and interplay of geometric shapes."

PT05 Aspen Post Office

1980, Copland, Hagman, Yaw. 235 Puppy Smith Rd. near Mill St.

A stark array of naked solar panels on top of a one-story, concrete block building with large glass panels may horrify fans of classical post offices. Some Postmodernists, however, fancy this example as suggesting a prototype style for the next generation of post offices—postal modern.

PT06 Pitkin County Courthouse

1891, William Quayle. 1987, rehabilitation, Gibson and Reno. 506 E. Main St. (northeast corner of Galena St.) (NR)

One of Colorado's oldest courthouses still in use blends Italianate and Second Empire influences. Art Nouveau calla lilies sprout from the mansard top of this building's crested, pilastered, pedimented, and fauxwindowed tower rising in a three-tiered pyramid. The design was blasted by an 1889 *Aspen Times* critic as an "abortive architectural aspiration" appealing only to "farmers coming to watch the swallows nesting in the gingerbread roof." The symmetrical, two-story body of the building is red brick, dressed with red sandstone trim around round-arched and square-headed windows. A silvery statue of Justice (minus her blindfold) stands in the entry pediment. The interior is in near-mint condition.

PT07　Hotel Jerome

1889. 1986, restoration, Caudill, Gustafson. 1987, addition, Hagman Yaw. 330 E. Main St. (northwest corner of S. Mill St.) (NR)

Round-arched upper windows under a frieze of recessed brick panels distinguish this three-story brick hotel, named for financier Jerome B. Wheeler, who bankrolled the $160,000 project. The hotel, with its balus-traded entry porch and a sacrosanct side-walk bench, has been the town gathering place since 1889. After the 1893 crash, a bartender bought it for back taxes and kept it open. The Paepckes leased the hotel in 1946 and began renovation. A $10 million expansion and restoration in 1986 converted the ninety modest rooms into twenty-one luxurious rooms and six suites. A sixty-six-room rear addition mirrors the original's rough sandstone trim, pink brick, and arched windows. Inside, Eastlake furniture, a pastiche of sixteen different floral wallpapers, rustic antler chandeliers, and Carrara marble bathrooms help the Jerome outshine even Aspen's newer luxury hotels, the Little Nell and the Ritz-Carlton.

PT08　Atkinson-Sardy House

c. 1892. 1980s, restoration and additions, Harry Teague. 128 E. Main St. (northeast corner of Aspen Ave.)

John W. Atkinson, who owned a brickyard at the base of Red Mountain, built his Queen Anne Style residence with walls four bricks thick. A widow's walk pokes through the cross-gabled, hipped roof beside a south side second-story porch with a bell-shaped cap. A round tower in the northwest corner borders the porch over the entry. Thomas J. Sardy, who ran a furniture store and mortuary discreetly separated by a curtain, bought the house in 1945. He worked with the Paepckes on Aspen's rejuvenation, helping to build the airport named for him.

Harry Teague added a twenty-room "carriage house." This spirited but sympathetic Neo-Queen-Anne addition uses similar red brick, sandstone trim, and shingled gable and bay ends to transform the corner property into a hotel screened by the exquisitely maintained house, garden, and evergreen trees.

PT09　Aspen Community Church (First Presbyterian Church, United Methodist Church)

1891. 200 E. Bleeker St. (northeast corner of Aspen St.) (NR)

This two-story Queen Anne Style church has a prominent battered three-story bell tower carrying an enclosed shingled belfry with louvered lancets beneath a graceful bell-shaped cap. Romanesque Revival detailing appears in walls of rough-faced sandstone from the Peach Blow quarries and large, radiating voussoirs. A truncated hipped roof has a dormer and parapeted gables extending above protruding bays on each street side, with a prominent round window on the entry facade. Above the ground-level offices and classrooms, the second-story sanctuary has semicircular pews with Neo-Gothic detailing like that in the woodwork and windows.

The church was built as the First Presbyterian Church by a congregation founded in 1886 by the Reverend H. S. Beavis. As Aspen shriveled to a town of only a few hundred, the Presbyterians and Methodists combined in 1920. Fourteen years later, a further consolidation led to its reorganization as the Aspen Community Church. This and St. Mary's Catholic Church, at 104 South Galena, are the last of Aspen's silver-age churches.

PT10 Given Institute for Pathobiology

1973, Harry Weese and Associates. 100 E. Francis St. (northeast corner of Garmisch St.)

The Paepckes donated this site for the University of Colorado's medical institute. The concrete-block building, one of Aspen's finest Modernist works, gives a playful rigor to a simple circle with angular extensions. Harry Weese, a distinguished Chicago Modernist, also designed the Lavatelli House at Snowmass and the Baird House in Aspen.

PT11 Waite House

1890. 234 W. Francis St. (northeast corner of 2nd St.) (NR)

Davis H. Waite, a schoolteacher and radical editor of *The Aspen Times,* was elected governor of Colorado on the Populist ticket in 1892. He shocked the wealthy power elite by siding with miners in bitter strikes, advocating the nationalization of businesses, and helping to make Colorado the first state to give women full voting rights. Waite returned to Aspen after one raucous term and lived in the two-story clapboard house until his death in 1900. Herbert Bayer was a later resident. In 1953 the house was sold to Robert O. Anderson, founder of Atlantic Richfield Company and longtime Aspen Institute chairman. The house now has additions and outbuildings wearing the same clapboard and shingled gables.

The Waite House is located in Aspen's West End, where silver-era cottages and mansions have been spruced up amid evolving architectural expressions of what constitutes appropriate restoration and infill. The Bruggerman residence (1987, Gibson and Reno), 401 Francis Street, is one of many attempts to update the Victorian idiom, while 120 East Francis Street (1880s; 1994 additions) is an example of a humble cottage turned into a mansion.

PT12 Bayer House

1950. 240 Lake Ave.

In the best tradition of the Modern Movement, this low, cinderblock house, now stuccoed, is simple and clean—two unadorned rectangular wings framing an interior courtyard. Closed to the street but open to the views beyond, it demonstrates the affinities between Modernism and traditional Japanese architecture.

PT13 Aspen Historical Society (Wheeler-Stallard House)

1888. 620 W. Bleeker St. (NR)

Jerome B. Wheeler's imposing, three-story Queen Anne house of red brick has a shake-shingle roof and distinctive Eastlake trim. Wheeler built the house for his wife, who still refused to budge from their Manitou Springs home. He gave Aspen the $90,000 mansion, its first smelter, its bank, and its opera house but lost most of his assets in the silver crash. In 1969 the Aspen Historical Society purchased the house as a museum and headquarters. The society, whose offices and archives are in the matching carriage house, offers house and town tours from the mansion, which occupies most of a tree-shaded block.

PT14 Webber-Paepcke House

1885. 442 W. Bleeker St. (NR)

This Second Empire home, in a block-long willow grove known as Pioneer Park, was built by Henry Webber, a shoe salesman who became a prominent businessman and a mayor of Aspen. His career was unhampered by rumors about the poisoning of his wife that circulated shortly before he married his niece. The Paepckes purchased the one-story brick mansard-roofed house as a summer home in 1945 and used the matching, attached carriage house to accommodate guest celebrities such as Albert Schweitzer and Walter Gropius.

PT15 Smith-Elisha House

1886. 320 W. Main St. (NR)

This asymmetrical collection of porches, bays, gables, and dormers rises three stories without benefit of a corner tower, the only piece missing from a picture puzzle of Queen elements. Mining man Eben Smith built this intriguing composition, which, with the matching clapboard carriage house, is now used as offices.

PT16 Hotel Lenado

1985, Harry Teague. 200 S. Aspen St. (southeast corner of Hopkins St.)

In pursuit of a regional style for the design of this hotel, Harry Teague used backwoods elements such as wooden poles, cheap siding, and bent twig furniture, which he helped select, cut, and install. He also had a hand in the masonry work on the fireplace in the 28-foot-high lobby. To blend his raw creation into the surrounding neighborhood of Victorian houses, he scaled and segmented the front facade with sunken terraces, stairways, porches, gables, and corner towers. Teague's composition combines high-tech, rustic, and Victorian elements with sophistication and wit.

PT17 Wheeler Opera House

1889, Willoughby J. Edbrooke. 330 E. Hyman St. (northwest corner of Mill St.) (NR)

Rough-faced Peach Blow sandstone walls and Romanesque Revival detailing distinguish this three-story corner landmark. A strong, banded cornice of smooth stone separates ground-floor storefront businesses from the tall, arcaded bays of the upper-level opera house. Aspen's early benefactor, Jerome B. Wheeler, lavished a fortune on the interior, and subsequent Aspenites have lionized it as proof of their early cultural proclivities. Willoughby Edbrooke, a Chicago architect noted for the design of the Old Post Office in Washington, D.C., and Denver's now-demolished Tabor Grand Opera House, worked on the Wheeler with his younger brother, Frank.

During Aspen's dim decades, the opera house was usually dark, and it suffered heavy fire damage. In 1949 the Paepckes leased it and had Herbert Bayer modernize it. Now owned by the city, it is gloriously resplendent, following a $4.5 million restoration which erased Bayer's work and other updatings to return the building to 1889. Decorative treatments include stenciling and wood graining by Grammar of Ornament, Denver. Reflecting Aspen's silver era, the elegant horseshoe balcony, gilded boxes, and leather seats shimmer beneath a huge chandelier and a beamed ceiling with silvery stars. On the more subdued exterior, Wheeler's storefront corner bank has become a splendiferous saloon with an adjacent storefront space housing Aspen's visitor information center.

PT18 City Hall (Armory)

1892. 130 S. Galena St. (northeast corner of Hopkins St.) (NR)

Aspen's factory-like armory, built in three months, hosted military drills by day and balls, festivals, and concerts at night. It served as an auditorium, gymnasium, Odd Fellows Hall, and roller rink before becoming City Hall in 1957. A soft red brick building trimmed in Peach Blow sandstone, it has a gable roof of corrugated sheet metal with hipped dormers. The second-story hall and first-floor storefronts have been carved up into three stories of small offices for city officials.

PT19 Elks Club (Webber Block)

1891. 1980s, renovation, Harry Teague. 219 S. Galena St. (northeast corner of Hyman Ave.)

Mayor Henry Webber's three-story business block has an angled corner entrance capped by a silvery dome. Peach Blow sandstone trim, half a million pressed red bricks, and a hefty metal cornice make this one of Aspen's finest landmarks. Innovative Harry Teague dutifully restored the exterior, then unleashed his creativity on a high-tech interior.

PT20.5 Aspen Mall, the Red Onion (the Brick Saloon)

PT21 Hemmeter House

PT22 The Little Nell

PT20 Aspen Mall

1970s, Hagman Yaw. 400 block of Hyman St., 300 and 400 blocks of Mill St., 400 block of Cooper St., 400 block of Galena St.

This five-block pedestrian mall is enlivened with native trees, sculpture, grass-lined watercourses, and a playground. In a mix ranging from Italianate to Postmodern, older structures abut recent ones that, encouraged by the local preservation ordinance, emulate but do not necessarily copy their elders. Mall shops include the Aspen Block (PT20.1, 1886) (NR), 301 South Galena, with an iron front, made by Keystone Ironworks in Kansas City, that rises to a corner tower with a sunburst and round arch inside an ornate pediment. Across the street, at 501 East Hyman, the Romanesque Revival Cowenhoven Block (PT20.2; 1890) (NR) showcases Peach Blow sandstone in the Silver City's finest hand-carved facade.

The Woods Building (PT20.3; 1887; 1959 rehabilitation, Fritz Benedict), 432 Hyman (northwest corner of Galena Street), is an early attempt at mixing old and new architecture. Benedict dressed up the old-timer with Neo-Victorian kickplates and transom windows as the front for a sunken mini-mall. Riede's City Bakery (PT20.4; 1885) (NR), 413 East Hyman, is one of only two remaining frame false-fronted buildings downtown. At Mill and Hyman, architect Travis Fulton and sculptor Nicholas De Wolf, an electrical engineer who helped develop microwaves, have created a valveless, computerized fountain. A block away on Hopkins, William Lipsey's Sculpture Garden is an unusual infill project, using earthworks, a fountain, and sculpture to evoke the jagged mountainscape.

The Red Onion, formerly the Brick Saloon (PT20.5; 1892, Thomas Latta, builder), 420 E. Cooper Avenue (NR), is an old-time saloon behind a Victorian storefront on the mall, where pugilists are confined these days to their portraits on the walls. Local architects Gibson and Reno rehabilitated the two-story red brick building, retaining the long, narrow barroom with its clay tile floor. The delicate Eastlake back bar rises to mansarded domes at either end, and the oak front bar is equally unusual for its Gothic arches fronting inlaid wooden flowers. Johnny Litchfield, a veteran of the Tenth Mountain Division and Camp Hale, bought the saloon and renamed it the Red Onion. Under any name it continues to be one of Aspen's most storied settings.

PT21 Hemmeter House

1972?. 1980s, remodeling, Hagman Yaw. 730 S. Galena St.

An ornate, freestanding, three-story elevator tower fronts this stepped house, which climbs a ski slope to its upper-level horizontal picture windows and balconies. Now hemmed in by condominiums, it reigned briefly as the house to end all houses in the Aspen contest for ever bigger, more palatial homes. California-Colorado-Hawaii developer and hotel magnate Chris Hemmeter razed a two-family condominium at the base of Aspen Mountain for a Postmodern mansion that architect Lawrence Yaw compared to Hemmeter's taste in hotel design, "very opulent, very ornate—explosive." Hemmeter sold it in 1988 for $16.3 million to the Marshall Field family of Chicago.

PT22 The Little Nell

1989, Hagman Yaw. 675 E. Durant St.

At the base of Aspen Mountain gondola lift, the Aspen firm of Hagman Yaw designed what was then the town's state-of-the-art luxury hotel. Named for a rich Aspen Mountain mine, this multigabled, dormered, and balconied facade is as pleasing to passers-by as to guests. Horseshoe-shaped to capture sunshine and mountain views, it shows how a large hotel can be tailored to fit a small, sensitive site. Pretentious by comparison is the six-story red brick and cast stone Ritz-Carlton Hotel (1992, Monarch and Dean), three blocks west on Durant, which parades as a late medieval manor house wrapped around courtyards. The Ritz compound re-

placed the town's first modern public lodging, the Aspen Inn (1962, Fritz Benedict and Herbert Bayer).

PT23 Aspen Mountain Ski Area

1938. South end of Aspen St.

Scandinavian miners brought skiing to Aspen, but commercial skiing did not begin until André Roche, a champion Swiss skier, proposed "a difficult course that will bring the world's greatest skiers to your door." WPA funds and labor helped build Roche Run's first lift, consisting of old steel cable and frame tram towers from the Little Annie Mine. The cable was attached to a Model A Ford engine and an eight-passenger wooden toboggan tow that resembled a rowboat. When the lift opened in January 1938, lift tickets cost 10 cents a ride or 50 cents a day. The boat tow was followed in 1946 by Lift 1, then the world's longest lift (7,904 feet). At the top of the mountain is Herbert Bayer's octagonal sun deck (1946). Aspen Mountain began to set international standards for ski areas, a trend continued in 1986 with installation of the Silver Queen Gondola. One of the boat tows, antique wooden chair lifts and tram cables, and the base of Lift 1, now National Register relics, are on display in Willoughby Park, 700 South Aspen Street, at the base of Aspen Mountain.

PT24 Benedict Building

1980s, Fritz Benedict. 1280 Ute Ave.

Hidden in an aspen grove, this one-story, raw wood, shed-roofed extension of its site is almost a nonbuilding, Along with the architect's office, it houses the Tenth Mountain Headquarters, which, among other things, operates eighteen backwoods cross-country ski huts, whose design Fritz Benedict oversaw.

Frederic (Fritz) Benedict, who studied under Frank Lloyd Wright, became acquainted with Aspen while a member of the army's Tenth Mountain Division ski troops. During a fifty-year romance with Aspen landscape and architecture that ended with his death in 1995, he developed, with his brother-in-law Herbert Bayer, an "Aspen style," exemplified by well-sited, low-slung Modernist structures of indigenous materials, notably wooden beams that often seem to fade into surrounding aspen groves. Benedict's work in Aspen ranges from the sod-roofed, low-slung Aspen Club Condominiums, 1450 Crystal Lake Road, to the Tipple Inn, 605 Dean Street, an old mine tipple site where Benedict made simple but handsome use of structural members as decorative elements.

PT25 Starwood

1962 and later. Old Cemetery Lane across Slaughter-house Bridge

Aspen's snazziest subdivision of multimillion dollar celebrity homes is a 1,000-acre enclave with an armed guard at the gate. Design standards required buried utilities and construction in materials and colors intended to match the semiarid terrain on the flank of Red Mountain. Approximately eighty homes, most hidden from their neighbors and many designed by notable architects, have been built over several decades. Lots alone sell for at least $1 million.

Bart Prince's 1992 house for Barbi Benton, the *Playboy* magazine celebrity, is a neo-Wrightian, organic composition of four pods crawling down a slope, with a dining room for 300 guests. Ted Conover, in *Whiteout: Lost in Aspen* (1991), takes readers to the 1980s home of Ritz-Carlton Hotel developer Mohammed Hadid:

Even in Aspen, $6 million buys a lot of house. It was a rectilinear mass of glass and stone, with four floors that sort of stepped down the steep mountainside and full-length balconies overlooking the valley. . . . A certain hardness still prevailed, enforced by all the glass, the many gold-plated fixtures and, especially, the marble floor. A creamy alabaster shade, it extended the length of the ground floor and was polished to a high luster. So solid and expansive was the floor that one could imagine it a natural outcropping from the mountain, responsible for the siting of the house, which had been blasted, chipped, planed, and polished down to its present perfect horizontal flatness.

PT26 Hines House

1983, Charles Moore and William Turnbull, Jr. 540 Shady Lane

Gerald Hines, the Texas developer well known as a patron of architecture, commis-sioned one of Aspen's most widely acclaimed new houses. Moore and Turnbull, who pioneered the Mineshaft Modern style, sited this home on Hunter Creek and built it with local materials around a huge spruce tree. Like many Aspen homes, this is a "party house" with many guest suites. Local architects consider it an important step in the development of an indigenous style that responds to both the setting and Aspen's mining town traditions.

PT27 Aspen Interfaith Chapel of the Prince of Peace

1969, Henighan and Gale. 70 Meadowood Dr.

The first landmark to greet anyone driving into Aspen from Glenwood Springs is said to have been inspired by wayfarers' chapels in the Alps. Its shingled spire becomes a hood over the openings of the stone bell tower. A happy wedding of stone, wood, and glass, it features stained glass windows in abstract designs by Jean Jacques Duval.

PT28 Aspen High School, Middle School, and Elementary School Complex

1965, 1972, 1991, Samuel J. Caudill. 446 Maroon Creek Rd.

Instead of sharp edges and rectangles, veteran Aspen architect Samuel Caudill used curves and circles borrowed from Native American structures, beneath domes that echo the surrounding mountains, for this complex of school buildings.

PT29 Holden-Marolt Ranch

1880s. Marolt Rd. near Castle Creek Rd. and Cemetery Lane

Part of this subdivided ranch is occupied by the Marolt Housing (1991, Harry Teague), Castle Creek Road and Cemetery Lane, a well-designed, low-budget dormitory and dining hall for seasonal workers. The Holden Silver Lixiviation Mill (1891) (NR) survives on Castle Creek Road near the bridge over Colorado 82 at the north end of town. Of this once large mill only the barnlike sampling works remains because it was converted to a barn on the Marolt Ranch. The barn was in turn converted to the Marolt Mining Museum in 1989 by the Aspen Historical Society.

PT30 Turner House

1982, John Lautner. 51 Heather Lane, off Castle Creek Rd.

John Lautner, a Los Angeles architect who is one of Frank Lloyd Wright's better-known apprentices, gave Aspen one of his free-form concrete houses. With its earth dome covered by grass, it epitomizes Lautner's propensity for curvilinear forms, the dynamic interaction of his buildings with the environment, and his inventiveness (a section of the living room pivots open to become an outdoor deck).

PT31 Aspen Music School

1880s, 1951. 1038 Castle Creek Rd.

The Aspen Music School started in an old mine structure and has had various additions. Taliesen graduates Fritz Benedict and Curtis Bessinger complemented the original low-slung, raw wood buildings clustered around ponds beside Castle Creek with simple frame and shake shingle construction. Low-pitched hipped roofs and balconies over the water lend the campus a Japanese tranquility prized by both Bauhaus and Wrightian schools.

PT32 Wildwood School

1980, Gibson and Reno. 27651 Colorado 82 (on the way to Independence Pass Rd.)

This fantasy preschool is a largely buried building with cavelike arched entries and windows, including one huge fisheye. The cavernous, organic interior is scaled to children, who play on top of the school as well as in it.

PT33 Sky View

1987–1990, Robert A. M. Stern

A notable example by a renowned contemporary practitioner in the traditional form of the American country house, this aerie combines a sympathy with its magnificent site with dramatic staging, lush interiors,

and every modern convenience. Located at the topmost reaches of Red Mountain, 1,200 feet above the town, the house commands a spectacular view of Aspen and the ski slopes. It is organized as a series of volumes in random-coursed sandstone block, stucco, and wood, with the principal rooms opening off a dramatic stair, revealing the view through twenty vertical feet of glazing that descends from the uphill north entrance. An angled wing to the west has three vaulted bays for guest suites overlooking a pool.

PT34 Independence Ghost Town and Independence Mill Site

1879–1890s. Colorado 82 (NR)

On the west side of 12,095-foot Independence Pass, prospectors found gold on July 4, 1879, in an alpine meadow near the headwaters of the Roaring Fork River. A rowdy town of several hundred residents survived as long as Independence Pass carried most of the traffic into Aspen. The pass toll road (1881) declined after the railroads arrived in 1887–1888. Attempts to revive the town under new names (Chipeta, Farewell, Sparkill, Mammoth City, and Mount Hope) faltered, although a few residents hung on until around 1900. Aspen Historical Society volunteers and the U.S. Forest Service have stabilized and roofed the remains of this ghost town, where ruins of a mill and several houses cling to the mountainside.

PT35 Ashcroft

1880–1912. 11 miles south of Aspen on Castle Creek Rd.

Silver strikes on Castle Creek in 1879 led to the founding of the first Pitkin County town. Ashcroft and its wagon road to Leadville smelters were important until 1887, when a railroad reached Aspen and it became the county's main smelter town. By 1890, Ashcroft had withered to twenty-five residents. Jack Leahey, an 1878 pioneer, poet, and self-appointed mayor, kept the town alive until his death in 1939. Ashcroft was a backdrop for a 1950s television series, *Sergeant Preston of the Yukon,* costarring the famous huskies raised by Stuart Mace, who revived the town as a haven for dog sledding and cross-country skiing. In 1974 the Aspen Historical

Society leased the townsite from the U.S. Forest Service and stabilized and roofed the structures left standing in a lush mountain meadow. This well-embalmed mining town contrasts sharply with the lavish new resorts and homes creeping up Castle Creek.

Redstone

John Cleveland Osgood, president of Colorado Fuel and Iron Company, built Redstone (1898, 7,180 feet) as a model company town where coal was made into coke for the furnaces in Pueblo. Remains of 144 of some 250 beehive ovens still line Colorado 133 in this Crystal River valley village framed by red sandstone cliffs.

For his experiment in paternalism, Osgood had CF&I's Sociological Department demolish existing shacks and shanties in 1902 and build Swiss chalets for the workers and their families. Theodore Boal and Frederick Harnois, architects of the Denver Country Club and of mansions for prominent Denverites, designed eighty-four cottages, an inn, a company store, a bachelors' lodge, a clubhouse (demolished), and Osgood's mansion. Each cottage varied in its design, color, and shingle and bargeboard frosting. Each had a lawn and vegetable patch. The Redstone Historical Museum, 364 Redstone Boulevard, is housed in a log cabin relocated from the rich Coal Basin district six miles west.

Redstone, coke ovens

PT36 Redstone Inn

1902, Boal and Harnois. 82 Redstone Blvd.

The centerpiece of John Osgood's crusade to improve workers' housing in Redstone was this forty-room boarding house for bachelor miners. Alpine-style half timbering and wood trim abound on three wings with clipped gable roofs, including a new west wing surrounding a courtyard dominated by a square clock tower. The inn, renovated and reopened in 1983, welcomes guests all year to its spacious parlors with large stone fireplaces and elegant reading, dining, and recreation rooms with oak furniture designed by Gustav Stickley. This inn had a clubhouse, theater, school, library, and hot springs plunge. Workers were expected to rise to this new environment: to dress for dinner and obey strict rules curbing profanity, gambling, and overindulgence.

PT37 Cleveholm Manor and Gatekeeper's Lodge

1902, Boal and Harnois. 18679 Pitkin County 133 (NR)

John Osgood built his own home a mile away from Redstone, up the Crystal River. The forty-two-room Tudor Revival mansion, completed in 1903 at a cost of $2.5 million, is an English manor house transplanted to a verdant mountain valley. It is built of big sandstone blocks quarried just across the river and half-timbered and shingled on the third story. Red sandstone with white sandstone trim and Tudor arches organize a fanciful, irregular composition. The lavish, well-maintained interior boasts fourteen onyx or marble fireplaces, solid mahogany woodwork, Tiffany lamps, and hand-tooled leather covering the library walls. Stone lions on gate pillars guard the 450-acre grounds, which once included a nine-hole golf course, a T-bar ski lift, and stables. A gazebo, gatehouse, and pumphouse survive. The south gatehouse has been moved to Grand Junction and opened as a bed and breakfast; the large greenhouse is now on the west side of Glenwood Springs, where its towering sandstone chimney may be seen from I-70. Osgood died at Cleveholm in 1926, twenty-three years after losing control of CF&I and Redstone to John D. Rockefeller. His home is now a splendid bed and breakfast inn.

PT37 Cleveholm Manor

Snowmass

Snowmass (1904, 6,899 feet), initially a railroad siding with livestock pens, became a post office community in 1904. The drive up scenic Snowmass Creek Valley passes scattered ranch houses, among them many old and new examples of log construction. In a spectacular mountain setting known for lavish, worldly resorts, Snowmass offers three otherworldly retreats built by idealists looking to better the human environment.

PT38 Rocky Mountain Institute

1984, Steven Conger. 1739 Snowmass Creek Rd.

This residential-office-research facility was built by many volunteers using local materials, organic forms, and active and passive solar systems. Physicist Amory Lovins and his wife, Hunter, a lawyer, founded the institute in 1982 to "foster the efficient and sustainable use of resources as a path to global security." A self-guided tour features experimental utilities, solar design, and a greenhouse in a serene and contemplative communal atmosphere.

PT39 St. Benedict's Monastery

1959, Brother Blaise Drayton. 1012 Monastery Rd. off Capitol Creek Rd., 2 miles south of Snowmass

Trappist monks (the Benedictine Order of Cistercians of Strict Observance) built the spartan green brick monastery and chapel on this 3,800-acre ranch along the headwaters of Capitol Creek. Inside the Neo-Romanesque compound, the chapel is a stark brick hall with no pews, only benches around the walls, and a minimalist altar, all under a high ceiling with raw wood beams. The monks support themselves by raising cattle, chickens, and sheep and selling their celebrated cookies. The public is welcome for mass and for morning and evening prayers, but otherwise the monks ask to be left in solitude.

PT40 Windstar Foundation

1980. 2317 Snowmass Creek Rd.

Singer John Denver, a longtime Aspen resident, founded this experimental facility to promote environmental concerns and pursue global peace. An existing ranch house was retrofitted as the solar demonstration and conference center. Buckminster Fuller designed the geodesic "biodome" (1983), where vegetables are grown year round. Other experimental shelters, including tipis, also adorn the grounds of Windstar.

PT41 Snowmass Village

1967, Fritz Benedict. 3 miles south of Snowmass

Fritz Benedict planned the original Snowmass Village for the Janss family, Los Angeles developers who also owned Sun Valley. Another Aspen architect, Samuel Caudill, has designed many of the retrofitted and new facilities, including the plaza, conference center, and Silvertree Lodge. Vacation homes are proliferating on every slope in sight. Some are notable, such as William Turnbull's Woodrun Place (1982), 425 Wood Run, and Harry Weese's Lavatelli residence (1969). A few old ranches and the Brush Creek Schoolhouse (1894), a clapboard one-room school used until 1943, survive from yesteryear.

PT42 Anderson Ranch Arts Center

1980, Harry Teague. 5263 Owl Creek Rd.

This ranch, named for its original owner, William Anderson, has been converted to a nonprofit educational foundation that teaches ceramics, painting, photography, printmaking, woodworking, and furniture design. An assortment of dilapidated log houses and barns, shoved aside by the developers of Snowmass Village, have taken refuge at the ranch. Since 1980, Aspen architect Harry Teague has restored and remodeled old structures and added new ones. "Unassertiveness and artistic messiness have been retained," *Architectural Record* put it in April 1989. Bark-sheathed porch columns, brightly painted windows, shake shingle, and metal roofs help to visually unite this offbeat campus.

PT43 Lipsey House

1982, William Lipsey. 2310 Juniper Hills Dr.

This local architect's version of an appropriate house for the Rockies is deliberately small and unassuming, conserving land, materials, and energy. The house is enlarged by clever interior and window design. Its

solar energy system does not detract from the handmade look of western ranch vernacular. Lipsey says he strove to "avoid high art pretensions" but admits that unpretentiousness could become a pretension in itself.

PT44 Snowmass Villas

1970, Ian Mackinlay and Henrick Bull. Brush Creek Rd.

These villas, stated *Architectural Record* (May 1970), "go beyond the Bavarian village fakery" of nearby Aspen and Vail by using innovations such as azure blue metal shed roofs that mirror the Colorado sky.

PT45 Spruce Lodge

1987–1991, Robert A. M. Stern. Old Snowmass Rd.

King of the hill is a huge, hotel-like estate, 9 miles up Old Snowmass Road from Colorado 82, designed for Walt Disney Company president Michael Eisner. The log lodge on a stone foundation combines the rustic forms of an Adirondack camp with a Rocky Mountain ranch. At the heart of the irregular plan is a timber-trussed living room with sandstone fireplace, French doors, and double-height windows framing views of the mountains and river.

Woody Creek

Woody Creek (1887, 7,400 feet), begun as a stop on the D&RG, did not become a post office town until 1920. The slab-sided, earthy Woody Creek Tavern, the ancient Woody Creek Schoolhouse, and trailer parks are a reality check for the resort upstream.

Mesa County (ME)

Grand Mesa—the world's biggest flat-topped mountain—gave its name to the county created in 1883. Ute was another name considered after the tribe was pushed out in 1881. Today few traces are left of the Utes except the trade beads which old-timers recover by screening sand from anthills. Euro-American settlers have transformed the dry country with irrigation ditches off the Colorado and

Gunnison rivers. The Grand River Ditch (1884, Matt Arch), a 35-foot-wide canal running 24 miles from Palisade to Fruita, made large-scale farms and orchards possible. Mesa has ranked high among Colorado counties in agricultural production since the early 1900s, gaining regional fame for its peaches. With the nuclear age, uranium became a cash crop, harvested recklessly in the 1950s and 1960s to the dismay of those now trying to clean up the radioactive mess.

Grand Junction, the county seat and metropolis of western Colorado, housed a third of the county's 1990 population of 93,145. Clifton has evolved from orchards to subdivisions, while the town cores of Collbran, Fruita, and Palisade remain more intact. Most of the county is undeveloped land, including parts of Grand Mesa and Uncompahgre national forests, Bureau of Land Management acreage, and the Colorado National Monument.

During the 1970s and early 1980s an oil shale boom fueled rapid county growth. Booms and busts in agriculture, uranium, and oil shale have created much modest worker housing, including bungalows and small, square frame houses with hipped roofs. When times were good, residents added on to these structures and installed rooftop evaporative swamp coolers to relieve the summer heat. Many original homes remain, often with traces of the water ditches and orchards which once dominated the area, and symmetrical globe willow trees, a fast-growing shade tree.

Grand Junction

The county seat, Grand Junction (1881, 4,586 feet), initially promoted as Denver West, was named for its site at the confluence of the Grand (renamed the Colorado in 1921) and Gunnison rivers. Following the removal of the Utes in 1881, George A. Crawford and others founded the town as a rail hub for the Denver & Rio Grande. The earliest pioneers lived in tents before constructing log cabins from cottonwoods growing along the river bottoms. Gunny sacks served as doors and oiled paper for windows; roofs were made of sod laced with cattails and rabbitbrush.

A lumber mill opened in 1882 and C. W. Kimball's brickyard soon afterward, enabling more permanent buildings to spring up along Colorado Avenue, the first main street. The D&RG's arrival in 1882 enabled Grand Junction to blossom as the regional supply center for a farming, ranching, and orchard region. Colorado's first sugar beet factory, opened in Grand Junction in 1899, became a uranium mill in the 1950s and

has since been demolished. The Prinster brothers' City Market grocery store, opened in the 1920s, is now a major regional chain, epitomizing Grand Junction's reign over a large western Colorado hinterland. Among Colorado cities, Grand Junction is second only to Denver in wholesale business.

Irrigation canals enabled Grand Junction, which boasts 354 days of sunshine a year, to become an oasis of green lawns, trees, and gardens. City fathers ordered the systematic planting of street trees throughout the city as sidewalks and curbing were installed. The city also honored its pioneer 1881 plat by establishing Emerson, Hawthorne, Washington, and Whitman parks. Newer parks include a riverfront greenway and Lincoln Park, with its 351-foot water slide, swimming pool, and golf course.

Brothers J. B. and W. C. Boyer designed many of Grand Junction's finer turn-of-the-century buildings, while Edward Chamberlin has done notable modern work. The oil shale boom of the 1970s is reflected in the new glass office buildings along Horizon Drive, which leads to the Walker Field Air-

Grand Junction

port (1982). Newer luxury homes can be found at the base of Colorado National Monument and on the north side of town.

A diverse regional economic base, the D&RG, the *Grand Junction Sentinel,* the Museum of Western Colorado, Mesa State College, and three hospitals have sustained Grand Junction as the largest city in western Colorado. Despite economic ups and downs, its population has grown steadily, decade by decade. A 1927 city plan by Denver planner Saco R. DeBoer anticipated a "city of at least 100,000." Grand Junction's 1990s boom may make that prediction come true for the metropolitan area.

ME01 Denver & Rio Grande Depot

1906, Henry J. Schlack; restoration, 1997–?, Edward Chamberlin. 119 Pitkin Ave. (southwest corner of 2nd St.) (NR)

The architect, brother of a D&RG vice president, also designed the railroad's Salt Lake City depot. This two story Beaux-Arts Neoclassical depot served both the Colorado Midland and the D&RG. Terracotta, colored and textured to look like local sandstone, is used for accent details on this beige brick edifice. Trackside, a two-story rounded bay contains a single-story entry portico. Square first-floor windows and round-arched second-story windows are set in recessed two-story bays divided by massive pilasters under a tile hipped roof. A 1980s restaurant addition has replaced a diner operated by the

D&RG. The once impressive oval waiting room had a double-height paneled ceiling with offices surrounding a mezzanine before the second floor was extended over the central space to expand the offices. The depot, now privately owned, retains its original golden oak woodwork, seating, and antique fixtures.

ME02 Museum of Western Colorado
(Whitman Elementary School)

1926, 1966. S. 4th St. (northeast corner of Ute Ave.)

This school, reopened as a museum in 1966, has tapestry brick panels to decorate the windowless west entry facade. The parking lot at the rear features one of the cast stone watering troughs that used to sit at the city's major intersections. The museum offers local history exhibits, a library, research collections, and tours of various sites, including Dinosaur Valley (ME03), Cross Orchards Museum (ME16), and the Rabbit Valley Dinosaur Quarry, a paleontologist's gold mine 24 miles west of Grand Junction on a marked I-70 exit.

ME03 Main Street Mall

1962, Robert Van Deusen. Between 2nd and 7th sts.

As Colorado's first main street mall project, this became a prototype for similar projects in Boulder, Denver, and other communities. Mature trees and raised landscape beds border a narrowed, curving street enlivened

ME01 Denver & Rio Grande Depot, c. 1910

by outdoor sculpture, fountains, and typical main street stalwarts—a classic, golden brick S. H. Kress and Company store with gilded trim and signage, at 546 Main, and the Decoesque Mesa Theater (1910; remodeled), 538 Main. Verner Z. Reed, Denver mining magnate, financed the Margery Building (1905), 519–527 Main Street, an elegant, two-story red brick with second-story bay windows beneath a rooftop balustrade. Next door is the two-story brick Montgomery Ward store, formerly the Fair Building (c. 1890, William Moyer). The First National Bank (1910), 115 North 5th Street (northwest corner of Main Street), is an imposing cornerstone for the mall. This five-story buff brick structure wears Neoclassical trim, including ornate first-floor pilasters, an exaggerated cornice, and antefixes. Across Main Street is a new Norwest Bank building with a gracefully curved glass entry facade mirroring a shiny chrome buffalo made of car bumpers. A grand stone arch from the demolished Canon Block is now a freestanding sculpture in the Norwest Bank parking lot.

On the former site of town founder George Crawford's home at 362 Main is the two-story, gray brick Reed Building (1908), which housed a J. C. Penney store. In 1985 it became Dinosaur Valley, a storefront branch of the Museum of Western Colorado that exhibits dinosaur skeletons and animated re-creations. Other buildings display terracotta Art Deco detail above newer, look-at-me storefronts.

ME04 Wayne N. Aspinall Federal Building (Post Office)

1915, James A. Wetmore, OSA. 400 Rood Ave. (northeast corner of 4th St.) (NR)

The post office moved to a Modernist edifice across the street in 1965, leaving various other federal agencies in this Beaux-Arts monument named for western Colorado's long-time U.S. representative. The three-story limestone building has an arcaded first floor with round-topped openings and tripartite, square-paned windows. The five arched bays on the east were added in a look-alike 1939 expansion. The cornice is topped by a balustraded parapet. Side elevations echo the main facade in general de-

sign, and a rear setback above the first floor helps light upper-level offices.

A 6-by-8-foot mural, *Harvest* (1940), by Denver artist Louise Emerson Ronnebeck, has recently been reinstalled after being lost for seventeen years in a warehouse. One of 1,100 murals commissioned for post offices by the Federal Works Agency's Section of Fine Arts, it depicts Ute Indians departing as white settlers arrive in western Colorado. It is now in the stairwell at the southwest corner of the building.

ME05 Grand Junction City Hall

1884, 1930s, 1975. N. 5th St., between Rood and White aves.

This city complex on the west half of a block shared with the Mesa County Courthouse is an architectural synthesis. The oldest section, on the south end, includes the first floor of the original Lowell Grade School. On the north end of the block, the WPA built a beige brick Moderne library, which was abandoned when the new Mesa County Library was completed. In 1975 a central section joined the two structures with remodeling that blends wire-cut brick, stucco, and glass. Tapestry brick panels like those used on another small WPA building in the complex add color and consistency to this effective integration of disparate buildings.

ME06 Mesa County Courthouse

1922, Eugene Groves. N. 6th St., between Rood and White aves.

Eugene Groves of Denver made the facade of the county courthouse a symmetrical exercise in Beaux-Arts aesthetics focusing on a grand entry with bronze doors. Smooth stone block rises two and one-half stories to a dentiled cornice. A molded cornice divides first and second levels and serves as a base for a recessed central section of the second floor, containing paired Ionic columns separating round-topped fanlight windows. The rhythm of these bays is continued across the first level and at the sides of the second level by flat pilasters that rise through the parapet. Behind is a fine buff brick addition (1974, Vanderwood and Henry) with large bays of tinted glass separated by raised brick bands.

ME06 Mesa County Courthouse

ME08.4 Moore House

ME08.6 Sickenberger House, c. 1925

ME07 **Colorado National Bank**

1985, Michael Barber Architecture. White to Rood aves. between 3rd and 5th sts.

This striking composition features an abstracted arcade of pink-tinted concrete that joins the main bank with a drive-in facility, then continues across North 4th Street to define a parking area. The rectangular buildings are faced with large, mirrored panels above bases of polished pink granite. This minimalist superblock complex responds creatively to neighboring ecclesiastical and government buildings and borrows its pink concrete color and stepped massing from the surrounding mesas.

ME08 **North Seventh Street Historic District**

1893–1929. 7th St. between Hill and Grand aves. (NRD)

A parkway whose grassy median sports antique acorn lampposts is lined with thirty-four homes that make up the county's best collection of historic dwellings. This part of the original city plat began to be developed with construction of the two-story frame Italianate Cyrus "Doc" Shores House (ME08.1; 1890), 327 North 7th Street, built as the home of a locally famous lawman. Town founder George Crawford moved from his original downtown dwelling to the more elegant Queen Anne house (1890) next door, at 337 North 7th St.

ME08.2 **R-5 High School** (Lowell School)

1925, Eugene Groves. 310 N. 7th St.

This school by a Denver architect is distinguished by yellow brick bands. The entrance has ornate columns, cross-paned windows, and an embellished overdoor. Roundels alternate with the arched windows on the second level.

ME08.3 **Bull House**

1906. 407 N. 7th St.

This two-story Mission Revival house of white brick has wide, overhanging eaves, low-pitched roofs, and a full-width front porch.

Its first-floor arcade, now enclosed, is reflected in the curvilinear parapet and attic windows.

ME08.4 Moore House

c. 1911. 433 N. 7th St.

John Moore, a prominent orchard and sugar beet farm owner, was the original owner of this stuccoed two-story house. The vernacular Mission Revival design incorporates hipped dormers, rounded parapets, and tripartite windows. The roof ends are decoratively bracketed, and beveled and leaded glass fills the rounded tops and upper sashes of twenty-five windows. Stone lions flanking the entry are recent, as are architecturally integrated rear additions.

ME08.5 Martin House

1923. 445 N. 7th St.

The Martin House is a two-story Craftsman dwelling with walls finished in Kelistone, a trade name for a mix of crushed quartz and fine pea gravel coated with stucco. The low gable roofs have wide eaves with prominent brackets. Heavy windowsills, caps, and lintels enforce the horizontal lines. The interior makes extensive use of golden oak in floors, stairs, and built-in furnishings.

ME08.6 Sickenberger House

1923. 710 Ouray Ave. (northeast corner of 7th St.)

The stucco and masonry exterior of this house exhibits strong horizontal emphasis in the broad porches and in porch and balcony railings similar to the sills and lintels. Eucalyptus panels the dining room and is used for beams in the living room, above swirl-textured plaster walls.

ME08.7 Ellison House

1921. 520 N. 7th St.

The Ellison House was built for the owner of a local lumber company who personally selected each board and supervised the meticulous detail incorporated in the construction. This frame bungalow has a full-width screened porch with tapered wood columns, a low gable roof with hipped gable ends, an attic dormer, bracketed eaves, and large, double-hung windows.

ME08.8 First Church of Christ Scientist

1929, J. Louis Ford. 535 N. 7th St.

This yellow and cream brick study in Neoclassical symmetry has a wide staircase rising to the portico, whose doors and flanking windows are framed by blind, round-arched recesses. Two stately Ionic columns support the porch beneath the dentiled cornice and pediment.

ME08.9 Talbert House

1907. 604 N. 7th St.

A granite stringcourse in the red brick at the first-story windowsill helps to hide the height of this three-story structure. Half-timbered roof and front porch gables add a Tudor touch. The interior features oak columns at the entrance to the parlor and a wide stairway baluster.

ME08.10 Brainerd House

1900. 605 N. 7th St.

This two-story clapboard Dutch Colonial has a characteristic gambrel roof and decorative shingles. The little house on the west corner of the lot, facing the side street, was originally the horse barn.

ME08.11 Moyer House

1905. 620 N. 7th St.

William Moyer was a successful banker and department store founder. A noted local philanthropist until the Depression, Moyer funded college tuition for local children, including novelist and playwright Dalton Trumbo, who portrayed life in Grand Junction in his novel *Eclipse*. Moyer's buff brick two-story house has sandstone trim and a double entry.

ME08.12 Murr House

1926. 639 N. 7th St.

The Murr House, although in the Craftsman style, departs somewhat from more standard designs in being built on pilings and including bedrooms on the first floor, eliminating the foyer, and moving the stairway to the rear of the house. The Flemish bond pattern of the brick (alternating headers and stretchers in each row) creates air space for insulation within the walls. Joints between the bricks are raked to create high relief. The intersecting gables are half timbered and roofed with the original slate.

ME08.13 Hottes House

1910. 707 N. 7th St.

This house incorporates several elements of Craftsman design: a river rock foundation, narrow clapboard siding, sandstone steps, large windows, bracketed face rafters, shingled gable ends, and sheltered attic windows.

Grandma & pa's house on Elm. st

ME09 Mesa State College

North Ave. to Elm St. between N. 12th St. and College St.

Established in 1925 in a former elementary school at the corner of 5th Street and Rood Avenue, Mesa State College has become a four-year college that enrolls some 4,000 students and occupies more than six blocks. The unpretentious campus is dominated by handsome modern beige brick buildings compatible with the original two-story, flat-roofed, golden brick Houston Hall (ME09.1; WPA, 1940). A building boom during the 1960s added many of the present twenty structures, including Tomlinson Library (1967), Walter Walker Fine Arts Center (1969), and the earth-sheltered W. W. Campbell College Center (1962). Several buildings are the work of Paul Atchison (see ME10).

ME10 Grand Junction High School

1940s, Paul Atchison. 1400 N. 5th St.

Denver architect Paul Atchison (1903–1985) specialized in Modernist, functional schools such as this. The harmonious grouping of two-story buildings in russet brick has banded jalousie windows topped by glass brick for better interior light. Covered walkways join the complex to a separate gymnasium and to an auditorium building that provides a hall for the Grand Junction Symphony.

ME11 Western Colorado Center for the Arts

1960s, Robert van Deusen; 1983, Edward Chamberlin. 1803 N. 7th St.

A leading Grand Junction architect redesigned this boxy 1960s concrete building to give it a more sculptural image. Rolling grass berms lap against the walls of the sculpture garden, which has a narrow slit entry. A strip of neon tube at the base of the complex is lit to signify an event in this privately constructed and maintained center that itself is modern art.

ME12 Gatehouse

1902, Boal and Harnois. 2502 N. 1st St. (southeast corner of Park Dr.)

The south gatehouse of Cleveholm Manor at Redstone in Pitkin County (PT37) was dismantled and moved in 1945 to Grand Junction to serve as a residence. Brothers Louis, Nunzio, and Vincent Grasso, Grand Junction's star stonemasons, relaid the building's large, quarry-face red and white sandstone blocks. The stone Tudor arches of the porch complement the vehicle gateway arch at the side of the house. Above the sandstone first floor, the stuccoed second floor has a half-timbered gable, and the flat roof of the porch serves as a small terrace for the second story.

ME13 State Home and Training School (Teller Institute for Indians)

1886. 2800 Rd. D

U.S. Senator Henry M. Teller helped open this school for Ute Indian children whose enrollment peaked in 1907 at 270 students. The 160-acre, tree-shaded campus was converted to a state home and training facility for the mentally and physically impaired in 1920. The pastoral campus is centered on the original two-story building of the Teller Institute with its two-story Doric portico. This noble and prevailing elder is surrounded by smaller new buildings of the same light-colored brick.

ME14 **Colorado National Monument**

1911. 2 miles southwest of Grand Junction via Colorado 340

John Otto, who lived as a hermit in Monument Canyon, long and loudly crusaded for designation of the towering sandstone sentinels overlooking the Colorado River valley near Grand Junction as a national monument. Otto was an eccentric brought before the courts three times for allegedly attempting to assassinate Colorado governors. Nevertheless, he found allies who helped win federal designation for this spectacular national monument. Otto became the first monument supervisor at a salary of $1 a month. With his burros and dynamite, he laid out many of the existing trails within the monument. Rimrock Drive, which follows one of Otto's foot trails, is a graceful, cliff-hanging highway with natural sandstone tunnels. Chunks of the handsome red stone serve as roadside retaining walls. This two-lane paved road was a project of the New Deal Civilian Conservation Corps, which paid unemployed young men $35 a week to build it.

ME14.1 **Visitors' Center**

1963. West entrance to Colorado National Monument

Red sandstone walls and low gable roofs form this contemporary Wrightian structure sited below the parking area and at the edge of the mesa. The center is the work of Grand Junction's famous stonemasons, the Grasso brothers.

ME14.2 **Chief Ranger's House**

1935, William G. Carnes. North side of the Visitors' Center

National Park Service architect William Carnes designed an unusually clean, handsome, gabled cottage that was skillfully executed by WPA labor in red sandstone excavated during the construction of Rimrock Road. This residence is part of the Saddlehorn Historic District (NRD), which includes the Saddlehorn Campground Comfort Station (1937, William G. Carnes). Sturdy sandstone chunks, which are stepped at the corners, and a cedar shingle gable roof with eaves and exposed rafter ends make this restroom a good example of rustic design. Even the original wrought iron hardware and plank doors survive. The historic district protects humbler service buildings, also characterized by red sandstone, red tile roofs, and labor-intensive WPA and CCC craftsmanship.

Clifton

In 1890 the D&RG built a station around which sprouted Clifton (1900, 4,710 feet), a fruit-growing town. In recent decades Clifton has become Grand Junction's fastest-growing suburb as orchards were bulldozed for the Coronado Shopping Mall and residential subdivisions.

ME15 **Kettle-Jens House** (Anderegg House)

c. 1907. 498 32 Rd. (NR)

The roofline, with its intersecting gables and pyramidal tower, distinguishes this Queen Anne house. Gable ends on the north, west, and east sides have recessed arches typical of the Shingle Style framing the second-story windows. After being moved to this site, the dwelling was restored during the 1970s, although synthetic siding still smothers the original clapboard.

ME16 **Cross Orchards Museum**

1909. 3073 F Rd. (NR)

On 243 acres acquired by heirs of the Red Cross Shoe fortune, the Red Cross Land and Fruit Company was formed in 1909 as a demonstration scientific orchard. Unimpressed, coddling moths and woolly aphids chewed up the profits of one of Colorado's largest apple orchards, which was subsequently subdivided and sold at auction in 1923. Farm buildings, including a huge, stepped-gabled barn, a blacksmith shop, a bunkhouse, and packing sheds, have been preserved in a 24-acre museum, which exhibits vintage road building equipment and horsedrawn farm machinery. The original farmhouse was razed, but the summerhouse stands. This branch site of the Museum of Western Colorado is now hemmed in by new subdivisions.

Ca. 1950-55 — Sold for ^$7,000,—

Palisade   *Palisade Peach Farm*

The famed peach orchards of Palisade (1891, 4,727 ft,) are planted on the sloping, well-drained land at the sheltered head of the Grand Valley. Between 1940 and 1960, Palisade produced a million bushels of peaches a year, but by the 1980s the figure had fallen to around 100,000 as orchards gave way to suburban growth.

ME17 Smith House

1899. 588 W. 1st St. (northeast corner of Elberta Ave.)

Queen Anne elements sparkle on this three-story dwelling, wrapped by a porch with grouped Ionic columns. The porch lines, pedimented entry, and ornamental brackets are repeated in the third-story overhanging gables and dormers. A wooden sunburst and a Palladian window bask in the facade gable end. Other fine homes on the street include John A. Port's two-story frame house (1905), at 398 West 1st Street, the first dwelling in Palisade to have indoor plumbing.

ME18 Palisade Livery Saloon

c. 1890. 215 Main St.

This two-story brick structure seems narrow because the first story is very tall and the building is 150 feet deep. The livery doors have been replaced by a storefront beneath upstairs windows with stone lintels and sills and a bracketed, pressed metal cornice. Inside, a 42-foot-long front bar stretches beyond a majestic mahogany back bar with tapered Ionic columns and a dentiled cornice echoing the front facade's oversailing cornice.

ME19 Bradshaw House

1908. 405 W. 1st St.

J. R. Bradshaw, a successful orchard owner and realtor, built one of the more substantial-looking homes along Palisade's main street. This two-and-one-half-story brick house has a hipped roof with projecting gables on east and north sides. A Corinthian-columned porch extends from the east bay across the north facade to end in a pedimented gable at the northwest corner above the entry. The sloping porch roof is supported by Composite columns atop a solid brick balustrade capped in stone. The clapboard barn has been converted to a four-car garage.

we were baptised here.

ME20 United Methodist Church

1907, Thomas P. Barber. 365 Main St.

Thomas Barber, a noted Colorado Springs architect, designed elegant Mission Revival churches like this throughout Colorado. Two domed towers rise above the curvilinear parapet on the asymmetrical facade. Round arches repeat in windows and doorways and in the open arches of the bell towers. Smaller windows flank the large, central stained glass window, which portrays Jesus conversing with the Samaritan women at the well. The beige brick walls are enhanced by narrow, battered buttresses.

ME21 Denver & Rio Grande Depot

c. 1907. Northwest corner of Peach Ave. and 3rd St.

This one-story Beaux-Arts Neoclassical depot resembling an enclosed pavilion has beige brick walls and large, recessed leaded glass windows under wide, bracketed eaves. A freight depot forms an elegant north wing, but a residence tacked onto the west side as a later addition spoils the picture.

ME22 Grand Valley Canal Dam

1916. 8 miles east of Palisade on I-70

This Colorado River dam feeds a 67-mile-long canal system that irrigates the Grand Valley, as the valley of the Colorado River between Palisade and the Utah border is called. The first set of imported German rollers (the huge cylinders that control the flow at the top of the dam) lies at the bottom of the Atlantic Ocean, part of a cargo sunk by British warships during World War I. Graceful arches above the seven German-made roller gates support a bridge and four tile-roofed towers containing the mechanisms to raise and lower the rollers. The dam diverts water into irrigation canals cut through sandstone cliffs. The $4.5 million project, the third roller dam in the United States, was begun in 1909 by the Bureau of Reclamation, but a clash between Secretary of the Interior Richard Ballinger and conservationist Gifford Pinchot held up the project for years.

ME23 Convicts' Bread Oven

1911. Colorado 65, 7.66 miles east of I-70 (NR)

Between 1899 and 1926 Colorado put prisoners to work building roads all across the state. A relic of that program is this concrete structure on a timber foundation, resembling an adobe oven, which was used to bake bread for the thirty-man road gangs and their guards. The roof is 4 feet high at the center, curving to 3 feet 3 inches at the walls. When the structure was hot, the coals were raked out and bread was inserted. The opening was sealed by a door and the round smoke hole in the roof was covered while the bread baked in the diminishing heat.

Collbran

Collbran (1891, 5,987 feet) was named for Henry Collbran of the Colorado Midland Railroad in the vain hope of attracting a rail line. A ranching town and former stage stop, It retains a quaint, false-fronted main street. The most impressive structures are the Collbran General Store (c. 1900), northwest corner of Main Street and Colorado 330, a two-story frame building with a dormered gambrel roof, and the clapboard Collbran Congregational Church (1903), 202 West High Street. The church has a diminutive rose window, fishscale shingles on the one fancy dormer, and various clapboard additions. A fine terracotta frieze inscribed with the name Stockman's Bank (1916), 124 Main Street (southwest corner of Short Street), crowns what is now the public library, a beige brick box with a round-arched entry flanked by round-arched windows with fanlights. The Collbran Auditorium (1910), northwest corner of Main Street and Colorado 330, is a large, barnlike frame structure with a curvilinear parapet topping the false

front. Built to host the Stockman's Ball, it is now used as a theater.

Whitewater

Whitewater (1883, 4,660 feet) is a ranching center named for rapids in the Gunnison River west of town. The barren badlands between Whitewater and Delta inspired a local wag to post a homemade sign, "Stinking Desert National Monument." The Bradbury Ranch (1895, Daniel Bradbury), 4614 U.S. 50, has a ranch house and outbuildings of local Dakota sandstone on the working ranch now operated by Walter Bradbury.

The former Whitewater Hotel (1888), 140 Short Street, a two-story frame building, has been converted to a private residence with an enclosed porch across its front. Next door to the east is the false-fronted frame Snider's General Store (1888), whose painted lettering remains just visible in the peeling facade. Coffman's Ranch (1884), 1 mile west of Whitewater, a two-story frame house with its gables decorated in fancy bargeboards and wood trim, was a pioneer cattle ranch and fruit farm in now ebbing Whitewater.

ME24 Land's End Shelter Cabin

1939, CCC. 10 miles east of Whitewater atop Grand Mesa on the Land's End Road

From Whitewater, the scenic Land's End dirt road twists up Grand Mesa to attain spectacular views. At the cliff top sits a rough shelter

with moss-covered native volcanic rock walls, a stone floor, and log ceiling beams. An observation deck overlooks the canyon lands of western Colorado. Nearby is a rustic stone eight-hole outhouse.

Fruita

Christened for the orchards that made Mesa County the fruit basket of Colorado, Fruita (1884, 4,498 feet) was platted by William E. Pabor, a D&RG publicist and one of Colorado's early proponents of agriculture. Pabor promoted Fruita as a producer of almonds, apricots, apples, grapes, nectarines, and peaches. Plagued by insect pests, alkali seepage, and over-irrigation, many of the orchards were removed during the 1920s and 1930s. A traffic circle at the intersection of Mesa and Aspen avenues defines a round park with a 15-foot-tall avocado-green *Tyrannosaurus rex* (1950s), constructed of stucco and restrained by a leg iron.

ME25 Fruita Junior High School

1936, Temple Hoyne Buell. Northwest corner of E. Pabor Ave. and N. Maple St.

American Architect and Architecture (October 1937) spotlighted this WPA Moderne beige brick, two-story school distinguished by its semicircular entry pavilion. Tall, narrow windows at the landing level illuminate the stairwell while window bands light the classrooms. Inside, innovative ramps replaced stairs, and lockers were recessed into the walls.

ME25 Fruita Junior High School

ME26 Fruita Library (Fruita Museum)

1938, WPA. 432 E. Aspen Ave.

Built as a museum, this tiny stone cottage with a red tile roof is now a miniature library that looks like the setting for a fairy tale.

ME27 Sacred Heart Catholic Church

1921, Nunzio Grasso, builder. 513 E. Aspen Ave. (northeast corner of Maple St.)

Nunzio Grasso, an Italian immigrant who became a stonemason in Grand Junction, built the walls and round arches of this church with blocks of rough-faced sandstone from the Little Book Cliffs Quarry. The church flaunts Florentine stained glass windows above and colored, leaded, and etched glass in the basement windows that came from its 1890 predecessor. Rose windows adorn the diminutive transepts. An oversized central tower has the entrance in its base.

Rio Blanco County   (RB)

Rio Blanco County (1889) is named for the White River, which flows through both Meeker and Rangely, the only sizable towns. Approximately 6,000 people reside in this rural county, which had a considerable prehistoric population. Among many pictographs, fortifications, and dwellings of the Fremont Culture, the Duck Creek Wickiup Village, 36 miles south of Meeker (NR), is the largest reported in Colorado. Archaeologists have excavated the remains of eleven wickiups, made of juniper or piñon poles braced against tree trunks. Wickiups were generally 4 to 6 feet high and 6 to 10 feet in diameter. The boughs or skins that would have covered these poles are gone, but thick mats of shredded juniper bark remain on the floors, along with fire pits.

The Utes, who also left art and artifacts at some of this county's many archaeological sites, here offered their last effective resistance to the white invasion of Colorado. They defeated Major Thomas Thornburgh and his troops near Yellow Jacket Pass, preventing them from rescuing Nathan Meeker at the White River Ute Indian Agency, where Meeker and ten civilian employees were slaughtered in 1879. Quick U.S. Army retaliation crushed the Utes, who were forcibly relocated to Utah and two small reservations in the southwest corner of Colorado.

Meeker

The county seat (1885, 6,249 feet) was named for Nathan Meeker, who was found after the Ute attack on the White River Ute Indian Agency with a barrel stave driven through his throat. After this bloody episode and the ouster of the Utes, an army cantonment here evolved into a pleasant, tree-shaded town, the hub of the White River valley, an unusually green and pastoral place by Colorado standards and a prosperous sheep, cattle, and hay raising area. The Flat Top Mountains in nearby White River National Forest are a hunting, fishing, and camping haven after the snow melts in June.

Meeker's main street might be a Hollywood set, with its antique acorn streetlamps and vintage hotel, cafe, bank, and drugstore. The beige sandstone used for many of these buildings is from the bluffs northwest of town. Conspicuously absent is a railroad station. No railroad ever reached Meeker, sparing it the usual pattern of speculation, boom-and-bust cycles, and industrial development. Very little has been demolished, and most buildings are still used in their original capacity. City Park, a rural riverside park, has three log cabins ranging from a 6-foot-high, dirt-roofed cabin to newer, larger models, all moved from outlying locations.

RB01 **Meeker Elementary School**

1939, WPA, Harry Pollard, construction superintendent. Main St. to Park Ave. between 4th and 5th sts.

WPA craftsmen shaped local sandstone for the exterior walls and trim of this Streamline Moderne school building. Alternating light and dark sandstone is used to subtly shape openings, stringcourses, and parapeted bays. This simple structure has aged beautifully, as has the Junior High School (1924, Robert K. Fuller), 555 Garfield Avenue, with its hammered, rough-faced sandstone walls rising to a slight parapet.

RB02 **Rio Blanco County Courthouse**

1933. Main to Park sts. between 5th and 6th sts.

One of the least pretentious and most pleasing Colorado courthouses, this horizontal, beige sandstone structure of two and one-half stories received closely matched additions in the 1950s. Many original fixtures survive, including the stainless steel lanterns on pilasters flanking the stepped entry pavilion.

RB03 **First National Bank**

c. 1904. Southwest corner of 5th and Main sts.

Unusually sensitive renovation marks this corner bank building, distinguished by a huge new round-arched entry reminiscent of Louis Sullivan's work. The beige brick of the old two-story bank is used for a new shell incorporating some of the old sandstone trim.

RB04 **Meeker Hotel**

1896, 1905, I. G. Mitchell. 560 Main St. (NR)

Round, fanlighted windows and a corbeled cornice distinguish this two-story, tripartite

RB04 Meeker Hotel

structure. The recessed center section with its wrought iron balcony was given matching wings in 1905. The inscription "R. S. Ball" on the entry parapet commemorates the original owner, Reuben S. Ball, who had a double fire wall of brick built into his hotel. The building remains relatively little changed outside. Inside, it is decorated with memorabilia from Vice President Theodore Roosevelt's stay during his 1901 hunting trip. I. G. Mitchell, a local carpenter-contractor, designed and built all three sections. Similar round-arched windows and fanlights suggest that he may have also constructed the two-story, red brick Odd Fellows Hall (1896) at 400 Main. Like the hotel, this hall has ornate brick trim, including first- and second-story corbeling, and brick pilas-

ters that spring into second-story brick arches.

RB05 A. Oldland and Company Store
(Hugus and Company Block)

1891. 1911, expansion and remodeling, William E. and Arthur A. Fisher. 574–594 Main St. (southeast corner of 6th St.)

This beige brick two-story commercial block with foundation and trim of local sandstone was built as part of a northwestern Colorado department store chain. It remains a department store with a wooden floor, 20-foot-high pressed metal ceiling, and golden oak display cabinets. Transomed storefronts and large, paired second-floor windows flood the store with daylight.

RB06 White River Cantonment

1882. 565 Park St.

The army post established after the Meeker massacre included primitive, low-slung barracks built with square nails and cottonwood logs. The old officers' quarters now houses the White River Museum. The parade grounds are occupied by the county courthouse (RB02). Another officers' quarters, 587 Park Street, became the office of the town newspaper, the *White River Review,* then the public library, and is now a private residence.

RB06 White River Cantonment

RB07 St. James Episcopal Church

1889. 386 4th St. (southeast corner of Park Ave.) (NR)

This picture-perfect Queen Anne Style church has a shingled, mansard-roofed open tower housing a bell from the Blymer Bell Foundry of Cincinnati. The church's rough block base and diminutive buttresses of tawny sandstone are topped with contrasting shingle cladding. Repetition of a triangle and Gothic arch motif in the facade promotes a subtle harmony, undisturbed by the sympathetic sandstone and shake-shingle addition.

RB08 Trappers Lake

53 miles east of Meeker on Rio Blanco County 8

This was the prototype for U.S. wilderness areas, thanks to U.S. Forest Service Recreation Engineer Arthur H. Carhart. Carhart, a pioneer landscape architect for the Forest Service, fought in the 1930s to persuade his superiors that roads and development should be banned on the shores of Colorado's second largest natural lake.

Coal mining magnate John C. Osgood hired W. L. Pattison to build the three Trappers Lake Cabins (1886), of hewn logs with notched corners, as a summer retreat. Two cabins remain, now used by the Colorado Division of Wildlife, which has made Trappers Lake a fish hatchery for native cutthroat trout. The north cabin, resting on a stone foundation, has boxed eaves and boxed bargeboard.

Rangely

Rangely (1884, 5,224 feet) remained a small ranching town until the 1902 opening of the Rangely Field, the sixth largest oil field in the United States. As the hub of oil production for northwestern Colorado, Rangely has become a jumble of quonset huts and other prefabricated construction. Main Street's old timers are the Nichols Store (1910) and the Queen Anne Style Nichols House (1920) behind the store. The Rangely Schoolhouse Museum (1913), 434 Main Street, is a one-room clapboard schoolhouse with an open bell tower and a boulder of oil shale on exhibit in the front yard. In contrast is the dramatic Postmodern Rangely High School (1986, Caudill, Gustafson and Associates), 234 Jones Avenue.

RB09 Kenney Ranch House

1893. 5 miles west of Rangely on Colorado 64

Bricks for this two-story Queen Anne house were made on site with antique equipment still on the grounds of this cattle and hay ranch. The dwelling flaunts Carpenter's Gothic trim in the oversized front gable and on the front porch.

RB10 Carrot Man Pictographs

11.6 miles south of Rangely on Rio Blanco County 23, then turn west on Moon Canyon Rd. and go .3 mile to a Bureau of Land Management sign by a rock overhang over a small gully

Among pecked and painted figures on this site under a rock overhang the elongated "carrot men" are most conspicuous. The pictographs (rock paintings), painted in red hematite on a stone outcropping, are distinctly anthropomorphic work of the Fremont Culture. (Illustration, p. 5)

RB11 Cañon Pintado

Colorado 139, 12 miles south of Rangely on Colorado 139 (NR)

A marked highway stop and sign welcome visitors to this unusually accessible Native American site, inhabited by Fremont people from approximately A.D. 500 to 1150. Along the self-guided Dragon Trail walking tour lie four pictographs and petroglyphs (rock carvings), seven rock shelters, and three granaries.

In 1776 the Dominguez-Escalante expedition marveled at these paintings, and Father Silvestre Escalante, in his diary, christened the area Cañon Pintado (painted canyon). A central figure is Kokopelli, the humpback flute player who also appears in Arizona and New Mexico rock art. A symbol of a vibrant and joyful Native American culture, Kokopelli has become a popular figure with modern-day southwestern artists.

Moffat County   (MF)

The Moffat Road, which began as the Denver, Salt Lake & Pacific and became the Denver & Rio Grande, never reached the last two destinations incorporated into its original name. But it did get to Craig, which became the county seat when the northwest corner of Colorado became Moffat County in 1911.

Since rail passenger service ended in the 1950s, U.S. 40 has kept people coming and going. The county's railroad and highway architecture are notable, although both routes are lined by dead and dying towns. Paralleling U.S. 40 are several abandoned stretches of the original route, the first paved transcontinental highway.

Second in size only to Las Animas County, Moffat is thinly settled with scattered cattle, hay, and sheep ranches. Coal, which initially attracted the railroad, is still a major industry. Monstrous open-pit mines such as the Trapper Mine south of Craig are served by new D&RG spur lines and hundred-car coal trains.

Oil and natural gas are likewise major products, and a 1950s and 1960s uranium boom also boosted the Maybell area. Tourism, particularly white water canoeing, kayaking, and rafting, as well as hunting, is a lively part of the economy. Dinosaur National Monument occupies more than 210,000 acres on the western edge of the county, spilling across the Utah line. Architectural gems there include the museum, visitors' center, and glass-enclosed fossil excavations. Several turn-of-the century homestead ranches have been preserved as National Register attractions within the national monument and in Brown's Park.

Craig

The county seat (1889, 8,113 feet) was named for the minister who started the handsome First Christian Church, 601 Yampa Avenue. Churches notwithstanding, Craig became a "yee-haw" Saturday night town for cowboys, railroad workers, and oilfield roughnecks, with stops such as the still rowdy White Horse Inn and Popular Bar. Yampa Avenue, the main north-south street, is a fairly intact turn-of-the-century commercial strip starting at the railroad depot and intersecting with Victory Way, as U.S. 40 in Craig was called in honor of U.S. 40's national designation as the Victory Highway. A now rare Ben Franklin dime store, in the original standard Streamline Moderne, is still in business at 6th and Yampa. East of town the U.S. 40 strip offers vintage roadside vernacular—a Dairy King and a drive-in theater, on U.S. 40 at 4th Street, now attended only by tumbleweeds, although the projection booth has been converted to a Wrightian residence.

Craig experienced a boom in the 1970s

Craig, Colorado-Ute Electric Association plant under construction

with the opening of the Colorado-Ute Electric Association power plant and a sharp increase in coal mining. Although originally platted as an orderly grid, it is now a sprawling town, dominated by signs for fast food, supermarket, and convenience chains. The horizon is pierced by the tallest smokestacks in Colorado—three 600-foot Colorado-Ute stacks (1967), complete with blinking red lights. Hillsides to the south are scarred by the Trapper strip mine, whose huge boom extracts coal from open-pit mines. Although topsoil and vegetation have been reinstated over mined-out swaths of the landscape, the spectacle is hardly picturesque.

MF01 Visitors' Center (Pullman Car *Marcia*)

MF01 **Visitors' Center** (Pullman Car *Marcia*)

1906, The Pullman Palace Car Company. 341 E. Victory Way at entrance to City Park (NR)

Beneath a drab, Pullman green exterior lies the exquisite private rail car of tycoon David H. Moffat, now protected by a Carpenter's Gothic train shed (1992, Robert Ralston). The car, donated by the D&RG to Craig in 1953, has African mahogany woodwork even for the berths tucked into the ceiling above stained and leaded glass windows, which are particularly fine in the water closet. Notable appointments include large leather chairs and couches, a ceiling-mounted brass compass, copper chandeliers, and a portrait of Moffat. With its observation platform, dining room, private rooms, servants' quarters, kitchen, and trunk room, this is a mansion

on wheels which Moffat named for his daughter.

MF02 **Museum of Northwestern Colorado** (State Armory)

1922, John J. Huddart. 590 Yampa Ave. (southwest corner of 6th St.)

Like most of the nineteen other state armories, this is a variant of a standard 1921 design attributed to Denver architect John J. Huddart. The two-story building on a rectangular plan shows a Mediterranean influence in its recessed central bay, with a pilaster-flanked, inset entry and arcaded second-story windows between twin square towers. In Craig, the tops of these towers were removed around 1950 because of problems with leaking. The two-story, yellow brick building with red brick trim has less terra-cotta ornament than most of its brother armories, although that material is used for an elegant side- and top-lighted entry and the building's identifying inscription. Behind a stepped parapet, the main roof is vaulted with a bowstring truss. The interior, converted to a museum in 1991, features a large exhibition space in the former drill hall, overlooked by a balcony.

MF03　Denver & Rio Grande Depot
(Denver & Salt Lake Depot)

1916, Joseph W. Roeschlaub, builder. 304 Yampa Ave.

This is a twin of the depot in Hayden, a single-story, red pressed brick Prairie Style station. In crowing about the new depot, *The Craig Empire,* October 11, 1916, concluded that "the work of removing the present 'depot' will be quite simple as all that will be necessary is for an engine to hook up to the two cars and move them down the track." Stripped of its red tile roof, the "new" depot is now abandoned and deteriorating.

MF04　Moffat County Courthouse

1917, William N. Bowman. 1963, Nixon and Jones. 221 W. Victory Way

A modern courthouse similar to Lester Jones's Usonian creation in Cañon City (Fremont County, FR16), this three-story, red brick cubistic composition has copper fascias and trim and recessed and cantilevered spaces. A look at the backside reveals how the newer structure incorporates and hides Bowman's original building of rough-faced sandstone.

Brown's Park

This broad valley on the Green River, also known as Brown's Hole, was a rendezvous point for fur trappers. Fort Davy Crockett (1838–1844), on the east bank of Green River in Brown's Park National Wildlife Refuge, was described by Thomas Jefferson Franham in 1839 as "a hollow square of one-story log cabins, with roofs and floors of mud constructed in the same manner as Fort William [Bent's Fort]. Around there we found the conical skin lodges of the squaws of white trappers." Only an archaeological site remains. Brown's Hole was also a hangout for outlaws such as Butch Cassidy (George Parker) and the Sundance Kid (Harry Longabough), who spent some time at the extant ranch of Anne Bassett, the queen of cattle rustlers.

MF05　Two-Bar Ranch

c. 1895. 1 mile south of Colorado 318 in Brown's Park National Wildlife Refuge (NR)

This is a remnant of the once vast cattle ranch of James S. Hoy with headquarters on the Little Snake River in Wyoming. By 1910 it had become a part of the extensive holdings of the Haley Livestock and Trading Company, one of the largest cattle operations in Colorado and Wyoming. Some of the original construction material may have been salvaged from Fort Davy Crockett. Today the buildings are deteriorated, with neither windows nor interior finish, but the hewn log bunkhouse and two-room ranch house continue to stand among several log outbuildings and pole corrals as remnants of the ranching past.

MF06　Old Ladore School

1910. 1.5 miles west of Colorado 318 beside the Green River in Brown's Park National Wildlife Refuge (NR)

A 50-by-30-foot hewn log schoolhouse with a hip-roofed open bell cupola and rear brick chimney commemorates efforts to civilize the wildest corner of Colorado. The school housed Saturday night dances and Sunday morning church services. Abandoned as a school in 1947, it is still used as a community center. Nearby lie the Ladore Cemetery and the log cabin built by Frank Myers to house children from outlying areas while school was in session.

Dinosaur

Dinosaur (1946, 5,900 feet), known as Artesia until 1966, caters to tourists headed for nearby Dinosaur National Monument with wonders such as the Dino Freeze Drive-In,

U.S. 40 and Colorado 64. This rural interpretation of a big-city fast food restaurant specializes in "dino-burgers" and huge frozen concoctions to help acclimate travelers to the high desert.

MF07 **Tourist Information Center**

1990, Michael Brendle Architects. U.S. 40 and Colorado 64

Reflecting prefabricated construction common in the area, this colored precast concrete structure has a corrugated, galvanized metal backside. The facade is decorated by three large panels of dinosaur glyphs mounted above the doors. Concrete fins protruding from the facade serve as exterior exhibit panels. This striking welcome station greets tourists on U.S. 40, which between Dinosaur and the Utah line offers only a few abandoned motels and cafes that are now sinking back into the sand and sagebrush.

Dinosaur National Monument

President Woodrow Wilson in 1915 set aside 80 acres around a dinosaur bone quarry in Utah as a national monument that was expanded into Colorado by President Franklin Roosevelt in 1938. Primarily semiarid land with extreme temperature fluctuations, the 326-square-mile site includes the spectacular canyons of the Yampa and Green rivers, which cut their way through the red, yellow, and beige sandstone to a rendezvous at Echo Park. This monument became a battlefield during the 1950s when conservationists stopped a Bureau of Reclamation dam, a victory celebrated by Wallace Stegner in *This Is Dinosaur* (1955).

Between about A.D. 1000 and 1150 the Fremont people lived here in pit houses and pecked petroglyphs into rock formations. In 1776 the Dominguez-Escalante expedition forded the Green River about two miles from the quarry site. Fossils excavated from the dinosaur bone quarry since 1908 have provided much insight into the Jurassic period.

MF08 **Quarry Visitor Center**

1958, Richard Hein of Ansen and Allen. Utah 149, 7 miles north of U.S. 40

A drastic departure from the National Park Service tradition of rustic styles is this International Style enclosure for the quarry. The San Francisco architect enclosed dinosaur bones and excavation tools with a butterfly roof and glass curtain walls that take advantage of the natural light. A drum-shaped concrete visitors' center serves as the entry. Accessibility for the disabled has required modifying stairs and ramps, but public spaces retain their original layouts and birch veneer paneling.

The museum complex includes the Douglass Workshop and Laboratory (1920) (NR), a small building, built into the hillside, of coursed rubblestone with a flat dirt roof. It commemorates Earl Douglass, a geologist, paleontologist, and botanist who discovered this rich dinosaur dig in 1908. Douglass excavated some 70,000 pounds of fossils for patron Andrew Carnegie's museum in Pittsburgh before active quarrying ended in 1924.

MF09 **Chew Ranch**

1902–early 1970s. U.S. 40, 2 miles east of the Utah line (NR)

Rancher Jack Chew homesteaded here on Pool Creek in 1910, building first a dugout, which still exists, then a hewn log ranch house (1940) and outbuildings with gable and shed roofs. His son Rial Chew ran the ranch until the 1960s. Now abandoned, the spread has been preserved as ruins within the Dinosaur National Monument, as an example of typical ranch architecture.

Lay

Several frame buildings survive in Lay (1881, 6,170 feet), including one barn with the town's name painted on the roof to attract passing pilots, a standard practice in the early decades of the air age.

MF10 **Edwin C. Johnson Boyhood Home**

1910. 6 miles west of Lay on the north side of U.S. 40

This one-room homestead shack has been transformed into a museum and memorial to one of Colorado's most enduring politicians, Edwin C. Johnson, governor (1933–1937 and 1955–1957) and U.S. senator (1937–1955). He arrived here from Kansas in 1910 with his family. Initially ill with tuberculosis, he responded to Colorado's salubrious climate. His daughter, Janet Johnson Howsam, and her husband Robert have turned the humble boyhood home into a homesteader's dream, complete with linoleum floor, plywood-paneled walls, and glass brick windows. To keep out coyotes and stray livestock, a 5-foot wrought iron and brick fence has been transplanted from a demolished Denver mansion. This astonishing fence eclipses the house and separates cut from uncut weeds in the memorial to Big Ed's earthy roots.

Routt County   (RT)

John L. Routt, Colorado governor from 1875 to 1879, gave his name to the county created in 1877. Gold initially attracted argonauts and gave birth to the towns of Clark, Columbine, and Hahns Peak. Coal—the black gold excavated at Oak Creek and many other communities—became the prime product after the 1908 arrival of the Denver, Salt Lake & Pacific Railroad (Moffat Road) in a county that often has led Colorado in coal production.

One of the highest and coolest counties, Routt averages a growing season of only about seventy-five days. Cattle and sheep ranching, haying, and a few cold-weather crops—wheat, potatoes, barley, oats, lettuce, and strawberries—have flourished. Ranches and farms, generally low-slung masonry or wood structures hunkered down against the weather, fit the rural mountain valley landscape.

Forty percent of the county lies within Routt National Forest, a recreational haven. In Steamboat Springs, one of the state's largest ski areas, over half the population has arrived since 1970, and almost 75 percent of the building stock is equally new. Variations of Alpine and Mineshaft Modern styles prevail around Steamboat Springs. Elsewhere in the county, many of the modest miners' homes and rustic ranches have metal roofs and little insulation, as residents have used cheap local coal not only to heat homes but also to melt heavy snow loads that have collapsed many a roof.

Steamboat Springs

The county seat (1875, 6,695 feet), at the junction of Soda Creek and the Yampa River, was established by James H. Crawford and named for the chugging sound of one of its more exuberant springs. Crawford and a group of investors platted a grid town which captured the county seat from the older mining town of Hahns Peak in 1894.

After the Moffat railroad arrived in 1909, Steamboat became one of the largest cattle and sheep shipping points in the United States. Haying and ranching were the main businesses until after World War II, when Steamboat boomed as a ski town celebrated for deep powder snow. Skiing had been the favorite local sport since the 1914 founding of the Steamboat Springs Winter Sports Club. Norwegian Carl Howelsen ("The Flying Norseman") laid out the Howelsen Hill Ski Jump and launched one of America's first winter carnivals, with cowboys skiing behind horses and the high school band marching on skis. Despite the quaint local festivities, travelers on U.S. 40 scurried past

Steamboat
Springs

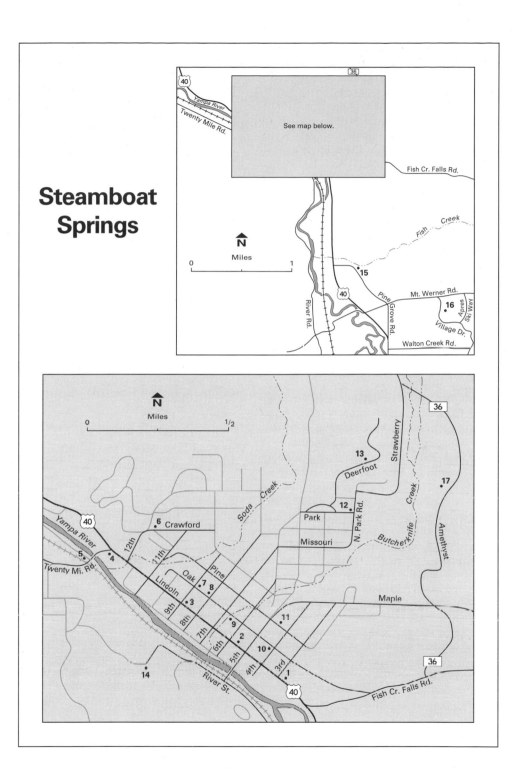

See map below.

Yamba River

Twenty Mile Rd.

Fish Cr. Falls Rd.

Fish Creek

N

Miles

0 — 1

15

River Rd.

Pine Grove Rd.

Mt. Werner Rd.

16

Apres Ski Way

Village Dr.

Walton Creek Rd.

N

Miles

0 — 1/2

36

Strawberry

13

Deerfoot

17

12

Park

N. Park Rd.

Butcher Knife Creek

Amethyst

Soda Creek

Missouri

40

Yampa River

6 Crawford

12th

11th

5

4

Twenty Mi. Rd.

Oak

Pine

Maple

Lincoln

7

8

9th

3

8th

9

7th

2

6th

5th

11

14

4th

3rd

10

1

River St.

40

Fish Cr. Falls Rd.

36

521

this ranching town located in a snow bowl averaging 164 inches a year. The town was so desperate for tourists that the Women's Club offered free baby sitting.

Population remained under 2,000 until the 1960s, when the ski business began to draw visitors. The population soared to 7,000 by the mid-1990s. Plans for the huge Catamount Lake Ski area, which has weathered local controversy and a U.S. Forest Service Environmental Impact Assessment, suggest that Steamboat Springs will keep bubbling. Despite the ski boom, no zoning ordinances until 1971, a lack of local preservation ordinances, and the opening of a Wal-Mart (1992), Steamboat has preserved much of its architectural heritage. This is evident along the stretch of U.S. 40 known as Lincoln Avenue, a 100-foot-wide main street once used for cattle drives. Some of the commercial structures, as well as outlying residences, exhibit the sandstone mined a mile south of town on the east shoulder of Emerald Mountain.

Among local stonemasons was the skier Carl Howelsen, whose craftsmanship is exemplified by the Furlong Building (c. 1920), 810 Lincoln Avenue, as well as the First National Bank in Craig, Moffat County (1918) and the Solandt Memorial Hospital in Hayden (1917). Local sandstone also enhances the First National Bank (1888), 803 Lincoln Avenue.

Notable Modernist work includes Denver architect Eugene Sternberg's Hillcrest Apartments (1959), 302 11th Street, and the Yampa Valley Electric Company (1956), 32 10th Street, the latter of Roman brick with ribbon windows, a flat roof, and a facade that showcases local stone. The Colorado Mountain College campus features polygonal red brick buildings (1967, Nixon and Jones) with flat, projecting roofs.

RT01 Steamboat Springs Health and Recreation Association Pool

1884. Northeast corner of U.S. 40 and 3rd St.

The original pool and frame bathhouse developed by town founder James Crawford has evolved into a large aquatic complex, designed by local architect Lincoln H. Jones. A 350-foot water slide—a fiberglass tube 4 feet in diameter—snakes down the hillside to discharge bathers into the pool. The restored historic source pool of this popular all-season watering hole is the starting point for a walking tour of seven of Steamboat's estimated 150 springs, which gush from the earth at temperatures ranging from 58 to 150 degrees F.

RT02 Routt County Courthouse

1923, Fuller and Fuller. 1982, annex, Lacey-Eidem and Associates. 522 Lincoln Ave.

In the Beaux-Arts tradition, this symmetrical, rectangular-plan building of yellow wirecut brick wears Neoclassical trim of Emerald Mountain sandstone and terracotta. The little-altered interior holds museum cases and photographs of the county's numerous pioneer schoolhouses. The original courthouse, at 928 Lincoln Avenue, began life as a rather plain two-story red brick commercial building, a use to which it has been returned.

RT03 Lyon Drug Store (Maxwell Building)

1908, Elmer Baer, builder. 840 Lincoln Ave. (northeast corner of 9th St.)

J. P. Maxwell, one of the founders of the Steamboat Springs Town Company, and Elmer Baer, a local contractor, put up this two-story red brick commercial building. Baer used local sandstone for stringcourses, a parapet cap, and Lincoln Avenue's most notable cornice and pediment.

RT04 Bud Werner Memorial Library

1967, Tor Westgaard. 1987, addition, William J. Rangitsch. 1289 Lincoln Ave.

The library's original building, a 3,500-square-foot modified A frame, was a chapel-shaped memorial to a local ski champion killed in 1964 by an avalanche in the Swiss Alps during motion picture filming. Sensitive enlargement came with a 6,500-square-foot rectangular addition to the west gable end. The entire structure has been resurfaced with horizontal redwood siding, while

RT04 Bud Werner Memorial Library

RT06 Crawford House

the profile and pointed-arch clerestory of the original building have been preserved. Just across the Yampa River is the hot spring for which the town is named.

RT05 Steamboat Springs Arts Council
(Denver & Rio Grande Depot)

1909, Frank E. Edbrooke. Twenty Mile Rd. near southwest corner of Lincoln Ave.

This symmetrically designed Beaux-Arts eclectic depot is two stories of brick with brick quoins, wooden bay windows, broad eaves, and scrolled Craftsman wooden brackets. Passenger service was discontinued in 1969, and in 1972 it became the home of the Steamboat Springs Council of the Arts and Humanities. The town converted the passenger waiting room to a gallery in 1987 and the baggage room to a theater and dance studio.

RT06 Crawford House

1894. 1184 Crawford Ave. (northeast corner of 12th St.)

James H. Crawford's house, with its hipped third-story dormers, is of rough-faced sandstone from nearby Emerald Mountain. The right half of the full-width front porch is surmounted by a triangular pediment over a large, round entry arch. Crawford served as Steamboat's first mayor, postmaster, school superintendent, and state legislator. The Crawford family plot in the Steamboat Springs cemetery has a large granite marker with a carving depicting this house.

RT07 St. Paul's Episcopal Church

1913, A. E. Gumprecht, builder. Northeast corner of Oak and 9th sts.

Carl Howelsen may have been the mason for this front-gabled chapel of local sandstone ashlar with handsome Gothic-arched doors and windows. The fine interior has exposed wood frame walls, open ceiling beams, a hand-carved golden oak altar, and miniature stained glass windows.

RT08 Tread of Pioneers Museum
(Campbell House)

1900, Ernest Campbell. 800 Oak St. (northwest corner of 8th St.)

The two-story frame house dressed in vernacular Carpenter's Gothic trim was moved here from 5th and Oak streets and reopened as a museum in 1959. First-story clapboard rises to a flared second story clad in shingle on this doll's house with half-timbered gable ends and porch pediments. Various rooms, including a new rear addition, are devoted to the cattle industry, mining, Native Americans, and skiing.

RT09 Christian Science Society Church

c. 1934. 641 Oak St.

This tiny log church with diagonal logs in the gable, bark trim, and an arched entry pediment reposes on a river rock foundation under a metal roof. A rustic character prevails also in the bare, log-walled interior.

RT10 Schaffnit House

1908, Elmer Baer, builder. 1983, restoration, Robert C. McHugh. 405 Oak St.

The steep-pitched metal roof on this Queen Anne Style house has lancet-arched fascias in the gable ends. Clapboard siding rises into the recessed areas created by the arches. The eaves have double scrolled brackets, and the spaces between the fascias and the roof are covered in bands of square and diamond-cut wood shingles. Henry Schaffnit, Jr., was a mayor of Steamboat Springs and backer of the *Steamboat Pilot*.

RT11 Steamboat Bed and Breakfast

c. 1905. 442 Pine St.

This two-story Georgian house with shiplap siding and three prominent attic dormers was built as a school for the First Congregational Church next door, which burned down in 1984. In the symmetrical facade, the hipped roof of the entry porch is centered between two bay windows.

RT12 Light House

1905, Elmer and Thomas Baer, builders. 204 Park Ave.

Francis Marion Light founded Light and Sons Western Wear (1905), 826–830 Lincoln Avenue, and made it the best-known emporium in northwestern Colorado. Light's Burma Shave–style mustard yellow highway signs extend even into northeastern Utah and southwestern Wyoming. A Missouri farmer and schoolteacher, Light arrived in Steamboat Springs with a wife, seven children, and a dog, who all helped staff the store. The Lights' two-story clapboard house complete with Tuscan porch posts may have been mail ordered from Sears, Roebuck. It sits on a hill as the centerpiece of the family ranch amid some surviving outbuildings in what is now the Deerfoot Artspark subdivision. A son, Wayne Light, author of *My First Eighty-One Years*, lived in the house after his father's death and sold off much of the surrounding acreage.

RT13 Robbins House

1986, Joseph Patrick Robbins. 720 Deerfoot Artspark Dr.

On a bank of Soda Creek behind the Light House, this four-story, Mineshaft Modern composition of redwood and river rock culminates in an arched cornice that conceals the top of a circular stairway. The house rises four stories from its low-lying site to catch the sun. Protruding shed-roofed bays house solar panels and large areas of glazing. Fanciful wooden cutout posts bracket the elevated walk to the entry. Other local works by the architect include a sensitive 1989 rehabilitation of the Chief Theater (1920s), 810 Lincoln Avenue.

RT14 Howelsen Hill Ski Area

1915, Carl Howelsen. 1370 Bob Adams Dr.

Colorado's pioneer ski area is named for the greatest single early promoter of the sport.

Carl Howelsen built the ski jump to promote the Steamboat Springs Winter Carnival, the oldest ski festival in the Rocky Mountains. Slalom and downhill courses were added in the late 1930s, and Olympic-sized 20-, 50-, 70-, and 90-meter jumps in 1975. Now a city park, the ski area is still used for local ski racing and jumping. The original lodge has been enlarged and improved by a 1992 design of Robert S. Ralston, who also designed the 1972 addition to blend with the 1934 boat tow structure.

RT15 **Pine Grove Restaurant** (Pine Grove Ranch Barn)

1910, Jerry McWilliams, builder. 1465 Pine Grove Rd.

Rancher Jerry McWilliams built this gambrel-roofed, board-and-batten barn of local pine. Sixty years later David Lindlow converted it to a restaurant, adding another barnlike wing and a round, silo-like two-story entry and stair for a Neo–Queen Anne look. The open-raftered second story contains a dance floor and dining areas and, like the entire building, is decorated with antiques, old photos, and other memorabilia of ranching days displayed on barnwood walls.

RT16 **Mt. Werner Ski Area**

1957; many additions. 1970, master plan, Kenneth R. White. 3 miles south of Steamboat Springs at Mt. Werner Rd. and Village Dr.

More than 25 miles of trails and lifts, including a $6 million high-speed quad lift, the Storm Peak Express (1992), crisscross this winter sports complex, now one of the state's largest single ski areas, with 2,500 skiable acres. Originally developed as Storm Peak, it was renamed for hometown Olympic champion Bud Werner. In 1969 local owners sold out to LTV, a Dallas conglomerate, which considerably enlarged the ski area and developed the nearby "village" of shops and condominiums.

Strawberry Park

This suburb (c. 1900) north of Steamboat Springs was named for the strawberry farms which once flourished there. Since the Perry Mansfield Arts Campus opened in 1913, it

has been an artists' haven and summer resort. The Strawberry Park Hot Springs, bubbling out of the earth at 150 degrees F. and into a half-dozen seminatural pools, attract bathers winter and summer.

RT17 **Strawberry Park Elementary School and Steamboat Springs Junior High School**

1981, Robert S. Ralston with William C. Muchow and Associates. Routt County 36, 1 mile north of Steamboat Springs .

This 12-acre campus includes the relocated and restored Fly Gulch Schoolhouse (c. 1900); a playground by Robert Leathers of Ithaca, New York, with his trademark wooden castles; and two Postmodern schools. The new schools are both single-story, rust-colored brick buildings with 30-foot-wide atrium "streets" flooded with natural light from clerestory windows.

RT18 **Crosby-Pascoe Cabin**

1882. Strawberry Park

Allegedly the oldest home in the county, this low-gabled house began as a hand-hewn cottonwood log cabin and now has two congenial additions. Moved in the 1960s from 7th and Pine downtown, it remains rustic and whimsical.

RT19 **Perry Mansfield Arts Campus**

1913, 1962. 40755 Routt County 36

Charlotte Perry and Portia Mansfield, two Smith College graduates who became dancers in New York City, founded one of America's oldest performing arts camps for young women in this semiwilderness area. On the wooded 88-acre campus students take courses in art, dance, music, theater, and recreation. The Julie Harris Theater (1962, Willard Sagel), named for one of the camp's most illustrious graduates, has some Wrightian hallmarks—a battered rubblestone base, bands of casement windows, and wide overhanging eaves converging in a prow. On this informal campus, dormitories, a general store, offices, and studios make up a quaint, in some cases dilapidated collection of slab, frame, and log buildings with corrugated metal roofs. The studios feature movable walls that open to catch summer light and breezes. Perry and Mansfield planned the 70-structure campus to blend into the surrounding aspen and evergreens, ordering contractors to spare every tree they possibly could.

Clark

Clark (1889, 7,721 feet), a stop named for stage operator Worthington Clark, became a ranching and mining center. The Clark School (1915), a stone and clapboard schoolhouse with an open belfry, does not hide its pedagogical origins although it has been remodeled as a private residence. Five miles north of Clark, the scenic drive along Routt County 42 on the west side of Steamboat Lake State Park rewards travelers with the Fetcher Brothers Ranch barn (c. 1890), a log barn with a rounded gable roof.

RT20 Brown Ranch

1906. 26230 Routt County 58 (at Routt County 129), 1 mile south of Clark

Sheep ranchers Margaret Brown and her husband purchased their first 160 acres on the Elk River in 1915. Margaret Brown's autobiography, *Shepherdess of the Elk River Valley* (1967), is one of few extensive accounts left by the many women who ran Colorado ranches. On moving to the ranch she wrote: "I shall never forget my happy feeling of possession and release as I rode over this small piece of pasture, fully adequate for the sheep and the lambing. On

the 21st of April, we moved the ewes into this place. There was a location cabin of one room and a shed lean-to, a good small horse barn of logs, a good chicken house and cow barn, a good sheep shelter, small but snug, and wonderful spring water."

Margaret Brown's husband died in 1918. She stayed on alone, raising enough hay often to help out neighbors during the long winters. By buying out the spreads of men who gave up, she expanded her ranch to 713 acres, which she ran until her death in 1965. Her hewn log ranch house sits on the bank of the Elk River amid rich hayfields and pastureland. Distinguished by three dormers in a steep-pitched, side-gable roof and a full-width screened front porch, it has ribbed metal roofing and chinked log construction that exemplify the local vernacular. To the original homestead cabin and ranch house, Brown added many of the outbuildings, such as a bunkhouse, an icehouse, and a tool shed, which are still used by her descendants.

RT21 Home Ranch

1978, Robert C. McHugh. 54880 Routt County 129

This neo-rustic dude ranch has traditional log and gable construction, metal roofs, exposed rafter ends, overhanging eaves, and river rock fireplaces and chimneys. Architect Robert McHugh studied the nearby Brown ranch house (RT20) for inspiration. The historic precedent is visible in the main

RT20 Brown Ranch House

lodge's two-story wings with steep, face-dormered gable roofs. Large, grouped windows and clerestories invite light inside. Around this central lodge, six similarly designed cabins are scattered across an aspen-blanketed hillside.

RT22 Moon Hill School

1913. Routt County 129, 3 miles south of Clark

The Elk Valley 4-H Club restored this one-room, lap-sided schoolhouse on a stone foundation with a Tuscan-columned front porch under a simple shed roof. The metal roof is crowned by an open cupola astride the ridge above the door. At the opposite end of the ridge, a square brick chimney completes the traditional form.

RT23 Columbine

1897–1967. Routt County 129, 6 miles north of Hahns Peak

Forest of aspen and pine is now creeping into this town of primitive log and slab homes served by a magnificent collection of outhouses. Named for the Columbine Gold Mine, the town was platted in 1897 by James R. Caron as an 11-acre grid superimposed on an 1881 gold camp. More than a dozen surviving log structures include a log barn saloon with a frame false front, a false-fronted general store, and an abandoned post office.

Hahns Peak

Routt County's oldest town, Hahns Peak (1862, 8,120 feet) was the county seat for thirty-three years until replaced by Steamboat Springs in 1912. Joseph Hahn, who found gold here in 1866, died of exposure before his camp boomed in 1874 and absorbed the nearby camps of Bug Town (later National City) and Poverty Bar. Placer mining quickly gave way to hydraulic mining, and scars from the process still disfigure Willow Creek and Poverty Bar on the northeast side of town, while the remains of a dredge lie in Bug Town. Today the dirt main street passes among an intriguing collection of slab, hewn log, and frame cabins with

some contemporary homes that make interesting use of local pine and spruce. Hahns Peak Village is a collection of about a dozen historic structures clustered along Main Street. The Withers Cabin (c. 1890s) is said to be the oldest structure in town.

Hahns Peak was returned to life with the establishment of Steamboat Lake State Recreation Area (1968) on the west side of town, which has sparked a recreational and second-home boom in this broad, mountain-rimmed valley. Atop bald, rocky, 10,839-foot Hahns Peak, the rock, timber, and cement Hahns Peak fire lookout tower (1924) has an open, skeletal, functional form that seems modern.

RT24 Hahns Peak Schoolhouse

1911. Main St. (NR)

In this one-room frame structure with an open bell tower, Augusta de Forrest, the first schoolmarm, taught grades one through twelve in her high-top shoes and ankle-length dress. After the school closed in 1942 this became a center for public meetings, dances, church services, card parties, and funerals. The coal shed and two 1911 privies survive, although the horse barn for student transport is gone. The restored school is now a museum owned and operated since 1973 by the Hahns Peak Area Historical Society along with the Hahns Peak Museum (1980, Robert S. Ralston) next door, an example of sensitively designed ghost town infill which provides a setting for the town's old steel-barred "bear trap" jail.

Hayden

Hayden (1875, 6,336 feet) was named for Ferdinand V. Hayden, the U.S. Geological Surveyor who camped near here while doing fieldwork for the first *Geological and Geographical Atlas of Colorado* (1877). Founded as a ranch center, Hayden became a rail town in 1913. This quaint, tree-shaded town in the picturesque Yampa River Valley served as the first county seat, from 1877 to 1879. The small frame house on Jefferson Avenue (U.S. 40) serves as the town hall. The largest of the three cast-stone houses (c. 1909) at Poplar and Washington streets is the three-story Hayden House (1909).

RT25 Congregational Church

1903. 1975, Robert S. Ralston. Northeast corner of U.S. 40 (Jefferson Ave.) and Spruce St.

This Queen Anne frame church has been tastefully expanded over the years. Ralston's addition and restoration set the original corner steeple beside the church as a dramatic freestanding sculpture.

RT26 Hayden Heritage Center (Denver & Rio Grande, Denver & Salt Lake Depot)

1918, Joseph W. Roeschlaub, builder. 300 W. Pearl St. (northeast corner of Poplar St.) (NR)

This rectangular, red brick, two-story building under a hipped terracotta tile roof typifies Denver & Salt Lake depot designs suggestive of the Prairie Style. An outside entrance provides access to the second-floor station agent's apartment. The ground-floor interior, relatively unchanged, features large wooden sash windows, wainscoting and plaster walls in the waiting room, and a telegraph office. After the D&RG acquired the line in 1947, it operated the depot until 1971, then donated the building to the town for use as a museum. The builder was a general contractor in Craig (Moffat County), where he designed a similar depot (MF03). Nearby, along the tracks at 198 Lincoln Avenue, is the Hayden Grain Company (1910s), the largest complex in town, evolved from a small frame freight office to

a geometric assortment of flat- and shed-roofed boxes and cylinders in sheet metal and wood frame.

RT27 Carpenter Ranch

1905. U.S. 40, 3 miles east of Hayden opposite Hayden Power Plant

Set far back from U.S. 40 in a lush meadow along the Yampa River are a large, two-story frame ranch house with several additions, a bungalow bunkhouse, and various barns. The complex, which started as a ranch in 1905 and was acquired by the Carpenter family in 1926, boasts Herefords "Better in Every Weigh." To preserve the 957-acre ranch, the Carpenter family, which owns it, has arranged future ownership and operation by the Nature Conservancy.

Farrington R. "Ferry" Carpenter tells his own story in *Confessions of a Maverick: An Autobiography* (1984). With a B.A. from Princeton and a Harvard Law School diploma, he chose to become a gentleman rancher. After the 1934 passage of the Taylor Grazing Act, he went to Washington as the Agriculture Department's first director of grazing. By balancing the interests of his fellow ranchers, conservationists, and the federal government, Carpenter implemented the plan to both use and conserve public lands despite the reservations of suspicious stockmen.

Oak Creek

Oak Creek (1907, 7,414 feet), laid out as a grid in Oak Creek Canyon, was named for the native gambel oak. It became the county's second largest town after the railroad arrived in 1909. Between the 1920s and the 1940s Oak Creek reigned as the most populous town in Routt County, peaking at almost 2,000, and as a coal mining hub. Thirteen bars, a lively red-light district, rambunctious union halls, and a boisterous Labor Day Parade marked the flush times.

With the closing of most area coal mines, this blue-collar town dwindled to a 1990 population of 673. Conveyor belts sheathed in corrugated metal climb the hillside 2 miles north on Colorado 131 at the Edna Coal Mine (1945), the oldest strip mine in

Colorado. Reminders of the more prosperous days include the frame ruins of the company town of Pinnacle (1900–1946), 1.25 miles southwest of Oak Creek off Routt County 25, where the Morrison Coal Company once maintained a community of fifty homes, a store, a dance hall, and a boarding house.

Oak Creek's main street (Colorado 131) is lined with 1920s buildings reflecting the town's heyday, including the false-fronted frame former United Mine Workers Hospital, northeast corner of Sharp Avenue. Bernard's Oak Creek Gas Station, 130 East Main Street, is a frame structure with a barrel-vaulted roof extending over the gas pumps. The Oak Creek Inn (c. 1908), 102 Bell Avenue, is a two-story clapboard boarding house. Other examples are the two-story sandstone Yampa Valley National Bank (1911, O. E. Davy, builder), southeast corner of Colfax Avenue and Sharp Street, and the two-story Beaux-Arts Neoclassical Oak Creek High School (1928, Temple Hoyne Buell), a once elegant beige brick building, now stuccoed.

RT28 Bell Mercantile

1910, Edward and Samuel Bell. 101–111 Moffat Ave. (southeast corner of Colorado 131) (NR)

Town founders Samuel and Edward Bell constructed this store on their ranch, and it became the town hub, serving as the company store for miners as well as a doctor's office and bank. The two-story frame struc-

RT30 Rock Creek Stage Station

ture on a concrete foundation retains its original shiplap siding, adorned with decades of advertising. A nearly flat roof drains to the rear and is punctuated by two original brick chimneys. Inside the recessed storefront entrance, the original bank safe remains, along with the pressed metal wall panels. A stairwell between the storefronts leads to the upstairs hotel.

RT29 Yellow Jacket Pass Stage Stop

c. 1900. 27775 Routt County 14, 16 miles south of Steamboat Springs

Yellow Jacket Pass was the pioneer route into the county from the railhead at Wolcott in Eagle County. This one-story cabin of chinked hewn logs with saddle-notched corners has a river rock foundation and chimney. Restored and well maintained, it has a fine interior of polished wooden beams, pine floors, and built-in cabinetry. After the railroad reached Routt County in 1908, this became a private home and later an inn. The Stagecoach Lake Recreation Area (1989), 2 miles south on Routt County 14, was named for this stage stop.

RT30 Rock Creek Stage Station

c. 1880. Routt National Forest Rd. 206 (Long Park Rd.), 1.3 miles east of Toponas off Colorado 134 on west side of Gore Pass (NR)

Animals were sheltered below and people above in this two-story structure of hand-hewn logs with V-notched joints. The station was a one-day trip from Steamboat Springs on the route to Georgetown via Gore and Berthoud passes. This doorless, windowless shell is significant for its large size and its picturesque site in a beautiful, lush, open meadow of the Rock Creek Valley.

Yampa

After beginning as a cluster of homesteads, Yampa (1894, 7,892 feet) emerged as a hub for the cattle, lumber, and coal industries. The still active Yampa Lumber Mill retains an old-fashioned horror for environmentalists—two of the metal cone kilns for burning sawdust that were once common throughout Colorado. The Amanda Fix House (c. 1890),

1st and Main streets, is a mansard-roofed Second Empire house that remains the fanciest residence in town. The Royal (formerly the Rio) Hotel (c. 1900), Moffat Avenue, is a large board-and-batten building behind a false front. The Van Camp Homestead Log Cabin (1883), Moffat Avenue, served as the Yampa Hotel, stage station, and livery for many years.

RT31 Antlers Bar

1896. Main St. and Moffat Ave.

This false-fronted frame structure began life as a saloon and has now been returned to that function after serving as a pool hall and soft drink store during Prohibition. Since 1933 Michael and Emily Benedict have operated the one-story tavern as an unreformed nineteenth-century western saloon. The stark white lap siding and plate glass exterior open to a bare plank floor and paneled walls with a collection of stuffed animals, artifacts, and barroom art, trophies, and humor. One ornate Victorian bar is for drinking and the other is a lunch counter in this long and lean watering hole.

RT32 Yampa Valley Women's Club

1903. 301 Main St.

This one-story frame bank has stuccoed walls, double-door transomed entry, a simple cornice, and a paneled frieze. After the bank failed in 1934, the Ladies Club of Yampa converted it to a library and the

RT33 Yampa Bible Church

Yampa Historical Society headquarters and museum, which retains the old vault and bank records.

RT33 Yampa Bible Church

c. 1889. Northwest corner of Moffat Ave. and Lincoln St.

Originally Congregational, this tall, lapsided church, dressed up with vernacular Greek Revival trim, has an open belfry in a corner tower with the entrance in its base and a large, two-story rear addition for offices and classrooms. The steep gable roof crossing over the sanctuary is repeated in the tower.

Delta County (DT)

After the Utes were expelled from the Gunnison and Uncompahgre river valleys in 1881, town builders, ranchers, and farmers arrived. Delta County was created one year later but developed slowly without the inducement of gold or silver. Slow growth meant a more stable population than those of the mercurial mining counties. Between 1900 and 1910, an irrigated farming boom roughly doubled the population to 13,000. Since then the county has grown slowly, reaching a population of 20,980 in 1990.

The Denver & Rio Grande Railroad, which built from Gunnison through Delta County to Grand Junction in 1881–1882, instigated the founding of many towns, including Delta, Hotchkiss, and Paonia. Along Surface Creek, the orchard towns of Austin, Cedaredge, and Eckert emerged. After 1900 cattle ranching became less important than irrigated farming. Irrigation enables Delta County to produce two-thirds of the state's apple crop, as well as apricots, cherries, nectarines, peaches, and plums.

To augment its agricultural base, Delta County has courted tourists, taking advantage of nearby Grand Mesa and the Black Canyon of the Gunnison National Monument. Big game hunting is another major draw, as locals and outsiders load up for elk, mule deer, and bear. The small towns of Delta and Paonia, which celebrate their heritage with lively murals and museums, have attracted refugees from urban areas.

Delta

The county seat (1883, 4,961 feet) was founded as Uncompahgre City by George Crawford and others. The 540-acre townsite was named for the river (un-come-PAH-gray: Ute for stinking or reddish water) but was renamed Delta when pronunciation problems impeded promotion. The new name suited the site at the junction of the Uncompahgre and Gunnison rivers. Delta is an oasis town dependent on irrigation, as it averages only about seven inches of precipitation a year.

Delta traces its roots to a fort established by Antoine Roubidoux, a French trapper from St. Louis, around 1826. Called Fort Roubidoux or Fort Uncompahgre, this log trading post survived until the Utes burned it in 1846. In 1991 the fort's log buildings were reconstructed as a living history museum in Delta's Confluence Park.

Delta is a progressive town of around 4,000 which won a 1992 All-American City Award. It has municipally owned power and water companies and fine county school and social service systems. With help from the National Trust for Historic Preservation, Delta undertook a Main Street facelift in the 1980s. Storefronts were restored, parking meters were removed, a mini-park was added, more than a hundred street trees were planted, and a dozen bright murals were painted in what is now promoted as "The City of Murals." Cowboy artist W. Richard Doherty of Delta began the mural proj-

ect with *Delta County Ark* (1987), showing males and females of twenty local wildlife species on the Moderne, beige brick Municipal Light and Power Company building (1937), 1223 South Main Street. Cedaredge watercolorist Connie Williams painted the rosy *Ute Country* (c. 1989) on the Sears, Roebuck store, 5th and Main, and *A Tribute to Agriculture* on the Delta Super Market, 6th and Main. Her *Delta County Labels* portrays local fruit brands on the Davis Clothing Company store, 401 Main.

The Delta County Courthouse (1957, Eugene D. Sternberg), 501 Palmer Street, is a low-slung, straightforward, Modernist composition of steel, brick, and glass. The Delta County History Museum (1989, Edward Chamberlin Associates), northwest corner of East 3rd and Meeker streets, incorporates an old firehouse in a new museum featuring the Jones Dinosaur Gallery and a "world class" butterfly collection.

Skyland (1943), 917 Dodge Street, is Delta's largest industrial plant and Colorado's largest fruit processor. It produces frozen, canned, and juiced products from apples, cherries, apricots, and peaches. The Adolph Coors Company built two large grain elevators here to store locally grown Moravian barley. One of Delta's best-known landmarks is the giant cottonwood, 85 feet high and 22 feet in circumference, known as the Ute Council Tree, Road 15.50 and Road G 96. Under its branches Chief Ouray and his tribesmen supposedly smoked the peace pipe with palefaces.

DT01 **Confluence Park**

1991. U.S. 50 and Gunnison River Dr.

Once a smelly wasteland housing the city dump, sewage sump, and Holly Beet Sugar Refinery (1920–1991), this is now a 305-acre park, with the Heddles Recreation Center (1992), Thunder Mountain Amphitheater (1991), a living history museum facsimile of Fort Roubidoux (1991), Horse Country Arena (1991), a large fishing, swimming, and boating lake, hiking trails, and a wildlife habitat. Three giant white cement towers, remnants of the demolished sugar plant, dominate the park and the townscape. New frame picnic shelters and a recycled steel highway bridge now used as pedestrian access to one of the islands in Confluence Lake add architectural interest.

DT03 First Methodist Church of Delta

DT02 **Delta Public Library**

1911, G. R. Femlee. 1984, addition, Dana Larson, Roubal and Associates. 536 Palmer St.

This mint-condition period piece is complete with large portraits of Andrew Carnegie and George Washington. An old-fashioned locked bookcase guards suspect literature. The Delta Brick and Tile Company provided the beige brick and tile for this miniature version of the standard Carnegie neo-Greek temple. Sharing the one-block site are an old, hand-hewn log jail (1894, W. R. Gale, builder) and the courthouse.

DT03 **First Methodist Church of Delta**

1910, Samuel A. Bullard. 199 E. 5th St. (northeast corner of Meeker St.) (NR)

Neo-Tudor arches and parapets prevail on this beige brick church with a foundation, capstone, and doorway and window trim of Windgate sandstone from nearby Escalante Canyon. A pyramidal roof with a central cupola rests on parapeted gables with crenelated towers at the streetside corners. The square sanctuary with stained glass from the Midland Glass Company of Omaha is an example of the so-called Akron plan popular around 1900. The Hinners eighteen-rank organ and the original ornately carved oak pews from the American Seating Company adorn the interior. The 1891 cornerstone is from an earlier church on the site.

DT04 **Garnethurst**

1896. 509 Leon St. (southwest corner of 5th St.) (NR)

Alfred Rufus King, a judge and mayor of Delta, built this 3,000-square-foot clapboard Queen Anne dwelling with gabled bays atop Garnet Mesa. A pedimented entry porch has slender classical columns and a turned balustrade. The paneled front door has leaded windows and a stained glass transom. Atop the porch is a smaller screened porch with fishscale shingles and decorative bargeboard and gable ornament. The interior has ornate hardware and wood moldings with designs of acorns, flowers, and crescents. Eastlake scrolled details on the staircase are highlighted by stained glass in a prominent circular balcony alcove. Some modifications date from 1910–1922, when the house was used as a hospital after the Kings moved to Denver.

DT05 **Egyptian Theater**

1928, Montana S. Fallis. 452 Main St. (NR)

Fascination with the 1920s excavation of King Tutankhamen's tomb inspired an architectural idiom that reached even small-town America. Fallis, the Denver architect who designed Denver's Mayan Theater, gave Delta one of Colorado's few surviving examples of Egyptomania. This theater's one-story Egyptian Deco facade is mostly intact, as are the two-story stage box in back of the

DT05 Egyptian Theater

building and sixteen carved Egyptian busts inside. "Delta County Ranks First in Everything with the Most Modern Theater in the Best Town in Colorado," crowed the *Delta County Independent* in a headline of September 28, 1928, followed by an article describing the Egyptian as "verily a treasure chest with jewel lights that gleam and glow all colors of the rainbow."

DT06 **Visitors' Center** (First National Bank)

1892. 1987, restoration. 301–305 Main St. (NR)

Delta stonemason John Jeffers constructed this Romanesque Revival red brick two-story bank trimmed with sandstone from nearby Escalante Canyon. The square, three-story mansard-roofed corner tower is Delta's skyscraper. After the last tenant, the Last Chance Saloon, closed, the town's foremost landmark was restored, from its pressed metal ceiling to the polished pink granite corner entry. It is now the Visitors' Center and Chamber of Commerce offices. Catercorner, at the northeast corner of Main and 4th streets, is the former Colorado Bank and Trust Company (1914), in similar stony Neoclassical garb, rehabilitated for use as City Hall.

DT07 **Post Office**

1938, Louis A. Simon, OSA; Harry B. Carter, consulting architect. 360 Meeker St. (northeast corner of 4th St.) (NR)

New Deal Moderne design is exemplified in this two-story, flat-roofed rectangular box of tan brick. The design employs symmetrical Beaux-Arts massing, but ornament was reduced to speed construction and lower costs. Colorado Yule marble trim includes three Art Deco–inspired floral spandrels, while the entry steps are granite. The little-altered interior features bas-relief panels (1942) by Mary B. Kittredge, who used clay from Brickyard Hill, site of the once large, now demolished Delta Brick and Tile Company. She mixed the clay with ocher for a burnt sienna color that complements the fluted oak paneling. Kittredge portrayed local cowboys on the south wall but on the north wall depicted maidens washing their feet, presumably in the Nile delta.

DT08 **Escalante Canyon Bridge**

1890, Bullen Bridge Company. Delta County 650R over the Gunnison River, 2 miles west of U.S. 50 (NR)

This quaint wagon bridge has a plank roadway and two 180-foot spans of pin-connected steel camelback through trusses. Twice moved, it is Colorado's oldest still-used state bridge. The Escalante Bridge, ranch, and creek are all named to commemorate Padre Silvestre Vélez de Escalante, the Spanish Franciscan missionary, explorer, and journal keeper of the Dominguez-Escalante expedition. That party provided the first written account and map of this region on a 1776 expedition that aimed to establish an overland route between Santa Fe, New Mexico, and Monterey, California. A dirt road continues up Escalante Creek and Canyon to the Uncompahgre Plateau, passing a few ranches, ruins of quarry sites, the Escalante Canyon Wildlife Area, and the Dry Mesa Dinosaur Quarry, which has yielded bones of fourteen species.

DT09 **Dry Fork Petroglyphs**

3 miles south of Escalante, west bank of Dry Fork of Escalante Creek

In soft, light-colored sandstone cliffs the Utes ground, pecked, and painted in mud human figures and horses, which the tribe acquired from the Spanish in the 1600s.

DT10 **Walker Homestead Stone Cabin**

1916, Harry Walker. 7 miles from the Escalante Bridge in Escalante Canyon

In a cottonwood grove beside Escalante Creek, this sturdy, windowless homestead house has rubble walls a foot thick made of local sandstone, volcanic stone, and field-stone. On the back side, the original mud mortar of the one-story cabin may still be seen.

DT11 **Captain Smith's Stone Cabin**

1911, Henry A. Smith. 18 miles from the Escalante Bridge in Escalante Canyon

Henry Smith, a Civil War veteran from Illinois, used local sandstone to build three walls of this tiny cabin around a sandstone monolith into whose smooth red face he carved a bed niche. Smith, who is said to have made his living as a tombstone carver, practiced on the nearby cliffs. His cabin was given a new shingle roof in the 1960s by the Youth Conservation Corps.

Cedaredge

Cedaredge (1894, 6,100 feet) was named for its location at the edge of Grand Mesa's Utah junipers, which easterners called cedar trees. North of Cedaredge on Grand Mesa, three rustic log and slab lodges serve tourists visiting the mesa's 280 lakes and reservoirs: Alexander Lakes Lodge (c. 1910), Grand Mesa Lodge, and Spruce Lake Lodge. In town, notable buildings include the Baptist Church (1905), northwest corner of Main

and 4th streets, a blond brick Queen Anne Style church with Gothic-arch cutouts in the square frame open bell tower.

DT12 **Community United Methodist Church**

1922. Northwest corner of 3rd and Aspen sts.

This unusual Craftsman church of local dark volcanic stone under a low-pitched roof has wide eaves and Craftsman brackets. The large, handsome complex on the site began with a bungalow parsonage (1918).

DT13 **Pioneer Town**

1990. Colorado 65 and 2nd St.

This village of two dozen historic structures was erected by the Surface Creek Valley Historical Society on the old Bar I Ranch site, whose only surviving structures are three silos (1918). Made of 2-by-6-inch boards stacked flat and standing 40 feet high, these sturdy eight- and nine-sided grain storage towers are the centerpiece of Pioneer Town. Structures moved in from elsewhere include the Cedaredge Jail, the Lizard Head Saloon, the First State Bank of Cedaredge, the Coalby Store (1910), and the Surface Creek Creamery. Antique tools and machines are also on exhibit in one of the state's more ambitious village reconstructions.

Donald and Inez Petersen, who funded Pioneer Town, also donated its Chapel of the Cross (1989). This exquisite board-and-

DT13 Pioneer Town, silos

batten variation on the white churches of the plains has a detached sanctuary end wall separated from the glazed gable end of the church by an outdoor courtyard. A copper roof, fine stained glass, exposed ceiling beams, and lovely landscaping are among the other refinements. Verticality is created by the pointed windows, batten stripes, and steep pitch of the gable roof.

Hotchkiss

Hotchkiss (1882, 5,357 feet) was named for founder Enos T. Hotchkiss, who introduced the first orchard to the area. His house and barn are on the south side of town, which retains several other pioneer structures, including the Bank of North Fork (1903), the Delta County Fairgrounds, and the Hotchkiss Museum, 180 South 2nd Street.

DT14 Hotchkiss Hotel

1897, Enos T. Hotchkiss, builder. 101 Bridge St. (Colorado 92) (NR)

The town founder built this two-story red brick hotel with bays divided by pilasters, commercial storefronts, and a corbeled brick cornice beneath a paneled brick parapet. Long the town hub, the hotel boasted rooms for fifty guests, a restaurant, a bar, a barbershop, hot baths, and a livery stable.

DT15 Hotchkiss National Fish Hatchery

1969. 3 miles east at Rd. 150 and Lane 3150 between the D&RG tracks and the North Fork of the Gunnison River

This modern complex includes a small visitors' center and a tank room, thirty-two outdoor raceways, and six mud-bottomed ponds. Hotchkiss annually raises about 1.2 million rainbow trout, nursing them from egg stage to 2-to-9-inch fingerlings.

DT16 Hanson's Castle (7X Ranch)

1905. 4 miles west of Hotchkiss on Colorado 92, turn right on Delta County 3100 and go 7 miles up Leroux Creek

Neo-Romanesque and Queen Anne elements dress up this ranch house of rough-faced local gray sandstone with red sand-

stone trim. The round tower with conical roof, second-story balcony, arched windows with voussoirs of contrasting stone, and roof-top balustrade gained this two-story square house local fame as a "castle." Now a private Hereford cattle ranch, the site includes an old two-story bunkhouse.

Orchard City

Orchard City (1965, 5,800 feet) was created in 1965 when the Orchard City Water District absorbed the three towns of Eckert, Cory, and Austin and much surrounding territory.

DT17 United Presbyterian Church of Eckert

1921. Main St. (Colorado 65)

Two stories of uncut, uncoursed rubblestone rise to a stepped parapet on the third-story square tower of this church, for which parishioners hauled thirty-three wagonloads of local dark volcanic rock. The well-crafted rustic church has carefully detailed door and window openings and fishscale shingle trim.

Paonia

Paonia (1882, 5,645 feet) was named by founder Samuel Wade for its many introduced peonies. The town is better known today for its sweet cherries, apricots, plums, pears, peaches, and grapes. Coal mining and tourism have allowed this town to flourish in recent decades, with a population climbing to more than 1,500. Of a dozen major coal mines in the area, only the Bear Mine at Somerset, the Cyprus (formerly the Westmorland), and West Elk still fill the large coal silos lining the D&RG tracks. The D&RG depot (1902), a single-story clapboard depot with plain board trim and a shingled trackside bay, was moved here in 1974.

Local artist Ginny Allen depicted community history in her mural for the Bear Building on Grand Avenue and a large mural of the Dominguez-Escalante expedition on the north side of the Cave Cafe, southwest cor-

Parker Boulch (sp?)
Victorian home to Plakes
ca? 1950

ner of 3rd Street and Grand Avenue. This picturesque town at the end of a spur road off Colorado 133 is a quiet, rural place surrounded by mountains. It has attracted writers and artists, including sculptors, who find Paonia's Lands End Sculpture Center one of Colorado's finest bronze foundries.

DT18 Bruce House

c. 1906. 1468 Colorado 133, 1 mile west of Paonia (NR)

Raymond Bruce built this large, two-story Queen Anne farmhouse himself, using clay from the basement excavation to make the bricks. Located on a prominent hill, the house is surrounded by orchards and a highway fruit stand.

DT19 Curtis Company Hardware

1902, Sidney Curtis, builder. 228 Grand Ave. (NR)

Delivered by horse and wagon, the bracketed metal cornice of this two-story brick store has a central arched pediment. Horses also brought in the cast iron storefront, made by Front Builders of St. Louis. One flat and one projecting second-story bay are framed in engaged Doric columns. Embossed metal panels with classical urn designs, a fleur-de-lis first-story frieze, and other classical ornament adorns the facade.

DT20 United Mine Workers of America No. 6417 Hall

1903. 226 Grand Ave.

This one-story hall of rough-faced sandstone with a round-arched entry flanked by Tuscan columns houses offices of the union for what has been the largest work group locally. Coal miners also have erected a memorial statue in Paonia Park to many colleagues killed and injured underground.

DT21 High Country News (Paonia Home and Farm Supply)

c. 1900. 1992, renovation, Peter Dobrovolny, 119 Grand Ave.

Ed and Betsy Marston, who moved to Colorado from New York City, took charge in 1958 of one of the best-known countercultural newspapers in the Rockies, a champion of small towns and rural areas. The journal moved into this old feed store, where architect Peter Dobrovolny of Basalt raised the ceiling to create clerestory windows and install high-tech utilities. The new frame false front with a stepped parapet looks as if it might be original.

DT22 Manor House Farm Bed and Breakfast

c. 1891. 41750 Lane 50, 1 mile east of Paonia

This hip-roofed frame farmhouse is set amid four acres of lawn, rose gardens, streams, and pastureland. The hostess, who was born and raised in Derbyshire, has designed the interior to reflect an English country inn. Second-story fenestration echoes the first-story enclosed porch.

DT23 Bowie School Museum

c. 1900. Colorado 187, 1 mile north of Paonia

A handsome two-room frame schoolhouse in use until 1958 is now operated as a museum by the North Fork of the Gunnison River Historical Society. The school was moved from Bowie, a typical coal mining town two miles northeast whose mine office and boarding house, like its mine, are now ruins.

Gunnison County   (GU)

Studded with 14,000-foot mountains and subjected to Colorado's coldest weather, this county is named for explorer John W. Gunnison, who also gave his name to the river. The Spanish had christened this tributary of the Colorado the Rio San Xavier before despairing of finding anything worthwhile in the rugged country through which it flows. Even Utes, and later mountain men, fled the Gunnison country during its fierce winters.

It took underground riches to lure settlers. Of the mining days little remains but prospect holes, log-ribbed mines, and more than sixty ghost towns. Gold and silver soon played out, but granite, marble, and coal sustained settlement a little longer. "White gold" in the form of plentiful snowfall has made winter sports as lucrative as summer tourism. Crested Butte, once a rich coal mining town, has been resurrected as a recreational haven with some 300 inches of snow a year. Elsewhere, quite a few ranchers survive by providing lodging for dudes, fishermen, and hunters. Gunnison, the county seat, is also a college town with a population frozen at around 5,000—half the county's residents.

Gunnison County builders wrestle with weather as well as with aesthetics. Sturdy log and granite structures with steep-pitched, snow-shedding metal roofs hunker down for the long winters. Colossal snowdrifts have made two-story outhouses and 20-foot-high clotheslines legendary.

Gunnison

The county seat (1876, 7,703 feet) originated as a cow camp to serve the nearby Los Pinos Ute Indian Agency. It is the coldest city in the nation, according to *Weatherwise* magazine, but is warmly defended by proud residents, who have branded the mountain on its south side with a *W* for Western State College. Locals claim this is the world's largest letter. It was installed in 1923 by students, including Effie Miller, who recalled years later: "We walked from the campus and took off our shoes and waded the river . . . measured and roped off the letter, gathered rocks and melted snow to mix the whitewash." The tougher the terrain, the harder Coloradans struggled to brand it as theirs—with painted rocks, mountaintop cairns, names carved into rocks and aspen trees, and, ultimately, with homes and businesses.

Since the Denver & Rio Grande arrived in 1882, Gunnison has been the principal town in this high-country county. Open irrigation ditches still line some of the gridded, tree-shaded streets. Smith's Opera House (1888), 100 North Boulevard, is a two-story Italianate brick building on the town's only parkway. Neither the parkway nor the opera house attracted the elite anticipated by boosters. The two-story frame commercial building at 2310 North Main Street is a rare Colorado example of the Italianate style executed in wood, complete with frame quoins and elaborately milled window trim. Hospitable landmarks include the two-story, lap-sided Mary Lawrence Bed and Breakfast (c. 1885), 601 Taylor Street, with milled Italianate trim and later Tuscan porch columns. Of the grandiose, four-story, Second Empire Style La Veta Hotel (1884), 219 South Boulevard at Gunnison Avenue, only the first story survives.

GU01 Pioneer Museum Park

Southeast corner of Tomichi Ave. (U.S. 50) and S. Adams St.

This museum compound includes facsimile Ute tipis, the 1871 log cabin which served as the area's first post office at the Los Pinos Ute Agency, and the one-room Paragon School (1905) with an elaborate two-story brick bell tower. The D&RG's Gunnison and Sargent depots and a six-car D&RG narrow-gauge train round out the collection. The museum also owns the Aberdeen Quarry (1879), 7 miles southwest on South Beaver Creek, which produced the gray granite skin of the Colorado State Capitol.

GU02 Western State College

1911. Between Colorado St., Georgia Ave., and Escalante Dr.

Founded as the Colorado State Normal School, WSC took its current name in 1923 when it was promoted to a liberal arts college. This state school has a steady enrollment of around 2,500 on a campus on the northeast side of Gunnison. The Clarence T. Hurst Science Hall (1962) houses the Hurst Museum, with exhibits, artifacts, and data on the college and the town.

GU02.1 Taylor Hall

1910, F. W. Cooper and G. B. Robertson

The first campus building has generally congenial additions made since the 1920s. The original hall, now the north wing, is a two-story pressed red brick Neoclassical building with a red sandstone ashlar ground floor and contrasting light sandstone trim. A prominent pedimented portico with Ionic columns commands the west facade, which overlooks both the campus and town.

GU02.2 Leslie J. Savage Library

1939, Temple Hoyne Buell (NR)

The library is the finest building on campus, a Spanish Colonial Revival beauty of white stucco with a red tile roof and arched windows. The Churrigueresque terracotta entry surround is adorned with the college seal, the lamp of learning, the microscope of science, the harp of music, and the scroll of literature. On the interior, restored in 1996, are a patterned particle board ceiling and Neo–Spanish Colonial oak furniture. The library set an elegant standard continued in Crawford Hall, to the west, and Ute Hall, on the south side of the campus quadrangle. Post–World War II buildings are bland, although the three-story library addition (1964) is more colorful and in scale with the exquisite library.

GU03 Fisher-Zugelder House and Smith Cottage

1881, Frederick Zugelder. 601 N. Wisconsin St. (northwest corner of Ruby Ave.) (NR)

Stonemason Frederick Zugelder used local beige sandstone with dressed edges for this two-story, L-plan house and matching cottage on an ample corner lot. Both buildings incorporate European revival forms in ver-

nacular interpretations. The exterior walls are double, with an air space for insulation. Even coursing on the most visible walls gives way to random courses on the north side and even to some rubble fieldstone in an upper gable end. Zugelder discovered, owned, and operated the Aberdeen Quarry, seven miles south of town on South Beaver Creek, which provided 280,000 cubic feet of granite for the Colorado State Capitol.

GU04 Gunnison Hotel (Webster Building)

1882. 229 N. Main St. (NR)

This three-story edifice has storefronts in three bays on the first floor, with a central recessed entrance. Above tall, double-hung upper-story windows is an opulent bracketed metal cornice. Flush stone bands at lintel levels add horizontal emphasis, and the lintels are carved with a curvilinear motif. Herman M. Webster built this to house his prospering dry goods business on the ground floor and family living quarters and hotel accommodations above.

GU05 Hartman Block

1881. 107 N. Main St.

This two-story Italianate building, stucco with a paneled stone frieze and a stone cornice, has a central, pedimented parapet. Town founder Alonzo Hartman, who arrived in 1872, started out as a rancher providing beef to the Los Pinos Ute Indian Agency. This elegant commercial block suggests that he prospered.

GU06 Gunnison Arts Council (Gunnison Hardware)

1887. 102 S. Main St. (southeast corner of Tomichi Ave. [U.S. 50]) (NR)

A two-story Italianate commercial edifice of rough sandstone block has a large, bracketed cornice punctuated with a pair of Gothic-arched pediments on the west facade. Paler sandstone is used for the surrounds of arched windows and quoins with dressed edges. Unsympathetic remodeling of the storefronts was reversed in the hardware store's 1993 conversion to the town arts center.

GU07 **Post Office**

1937, Louis A. Simon, OSA. 200 N. Wisconsin St. (northeast corner of Virginia Ave.)

Inside this one-story, beige brick, New Deal Moderne monument is Ila McAfee Turner's 1940 mural, *The Wealth of the West*, depicting a cattle drive across the Gunnison River, where an old prospector and his burrow are panning while a fly fisherman tests the waters. This colorful mural captures the Gunnison country's purple sagebrush hills, turquoise water, and dark evergreens. The interior still has the original terrazzo floor, gray marble wainscoting, and white Colorado Yule marble trim, but a new, dark-colored tubular entry canopy is out of place.

GU08 **Municipal Building**

1931, Mountjoy and Frewen. Southwest corner of Virginia Ave. and N. Wisconsin St.

Iron flower planters were built into this two story concrete Art Deco town hall. Recessed windows are separated by vertical piers topped by panels with a foliage motif. The south end of the building was originally a fire station.

GU09 **Blackstock-O'Leary Elementary School**

1926, Mountjoy and Frewen. 225 N. Pine St.

This Neoclassical school building is symmetrical in design, flanked by perpendicular flat-roofed wings on its west side. Yellow brick provides a good background for the red tile cross-gable roof and the terracotta trim, seen in relief banding and sills, molded cornices, and entry surrounds. Paired entrances are offset in the side wings, topped by round-arched transoms and flanked by fluted columns with Corinthian capitals. Brick detailing appears in corbeled, arcaded friezes on the gable ends, recessed banding in the base, and corner piers.

GU10 **Church of the Good Samaritan**

1882. Southwest corner of Pine St. and Virginia Ave.

An Episcopal congregation built and maintains the town's oldest and finest church, a vernacular Gothic Revival edifice of stone with stained glass lancets and a rose window.

The gable roofs of the new parish hall and office relate to the church, and a masonry wall ties the new and old together.

GU11 **San Ildefonso House**

c. 1938. 509 W. Virginia Ave.

This tiny (300-square-foot) Pueblo Revival house is one of several, including the studio to the east, built by Indians from San Ildefonso Pueblo in New Mexico. The Indians came north in the summers to make and sell jewelry at Ender's Hardware across the street. Under cement stucco, restorer Bruce Hoffman found the original mud plaster applied over chicken wire fastened to the adobe bricks by nails driven through bottle caps. The irregular massing, bulging parapets, vigas, and appealing simplicity of the Pueblo Revival style are captured here in miniature.

GU12 **Hartman Castle**

1885. 277 Gunnison County 38, 1 mile southwest of Gunnison, southwest of the airport

Gunnison's most distinctive historic house, this Queen Anne Style castle commanded a 2,000-acre ranch homesteaded in 1875 by Alonzo Hartman. Hartman, who, with Sylvester Richardson, founded Gunnison, called his home Dos Rios for its site at the junction of the Gunnison and Tomichi rivers. Atop a stone base, the brick first floor and shingled second story look like a small appendage to the massive, three-story central tower with its smaller, conical-capped belvedere. Seven leaded and stained glass windows of decreasing size climb the first story of the circular tower. Inside, ornate white oak woodwork is among the many rich construction details. Hartman also built the brick barn (1889) and his earlier L-shaped, one-and-one-half-story house (c. 1880) with vertical, horizontal, and herringbone lap siding.

GU13 **Blue Mesa Reservoir**

1963. 11 miles west of Gunnison on U.S. 50

The largest lake in Colorado and the surrounding Curecanti National Recreation Area originated with the Blue Mesa Dam (1963), a 342-foot-high earthen structure.

Below it are the Morrow Point Dam (1971), the first large double-curvature, thin-arch concrete dam in the United States, and Crystal Dam, forming a trio of recreational reservoirs on the Gunnison River.

Crested Butte

The once grimy coal mining town of Crested Butte (1878, 8,885 feet) (NRD) has been reborn as one of Colorado's slickest resorts. The street grid is laid out in a beautiful mountain valley named for the most prominent of many nearby peaks, whose top resembles a cock's comb. In 1881, the town became the D&RG's rail hub for even more remote mining towns in the surrounding Elk Mountains. Platted and promoted by sawmill owner Howard F. Smith, Crested Butte remains a town of largely frame buildings.

Rubble piles at the corner of 3rd Street and Belleview Avenue are all that remains of the long line of 150 kilns at the base of Big Mine Hill. After the last coal producer, the Big Mine, closed in 1952, Crested Butte looked like a goner. It slumbered until 1966, when the Mount Crested Butte Ski Area opened on the former Malensk Ranch, reinforcing a winter sports tradition traceable to the 1886 founding of the Crested Butte Snow Shoe and Toboggan Club. Because the ski area is three miles north of town and behind a mountain, Crested Butte was spared some of the intense development that has transformed Aspen, Breckenridge, and Telluride. Many nineteenth-century structures survive, albeit with often fanciful restorations and additions. Behind the wonderful scrolled wrought iron arch of the Crested Butte Cemetery (1879), tombstones tell of the short, hard, and dangerous lives of immigrant miners. The cemetery chapel contains the elaborate wooden altar, statues, and altar from St. Patrick's Catholic Church, now empty and for sale at 108 Maroon Avenue.

The Crested Butte Historic District (NRD) is roughly bounded by Whiterock and Maroon avenues, between 1st and 8th streets.

New buildings within the district, such as the Crested Butte Brew Pub (1991), 226 Elk Avenue, the Crested Beauty Bed and Breakfast Inn (1992, Alex Ortiz), 329 Whiterock Avenue, and the fire station (1974), 306 Maroon Avenue, all play on traditional massing and materials.

GU14 Crested Butte Mountain Heritage Museum (Denver & Rio Grande Depot)
1881. 724 Elk Ave.

Crested Butte's former depot, a standard D&RG Queen Anne model similar to those at Creede, Wagon Wheel Gap, and elsewhere, has living quarters above the waiting room. Vertical siding rises to the first-floor sills, with horizontal siding above. The steep-pitched roof has flared eaves with large, curved brackets, offsetting shingled, full-height dormers with sunburst motifs in the gable peaks. After the spur line from Gunnison was abandoned in 1954, the station was converted to a community center and a home for the Crested Butte Mountain Heritage Museum.

GU15 Condominiums (Mule Barns)
1890s; 1980, Bruce Robertson. 709 Maroon Ave.

The central portion of this former home for 100 working mine mules was moved into town and expanded into condominiums. The barn's tall, narrow profile is almost a caricature of its former self. Two doors east and far less altered is the Colorado Fuel and Iron Company mine superintendent's two-story frame Queen Anne dwelling (c. 1888).

GU16 Community Library (Rock Schoolhouse)
1893. 1993, restoration, Michael Holland, Bill Rosenberry, and Nan Lumb. Southeast corner of Maroon Ave. and 5th St.

This two-story school building of coursed, rough-faced stone has a square front bay centered between separate boys' and girls' entrances that are more typical of eastern schools of the day than of those in western communities. The two entrances are sheltered by bracketed canopies. Paneled doors have glazed transoms set beneath blind arches. The central bay rises to a shingled mansard topped by an open cupola with a shingled, bell-shaped cap and a weathervane. The schoolhouse is grouped on a cul-de-sac with the two-story brick high school (1927) and the contemporary frame middle school (1991) with sandstone block colored to match the sandstone of the Rock Schoolhouse.

GU17 Union Congregational Church

1883. 403 Maroon Ave. (northeast corner of 4th St.)

Eastlake trim adorns this frame, front-gabled Carpenter's Gothic church. The lovely square corner tower tapers to an open bell cupola with an arched cutout, elaborate brackets, and a balustrade. Horizontal clapboard siding contrasts with vertical trim boards. A tripartite lancet group high in the front wall corresponds to three double-hung windows at the first-floor level. The entry is protected by a Gothic-arched canopy and the bargeboard is decorated with trefoil cutouts.

GU18 Mihelich Conoco Station and Hardware Store

1883. 329 Elk Ave. (northwest corner of 4th St.)

This remnant of the old blue-collar coal town has a 1902 potbellied stove and the ultimate wall trophy, the 1899 World Record Wapiti—a twelve-point elk taken in nearby Dark Canyon. A typical bracketed frame false front and glass storefront still predominate despite many design concessions to twentieth-century pragmatism and tourism, such as the gasoline pumps.

GU19 Colorado Fuel and Iron Company Store

1937. 303 Elk Ave. (northeast corner of 3rd St.)

CF&I, which owned and operated many of the area's coal mines, built and operated this stuccoed masonry store with its distinctive curvilinear parapet. When CF&I closed the Big Mine in 1952, it also closed this store, since reopened as a mini–shopping mall. In the rear alley is the famous two-story outhouse—supposedly a response to the snowdrifts that persist in shady places until May.

GU20 Stefanic's General Store

1893. 228 Elk Ave.

This two-story frame false-fronted store has what may be the original plate glass storefront. Asphalt "brick" siding has been tacked on to the second story, which flaunts three pedimented Neoclassical windows.

GU21 Old City Hall

1883, Jacob Kochevar, builder. 132 Elk Ave. (southwest corner of 2nd St.)

Crowned by a square, open bell tower, this two-story frame false-fronted building with a central, arched entry housed the town hall and fire department until 1952. One of the most picturesque structures in a picturesque town, it has shiplap siding and distinctive round arches that form a motif on the flush board facade cut to look like ashlar masonry. The old stone jailhouse (c. 1883) sits behind at 409 2nd Street.

GU22 Forest Queen Hotel

1890. 129 Elk Ave. (northwest corner of 2nd St.)

This two-story frame building beside Coal Creek has a false front with a cornice supported by carved brackets and a paneled frieze. A four-bay storefront has a separate entrance for the hotel on the right and a recessed entry between large glazed bays, now enclosed for a vestibule. Wooden corner pilasters above echo the pilasters dividing the first-floor bays. Little altered since the 1880s, when it served as a general store, the Forest Queen was a bar and brothel before its reformation as a hotel and restaurant. Interior highlights include a high wooden ceiling and an antique safe and back bar.

GU23 **Kochevar Saloon**

1899, Jacob Kochevar and Son, builders. 127 Elk Ave.

A symmetrical false front with a decorative bracketed cornice hides a deep, front-gabled structure. The three-bay storefront has double doors in the central recessed entry. The upper facade has three tall, double-hung windows with three smaller double-hung windows above spaced closer to each other, creating the illusion of a third story. Underneath the clapboard lie hand-hewn square timbers. Jacob Kochevar, a skilled Croatian carpenter, constructed various houses and businesses in town, as well as the Old City Hall (GU21), across the street. Both the exterior and the front barroom are well preserved.

GU24 **Elk Mountain Lodge** (CF&I Boarding House)

1919. 200 Gothic Ave. (northwest corner of 2nd St.)

Until the 1950s some sixty-five coal miners lived in this rectangular, two-story stuccoed concrete building with a concrete foundation and a metal hipped roof. A full-width enclosed porch now wraps around the southeast corner, and a newer shed addition lies on the east. The lack of trim and detail suggests the utilitarian origins of what has become a tourist lodge.

Other company housing immediately to the west includes two stuccoed concrete-block supervisors' houses (1922), with hipped and truncated metal roofs. Four front-gabled frame bungalows (1926) have clapboard siding and square-cut wood shingles in the gable ends. All but one have lost their recessed, full-width front porches.

GU25 **Crested Butte Club Victorian Hotel and Spa** (Croatian Hall)

1885; 1989. 512 2nd St.

Croatian coal miners relied on this former lodge not only for food, drink, and lodging, but also for sick benefits, burials, and prayers of the Croatian St. Barbara Society, named for the patron saint of miners. Such consolations were needed in the accident-prone coal industry; frequent tragedies included an explosion in Crested Butte's Jokerville Mine that killed sixty men. In 1902 this building was rolled on logs from Elk Avenue to its present site. The restored corrugated sheet metal false front incorporates the original storefront and recessed entry to what remains a first-floor saloon. The upstairs has been converted to seven elegantly furnished guest rooms with such amenities as a racquetball court, an aerobics room, steam baths, and a giant hot tub.

GU26 **Ski Lodge at Mount Crested Butte**

1965, Bruce Alonzo Goff. 33 Whetstone Rd.

One of Frank Lloyd Wright's best-known disciples designed this lodge as a two-story frame cone with shingle cladding and vertical bands of windows. A low, cylindrical base houses sleeping spaces, leaving room for common areas in the dramatically shaped upper story topped by a cylindrical steel chimney with a unique forked finial. Many newer surrounding residences have somewhat diluted the impact of Goff's structure, but it remains prominent on the open east slope above the ski village center.

GU27 **Gothic**

1879–1914. 7.5 miles north of Crested Butte via Gothic Rd. (National Forest Service Rd. 317)

This mining camp borrowed its name from nearby Mt. Gothic, whose rock formations were likened by Hayden Survey topographer Henry Gannett to a cathedral's pinnacles and flying buttresses. Several hundred people lived here during the 1880s, but only five buildings remain of their log and frame city. The well-preserved, two-story, false-fronted town hall (c. 1880) is now a visitor information center and general store.

GU30 Colorado-Yule Marble Quarry, early twentieth century

GU28 Rocky Mountain Biological Laboratory

1925. Gothic Rd.

This laboratory amid the ruins of the old mining town began with the purchase of Gothic by John C. Johnson, a biology professor at Western State College. An international contingent of scholars gather here each summer to focus on biological and environmental issues at what has become one of America's premier Alpine field stations. The Oh-Be-Joyful and Swallow's Nest houses date from the early 1880s, and the Ore House and the Mammal and Parasitology Laboratory were built by T. K. Dissette in a 1914 attempt to revitalize the town. Laboratory personnel constructed nineteen additional buildings in the 1920s and 1930s, using the town's log and frame vernacular and, in some cases, lumber from collapsed buildings.

Marble

Marble (1890, 7,950 feet) is near the place on Yule Creek, along the headwaters of the Crystal River, where George Yule found an outcropping of high-grade white marble in 1874. Marble's quarriers exhibited their 99-percent-pure calcium carbonate at the World's Columbian Exposition of 1893, where the popularity of the classical buildings helped create a national market for the fine Carrara-like marble. Mule sleds were used to haul the stone to the D&RG railhead

in Carbondale until the Crystal River & San Juan Railroad reached Marble in 1906. The town produced the largest single chunk of marble ever quarried in the United States, used for the Tomb of the Unknown Soldier in Arlington, Virginia.

Colorado briefly rivaled Vermont and Tennessee for marble production before Marble's quarries closed in 1941. They reopened on a limited scale in 1991 as builders once again began to fancy this fine native stone. The dirt-streeted, fading town has been partly repossessed by aspen and conifers. Buildings are few and far between; most of the town has been wiped out by avalanches and mudslides, which have sometimes left exposed marble foundations as souvenirs. Today only a handful of residents live year round in a town that once housed some 1,300 people.

GU29 Colorado Yule Marble Company Mill Site

Park and W. 3rd sts. (NR)

John C. Osgood opened this mill to refine the snowy white stone that George Yule had discovered. Nearby, the Mormon church also established the smaller White Marble Company quarry, and eastern stockholders opened the Strauss Quarry. Several marble-clad ruins, including six storage shed towers, remain of Osgood's operation.

GU30 Colorado Yule Marble Quarry

1880s. 4 miles south of Marble on Yule Creek Rd.

In 1990 the revived Colorado Yule Marble Company, headquartered in Denver, took a seventy-year lease from the Vermont Marble Company, which had owned the main quarry since the old Colorado Yule Marble Company (1905) went out of business in 1941. This huge underground quarry has provided stone for more than seventy-five structures in the United States, which are listed in *Marble, Colorado: City of Stone* (1970), by Duane Vandenbusche and Rex Myers. A steep, scenic dirt road leads to the fenced quarry, where tours are by special permission.

GU31 Marble Historical Society Museum (Marble High School)

1910. 412 W. Main St. (NR)

Marble's old high school, with its marble foundation and stout, square porch posts, is the largest building in town. The gabled entry porch of the building, topped by an open bell cupola, is echoed by the triangular dormer behind it. Bungalow and Craftsman elements are apparent in the two-story, side-gabled structure over a full basement on a U plan. Shiplap siding is decorated on the front with half timbering in the porch and dormer gable ends. The large windows, symmetrically arranged, have a nine-over-one double-hung sash configuration, with small, multipane units tucked under the eaves. The school is painted green and white, the Colorado Yule Marble Company colors, which are also appropriate for the woodsy setting.

GU32 Marble Town Hall

c. 1908. 407 W. Main St. (NR)

This is the largest model of several company homes provided by the Colorado Yule Marble Company. Distinguished by a gambrel roof, overhanging eaves, and exposed rafter ends, it has an inset, open, full-width porch. Moved from its original site on State Street and renovated as the town hall in the late 1960s, the wooden building has no foundation but does have a new metal roof.

GU33 Parry House

1891, William D. Parry, builder. 115 W. Main St. (NR)

William Parry, a Welsh miner who helped found the town of Marble, built his front-gabled, one-and-one-half-story house on a stone foundation. It is sheathed in board-and-batten siding and has decorative shingles and bargeboard and a full-width porch. Scattered outbuildings are connected by wooden sidewalks.

GU34 St. Paul's Community Church

1886; moved 1910. 123 State St. (northeast corner of W. 2nd St.) (NR)

Moved here from Aspen, this little Gothic Revival frame church with a steep-pitched roof has a marble cross inlaid in the concrete entryway. A cross-gabled wing at the rear, finished in board and batten, added two rooms and a recess for the chancel, creating a T plan. In 1911 a belfry was added above the protruding entry vestibule to accommodate a 500-pound bell cast by Moncy Bell Company, Troy, New York. The clapboard shell is graced with lancet windows that shed light on a well-preserved interior.

GU35 Crystal River Powerhouse

1892. Gunnison County 3, 7 miles southeast of Marble (NR)

One of Colorado's most photographed buildings generated electricity for nearby mines. This steep-gabled log structure perched on a rock outcropping in the Crystal River consists of a round-log compressor house attached to a single-story board-and-batten gear house. A penstock of rough-milled 6-inch-square cross braces on 12-by-12-inch vertical beams descends directly to the river from below the gear house. The operation closed in 1917, and the mechanical equipment, water wheel, and dam are gone, but the stabilized powerhouse remains.

Pitkin

Pitkin (1879, 9,000 feet) sprang up as a silver mining town named for Colorado governor Frederick W. Pitkin. The 1904 Pitkin Hotel (Masonic Block), 329 Main Street, and the tiny Denver, South Park & Pacific depot (1882) at the northeast corner of State and 6th streets, with its oversized, bracketed roof, have been restored. Built into a south-facing hill, the Pitkin City Hall (1900), 400 4th Street (NR), has a stone first floor with a lap-sided second story and an open bell tower. This quaint town in a remote, picturesque mountain valley is watered by open irrigation ditches between the street and plank sidewalks along Main Street. Survivors include a false-fronted assay office (1881) and mercantile building, as well as the gabled Queen Anne Style Community Church.

GU36 Alpine Tunnel

1881. 19 miles northeast of Pitkin via Quartz Creek Rd.

Horseshoe arches of 12-by-12-inch California redwood timbers still support this tunnel cut beneath the Continental Divide at 11,600 feet for the Denver, South Park & Pacific Railroad. Nominally headed for the Pacific, this narrow-gauge line exhausted its funds and energy digging the first tunnel under Colorado's Continental Divide and never got beyond Gunnison County. Aban-doned in 1910 and sealed off, the tunnel is celebrated in a two-room museum in the restored West Portal Depot. Tunnel Gulch Tank has been restored along an auto road using the twisting roadbed of the DSP&P. The Palisades, a 33-foot-high, 452-foot-long, hand-fitted stone retaining wall two-and-one-half feet thick allowed the trains to cross the face of a sheer granite cliff. Dry-laid rubble cut from the cliff widened a narrow natural shelf to accommodate the track. This is perhaps the largest example of stone railroad construction in the American West.

Tincup

Gold panned out of East Willow Creek in a tin cup gave birth to Tincup (1880, 10,160 feet), one of Colorado's most picturesque "ghost towns." Set in a lush mountain meadow, this quaint, dirt-streeted log and frame town is well maintained by a summer community who annually condemn one of their number to winter there to guard the town. In 1900, 264 residents sustained two newspapers and numerous saloons, but fires in 1906 and 1913 hastened the town's decline. By 1917 it was abandoned during the long winter. Approximately fifty structures, most constructed between 1879 and 1910, survive, many of them native pine log cabins chinked with the local gray clay. Log interiors were smoothed so the cabins could be insulated with newspaper or muslin. The

Tincup

Tincup Store (c. 1905) was the first headquarters for the Gunnison National Forest. Frenchy's Restaurant (1984), northwest corner of Grand Avenue and Main Street, is a new log cabin built to look old. The cemetery in the nearby forest includes both wrought iron and log fences to protect family plots.

GU37 **Town Hall**

1903. Northwest corner of Grand and Washington aves.

Tincup's Queen Anne town hall is its most conspicuous and photographed structure.

The lap-sided, front-gabled building has twin corner entries, also gable-roofed, one surmounted by a closed bell tower. It still functions as the town hall and community center.

GU38 **Jail**

1890s. End of Walnut St.

A low-slung, hewn log structure with a metal roof, heavy timber shutters, and steel-barred windows, the Tincup jail has ceiling logs that extend through the front gable and dovetailed log walls that project beyond the corners. Even the outhouse has an outside lock.

Hinsdale County   (HN)

Hinsdale County, founded in 1874 and named for politician George A. Hinsdale, first chose San Juan City as a county seat. Both San Juan City and the current county seat, Lake City, followed the western custom of kiting, or adding "city" to a name as a tail is added to a kite. The extension, it was thought, made a town sound bigger and gave it a better chance to fly.

Three national forests (Rio Grande, San Juan, and Uncompahgre) and the Bureau of Land Management embrace more than 95 percent of this mountainous county, whose population peaked at 1,609 residents in 1900. A silver boom in the 1870s and the arrival of the D&RG in 1889 swelled growth, but the 1893 devaluation of silver snuffed booster hopes permanently. Of fifteen ghost towns in the county, the best-preserved is Carson, accessible only via a rough four-wheel-drive route. With a 1990 population of 467, Hinsdale boasts of being the least populous county in Colorado and one of the smallest in the United States. Since the 1920s the population of the entire county has been under 500, almost all concentrated in or near Lake City, the only live town.

Lake City

The county seat (1875, 8,671 feet) was founded by Enos T. Hotchkiss as a stop on his toll road between Saguache and the new gold rush town of Howardsville. Hotchkiss lingered at Lake City after he discovered the Golden Fleece lode. He platted the town on the usual grid, in the valley where Henson Creek joins the Lake Fork of the Gunnison River. The remote town, isolated by high peaks, was named for nearby Lake San Cristobal, the third largest natural lake in Colorado.

The boom-and-bust cycles of most mining towns were accentuated in Lake City. During the initial 1877 boom an estimated 136 buildings were completed, including two smelters, the courthouse, and a dozen businesses. A second boom in the 1880s produced a now-vanished brick school (1881, Robert S. Roeschlaub), the Hough Block, and a number of stylish brick residences. The 1893 depression nearly drowned Lake City, although the D&RG spur line remained until 1933. Now primarily a summer town, Lake City has installed plank sidewalks and preserved many of its silver-era structures. Stone and false-fronted frame buildings, generally in the Italianate style, characterize a well-preserved business district. Lake City remains one of Colorado's most scenic mining towns with local preservation guidelines as well as National Register Historic District designation.

HN01 **Hinsdale County Museum** (Finley Block)

1877. 130 Silver St. (southeast corner of 2nd St.)

Henry Finley, the president of the Lake City Town Company, had this one-story store built with both dressed and rough stone. The facade has three elliptical-arched front openings, the center one being a recessed doorway. As the first stone edifice in town, the Finley Block marked Lake City's graduation from the tent, log, and frame stage of town building. Celebrated as the "Stone Trade Palace," the building served as the Odd Fellows hall for decades until 1974, when the Hinsdale County Historical Society converted it to a museum. This jewel retains its large storefront windows, double-

HN03 First National Bank of Lake City (Miners and Merchants Bank)

bracketed metal cornice, and interior hardwood floors and pressed metal ceiling.

HN02 **Drugstore**

1876. 227 Silver St.

Swivel stools at the marble soda fountain are still in use in this extraordinarily well-preserved pharmacy. The frame Italianate storefront provides a good preview of the antique Eastlake display cases, medicine cabinets, and bottle racks inside.

HN03 **First National Bank of Lake City** (Miners and Merchants Bank)

c. 1877, George Bauer and John Schultz, builders. 231 Silver St. (southwest corner of 3rd St.)

John S. Hough hired George Bauer and John Schultz, stonemasons from Del Norte in Rio Grande County and brothers-in-law, to build this two-story stone bank building with a wooden cornice supported by scalloped and scrolled brackets. They used dressed local stone for the pilasters between arched windows with oversized keystones. Inside, skillful mortise-and-tenon joints distinguish the construction, as do the thick brick walls of a walk-in vault, hardwood floors, and a pressed metal ceiling. The Thatcher brothers of Pueblo took over the bank after its initial failure and operated it until 1904, when the Bank Exchange Saloon moved in. Nowadays this splendid structure houses the First National Bank of Lake City and the newspaper—the tiny, venerable *Hinsdale County Silver World.*

HN04 **Town Hall** (Opera House–Armory)

1883. 230 3rd St. (southeast corner of Bluff St.)

Three 9-foot-high doors distinguish the brick facade of this stone opera house with a 16-by-22-foot stage. Sandstone keystones ornament the arched openings, while large timber trusses installed after an 1886 roof collapse support the main hall, which now has two wings. The Pitkin Guards of the state militia headquartered here, but the building also served for shows, dances, and as a roller skating rink. Most recently it has been a community center and the town hall.

HN05 Hough Block

1880, John S. Hough. Silver St. (northeast corner of 3rd. St.)

The local brick construction of the Hough Block is highlighted by native sandstone trim and a cast iron storefront from T. R. Pullis and Sons, St. Louis. The store has been in continuous use since it opened, selling everything from hardware to liquor, with offices upstairs. The subterranean Hole-in-the-Wall Saloon contains wildlife dioramas, ranging from a lurking raccoon to a howling coyote.

HN06 First Baptist Church

1891. Bluff St. (west end of 4th St.)

Exuberant pediments and scrolled wooden trim shine on this Queen Anne church with lap siding and Carpenter's Gothic detailing. The 45-foot steeple culminates in a weathervane finial with a cutout cross. Fine leaded and stained glass windows grace a sanctuary that seats over a hundred on folding opera chairs. Volunteers completely restored the church and installed a new metal roof for the building's centennial.

HN07 Frank House

1880, Jacob J. Frank. 430 Silver St.

Jacob Frank, the village blacksmith, apparently designed and built this story-and-a-half hand-hewn log cabin for his family. A smaller, one-story cabin attached at the rear enlarges the rustic dwelling and adds a brick chimney. The cabin is one of the few survivors from the town's mining camp stage.

HN08 Kohler House

1881, Henry Kohler. Northwest corner of Silver St. and 5th St.

Henry Kohler, the town druggist, built a small, L-shaped Queen Anne cottage of stone faced in ornate local brickwork. The house is distinguished by Ionic porch columns (1911) and round-arched windows with shutters. Kohler later moved to Denver and, with partner Frank McLister, founded the largest paint plant in the Rockies, the Komac Paint Company.

HN09 Marsh House

1893, Jefferson J. Marsh. 608 Gunnison Ave.

Marsh, an amateur architect and professional builder, designed his own lap-sided Queen Anne home as well as the more extravagant Youmans-Carey House next door. A well-proportioned wraparound veranda leads to a pedimented corner entry. Spoolwork, Eastlake balusters, shinglework, cutout gable end trim, and a second-story balcony over the south side bay enhance this well-preserved example of Carpenter's Gothic. Its fanciful, lacy nature belies its history as the county pest house during the 1918 influenza epidemic. Elegantly restored, it is a splendid picture in sedate gray and white paint.

HN10 Youmans-Carey House

1895, Jefferson J. Marsh, builder. 600 Gunnison Ave.

Originally rainbow hues of green, yellow, and blue highlighted details on the fanciest house in Lake City. Sawmill owner Harry Youmans had the town's leading contractor build this Carpenter's Gothic showplace. Eastlake trim decorates the unusual corner entry porch, which is topped by a little octagonal tower. First- and second-story bays and porches are adorned with ornate wooden brackets, balcony trim, bargeboards, and cutout gable ends. Between the first and second stories, the shiplap siding alternates

HN07 Frank House (left)
HN10 Youmans-Carey House (right)

HN12 Presbyterian Church, manse (below, left)
HN13 Hinsdale County Courthouse (below, right)
HN16 Capitol City (bottom)

with wood panels and a shingle skirt. Saloonkeeper Alex Carey bought the house around 1900. His heirs have restored it from the stone foundation to the finial atop the entry tower.

HN11 Hough House

1877, John S. Hough. 500 Gunnison Ave.

Unlike the Kohler House, this L-shaped clapboard cottage with modest additions has a period porch, as well as a fine square bay window. John Hough, the 1876 Democratic candidate for governor of Colorado, was the town's leading civic and commercial entrepreneur. He also built the Miners and Merchants Bank (HN03) and the Hough Block (HN05) in downtown Lake City.

HN12 Presbyterian Church

1876, George Darley. 1988, restoration and additions. 431 5th St.

The Reverend George Darley, a skilled carpenter, built his own church and an adjacent two-story manse to help keep succeeding Presbyterian ministers happy in isolated Lake City. The white clapboard church with pedimented lintels was a typical country church until 1882, when its vernacular Second Empire tower was added. This 60-foot bell tower has shingles and eight lancet louvers beneath a graceful, soaring spire. The original side doors of the tower base could not accommodate funeral caskets and had to be augmented by a double central door. Darley, Colorado's most prominent pioneer Presbyterian minister, published an autobiography, *Pioneering in the San Juans* (1899). His brother Alex, also a minister, guided this church through the 1880s. The oldest church on the Western Slope retains its original pews and pulpit, illuminated by newer, stained glass windows.

The clapboard L-shaped manse (1879, George Darley), 429 Gunnison Avenue (southwest corner of 5th Street), is likewise an exercise in vernacular Second Empire detailing with its pedimented and bracketed lintels, double windows, and double quatrefoil cutout in the front gable end. Darley's painstaking carpentry paid off: ministers have lived here to this day. Darley also built a Presbyterian church in Ouray and another

in Del Norte, where he also worked to build the Presbyterian College of the Southwest.

HN13 Hinsdale County Courthouse

1877. 137 Henson St.

In this simple, two-story courthouse with a front gable and lap siding, Alfred Packer, Colorado's most notorious criminal, was tried and convicted of murder compounded by cannibalism. "Packer," the judge supposedly said after condemning him to be hanged: "You son of a bitch, there were only seven Democrats in Hinsdale County, and you ate five of them." The courtroom, up a curved staircase, is little changed. The downstairs hallway holds historical exhibits. Outside, sawn brackets around the eaves and lintel moldings provide chaste ornament for one of the state's least ostentatious courthouses.

HN14 St. Rose of Lima Catholic Church

1878, George Campbell, builder. 1987, restoration. 123 Park St. (NR)

Tiny Gothic-arched windows and a blind rose window decorate the shingled steeple and bell tower of this clapboard Carpenter's Gothic church. Local carpenter George Campbell prepared plans for a $2,500 church, which was scaled down to this 32-by-55-foot, $1,200 building. The 1987 restoration removed the original plaster and lath interior and the adobe bricks which had been built into the walls as insulation.

HN15 Foote House

1882. 1980s, renovation. 125 Park St.

Italianate massing and some detailing survive on this altered two-story brick house, considered the handsomest and most expensive ($4,000) house in town when Stephen C. Foote built it. Square, diamond, and fishscale shingling cover the mansard roof and help to integrate various additions, including a Neo-Victorian two-car garage.

HN16 Capitol City

1877–1920. 10 miles west of Lake City on Henson Creek Rd. (Hinsdale County 20)

This would-be capital of Colorado is sited in a broad mountain valley. Founder George S. Lee platted an ambitious 200-acre townsite and built his large brick house as a "governor's mansion." Lee incorporated what he claimed would soon be a city of thousands. Census records show a peak population of 59 in 1910, although Capitol City boosters contend that it reached 500 between the ten-year counts. Capitol City's fantasy of displacing Denver was still alive in 1895, when *The Resources and Mineral Wealth of Hinsdale County* boasted that it had "all the appearances of a metropolitan town . . . is situated in the richest belt of Southern Colorado" and had "produced several million dollars worth of ore when silver and lead were at fair prices." Today an easily drivable dirt road leads to a restored post office of hewn, V-notched logs, one old cabin, and a few new log summer homes. The "governor's mansion," like Lee's state capital dream, has vanished.

HN17 Rose Lime Kiln

1881, Samuel Tarkington, builder. Beside Henson Creek on Henson Creek Rd. (Hinsdale County 20), 12 miles west of Lake City

Capitol City financier and developer George S. Lee built this kiln in anticipation of a building boom that never transpired. Named for his daughter, the kiln extracted lime through heat calcination to be used in lime mortar and in chinking for log buildings. Abandoned in 1882, the 44-foot-tall structure consists of a central, rectangular chimney with attached furnaces at the base and a battered central section reinforced with external steel rods at stress points. Lee used brick and stone from local sources and designed the kiln so that fuel and lime never touched. Limestone was introduced in the upper part of the chimney and heated to 1,000 degrees as it descended until the lime accumulated in the bottom five feet of the chimney, then was cooled and removed through a metal hopper.

Archuleta County (AA)

State Senator Antonio D. Archuleta introduced the bill to create the county named for him in 1885. Most of this mountainous county is either in San Juan National Forest or part of the Southern Ute Reservation, which occupies its southwest quadrant. The Denver & Rio Grande reached Pagosa Springs in 1881 and began shipping out cattle, sheep, and timber. Forests of giant ponderosa pines and Englemann spruce made Archuleta County the state's largest lumber producer by 1900. The modern economy is supported by production of oil, sand, and gravel as well as by agriculture, lumbering, and recreation, with the last predominant. Vernacular architecture, Anglo and Hispanic, prevails.

Pagosa Springs

The county seat (1878, 7,079 feet) took its name from the Ute word for "boiling water" or "healing water." Ute legends speak of a plague that fell upon the tribe. In desperation, they held a council on the banks of the San Juan River. The Utes danced and prayed around a huge bonfire until, exhausted, they slept. Upon awakening the Indians found, in place of the bonfire, the steaming waters of the Great Pagosa. After they bathed in and drank the water the Utes were cured.

Colorado's largest natural hot springs also attracted white hunters and prospectors. By 1876 placer claims and cabins rimmed the main spring. One square mile surrounding the principal spring was staked out as a townsite in 1877 and platted in 1883. Fort Lewis was established at Pagosa Springs in 1878 to protect the interlopers from the Utes, but was moved to a site near Durango in 1880.

With a population of just over 1,200, Pagosa Springs is the only sizable community in a county of about 5,500 residents. Thanks to a $1.3 million Department of Energy grant in 1979, many downtown buildings are on a municipal geothermal energy circuit. Other buildings have their own private geothermal systems. During the early 1990s the town constructed a landscaped river walk with paved paths, a restroom gazebo, and covered picnic tables. A modern resort and condominium community three miles west of town on U.S. 160 includes the picturesque, hewn log Six Mile Ranch Cabin (1891).

AA01 Rolling Pin Bakery Cafe

1906. 214 Pagosa St. (U.S. 160)

This Craftsman bungalow is made of smooth cast stone blocks, with porch columns of the same material, on a rough-faced cast stone base. Wide eaves with sawn brackets now shelter the outdoor deck of a cafe and bakery.

AA02 Pagosa Springs Middle School

1924, Leo Des Jardins Company. 310 Pagosa St.

Multishaded orange brick banding and trim highlight this symmetrical, two-story beige brick former high school, which is on the city's geothermal circuit. Paired entrances are located in slightly protruding side wings under heavily bracketed porticos, in bays that rise to hexagonal caps, giving the impression of towers.

Next to the middle school is the Pagosa Springs High School (1954, Wheeler and Lewis; 1982, Lescher and Mahoney), a series of interlocking bays extending east and south from a taller, low-gabled original wing. Both newer structures have flat roofs and single-story elevations in painted concrete block and share a polygonal entry lobby that focuses on a sunken conversation pit.

AA03 Great Pagosa Hot Spring

Hot Springs Rd. at San Juan Ave.

The largest hot spring in the state (136 degrees F.) flows into a pool about 75 feet in diameter. The Big Pagosa is fenced to keep out daredevils and has outdoor interpretive markers. The adjacent commercial hot springs has channeled other hot springs into a series of sculpted concrete pools descending a slope to the river, allowing patrons to stew over a wonderful view of the San Juan River and the San Juan Mountains beyond.

AA04 Post Office

1993. Hot Springs Rd. across from the Great Pagosa Hot Spring

In a departure from postal service functionalism, this festive post office playfully reinterprets the observation towers of old Fort Lewis. The loading dock drew inspiration from the town's gabled D&RG depot, now gone.

AA05 Pagosa Hotel

c. 1900. 416–424 Pagosa St.

The town's large old two-story hotel now houses a cinema and shops in the ground-floor storefronts, with a central staircase entry leading to upstairs offices. A low, arched parapet distinguishes this otherwise plain brick hotel overlooking the river.

AA06 Archuleta County Courthouse

1928, Eugene G. Groves. 455 Pagosa St.

Archuleta County's third courthouse, a Denver architect's design, uses naturally heated water from a 170-foot-deep artesian well pumped through a heat exchanger to an otherwise standard system of hot water radiators. When constructed, it was considered one of the most advanced geothermal buildings in the country. Subsequent additions to the original two-story structure have greatly enlarged the original space. By extending the structure down a bank to the San Juan River, the county added basement space exposed on the south and fronting the new river walk. The whole is united by a stucco coating with raised horizontal banding and grouped windows with arched surrounds. Contrasting vertical piers visually divide the long facade into bays.

AA06 Archuleta County Courthouse

AA07 **Ruby M. Sisson Memorial Library**

1989, George King. Southwest corner of Pagosa and 7th sts.

The library is nestled into a hillside and bermed with banks of native plants on the north and east, with a lower level of the L plan exposed by glazing at the northwest corner. The mass of the dark gray standing-seam metal roof dominates the design with its horizontal emphasis. The handsome oak entry to the upper level on the south has a generous porte-cochère. The narrow windows are grouped between bands of raised courses in the rough cinderblock walls, under wide, overhanging eaves.

AA08 **Echo Manor Inn**

c. 1970–1990. 3360 Archuleta County 84, 3 miles south of Archuleta

Locally known as "the castle," the Echo Manor Inn looks more like a homemade, vernacular version of a Charles Platt country manor. Inspired by a trip to Disneyland, the original owner made many additions to what began as a simple A-frame house. Its A-frame origins are commemorated by the steep pitches of the multiple shingled gables and dormers. A uniform stucco finish adds some cohesion, but the multilevel interior is erratic. A subsequent owner converted this Tudoresque fantasy into a bed and breakfast.

AA09 **Chimney Rock Archaeological Area**

17 miles west of Pagosa Springs via U.S. 160, then south 3 miles on Colorado 151 (NRA)

The U.S. Forest Service offers archaeological tours of the ruins atop the 1,200-foot hill crowned by Chimney Rock. At this spectacular site, possibly a religious shrine, prehistoric Coloradans built the northeastern outpost of Anasazi culture. It represents both Chaco- and Mesa Verde–type cliff dweller constructions. Kivas, rectangular pueblo houses, and other ruins line the hilltop site of this prominent natural landmark near the Piedra River. Excavations since the 1920s have focused on this site as the easternmost of the cliff dweller settlements. Like the Anasazi at Mesa Verde, these Indians abandoned their village in the thirteenth century, apparently to resettle in Rio Grande River pueblos. Taos Pueblo Indians in New Mexico attach religious significance to Chimney Rock, likening its massive twin stone pinnacles to twin war gods. More than 200 architectural structures indicate that hundreds of Native Americans lived here, with a peak construction era from around 900 to 1125.

La Plata County (LP)

La Plata County (1874) takes its name from the La Plata (Spanish for silver) Mountain Range, where Spaniards discovered silver in the 1700s. Other minerals also lay in the rugged, snowy mountains in the northern part of the county, while the broad mesas and river valleys in the south fostered agriculture. Water resources include the Animas, Los Pinos, La Plata, and Florida rivers and their tributaries, and Electra Lake, Lemon Dam (1964), and Vallecito Reservoir (1941, WPA). The San Juan National Forest occupies nearly all of the northern half of the county, and the Southern Ute Indian Reservation occupies much of the southern half, with a narrow band of land in between containing Durango, the county seat. This prosperous town of more than 13,000 and its growing suburbs house about half the county's 33,000 residents.

An 1870s gold rush first brought in settlers, but development awaited the 1881 arrival of the Denver & Rio Grande Railroad. Not only gold, but silver, coal, oil, gas, vanadium, and uranium have helped make this the richest county in southwestern Colorado. Agriculture and recreation, including hunting, fishing, and skiing, provide the modern-day economic base.

Durango

The county seat (1880, 6,512 feet) was founded by the D&RG just south of then thriving Animas City (c. 1877), which soon was eclipsed and annexed by the railroad town. Animas City lay on the river the Spanish named for lost souls (El Río de Las Animas Perdidas), and when Durango arose two miles downstream it was indeed doomed. William J. Palmer, Alexander C. Hunt, and other D&RG town promoters named Durango after the city in Mexico which they hoped the railroad would reach someday. In the Colorado town, the railroad controlled the land, a smelter site, and nearby coalfields.

D&RG vice president Dr. William A. Bell laid out a planned community, like the D&RG town of Colorado Springs. He platted Durango with two parks, a county court-house site, church sites, and the 3rd Avenue Parkway residential district on the bluff east of town. By 1890 horsedrawn trolleys clanged up and down Main Avenue. The "sagebrush metropolis," cheered *The Durango Record*'s feisty editor Caroline Romney, "is really attaining metropolitan proportions."

Coal-rich Durango boomed as the smelter city of the San Juans, replacing Parrot City as the county seat in 1881. The San Juan Smelter (1881) processed silver and gold ores and later uranium. The later use led the Environmental Protection Agency to demolish the huge brick stack in 1988, remove radioactive dirt from its base, and promote the return of vegetation burned off Smelter Mountain. Since the smelter closed in 1963, Durango has concentrated on tourism. Fort Lewis College, established in 1933, is the town's single largest employer, followed by

Durango, 1880s; Strater Hotel in left background

the Durango-Silverton Narrow Gauge Railroad.

The railroad, which draws some 200,000 passengers a year, has kept Main Avenue the center of activity in Durango, eclipsing even the new, dun-colored Durango Mall south of town. Both Main Avenue and the Third Avenue Residential District between 5th and 15th streets have been set aside as National Register Historic Districts. Durango's suburbs now sprawl northward for 11 miles along U.S. 550 to Hermosa, and along U.S. 160 westward toward Hesperus and eastward to Bayfield.

LP01 Durango-Silverton Narrow Gauge Depot (Denver & Rio Grande Depot)

1882, J. H. Ernest Waters. 479 Main Ave. (NR)

The D&RG's distinctive pale yellow and chocolate brown colors shine on this debonair depot, a clapboard affair with a second-story central pavilion and side-gabled wings. J. H. Ernest Waters, an English mining engineer, designed the depot, and Charles Walker supervised construction. Tongue-in-groove wainscoting added in 1935 cut off the lower half of the pedimented windows, according to long-time stationmaster Amos Cordova. The well-maintained passenger depot and its gift shop serve the tourist armies boarding America's most celebrated narrow-gauge steam excursion train.

A lawn and flower gardens grace the depot's front yard, and in back is a fabulous collection of antique or restored railroad shops and yards that can repair or fabricate every piece necessary to keep the railroad rolling. The old turntable (1884, Detroit Ironworks) is still in use although upgraded from the original manual operation. A February 10, 1989, fire destroyed the historic roundhouse and shops, but they were quickly restored in reproduction structures which visitors can tour for a fee.

The Durango-Silverton Narrow Gauge Railroad is not a restoration, but a never-abandoned anachronism in use since 1882. D&RG engineer Thomas Wigglesworth oversaw construction of the 54 miles from Durango up the Animas River canyon to Silverton, in San Juan County. Despite the torturous mountain terrain, Wigglesworth achieved a maximum grade of 2.5 percent (a 2.5-foot elevation gain in 100 feet of track). He also used all-steel track, instead of the iron track previously used by the D&RG. Narrow shelves were cut into rock cliffs 400 feet above the Animas River gorge for this cliff-hugging railroad. The D&RG continued service between Durango and Silverton until 1981, when Charles Bradshaw bought the line and upgraded it. The line has been designated both a National Historic Landmark and a National Historic Civil Engineering Landmark.

LP02 Strater Hotel

1888, Paul Geier. 699 Main Ave. (southwest corner of 7th St.) (NR)

The Strater Hotel, opened during Durango's first boom, glories in Victorian excess, starting with its overblown cornice, two-story oriel windows, and hand-carved white sandstone frosting. Henry M. Strater erected the four-story, red brick hotel and four years later constructed the three-story Columbian Hotel (1892) next door. After the crash of 1893 crushed Strater, his two hotels were consolidated. Subsequent owners, the Barker family, have restored and greatly improved the hotel. They have endowed the lobby, dining rooms, meeting rooms, the Diamond Belle Saloon, and the ninety-three guest rooms with antique furnishings, including what they claim is the world's largest collection of American Victorian walnut antiques.

Louis L'Amour, once the world's best-selling western novelist, always asked for room 222, above the Diamond Belle Saloon, where the honky tonk atmosphere set the mood for his sentimental romances of the Old West. Room 222, like many others, is lavishly decorated with flocked wallpaper and window treatments which consume 30 yards of plush velvet at each window.

LP03 Newman Block

1892. 801–813 Main Ave. (northwest corner of 8th St.) (NR)

Red sandstone ashlar blocks from Ramsey's Quarry near Dolores give this three-story Romanesque Revival building a masonry monumentality. Pioneer miner, merchant, and state senator Charles Newman dressed up his corner edifice with cast iron storefronts and a pressed metal frieze with bas-relief garlands. Acanthus leaf capitals frame the leaded and frosted glass storefront transom. The Newman Block, home to store-front retail uses and upper-story offices, shares its block with some artful infill. Next door to the north, the Main Mall (1976, Richard D. Walker and Associates), 835 Main, uses fine contemporary brickwork for a facade animated by a dramatic cornice, corbeling, recessed two-story round-arched windows, bays, and a recessed entrance. Walker, a Durango architect, used textured burnt orange and blue-tinged bricks in this modern structure that acknowledges the legacy of Victorian buildings destroyed by fire.

LP04 Burns National Bank

1892. 900 Main Ave. (northeast corner of 9th St.)

Distinctive rosy purple sandstone, probably from Silverton, faces this splendid two-story bank building with a rounded corner. Colossal round arches frame the street-level windows, while stout, polished colonnettes with Byzantine capitals support the round entry arch of rough stone. The rosy purple stone is used for the dentiled cornice above second-story round-arched windows inset in rectangles. A first-rate east addition (1978, John Pomeroy) uses the same fenestration in a red brick facade and underlines the round-arch theme in an abstract marquee and corner tower, both executed in boxcar siding. The interior has been radically remodeled and modernized.

LP05 First National Bank

1892, John F. Bell, builder. 901 Main Ave. (northwest corner of 9th St.)

In brick, quarry-face stone, and cast iron, this two-story Romanesque Revival bank replaced an 1882 bank destroyed by fire. Brick corbeling and weaving patterns culminate in the flared brick parapet. When federal bank inspectors questioned the location of the region's only national bank in 1985, bank president Alfred Camp shot back that the First had "the most central and desirable corner in Durango." Uncle Sam may have been concerned that the rest of the 900 block was part of Durango's bar and brothel district.

LP06 Central Hotel

1892. 975 Main Ave. (southwest corner of 10th St.)

One of the most striking structures on Main Avenue, this narrow, three-story Italianate hotel has a mansard fourth floor with prominent dormers. Its red brick skin contrasts with white stone trim in hand-carved floral patterns. On the first floor is the El Rancho Bar, where twenty-year-old Jack Dempsey, the future heavyweight world champion, supposedly knocked out Andy Mally in the tenth round. A mural on the side of the building commemorates that bout, while a large mural over the pool tables celebrates more recent exploits of regulars.

LP07 Main Avenue Furnishings (Balthasar Kern Saloon)

1889. 1015 Main Ave.

Durango businessmen sought the same stylish garb for their buildings as their peers in Denver, Chicago, St. Louis, and San Francisco. The Kern family had the Mesker Brothers of St. Louis provide their two-story, cast iron storefront. Colored glass squares frame the large transom windows, while the iron facade sprouts into rosettes, medallions, Ionic capitals, and a bracketed cornice on this fine Italianate emporium.

LP08 Office Building (Post Office)

1928, James A. Wetmore, OSA; F. M. Beadreau, local construction engineer. 1060 Main Ave. (NR)

LP07 Main Avenue Furnishings (Balthasar Kern Saloon)

Georgian Revival style is exemplified by this golden brick post office, now happily restored for offices. Grand, round-arched openings with fanlights make the facade a study in symmetry. Three diminutive third-story pedimented dormers hide behind a rooftop balustrade. In the elegant interior many original fixtures, including the marble stairs, basement vault, and golden oak and brass elevator cab, survive, as does the U-shaped plan. Original architectural drawings are displayed as part of a lobby exhibit on the building's construction.

LP09 La Plata County Courthouse

1959, C. Francis Pillsbury. 1989, Caudill Gustafson Ross and Associates. 1060 E. 2nd Ave. (between 10th and 11th sts.)

Durangoans razed their old (1892) Italianate stone courthouse after Francis Pillsbury, a Denver architect, designed a two-story, orange brick, rectilinear wing that was left freestanding. Thirty years later a team of Aspen architects added another wing in the same boxy form as Pillsbury's work with a contemporary version of a dentiled cornice in metal, recessed windows, and a second

story of slightly cantilevered cubes. They tied the wings together and gave the full-block complex a distinctive entry through a central, three-story Neo-Victorian bell tower crowned with a wrought iron crest. The old courthouse bell and Seth Thomas clock were repaired by Durango automobile mechanic Tony Ferdinando and installed in the tower.

LP10 Carnegie Library

1907, William E. and Arthur A. Fisher. 1967, addition, George King. 1993, restoration and addition, R. Michael Bell. 1188 E. 2nd Ave. (southeast corner of 12th St.)

Broad eaves give a Prairie Style horizontality to this one-story Beaux-Arts Mediterranean Revival library with a creamy stucco exterior and a red tile roof. A 1967 south addition in burnt orange brick clashed with the original. Durango architect Michael Bell came up with a fine solution: his new entry hides the 1967 eyesore and uses cream-colored stucco walls with cast stone banding that matches the original jewel box.

LP11 School Administration Building (Durango High School)

1916, Charles S. Thomas and Thomas MacLaren. 2nd Ave. and E. 12th St.

Two prominent Colorado Springs architects designed this Beaux-Arts Mediterranean Revival high school, dressing the three-story building in beige brick with creamy terracotta trim. A curvilinear parapet over the central, round-arched entry is echoed by the terracotta entry surround. This virtually unaltered building is enhanced by a front yard rose garden and landscaped grounds that flow westward into the grassy city park on Main Avenue.

LP12 3rd Avenue Residential District

3rd Ave. between E. 5th and 15th sts. (NRD)

Durango's historic residential district is a veritable catalog of 1880s to 1920s homes, ranging from mansions such as the Amy House (LP12.3), the neighboring Wilson-Perking House (1892), and the fine, half-timbered, two-story Craftsman house at 1215 3rd Avenue, to modest cottages and bungalows such as saloonkeeper James Barrie's house (c. 1885), 1131 3rd Avenue, with a later metal roof and asbestos siding that do not conceal the graceful shape of the original cottage. Third Avenue is a tree-lined parkway with a median, generous setbacks, and planting strips that has generally inspired attractive landscaping of even the most modest dwellings.

LP12.1 First Presbyterian Church

1890, L. H. Volk and Sons. 1161 3rd Ave. (southwest corner of E. 12th St.) (NR)

Brooklyn, New York, architects made this church a pretty Queen Anne picture. They specified rough-faced native sandstone for walls rising to a shake shingle hood and bell

tower. Round arches are repeated in the stained glass windows, the entries, and the graceful bell tower.

LP12.2 Wigglesworth House

1883, Charles Bayles, builder. 1154 3rd Ave.

William Hudson Wigglesworth, the son of D&RG surveyor Thomas Wigglesworth, was a Durango town manager who built this two-story vernacular Colonial Revival house. Its muted details include the stone foundation, shed dormers, miniature roof brackets, and ball finials on the side gable ends.

LP12.3 Hood Mortuary (Amy House)

1888, Little and O'Connor. 1261 3rd Ave. (southwest corner of E. 13th St.)

Ernest Amy, manager of the San Juan Smelter, hired New York architects and spent $50,000 to build Durango's finest home, hoping to lure his wife west from New York City. Durango newspapers compared it to "a New York City Mansion" and cited it as proof "that Durango is no mushroom city." Durango's first all-electric house, it had 25-watt light fixtures in every room. Notwithstanding heroic architectural efforts, Amy's wife did not like Durango and persuaded him to go back to New York after the crash of 1893.

A sophisticated specimen that would be at

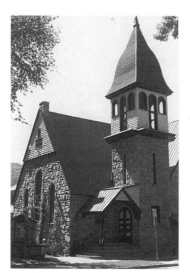

LP12.1 First Presbyterian Church
LP12.3 Hood Mortuary (Amy House)

La Plata County (LP) 559

home in Newport or Providence, the house displays the polygonal dormers, bands of multipane windows, round arches, rough stone, rustic shingles, and tall, ornate chimneys characteristic of the Shingle Style. It is dominated by a round, three-story corner tower with a nipple finial. This bulging, oversized tower contains a first-floor parlor and a second-story library, now the best-preserved room in the house. Contrasting with the shingle skin of the tower and second story is the local tawny sandstone, used in rough ashlar blocks, for the first story. Inside, cherry wood paneling prevails on the first floor with pine for the third-story servant's quarters. Slight interior modifications in what is now an elegant funeral home include a chapel and casket display rooms.

LP13 La Plata County Fairgrounds

1890s. 1935, stables and grandstand, WPA. Northwest corner of Main Ave. and E. 25th St. (NR)

Tawny local sandstone forms the walls, bandstand support, and entry gateway for this rodeo and fairgrounds. A stone wall stretching for three blocks along Main Avenue is the back wall for adobe brick stables. They face the large grandstand, a frame affair built on stout stone pillars. Amid sprawling Main Avenue development, this relic of the 1930s somehow survives, despite intense development pressure, as perhaps Colorado's finest WPA-built county fairgrounds.

LP14 Animas School Museum

1906. 3065 W. 2nd Ave. (southwest corner of 31st St.)

Since 1980 the La Plata County Historical Society Museum has occupied this three-story sandstone building on spacious, landscaped grounds. The Cummins family, local masons, probably built the school using sandstone quarried from the bluff just behind the site. They laid the rough-cut, quarry-face stone, colored in warm, tawny tones, in regular courses with subtle banding. One schoolroom has been restored as a 1908 setting for time-tripping schoolchildren.

LP15 Fort Lewis College

1956, James M. Hunter Associates. College Hill

James Hunter, a Boulder architect, provided the master plan and designed the early buildings for Fort Lewis College, which is spectacularly sited on a high mesa on the eastern edge of Durango. Most buildings on this sprawling young campus are made of tawny native sandstone. With some 4,300 students, the college is Durango's second biggest industry after tourism. Begun as a military post in Pagosa Springs during the 1880s, this was an Indian school, a high school, and a junior college before it became a four-year college in 1962. The most spectacular structure, Hunter's McPherson Chapel (1959), is a geometric abstraction with a large prow aimed heavenward above an angular stained glass wall, a design reminiscent of Frank Lloyd Wright's Madison, Wisconsin, Unitarian church. Dramatically sited on the edge of the mesa overlooking Durango, it is tied to its site by rough-faced ashlar walls of local sandstone.

Bayfield

Bayfield (1889, 6,900 feet), called Los Pinos until 1899, is a quaint rural town 10 miles east of Durango in a grove of cottonwoods and willows on the Los Pinos River, at the northern edge of the Southern Ute Indian Reservation. The main street, Mill Street, is lined with clapboard and pressed metal false fronted buildings. An old stone town hall has a horseshoe set into its identifying inscription. The stone library across the street is made of the same local sandstone. Nearby attractions include the Rommer Ranch (1878) and the Zabel Canyon Indian Ruins (NR).

Ignacio

Ignacio (1882, 6,432 feet) was named for a Ute Indian chief who led the tribe from the 1880s until his death in 1912. This is the headquarters of the Southern Ute Indian Reservation, which houses the Southern Ute Boarding School (1902) and a former hospital (1933) and girls' dormitory (1930) that are now part of the Tribal Affairs Office Complex. The town was platted in 1910 when whites purchased the land from the tribe. Across the street from the Tribal Affairs Complex, Colorado 172 and La Plata County 314, is the Sky Ute Lodge (1971), a motel, restaurant, museum, community center, and gallery remodeled in 1993 to include a casino.

San Juan County   (SA)

San Juan County (1876), in the heart of the San Juan Mountains, has "three months of winter and nine months of mighty late fall." The growing season averages only fourteen days in Silverton, the county seat, and the county does not have a single farm. Even sheep and cattle only summer here. It took gold, lead, copper, and zinc mining to lure people into this two-mile-high county, where three-fourths of the land is in national forests or wilderness areas. From a peak of 3,063 in 1910, the population has dwindled to less than 500 souls, nearly all of whom live in Silverton, the sole survivor of some sixteen mining towns.

Silverton

The county seat (1874, 9,318 feet) has been preserved by its economic poverty and geographic isolation as a quaint mining town used as a set for many films, including *Naked Spur, Ticket to Tomahawk,* and *Maverick Queen.* After a false start with an 1860 gold humbug, the town blossomed in the 1870s. The Greene Smelter (1874) briefly made Silverton the smelting capital of southwestern Colorado until the railroad arrived in 1882 and carted off Silverton's rich ores to the San Juan Smelter in Durango. By shifting to gold and other metals, Silverton survived the 1893 silver crash. Mining fed the town and the county until 1991, when the Sunnyside Mine closed. Afterward the mining industry hit rock bottom, but Silverton still prides itself on being "the mining town that never quit."

Many of the remote mines above Silverton are accessible only by foot, mountain bike, or four-wheel drive. Even the Denver & Rio Grande, which built the Durango-Silverton line, refused to build up the Animas River to Animas Forks, up Cement Creek to Gladstone, or up Mineral Creek to Chattanooga and Red Mountain. So Otto Mears, a leading entrepreneur of the San Juans, undertook that gamble, with three baby lines that crawled up to timberline mining camps and enabled Silverton to puff itself as the "Narrow Gauge Capital of the World." Tourism is the mother lode today, and the Durango-Silverton Narrow Gauge Railroad disgorges some 2,000 summer tourists daily. Motorists reach Silverton from Ouray and Durango by U.S. 550, the "Million Dollar Highway" (see Ouray County, OR26).

Silverton, snuggled into a picturesque mountain valley surrounded by snowcapped mountains, has a National Historic Landmark designation. The commercial district, which has seen little new construction since 1910, includes several livery stables. Of the notorious red-light district on Blair Street, some of the former bordellos survive, most notably the Welcome Saloon (1883; 1909), 1161 Blair, and the Shady Lady Bar (c. 1900), 1154 Blair. "Chippies" from Blair Street sometimes toured outlying mining towns if business was slow, riding up to boarding houses in tram ore buckets. Fines levied on bordellos, bars, and speakeasies sustained the town coffers, so Silverton did not levy the heavy property taxes which led people in other mining towns to demolish their buildings during hard times to avoid payment. Hospitable landmarks include the Alma House (1902), 220 East 10th Street, which Bridget Hughes opened as a miners' boarding house. Built of rough local granite blocks with a frame, dormered second story,

Silverton

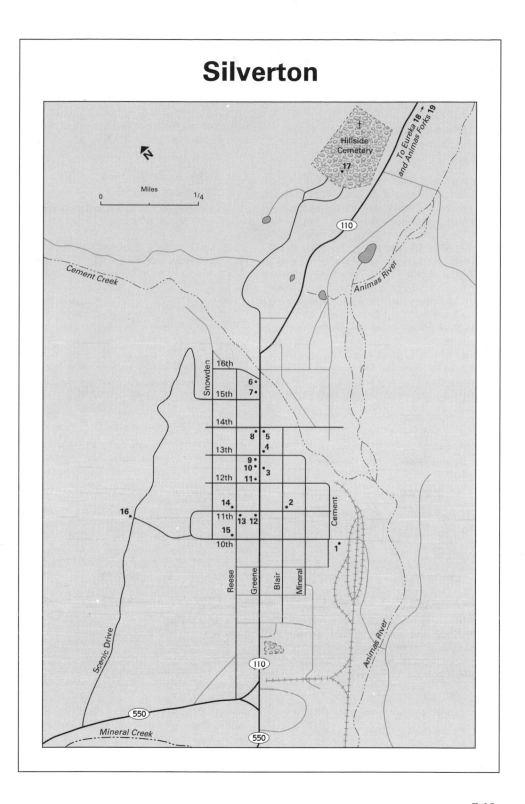

it was restored in the 1980s as a bed and breakfast, as was the Queen Anne Style Wingate House (1886, Emma Harris), 1045 Snowden Street.

SA01 Durango-Silverton Narrow Gauge Depot (Denver & Rio Grande Depot)

1882. East end of 10th St. (NR)

This standard clapboard depot with a gable roof and pedimented windows and doorways was restored during the 1970s by the San Juan County Historical Society. Since 1982 it has been used as a depot and ticket office by the Durango-Silverton Narrow Gauge Railroad. Next door, at 441 10th Street, is the frame depot (1890) which Otto Mears built for his Silverton Railroad. It contains the ticket office and stationmaster's quarters; a later addition housed the depot for another of Mears's narrow-gauge lines, the Silverton Northern Railroad. The SN operated a rail bus (a custom-made contraption with a 1916 Cadillac V-8 engine) between Silverton and Animas Forks until 1936 and to Eureka until 1942. One of these auto-rail hybrids, the Casey Jones, is on display behind the jail museum (SA06).

SA02 Bent Elbow Saloon (Florence Saloon)

1907. 1114 Blair St. (corner of 11th St.)

The Italian builders and original co-owners of this saloon named it for the city in their native Tuscany. The two-story clapboard box sheathed in pressed metal "brick" retains its pressed metal cornice and original storefront with a recessed entry under a new balcony. Now a Hollywoodish invitation to tourists, the saloon once staged mock shootouts and hangings. Inside, not only the ceiling but the walls are clad in pressed metal. The Brunswick Balke Collender back bar was "Union Made by Amalgamated Woodworkers of America."

SA03 Teller House (Fischer Building)

1896, Charles Fischer, builder. 1250 Greene St.

Silverton's brewer, Charles Fischer, erected this double-front, two-story brick building with storefront space below and guest rooms

for the Teller House hotel above. The fine Eastlake wooden trim and the battered oak bar are notable. The Teller House, now a bed and breakfast with a bakery on the ground floor, retains much of its original interior, including doors enclosing the central stairway with its original skylight and boxcar paneling.

SA04 Pickle Barrel (Sherwin and Houghton Store)

1880, George Bauer and John Schultz, stonemasons. 1304 Greene St. (southeast corner of 13th St.)

Stonemasons George Bauer and John Schultz of Del Norte built this gem with the help of local carpenters Emile Homann and George Swan. They used local gray granite for the walls and an unusual stone false front with a tiny wooden bracketed cornice. Rough-cut granite blocks form the uncoursed walls, inside and out, of this one-story commercial building with its original triple-arch plate glass storefront, hardwood floors, and 12-foot-high ceilings.

SA05 Town Hall

1908, Silas W. Smith. 1360 Greene St. (corner of 14th St.)

A silvery, egg-shaped dome caps the open bell tower of this two-story building with a second-story balcony under a Neoclassical pediment supported by paired Ionic columns. Built of Silverton's distinctive local rosy-purple sandstone, it was restored in the 1970s, then re-restored after a Thanksgiving weekend fire in 1992 caused by a heating system that kept snow off the roof. The original town hall and fire station (1883), with a hook and ladder carved over the door, still stands at 1245 Blair Street.

SA06 **San Juan County History Museum** (San Juan County Jail)

1902. 16th and Greene sts.

A three-story brick box with the jailer's quarters on the first floor and cells above served as a shelter for indigents during Silverton's drowsy decades. The interior, and perhaps the exterior, are a standard design from the Pauley Jail Building and Manufacturing Company, St. Louis, which included one woman's cell and a never-finished padded cell. The original state-of-the-art steel cells, complete with leg irons and ball, are now part of the county museum, which moved into the jail in 1965. The predecessor jail (1883), 1361 Greene Street, is a structure of 2-by-6-inch boards laid flat.

SA07 **San Juan County Courthouse**

1907, James Murdoch. 1567 Greene St. (Courthouse Square)

A gold-colored dome crowns this Georgian Revival monument, sited on a grassy square block shared by the San Juan County History Museum and the San Juan County Historical Society Archives and Research Center (1994). On the courthouse lawn is a monument imbedded with ore specimens from fifty-one local mines. Native gray sandstone was used for the foundation as well as the trim of this two-story structure of pressed gray brick, capped by a square tower with an elongated, open bell cupola. Paired Doric columns of cast stone support the entry porticos. The interior is pristine, with the original hexagonal tile mosaic floors, oak woodwork, high ceilings, signage, fixtures, and a treasury of maps showing mining claims and the original town plat.

SA08 **Wyman Hotel** (Wyman Building)

1902, Louis Wyman. 1371 Greene St. (corner of 14th St.)

Louis Wyman arrived in San Juan County in 1885 with fifteen burros and by 1900 had over a hundred pack animals, forty-five employees, and the county's largest freighting firm. Every month he bought nineteen boxcars of hay and grain and delivered some 1,500 tons of ore to the D&RG depot. To celebrate his burro-borne empire, he built this two-story corner building, of rosy-purple local sandstone from the Wyman Quarry on South Mineral Creek. The truncated corner entry rises to a parapet framing a bas-relief of a burro—a pet whose portrait Wyman carved himself. After serving as offices, a general store, and a lodge hall, the edifice had become a parking garage before restoration as the Wyman Hotel in the early 1990s by Donald Stott, who found original construction of 3-by-12 beams and 24-inch-thick stone walls, with skylights that could "stand up to the 21 feet of snow we get each winter in Silverton."

SA09 **Posey and Wingate Building**

1880, George Bauer and John Schultz, stonemasons. 1269 Greene St. (corner of 13th St.)

One of the oldest commercial brick structures in western Colorado was built as a hardware store by Oliver P. Posey and John W. Wingate. The ornate, two-story edifice has a cast iron storefront (T. B. Pullis and Sons, St. Louis) with Corinthian columns. After housing Posey and Wingate's store and the San Juan County Bank, the building became the First National Bank of Silverton. The bank vault is still located in a building whose fine, round-arched windows on 13th Street now frame a lively, high-ceilinged saloon.

SA10 **Silverton Standard and Miner**

1875, George Wright, builder. 1257 Greene St.

By tracing its roots to the *La Plata Miner,* established in 1875, the *Silverton Standard and Miner* claims to be the oldest continuously published newspaper in western Colorado. This small clapboard building houses a cylinder press (R. Hoe and Company, New York, 1830), once used to publish Ouray's *Solid Muldoon* as well as the *Standard and Miner.* Opened as a saloon, the building later saw stints as a dry goods, a cafe, a tailor shop, and a barbershop before the newspaper moved in, along with a bookstore, in 1952.

SA11 Grand Imperial Hotel

SA11 **Grand Imperial Hotel**

1883, John Griswold. 1219 Greene St. (corner of 12th St.)

Boosters of out-of-the-way towns like Silverton built grand hotels to bring the world, or at least some investors, into town. Englishman Charles S. Thomson built this grand hotel, a two-story Italianate building with a mansard third story and prominent battery of gabled dormers. Wrought iron columns separate first-floor plate glass storefronts. Above a first story of square-cut, irregularly coursed ashlar are a second story faced in brick with rhythmical rows of arched windows and a third story with rounded dormers set in diamond-patterned sheet metal. The county courthouse occupied the second floor for several years before the present courthouse was completed. In 1950 Winfield Morton of Dallas, Texas, bought the hotel for $60,000 and spent $369,000 to convert its fifty-six rooms and three bathrooms into forty-two rooms with baths. Resplendent with Victorian fixtures, it is now a forty-room hotel with first-floor lobby, shops, dining rooms, and a splendid saloon whose cherry back bar has diamond dust mirrors set in three ornate arches springing from Corinthian capitals. Saloon hall commotion is quieted somewhat by new pressed metal ceilings from the venerable W. T. Norman Sheet Metal Manufacturing Company of Missouri. These shiny ceilings brighten the common rooms with reflected light and reflect sound down and away from upstairs sleeping rooms.

SA12 **American Legion Post** (Western Federation of Miners Union Hall)

1901. 1069 Greene St. (corner of 11th St.)

Members of the Western Federation of Miners (WFM) donated labor to build this brick edifice with an open second-story hall, only to be evicted during the 1903–1904 strikes. Subsequently their hall housed a store, a funeral home, and various saloons and lodges. Brick pilasters and cast iron columns front the recessed entry and storefronts. Elongated second-story windows with round tops have stone trim beneath a bracketed metal cornice. In 1948 the AFL-CIO sold the hall to the American Legion, but in 1989 the upstairs hall came back to life as the Miners Union Theater. A small, square tower atop the corner entry and a flagpole make this hall easy to find.

The WFM also built the Miners' Hospital (1907), 1325 Snowden Street, on the site of the pioneer cabin of Francis M. Snowden, a founder of Silverton. The hospital, a dreary red brick building on a rough stone foundation, later became headquarters for Standard Metals, Sunnyside Gold, Echo Bay Mines, and other operators of the Sunnyside Mine.

SA13 **United Church of Silverton**

1880, Harlan P. Roberts, builder. 1060 Reese St. (corner of 11th St.)

The oldest Congregational church on the Western Slope did not complete its steep,

SA13 United Church of Silverton

shingle-clad steeple with a weathervane finial until 1892. Pastor Roberts and his flock built this vernacular Carpenter's Gothic church. The matching clapboard parsonage (1884) wears Neoclassical trim instead of the Gothic reserved for the church.

SA14 **Silverton Public Library**

1906, John F. Wing and Marshall S. Mahurin. 11th and Reese sts.

The original men's reading room survives in the stone-walled basement of one of Colorado's best-preserved Carnegie libraries. The original golden oak card catalog and woodwork, as well as portraits of Andrew Carnegie and Charles Darwin, still adorn this tiny sanctuary. The Fort Wayne, Indiana, architects, John Wing and Marshall Mahurin, provided plans implemented by local contractor Thomas G. Edwards.

SA15 **St. Patrick's Catholic Church**

1905, Frederick W. Paroth. 1005 Reese St. (corner of 10th St.)

A Denver architect who did much work for the Denver Catholic Diocese designed this brown brick, stone-trimmed building. It re-

placed a frame church (1884) erected a block farther up 10th Street. Italian and Tyrolean miners donated much of the masonry work and helped construct the rectory (1906) next door. The large, square, open bell tower with a ball finial and Celtic cross and the corner minarets are the only surprises on this otherwise standard Romanesque Revival church with its round-arched openings, rose windows, buttresses, and rough stone foundation. Much love and attention has been spent on this church, despite dwindling resources and membership, as Nellie M. Hill recounts in *High Country Parish* (1984).

SA16 **Christ of the Mines Shrine**

1959. Scenic Dr. and 10th St.

Silverton's fortunes fell to an all-time low in the 1950s when the D&RG suspended year-round operations to become a summer-only passenger operation and the Shenandoah-Dives, the largest mine in the county, closed. Rather than mourn their unemployment, members of the Catholic Men's Club at St. Patrick's Church and Father Joseph Halloran undertook this shrine. The county donated the site and volunteers used old stone from Charles Fischer's abandoned Silverton

SA15 St. Patrick's Catholic Church

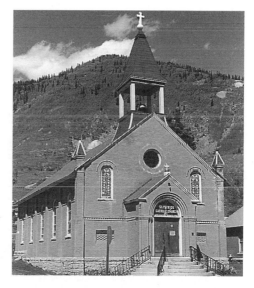

Brewery to make a base and a grotto for the statue.

The whole town donated labor, supplies, and money to buy and install the 5-ton, 12-foot-high Carrara marble Christ, with arms uplifted to bless Silverton and its mines. Shortly after the shrine's 1959 dedication, the Standard Metals Corporation reopened the Sunnyside Mine, and Florida citrus baron Charles Bradshaw revived the Durango-Silverton Narrow Gauge Railroad, which has been Silverton's lifeline since its construction in 1882.

SA17 Hillside Cemetery

1873. .5 mile northeast of Silverton off Colorado 110

A "Dead End" sign leads to Silverton's only cemetery. On a hill overlooking the town, this burial ground invaded by aspen and wildflowers contains stone markers commemorating in various languages the short and dangerous lives of mining town residents. *The Story of Hillside Cemetery, 1873–1988* (San Juan County Historical Society, 1989) contains biographical sketches of nearly all the 1,100 people buried here.

SA18 Eureka

1875–1942. 9 miles northeast of Silverton via Colorado 110 and Engineer Pass Rd.

Beyond Hillside Cemetery, Colorado 110 follows the Animas River to some spectacular

ghost towns and mining ruins. Five miles above Silverton lie relics of the original county seat of Howardsville (1874–1939), where the Old Hundred Mine offers a tram car tour. Another 5 miles up the road, Eureka, the county's only company town, is littered with the huge cement foundations of mills. Among these skeletons stepping up steep mountainsides are various concrete ruins of the Sunnyside Mill, a major gold, silver, lead, and zinc producer from 1873 until 1991. Archimedes must have smiled upon Eureka: More than $50 million in precious metals flowed out of this town and some 200 miners lived here as late as the 1930s, when Eureka's precipitous decline began. Eureka was dismantled and its homes moved to, among other places, Silverton, Durango, and the Idarado Mine on Red Mountain Pass.

SA18 Eureka, Sunnyside Mill, c. 1910

SA19 Animas Forks

SA19 **Animas Forks**

1875–1915. 13 miles northeast of Silverton on Engineer Pass Rd.

Accessible only by four-wheel drive, this is one of Colorado's premier ghost towns, with a breathtaking, 11,200-foot-high site at the confluence of the north and west forks of the Animas River. The town once boasted some 200 residents and a plank sidewalk main street with several hotels, saloons, and the highest newspaper in the United States, *The Animas Forks Pioneer.* The stout old jail (1882), made of 2-by-6-inch planks stacked flat to create stronger walls, survives. So does the William D. Duncan House (1879; stabilized, 1987–1988), with its prominent bay window, at the northwest end of Main Street. The San Juan County Historical Society and Bureau of Land Management have undertaken to preserve Animas Forks and some of the surrounding mines and mills. Among many ruins are the concrete foundation of the three-story Gold Prince Boarding House; the skeleton of the Gold Prince's steel-frame concentrating mill, measuring 363 by 184 feet; and ruins of the 12,600-foot-long tramway with steel cables suspended from thirty-three towers to the Gold Prince Mine in Placer Gulch. Little remains of the Silverton Northern's 50-foot turntable (1904), where railroad locomotives were turned for the trip back to Silverton.

Ouray County (OR)

This mountainous realm is drained by the Uncompahgre River and its tributaries, which water ranches and farms in the relatively flat northern half of the county. The mountainous southern half, consisting of the lofty Sneffels and Courthouse ranges, lies largely within the Uncompahgre National Forest.

Ouray, the peacemaking Ute chief, is commemorated by the name the county took when formed in 1877. Gold discoveries had lured prospectors after the Utes were dispossessed in 1873. Silver had become more important by the 1880s, but, with the crash of 1893, fortune seekers refocused on gold. The county's last two great mines, the Idarado and the Camp Bird, both closed by the 1980s.

David Day, the founding editor of Ouray's wonderfully witty newspaper, the *Solid Muldoon,* maintained as early as the 1880s that tourism was a resource to be mined. Despite Day's prodding, the county did not seriously begin to court tourists until the 1920s, when the town of Ouray built the municipal hot springs pool and bathhouse (OR03). By then the county had more ghost towns than live ones. Today, of twenty-four post office towns, only Ouray and Ridgway are still active.

The county population peaked at 7,000 by the early 1890s with about half that number in Ouray. Since the 1893 silver crash, populations in both the town and the county have shrunk; Ouray town stabilized at around 700 residents and the county at about 3,000. Recent growth has been largely centered in Ridgway, where fashion clothier Ralph Lauren, actor Dennis Weaver, and other celebrities have taken to gentleman ranching. Lauren, who can sometimes be seen driving around the area in designer jeans and an old pickup truck, was lauded by *Vanity Fair* as "a real godsend to Ouray County. He set the tone for the new look of it." Weaver promotes environmentalism and operates the Big Barn Dance Hall in Ridgway.

Ouray, c. 1910

Ouray

Ouray (1875, 7,706 feet), the county seat and only sizable town, was started by prospectors from Silverton who found silver along the Uncompahgre River near its confluence with Oak and Canyon creeks. Francis Carney, owner of the Blake Placer at the north end of town, did not find gold or silver but did discover a good clay for brick. He opened a brickyard on the site that produced fine and inexpensive building material. Carney also developed considerable skill as a mason and contractor for such structures as the courthouse, the hospital, the St. Elmo Hotel, the Western Hotel, and the Wright Opera House.

Transportation enabled the county to ship out its products at a profit. The Red Mountain and Uncompahgre Canyon toll road, which later became U.S. 550, the so-called

Million Dollar Highway (OR26), reached Ouray from Silverton in 1886. The Denver & Rio Grande arrived from Montrose a year later. Although set back by the 1893 silver crash, the town shifted to gold, relying on the Camp Bird, Revenue, Virginius, and other auriferous treasure troves.

A National Register Historic District encompasses 331 structures and most of the town between Oak and 5th streets and 3rd and 8th avenues. The brothels, gambling joints, and theaters that once made up a formidable vice district are gone, as is the brewery, whose stone ruins now serve as a picnic ground.

Despite a raucous past, Ouray has become genteel. Quiet, tree-shaded dirt streets are lined by well-kept Victorian homes. The city and several motels have harnessed hot springs to heat their buildings. From the beginning, Ouray was not just another "git

Ouray

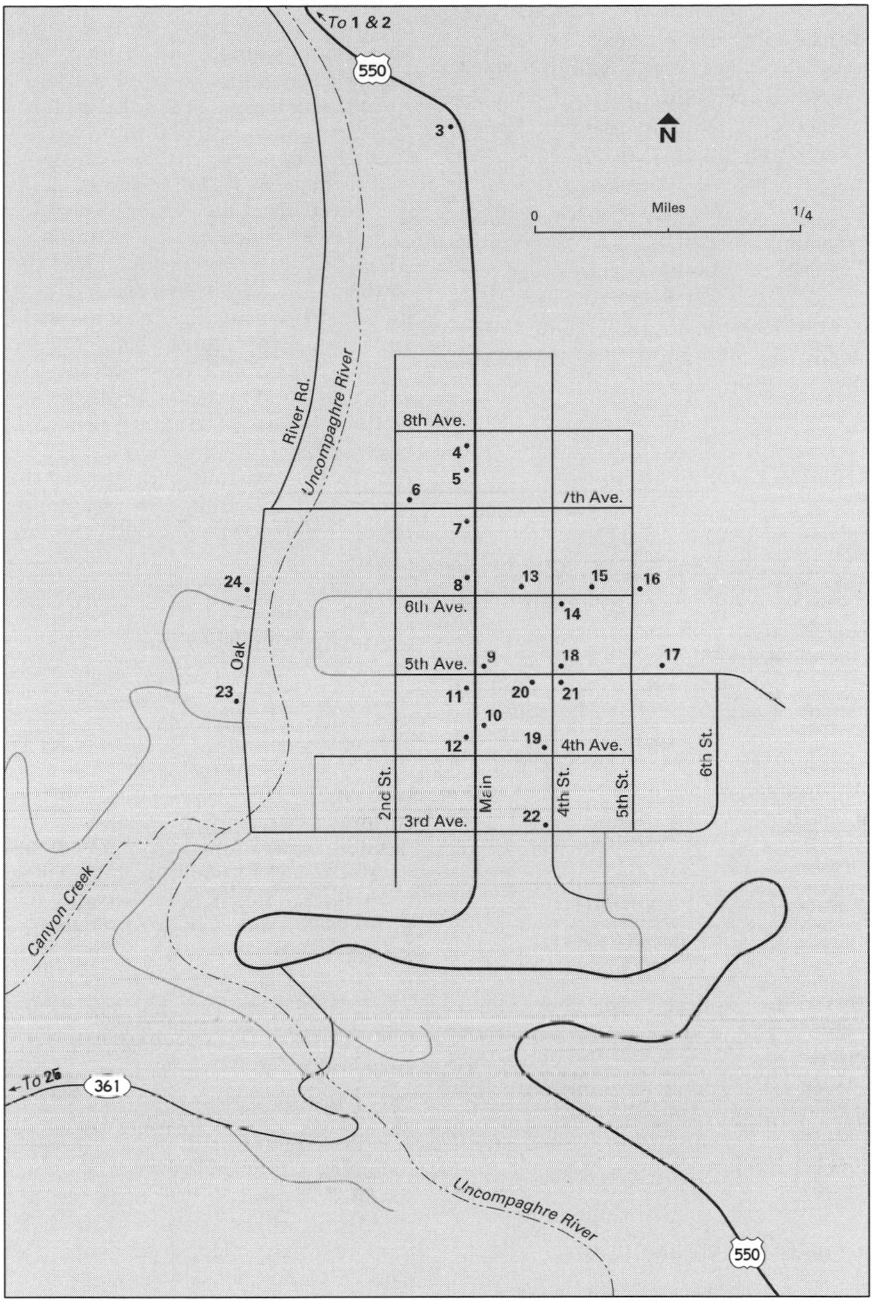

To 1 & 2

550

3

N

Miles
0   1/4

River Rd.

Uncompaghre River

8th Ave.

4
5

6

7th Ave.

7

24

8   13   15   16

6th Ave.   14

Oak

5th Ave.   9   18   17

23

11   20   21

10

12   19   4th Ave.

2nd St.

Main

4th St.

5th St.

6th St.

3rd Ave.   22

Canyon Creek

To 26   361

Uncompaghre River

550

569

and get out" mining town. It strove for architectural prominence and permanence by building in brick and stone. "Ouray, though a mining town," as Mae Lacy Baggs put it in *Colorado: The Queen Jewel of the Rockies* (1918), "takes its dignity very seriously."

Ouray also takes its recreation seriously. Numerous hiking and jeep trails start in town, including paths to the Box Canyon and lower and upper Cascade Falls. Near the upper falls lie the metal-roofed remains of the Chief Ouray Mine boarding house and machine shop. On Main Street (U.S. 550), some old dwellings have been converted to bed and breakfast inns: Main Street House, 334 Main; 1898 House (1898), 322 Main; and the hewn log Miner's Cabin (1889), 318 Main.

OR01 Ouray County Poorhouse

1892. 5 miles north of Ouray, northeast corner of Cutler Creek and U.S. 550 at Bar C Ranch

George Jackson built his three-story red brick house in the Second Empire style, using light stone for the elaborate quoins and window treatment. Various porches, large bays, and attic rooms under a mansard roof made it large enough to be converted in 1914 to the county poor farm, which housed indigents. Now a vacant relic, it seems forgotten in a grove of trees inside a horse pasture.

OR02 Bachelor-Syracuse Mine

1884. Dexter Creek Rd. (Ouray County 14), 2 miles north of Ouray at U.S. 550 and Ouray County 14

Tourists can dine here better than miners ever did and board the original electric "trammer" for a tour 3,350 horizontal feet into Gold Hill, a gold and silver treasure chest first discovered in 1884 by three bachelors. Much of the original mine and equipment is on exhibit.

OR03 Ouray Hot Springs Pool

1926. Main St. at north entrance to town (NR)

For centuries Ute Indians resorted to the numerous hot springs in the Ouray area to soak away their aches and pains. The hot water kept nearby plants green all winter, attracting wild game, which provided an additional reason to seek out the springs. Bone-chilled, rheumatic miners sought out the magical waters as a cure for everything from miner's lung to impotence. The odorless water is piped in from a Box Canyon spring, which flows out of the ground at 156 degrees F., then is mixed with cold water for a small pool where bathers can soak at 101 to 115 degrees F. Three larger pools have incrementally cooler water, with the largest and coolest roped for lap swimming.

Tent cabanas which once lined the edge of the pool have been replaced by a bathhouse (1974), but the main pool, built in 1926, remains—a huge 250-by-150 foot oval ranging from 2 to 9 feet in depth. A smaller, adjacent pond, created by flooding some of the clay pits of Francis Carney's former brickyard, keeps goldfish in warm water year round. The spacious park around the pool features a bandstand, a visitors' center, and restored narrow-gauge D&RG caboose 0575 (1886).

OR04 Silver Nugget Cafe

1898, J. L. Murphy. 740 Main St. (southwest corner of 8th Ave.)

This corner commercial block retains its cast iron columns and a plate glass storefront beneath a fancy cornice. It opened, according to an 1898 newspaper account, as "a saloon with a female rooming attachment on the second floor." In 1992 the upstairs bordello reopened as a bed and breakfast with seven small bedrooms, a bath, and a parlor.

OR05 Pricco's Restaurant (Cascade Grocery)

1903. 736 Main St.

The Pricco family still owns this single-story Italianate structure built for Dominick Fausonne and Joseph Pricco. It has a classic storefront, with a recessed central doorway flanked by large glass panes beneath a bracketed cast iron cornice with a garland frieze. New face brick and an outside dining deck have been added to what is now Pricco's Restaurant.

OR06 **Western Hotel**

1891, John Johnstone and Frederick Mayol. 210 7th Ave., 1 block west of Main St.

Rising three stories, this large frame hotel covered in shiplap siding has a full-length front porch with a rooftop balustrade that becomes a second-story balcony. Francis Carney laid the stone and brick foundation, but carpenters probably installed the elaborate boxed cornice and false pedimented front. The expansive plate glass on the first floor has elongated transoms and ornate side lights. The first floor has a large dining room, saloon, and sample rooms where drummers (traveling salesmen) displayed their wares.

Stable management and electricity came in 1897 when the Western was taken over by Denver hoteliers William Holt and H. P. Foster, whose names still decorate the pediment. The hotel became a home for many miners, while tourists gravitated to the more elegant Beaumont. Maria "Ma" Flor, who ran the hotel from 1916 to 1961, welcomed even the poorest and sickest miners and never let anyone leave hungry. After it was closed, then used as a museum and as a jeep rental, the Western reopened in 1982 as a fifty-room hotel with a first-floor restaurant and saloon.

OR07 **Buckskin Trading**

1989, David Westfall. 636 Main St.

This new "Victorian" is very sympathetic to its elderly neighbors. One modern touch— a third-story penthouse—is recessed and inconspicuous. A few doors away, at 630 Main Street, less successful modernization transformed the old Chipeta Theater into the Chipeta Emporium (1991). The theater is now hidden behind a grandiose three-story facade with a gaudy paint scheme, Palladian windows, sunburst pattern woodwork, and other pseudo-Victorian gingerbread of a Disneylandish mini-mall.

OR08 **Outlaw Bar**

1876. 610 Main St.

This western bar, museum, and restaurant is a treat in many ways, although the dim wagon-wheel chandeliers make it hard to inspect all the antiques, stuffed animals, and hats (including John Wayne's Stetson, captured while he was in nearby Ridgway filming *True Grit*). Taverns with various names have been here since 1876, most notably The Miners Pick, a notorious hangout for miners. The front facade retains the old metal cornice and rough stone foundation, but the storefront has been updated.

OR09 **Beaumont Hotel**

1887, Otto Bulow. 501 Main St. (northeast corner of 5th Ave.) (NR)

The architect of this hotel employed mansarded French, Italianate, and Romanesque Revival elements without loosing a sense of harmony in what might be cataloged as a Second Empire structure. The three-story brick building has a square corner tower and mini-towers capping the ends of its two wings. The steep-pitched slate roof is punctuated by Chateauesque dormers and capped with ornate finials and a weathervane dated 1886. The storefront spaces once housed the town's first bank and Western Union offices.

Gentlemen entered the hotel on Main Street and ladies on 5th Avenue. Inside, a grand staircase of solid oak climbs a central atrium with balconies on each floor, beneath a skylight and orchestra gallery. Over the years the Beaumont has lost many of its fine original furnishings and stooped to white paint and neon signs to capture commerce.

In 1998 Mary and Dan King bought the Beaumont at auction for $850,000 and spent $6 million to restore it as a hotel with street-level shops.

OR10 Elks Lodge

1904, Reynolds and Kullerstrand; E. H. Powell. 421 Main St.

Erected on the sites of Wing Kee's Laundry and Jesse Neumann's saloon, this two-story clubhouse of polished brick features a two-lane bowling alley, a billiard hall, a banquet room, and a 35-by-60-foot lodge hall. Three local contractors erected this eclectic edifice. Italianate windows, a mini-mansard roof with roundel windows, and a third-story cherub face grace the front facade, which culminates in a corner tower sprouting into an Art Nouveau outdoor chandelier. Some 300 "wearers of the antlers" helped lay the cornerstone for lodge 492 on July 31, 1904. The Elks Club, virtually unchanged inside and out, is a stately monument to one of the fraternal orders that were surrogate families to single miners.

OR11 Wright Opera House

1888. 480 Main St.

Ouray's opera house has an extraordinary two-story cast iron storefront, a design patented in 1887 by Mesker Brothers of St. Louis. By the late 1880s a wide variety of ornate fronts could be mail ordered from the Meskers, who shipped half a million catalogs a year to prospective customers nationwide. This front has Corinthian pilasters, a balcony with a transomed, stained glass window, a cornice, and a pediment. The elaborate design typifies the tendency throughout America at the time to combine machine-age building technology with classical forms.

Edward Wright, part owner of the Wheel of Fortune Mine, built the opera house during Ouray's flush times. First-floor stores helped support the second-floor opera hall. After the palmy days, the opera house was converted to a community center, then was used as the high school auditorium and basketball court, heated by stoves at either end. In recent decades it housed a garage

OR11 Wright Opera House

before becoming headquarters for a jeep tour outfit.

Next to the opera house, at the southwest corner of Main Street and 5th Avenue, is the Wright Building (1881), Ouray's oldest commercial building. This two-story clapboard structure with pedimented windows shows the scars of age, despite the flashy pink and white paint of the current occupant, the Ouray Candy Company. The quirky north facade features a potpourri of pedimented windows, doors, and a metal-sheathed, three-story rear addition.

OR12 St. Elmo Hotel

1898, Francis Carney. 426 Main St.

Catherine "Kittie" O'Brien Porter Heit had Francis Carney construct this neat brick hotel. Round-arched first-floor openings are juxtaposed with second-floor windows that have Italianate, segmental-arched tops. Once a humble, $1-a-night hotel for miners, the St. Elmo was rehabilitated in the 1980s as a bed and breakfast, offering elegant Victorian accommodations and Continental cuisine in the Bon Ton, as Kittie first called the dining room a century ago.

OR13 City Hall

1900, Francis Carney. 1989, Hall and Associates Restoration. 220 6th Ave., between Main and 4th sts. (NR)

Francis Carney built and may have designed Ouray's one-story brick and stone town hall with a basement jail. The following year he added a second-floor library, gymnasium, and meeting hall donated by Camp Bird mining magnate Thomas F. Walsh. Ignoring the original Romanesque Revival structure, Walsh insisted on a Neoclassical second floor. The superstructure and bell tower are Ouray's answer to Independence Hall in Philadelphia.

Following a 1950 fire, the city hall was rebuilt as a hideous stucco lump with an unwieldy metal tower adorned by a siren, antenna, bells, and a grim-looking Christmas star outlined in light bulbs. In 1989 citizens raised $110,000 to restore the city hall to respectability. The Walsh Library, with its golden oak furnishings and fine mining and natural history book collection, has been moved downstairs. The front facade, with a granite base and brick above, has been revived with the help of precast stone trim to match the original granite and sandstone. To minimize maintenance, anodized gold aluminum was used to sheathe the hexagonal dome and Fypon, a molded plastic, for the pilasters, pediment, brackets, and urn finials on the gold-colored dome. The synthetic tower could not support the brass bell that Walsh gave the town; it had to be mounted on a new pedestal in front of the building.

OR14 **Ouray County Courthouse**

1888, Frank E. Edbrooke. 541 4th St. (southeast corner of 6th Ave.)

Francis Carney constructed this courthouse designed by Colorado's foremost nineteenth-century architect. The brick walls and cut stone trim, noted Ouray's *Solid Muldoon* (August 10, 1888), "are all home productions with the exception of the finishing lumber, which comes from Chicago." Fine brick walls flare into a corbeled cornice. A third-story tower above the pediment of the entry portico is the main attraction. Its large, square belfry has triple round-arched openings beneath a bell-shaped roof topped by a ball finial.

The courthouse was dedicated in April 1889, according to the *Solid Muldoon,* "in strict accord with western custom," with the help of "a keg of hand-made inspiration, several cases of Milwaukee enthusiasm and divers and various brands of pure Havanas."

Initially, both city and county officials used the building, which housed the county court, city council, and fire wagons. Behind the courthouse the old jail remains, in a stout granite and brick two-story building. Inside this unusual courthouse are many original fixtures, from golden oak wainscoting and trim to a famous jury box equipped with rocking chairs. Courtroom spectators sit in some 150 cast iron chairs. Small towns needed such extensive seating, as trials not only provided free dramatic entertainment but also allowed townsfolk to window shop for lawyers.

OR15 **Ouray County Historical Museum** (St. Joseph Hospital)

1887, Francis Carney, contractor. 420 6th Ave.

Editor David Day of the *Solid Muldoon* raised about $5,000 and St. Patrick's Catholic Church next door provided the site for this hospital opened by the Sisters of Mercy. Carney used large, rough-faced blocks from nearby Limestone Hill to erect a sturdy, two-story Italianate building with a full basement. Inside, Mother Mary Michael Cummings and her nuns offered spiritual as well as physical care, redirecting the soul of many a hardened miner. After the sisters left, it became a private hospital and, in 1971, the Ouray County Historical Museum. Three floors and twenty-seven rooms house various exhibits devoted to medical, mining, and local history. Two rough-hewn log cabins (1870s) have been transplanted to the museum grounds.

OR16 **Wiesbaden Hot Springs Spa and Lodge**

1879, 1947. 625 5th St.

The Ute chief Ouray supposedly soaked in the hot springs that make this one of Ouray's finest geothermal complexes. The Wiesbaden proudly displays an 1886 William H. Jackson photo of an adobe hut, which stood on the hill behind the Wiesbaden, alleged to be one of Chief Ouray's homes. The original frame structure, Mother Buchanan's Bath House, is now the rear appendage of a modernized nineteen-room lodge of natural wood and glass under a shake shingle roof. Three hot springs heat a natural rock sauna, vapor cave, soaking pool (110 degrees F.), and outdoor swimming pool (105 degrees F.).

OR17 **Kullerstrand House**

1898, George E. Kullerstrand. 510 5th Ave.

Spindles, bargeboard, a turret, and finials grace this Queen Anne house with a second-story recessed corner porch and corner tower capped by a lightning rod. Inside, George Kullerstrand, a prominent contractor, indulged his hobby of installing ornately carved and inlaid woodwork, including built-in storage.

OR18 **Ashley House**

1891. 505 4th St. (northeast corner of 5th Ave.)

Dr. W. W. Ashley's gracefully aging Queen Anne house is the town's show home and a catalog collection of gingerbread trim. Its rich detail includes an oak leaf frieze on the front bay window and the elaborate porch with its spindles, beading, cutouts, and hanging pendants. The matching garage has a granite foundation and shingle-skirted second story. Seven different styles of shingles adorn the house, but excessive detail is relieved by the harmonious massing: the front

facade enlarges upon a bay window in repeated rectangles.

OR19 **First Presbyterian Church**

1890. 4th Ave. (northwest corner of 4th St.)

This shingled Queen Anne Style church was restored in 1986 behind a large construction sign reading "GOD AT WORK." The Reverend George M. Darley, Colorado's most prominent pioneer Presbyterian minister, founded the congregation in 1877 and spearheaded erection of this building twenty-three years later, using plans furnished by the Presbyterian Erection Board in Philadelphia. The church has suffered heavy fire damage, additions, and alterations, including installation of a steeple for the schoolhouse bell after the town's original school was demolished in 1938. Palladian windows and a red metal roof help unify somewhat disparate parts.

OR20 **St. John's Episcopal Church**

1880. 329 5th Ave. (southwest corner of 4th St.)

Ouray's oldest ecclesiastical edifice contains an antique wooden altar screen and wainscoting made of timber recycled from the Revenue mine. "Cousin Jacks," Cornish miners noted for their expert masonry work, are said to have built this stone church. The old asphalt roof has been replaced by corrugated metal better able to shed snow. It is a simple, dark, low building—the base of what was to have been a much larger church before the silver crash of 1893 sank Ouray's high hopes. The lovely stained glass windows (1988, Virginia Laycock) portray "God's gift to Ouray." The attached parish hall (1976) does not distract from this simple sanctuary inspired by English country churches.

OR21 **Hurlburt House**

1894, George R. Hurlburt. 445 4th St. (southeast corner of 5th Ave.)

George Hurlburt, one of the bachelor miners who discovered the Bachelor-Syracuse Mine, built this one-story cottage. After his 1894 marriage he transformed it into a spacious Queen Anne dwelling with touches of elegance—parquet floors, the balustraded porch, and a fine wrought iron fence.

OR22 Tanner House

1896, R. D. Coleman. 300 4th St. (northwest corner of 3rd Ave.)

A Philadelphia architect designed this gambrel-roofed, two-story cottage with prominent dormers, leaded Palladian windows, curved bay windows of prismatic Italian glass, and a Queen Anne porch. The stamped metal wreath and garlands in the front porch pediment are repeated in wood on the front door.

OR23 Wright-Gregory House

1878, Edward McIntyre. 442 Oak St.

George Wright, brother of Edward, who built the Wright Building and the opera house, bought this two-story, hand-hewn log house for his bride of nineteen, Lenora. Wright had Edward McIntyre, who had built the home a year earlier, cover the hewn logs with siding and add dormer windows and the living room bay. Doris Gregory, an educator who has written numerous books on Ouray County history, has long resided in this well-preserved, picturesque home.

OR24 Wheeler House

1882. 602 Oak St.

Major Willard D. Wheeler arrived in Ouray in 1876 as the agent for the Uncompahgre Indian Agency. Meanwhile his brother, Lieutenant George M. Wheeler, supervised the famed Wheeler Geographic Survey, which first thoroughly explored, mapped, and reported on much of the American West. Willard founded the Bank of Ouray and presided over the Ouray Water Works. Over the years his hewn log home evolved into a charming cottage with a shingled second story.

Other Oak Street homes between the 3rd Avenue and 7th Avenue bridges range from a pioneer prefabricated house (1889) at 322 Oak to 1960s A frames, from cute Swiss ersatz to a 1980s log house. Representative homes include the Larsen House (c. 1901), 306 Oak, originally the home of a Swedish miner, and the Kimball House (1900), 516 Oak, a countrified foursquare with a unique lookout that uses the old opera house fire escape as stairs mounting a side yard boulder.

OR25 Camp Bird Mine

6 miles west of Ouray on Ouray County 361 at junction of Canyon and Imogene creeks

Thomas J. Walsh, an Irish carpenter who reworked old silver claims, found high-grade gold ore and spent $20,000 to buy claims which he consolidated and named the Camp Bird, for the camp-robbing gray jays who snatched his grub. After extracting millions in gold ore, Walsh sold his holdings to a British firm for another $5.2 million. The new owners built the large, Queen Anne Style mine manager's house (1903), a genteel apparition sitting at the edge of immense tailing ponds. Walsh's daughter, Washington socialite Evalyn Walsh McLean, acquired the Hope Diamond and described the family's wealth and tragedy in *Father Struck It Rich* (1936).

OR26 Million Dollar Highway

1924. U.S. 550, Ouray to Durango

This 70-mile stretch of U.S. 550 is a two-lane road, often without guardrails, that slithers up the Uncompahgre Canyon to Red Mountain Pass, plunges down into Silverton, and then climbs Molas Pass for the long descent to Durango. At many points this hair-raising highway follows the original toll road, a cliff-hanging wonder opened in 1889. The modern, paved highway allegedly (1) cost $1 million to build, (2) was constructed on a roadbed made of rich mine tailings, or (3) caused travelers to swear they would not take the road again, even for a million dollars. Another million may have been spent trying to control the Riverside Slide, the most murderous avalanche in Colorado. The Riverside Avalanche Chute (1985) is a concrete highway tunnel overpass for snow slides, which here have killed at least five people and demolished a rotary snowplow.

OR27 Red Mountain

1883–1913. U.S. Forest Service Rd. 886, 2 miles south of Ironton and U.S. 550

The town of Red Mountain (with three townsites about one mile apart) originated with silver strikes in the valley below the mountains known by that name—three pyramidal peaks with bright slopes of oxidized iron. The *Solid Muldoon* reported on March 9, 1883: "Five weeks ago the site where Red Mt. now stands was woodland covered with heavy spruce timber. Today, hotels, printing offices, groceries, meat markets, a telephone office, saloons, and dance houses are up and booming. . . ." By 1913 the town gave up its ghost—and its post office—but it has been immortalized in David Lavender's historical novel *Red Mountain*. Following decades of fire and ice, little remains except the dilapidated shaft houses of the two largest mines, the National Belle and the Yankee Girl. Along U.S. 550 on the south side of Red Mountain Pass the giant, century-old Idarado Mine, complete with company housing, offices, and loading apparatus, is largely intact, awaiting a revival.

Ridgway

Ridgway (1891, 6,985 feet), named for Rio Grande Southern construction superintendent Robert M. Ridgway, emerged as a rail and ranching hub where the Rio Grande Southern joined the D&RG. Rip-roaring cowboys raced down Main Street on Saturday nights, starting a tradition continued by rodeo riders at Ridgway's Ouray County Fairgrounds, whose racetrack dates to 1892.

Most of the original town is gone, destroyed by fires in the 1930s, although the old stone town hall, firehouse, and jail survive. Rio Grande Southern rail service, prolonged by use of the hybrid vehicles known as Galloping Geese, kept Ridgway alive. After the RGS ran into financial straits, these contraptions, which were cheaper to build and maintain than conventional rolling stock, carried passengers, mail, and freight along the Rio Grande Southern route between Durango, Telluride, Dolores, and Ridgway from the 1930s until 1952. A "goose" consisted of an automobile engine fitted into a narrow-gauge cab with a homemade "bus" attached behind it and a distinctive horn that sounded like a honking goose. When the engine overheated its hood flaps would be opened, giving the goose what looked like wings. The first Galloping Goose was constructed in Ridgway in 1931, using a Buick Master Six touring car, railroad wheels, and a cowcatcher.

So little was left of Ridgway in 1956 that the Dallas Creek Project planned to bury the burned-out town in a watery grave. But neither fire nor the proposed flood could sink this town. Ridgway rebounded in the 1980s, when slick new developments cropped up beside antique structures as the town became fashionable. Celebrating its rebirth, in 1988 the "Gateway to the San Juans" built a new town hall, community center, and fire station. On the dirt streets, scattered mobile homes and movie prop buildings intermingle with authentic old-timers in a peculiar National Register Historic District. The Ridgway Land Company's planned "historical commercial park," Trail Town, adds to the confusion of styles and eras.

Jeans, boots, pearl-buttoned shirts, and western hats are still a common sight but now tend to be designer brands. The beautiful mountain-rimmed lower Uncompahgre Valley has become a haven for gentlemen ranchers. These urban cowboys included the founder of Continental Airlines, Robert Six, a fast-drawing six-shooter buff who built a ranch on Cow Creek. Fashion designer Ralph Lauren owns a 20,000-acre ranch with a fancy log house on Dallas Meadows.

OR28 Rio Grande Southern Depot

1890. 321 N. Railroad St.

RGS Superintendent Robert Ridgway selected the site for a depot that greeted rail passengers until 1952. It has been moved two blocks and converted to a private home with a two-car garage. The steep gable roof and Queen Anne tower survive on a long, rectangular structure with a bracketed overhang covering what was once the station platform. For the 1961 film *How the West Was*

Won, the depot was dressed up in additional Queen Anne ornament to play the part of the Independence Hotel, but has since lost most of its movie makeup. The Rio Grande Southern yards near here once employed fifty men, who worked at a five-bay roundhouse (now gone), two-story office, and shops where the famed flock of Galloping Geese were built and maintained.

OR29 Bank of Ridgway

1911. 521–523 Clinton St.

This typical two-story commercial brick structure with rough red sandstone trim, cornice, and parapet was erected by Amos Walther after he bought the bank that Otto Mears, Frederick Walsen, and other town founders launched in 1891. Over the years it has housed the post office and the Ridgway Pharmacy, the telephone company, and numerous offices and businesses. It was restored and refurnished in 1991 for retail use.

OR30 Old Reliable Store

1892. Northwest corner of Lena and Sherman sts.

Francis B. Hockley opened this emporium in 1892 and ran it until 1948. The one-story brick corner building, dressed up with a shake shingle porch for the film *True Grit,* has become an import clothing store.

OR31 Sunridge (Weaver House)

1989, Michael Reynolds. 4 miles west of Ridgway, Ouray County 24 and Ouray County 21 on Dallas Creek

Dennis Weaver, the limping deputy sheriff of the TV series *Gunsmoke,* and his wife, Gerry, hired a Taos, New Mexico, architect to design an "Earthship" of recycled waste and adobe with over 3,000 mud-filled tires and 15,000 aluminum cans. All this trash is hidden under the adobe skin of this 6,000-square-foot, $300,000 multilevel house. The glass south face is at an angle to catch the winter sun. Tipis in the front yard are a memorial to earlier residents. Largely sunken into a south-facing slope, this is a well-disguised celebrity mansion. Michael Reynolds, a leading proponent of earth architecture, solar energy, and recycled materials, elaborates on his ideas in his book *A Coming of Wizards: A Manual of Human Potential* (1988). His house for Weaver is perhaps the best known of about one hundred such dwellings in Colorado.

Montrose County (MO)

Montrose County (1882) is generally dry, broken tableland, with the notable exceptions of the Black Canyon of the Gunnison National Monument, Uncompahgre National Forest, and the settled valleys of the Gunnison, San Miguel, and Uncompahgre rivers. After the Ute Removal farmers, ranchers, and miners moved into the county, which is one of Colorado's richer agricultural regions.

The Ute Indian Museum in Montrose commemorates that tribe's presence. Nothing remains of Fort Crawford, an 1880s U.S. Army cantonment on the Uncompahgre River, eight miles south of Montrose, established to police the Utes. Sodbusters prospered after the 1909 completion of one of the nation's first major

Bureau of Reclamation projects, the Gunnison Tunnel. The water it carries turned sagebrush and alkali flats into productive croplands. Some pioneer ranches and farms survive, as do distinctive onion cellars, built with heavy ponderosa pine logs and bermed earth. Cattle, sheep, apple orchards, hay, sweet corn, potatoes, onions, and alfalfa have been important to the economy.

Mining continued well into the twentieth century, with discovery of rich uranium and vanadium deposits in western Montrose county. "Uranium fever" swept the county between the 1940s and the 1960s. The fever subsided almost as suddenly as it came, leaving the toxic ghost towns of Uravan and Vancorum, modern-era ruins of crumbling asphalt streets and shacks with linoleum floors. Older towns such as Olathe survive, with vernacular architecture in wood, brick, adobe, and local sandstone, as well as prefabricated construction. In this rural county, only about a third of the 25,000 residents live in the county seat and single city, Montrose.

Montrose

The county seat (1882, 5,794 feet) was named by town company president Joseph Selig for the Duke of Montrose in Sir Walter Scott's novel *The Legend of Montrose* (1819). This is a growing community with a diversified economy that combines agriculture, mining, service industries, and tourism, sweetened by Russell Stover Candies, which moved its main plant here in the 1970s from Denver.

Montrose's agricultural roots are obvious in many venerable storage and processing facilities along the tracks near the former D&RG depot, now the county historical museum. Its commercial role is reflected in several solid blocks of two-story business buildings along Main Street (U.S. 50), where masonry upper stories with brick corbeling and metal cornices survive above generally altered storefronts.

MO01 **Montrose County Historical Museum** (Denver & Rio Grande Depot)

1912. 21 N. Rio Grande Ave. (northwest corner of Main St. [U.S. 50]) (NR)

MO01 Denver & Rio Grande Depot, 1920s

This two-story rectangular depot in the Mission Revival style has a low hipped roof of red tile with wide, overhanging eaves. Similar tile roofs with the same pitch cover arcaded platforms on three sides and an enclosed baggage wing on the north. The concrete foundation rises into walls finished smooth to sill height. Walls above are slightly recessed and finished in a rough stucco. Stepped parapets over the entry doors are echoed in curvilinear parapets in the main roof above a bay with a half-elliptical, tripartite window. The depot grounds are now guarded by a chain-link fence that encloses the museum collection, including a furnished homesteader's cabin and a country store.

MO03 Montrose County Courthouse

MO02 **Carriage Works**

1895, William Diehl, builder. 237 N. Cascade Ave. (southwest corner of N. 3rd St.)

"Studebaker Bill" Diehl built this 21-by-57-foot barnlike structure, just north of his surviving 1885 frame house, to repair wagons and farm machinery and sell Studebaker wagons. The dilapidated two-story frame building with boarded-up windows has the only remaining unaltered false front in Montrose. The front is covered in shiplap siding, while the other walls are vertical boards. A blacksmith forge remains, although its chimney has collapsed. Seventeen-year-old Jack Dempsey is said to have trained in one of the back rooms for his first big fight in 1912 at the Montrose Masonic temple before becoming the world champion heavyweight (1919–1926).

MO03 **Montrose County Courthouse**

1922, William N. Bowman. 300 S. 1st St. (NR)

Mules hauled blocks of tan sandstone from the local Kaleway Quarry to complete the walls of this Neoclassical edifice. Rough-faced stone is used for the walls of the first three stories. Smooth stone is employed for the fourth, as well as for the entry bay and for quoins and banding. A grand staircase climbs to three pairs of transomed doors set between two-story Doric columns supporting a shallow portico. A sympathetic WPA addition, a lawn, and trees fill out the half-block site.

MO04 **Post Office**

1931–1932, James A. Wetmore, OSA. 321 S. First St. (NR)

How well terracotta could mimic stone is demonstrated in this Italian Renaissance Revival post office of reinforced concrete and hollow tile, which appears to be a scaled-down version of a two-story design. A gray terracotta skin that looks—and even feels—like limestone was supplied by the Northwestern Terra Cotta Company of Denver. The blocks are clearly defined by wide spacing and raked mortar. Under a low hipped roof of Roman tile, the one-story rectangular building has five bays with round-arched and fanlighted windows and doors. Oversized keystones denote the three arches that form the entrance, and oversized spiked lanterns flank the doors. Real limestone appears as wainscoting in the tile-floored lobby.

MO05 **Fox Theater**

1920s. 23 S. Cascade Ave.

An onion dome and parody of a minaret top this two-story masonry box, now devoid of any further decoration to carry the theme. Recently divided into three screening rooms inside, it has also been altered in back, where the much rearranged masonry of the alley walls looks like a remodeler's jigsaw puzzle.

MO06 Montrose City Hall

1926. 433 S. 1st St. (NR)

A mini–civic center of narrow lawns, tiny plazas, a pool featuring the bell and anchor of the decommissioned USS *Montrose,* and public sculpture surrounds this two-story masonry building on a concrete foundation. Its walls are faced in yellow brick. Contrasting red brick is used for quoins and intermixed in courses of stretcher and Flemish bond to form geometric patterns, primarily in spandrels, adding a distinct vertical Art Deco element. A decorative band above the second-story windows acts as a frieze and adds a classical note. The parapet fronting a flat roof resembles a battlement, with crenelations near the corners. The irregular structure was originally built to house both City Hall and the City Library, explaining the two main entrances. The street east of City Hall has been closed off to form a plaza shared by a sister building, the two-story Firehouse No. 1 (c. 1910) to the north. Now converted to city offices, the firehouse has been joined to City Hall by an enclosed elevated crossover above a narrow band of lawn.

MO07 Masonic Temple

1911. 509–511 E. Main St.

Above a storefront with recessed entries, four stout Doric columns flank an inset portico in this fraternal temple. Its domed second-story hall hosted some of the 100 boxing matches Jack Dempsey fought between 1912 and 1914. The Masons have moved out, and their hall now houses jazzercise sessions.

MO08 United Methodist Church of Montrose

1917; 1991 addition, Patrik Davis Associates. 19 S. Park Ave. (northeast corner of S. 1st St.)

Square corner towers flank a metal dome on this yellow brick Neo-Romanesque church. Patrik Davis, a Montrose architect, recom-

MO08 United Methodist Church of Montrose

bined these elements in an innovative educational and social wing to the east, which uses a yellow brick closely matching the original. A rough cinderblock base complements the original sandstone foundation. The polygonal bay reappears as a stuccoed bridge between the buildings, with various cross motifs incorporated into glass block fenestration. The tower is recreated around the new entrance and finished in rose stucco, using the distinctive stepped parapet profile. A round "rose" window, set in a diamond shape and trimmed in contrasting brick, incorporates a Celtic cross using three types of glass block.

MO09 Lathrop House

1902. 718 E. Main St. (NR)

This two-story Queen Anne house has that style's typical asymmetrical massing, with a multigable roof, decorative porches, and paneled gable ends. It also wears classical elements such as a porch roof pediment, Tuscan columns, and a Palladian window. A full-width front porch incorporates a conical roof in the northeast corner, where a full-blown example of the style would have a two- or three-story tower. John V. Lathrop came from Kansas in 1890 and opened the Lathrop Hardware Store, which remains in operation. His wife Emma's uncle designed what she claimed was the largest and costliest ($10,000) house in town. Returned to single-family use after service as multifamily housing in the 1930s and as a restaurant in the 1970s, the dwelling has a restored, shiplap-sided exterior on a local stone foundation. The interior retains the original spindled oak staircase, columned oak fireplace, sideboard with beveled mirror, and columns dividing the formal front parlor from the less formal family back parlor.

MO10 Uncompahgre Valley Water Users Association Offices (U.S. Bureau of Reclamation)

1905. 601 N. Park Ave. (NR)

Disguised as an overgrown foursquare in deference to the surrounding residential neighborhood, this two-and-one-half-story office building housed some of the first U.S. Bureau of Reclamation workers in Colorado. The large turbine drum on the front lawn is a souvenir of one of the bureau's first major projects—the Gunnison Tunnel (MO16; 1909).

MO11 Montrose Regional Airport

1988, Patrik Davis Associates. 2100 Airport Rd.

Local architect Patrik Davis designed the Montrose airport terminal to greet visitors with small-town hospitality. A two-sided fireplace is the centerpiece of the passenger seating area, which has a tile floor patterned with the Ute pictogram for travel and a high, skylighted ceiling of knotty pine. The walls are earthy, ground-face cinderblock, and natural-finished glue-laminated beams extend over wide walkways. The gable roof has skylights and dormers decorated with the Hopi good luck symbol.

MO12 Townsend House

c. 1888. 222 S. 5th St. (NR)

Capped by roofline cresting and a Tudor-esque chimney, this two-and-one-half-story Queen Anne dwelling of pinkish brown brick has a steep, multigable roof covered in its original copper and zinc. The unusually attractive and well-preserved house harmoniously blends rich details: Eastlake barge-

board and cutouts on the gable ends, a small second-story porch over the entry with turned posts and balustrade echoing those of the larger first-story porch below, and mature landscaping behind a wrought iron spearhead fence. Businessman and banker Thomas B. Townsend manufactured the bricks at his Montrose factory.

MO13 Pediatric Associates

1993, Patrik Davis Associates. 947 S. 5th St. (northwest corner of Lot Ave.)

When asked to expand a plain brick building with a stucco box, the architect invoked artistic license and created a grouping of angled, rectangular bays, "like children's building blocks scattered across the site." However, the addition is scaled to blend with the site and the parent building, whose dark red brick it matches while also using some contrasting pale pink stucco. Window sunscreens of copper tubing add a useful and playful note.

MO14 Montrose Pavilion

1991, Patrik Davis Associates. 1800 Pavilion Dr. (south from Niagara Rd.)

Classical Tuscan columns, balustrades, and porticos—all of precast concrete—add class to this $3.5 million convention and special events complex. Some 30,000 square feet in a U plan include a 602-seat auditorium theater connected by a glazed gallery to meeting rooms, a banquet hall, a ballroom, and a senior center. Sited in southeast Montrose on 15 acres, the gray stuccoed building looks south, to the San Juan Mountains. A paved and planted court between the wings serves for outdoor weddings and receptions. A glass pyramid above the auditorium that glows when the pavilion is open serves as a beacon. Another cost-effective yet elegant public building by Davis is the Aquatic Center (1987), northeast corner of Rio Grande Avenue and South 9th Street, an oversize cinderblock box with a terne gable roof and a water slide and fenced sun deck on the south.

MO15 Ute Indian Museum

1956, Dudley T. Smith. 1996 addition, Edward Chamberlin. 17253 Chipeta Dr., 2 miles south of Montrose on U.S. 550

This museum of painted cinderblock forming flat-roofed boxes of varying heights celebrates the Utes and their culture. Exhibits in two 20-by-40-foot galleries display, among other artifacts, the collection of Thomas McKee, a local photographer who documented tribal life during the 1890s. The museum honors the famous Ute chief, Ouray (d. 1880), and his wife, Chipeta. Sited on a hilltop near the willow-lined banks of the Uncompahgre River, the 6-acre site, once part of Ouray's 400-acre farm, includes a park, Chipeta's grave, and a marker for the Dominguez-Escalante expedition of 1776, whose members found the Utes to be an attractive and friendly people. The Ouray Springs, on the grounds, are covered with a cement tipi (1924), donated by the Daughters of the American Revolution.

MO16 Gunnison Tunnel

1909. Off U.S. 50, 6.5 miles east of Montrose on Montrose County 348 (Miguel Rd.) (NR)

Unemployed miners started digging at either end of this tunnel, part of the Bureau of Reclamation's $3 million Uncompahgre Valley Project. It is 10 feet by 12 feet, 5.8 miles long, and two-thirds concrete lined, with the upstream portion cut through solid rock. It carries water from a deep gorge of the Gunnison River under Vernal Mesa to the 12-mile-long South Canal, which flows into the Uncompahgre River. From the Uncompahgre, water is channeled into a network of canals irrigating 146,000 acres in Delta, Montrose, and Ouray counties. President William Howard Taft presided at the grand opening ceremonies in 1909. As the first major U.S. transmontane irrigation system and the longest U.S. irrigation canal when built, it has been designated a National Historic Civil Engineering Landmark.

MO17 Black Canyon of the Gunnison National Monument

1933. 15 miles east of Montrose via U.S. 50 and Colorado 347

Thanks to sheer, 1,000-foot-high walls and difficult access, as well as the National Monument designation, the 53-mile-long gorge cut by the Gunnison River has been preserved in its wild state. The river drops an average of 95 feet per mile, one of the steepest fall rates for a North American river. The deepest and most spectacular 12 miles lie within the National Monument's dark gray walls of gneiss and schist with pinkish crystalline granite bands. Abraham Lincoln Fellows, in his diary from the 1901 survey of the gorge, wrote, "Our surroundings were of the wildest possible description. The roar of the waterfalls was constantly in our ears, and the walls of the canyon, towering a half mile in height above us, were seemingly vertical. Occasionally a rock would fall from one side or the other, with a roar and crash, exploding like a ton of dynamite when it struck bottom, making us think our last day had come."

Bedrock

Bedrock (1883, 4,970 feet) is the hub of the Paradox Valley, a remote, arid valley 30 miles long and 3 miles wide, so named because the Dolores River crosses it at right angles rather than flowing through it. Scrawny cattle graze around abandoned uranium mines outside the town, which is noted for its adobe schoolhouse (1900) and quaint general store.

MO18 Bedrock Store

1882, James P. Galloway. 9812 Colorado 90

This antique rural general store, post office, gas station, and town center has a first story of native sandstone rubble set in concrete, a second story of clapboard with a false front, and a sheet metal roof. It is heated by a potbellied stove and has wooden floors and display cases, a loafers' bench in front, and an outhouse in back. This relic of the nineteenth-century town also has a second-story balcony and a shady porch below for surveying a bleak foreground enriched by distant views of the snowcapped Manti La Sal and San Juan Mountains.

Cimarron

MO19 **Narrow-Gauge Trestle** (Denver & Rio Grande Bridge 259)

1880s. 1 mile from U.S. 50, on Montrose County Q83 at the west edge of Cimarron (NR)

Cimarron (1883, 6,900 feet) was once the location of a four-span railroad bridge over the Cimarron River and a huge livestock loading hub, as well as an important maintenance stop for the Denver & Rio Grande. Nearly all the wooden shop and roundhouse facilities are gone. All that remains of the bridge are 119 feet composed of two pin-connected Pratt trusses with L-shaped girders of sheet steel tied with 8-inch-square wooden decking. Other bridges, as well as most of the roadbed, have been displaced by the reservoirs of the Blue Mesa and Morrow Point dams. This remnant in a rugged, remote canyon is a noteworthy fragment of an engineering and construction feat. It also speaks of the larger search for a rail route west, beginning with the epic railroad survey of Captain John W. Gunnison in 1853. The National Park Service and the town of Montrose have placed an engine, boxcar, and caboose on the bridge segment, backed by the dark canyon walls. At the mouth of the canyon, D&RG freight and stock cars are on exhibit at a small, plank-sided visitors' center.

MO20 **Morrow Point Dam**

1971, Bureau of Land Management. 1 mile northeast of Cimarron on Rd. Q83

The first large double-curvature, thin-arch dam built in the United States is 469 feet high and 740 feet long, with a 52-foot-wide base tapering to 12 feet at the crest. The dramatic free falling spillway is three times the height of Niagara Falls, and the underground power plant has a 120,000-kilowatt capacity.

MO21 **School District No. 6 Schoolhouse**

1921. 2 miles east of Cimarron on U.S. 50

A single-story Mission Revival school of yellow brick with a curvilinear parapet over its protruding, round-arched entrance is sited on a hill overlooking U.S. 50 from the north.

The slope in front has been cut away to create a garage entrance into the basement in what is now a private residence.

Naturita

Naturita (1882, 5,431 feet) was formerly named Chipeta for the wife of Chief Ouray. Between 1898 and 1928, ores taken from this region accounted for half the world's supply of radium. The U.S. Vanadium Company mill processed both uranium and vanadium. The town's hot history is exhibited at the Naturita Schoolhouse Museum.

Nucla

Nucla (1904, 5,862 feet), begun as a socialist commune by the New Utopian Community Land Association, incorporated in 1894. Shares were sold throughout the country, and a 15-mile-long gravity-fed canal was constructed to bring water to the area. By the 1920s, as Ellen Peterson explains in *The Spell of the Tabeguache* (1957), the Colorado Co-operative, which ran Nucla, was little more than a water company, and the businesses and neat frame bungalows were in private hands. One of the few remnants of the original plan is the one-story, brick false-fronted Colorado Co-operative Company store (c. 1900) at the upper end of an unusually broad main street. Nuclans may have second thoughts about a capitalist economy as they survey the open-pit Peabody Coal Mine at the upper end of Main Street and the ruins of the Union Carbide mill, closed in 1982. The coal is pulverized and fluidized to fuel Nucla's power plant in an innovative process for economically reducing pollution.

Uravan

Uravan (1936, 4,990 feet) is a spooky relic of the atomic age, a latter-day boom town where a uranium and vanadium mill are now decaying. The U.S. Vanadium Company developed the town. It was later run by the

Union Carbide Corporation, which closed its operations in 1984. Uravan appeared on the Environmental Protection Agency Superfund list two years later. Cleanup continues, and this burned-out town in search of resurrection has offered itself as a regional dump site for radioactive waste.

MO22 **Hanging Flume**

1891, N. P. Turner. 5.7 miles northwest of Uravan on Colorado 141 at the confluence of the Dolores and San Miguel rivers (NR)

Gold placer miners at Mesa Creek constructed this aqueduct to divert some of the San Miguel River to their diggings. The 6-foot-wide-by-4-foot-deep flume clings to the canyon walls 100 to 150 feet above the river and 200 to 500 feet below the rims of the San Miguel River and Dolores River canyons. Sills were fastened to the cliff by iron pins and supported by cantilevered timbers, also pinned to the cliff. From these sills workers were lowered in baskets to hand drill pinholes for the flume. The flume itself was then used to bring workers and supplies to the construction site. The flume, completed at a cost of $100,000, carried over 80 million gallons of water per day. Maintenance was a constant problem, and the flume was abandoned in 1893. Neighboring ranchers took much of the lumber, but sections are still visible along Colorado 141.

San Miguel County (SM)

San Miguel County (1883) ranges from snow-packed mountains on its eastern boundary to arid, high-country plateaus on its Utah border. Its buildings vary from deluxe ski ranches in Telluride to gentlemen's ranches on Wilson Mesa, to working ranches around Norwood. Nearly 75 percent of the population lives in the Telluride area, where recent booms have brought the county population to 4,000, still 1,200 short of its 1900 population. Norwood is the only incorporated town in the entire western two-thirds of San Miguel County.

The county was named after the river, whose headwaters are in the snow-packed mountains above Telluride. The discovery of gold in the 1870s first attracted miners, and gold continued to be the main attraction, augmented by silver, copper, and lead. The Idarado Mining Company, which ultimately owned most mines in the Telluride district, did not close until 1978.

Telluride

The county seat (1878, 8,750 feet), born amid a gold strike, boomed again as a ski resort a century later. The town's Victorian architecture, world-class skiing, and summer festivals have attracted a sophisticated population. *Megatrends* author John Naisbitt has built a "mega-cabin," and Hollywood stars have bought old Victorian homes or built new ones in a town often described as the up and coming rival of Aspen.

Although mines operated until the 1970s, their twentieth-century production never matched that of the nineteenth-century boom. Between the 1920s and the 1970s Telluride stagnated, with very little new construction. Poverty preserved the town, as did its remote location at the dead end of a country road. The isolation came to an end in 1969, when Joseph T. Zoline, a plastics manufacturer from Beverly Hills, California, announced plans to build the Telluride Ski Area. Within months property values jumped 150 percent. Newcomers streamed in, mostly monied transplants from other parts of the country. A summertime series of bluegrass, jazz, film, wine, and mushroom festivals also helped turn the town into a popular summer destination.

Telluride

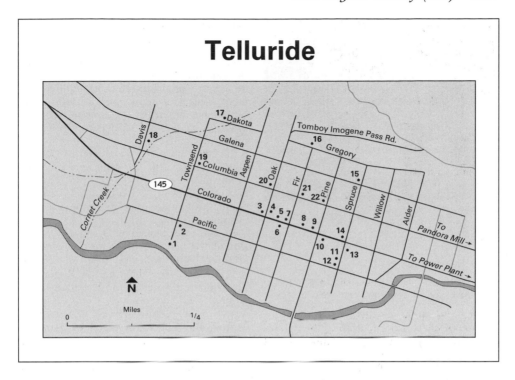

Old downtown Telluride was designated a National Historic Landmark District in 1961, and a 1974 local preservation ordinance restricts alterations, new construction, and demolition within the historic district. The town's Historic and Architectural Review Commission guidelines include a 35-foot height limit, setback requirements, and a ban on raw redwood in favor of painted frame. The "typical" Telluride house is a gabled frame building with simple ornamentation. Many of these modest houses have been overwhelmed with added towers, bay windows, and decorative shingling, which met the new construction guidelines for size, scale, and material but obscured the original design.

Despite ever-mounting development pressures, Telluride has managed to hang on to much of its historic architecture. The main street, Colorado Avenue, supposedly built extra wide to accommodate the turnaround of mule trains, continues to be the commercial center and has retained many original buildings. Telluride's better residences, hos-

pitals, churches, and schools occupy the sunny northern hillside. In the mining era engineers or managers from the East Coast or England lived here, while Italian and Irish families lived down the hill. On less desirable, lower land south of Colorado Avenue lived Telluride's laborers, many of whom were Scandinavian, in a neighborhood bordering the San Miguel River and the railroad tracks.

SM01 San Juan Brew Pub (Rio Grande Southern Depot)

1891. 1991, Charles Cunliffe End of S. Townsend Ave.

San Miguel County had gutted this lap-sided Queen Anne Style depot for heavy equipment storage. Charles Cunliffe, an Aspen architect, put it back together again and doubled the space to accommodate a basement microbrewery. The old depot now has a saloon inside and a beer garden in back on the San Miguel River.

SM01 San Juan Brew Pub (Rio Grande Southern Depot)

SM02 **Swede-Finn Hall**

1899. 1992, restoration, Mathew Allen. 472 W. Pacific Ave. (southeast corner of Townsend Ave.)

Finns who spoke Swedish as a result of Sweden's 700-year occupation of their country built this old-fashioned clapboard hall with double-pane sash windows and a hardwood floor. During Prohibition it became the Swede-Finn Temperance Hall. Restoration has left it a large, primitive hall whose beauty is in the fine woodwork, complemented by the streamlined classicism of the new cherry wood bar. Pacific Avenue between Townsend Street and Oak Street, the heart of the neighborhood once occupied by Finnish miners, still contains the Finn Town Flats (a boarding house) and Finn Hall, a meeting hall (1896), 440 West Pacific Avenue.

SM03 **San Miguel County Courthouse**

1887. 301 W. Colorado Ave. (northwest corner of Oak St.)

A central, three-story brick clock tower distinguishes this two-story Italianate building, which incorporates red bricks from the first county courthouse. Over the years the courthouse hosted dances, lectures, community meetings, shows, revivals, fairs, and religious services. The one-story stone county jail is on the west side of the courthouse, and a Rio Grande Southern Galloping Goose, a hybrid passenger car and locomotive, nests on the courthouse lawn.

SM04 **Sheridan Opera House**

1913. 110 N. Oak St. (NR)

The Sheridan Opera House, originally for theater and vaudeville performances, now houses the Telluride International Film Festival. Typical of many period commercial buildings, the drab, three-story, red brick building has a flat roof, corbeled brick cornice, and arched openings. Of more interest is the 200-seat interior, restored in 1972 to its Gilded Age sparkle. The seats were originally removable to make a dance floor. The theater's roll curtain, which depicts a Venetian scene, was hand painted in tempera by western painter John Erickson.

In 1985 the Sheridan Opera House was remodeled again, this time by Phoenix architect Peter Johnson. Johnson's facelift and addition were defended by Roger Neville Williams, owner of the Sheridan Opera House, who contended: "This building wasn't pretty before. It was a turn-of-the-century building constructed by a mining engineer." Despite approval by the Historic and Architectural Review Commission, many residents felt the addition, with its brick piers and vertical glass panels, was insensitive to the original. Many were also outraged that the remodeling had covered up a cherished piece of Telluride history—an old brick wall bearing the faded painted message: "Opera House Picture Show every evening—Admission ten cents and 15 cents." The historic "SHOW" sign, outlined in light bulbs, remains, although the marquee disappeared during the remodeling.

SM05 **New Sheridan Hotel**

1896, Gus Brickson and Max Hipplen, builders. 231–235 W. Colorado Ave. (NR)

This two-story red brick building, with a third floor added in 1899, is enhanced by ornate primary and secondary metal cornices and six arched windows on both the second and third floors. The front entrance has large display windows flanked by cast iron columns.

The bar originally featured calfskin-covered walls, while the restaurant advertised velvet-curtained booths equipped with telephones which diners used to order meals. Unfortunately many of the original Victorian furnishings were sold to Knott's Berry Farm, the Southern California amusement park, although a 30-foot-long mirror framed in Corinthian columns still reflects the surviving Austrian cherry wood bar. The hotel's patrons included Lillian Gish, Sarah Bernhardt, and Colorado's three-time choice for U.S. president, William Jennings Bryan, who delivered one of his silverite speeches in front of the hotel for Telluride's July 4, 1903, celebration. During the labor wars of 1903–1904, the New Sheridan Hotel was commandeered by the Colorado National Guard as its headquarters for suppressing striking miners. Since then it has been rehabilitated for modern-day travelers.

SM06 Pekkarine Building

1880s. 222 W. Colorado Ave. (between Oak and Fir sts.)

A successful Finnish immigrant built this two-story brick building, where he opened a boot shop in the basement, a mercantile on the first floor, and family apartments on the second floor. Although architecturally undistinguished, it is one of the oldest, least altered Colorado Avenue buildings.

SM07 Old Elks Club (First National Bank)

1892. 201–211 W. Colorado Ave. (northwest corner of Fir St.)

Massive corner entry arches distinguish this Romanesque Revival gem, the handsomest building in town. Rough-faced sandstone gives way at the entrance to slender, polished granite half columns. Projections suggesting a square tower further emphasize the entry. Unfortunately someone has tried to enhance the soft natural glow of the local sandstone with purple paint.

SM08 Mahr Building

1892, Andrew and B. M. Mahr, builders. 129–131 W. Colorado Ave.

Telluride's only all-metal-clad facade is on the two-story Mahr Building. It replaced the one-story, wood-frame San Miguel Valley Bank building, which had the distinction of being the first bank to be robbed by Butch Cassidy, in 1886. The money was never recovered. The Italianate cast iron facade bears the inscription: "Mesker Bros., Front Builders, St. Louis, Mo., Pat. Oct 4 '87." The galvanized iron panels on the second story form eight small columns surrounding four narrow windows. The overhanging cor-

SM07 Old Elks Club (First National Bank)

SM08 Mahr Building

nice has decorative brackets, panels, and finials.

SM09 Bank of Telluride

c. 1893. 109 W. Colorado Ave.

Telluride's only example of Neoclassical architecture has two large, fluted Ionic columns in terracotta supporting a terracotta entablature embellished with dentils, moldings, and a pediment. Bank president Charles "Buck" Waggoner made national headlines in 1929 when he multiplied his bank's assets at the expense of six New York banks. "A seedy country banker swindles six New York banks out of $500,000," declared the *New York Times* headline. Waggoner used the money to pay off the Bank of Telluride's debts, ensuring that his depositors did not lose any money, but was convicted and imprisoned for bank fraud.

SM10 Nunn and Wrench Building

1899. 100–114 E. Colorado Ave.

Lucien L. Nunn, whose utility company supplied electricity to local mines and mills, and A. M. Wrench erected this unusually large one-story red brick building with five storefronts under a decorative metal cornice. Several store interiors retain original architectural details, including pressed metal ceilings and walls. Nunn's house, at the northwest corner of Aspen Street and Columbia Avenue, also survives.

SM11 Senate Saloon

c. 1896. 125 S. Spruce Ave.

Starting out as a respectable boarding house, the Senate evolved into a notorious saloon where Pacific Avenue prostitutes flaunted their finery. The simple brick one-story box on a stone foundation rising to windowsill level was restored in the 1960s as a bar and restaurant under the original name. It retains the brass footrail, spittoons, pressed metal ceiling, and plank floor of the original interior but never regained a second story lost to fire.

SM12 The Cribs

1890s. 121, 123, 125–127 E. Pacific Ave. (northwest corner of Spruce St.) (NR)

As in most predominately male mining districts, prostitution flourished in Telluride. Of twenty-six houses of ill repute, these three simple, lap-sided, front-gabled cottages remain. Small, two-room brothels like these once lined the eastern end of Pacific Avenue, wall-to-wall with the town's saloons and gambling halls. These humble "cribs" were usually torn down as mining towns became more "civilized." These are among the few of the kind surviving anywhere in the nation. At the east end of the row, at the northwest corner of Pacific Avenue and Spruce Street, a more elaborate "female boarding house" occupied the upper story of the Silver Bell Saloon and Dance Hall (1890; 1986 restoration, David W. Petersen). This simple, two-story clapboard box is now a tiny school for the arts. In 1979 the National Trust for Historic Preservation purchased the three rare cribs and sold them, with protective covenants, to the town of Telluride, which has rehabilitated them as low-income housing.

SM13 Wilkinson Public Library (Jail)

1887. 1987, renovation and addition, Gibson and Reno. 100 S. Spruce Ave.

Telluride's old, 800-square-foot stone jail was enlarged with a 4,000-square-foot addition and converted to the town library. The addition leaves the jail as the more prominent wing of an L-shaped building enclosing two sides of a courtyard, entered through a new stone and wood archway with built-in benches. The open-beam gable on this archway reflects the pedimented gable dormers of the new metal-roofed, red brick library building and the open beams of the Postmodern interior.

SM14 Roma Bar

1880s. 133 E. Colorado Ave. (northwest corner of Spruce St.)

One wild night, some think, the jam-packed Roma Bar fell into the basement. Actually it was carefully moved downstairs piece by piece, allowing a much higher roof and atrium to capture some of the barroom racket. Supposedly the rubblestone basement walls conceal a tunnel to nearby St. Patrick's Church, dug to supply the Roma with sacramental wine during Prohibition. An 1860 Brunswick-Balke-Collender carved walnut back bar with 12-foot French mirrors graces this lively tavern. The round arches of the bar mirrors are reflected in new wall mirrors, which help to visually enlarge the tiny, crowded space.

SM15 St. Patrick's Catholic Church

1896. 301 N. Spruce St. (northwest corner of E. Galena Ave.)

Telluride's best example of Gothic Revival architecture is a chapel with a steeply pitched front gable, clapboard siding, Gothic-arched windows, and an unusually elongated gabled bell tower. The surrounding "Catholic Hill" neighborhood attracted many Italians and Austrians. The wooden Stations of the Cross, hand carved in Tyrol, are one of the few ornate touches in a simple frame interior with well-worn pews and humble, frosted glass windows.

SM16 San Miguel County Historical Society Museum (Hospital)

1895. 201 W. Gregory Ave. (north end of Fir St.)

Dr. H. C. Hall had this two-story hospital constructed with large blocks of native sandstone. A metal hipped roof forms a pediment over the entry that is repeated in the smaller pediments of two rooftop dormers. The hospital closed in 1964, to reopen two years later as the county history museum.

SM17 Naisbitt-Aburdene House

1987, Theodore R. Brown. 459 W. Dakota Ave. (west bank of Cornet Creek)

Selecting for their own home not futuristic but historic design themes, futurologists John Naisbitt and Patricia Aburdene, the authors of *Megatrends* (1982) and *Megatrends 2000* (1990), asked a San Francisco architect to use natural elements reflecting the local vernacular. Brown responded with a two-story house of lodgepole pine, cantilevered over Cornet Creek and terraced to reflect the strata of the surrounding Rockies. The creek is brought into the plan with a bridge that serves as the main entry, and stones from the creek bed are incorporated into the concrete foundation. Multiple dormers and gables adorned with prominent log bargeboards and projecting log vigas, as well as log decks, make this a prickly-looking composition, culminating in an octagonal tower observatory with a carved log finial. The architect drew inspiration not only from the site, but also from old mining camps, whose rusty metal roofs suggested the corrugated Cor-ten steel used here. The house, which was featured in the June 1989 issue of *Architectural Digest*, is a good specimen of neo-rustic design.

SM18 Peach House

1977, Jack Para. 260 N. Davis St.

Jack Para collaborated with Telluride artist Edward Wiener to construct this vividly colored, comic-strip version of a two-story frame Queen Anne house. Peachy paint is complemented by a wild range of trim colors in this example of high neo-Victorian with updated Carpenter's Gothic trim.

SM19 Elementary School–Community Center (High School)

1896. 423 W. Columbia Ave. (northeast corner of Townsend Ave.)

Poor brickwork led to the collapse of an 1895 school, rebuilt as this two-story red brick and tan sandstone edifice notable for its central bay, whose round-arched entry is repeated in second-story and gable windows. A Quonset hut (1949) erected as a gymnasium has been the community center since

1967. A large rear addition (c. 1900) matches the original, even to a twin rooftop cupola.

SM20 Davis-Waggoner House

1899. 207 N. Oak St. (northwest corner of Columbia Ave.)

This large foursquare has a typical attic dormer and twin second-story windows. Dentils and quoins emphasize the symmetrical composition on a rectangular plan. This beautifully maintained specimen wears red brick with white wooden trim, including latticework under the Tuscan-columned porch. Constructed for Edwin L. Davis, it is one of old Telluride's finest residences, although it would be a typical home in many Denver neighborhoods. Charles "Buck" Waggoner, president of the Bank of Telluride, later lived here.

SM21 Town Hall

1883. 135 W. Columbia Ave. (northeast corner of N. Fir St.)

This one-story, lap-sided building with a fire tower added later was built as the town's first school. The tower's height provided not only a good lookout, but also space to allow fire hoses to be hung out to dry.

SM22 Miners Union Hospital

1902. 1973, renovation, Robert Garber. 107 W. Columbia Ave. (northwest corner of Pine St.)

The Western Federation of Miners, a powerful presence in Telluride during the labor strikes of 1901–1904, built this hospital, heralded as "the best designed and most thoroughly equipped hospital in southern Colorado." Of the union labor employed in construction, the WFM boasted: "Every stroke of work on the building was done by union men, and the highest wages were paid."

The boxy, three-story edifice has a basement and trim of local Deep Creek sandstone, brick quoins, and hipped dormers in a hipped roof. Above the basement union hall, the hospital stories were constructed of pressed brick from Durango. After the union was chased out of town in 1904, the hospital closed, then reopened as a post office, offices, and an Odd Fellows hall. In 1973 it was rehabilitated as apartments with a laundromat in the old union hall.

SM23 The Peaks Penthouse and Condominiums (Doral Telluride Resort and Spa)

1992, Anthony Pellecchia Associates. Atop Country Club Dr., Telluride Mountain Village, 8 miles southwest of Telluride

Toniest of all the Telluride accommodations, this $90 million Postmodern monument of concrete is dressed up with copper roofs and chimney pots. Eight-to-ten-story buildings crowd a spectacular site on the edge of the Telluride Ski Area. Asked to design a 465,000-square-foot hotel complex on a 5.5-acre site, the architects tried to lessen its impact by making it look like a cluster of separate buildings rather than a monolith. They also strove to tie it to the environment by using red sandstone at ground level, but failed to bring this monster to earth.

SM24 Pandora Mill

1880s; many additions. 2 miles southeast at east end of Columbia Ave.

Much of the Smuggler-Union Mining Company's giant Pandora Mill survives, but not the surrounding company town, tram terminals, mine tunnels, offices, and boarding houses. This rusty remnant of yesterday's industry at first glance resembles a Mineshaft Modern condominium, with its industrial glass walls and corrugated and skylighted metal roof. Built as a gravity flow mill, it steps down the hillside under shed roofing. During a century of operations it proved to be a Pandora's box, creating the huge mill waste mountains which Telluride has been struggling to detoxify and revegetate.

SM25 Smuggler-Union Hydroelectric Power Plant

1907. 1.8-mile hike or four-wheel drive ride from Pandora Mill (NR)

This unlikely apparition is spectacularly sited atop 365-foot Bridal Veil Falls, the longest waterfall in Colorado. Buckeley Wells, the manager of the Smuggler-Union Mining Company, supposedly chose the site and worked with architects to design a handsome plant with a stone foundation and steeply gabled and dormered frame superstructure that give it a domestic appearance. On the waterfall side, a two-story bay rises abruptly out of the base to a polygonal roof. Although power plants are often eyesores, this one is most photogenic.

SM26 Tomboy Mine

1880–1927. 5 miles northeast of Telluride on Imogene Pass Rd.

Several hundred people lived here, in the 11,500-foot glacial cirque known as Savage Basin, during the Tomboy Mine's peak years, between the 1890s and World War I. A 200-ton stamp mill crushed ore delivered by an aerial tram that climbed 3,100 feet into the surrounding hills to reach ore bodies. A large boarding house, a store, 100 residences, a YMCA, and even a tennis court occupied the site where only concrete and brick ruins linger today. For a firsthand account of life at the Tomboy, see Harriet Fish Backus, *Tomboy Bride* (1969).

SM27 Fort Peabody

1903, Colorado State Militia. 7 miles east of Telluride atop Imogene Pass

The union-bashing Colorado State Militia built this rock hut to keep union miners from traveling to Telluride, where scab laborers had been recruited during the bloody 1903–1904 labor wars. Governor James Peabody used such structures and the state militia to crush the Western Federation of Min-

ers. At 13,114 feet, Imogene is one of the highest drivable passes, open only a few months each year but well worth the trip for the scenery and a wealth of mining ruins.

SM28 Ames Generating Plant

1891, Lucien L. Nunn. U.S. Forest Service Rd. 625, 12 miles southwest of Telluride

This Neoclassical stone building housed the world's first generating station to produce and transmit alternating current for industrial use. It still provides power for Telluride. The noted western historian David Lavender, a Telluride native, described how locals marveled at Nunn's powerhouse in *The Rockies* (1968):

Every Sunday afternoon during good weather people rode by train and carriage from Telluride to see the generator start up. . . . Electric arcs jumped six feet when the switches were thrown. A deep-throated hum filled the tiny room, and after the display was over, some popeyed miner always asked how long it took the alternating current to rush up the hill to the Gold King, give the armature a twist, and return. By dark, maybe? When told, the questioners were invariably indignant: 186,000 miles a second? Whose leg are you trying to pull, mister?

Norwood

Norwood (1885, 7,014 feet) is the hub of San Miguel County's ranching and farming industries. The hardware store, located on Grand Avenue, the main street, is an excellent example of the town's early commercial architecture. Norwood's oldest building may be the Henry Copp Cabin (c. 1886). Once the post office and general store, it was recycled in 1999 as a community center. The old Norwood School has become a Masonic temple, and a log cabin serves as the town hall.

SM29 Lone Cone Bar

1932. 1580 Grand Ave.

Built after a fire consumed the original building, this cinderblock structure envelops a magnificent old Brunswick Empire back bar standing 10 feet high with a pink marble base and a brass footrail. It and a companion front bar and liquor cabinet, also dating to the 1890s, were hauled in from Silverton during the 1940s.

SM30 Back Narrows Inn (Western Hotel)

1888. 1550 Grand Ave.

When Norwood voted for incorporation in 1905, the election took place in this two-story frame hotel with a recessed, full-length front porch. Known earlier as the Western Hotel or Royer's Hotel, it is connected by a newer bridge building to an annex, a lap-sided foursquare.

Dolores County   (DL)

Dolores County (1881) originated with a silver strike at Rico, which became the first county seat. The Dolores River, named by explorer Juan Maria de Rivera to commemorate the sorrows of the Virgin Mary (El Río de Nuestra Señora de los Dolores), cuts a miniature Grand Canyon in San Juan National Forest, which covers about half the county. Although mining created the county, it soon became more dependent on farming, ranching, lumbering, and recreation. Dunton, a mining and smelter town, has been sustained by its hot springs resort of antique log buildings. With a uranium boom in the Dove Creek area, the county population peaked in the 1960s at some 2,200.

Dove Creek

The county seat (1915, 6,843 feet), named for the creek where pioneers found wild doves, is a small agricultural town that boomed during the 1950s but fizzled with the collapse of the uranium market. Returning to its agrarian roots, Dove Creek now puffs itself as "The Pinto Bean Capital of the World." Anasazi beans, a new hybrid, became a gourmet food in the early 1990s. Some 700 residents—about half the county's population—live here. Dove Creek has a few notable structures, such as the remains of a cabin once inhabited by Zane Grey, the western novelist who drew inspiration from the surrounding landscape for his novel *Riders of the Purple Sage*.

Rico

Born with a silver spoon in its mouth, Rico (1879, 8,827 feet) has been malnourished since the 1893 silver crash. Prospectors began poking around in the late 1860s, but

did not make significant silver strikes until 1879. The silver bonanza spurred Otto Mears's Rio Grande Southern railroad to build a narrow-gauge line over Lizard Head Pass, and in 1890 Rico's population peaked at around 1,200. Rico's long decline enabled prosperous farmers at the county's west end to vote for moving the county seat to Dove Creek in 1944. In 1953 discovery of iron pyrites, used to make sulfuric acid, led to construction of the Ramco sulfuric acid plant near Rico. Toxic fumes and waste from the plant killed aspen trees and polluted the upper Dolores River before the plant closed in 1962. Today, Rico is liveliest in summer, when tourists stop to gawk at this ghostly mining town. The coke ovens a mile south of town on Colorado 145 are reminders of Rico's richer days.

DL01 **Dey Building**

1892. Glasgow Ave. (Colorado 145)

This two-story commercial edifice speaks eloquently of the area's skilled stonemasons and fine stone. The sandstone front flaunts

DL01 Dey Building

This clapboard church is distinguished by round-arched windows repeated in the entry, the base and louvered windows of the bell tower, the sanctuary, and a tiny Palladian window in the front gable.

DL04 **Kaufman House**

1891–1892, Frank L. Hill. 1990s, restoration. Silver St. (north of Mantz Ave.) (NR)

This two-story box with a flat roof may be the only masonry residence in a frame town. Panels in the brick walls on the south and east adorn distinctive bays. An elaborate wooden cornice on the east originally extended along the south side as well, and a porch once sheltered the first floor along the south and west sides.

DL05 **Atlantic Cable Mine**

1878. West side of Colorado 145 at the north end of town

In 1878 John Glasgow and others located this claim, later consolidated with others as the Dolores Silver Mining Company. The headframe and shaft remain visible today. The mine produced substantial silver, zinc, lead, and copper until the 1940s.

Romanesque Revival detail, with an arcaded second story, a bracketed cornice, and a pediment. Uncoursed rubblestone forms side walls, now visible with the demise of neighboring buildings. The ground-floor storefront is asymmetrically arranged with recessed entries for both levels on the left. Once the Metropole Bar occupied the first floor, which since 1939 has housed the Enterprise Cafe and Bar.

DL02 **Town Hall** (Dolores County Courthouse)

1893. Northeast corner of Commercial and Mantz sts. (NR)

A rectangular, symmetrical structure, this two-story courthouse has cross-gabled wings on a granite foundation and a raised basement. Red pressed brick from Durango is trimmed in rough red sandstone from the Cutler Quarry, 18 miles south of Rico. The central entry is at the base of a protruding, square, three-story tower with a pyramidal cap flanked by hipped dormers. The arches, rough-faced stone, and verticality of the most imposing building in town hint at the Richardsonian Romanesque style.

DL03 **Rico Community Church** (Congregational Church)

1891. 1993, restoration. Silver St.

DL03 Rico Community Church (Congregational Church)

Montezuma County   (MT)

The county established in 1889 in the southwestern corner of Colorado is rich in prehistoric ruins, including the first United Nations–designated World Heritage site in the United States—Mesa Verde National Park. As the county's name suggests, its fabulous cliff dwellings were not initially credited to local Native Americans but to the Aztecs of Mexico. Ironically, the county seat was named for Montezuma's nemesis, Hernando Cortés.

The Anasazi (Navajo for "ancient ones" or "ancient enemies"), not the Aztecs, built these stone cities into canyon walls. Then, like the builders of the tower of Babel, they disappeared, leaving ruins for moderns to ponder. Thousands of other prehistoric sites scattered around the county make it heaven on earth for archaeologists and prehistory buffs.

Native Americans still occupy the southern half of this county, which has one of Colorado's two Indian reservations—the Ute Mountain Ute Reservation, whose hub is at Towaoc. Utes made up roughly a quarter of the 18,672 residents of Montezuma County in 1990. Archaeologists, who have determined the age of structures by using dendrochronology, or dating of tree rings, in the roof beams, estimate that twice as many people lived in the area during the golden age of the Anasazi, A.D. 900–1200.

Settlement by U.S. citizens began in the 1880s with the arrival of ranching, irrigation, and dry-land farming. Apples, apricots, grapes, and potatoes were major crops, eclipsed in recent years by pinto beans, most notably the popular, multicolored, gourmet Anasazi bean. Early settlers did a little hard-rock mining, but the 1950s emergence of uranium and oil industries was more important.

Tourism focuses on Mesa Verde, the first national park (1906) established primarily to preserve architectural rather than natural resources. Anasazi buildings at Mesa Verde are Colorado's greatest architectural legacy. While the prehistoric cliff dwellings are the most remarkable Native American structures surviving in the United States, many of the National Park Service buildings are admirable examples of the Pueblo Revival Style.

Cortez

Cortez (1887, 6,200 feet) was laid out in 1886 by M. J. Mack, engineer for the Montezuma Valley Water Supply Company, as the county seat and commercial hub. The first house and school were constructed in 1887. One of the few county seats never served by a railroad, Cortez remained a small town although tourism grew after the creation of Mesa Verde National Park in 1906. The town has several archaeological research centers and museums. Much strip development has come to line U.S. 160, the main street of this town of some 7,000 residents. Some of the oldest downtown landmarks are built of a dusty-colored sandstone quarried nearby in Crow Canyon.

MT01 Colorado Welcome Center

1987, Dean Brookie. 928 E. Main St. (northwest corner of Mildred Rd. in City Park)

This inviting information center and mini-museum is a viga-studded, two-story stucco hybrid that borrows from the International

Style as well as the Pueblo Revival. Dean Brookie, a Durango architect, used shapes, including a round tower and oddly angled rooms, suggested by the Mesa Verde ruins.

MT02 Montezuma Valley National Bank

1907. Northeast corner of Main and Market sts.

Wearing the classical garb preferred by bankers, this symmetrical, one-story building of rough-faced sandstone boasts decorative stamped metal for the banding and the corner entry pediment. This sedate bank slips out of character inside, where it revels in chandeliers and red flocked wallpaper.

MT03 Cortez University of Colorado Center, Museum, and Cultural Park

c. 1900. 25 N. Market St.

Built as the steel-frame, brick, and stucco E. R. Lamb Mercantile, this building is distinguished by a second-story cast iron front from Mesker Brothers of St. Louis. This metal false front exults in florid metal pilasters, corbeling, garlanded friezes, bas-relief panels, and an exuberant cornice. A trompe-l'oeil mural of modern-day Pueblo Indian life covering the entire north wall helps to integrate a Victorian business block with its newer storefront additions—fake vigas, log-columned porch, and balcony. The adjacent cultural park contains a reconstructed hogan, tipi, and dance arena. The University of Colorado has long been the major sponsor of local archaeological research and in 1987 opened this educational outreach center and museum in cooperation with the city of Cortez. Despite additions, this building maintains more of its integrity than its neighbor at 10 West Main Street, the Wilson Drug Building, formerly the Stoneblock Building (1889), a once impressive two-story stone business block now diminished by a stuccoed pediment, glass block storefront, and aluminum awnings.

MT04 Ertel Funeral Home

1936, Walter H. Simon. 42 N. Market St.

Like many southwestern business buildings, this one blends Spanish Colonial Revival, Mission Revival, and Pueblo Revival styles, combining battered stucco walls and vigas with a bell niche, wrought iron trim, and a red tile roof. John Walter Ertel built this as a funeral parlor. It is well preserved on the exterior, although modified inside to keep up with advances in mortuary science.

MT05 Cortez School Administration Building

1930s, WPA?. 121 E. 1st St.

One of the few handsome, unaltered edifices in town is sheathed in rusticated local sandstone trimmed in the same stone. A grand, round-arched entry and stepped parapet are among the most appealing of several discreet details. Originally a school, it is now the administrative headquarters of the school district.

MT06 Crow Canyon Archaeological Center

1979. 4 miles northwest of Cortez via U.S. 666 and Montezuma County L to 23390 Montezuma County K

The two-story Crow Canyon Lodge (1982) and the three-story research and educational center (1989), Neo–Pueblo Revival structures of stucco and squared logs, are the hubs of a complex which allows students and amateurs a chance to practice archaeological techniques. Ten squared log, hexagonal hogans (1980s) provide additional housing for participants in digs at various nearby sites, including Sand Canyon Pueblo, a thirteenth-century complex of more than 400 rooms, kivas, and towers.

MT07 Kelly Place Bed and Breakfast

1966, Jared Morse. 1980s, additions. 14663 Montezuma County G (McElmo Canyon Rd.), 10 miles west of Cortez

George Kelly, a horticulturist who did much statewide to promote use of native plants in landscaping, worked with the architect on this stone and stucco Southwestern Style home. The U-shaped structure is wrapped around a south-facing courtyard and walled garden. Despite additions, most noticeably a second story on the east wing, it retains much of its original Pueblo Revival charm. The 100-acre site contains both native and introduced plants, not to mention Anasazi ruins, at what is now a bed and breakfast inn and educational center.

MT08 Hovenweep National Monument

25 miles west of Cortez via Montezuma County G (McElmo Canyon Rd.)

Hovenweep (Ute for deserted valley) consists of widely scattered Anasazi structures in Colorado and Utah, including square, round, and oval masonry towers and one D-shaped one built near springs. These smooth masonry structures are reminiscent of medieval European fortifications, but openings in the Hovenweep towers may have been for astronomical observation rather than for defensive purposes. Designated a national monument in 1923, Hovenweep has a visitors' center (in Utah, 16 miles east of Hatch) and five major sites.

Dolores

Dolores (1878, 6,936 feet) was named for El Río de Nuestra Señora de los Dolores (river of our lady of sorrows). This was a railroad town served by the Rio Grande Southern. Many nineteenth-century railroad-era structures survive, in various states of disuse. Pleasant's Old West Antiques, 400 Central Avenue, includes a museum specializing in old printing equipment. The Village Blacksmith is still at work at 11th Street and Colorado 145. Architecturally, this town's wonders range from the abandoned Chateau Style Del Rio Hotel to the pressed metal facade of the Hollywood Saloon, which resembles a western movie set.

MT09 Rio Grande Southern Depot Museum

1993, Richard L. Dorman. In Flanders Park, 420 Railroad Ave. (Colorado 145), northwest corner of S. 5th St.

Richard Dorman, a Santa Fe architect, faithfully reincarnated the classic Queen Anne Style depot lost to a fire. The steep-pitched, cross-gabled upper story contains the stationmaster's quarters, with freight and passenger services below. The new depot is a

fine nest for Galloping Goose No. 5, one of the famed flock of seven hybrid rail and motor vehicles. Goose No. 5 initially had a 1925 Pierce Arrow engine attached to a Wayne bus.

MT10 Rio Grande Southern Hotel

1893, E. L. Wilbur. 101 S. 5th St. (southeast corner of Central Ave.) (NR)

This recently restored frame hotel consists of a two-story original structure with a smaller 1902 frame addition. It was stuccoed to comply with a new ordinance after a 1913 fire that claimed the hotel's icehouse and stables, along with other downtown buildings. The third-story gables retain their original bargeboard and wood shingles in an alternating square and fishscale pattern beneath a sunburst. In contrast to the Queen Anne facade, the other three walls are plain-Jane stuccoed planks.

MT11 Exon Mercantile Company

1896, William James Exon. 315 Central Ave. (northwest corner of 4th St.)

The typical corbeled brick facade and transomed glass storefronts of this relic are little altered. The typical stepped-down side walls hide a slightly pitched roof descending to a collection of stone and corrugated metal sheds at the rear.

MT12 Anasazi Heritage Center

1988, Curt Lamprecht and Gayle Erickson, Bureau of Reclamation architects. 27501 Colorado 184, 2 miles west of Dolores

Built as part of the mitigation for many Anasazi sites drowned by the huge McPhee Reservoir project, this $4.8 million, state-of-the-art museum preserves and exhibits some of the artifacts salvaged from what is now Colorado's second largest lake. Stone from cuts for the McPhee Dam went into the walls of the Neo–Pueblo Revival complex. The structure is a one-story semicircle, designed to catch sunlight, which is visually extended into a circle by an open-beam pergola and curving walls. The 40,500-square-foot museum houses not only artifacts, but also archives, a theater, a conference center, a library, hands-on exhibits, and a full-scale reconstructed pit house. Trails lead to the nearby Dominguez and Escalante ruins, two important excavated Anasazi sites first discovered in 1776 by Fathers Dominguez and Escalante. The Escalante ruin is notable as an example of Chaco Canyon–type masonry, consisting of stone blocks alternating with bands of smaller stones, or spalls, enclosing a core of sandstone rubble.

Mancos

Mancos (1877, 6,993 feet) was named for the Mancos (Spanish for one-handed) River by members of the Dominguez-Escalante expedition after one of their party fell from his horse and injured his arm. Initially a ranching community, it became a tourist town catering to visitors at nearby Mesa Verde National Park. Boyle Park, at the east end of Main Street, contains a stout, two-cell jail (1895), built of two-by-six boards laid flat. Vintage Main Street buildings include the Columbine Bar (1902). On U.S. 160, 3 miles west of town, sagebrush flats surround the Hogan Trading Post, with fake Plains Indians tipis amid telephone-pole-sized arrows.

MT13 **Bauer Bank Building**

1905, George Bauer. Southwest corner of Main St. (U.S. 160) and Grand Ave.

Basement and first-floor sandstone support a brick upper story on this Italianate commercial building with basement frontage in the rear along the Mancos River. Although a corrugated metal front hides the original

storefronts, the edifice is still noteworthy for its bracketed metal cornice with serpentine and fleur-de-lis designs in the frieze and its third-story roundel windows.

MT14 **Bauer Mansion**

1889, George Bauer. 102 Bauer Ave. (northwest corner of N. Main St.)

George Bauer opened the first store and first bank in Montezuma County. He built this two-and-one-half-story house of soft red brick with smooth sandstone quoins and flattened-arch windows. Between 1919 and 1952, when it served as a hospital, alterations were made to this Italianate residence, now a bed and breakfast inn.

MT15 **Wrightsman Hotel**

1903, J. D. Wrightsman. N. Mesa St. (southwest corner of Bauer Ave.)

This pastiche of Queen Anne, Tudor Revival, and Romanesque Revival elements includes unusual fanlighted eyebrow dormers, half timbering, and oriel windows. Well maintained behind an elegant wrought iron fence on spacious grounds, the two-and-one-half-story house of rough-faced stone has suffered few alterations since its 1910 conversion to a hotel.

MT16 **Mancos High School**

1909, W. L. Morse and David Ramsey. 301 Grand Ave. (U.S. 160) (NR)

This fine, formal school building is sheathed in tawny local sandstone. The rectangular, three-story building with a central entry bay

rising into an open, mansarded bell tower has undistracting additions.

MT17 United Methodist Church

1880s, 1920s?. Northeast corner of Grand Ave. (U.S. 160) and Oak St.

With unusual flourish, a curvilinear parapet fronts this Mission Revival church, culminating in an open belfry with a domed cap. Smooth stucco walls emphasize the molded detail along the parapet, and an arcaded portico protects the entrance. An aging brick rear chimney suggests that this was an old brick church "southwesternized" in more recent decades. Unusually tasteful design extends to the front yard sculpture—three crosses made of steel I beams.

MT18 Veterans of Foreign Wars Post (Mancos Opera House)

1910, A. J. Ames and George D. Woods. 136 W. Grand Ave (northeast corner of Mesa St.) (NR)

Despite a three-story facade of brick with sandstone trim, this is actually a two-story building with the high-ceilinged VFW hall on the first floor. Upstairs, the town's largest commercial building housed the Checkerboard Ballroom, so called for the numbered squares painted on the floor. When the music—provided by local bands such as the Slumber Wreckers—stopped, a number was called and a prize awarded to whomever stood on that numbered square. The hall, which holds 300, has served for basketball games and high school graduations, as well as for live performances and movies. The relatively modest trim, corbeling, and stepped corner parapets typify twentieth-century restraint rather than nineteenth-century exuberance.

MT19 Ohio Blue Tip Match Company

1947. Grande Ave. (U.S. 160), 5 miles west of town

Belching smokestacks and screeching whistles announce the town's major industry, which annually whittles some four million board feet of aspen trees into matchsticks. These are shipped to Wadsworth, Ohio, and coated with combustible phosphorous tips, dyed blue.

Mesa Verde National Park

Mesa Verde National Park (1906, 8,000 feet) takes its name from the green tablelands with architectural ruins left by the Anasazi, a people who arrived several thousand years ago. They became a settled, corn-raising people who built extensive communities. Pit houses, the earliest known Anasazi dwellings, date to the Basketmaker period, beginning around 1800 B.C., when, according to research using carbon dating, corn was first cultivated. These shallow recesses in the ground had become almost entirely subterranean pits by A.D. 800. Inside were benches built into the walls around a central fireplace and a stone deflector-ventilator shaft. Roofs were log and brush. As the culture advanced, the pit houses became the ceremonial kivas of Pueblo villages and cliff dwellings. These kivas retained the sunken circular shape with an antechamber, a central firepit, a stone deflector, and a *sipapu*, or spirit hole, symbolizing a spiritual connection with Mother Earth. Kivas generally have six to eight masonry piers rising out of the peripheral benches for roof support. Entry was through a small roof hatchway, as in early pit houses.

From subterranean mud, stone, and stick pit houses the Anasazi advanced to aboveground masonry pueblos with multiple rooms. Their stout masonry construction rose two, three, and even four stories. Pueblo-era masonry work consisted of large, well-shaped stones set into thick mud mortar. Small stones, or spalls, were shoved into the mortar to make it more compact. Later Pueblo-era buildings are notable for their smooth surfaces and clean, sharp lines, best seen at Far View Ruins (MT23). Stones were carefully chosen for size and, in the case of the park's fifty-seven towers, shaped to form circular walls. Uneven sandstone walls were pounded and pecked smooth with harder riverbed hammerstones. This "pecking" left an even but dimpled wall surface. Drywall construction can be found, especially in storage chambers. Interior walls were given less attention, merely plastered with mud and sometimes painted with orange-red designs in geometric or animal motifs. Although the Anasazi occasionally experimented with mud bricks reinforced by dried grasses, bark, or yucca leaves, these are different from the adobe bricks introduced by the Spanish.

Single-coursed masonry (900–1100) evolved into double-coursed masonry (1100–1300). A basket-making culture became a pottery-making one. Artifacts reveal that one of the most advanced Indian civilizations north of Mexico developed an elaborate cultural and religious life. Discoveries range from flutelike instruments made of bones to marked bones possibly used as dice for gambling. The most notable artifacts are the ornate pottery in various designs, sizes, and shapes.

During their golden age, roughly A.D. 1100 to 1275, the Mesa Verdeans moved from the mesa-top pueblos to cliff dwellings several hundred feet under the cliff ledges and above the valley floors. Archaeologists speculate that they made this move for defensive, religious, or climate-control purposes. To build these stone cliff cities, the Native Americans carefully sized and sometimes shaped native sandstone blocks, as they had for the earlier towers. Roofs consisted of log beams with cross layers of sticks topped by mud. The cliff dwellings had no standard floor plans but were fitted to the cliffs. Doors are usually two to three feet above the floor and sometimes T-shaped. Windows were rare and little more than peepholes. Buildings were terraced, with the largest areas on the lowest floors. For reasons still debated but probably at least partly because of drought and crop failure, the Mesa Verdeans abandoned these early-day condominiums during the great drought of 1275–1300.

Spanish explorers first reported on the Mesa Verde ruins. The Hayden Survey of the 1870s also described some of the ruins, which were first photographed by survey cameraman William Henry Jackson. More extensive discoveries and the beginning of tourism and artifact collecting began in the 1880s with expeditions organized by local ranchers, the Wetherill family of Mancos.

Gustav Nordenskiöld, a Swede, conducted the first scientific survey and carted off artifacts to Scandinavia. Growing concern about the loss of artifacts and the need to preserve the ruins led to the creation of Mesa Verde National Park in 1906. Passage of the Federal Antiquities Act the same year made it a crime to remove artifacts from public lands. Today visitors see stabilized and sometimes partly reconstructed ruins of an astonishing prehistoric culture.

MT20 Far View Visitor Center

1965, Joseph P. Marlow. On Ruins Rd., 14 miles from park entrance

This starting point for park tours is a circular stone structure, a modern-day rendition of a huge kiva. An entry ramp tunneling under the highway suggests the subterranean entries to kivas and pit houses. Nearby is the only overnight accommodation (other than Morefield Village Camp Ground) in the park, Far View Motor Lodge (1965, Barker, Rinker, Seacat). It consists of simple, one- and two-story detached units of glass and vertical clapboard on frame raised on concrete stilts. The motel rooms have outside decks and flattened, V-shaped roofs flared to accentuate the fine views.

MT21 Long House

1200–1300. Wetherill Mesa Rd., side trip from Far View Visitor Center (summer only)

Named for its long central plaza and rows of small, low-ceilinged rooms, the Long House is second only to Cliff Palace (MT28) in size. The "Great Kiva" is a large sunken court with five small rectangular, masonry-lined pits which may have been covered with animal skins for use as foot drums like those found in modern-day Pueblo Indian kivas in New Mexico.

MT22 Step House

600–1200 On Wetherill Mesa

This ruin contains both early pit houses and later surface dwellings. Aboriginal steps leading to the main cave dwelling facilitated early excavation. Here walls were made with mud plaster decorated with paintings of bighorn sheep.

MT23 **Far View House**

1100–1300. On the Chapin Mesa loop drive (open year round)

In one of the most extensive mesa-top pueblos in the park, the Anasazi used stone tools to hammer rocks into smooth, curved, or straight walls. Attached apartments rising as high as three stories are held together with mortar strengthened by rock and potsherds, making this an especially fine example of masonry construction. Several thousand tons of rock and timber were brought in by people who did not use wheels. Far View House itself is a large, rectangular pueblo consisting of some forty ground-floor rooms and five kivas. Many of the kivas and pueblos here are more akin in construction and layout to those in Chaco Canyon National Monument in New Mexico than to other villages at Mesa Verde. Nearby is a large circular depression known as Mummy Lake, perhaps a prehistoric reservoir for this large village.

Jesse W. Fewkes, an archaeologist from the Smithsonian, began excavation and stabilization of the Far View group in 1916. Fewkes reinforced walls, rebuilt some of them, and capped many with cement, believing that "unless the walls are protected they will fall in a few years into piles of stone." Later the National Park Service abandoned this policy of reconstruction in favor of a stricter preservation policy.

MT24 **Mesa Verde National Park Administrative District (NHL)**

Jesse Nusbaum, the son of a pioneer bricklayer in Greeley, was the superintendent of Mesa Verde National Park during much of the 1920s, 1930s, and 1940s. He became an exponent of the Pueblo Revival style after working with Mary Coulter, an architect who designed restaurants and hotels for the Santa Fe Railroad. Nusbaum also consulted with his friend, the Santa Fe architect John Gaw Meem, before designing much of the headquarters complex. Nusbaum was an archaeologist and amateur architect who earlier worked with Meem in Santa Fe, where

Meem's projects included the restoration of the Palace of the Governors and the design of the Santa Fe Art Museum. At Mesa Verde, Nusbaum, with some assistance from his wife, Eileen, made rough designs for headquarters buildings which were refined by park service architects.

The Nusbaums initially lived in a tent while supervising Navajo Indians who constructed many of the park facilities. Navajos, who still do much of the work in the park, also built for themselves seven rock hogans and a sweat lodge, off limits to visitors. Also off limits is one of the least altered Nusbaum buildings, the 1930s ranger dormitory, now the park research library.

Jesse Nusbaum interested John D. Rockefeller, Jr., in financing extensive digs at key sites around the park, although a great many remain unexplored. Even after leaving Mesa Verde to direct the Laboratory of Anthropology in Santa Fe, Nusbaum continued to review construction drawings for additions and alterations to the Mesa Verde complex. The result is a headquarters complex of consistently fine Pueblo Revival buildings that represent the first National Park Service use of indigenous architecture. During a period when native culture was still little respected and the Pueblo Revival style was just coming to be appreciated, Mesa Verde introduced the style to millions of park visitors.

Nusbaum's elegant, horizontal structures mirror the natural forms of the mesa country as well as the prehistoric ruins. Native sandstone wall courses have flush mud mortar that gives the 18-inch thick, battered walls a smooth appearance. The load-bearing walls support peeled log vigas which project through the masonry to the exterior. The vigas on the interior support half-round sapling or split wood slats (latías: Spanish, little legs). Low, irregular parapets edge the flat roofs. Adz marks texture exterior door and window woodwork. Interiors have distinctive plaster walls, sandstone floors, *bancos* (built-in benches), and corner fireplaces.

Sensitive landscaping with local sandstone walks and native plants (piñon pine, rabbitbrush, yucca, gambel oak, Indian paintbrush) integrates the park buildings into the scene without jarring visitors from their contemplation of prehistoric marvels. Frederick Law Olmsted, Jr., on a 1924 tour, called

MT23 Far View House (far left)

MT24.1 Spruce Tree Point Museum, exterior detail (left) and west elevation drawing (below)

MT24.2 Chief Ranger Station (above, left)

MT24.4 Superintendent's Residence (above, right)

MT28 Cliff Palace (right)

Nusbaum's work "among the finest and most appropriate in the National Park Service."

MT24.1 Spruce Tree Point Museum

1923, 1936, Jesse Nusbaum

Peeled log porch posts with bracketed and scrolled capitals distinguish the one-story stone facade of this Pueblo Revival museum. A central courtyard featuring native vegetation brings light into the interior, as do the original wood-sash windows. Inspired by Spanish Colonial churches, the museum's auditorium includes a rear balcony (choir loft) and double entry doors. The high ceiling is formed by latías supporting smaller latías running parallel to the main vigas in traditional Pueblo Revival style. Inside, the style is also evident in the heavily textured walls and other details. The exhibits include exquisite 1930s dioramas as well as Anasazi artifacts, such as crutches, which suggest compassion for the old and disabled.

MT24.2 Chief Ranger Station

1927, Jesse Nusbaum

Built as a community house and natural history museum just south of the history museum, this cliff-hanger overlooks the Spruce Tree House ruins (MT25) across the canyon. Its observation porch enriches the experience with a stone floor, handmade wooden benches, and viga ceiling. Like many other buildings in this complex, it is built of rough-cut, regularly coursed local sandstone and cement with a low parapet roof and Pueblo Revival detailing.

MT24.3 Park Headquarters

1923, Jesse Nusbaum. 1940, additions

The original small, three-room office just south of the Chief Ranger Station has been expanded to 2,000 square feet but remains a fine example of Pueblo Revival massing and detail. Peeled log posts have zigzag capitals, while the battered sandstone walls are enlivened by vigas and hewn log window and door surrounds.

MT24.4 Superintendent's Residence

1921, Jesse Nusbaum. 1930s, additions

Sited spectacularly on the rim of Spruce Tree Canyon, the superintendent's residence echoes the ruins across the canyon by incorporating some peck-marked stones that were once part of prehistoric structures and a distinctive Anasazi T-shaped doorway in the basement wall. Three-foot-thick masonry walls survive, although the corner fireplaces have been removed and the open-beam ceiling has been sealed.

MT24.5 Post Office

1923, Jesse Nusbaum

This structure on the south side of the superintendent's driveway was originally a tiny comfort station tucked into the rock. Pueblo Revival details include the original recessed wooden entry, latía roofing, window frames, and the *banco* in the lobby.

MT24.6 Spruce Tree Terrace Restaurant (Eileen Nusbaum Hospital)

1926, Jesse Nusbaum

The hospital opened and operated by Jesse Nusbaum's wife is now a Pueblo Revival restaurant with outdoor patio dining and a large gift shop. The original one-story stone hospital has been reconfigured and expanded considerably.

MT25 Spruce Tree House

1200–1300

Immediately below the National Park Service complex is the most accessible Mesa Verde cliff dwelling. A self-guided tour leads to eight kivas and over 100 rooms built into this natural cave, which is 216 feet long and 89 feet deep at its widest. Little stabilization was needed here, and the ruin is about 90 percent original. One three-story masonry wall has a colored plaster geometric design. Also open to visitors is a reconstructed, covered kiva, with its characteristic six pilasters and banquettes on the round periphery and its central *sipapu*, firepit, and deflector.

MT26 Square Tower House

1200–1300

The four-story tower gave this ruin its name. Originally the complex had more than eighty rooms, of which sixty rooms and seven kivas may be seen today.

MT27 Sun Temple

1200–1300

This D-shaped structure is 121 feet long, 64 feet wide, and 11 feet high, with twenty-four rooms, three kivas, and a kiva court. The walls are 2 feet thick and 11 to 14 feet high. Anthropologists speculate that this edifice served religious purposes.

MT28 Cliff Palace

c. 1209–1270s

With 217 rooms and 23 kivas that perhaps accommodated 300 residents, Cliff Palace is the largest North American cliff dwelling— 80 feet high, 80 feet deep, and 200 feet long. Fourteen connected storage rooms built into the roof of the cave kept food and other materials cool, dry, and out of the reach of children, dogs, and domesticated turkeys. To reach such remote parts of the cliff dwellings, the Mesa Verdeans used log ladders and toeholds and handholds carved into the rock. Vigas extending through the masonry walls and murals in zigzag motifs are also notable. Here it is possible to see the small chinking stones fitted into the mortar in the hammered sandstone masonry, traces of the original pinkish-brown plaster, and painted Anasazi wall designs.

MT29 Balcony House

c. 1190–1282

Tight crawl spaces, long ladders, and stone toeholds and footholds make this a memorable and strenuous tour. Tucked under a sandstone overhang 600 feet above the val ley floor, Balcony House contains about forty rooms and is notable for its fine original plaster, courtyards, and stone balconies.

Towaoc

The Utes named Towaoc (1915, 5,800 feet) with their word for "all right" or "just fine" (pronounced *toy yak*). As the headquarters for the Ute Mountain Utes (originally the Weminuche Ute band), the town also serves as the gateway to the Ute Mountain Tribal Park (MT30), which is twice the size of Mesa Verde National Park. The old pottery building and gift shop, 3 miles east of town at U.S. 160 and U.S. 166, have been remodeled into a slick, streamlined, Neo–Pueblo Revival casino (1992). The old brick Ute Mountain Boarding School (1919) now houses the Bureau of Indian Affairs, the tribal library, and tribal offices. The Tribal Affairs Building (1889) is a two-story, S-plan structure, stuccoed in adobe style.

Not until oil discoveries on the reservation in the 1950s did all Mountain Utes have enough money to move out of tents and hogans into standard housing units. "We'll all live like white men," lamented spiritual leader Terry Knight. "We'll live in square houses and pay mortgages."

MT30 Ute Mountain Ute Tribal Park

Junction of U.S. 160 and U.S. 666

This 125,000-acre tract, whose Native American ruins were first excavated in 1913 by Earl Morris, has been left "wild." The park contains unreconstructed Ute and Anasazi ruins. Tours must be accompanied by Ute guides and may be arranged through the Ute Mountain Ute Tribal Park Secretary.

Bibliography

Little has been published on Colorado, or even on Rocky Mountain, architecture. The state lacks any book-length overview of its architectural history, and the only biographies of major architects available are Francine Haber, Kenneth R. Fuller, and David N. Wetzel, *Robert S. Roeschlaub: Architect of the Emerging West* (Denver: Colorado Historical Society, 1988), and Carl D. Sheppard, *Creator of the Santa Fe Style: Isaac Hamilton Rapp, Architect* (Albuquerque: University of New Mexico Press, 1988).

A good brief overview is Devon Carlson and Olga Jackson, *Architecture: Colorado* (Denver: Colorado Chapter, American Institute of Architects, 1966). Also helpful are Sandra Dallas's highly readable, well-illustrated works, including *Colorado Homes* (Norman: University of Oklahoma Press, 1986), and *Gaslights and Gingerbread: Colorado's Historic Homes* (Denver: Sage Books, 1965). Sarah J. Pearce, *A Guide to Colorado Architecture* (Denver: Colorado Historical Society, 1983) is instructive and a good starting place.

National Register records of the State Historic Preservation Office at the Colorado History Museum provide information on many individual buildings and districts. Communities with local landmark designations often have files, usually maintained by their planning offices. The annual awards presented by the Denver and Colorado chapters of the American Institute of Architects provide a list of some of the more notable contemporary structures.

E. Steve Cassells's *The Archaeology of Colorado* (Boulder: Johnson Books, 1983) surveys the evidence and theories advanced to date about prehistoric peoples and their buildings. A survey of Colorado's Native American architecture is lacking, but Robert Adams portrays selected Hispanic structures in *The Architecture and Art of Early Hispanic Colorado* (Denver: Colorado Historical Society, 1974).

Denver is covered in some depth in Richard D. Brettell, *Historic Denver: The Architects and the Architecture, 1858–1893* (Denver: Historic Denver, Inc., 1973) and in a sequel, Thomas J. Noel and Barbara S Norgren, *Denver: The City Beautiful and Its Architects, 1893–1941* (Denver: Historic Denver, Inc., 1987), which includes a biographical dictionary of major architects. Many communities are covered by walking tour booklets, which range widely in format, detail, and accuracy.

An excellent inspection of Colorado's landscape is Kenneth I. Helphand's *Colorado: Visions of an American Landscape* (Niwot: Colorado Chapter of the American Society of Landscape Architects/Roberts Rinehart, 1992).

GENERAL WORKS

Baron, Robert C., Stephen J. Leonard, and Thomas J. Noel, eds. *Thomas Hornsby Ferril and the American West.* Golden: Fulcrum Publishing, 1996.

Benson, Maxine. *1001 Colorado Place Names.* Topeka: University Press of Kansas, 1994.

Colorado Atlas and Gazetteer. Freeport, Maine: DeLorme Mapping, 1991.

Francaviglia, Richard V. *Hard Places: Reading the Landscape of America's Historic Mining Districts.* Iowa City, Iowa: University of Iowa Press, 1991.

Freed, Elaine. *Preserving the Great Plains and the Rocky Mountains.* Albuquerque: University of New Mexico Press, 1992.

Herbst, Rebecca, and Vicki Rottman, eds. *Historic Bridges of Colorado.* Denver: Colorado Department of Highways, 1986.

Mahar-Keplinger, Lisa. *Grain Elevators.* Princeton, N.J.: Princeton University Press, 1993.

McAlester, Virginia and Lee. *A Field Guide to American Houses.* New York: Alfred A. Knopf, 1988.

Messinger, Jean Goodwin, and Mary Jane Massey Rust. *Faith in High Places: Historic Country Churches of Colorado.* Boulder: Roberts Rinehart Publishing, 1995.

Nabokov, Peter, and Robert Easton. *Native American Architecture.* New York: Oxford University Press, 1989.

Noel, Thomas J., Paul F. Mahoney, and Richard E. Stevens. *Historical Atlas of Colorado.* Norman: University of Oklahoma Press, 1994.

Stoehr, C. Eric. *Bonanza Victorian: Architecture and Society in Colorado Mining Towns.* Albuquerque: University of New Mexico Press, 1975.

Warren, Scott and Beth, *Victorian Bonanza: Victorian Architecture of the Rocky Mountain West.* Flagstaff, Arizona: Northland Press, 1989.

The WPA Guide to 1930s Colorado. With a new introduction by Thomas J. Noel. Lawrence: University Press of Kansas, 1987.

REGIONS

Arkansas River

Davis, Clyde Byron. *The Arkansas.* New York: Farrar & Rinehart, 1940.

Sherow, James Earl. *Watering the Valley: Development along the High Plains Arkansas River, 1870–1950.* Topeka: University Press of Kansas, 1990.

Simmons, Virginia McConnell. *The Upper Arkansas: A*

Mountain River Valley. Boulder: Pruett Publishing Company, 1990.

Colorado River

Fradkin, Philip L. *A River No More: The Colorado River and the West.* New York: Alfred A. Knopf, 1981.

Vandenbusche, Duane, and Duane A. Smith. *A Land Alone: Colorado's Western Slope.* Boulder: Pruett Publishing Company, 1981.

Waters, Frank. *The Colorado.* New York: Rinehart and Company, 1946.

Rio Grande

Cobos, Rubén. *A Dictionary of New Mexico and Southern Colorado Spanish.* Santa Fe: Museum of New Mexico Press, 1983.

Gilpin, Laura. *The Rio Grande: River of Destiny.* New York: Duell, Sloan and Pierce, 1949.

Griswold, P. R. *Rio Grande along the Rio Grande.* Denver: The author, 1986.

Horgan, Paul. *Great River: The Rio Grande in North American History.* New York: Rinehart and Company, 1954. 2 vols.

The San Luis Valley Historian. Alamosa: The San Luis Valley Historical Society, 1968–present. (Articles on specific buildings and communities.)

Simmons, Virginia McConnell. "Hispanic Place Names of the San Luis Valley," *The San Luis Valley Historian* 23 (1991).

———. *The San Luis Valley: Land of the Six Armed Cross.* Boulder: Pruett Publishing Company, 1979.

Stedman, Myrtle. *Rural Architecture of Northern New Mexico and Southern Colorado.* Santa Fe: Sunstone Press, 1989.

Tushar, Olibama Lopez. *The People of "El Valle."* Pueblo: El Escritorio, 1992. 2nd ed.

South Platte River

Monahan, Doris. *Destination Denver City: The South Platte Trail.* Athens, Ohio: The Swallow Press, 1985.

Probst, Nell Brown. *Forgotten People: A History of the South Platte Trail.* Boulder: Pruett Publishing Company, 1979.

COUNTIES
Adams

Marcy, Richard, and William O'Connor, eds. *Forgotten Past of Adams County.* Thornton High School, n.d.

Miller, Barbara, and Gail Schatz. *Images of Aurora: Architecture and Lifestyles.* Aurora: Aurora Public Schools, 1982.

Wagner, Albin. *Adams County: Crossroads of the West* (booklet). Brighton: Adams County Commissioners, 1977.

Alamosa

Feitz, Leland. *Alamosa.* Colorado Springs: Little London Press, 1976.

Arapahoe

Colorado Plains. Strasburg: Comanche Crossing Historical Society, 1984.

Keller, Carolyn K. "Exploring Architecture in Arapahoe County, 1860–1995." M.A. thesis, University of Colorado at Denver, 1993.

Englewood, Colorado: Its People and History, 1903–1993. Englewood: Englewood Historical Society, 1993.

McQuarie, Robert J., and C. W. Buchholtz. *Littleton, Colorado: Settlement to Centennial.* Littleton: Littleton History Museum, 1990.

Mehls, Steve, Carol Drake, and James E. Fell, Jr. *Aurora: Gateway to the Rockies.* Evergreen: Cordillera Press, 1985.

Miller, Barbara, and Gail Schatz. *Images of Aurora: Architecture and Lifestyles.* Aurora: Aurora Public Schools, 1982.

Archuleta

Chappell, Gordon S. *Logging Along the Denver & Rio Grande.* Golden: Colorado Railroad Museum, 1971.

Eddy, Frank W. *Archaeological Investigations at Chimney Rock Mesa: 1970–1972.* Boulder: Colorado Archaeological Society, 1977.

Lister, Florence C. *In The Shadow of the Rocks: Archaeology of the Chimney Rock District in Southeastern Colorado.* Niwot: University Press of Colorado, 1993.

Baca

Baca County Historical Society. *Baca County.* Lubbock, Texas: Specialty Publishing Company, 1983.

Osteen, Ike. *A Place Called Baca.* Chicago: Adams Press, 1979.

Pearson, Jeff and Jessica, with photographs by John Manos. *No Time But Place: A Prairie Pastoral.* New York: McGraw-Hill, 1980.

Boulder

Barker, Jane Valentine. *Historic Homes of Boulder County.* Boulder: Pruett Publishing Company, 1979.

Deno, Bill. *Body and Soul: Architectural Style at the University of Colorado at Boulder.* Boulder: University of Colorado, 1994.

Lafayette, Colorado: Treeless Plain to Thriving City, 1889–1989. Lafayette Historical Society, 1990.

Pettem, Silvia. *Boulder: Evolution of a City.* Niwot: University Press of Colorado, 1994.

Pettem, Silvia. *Guide to Historic Western Boulder County.* Evergreen: Cordillera Press, 1989.

Runnells, Donald D. *Boulder: A Sight to Behold.* Boulder: Estey Printing, 1976.

Smith, Phyllis. *A Look at Boulder from Settlement to City.* Boulder: Pruett Publishing Company, 1981.

Chaffee

Anderson, Peter. *From Gold to Ghosts: A History of St. Elmo. Colorado.* Gunnison: B & B Printers, 1983.

Everett, George C., and Dr. Wendell F. Hutchinson. *Under the Angel of Shavano.* Denver: Golden Bell Press, 1963.

Shaputis, June, and Susanna Kelly, eds. *A History of Chaffee County.* Marcelline, Missouri: Wadsworth Publishing Company, 1982.

Swift, Kim. *Heart of the Rockies: A History of the Salida Area.* Colorado Springs: Century One Press, 1980.

Cheyenne

Hogan, Marion A. *Kit Carson, Colorado.* . . . Kit Carson: Kit Carson Historical Society, 1974.

Clear Creek

History of Clear Creek County. Idaho Springs: Historical Society of Idaho Springs, 1986.

Mead, Jay, ed. *Silver Plume Walking Tour.* Silver Plume: People for Silver Plume, c. 1985.

Neeley, Cynthia C., Walter R. Borneman, and Christine A. Bradley. *Guide to the Georgetown Silver Plume Historic District.* Evergreen: Cordillera Press, 1986.

Conejos

Mead, Frances Harvey. *Conejos County.* Colorado Springs: Century One Press, 1984.

Costilla

Valdez, Arnold A. and Maria A. *The Culebra River Villages of Costilla County: Village Architecture and Its Historical Context, 1851–1940.* Denver: Colorado Historical Society Preservation Office, 1991.

Custer

Dodds, Joanne West. *Custer County.* Pueblo: Pueblo Regional Library, 1992.

Turk, Gayle. *Wet Mountain Valley.* Colorado Springs: Little London Press, 1975.

Delta

Austin, Hazel Baker. *Surface Creek Country.* Delta: Delta County Independent, 1977.

Delta County Independent. Annual Tourist Guide.

Rockwell, Wilson. "Delta County: The Formative Years." Typescript, Delta Public Library.

Denver

Abrams, Jeanne E. *Historic Jewish Denver.* Denver: Rocky Mountain Jewish Historical Society, 1982.

American Institute of Architects, Denver Chapter. *Newsletter* and annual awards.

Bakke, Diane, and Jackie Davis. *Places around the Base: A Historic Tour of the Coors Field Neighborhood.* Englewood: Westcliffe Publishers, Inc., 1995.

City Club of Denver. *Art in Denver.* Denver: Denver Public Library, 1928.

Dallas, Sandra. *Cherry Creek Gothic: Victorian Architecture in Denver.* Norman: University of Oklahoma Press, 1970.

Davis, Sally, and Betty Baldwin. *Denver Dwellings and Descendants.* Denver: Sage Books, 1963.

Denver Landmark Preservation Commission. List of Individual and District Designations. On file in Denver Planning Office.

———. *Historic Buildings Inventory.* Denver: Denver Planning Office, rev. 1981.

Etter, Carolyn and Don D. *The Denver Zoo: A Centennial History.* Boulder: Roberts Rinehart, 1995.

Etter, Don D. *Denver Going Modern.* Denver: Graphic Impressions, Inc., 1977.

———. *Denver's Park and Parkway System.* Denver: Colorado Historical Society National Register Nomination, 1986.

———. *University Park: Four Walking Tours.* Denver: Graphic Impressions, Inc., 1974.

Forest, Kenton, Gene McKeever, and Raymond McAllister. *History of the Public Schools of Denver: A Brief History and Complete Building Survey.* Denver: Tramway Press, Inc., 1989.

Gleason, Barbara. *The Lower Downtown Historic District.* Denver: Denver Museum of Natural History and Historic Denver, Inc., 1955.

Haber, Francine, Kenneth R. Fuller, and David R. Wetzel. *Robert S. Roeschlaub: Architect of the Emerging West, 1843–1923.* Denver: Colorado Historical Society, 1988.

Kohl, Edith Eudora. *Denver's Historic Mansions.* Denver: Sage Books, 1957.

Leonard, Stephen J., and Thomas J. Noel. *Denver: Mining Camp to Metropolis.* Niwot: University Press of Colorado, 1990.

Murphy, Jack A. *A Geographic Tour of Historic Buildings and Monuments in Denver, Colorado.* Denver: Denver Museum of Natural History and Historic Denver, Inc., 1995.

Musick, G. Meredith, Sr. *Wayfarer in Architecture.* Denver: privately printed, 1976.

Noel, Thomas J. *Denver Landmarks and Historic Districts: A Pictorial Guide.* Foreword by Wellington Webb. Niwot: University Press of Colorado, 1996.

Noel, Thomas J. *Denver's Larimer Street: Main Street, Skid Row, and Urban Renaissance.* Denver: Historic Denver, Inc., 1982.

———. *Richthofen's Montclair: A Pioneer Denver Suburb.* Boulder: Pruett Publishing Company, 1978.

Noel, Thomas J., and Barbara J. Norgren. *Denver: The City Beautiful and Its Architects, 1893–1941.* Denver: Historic Denver, Inc., 1987.

Smiley, Jerome C. *History of Denver.* Denver: Times-Sun Publishing Company, 1901.

West, William A. *Curtis Park: A Denver Neighborhood.* Boulder: Colorado Associated University Press, 1980.

Wiberg, Ruth E. *Rediscovering Northwest Denver: Its History, Its People, Its Landmarks.* Niwot: University Press of Colorado, 1995.

Wilk, Diane. *A Guide to Denver's Architectural Styles and Terms.* Denver: Denver Museum of Natural History and Historic Denver, Inc., 1995.

———. *The Wyman Historic District.* Denver: Denver Museum of Natural History and Historic Denver, Inc., 1995.

Douglas

Appleby, Susan. "Douglas County: A History and Guide to Cultural Resources." M.A. thesis, University of Colorado at Denver, 1995.

Lowenberg, Robert. *Castle Rock: A Grass Roots History.* Castle Rock: Lowenberg Publishers, 1980.

Our Heritage: People of Douglas County. Castle Rock: Douglas County Historical Book Committee, 1982.

Marr, Josephine L. *Douglas County: A Historical Journey.* Gunnison: B & B Printers, 1983.

Eagle

Braun, Thomas A., and Jeffery T. Winston, "The Vail Village Urban Design Guide Plan," *Urban Design Review* 9 (1986).

Coquoz, Renee L. *The Invisible Men of Skis: The Story of the Construction of Camp Hale. . . .* Boulder: Johnson Publishing Company, 1970.

Dallas, Sandra. *Vail.* Boulder: Pruett Publishing Company, 1969.

Danielson, Clarence L. and Ralph W., *Basalt: Colorado Midland Town.* Boulder: Pruett Publishing Company, 1965.

Knight, MacDonald, and Leonard Hammock. *Early Days on the Eagle.* Eagle: The authors, 1965.

Roberts, Jack. *The Amazing Adventures of Lord Gore.* Denver: Sundance Books, 1977.

Simonton, June. *Beaver Creek: The First One Hundred Years.* Beaver Creek: Beaver Creek Resort Company, 1980.

Simonton, June. *Vail: Story of a Colorado Mountain Valley.* Dallas: Taylor Publishing Company, 1987.

Elbert

Corbett, Ethel Rae. *Western Pioneer Days.* Denver: Reliable Graphics, Inc., 1974.

Gabehart, Margee. *Elbert County History.* Dallas: Curtis Media Corporation, 1989.

Holt, Kittie. *The Rise and Fall of a Town.* Denver: Riverside Print Company, 1975.

Matthews, Carl F. *Early Days Around the Divide.* St. Louis: Sign Book Company, 1969.

Thom, Kay, et al. *The History of Elbert County.* Simla: Simla High School, 1959.

El Paso

Abele, Deborah Edge. *The Westside: An Introduction to Its History and Architecture.* Colorado Springs: City of Colorado Springs, c. 1983.

Bruegmann, Robert, ed. *Modernism at Midcentury: The Architecture of the U.S. Air Force Academy.* Chicago: University of Chicago Press, 1994.

Burgess, Mary E., and Ruth Shaw. *Pilgrimage into the Past: A Tour of Area Landmarks.* Colorado Springs: Landmark Council of the Pikes Peak Region, 1978.

Colorado Springs Fine Arts Center: A History and Selections from the Permanent Collections. Colorado Springs: Colorado Springs Fine Arts Center, 1986.

Finlay, George. *Colorado Springs: A Guide Book Describing the Rock Formations in the Vicinity of Colorado Springs.* Colorado Springs: The Out West Company, 1906.

Freed, Elaine. *Historic Sites and Structures: El Paso County, Colorado.* Colorado Springs: El Paso County Commissioners, 1977.

Hetzler, Rosemary, and John Hetzler. *Colorado Springs and The Pikes Peak Country: A Pictorial History.* Norfolk, Va.: The Donning Co., 1981.

Hirsch, Susan L. *Old Colorado City Historic Inventory.*

Colorado Springs: City Planning Department, c. 1985.

Naeve, Milo M. *A Century of Building in the Pikes Peak Region.* Colorado Springs: Colorado Springs Fine Arts Center, 1972.

Ormes, Manley Dayton. *The Book of Colorado Springs.* Colorado Springs: The Dentan Printing Co., 1933.

Pearring, Joanne, and John Pearring. *The Walking Tour: An Historical Guide to Manitou Springs.* Manitou Springs: Text Pros, 1983.

Sprague, Marshall. *Newport in the Rockies: The Life and Good Times of Colorado Springs.* Denver: Sage Books, 1961.

Fremont

Campbell, Rosemae Wells. *From Trappers to Tourists: Fremont County, 1830–1950.* Palmer Lake: The Filter Press, 1972.

Chapman, Joe. *The Royal Gorge.* Cañon City: The Royal Gorge Co., 1965.

Fisher, Cara D. *About the Avenues.* Cañon City: Fremont-Custer Historical Society, Inc., 1987.

Fisher, Cara D., and Elinor M. McGinn. *If the Walls Could Speak.* Cañon City: Fremont-Custer Historical Society, Inc., 1984.

Garfield

Gulliford, Andrew. *Boomtown Blues: Colorado Oil Shale, 1885–1985.* Niwot: University Press of Colorado, 1989.

———. *Garfield County, Colorado, 1883–1983.* Glenwood Springs: Grand River Museum Alliance, 1983.

Rifle Shots: The Story of Rifle, Colorado. Rifle: Rifle Reading Club, 1973.

Urquhart, Lena M. *Glenwood Springs: Spa in the Mountains.* Glenwood Springs: Taylor Publishing Company, 1970.

Gilpin

Axford, H. William. *Gilpin County Gold: Peter McFarlane, 1848–1929.* Chicago: Sage Books, 1976.

Granruth, Alan. *A Guide to Downtown Central City, Colorado.* N.p.: 1989.

Hollenback, Frank. *Central City and Black Hawk: Then and Now.* Denver: Swallow Press, 1961.

Leyendecker, Liston E. *Washington Hall: Gilpin County's Oldest Courthouse.* Colorado State University (Fort Collins) Cooperative Extension Service Historical Bulletin no. 1, 1976.

Leyendecker, Liston E., and Edward D. White, Jr. *Little Kingdom Master Plan.* Denver: Colorado Historical Society, 1975.

Pearce, Sarah J., and Christine Pfaff. *Guide to Historic Central City and Black Hawk.* Evergreen: Cordillera Press, 1987.

Grand

Black, Robert C., III. *Island in the Rockies: The History of Grand County, Colorado to 1930.* Boulder: Pruett Publishing Company, 1969.

Buchholtz, C. W. *Rocky Mountain National Park: A*

History. Boulder: University Press of Colorado, 1983.

Cairns, Mary Lyons. *Grand Lake in the Olden Days*. Denver: World Press, 1971.

———. *Grand Lake: The Pioneers*. Denver: World Press, 1946.

Grand County Historical Association Journal. 1980–present.

Hess, Karl, Jr. *Rocky Times in Rocky Mountain National Park*. Niwot: University Press of Colorado, 1993.

Reich, Alice, and Thomas J. Steele, S.J. *Fraser Haps and Mishaps: The Diary of Mary E. Cozens*. Denver: Regis College Press, 1990.

Gunnison

McCoy, Dell. *The Crystal River Pictorial*. Denver: Sundance, 1972.

Mumey, Nollie. *History of Tincup, Colorado*. Boulder: Johnson Publishing Company, 1963.

Schader, Conrad F. *Colorado's Alluring Tincup*. Golden: Regio Alto Publishers, 1992.

Sibley, George. *A Crested Butte Primer*. Gunnison: B & B Printers, 1972.

Smith, Duane A. *When Coal Was King: A History of Crested Butte, Colorado, 1880–1952*. Golden: Colorado School of Mines, 1974.

Vandenbusche, Duane. *The Gunnison Country*. Gunnison: B & B Printers, 1980.

Vandenbusche, Duane, and Rex Myers. *Marble, Colorado: City of Stone*. Denver: Golden Bell Press, 1970.

Hinsdale

Houston, Grant. *Lake City Reflections*. Lake City: The author, 1976.

An Official Guide to Historic Homes, Lake City, Colorado. Lake City: Hinsdale County Historical Society, c. 1990.

Wright, Carolyn and Clarence. *Tiny Hinsdale of the Silvery San Juan*. Denver: Big Mountain Press, 1964.

Huerfano

Nardine, Henry. *In the Shadows of the Spanish Peaks: A History of Huerfano County, Colorado*. N.p.: Published by the author, 1988.

Owens, Robert Perchy. *Huerfano Valley As I Knew It*. Cañon City: Published by the author, 1975.

Jackson

Gresham, Hazel. *North Park*. Steamboat Springs: The Steamboat Pilot, 1975.

Jefferson

Arvada Just Between You and Me, 1904–1941. Arvada: Arvada Historical Society, 1985.

Historically Jeffco. Morrison: Jefferson County Historical Commission, 1987–present. Quarterly magazine.

More Than Gold . . . Arvada. Arvada: Arvada Historical Society, 1976.

Scheunemann, Toni L. *The Foothills Art Center*. Golden: Foothills Art Center, 1992.

Sternberg, Barbara and Gene. *Evergreen: Our Mountain Community*. Boulder: Johnson Publishing Company, 1987.

Wilcox, Patricia K., ed. *Lakewood, Colorado: An Illustrated Biography*. Lakewood: Lakewood Twenty-Fifth Anniversary Commission, 1994.

———, ed. *76 Centennial Stories of Lakewood*. Lakewood: Lakewood Historical Society, 1976.

Kiowa

Teal, Roberta, and Betty Jacobs. *Kiowa County*. Boulder: Johnson Publishing Company/Kiowa County Bicentennial Committee, 1976.

Lake

Blair, Edward. *Leadville: Colorado's Magic City*. Boulder: Pruett Publishing Company, 1980.

Voynich, Stephen M. *Climax: The History of Colorado's Climax Molybdenum Mine*. Missoula: Mountain Press Publishing Company, 1996.

Weier, Darlene Godat. *Leadville's Ice Palace: Colossus in the Colorado Rockies*. Lakewood: Ice Castle Editions, 1994.

La Plata

Smith, Duane A. *Guide to Historic Durango and Silverton*. Evergreen: Cordillera Press, 1988.

———. *Rocky Mountain Boom Town: A History of Durango*. Albuquerque: University of New Mexico Press, 1980.

Larimer

Fleming, Barbara Allbrandt. *Fort Collins: A Pictorial History*. Norfolk, Va.: The Donning Co., 1985.

Sundberg, Wayne. *Historic Fort Collins*. Fort Collins: Old Army Press, 1975.

Watrous, Ansel. *History of Larimer County, Colorado*. Fort Collins: Courier Printing and Publishing Co., 1911; reprinted 1972 by Old Army Press of Fort Collins.

Las Animas

Stokes, Gerald H. *A Walk through the History of Trinidad*. Trinidad: Trinidad Historical Society, 1986, 1991.

Taylor, Morris. *Trinidad*. Trinidad: Trinidad Historical Society, 1976.

Lincoln

Cooley, Dale. *A Brief History of Limon, Colorado*. Limon: Limon Leader, 1978.

Lincoln County from the Beginning to 1940. Hugo: Lincoln County Historical Society, c. 1976.

Logan

Conklin, Emma Burke. *History of Logan County, Colorado*. Denver: Welch-Haffner Printing Company, 1928.

Sterling Centennial: Logan County Family History. Sterling: Centennial Committee, 1984.

Wells, Dale. *The Logan County Ledger*. Sterling: Logan County Historical Society, 1976.

Mesa

Barcus, Earlyanne, et al. *Echoes of a Dream*. Fruita: Lower Valley Heritage Group, 1983.

Fishell, Dave, *The Grand Heritage: A Photographic History of Grand Junction, Colorado*. Norfolk, Virginia: The Donning Company, 1985.

Journal of the Western Slope. Quarterly magazine, Mesa State College, 1985–present.

Kania, Alan J. *John Otto of Colorado National Monument*. Boulder: Roberts Rinehart, Inc., 1984.

McCreanor, Emma. *Mesa County: A 100 Year History*. Grand Junction: The Museum of Western Colorado, 1986.

Underwood, Kathleen. *Grand Junction: Town Building on the Colorado Frontier*. Albuquerque: University of New Mexico Press, 1987.

Young, Helen Hawxhurst. *The Skin and Bones of Plateau Valley History*. Grand Junction: Wilson and Young Printers, 1976.

Moffat

Burroughs, John Rolfe. *Where the Old West Stayed Young*. New York: Bonanza Books, 1962.

Kouris, Diana Allen. *The Romantic and Notorious History of Brown's Park*. Greybull, Wyoming: Wolverine Press, 1988.

Stegner, Wallace, ed. *This Is Dinosaur: Echo Park Country and Its Magic Rivers*. New York: Alfred A. Knopf, 1955.

Montezuma

Lange, Frederick W. *Cortez Crossroads: A Guide to the Anasazi Heritage and Scenic Beauty of the Four Corners Region*. Boulder: Johnson Books, 1989.

Smith, Duane A. *Mesa Verde National Park: Shadows of the Centuries*. Topeka: University Press of Kansas, 1988.

Watson, Don. *Indians of the Mesa Verde*. Mesa Verde: Mesa Verde Museum Association, 1961.

Montrose

Freeman, Ira S. *A History of Montezuma County*. Boulder: Johnson Publishing Company, 1958.

Morgan

Rickel, Wesley K., ed. *One Hundred Eleven Trees: A Compilation of Biographies*. Fort Morgan: Fort Morgan Heritage Foundation, 1976.

Fort Morgan High School students. *Windows to the Past: Reflections of the Future*. Fort Morgan: Fort Morgan Heritage Foundation, 1994.

Otero

Thorson, George A., et al. *Bent's Old Fort*. Denver: Colorado Historical Society, 1977.

Ouray

Benham, Jack L. *Camp Bird and the Revenue*. Ouray: Bear Creek Publishing Company, 1980.

Gregory, Doris H. *History of the Wright Opera House*. Long Beach, Calif.: Cascade Publications, 1983.

————. *Houses on Oak Street: A Walk into History*. Long Beach, Calif.: Cascade Publications, 1982.

————. *Ouray's Beaumont Hotel: A Century of Ouray's History*. Long Beach, Calif.: Cascade Publications, 1989.

————. *The Town That Refused to Die: Ridgway, Colorado, 1890–1991*. Long Beach, Calif.: Cascade Publications, 1991.

Gregory, Marvin, and P. David Smith, *The Million Dollar Highway*. Ouray: Wayfinder Press, 1986.

Park

Amitrani, Eugene J. *A Town is Born: The Story of South Park City*. Fairplay: South Park City, 1982.

Dyer, Mary. *Echoes of Como, Colorado, 1879–1973*. Dillon: D & L Printing, 1974.

McConnell, Virginia. *Bayou Salado: The Story of South Park*. Denver: Sage Books, 1966.

Phillips

Phillips County Historical Society. *Those Were The Days. . . .* Holyoke: Holyoke Enterprise Printing Co., 1993.

Pitkin

Allen, James S. *The Romance of Commerce and Culture: Capitalism, Modernism and the Chicago-Aspen Crusade for Cultural Reform*. Chicago: University of Chicago Press, 1983.

Aslet, Clive, ed. *The American Houses of Robert A. M. Stern*. New York: Rizzoli International Publications, Inc., 1991.

Hopton, Heather, and Lilo Shuldener. *Aspen's Early Days: A Walking Tour*. Boulder: Johnson Publishing Company/Aspen Historical Society, 1975.

Hyman, Sidney. *The Aspen Ides*. Norman, Oklahoma: University of Oklahoma Press, 1975.

Pearce, Sarah J., and Roxanne Eflin. *Guide to Historic Aspen and the Roaring Fork Valley*. Evergreen: Cordillera Press, 1990.

Pueblo

Bryan, Ray. *Four Historic Walking Tours of Pueblo, Colorado*. Pueblo: Pueblo Regional Library, 1980.

Dodds, Joanne West. *Pueblo: A Pictorial History*. Norfolk, Va.: Donning, 1982.

————. *They All Come to Pueblo: A Social History*. Virginia Beach, Va.: The Donning Company, 1994.

Rio Blanco

Bury, Susan, ed. *This is What I Remember: By and About the People of the White River Country*. Meeker: Rio Blanco County Historical Society, 1972.

Sprague, Marshall. *Massacre: The Tragedy at White River*. Boston: Little, Brown, 1957.

Rio Grande

Riggenbach, Emma M. *A Bridge to Yesterday*. Monte Vista: High Valley Press, 1982.

Welcome to Historic Del Norte: A Walking Tour. Del Norte: Del Norte Centennial Committee, 1975.

Routt

Burroughs, John Rolfe. *Steamboat in the Rockies*. Fort Collins: Old Army Press, 1974.

The Historical Guide to Routt County. Steamboat Springs: Tread of Pioneers Museum, 1979.

Stevenson, Thelma V. *Historic Hahns Peak*. Fort Collins: Robinson Press, 1976.

Towler, Sureva. *History of Skiing in Steamboat Springs*. Denver: Frederic Printing, 1987.

San Juan

Bird, Allan G. *Bordellos of Blair Street*. Grand Rapids, Mich.: The Other Shop, 1987.

———. *Silverton Then and Now*. Englewood: Access Publishers, 1990.

Nossaman, Allen. *Many More Mountains*. 2 vols. Denver: Sundance Books, 1989, 1993.

Sloan, Robert E., and Carl A. Skowronski. *The Rainbow Route*. Silverton: Sundance Publications, 1975.

San Miguel

Fetter, Richard L. and Suzanne. *Telluride: From Pick to Powder*. Caldwell, Idaho: The Caxton Printers, 1979.

Summit

Dempsey, Stanley, and James E. Fell, Jr. *Mining the Summit: Colorado's Tenmile District*. Norman: University of Oklahoma Press, 1986.

Ellis, Erl H. *The Gold Dredging Boats around Breckenridge, Colorado*. Boulder: Johnson Publishing Company, 1967.

Emore, Anna. *Dillon: The Blue River Wonderland*. Dillon: Summit Historical Society, 1983.

Fiester, Mark. *Blasted, Beloved Breckenridge*. Boulder: Pruett Publishing Company, 1973.

Gilleland, Mary Ellen. *Summit*. Silverthorne: Alpenrose Press, 1980.

Pritchard, Sandra F. *Roadside Summit I: A Natural Landscape*. Dillon: Summit Historical Society, 1988.

———. *Roadside Summit II: The Human Landscape*. Dillon: Summit Historical Society, 1992.

Sharp, Verna. *A History of Montezuma, Sts. John, and Argentine: Early Mining Camps of Summit County*. Dillon: Summit Historical Society, 1971.

Teller

Cafky, Morris. *Rails around Gold Hill*. Denver: Rocky Mountain Railroad Club, 1955.

Feitz, Leland. *Ghost Towns of the Cripple Creek District*. Colorado Springs: Little London Press, 1974.

Levine, Brian. *Cripple Creek: City of Influence*. Cripple Creek: Cripple Creek Historic Preservation Department, 1994.

Levine, Brian. *A Guide to the Cripple Creek–Victor Mining District*. Colorado Springs: Century One Press, 1987.

Munn, Bill. *A Guide to the Mines of the Cripple Creek District*. Colorado Springs: Century One Press, 1984.

Sprague, Marshall. *Money Mountain*. Boston: Little, Brown, 1953.

Washington

Hawthorne, Roger. *In the Footpaths of Time: Walking Tour of Historical Otis*. Otis: Town of Otis Recreation Department, 1986.

One Hundred Years in Pictures: Akron, 1882–1982. Akron: Washington County Museum Association, 1982.

Weld

Boyd, Davis. *A History: Greeley and the Union Colony of Colorado*. Greeley: Greeley Tribune, 1890.

Shwayder, Carol Rein. *Weld County Old and New*. Greeley: Unicorn Ventures, 1983.

White, Nadine. *A Stroll around Historic Eaton*. Eaton: Nadine White, 1991.

Yuma

Russell, Mrs. Hal. *Settler Mac and the Charmed Quarter Section*. Denver: Sage Books, 1956.

Yuma County Historical Society. *Action on the Plains* and *Yuma Album of Action on the Plains*. Yuma: Pioneer Printing, 1971, 1981.

Glossary

AIA See AMERICAN INSTITUTE OF ARCHITECTS.

abacus The top member of a column capital. In the Doric order, it is a flat block, square in plan, between the echinus of the capital and the architrave of the entablature above.

Academic Gothic See COLLEGIATE GOTHIC.

acroterium, acroterion (plural: acroteria) **1** A pedestal for a statue or similar decorative feature at the apex or at the lower corners of a pediment. **2** Any ornamental feature at these locations.

Adamesque A mode of architectural design, with emphasis on interiors, reminiscent of the work of the Scottish architects Robert Adam (1728–1792) and his brother James (1732–1794). It is characterized by attenuated proportions, bright color, and elegant linear detailing. Adamesque interiors, as one aspect of the broader Neoclassical movement, became popular in the late eighteenth century in Britain, Russia, and elsewhere in northern Europe. Simplified versions of these interiors began to be seen in the United States around the year 1800 in the work of Charles Bulfinch (1763–1844) and Samuel McIntire (1757–1811). Adamesque interiors, often emulating original Adam designs, were again popular in the 1920s. See also the related term FEDERAL.

aedicule, aedicular An exterior niche, door, or window, framed by columns or pilasters and topped by an entablature and pediment. Meaning has been extended to a smaller-scale representation of a temple front on an interior wall. Distinguished from a tabernacle (definition 1), which usually occurs on an interior wall. See also the related term NICHE.

Aesthetic movement A late nineteenth-century movement in interior design and the decorative arts, emphasizing the application of artistic principles in the production of objects and the creation of interior ensembles. Aesthetic movement works are characterized by a broad eclecticism of materials and styles (especially the exotic) and by a preference for "conventionalized" (i.e., stylized) ornament, rather than naturalistic. The movement flourished in Britain from the 1850s through the 1870s and in the United States from the 1870s through the 1880s. Designers associated with the movement include William Morris (1834–1896) in England and Herter Brothers (1865–1905) in America. The Aesthetic movement evolved into and overlapped with the Art Nouveau and the Arts and Crafts movement. See also the related term QUEEN ANNE (definition 4).

ambulatory A passageway around the apse of a church, allowing for circulation behind the sanctuary.

American Adam Style See FEDERAL.

American bond See COMMON BOND.

American Foursquare See FOURSQUARE HOUSE.

American Institute of Architects (AIA) The national professional organization of architects, established in New York in 1857. The first national convention was held in New York in 1867, and at that meeting, provision was made for the creation of local chapters. In 1889, the American Institute of Architects absorbed the independent Chicago-based Western Association of Architects (established 1884). The headquarters of the national organization moved from New York to Washington in 1898.

American Renaissance Ambiguous term. See instead BEAUX-ARTS CLASSICISM, COLONIAL REVIVAL, FEDERAL REVIVAL.

Anglo-Palladianism, Anglo-Palladian An architectural movement in England motivated by a reaction against the English Baroque and by a rediscovery of the work of the English Renaissance architect Inigo Jones (1573–1652) and the Italian Renaissance architect Andrea Palladio (1508–1580). Anglo-Palladianism flourished in England (c. 1710s–1760s) and in the British North American colonies (c. 1740s–1790s). Key figures in the Anglo-Palladian movement were Colen Campbell (1676–1729) and Richard Boyle, Lord Burlington (1694–1753). Sometimes called Burlingtonian, Palladian Revival. See also the more general term Palladianism and the related terms GEORGIAN PERIOD, JEFFERSONIAN.

antefix In classical architecture, a small upright decoration at the eaves of a roof, originally devised to hide the ends of the roof tiles. Also, a similar ornament along the ridge of the roof.

anthemion (plural: anthemions) A Greek ornamental motif based upon the honeysuckle or palmette. It may appear as a single element on an antefix or as a running ornament on a frieze or other banded feature.

antiquity The broad epoch of Western history preceding the Middle Ages and including such ancient civilizations as Egyptian, Greek, and Roman.

apse, apsidal A semicircular or polygonal feature projecting as a major element from an important interior space, especially at the chancel end of a church. Distinguished from an exedra, which is a semicircular or polygonal space, usually containing a bench, in the wall of a garden or nonreligious building. A substantial apse in a church, containing an ambulatory and radiating chapels, is called a chevet. The terms apse and chevet are used to describe the *form* of the end of the church containing the altar, while the terms chancel, choir, and sanctuary are used to describe the liturgical *function* of this end of the church and the spaces within it. Less substantial projections in nonreligious buildings are called bays if polygonal or bowfronts if curved.

arbor 1 An openwork structure covered with climbing plants. Distinguished from a trellis, which is generally a simpler, more two-dimensional structure, often attached to a wall. Distinguished from a pergola, which is an openwork structure supported by a colonnade, creating a shaded walk. **2** A grouping of closely planted trees or shrubs, trained together and self-supporting.

arcade 1 A series of arches, carried on columns or piers or other supports. **2** A covered walkway, one side of which is part of a building, while the other is open, as a series of arches, to the exterior. **3** In the nineteenth and early twentieth centuries, an interior street or other extensive space lined with shops and stores.

arch A curved construction that spans an opening. (Some arches may be flat or triangular, and many have a complex or compound curvature.) A masonry arch consists of a series of wedge-shaped parts (voussoirs) that press together toward the center while being restrained from spreading outward by the surrounding wall or the adjacent arch.

architrave 1 The lowest member of a classical entablature. **2** The moldings on the face of a wall around a doorway or other opening. Sometimes called the casing. Distinguished from the jambs, which are the vertical linings perpendicular to the wall planes at the sides of an opening. Distinguished from surround, a term usually applied to the entire door or window frame considered as a unit.

archivolt The group of moldings following the shape of an arched opening.

arcuation, arcuated Construction using arches.

Art Deco A decorative style stimulated by the 1925 Exposition Internationale des Arts Décoratifs et Industriels Modernes, held in Paris. As the first phase of the Moderne, Art Deco is characterized by sharp angular and curvilinear forms, by a richness of materials (including polished metal, stone, and exotic woods), and by an overall sleekness of design. The style was often used in the commercial and residential architecture of the 1930s (e.g., skyscrapers, hotels, apartment buildings). Sometimes called Art Deco Moderne, Deco, Jazz Moderne, Zigzag Moderne, Zigzag Modernistic. See also the more general term MODERNE and the related terms MAYAN REVIVAL, PWA MODERNE, STREAMLINE MODERNE.

Art Moderne See MODERNE.

Art Nouveau A style in architecture, interior design, and the decorative arts that flourished principally in France and Belgium in the 1890s. The Art Nouveau is characterized by undulating and whiplash lines and by sensuous organic forms. The Art Nouveau in Britain and the United States evolved from and overlapped with the Aesthetic movement.

Arts and Crafts A late nineteenth- and early twentieth-century movement in interior design and the decorative arts, emphasizing the importance of hand crafting for everyday objects. Arts and Crafts works are characterized by rectilinear geometries and high contrasts between figure and ground, and the furniture often features expressed construction. The term originated with the Arts and Crafts Exhibition Society, founded in England in 1888. Designers associated with the movement include C. F. A. Voysey (1857–1941) in England and the brothers Charles S. Greene (1868–1957) and Henry M. Greene (1870–1954) in America. The Arts and Crafts movement evolved from and overlapped with the Aesthetic movement. For a more specific term, used in the United States after 1900, see also CRAFTSMAN.

ashlar Squared blocks of stone that fit tightly against one another.

atelier 1 A studio where the fine arts, including architecture, are taught. Applied particularly to the offices of prominent architects in Paris who provided design training to students enrolled in or informally attached to the Ecole des Beaux-Arts. By extension, any working office where some organized teaching is done. **2** A place where artworks or handicrafts are produced by skilled workers. **3** An artist's studio or workshop.

attic 1 The area beneath the roof and above the main stories (or story) of a building. Sometimes called a garret. **2** A low story above the entablature, often a blocklike mass that caps the building.

axis An imaginary center line to which are referred the parts of a building or the relations of a number of buildings to one another.

axonometric drawing A pictorial drawing using axonometric projection, in which horizontal lines that are perpendicular in an object, building, or space are drawn as perpendicular (usually at two 45–degree angles from the vertical, or at complementary angles of 30 and 60 degrees). Consequently, all angular and dimensional relationships in plan remain the same in the drawing as in the thing depicted. Sometimes called an axon or an axonometric. See also the related terms ISOMETRIC DRAWING, PERSPECTIVE DRAWING.

balloon frame construction A system of light frame construction in which single studs extend the full height of the frame (commonly two stories), from the foundation to the roof. Floor joists are fastened to the sides of the studs. Structural members are usually sawn lumber, ranging from two-by-fours to two-by-tens, and are fastened with nails. Sometimes called balloon framing. The technique, developed in Chicago and other boomtowns of the 1830s, has been largely replaced in the twentieth century by platform frame construction.

baluster One of a series of short vertical members, often vase-shaped in profile, used to support a handrail for a stair or a railing. Balusters that are thinner and simpler in profile are sometimes called banisters.

balustrade A series of balusters or posts supporting a rail or coping across the top (and sometimes resting on a lower rail). Balustrades are often found on stairs, balconies, parapets, and terraces.

band course Ambiguous term. See instead BAND MOLDING or STRINGCOURSE.

band molding In masonry or frame construction, any horizontal flat member or molding or group of moldings projecting slightly from a wall and marking a division in the wall. Not properly a synonym for band course. Simpler horizontal bands in masonry are generally called stringcourses.

bandstand A small pavilion, usually polygonal or circular in plan, designed to shelter bands during public concerts in a garden, park, green, or square. See also the related terms GAZEBO, KIOSK.

banister 1 Corrupted spelling of baluster, in use since about the seventeenth century. Now occasionally used for balusters that are thinner and simpler in profile than classical vase-shaped balusters. 2 Improperly used to mean the handrail of a stair.

bargeboard An ornate fascia board that is attached to the sloping edges (verges) of a roof, covering the ends of the horizontal roof timbers (purlins). Bargeboards are usually ornamented with carved, turned, or jigsawn forms. Sometimes called gableboards, vergeboards. Less ornate boards along the verges of a roof are simply called fascia boards.

Baroque A style of art and architecture that flourished in Europe and colonial North American during the seventeenth and eighteenth centuries. Although based on the architecture of the Renaissance, Baroque architecture was more dynamic, with circles frequently giving way to ovals, flat walls to curved or undulating ones, and separate elements to interlocking forms. It was a monumental and richly three-dimensional style with elaborate systems of ornamental and figural sculpture. See also the related terms RENAISSANCE, ROCOCO.

Baroque Revival See NEO-BAROQUE.

barrel vault A vaulted roof or ceiling of semicircular or semielliptical cross section, forming a tunnellike enclosure over an apartment, corridor, or similar space.

Barryesque Term applied to Italianate buildings showing the influence of the English architect Sir Charles Barry (1795–1860), who introduced a derivative form of the Italian High Renaissance palazzo in his Travelers Club in London, 1829–1832. The style was brought to the United States by the Scottish-trained architect John Notman (1810–1865) and was popular from the late 1840s through the 1860s, especially for institutional and government buildings. Distinguished from the Italian Villa Style, which has the northern Italian rural vernacular villa as its prototype. See also the more general term ITALIANATE.

basement 1 The lowest story of a building, either partly or entirely below grade. 2 The lower part of the walls of any building, usually articulated distinctly from the upper part of the walls.

batten 1 A narrow strip of wood applied to cover a joint along the edges of two parallel boards in the same plane. 2 A strip of wood fastened across two or more parallel boards to hold them together.

Sometimes called a cross batten. See also the related term BOARD-AND-BATTEN SIDING.

battered (adjective). Inclined from the vertical. A wall is said to be battered or to have a batter when it recedes as it rises.

battlement, battlemented See CRENELATION.

Bauhaus 1 Work in any of the visual arts by the faculty and students of the Bauhaus, the innovative design school founded by Walter Gropius (1883–1969) and an active force in German modernism from 1919 until 1933. 2 Work in any of the visual arts by the former faculty and students of the Bauhaus, or by individuals influenced by them. See also the related terms INTERNATIONAL STYLE, MIESIAN.

bay 1 The interval between two recurring members. A facade is frequently measured by window bays, a skeletal frame by structural bays. 2 A polygonal or curved unit of one or more stories, projecting from the wall and usually containing grouped windows (bay windows) on each story. See also the more specific term BOWFRONT.

bay window The horizontally grouped windows in a projecting bay (definition 2), or the projecting bay itself, if it is not more than one story. Distinguished from an oriel, which does not rise from the foundation and has a suspended rather than rooted appearance. A semicircular or semielliptical bay window is called a bow window. A bay window with a central section of plate glass in a late nineteenth-century commercial building is called a Chicago window.

beam A structural spanning member of stone, wood, iron, steel, or reinforced concrete. See also the more specific terms GIRDER, I-BEAM, JOIST.

bearing wall A wall that is fully structural, carrying the load of the floors and roof all the way to the foundation. Sometimes called a supporting wall. Distinguished from curtain wall. See also the related term LOAD-BEARING.

Beaux-Arts Historicist design on a monumental scale, as taught at the Ecole des Beaux-Arts in Paris throughout the nineteenth century and early twentieth century. The term Beaux-Arts is generally applied to an eclectic Roman-Renaissance-Baroque architecture of the 1850s through the 1920s, disseminated internationally by students and followers of the Ecole des Beaux-Arts. As a general style term Beaux-Arts connotes an academically grounded discipline for historical eclecticism, rather than one single style, as well as the disciplined development of a *parti* into a fully visualized design. More specific style terms include Néo-Grec (1840s–1870s) and Beaux-Arts classicism (1870s–1930s). See also the related terms NEOCLASSICISM, for describing Ecole-related work from the 1790s to the 1840s, and SECOND EMPIRE, for describing the work from the 1850s to the 1880s.

Beaux-Arts classicism, Beaux-Arts classical Term applied to eclectic Roman-Renaissance-Baroque architecture and urbanism after the Néo-Grec and Second Empire phases, i.e., from the 1870s through the 1930s. Sometimes called Classic Revival, Classical Revival, McKim classicism, Neoclassical Revival. See also the more general term BEAUX-ARTS and the related terms CITY BEAUTIFUL MOVEMENT, PWA MODERNE.

belfry A cupola, turret, or room in a tower where a bell is housed.

bell cote A small gabled structure astride the ridge of a roof, which shelters a bell. It is usually close to the front wall plane of the building.

belt course See STRINGCOURSE.

belvedere 1 Any building, especially a pavilion or shelter, that is located to take advantage of a view. See also the related term GAZEBO. **2** See CUPOLA (definition 2).

blind (adjective) Term applied to the surface use of elements that would otherwise articulate an opening but where no opening exists. Used in such combinations as blind arcade, blind arch, blind door, blind window.

board-and-batten siding A type of siding for wood frame buildings, consisting of wide vertical boards with narrow strips of wood (battens) covering the joints. (In rare instances, the battens may be fastened behind the joints. If the gaps between boards are wide and the back battens approach the width of the outer boards, the siding is called board-on-board.) See also the related term BATTEN.

board-on-board siding A type of siding for wood frame buildings, consisting of two layers of vertical boards, with the outer layer of boards covering the wide gaps between the boards of the inner layer.

bowfront A semicircular or semielliptical bay (definition 2).

bow window A semicircular or semielliptical bay window.

brace A single wooden or metal member placed diagonally within a framework or truss or beneath an overhang. Distinguished from a bracket, which is a more substantial triangular feature, and from a strut, which is essentially a post set in a diagonal position.

braced frame construction A combination of heavy and light timber frame construction, in which the principal vertical and horizontal framing members (posts and girts) are fastened by mortise and tenon joints, while the one-story-high studs are nailed to the heavy timber frame. The overall frame is made more rigid by diagonal braces. Sometimes called braced framing.

bracket Any solid, pierced, or built-up triangular feature projecting from the face of a wall to support a projecting element, like the top member of a cornice or the verges or eaves of a roof. Brackets are frequently used for ornamental as well as structural purposes. Distinguished from a brace, which is a simple barlike structural member. Distinguished from the more specific term console, which has a height greater than its projection from the wall. See also the related term CORBEL.

Bracketed Style A nineteenth-century term for Italianate.

brick bonds, brickwork See the more specific terms COMMON BOND, ENGLISH BOND, FLEMISH BOND, RUNNING BOND.

British colonial A term applied to buildings, towns, landscapes, and other artifacts from the period of actual British colonial occupation of large parts of eastern North American (c. 1607–1781 for the United States; c. 1750s–1867 for much of Canada). The British colonial period saw the introduction into the New World of various regional strains of English and Scotch-Irish folk culture, as well as high-style Anglo-European Renaissance, Baroque, and Neoclassical design. Sometimes called English colonial. Loosely called colonial or Early American. See also the related term GEORGIAN PERIOD.

Brutalism An architectural style of the 1950s through 1970s, characterized by complex massing and by a frank expression of structural members, elements of building systems, and materials (especially concrete). Some of the work of Paul Rudolph (born 1918) is associated with this style. Sometimes called New Brutalism.

bungalow A low one- or one-and-one-half-story house of modest pretensions with a low-pitched gable or hipped roof, a conspicuous porch, and projecting eaves. This house type was a popular builders' type from around 1900 to 1930. The term bungalow was also loosely applied to any vernacular building of a semirustic nature, including vacation cottages and lodges.

Burlingtonian See ANGLO-PALLADIANISM.

buttress An exterior mass of masonry bonded into a wall that it strengthens or supports. Buttresses often absorb lateral thrusts from roofs or vaults.

Byzantine Term applied to the art and architecture of the Eastern Roman Empire centered at Byzantium (i.e., Constantinople, Istanbul) from the early 500s to the mid-1400s. Byzantine architecture is characterized by massive domes, round arches, richly carved capitals, and the extensive use of mosaic.

Byzantine Revival See NEO-BYZANTINE.

campanile In Italian, a bell tower. While usually free-standing in medieval and Renaissance architecture, it was often incorporated as a prominent unit in the massing of picturesque nineteenth-century buildings.

cantilever A beam, girder, slab, truss, or other structural member that projects beyond its supporting wall or column.

cap A canopy, ledge, molding, or pediment over a window. Sometimes called a window cap. Distinguished from a hood, which is a similar feature over a door. See also the related term HEAD MOLDING.

capital The moldings and carved enrichment at the top of a column, pilaster, pier, or pedestal.

Carpenter's Gothic Term applied to a version of the Gothic Revival (c. 1840s–1870s), in which Gothic motifs are adapted to the kind of wooden details that can be produced by lathes, jigsaws, and molding machines. Sometimes called Carpenter Gothic, Gingerbread Style, Steamboat Gothic. See also the more general term GOTHIC REVIVAL.

carriage porch SEE PORTE-COCHÈRE.

casement window A window that opens from the side on hinges, like a door, out from the plane of the wall. Distinguished from a double-hung window.

casing See ARCHITRAVE (definition 2).

cast iron Iron shaped by a molding process, generally strong in compression but brittle in tension. Distinguished from wrought iron, which has been forged to increase its tensile properties.

cast iron front An architectural facade made of prefabricated molded iron parts, often markedly skeletal in appearance with extensive glass infilling. Prevalent from the late 1840s to the early 1870s.

castellated Having the elements of a medieval castle, such as crenelation and turrets.

cavetto cornice See COVED CORNICE.

cement A mixture of burnt lime and clay with water, which hardens permanently when dry. When a fine aggregate of sand is added, the cement may be used as a mortar for masonry construction or as a plaster or stucco coating. When a coarser aggregate of gravel or crushed stone is added, along with sand, the mixture is called concrete.

chamfer The oblique surface formed by cutting off a square edge at an equal angle to each face.

chancel 1 The end of a Roman Catholic or High Episcopal church containing the altar and set apart for the clergy and choir by a screen, rail, or steps. Usually the entire east end of a church beyond the crossing. In churches that have a long chancel space, the part of the chancel between the crossing and the apse, where the singers participate in the service, is called the choir. The innermost part of the chancel, containing the principal altar, is called the sanctuary. **2** In less extensive Catholic and Episcopal churches, the terms chancel and choir are often used interchangeably to mean the entire eastern arm of the church.

Chateauesque A term applied to masonry buildings from the 1870s through the 1920s in which stylistic references are derived from early French Renaissance chateaux, from the reign of Francis I (1515–1547) or even earlier. Sometimes called Chateau Style, Chateauesque Revival, Francis I Style, François Premier.

chevet In large churches, particularly those based upon French Gothic precedents, a substantial apse surrounded by an ambulatory and often containing radiating chapels.

Chicago School A diverse group of architects associated with the development of the tall (i.e., six- to twenty-story), usually metal frame commercial building in Chicago during the 1880s and 1890s. William Le Baron Jenney, Burnham and Root, and Adler and Sullivan are identified with this group. Sometimes called Chicago Commercial Style, Commercial Style. See also the related term PRAIRIE SCHOOL.

Chicago window A tripartite oblong window in which a large fixed center pane is placed between two narrow sash windows. Popularized in Chicago commercial buildings of the 1880s–1890s. See also BAY WINDOW.

chimney girt In timber frame construction, a major wooden beam that passes across the breast of the central chimney. It is supported at its ends by the longitudinal girts of the building and sometimes carries one end of the summer beam.

choir 1 The part of a Roman Catholic or High Episcopal church where the singers participate in the service. Usually the space within the chancel arm of the church, situated between the crossing to the west and the sanctuary to the east. **2** In less extensive Catholic and Episcopal churches, the terms choir and chancel are often used interchangeably to mean the entire eastern arm of the church.

Churrigueresque Term applied to Spanish and Spanish colonial Baroque architecture resembling the work of the Spanish architect José Benito de Churriguera (1665–1725) and his brothers. The style is characterized by a freely interpreted assemblage of such elements as twisted columns, broken pediments, and scroll brackets. See also the related term SPANISH COLONIAL.

cinquefoil A type of Gothic tracery having five parts (lobes or foils) separated by pointed elements (cusps).

City Beautiful movement A movement in architecture, landscape architecture, and planning in the United States from the 1890s through the 1920s, advocating the beautification of cities in the image of some of the most urbane places of the time: the world's fairs. City Beautiful schemes emphasized civic centers, boulevards, and waterfront improvements, and sometimes included comprehensive metropolitan plans for parks, parkways, and transportation facilities. See also the related term BEAUX-ARTS CLASSICISM.

clapboard A tapered board that is thinner along the top edge and thicker along the bottom edge, applied horizontally with edges overlapping to provide weathertight siding on a building of wood construction. Early clapboards were split (rived, riven) and were used for barrel staves and for wainscoting. The term now applies to any beveled siding board, whether split or sawn, rabbeted or not, regardless of length or width. (The term is sometimes applied only to a form of bevel siding used in New England, about four feet long and quarter-sawn.) Sometimes called weatherboards.

classical orders See ORDER.

classical rectangle See GOLDEN SECTION.

Classical Revival Ambiguous term, suggesting (1) Neoclassical design of the late eighteenth and early nineteenth centuries, including the Greek Revival; or (2) Beaux-Arts classical design of the late nineteenth and early twentieth centuries. Sometimes called Classic Revival. See instead BEAUX-ARTS CLASSICISM, GREEK REVIVAL, NEOCLASSICISM.

classicism, classical, classicizing Terms describing

the application of principles or elements derived from the visual arts of the Greco-Roman era (seventh century B.C. through fourth century A.D.) at any subsequent period of Western civilization, but particularly since the Renaissance. More a descriptive term for an approach to design and for a general cultural sensibility than for any particular style. See also the related term NEOCLASSICISM.

clerestory A part of a building that rises above the roof of another part and has windows in its walls.

clipped gable roof See JERKINHEAD ROOF.

coffer A recessed panel, usually square or octagonal, in a ceiling. Such panels are also found on the inner surfaces of domes and vaults.

collar beam A horizontal tension member in a pitched roof connecting opposite rafters, generally halfway up or higher. Its function is to tie the angular members together and prevent them from spreading.

Collegiate Gothic 1 Originally, a secular version of English Gothic architecture, characteristic of the older colleges of Oxford and Cambridge. **2** A secular version of Late Gothic Revival architecture, which became a popular style for North American colleges and universities from the 1890s through the 1920s. Sometimes called Academic Gothic.

colonial 1 Not strictly a style term, but a term for the entire period during which a particular European country held political dominion over a part of the Western Hemisphere, Africa, Asia, Australia, or Oceania. See also the more specific terms BRITISH COLONIAL, DUTCH COLONIAL, FRENCH COLONIAL, SPANISH COLONIAL. **2** Loosely used to mean the British colonial period in North American (c. 1607–1781 for the United States; c. 1750s–1867 for much of Canada).

Colonial Revival Generally understood to mean the revival of forms from British colonial design. The Colonial Revival began in New England in the 1860s and continues nationwide into the present. Sometimes called Neo-Colonial. See also the more specific term GEORGIAN REVIVAL and the related terms FEDERAL REVIVAL, SHINGLE STYLE.

colonnade A series of freestanding or engaged columns supporting an entablature or simple beam.

colonnette A diminutive, often attenuated, column.

colossal order See GIANT ORDER.

column 1 A vertical supporting element, usually cylindrical and slightly tapering, consisting of a base (except in the Greek Doric order), shaft, and capital. See also the related terms ENTABLATURE, ENTASIS, ORDER. **2** Any vertical supporting element in a skeletal frame.

Commercial Style See CHICAGO SCHOOL.

common bond A pattern of brickwork in which every fifth or sixth course consists of all headers, the other courses being all stretchers. Sometimes called American bond. Distinguished from running bond, in which no headers appear.

Composite order An ensemble of classical column and entablature elements, particularly characterized by large Ionic volutes and Corinthian acanthus leaves in the capital of the column. See also the more general term ORDER.

concrete An artificial stone made by mixing cement, water, sand, and a coarse aggregate (such as gravel or crushed stone) in specified proportions. The mix is shaped in molds called forms. Distinguished from cement, which is the binder without the aggregate.

console A type of bracket with a scroll-shaped or S-curve profile and a height greater than its projection from the wall. Distinguished from the more general term bracket, which is usually applied to supports whose projection and height are nearly equal. Distinguished from a modillion, which usually is smaller, has a projection greater than its height (or thickness), and appears in a series, as in a classical cornice.

coping The cap or top course of a wall, parapet, balustrade, or chimney, usually designed to shed water.

corbel A projecting stone that supports a superincumbent weight. In medieval architecture and its derivatives, a support for such major features as vaulting shafts, vaulting ribs, or oriels. See also the related term BRACKET.

corbeled construction Masonry that is built outward beyond the vertical by letting successive courses project beyond those below. Sometimes called corbeling.

corbeled cornice A cornice made up of courses of projecting masonry, each of which extends farther outward than the one below.

Corinthian order An ensemble of classical column and entablature elements, particularly characterized by acanthus leaves and small volutes in the capital of the column. See also the more general term ORDER.

cornice The crowning member of a wall or entablature.

Corporate International Style A term, not widely used, for curtain wall commercial, institutional, and governmental buildings since the Second World War, which represent a widespread adoption of selected International Style ideas from the 1920s. See also the more general term INTERNATIONAL STYLE.

Corporate Style An architectural style developed in the early industrial communities of New England during the first half of the nineteenth century. This austere but graceful mode of construction was derived from the red-brick Federal architecture of the early nineteenth century and is characterized by the same elegant proportions, cleanly cut openings, and simple refined detailing. The term was coined by William Pierson in the 1970s. Not to be confused with Corporate International Style.

cottage 1 A relatively modest rural or suburban dwelling. Distinguished from a villa, which is a more substantial and often more elaborate dwelling. **2** A seasonal dwelling, regardless of size, especially one located in a resort community.

cottage orné A rustic building in the romantic, picturesque tradition, noted for such features as bay windows, oriels, ornamented gables, and clustered chimneys.

course A layer of building blocks, such as bricks or stones, extending the full length and thickness of a wall.

coved ceiling A ceiling in which the transition between wall and ceiling is formed by a large concave panel or molding. Sometimes called a cove ceiling.

coved cornice A cornice with a concave profile. Sometimes called a cavetto cornice.

Craftsman A style of furniture and interior design belonging to the Arts and Crafts movement in the United States, and specifically related to *The Craftsman* magazine (1901–1916), published by Gustav Stickley (1858–1942). Some entire houses known to be derived from this publication can be called Craftsman houses. See also the more general term ARTS AND CRAFTS.

crenelation, crenelated A form of embellishment on a parapet consisting of indentations (crenels or embrasures) alternating with solid blocks of wall (merlons). Virtually synonymous with battlement, battlemented; embattlement, embattled.

cresting An ornamental strip or fencelike feature, usually of metal or tile, along the ridgeline or summit of a roof.

crocket In Gothic architecture, a small ornament resembling bunched foliage, placed at intervals on the sloping edges of gables, pinnacles, or spires.

crossing In a church with a cruciform plan, the area where the arms of the cross intersect; specifically, the space where the transept crosses the nave and chancel.

cross rib See LIERNE.

cross section See SECTION.

crown The central, or highest, part of an arch or vault.

crown molding The highest in a series of moldings.

crowstep Any one of the progressions in a gable that ascends in steps rather than in a continuous slope.

cruciform In the shape of a cross. Usually used to describe the ground plans of buildings. See also the more specific terms GREEK CROSS, LATIN CROSS.

cupola 1 A small domed structure on top of a belfry, steeple, or tower. **2** A lantern, square or polygonal in plan, with windows or vents, which is located at the summit of a roof. Sometimes called a belvedere. Distinguished from a skylight, which is a lesser feature located on the slope of a roof. **3** In historic English usage, synonymous with dome. A dome is now understood to be a more substantial feature.

curtain wall In skeleton frame or reinforced concrete construction, a thin nonstructural cladding of stone, brick, terra cotta, glass, or metal veneer. Distinguished from bearing wall. See also the related term LOAD-BEARING.

cusp The pointed, roughly triangular intersection of the arcs of lobes or foils in the tracery of windows, screens, or panels.

dado A broad decorative band around the lower portion of an interior wall, between the baseboard and dado rail or cap molding. (The term is often applied to this entire zone, including baseboard and dado rail.) The dado may be painted, papered, or covered with some other material, so as to have a different treatment from the upper zone of the wall. Dado connotes any continuous lower zone in a room, equivalent to a pedestal. A wood-paneled dado is called a wainscot.

Deco. See ART DECO.

dentil, denticulated A small ornamental block forming one of a series set in a row. A dentil molding is composed of such a series.

dependency A building, wing, or room, subordinate to, or serving as an adjunct to a main building. A dependency may be attached to or detached from a main building. Distinguished from an outbuilding, which is always detached.

diaper An overall repetitive pattern on a flat surface, especially a pattern of geometric or representational forms arranged in a diamond-shaped or checkerboard grid. Sometimes called diaper work.

discharging arch See RELIEVING ARCH.

dome A major hemispherical or curved roof feature rising from a circular, polygonal, or square base. Distinguished from a cupola, which is a smaller, usually subordinate, domical element.

Doric order An ensemble of classical column and entablature elements, particularly characterized by the use of triglyphs and metopes in the frieze of the entablature. See also the more general term ORDER.

dormer A roof-sheltered window (or vent), usually with vertical sides and front, set into a sloping roof. Sometimes called a dormer window.

dosseret See IMPOST BLOCK.

double-hung window A window consisting of a pair of frames, or sashes, one above the other, arranged to slide up and down. Their movement is sometimes stabilized by a system of cords and counterbalancing weights contained in narrow boxing at each side of the window frame. Sometimes called guillotine sash.

double-pen In vernacular architecture, particularly houses, a term applied to a plan consisting of two rooms side by side or separated by a hallway.

double-pile In vernacular architecture, particularly houses, a term applied to a plan that is two rooms deep and any number of rooms wide.

drip molding See HEAD MOLDING.

drum 1 A cylindrical or polygonal wall zone upon which a dome rests. **2** One of the cylinders of stone that form the shaft of a column.

Dutch colonial A term applied to buildings, towns, landscapes, and other artifacts from the period of actual Dutch colonial occupation of the Hudson River valley and adjacent areas (c. 1614–1664). Meaning has been extended to apply to the artifacts of Dutch ethnic groups and their descendants, even into the early nineteenth century.

Dutch Colonial Revival The revival of forms from design in the Dutch tradition.

ear A slight projection just below the upper corners of a door or window architrave or casing. Sometimes called a shouldered architrave.

Early American See BRITISH COLONIAL.

Early Christian A style of art and architecture in the Mediterranean world that was developed by the early Christians before the fall of the Western Roman Empire, derived from late Roman art and architecture and leading to the Romanesque (early fourth to early sixth century).

Early Georgian period Not strictly a style term, but a term for a period in British and British colonial history approximately coinciding with the reigns of George I (1714–1727) and George II (1727–1760). See also the related term LATE GEORGIAN PERIOD.

Early Gothic Revival A term for the Gothic Revival work of the late eighteenth to the mid-nineteenth century. See also the related term LATE GOTHIC REVIVAL.

Eastlake A decorative arts and interior design term of the 1860s and 1880s sometimes applied to architecture. Named after Charles Locke Eastlake (1836–1906), an English advocate of the application of Gothic principles of construction and design, rather than mere Gothic elements. Characterized by simplicity and solidity of forms, which are sometimes embellished with chamfered, turned, or incised details. Sometimes called Eastlake Gothic, Modern Gothic. See also the related term QUEEN ANNE.

eaves The horizontal lower edges of a roof plane, usually projecting beyond the wall below. Distinguished from verges, which are the sloping edges of a roof plane.

echinus A heavy molding with a curved profile placed immediately below the abacus, or top member, of a classical capital. Particularly prominent in the Doric and Tuscan orders.

eclecticism, eclectic A sensibility in design, prevalent since the eighteenth century, involving the selection of elements from a variety of sources, including historical periods of high-style design (Western and non-Western), vernacular design (Western and non-Western), and (in the twentieth century) contemporary industrial design. Distinguished from historicism and revivalism by drawing upon a wider range of sources than the historical periods of high-style design.

Ecole, Ecole des Beaux-Arts See BEAUX-ARTS.

Egyptian Revival Term applied to eclectic works or elements of those works that emulate forms in the visual arts of ancient Egyptian civilization.

elevation A drawing (in orthographic projection) of an upright, planar aspect of an object or building. The vertical complement of a plan. Sometimes loosely used in the sense of a facade view or any frontal representation of a wall, whether photograph or drawing, whether measured to scale or not.

Elizabethan Manor Style See NEO-TUDOR.

Elizabethan period A term for a period in English history coinciding with the reign of Elizabeth I (1558–1603). See also the more general term TUDOR PERIOD and the related term JACOBEAN PERIOD for the succeeding period.

embattlement, embattled See CRENELATION.

encaustic tile A tile decorated by a polychrome glazed or ceramic inlay pattern.

engaged column A half-round column attached to a wall. Distinguished from a free-standing column by seeming to be built into the wall. Distinguished from a pilaster, which is a flattened column. Distinguished from a recessed column, which is a fully round column set into a nichelike space.

English bond A pattern of brickwork in which the bricks are set in alternating courses of stretchers and headers.

English colonial See BRITISH COLONIAL.

English Half-timber Style See NEO-TUDOR.

entablature In a classical order, a richly detailed horizontal member resting on columns or pilasters. It is divided horizontally into three main parts. The lowest is the architrave (definition 1), the structural part, and is generally an unornamented continuous beam or series of beams. The middle part is the frieze (definition 1), which is generally the most freely ornamented part. The uppermost is the cornice. Composed of a sequence of moldings, the cornice overhangs the frieze and architrave and serves as a crown to the whole. Each part has the moldings and decorative treatment that are characteristic of the particular order, but modern adaptations often alter canonical details. See also the related terms COLUMN, ORDER.

entablature block A block bearing the canonical elements of a classical entablature on three or all four sides, placed between a column capital and a feature above, such as a balcony or ceiling. Distinguished from an impost block, which has the form of an inverted truncated pyramid and detailing typical of medieval architecture.

entasis The slight convex curving of the vertical profile of a tapered column.

exedra A semicircular or polygonal space usually containing a bench, in the wall of a garden or a building other than a church. Distinguished from a niche, which is usually a smaller feature higher in a wall, and from an apse, which is usually identified with churches.

exotic revivals A term occasionally used to suggest a distinction between revivals of European styles (e.g., Greek, Gothic Revivals) and non-European styles (e.g., Egyptian, Moorish Revivals). See also the more specific terms EGYPTIAN REVIVAL, MAYAN REVIVAL, MOORISH REVIVAL.

extrados The outer curve or outside surface of an arch. See also the related term INTRADOS.

eyebrow dormer A low dormer with a small segmental window or vent but no sides. The roofing warps or bows over the window or vent in a wavy line.

facade An exterior face of a building, especially the principal or entrance front. Distinguished from an elevation, which is an orthographic drawing of a building face.

false half-timbering A surface treatment that simulates half-timber construction, consisting of a lattice of broad boards and stucco applied as an exterior veneer on a building of masonry or wood frame construction. Most commonly seen in domestic architecture from the late nineteenth century onward.

fanlight A semicircular or semielliptical window over a door, with radiating mullions in the form of an open fan. Sometimes called a sunburst light. See also the more general term TRANSOM (definition 1) and the related term SIDE LIGHT.

fan vault A type of Gothic vault in which the primary ribs all have the same curvature and radiate in a half circle around the springing point.

fascia 1 A plain, molded, or ornamented board that covers the horizontal edges (eaves) or sloping edges (verges) of a roof. Distinguished from the more specific term bargeboards, which are ornate fascia boards attached to the sloping edges of a roof. Distinguished from a frieze (definition 2), which is located at the top of a wall. **2** One of the broad continuous bands that make up the architrave of the Ionic, Corinthian, or Composite order.

Federal A version of Neoclassical architecture in the United States popular from New England to Virginia, and in other regions influenced by the Northeast. It flourished from the 1790s through the 1820s and is found in some regions as late as the 1840s. Sometimes called American Adam Style. Not to be confused with Federalist. See also the related terms JEFFERSONIAN, ROMAN REVIVAL.

Federal Revival Term applied to eclectic works (c. 1890s–1930s) or elements of those works that emulate forms in the visual arts of the Federal period. Sometimes called NeoFederal. See also the related terms COLONIAL REVIVAL, GEORGIAN REVIVAL.

Federalist Name of an American political party and the era it dominated (c. 1787–1820). Not to be confused with Federal.

fenestration Window treatment: arrangement and proportioning.

festoon A motif representing entwined leaves, flowers, or fruits, hung in a catenary curve from two points. Distinguished from a swag, which is a motif representing a fold of drapery hung in a similar curve. See also the more general term GARLAND.

fillet 1 A relatively narrow flat molding. **2** Any thin band.

finial A vertical ornament placed upon the apex of an architectural feature, such as a gable, turret, or canopy. Distinguished from a pinnacle, which is a larger feature, usually associated with Gothic architecture.

fireproofing In metal skeletal framing, the wrapping of structural members in terra-cotta tile or other fire-resistant material.

flashing A strip of metal, plastic, or various flexible compositional materials used at roof valleys and ridges and at chimney corners to keep water out. Any similar material used to protect door and window heads and sills.

Flemish bond A pattern of brickwork in which the stretchers and headers alternate in the same row and are staggered from one row to the next. Because this creates a more animated texture than English bond, Flemish bond was favored for front facades and more elegant buildings.

Flemish gable A gable whose upper slopes ascend in steps rather than in a straight line. These steps may be rectilinear or curved, or a combination of both.

fluting, fluted A series of parallel grooves or channels (flutes), usually semicircular or semielliptical in plan, that accentuate the verticality of the shaft of a column or pilaster.

flying buttress In Gothic architecture a spanning member, usually in the form of an arch, that reaches across the open space from an exterior buttress pier to that point on the wall of the building where the thrusts of the interior vaults are concentrated. Because of its arched construction, a flying buttress exerts a counterthrust against the pressure of the vaults contained by the vertical strength of the buttress pier.

foliated (adjective). In the form of leaves or leaflike shapes.

folk Not a style term in itself, but a descriptive term, applicable to all the visual arts and all styles and periods. Applied to (1) a regional, often ethnic, tradition in which continuities through the years in the overall appearance of artifacts (including buildings) are more important than changes in stylistic embellishment; (2) the work of individual artists and artisans unexposed to or uninterested in prevailing or avant-garde ideals of form and technique. Approximate synonyms include anonymous, naive, primitive, traditional. For architecture, see also the more general term VERNACULAR and the related term POPULAR.

four-part vault See QUADRIPARTITE VAULT.

foursquare house A hipped-roof, two-story house with four principal rooms on each floor and a symmetrical facade. It usually has a front porch across the full width of the house and one or more large dormers on the roof. A common suburban house type from the 1890s to the 1920s. Sometimes called American Foursquare, Prairie Box.

frame construction, frame See BRACED FRAME CONSTRUCTION, LIGHT FRAME CONSTRUCTION (BALLOON FRAME CONSTRUCTION, PLATFORM FRAME CONSTRUCTION), SKELETON CONSTRUCTION, TIMBER FRAME CONSTRUCTION.

Francis 1 style See CHATEAUESQUE.

François Premier See CHATEAUESQUE.

French colonial A term applied to buildings, towns, landscapes, and other artifacts from the period of actual French colonial occupation of large parts of eastern North American (c. 1605–1763). The term is extended to apply to the artifacts of French ethnic groups and their descendants, well into the nineteenth century.

French Norman A style associated since the 1920s with residential architecture based on rural houses of the French provinces of Normandy and Brittany. While not a major revival style, it is characterized by asymmetrical plans, round stair towers with conical roofs, stucco walls, and steep hipped roofs. Sometimes called Norman French.

fret An ornament, usually in series, as a band or field, consisting of a latticelike interlocking of right-angled linear elements.

frieze 1 The broad horizontal band that forms the central part of a classical entablature. **2** Any long horizontal band or zone, especially one that has a chiefly decorative purpose, located at the top of a wall. Distinguished from a fascia, which is attached to the horizontal edge of a roof.

front gabled Term applied to a building whose principal gable end faces the front of the lot or some feature like a street or open space. Sometimes called gable front. Distinguished from side gabled.

gable The wall area immediately below the end of a gable, gambrel, or jerkinhead roof.

gableboard See BARGEBOARD.

gable front See FRONT GABLED.

gable roof A roof in which the two planes slope equally toward each other to a common ridge. Sometimes called a pitched roof.

gambrel roof A roof that has a single ridgepole but a double pitch. The lower plane, which rises from the eaves, is rather steep. The upper plane, which extends from the lower plane to the ridgeline, has a flatter pitch.

garland A motif representing a rope of entwined leaves, flowers, ribbons, or drapery, regardless of its shape or position. It may be formed into a wreath, festoon, or swag, or follow the outline of a rectilinear architectural element.

garret See ATTIC (definition 1).

gauged brick A brick that has been cut or rubbed to a uniform size and shape.

gazebo A small pavilion, usually polygonal or circular in plan and serving as a garden or park shelter. Distinguished from a kiosk, which generally has some commercial or public function. See also the related terms BANDSTAND, BELVEDERE (definition 1).

General Grant Style See SECOND EMPIRE.

Georgian period A term for a period in British and British colonial history, and not, in architecture or the other visual arts, a sufficiently specific style term. The Georgian period begins with the coronation of George I in 1714 and extends until about 1781 in the area that became the United States (and in Britain, until the death of George IV in 1830). See also the related terms ANGLO-PALLADIANISM, BRITISH COLONIAL.

Georgian plan See DOUBLE-PILE plus DOUBLE-PEN (i.e., a four-room plan with central hallway).

Georgian Revival A revival of Georgian period forms—in England, from the 1860s to the present, and in the United States, from the 1880s to the present. Sometimes called Neo-Georgian. See also the more general term COLONIAL REVIVAL and the related term FEDERAL REVIVAL.

giant order A composition involving any one of the five principal classical orders, in which the columns or pilasters are nearly as tall as the height of the entire building. Sometimes called a colossal order. See also the more general term ORDER.

Gingerbread Style See CARPENTER'S GOTHIC.

girder A major horizontal spanning member, comparable in function to a beam, but larger and often built up of a number of parts. It usually runs at right angles to the beams and serves as their principal means of support.

girt In timber frame construction, a horizontal beam at intermediate (e.g., second-floor) level, spanning between posts.

glazing bar See MUNTIN.

golden section Any line divided into two parts so that the ratio of the longer part to the shorter part equals the ratio of the length of the whole line to the longer part: $a/b - (a+b)/a$. This ratio is approximately 1.618:1. A golden rectangle, or classical rectangle, is a rectangle whose long side is related to the short side in the same ratio as the golden section. It is proportioned so that neither the long nor the short side seems to dominate. In a Fibonacci series (i.e., 1, 2, 3, 5, 8, 13, . . .), the sum of the two preceding terms gives the next. The higher one goes in such a series, the closer the ratio of two sequential terms approaches the golden section.

Gothic An architectural style prevalent in Europe from the twelfth century into the fifteenth in Italy (and into the sixteenth century in the rest of Europe). It is characterized by pointed arches and ribbed vaults and by the dominance of openings over masonry mass in the wall. The Gothic was preceded by the Romanesque and followed by the Renaissance.

Gothic Revival A movement in Europe and North America devoted to reviving the forms and the spirit of Gothic architecture and the allied arts. It originated in the mid-eighteenth century. Sometimes called the Pointed Style in the nineteenth century, and sometimes called Neo-Gothic. See also the more specific terms CARPENTER'S GOTHIC, EARLY GOTHIC REVIVAL, HIGH VICTORIAN GOTHIC, LATE GOTHIC REVIVAL.

Grecian A nineteenth-century term for Greek Revival.

Greek cross A cross with four equal arms. Usually used to describe the ground plan of a building. See also the more general term CRUCIFORM.

Greek Revival A movement in Europe and North American devoted to reviving the forms and the spirit of Classical Greek architecture, sculpture, and decorative arts. It originated in the mid-eighteenth century, culminated in the 1830s, and continued into the 1850s. Sometimes called Grecian in the nineteenth century. See also the more general term NEOCLASSICAL.

groin The curved edge formed by the intersection of two vaults.

guillotine sash See DOUBLE-HUNG WINDOW.

HABS See HISTORIC AMERICAN BUILDINGS SURVEY.

HAER See HISTORIC AMERICAN ENGINEERING RECORD.

half-timber construction A variety of timber frame construction in which the framing members are exposed on the exterior of the wall, with the spaces between timbers being filled with wattle-and-daub (i.e., woven lath and plaster) or masonry materials, such as brick or stone. These masonry materials may also be covered with stucco. Sometimes called half-timbered construction.

hall-and-parlor house, hall-and-parlor plan A double-pen house (i.e., a house that is one room deep and two rooms wide). Usually applied to houses without a central through-passage, to distinguish from hall-passage-parlor houses.

hall-passage-parlor house, hall-passage-parlor plan A two-room house with a central through-passage or hallway.

hammerbeam A short horizontal beam projecting inward from the foot of the principal rafter and supported below by a diagonal brace tied into a vertical wall post. The hammer beams carry much of the load of the roof trussing above. Hammer beam trusses, which could be assembled using a series of smaller timbers, were often used in late medieval England instead of conventional trusses, which required long horizontal tie beams extending across an entire interior space.

haunch The part of the arch between the crown or keystone and the springing.

header A brick laid across the thickness of a wall, so that the short end of the brick shows on the exterior.

head molding A molding or set of moldings designed to shelter and embellish the top of a door or window. Sometimes called a drip molding. See also the related terms CAP (for windows) and HOOD (for doors).

heavy timber construction See TIMBER-FRAME CONSTRUCTION.

high style or high-style (adjective) Not a style term in itself, but a descriptive term, applicable to all the visual arts and all styles and periods. Applied to the works of the masters and their schools and disciples, usually reflecting a cosmopolitan awareness of traditions beyond a particular place or time. Usually contrasted with vernacular (including the folk and popular traditions).

high tech Term applied to architecture in which building materials and elements of building systems are used to celebrate contemporary technology. Elemental geometric forms, primary colors, and metallic finishes are used to heighten the technological imagery.

High Victorian Gothic A version of the Gothic Revival that originated in England in the 1850s and spread to North American in the 1860s. Characterized by polychromatic exteriors inspired by the medieval Gothic architecture of northern Italy. Sometimes called Ruskin Gothic, Ruskinian Gothic, Venetian Gothic, Victorian Gothic. See also the more general term GOTHIC REVIVAL.

hipped gable roof See JERKINHEAD ROOF.

hipped roof A roof that pitches inward from all four sides. The edge where any two planes meet is called the hip.

Historic American Buildings Survey (HABS) A branch of the National Park Service of the United States Department of the Interior, established in 1933 to produce detailed documentation of American architecture. HABS documentation typically includes historical and architectural data, photographs, and measured drawings, and is deposited in the Prints and Photographs Division of the Library of Congres. See also the related term HISTORIC AMERICAN ENGINEERING RECORD.

Historic American Engineering Record (HAER) A branch of the National Park Service of the United States Department of the Interior, established in 1969 to produce detailed documentation of sites and structures associated with industry, transportation, and other areas of technology. See also the related term HISTORIC AMERICAN BUILDINGS SURVEY.

historicism, historicist, historicizing A type of eclecticism prevalent since the eighteenth century, involving the use of forms from historical periods of high-style design (usually in the Western tradition) and, occasionally, from favored traditions of vernacular design (such as the various colonial traditions in the United States). Historicist influences are designated by the use of the prefix Neo- with a previous historical style (e.g., Neo-Baroque). Distinguished from the more general term eclecticism, which draws upon a wider range of sources in addition to the historical. See also the more specific term REVIVALISM.

hollow building tile A hollow terracotta building block used for constructing exterior bearing walls of buildings up to about three stories, as well as interior walls and partitions.

hood A canopy, ledge, molding, or pediment over a door. Distinguished from a cap, which is a similar feature over a window. Sometimes called a hood molding. See also the related term HEAD MOLDING.

horizontal plank frame construction A system of wood construction in which horizontal planks are set or nailed into the corner posts of a timber frame building. There are, however, no studs or intermediate posts connecting the sill and the plate. See also the related term VERTICAL PLANK FRAME CONSTRUCTION.

hung ceiling See SUSPENDED CEILING.

hyphen A subsidiary building unit, often one story, connecting the central block and the wings or dependencies.

I-beam The most common profile in steel structural shapes (although it also appears in cast iron and in reinforced concrete). Used especially for spanning elements, it is shaped like the capital letter I to make the most efficient use of the material consistent with a shape that permits easy assemblage. The vertical face of the I is the web. The horizontal faces are the flanges. Other standard shapes for steel framing elements are Hs, Ts, Zs, Ls (known as angles), and square-cornered Us (channels).

I-house A two-story house, one room deep and two rooms wide, usually with a central hallway. The I-house is a nineteenth-century descendant of the hall-and-parlor houses of the colonial period. The term is commonly applied to the end-chimney houses of the southern and mid-Atlantic traditions. The term most likely derives from the resemblance between the tall, narrow end walls of these houses and the capital letter *I*.

impost The top part of a pier or wall, upon which rests the springer or lowest voussoir of an arch.

impost block A block, often in the form of an inverted truncated pyramid, placed between a column capital and the lowest voussoirs of an arch above. Distinguished from an entablature block, which has the details found in a classical entablature. Sometimes called a dosseret or supercapital.

in antis Columns in antis are placed between two projecting sections of wall, in an imaginary plane connecting the ends of the two wall elements.

intermediate rib See TIERCERON.

International Style A style that originated in the 1920s and flourished into the 1970s, characterized by the expression of volume and surface and by the suppression of historicist ornament and axial symmetry. The term was originally applied by Henry-Russell Hitchcock and Philip Johnson to the new, nontraditional, mostly European architecture of the 1920s in their 1932 exhibition at the Museum of Modern Art and in their accompanying book, *The International Style*. Also called International, International Modern. See also the more specific term CORPORATE INTERNATIONAL STYLE and the related terms BAUHAUS, MIESIAN, SECOND CHICAGO SCHOOL.

intrados The inner curve or underside (soffit) of an arch. See also the related term EXTRADOS.

Ionic order An ensemble of classical column and entablature elements, particularly characterized by the use of large volutes in the capital of the column. See also the more general term ORDER.

isometric drawing A pictorial drawing using isometric projection, in which all horizontal lines that are perpendicular in an object, building, or space are drawn at 60–degree angles from the vertical. Consequently, a single scale can be used for all three dimensions. Sometimes called an isometric. See also the related terms AXONOMETRIC DRAWING, PERSPECTIVE DRAWING.

Italianate 1 A general term for an eclectic Neo-Renaissance and Neo-Romanesque style, originating in England and Germany in the early nineteenth century and prevalent in the United States between the 1840s and 1880s, not only in houses but also in Main Street commercial buildings. The Italianate is characterized by prominent window heads and bracketed cornices. Called the Bracketed Style in the nineteenth century. See also the more specific terms BARRYESQUE, ITALIAN VILLA STYLE, and the related terms RENAISSANCE REVIVAL, ROUND ARCH MODE, SECOND EMPIRE. **2** A specific term for Italianate buildings that are predominantly symmetrical in plan and elevation. Distinguished from Barryesque, which is applied to more formal institutional and governmental buildings.

Italian Villa Style A subtype of the Italianate style

(definition 1), originating in England and Germany in the early nineteenth century and prevalent in the United States between the 1840s and 1870s, mostly in houses, but also churches and other public buildings. The style is characterized by asymmetrical plans and elevations, irregular blocklike massing, round arch arcades and openings, and northern Italian Romanesque detailing. Larger Italian Villa buildings often had a campanile-like tower. Distinguished from the more symmetrical Italianate style (definition 2) by having the northern Italian rural vernacular villa as prototype.

jacal (plural: jacales) A small hut with walls consisting of vertical poles, often plastered with mud.

Jacobean period A term for a period in British history coinciding with the rule of James I (1603–1625). See also the related term ELIZABETHAN for the immediately preceding period, which itself is part of the Tudor period.

Jacobethan Revival See NEO-TUDOR.

jamb The vertical side face of a door or window opening, amounting to the full thickness of the wall, and usually enriched with paneling, moldings, or jamb shafts (which are engaged columns set into a splayed, or angled, jamb). In an opening containing a door or window, the jamb is distinguished from the reveal, which is the portion of wall thickness between the door or window frame and the outer surface of the wall. (In an opening without a door or window, the terms jamb and reveal are used interchangeably.) Also distinguished from an architrave (definition 2), which consists of the moldings on the face of a wall around the opening.

Jazz Moderne See ART DECO.

Jeffersonian A personal style of Neoclassicism identified with the architecture of Thomas Jefferson (1743–1826), derived in part from Palladian ideas and in part from Imperial Roman prototypes. The style had a limited influence in the piedmont of Virginia and across the Appalachians into the Ohio River valley. Sometimes called Jeffersonian Classicism. See also the related terms ANGLO-PALLADIANISM, FEDERAL, ROMAN REVIVAL.

jerkinhead roof A gable roof in which the upper portion of the gable end is hipped, or inclined inward along the ridgeline, forming a small triangle of roof surface. Sometimes called a clipped gable roof or hipped gable roof.

joist One of a series of small horizontal beams that support a floor or ceiling.

keystone The central wedge-shaped stone at the crown of an arch.

king post In a truss, the vertical suspension member that connects the tie beam with the apex of opposing principal rafters.

kiosk Originally, a Turkish summer palace. Since the nineteenth century, the term has been applied to any small pavilion or stand, usually found in public gardens, parks, streets, and malls, where it serves some commercial or public function. Distinguished from a gazebo, which may be found in public or private gardens or parks, but which usually serves as a sheltered resting place. See also the related term BANDSTAND.

label 1 A drip molding, over a square-headed door or window, which extends for a short distance down each side of the opening. **2** A similar vertical downward extension of a drip molding over an arch of any form. Sometimes called a label molding.

label stop 1 An L-shaped termination at the lower ends of a label. **2** Any decorative boss or other termination of a label.

lancet arch An arch generally tall and sharply pointed, whose centers are farther apart than the width or span of the arch.

lantern 1 The uppermost stage of a dome, containing windows or arcaded openings. **2** Any feature, square or polygonal in plan and usually containing windows, rising above the roof of a building. The square structures that serve as skylights on the roofs of nineteenth-century buildings—particularly houses—were also called lantern lights—and, in Italianate and Second Empire buildings, came to be called cupolas.

Late Georgian period Not strictly a style term, but a term for a period in British and British colonial history approximately coinciding with the reigns of George III (1760–1820) and George IV (1820–1830). In the United States, the Late Georgian period is now understood to end sometime during the Revolutionary War (1775–1781) and to be followed by the Federal period (c. 1787–1820). In Britain, the Late Georgian period includes the Regency period (1811–1820s). See also the related term EARLY GEORGIAN PERIOD.

Late Gothic Revival A term for the Gothic Revival work of the late nineteenth and early twentieth centuries. See also the more specific term COLLEGIATE GOTHIC (definition 2) and the related term EARLY GOTHIC REVIVAL.

lath A latticelike, continuous surface of small wooden strips or metal mesh nailed to walls or partitions to hold plaster.

Latin cross A cross with one long and three short arms. Usually used to describe the ground plans of Roman Catholic and Protestant churches. See also the more general term CRUCIFORM.

latía Also *latilla* (Spanish for little log). Small peeled poles used as lath in beamed ceilings, often laid in a herringbone fashion across room beams.

leaded glass Panes of glass held in place by lead strips, or cames. The panes, clear or stained, may be of any shape.

lean-to roof. See SHED ROOF.

lierne In a Gothic vault, a short ornamental rib connecting the major transverse ribs and the secondary tiercerons. Sometimes called a cross rib or tertiary rib.

light frame construction A type of wood frame construction in which relatively light structural members (usually sawn lumber, ranging from two-by-fours to two-by-tens) are fastened with nails. Distin-

guished from timber frame construction, in which relatively heavy structural members (hewn or sawn timbers, measuring six by six and larger) are fastened with mortise-and-tenon joints. See the more specific terms BALLOON FRAME CONSTRUCTION, PLATFORM FRAME CONSTRUCTION.

lintel A horizontal structural member that supports the wall over an opening or spans between two adjacent piers or columns.

living hall In Queen Anne, Shingle Style, and Colonial Revival houses, an extensive room, often containing the entry, the main staircase, a fireplace, and an inglenook.

load-bearing Term applied to a wall, column, pier, or any vertical supporting member, constructed so that all loads are carried to the ground through the wall, column, or pier. See also the related terms BEARING WALL, CURTAIN WALL.

loggia 1 A porch or open-air room, particularly one set within the body of a building. **2** An arcaded or colonnaded structure, open on one or more sides, sometimes with an upper story. **3** An eighteenth- and nineteenth-century term for a porch or veranda.

Lombard A style term applied in the United States in the mid-nineteenth century to buildings derived from the Romanesque architecture of northern Italy (especially Lombardy) and the earlier nineteenth-century architecture of southern Germany. Characterized by the use of brick, for both structural and ornamental purposes. Also called Lombardic. See also the related term ROUND ARCH MODE.

lunette 1 A semicircular area, especially one that contains some decorative treatment or a mural painting. **2** A semicircular window in such an area.

Mannerism, Mannerist 1 A phase of Renaissance art and architecture in the mid-sixteenth century, characterized by distortions, contortions, inversions, odd juxtapositions, and other departures from High Renaissance canons of design. **2** (Not capitalized) A sensibility in design, regardless of style or period, characterized by a knowledgeable violation of rules and intended as a comment on the very nature of convention.

mansard roof A hipped roof with double pitch. The upper slope may approach flatness, while the lower slope has a very steep pitch, sometimes flaring in a concave curve (or swelling in a convex curve) as it comes to the eaves. This lower slope usually has windows, and the area under the roof often amounts to a full story. The name is a corruption of that of François Mansart (1598–1666), who designed roofs of this type, which was revived in Paris during the Second Empire period.

Mansard Style, Mansardic See SECOND EMPIRE.

masonry Construction using stone, brick, block, or some other hard and durable material laid up in units and usually bonded by mortar.

massing The grouping or arrangement of the primary volumetric components of a building.

Mayan Revival Term applied to eclectic works or

elements of those works that emulate forms in the visual arts of the Maya civilization of Central America. See also the related term ART DECO.

McKim classicism, McKim classical Architecture of, or in the manner of, the firm of McKim, Mead and White, 1890s–1920s. See BEAUX-ARTS CLASSICISM.

medieval Term applied to the Middle Ages in European civilization between the age of antiquity and the age of the Renaissance (i.e., mid-400s to mid-1400s in Italy; mid-400s to late 1500s in England). In architecture and the other visual arts, the medieval period included the end of the Early Christian period, then the Byzantine, the Romanesque, and the Gothic styles or periods.

Mediterranean Revival A style generally associated since the early twentieth century with residential architecture based on Italian villas of the sixteenth century. While not a major revival style, it is characterized by symmetrical arrangements, stucco walls, and low-pitch tile roofs. Sometimes called Mediterranean Villa, Neo-Mediterranean. See also the related term SPANISH COLONIAL REVIVAL.

metope In a Doric entablature, that part of the frieze which falls between two triglyphs. In the Greek Doric order the metopes often contain small sculptural reliefs.

Middle Ages See MEDIEVAL.

Miesian Term applied to work showing the influence of the German American architect Ludwig Mies van der Rohe (1886–1969). See also the related terms BAUHAUS, INTERNATIONAL STYLE, SECOND CHICAGO SCHOOL.

Mineshaft Modern A type of Postmodern architecture referring to tall, vertical open spaces such as those found in mineshafts. The term was coined by David Gebhart in the 1960s to describe work of Charles Moore and William Turnbull at Sea Ranch Condominium No. 1. Sometimes called Mine Shack Modern for its use of shed roofs, makeshift composition, and diagonal board sheathing.

Mission Revival A style originating in the 1890s, and making use of forms and materials from the Spanish and Mexican mission architecture of the eighteenth and early nineteenth centuries. Not to be confused with Mission furniture of the Arts and Crafts movement. See also the more general term SPANISH COLONIAL REVIVAL.

modern Ambiguous term, applied in various ways during the past century to the history of the visual arts and world history generally: (1) from the 1910s to the present (see also the more specific terms BAUHAUS, INTERNATIONAL STYLE; (2) from the 1860s, 1870s, 1880s, or 1890s to the present; (3) from the Enlightenment or the advent of Neoclassicism or the industrial revolution, c. 1750, to the present; (4) from the Renaissance in Italy, c. 1450, to the present.

Modern Gothic See EASTLAKE.

Moderne A term applied to a wide range of design work from the 1920s through the 1940s, in which aspects of traditionalism and modernism coexist and in which eclecticism (from a historical, exotic, or machine aesthetic) is inseparable from the urge for stylization. Sometimes called Art Moderne, Modernistic. See also the more specific terms ART DECO, PWA MODERNE, STREAMLINE MODERNE.

modillion One of a series of small, thin scroll brackets under the projecting crown molding of a classical cornice. It is found in the Corinthian and Composite orders. Distinguished from a console, which usually is larger and has a height greater than its projection from the wall.

molding A running surface composed of parallel and continuous sections of simple or compound curves and flat areas.

monitor An extensive shed-roofed feature on a roof, containing a band of windows or vents. It may be located along one of the roof slopes (a trap-door monitor) or along the ridgeline (a clerestory monitor), and it usually runs the entire length of the roof. Distinguished from a skylight, which is a low-profile or flush-mounted feature in the plane of the roof.

Moorish Revival Term applied to eclectic works or elements of those works that emulate forms in the visual arts of those parts of North Africa and Spain under Muslim domination from the seventh through the fifteenth century. See also the related term ORIENTAL REVIVAL.

mortar A mixture of cement or lime with water and a fine aggregate of sand used to secure bricks or stones in masonry construction.

mortise-and-tenon joint A timber framing joint that is made by one member having its end shaped into a projecting piece (tenon) that fits exactly into a hole (mortise) in the other member. Once joined, the pieces are held together by a peg that passes through the tenon.

mullion 1 A post or similar vertical member dividing a window into two or more units, or lights, each of which may be further subdivided (by muntins) into panes. 2 A post or similar vertical member dividing a wall opening into two or more contiguous windows.

muntin One of the small vertical or horizontal members that hold panes of glass within a window or glazed door. Distinguished from a mullion, which is a heavier vertical member separating paired or grouped windows. Sometimes called a glazing bar, sash bar, or window bar.

mushroom column A reinforced concrete column that flares at the top in order to counteract shear stresses in the vicinity of the column.

National Register of Historic Places A branch of the National Park Service of the United States Department of the Interior, established by the National Historic Preservation Act of 1966, to maintain files of documentation on districts, sites, buildings, structures, and objects of national, state, or local significance. Properties listed on the National Register are afforded administrative—and, ultimately, judicial—review in instances where projects funded or assisted by federal agencies might have an impact on the historic property. Properties listed on the register may also be eligible for certain tax benefits.

nave **1** The entire body of a church between the entrance and the crossing. **2** The central space of a church, between the side aisles, extending from the entrance end to the crossing.

Neo-Baroque Term applied to eclectic works or elements of those works that emulate forms in the visual arts of the Baroque style or period. Sometimes called Baroque Revival.

Neo-Byzantine Term applied to eclectic works or elements of those works that emulate forms in the visual arts of the Byzantine style or period. Sometimes called Byzantine Revival.

Neoclassical Revival See BEAUX-ARTS CLASSICISM.

Neoclassicism, Neoclassical A broad movement in the visual arts which drew its inspiration from ancient Greece and Rome. It began in the mid-eighteenth century with the advent of the science of archeology and extended into the mid-nineteenth century (in some Beaux-Arts work, into the 1930s; in some Postmodern work, even into the present). See also the related terms BEAUX-ARTS, BEAUX-ARTS CLASSICISM, CLASSICISM, AND THE MORE SPECIFIC TERMS GREEK REVIVAL, ROMAN REVIVAL.

Neo-Colonial See COLONIAL REVIVAL.

Neo-Federal See FEDERAL REVIVAL.

Neo-Georgian See GEORGIAN REVIVAL.

Neo-Gothic Term applied to eclectic works or elements of those works that emulate forms in the visual arts of the Gothic style or period. The cultural movement that produced so many such works in the eighteenth, nineteenth, and twentieth centuries is called the Gothic Revival, though that term covers a wide range of work.

Néo-Grec An architectural style developed in connection with the Ecole des Beaux-Arts in Paris during the 1840s and characterized by the use of stylized Greek elements, often in conjunction with cast iron or brick construction. See also the more general term BEAUX-ARTS.

Neo-Hispanic See SPANISH COLONIAL REVIVAL.

Neo-Mediterranean See MEDITERRANEAN REVIVAL.

Neo-Norman Term applied to eclectic works or elements of those works that emulate forms in the visual arts of the eleventh- and twelfth-century Romanesque of Norman France and Britain.

Neo-Palladian See PALLADIANISM.

Neo-Renaissance Term applied to eclectic works or elements of those works that emulate forms in the visual arts of the Renaissance style or period. The mid- to late nineteenth-century cultural movement that produced so many such works is called the Renaissance Revival, though that term covers a wide range of work.

Neo-Romanesque Term applied to eclectic works or elements of those works that emulate forms in the visual arts of the Romanesque style or period. The mid-nineteenth-century cultural movement that produced so many such works is called the Romanesque Revival, though that term covers a wide range of work.

Neo-Tudor Term applied to eclectic works or elements of those works that emulate forms in the visual arts of the Tudor period. Sometimes loosely called Elizabethan Manor Style, English Half-timber Style, Jacobethan Revival, Tudor Revival.

New Brutalism See BRUTALISM.

New Formalism A style prevalent since the 1960s, characterized by symmetrical arrangements, rich materials (marble cladding, metal grillework), and stylized classical (even Gothic) detailing. Architects associated with this style include Philip Johnson (born 1906), Edward Durell Stone (1902–1978), and Minoru Yamasaki (born 1912).

newel post A post at the head or foot of a flight of stairs, to which the handrail is fastened. Newel posts occur in a variety of shapes, in profile and cross section, and are generally more substantial elements than the individual balusters that support the handrail.

niche A recess in a wall, usually designed to contain sculpture or an urn. A niche is often semicircular in plan and surmounted by a half dome or shell form. See also the related terms AEDICULE, TABERNACLE (definition 1).

nogging Brickwork that fills the spaces between members of a timber frame wall or partition.

Norman French See FRENCH NORMAN.

octagon house A rare house type of the 1850s, based on the ideas of Orson Squire Fowler (1809–1887), who argued for the efficiencies of an octagonal floor plan. Sometimes called octagon mode.

oculus A circular opening in a ceiling or wall or at the top of a dome.

ogee arch A pointed arch formed by a pair of opposing S-shaped curves.

order The most important constituents of classical architecture are the orders, first developed as a structural-aesthetic system by the ancient Greeks. An order has two major components. A column with its capital is the main vertical supporting member. The principal horizontal member is the entablature. The Greeks developed three different types of order, the Doric, Ionic, and Corinthian, each distinguishable by its own decorative system and proportions. All three were taken over and modified by the Romans, who added two orders of their own, the Tuscan, which is a simplified form of the Doric, and the Composite, which is made up of elements of both the Ionic and the Corinthian. The Romans often used the orders as a structural system in the same manner as the Greeks. Unlike the Greeks, however, they also applied them as decoration to the surfaces of walls that were supported by other means. Sometimes called classical orders. See also the related terms COLUMN, ENTABLATURE, GIANT ORDER, SUPERPOSITION (definition 1).

oriel A projecting polygonal or curved window unit of one or more stories, supported on brackets or corbels. Sometimes called an oriel window. Distinguished from a bay window, which rises from the foundation and has a rooted rather than a suspended appearance. However, a multistory projection in a tall building, whether cantilevered out or built from the foundation, is called a projecting bay or a unit of bay windows.

Oriental Revival Ambiguous term, suggesting eclectic influences from any period in any culture in the "Orient," or Asia, including Turkish, Persian, Indian, Chinese, and Japanese, as well as Arabic (even the Moorish of North Africa and Spain). Sometimes called Oriental style. See also the related term MOORISH REVIVAL.

orthographic projection A system of visual representation in which all details on or near some principal plane, object, building, or space are projected, to scale, onto the parallel plane of the drawing. Orthographic projection thus flattens all forms into a single two-dimensional picture plane and allows for an exact scaling of every feature in that plane. Distinguished from pictorial projection, which creates the illusion of three-dimensional depth. See also the more specific terms ELEVATION, PLAN, SECTION.

outbuilding A building subsidiary to and completely detached from another building. Distinguished from a dependency, which may be attached or detached.

overhang The projection of part of a structure beyond the portion below.

PWA Moderne A synthesis of the Moderne (i.e., Art Deco or Streamline Moderne) with an austere late type of Beaux-Arts classicism, often associated with federal government buildings of the 1930s and 1940s during the Public Works Administration. See also the more general term MODERNE and the related terms ART DECO, BEAUX-ARTS CLASSICISM, STREAMLINE MODERNE.

Palladianism, Palladian Work influenced by the Italian Renaissance architect Andrea Palladio (1508–1580), particularly by means of his treatise, *I Quattro Libri dell'Architettura* (*The Four Books of Architecture*, originally published in 1570 and disseminated throughout Europe in numerous translations and editions until the mid-eighteenth century). The most significant flourishing of Palladianism was in England, from the 1710s to the 1760s, and in the British North American colonies, from the 1740s to the 1790s. Sometimes called Neo-Palladian, Palladian classical. See also the more specific term ANGLO-PALLADIANISM.

Palladian motif A three-part composition for a door or window, in which a round-headed opening is flanked by lower flat-headed openings and separated from them by columns, pilasters, or mullions. The flanking sections, and sometimes the entire unit, may be blind (i.e., not open).

Palladian Revival See ANGLOPALLADIANISM.

Palladian window A window subdivided as in the Palladian motif.

parapet A low wall at the edge of a roof, balcony, or terrace, sometimes formed by the upward extension of the wall below.

pargeting Elaborate stucco or plasterwork, especially an ornammental finish for exterior plaster walls, sometimes decorated with figures in low relief or indented. Found in late medieval, Queen Anne, and period revival buildings. Sometimes called parging, pargework. See also the more general term STUCCO.

parquet Inlaid wood flooring, usually set in simple geometric patterns.

parti The essential solution to an architectural program or problem; the basic concept for the arrangement of spaces, before the development and elaboration of the design.

patera (plural: paterae) A circular or oval panel or plaque decorated with stylized flower petals or radiating linear motifs. Distinguished from a roundel, which is always circular.

pavilion 1 A central or corner unit that projects from a larger architectural mass and is usually accented by a special treatment of the wall or roof. **2** A detached or semidetached structure used for specialized activities, as at a hospital. **3** In a garden or fairground, a temporary structure or tent, usually ornamented.

pediment 1 In classical architecture, the low triangular gable end of the roof, framed by raking cornices along the inclined edges of the roof and by a horizontal cornice below. **2** In Renaissance and Baroque and later classically derived architecture, the triangular or curvilinear culmination of a prominent part of a facade. **3** A similar but smaller-scale feature over a door or window. It may be triangular or curvilinear.

pendentive A concave surface in the form of a spherical triangle that forms the structural transition from the square plan of a crossing to the circular plan of a dome.

pergola A structure with an open wood framed roof, often latticed, and supported by a colonnade. It is usually covered by climbing plants, such as vines or roses, and provides shade for a garden walk or a passageway to a building. Distinguished from arbors or trellises, which are less extensive accessory structures lacking the colonnade.

period house Term applied to suburban and country houses in which period revival styles are dominant.

period revival Term applied to eclectic works—particularly suburban and country houses—of the first three decades of the twentieth century, in which a particular historical or regional style is dominant. See also the more specific terms COLONIAL REVIVAL, DUTCH COLONIAL REVIVAL, GEORGIAN REVIVAL, NEO-TUDOR, SPANISH COLONIAL REVIVAL.

peripteral (adjective) Surrounded by a single row of columns.

peristyle A range of columns surrounding a building or an open court.

perspective drawing A pictorial drawing representing an object, building, or space, as if seen from a single vantage point. The illusion of three dimensions is created by using a system based on the optical laws of converging lines and vanishing points. See also the related terms AXONOMETRIC DRAWING, ISOMETRIC DRAWING.

piano nobile (plural: piani nobili) In Renaissance and later architecture, a floor with formal reception, living, and dining rooms. The principal and often tallest story in a building, usually one level above the ground level.

piazza 1 A plaza or square. **2** An eighteenth- and nineteenth-century term for a porch or veranda.

pictorial projection A system of visual representation in which an object, building, or space is projected onto the picture plane in such a way that the illusion of three-dimensional depth is created. Distinguished from orthographic projection, in which the dimension of depth is excluded. See also the more specific terms AXONOMETRIC DRAWING, ISOMETRIC DRAWING, PERSPECTIVE DRAWING.

picturesque An aesthetic category in architecture and landscape architecture in the late eighteenth and early nineteenth centuries. It is characterized by relationships among buildings and landscape features that evoke the qualities of landscape paintings, in which the eye is led past a variety of forms and spaces into the distance and the mind is led to contemplate a sense of age (by means of ruins, fallen trees, weathered rocks, and mossy surfaces on all of these). In actual settings, asymmetrical and eclectic buildings, indirect approaches, and contrasting clusters of plantings heighten the experience of the picturesque.

pier 1 A freestanding mass, supporting a concentrated load from an arch, a beam, a truss, or a girder. While generally rectilinear in plan, piers in buildings based upon medieval precedents are often curvilinear in plan. **2** An upright portion of a wall that performs a columnar function. The pier may be continuous with the plane of the wall, or it may be distinguished from the plane of the wall to give it a columnlike independence.

pier and spandrel. A type of skeletal wall organization in which the vertical metal columns (and their square-cornered cladding) project in front of the plane of windows and their spandrel panels. The spandrel panels may be exposed structural spanning members. More often they provide decorative covering for the structure.

pilaster 1 A flattened column, with or without fluting, that is attached to a wall. It is usually finished with the same capital and base as a freestanding column. **2** Any narrow, vertical strip attached to a wall. Distinguished from an engaged column, which has a convex curvature.

pillar Ambiguous term, often used interchangeably with column, pier, or post. See instead one of those terms. (Although the term pillar is sometimes applied to columns that are square in plan, the term pier is preferable.)

pinnacle In Gothic architecture, a small spirelike element providing an ornamental finish to the high-est part of a buttress or roof. It has a slender pyramidal or conical form and is often articulated with crockets or ribs and is topped by a finial. Distinguished from a finial, which is a smaller feature appearing by itself.

pitched roof See GABLE ROOF.

plan A drawing (in orthographic projection) representing all or part of an object, building, or space, as if viewed from directly above. A floor plan is a drawing of a horizontal cut through a building, usually at the level of the windows, showing the configuration of walls and openings. Other types of plans may illustrate ceilings, roofs, structural elements, and mechanical systems.

plank construction General term. See instead the more specific terms HORIZONTAL PLANK FRAME CONSTRUCTION, VERTICAL PLANK CONSTRUCTION.

plate 1 In timber frame construction, the topmost horizontal structural member of a wall, to which the roof rafters are fastened. **2** In platform and balloon frame construction, the horizontal members to which the tops and bottoms of studs are nailed. The bottom plate is sometimes called the sill plate or sole plate.

Plateresque Term applied to Spanish and Spanish colonial Renaissance architecture from the early sixteenth century onward, in which the delicate, finely sculptured detail resembles the work of a silversmith *(platero)*. See also the related term SPANISH COLONIAL.

platform frame construction A system of light frame construction in which each story is built as an independent unit and the studs are only one story high. The floor joists of each story rest on the top plates of the story below, and the bearing walls or partitions rest on the subfloor of each floor unit or platform. Platform framing is easier to construct and more rigid than balloon framing and has become the common framing method in the twentieth century. Structural members are usually sawn lumber, ranging from two-by-fours to two-by-tens, and are fastened with nails. Sometimes called platform framing, western frame, western framing.

plinth The base block of a column, pilaster, pedestal, dado, or door architrave.

Pointed Style A nineteenth-century term for Gothic Revival.

polychromy, polychromatic, polychrome A many-colored treatment, especially the combination of materials in various colors or the application of surface color, to articulate wall and roof planes and to highlight structure.

popular A term applied to vernacular architecture influenced by such publications as books of the orders, builders' guides, style books, pattern books, mail-order catalogs, architectural periodicals, and household magazines. Architecture in the popular tradition may be built according to commercially available plans or from widely distributed components; or it may be built by local practitioners (architects, builders, contractors) emulating buildings that are represented in publications. The distinction between popular architecture and high-style architecture by lesser-known architects depends on one's point of view with regard to the division between vernacular and high-style. See also the more general term VERNACULAR and the related term FOLK.

porch A structure attached to a building to shelter an entrance or to serve as a semienclosed sitting, working, or sleeping space. Distinguished from a portico, which is either a pedimented feature at least one story in height supported by classical columns or a more extensive colonnaded feature.

porte-cochère A porch projecting over a driveway and providing shelter to people leaving a vehicle and entering a building or vice versa. Also called a carriage porch.

portico 1 A porch at least one story in height consisting of a low-pitched roof supported on classical columns and finished in front with an entablature and pediment. **2** An extensive porch supported by a colonnade.

post A vertical supporting element, either square or circular in plan. Posts are the integral vertical members of a frame or truss, whether of wood or metal. Posts may also carry fences or gates, or may serve as freestanding markers (e.g., mileposts).

post-and-beam construction A structural system in which the main support is provided by vertical members (posts) carrying horizontal members (beams or lintels). Sometimes called post and girt construction, post and lintel construction, trabeation, trabeated construction.

Postmodernism, Postmodern A term applied to work that involves a reaction against the ideas and works of various twentieth-century modern movements, particularly the Bauhaus and the International Style. Postmodern work makes use of historicism, yet the traditional elements are often merely applied to buildings that, in every other respect, are products of modern movement design. The term is also applied to works that are attempting to demonstrate an extension of the principles of various modern movements.

Prairie Box See FOURSQUARE HOUSE.

Prairie School, Prairie Style A diverse group of architects working in Chicago and throughout the Midwest from the 1890s to the 1920s, strongly influenced by Frank Lloyd Wright and to a lesser degree by Louis Sullivan. The term is applied mainly to domestic architecture. An architect is said to belong to the Prairie School; a work of architecture is said to be in the Prairie Style. Sometimes called Prairie, for short. See also the related terms CHICAGO SCHOOL, WRIGHTIAN.

pre-Columbian Term applied to the major cultures of Latin American (e.g., Aztec, Maya, Inca) that flourished prior to the discovery of the New World by Columbus in 1492 and the Spanish conquests of the sixteenth century. Distinguished from North American Indian, which is generally applied to indigenous cultures within the area that would become the United States and Canada.

pressed metal Thin sheets of metal (usually galvanized or tin-plated iron) stamped into patterned panels for covering ceilings and exterior and interior walls or into molding profiles and other details for assembly into exterior and interior cornices. Loosely called pressed tin or stamped metal. Prevalent from the 1870s through the 1920s.

program The list of functional, spatial, and other requirements that guides an architect in developing a design.

proscenium In a recessed stage, the area between the orchestra and the curtain.

proscenium arch In a recessed stage, the enframement of the opening.

prostyle Having a columnar portico in front, but not on the sides and rear.

provincialism, provincial Term applied to work in an isolated area (such as a province of a cosmopolitan center or a colony of a mother country), where traditional practices persist, with some awareness of what is being done in the cosmopolitan center or the homeland.

Pueblo Revival Twentieth-century style influenced by Native American (Pueblo and Anasazi) architecture. Characteristics include stepped, irregular massing, blunt or rounded shapes, flat roofs, and protruding roof beams, or vigas. The style sometimes incorporates Mission Revival features such as rounded parapets, tile, and wrought iron.

purlin In roof construction, a structural member laid across the principal rafters and parallel to the wall plate and the ridge beam. The light common rafters to which the roofing surface is attached are fastened across the purlins. See also the related term RAFTER.

pylon 1 Originally, the gateway facade of an Egyptian temple complex, consisting of a truncated broad pyramidal form with battered (inclined) wall surfaces on all four sides, or two truncated pyramidal towers flanking an entrance portal. **2** Any towerlike structure from which bridge cables or utility lines are suspended.

quadripartite vault A vault divided into four triangular sections by a pair of diagonal ribs. Sometimes called a four-part vault.

quarry-faced See ROCK-FACED.

quatrefoil A type of Gothic tracery having four parts (lobes or foils) separated by pointed elements (cusps).

Queen Anne Ambiguous but widely used term. **1** In architecture, the Queen Anne Style is an eclectic style of the 1860s through 1910s in England and the United States, characterized by the incorporation of forms from postmedieval vernacular architecture and the architecture of the Georgian period. Sometimes called Queen Anne Revival. See also the more specific term SHINGLE STYLE and the related terms EASTLAKE, STICK STYLE. **2** In architecture, the original Queen Anne period extends from the late seventeenth into the early eighteenth century. **3** In the decorative arts, the Queen Anne Style and period properly refer to work of the early eighteenth century during the reign of Queen Anne (1702–1714), i.e., after William and Mary and before Georgian). **4** In the decorative arts, eclectic work of the 1860s to 1880s is properly referred to as Queen Anne Revival. See also the related term AESTHETIC MOVEMENT.

quoin One of the bricks or stones laid in alternating directions, which bond and form the exterior corner of a building. Sometimes simulated in wood or stucco.

rafter One of the inclined structural members of a roof. Principal rafters are primary supporting elements spanning between the walls and the apex of the roof and carrying the longitudinal purlins. Common rafters are secondary supporting elements fastened onto purlins to carry the roof surfacing. See also the related term PURLIN.

raking cornice A cornice that finishes the sloping edges of a gable roof, such as the inclined sides of a triangular pediment.

random ashlar A type of masonry in which squared and dressed blocks are laid in a random pattern rather than in straight horizontal courses.

recessed column A fully round column set into a nichelike space only slightly larger than the column. Distinguished from an engaged column, which appears to be built into the wall.

reentrant angle An acute angle created by the juncture of two planes, such as walls.

refectory A dining hall, especially in medieval architecture.

regionalism 1 The sum of cultural characteristics (including material culture, language) that define a geographic region, usually extending beyond a single state or province, and coinciding with one or more large physiographic areas. **2** The conscious use, within a region, of forms and materials identified with that region, creating an architecture that is in keeping with the historical architecture of the region, and even a distinctive new regional style.

register A horizontal zone of a wall, altarpiece, or other vertical feature. Usually synonymous with story, but more inclusive, allowing for the description of zones with no corresponding interior spaces.

relieving arch An arch, usually of masonry, built over the lintel of an opening to carry the load of the wall above and relieve the lintel of carrying such load. Sometimes called a discharging arch or safety arch.

Renaissance The period in European civilzation identified with a rediscovery or rebirth *(rinascimento)* of classical Roman (and to a lesser extent, Greek) learning, art, and architecture. Renaissance architecture began in Italy in the mid–1400s (Early Renaissance) and reached a peak in the early to mid–1500s (High Renaissance). In England, Renaissance architecture did not begin until the late 1500s or early 1600s. The Renaissance in art and architecture was preceded by the Gothic and followed by the Baroque.

Renaissance Revival 1 In architecture, applied to *(a)* Italianate work of the 1840s through 1880s and *(b)* Beaux-Arts classical work of the 1880s through 1920s. **2** In the decorative arts, an eclectic furniture style incorporating a variety of Renaissance, Baroque, and Néo-Grec architectural motifs and utilizing wood marquetry, incised lines (often gilded), and ormolu and porcelain ornaments. Sometimes called Neo-Renaissance.

rendering Any drawing, whether orthographic (plan, elevation, section) or pictorial (perspective), in which shades and shadows are represented.

reredos A screen or wall at the back of an altar, usually with architectural and figural decoration.

return The continuation of a molding, cornice, or other projecting member, in a different direction, as in the horizontal cornice returns at the base of the raking cornices of a triangular pediment.

reveal 1 The portion of wall thickness between a door or window frame and the outer face of the wall. **2** Same as jamb, but only in an opening without a door or window.

revival, revivalism A type of historicism prevalent since the eighteenth century, involving the adaptation of historical forms to contemporary functions. Distinguished from a more pervasive historicism by an ideological conviction that sought to rationalize the choice of a historical style according to the values of the historical period that produced it. (The Gothic Revival, for instance, was associated with the Christianity of the Middle Ages.) Revival works, therefore, tend to invoke a single historical style. More hybrid works are manifestations of a less dogmatic historicism or eclecticism. See also the more general terms HISTORICISM, ECLECTICISM.

rib The projecting linear element that separates the curved planar cells (or webs) of vaulting. Originally these were the supporting members for the vaulting, but they may also be purely decorative.

Richardsonian Term applied to any work showing the influence of the American architect Henry Hobson Richardson (1838–1886). See the note under the more limiting term RICHARDSONIAN ROMANESQUE.

Richardsonian Romanesque Term applied to Neo-Romanesque work showing the influence of the American architect Henry Hobson Richardson (1838–1886). While many of Richardson's works make eclectic use of round arches and Romanesque details, many of his works show a creative eclecticism that transcends any particular historical style. The term Richardsonian, therefore, is a more inclusive term for the work of his followers than Richardsonian Romanesque—a term that continues to be widely used. Sometimes called Richardson Romanesque, Richardsonian Romanesque Revival.

ridgepole The horizontal beam or board at the apex of a roof, to which the upper ends of the rafters are fastened. Sometimes called a ridge beam, ridgeboard, ridge piece.

rinceau An ornamental device consisting of a sinuous and branching scroll elaborated with leaves and other natural forms.

rock-faced Term applied to the rough, unfinished face of a stone used in building. Sometimes called quarry-faced, rough-faced.

Rococo. A late phase of the Baroque, marked by elegant reverse-curve ornament, light scale, and delicate color. See also the related term BAROQUE.

Romanesque A medieval architectural style which reached its height in the eleventh and twelfth centuries. It is characterized by round arched construction and massive masonry walls. The Romanesque was preceded by the Early Christian and Byzantine periods in the eastern Mediterranean world and by a variety of localized styles and periods in northern and western Europe; it was followed throughout Europe by the Gothic.

Romanesque Revival Applied to (1) Rundbogenstil and Round Arch work in the United States as early as the 1840s and (2) Richardsonian Romanesque work into the 1890s (later in some areas). Sometimes called Neo-Romanesque.

Roman Revival A term, not widely accepted, for a version of Neoclassicism involving the use of forms from the visual arts of the Imperial Roman period. Applied to various works in Italy, England, and the United States, where it is most clearly visible in the architecture of Thomas Jefferson. See also the related terms FEDERAL, JEFFERSONIAN, NEOCLASSICISM.

rood screen An ornamental screen that serves as a partition between the crossing and the chancel or choir of a church.

rosette A circular floral ornament similar to an open rose.

rotunda 1 A circular hall in a large building, especially an area beneath a dome or cupola. 2 A building round both inside and outside, usually domed.

Round Arch mode The American counterpart of the German Rundbogenstil, characterized by the predominance of round arches, whether these are accentuated by Romanesque or Renaissance detailing or left as simple unadorned openings. See also the related terms ITALIANATE, LOMBARD, RUNDBOGENSTIL.

roundel. A circular panel or plaque. Distinguished from a patera, which is oval shaped.

rough-faced See ROCK-FACED.

rubble masonry A type of masonry utilizing uncut or roughly shaped stone, such as fieldstone or boulders.

Rundbogenstil Literally, "round arch style," a historicist style originating in Germany in the 1820s and spreading to Britain and the United States from the 1840s through the 1860s. It is characterized by an eclectic combination of Romanesque and Renaissance elements. See also the related term ROUND ARCH MODE.

running bond A pattern of brickwork in which only stretchers appear, with the vertical joints of one course falling halfway between the vertical joints of adjacent courses. Sometimes called stretcher bond. Distinguished from common bond, in which every fifth or sixth course consists of all headers.

Ruskin Gothic, Ruskinian Gothic. See HIGH VICTORIAN GOTHIC.

rustication, rusticated Masonry in which the joints are emphasized by narrow recessed channels or grooves outlining each block. Sometimes simulated in wood or stucco.

sacristy A room in a church where liturgical vessels and vestments are kept.

safety arch See RELIEVING ARCH.

sanctuary 1 The part of a church that contains the principal altar. Usually the innermost space within the chancel arm of the church, situated to the east of the choir. 2 Loosely used to mean a place of worship, a sacred place.

sash Any framework of a window. It may be movable or fixed. It may slide in a vertical plane (as in a double-hung window) or may be pivoted (as in a casement window).

sash bar See MUNTIN.

Secession movement The refined classicist Austrian (Viennese) version of the Art Nouveau style, so named beause the artists and architects involved seceded from the official Academy in 1897. Josef Hoffmann (1870–1956) is the architect most frequently mentioned in association with this movement.

Second Chicago School A term sometimes applied to the International Style in Chicago from the 1940s to the 1970s, particularly the work of Mies van der Rohe. See also the related terms INTERNATIONAL STYLE, MIESIAN.

Second Empire Not strictly a style term but a term for a period in French history coinciding with the rule of Napoleon III (1852–1870). Generally applied in the United States, however, to a phase of Beaux-Arts governmental and institutional architecture (1850s–1880s) as well as to countless hybrids of Beaux-Arts and Italianate forms in residential, commercial, and industrial architecture (1850s–1880s). Sometimes called General Grant Style, Mansard Style, Mansardic. See also the related terms BEAUX-ARTS, ITALIANATE (definition 1).

section A drawing (in orthographic projection) representing a vertical cut through an object, building, or space. An architectural section shows interior relationships of space and structure, and may also include mechanical systems. Sometimes called a cross section.

segmental arch An arch formed on a segmental curve. Its center lies below the springing line.

segmental curve A curve that is a segment (i.e., less than half the circumference) of a circle or an ellipse. The baseline of the curve is a chord measuring less than the diameter of the larger circle from which the segment is taken.

segmental pediment A pediment whose top is a segmental curve.

segmental vault A vault whose cross section is a segmental curve. A dome built on segmental curves is called a saucer dome.

setback 1 In architecture, particularly in the design of tall buildings, a series of upper stories that are stepped back to allow more sunlight to reach the streets. **2** In planning, the amount of space between the lot line and the perimeter of a building.

shaft The tall part of a column between the base and the capital.

shed roof A roof having only one sloping plane. Sometimes called a lean-to roof.

Shingle Style A term applied primarily to American domestic architecture of the 1870s through the 1890s, in which broad expanses of wood shingles dominate the exterior roof and wall planes. Rooms open widely into one another and to the outdoors, and the ample living hall or stair hall is often the dominant feature of the interior. The term was coined in the 1940s by Vincent Scully for a series of seaside and suburban houses of the northeastern United States. The Shingle Style is a version of the Anglo-American Queen Anne Style. See also the related terms COLONIAL REVIVAL, STICK STYLE.

shouldered architrave See EAR.

side gabled Term applied to a building whose gable ends face the sides of a lot. Distinguished from front gabled.

side light A framed area of fixed glass alongside a door or window. See also the related term FANLIGHT.

sill course In masonry, a stringcourse set at window-sill level, usually differentiated from the wall by its greater projection, its finish, or its thickness. Not applicable to frame construction.

sill plate See PLATE (definition 2).

skeleton construction, skeleton frame A system of construction in which all loads are carried to the ground through a rigid framework of iron, steel, or reinforced concrete. The exterior walls are curtain walls (i.e., not load-bearing).

skylight A window in a roof, specifically one that is flush with the roof plane or only slightly protruding. Distinguished from a cupola (definition 2), which is a major centralized feature at the summit of a roof. Distinguished from a monitor, which is an extensive roof feature containing a band of windows or vents.

soffit The exposed underside of any overhead component, such as an arch, beam, cornice, or lintel. See also the related term INTRADOS.

sole plate See PLATE (definition 2).

space frame A series of trusses placed side by side and joined to one another by triangulated rods, tubes, or beams, so that the individual planar trusses are united into a three-dimensional structural framework. Often used in roof structures requiring long spans.

spandrel 1 The quasi-triangular space between two adjoining arches and a line connecting their crowns, or between an arch and the columns and entablature that frame it. **2** In skeletal construction, the wall area between the top of a window and the

sill of the window in the story above. Sometimes called a spandrel panel.

Spanish colonial A term applied to buildings, towns, landscapes, and other artifacts from the various periods of actual Spanish colonial occupation in North American (c. 1565–1821 in Florida; c. 1763–1800 in Louisiana and the Lower Mississippi valley; c. 1590s–1821 in Texas and the southwestern United States; c. 1769–1821 in California). The term is extended to apply to the artifacts of Hispanic ethnic groups (e.g., Mexicans, Puerto Ricans, Cubans) and their descendants, even into the early twentieth century. See also the related terms CHURRIGUE-RESQUE, PLATERESQUE.

Spanish Colonial Revival The revival of forms from Spanish colonial and provincial Mexican design. The Spanish Colonial Revival began in Florida and California in the 1880s and continues nationwide into the present. Sometimes called Neo-Hispanic, Spanish Eclectic, Spanish Revival. See also the more specific term MISSION REVIVAL and the related term MEDITERRANEAN REVIVAL.

spindle A turned wooden element, thicker toward the middle and thinner at either end, found in arch screens, porch trim, and other ornamental assemblages. Banisters (i.e., thin, simple balusters) may be spindle-shaped, but the term spindle, when used alone, usually connotes shorter elements.

spire A slender pointed element surmounting a building. A tall, attenuated pyramidal form with any number of thin triangular faces that are unbroken or articulated only with crockets, pinnacles, or small dormers. Distinguished from a steeple, which is divided into stages and which may be topped with a spire.

splay The slanting surface formed by cutting off a right-angle corner at an oblique angle to one face. A reveal at an oblique angle to the exterior face of the wall.

springing, springing line, springing point The line or point where an arch or vault rises from its supports and begins to curve. Usually the juncture between the impost of the support below and the springer, or first voussoir, of the arch above.

squinch An arch, lintel, or corbeling, built across the interior corner of two walls to form one side of an octagonal base for a dome. This octagonal base serves as the structural transition from a square interior crossing space to an octagonal or round dome.

stair A series of steps, or flights of steps connected by landings, which connects two or more levels or floors.

staircase The ensemble of a stair and its enclosing walls. Sometimes called a stairway.

stair tower A projecting tower or other building block that contains a stair.

stamped metal See PRESSED METAL.

Steamboat Gothic See CARPENTER'S GOTHIC.

steeple 1 A tall structure rising from a tower, consisting of a series of superimposed stages diminishing in plan, and usually topped by a spire or small cupola. Distinguished from a spire, which is not divided into stages. **2** Less commonly used to mean the whole of the tower, from the ground to the top of the spire or cupola.

stepped gable A gable in which the wall rises in a series of steps above the planes of the roof.

stereotomy The science of cutting three-dimensional shapes from stone, such as the units that make up a carefully fitted masonry vault.

Stick Style A term applied primarily to American domestic architecture of the 1850s through the 1870s, in which exterior wall planes are subdivided into bays and stories outlined by narrow boards called "stickwork." The term was coined by Vincent Scully in the 1940s for a series of houses with clearly articulated wall panels and sticklike porch supports and eaves brackets. Sources include the English and German picturesque traditions, as well as the French rationalist tradition. See also the related terms QUEEN ANNE, SHINGLE STYLE.

story (plural: stories). The space in a building between floor levels. British spelling is storey, storeys. Sometimes called a register, a more inclusive term applied to horizontal on a vertical plane zones that do not correspond to actual floor levels.

Streamline Moderne A later phase of the Moderne, popular in the 1930s and 1940s and characterized by stucco surfaces with rounded corners, by horizontal banding, overhangs, and window groupings, and by other details suggestive of modern Machine Age aerodynamic forms. Sometimes called Streamline Modern, Streamline Modernistic. See also the more general term MODERNE and the related terms ART DECO and PWA MODERNE.

stretcher A brick laid the length of a wall, so that the long side of the brick shows on the exterior.

stretcher bond See running bond.

string In a stair, an inclined board that supports the ends of the steps. Sometimes called a stringer.

stringcourse In masonry, a horizontal band, generally narrower than other courses, extending across the facade of a building and in some instances encircling such features as pillars or columns. It may be flush or projecting; of identical or contrasting material; flat, molded, or richly carved. Not applicable to frame construction. Sometimes called a band course or belt course. More elaborate horizontal bands in masonry or frame construction are generally called band moldings.

strut A column, post, or pole that is set in a diagonal position and thus serves as a stiffener by triangulation. Distinguished from a brace, which is usually a shorter bracketlike member.

stucco 1 An exterior plaster finish, usually textured, composed of portland cement, lime, and sand, which are mixed with water. **2** A fine plaster used for decorative work or moldings. See also the more specific term PARGETING.

stud One of the vertical supporting elements in a wall, especially in balloon and platform frame con-

struction. Studs are relatively lightweight members (usually two-by-fours).

Sullivanesque Term applied to work showing the influence of the American architect Louis Henry Sullivan (1856–1924).

sunburst light See FANLIGHT.

supercapital See IMPOST BLOCK.

supercolumniation See SUPERPOSITION (definition 1).

superimposition, superimposed See SUPERPOSITION.

superposition, superposed 1 The use of an ensemble of the classical orders, one above the other, as the major elements articulating a facade. When this is done, the Doric, considered the simplest order, is used on or near the ground story. The Ionic, considered more complex, comes next; and the Corinthian, considered the most complex, is used at the top. Sometimes the Tuscan order or rusticated masonry may be used for the ground story beneath the Doric order, and the Composite order may be used above the Corinthian order. Sometimes called supercolumniation, superimposition. See also the related term ORDER. **2** Less commonly, any vertical relationship of architectural elements (e.g., windows, piers, colonnettes) in any style or period.

superstructure A structure raised upon another structure, as a building upon a foundation, basement, or substructure.

Supervising Architect The Supervising Architect of the United States Treasury Department, whose office was responsible for the design and construction of all major federal government buildings (such as courthouses, customhouses, and post offices) from the 1850s through the 1930s. The Office of the Supervising Architect was formally established by Congress in 1864 and lasted until 1939, when its functions were absorbed into the Public Buildings Administration (and in 1949, into the General Services Administration).

supporting wall See BEARING WALL.

surround An encircling border or decorative frame around a door or window. Distinguished from architrave (definition 2), a term usually applied to the frame around an opening when considered as a series of relatively flat face moldings.

suspended ceiling A ceiling suspended from rodlike hangers below the level of the floor above. The interval between the floor slab above and the suspended ceiling often serves as a space for ducts, utilities, and air circulation. Sometimes called a hung ceiling.

swag A motif representing a suspended fold of drapery hanging in a catenary curve from two points. Distinguished from a festoon, which is a motif representing entwined leaves, flowers, or fruits, hung in a similar curve. See also the more general term GARLAND.

tabernacle 1 A niche or recess, usually on an interior wall, framed by columns or pilasters and topped by an entablature and pediment. Distinguished from an aedicule, which more often occurs on an exterior wall. See also the related term NICHE. **2** In the Jewish religion, a portable sanctuary. **3** In Protestant denominations, a large auditorium church.

terracotta A hard ceramic material used for (1) fireproofing, especially as a fitted cladding around metal skeletal construction; or (2) an exterior or interior wall cladding, which is often glazed and multicolored.

Territorial Style An early to mid-nineteenth-century vernacular style typical of the territorial period in the southwestern United States, i.e., the years between U.S. acquisition from Mexico and statehood. The style combines traditional Spanish colonial adobe construction with superimposed Anglo-influenced elements and materials (pitched roofs, columned porches, shingles, milled lumber, fired brick) and Greek Revival wood details, including door and window pediments.

tertiary rib See LIERNE.

thermal window A large lunette window similar to those found in ancient Roman baths *(thermae)*. The window is subdivided into three to five parts by vertical mullions. Sometimes called a *thermae* window.

three-hinged arch An arch in two major segments anchored with cylindrical "hinge" pins at either end and at the crown. Movement within the arch, caused by temperature changes, the torsion of wind movements, or other forces, can be absorbed by the movement of the arch around the pins, thereby avoiding stresses that would occur in the structural frame if the arches were fixed.

tie beam A horizontal tension member that ties together the opposing angular members of a truss and prevents them from spreading.

tier A group of stories or any zone of architectural elements arranged horizontally.

tierceron In a Gothic vault, a secondary rib that rises from the springing to an intermediate position on either side of the diagonal ribs. Sometimes called an intermediate rib.

tie rod A metal rod that spans the distance between two structural members and, by its tensile strength, restrains them against tendencies to collapse outward.

timber frame construction, timber framing A type of wood frame construction in which heavy timber posts and beams (six-by-sixes and larger) are fastened using mortise and tenon joints. Sometimes called heavy timber construction. Distinguished from light frame construction, in which relatively light structural members (two-by-fours to two-by-tens) are fastened with nails.

trabeation, trabeated construction. See POST AND BEAM CONSTRUCTION.

tracery Decoration within an arch or other opening, made up of narrow curvilinear bands or more elaborately molded strips. In Gothic architecture, the curved interlocking stone bars that contain the leaded stained glass.

transept The lateral arm of a cross-shaped church, usually between the nave (the area for the congregation) and the chancel (the area for the altar, clergy, and choir).

transom 1 A narrow horizontal window unit, either fixed or movable, over a door. Sometimes called a transom light. See also the more specific term fanlight. **2** A horizontal bar, as distinguished from a vertical mullion, especially one crossing a door or window opening near the top.

transverse rib In a Gothic vault, a rib at right angles to the ridge rib.

trefoil A type of Gothic tracery having three parts (lobes or foils) separated by pointed elements (cusps).

trellis Any open latticework made of strips of wood or metal crossing one another, usually supporting climbing plants. Distinguished from an arbor, which is generally a more substantial yet compact three-dimensional structure, and from a pergola, which is a more extensive colonnaded structure.

triforium In a Gothic church, an arcade in the wall above the arches of the nave, choir, or transept and below the clerestory window.

triglyph One of the slightly raised blocks in a Doric frieze. It consists of three narrow vertical bands separated by two V-shaped grooves.

triumphal arch 1 A freestanding arch erected for a victory procession. It usually consists of a broad central arched opening, flanked by two smaller bays (usually with open or blind arches). The bays are usually articulated by classical columns, supporting an entablature and a high attic. **2** An similar configuration applied to a facade to denote a monumental entryway.

truss A rigid triangular framework made up of beams, posts, braces, struts, and ties and used for the spanning of large spaces. The major horizontal or inclined members are called chords. The connecting vertical and diagonal elements are called the web members.

Tudor arch A low-profile arch characterized by two pairs of arcs, one pair of tight arcs at the springing, another pair of broad (nearly flat) arcs at the apex or crown.

Tudor period A term for a period in English history coinciding with the rule of monarchs of the house of Tudor (1485–1603). Tudor period architecture is Late Gothic, with only hints of the Renaissance. See also the more specific term ELIZABETHAN PERIOD for the end of this period, and the related term JACOBEAN PERIOD for the succeeding period.

Tudor Revival See NEO-TUDOR.

turret A small towerlike structure, often circular in plan, built against the side or at an exterior or interior corner of a building.

Tuscan order An ensemble of classical column and entablature elements, similar to the Roman Doric order, but without triglyphs in the frieze and without mutules (domino-like blocks) in the cornice of the entablature. See also the more general term ORDER.

tympanum (plural: tympana) **1** The triangular or segmental area enclosed by the cornice moldings of a pediment, frequently ornamented with sculpture. **2** Any space similarly delineated or bounded, as between the lintel of a door or window and the arch above.

umbrage A term used by Alexander Jackson Davis (1803–1892) as a synonym for veranda, the implication being a shadowed area.

vault An arched roof or ceiling, usually constructed in brick or stone, but also in tile, metal or concrete. A nonstructural plaster ceiling that simulates a masonry vault.

Venetian Gothic See HIGH VICTORIAN GOTHIC.

veranda A nineteenth-century term for porch. Sometimes spelled verandah.

vergeboard See BARGEBOARD.

verges The sloping edges of a gable, gambrel, or lean-to roof, usually projecting beyond the wall below. Distinguished from eaves, which are the horizontal lower edges of a roof plane.

vernacular Not a style in itself, but a descriptive term, applicable primarily to architecture, covering the vast range of ordinary buildings that are produced outside the high-style tradition of well-known architects. The vernacular tradition includes the folk tradition of regional and ethnic buildings whose forms (plan and massing) remain relatively constant through the years, in spite of stylistic embellishments. The term vernacular architecture is often used as if it meant only folk architecture. However, the vernacular tradition in architecture also includes the popular tradition of buildings whose design was influenced by such publications as books of the orders, builders' guides, style books, pattern books, mail-order catalogs, architectural periodicals, and household magazines. Usually contrasted with high-style. See also the more specific terms FOLK, POPULAR.

vertical plank construction A system of wood construction in which vertical planks are set or nailed into heavy timber horizontal sills and plates. A building so constructed has no corner posts and no studs. Two-story vertical plank buildings have planks extending the full height of the building, with no girt between the two stories. Second-floor joists are merely mortised into the planks. Distinguished from the more specific term vertical plank frame construction, in which there are corner posts.

vertical plank frame construction A type of vertical plank construction, in which heavy timber corner posts are introduced to provide support for the plate, to which the tops of the planks are fastened. See also the related term HORIZONTAL PLANK FRAME CONSTRUCTION.

vestibule A small entry hall between the outer door and the main hallway of a building.

Victorian Gothic See HIGH VICTORIAN GOTHIC.

Victorian period A term for a period in British, British colonial, and Anglo-American history, and not, in architecture or the other visual arts, a sufficiently specific style term. The Victorian period extended across eight decades, from the coronation of Queen Victoria in 1837 to her death in 1901. See instead EASTLAKE, GOTHIC REVIVAL, GREEK REVIVAL, QUEEN ANNE, SHINGLE STYLE, STICK STYLE and other specific style terms.

Victorian Romanesque Ambiguous term. See instead RICHARDSONIAN ROMANESQUE, ROMANESQUE REVIVAL, ROUND ARCH MODE.

viga Spanish for a log or beam supporting the roof and projecting beyond the wall surface.

villa 1 In the Roman and Renaissance periods, a suburban or rural residential complex, often quite elaborate, consisting of a house, dependencies, and gardens. **2** Since the eighteenth century, any detached suburban or rural house of picturesque character and some pretension. Distinguished from the more modest house form known as a cottage.

volute 1 A spiral scroll, especially the one that is a distinctive feature of the Ionic capital. **2** A large scroll-shaped buttress on a facade or dome.

voussoir A wedge-shaped stone or brick used in the construction of an arch. Its tapering sides coincide with radii of the arch.

wainscot A decorative or protective facing, usually of wood paneling, applied to the lower portion of an interior partition or wall. Distinguished from a dado, which is the zone at the base of a wall, regardless of the material used to cover it. Wainscot properly connotes woodwork. Sometimes called wainscoting.

water table 1 In masonry, a course of molded bricks or stones set forward several inches near the base of a wall and serving as the cap of the basement courses. **2** In frame construction, a ledge or projecting molding just above the foundation to protect it from rainwater. **3** In masonry or frame construction, any horizontal exterior ledge on a wall, pier, or buttress. Often sloped and provided with a drip molding to prevent water from running down the face of the wall below.

weatherboard See CLAPBOARD.

weathering The inclination given to the upper surface of any element so that it will shed water.

web 1 The relatively thin shell of masonry between the ribs of a ribbed vault. **2** The portion of a truss between the chords, or the portion of a girder or I-beam between the flanges.

western frame, western framing See PLATFORM FRAME CONSTRUCTION.

winder A step, more or less wedge-shaped, with its tread wider at one end than the other.

window bar See MUNTIN.

window cap See CAP.

window head A head molding or pedimented feature over a window.

Wrightian Term applied to work showing the influence of the American architect Frank Lloyd Wright (1867–1959). See also the related term PRAIRIE SCHOOL.

wrought iron Iron shaped by a hammering process, to improve the tensile properties of the metal. Distinguished from cast iron, a brittle material, which is formed in molds.

Zigzag Moderne, Zigzag Modernistic See ART DECO.

Illustration Credits

Photos not otherwise credited are by or from the collection of Thomas J. Noel.

INTRODUCTION
Page 5, Rick Athearn; **p. 9,** Denver Public Library/ Western History Department **p. 11,** Library of Congress; **p. 12,** Amon Carter Museum (Mazzulla Collection); **p. 13,** Denver Public Library/Western History Department; **p. 15,** Amon Carter Museum (Mazzulla Collection); **p. 16 (bottom),** Colorado Historical Society; **p. 22,** Denver Public Library/Western History Department; **p. 26,** John Gaw Meem Archives, Zimmerman Library, University of New Mexico

DENVER
DV001, DV002 Colorado State Archives; **DV004** William Taylor; **DV009** Denver Public Library/Western History Department (L. C. McClure); **DV010** Photo by Otto Roach; **DV011** Colorado Historical Society; **DV020** Denver Public Library/Western History Department (L. C. McClure); **DV022, DV023, DV024** Roger Whitacre; **DV025** Amon Carter Museum (Mazzulla Collection); **DV028** State Historical Society of Colorado; **DV034** James Baca; **DV037** Glenn Cuerden; **DV040** Roger Whitacre; **DV046** Denver Center for the Performing Arts (Roger Whitacre); **DV046.1** Denver Public Library/Western History Department; **DV050** Roger Whitacre; **DV060** Denver Public Library/Western History Department; **DV065** Michael Gamer; **DV076** Roger Whitacre; **DV077** Colorado Historical Society; **DV082** Glenn Cuerden; **DV087** The Denver Catholic Register/Archdiocese of Denver Archives; **DV091** Roger Whitacre; **DV092** Sandra Dallas Atchison; **DV093** Roger Whitacre; **DV097** Denver Public Library/Western History Department (L. C. McClure); **DV098** Roger Whitacre; **DV102** Glenn Cuerden; **DV104, DV109** Roger Whitacre; **DV122** Hank Toll; **DV125** Colorado Historical Society; **DV132** Glenn Cuerden; **DV134** *Denver Municipal Facts* (drawing by A. O. Ahlberg); **DV136.3, DV145** Glenn Cuerden; **DV147** Roger Whitacre; **DV155** Denver Public Library/Western History Department (Orin Sealy); **DV168** C. W. Fentress, J. H. Bradburn and Associates; **DV183** Denver Public Library/Western History Department; **DV185** Barbara Norgren; **DV186** Denver Public Library/Western History Department (L. C. McClure) **DV192** James Baca; **DV208** Roger Whitacre; **DV214** Denver Archdiocese Archives/Roy C. Hyskell; **DV215** Denver Public Library/Western History Department; **DV216** Four Mile House Historic Park

ADAMS COUNTY
AM09, AM16 Glenn Cuerden

ARAPAHOE COUNTY
AH01, AH03, AH05 Littleton Historical Museum; **AH08** Steven Scott; **AH09** Littleton Historical Museum; **AH26.4** Roger Whitacre; **AH37** Rocky Mountain Prestress, Inc. **AH41** Glenn Cuerden

DOUGLAS COUNTY
DA01 Greg Hursley

JEFFERSON COUNTY
JF15 Roger Whitacre; **JF16.3** Denver Public Library/ Western History Department; **JF23** Historic American Buildings Survey; **JF26** Center for Judaic Studies, University of Denver; **JF34** Nick Wheeler; **JF38, JF39** Denver Public Library/Western History Department; **JF42** Glenn Cuerden

BOULDER COUNTY
BL22.5 Colorado Historical Society; **BL22.7** J. Martin Natvig; **BL33** James Baca

GILPIN COUNTY
GL11 Louise Pote; **GL17** Glenn Cuerden; **GL24** Historic American Buildings Survey

CLEAR CREEK COUNTY
CC01 Historic American Buildings Survey (drawing); **CC07** Ira Gay Sealy; **CC09** Glenn Cuerden; **CC10** Otto Roach; **CC22** Historic American Buildings Survey

PARK COUNTY
PK04 Glenn Cuerden; **PK12** Photo by Margaret Kountze Berger; **PK15** Colorado Historical Society

LARIMER COUNTY
LR01.7, LR01.9, LR09, LR15, LR19 Fort Collins Public Library

WELD COUNTY
WE22.5 Denver Public Library/Western History Department; **WE23, WE24** Thomas H. Simmons; **WE37** Reif Heck

MORGAN COUNTY
MR13 Andrew Gulliford

LOGAN COUNTY
LO01, LO04 Denver Public Library/Western History Department; **LO10** Archdiocesan Archives, Denver

EL PASO COUNTY
EP07 Penrose Public Library/Western History Department; **EP12, EP21** Penrose Public Library/Western History Department; **EP22** Ron Johnson; **EP34.1** Colorado Springs Pioneers Museum/Starsmore Center for Local History; **EP34.4, EP45, EP50** Penrose Public Library/Western History Department; **EP53** Denver Public Library/Western History Department (L. C. McClure);**EP56, EP58, EP65** Penrose Public Library/Western History Department; **EP68** Zimmerman Library, University of New Mexico (Roy C. Hyskell; **EP69** The Colorado College Library

PUEBLO COUNTY
PE03 Glenn Cuerden; **PE05** Edwin L. Dodds; **PE06** Pueble Regional Library; **PE08, PE10** Edwin L. Dodds **PE26** Edwin L. Dodds; **PE30** Pueblo Regional Library; **PE31** Denver Public Library/Western History Department (photo by Sandra Dallas Atchison); **PE40** Edwin L. Dodds

TELLER COUNTY
TL29 Denver Public Library/Western History Department

FREMONT COUNTY
FR04 Jackson Thode Collection (photo by George L. Beam)

CHAFFEE COUNTY
CF25 Colorado Springs Pioneers Museum/Starsmore Center for Local History

LAKE COUNTY
LK16 Denver Public Library/Western History Department (photo by Muriel S. Wolle); **LK20** Courtesy Amon Carter Museum (Mazzulla Collection)

CUSTER COUNTY
CR05 Rick Athearn

LAS ANIMAS COUNTY
LA09 Glenn Aultman; **LA10** Denver Public Library/ Western History Department (photo by Sandra Dallas Atchison); **LA17, LA22** Glenn Aultman

PROWERS COUNTY
PW03 Reif Heck; **PW11** Denver Public Library/Western History Department

CHEYENNE COUNTY
CH01 Denver Public Library/Western History Department

COSTILLA COUNTY
CT04, CT08, CT16, CT21 Virginia Simmons

SAGUACHE COUNTY
SH23 Keith Bean

GRAND COUNTY
GA05 Colorado Historical Society

EAGLE COUNTY
Page 467 Unnumbered photo: Glenn Cuerden

PITKIN COUNTY
PT20.5 Mary Eshbaugh Hayes; **p. 499** Unnumbered photo: Glenn Cuerden

MESA COUNTY
ME01 Colorado Historical Society (photo by George L. Beam); **ME08.6** Frank Dean

RIO BLANCO
RB06 Denver Public Library/Western History Department

MOFFAT COUNTY
Page 517 Unnumbered photo: Glenn Cuerden; **MF01** Colorado Historical Society

ROUTT COUNTY
RT04 Ken Proper; **RT06** Denver Public Library/ Western History Department; **RT10** Ken Proper

DELTA COUNTY
DT05 Colorado Historical Society

GUNNISON COUNTY
GU30 Denver Public Library/Western History Department (photo by George L. Beam)

LA PLATA COUNTY
Page 554 Unnumbered photo: Amon Carter Museum (Mazzulla Collection)

SAN JUAN COUNTY
SA18 Denver Public Library/Western History Department; **SA19** Joseph Collier

OURAY COUNTY
Page 568 Unnumbered photo: Denver Public Library/Western History Department (L. C. McClure); **OR29** Glenn Cuerden

MONTROSE COUNTY
MO01 Colorado Historical Society; **MO03** Glenn Cuerden

SAN MIGUEL COUNTY
SM11 Denver Public Library/Western History Departmen (photo by Muriel S. Wolle)

MONTEZUMA COUNTY
MT24.1 Historic American Buildings Survey (drawing, Kevin Speece, Roger Muzia); **MT28** Denver Public Library/Western History Department (photo by Jesse Nusbaum)

Index

Pages with illustrations are indicated in **bold**.

A

Abels, Gale, and Associates: Student Art Gallery (Emmanuel Sherith Israel Chapel) renovation, Denver, 70

Abo, Ronald K.: Town Hall renovation, Castle Rock, 144; Union Pacific Depot restoration, Sterling, 257

Abriendo Inn (Walter House), Pueblo, 325

Acacia Park, Colorado Springs, 284, 289

Acme Building, Cañon City, 343

Adams, Alva (Colorado governor), 118, 324, 385

Adams Avenue District, South Pueblo, 323

Adams Mark Hotel (Zeckendorf Plaza), Denver, 49

Adams State College, 408–409

Adelaide Bridge, Fremont County, 348

Adobe: construction, 4, 10–11, 18, 33, 280, 313, 401–405 passim, 406, 411, 598; examples, 161, 244, 249, 327, 372, 373, 378–379, 389, 392–393, 410, 411–424 passim, 427, 431–432, 438, 439, 443, 511, 539, 577

Ady Terrace (Tremont Apartments), Denver, 51

Agate, 274–275; Community Church, 274; Hotel, 275

Aiken, William: Old Federal Building (Post Office), Pueblo, **316**

Air Force Academy. *See* U.S. Air Force Academy

Akron, 270–272; Public Library, 271

Alamo Hotel, Colorado Springs, 288

Alamosa, 405–409; Senior Center (Hunt House), 407; Visitors' Center, 407

Aldine Apartments, Denver, 83

Allen and Phillip Architects, Inc.: West Park Place, Westminster, 124

Allen, Mathew: Swede-Finn Hall restoration, Telluride, 586

Allenspark, 182

Allied Architects: City and County Building, Denver, 46, **47**, 48

All Saints Lutheran Church of Eben-Ezer, Brush, 254

All Souls Unitarian Church, Colorado Springs, 296

Alma, 213–215; Fire House and Mining Museum, 215

Alpine Hose Company No. 2, Georgetown, **203**–204

Alpine Standard station, Vail, **469**

Alpine Style, 28, 238, 310, 469, 471, 473, 474, 476, 487, 499, 520

Alpine Tunnel, Gunnison County, 545

Alpine Visitor Center, Grand County, 457

Altman, 329

Amache Japanese Relocation Camp site, Granada, **386**

American Beet Sugar Plant, Rocky Ford, 395

American Furniture Company (Mechanics and Masonic Hall), Pueblo, 315

American Institute of Architects (AIA), 29, 30, 150, 162

American Legion halls and posts: Center, 440; Silverton, 564

American Medical Center (Jewish Consumptive Relief Society), Lakewood, 158

American Mountaineering Center (Golden High School), Golden, 151

American National Bank, Leadville, 363–364

American Numismatic Association Museum, Colorado Springs, 294

American Smelting and Refining Company, 110, 380; Globeville Plant, Denver, 110

American Woodmen Building, Denver, 84

Ames, A. J.: Veterans of Foreign Wars Post, Mancos, 598

Ames Generating Plant, San Miguel County, 591

Amtrak depots: Glenwood Springs, 481; Greeley, 243; Granby, 453

Amy House, Durango, 558

Anaconda, Teller County, 334

Anasazi building and habitation, 6, 8, 10, 447, 553, 592, 594, 596–603

Anasazi Heritage Center, Dolores, 596–597

Anderson, C. J.: United Methodist Church, Monte Vista, 430

Anderson, David: Lumber Baron Bed and Breakfast restoration, Denver, 106

Anderson and DeBartelo: National Renewable Energy Research Facility, Golden, 151

Anderson House, Fort Collins, 231

Anderson, Mason, Dale, 91, 264; Tropical Discovery, Denver

Zoological Gardens, 91; Wray Elementary and High School, 264

Anderson Ranch Arts Center, Pitkin County, 501

Anderson's Hardware, Fort Collins, 231

Andrews and Anderson: Loveland Block/Territorial Capitol renovation, Golden, 152

Andrews House, Fort Collins, **230**

Andrews, Jacques and Rantoul, 58, 59, 294; Boston Building, Denver, 59; Equitable Building, Denver, 58–**59**; Palmer Hall, The Colorado College, 294

Andrews-McHugh House, Fort Collins, 230

Anholtz Farmhouse, Vail, 472

Animas City, 554

Animas Forks, 560, 562, **566**, 567

Animas School Museum, Durango, 559

Annex Building–Opera House, Cañon City, 342–343

Annunciation Catholic Church, Leadville, 365

Ansen and Allen: Quarry Visitor Center, Dinosaur National Monument, 519

Antelope Springs, Mineral County, 436

Anthony, Emmett: Odd Fellows Hall, Denver, 60; Sacred Heart Church, Denver, 64

Antlers Bar, Yampa, 530

Antlers Doubletree Hotel, Colorado Springs, 290

Antlers Hotel, Colorado Springs (demolished), 282, 290, 294, 297

Antlers Hotel, Colorado Springs (demolished), 282, 290, 294, 297

Antlers School, Silt, 486

Antonito, 418, 419–421

Aquatic Center, Montrose, 581

Arabian Horse Center, Westminster, 123

Arapahoe Acres, Englewood, 129

Arapahoe Community College, Littleton, 126

Arapahoe Greenway, Littleton, 124, 127–128

Arapaho Indian sites, Boulder, 182

Arcadia Park, Colorado Springs, 23

Architects Collaborative, The: Martin Marietta Astronautics, Lakewood, 160

Architects' Small House Service Bureau Model House, Denver, 89

Architecture One: Taco Bell (Mawson House), Fort Collins, 228–229

Argo Mill, Idaho Springs, 210

639